University Casebook Series

March, 1991

ACCOUNTING AND THE LAW, Fourth Edition (1978), with Problems Pamphlet (Successor to Dohr, Phillips, Thompson & Warren)

George C. Thompson, Professor, Columbia University Graduate School of Business.
Robert Whitman, Professor of Law, University of Connecticut.
Ellis L. Phillips, Jr., Member of the New York Bar.
William C. Warren, Professor of Law Emeritus, Columbia University.

ACCOUNTING FOR LAWYERS, MATERIALS ON (1980)

David R. Herwitz, Professor of Law, Harvard University.

ADMINISTRATIVE LAW, Eighth Edition (1987), with 1989 Case Supplement and 1983 Problems Supplement (Supplement edited in association with Paul R. Verkuil, Dean and Professor of Law, Tulane University)

Walter Gellhorn, University Professor Emeritus, Columbia University.
Clark Byse, Professor of Law, Harvard University.
Peter L. Strauss, Professor of Law, Columbia University.
Todd D. Rakoff, Professor of Law, Harvard University.
Roy A. Schotland, Professor of Law, Georgetown University.

ADMIRALTY, Third Edition (1987), with Statute and Rule Supplement

Jo Desha Lucas, Professor of Law, University of Chicago.

ADVOCACY, see also Lawyering Process

AGENCY, see also Enterprise Organization

AGENCY—PARTNERSHIPS, Fourth Edition (1987)

Abridgement from Conard, Knauss & Siegel's Enterprise Organization, Fourth Edition.

AGENCY AND PARTNERSHIPS (1987)

Melvin A. Eisenberg, Professor of Law, University of California, Berkeley.

ANTITRUST: FREE ENTERPRISE AND ECONOMIC ORGANIZATION, Sixth Edition (1983), with 1983 Problems in Antitrust Supplement and 1990 Case Supplement

Louis B. Schwartz, Professor of Law, University of Pennsylvania.
John J. Flynn, Professor of Law, University of Utah.
Harry First, Professor of Law, New York University.

BANKRUPTCY, Second Edition (1989), with 1990 Case Supplement

Robert L. Jordan, Professor of Law, University of California, Los Angeles.
William D. Warren, Professor of Law, University of California, Los Angeles.

BANKRUPTCY AND DEBTOR–CREDITOR LAW, Second Edition (1988)

Theodore Eisenberg, Professor of Law, Cornell University.

BUSINESS CRIME (1990)

> Harry First, Professor of Law, New York University.

BUSINESS ORGANIZATION, see also Enterprise Organization

BUSINESS PLANNING, Temporary Second Edition (1984)

> David R. Herwitz, Professor of Law, Harvard University.

BUSINESS TORTS (1972)

> Milton Handler, Professor of Law Emeritus, Columbia University.

CHILDREN IN THE LEGAL SYSTEM (1983) with 1990 Supplement (Supplement edited in association with Elizabeth S. Scott, Professor of Law, University of Virginia)

> Walter Wadlington, Professor of Law, University of Virginia.
> Charles H. Whitebread, Professor of Law, University of Southern California.
> Samuel Davis, Professor of Law, University of Georgia.

CIVIL PROCEDURE, see Procedure

CIVIL RIGHTS ACTIONS (1988), with 1990 Supplement

> Peter W. Low, Professor of Law, University of Virginia.
> John C. Jeffries, Jr., Professor of Law, University of Virginia.

CLINIC, see also Lawyering Process

COMMERCIAL AND DEBTOR–CREDITOR LAW: SELECTED STATUTES, 1990 EDITION

COMMERCIAL LAW, Second Edition (1987)

> Robert L. Jordan, Professor of Law, University of California, Los Angeles.
> William D. Warren, Professor of Law, University of California, Los Angeles.

COMMERCIAL LAW, Fourth Edition (1985), with 1990 Case Supplement

> E. Allan Farnsworth, Professor of Law, Columbia University.
> John Honnold, Professor of Law, University of Pennsylvania.

COMMERCIAL PAPER, Third Edition (1984), with 1990 Case Supplement

> E. Allan Farnsworth, Professor of Law, Columbia University.

COMMERCIAL PAPER, Second Edition (1987) (Reprinted from COMMERCIAL LAW, Second Edition (1987))

> Robert L. Jordan, Professor of Law, University of California, Los Angeles.
> William D. Warren, Professor of Law, University of California, Los Angeles.

COMMERCIAL PAPER AND BANK DEPOSITS AND COLLECTIONS (1967), with Statutory Supplement

> William D. Hawkland, Professor of Law, University of Illinois.

COMMERCIAL TRANSACTIONS—Principles and Policies, Second Edition (1991)

> Alan Schwartz, Professor of Law, Yale University.
> Robert E. Scott, Professor of Law, University of Virginia.

COMPARATIVE LAW, Fifth Edition (1988)

> Rudolf B. Schlesinger, Professor of Law, Hastings College of the Law.
> Hans W. Baade, Professor of Law, University of Texas.
> Mirjan P. Damaska, Professor of Law, Yale Law School.
> Peter E. Herzog, Professor of Law, Syracuse University.

COMPETITIVE PROCESS, LEGAL REGULATION OF THE, Fourth Edition (1990), with 1989 Selected Statutes Supplement

Edmund W. Kitch, Professor of Law, University of Virginia.

Harvey S. Perlman, Dean of the Law School, University of Nebraska.

CONFLICT OF LAWS, Ninth Edition (1990)

Willis L. M. Reese, Professor of Law, Columbia University.

Maurice Rosenberg, Professor of Law, Columbia University.

Peter Hay, Professor of Law, University of Illinois.

CONSTITUTIONAL LAW, Eighth Edition (1989), with 1990 Case Supplement

Edward L. Barrett, Jr., Professor of Law, University of California, Davis.

William Cohen, Professor of Law, Stanford University.

Jonathan D. Varat, Professor of Law, University of California, Los Angeles.

CONSTITUTIONAL LAW, CIVIL LIBERTY AND INDIVIDUAL RIGHTS, Second Edition (1982), with 1989 Supplement

William Cohen, Professor of Law, Stanford University.

John Kaplan, Professor of Law, Stanford University.

CONSTITUTIONAL LAW, Eleventh Edition (1985), with 1990 Supplement (Supplement edited in association with Frederick F. Schauer, Professor, Harvard University)

Gerald Gunther, Professor of Law, Stanford University.

CONSTITUTIONAL LAW, INDIVIDUAL RIGHTS IN, Fourth Edition (1986), (Reprinted from CONSTITUTIONAL LAW, Eleventh Edition), with 1990 Supplement (Supplement edited in association with Frederick F. Schauer, Professor, Harvard University)

Gerald Gunther, Professor of Law, Stanford University.

CONSUMER TRANSACTIONS, Second Edition (1991), with Selected Statutes and Regulations Supplement

Michael M. Greenfield, Professor of Law, Washington University.

CONTRACT LAW AND ITS APPLICATION, Fourth Edition (1988)

Arthur Rosett, Professor of Law, University of California, Los Angeles.

CONTRACT LAW, STUDIES IN, Third Edition (1984)

Edward J. Murphy, Professor of Law, University of Notre Dame.

Richard E. Speidel, Professor of Law, Northwestern University.

CONTRACTS, Fifth Edition (1987)

John P. Dawson, late Professor of Law, Harvard University.

William Burnett Harvey, Professor of Law and Political Science, Boston University.

Stanley D. Henderson, Professor of Law, University of Virginia.

CONTRACTS, Fourth Edition (1988)

E. Allan Farnsworth, Professor of Law, Columbia University.

William F. Young, Professor of Law, Columbia University.

CONTRACTS, Selections on (statutory materials) (1988)

CONTRACTS, Second Edition (1978), with Statutory and Administrative Law Supplement (1978)

Ian R. Macneil, Professor of Law, Cornell University.

COPYRIGHT, PATENTS AND TRADEMARKS, see also Competitive Process; see also Selected Statutes and International Agreements

COPYRIGHT, PATENT, TRADEMARK AND RELATED STATE DOCTRINES, Third Edition (1990), with 1989 Selected Statutes Supplement and 1981 Problem Supplement

Paul Goldstein, Professor of Law, Stanford University.

COPYRIGHT, Unfair Competition, and Other Topics Bearing on the Protection of Literary, Musical, and Artistic Works, Fifth Edition (1990), with 1990 Statutory Supplement

Ralph S. Brown, Jr., Professor of Law, Yale University.
Robert C. Denicola, Professor of Law, University of Nebraska.

CORPORATE ACQUISITIONS, The Law and Finance of (1986), with 1990 Supplement

Ronald J. Gilson, Professor of Law, Stanford University.

CORPORATE FINANCE, Third Edition (1987)

Victor Brudney, Professor of Law, Harvard University.
Marvin A. Chirelstein, Professor of Law, Columbia University.

CORPORATION LAW, BASIC, Third Edition (1989), with Documentary Supplement

Detlev F. Vagts, Professor of Law, Harvard University.

CORPORATIONS, see also Enterprise Organization

CORPORATIONS, Sixth Edition—Concise (1988), with 1990 Case Supplement and 1990 Statutory Supplement

William L. Cary, late Professor of Law, Columbia University.
Melvin Aron Eisenberg, Professor of Law, University of California, Berkeley.

CORPORATIONS, Sixth Edition—Unabridged (1988), with 1990 Case Supplement and 1990 Statutory Supplement

William L. Cary, late Professor of Law, Columbia University.
Melvin Aron Eisenberg, Professor of Law, University of California, Berkeley.

CORPORATIONS AND BUSINESS ASSOCIATIONS—STATUTES, RULES, AND FORMS (1990)

CORRECTIONS, SEE SENTENCING

CREDITORS' RIGHTS, see also Debtor-Creditor Law

CRIMINAL JUSTICE ADMINISTRATION, Fourth Edition (1991)

Frank W. Miller, Professor of Law, Washington University.
Robert O. Dawson, Professor of Law, University of Texas.
George E. Dix, Professor of Law, University of Texas.
Raymond I. Parnas, Professor of Law, University of California, Davis.

CRIMINAL LAW, Fourth Edition (1987)

Fred E. Inbau, Professor of Law Emeritus, Northwestern University.
Andre A. Moenssens, Professor of Law, University of Richmond.
James R. Thompson, Professor of Law Emeritus, Northwestern University.

CRIMINAL LAW AND APPROACHES TO THE STUDY OF LAW, Second Edition (1991)

John M. Brumbaugh, Professor of Law, University of Maryland.

CRIMINAL LAW, Second Edition (1986)

Peter W. Low, Professor of Law, University of Virginia.
John C. Jeffries, Jr., Professor of Law, University of Virginia.
Richard C. Bonnie, Professor of Law, University of Virginia.

CRIMINAL LAW, Fourth Edition (1986)

Lloyd L. Weinreb, Professor of Law, Harvard University.

CRIMINAL LAW AND PROCEDURE, Seventh Edition (1989)

Ronald N. Boyce, Professor of Law, University of Utah.
Rollin M. Perkins, Professor of Law Emeritus, University of California, Hastings College of the Law.

CRIMINAL PROCEDURE, Third Edition (1987), with 1990 Supplement

James B. Haddad, Professor of Law, Northwestern University.
James B. Zagel, Chief, Criminal Justice Division, Office of Attorney General of Illinois.
Gary L. Starkman, Assistant U. S. Attorney, Northern District of Illinois.
William J. Bauer, Chief Judge of the U.S. Court of Appeals, Seventh Circuit.

CRIMINAL PROCESS, Fourth Edition (1987), with 1990 Supplement

Lloyd L. Weinreb, Professor of Law, Harvard University.

DAMAGES, Second Edition (1952)

Charles T. McCormick, late Professor of Law, University of Texas.
William F. Fritz, late Professor of Law, University of Texas.

DECEDENTS' ESTATES AND TRUSTS, Seventh Edition (1988)

John Ritchie, late Professor of Law, University of Virginia.
Neill H. Alford, Jr., Professor of Law, University of Virginia.
Richard W. Effland, late Professor of Law, Arizona State University.

DISPUTE RESOLUTION, Processes of (1989)

John S. Murray, President and Executive Director of The Conflict Clinic, Inc., George Mason University.
Alan Scott Rau, Professor of Law, University of Texas.
Edward F. Sherman, Professor of Law, University of Texas.

DOMESTIC RELATIONS, see also Family Law

DOMESTIC RELATIONS, Second Edition (1990)

Walter Wadlington, Professor of Law, University of Virginia.

EMPLOYMENT DISCRIMINATION, Second Edition (1987), with 1990 Supplement

Joel W. Friedman, Professor of Law, Tulane University.
George M. Strickler, Professor of Law, Tulane University.

EMPLOYMENT LAW, Second Edition (1991), with Statutory Supplement

Mark A. Rothstein, Professor of Law, University of Houston.
Andria S. Knapp, Visiting Professor of Law, Golden Gate University.
Lance Liebman, Professor of Law, Harvard University.

ENERGY LAW (1983) with 1986 Case Supplement

Donald N. Zillman, Professor of Law, University of Utah.
Laurence Lattman, Dean of Mines and Engineering, University of Utah.

ENTERPRISE ORGANIZATION, Fourth Edition (1987), with 1987 Corporation and Partnership Statutes, Rules and Forms Supplement

Alfred F. Conard, Professor of Law, University of Michigan.
Robert L. Knauss, Dean of the Law School, University of Houston.
Stanley Siegel, Professor of Law, University of California, Los Angeles.

ENVIRONMENTAL POLICY LAW 1985 Edition, with 1985 Problems Supplement (Supplement in association with Ronald H. Rosenberg, Professor of Law, College of William and Mary)

Thomas J. Schoenbaum, Professor of Law, University of Georgia.

EQUITY, see also Remedies

EQUITY, RESTITUTION AND DAMAGES, Second Edition (1974)

Robert Childres, late Professor of Law, Northwestern University.
William F. Johnson, Jr., Professor of Law, New York University.

ESTATE PLANNING, Second Edition (1982), with 1985 Case, Text and Documentary Supplement

David Westfall, Professor of Law, Harvard University.

ETHICS, see Legal Profession, Professional Responsibility, and Social Responsibilities

ETHICS OF LAWYERING, THE LAW AND (1990)

Geoffrey C. Hazard, Jr., Professor of Law, Yale University.
Susan P. Koniak, Professor of Law, University of Pittsburgh.

ETHICS AND PROFESSIONAL RESPONSIBILITY (1981) (Reprinted from THE LAWYERING PROCESS)

Gary Bellow, Professor of Law, Harvard University.
Bea Moulton, Legal Services Corporation.

EVIDENCE, Sixth Edition (1988 Reprint), with 1990 Case Supplement (Supplement edited in association with Roger C. Park, Professor of Law, University of Minnesota)

John Kaplan, Professor of Law, Stanford University.
Jon R. Waltz, Professor of Law, Northwestern University.

EVIDENCE, Eighth Edition (1988), with Rules, Statute and Case Supplement (1990)

Jack B. Weinstein, Chief Judge, United States District Court.
John H. Mansfield, Professor of Law, Harvard University.
Norman Abrams, Professor of Law, University of California, Los Angeles.
Margaret Berger, Professor of Law, Brooklyn Law School.

FAMILY LAW, see also Domestic Relations

FAMILY LAW Second Edition (1985), with 1991 Supplement

Judith C. Areen, Professor of Law, Georgetown University.

FAMILY LAW AND CHILDREN IN THE LEGAL SYSTEM, STATUTORY MATERIALS (1981)

Walter Wadlington, Professor of Law, University of Virginia.

FEDERAL COURTS, Eighth Edition (1988), with 1990 Supplement

Charles T. McCormick, late Professor of Law, University of Texas.
James H. Chadbourn, late Professor of Law, Harvard University.
Charles Alan Wright, Professor of Law, University of Texas, Austin.

FEDERAL COURTS AND THE FEDERAL SYSTEM, Hart and Wechsler's Third Edition (1988), with 1989 Case Supplement, and the Judicial Code and Rules of Procedure in the Federal Courts (1989)

Paul M. Bator, Professor of Law, University of Chicago.

Daniel J. Meltzer, Professor of Law, Harvard University.

Paul J. Mishkin, Professor of Law, University of California, Berkeley.

David L. Shapiro, Professor of Law, Harvard University.

FEDERAL COURTS AND THE LAW OF FEDERAL–STATE RELATIONS, Second Edition (1989), with 1990 Supplement

Peter W. Low, Professor of Law, University of Virginia.

John C. Jeffries, Jr., Professor of Law, University of Virginia.

FEDERAL PUBLIC LAND AND RESOURCES LAW, Second Edition (1987), with 1990 Case Supplement and 1990 Statutory Supplement

George C. Coggins, Professor of Law, University of Kansas.

Charles F. Wilkinson, Professor of Law, University of Oregon.

FEDERAL RULES OF CIVIL PROCEDURE and Selected Other Procedural Provisions, 1990 Edition

FEDERAL TAXATION, see Taxation

FOOD AND DRUG LAW (1980), with Statutory Supplement

Richard A. Merrill, Dean of the School of Law, University of Virginia.

Peter Barton Hutt, Esq.

FUTURE INTERESTS (1970)

Howard R. Williams, Professor of Law, Stanford University.

FUTURE INTERESTS AND ESTATE PLANNING (1961), with 1962 Supplement

W. Barton Leach, late Professor of Law, Harvard University.

James K. Logan, formerly Dean of the Law School, University of Kansas.

GOVERNMENT CONTRACTS, FEDERAL, Successor Edition (1985), with 1989 Supplement

John W. Whelan, Professor of Law, Hastings College of the Law.

GOVERNMENT REGULATION: FREE ENTERPRISE AND ECONOMIC ORGANIZATION, Sixth Edition (1985)

Louis B. Schwartz, Professor of Law, Hastings College of the Law.

John J. Flynn, Professor of Law, University of Utah.

Harry First, Professor of Law, New York University.

HEALTH CARE LAW AND POLICY (1988)

Clark C. Havighurst, Professor of Law, Duke University.

HINCKLEY, JOHN W., JR., TRIAL OF: A Case Study of the Insanity Defense (1986)

Peter W. Low, Professor of Law, University of Virginia.

John C. Jeffries, Jr., Professor of Law, University of Virginia.

Richard C. Bonnie, Professor of Law, University of Virginia.

INJUNCTIONS, Second Edition (1984)

Owen M. Fiss, Professor of Law, Yale University.

Doug Rendleman, Professor of Law, College of William and Mary.

INSTITUTIONAL INVESTORS, (1978)

David L. Ratner, Professor of Law, Cornell University.

UNIVERSITY CASEBOOK SERIES—Continued

INSURANCE, Second Edition (1985)

> William F. Young, Professor of Law, Columbia University.
> Eric M. Holmes, Professor of Law, University of Georgia.

INSURANCE LAW AND REGULATION (1990)

> Kenneth S. Abraham, University of Virginia.

INTERNATIONAL LAW, see also Transnational Legal Problems, Transnational Business Problems, and United Nations Law

INTERNATIONAL LAW IN CONTEMPORARY PERSPECTIVE (1981), with Essay Supplement

> Myres S. McDougal, Professor of Law, Yale University.
> W. Michael Reisman, Professor of Law, Yale University.

INTERNATIONAL LEGAL SYSTEM, Third Edition (1988), with Documentary Supplement

> Joseph Modeste Sweeney, Professor of Law, University of California, Hastings.
> Covey T. Oliver, Professor of Law, University of Pennsylvania.
> Noyes E. Leech, Professor of Law Emeritus, University of Pennsylvania.

INTRODUCTION TO LAW, see also Legal Method, On Law in Courts, and Dynamics of American Law

INTRODUCTION TO THE STUDY OF LAW (1970)

> E. Wayne Thode, late Professor of Law, University of Utah.
> Leon Lebowitz, Professor of Law, University of Texas.
> Lester J. Mazor, Professor of Law, University of Utah.

JUDICIAL CODE and Rules of Procedure in the Federal Courts, Students' Edition, 1989 Revision

> Daniel J. Meltzer, Professor of Law, Harvard University.
> David L. Shapiro, Professor of Law, Harvard University.

JURISPRUDENCE (Temporary Edition Hardbound) (1949)

> Lon L. Fuller, late Professor of Law, Harvard University.

JUVENILE, see also Children

JUVENILE JUSTICE PROCESS, Third Edition (1985)

> Frank W. Miller, Professor of Law, Washington University.
> Robert O. Dawson, Professor of Law, University of Texas.
> George E. Dix, Professor of Law, University of Texas.
> Raymond I. Parnas, Professor of Law, University of California, Davis.

LABOR LAW, Eleventh Edition (1991), with 1991 Statutory Supplement

> Archibald Cox, Professor of Law, Harvard University.
> Derek C. Bok, President, Harvard University.
> Robert A. Gorman, Professor of Law, University of Pennsylvania.
> Matthew W. Finkin, Professor of Law, University of Illinois.

LABOR LAW, Second Edition (1982), with Statutory Supplement

> Clyde W. Summers, Professor of Law, University of Pennsylvania.
> Harry H. Wellington, Dean of the Law School, Yale University.
> Alan Hyde, Professor of Law, Rutgers University.

MASS MEDIA LAW, Fourth Edition (1990)

Marc A. Franklin, Professor of Law, Stanford University.
David A. Anderson, Professor of Law, University of Texas.

MUNICIPAL CORPORATIONS, see Local Government Law

NEGOTIABLE INSTRUMENTS, see Commercial Paper

NEGOTIATION (1981) (Reprinted from THE LAWYERING PROCESS)

Gary Bellow, Professor of Law, Harvard Law School.
Bea Moulton, Legal Services Corporation.

NEW YORK PRACTICE, Fourth Edition (1978)

Herbert Peterfreund, Professor of Law, New York University.
Joseph M. McLaughlin, Dean of the Law School, Fordham University.

OIL AND GAS, Fifth Edition (1987)

Howard R. Williams, Professor of Law, Stanford University.
Richard C. Maxwell, Professor of Law, University of California, Los Angeles.
Charles J. Meyers, late Dean of the Law School, Stanford University.
Stephen F. Williams, Judge of the United States Court of Appeals.

ON LAW IN COURTS (1965)

Paul J. Mishkin, Professor of Law, University of California, Berkeley.
Clarence Morris, Professor of Law Emeritus, University of Pennsylvania.

PENSION AND EMPLOYEE BENEFIT LAW (1990)

John H. Langbein, Professor of Law, University of Chicago.
Bruce A. Wolk, Professor of Law, University of California, Davis.

PLEADING AND PROCEDURE, see Procedure, Civil

POLICE FUNCTION, Fifth Edition (1991)

Reprint of Chapters 1–10 of Miller, Dawson, Dix and Parnas's CRIMINAL
JUSTICE ADMINISTRATION, Fourth Edition.

**PREPARING AND PRESENTING THE CASE (1981) (Reprinted from THE LAW-
YERING PROCESS)**

Gary Bellow, Professor of Law, Harvard Law School.
Bea Moulton, Legal Services Corporation.

PROCEDURE (1988), with Procedure Supplement (1989)

Robert M. Cover, late Professor of Law, Yale Law School.
Owen M. Fiss, Professor of Law, Yale Law School.
Judith Resnik, Professor of Law, University of Southern California Law Center.

**PROCEDURE—CIVIL PROCEDURE, Second Edition (1974), with 1979 Supple-
ment**

The late James H. Chadbourn, Professor of Law, Harvard University.
A. Leo Levin, Professor of Law, University of Pennsylvania.
Philip Shuchman, Professor of Law, Cornell University.

PROCEDURE—CIVIL PROCEDURE, Sixth Edition (1990)

Richard H. Field, late Professor of Law, Harvard University.
Benjamin Kaplan, Professor of Law Emeritus, Harvard University.
Kevin M. Clermont, Professor of Law, Cornell University.

PROCEDURE—CIVIL PROCEDURE, Fifth Edition (1990)

Maurice Rosenberg, Professor of Law, Columbia University.
Hans Smit, Professor of Law, Columbia University.
Rochelle C. Dreyfuss, Professor of Law, New York University.

PROCEDURE—PLEADING AND PROCEDURE: State and Federal, Sixth Edition (1989), with 1990 Case Supplement

David W. Louisell, late Professor of Law, University of California, Berkeley.
Geoffrey C. Hazard, Jr., Professor of Law, Yale University.
Colin C. Tait, Professor of Law, University of Connecticut.

PROCEDURE—FEDERAL RULES OF CIVIL PROCEDURE, 1990 Edition

PRODUCTS LIABILITY AND SAFETY, Second Edition, (1989), with 1989 Statutory Supplement

W. Page Keeton, Professor of Law, University of Texas.
David G. Owen, Professor of Law, University of South Carolina.
John E. Montgomery, Professor of Law, University of South Carolina.
Michael D. Green, Professor of Law, University of Iowa

PROFESSIONAL RESPONSIBILITY, Fifth Edition (1991), with 1991 Selected Standards on Professional Responsibility Supplement

Thomas D. Morgan, Professor of Law, George Washington University.
Ronald D. Rotunda, Professor of Law, University of Illinois.

PROPERTY, Sixth Edition (1990)

John E. Cribbet, Professor of Law, University of Illinois.
Corwin W. Johnson, Professor of Law, University of Texas.
Roger W. Findley, Professor of Law, University of Illinois.
Ernest E. Smith, Professor of Law, University of Texas.

PROPERTY—PERSONAL (1953)

S. Kenneth Skolfield, late Professor of Law Emeritus, Boston University.

PROPERTY—PERSONAL, Third Edition (1954)

Everett Fraser, late Dean of the Law School Emeritus, University of Minnesota.
Third Edition by Charles W. Taintor, late Professor of Law, University of Pittsburgh.

PROPERTY—INTRODUCTION, TO REAL PROPERTY, Third Edition (1954)

Everett Fraser, late Dean of the Law School Emeritus, University of Minnesota.

PROPERTY—FUNDAMENTALS OF MODERN REAL PROPERTY, Second Edition (1982), with 1985 Supplement

Edward H. Rabin, Professor of Law, University of California, Davis.

PROPERTY, REAL (1984), with 1988 Supplement

Paul Goldstein, Professor of Law, Stanford University.

PROSECUTION AND ADJUDICATION, Fourth Edition (1991)

Reprint of Chapters 11–26 of Miller, Dawson, Dix and Parnas's CRIMINAL JUSTICE ADMINISTRATION, Fourth Edition.

PSYCHIATRY AND LAW, see Mental Health, see also Hinckley, Trial of

PUBLIC UTILITY LAW, see Free Enterprise, also Regulated Industries

REAL ESTATE PLANNING, Third Edition (1989), with Revised Problem and Statutory Supplement (1991)

Norton L. Steuben, Professor of Law, University of Colorado.

REAL ESTATE TRANSACTIONS, Revised Second Edition (1988), with Statute, Form and Problem Supplement (1988)

Paul Goldstein, Professor of Law, Stanford University.

RECEIVERSHIP AND CORPORATE REORGANIZATION, see Creditors' Rights

REGULATED INDUSTRIES, Second Edition, (1976)

William K. Jones, Professor of Law, Columbia University.

REMEDIES, Second Edition (1987)

Edward D. Re, Chief Judge, U. S. Court of International Trade.

REMEDIES, (1989)

Elaine W. Shoben, Professor of Law, University of Illinois.
Wm. Murray Tabb, Professor of Law, Baylor University.

SALES, Second Edition (1986)

Marion W. Benfield, Jr., Professor of Law, University of Illinois.
William D. Hawkland, Chancellor, Louisiana State Law Center.

SALES AND SALES FINANCING, Fifth Edition (1984)

John Honnold, Professor of Law, University of Pennsylvania.

SALES LAW AND THE CONTRACTING PROCESS, Second Edition (1991)

(Reprinted from Commercial Transactions, Second Edition (1991)
Alan Schwartz, Professor of Law, Yale University.
Robert E. Scott, Professor of Law, University of Virginia.

SECURED TRANSACTIONS IN PERSONAL PROPERTY, Second Edition (1987) (Reprinted from COMMERCIAL LAW, Second Edition (1987))

Robert L. Jordan, Professor of Law, University of California, Los Angeles.
William D. Warren, Professor of Law, University of California, Los Angeles.

SECURITIES REGULATION, Sixth Edition (1987), with 1990 Selected Statutes, Rules and Forms Supplement and 1990 Cases and Releases Supplement

Richard W. Jennings, Professor of Law, University of California, Berkeley.
Harold Marsh, Jr., Member of California Bar.

SECURITIES REGULATION, Second Edition (1988), with Statute, Rule and Form Supplement (1988)

Larry D. Soderquist, Professor of Law, Vanderbilt University.

SECURITY INTERESTS IN PERSONAL PROPERTY, Second Edition (1987)

Douglas G. Baird, Professor of Law, University of Chicago.
Thomas H. Jackson, Dean of the Law School, University of Virginia.

SECURITY INTERESTS IN PERSONAL PROPERTY (1985) (Reprinted from Sales and Sales Financing, Fifth Edition)

John Honnold, Professor of Law, University of Pennsylvania.

SELECTED STANDARDS ON PROFESSIONAL RESPONSIBILITY, 1991 Edition

UNIVERSITY CASEBOOK SERIES—Continued

SELECTED STATUTES AND INTERNATIONAL AGREEMENTS ON UNFAIR COMPETITION, TRADEMARK, COPYRIGHT AND PATENT, 1989 Edition

SELECTED STATUTES ON TRUSTS AND ESTATES, 1991 Edition

SOCIAL RESPONSIBILITIES OF LAWYERS, Case Studies (1988)

Philip B. Heymann, Professor of Law, Harvard University.
Lance Liebman, Professor of Law, Harvard University.

SOCIAL SCIENCE IN LAW, Second Edition (1990)

John Monahan, Professor of Law, University of Virginia.
Laurens Walker, Professor of Law, University of Virginia.

TAXATION, FEDERAL INCOME (1989)

Stephen B. Cohen, Professor of Law, Georgetown University

TAXATION, FEDERAL INCOME, Second Edition (1988), with 1990 Supplement (Supplement edited in association with Deborah H. Schenk, Professor of Law, New York University)

Michael J. Graetz, Professor of Law, Yale University.

TAXATION, FEDERAL INCOME, Sixth Edition (1987)

James J. Freeland, Professor of Law, University of Florida.
Stephen A. Lind, Professor of Law, University of Florida and University of California, Hastings.
Richard B. Stephens, late Professor of Law Emeritus, University of Florida.

TAXATION, FEDERAL INCOME, Successor Edition (1986), with 1990 Legislative Supplement

Stanley S. Surrey, late Professor of Law, Harvard University.
Paul R. McDaniel, Professor of Law, Boston College.
Hugh J. Ault, Professor of Law, Boston College.
Stanley A. Koppelman, Professor of Law, Boston University.

TAXATION, FEDERAL INCOME, OF BUSINESS ORGANIZATIONS (1991)

Paul R. McDaniel, Professor of Law, Boston College.
Hugh J. Ault, Professor of Law, Boston College.
Martin J. McMahon, Jr., Professor of Law, University of Kentucky.
Daniel L. Simmons, Professor of Law, University of California, Davis.

TAXATION, FEDERAL INCOME, OF PARTNERSHIPS AND S CORPORATIONS (1991)

Paul R. McDaniel, Professor of Law, Boston College.
Hugh J. Ault, Professor of Law, Boston College.
Martin J. McMahon, Jr., Professor of Law, University of Kentucky.
Daniel L. Simmons, Professor of Law, University of California, Davis.

TAXATION, FEDERAL INCOME, OIL AND GAS, NATURAL RESOURCES TRANSACTIONS (1990)

Peter C. Maxfield, Professor of Law, University of Wyoming.
James L. Houghton, CPA, Partner, Ernst and Young.
James R. Gaar, CPA, Partner, Ernst and Young.

TAXATION, FEDERAL WEALTH TRANSFER, Successor Edition (1987)

Stanley S. Surrey, late Professor of Law, Harvard University.
Paul R. McDaniel, Professor of Law, Boston College.
Harry L. Gutman, Professor of Law, University of Pennsylvania.

UNIVERSITY CASEBOOK SERIES—Continued

TAXATION, FUNDAMENTALS OF CORPORATE, Second Edition (1987), with 1989 Supplement

Stephen A. Lind, Professor of Law, University of Florida and University of California, Hastings.
Stephen Schwarz, Professor of Law, University of California, Hastings.
Daniel J. Lathrope, Professor of Law, University of California, Hastings.
Joshua Rosenberg, Professor of Law, University of San Francisco.

TAXATION, FUNDAMENTALS OF PARTNERSHIP, Second Edition (1988)

Stephen A. Lind, Professor of Law, University of Florida and University of California, Hastings.
Stephen Schwarz, Professor of Law, University of California, Hastings.
Daniel J. Lathrope, Professor of Law, University of California, Hastings.
Joshua Rosenberg, Professor of Law, University of San Francisco.

TAXATION, PROBLEMS IN THE FEDERAL INCOME TAXATION OF PARTNERSHIPS AND CORPORATIONS, Second Edition (1986)

Norton L. Steuben, Professor of Law, University of Colorado.
William J. Turnier, Professor of Law, University of North Carolina.

TAXATION, PROBLEMS IN THE FUNDAMENTALS OF FEDERAL INCOME, Second Edition (1985)

Norton L. Steuben, Professor of Law, University of Colorado.
William J. Turnier, Professor of Law, University of North Carolina.

TORT LAW AND ALTERNATIVES, Fourth Edition (1987)

Marc A. Franklin, Professor of Law, Stanford University.
Robert L. Rabin, Professor of Law, Stanford University.

TORTS, Eighth Edition (1988)

William L. Prosser, late Professor of Law, University of California, Hastings.
John W. Wade, Professor of Law, Vanderbilt University.
Victor E. Schwartz, Adjunct Professor of Law, Georgetown University.

TORTS, Third Edition (1976)

Harry Shulman, late Dean of the Law School, Yale University.
Fleming James, Jr., Professor of Law Emeritus, Yale University.
Oscar S. Gray, Professor of Law, University of Maryland.

TRADE REGULATION, Third Edition (1990)

Milton Handler, Professor of Law Emeritus, Columbia University.
Harlan M. Blake, Professor of Law, Columbia University.
Robert Pitofsky, Professor of Law, Georgetown University.
Harvey J. Goldschmid, Professor of Law, Columbia University.

TRADE REGULATION, see Antitrust

TRANSNATIONAL BUSINESS PROBLEMS (1986)

Detlev F. Vagts, Professor of Law, Harvard University.

TRANSNATIONAL LEGAL PROBLEMS, Third Edition (1986) with 1991 Revised Edition of Documentary Supplement

Henry J. Steiner, Professor of Law, Harvard University.
Detlev F. Vagts, Professor of Law, Harvard University.

TRIAL, see also Evidence, Making the Record, Lawyering Process and Preparing and Presenting the Case

UNIVERSITY CASEBOOK SERIES—Continued

TRUSTS, Fifth Edition (1978)

George G. Bogert, late Professor of Law Emeritus, University of Chicago.
Dallin H. Oaks, President, Brigham Young University.

TRUSTS AND ESTATES, SELECTED STATUTES ON, 1991 Edition

TRUSTS AND SUCCESSION (Palmer's), Fourth Edition (1983)

Richard V. Wellman, Professor of Law, University of Georgia.
Lawrence W. Waggoner, Professor of Law, University of Michigan.
Olin L. Browder, Jr., Professor of Law, University of Michigan.

UNFAIR COMPETITION, see Competitive Process and Business Torts

WATER RESOURCE MANAGEMENT, Third Edition (1988)

The late Charles J. Meyers, formerly Dean, Stanford University Law School.
A. Dan Tarlock, Professor of Law, IIT Chicago-Kent College of Law.
James N. Corbridge, Jr., Chancellor, University of Colorado at Boulder, and
    Professor of Law, University of Colorado.
David H. Getches, Professor of Law, University of Colorado.

WILLS AND ADMINISTRATION, Fifth Edition (1961)

Philip Mechem, late Professor of Law, University of Pennsylvania.
Thomas E. Atkinson, late Professor of Law, New York University.

WRITING AND ANALYSIS IN THE LAW, Second Edition (1991)

Helene S. Shapo, Professor of Law, Northwestern University
Marilyn R. Walter, Professor of Law, Brooklyn Law School
Elizabeth Fajans, Writing Specialist, Brooklyn Law School

University Casebook Series

THE LAW AND ETHICS
OF LAWYERING

By

GEOFFREY C. HAZARD, JR.
Sterling Professor of Law, Yale Law School

and

SUSAN P. KONIAK
Assistant Professor of Law
University of Pittsburgh School of Law

Westbury, New York
THE FOUNDATION PRESS, INC.
1990

Library of Congress Cataloging-in-Publication Data

Hazard, Geoffrey C.

   The law and ethics of lawyering / by Geoffrey C. Hazard, Jr. and
Susan P. Koniak.

      p.   cm. — (University casebook series)

   ISBN 0–88277–786–6

   1. Legal ethics—United States—Cases. 2. Lawyers—United States
—Discipline—Cases. I. Koniak, Susan P. II. Title. III. Series.

KF306.A4H39 1990

174'.3'0973—dc20

90–2764

CIP

H. & K. Law & Ethics of Lawyering UCB

1st Reprint—1991

To the memory of our friend Robert M. Cover

*

PREFACE

This book seeks to fulfill its title. Thus, first of all it contains cases. Cases are at the same time sources of legal doctrine in the law governing law practice, a mirror of the minds of judges in interpreting what lawyers do, and "war stories" of difficult situations that lawyers confront. This book also contains statutes and rules of professional conduct. Statutes reflect public sentiment about right and wrong in transactions in which lawyers are involved, such as managing business enterprise, buying and selling property, administering criminal justice, and paying taxes. The rules of professional conduct are formulated primarily through the authorship of lawyers. Hence, those rules are a mirror of the minds of lawyers in interpreting their own work. All of these legal sources project visions of the practice of law, but the visions are not the same. Therein lies an important part of the tale.

The book also contains source materials on ethics and morals, from Plato and since. The practice of law is not fully intelligible without reference to these great philosophical issues in ethics and to ethical standards of the community at large. Community ethical standards inform the minds of clients and opposite parties with whom a lawyer deals, the minds of officials and other lawyers with whom lawyers must work, and the minds of jurors, judges and disciplinary committees before whom a lawyer may be called to account. Neither is the practice of law fully intelligible without reference to the inner mind of each of us who engages in law practice. Every act a lawyer does, or fails to do, appears somehow in her own mind's eye. The accumulation of these impressions is not only professional experience but personal identity as well. Every lawyer should continually ask herself: what kind of memories will this leave with me. Contemplating the morality of practicing law does not come too soon in law school. Indeed if not started then it may come too late, or never.

The materials in the book also reflect the variousness of lawyers' situations in practice. Some of the cases and rules involve big firm corporate practice. Others involve small firm lawyers and sole practitioners and such transactions as drafting a will, handling a divorce, or defending a criminal accused. Situation in practice makes a difference in the kind of matters a lawyer handles and therefore the kind of ethical problems she encounters. Situation in practice also makes a difference in the kinds of political, economic and moral resources a lawyer has for dealing with ethical problems. In these respects, lawyers are very different from each other. Yet they are alike in being governed by a common body of law and professional lore and being obliged, in the end, to resolve ethical dilemmas alone on the basis of personal judgment.

The book covers a wide range not only in the foregoing respects but in fields of legal subject matter. We include distillates of criminal law and procedure, civil procedure, evidence law, tort law, contract law, securities law, and corporation law, and make reference to tax law and the law of wills, estate planning, and marital dissolution. This cannot be avoided if the problems of legal ethics are to be adequately comprehended. The stuff of law practice includes all legal subjects, and law practice performed competently and ethically requires dealing with unfamiliar areas of law. In the "pervasive method" of teaching legal ethics, ethical problems are implanted in the context of a body of some other law in some other course. This book represents the "pervasive method" in reverse.

G.C.H., Jr.
S.P.K.

January, 1990

ACKNOWLEDGEMENTS

We thank the hundreds of students and lawyers in our professional experience who have helped us to try and understand this subject. Special thanks go to Roger C. Cramton of Cornell Law School, whose detailed comments on an earlier draft of this book were extremely helpful. We thank LuAnn Driscoll, Ruth Jencks, Karen Knochel, Darleen Mocello, Carolyn Rohan, Barbara Salopek, and Hillary Sonet, who have typed various portions of this manuscript. We thank Kathleen C. Cleary, Andrew B. Klaber, Kristen A. Lee, Daniel Lee and Lauren Schlecker, research assistants at the Law School of the University of Pittsburgh, who have worked so earnestly on the completion of this project. Especially, we thank Margaret M. Egler, J.D. 1988, University of Pittsburgh, for her tireless efforts, her critical eye, her good spirit and her sincere dedication to this project.

We thank each other for a lovely law partnership.

G.C.H., Jr.
S.P.K.

Having completed this, my first major work, I must acknowledge my personal debt to my parents, Morris and Esther Koniak, whose love for each other and their children is an important source of my faith; to my brother Jay, whose perseverance and good cheer in facing many hardships inspires me; to Michael E. Robinson, my friend, who worked beside me through many a wee hour of the morning and whose insight, generosity and patience were invaluable throughout this project; and to my other close friends, who understand how much they mean to me despite this brief and collective reference. Finally, I thank John D. Geanakoplos, whom I cherish for all he is. By helping me believe in myself, he made this book possible.

S.P.K.

ACKNOWLEDGEMENTS

American Bar Association, Formal Opinion 352 (July 7, 1985). Copyright © by the American Bar Association and reprinted with its permission.

Association of the Bar of the City of New York, Committee on Professional and Judicial Ethics, Inquiry Reference 80–23. Reprinted with permission.

Derrick A. Bell, Jr., Serving Two Masters: Integration Ideals and Client Interests in School Desegregation Litigation, 85 Yale L.J. 470 (1976). Reprinted with permission of the Yale Law Journal Company and Fred B. Rothman & Company.

Sissela Bok, Lying: Moral Choice in Public and Private Life (1978). Copyright © 1978 by Sissela Bok and reprinted with her permission and the permission of Pantheon Books.

Sissela Bok, Secrets (1982). Copyright © 1983 by Sissela Bok and reprinted with her permission and the permission of Pantheon Books.

Louis D. Brandeis, The Opportunity in the Law (1905), in Brandeis, Business: a Profession (1914).

Kathleen F. Brickey, Tainted Assets and the Right to Counsel—The Money Laundering Conundrum, 66 Wash.U.L.Q. 47 (1988). Reprinted with permission.

John C. Coffee, Jr., Understanding the Plaintiff's Attorney: The Implications of Economic Theory for Private Enforcement of Law Through Class and Derivative Actions, 86 Col.L.Rev. 669 (1986). Reprinted with permission.

Robert M. Cover, Violence and the Word, 95 Yale L.J. 1601 (1986). Reprinted with permission of the Yale Law Journal Company and Fred B. Rothman & Company.

Norman Dorsen and Leon Friedman, Disorder in the Courtroom (1973). Copyright © 1973 by Association of the Bar of the City of New York. Reprinted with permission.

Federal Bar Association, Professional Ethics Committee, Opinion 73–1: The Government Client and Confidentiality, 32 Fed.B.J. 71 (1973). Reprinted with permission of the Federal Bar Association and the Federal Bar Journal.

Monroe H. Freedman, Perjury The Lawyer's Trilemma, 1 Litigation 26 (No. 1 Winter, 1975). Reprinted with permission of the Section of Litigation, American Bar Association.

James J. Fuld, Lawyers' Standards and Responsibilities in Rendering Opinions, 33 Bus.Law. 1295 (1978). Copyright © 1978 by the American Bar Association and reprinted with its permission and the permission of its Section of Business Law. All rights reserved.

William J. Genego, The Future of Effective Assistance of Counsel: Performance Standards and Competent Representation, 22 American

Crim.L.Rev. 181 (1984). Copyright © 1984 jointly by American Criminal Law Review and the author and reprinted with the permission of both.

Carol Gilligan, In a Different Voice (1982). Copyright © 1980 by Carol Gilligan. Reprinted with permission of the publisher Harvard University Press.

Erving Goffman, Asylums: Essays on the Social Situation of Mental Patients and Other Inmates (1961). Copyright © 1961 by Erving Goffman. Reprinted with permission.

Robert W. Gordon, The Ideal and the Actual in the Law, in Gawalt, ed., the New High Priests: Lawyers in Post–Civil War America (1984). Reprinted with permission.

Geoffrey C. Hazard, Jr., Disciplinary Process Needs Major Reform, National Law Journal, August 1, 1988, p. 13. Reprinted with permission.

Geoffrey C. Hazard, Jr., Ethics in the Practice of Law (1978). Reprinted with permission of Yale University Press.

Geoffrey C. Hazard, Jr., How Far May a Lawyer Go in Assisting a Client in Legally Wrongful Conduct?, 35 U.Miami L.Rev. 669 (1981). Reprinted with the permission of the University of Miami Law Review.

Geoffrey C. Hazard, Jr., Permissive Affirmative Action on Behalf of Blacks, 1987 U. Copyright 1987 University of Illinois Law Review, Board of Trustees of the University of Illinois. Reprinted with permission.

Geoffrey C. Hazard, Jr., Rectification of Client Fraud: Death and Revival of a Professional Norm, 33 Emory L.J. 271 (1984). Reprinted with permission of the Emory Law Journal.

Geoffrey C. Hazard, Jr., Securing Courtroom Decorum, 80 Yale L.J. 433 (1970). Reprinted with permission of the Yale Law Journal Company and Fred B. Rothman & Company.

Geoffrey C. Hazard, Jr., Triangular Lawyer Relationships: An Exploratory Analysis, 1 Geo.J. of Leg. Ethics 15 (1987). Reprinted with permission of the Georgetown Journal of Legal Ethics.

Kenney F. Hegland, Moral Dilemmas in Teaching Trial Advocacy, 32 J. of Leg.Ed. 69 (1982). Reprinted with permission of the author and the Journal of Legal Education.

Ronald L. Hirsch, Are You on Target?, The Barrister Magazine, Vol. 12, No. 1, p. 17. Reprinted with permission.

Oliver W. Holmes, The Path of Law in Collected Legal Papers (1920), also appears 10 Harv.L.Rev. 457 (1897).

David Hoffman, A Course in Legal Study (1836).

Robert Keeton, Trial Tactics and Methods (2d ed. 1973). Copyright © 1973 by Little, Brown and Company and reprinted with its permission.

Athelia Knight and Joseph Bouchard, Lawyer Refuses to Reveal Name of Child Moslester, Washington Post, January 13, 1980, p. D3. Reprinted with permission.

Steven C. Krane, The Attorney Unshackled: SEC Rule 2(e) Violates Clients' Sixth Amendment Right to Counsel, 57 Notre Dame Lawyer 50 (1981). Copyright © 1981 by Notre Dame Law Review, University of Notre Dame. Reprinted with permission.

Charles R. Lawrence III, The Id, the Ego and Equal Protection: Reckoning with Unconscious Racism, 39 Stan.L.Rev. 317 (1987). Copyright © 1987 by the Board of Trustees of the Leland Stanford Junior University. Reprinted with permission.

Luban, Paternalism and the Legal Profession, 1981 Wis.L.Rev. 454. Reprinted with the permission of the Wisconsin Law Review.

Merton E. Marks, The Lawyers and the Realtors, 49 ABA J. 139 (1963).

T. McPike and Mark Harrison, Lawyer Discipline Since 1970, in ALI–ABA, Law Practice Quality Evaluation: An Appraisal of Peer Review and other Measures to Enhance Professional Performance (September 10–12, 1987). Reprinted with permission of the American Law Institute—American Bar Association Committee on Professional Education.

Plato, Gorgias in the Dialogues of Plato, translated by Benjamin Jowett (1898). Copyright © 1898 by D. Appleton and Company.

Deborah L. Rhode, Class Conflicts in Class Actions, 34 Stan.L.Rev. 1183 (1982). Copyright © 1982 by the Board of Trustees of the Leland Stanford Junior University. Reprinted with permission.

Deborah L. Rhode, Perspectives on Professional Women, Stan.L. Rev. 1163 (1988). Copyright © 1988 by the Board of Trustees of the Leland Stanford Junior University. Reprinted with permission.

Douglas E. Rosenthal, Lawyer and Client, Who's in Charge? Copyright © 1974 by the Russell Sage Foundation and reprinted with its permission.

Eric Schnapper, Legal Ethics and the Government Lawyer, 32 The Record 649 (1979).

Geraldine Segal, Blacks in the Law (University of Pennsylvania Press 1985). Reprinted with permission.

William H. Simon, The Ideology of Advocacy, 1978 Wisconsin Law Review 30. Copyright © 1978 Wisconsin Law Review. Reprinted with the permission of the Wisconsin Law Review.

Harlan Fiske Stone, The Public Influence of the Bar, 48 Harv.L.Rev. 1 (1934). Reprinted with permission of the Harvard Law Review.

Richard H. Underwood, Adversary Ethics: More Dirty Tricks, 6 Am.J. Trial Advoc. 265 (Fall 1982). Copyright © 1982 by American Journal of Trial Advocacy, Cumberland School of Law of Samford University, Birmingham, Alambama and reprinted with its permission. All rights reserved.

ACKNOWLEDGEMENTS

Richard Wasserstrom, Lawyers as Professionals: Some Moral Issues, 5 Human Rights 1 (1975). Reprinted with permission.

*

SUMMARY OF CONTENTS

TABLE OF CONTENTS

TABLE OF CONTENTS

TABLE OF CONTENTS

Page

TABLE OF CONTENTS

TABLE OF CASES

Principal cases are in italic type. Non-principal cases are in roman type. References are to Pages.

li

*

TABLE OF OTHER AUTHORITIES

TABLE OF OTHER AUTHORITIES

TABLE OF OTHER AUTHORITIES

TABLE OF OTHER AUTHORITIES

THE LAW AND ETHICS
OF LAWYERING

*

Chapter I

THE RELATIONSHIP OF LAW, THE LAWYER, AND ETHICS

A. INTRODUCTION

GEOFFREY C. HAZARD, Jr., ETHICS IN THE PRACTICE OF LAW (1978)

pp. 1–3, 11–14, 19–21.*

In much of literature the idea of an ethical lawyer is regarded as a contradiction in terms. Thus Shakespeare: "quiddities . . . and tricks;" "the first thing we do, let's kill all the lawyers." Thus Burke: "It is not what a lawyer tells me I may do; but what humanity, reason, and justice, tell me I ought to do." Thus Sandburg: "Why is there always a secret singing when a lawyer cashes in?" Thus Judge Learned Hand: "About trials hang a suspicion of trickery and a sense of a result depending upon cajolery or worse." Folklore and popular opinion similarly reflect deep, probably ineradicable suspicion of lawyers' honesty and integrity. Even within the legal profession an ethically exemplary lawyer is probably taken to be an idealization rather than a descriptive category.

This book, however, is about an ethical lawyer. It assumes that someone can be ethical while being a lawyer, but is an inquiry into the sense and context in which this assumption might be sustained. The inquiry ought therefore to begin by stating what is meant by *ethics*. As used here, *ethics* refers to imperatives regarding the welfare of others that are recognized as binding upon a person's conduct in some more immediate and binding sense than *law* and in some more general and impersonal sense than *morals*. This definition is narrower than those of the philosophers. At least in some such definitions, law, morals, and ethics are a part of a general subject that includes all aspects of the concept of obligation. Moreover, among the various systems of ethics there are ones that deny the existence or even the intelligibility of an imperative regarding the welfare of others. In these systems, the sense of self is the only thing that can or should be given regard or, indeed, the only thing that can be said to exist. But in these systems it also seems impossible coherently to condemn another person's conduct as unethical, which is the problem that both lawyers and their ethical critics are concerned with. So, while acknowledging the place in the philosophical universe of what are termed ethical egoism and radical ethical passivity, our concern here is with the relationships between rules that are believed to exist and the conduct they are thought to refer to.

Even when this is taken as a place of beginning, there remain serious questions as to what ethical rules are all about. For example, they can be regarded as moral sentiments that have attained a certain publicity and formality but which remain matters of personal taste and conviction, like preferences in art. On the other hand, they can be regarded as a subspecies of legislation—rules that differ from law only in that their enforcement is relatively informal. On another plane, ethics can be considered a process of subjective deliberation leading to a decision about what one ought to do, or as an interpersonal exchange establishing what a group will say one should have done. Perhaps in the world of acting, judging, and being judged, ethics is best regarded as all of these—deliberation about how one should act given the existence of rules established by a consensus that one shares substantially if not unreservedly. But if this is ethics, how does it differ from law? Is it not simply a subspecies of legislation, having the sanction of authority and the pragmatic value of protecting order and autonomy, but not entailing any special moral obligation?

This leads to a second problem, peculiar to legal ethics. A lawyer is a legal technician. His training demythologizes the law and exposes his mind to the ambiguities of its commands, the frequently specious character of its policy, and the frailties of its interpreters. His professional function consists largely of providing counsel for clients about how to escape or mitigate the incidence of the law's obligations, or, if he is in law enforcement or activist law reform, on how to make the incidence of the law enforcement broader and deeper. The essence of these activities is the manipulation of governmental authority and the language and social processes through which that authority is exercised. The lawyer as counsellor gives at least lip service to the idea that the law's obligations are real, but he is bound to advise on the extent to which they are mere formalities or even less. What view should he take of rules that address his own conduct? Are they legal regulations whose burdens he may minimize or obviate by technical advice delivered professionally to himself, or are they strictures of conscience whose only meaning is in their observation?

Finally, the notion of ethics as applied to lawyers entails the difficulty, common to all professions, arising from the fact that there is a client in the picture. Ethics, seriously discussed as in philosophy, usually speak in terms that require treating all other persons on an equal footing. That is, their norms are cast as universals in which in principle every "other" is entitled to equal respect and consideration in the calculation of the actor's alternatives and course of action. On the other hand, professional ethics give priority to an "other" who is a client and in general require subordination of everyone else's interests to that of the client. Indeed, the central problem in professional ethics can be described as the tension between the client's preferred position resulting from the professional connection and the position of equality that everyone else is accorded by general principles of morality and legality.

. . .

. . . If the profession were uniformly an elite, it would be unlikely to have adopted a formal code and so the problem of disobeying it would not arise. Our relatively heterogeneous legal profession, however, seems to require positive legislation to resolve questions of conduct about which there is not a consensus. But positive legislation is inevitably simplistic to some degree, and thus an incomplete guide in delicate situations. A truly conscientious and self-confident practitioner would not feel bound to follow the letter of the law when his personal judgment dictated a different course. Hence, the concept of a principled violation of the rules of ethics introduces what is in fact a triple standard—conscience for some, code for others, and lip-service for still others. The point is not that this is a desirable state of affairs, but a state of affairs that necessarily results from the admission that conduct can be at the same time unlawful and right. And this returns us to the relativistic conception of ethics with which [many people begin.]

Another aspect of the question whether there can be an ethical lawyer appears in the disjunction of two ideas, one concerning the idea of "being" ethical and the other concerning the professional functions of lawyers.

As to the idea of being ethical: Ethical rules, like legal and moral rules, combine an element of approval or disapproval with an element of neutrality. The element of approval or disapproval is clear enough: Stealing is bad, betraying a trust is bad, being an accomplice to a crime is bad; fulfilling a contract is good, being helpful to the poor is good, paying the due amount of one's taxes is good, etc. The element of neutrality is less apparent. It arises from the fact that the approving or disapproving statements in ethical rules (or legal or moral rules) are expressed in categorical and abstract terms, referring not to specific instances but to types of instances. Thus, rules condemn stealing without indicating whether an individual instance of behavior *is* stealing, and approve fulfilling a contract without indicating that a specific contract was fulfilled. Rules go on to provide definitions of the kinds of things that are condemned and approved. The definitions can be more or less particularized. But no matter how particularized, the definitions are generalizations that apply to all situations coming within their terms. In the Biblical phrase, a rule is "no respecter of persons," that is, it is neutral among them.

To say that a particular person is "ethical" or "unethical," however, is to make a very particularized statement—indeed an intensely personal one. What is meant by such a statement is not that the person was or was not governed by ethical rules, but that he conducted himself in a way that displays a good or bad attitude or predisposition toward conformity to rules. The evaluation of a person's ethical standing is based on the assumption that he has had a choice between obedience and violation and that he reveals himself in the choices he makes.

Judgments of a person's ethical nature are of course tempered by recognition of special circumstances. Although the rules of behavior are framed in universal terms, only in a rigorous system taken seriously is there an expectation that they will be applied in that way. In folk ethics it is accepted that a person owes one kind of duty to a member of his family (or village or working group) and another to those with whom his relationship is more remote. However, when the possibility of such discrimination is sanctioned, it immediately opens up all kinds of questions along at least two lines: How does one rank the various "others" (spouse, child, cousin, next-door neighbor, fellow worker, compatriot, etc.) and how does one rank different kinds of obligations (to refrain from killing, to refrain from stealing, to forbear, to counsel forbearance by others, to come to another's aid, to sacrifice one's self for another, etc.). These questions pose great philosophic difficulties for all universalistic ethical conceptions, a fact that may explain why these conceptions are usually expressed in wholly abstract terms. They pose similar difficulties in practical application, so that folk ethics is a mishmash of homilies, legalistic formulations of various duty relationships, and resignation to subjective ethical choice.

We lead our daily lives by making ethical discriminations in these terms, but we are left defenseless against charges of inconsistency, casuistry, and discrimination. The burden of these charges can be lifted by attributing responsibility to the force of circumstances. Thus we say that no one volunteers to have to distinguish between his spouse and child, employer and customer, or neighbor and the building inspector. When events conscript us into doing so, we make ethical distinctions because we must in order to continue to function. At the level of principle, therefore, ethics consists of universals, while at the level of application it is a complicated scheme of excuses based on practical necessity.

The rules governing a lawyer's office are neither. They are not universal because they give a preferred position to clients; the office of lawyer begins with having to make distinctions among persons. At least in an immediate sense, they are not based on practical necessity, for no one is compelled to become a lawyer and, ordinarily at least, no lawyer is compelled to take a particular case. While in some situations a lawyer is supposed to act with perfect neutrality among others, a lawyer usually intervenes in relationships between others with a predisposition to treat the one who is his client with greater solicitude than he treats the other, regardless of the merits of their respective positions.

According to any "nonlegal" ethics, intervention on these terms is difficult to justify. It violates the principle of equal treatment inherent in all forms of universalist ethics. It lacks the involuntarism that is present in the ethical dilemmas of everyday life. For the lawyer does not merely encounter choices between the conflicting interests of others but makes a business out of such encounters, and takes partisan positions for money. Thus, his vocation violates the concepts of ethics held both by philosophers and in folklore. On this analysis, the idea of an ethical lawyer is therefore an impossibility.

. . .

The Code of Professional Responsibility [and the Model Rules of Professional Conduct] govern several matters that are very important to the public interest but irrelevant to [ethics as such.]. These include:

— Rules regulating competition among lawyers (advertising, solicitation, etc.), which are subsumed under the rubric of assisting "the legal profession in fulfilling its duty to make legal counsel available."

— Rules regulating competition from outside the profession. The substance of these rules is that lawyers should prevent nonlawyers from doing anything that is the "practice of law," whatever that may include.

— Rules requiring that a lawyer practice competently. Technical competence is presupposed in the present discussion.

— Certain special rules having to do with lawyers who hold public office, whose substance is that a lawyer should not use public office for the benefit of private clients, or take bribes.

Putting these aside, the Code [and the] [R]ules of [P]rofessional [C]onduct deal with essentially three problems:

— Confidentiality: What matters learned by a lawyer should he treat as secret, and from whom, and under what conditions may the secrecy be lifted?

— Conflict of interest: When and to what extent is a lawyer prohibited from acting because there is a conflict of interest between his clients or between himself and a client?

— Prohibited assistance: What kinds of things is a lawyer prohibited from doing for a client?

These are all tough problems, and not only for lawyers. What is perhaps not fully appreciated, by lawyers and laymen alike, is that similar problems arise in everyday life. If this fact were appreciated by lawyers, they might be able to perceive and to discuss the problems free of the introverted assumption that lawyers alone can appreciate their complex and stressful nature. If laymen recognized the similarity, they might regard the lawyers' ethical dilemmas with greater comprehension and perhaps even greater sympathy.

Many illustrations might be suggested from other walks of life, at work and at home, of problems involving confidentiality, conflict of interest, and prohibited assistance. A few will suffice to make the point. Thus, regarding confidentiality: What should a parent do who knows that his child has stolen something from a store? A pediatrician who discovers physical abuse of a child by its parents? A teacher who finds out that a student has been using drugs? An accountant who knows that his client is understating income for tax purposes? Regarding conflict of interest: Does a parent send a healthy child to college rather than send a sick one to the Mayo Clinic? A plant manager trim on safety systems to keep his company financially afloat? A doctor order hospitalization because medical insurance will not otherwise cover the patient? A supervisor commend a subordinate who may become a rival? Regarding prohibited assistance: Do you help a friend by lying to the police? Omit adverse information when asked to evaluate a former student or employee? Help sell stock that may be overvalued? Maintain the "character of a neighborhood" by not renting to a black?

If there is any peculiarity about these problems as they are confronted by lawyers, it is that a lawyer confronts them every day and is supposed to resolve them in a fashion that is compatible with a conception of his professional role. The [ethics codes] undertake to tell him how he should do so.

.   .   .

B. WHO AMONG US?

SPAULDING v. ZIMMERMAN

Supreme Court of Minnesota, 1962.
263 Minn. 346, 116 N.W.2d 704.

THOMAS GALLAGHER, JUSTICE.

Appeal from an order of the District Court of Douglas County vacating and setting aside a prior order of such court dated May 8, 1957, approving a settlement made on behalf of David Spaulding on March 5, 1957, at which time he was a minor of the age of 20 years; and in connection therewith, vacating and setting aside releases executed by him and his parents, a stipulation of dismissal, an order for dismissal with prejudice, and a judgment entered pursuant thereto.

The prior action was brought against defendants by Theodore Spaulding, as father and natural guardian of David Spaulding, for injuries sustained by David in an automobile accident, arising out of a collision which occurred August 24, 1956, between an automobile driven by John Zimmerman, in which David was a passenger, and one owned by John Ledermann and driven by Florian Ledermann.

On appeal defendants contend that the court was without jurisdiction to vacate the settlement solely because their counsel then possessed information, unknown to plaintiff herein, that at the time he was suffering from an aorta aneurysm which may have resulted from the accident, because (1) no mutual mistake of fact was involved; (2) no duty rested upon them to disclose information to plaintiff which they could assume had been disclosed to him by his own physicians; (3) insurance limitations as well as physical injuries formed the basis for the settlement; and (4) plaintiff's motion to vacate the order for settlement and to set aside the releases was barred by the limitations provided in Rule 60.02 of Rules of Civil Procedure.[1]

After the accident, David's injuries were diagnosed by his family physician, Dr. James H. Cain, as a severe crushing injury of the chest with multiple rib fractures; a severe cerebral concussion, probably with petechial hemorrhages of the brain; and bilateral fractures of the clavicles. At Dr. Cain's suggestion, on January 3, 1957, David was examined by Dr. John F. Pohl, an orthopedic specialist, who made X-ray studies of his chest. Dr. Pohl's detailed report of this examination included the following:

> ". . . The lung fields are clear. The heart and aorta are normal."

Nothing in such report indicated the aorta aneurysm with which David was then suffering. On March 1, 1957, at the suggestion of Dr. Pohl, David was examined from a neurological viewpoint by Dr. Paul S. Blake, and in the report of this examination there was no finding of the aorta aneurysm.

In the meantime, on February 22, 1957, at defendants' request, David was examined by Dr. Hewitt Hannah, a neurologist. On February 26, 1957, the latter reported to Messrs. Field, Arveson, & Donoho, attorneys for defendant John Zimmerman, as follows:

> "The one feature of the case which bothers me more than any other part of the case is the fact that this boy of 20 years of age has an aneurysm, which means a dilatation of the aorta and the arch of the aorta. Whether this came out of this accident I cannot say with any degree of certainty and I have discussed it with the Roentgenologist and a couple of Internists. . . . Of course an aneurysm or dilatation of the aorta in a boy of this age is a serious matter as far as his life. This aneurysm may dilate further and it might rupture with further dilatation and this would cause his death.
>
> "It would be interesting also to know whether the X-ray of his lungs, taken immediately following the accident, shows this dilatation or not. If it was not present immediately following the accident and is now present, then we could be sure that it came out of the accident."

---

1. Rule 60.02 of Rules of Civil Procedure provides in part:

"On motion . . . the court may relieve a party . . . from a final . . . order, or proceeding for the following reasons: (1) Mistake, inadvertence, surprise, or excusable neglect; (2) newly discovered evidence which by due diligence could not have been discovered in time to move for a new trial under Rule 59.03; (3) fraud (whether . . . intrinsic or extrinsic), misrepresentation, or other misconduct of an adverse party; . . . or (6) any other reason justifying relief from the operation of the judgment. The motion shall be made within a reasonable time, and for reasons (1), (2), and (3) not more than one year after the judgment, order, or proceeding was entered or taken. . . . This rule does not limit the power of a court to entertain an independent action to relieve a party from a judgment, order, or proceeding, . . . or to set aside a judgment for fraud upon the court."

Prior to the negotiations for settlement, the contents of the above report were made known to counsel for defendants Florian and John Ledermann.

The case was called for trial on March 4, 1957, at which time the respective parties and their counsel possessed such information as to David's physical condition as was revealed to them by their respective medical examiners as above described. It is thus apparent that neither David nor his father, the nominal plaintiff in the prior action, was then aware that David was suffering the aorta aneurysm but on the contrary believed that he was recovering from the injuries sustained in the accident.

On the following day an agreement for settlement was reached wherein, in consideration of the payment of $6,500, David and his father agreed to settle in full for all claims arising out of the accident.

Richard S. Roberts, counsel for David, thereafter presented to the court a petition for approval of the settlement, wherein David's injuries were described as:

> ". . . severe crushing of the chest, with multiple rib fractures, severe cerebral concussion, with petechial hemorrhages of the brain, bilateral fractures of the clavicles."

Attached to the petition were affidavits of David's physicians, Drs. James H. Cain and Paul S. Blake, wherein they set forth the same diagnoses they had made upon completion of their respective examinations of David as above described. At no time was there information disclosed to the court that David was then suffering from an aorta aneurysm which may have been the result of the accident. Based upon the petition for settlement and such affidavits of Drs. Cain and Blake, the court on May 8, 1957, made its order approving the settlement.

Early in 1959, David was required by the army reserve, of which he was a member, to have a physical checkup. For this, he again engaged the services of Dr. Cain. In this checkup, the latter discovered the aorta aneurysm. He then reexamined the X rays which had been taken shortly after the accident and at this time discovered that they disclosed the beginning of the process which produced the aneurysm. He promptly sent David to Dr. Jerome Grismer for an examination and opinion. The latter confirmed the finding of the aorta aneurysm and recommended immediate surgery therefor. This was performed by him at Mount Sinai Hospital in Minneapolis on March 10, 1959.

Shortly thereafter, David, having attained his majority, instituted the present action for additional damages due to the more serious injuries including the aorta aneurysm which he alleges proximately resulted from the accident. As indicated above, the prior order for settlement was vacated. In a memorandum made a part of the order vacating the settlement, the court stated:

> "The facts material to a determination of the motion are without substantial dispute. The only disputed facts appear to be

whether . . . Mr. Roberts, former counsel for plaintiff, discussed plaintiff's injuries with Mr. Arvesen, counsel for defendant Zimmerman, immediately before the settlement agreement, and, further, whether or not there is a causal relationship between the accident and the aneurysm.

"Contrary to the . . . suggestion in the affidavit of Mr. Roberts that he discussed the minor's injuries with Mr. Arvesen, the Court finds that no such discussion of the specific injuries claimed occurred prior to the settlement agreement on March 5, 1957.

". . . the Court finds that although the aneurysm now existing is causally related to the accident, such finding is for the purpose of the motions only and is based solely upon the opinion expressed by Dr. Cain (Exhibit 'F'), which, so far as the Court can find from the numerous affidavits and statements of fact by counsel, stands without dispute.

. . .

"The mistake concerning the existence of the aneurysm was not mutual. For reasons which do not appear, plaintiff's doctor failed to ascertain its existence. By reason of the failure of plaintiff's counsel to use available rules of discovery, plaintiff's doctor and all his representatives did not learn that defendants and their agents knew of its existence and possible serious consequences. Except for the character of the concealment in the light of plaintiff's minority, the Court would, I believe, be justified in denying plaintiff's motion to vacate, leaving him to whatever questionable remedy he may have against his doctor and against his lawyer.

"That defendants' counsel concealed the knowledge they had is not disputed. The essence of the application of the above rule is the character of the concealment. Was it done under circumstances that defendants must be charged with knowledge that plaintiff did not know of the injury? If so, an enriching advantage was gained for defendants at plaintiff's expense. There is no doubt of the good faith of both defendants' counsel. There is no doubt that during the course of the negotiations, when the parties were in an adversary relationship, no rule required or duty rested upon defendants or their representatives to disclose this knowledge. However, once the agreement to settle was reached, it is difficult to characterize the parties' relationship as adverse. At this point all parties were interested in securing Court approval. . . .

"When the adversary nature of the negotiations concluded in a settlement, the procedure took on the posture of a joint application to the Court, at least so far as the facts upon which the Court could and must approve settlement is concerned. It is here that the true nature of the concealment appears, and defendants' failure to act affirmatively, after having been given a copy of the application for approval, can only be defendants' decision to take a calculated risk that the settlement would be final. . . .

1. The principals applicable to the court's authority to vacate settlements made on behalf of minors and approved by it appear well established. With reference thereto, we have held that the court in its discretion may vacate such a settlement, even though it is not induced by fraud or bad faith, where it is shown that in the accident the minor sustained separate and distinct injuries which were not known or considered by the court at the time settlement was approved . . .

2. From the foregoing it is clear that in the instant case the court did not abuse its discretion in setting aside the settlement which it had approved on plaintiff's behalf while he was still a minor. It is undisputed that neither he nor his counsel nor his medical attendants were aware that at the time settlement was made he was suffering from an aorta aneurysm which may have resulted from the accident. The seriousness of this disability is indicated by Dr. Hannah's report indicating the imminent danger of death therefrom. This was known by counsel for both defendants but was not disclosed to the court at the time it was petitioned to approve the settlement. While no canon of ethics or legal obligation may have required them to inform plaintiff or his counsel with respect thereto, or to advise the court therein, it did become obvious to them at the time, that the settlement then made did not contemplate or take into consideration the disability described. This fact opened the way for the court to later exercise its discretion in vacating the settlement and under the circumstances described we cannot say that there was any abuse of discretion on the part of the court in so doing under Rule 60.02(6) of Rules of Civil Procedure. . . .

Questions and Comments

What was Zimmerman's duty to Spaulding? What responsibility did the defense-paid doctor have to Spaulding? What were Zimmerman's lawyers' responsibilities to Zimmerman? To the doctor they hired? To Spaulding?

Fed.R.Civ.P. 35(a) provides that upon motion showing good cause the court may order a party to submit to a physical or mental examination. Rule 35(b) provides that the medical report from any such examination (or any examination agreed to by the parties without court order) shall be supplied to the party examined upon that party's request. There are similar state rules.

Spaulding's lawyers could have obtained a copy of the defense expert's report, if they had asked the right questions or made the right motions. Does the negligence of Spaulding's lawyers (or of his doctor) excuse or mitigate the silence of Zimmerman's lawyers (or the doctor they hired)?

The trial court said that but for Spaulding's minority, the court would have left Spaulding to seek redress against his doctor and his lawyer. The appeals court apparently agrees with this statement.

Does this game-like framework lose sight of David Spaulding? Notice that the court does not base its ruling on the seriousness of the undisclosed facts but on Spaulding's minority. Why?

In Brown v. County of Genesee, 872 F.2d 169 (6th Cir.1989), an employment discrimination case, during settlement negotiations plaintiff Brown through her lawyer made it clear to defense counsel that Brown "would not settle unless [she] were paid at a rate of pay she would have received had she been hired on June 16, 1982." Both Brown and her lawyers believed the highest rate of pay to which this condition would entitle her was Step C pay, and thus they settled for Step C pay. In fact, she would have been eligible for Step D pay, which was higher. At the time of settlement, defense counsel "did not know, but he believed it probable that Brown and her counsel" mistakenly believed that Step C was the ceiling for employees hired on June 16, 1982. He said nothing to correct their mistaken belief. The district court vacated the settlement, but the Sixth Circuit reversed, holding that "absent some misrepresentation or fraudulent conduct, [the defendant] had no duty to advise [Brown or her counsel] of any such factual error. . . ." The court pointed out that Brown's counsel could have discovered the correct information about the pay scales from examining public documents or by asking the right questions in discovery. "The failure of Brown's counsel . . . cannot be imputed to the [defendant] as unethical or fraudulent."

Fed.R.Civ.P. 26(e) provides that a party is not required to supplement a response made in discovery to include information later acquired as long as the response was complete when made. The rule then lists several exceptions to this general statement. Consider some of these exceptions. There is a duty to seasonably supplement any response concerning the substance of expert testimony expected to be offered at trial, Rule 26(e)(1)(B). There is a duty to seasonably amend any response, if the party learns it was based on information that the party knew was incorrect at the time the statement was made, Rule 26(e)(2)(A). There is a duty to seasonably amend any response if the party learns that, although correct when made, "the circumstances are such that a failure to amend the response is in substance a knowing concealment." The Advisory Committee Notes explain that the latter two exceptions are designed to cover situations in which the "lawyer obtains actual knowledge that a prior response is incorrect" but that they do not impose a continuing obligation to check prior answers. All answers must, however, be supplemented if the court so orders *or if the opposing party makes a new discovery request for supplemental answers,* Rule 26(e)(3). Moreover, under Rule 26(g), a lawyer must sign all discovery requests and responses. This signature constitutes a warranty that *after reasonable inquiry,* the lawyer believes that the paper is, inter alia, in compliance with the discovery rules. False answers, whether knowingly or negligently made, are not in compliance with the discovery rules.

These rules provide no help to the Spauldings or Browns of this world, whose lawyers fail to ask the right questions.

Introduction to the Ethical Codes

Three times in its history the American Bar Association has issued a model code for regulation of the conduct of lawyers. The ABA is a voluntary organization of lawyers and as such its actions do not have the force of law. However, the ABA has long been recognized as the leading national organization of lawyers, and it has enjoyed success in convincing state courts, state legislatures, federal courts and federal agencies to adopt some form of its model codes, giving the codes, as so adopted, the effect of law.

The Canons of Professional Ethics, which are alluded to in the opinion of the trial court in *Spaulding,* were adopted by the American Bar Association in 1909. The Canons owed a great debt to the work of David Hoffman and George Sharswood whose published lectures on ethics in the 1800's were the basis for ethical codes for lawyers. Alabama was the first jurisdiction to adopt a formal code of ethics, Alabama Canons of Ethics (1887), which codified Sharswood's work. By the time the ABA's Canons were adopted a number of other states had promulgated formal rules. Apart from these formal rules by the states and the ABA, regulation of the profession was left to common law with occasional statutory pronouncements.

The ABA's Canons originally numbered 32, but by the end of the 1930's there were 47. Even at 47, the Canons were brief, written in broad language with a high moral tone. See the provisions quoted below. Criticism of the Canons centered on the need for more specificity. Despite their ambiguities, the Canons were widely recognized and were still in force in 1962 when *Spaulding* was decided.

In 1964, Lewis F. Powell, Jr., then President of the ABA, appointed a committee to examine the Canons and suggest revisions. This committee proposed The Code of Professional Responsibility, which the ABA adopted in 1969. Some form of the Model Code thereafter was adopted by almost every state. Most federal courts adopted the Model Code by local court rule. Note that the federal courts are not required to abide by the version of the Code adopted in the state in which they sit. Under Fed.R.Civ.P. 83, the federal district courts may establish their own rules for lawyers practicing in the district. See, e.g., United States v. Walsh, 699 F.Supp. 469, 472 (D.N.J.1988) (*Model* Rule 1.11 applies in district court not Rule 1.11 as amended in New Jersey's version of the Rules). Most United States District Courts, however, adopt the rules in effect in the states in which they sit.

The 1969 Code has a much more complicated format than the 1909 Canons. The Code contains nine Canons, which function as chapter headings. Under each Canon there are both Ethical Considerations and Disciplinary Rules. The Preamble and Preliminary Statement of the Code explains its structure as follows:

> The Canons are statements of axiomatic norms, expressing in general terms the standards of professional conduct expected of lawyers in their relationships with the public, with the legal system, and with the legal profession. They embody the general concepts from which the Ethical Considerations and the Disciplinary Rules are derived.

> The Ethical Considerations are aspirational in character and represent the objectives toward which every member of the profession should strive. They constitute a body of principles upon which the lawyer can rely for guidance in many specific situations.

> The Disciplinary Rules, unlike the Ethical Considerations, are mandatory in character. The Disciplinary Rules state the minimum level of conduct below which no lawyer can fall without being subject to disciplinary action . . . An enforcing agency, in applying the Disciplinary Rules, may find interpretive guidance in the basic principles embodied in the Canons and in the objectives, reflected in the Ethical Considerations.

In fact, the structure of the Code is not as clear as this statement suggests. For example, while the Ethical Considerations are supposed to be aspirational statements, some sound like commands, e.g., EC 5–15 "A lawyer should never . . ." Other ECs elaborate the Disciplinary Rules by providing concrete examples of what they mean, see, e.g., EC 3–8 and 5–24. Not surprisingly, courts and bar disciplinary bodies have often applied Ethical Considerations as if they were Disciplinary Rules.

Aside from problems of structure, the Model Code has been criticized for embodying outdated assumptions about what lawyers do and how they do it. The Code primarily reflects a vision of lawyers in the courtroom—equal advocates competing under the watchful eye of a judge, who stands ready to correct overzealousness of either party. This vision provides little practical guidance to the lawyer as negotiator, draftsman or counselor, or even in pretrial matters. The Code also envisions lawyers operating in practice alone or with a few partners, equal in status and responsibility. Of course, today lawyers practice in large organizations—large law firms, government offices, corporations—with hierarchical structures in which lawyers at various levels have different degrees of responsibility and control over their work. Finally, the Code imagines the client as an individual, not a collection of individuals and not an inanimate legal entity such as a corporation or a government agency. The lawyer representing a corporation or a class is left with little enlightenment on such basic issues as the identity of the client.

In 1977, ABA President William Spann appointed a Commission on the Evaluation of Professional Responsibility to recommend changes in the Code of Professional Responsibility. This Commission was popularly known as the Kutak Commission after its Chairman Robert J.

Kutak. The Kutak Commission concluded that a new formulation was needed with a cleaner structure and based on a modern conception of the lawyer's role. The Kutak Commission, unlike the committee which drafted the Model Code, worked largely in the open: it held public hearings and circulated its working drafts to the bar and public alike for comment. The resulting debate over the professional responsibility of lawyers was unprecedented in scope and intensity. In 1983, the ABA House of Delegates, after amending several key provisions of the Kutak final draft, adopted the Model Rules of Professional Conduct, with a recommendation to the states and to the federal courts and agencies that the Model Rules replace their respective versions of the Model Code.

The format of the Model Rules follows that used by the Restatements of Law produced by the American Law Institute: black letter rules followed by explanatory comments. The Rules also reflect a more modern concept of the lawyer's role. For example, M.R. 1.13 addresses the lawyer who represents an entity as distinct from an individual; M.R. 2.1 addresses the lawyer as advisor; M.R. 2.2, the lawyer as intermediary; M.R. 2.3, the lawyer as evaluator of a matter for the use of third parties; M.R. 5.1 describes the responsibilities of a partner or supervisory lawyer; M.R. 5.2 is the counterpart rule for the lawyer who is a subordinate.

As of June 1989, over one-half of the states had adopted some version of the Model Rules. Some states, for example New York, North Carolina, Oregon and Virginia, have decided to retain their version of the Code—often with at least some adjustments based on provisions in the Model Rules. The federal courts, including the Supreme Court, cite the Model Rules and the Model Code as authority in decisions concerning lawyer's professional conduct.

The ABA has generated two other important sets of rules governing the conduct of lawyers: the ABA Standards Relating to the Administration of Criminal Justice and the Model Code of Judicial Conduct. In most jurisdictions the Standards do not have the same force of law as the versions of the Model Code or Model Rules. However, they are frequently relied on by state and federal courts as authority for the proper standard of conduct for prosecutors and defense counsel. The Code of Judicial Conduct applies to judges and has been adopted in most states and the federal courts. Its regulation of judges imposes controls on relationships between judges and lawyers.

The ABA Standing Committee on Ethics and Professional Responsibility issues formal and informal opinions on ethical questions. These opinions do not have the force of law but they are sometimes cited by courts. In theory a Formal Opinion responds to a question of general interest, while an Informal Opinion is a response to a question "comparatively narrow in scope." ABA, Opinions of the Committee on Professional Ethics 6 (1967); ABA Standing Committee on Ethics and Professional Responsibility, Rules of Procedure 3.

State and local bars also issue similar ethics opinions. Some states publish annotated editions of the state ethical code that include state and local ethics opinions. State and local bar ethics opinions may provide guidance and at least are usually a good defense to a disciplinary charge, but they do not have the status of law. Court decisions are the only truly authoritative interpretation of ethics rules. When court precedent conflicts with a bar opinion, the court's opinion governs.

The Ethical Rules and *Spaulding*

Read the following provisions of the Canons and their counterparts in the Code and Rules. The court in *Spaulding* stated that no canon of ethics was violated by the lawyers. Do you agree?

Canon 15. How Far a Lawyer May Go in Supporting a Client's Cause

Nothing operates more certainly to create or to foster popular prejudice against lawyers as a class, and to deprive the profession of that full measure of public esteem and confidence which belongs to the proper discharge of its duties than does the false claim, often set up by the unscrupulous in defense of questionable transactions, that it is the duty of the lawyer to do whatever may enable him to succeed in winning his client's cause.

. . .

The lawyer owes "entire devotion to the interest of the client, warm zeal in the maintenance and defense of his rights and the exertion of his utmost learning and ability," to the end that nothing be taken or be withheld from him, save by the rules of law, legally applied. . . . But it is steadfastly to be borne in mind that the great trust of the lawyer is to be performed within and not without the bounds of the law. The office of attorney does not permit, much less does it demand of him for any client violation of law or any manner of fraud or chicane. He must obey his own conscience and not that of his client.

――――――

Canon 22. Candor and Fairness

The conduct of the lawyer before the Court and with other lawyers should be characterized by candor and fairness.

It is not candid or fair for the lawyer knowingly to misquote the contents of a paper, the testimony of a witness, the language or the argument of opposing counsel, or the language of a decision or a textbook . . .

It is unprofessional and dishonorable to deal other than candidly with the facts in taking the statements of witnesses, in drawing affidavits and other documents, and in the presentation of causes.

. . .

These and all kindred practices are unprofessional and unworthy of an officer of the law charged, as is the lawyer, with the duty of aiding in the administration of justice.

Compare DR 7–102(A); and M.R. 3.3 and 4.1.

Canon 31. Responsibility for Litigation

No lawyer is obliged to act either as advisor or advocate for every person who may wish to become his client. He has the right to decline employment. Every lawyer upon his own responsibility must decide what employment he will accept as counsel, what causes he will bring into Court for plaintiffs, what cases he will contest in Court for defendants. The responsibility for advising as to questionable transactions, for bringing questionable suits, for urging questionable defenses, is the lawyer's responsibility. He cannot escape it by urging as an excuse that he is only following his client's instructions.

Canon 37. Confidences of a Client

It is the duty of a lawyer to preserve his client's confidences. This duty outlasts the lawyer's employment and extends as well to his employees . . .

. . . The announced intention of a client to commit a crime is not included within the confidences which he is bound to respect. He may properly make such disclosures as may be necessary to prevent the act or protect those against whom it is threatened.

Compare DR 4–101 and M.R. 1.6.

Canon 41. Discovery of Imposition and Deception

When a lawyer discovers that some fraud or deception has been practiced, which has unjustly imposed upon the court or a party, he should endeavor to rectify it; at first by advising his client, and if his client refuses to forego the advantage thus unjustly gained, he should promptly inform the injured person or his counsel, so that they may take appropriate steps.

Compare DR 7–102(B) and M.R. 1.2(d), 1.6 and 3.3.

Canon 44. Withdrawal From Employment as Attorney or Counsel

The right of an attorney or counsel to withdraw from employment, once assumed, arises only from good cause. Even the desire or consent of the client, is not always sufficient. The lawyer should not throw up the unfinished task to the detriment of his client except for reasons of honor or self-respect. If the client insists upon an unjust or immoral course in the conduct of his case, or if he persists over the attorney's remonstrance in presenting frivolous defenses, . . . the lawyer may be warranted in withdrawing on due notice to the client, allowing him time to employ another lawyer. . . .

Compare DR 2–110 and M.R. 1.16.

C. PERSPECTIVES ON THE MORALITY OF THE LAWYER'S ROLE

The Lawyer as Friend?

In examining the question, "Can a lawyer be a good person?", Professor Charles Fried has sought to justify the lawyer's disregard for the interests of others by drawing an analogy to friendship.

> [M]y analogy shall be to friendship, where the freedom to choose and to be chosen expresses our freedom to hold something of ourselves in reserve, in reserve even from the universalizing claims of morality. These personal ties and the claims they engender may be all-consuming, as with a close friend or family member, or they may be limited, special-purpose claims, as in the case of the client or patient. The special-purpose claim is one in which the beneficiary, the client, is entitled to all the special consideration *within* the limits of the relationship which we accord to a friend or a loved one. It is not that the claims of the client are less intense or demanding: they are only more limited in their scope. After all, the ordinary concept of friendship, provides only an analogy. . . .
>
> · · ·
>
> If [however] personal integrity lies at the foundation of the lawyer's right to treat his client as a friend, then surely consideration for personal integrity—his own and others'—must limit what he can do in friendship. Consideration for personal integrity forbids me to lie, cheat, or humiliate, whether in my own interests or those of a friend, so surely they prohibit such conduct on behalf of a client, one's legal friend. . . .
>
> · · ·
>
> . . . Fried, The Lawyer as Friend: The Moral Foundations of the Lawyer–Client Relation, 85 Yale L.J. 1060, 1071, 1083 (1976).

There are distinctions between lawyers and "real" friends, e.g., lawyers unlike friends are paid and are granted a special franchise by the state to give legal advice; and friendship is an "open" contract that the parties are continuously free to redefine or revoke. Do these distinctions suggest different moral responsibilities for lawyers?

What would a good friend of Zimmerman's have advised him to do?

For a critique of Fried's analogy to friendship, see Dauer & Leff, Correspondence, 85 Yale L.J. 573 (1977). Also see Simon, The Ideology of Advocacy, 1978 Wis.L.Rev. 29, 108 (stating that Fried's portrayal of the lawyer-client relationship resembles prostitution more than friendship).

RICHARD WASSERSTROM, "LAWYERS AS PROFESSIONALS: SOME MORAL ISSUES"
5 Human Rights 1 (1975).*

In this paper I examine two moral criticisms of lawyers which, if well-founded, are fundamental. . . .

The first criticism centers around the lawyer's stance toward the world at large. The accusation is that the lawyer-client relationship renders the lawyer at best systematically amoral and at worst more than occasionally immoral in his or her dealings with the rest of mankind.

The second criticism focuses upon the relationship between the lawyer and the client. Here the charge is that it is the lawyer-client relationship which is morally objectionable because it is a relationship in which the lawyer dominates and in which the lawyer typically, and perhaps inevitably, treats the client in both an impersonal and a paternalistic fashion.

. . .

Although I am undecided about the ultimate merits of either criticism, I am convinced that each is deserving of careful articulation and assessment, and that each contains insights that deserve more acknowledgment than they often receive. My ambition is, therefore, more to exhibit the relevant considerations and to stimulate additional reflection, than it is to provide any very definite conclusions.

I.

. . . [T]he first issue I propose to examine concerns the ways the professional-client relationship affects the professional's stance toward the world at large. The primary question that is presented is whether there is adequate justification for the kind of moral universe that comes to be inhabited by the lawyer as he or she goes through professional life. For at best the lawyer's world is a simplified moral world; often it is an amoral one; and more than occasionally, perhaps, an overtly immoral one.

. . .

. . . [O]ne central feature of the professions in general and of law in particular is that there is a special, complicated relationship between the professional, and the client or patient. For each of the parties in this relationship, but especially for the professional, the behavior that is involved is to a very significant degree, what I call, role-differentiated behavior. . . .

. . .

. . . [W]here the attorney-client relationship exists, it is often appropriate and many times even obligatory for the attorney to do things that, all other things being equal, an ordinary person need not, and should not do. What is characteristic of this role of a lawyer is the lawyer's required indifference to a wide variety of ends and consequences that in other contexts would be of undeniable moral significance. Once a lawyer represents a client, the lawyer has a duty to make his or her expertise fully available in the realization of the end sought by the client, irrespective, for the most part, of the moral worth to which the end will be put or the character of the client who seeks to utilize it. Provided that the end sought is not illegal, the lawyer is, in essence, an amoral technician whose peculiar skills and knowledge in respect to the law are available to those with whom the relationship of client is established. The question, as I have indicated, is whether this particular and pervasive feature of professionalism is itself justifiable. At a minimum, I do not think any of the typical, simple answers will suffice.

One such answer focuses upon and generalizes from the criminal defense lawyer. . . . The received view within the profession (and to a lesser degree within the society at large) is that having once agreed to represent the client, the lawyer is under an obligation to do his or her best to defend that person at trial, irrespective, for instance, even of the lawyer's belief in the client's innocence. . . .

But . . . the irrelevance of the guilt or innocence of an accused client by no means exhausts the altered perspective of the lawyer's conscience, even in criminal cases. For in the course of defending an accused, an attorney may have, as a part of his or her duty of representation, the obligation to invoke procedures and practices which are themselves morally objectionable and of which the lawyer in other contexts might thoroughly disapprove. And these situations, I think, are somewhat less comfortable to confront. For example, in California, the case law permits a defendant in a rape case to secure in some circumstances an order from the court requiring the complaining witness, that is the rape victim, to submit to a psychiatric examination before trial.[2] For no other crime is such a pretrial remedy available. In no other case can the victim of a crime be required to undergo psychiatric examination at the request of the defendant on the ground that the results of the examination may help the defendant prove that the offense did not take place. I think such a rule is wrong and is reflective of the sexist bias of the law in respect to rape. . . . Nonetheless, it appears to be part of the role-differentiated obligation of a lawyer for a defendant charged with rape to seek to take advantage of

2. Ballard v. Superior Court, 64 Cal.2d 159, 410 P.2d 838, 49 Cal.Rptr. 302 (1966).

this particular rule of law—irrespective of the independent moral view he or she may have of the rightness or wrongness of such a rule.

Nor, it is important to point out, is this peculiar, strikingly amoral behavior limited to the lawyer involved with the workings of the criminal law. Most clients come to lawyers to get the lawyers to help them do things that they could not easily do without the assistance provided by the lawyer's special competence. . . .

And in each case, the role-differentiated character of the lawyer's way of being tends to render irrelevant what would otherwise be morally relevant considerations. Suppose that a client desires to make a will disinheriting her children because they opposed the war in Vietnam. Should the lawyer refuse to draft the will because the lawyer thinks this a bad reason to disinherit one's children? Suppose a client can avoid the payment of taxes through a loophole only available to a few wealthy taxpayers. Should the lawyer refuse to tell the client of a loophole because the lawyer thinks it an unfair advantage for the rich? Suppose a client wants to start a corporation that will manufacture, distribute and promote a harmful but not illegal substance, e.g., cigarettes. Should the lawyer refuse to prepare the articles of incorporation for the corporation? In each case, the accepted view within the profession is that these matters are just of no concern to the lawyer *qua* lawyer. The lawyer need not of course agree to represent the client (and that is equally true for the unpopular client accused of a heinous crime), but there is nothing wrong with representing a client whose aims and purposes are quite immoral. And having agreed to do so, the lawyer is required to provide the best possible assistance, without regard to his or her disapproval of the objective that is sought.

The lesson, on this view, is clear. The job of the lawyer, so the argument typically concludes, is not to approve or disapprove of the character of his or her client, the cause for which the client seeks the lawyer's assistance, or the avenues provided by the law to achieve that which the client wants to accomplish. . . . And the difficulty I have with all of this is that the arguments for such a way of life seem to be not quite so convincing to me as they do to many lawyers. I am, that is, at best uncertain that it is a good thing for lawyers to be so professional—for them to embrace so completely this role-differentiated way of approaching matters.

. . .

. . . [F]or most lawyers, most of the time, pursuing the interests of one's clients is an attractive and satisfying way to live in part just because the moral world of the lawyer is a simpler, less complicated, and less ambiguous world than the moral world of ordinary life. . . .

But there is, of course, also an argument which seeks to demonstrate that it is good and not merely comfortable for lawyers to behave this way.

It is good, so the argument goes, that the lawyer's behavior and concomitant point of view are role-differentiated because the lawyer *qua* lawyer participates in a complex institution which functions well only if the individuals adhere to their institutional roles.

For example, when there is a conflict between individuals, or between the state and an individual, there is a well-established institutional mechanism by which to get that dispute resolved. That mechanism is the trial in which each side is represented by a lawyer whose job it is both to present his or her client's case in the most attractive, forceful light and to seek to expose the weaknesses and defects in the case of the opponent.

When an individual is charged with having committed a crime, the trial is the mechanism by which we determine in our society whether or not the person is in fact guilty. Just imagine what would happen if lawyers were to refuse, for instance, to represent persons whom they thought to be guilty. . . . The private judgment of individual lawyers would in effect be substituted for the public, institutional judgment of the judge and jury. The amorality of lawyers helps to guarantee that every criminal defendant will have his or her day in court.

· · ·

Nor is the amorality of the institutional role of the lawyer restricted to the defense of those accused of crimes. . . . The attorney may think it wrong to disinherit one's children because of their views about the Vietnam war, but here the attorney's complaint is really with the laws of inheritance and not with his or her client. The attorney may think the tax provision an unfair, unjustifiable loophole, but once more the complaint is really with the Internal Revenue Code and not with the client who seeks to take advantage of it. . . . If lawyers were to substitute their own private views of what ought to be legally permissible and impermissible for those of the legislature, this would constitute a surreptitious and undesirable shift from a democracy to an oligarchy of lawyers. For given the fact that lawyers are needed to effectuate the wishes of clients, the lawyer ought to make his or her skills available to those who seek them without regard for the particular objectives of the client.

· · ·

As I indicated earlier, I do believe that the amoral behavior of the *criminal* defense lawyer is justifiable. But I think that [justification] depends at least as much upon the special needs of an accused as upon any more general defense of a lawyer's role-differentiated behavior. As a matter of fact I think it likely that many persons such as myself have been misled by the special features of the criminal case. Because a deprivation of liberty is so serious, because the prosecutorial resources of the state are so vast, and because, perhaps, of a serious skepticism about the rightness of punishment even where wrongdoing has occurred, it is easy to accept the view that it makes sense to charge the defense counsel with the job of making the best possible case for the accused—without regard, so to speak, for the merits. This coupled with the fact that it is an adversarial proceeding succeeds, I think, in justifying the amorality of the criminal defense counsel. But this does not, however, justify a comparable perspective on the part of lawyers generally. Once we leave the peculiar situation of the criminal defense lawyer, I think it quite likely that the role-differentiated amorality of the lawyer is almost certainly excessive and at times inappropriate. . . .

Moreover, even if I am wrong about all this, four things do seem to me to be true and important.

First, all of the arguments that support the role-differentiated amorality of the lawyer on institutional grounds can succeed only if the enormous degree of trust and confidence in the institutions themselves is itself justified. . . . To the degree to which the institutional rules and practices are unjust, unwise or undesirable, to that same degree is the case for the role-differentiated behavior of the lawyer weakened if not destroyed.

Second, it is clear that there are definite character traits that the professional such as the lawyer must take on if the system is to work. What is less clear is that they are admirable ones. Even if the role-differentiated amorality of the professional lawyer is justified by the virtues of the adversary system, this also means that the lawyer *qua* lawyer will be encouraged to be competitive rather than cooperative; aggressive rather than accommodating; ruthless rather than compassionate; and pragmatic rather than principled. . . . It is surely neither accidental nor unimportant that these are the same character traits that are emphasized and valued by the capitalist ethic—and on precisely analogous grounds. Because the ideals of professionalism and capitalism are the dominant ones within our culture, it is harder than most of us suspect even to take seriously the suggestion that radically different styles of living, kinds of occupational outlooks, and types of social institutions might be possible, let alone preferable.

Third, there is a special feature of the role-differentiated behavior of the lawyer that distinguishes it from the comparable behavior of other professionals. What I have in mind can be brought out through the following question: Why is it that it seems far less plausible to talk critically about the amorality of the doctor, for instance, who treats all patients irrespective of their moral character than it does to talk critically about the comparable amorality of the lawyer? . . .

. . . The lawyer lives with and within a dilemma that is not shared by other professionals. If the lawyer actually believes everything that he or she asserts on behalf of the client, then it appears to be proper to regard the lawyer as in fact embracing and endorsing the points of view that he or she articulates. If the lawyer does not in fact believe what is urged by way of argument, if the lawyer is only playing a role, then it appears to be proper to tax the lawyer with hypocrisy and insincerity. To be sure, actors in a play take on roles and say things that the characters, not the actors, believe. But we know it is a play and that they are actors. The law courts are not, however, theaters, and the lawyers both talk about justice and they genuinely seek to persuade. The fact that the lawyer's words, thoughts, and convictions are, apparently, for sale and at the service of the client helps us, I think, to understand the peculiar hostility which is more than occasionally uniquely directed by lay persons toward lawyers. . . .

Fourth, . . . we do pay a social price for that way of thought and action. For to become and to be a professional, such as a lawyer, is to incorporate within oneself ways of behaving and ways of thinking that shape the whole person. It is especially hard, if not impossible, because of the nature of the professions, for one's professional way of thinking not to dominate one's entire adult life. . . . In important respects, one's professional role becomes and is one's dominant role, so that for many persons at least they become their professional being. This is at a minimum a heavy price to pay for the professions as we know them in our culture, and especially so for lawyers. Whether it is an inevitable price is, I think, an open question, largely because the problem has not begun to be fully perceived as such by the professionals in general, the legal profession in particular, or by the educational institutions that train professionals.

II.

The role-differentiated behavior of the professional also lies at the heart of the second of the two moral issues I want to discuss, namely, the character of the interpersonal relationship that exists between the lawyer and the client. As I indicated at the outset, the charge that I want to examine here is that the relationship between the lawyer and the client is typically, if not inevitably, a morally defective one in which the client is not treated with the respect and dignity that he or she deserves.

. . .

. . . [O]ne pervasive, and I think necessary, feature of the relationship between any professional and the client or patient is that it is in some sense a relationship of inequality. This relationship of inequality is intrinsic to the existence of professionalism. For the professional is, in some respects at least, always in a position of dominance vis-à-vis the client, and the client in a position of dependence vis-à-vis the professional. . . .

To begin with, there is the fact that one characteristic of professions is that the professional is the possessor of expert knowledge of a sort not readily or easily attainable by members of the community at large. Hence, in the most straightforward of all senses the client, typically, is dependent upon the professional's skill or knowledge because the client does not possess the same knowledge.

Moreover, virtually every profession has its own technical language, a private terminology which can only be fully understood by the members of the profession. The presence of such a language plays the dual role of creating and affirming the membership of the professionals within the profession and of preventing the client from fully discussing or understanding his or her concerns in the language of the profession.

. . .

In addition, because the matters for which professional assistance is sought usually involve things of great personal concern to the client, it is the received wisdom within the professions that the client lacks the perspective necessary to pursue in a satisfactory way his or her own best interests, and that the client requires a detached, disinterested representative to look after his or her interests. . . .

Finally, as I have indicated, to be a professional is to have been acculturated in a certain way. It is to have satisfactorily passed through a lengthy and allegedly difficult period of study and training. It is to have done something hard. Something that not everyone can do. Almost all professions encourage this way of viewing oneself; as having joined an elect group by virtue of hard work and mastery of the mysteries of the profession. In addition, the society at large treats members of a profession as members of an elite by paying them more than most people for the work they do with their heads rather than their hands, and by according them a substantial amount of social prestige and power by virtue of their membership in a profession. It is hard, I think, if not impossible, for a person to emerge from professional training and participate in a profession without the belief that he or she is a special kind of person, both different from and somewhat better than those nonprofessional members of the social order. It is equally hard for the other members of society not to hold an analogous view of the professionals. And these beliefs surely contribute, too, to the dominant role played by a professional in any professional-client relationship.

. . .

. . . . It is, I believe, indicative of the state of legal education and of the profession that there has been to date extremely little self-conscious concern even with the possibility that these dimensions of the attorney-client relationship are worth examining—to say nothing of being capable of alteration. That awareness is, surely, the prerequisite to any serious assessment of the moral character of the attorney-client relationship as a relationship among adult human beings.

. . .

Questions and Comments

How would Wasserstrom have a lawyer deal with Zimmerman to accord him the "respect and dignity that he . . . deserves"?

Wasserstrom accepts the role-based morality of the criminal defense lawyer, while rejecting such morality for lawyers in other situations. Are his arguments distinguishing the criminal lawyer persuasive? Are not his arguments against the role-morality of other lawyers equally applicable to the criminal defense lawyer? For example: Is trust and confidence in the criminal justice system more warranted than trust and confidence in the civil system? Should we be less concerned with the character traits that are nourished by role-morality in criminal defense lawyers than in civil lawyers?

Suppose Zimmerman was a criminal defendant who possessed knowledge which, if disclosed, would save another's life but result in Zimmerman's imprisonment. Would the morality of his lawyer's action in keeping the information secret be different than in the civil case? Suppose a criminal defendant confesses to her lawyer that she has committed a crime for which someone else is due to be executed. How is that situation different from the one presented in *Spaulding?*

In Nebraska v. Harper, 214 Neb. 911, 336 N.W.2d 597 (1983), cert. denied, 465 U.S. 1013 (1984), Harper, who had been convicted of poisoning several people, claimed that his trial counsel had provided ineffective representation because the lawyer had "permitted" Harper to tell the court the kind of poison he had administered to victims who were still alive. This disclosure permitted the victims to get appropriate medical treatment. The trial court allowed the disclosure but excluded from evidence the fact that Harper provided this information. In rejecting the claim of ineffective assistance of counsel. The court said:

> [R]efusal . . . to disclose would have only served as an aggravating circumstance. To now suggest that [the lawyer] should not have permitted Harper to disclose . . . is totally without basis. The lives of three individuals hung in the balance. Effective assistance of counsel does not require such callous behavior as [now] suggested by Harper.

336 N.W.2d at 600.

Wasserstrom describes the lawyer's moral universe as defined by client interests and restricted only by the dictates of law. He says that conduct permissible under law includes immoral behavior that should not be condoned. His argument assumes that the boundary between lawful and unlawful conduct is discernible, discerned and respected by most lawyers. The problem, according to Wasserstrom and most other commentators on this subject, is not that lawyers are lawless but that compliance with law does not ensure "moral" behavior. Yet Wasserstrom acknowledges, in a part of his article not reprinted here, that the Watergate scandal, which involved many lawyers, was a major factor in the renewed concern about lawyer's ethics. What those lawyers did, however, was not merely immoral but illegal. Does the amorality of lawyer's role-differentiated behavior lead to lawlessness?

The Perspective of the Bad Man

OLIVER WENDELL HOLMES, THE PATH OF LAW
COLLECTED LEGAL PAPERS (1920)

pp. 167–169, 171–175
Appears also in 10 Harv.L.Rev. 457–462 (1897).

When we study law we are not studying a mystery but a well-known profession. We are studying what we shall want in order to appear before judges, or to advise people in such a way as to keep them out of court. The reason why it is a profession, why people will pay lawyers to argue for them or to advise them, is that in societies like ours the command of the public force is intrusted to the judges in certain cases, and the whole power of the state will be put forth, if necessary, to carry out their judgments and decrees. People want to know under what circumstances and how far they will run the risk of coming against what is so much stronger than themselves, and hence it becomes a business to find out when this danger is to be feared. The object of our study, then, is prediction, the prediction of the incidence of the public force through the instrumentality of the courts.

. . . If you want to know the law and nothing else, you must look at it as a bad man, who cares only for the material consequences which such knowledge enables him to predict, not as a good one, who finds his reasons for conduct, whether inside the law or outside of it, in the vaguer sanctions of conscience. The theoretical importance of the distinction is no less, if you would reason on your subject aright. The law is full of phraseology drawn from morals, and by the mere force of language continually invites us to pass from one domain to the other without perceiving it, as we are sure to do unless we have the boundary constantly before our minds. . . .

The confusion with which I am dealing besets confessedly legal conceptions. Take the fundamental question. What constitutes the law? You will find some text writers telling you that it is something different from what is decided by the courts of Massachusetts or England, that it is a system of reason, that it is a deduction from principles of ethics or admitted axioms or what not, which may or may not coincide with the decisions. But if we take the view of our friend the bad man we shall find that he does not care two straws for the axioms or deductions, but that he does want to know what the Massachusetts or English courts are likely to do in fact. I am much of his mind. The prophecies of what the court will do in fact, and nothing more pretentious, are what I mean by the law.

Take again a notion which as popularly understood is the widest conception which the law contains—the notion of legal duty, to which already I have referred. We fill the word with all the content which we draw from morals. But what does it mean to a bad man? Mainly, and in the first place, a prophecy that if he does certain things he will be subjected to disagreeable consequences by way of imprisonment or compulsory payment of money. But from his point of view, what is the difference between being fined and being taxed a certain sum for doing, a certain thing? . . .

Questions and Comments

Holmes says the bad man's perspective is necessary "if you want to know the law and *nothing else.* . . ." What are the consequences for the lawyer of adopting this perspective? Is it possible to keep the bad man's perspective in one's office and not have it intrude on the rest of one's life? What are the consequences of this view for the client?

How would Holmes have advised Zimmerman's lawyers to counsel Zimmerman?

Holmes' "bad man" presumably would be interested not only in what the courts of Massachusetts would say but also in the likelihood that a prosecutor or private person would bring his actions before a court. If the courts would hold the client liable, but the local prosecutor is unlikely to discover the violation, should the lawyer so inform the client? How should the likelihood of prosecution affect the advice the lawyer gives the client? If Holmes' lawyer found out that the judge could be bought, should she tell her client this too?

A Critique of the Bad Man's Perspective

WILLIAM H. SIMON, "THE IDEOLOGY OF ADVOCACY: PROCEDURAL JUSTICE AND PROFESSIONAL ETHICS"
1978 Wis.L.Rev. 30, 39–41, 53, 55–58.*

THE LAWYER AS CHAMPION (THE WAR OF ALL AGAINST ALL)

. . .

The fullest justification of the Ideology of Advocacy rests on Positivist legal theory. The term Positivist is used here to refer to the kind of theory which emphasizes the separation of law from personal and social norms, the connection of law with the authoritative application of force, and the systematic, objective character of law.[24] Positivism was the basis of the profession's conception of advocacy in the late 19th and early 20th centuries, and it is still an important component of the professional self-image of some lawyers, despite its repudiation in most areas by the intellectual leaders of the bar. Even lawyers who reject Positivism as a general jurisprudential theory are sometimes prone to fall back on it when justifying their professional roles.

24. See, e.g., J. Austin, The Province of Jurisprudence Determined (Hart ed. 1954); H. Hart, The Concept of Law (1961) . . . Holmes, The Path of the Law, 10 Harv.L.Rev. 457 (1897) . . . Kelsen, The Pure Theory of Law: Its Methods and Fundamental Concepts, (pts. 1–2) 50 L.Q.Rev. 474 (1934) and 51 L.Q.Rev. 517 (1935).

. . .

A. Positivist Advocacy

The Positivist theory is constructed on the philosophical foundation laid by Thomas Hobbes.[25] In the Positivist view, society is an aggregate of egoistic individuals each pursuing his own ends. Government is an artificial creation, the basic function of which is to remedy the disorder which would result if the natural centrifugal tendencies of society went unchecked. . . .

Ends are natural, individual, subjective, and arbitrary. Social norms result from the random convergence of individual ends. By contrast, it is possible to construct a system of rules which is artificial, impersonal, objective, and rational. The best way to provide order is to create a sovereign (e.g., monarch, legislature, party) which is neutral toward the various ends of the citizens and which acts through rules. Rules will give a regularity to social life and thus eliminate uncertainty. Oppression will be eliminated once power is concentrated in the hands of a neutral ruler. An obstacle remains. The legitimacy of the sovereign rests solely on the unique end of order which all share. Yet, from the point of view of each citizen, this end extends only to the orderly behavior of the others. People will constantly be tempted to violate the rules in order to pursue their own individual ends. No one will be willing to pay the price of resisting such temptation without some assurance that the others will also obey. The solution is to have the rules provide for the administration of rewards and punishments in a manner calculated to insure general obedience.

The rules will define for each citizen a private sphere of autonomy. Within this sphere, he need not account to anyone for his actions. So long as he remains within his sphere, he need not fear coercion by the sovereign. The sovereign's enforcement of the rules against the other citizens will insure that they do not trespass within his sphere. Where disputes arise, they must be resolved in accordance with the rules. Since the sovereign cannot itself apply the rules to every particular dispute, it must appoint judges to act on its behalf. It is important that the judges apply the rules with impersonal regularity. They must not refer to their own personal ends. . . . The system enables the judge to reason from the general prescriptions of the rules to particular results. The judge applies the rules to the factual premises of the given situation. The disposition of the case is dictated by the system. The judge has no discretion; he is bound by the system.

The need for lawyers in the Positivist theory arises from the strangeness of the law. Since the legal system is independent of personal ends and social norms, its prescriptions often appear alien. They may be very complicated, and the sovereign may find it convenient to express them in an esoteric language. Thus, the rules are not easily apprehensible. But the individual needs to know how he can

---

25. T. Hobbes, Leviathan (1651). See, L. Fuller, The Law in Quest of Itself 19–26 (1940) . . . R. Unger, Knowledge and Politics, 5, 37–38 (1975) . . .

further his ends without causing the sovereign to intervene with sanctions. Otherwise, he will be in the very state of uncertainty that government was supposed to remedy. Moreover, if other citizens can gain a superior understanding of the rules, they can use this knowledge to oppress him by maneuvering him into situations where sovereign power will operate to his disadvantage. The solution is to create a class of legal specialists and to require its members to serve every citizen regardless of his ends.

The function of the lawyer is to explain how, and under what circumstances, the sovereign will intervene in his client's life. The lawyer enables his client to pursue his ends effectively by predicting the likelihood of assistance or sanction which attaches to alternative courses of action. He does so by the same type of systematic reasoning which the judge uses to decide cases. From another perspective, this function can be described as informing the client of his rights. A right is an opportunity to invoke or resist the force of the sovereign in a certain way. Rights are defined by the rules of the legal system.

. . .

B. *The Critique of Positivist Advocacy*

. . .

. . . Positivism fails to show that the lawyer can enhance his client's autonomy. Rather, it appears from Positivism's own premises that the lawyer who adheres to the Positivist version of the Ideology of Advocacy must end by subverting his client's autonomy . . .

The Positivist version of the Ideology of Advocacy focuses on the person for whom the law is a mystery. Such a person, even if conscious of and articulate about his ends, would not know which aspects of them the lawyer would need to understand in order to gauge the impact of the legal system on his life. In order to isolate these aspects, he would need the legal knowledge for which he relies on his lawyer. The lawyer, on the other hand, has no reliable way of learning the client's ends on his own . . . [An underlying assumption of Positivism is that the client's] ends are subjective, individual, and arbitrary, [and that therefore] the lawyer has no access to them.[56] . . . [It then follows that] any attempt to [ask] . . . the client [about] . . . his ends or to interpret the client's ambiguous replies will necessarily involve the intrusion of the lawyer's own ends. Thus, consciously or not, the Positivist lawyer is faced with a dilemma: On the one hand, he cannot give intelligible advice to his client without referring to [what the client wants, i.e., the client's] ends; on the other hand, he cannot refer to ends without endangering the client's autonomy, and thus, undermining the basic purpose of his role.

56. Cf. S. Wolin, Politics and Vision: Continuity and Innovation in Western Political Thought 341 (1960) ("The basic assumption [of liberal political thought], that each was the best judge of his own interests, rested squarely on the belief that no individual could truly understand another.").

. . .

. . . [The Positivist Lawyer resolves this dilemma by imputing ends to the client.] The ends which Positivism imputes are derived from the basic Positivist premise of egoism, but they go beyond this initial premise to emphasize characteristics of extreme selfishness. The specific ends most often imputed are the maximization of freedom of movement and the accumulation of wealth.

. . .

. . . The client of whom Positivism is most solicitous is the naive person, face to face with the alien force of the state, threatened with a massive disruption of his life. Confronted with the need to act in this strange situation, the client must make sense of it as best he can. The lawyer puts himself forth quite plausibly as the client's best hope of mastering his predicament. If he is to avoid being overwhelmed by chaos, he must acquiesce in his lawyer's definition of the situation. He must think in a manner which gives coherence to the advice he is given. He may begin to do this quite unconsciously. If he is at all aware of the change, he is likely to see it as a defensive posture forced on him by the hostile intentions of opposing parties . . . His only strategy of survival requires that he see himself as the lawyers and the officials see him, as an abstraction, a hypothetical person with only a few crude, discrete ends.[61] He must assume that his subtler ends, his long-range plans, and his social relationships are irrelevant to the situation at hand. This is the profound and unintended meaning of Holmes's remark:

> If you want to know the law and nothing else, you must look at it as a bad man, who cares only for the material consequences which such knowledge enables him to predict, not as a good one, who finds his reasons for conduct, whether inside the law or outside of it, in the vaguer sanctions of conscience.

The role of the bad man, conceived as an analytical device for the lawyer, becomes, under pressure of circumstances, a psychological reality for the client.

. . .

Despite its complete irrationality, this Positivist strategy [of imposing ends on the client] has become so widely accepted that many lawyers have come to equate the manipulation of the client . . . with neutral advice to the client on his rights. For instance, lawyers constantly express astonishment at the willingness of intelligent laymen, aware of their rights, to make inculpatory statements to the authorities. They can think of no other explanation for this phenomenon besides confusion or pressure from the interrogators, and they thus

61. On the process by which an individual comes to accept the others' definition of his situation, see J. Sartre, Being and Nothingness 55–67, 252–302 (Barnes trans. 1952) . . . Goffman, The Moral Career of the Mental Patient, in Asylums: Essays on the Social Situation of Mental Patients and Other Inmates 127–169 (1961) . . . Lukacs, Reification and the Consciousness of the Proletariat, in History and Class Consciousness 83–110 (Livingstone trans. 1971) . . . .

conclude that no one can be expected to make an "informed decision" on such matters without the assistance of counsel. But the lawyer's assistance does not take the form of neutral information or the alleviation of pressure. Along with his knowledge of the law, the lawyer brings his own prejudices and his own psychological pressures. These derive from the conception of the roles of lawyer and client which is implicit in Positivism generally and in the strategy of imputed ends. As Justice Jackson put it, "[A]ny lawyer worth his salt will tell the suspect in no uncertain terms to make no statement to the police under any circumstances." [66] The Positivist lawyer is not an advisor, but a lobbyist for a peculiar theory of human nature.

. . .

Questions

The Positivist interpretation of law was in part a reaction to a Natural Law interpretation which held that law expresses inevitable and therefore "natural" justice. Does the legal system deliver natural justice? Or, at best, moderately effective controls on "bad men"? If the latter, shouldn't a lawyer advise her client on that basis? Every sensitive person wishes for more caring conduct toward others than the "bad man" delivers. But how can legal process deliver or compel such conduct? Can you pursue a vocation that, generally speaking, is not a "caring profession," like medicine or teaching?

Other material on the morality of the lawyer's role and relationship with clients include: Rosenthal, Lawyer & Client: Who's In Charge? (1974); Goldman, The Moral Foundations of Professional Ethics, ch. 3 (1980); Kaufman, Book Review, 94 Harv.L.Rev. 1504 (1981) (reviewing Goldman); Luban, The Good Lawyer: The Lawyers' Roles and Lawyers' Ethics (1984) (collection of articles on the morality of the lawyer's role); Schneyer, Moral Philosophy's Standard Misconception of Legal Ethics, 1984 Wis.L.Rev. 1529; Pepper, The Lawyer's Amoral Ethical Role: A Defense, A Problem and Some Possibilities, 1986 Am.B. Found.Res.J. 613; Shaffer, Legal Ethics and the Good Client, 36 Cath. U.L.Rev. 319 (1987); Simon, Ethical Discretion in Lawyering, 101 Harv. L.Rev. 1083 (1988).

CAROL GILLIGAN, IN A DIFFERENT VOICE (1982)
pp. 25–29.*

The dilemma that these eleven-year-olds were asked to resolve was one in the series devised by [Lawrence] Kohlberg to measure moral

---

66. Watts v. Indiana, 338 U.S. 49, 59 (1949); cf. Justice Jackson's remark on his experience of civil practice in Jamestown, N.Y., ". . . . a lawyer there, if he was consulted on a matter, usually dominated the matter, no matter who the businessman was." E. Gerhart, America's Advocate: Robert M. Jackson 63 (1958).

development in adolescence by presenting a conflict between moral norms and exploring the logic of its resolution. In this particular dilemma, a man named Heinz considers whether or not to steal a drug which he cannot afford to buy in order to save the life of his wife. In the standard format of Kohlberg's interviewing procedure, the description of the dilemma itself—Heinz's predicament, the wife's disease, the druggist's refusal to lower his price—is followed by the question, "Should Heinz steal the drug?" The reasons for and against stealing are then explored through a series of questions that vary the parameters of the dilemma in a way designed to reveal the underlying structure of moral thought.

Jake, at eleven, is clear from the outset that Heinz should steal the drug. Constructing the dilemma, as Kohlberg did, as a conflict between the values of property and life, he discerns the logical priority of life and uses that logic to justify his choice.

For one thing, a human life is worth more than money, and if the druggist only makes $1,000, he is still going to live, but if Heinz doesn't steal the drug, his wife is going to die (*Why is life worth more than money?*) Because the druggist can get a thousand dollars later from rich people with cancer, but Heinz can't get his wife again. (*Why not?*) Because people are all different and so you couldn't get Heinz's wife again.

Asked whether Heinz should steal the drug if he does not love his wife, Jake replies that he should, saying that not only is there "a difference between hating and killing," but also, if Heinz were caught, "the judge would probably think it was the right thing to do." Asked about the fact that, in stealing, Heinz would be breaking the law, he says that "the laws have mistakes and you can't go writing up a law for everything that you can imagine."

· · ·

[In contrast to Jake's answers are Amy's.] Asked if Heinz should steal the drug, she replies . . .

Well, I don't think so. I think there might be other ways besides stealing it, like if he could borrow the money or make a loan or something, but he really shouldn't steal the drug—but his wife shouldn't die either.

Asked why he should not steal the drug, she considers neither property nor law but rather the effect that theft could have on the relationship between Heinz and his wife:

If he stole the drug, he might save his wife then, but if he did, he might have to go to jail, and then his wife might get sicker again, and he couldn't get more of the drug, and it might not be good. So, they should really just talk it out and find some other way to make the money.

Seeing in the dilemma not a math problem with humans but a narrative of relationships that extends over time. Amy envisions the wife's continuing need for her husband and the husband's continuing concern for his wife and seeks to respond to the druggist's need in a way that would sustain rather than sever connection. . . . Since Amy's moral judgment is grounded in the belief that "if somebody has something that would keep somebody alive, then it's not right not to give it to them," she considers the problem in the dilemma to arise not from the druggist's assertion of rights but from his failure of response.

. . . Failing to see the dilemma as a self-contained problem in moral logic, she does not discern the internal structure of its resolution; . . . she constructs the problem differently. . . .

Instead, seeing a world comprised of relationships rather than people standing alone, a world that coheres through human connection rather than through systems of rules, she finds the puzzle in the dilemma to lie in the failure of the druggist to respond to the wife. Saying that "it is not right for someone to die when their life could be saved," she assumes that if the druggist were to see the consequences of his refusal to lower his price, he would realize that "he should just give it to the wife and then have the husband pay back the money later." Thus she considers the solution to the dilemma to lie in making the wife's condition more salient to the druggist or, that failing, in appealing to others who are in a position to help.

Just as Jake is confident the judge would agree that stealing is the right thing for Heinz to do, so Amy is confident that, "if Heinz and the druggist had talked it out long enough, they could reach something besides stealing." . . .

Questions

How would Jake analyze the moral predicament of the lawyers in *Spaulding*? How would Amy? Can you improve on their analyses?

D. PITFALLS FOR THE UNWARY

Shaping and Using Law and Facts

Both legal education and legal practice attune lawyers to the ambiguity of law and facts. The first year law student who reads the proverbial statute prohibiting vehicles in the park * might think she knows what the statute means, but the law professor quickly demonstrates how slippery words can be. Does the statute include motorcycles? Bicycles? Baby carriages? An Army truck used as a war memorial? A similar process occurs in law firms where new associates find out how many ways there are to characterize their client's behavior. Facts that seem clearly to show negligence reemerge under a partner's skillful hands as facts demonstrating great care and caution. Taking advantage of ambiguity that exists, and creating

* H.L.A. Hart, *The Concept of Law* 121 (1961).

ambiguity where none was seen before, are skills that every lawyer cultivates. There is, however, some line beyond which exercise of these skills can lead to trouble.

In In the Matter of Krueger, 103 Wis.2d 192, 307 N.W.2d 184 (1981), the client, while living in Illinois, retained Krueger, a Wisconsin lawyer, to represent him in a divorce proceeding. Krueger counseled the client to rent a room in Wisconsin to satisfy the residency requirement for a divorce action under Wisconsin law. The client did so for two weeks. Krueger thereafter filed a divorce petition for the client alleging that the client had been a resident of Wisconsin for more than six months and of the county in question for more than 30 days. The court-appointed referee found that the client initially gave Krueger some reason to believe that he could meet Wisconsin's residency requirements and "that diverse opinions could exist concerning the client's residency at the time the action was commenced." Krueger did not tell his client to testify falsely but did tell him how to "manifest an intention to continue his Wisconsin residency, despite the presence of facts indicating a specific intention to abandon a Wisconsin domicile . . . ." Krueger was publicly reprimanded for unprofessional conduct. What did he do wrong? Should Krueger have refused to tell the client what the courts would consider to be evidence of an intention to stay in Wisconsin once he had reason to believe the client would not stay? Is it proper to keep such information from a client?

Legal philosophy also generally interprets law as uncertain and malleable. Most forms of legal positivism asserted that law in its various forms—statutory, common and natural—was discoverable, i.e., had an inherent meaning apart from the will of its reader or interpreter. Judges could be right or wrong about what the law was. Positivism was supplanted as the dominant jurisprudential perspective by legal realism, which understood law as "what courts do". Law was what judges said it was; the lawyer's job was to predict what that might be. See the Holmes' excerpt printed above. What judges did and would do—in other words, what the law was and would be—could be understood as a function of the societal values held by judges, who as products of their environment would act consistent with historical and cultural norms. Understanding those norms, the values of the society that produced judges, was the key to understanding law. Critical Legal Studies takes the realist critique of positivism one step further. Law is to be understood as the product of neither rational thought nor shared societal values. Law is power exercised by judges as state officials. Their will, their commitment to their own values and the use of power, is what determines the content of law. If law is the exercise of power or a prediction of what courts will do, why was Krueger wrong to help his client understand and act in a way that would produce a more favorable ruling by the courts?

How does a lawyer interpret the requirement of Canon 7 of the Model Code that representation of a client remain "within the bounds of the law," when many modern concepts of law refute the notion that it has bounds?

Where is the line between presenting evidence in the light most favorable to one's client, permitted under EC 7–6, and making false statements about the facts, prohibited by DR 7–102(5) and M.R. 3.3?

Lawyers' Immunity from Law's Prohibitions

Introductory Note

When lawyers are acting not as advocates but as counselors, advisors, negotiators etc., the law treats them very much as it treats laypeople performing similar roles. Hence, lawyers most of the time are governed by the law that applies to all people regardless of profession. The exception is the advocate, who does not act in the real world but in a staged world with its own set of rules—the theater of a court—where the lawyer is governed by the special rules governing the theater.

The paradigm of the trial lawyer suggests that lawyers as such enjoy some general immunity from the strictures of the law. This is not so. The suspension of the general law (and the substitution of special rules) for the advocate arises not from membership in the profession but from the courtroom theater and the lawyer's part in it.

The fact that the advocate operates under special rules is a source of confusion for many lawyers and an excuse for misconduct by others.* The extent to which laws of general application apply to lawyers outside the courtroom will be considered in depth in the next chapter. The special rules that govern the advocate in court are considered in Chapter 5. The following case examines the line between the paradigms of in-court behavior and office conduct.

COMMONWEALTH v. STENHACH
Superior Court of Pennsylvania, 1986.
356 Pa.Super. 5, 514 A.2d 114, appeal denied, 517 Pa. 589, 534 A.2d 769 (1987).

HESTER, JUDGE:

Two criminal defense attorneys have appealed from convictions for hindering prosecution and tampering with evidence arising from their conduct while representing a defendant in a murder trial. Appellants George and Walter Stenhach were young public defenders appointed to represent Richard Buchanan, a man charged with first degree murder. Following Buchanan's directions, appellants recovered a rifle stock used in the homicide. Allegedly believing that disclosure of the rifle stock

---

* "One of the least supportable excesses of M. Freedman, Lawyer's Ethics in an Adversary System (1975), is the extension of arguments for client-oriented lawyer action from the area of advocacy to the entirely different field of client counseling. As a glaring example, arguments for a lawyer's exclusive focus on the interests of his or her client that Professor Freedman develops, in the context of the criminal defense function, he then applies without qualification to lawyers who advise clients about non-criminal law matters when issuing securities, id. at 20–24." Wolfram, Modern Legal Ethics (1986) § 13.3.4 n. 45 at 697.

would be legally and ethically prohibited, appellants did not deliver it to the prosecutor until ordered to do so by the court during the prosecution's case. After Buchanan's conviction of third degree murder, appellants were charged with hindering prosecution, 18 Pa.C.S. § 5105(a)(3), tampering with physical evidence, § 4910(1), criminal conspiracy, § 903, and criminal solicitation, § 902. A jury found both appellants guilty of hindering prosecution, a third degree felony, and tampering, a second degree misdemeanor. In addition, George was convicted of solicitation, and Walter of conspiracy. Each was sentenced to twelve months probation and a fine of $750.

Their appeal raises questions relating to the interplay of the fifth and sixth amendments to the United States Constitution, the statutory attorney-client privilege, and the Pennsylvania Code of Professional Responsibility, in which appellants challenge their duty to deliver evidence to the prosecution. Appellants also raise a due process challenge to the criminal statutes which prohibit hindering prosecution and tampering with evidence when these statutes are applied to criminal defense attorneys, claiming the statutes are unconstitutionally overbroad; the statutory defense of justification; and allegations of numerous trial errors in evidentiary and other rulings. Amicus curiae briefs by the Pennsylvania Trial Lawyers Association, the National Association of Criminal Defense Lawyers and the Public Defender Association of Pennsylvania all support reversal of the judgments of sentence.

We reject appellants' argument that their retention of physical evidence was proper under existing law. We hold, however, that the statutes under which they were convicted are unconstitutionally overbroad as applied to criminal defense attorneys. Accordingly, we do not address appellants' claims of trial error, but order appellants discharged.

Background

In March, 1982, Theodore Young was killed in Potter County. The following day Richard Buchanan and an accomplice were arrested and charged with first degree murder. Appellant George Stenhach, part-time Public Defender of Potter County, undertook Buchanan's defense immediately. He petitioned for appointment of an investigator to assist in Buchanan's defense, and former police officer Daniel Weidner was appointed as Buchanan's investigator. During a confidential conference among Stenhach, Weidner and Buchanan, Buchanan described the death of Theodore Young. He said that Young had attacked him with two knives and that during the attack, Young had died after he was shot, hit by Buchanan's car, then struck by Buchanan's rifle, causing the stock of the rifle to break off. Buchanan and his accomplice had then disposed of the weapons and other items relating to Young's death. During the conference, Weidner and Buchanan prepared a map identifying the location of some of these items.

Appellant Walter Stenhach, George's younger brother, was practicing law in partnership with George, and assisted in Buchanan's defense. Appellants George and Walter Stenhach had graduated from law school in 1978 and 1980, respectively, and had been admitted to practice in Pennsylvania in 1979 and 1981. They discussed the information received from Buchanan, and decided to pursue the theory of self-defense and to attempt to gather evidence supporting that theory. Accordingly, they ordered Weidner to search for the items Buchanan had described, and to retrieve as many as he could find.

On the same day, Weidner found the broken rifle stock and brought it back to appellants' office. He did not find the barrel, which was eventually discovered by the prosecutor and introduced into evidence at Buchanan's trial. Weidner was unable to locate the knives allegedly used by the victim, and no knives were ever found. When Weidner delivered the rifle stock to appellants, they stored it inside a paper bag in a desk drawer in their office.

Weidner had been a police officer for twenty years and was performing his first defense investigation in the Buchanan case. He expressed his concern as many as twenty times during the five months before Buchanan's trial that appellants were violating the law by withholding the rifle stock. Based on their research of case law, the Constitution, Pennsylvania statutes and the Pennsylvania Code of Professional Responsibility, appellants repeatedly told Weidner that the weapon was protected by the attorney-client privilege and that Weidner and appellants had a legal duty to preserve Buchanan's confidential communications which led to discovery of the weapon.

On the fourth day of Buchanan's murder trial, during an in-camera hearing, the prosecutor questioned Weidner about the rifle stock. Appellants objected on the ground that an answer would violate the attorney-client privilege. The trial judge overruled the objection, holding the privilege inapplicable to physical evidence, and ordered Weidner to answer. After Weidner testified how he had located and retrieved the rifle stock, the judge ordered its production, and appellants brought it from their office. The stock was not entered into evidence during Buchanan's trial by the prosecution or by the defense.

After Buchanan's conviction, the prosecutor, District Attorney Leber, charged appellants with hindering prosecution and tampering with evidence for withholding the rifle stock. Due to Leber's role as a prospective witness against appellants, a prosecutor was appointed by the state attorney general's office.

At appellants' trial, the primary witnesses for the Commonwealth were Buchanan, Leber and Weidner. Due to Buchanan's invocation of his fifth amendment privilege while his conviction was on direct appeal, the trial court allowed the transcript of Buchanan's testimony in his murder trial to be read into evidence against appellants to establish the evidentiary nature of the rifle stock in question. Leber testified concerning its concealment, its production, and the effect on the prosecution of Buchanan. Weidner testified about discovery and seizure of the evidence as well as appellants' acts and statements regarding continuing retention of the weapon after its discovery.

Appellants in turn testified about the various authorities which allegedly justified their belief that they were obligated to retain the rifle stock to protect their client. They attempted to offer the expert testimony of law professor John Burkoff to establish a justification defense based on the ethical standards applicable to attorney conduct. The trial judge did not permit Burkoff to testify, nor did he instruct the jury on the defense of justification.

Following conviction and sentencing, this appeal was filed. Appellants argue four issues. First, they challenge the trial court's interpretation of the statutes as requiring production of the physical evidence without a court order. Second, they argue they were denied due process of law in that the hindering prosecution and evidence tampering statutes are unconstitutionally vague or overbroad as applied to defense attorneys when literal compliance would require them to violate their statutory, ethical and constitutional duties to their clients. Third, they claim the trial court erred in refusing to permit presentation of a justification defense. Fourth, they argue that the trial court committed reversible error [in failing to sustain a number of appellants' objections]. . . .

Duty to Deliver

Appellants' first argument is that they had no duty to turn over the rifle stock to the prosecutor until ordered to do so by the court. We reject this argument. Although we have no Pennsylvania cases on point, the decisions in other jurisdictions appear to be virtually unanimous in requiring a criminal defense attorney to deliver physical evidence in his possession to the prosecution without court order. It is true that most of the cases arose in the context of appeals from criminal convictions challenging the effectiveness of counsel who had turned over physical evidence, or in the context of litigation of discovery orders or in the context of contempt proceedings against attorneys who failed to produce evidence. The sole case in which an attorney was charged with a criminal offense resulted in the only holding that the concealed evidence was protected by the attorney-client privilege. We join the overwhelming majority of states which hold that physical evidence of crime in the possession of a criminal defense attorney is not subject to a privilege but must be delivered to the prosecution.

. . .

Turning to the law in other jurisdictions, we note the much-quoted case of State v. Olwell, 64 Wash.2d 828, 394 P.2d 681 (1964). A criminal defense attorney had been held in contempt of court following his refusal to answer questions or produce weapons at a coroner's inquest, in defiance of a subpoena duces tecum. The appellate court reversed the finding of contempt, holding that the subpoena was defective on its face for invading the confidential relationship between attorney and client so that refusal to testify against the client was not contemptuous. Id. at 833, 394 P.2d 681. The court went on to state that the attorney was required to produce the weapon on his own motion, and that the jury was not to learn the source of the evidence.

We do not, however, by so holding, mean to imply that evidence can be permanently withheld by the attorney under the claim of the attorney-client privilege. Here, we must consider the balancing process between the attorney-client privilege and the public interest in criminal investigation. We are in agreement that the attorney-client privilege is applicable to the knife held by appellant, but do not agree that the privilege warrants the attorney, as an officer of the court, from withholding it after being properly requested to produce the same. The attorney should not be a depository for criminal evidence (such as a knife, other weapons, stolen property, etc.), which in itself has little, if any, material value for the purposes of aiding counsel in the preparation of the defense of his client's case. Such evidence given the attorney during legal consultation for information purposes and used by the attorney in preparing the defense of his client's case whether or not the case ever goes to trial, could clearly be withheld for a reasonable period of time. It follows that the attorney, after a reasonable period, should, as an officer of the court, on his own motion turn the same over to the prosecution.

We think the attorney-client privilege should and can be preserved even though the attorney surrenders the evidence he has in his possession. The prosecution, upon receipt of such evidence from an attorney, where charge against the attorney's client is contemplated (presently or in the future), should be well aware of the existence of the attorney-client privilege. Therefore, the state when attempting to introduce such evidence at the trial, should take extreme precautions to make certain that the source of the evidence is not disclosed in the presence of the jury and prejudicial error is not committed. By thus allowing the prosecution to recover such evidence, the public interest is served, and by refusing the prosecution an opportunity to disclose the source of the evidence, the client's privilege is preserved and a balance is reached between these conflicting interests.

Id. at 833–34, 394 P.2d 681. We have quoted at length from *Olwell* because most of the cases which follow cite or quote it and raise the same issues addressed in the above passage.

People v. Meredith, 29 Cal.3d 682, 175 Cal.Rptr. 612, 631 P.2d 46 (1981), reached similar conclusions. A murder defendant told his attorney where he had abandoned physical evidence of the crime. The attorney's investigator retrieved the evidence, the attorney examined it and then turned it over to the police, and the evidence was admitted at trial along with testimony of the investigator describing the location of the evidence. On appeal from his conviction, the defendant conceded the admissibility of the physical evidence, but challenged the admissibility of the testimony regarding its location. The court held that the testimony did not violate the attorney-client privilege. "When defense counsel alters or removes physical evidence, he necessarily deprives the prosecution of the opportunity to observe that evidence in its original condition or location. . . . To extend the attorney-client privilege to a case in which the defense removed evidence might encourage defense counsel to race the police to seize critical evidence." Id. 175 Cal.Rptr. at 612, 631 P.2d at 46.

In People v. Lee, 83 Cal.Rptr. 715, 3 Cal.App.3d 514 (1970), the court also concluded that physical evidence in the possession of an attorney was not privileged. . . .

Morrell v. State, 575 P.2d 1200 (Alaska Supreme Ct.1978), is another direct appeal from a criminal conviction raising the issue of ineffectiveness of trial counsel following his delivery of incriminating physical evidence to the police. A third party had discovered the evidence and brought it to the attorney. Unsure of his duties, he sought guidance from the ethics committee of the state bar association. The committee advised him to return the evidence to the finder, explaining the laws pertaining to concealment of evidence. Counsel did so, and assisted the third party in delivering the evidence to the police. The court held that counsel was not ineffective, stating:

> As [appellant] notes, authority in this area is surprisingly sparse. The existing authority seems to indicate, however, that a criminal defense attorney has an obligation to turn over to the prosecution physical evidence which comes into his possession, especially where the evidence comes into the attorney's possession through acts of a third party who is neither a client of the attorney nor an agent of a client. After turning over such evidence, an attorney may have either a right or a duty to remain silent as to the circumstances under which he obtained such evidence. . . .

Id. at 1207. After reviewing cases involving duties of attorneys in possession of incriminating physical evidence, the court summarized their holdings.

> From the foregoing cases emerges the rule that a criminal defense attorney must turn over to the prosecution real evidence that the attorney obtains from his client. Further, if the evidence is obtained from a non-client third party who is not acting for the client, then the privilege to refuse to testify concerning the manner in which the evidence was obtained is inapplicable.

Id. at 1210.

Another case in which defense counsel, who had received physical evidence incriminating his client from a third party, sought the advice of the state bar association ethics committee is Hitch v. Pima County Superior Court, 146 Ariz. 588, 708 P.2d 72 (Supreme Ct.1985). The committee's opinion advised him he had a legal obligation to deliver the evidence to the prosecution. He informed the court of the evidence and the ethics committee opinion, whereupon the court ordered him to turn over the evidence and to withdraw from the case. His client, prior to trial, appealed that order.

The Arizona Supreme Court, referring to "Ethical Standard to Guide [A Lawyer] Who Receives Physical Evidence Implicating His Client in Criminal Conduct," proposed by the Ethics Committee of the Criminal Justice Section of the American Bar Association, 29 Crim.L. Rptr. 2465–66 (August 26, 1981), held that the attorney might return the evidence to its source if he could do so without destroying the evidence, or he must turn it over to the prosecution. Counsel's reasonable belief that the third-party source, a friend of the client, might cause destruction or concealment of the evidence necessitated its delivery to the prosecution. The court also rejected the procedure utilized in the District of Columbia whereby such evidence is given to the local bar association for subsequent delivery to the prosecutor. The court believed that such anonymous transmittal would frequently destroy the evidentiary significance of the physical item, which often depends upon where and under what circumstances it was found. Citing People v. Nash, 110 Mich.App. 428, 447, 313 N.W.2d 307, 314 (1981), the court stated that "it is simpler and more direct for defendant's attorney to turn the matter over to the state as long as it is understood that the prosecutor may not mention in front of the jury the fact that the evidence came from the defendant or his attorney." *Hitch,* supra, 708 P.2d at 79. Finding no dereliction in the attorney's representation of his client, the court held that he need not withdraw unless "the client [believes] his attorney no longer has his best interest in mind." Id.

The only case we have found involving criminal prosecution of an attorney for failure to deliver physical evidence is People v. Belge, 83 Misc.2d 186, 372 N.Y.S.2d 798 (1975). Representing a murder defendant and relying on an insanity defense, counsel investigated his client's claim that he had committed other murders and discovered one of the bodies hidden in a cemetery. He left the body *in situ* and did not reveal his discovery until his client's trial. After the murder trial, counsel was indicted for the offenses of failure to assure that a decent burial be accorded the dead and failure to report to authorities the death of a person without medical attendance. Not surprisingly,

> Public indignation reached the fever pitch. . . . A hue and cry went up from the press and other news media. . . . However, the [Constitution] attempts to preserve the dignity of the individual and to do that guarantees him the services of an attorney who will bring to the bar and to the bench every conceivable protection from the inroads of the state against such rights as are vested in the [C]onstitution for one accused of crime. Among those substantial constitutional rights is that a defendant does not have to incriminate himself. His attorneys were bound to uphold that concept and [to] maintain what has been called a sacred trust of confidentiality.

372 N.Y.S.2d at 801–02. The court held that counsel had "conducted himself as an officer of this Court with all the zeal at his command to protect the constitutional rights of his client," id. at 803, and dismissed the indictment.

The court did state, however, that the attorney's conduct in balancing his client's rights against the public interest in the administration of justice was, "in a sense, obstruction of justice." The court believed the grand jury was "grasping at straws," and that if instead of charging the attorney with violation of a "pseudo-criminal statute," it had charged him with obstruction of justice under a proper statute, the court would have been faced with a much more difficult decision. Id.

With the exception of *Belge,* id., the foregoing cases provide a consistent body of law, which we adopt. To summarize, a criminal defense attorney in possession of physical evidence incriminating his client may, after a reasonable time for examination, return it to its source if he can do so without hindering the apprehension, prosecution, conviction or punishment of another and without altering, destroying or concealing it or impairing its verity or availability in any pending or imminent investigation or proceeding. Otherwise, he must deliver it to the prosecution on his own motion. In the latter event, the prosecution is entitled to use the physical evidence as well as information pertaining to its condition, location and discovery but may not disclose to a fact-finder the source of the evidence. We thus reject appellants' contention that their conduct was proper and that they had no duty to deliver the rifle stock to the prosecution until they were ordered to do so.

Due Process: Overbreadth

Appellants' second argument is that the statutes against hindering prosecution and tampering with evidence are unconstitutionally vague or overbroad as applied to attorneys engaged in the representation of criminal defendants, and hence their enforcement against appellants was a denial of due process. We agree. Our discussion of appellants' first argument, while holding that defense attorneys have an affirmative duty to deliver physical evidence to the prosecution, clearly demonstrates that there are conflicting concerns facing defense attorneys in possession of incriminating physical evidence. Moreover, we are not aware of *any* case in *any* state in which an attorney was convicted of a crime for conduct similar to that of appellants. . . .

Both overbroad and vague statutes deny due process in two ways: they do not give fair notice to people of ordinary intelligence that their contemplated activity may be unlawful, and they do not set reasonably clear guidelines for law enforcement officials and courts, thus inviting arbitrary and discriminatory enforcement. . . .

We hold that the statutes at issue in this case are overbroad when applied to attorneys representing criminal defendants. The literal language of each section is relatively clear. Section 5105(a)(3) states that a person is guilty of hindering prosecution "if, with intent to hinder the . . . conviction . . . of another for crime, he . . . conceals . . . evidence of the crime . . . regardless of its admissibility in evidence. . . ." Section 4910 provides that a person is guilty of tampering with physical evidence "if, believing that an official proceeding . . . is pending . . ., he . . . conceals or removes any record, document or thing with intent to impair its verity or availability in such proceeding. . . ." The clarity of the language is delusive, for it prohibits conduct which cannot constitutionally be prohibited along with conduct which clearly can. In certain circumstances, an attorney might conceal evidence with the intent of impairing its availability in his client's criminal trial and with the intent of hindering his client's conviction.

An example of such circumstances might involve an attorney whose client gives him a handwritten account of involvement in the crime he is charged with committing. If the attorney were to destroy the statement or retain it in his file, he would be guilty of violating the literal terms of the statutes against hindering prosecution and tampering with evidence. Yet no one would suggest the attorney should give the document to the prosecutor; indeed, to do so would be an egregious violation of the attorney's duties to his client.

The functions of the attorney counseling a criminal defendant have a constitutional dimension. In opposing unreasonable searches and seizures, in preventing self-incrimination and in rendering effective assistance of counsel, the defense attorney is charged with the protection of fourth, fifth and sixth amendment rights. In performing these functions, the defense attorney might run afoul of the statutes against hindering prosecution and tampering with evidence; thus he may not have adequate notice of what conduct might be a crime, and he is subject to the threat of arbitrary and discriminatory prosecution.

Beyond the obvious example stated above, there is little or no guidance for an attorney to know when he has crossed the invisible line into an area of criminal behavior. There are no prior cases in this jurisdiction in which a criminal defense attorney has been convicted of violating these statutes. We have discussed many of the similar cases from other jurisdictions, none of which addresses the precise issues facing us in this case. Although we focused on the uniformity we found in those cases as to disposition of physical evidence, they express a great deal of doubt and reflect great diversity as to the grayer areas of ethical usage of evidence of all sorts. Attorneys face a distressing paucity of dispositive precedent to guide them in balancing their duty of zealous representation against their duty as officers of the court. Volumes are filled with other potential sources of guidance, such as ethical codes and comments thereto, both proposed and adopted, advisory opinions by ethics committees and myriad articles in legal periodicals. The plethora of writings exemplifies the profession's concern with the problem, and although they may help to clarify some of the issues, they fail to answer many of the difficult questions in this area of legal practice.

In the cases discussed in the preceding section, we find many statements which belie the seeming consistency in their approach to the problem. *People v. Belge,* supra, of course, dismissing the indictment against an attorney who had withheld evidence, focused on the rights of a criminal defendant rather than the society's interest in criminal law enforcement:

> A trial is in part a search for truth, but it is only partly a search for truth. The mantle of innocence is flung over the defendant to such an extent that he is safeguarded by rules of evidence which frequently keep out absolute truth, much to the chagrin of juries. Nevertheless, this has been a part of our system since our laws were taken from the laws of England and over these many years has been found to best protect a balance between the rights of the individual and the rights of society.

Belge, supra, 372 N.Y.S.2d at 801. Another example is *In re Gartley,* supra, wherein this court stated:

> Not only is effective assistance of counsel a constitutional mandate, it is also necessary to an adversary system of justice. Assuredly, counsel's assistance can be made safely and readily available only when the client is free from the apprehension of disclosure.

. . .

Finally, *Hitch v. Pima County Superior Court,* supra, although holding that an attorney has a duty to deliver incriminating evidence to the prosecutor, added:

> We note also that the lawyer's role as a zealous advocate is an important one, not only for the client but for the administration of justice. We have chosen an adversary system of justice in which, in theory, the state and the defendant meet as equals—"strength against strength, resource against resource, argument against argument." United States v. Bagley, [473 U.S. 667, 694] n. 2, 105 S.Ct. 3375, 3390 n. 2, 87 L.Ed.2d 481, 486 n. 2 (1985) (Marshall, J., dissenting). In order to close the gap between theory and practice and thereby ensure that the system is working properly, a defendant must have an attorney who will fight against the powerful resources of the state. It is only when this occurs that we can be assured that the system is functioning properly and only the guilty are convicted.

Hitch, supra, 708 P.2d at 76.

Two cases cited in the previous section involved attorneys who had sought advisory opinions from ethics committees when confronted with problems related to disposition of physical evidence. Their action was salutory, but underscores the dilemma facing criminal defense attorneys in similar situations. Not only is the resort to guidance from an ethics committee a time-consuming process,[2] it is a process totally inconsistent with the precision which must attend a valid criminal statute to inform its subjects of what specific behavior is proscribed.

Another symbol of the dilemma is its extensive treatment in legal periodicals. Of the many articles which have been cited by the parties in this case, we have found several to be helpful and noteworthy.[3] Nonetheless, the writings exemplify a variety of approaches and suggestions, and indicate that an evidentiary problem related to incriminating evidence might arise in divers contexts in the representation of criminal defendants. It is not incumbent upon attorneys to digest the legal periodicals in order to conform their conduct to a criminal statute. The statutes involved in this case embrace conduct which is constitutionally protected as well as conduct which may validly be prohibited, and there is no line between the two which can be ascertained with any assurance whatsoever.

Even if it were possible, it is not the function of this court to provide an advisory opinion as to various examples of attorney conduct not involved in this case which might or might not violate the statutes we are reviewing. We note that other jurisdictions have enacted criminal statutes which address the unique role of defense attorneys in the administration of criminal justice and do not subject them to rules identical with those applicable to the public. *See* Clark v. State, 159 Tex.Cr.R. 187, 261 S.W.2d 339, cert. denied, 346 U.S. 855, 74 S.Ct. 69, 98 L.Ed. 369 (1953) (statute specifically excluded from liability one who aids an offender in preparing his defense). We note, also, as the Pennsylvania Supreme Court iterated in *Estate of Pedrick*, that the courts have the power, outside the context of criminal sanctions, to regulate the conduct of attorneys practicing before them, and that the Pennsylvania Supreme Court has established a Disciplinary Board together with comprehensive rules for dealing with apparent attorney misconduct. 505 Pa. [530,] 542, 482 A.2d [215,] 221.

For these reasons, we hold that the statutes which prohibit hindering prosecution and tampering with physical evidence are unconstitutionally overbroad when applied to attorneys representing criminal defendants.

2. The court in *Hitch,* supra, explained the result of seeking advice in that case:

We note that the prosecution in this matter has been delayed for over a year while this issue is being resolved. We believe that the recourse to the State Bar Ethics Committee, while proper and commendable, resulted in an excessive delay. We hope that in the future the State Bar Ethics Committee will be more prompt in responding to requests for opinions when, as here, a criminal prosecution is held in abeyance awaiting the opinion of the Committee.

Id. 708 P.2d at 79 n. 3.

3. See Comment, Ethics, Law and Loyalty: The Attorney's Duty to Turn Over Incriminating Physical Evidence, 32 Stan.L.Rev. 977 (1980); Comment, The Right of a Criminal Defense Attorney to Withhold Physical Evidence Received from His Client, 38 U.Chi.L.Rev. 211 (1970); Comment, Disclosure of Incriminating Physical Evidence; The Defense Attorney's Dilemma, 52 U.Colo.L.Rev. 419 (1981).

Accordingly, the judgments of sentence are vacated and appellants discharged.

Questions and Comments

Did the Lawyers in **Stenhach** *Commit a Crime?*

The court rejects the argument that the lawyers had no duty to turn over the evidence. The court not only "adopts" the rule of other jurisdictions that the lawyer has a responsibility under the ethics rules to turn over incriminating physical evidence, but speaks as if this duty was in force at the time the lawyers in this case acted. Why is the court confident that lawyers can observe the line between ethical and unethical conduct but not between criminal and legal conduct? Why isn't the court concerned about the potential "chilling effect" of the discipline rules?

The lawyers claimed that they had conducted exhaustive research and concluded they were "obligated" to retain the rifle stock. However, as the court's review of the case law shows, all the decided cases, with the exception of *Belge,* had held that there was a duty to turn over such evidence. Despite the consistency of court decisions in this area, lawyers have long been confused about their duties as to incriminating physical evidence. In In re Ryder, 263 F.Supp. 360 (E.D.Va.1967), aff'd, 381 F.2d 713 (4th Cir.1967), a seminal case, the lawyer was disciplined for removing a sawed-off shot gun and the proceeds of a bank robbery from his client's safe deposit box and placing these items in a safe deposit box under his own name. Ryder had consulted with several other lawyers, including a former judge, asking what he should do with this evidence. All those consulted were uncertain, but none recommended the "correct" course of conduct, i.e., turning the evidence over to the police. Neither did any suggest that Ryder might be criminally liable as an accomplice for retaining and concealing money stolen from the bank. The confusion might be attributed to the fact that *Ryder* was one of the first decided opinions on this question, but this answer does not explain the failure to consider the larceny statute as potentially applicable. This failure seems attributable to the assumption that lawyers are immune from laws of general applicability. Second and more critical, *Ryder* does not explain the continuing confusion of lawyers like the Stenhach brothers. In 1980, a commentator wrote:

> The attorney [in possession of incriminating physical evidence] has little guidance on how to resolve [the conflicting responsibilities as an officer of the court and to the client]. Neither the attorney-client privilege nor ethical rules nor statutes nor constitutional doctrines give a clear signal to the attorney seeking both to maintain loyalty to her client and to be properly candid with the court. The attorney in possession of incriminating physical evidence confronts a series of rules most of which indicate the importance of the value of loyalty to the client but none of which quite

provides the loyal attorney with a *safe harbor* from discipline or criminal penalties.

Note, Ethics, Law, and Loyalty: The Attorney's Duty to Turn Over Incriminating Physical Evidence, 32 Stan.L.Rev. 977, 980 (1980) (emphasis added).

Recent articles continue to bemoan the confusion in this area. See, e.g., Lefstein, Incriminating Physical Evidence, The Defense Attorney's Dilemma, and the Need for Rules, 64 N.C.L.Rev. 897 (1986). The confusion may have less to do with conflicting legal standards, however, than with a perceived conflict between what the law actually requires and what lawyers believe to be their duty, i.e., not to betray their clients.

Incriminating Evidence

DR 7–102(A)(4) of the Code provides: ". . . a lawyer shall not conceal or knowingly fail to disclose that which he is required by law to reveal"; and DR 7–109(A) states: "A lawyer shall not suppress any evidence that he or his client has a legal obligation to reveal or produce." Finally, DR 7–102(A)(8): "a lawyer shall not knowingly engage in other illegal conduct or conduct contrary to a Disciplinary Rule." Hence, the Code position is clearly that on this issue (as on all others, DR 7–102(A)(8)), "other law" "trumps" the general duty of loyalty to the client.

The Rules come out in the same place. M.R. 3.4(a): "A lawyer shall not *unlawfully* obstruct another party's access to evidence, or *unlawfully* alter, destroy or conceal a document or other material having potential evidentiary value. A lawyer shall not counsel or assist another person to do any such act." (emphasis added).

The question then is: What does law require?

First, there are criminal laws on the concealment and destruction of evidence. All jurisdictions have made the concealment or destruction of evidence criminal, although the circumstances that trigger the statutes vary from one state to another. Some states prohibit destruction only when the person "knows" a proceeding is ongoing or about to be instituted; others prohibit destruction when the person "believes" one is pending or about to be instituted; and others prohibit destruction with intent to prevent the production of the evidence. See, e.g., Model Penal Code § 242.3 (1962); 18 U.S.C. § 1000; West's Ann.Cal.Pen.Code § 135; Minn.Stat.Ann. § 609.63(1), (7); N.Y.—McKinney's Penal Law § 205.50. Few of these statutes make exception for lawyers. But see Clark v. State, 159 Tex.Crim. 187, 261 S.W.2d 339 (1953), cert. denied, 346 U.S. 855 (1953) (Texas concealment statute contains an exclusion for lawyers), and the approval of this approach in *Stenhach.*

Contraband statutes, which make the possession of certain items illegal, exist in all jurisdictions and make no exceptions for criminal defense lawyers.* See, e.g., Model Pen.Code § 5.06–.07 (1962) (possession of criminal instruments and weapons); West's Ann.Cal.Pen.Code § 12020 (Supp.1980) (possession of illegal weapons); West's Ann.Cal. Health & Safety Code § 11377 (Supp.1980) (possession of drugs and controlled substances); Uniform Controlled Substances Act § 401(c).

The case law, as pointed out in *Stenhach,* is unanimous in holding that the ethics rules, read in conjunction with the concealment and contraband laws, require disclosure. But see Stenhach II, discussed below. There is some question as *Stenhach* demonstrates, whether courts will uphold the use of criminal sanctions against criminal defense lawyers whose conduct violates these laws, but none that lawyers may be disciplined for such conduct under the ethics rules.

Case Law on the Lawyer's Obligations as to Incriminating Evidence

The general rule is that a lawyer must not act or assist in the destruction or unlawful concealment ** of evidence. This means that a lawyer must not take affirmative steps to conceal evidence, such as those taken by the lawyers in *Stenhach.* It also means that once a lawyer has possession of evidence, she must not return the evidence to its source (whether that is the client or a third party) if the lawyer has reason to believe that by doing so the evidence will be destroyed, unlawfully concealed or that the chain of evidence will thereby be broken. The lawyer should deliver the evidence to the prosecution. See, e.g., Hitch v. Pima County Court, 146 Ariz. 588, 708 P.2d 72 (1985); People v. Meredith, 29 Cal.3d 682, 631 P.2d 46 (1981). If a lawyer leaves evidence where she found it, she cannot be compelled to reveal information gained from privileged communication. However, once the evidence is taken from its original resting place thereby destroying the chain of evidence, the privilege is destroyed and the lawyer must turn the evidence over to the prosecution.

Are there ever situations when a lawyer may return the evidence to its source rather than turning it over to the prosecution? In light of the risk of subsequent destruction or concealment, the majority of jurisdictions require the lawyer to hand over to the proper authorities *all* physical evidence.*** See, e.g., State ex rel. Sowers v. Olwell, 64

* At least one commentator has suggested that the contraband statutes be amended to provide an exception for lawyers. Note, Ethics, Law, and Loyalty: The Attorney's Duty to Turn Over Incriminating Physical Evidence, 32 Stan.L.Rev. 977, 995 (1980). This commentator also suggests an exception for lawyers under the concealment and destruction of evidence statutes, arguing that the lawyer's duty of loyalty to the client should preclude having to provide the prosecution with physical evidence.

** The word "unlawful" distinguishes what might be called "lawful concealment", i.e., the legal steps an attorney may take to suppress evidence inadmissible under the evidence rules or obtained through a violation of the client's constitutional rights; or the legal steps a lawyer may take to prevent the opposing party in a civil case from gaining access to privileged material.

*** Throughout this discussion we are speaking of *physical* evidence. A bright line exists between the lawyer's possession of physical evidence and her knowledge of testimonial evidence. The lawyer has a duty to keep the testimonial evidence of past criminal activity confidential.

Wash.2d 828, 394 P.2d 681 (1964); People v. Lee, 3 Cal.App.3d 514, 83 Cal.Rptr. 715 (1970); Morrell v. State, 575 P.2d 1200 (Alaska 1978).

There are two caveats to this rule. The first concerns evidence created in the preparation of the defense, such as a statement by the defendant prepared for the lawyer on what the defendant knew about the bank's security system. These are privileged communications between client and lawyer and are not considered physical evidence under this rule. The fact that certain communications between client and lawyer are in physical form does not change their status as communications. However, if the written statement was not prepared to assist in the defense, e.g., the client kept a journal of her criminal activities, it is physical evidence that the lawyer would have a duty to hand over to the prosecution. See, e.g., Morrell v. State, 575 P.2d 1200 (Alaska 1978) (third party gave lawyer kidnap plans written out by the defendant; lawyer acted properly in returning the plans to the third party and advising him to turn them over to the police). Accord: State v. Carlin, 7 Kan.App.2d 219, 640 P.2d 324 (1982) (lawyer ordered to surrender an incriminating tape recording made by the client). Second, some courts have held that evidence that the state could not compel the defendant to produce against her will, if given to the lawyer by the client, need not be turned over to the authorities by the lawyer. See, e.g., State v. Superior Court, 128 Ariz. 253, 625 P.2d 316 (1981). In fact, the *Ryder* court in dicta appeared to be of this view. The court stated that if the evidence in Ryder's possession had not been a fruit or instrumentality of the crime but instead "merely evidentiary articles," Ryder could not be compelled to produce them. This opinion was based on the premise that "merely evidentiary articles" could not be seized from the defendant himself by compulsion of law. The "mere evidence" rule was repudiated by the Supreme Court in Warden v. Hayden, 387 U.S. 294, 306–307, 87 S.Ct. 1642, 1649–50 (1967).

Generally, it is said that the lawyer may retain the evidence for a "reasonable" period of time. As long as the defense then stipulates to the "chain of possession, location or condition of the evidence," the prosecution may not disclose to the jury from whom or in what manner the evidence was obtained. People v. Meredith, supra 631 P.2d at 54; see also *Olwell,* supra. The rationale for this restriction on the prosecution is that while the physical evidence itself is not privileged, the delivery to the lawyer is a privileged communication, which should not be revealed to the jury. On the other hand, the defendant should not be permitted to "destroy" the evidence (by destroying its usefulness) and that would be the result if the defense failed to stipulate to its original location and source. As the court in *People v. Meredith* expressed it:

> To bar admission of testimony concerning the original condition and location of the evidence . . . permits the defense to "destroy" critical information; it is as if . . . the wallet in this case bore a tag bearing the words "located in the trash can by Scott's resi-

dence," and the defense by taking the wallet, destroyed this tag. 631 P.2d at 53.

The District of Columbia has a unique rule: The lawyer must hand the evidence over to the District of Columbia Bar Counsel, who in turn is obliged to give the evidence to the prosecuting authorities without revealing its source. Other courts have rejected this rule because it may result in erasing the chain of evidence so completely as to render the evidence meaningless. See Hitch v. Pima County, 146 Ariz. 588, 708 P.2d 72, 78–79:

> Not all items have evidentiary significance in and of themselves. In this case, for instance, the watch is not inculpatory per se; rather, it is the fact that the [victim's] watch was found in defendant's jacket that makes the watch material evidence. By returning the watch anonymously to the police, this significance is lost. Assuming investigating officials are even able to determine to what case the evidence belongs, they may never be able to reconstruct where it was originally discovered or under what circumstances.

Do the rules change when a lawyer obtains the evidence from a third party rather than from the client or from the client's agent? When the source is the client or the client's agent, the attorney-client privilege prevents the prosecution from compelling the lawyer to testify as to the origin of the evidence as long as there is the appropriate stipulation from the defense. However, when the source is a third party, some courts hold that the privilege is inapplicable. See, e.g., *Olwell,* supra. But see *Hitch v. Pima,* supra (prosecution may not reveal source of evidence which lawyer obtained from a third party provided the defense makes the appropriate stipulations). [The lawyer's responsibilities as to evidence in civil cases is discussed in Chapter 5 below.]

Given this case law, how could the lawyers in *Stenhach* have conducted extensive research, as they testified, and reached the conclusion they did? Apparently they approached their research with the goal of building a legal argument to justify the retention of the rifle stock. What question might they have asked instead?

The Buried Bodies Case:

People v. Belge, 50 A.D.2d 1088, 376 N.Y.S.2d 771 (4th Dept.1975), aff'd, 41 N.Y.2d 60, 359 N.E.2d 377 (1976).

This case has gained a special place in the annals of legal ethics. The client, Robert Garrow, was charged with murder. He confessed to his lawyers, Belge and Armani, that he had committed the crime charged and that he had committed three other murders as well. The bodies of two of these victims had not yet been discovered by the police. Following Garrow's directions, the two lawyers found the bodies of Alicia Hauk, a 16 year-old high school student who had disappeared a month earlier, and Susan Petz, a 21 year-old Boston University journalism student. Susan Petz had disappeared after going camping with Dan Porter, who was the third murder victim and whose body had already been discovered by the police. The lawyers photographed the bodies of Alicia Hauk and Susan Petz, but told no one of their discovery.

Ms. Petz' family, knowing that their daughter's camping partner had been murdered, feared that she too was dead. On hearing that Garrow was charged with a murder in the Adirondacks, they thought he might know whether their daughter was alive or not. They went to Belge and Armani and pleaded for knowledge about their daughter, but the lawyers remained silent. The lawyers had offered to help police solve the Petz and Hauk cases in exchange for a plea bargain promise that Garrow would be committed to a mental hospital.

Community outrage over the case resulted in criminal charges against one of the lawyers for violating a New York law requiring a decent burial for the dead and the reporting of any death that occurs without medical attention. The trial court granted a motion to dismiss based on attorney-client privilege. On appeal, the court affirmed holding that the privilege "effectively shielded the defendant attorney from his actions which would otherwise have violated the Public Health Law." The court, however, went on to express its "serious concern" with the argument that the privilege is absolute. "We believe that an attorney must protect his client's interests, but also must observe basic human standards of decency, having due regard to the need that the legal system accord justice to the interests of society and its individual members." 376 N.Y.S.2d 771, 772.

After the court's decision, the Committee on Professional Ethics of the New York State Bar Ass'n issued an opinion, No. 479, stating that the lawyer's silence was required by the ethical rules.

The court in *Stenhach* notes that *Belge,* the only case to hold there was no duty to turn over physical evidence, was also the only case to involve criminal prosecution of the lawyers. *Belge,* however, is distinguishable on other grounds. The lawyers in that case never had possession of the evidence. They looked at the bodies in their original resting place and left them there. They did nothing to conceal or alter the evidence.

Did the lawyers in *Belge* act immorally?

Why Aren't Lawyers Prosecuted for Concealing Evidence?

Prosecutors have shown little interest in prosecuting lawyers for violating the evidence or contraband statutes. While there may be many reasons for this, including collegial sympathy, the primary reasons include: (1) Most of the evidence statutes require proof of "specific" or "willful" intent, e.g., intent to hinder the prosecution, and prosecutors appreciate that lawyers will claim to have concealed with intent to fulfill their professional responsibility; (2) Prosecutorial discretion is exercised against prosecution where the violator acted without malicious intent or bad faith, even if the statute does not require evil purpose; and (3) Prosecutors may share the assumption that lawyers are somehow immune from liability.

Stenhach II

In Office of Disciplinary Counsel v. Stenhach, No. 479, slip op. at 25–27 (Pa.Supr.Ct.Disciplinary Board Aug. 8, 1989) the board unanimously refused to discipline the Stenhach brothers for their conduct in the principal case.

As stated by the Supreme Court in Office of Disciplinary Counsel v. Keller, 509 Pa. 573, 579, 506 A.2d 872, 875 (1986), the primary purpose of our system of lawyer discipline is to protect the public from unfit attorneys and to maintain the integrity of the legal system. The conduct of Respondents in this case did not and could not in any way defeat this primary purpose, namely protecting the public from unfit attorneys. Respondents made a good faith effort to balance their duties to their client against their duties owed to the court as an officer. By retaining the evidence, Respondents protected their client's constitutional rights and by not tampering or destroying the evidence and keeping the evidence where it could be readily recovered upon lawful request, Respondents served their duty to the court. Respondents relied on Ethical Consideration 7–3 and resolved in favor of their client doubts as to the bounds of the law. The only thing Respondents can be accused of is zealously defending their client. However, the zealous advocate is necessary to an adversary system of justice . . .

A review of the facts found by the Hearing Committee will demonstrate that maintenance of the integrity of the legal system did not require the Respondents to turn over the evidence to the District Attorney. The District Attorney knew or should have known that the Respondent had knowledge of or may have acquired physical evidence of the crime. The District Attorney did not make any requests to the Respondents to turn over evidence before the trial. More importantly, a conviction was obtained without the use of the rifle stock as evidence; and the District Attorney chose not to put the rifle stock into evidence after the Respondents delivered it to the court, despite the fact the District Attorney had the means to do so. Thus, the integrity of the legal system was maintained because there was no reason to believe the evidence was of importance to the resolution of a disputed fact or the successful prosecution of Respondent's client.

Does this clarify the rule on incriminating evidence in Pennsylvania? In *Stenhach II*, the board makes much of how uncertain the lawyer's duty as to incriminating evidence was in Pennsylvania prior to *Stenhach I*, and concludes that it was therefore proper for the lawyers to have "resolved in favor of their client doubts as to the bounds of the law." Is the law still uncertain? Is the rule in Pennsylvania after

Stenhach II that a lawyer may retain incriminating evidence so long as it is not too incriminating? Since the time that the Stenhach brothers acted, a version of the Model Rules has become effective in Pennsylvania. Pennsylvania's version of M.R. 3.4(a) is substantially similar to the Model Rules' version. Does this clarify the rule in Pennsylvania?

We believe that *Stenhach II* notwithstanding, a lawyer in Pennsylvania who acts as Ryder did, i.e., retains possession of contraband or the proceeds of a crime, or for that matter one who retains the murder weapon or any other material evidence that incriminates the client, runs a serious risk of being disciplined for such conduct. If we are right, what explains *Stenhach II*?

Chapter II

CONFORMITY TO THE LAW

A. CRIMINAL LAW

Fraud

UNITED STATES v. BENJAMIN

United States Court of Appeals, Second Circuit, 1964.
328 F.2d 854.

FRIENDLY, CIRCUIT JUDGE.

This appeal concerns another of those sickening financial frauds which so sadly memorialize the rapacity of the perpetrators and the gullibility, and perhaps also the cupidity, of the victims. It is unusual in that the vehicle, American Equities Corporation, owned nothing at all—and, in a happier sense, in that the SEC was able to nip the fraud quite early in the bud. The appellants are Milton Mende, the principal promoter, Martin Benjamin, his lawyer, and Bernard Howard, a certified public accountant. After trial in the District Court for the Southern District of New York before Judge Palmieri without a jury, all three were convicted of conspiring willfully by use of interstate commerce to sell unregistered securities and to defraud in the sale of securities, in violation of the Securities Act of 1933, §§ 5(a) and (c), and 17(a), 15 U.S.C. §§ 77e(a) and (c), and 77q(a), sections which are implemented criminally by § 24 of the Act, 15 U.S.C. § 77x. Mende and Benjamin were convicted also on three substantive counts for using the mails in furtherance of the fraudulent schemes in violation of 18 U.S.C. § 1341. As their sentences on the latter counts were the same as those on the conspiracy count and run concurrently with them, and as we are satisfied that their conspiracy conviction was proper, we need not concern ourselves with the mail fraud counts. Lawn v. United States, 355 U.S. 339, 362, 78 S.Ct. 311, 2 L.Ed.2d 321 (1958).

Since the principal claim of Howard and Benjamin relates to the sufficiency of the evidence against them, it is necessary to give some description of what went on. The scheme began in December, 1960, when Mende, then in Nevada, arranged to be put in touch with a Reno attorney, McDonald, who was reported to have some "old corporations prior to 1933" for sale. Mende's interest in corporations of such vintage was due to § 3(a)(1) of the Securities Act of 1933, 15 U.S.C. § 77c(a)(1), which confers an exemption from the need for registration on

"Any security which, prior to or within sixty days after May 27, 1933, has been sold or disposed of by the issuer or bona fide offered to the public, but this exemption shall not apply to any new offering of any such security by an issuer or underwriter subsequent to such sixty days."

He was especially attracted by a 1919 shell, then bearing the rather appropriate name of Star Midas Mining Co., Inc. Authorized to issue 1,500,000 shares with a par value of 10¢ per share, Star Midas had approximately 964,000 shares outstanding, nearly all owned by a so-called "Mahoney group." It had no assets. After arranging to purchase the Mahoney holdings for $5,000 plus a $1,500 fee, Mende instructed McDonald to change the corporate name to American Equities Corporation and to increase the authorized capital to $1,500,000 by raising the par value to $1 per share. Before closing the purchase, the funds for which were not yet available, Mende, with McDonald's cooperation, bought stock certificates and a seal reflecting these changes. The purchase was not completed until February 23, 1961, when McDonald, having previously caused appropriate resolutions to be adopted and new officers and directors of Mende's selection to be named, turned over to Reiss and Kovaleski, as Mende's representatives, the books and records of the corporation and stock certificates for the 890,000 shares owned by the selling group. At this time the name of the corporation was changed.

Mende had not waited to acquire the American Equities shares before starting to sell them. In mid-January, 1961, he ordered an additional supply of stock certificates from a Los Angeles printer. By entering a bid to buy shares he arranged for American Equities to appear in the pink and white sheets of the National Quotation Service at a price of something over $5 per share. Robert Drattell, president of Lawrence Securities, Inc., which was inactive because of financial difficulties, testified that Benjamin then sought to interest him in selling shares of a corporation whose alleged assets corresponded with those later shown in statements of American Equities. Benjamin indicated that if Drattell would cooperate, he might be in a position to find some way to make capital available to Lawrence Securities. Later in January, Benjamin had Drattell come to a New York hotel to meet Mende, who told Drattell and Reiter, another broker, in Benjamin's presence, that American Equities "was a holding corporation that had property, various types of property all over the United States, assets of about six and a half million dollars, liabilities of about three million dollars." Mende whetted Drattell's appetite, as Benjamin had already done, by indicating he would help to get Lawrence Securities back on its feet. Drattell said he "would need letters of opinion" and "certified financial statements," and also would need to see the transfer records which, Mende told him, were kept by "a certified public accountant out on the Coast."

Benjamin speedily filled one of Drattell's demands by handing him a signed opinion, dated January 28, 1961, headed "To Whom It May Concern: American Equities Corporation." It recited that the corporation was organized in May, 1919, "and there was at that time issued to the public, 963,067 Shares." It went on to say that in Benjamin's opinion "the aforesaid shares are presently free and tradeable pursuant to" § 3(a)(1) of the Securities Act which it quoted, and reiterated:

> "In view of the foregoing section, and further in view of the fact that the original issuance of the 963,067 Shares in May of 1919, falls directly within Section 3(1) of the Securities Act of 1933, and is therefore, in my opinion, free and tradeable." [sic]

On January 28, Benjamin with Reiter and another broker, Parks, went to Los Angeles. Mende gave 4,000 shares of American Equities to Parks and 20,000 shares to Reiter, and also handed Reiter 5,000 shares to be given to Drattell. The latter used these to obtain from the Empire Trust Company a $12,500 loan, $3,500 of which went to bolstering Lawrence Securities' depleted capital account and the balance to Reiter, Mende and Mende's wife; Drattell sent a confirmation, dated January 31, 1961, of the "purchase" of these 5,000 shares for $9,000 to "Martin Benjamin Trustee." Later, after Drattell had gone to California to view some of the supposed assets of American Equities, he and Benjamin visited the office of Reiss, the transfer agent, where Benjamin prepared two letters. One, signed by Reiss, advised as to the 5,000 shares given to Drattell "that said certificates is free stock and is not investment stock"; [1] the second, dated back to January 31, and signed by "Martin Benjamin Trustee," purported to evidence the "sale" of the 5,000 shares for $9,000 and directed the distribution to Reiter and Mrs. Mende that had already been made.

Reiter and Parks had also brought from California copies of a paper with a printed cover entitled "American Equities Corporation." This contained an unidentified "Pro Forma Balance Sheet" as of November 30, 1960, in fact prepared by Reiss,[2] and a sheet of descriptive material, a draft of which the judge could reasonably have found to have been written out by Benjamin. The first numbered paragraph of this recited that American Equities was "a diversified investment company formed in the State of Nevada in 1919" and that its holdings consisted of "8 Apartment Houses, 2 Hotels, 2 Office Buildings (all located in Detroit area, Michigan)" with a "gross income from the properties" of $1,061,406.51 and net income of $200,000. This was completely false; the company owned no real estate in Detroit or elsewhere. Three subsequent paragraphs gave facts and figures as to the Outpost Inn, in Arizona, Biesmeyer Boat & Plastic Co., also of Arizona, and Stanford Trailer and Marine Supply Co., of California; the description did not say just what was American Equities' interest in these companies and the only elucidation in the balance sheet was in a note indicating that the price of the Outpost Inn would be $71,000 in cash and a $79,000 note, the former being separately shown as a liability. In fact, no arrangements of any kind had been made as to the Outpost Inn, and the owner of Biesmeyer testified that in December,

---

1. By what Drattell assumed to have been a Freudian slip, the word "not" was originally typed "hot."

2. Reiss was also convicted of conspiracy but has not prosecuted an appeal.

1960, he had agreed to give Mende an option for a down payment of $10,000 which was never made; we are not informed as to Stanford Trailer and Marine. Finally the description stated that American Equities "has acquired a working interest of 68% of the California Molded Products," whose 1961 sales were estimated at $2,000,000 with a gross profit margin "in excess of 30.1% with a potential of 32% by April, 1961," and that American Equities was negotiating to acquire still other companies, one "doing in excess of $20,000,000.00 annually." In fact, and to Benjamin's knowledge, American Equities had not acquired any interest in California Molded Products; all it had was a month's option, dated January 16, 1961, to acquire 68% of the stock for $145,000.

In mid-January, Benjamin invited Howard, a certified public accountant who had served Benjamin and his clients, to do some work for American Equities. Howard testified he received the November 30, 1960, "Pro Forma Balance Sheet," a yellow handwritten sheet of paper listing certain real estate holdings in Detroit, and balance sheets of corporations which Mende and Benjamin claimed were "owned or controlled" by American Equities. From these materials and without any examination of books and records, he prepared a paper dated February 10, 1961, and on the following day gave copies of this to Mende who handed one to Reiter. The latter testified that this was in Howard's presence.

The paper has a cover, on the stationery of Howard as a Certified Public Accountant, which bears the legend:

AMERICAN EQUITIES CORPORATION
DECEMBER 31, 1960

AUDITORS REPORT

This is followed by a two-page letter in which Howard advises the company that "After an examination of the books and records of the diversified holdings of your corporation for the period ended December 31, 1960," he is submitting a report of the company as at that date, consisting of "Exhibit 'A'—Pro-forma Balance Sheet as at December 31, 1960." Next comes a section entitled "COMMENTS" informing the company that it is "a diversified investment corporation with the following holdings." These were substantially the same as in the description accompanying the November 30 statement, with the Outpost Inn, Biesmeyer, Stanford and also California Molded Products now clearly listed among them. The comment on California Molded Products anticipates 1961 sales of $2,000,000 with gross profit margin in excess of 30% and a net of better than 4%, but omits to limit the company's interest in these riches to 68%, the most that was claimed by the November 30 balance sheet. The comments say that "The statement which is pro-forma includes the disposition of $500,000 which a group of stockholders propose to advance to the corporation as a long term loan"; that $150,000 of this was to be advanced to subsidiaries for working capital and $71,000 "to repay an officer for the purchase of the assets of the Outpost Inn, Inc."; that "The assets are shown at actual cost and are calculated at the most conservative value," although "A recent appraisal of the real estate in Detroit shows an increase of approximately $2,500,000.00 over book value, which has not been reflected in the statement"; that "The accounts receivable, loans receivable, loans payable, and mortgages payable were not verified by direct communication" and inventories were taken as submitted by the management; and, finally, that "The statement reflects an accurate and true picture of the corporation's net worth after taking into consideration the proposed loan by the officers." The "Pro–Forma Balance Sheet as at December 31, 1960" showed total assets of $7,769,657.11 and a net worth of $3,681,049.70—this including $963,067.00 in the capital stock account. Howard received $200 for his two days of service in preparing the report.

. . .

American Equities stock continued to be sold until March 22, 1961, when, as a result of the SEC's action, trading stopped.

Howard's principal claim is that the evidence against him was insufficient to show the state of mind required for a criminal conviction. He says he was performing an accountant's duties innocently if inefficiently—and for a negligible compensation, that he sheltered himself with the label "pro forma," and that he did not know his reports were to help in stock peddling but thought they were to be used solely for management purposes. His own testimony belies the last claim; he admitted knowing that the promoters intended to use the stock as collateral for loans or as part of or collateral for the purchase price in various acquisitions and that his statements were shown to prospective lenders or sellers. Since his reports were little more than a regurgitation of material handed him by the "management" and related to properties that, as he had reason to know, were not owned, the judge could properly have regarded his claim that he thought them needed for "management" purposes as incredible in the last degree. But the evidence we have summarized shows directly that he knew his reports were being used with brokers who were selling the stock. Drattell, whom he knew to be a broker interested in American Equities, telephoned him in regard to his reports, and, on Reiter's testimony, he saw Mende hand a copy of his first report to Reiter whom he knew to be similarly interested.

The argument that reports which depicted American Equities as owner of properties and companies it neither owned nor had any firm arrangements to acquire were not false because they were stated to be "pro forma" involves a complete misconception of the duties of an accountant in issuing a report thus entitled. Although pro forma statements "purport to give effect to transactions actually consummated or expected to be consummated at a date subsequent to that of the date of the statements," "auditors consider it proper to submit their report and opinion on such statements only when the nature of the transactions effected is clearly described in the statements, and when satisfactory evidence of their bona fides is available, such as actual subsequent consummation or signed firm contracts." Montgomery, Auditing Theory and Practice (6th ed. 1940), 62–63; see also Prentice-Hall Encyclopedic Dictionary of Business Finance (1960), 485. It would be insulting an honorable profession to suppose that a certified public accountant may take the representations of a corporation official as to companies it proposes to acquire, combine their balance sheets without any investigation as to the arrangements for their acquisition or suitable provision reflecting payment of the purchase price, and justify the meaningless result simply by an appliqué of two Latin words.

It is true that the Government had not merely to show that the statements were false but to present evidence from which the judge could be convinced beyond reasonable doubt of Howard's culpable state of mind. But, as Judge Hough said for this court years ago, "when that state of mind is a knowledge of false statements, while there is no allowable inference of knowledge from the mere fact of falsity, there are many cases where from the actor's special situation and continuity of conduct an inference that he *did* know the untruth of what he said or wrote may legitimately be drawn." Bentel v. United States, 13 F.2d 327, 329 (2 Cir.), cert. denied sub nom., Amos v. United States, 273 U.S. 713, 47 S.Ct. 109, 71 L.Ed. 854 (1926). Any accountant must know that his obligations in certifying "pro forma" statements are not satisfied by any such arithmetical exercise as Howard performed. But, as our description of the reports has indicated, there were further false assertions, some of them clearly known to Howard to be such; these constituted a basis for holding him [sic] that was independent of the falsity of the total report, as well as for discrediting his assertions of ignorance as to what was required of him. The Michigan real estate was represented to Howard not as properties to be acquired but as already owned; he claimed to have seen deeds for these properties but admitted that American Equities was not named as grantee. The statements that certain assets had not been "verified by direct communication" implied that with this qualification all assets had been verified by suitable means; they had not been. Howard made no examination of American Equities' books, which, indeed, were not available when he rendered his first report; even a most cursory inspection would have revealed that nothing had been paid when the capital stock account was written up ten-fold. His statement purported to reflect "an accurate and true picture of the corporation's net worth after taking into consideration the proposed loan by the officers"; at best it would have been accurate only if the corporation had had at least some contractual basis for the assertion of ownership, and even then only if proper provision had been made for the cost. The inclusion as an asset of over $700,000 of "Unrecovered Development Costs" of a dormant mining company known to have been through insolvency proceedings was wholly indefensible. Perhaps most damning of all was the making of a profit and loss statement including a positive assertion that the six companies were "acquired within the last few months," when Howard knew that at least some of them had not been acquired at all.

. . . Judge Learned Hand said in a similar context, ". . . the cumulation of instances, each explicable only by extreme credulity or professional inexpertness, may have a probative force immensely greater than any one of them alone." United States v. White, 124 F.2d 181, 185 (2 Cir.1941).

In fact, however, the Government was not required to go that far. "Willful," the Supreme Court has told us, "is a word of many meanings, its construction often being influenced by its context." Spies v. United States, 317 U.S. 492, 497, 63 S.Ct. 364, 367, 87 L.Ed. 418 (1943), citing United States v. Murdock, 290 U.S. 389, 394–396, 54 S.Ct. 223, 78 L.Ed. 381 (1933). We think that in the context of § 24 of the Securities Act as applied to § 17(a), the Government can meet its burden by proving that a defendant deliberately closed his eyes to facts he had a duty to see, compare Spurr v. United States, 174 U.S. 728, 19 S.Ct. 812, 43 L.Ed. 1150 (1899) and American Law Institute, Model Penal Code, § 2.02(7), commentary in Tent.Draft No. 4, pages 129–30 (1955), or recklessly stated as facts things of which he was ignorant. Judge Hough so ruled in Bentel v. United States, supra; although that case and the similar ruling in Slakoff v. United States, 8 F.2d 9 (3 Cir.1925), were under the mail fraud statute, § 215 of the then Criminal Code, 35 Stat. 1130 (1909), the ancestor of 18 U.S.C. § 1341, which does not use the term "willfully," the Congress that passed the Securities Act scarcely meant to make life easier for defrauders. Other circuits have gone further and have held the willfulness requirement of the Securities Act to be satisfied in fraud cases by proof of representations which due diligence would have shown to be untrue. Stone v. United States, 113 F.2d 70, 75 (6 Cir.1940); United States v. Schaefer, 299 F.2d 625, 629, 632 (7 Cir.), cert. denied, 370 U.S. 917, 82 S.Ct. 1553, 8 L.Ed.2d 497 (1962). In our complex society the accountant's certificate and the lawyer's opinion can be instruments for inflicting pecuniary loss more potent than the chisel or the crowbar. Of course, Congress did not mean that any mistake of law or misstatement of fact should subject an attorney or an accountant to criminal liability simply because more skillful practitioners would not have made them. But Congress equally could not have intended that men holding themselves out as members of these ancient professions should be able to escape criminal liability on a plea of ignorance when they have shut their eyes to what was plainly to be seen or have represented a knowledge they knew they did not possess. . . .

Much of what we have said as to Howard is relevant also to Benjamin's claim of insufficiency of the evidence as to his culpable state of mind. Benjamin brought Howard into the scheme; he had written out the list of assets which Howard later used in his first report; as Howard testified, Benjamin had told him to take the statements of the various companies "and just put them into a consolidated form"; and his work in connection with several of the proposed "acquisitions" gave him actual knowledge of the falsity both of the November 30 statement and of Howard's reports. But there was much more than this. His opinion letter made a positive statement that he believed all the shares of American Equities were exempt from registration, although he must have known that control of the corporation, not yet even named "American Equities Corporation," was being acquired by Mende and that the statute explicitly denied exemption to any new offerings by persons in control, a limitation of which his testimony before the SEC showed he was well aware. Yet there is abundant evidence that Benjamin knew Mende was putting American Equities shares on the market. Among the instances was the transaction outlined above with Drattell in late January wherein Benjamin received a confirmation of a purchase of 5,000 shares from "Martin Benjamin Trustee" for $9,000—at a time when the pink sheets were quoting the stock at $5 per share or more—and the distribution of part of the proceeds to Mende and his wife; yet Benjamin prepared a letter whereby the transfer agent certified these shares to be "free stock and . . . not investment stock." In another transaction, not previously mentioned, wherein Mende had a nominee, Mrs. Tanner, sell American Equities shares to relatives and friends of Paul Reicher, her father, on a basis whereby she retained $2 per share for her pains, she received a letter signed by "Martin Benjamin Trustee" acknowledging the sale of 11,000 shares to her and the receipt of $4.75 per share. Benjamin's role was far more than that of an attorney. He told Drattell he was acting as a "trustee" for some of the principals and, when Drattell sought elucidation, explained that "as a trustee and as an attorney . . . licensed in the State of New York, . . . he was not obligated to reveal any of the sources and it is enough for anyone to accept a legal document from a trustee who was an attorney and the trustee was not required to reveal the source of the legal document or who the principals were behind the legal document"—surely a novel contribution to the law of trusts. His proffer of financial aid if Drattell would undertake some distribution of American Equities afforded further basis for inferring knowledge of the intended fraud, as did his efforts falsely to minimize Mende's role when he and others were examined by the SEC. This and other evidence made a case at least as strong as that held sufficient with respect to another lawyer in United States v. Crosby, 294 F.2d 928, 938 (2 Cir.1961), cert. denied sub nom. Mittelman v. United States, 368 U.S. 984, 82 S.Ct. 599, 7 L.Ed.2d 523 (1962).

Howard and Benjamin make the complaint, standard in appeals of this sort and buttressed by the inevitable citation of Kotteakos v. United States, 328 U.S. 750, 66 S.Ct. 1239, 90 L.Ed. 1557 (1946), that although the indictment alleged a single conspiracy, the proof showed separate ones to sell unregistered securities and to defraud. The argument could not avail Benjamin in any event since the evidence clearly implicated him in both aspects of the scheme. See United

States v. Agueci, 310 F.2d 817, 827–828 (2 Cir.1962), cert. denied, 372
U.S. 959, 83 S.Ct. 1016, 10 L.Ed.2d 12 (1963). But the point is wholly
without merit. The fraudulent acts and the unlawful failure to register
information which would uncover them were essential steps in a single
scheme to dupe; the limited scope of Kotteakos was explained in
Blumenthal v. United States, 332 U.S. 539, 558–559, 68 S.Ct. 248, 92
L.Ed. 154 (1947) and its inapplicability to an integrated financial fraud
like this was affirmed by us in United States v. Crosby, supra, 294 F.2d
at 944–945. It is thus immaterial that the evidence may not have
shown awareness by Howard of the part of the scheme that involved
the sale of unregistered shares, United States v. Agueci, supra, and
cases there cited.

Mende, as the central figure in the scheme, has not challenged the
sufficiency of the evidence introduced against him. He raises several
points on appeal; all seem so patently without substance as not to
require discussion. We here mention only his claim that McDonald's
testimony should have been excluded under the attorney-client privilege, and we do that solely to state its complete lack of merit. The
relation between Mende and McDonald was not that of client and
attorney but of buyer and seller; what Mende was seeking from
McDonald was not legal advice but a pre–1933 corporate shell.

Affirmed.

Notes on Benjamin
Questions and Comments

Benjamin's criminal liability is based on activities, such as drafting
an opinion letter and trying to minimize Mende's role when examined
by the SEC, that are routinely undertaken by lawyers. What made
these acts criminal?

A basic premise of criminal law is that bad acts alone are not
enough to establish criminal liability; the actor must also have had a
culpable state of mind, the *mens rea*. There are various states of mind
that might be sufficient for criminal liability. Some crimes require a
specific intent to do harm; others provide that negligence satisfies the
mens rea component. Strict liability offenses are the exception.

The crimes charged against Howard and Benjamin were not strict
liability crimes. They required some level of *mens rea*. What state of
mind did the government have to prove to establish the requisite *mens
rea*?

What distinguishes mere incompetence or misplaced confidence in
a client's representations from the conduct of Howard and Benjamin?

What a Lawyer "Knows"

In *Benjamin* it is clear that the lawyer through his actions facilitated the criminal scheme. The question is whether the lawyer did so with a culpable state of mind. Some jurisdictions hold that for a person to be guilty of aiding and abetting another's criminal conduct mere knowledge of the other's purpose is not enough: he must associate himself with the venture, participate in it as something he desires to bring about, and seek by his acts to make it succeed. See United States v. Peoni, 100 F.2d 401 (2d Cir.1938). Others hold that knowledge or reason to know of the other's intent to commit a crime is sufficient to establish the *mens rea.* See, e.g., Mowery v. State, 132 Tex.Cr. 408, 105 S.W.2d 239 (1937).* Even where more than mere knowledge is required, the intent to facilitate the commission of the crime may be inferred from the actor's knowledge that the principal would use the aid to commit a crime. The question of what a lawyer knows about his client's criminal purpose is therefore critical.

Moreover, both the Model Code and the Model Rules make it unethical for a lawyer to facilitate a client's criminal or fraudulent purpose. The formulation in DR 7–102(A)(7) is: "counsel or assist his client in conduct that the lawyer knows to be illegal or fraudulent." The formulation in M.R. 1.2(d) is: "counsel a client to engage, or assist a client, in conduct that the lawyer knows is criminal or fraudulent." Does the reach of these formulations differ? When will a lawyer be held to have known that her client is engaged in or contemplating criminal activity?

Benjamin suggests that lawyers (and accountants) have a greater responsibility to know what their clients are about than nonprofessionals in similar situations. This greater responsibility is grounded on the assumption that lawyers (and other similarly situated professionals) have a greater familiarity with the applicable legal limits and thus have a greater sensitivity to facts that suggest those limits are being transgressed. This kind of assumption runs counter to that suggested by the paradigm of the criminal defense lawyer, who is permitted, indeed expected, to act in court as if the client was innocent no matter what reasons the lawyer may have to believe or know otherwise. Relying on the criminal defense paradigm, lawyers are fond of saying that their job is not to judge the client but to believe in her. However, as *Benjamin* makes clear, lawyers acting as counselors or advisors who "shut their eyes to what was plainly to be seen," or represent that they know something that they do not know, not only act improperly: they risk criminal sanctions.** See also People v. Zelinger, 179 Colo. 379, 504 P.2d 668 (1972) (lawyer failed to inquire into whether the car received as a fee was stolen property).

---

* For a general discussion of the various mental states required for accomplice liability see LaFave and Scott, Criminal Law 2d ed. (1986) § 6.7(b) at 579.

** What the lawyer as advocate "knows" about the truthfulness of her client's assertions is discussed in chapter 5 below.

What a Lawyer Does—The Actus Reus

A corollary to the principle that bad acts alone are insufficient for criminal liability is that bad thoughts without an act are also insufficient. For criminal liability to attach, there must be an act (actus reus) performed with the required culpable state of mind.

As *Benjamin* shows, an act routine in law practice may constitute the actus reus. The giving of advice may itself be sufficient to constitute the actus reus and will result in criminal liability when the required culpable state of mind is present (which may be mere knowledge that the client intends to use the advice to further a criminal purpose). See, e.g., United States v. Feaster, 843 F.2d 1392 (6th Cir.), cert. denied, 109 S.Ct. 244 (1988) (unreported opinion, text available on WESTLAW) (lawyer advised undercover agent, posing as client, on how to avoid paying taxes; properly charged with aiding preparation of false return); and United States v. Perlstein, 126 F.2d 789 (3d Cir.1942), cert. denied, 316 U.S. 678 (1942) (lawyer who advised client to destroy documents if a proceeding was instituted, guilty of conspiracy to obstruct future judicial proceeding).

Consider the Following Description on What Constitutes Assistance From Kadish, Complicity, Cause and Blame: A Study in the Interpretation of Doctrine, 73 Calif.L.Rev. 323, 343 (1985):

Various terms are used to capture the central notions of assistance and influence. Assistance is sometimes expressed as helping, aiding, or abetting. Liability never turns, however, on the choice among these terms. All embrace ways in which one person may help another commit a crime, including furnishing means, whether material or informational, providing opportunities, and lending a helping hand in preparation or execution. Influence is expressed in a greater variety of terms, sometimes with overlapping meanings, sometimes with different connotations. *Advise,* like counsel, imports offering one's opinion in favor of some action. *Persuade* is stronger, suggesting a greater effort to prevail on a person, or counseling strongly. *Command* is even stronger, implying an order or direction, commonly by one with some authority over the other. *Encourage* suggests giving support to a course of action to which another is already inclined. *Induce* means to persuade, but may suggest influence beyond persuasion. *Procure* seems to go further, suggesting bringing something about in the sense of producing a result. *Instigate* as well as *incite* suggest stirring up and stimulating, spurring another to a course of action. *Provoke* is roughly equivalent to incite, with the added sense of producing a response by exploiting a person's sensitivities. *Solicit* is generally equivalent to incite in legal usage, although in common usage it suggests simply asking or proposing.

These differences in emphasis and connotation rarely have legal significance. All of these terms describe ways of influencing a person to choose to act in a particular way and therefore constitute a ground of complicity. Occasionally, however, the precise form of influence affects the legal conclusion, most often where statutes employ one or more of these terms restrictively.

For cases imposing discipline for aiding and abetting the unlawful activity of a client, see People v. Kenelly, 648 P.2d 1065 (Colo.1982) (lawyer fashioned an agreement whereby client would receive money in return for being unavailable to testify at a criminal trial); In re La Duca, 62 N.J. 133, 299 A.2d 405 (1973) (lawyer aided client in extorting ransom for the return of stolen property). Drafting documents with unlawful terms may also constitute assisting in illegal conduct. See, e.g., In re Giordano, 49 N.J. 210, 229 A.2d 524 (1957) (usurious loan contract).

Hypothetical *

A partner hands you, a new associate in the firm, a list of countries, all with favorable climates, and asks you to prepare a memo on the extradition policy of each, particularly their policy on extraditing people to the United States who have been accused of securities law violations.

Would preparing the memo subject you to prosecution for aiding and abetting a violation of the securities law or the escape of a fugitive or obstructing justice—if it turns out that the client is under indictment (or has recently been convicted) for violating the securities laws? What rules or code provisions are implicated? What questions, if any, should you (would you) ask? Are M.R. 5.1 and 5.2 of any assistance here?

Other White Collar Crimes

In addition to possible prosecution as an aider or abettor of the crime in which the client may be engaged, a lawyer who suspects that her client is engaged in criminal activity must be concerned with liability under other criminal statutes. The following notes describe some of the crimes for which lawyers risk exposure.

Conspiracy

In addition to substantive offenses, Benjamin was convicted of conspiracy to commit the substantive offenses. The core of any conspiracy charge is the *agreement* to do something unlawful (or something lawful through unlawful means). The agreement, however, need not be proved through direct evidence, nor must the agreement be explicit. A tacit understanding to do something illegal in concert with others will

* This hypothetical is based on the experience of an associate in the international law department of a large firm.

suffice, and a tacit agreement may be proved by showing that two or more people acted in a way that permits the inference they had some form of agreement.   Direct Sales Co. v. United States, 319 U.S. 703, 63 S.Ct. 1265 (1943).   On conspiracy see generally LaFave and Scott, Criminal Law 2d ed. (1986) §§ 6.4–6.5.   Successful withdrawal from a conspiracy requires an "affirmative act bringing home the fact of [one's] withdrawal to [one's] confederates."   Loser v. Superior Court, 78 Cal. App.2d 30, 177 P.2d 320 (1947).   Disclosing the conspiracy to authorities is obviously the most effective way to meet this test.   Conspiracy may also be a tort.   See, e.g., Hartford Accident and Indemnity Co. v. Sullivan, 846 F.2d 377 (7th Cir.1988) (lawyer liable for civil conspiracy when the lawyer: (1) prepared materially misleading documents to secure a bank loan for a partnership in which the lawyer was a member; (2) knew that the misleading information was being used to secure new loans; and (3) benefitted from the money fraudulently obtained, which was used to pay a debt of the partnership).

Mail Fraud

The mail and wire fraud statutes, 18 U.S.C. §§ 1341, 1343, prohibit the use of the mail or of electronic transmissions to execute "any scheme or artifice to defraud, or for the purpose of obtaining money or property by false or fraudulent pretenses . . ."   The material mailed need not itself be false as long as it aids the execution of a fraud. United States v. Talbott, 590 F.2d 192 (6th Cir.1978); United States v. Reid, 533 F.2d 1255 (D.C.Cir.1976).   Mailings occurring after receipt of the goods or money obtained by fraud are covered if they "were designed to lull the victims into a false sense of security, postpone their ultimate complaint to the authorities, and therefore make the apprehension of the defendants less likely than if no mailings had taken place."   United States v. Maze, 414 U.S. 395, 403, 94 S.Ct. 645, 650 (1974).

Until 1987, the mail and wire fraud statutes had been interpreted by the Courts of Appeals as reaching fraudulent schemes to deprive people of "intangible rights" as well.   For example, the mail fraud statute was frequently used to convict corrupt state and federal government officials (many of them lawyers) for defrauding citizens of their right to the honest service of their governmental officials.   United States v. Holzer, 816 F.2d 304 (7th Cir.1987) (county judge); United States v. Diggs, 198 U.S.App.D.C. 255, 613 F.2d 988 (1979) (Congressman); United States v. Mandel, 591 F.2d 1347 (4th Cir.1979) (governor); United States v. Classic, 35 F.Supp. 457 (E.D.La.1940) (election commissioner).

Typically, these cases involved a government official who had used his or her office for personal gain rather than to further the public interest.   Private persons were also prosecuted for schemes involving the corruption of public servants.   See, e.g., United States v. Rauhoff, 525 F.2d 1170 (7th Cir.1975) (bribing state secretary of state).   Another "intangible right" was the public's right to an honest election process, see, e.g., United States v. Girdner, 754 F.2d 877 (10th Cir.1985); and United States v. Clapps, 732 F.2d 1148 (3d Cir.), cert. denied, 469 U.S. 1085 (1984) (convictions for using the mails to falsify votes). Employees and union officials who accepted kickbacks or used confidential information for personal gain were also prosecuted under the "intangible rights" theory. See, e.g., United States v. Bryza, 522 F.2d 414 (7th Cir. 1975).

In McNally v. United States, 483 U.S. 350, 107 S.Ct. 2875 (1987), the Supreme Court rejected this line of cases holding that the mail and wire fraud statutes did not cover schemes to defraud people of intangible rights, but instead were limited to property interests. Congress responded by amending the mail fraud statute to overturn *McNally*. See 18 U.S.C. § 1346 (1988) ("the term 'scheme or artifice to defraud' includes a scheme or artifice to deprive another of the intangible right of honest services").

Before Congress acted, the Supreme Court itself gave the fraud statutes a broader reading. Carpenter v. United States, 484 U.S. 19, 108 S.Ct. 316 (1987) involved the activities of Winans, the Wall Street Journal's "Heard on the Street" columnist, in a scheme with two securities brokers. Winans would give the brokers advance notice of his column. The brokers and their client bought and sold securities based on the probable impact of the column on the market. The defendants were convicted of violating the federal securities laws and the mail and wire fraud statutes. The Supreme Court was divided 4–4 on the securities law convictions, but unanimously affirmed the convictions for fraud. The defendants argued that under *McNally* their scheme did not deprive the Wall St. Journal of property. The court rejected this argument:

> Petitioners argue that the Journal's interest in prepublication confidentiality for the "Heard" columns is no more than an intangible consideration outside the reach of § 1341; nor does that law, it is urged, protect against mere injury to reputation. This is not a case like *McNally*, however. . . . Here, the object of the scheme was to take the Journal's confidential business information—the publication schedule and contents of the "Heard" column—and its intangible nature does not make it any less 'property' protected by the mail and wire fraud statutes. *McNally* did not limit the scope of § 1341 to tangible as distinguished from intangible property rights.

Carpenter 108 S.Ct. at 320.

Lawyers continually are in possession of confidential information belonging to their clients and to third parties. The unauthorized use of such information for personal gain violates the federal fraud statutes whenever the mail, a telephone or any other electronic transmission is used in the course of the scheme. See, e.g., United States v. Grossman, 843 F.2d 78 (2d Cir.1988), cert. denied, 109 S.Ct. 864 (1989). Lawyers often represent clients who possess confidential information. If the lawyer knows that a client is using such information for personal gain, and affords substantial assistance in executing the client's plan, the lawyer risks prosecution as an aider and abettor. See also United States v. Bronston, 658 F.2d 920 (2d Cir.1981) (lawyer deprived his firm's client of honest services by representing another client whose interests directly conflicted).

RICO

The Racketeer Influenced and Corrupt Organizations Act (RICO), 18 U.S.C. §§ 1961–68 (1982 & Supp. III 1985), defines "racketeering" acts to include not only murder and kidnapping but mail, wire and securities fraud. The inclusion of these latter "white-collar" crimes gives the statute a reach far beyond its original target, the "mob." RICO authorizes civil remedies as well as criminal sanctions. A private party who brings suit to redress injury resulting from prohibited conduct under RICO is entitled to treble damages, the cost of suit and attorneys' fees.

RICO prohibits, in any enterprise affecting interstate commerce: (1) investing income derived from a pattern of racketeering; (2) acquiring or maintaining an interest through a pattern of racketeering; (3) participating in the enterprise's affairs through a pattern of racketeering; and (4) conspiring to engage in any of these activities. To establish a "pattern" of racketeering, it is necessary to show two acts of racketeering and the threat of continuing racketeering activity. Given the definition of racketeering acts, two instances of mail or wire fraud would satisfy the "two act" requirement. In Sedima, S.P.R.L. v. Imrex Co., 473 U.S. 479, 105 S.Ct. 3275 (1985), the Supreme Court refused to interpret RICO as requiring a criminal conviction to support civil RICO liability. It did, however, indicate that " '[p]roof of two acts . . . without more does not establish a pattern . . . [C]ontinuity plus relationship [are what] produce a pattern.' " 473 U.S. at 496 n. 14.

Not surprisingly the wide reach of RICO has engendered much criticism by lawyers in corporate practice.* In August 1986, the ABA House of Delegates passed resolutions urging Congress to change the definition of racketeering activity and to require a criminal RICO conviction as a condition precedent to civil RICO liability. See also Lynch, RICO: The Crime of Being a Criminal, Parts I & II, 87 Colum.L. Rev. 661, Parts III & IV, 87 Colum.L.Rev. 920 (1987); Note, Civil RICO

---

* "In practice, [civil RICO] frequently has been invoked against legitimate businesses in ordinary commercial settings. . . . [T]he ABA Task Force that studied civil RICO found that 40% of the reported cases involved securities fraud, 37% involved common-law fraud in a commercial or business setting. Many a prudent defendant, facing ruinous exposure, will decide to settle even a case with no merit. It is thus not surprising that civil RICO has been used for extortive purposes, giving rise to the very evils that it was designed to combat." Report of the Ad Hoc Civil RICO Task Force of the ABA Section of Corporation, Banking and Business Law 69 (1985).

"Only 9% of all civil RICO cases have involved allegations of criminal activity normally associated with professional criminals. The central purpose that Congress sought to promote through civil RICO is now a mere footnote." Sedima, S.P.R.L. v. Imrex Co., 473 U.S. 479, 506 (1985) (Marshall, J., dissenting).

is a Misnomer . . ., 100 Harv.L.Rev. 1288 (1987). But see Goldsmith, Civil RICO Reform: The Basis for a Compromise, 71 Minn.L.Rev. 827 (1987) (describing the criticism of RICO as overstated and proposing a moderate revision). Congress has been considering various proposals to limit the statute's scope.

United States v. Teitler, 802 F.2d 606 (2d Cir.1986), affirmed the conviction of two lawyers for mail fraud; for conspiring to conduct the affairs of an enterprise through a pattern of racketeering; and for conducting the affairs of an enterprise through racketeering. The enterprise was their law firm.

> [T]he method of operation employed by the enterprise included the creation of false documents and the encouragement of perjury by the firm's clients in order to inflate their injuries and expenses so as to obtain better settlements in negligence lawsuits brought by the firm . . . [T]he fraud took several forms—creation of false medical bills, submission of false affidavits to document housekeeping services that were never rendered and lost wages that were never earned; referral of clients to doctors who provided backdated bills and exaggerated medical reports; and procurement of false testimony at trials and examinations before trial . . . Further, when a grand jury investigation was underway, defendants Norman Teitler, head of the firm, and Maureen Murphy, an employee, allegedly tried to induce false testimony before the grand jury.

> 808 F.2d at 609.

Obstruction of Justice

This crime was the central charge against the Watergate defendants, many of whom were lawyers. See United States v. Haldeman, 559 F.2d 31 n. 2, n. 3 (D.C.Cir.1976). The federal obstruction of justice statute, 18 U.S.C. § 1503, provides: "Whoever corruptly . . . endeavors to influence, intimidate, or impede any . . . officer . . . of any court of the United States . . . in the discharge of his duty . . . or corruptly . . . influences, obstructs or impedes, or endeavors to influence, obstruct, or impede, the due administration of justice, shall be fined . . . or imprisoned . . . or both." The means used to obstruct justice need not in themselves be unlawful. See United States v. Cintolo, 818 F.2d 980 (1st Cir.1987) (lawyer convicted of obstructing justice even though conduct on which charge was based, i.e., advising a client, was not itself unlawful). The crime of obstruction of justice "reaches all corrupt conduct capable of producing an effect that prevents justice from being duly administered, regardless of the means employed." United States v. Silverman, 745 F.2d 1386, 1393 (11th Cir. 1984); see also State v. Cogdell, 273 S.C. 563, 257 S.E.2d 748, 750 (1979).

Conduct commonly treated as obstruction of justice includes: attempt to alter or prevent the testimony of a witness, United States v. Tedesco, 635 F.2d 902, 907 (1st Cir.1980), cert. denied, 452 U.S. 962 (1981); interference with a grand jury investigation, United States v.

Walasek, 527 F.2d 676 (3d Cir.1975), and United States v. Teitler supra; and the destruction of evidence that is being sought by a court or grand jury, United States v. Faudman, 640 F.2d 20 (6th Cir.1981).

In *Cintolo,* supra, the lawyer advised his client to refuse to testify before the grand jury even though the client had a valid grant of immunity. The prosecution introduced tape-recorded conversations between the lawyer and others that revealed the lawyer's purpose was to keep the grand jury from finding out about the criminal activities of others, some of whom were also apparently represented by the lawyer-defendant. In fact, the lawyer regularly reported on his client's inclination to testify and was aware of plans to kill the "client" should he decide to testify.

[M]eans, though lawful in themselves, can cross the line of illegality if (i) employed with a corrupt motive, (ii) to hinder the due administration of justice, so long as (iii) the means have the capacity to obstruct.

The appellant and amici [The Massachusetts Association of Criminal Defense Lawyers and National Network for the Right to Counsel] pay lip service to this principle, but maintain that different considerations come into play where criminal defense lawyers are concerned. In those [situations], they assert, a corrupt motive may not be found in conduct which is, itself, not independently illegal. . . .

[T]he conversion of innocent acts to guilty ones by the addition of improper intent—is what this case is all about. . . . Nothing in the caselaw . . . suggests that lawyers should be plucked gently from the madding crowd and sheltered from the rigors of 18 U.S.C. § 1503 . . .

818 F.2d at 992–93, 995–96.

Foreign Corrupt Practices Act

The Foreign Corrupt Practices Act (FCPA) requires that companies whose securities are publicly traded maintain accounts that "in reasonable detail, accurately and fairly reflect the transactions and dispositions of the assets of the issuer . . . in conformity with generally accepted accounting principles . . . ." 15 U.S.C. § 78m(b)(2)–(3). FCPA requires corporate disclosure as a deterrent to foreign bribes, but its most significant provision is a "books and records" provision. This provision "gives the SEC authority over the entire financial management and reporting requirements" of publicly held corporations in the United States. See SEC v. World–Wide Coin Investments, 567 F.Supp. 724, 746 (N.D.Ga.1983).

Section 13(b)(2)(a) of the FCPA provides that every issuer of registered securities shall "make and keep books, records and accounts which, in reasonable detail, accurately and fairly reflect the transactions and dispositions of the assets of the issuer." Section 13(b)(2)(b) requires issuers to maintain a system of internal accounting controls that meets certain specifications. Rule 13b2–1 promulgated by the SEC under these sections provides: "No person shall, directly or indirectly, falsify or cause to be falsified, any book [or] record subject to § 13(b)(2)(a)."

There is no scienter requirement. See *Worldwide,* supra (rejecting any scienter requirement as contrary to the plain language of the statute and its purpose). For an analysis of the Act, see Porrata–Doria, Amending the Foreign Corrupt Practices Act of 1977: Repeating the Mistakes of the Past?, 38 Rutgers L.Rev. 29 (1985).

Paying Lawyers With the Proceeds of Crime

Introductory Note

Brickey, "Tainted Assets and the Right to Counsel—The Money Laundering Conundrum," 66 Wash.U.L.Q. 47, 47–49 (1988), provides a concise summary of the problem:

> If you asked criminal lawyers across the country what the major concern of the criminal defense bar is today, they would reply that the most pressing concern is an "intolerable Sixth Amendment crisis" created by government intrusions into the attorney-client relationship. . . .

> Item one: The practice of issuing subpoenas to attorneys summoning them to provide the grand jury with financial information that relates to their clients. The government wants to know the amount of the fee paid for the lawyer's representation, the manner in which it was paid (i.e., was it a large amount of cash), and the identity of the payor (i.e., is your client carrying around all of this cash, or did you obtain it from some third party benefactor).

> The reason the government seeks fee information from the lawyer is item two. The Racketeer Influenced and Corrupt Organizations Act (RICO) [supra] and the Continuing Criminal Enterprise Statute (CCE) [21 U.S.C. § 848]. These federal racketeering and drug laws require forfeiture of assets acquired directly or indirectly through specified criminal activity. Fee information the government obtains from the lawyer may thus provide evidence that their clients have assets subject to forfeiture. To compound the problem, a prosecutor who decides to pursue forfeiture of those assets may seek a pre-trial restraining order to prevent the client from transferring them to anyone—including his lawyer. The prosecutor may also notify the lawyer that all tainted assets, including those already paid as a fee for legal services, may be forfeited upon the client's conviction.

> Item three is a relatively new provision in the Internal Revenue Code, [26 U.S.C. § 6050(I)]. Section 6050I requires every person who receives more than $10,000 in cash in connection with a trade or business to file a report with the Internal Revenue Service. The implementing regulations make clear that lawyers are engaged in a trade or business for purposes of the reporting requirement. Thus, a

lawyer may be required to inform the government that client X paid a $100,000 fee in cash on the fourth of July.

And what if the lawyer has reason to know that some or all of the fee is derived from the client's criminal activity? That brings us to item four. A new federal money laundering statute [18 U.S.C. § 1957] makes it a crime knowingly to engage in a monetary transaction with a financial institution if the amount of the transaction exceeds $10,000 and the funds are derived from specified criminal activity. Thus, if the lawyer knows that the client's money comes from an illicit source, the lawyer cannot deposit the $100,000 fee in the bank without committing a crime.

Subpoenaing Lawyers Before Grand Juries*

In recent years, the number of criminal defense lawyers being subpoenaed before grand juries has risen dramatically. The impetus is the forfeiture provisions of RICO and CCE.

A 1985 survey indicated that the Government had questioned the source of the lawyer's fees in one or more cases of 21 percent of the lawyers responding, and had sought to disqualify 26 percent of the lawyers responding in one or more of their cases. Genego, Risky Business: The Hazards of Being a Criminal Defense Lawyer, 1 Crim. Just. 1 (1986). See also United States v. Klubock, 832 F.2d 664 (1st Cir. 1987) (en banc) (Government admission that in the 306 to 463 criminal cases filed in the District of Massachusetts per year, 50 to 100 attorney subpoenas are served).

As stated in In re Grand Jury Investigation (Sturgis), 412 F.Supp. 943, 945–946 (E.D.Pa.1976):

. . . The dangers and disadvantages of the practice have been demonstrated in [various] cases . . . The practice permits the government by unilateral action to create the possibility of a conflict of interest between the attorney and client, which may lead to a suspect's being denied his choice of counsel by disqualification. The very presence of the attorney in the grand jury room, even if only to assert valid privileges, can raise doubts in the client's mind as to his lawyer's unfettered devotion to the client's interests and thus impair or at least impinge upon the attorney-client relationship.

The increased use of grand jury subpoenas has generated much comment, almost all of it negative. See, e.g., Suni, Subpoena to Criminal Defense Lawyers: A Proposal for Limits, 65 Or.L.Rev. 215 (1986); Peirce & Colamarino, Defense Counsel as a Witness for the Prosecution: Curbing the Practice of Issuing Grand Jury Subpoenas to Counsel for Targets of Investigations, 36 Hastings L.J. 821 (1985); Zwerling, Federal Grand Juries v. Attorney Independence and the Attorney–Client Privilege, 27 Hastings L.J. 1263 (1976); Note, Grand

---

* On the general rule that fee information and client identity are not covered by the attorney client privilege and the limited exceptions to that rule, see United States v. Hodge & Zweig, printed in Chapter 4 below, and the notes following it.

Jury Subpoenas of a Target's Attorney: The Need for a Preliminary Showing, 20 Ga.L.Rev. 747 (1986). For a debate on the issue see Merkle/Moscarino, At Issue: Are Prosecutors Invading the Attorney–Client Relationship?, 71 A.B.A.J. 38 (1985).

One proposal would require the prosecutor to obtain judicial approval before issuing the subpoena. In 1986, the ABA House of Delegates approved a resolution urging state and federal authorities to adopt this approach through rules of court, statutes or case law. A 1988 resolution by the ABA proposed: that there be an adversarial proceeding before the judge could grant approval for the subpoena; that the government show that the evidence is "essential" to a grand jury investigation; and that the subpoena list with particularity the information sought. Finally, the ABA resolution would require that the prosecutor show not only that there is no feasible alternative, but that "all reasonable attempts to obtain the information from" other sources have failed.

In 1985 the Justice Department issued internal guidelines in the United States Attorney's Manual, entitled "Policy with Regard to the Issuance of Grand Jury or Trial Subpoena to Attorneys for Information Relating to the Representation of Clients." They require the Assistant Attorney General of the Criminal Division of the Justice Department to authorize any such subpoena. The prosecutor must make "all reasonable attempts" to obtain the information from other sources before subpoenaing the lawyer "*unless* such efforts would compromise a criminal investigation . . . or would impair the ability to obtain such information from [the] lawyer" (emphasis added). The text of these guidelines is reprinted in In re Grand Jury Subpoena to Attorney (Under Seal), 679 F.Supp. 1403, 1408 n. 15 (N.D.W.Va.1988).

Most courts have refused to require the prosecutor to show need and relevance, in an ex parte proceeding or otherwise, before subpoenaing a lawyer to testify before a grand jury on client matters. See United States v. Perry, 857 F.2d 1346 (9th Cir.1988) (collecting cases); In re Grand Jury Subpoena (Slotnick), 781 F.2d 238 (2d Cir.1985) (en banc), cert. denied, 475 U.S. 1108 (1986). These courts have emphasized the importance of the grand jury's investigative role. Prior court approval is not required before any other witness is called before the grand jury, see Branzburg v. Hayes, 408 U.S. 665, 92 S.Ct. 2646 (1972) (rejecting argument that government make a special showing of need before calling journalists before the grand jury).

The argument that the Sixth Amendment right to counsel requires special procedures for lawyers has been consistently rejected. See, e.g., United States v. Perry, 857 F.2d 1346 (9th Cir.1988). The ground is that the Sixth Amendment does not attach during the investigatory stages of a grand jury investigation; it attaches only after adversary proceedings have been instituted. United States v. Gouveia, 467 U.S. 180, 185, 104 S.Ct. 2292, 2295 (1984).

Not all courts share the majority view outlined above. In In re Special Grand Jury No. 81-1 (Harvey), 676 F.2d 1005 (4th Cir.1982), withdrawn on other grounds 697 F.2d 112, the court held that the Government was required to make a preliminary showing of relevance and need before issuing a grand jury subpoena to a lawyer whose client was a target of the investigation. See also In re Grand Jury Subpoena to Attorney (Under Seal), 679 F.Supp. 1403 (N.D.W.Va.1988) (relying in part on *No. 81–1*).

A victory for the critics of present practice was achieved in United States v. Klubock, 832 F.2d 664 (1st Cir.1987) (en banc). The Massachusetts Bar Association proposed and the Supreme Judicial Court of Massachusetts in 1986 adopted an ethical rule, Prosecutorial Function 15 (PF 15), SJC Rule 3:08, which states: "It is unprofessional conduct for a prosecutor to subpoena an attorney to a grand jury without prior judicial approval . . . where the prosecutor seeks to compel the attorney/witness to provide evidence . . . [about a client]."

This rule, also adopted by the United States District Court for Massachusetts, was challenged by federal prosecutors who claimed: 1) that as an attempt by state authorities to control federal prosecutors it violated the Supremacy Clause of the Constitution; 2) that the District Court lacked the power to promulgate the rule because it effected a substantial change in grand jury practice—a change that should be made by amending the Federal Rules of Criminal Procedure or by separate Congressional enactment; and 3) that the rule as a matter of policy is so unwise that the Court of Appeals should exercise its supervisory powers to invalidate it.

An evenly divided en banc opinion affirmed the panel decision upholding the rule. But see The Florida Bar re Amendments to the Rules Regulating the Florida Bar, 519 So.2d 971 (Fla.1987) (refusing to adopt a similar rule); and In re Nackson, 114 N.J. 527, 555 A.2d 1101 (1989) (same).

Forfeiture of Crime Proceeds

The forfeiture provisions of RICO and CCE were enhanced by the Comprehensive Crime Control Act of 1984. Forfeiture now may relate back to the date of the criminal conduct that is the predicate of the forfeiture. See 18 U.S.C. § 1963(c); 21 U.S.C. § 853(c). Suppose that a crime such as sale of narcotics occurs on June 1, the defendant is arrested on September 1, and that defendant retains a lawyer on September 3 on the basis of a cash fee. The Government may demand forfeiture of the cash on the basis that it was realized from the illegal sale on June 1. An asset is not insulated from forfeiture by being transferred to a third party. If the conditions of forfeiture can be established, money paid the lawyer on September 3, has to be remitted to the government, leaving no fee money for defense, unless the lawyer can show that he was a bona fide purchaser *and* that he had no reason to know the money was proceeds from criminal conduct. Moreover, the government may seek forfeiture not only at the inception of the representation but after the criminal proceeding that results in conviction. This makes it financially very risky for a private criminal defense lawyer to take a case where the fee money may be subject to forfeiture, as it may well be in any narcotics case and many RICO cases. See generally Ass'n Bar City of New York, Committee on Criminal Advocacy, The Forfeiture of Attorney Fees in Criminal Cases: A Call for Immediate Remedial Action, 41 The Record 469 (1986); Cloud, Forfeiting Defense Attorneys' Fees, 1987 Wis.L.Rev. 1.

In 1989, the Supreme Court in two 5–4 decisions held that the forfeiture provisions did not exempt assets used to pay an attorney; that the defendant's assets may be frozen before conviction based on a finding of probable cause to believe that the assets are forfeitable, United States v. Monsanto, 109 S.Ct. 2657 (1989); and that forfeiture of attorney's fees does not violate the defendant's Sixth Amendment right to counsel or Fifth Amendment right to due process, Caplin & Drysdale v. United States, 109 S.Ct. 2646 (1989).

> Whatever the full extent of the Sixth Amendment's protection of one's right to retain counsel of his choosing, that protection does not go beyond "the individual's right to spend his own money to obtain the advice and assistance of . . . counsel." . . . A defendant has no Sixth Amendment right to spend another person's money for services rendered by an attorney, even if those funds are the only way that that defendant will be able to retain the attorney of his choice. A robbery suspect, for example, has no Sixth Amendment right to use funds he has stolen from a bank to retain an attorney to defend him if he is apprehended. The money, though in his possession, is not rightfully his; the government does not violate the Sixth Amendment if it seizes the robbery proceeds, and refuses to permit the defendant to use them to pay for his defense. "(N)o lawyer, in any case, . . . has the right to accept stolen property, or . . . ransom money, in payment of a fee . . . The privilege to practice law is not a license to steal." Laska v. United States, 82 F.2d 672, 677 (10th Cir.1936).

>   · · ·

> . . . [T]he Court of Appeals put it aptly: "The modern day Jean Valjean must be satisfied with appointed counsel. Yet the drug merchant claims that his possession of huge sums of money . . . entitles him to something more. We reject this contention, and any notion of a constitutional right to use the proceeds of crime to finance an expensive defense." 837 F.2d, at 649. . . .

> *Caplin,* supra, 109 S.Ct. at 2652, 2655.

Justice Blackmun, for himself and Justices Brennan, Marshall and Stevens, dissented in both cases. In *Caplin,* he wrote:

> The right to retain private counsel serves to foster the trust between attorney and client that is necessary for the attorney to be a truly effective advocate. . . . When the Government insists

upon the right to choose the defendant's counsel for him, that relationship of trust is undermined: counsel is too readily perceived as the Government's agent rather than his own. . . .

The right to retain private counsel also serves to assure some modicum of equality between the Government and those it chooses to prosecute. The Government can be expected to "spend vast sums of money . . . to try defendants accused of crime," *Gideon v. Wainwright,* 372 U.S., at 344, and of course will devote greater resources to complex cases in which the punitive stakes are high. Precisely for this reason, "there are few defendants charged with crime, few indeed, who fail to hire the best lawyers they can get to prepare and present their defenses." Ibid. But when the Government provides for appointed counsel, there is no guarantee that levels of compensation and staffing will be even average. Where cases are complex, trials long, and stakes high, that problem is exacerbated. "Despite the legal profession's commitment to pro bono work," . . . even the best-intentioned of attorneys may have no choice but to decline the task of representing defendants in cases for which they will not receive adequate compensation. . . . Over the long haul, the result of lowered compensation levels will be that talented attorneys will "decline to enter criminal practice . . . This exodus of talented attorneys could devastate the criminal defense bar." Winick, Forfeiture of Attorneys' Fees under RICO and CCE and the Right to Counsel of Choice: the Constitutional Dilemma and How to Avoid It, 43 U.Miami L.Rev. 765, 781 (1989). Without the defendant's right to retain private counsel, the Government too readily could defeat its adversaries simply by outspending them.

Caplin, Blackmun, J., dissenting 109 S.Ct. at 2672–73.

Money Laundering and Attorneys' Fees

As noted in the Brickey excerpt above, the money laundering statute makes it a crime knowingly to engage in a monetary transaction with a financial institution for any amount over $10,000 that is derived from specified criminal activity. In 1988, before the decision in *Caplin,* supra, Congress amended the money laundering statute, 18 U.S.C. 1957(f)(1), to provide that:

[T]he term "monetary transaction" . . . does not include any transaction necessary to preserve a person's right to representation as guaranteed by the sixth amendment to the Constitution.

After *Caplin,* what, if anything, does this amendment mean?

Prepaid Legal Services for Drug Dealers

On July 20, 1989, the Wall St. Journal reported on p. B5 that an attorney in Florida had been convicted of conspiracy to import marijuana and conspiracy to defraud the Internal Revenue Service by concealing the proceeds of narcotics law violations. According to the government's case, the lawyer collected his fee from his clients before they took off on their drug smuggling trips. He charged $10,000 for each person on board the boat, and if no one was caught he kept the money. If anyone was arrested, he was obliged to represent them without further charge.

Conduct Prejudicial to the Administration of Justice: M.R. 8.4(d) and DR 1–102(A)(5)

Note on In re Masters

In In re Masters, 91 Ill.2d 413, 438 N.E.2d 187 (1982), Masters, a former State's attorney, advised his client, a corporation, to pay extortion demands made by an agent of the Iron Worker's Union, William Arambasich. From his years as State's Attorney Masters was familiar with Arambasich's reputation for violence. He had even worked to persuade several of Arambasich's victims to testify against him but to no avail. Arambasich made his extortion demand to the client by placing a gun on a foreman's desk, demanding $1,000 every six months and threatening to "shut down the job if it wasn't paid," indicating that people would be physically harmed in the process. Masters not only advised his client to comply with Arambasich's demands, but also he volunteered to deliver the money. His role as a deliveryman continued for more than four years.

Masters and his client finally agreed that the payments should stop. Masters called Arambasich and told him that no more money would be paid. Masters received a grant of immunity from criminal prosecution in exchange for testimony against Arambasich.

In disciplinary proceedings, Masters was charged with violating the Illinois counterparts to Model Code DR 7–102(A)(3), knowingly failing to disclose that which he is required by law to reveal; DR 7–102(A)(7), counseling or assisting one's client in illegal activity; DR 1–102(A)(3) and (4), engaging in conduct involving fraud, deceit and moral turpitude; and DR 1–102(A)(5) and (6), engaging in conduct prejudicial to the administration of justice. Masters argued that his advice, given in good faith, to cooperate with the extortionist under the threat of serious physical injury, and his failure to report the matter to the authorities given these circumstances, should not be grounds for discipline.

In rejecting these arguments, the court said: ". . . As an attorney [and as] former State's Attorney, [Masters] was certainly aware . . . that the proper course of conduct was to report the extortion demand to the appropriate authorities. For a lawyer of [his] demonstrated ability and standing at the bar to serve as the conduit through which funds were passed from the alleged victim to the extortionist was unprofessional and unseemly and served to bring the legal profession into disrepute." Id. 438 N.E.2d at 193.

Questions and Comments

If Masters were not involved in the payoffs personally but knew that his client had been paying Arambasich for four years, would the court have disciplined him? Should lawyers have a general duty to report crimes? See ABA Informal Op. 1210 (1972) (discussing the duty of lawyers to report crimes when knowledge is based on unprivileged sources).

The prohibition on engaging in conduct prejudicial to the administration of justice is generally invoked in situations similar to those chargeable as obstruction to justice. See, e.g., Florida Bar v. Simons, 391 So.2d 684 (Fla.1980) (advising clients to testify falsely); People v. Kenelly, 648 P.2d 1065 (Colo.1982) (paying witness to be unavailable to testify); In re Barrett, 88 N.J. 450, 443 A.2d 678 (1982) (threatening criminal prosecution and altering documents).

But it has been used by the courts in other contexts, for example, State v. Nelson, 210 Kan. 637, 504 P.2d 211 (1972) (lawyer's false statements about a judicial officer); In re Howe, 257 N.W.2d 420 (N.D. 1977) (lawyer's false statements to bar admissions authorities); People v. Kane, 638 P.2d 253 (Colo.1981) (lawyer's failure to appear at a contempt hearing for his failure to make child support payments). This provision has been criticized as overbroad and vague. See Weckstein, Maintaining the Integrity and Competence of the Legal Profession, 48 Tex.L.Rev. 267, 275–276 (1970); and Comment, ABA Code of Professional Responsibility: Void for Vagueness?, 57 N.C.L.Rev. 671, 685 (1971). But it has nevertheless been upheld by the courts. Howell v. State Bar of Texas, 843 F.2d 205 (5th Cir.1988); In re Keiler, 380 A.2d 119, 126 n. 7 (D.C.App.1977); Office of Disciplinary Counsel v. Campbell, 463 Pa. 472, 482, 345 A.2d 616, 621–22 (1975) (DR 1–102(A)(5) arguably vague but clear as applied to case at bar), cert. denied, 424 U.S. 926 (1976). Is it broader or vaguer than the federal obstruction of justice statute?

In re Corboy, 124 Ill.2d 29, 528 N.E.2d 694 (1988), involved a loan by several Chicago lawyers to a Cook County Circuit Judge, solicited by a lawyer who was a mutual acquaintance but who, it turned out, was also an accomplice in illegal payments received by the judge for fixing the criminal calendar. The loan was represented to be for a hospital bill for the judge's mother, and there was no evidence that the lawyers making the loan knew of the judge's corrupt activities. The funds were transmitted by checks payable to the judge, who did not use them to pay the hospital bill. Illinois Rule 7–110(a), corresponding to DR 7–110(A), provides that a lawyer may not "give or lend anything of value" to a judge. The Illinois Supreme Court held that the rule is a "per se" prohibition that does not require a corrupt purpose, although, when read with Code of Judicial Conduct Rule 5(C)(4), it does not prohibit gifts implicit in "ordinary social hospitality." The loan to the judge was held a violation of Rule 7–110(a) and was said also to be a violation of Model Rule 8.4(f), which provides that a lawyer shall not "knowingly assist a judge . . . in conduct that is a violation of applicable rules of judicial conduct or other law." However, no sanction was imposed upon the respondents because they "acted without the guidance of precedent or settled opinion, and there was, apparently, considerable belief among members of the bar that they had acted properly."

B. TORT LAW

GREYCAS, INC. v. PROUD

United States Court of Appeals, Seventh Circuit, 1987.
826 F.2d 1560.

POSNER, CIRCUIT JUDGE.

Theodore S. Proud, Jr., a member of the Illinois bar who practices law in a suburb of Chicago, appeals from a judgment against him for $833,760, entered after a bench trial. The tale of malpractice and misrepresentation that led to the judgment begins with Proud's brother-in-law, Wayne Crawford, like Proud a lawyer but one who devoted most of his attention to a large farm that he owned in downstate Illinois. The farm fell on hard times and by 1981 Crawford was in dire financial straits. He had pledged most of his farm machinery to lenders, yet now desparately needed more money. He approached Greycas, Inc., the plaintiff in this case, a large financial company headquartered in Arizona, seeking a large loan that he offered to secure with the farm machinery. He did not tell Greycas about his financial difficulties or that he had pledged the machinery to other lenders, but he did make clear that he needed the loan in a hurry. Greycas obtained several appraisals of Crawford's farm machinery but did not investigate Crawford's financial position or discover that he had pledged the collateral to other lenders, who had perfected their liens in the collateral. Greycas agreed to lend Crawford $1,367,966.50, which was less than the appraised value of the machinery.

The loan was subject, however, to an important condition, which is at the heart of this case: Crawford was required to submit a letter to Greycas, from counsel whom he would retain, assuring Greycas that there were no prior liens on the machinery that was to secure the loan. Crawford asked Proud to prepare the letter, and he did so, and mailed it to Greycas, and within 20 days of the first contact between Crawford and Greycas the loan closed and the money was disbursed. A year later Crawford defaulted on the loan; shortly afterward he committed suicide. Greycas then learned that most of the farm machinery that Crawford had pledged to it had previously been pledged to other lenders.

The machinery was sold at auction. The Illinois state court that determined the creditors' priorities in the proceeds of the sale held that Greycas did not have a first priority on most of the machinery that secured its loan; as a result Greycas has been able to recover only a small part of the loan. The judgment it obtained in the present suit is the district judge's estimate of the value that it would have realized on its collateral had there been no prior liens, as Proud represented in his letter.

That letter is the centerpiece of the litigation. Typed on the stationery of Proud's firm and addressed to Greycas, it identifies Proud as Crawford's lawyer and states that, "in such capacity, I have been asked to render my opinion in connection with" the proposed loan to Crawford. It also states that "this opinion is being delivered in accordance with the requirements of the Loan Agreement" and that

> I have conducted a U.C.C., tax, and judgment search with respect to the Company [i.e., Crawford's farm] as of March 19, 1981, and except as hereinafter noted all units listed on the attached Exhibit A ("Equipment") are free and clear of all liens or encumbrances other than Lender's perfected security interest therein which was recorded March 19, 1981 at the Office of the Recorder of Deeds of Fayette County, Illinois.

The reference to the lender's security interest is to Greycas's interest; Crawford, pursuant to the loan agreement, had filed a notice of that interest with the recorder. The excepted units to which the letter refers are four vehicles. Exhibit A is a long list of farm machinery—the collateral that Greycas thought it was getting to secure the loan, free of any other liens. Attached to the loan agreement itself, however, as Exhibit B, is another list of farm machinery constituting the collateral for the loan, and there are discrepancies between the two lists; . . .

Proud never conducted a search for prior liens on the machinery listed in Exhibit A. His brother-in-law gave him the list and told him there were no liens other than the one that Crawford had just filed for Greycas. Proud made no effort to verify Crawford's statement. The theory of the complaint is that Proud was negligent in representing that there were no prior liens, merely on his brother-in-law's say-so. No doubt Proud *was* negligent in failing to conduct a search, but we are not clear why the *misrepresentation* is alleged to be negligent rather than deliberate and hence fraudulent, in which event Greycas's alleged contributory negligence would not be an issue (as it is, we shall see), since there is no defense of contributory or comparative negligence to a deliberate tort, such as fraud. Proud did not merely say, "There are no liens"; he said, "I have conducted a U.C.C., tax, and judgment search"; and not only is this statement, too, a false one, but its falsehood cannot have been inadvertent, for Proud knew he had not conducted such a search. The concealment of his relationship with Crawford might also support a charge of fraud. But Greycas decided, for whatever reason, to argue negligent misrepresentation rather than fraud. It may have feared that Proud's insurance policy for professional malpractice excluded deliberate wrongdoing from its coverage, or may not have wanted to bear the higher burden of proving fraud, or may have feared that an accusation of fraud would make it harder to settle the case—for most cases, of course, are settled, though this one has not been. In any event, Proud does not argue that either he is liable for fraud or he is liable for nothing.

He also does not, and could not, deny or justify the misrepresentation; but he argues that it is not actionable under the tort law of Illinois, because he had no duty of care to Greycas. (This is a diversity case and the parties agree that Illinois tort law governs the substantive issues.) He argues that Greycas had an adversarial relationship with Proud's client, Crawford, and that a lawyer has no duty of straight dealing to an adversary, at least none enforceable by a tort suit. In so arguing, Proud is characterizing Greycas's suit as one for professional malpractice rather than negligent misrepresentation, yet elsewhere in his briefs he insists that the suit was solely for negligent misrepresentation—while Greycas insists that its suit charges both torts. Legal malpractice based on a false representation, and negligent misrepresentation by a lawyer, are such similar legal concepts, however, that we have great difficulty both in holding them apart in our minds and in understanding why the parties are quarreling over the exact characterization; no one suggests, for example, that the statute of limitations might have run on one but not the other tort. So we shall discuss both.

Proud is undoubtedly correct in arguing that a lawyer has no general duty of care toward his adversary's client; it would be a considerable and, as it seems to us, an undesirable novelty to hold that every bit of sharp dealing by a lawyer gives rise to prima facie tort liability to the opposing party in the lawsuit or negotiation. The tort of malpractice normally refers to a lawyer's careless or otherwise wrongful conduct toward his own client. Proud argues that Crawford rather than Greycas was his client, and although this is not so clear as Proud supposes—another characterization of the transaction is that Crawford undertook to obtain a lawyer for Greycas in the loan transaction—we shall assume for purposes of discussion that Greycas was not Proud's client.

Therefore if malpractice just meant carelessness or other misconduct toward one's own client, Proud would not be liable for malpractice to Greycas. But in Pelham v. Griesheimer, 92 Ill.2d 13, 64 Ill.Dec. 544, 440 N.E.2d 96 (1982), the Supreme Court of Illinois discarded the old common law requirement of privity of contract for professional malpractice; so now it is possible for someone who is not the lawyer's (or other professional's) client to sue him for malpractice. The court in *Pelham* was worried, though, about the possibility of a lawyer's being held liable "to an unlimited and unknown number of potential plaintiffs," . . . so it added that "for a nonclient to succeed in a negligence action against an attorney, he must prove that the primary purpose and intent of the attorney-client relationship itself was to benefit or influence the third party," . . . That, however, describes this case exactly. Crawford hired Proud not only for the primary purpose, but for the sole purpose, of influencing Greycas to make Crawford a loan.

The case is much like Brumley v. Touche, Ross & Co., 139 Ill.App.3d 831, 836, 93 Ill.Dec. 816, 819–20, 487 N.E.2d 641, 644–45 (1985), where a complaint that an accounting firm had negligently prepared an audit report that the firm knew would be shown to an investor in the audited corporation and relied on by that investor was held to state a claim for professional malpractice. In Conroy v. Andeck Resources '81 Year–End Ltd., 137 Ill.App.3d 375, 389–91, 92 Ill.Dec. 10, 21–22, 484 N.E.2d 525, 536–37 (1985), in contrast, a law firm that represented an offeror of securities was held not to have any duty of care to investors. The representation was not intended for the benefit of investors. Their reliance on the law firm's using due care in the services it provided in connection with the offer was not invited. Cf. Barker v. Henderson, Franklin, Starnes & Holt, 797 F.2d 490, 497 (7th Cir.1986).

All this assumes that *Pelham* governs this case, but arguably it does not, for Greycas, as we noted, may have decided to bring this as a suit for negligent misrepresentation rather than professional malpractice. We know of no obstacle to such an election; nothing is more common in American jurisprudence than overlapping torts.

The claim of negligent misrepresentation might seem utterly straightforward. It might seem that by addressing a letter to Greycas intended (as Proud's counsel admitted at argument) to induce reliance on the statements in it, Proud made himself prima facie liable for any material misrepresentations, careless or deliberate, in the letter, whether or not Proud was Crawford's lawyer or for that matter anyone's lawyer. Knowing that Greycas was relying on him to determine whether the collateral for the loan was encumbered and to advise Greycas of the results of his determination, Proud negligently misrepresented the situation, to Greycas's detriment. But merely labeling a suit as one for negligent misrepresentation rather than professional malpractice will not make the problem of indefinite and perhaps excessive liability, which induced the court in *Pelham* to place limitations on the duty of care, go away. So one is not surprised to find that courts have placed similar limitations on suits for negligent misrepresentation—so similar that we are led to question whether, . . . these really are different torts, at least when both grow out of negligent misrepresentations by lawyers. For example, the *Brumley* case, which we cited earlier, is a professional-malpractice case, yet it has essentially the same facts as Ultramares Corp. v. Touche, Niven & Co., 255 N.Y. 170, 174 N.E. 441 (1931), where the New York Court of Appeals, in a famous opinion by Judge Cardozo, held that an accountant's negligent misrepresentation was not actionable at the suit of a lender who had relied on the accountant's certified audit of the borrower.

The absence of a contract between the lender and the accountant defeated the suit in *Ultramares*—yet why should privity of contract have been required for liability just because the negligence lay in disseminating information rather than in designing or manufacturing a product? The privity limitation in products cases had been rejected, in another famous Cardozo opinion, years earlier. See MacPherson v.

Buick Motor Co., 217 N.Y. 382, 111 N.E. 1050 (1916). Professor Bishop
suggests that courts were worried that imposing heavy liabilities on
producers of information might cause socially valuable information to
be underproduced. See Negligent Misrepresentation Through Econo-
mists' Eyes, 96 L.Q.Rev. 360 (1980). Many producers of information
have difficulty appropriating its benefits to society. The property-
rights system in information is incomplete; someone who comes up
with a new idea that the law of intellectual property does not protect
cannot prevent others from using the idea without reimbursing his
costs of invention or discovery. So the law must be careful not to weigh
these producers down too heavily with tort liabilities. For example,
information produced by securities analysts, the news media, academi-
cians, and so forth is socially valuable, but as its producers can't
capture the full value of the information in their fees and other
remuneration the information may be underproduced. Maybe it is
right, therefore—or at least efficient—that none of these producers
should have to bear the full costs. . . . At least that was once the
view; and while *Ultramares* has now been rejected, in Illinois as
elsewhere—maybe because providers of information are deemed more
robust today than they once were or maybe because it is now believed
that auditors, surveyors, and other providers of professional services
were always able to capture the social value of even the information
component of those services in the fees they charged their clients—a
residuum of concern remains. So when in Rozny v. Marnul, 43 Ill.2d
54, 250 N.E.2d 656 (1969), the Supreme Court of Illinois, joining the
march away from *Ultramares,* held for the first time that negligent
misrepresentation was actionable despite the absence of a contract, and
thus cast aside the same "privity of contract" limitation later overruled
with regard to professional malpractice in *Pelham,* the court was
careful to emphasize facts in the particular case before it that limited
the scope of its holding—facts such as that the defendant, a surveyor,
had placed his "absolute guarantee for accuracy" on the plat and that
only a few persons would receive and rely on it, thus limiting the
potential scope of liability. . . .

Later Illinois cases, however, influenced by section 552 of the
Second Restatement of Torts (1977), state the limitation on liability for
negligent misrepresentation in more compact terms—as well as in
narrower scope—than *Rozny.* These are cases in the intermediate
appellate court, but, as we have no reason to think the Supreme Court
of Illinois would reject them, we are bound to follow them. . . . They
hold that "one who in the course of his business or profession supplies
information for the guidance of others in their business transactions" is
liable for negligent misrepresentations that induce detrimental reliance. . . . Whether there is a practical as distinct from a merely
semantic difference between this formulation of the duty limitation and
that of *Pelham* may be doubted but cannot change the outcome of this
case. Proud, in the practice of his profession, supplied information (or
rather misinformation) to Greycas that was intended to guide Greycas

in commercial dealings with Crawford. Proud therefore had a duty to use due care to see that the information was correct. He used no care.

Proud must lose on the issue of liability even if the narrower, *ad hoc* approach of *Rozny* is used instead of the approach of section 552 of the Restatement. Information about the existence of previous liens on particular items of property is of limited social as distinct from private value, by which we mean simply that the information is not likely to be disseminated widely. There is consequently no reason to give it special encouragement by overlooking carelessness in its collection and expression. Where as in this case the defendant makes the negligent misrepresentation directly to the plaintiff in the course of the defendant's business or profession, the courts have little difficulty in finding a duty of care. Prosser and Keeton on the Law of Torts . . . § 107, at p. 747.

There is no serious doubt about the existence of a causal relationship between the misrepresentation and the loan. Greycas would not have made the loan without Proud's letter. Nor would it have made the loan had Proud advised it that the collateral was so heavily encumbered that the loan was as if unsecured, for then Greycas would have known that the probability of repayment was slight. Merely to charge a higher interest rate would not have been an attractive alternative to security; it would have made default virtually inevitable by saddling Crawford with a huge fixed debt. To understand the astronomical interest rate that is required to make an unsecured loan a paying proposition to the lender when the risk of default is high, notice that even if the riskless interest rate is only 3 percent, the rate of inflation zero, the cost of administering the loan zero, and the lender risk-neutral, he still must charge an annual interest rate of 106 percent if he thinks there is only a 50 percent chance that he will get his principal back.

Proud argues, however, that his damages should be reduced in recognition of Greycas's own contributory negligence, which, though no longer a complete defense in Illinois, is a partial defense, renamed "comparative negligence." . . . It is as much a defense to negligent misrepresentation as to any other tort of negligence. . . . On the issue of comparative negligence the district court said only that "defendant may have proved negligence upon the part of plaintiff but that negligence, if any, had no causal relationship to the malpractice of the defendant or the damages to the plaintiff." This comment is not easy to fathom. If Greycas was careless in deciding whether to make the loan, this implies that a reasonable investigation by Greycas would have shown that the collateral for the loan was already heavily encumbered; knowing this, Greycas would not have made the loan and therefore would not have suffered any damages.

But we think it too clear to require a remand for further proceedings that Proud failed to prove a want of due care by Greycas. Due care is the care that is optimal given that the other party is exercising due care. . . . It is not the higher level of care that would be optimal if potential tort victims were required to assume that the rest of the world was negligent. A pedestrian is not required to exercise a level of care (e.g., wearing a helmet or a shin guard) that would be optimal if there were no sanctions against reckless driving. Otherwise drivers would be encouraged to drive recklessly, and knowing this pedestrians would be encouraged to wear helmets and shin guards. The result would be a shift from a superior method of accident avoidance (not driving recklessly) to an inferior one (pedestrian armor).

So we must ask whether Greycas would have been careless not to conduct its own UCC search had Proud done what he had said he did—conduct his own UCC search. The answer is no. The law normally does not require duplicative precautions unless one is likely to fail or the consequences of failure (slight though the likelihood may be) would be catastrophic. One UCC search is enough to disclose prior liens, and Greycas acted reasonably in relying on Proud to conduct it. Although Greycas had much warning that Crawford was in financial trouble and that the loan might not be repaid, that was a reason for charging a hefty interest rate and insisting that the loan be secured; it was not a reason for duplicating Proud's work. It is not hard to conduct a UCC lien search; it just requires checking the records in the recorder's office for the county where the debtor lives. See Ill.Rev.Stat. ch. 26, ¶ 9–401. So the only reason to backstop Proud was if Greycas should have assumed he was careless or dishonest; and we have just said that the duty of care does not require such an assumption. Had Proud disclosed that he was Crawford's brother-in-law this might have been a warning signal that Greycas could ignore only at its peril. To go forward in the face of a known danger is to assume the risk. . . . But Proud did not disclose his relationship to Crawford.

The last issue concerns the amount of damages awarded Greycas. . . .

. . .

. . . [T]he judge was, if anything, unduly generous to Proud, in giving Greycas only the value of the collateral on the date of default, rather than the unpaid principal of the loan. But for Proud's misrepresentations, Greycas would not have made the loan, so its damages are not just the collateral but the entire uncollectable portion of the loan together with the interest that the money would have earned in an alternative use . . . We therefore conclude that the realizable value of Greycas's collateral on the date of Crawford's default was a real loss.

A final point. The record of this case reveals serious misconduct by an Illinois attorney. We are therefore sending a copy of this opinion to the Attorney Registration and Disciplinary Commission of the Supreme Court of Illinois for such disciplinary action as may be deemed appropriate in the circumstances.

Affirmed.

BAUER, CHIEF JUDGE, concurring.

I am in agreement with the majority opinion. I believe that Proud would be liable without reference to legal malpractice or negligent misrepresentation. The evidence in this case indicates that he is guilty of fraud or intentional misrepresentation. He was lying when he represented that he had made U.C.C., tax and judgment searches on his brother-in-law's farm. He intended the misrepresentation to induce Greycas to make a loan to his brother-in-law; Greycas justifiably relied upon the misrepresentation in making the loan and was injured as a result. Under these facts, Proud's misrepresentation was indefensible.

Questions and Comments

In discussing comparative negligence the court points out that "[a] pedestrian is not required to exercise a level of care (e.g. wearing a helmet) that would be optimal if there were no sanctions against reckless driving." Yet later the court suggests that if Proud had disclosed to Greycas that he was Crawford's brother-in-law, "this might have been a warning signal that Greycas could ignore only at its peril. To go forward in the face of a known danger is to assume the risk." Making false statements is unethical whether or not they are made on behalf of one's brother-in-law. If made with intent to defraud, they are fraudulent regardless of the relationship between the maker and the party he is "helping." Why then should a third party be required to see the relationship as a warning signal?

In Greyhound Leasing & Financial Corp. v. Norwest Bank of Jamestown, 854 F.2d 1122 (8th Cir.1988), as in *Greycas,* the lender, Greyhound, required a lawyer's opinion letter stating that the farm equipment securing the loan was unencumbered; it wanted a lawyer from the farmer's own locality to write the letter because a local lawyer would be more likely to be familiar with the farmer's business activities. The lawyer wrote a letter stating that he was "not aware of any liens or encumbrances . . . created or suffered by the lessee nor have they [sic] granted or conveyed any liens or encumbrances of any nature with respect thereto." In fact, almost all of the equipment was encumbered by at least one lien. The lawyer was told by his client that all of the equipment was brand new and not yet "owned or possessed by him." He also had documents prepared by Greyhound which asserted that the equipment was new. The equipment was, however, not new. Relying on the word of his client and the documents sent by Greyhound, the lawyer did not conduct a lien search before signing the opinion letter because in North Dakota one cannot create a valid lien on farm equipment until it is "owned or possessed." Shortly after the loan money was paid over, the farmer filed bankruptcy. Greyhound found itself with virtually no collateral and a bankrupt debtor; it filed suit against the lawyer. The district court held for the lawyer on two grounds: first, the letter only gave the lawyer's personal assurance that there were no liens and was therefore not a misrepresentation; and second, even if the letter constituted negligent misrepresentation, Greyhound's negligence exceeded that of the lawyer and thus under North Dakota's doctrine of contributory negligence Greyhound could not recover.

The Court of Appeals affirmed on the second ground. Assuming arguendo, that the letter was a negligent misrepresentation, it held that Greyhound's negligence was greater. First, Greyhound was negligent when, knowing the equipment was not new, it prepared documents that stated otherwise in order to gain a tax benefit. Second, Greyhound was negligent in failing to make its own independent investigation of the lien situation:

> Greyhound claims to have paid out $1 million in reliance on the opinion of a lawyer whom it never contacted or instructed and to whom it arranged the transmittal of seriously inaccurate documents. It devised for the lawyer to sign a most equivocal form of opinion letter which does not clearly set forth the representation which Greyhound now says it thought it was getting from the lawyer, and relied upon it. It seems to us eminently reasonable to hold, as the trial judge did, that under the circumstances, Greyhound had an independent obligation to investigate the existence of liens.

Id. at 1125.

Is this consistent with the reasoning in *Greycas*?

If Greyhound had not known that the equipment was old, would the ambiguous language of the opinion letter have shielded the lawyer from a claim of negligent misrepresentation? In addition to the language quoted above, the opinion letter prefaced each paragraph with this sentence: "We have conducted such investigations as we deemed necessary, in order to render the opinions set forth below." Does this strengthen the claim that the letter constituted negligent misrepresentation?

Negligent Misrepresentation

Case Law

In Roberts v. Ball, Hunt . . ., 57 Cal.App.3d 104, 128 Cal.Rptr. 901 (1976), the firm's client needed a loan. To get the loan, the client, a partnership, asked the Ball, Hunt firm to prepare an opinion letter that the client could show to its potential creditor. The letter stated that the fourteen partners of the client-partnership were all general partners. To the creditor, Roberts, this assurance was critical because general partners are liable for the debts of the partnership in the event of default. The firm prepared the letter knowing its intended use. The client gave the letter to Roberts, who, relying on the letter, made the loan. When the partnership defaulted, thirteen of the fourteen partners defended a suit brought against them by Roberts by claiming to be only limited partners. Roberts sued the firm for fraud and negligent misrepresentation, claiming that at the time the firm drafted the letter it knew that several of the partners believed they were limited and not general partners and were asserting that position in partnership meetings. According to Roberts, the firm had a duty to disclose these material facts in the opinion letter.

The firm's defense was that it had no intent to deceive and thus was not liable for fraud. The court agreed that the complaint failed to state a cause of action for fraud because there was no allegation of intent to deceive, but held that the firm could be liable for negligent misrepresentation. California, the court stated, rejects the "traditional view . . . that an attorney may not . . . be held liable to third persons [for negligence] because he is not in privity with them, and owes them no duty to act with care." To determine whether a lawyer is liable to someone not a client:

> involves the balancing of various factors, among which are the extent to which the transaction was intended to affect the plaintiff, the foreseeability of harm to him, the degree of certainty that the plaintiff suffered injury, the closeness of the connection between the defendant's conduct and the injury suffered, and the policy of preventing future harm.

Roberts, 128 Cal.Rptr. at 905, citing Lucas v. Hamm, 364 P.2d 685, 687 (1962) (reprinted in chapter 3 below).

Felts v. National Account System Association, 469 F.Supp. 54 (N.D. Miss.1978), involved the sale of unregistered securities by materially false and misleading advertisements and other false documents. Purchasers of the securities brought suit against the offerer's lawyer based on the lawyer's failure to verify or investigate the facts.

> The plaintiffs here were foreseeable and intended third party beneficiaries of [the lawyer's] legal services and skill. It was foreseeable (and, indeed, known) to [the lawyer] . . . that the plaintiffs and all purchasers of these securities would rely on him. [The lawyer] voluntarily assumed a relationship not only with [the issuer] but also with the purchasers of these securities. The law and public policy require that the attorney exercise his position of trust and superior knowledge responsibly so as not to adversely affect persons whose rights and interests are certain and foreseeable.

> Id. at 68.

See also Bradford Securities Processing Services Inc. v. Plaza Bank & Trust, 653 P.2d 188 (Okl.1982) (bond counsel who negligently misrepresented the value and nature of bonds held liable to all foreseeable plaintiffs).

With *Felts* and *Bradford* compare Astor Chauffeured Limousine Co. v. Runnfeldt Investment Corp., 1988 WL 101267 (N.D.Ill.) (not reported in F.Supp.) (applying Illinois law). In *Astor* the court held that the seller's lawyer was not liable to the purchasers of stocks who had relied on the lawyer's negligent misrepresentations because "the duties involved [in representing the seller of stocks], including negotiations and drafting of contractual agreements . . . [are] clearly adversarial in nature" and were not intended directly to benefit the purchasers. See the discussion of "adversarial" relationships in *Greycas.*

Relaxation of the Requirement of Privity

All these cases represent departures from the traditional rule that a lawyer is only liable for negligence to those in privity of contract with the lawyer. Many jurisdictions, perhaps a majority, still purport to adhere to the traditional rule. Apparently, the first case to enunciate the privity rule was Robertson v. Fleming, 4 Macq.H. of L.Cas. 167 (House of Lords, Scottish Appeals, 1861); it was restated in Fish v. Kelly, 17 C.B. (N.S.) 194 (Common Bench 1864). The most authoritative early pronouncement in this country was in National Savings Bank v. Ward, 100 U.S. 195 (1880), which involved facts strikingly similar to those in *Greycas.* The lawyer was negligent in conducting a title search and failed to find a prior conveyance; a bank loaned the client money based on the lawyer's opinion letter that the title was good. The Supreme Court held that the lawyer was not liable to the bank because the bank was not in privity with the lawyer.

New York adheres to the traditional rule. For example, in Grassi v. Tatavito Homes, Inc., 90 A.D.2d 479, 454 N.Y.S.2d 471 (2d Dept.1982), aff'd, 58 N.Y.2d 1038, 448 N.E.2d 1356 (1983), the court held that the attorney for the seller in a sale of property could not be held liable to the buyer for his negligent misrepresentation that the seller owned the property and had title insurance. "Absent privity," the court stated, the attorney "is not liable for simple negligence." 454 N.Y.S.2d at 472. For a case with facts similar to those in *Greycas* and *Greyhound,* see Council Commerce Corp. v. Schwartz, Sachs & Kamhi, P.C., 144 A.D.2d 422, 534 N.Y.S.2d 1 (2d Dept.1988), appeal denied, 74 N.Y.2d 606, 543 N.E.2d 85 (1989) (applying traditional rule: lawyers not liable to lender).

Nevertheless, even in New York lawyers have been held liable to nonclients for negligent misrepresentation when the purpose of the legal opinion was that the third parties rely on the lawyer's statements. See Crossland Savings FSB v. Rockwood Insurance Co., 700 F.Supp. 1274 (S.D.N.Y.1988) (collecting New York cases to this effect). In *Crossland,* the court reconciled these cases with the traditional rule as follows: "When a lawyer at the direction of her client prepares an opinion letter, which is addressed to the third party or which expressly invites the third party's reliance, she engages in a form of limited representation [of that third party]." Id. at 1282, quoting 1 Hazard & Hodes, The Law of Lawyering 320 (1987). See also the statement in *Greycas* that Proud's client might be said to have been the lender.

The lawyer's liability to third parties for professional malpractice is discussed in Chapter 3 along with liability to clients for malpractice.

Intentional Torts

Overview

As both the majority and concurrence in *Greycas* point out, the lawyer could have been sued for fraud instead of negligent misrepresentation and malpractice. Proud said he conducted a U.C.C., tax and judgment search when he had not, and he lied with the intent of separating Greycas from its money—fraud.

Generally, a lawyer has no privilege to commit intentional torts against third parties in the course of representing a client or to assist the client in committing intentional torts against third parties. The most notable exception to this rule is the lawyer's absolute privilege to utter defamatory statements in court or reasonably related to court proceedings. The privilege covers written and oral statements. The qualified privilege to make statements intended to protect the interests of others, which applies to all fiduciaries, also extends to lawyers. See, e.g., Pelagatti v. Cohen, 370 Pa.Super. 422, 536 A.2d 1337 (1987) (discussing both the absolute and qualified privilege); and Dano v. Royal Globe Ins. Co., 59 N.Y.2d 827, 451 N.E.2d 488 (1983). See Chapter 5 below, in which the lawyer's tort liability for conduct connected to litigation is discussed along with other legal limits on the advocate's conduct of litigation or an appeal.

For the intentional torts of fraud and misrepresentation, the plaintiff must show that the lawyer intended to deceive and that the plaintiff was one of a class of people that the lawyer might reasonably have foreseen being taken in. There is no requirement of a special duty or relationship. If the lawyer honestly believed that the communication was truthful, she lacked the intent necessary for fraud unless her belief was reckless.

Fraudulent intent may be shown by a reckless disregard for the truth or falsity of the proposition asserted. For example, in In re Flight Transportation Corporation Securities Litigation, 593 F.Supp. 612 (D.Minn.1984), the court held that the purchasers of securities stated a cause of action for common law fraud against the law firm that had represented the underwriters of the securities by alleging: (1) that the firm, knowingly or in reckless disregard of the facts, had made or aided others to make untrue statements of material facts and had omitted to state other material facts necessary in order to make the statements made not misleading; (2) that the purchasers had relied on these statements; and (3) that the firm by preparing the alleged fraudulent prospectuses had assumed a duty to prospective purchasers.

May a lawyer ever safely rely on her client's assertions without some independent verification of the facts?

> It is claimed that a lawyer is entitled to rely on the statements of his client and that to require him to verify their accuracy would

set an unreasonably high standard. This is too broad a generalization. It is all a matter of degree. To require an audit would
obviously be unreasonable. On the other hand, to require a check
of matters easily verifiable is not unreasonable. Even honest
clients can make mistakes.

Seidel v. Public Service Co. of New Hampshire, 616 F.Supp.
1342, 1362 (D.N.H.1985), quoting Escott v. Bar Chris Constr. Co.,
283 F.Supp. 643, 690 (S.D.N.Y.1968).

See also Stokes v. Lokken, 644 F.2d 779 (8th Cir.1981) (lawyer who
recklessly relies on information provided by client may be liable for
fraud); and Ames Bank v. Hahn, 205 Neb. 353, 287 N.W.2d 687 (1980)
(lawyer may be liable for misrepresentation for making statement
without any knowledge as to whether it is true).

Note on Newburger, Loeb & Co., Inc. v. Gross

In Newburger, Loeb & Co., Inc. v. Gross, 563 F.2d 1057 (2d Cir.
1977), the lawyers were held liable for assisting their clients in intentionally tortious conduct. The law firm, Finley Kumble, through its
partner Robert Persky, represented several general partners in a failing brokerage firm. Persky helped implement a plan to transfer the
partnership's assets to a newly formed corporation against the wishes of
some of the brokerage firm's other partners. The assets were transferred in violation of New York law, which requires that all partners
consent to the transfer unless the partnership agreement expressly
provides otherwise. The transfer of assets required an opinion letter
stating that the partnership had the authority to make the transfer.
Persky issued this letter, after another law firm had declined to do so.
The letter purported to construe the partnership agreement to give the
partners a right to transfer the assets without the consent of other
partners. The court found "simply no language in the partnership
agreement" that could legitimately be construed in this manner, and
held the transfer to be a conversion.

Finley Kumble claimed that because it was acting in its professional capacity, it was immune from suit by third parties for having given
its clients bad advice. The court rejected this defense:

Under New York law an attorney generally cannot be held
liable to third parties for actions taken in furtherance of his role
unless it is shown that he 'did something either tortious in character or beyond the scope of his honorable employment.' Dallas v.
Fassnacht, 42 N.Y.S.2d 415, 418 (Sup.Ct.N.Y. County 1943). Thus,
while an attorney is privileged to give honest advice, even if
erroneous, and generally is not responsible for the motives of his
clients, admission to the bar does not create a license to act
maliciously, fraudulently, or knowingly to tread upon the legal
rights of others.

. . .

The issue here is simply whether [the trial judge] was warranted in finding that Persky had violated that standard.

. . .

[The trial judge] found that "[w]ithout question, Persky was at the heart of this entire matter, guiding the entire plan, carrying threats to the dissidents and knowingly counseling, advising and instituting baseless and fraudulent lawsuits to achieve the [clients'] goal." . . . [I]nter alia, Persky was responsible for: (1) manipulating the settlement and assertion of [baseless claims]; (2) threatening the [other partners] with [litigation] in bad faith; (3) [making allegations about one of the other partner's in a complaint] in disregard for the truth, thereby needlessly vilifying [him]; (4) issuing a false opinion letter . . . thereby furthering the transfer in violation of the rights [of the other partners]; and (5) inducing and participating in the partners' breach of fiduciary obligation to [the other partners]. We find that the record supports the conclusion that Persky went "beyond his honorable employment" and the district court's finding of liability.

Newburger, 563 F.2d at 1080.

Persky's opinion letter said the general partners could transfer the partnership assets without the limited partners' consent. He reasoned that the provisions granting the general partners the power to terminate the partnership included the power to transfer assets. Is this a plausible argument?

In Yoggerst v. Stewart, 623 F.2d 35 (7th Cir.1980), the court, citing *Newburger,* held "an attorney, offering advice in good faith is not liable for the torts of a client." The facts in *Yoggerst* indicated that the lawyer did not know and had no reason to know that his client would use his advice to engage in tortious activity.

In Worldwide Marine Trading Corp. v. Marine Transport Service Inc., 527 F.Supp. 581 (E.D.Pa.1981), the court held that the lawyer's activities did not amount to culpable participation in his client's tortious interference with contract or violation of the antitrust laws.

The court said that, unless the lawyer was a "stakeholder" in the alleged conspiracy, the lawyer:

must [have done] more than be present at the scene, and indeed must [have done] more than merely advise. . . .

There is an important societal interest in protecting the lawyer from third-party lawsuits, and thus in requiring a showing of a knowingly fraudulent or tortious action by the lawyer before permitting third-party recovery from the lawyer. . . . A lawyer must be able to act decisively on behalf of his client, without fearing that he will provide "the deep pocket" in subsequent litigation. If his advice and activity are wrong or negligent, he is already exposed by virtue of his duty to his client. In the context of this case, for example, if plaintiffs prevail, [the lawyer] may have some cause to fear that certain defendants [his former clients] will proceed against him.

527 F.Supp. at 581.

For a recent case, holding a lawyer liable for assisting in the intentional breach of fiduciary duties, see Whitfield v. Lindemann, 853 F.2d 1298 (5th Cir.1988), cert. denied, 109 S.Ct. 2428 (1989) (liability of lawyer is not limited to amount of personal gain). The special responsibilities of lawyers who represent fiduciaries is taken up in Chapter 9 below.

GEOFFREY C. HAZARD, Jr., "HOW FAR MAY A LAWYER GO IN ASSISTING A CLIENT IN UNLAWFUL CONDUCT?"
35 U. of Miami L.Rev. 669 (1981).*

. . .

The general question to be considered is: How far may a lawyer lawfully go in providing assistance to a client that might enable the client to carry out an act that is to some degree illegal?

. . .

. . . The services that a lawyer can provide cover a wide spectrum, regardless of the client purposes that may be involved. At one end of the spectrum is simply advice as to what the law "is," without specific aid or encouragement to the client. It is not easy to provide advice that is neutral with respect to the purposes implicit in the request for advice. Nevertheless, it is possible to give unsuggestive advice, and doing so is the least instrumental form of assistance that a lawyer can provide a client. At the other end of the spectrum of lawyer assistance is pure instrumentalism—the lawyer's physical execution of a purpose that the client would like to realize but cannot or will not actually execute himself. One example would be a lawyer who serves as "bagman" in an illegal payoff for a client who wishes to remain behind the scenes.

At the least instrumental end of the spectrum, the lawyer merely provides the client with an expert definition of the limits of the law, leaving it to the client to consider whether those limits should be transgressed. At the other end of the spectrum, the lawyer personally provides the means without which the client could not achieve the illicit purpose. The law clearly sanctions providing assistance at the least instrumental end of this spectrum. The law clearly prohibits conduct at the other end. But what about forms of conduct that fall within these extremes? Obviously, the farther we move away from simple, unsuggestive advice, and the closer we move toward active assistance, the farther we get from what the law encourages and permits and the closer we get to what the law abhors and proscribes. The questions raised by conduct falling in the middle of the spectrum, however, are difficult, and the answers are usually qualified. What advice should the lawyer give about the limits of the law of fraud or breach of fiduciary duty to a client who has fiduciary obligations but shows signs of being self-interested? What about a client who requests his attorney to prepare documents for a transaction whose factual particulars the client refuses to disclose but the lawyer has reason to suspect? What about a client who asks his lawyer to make frequent, but unscheduled, deposits of very large sums of cash in bank accounts bearing fictitious names? In the latter case, what if the city is Miami in 1981, and the client is twenty-four years of age?

. . .

It is rare that the lawyer fully knows a client's purposes or fully anticipates the ways in which the client might make use of the lawyer's services. Indeed, the client himself often does not fully realize his purposes until the moment of choice has come and gone. Furthermore, a lawyer does not learn of a client's purposes in a continuous narrative. Rather, revelation comes in fragments, often beginning in the historical middle rather than at the historical beginning. As the matter unfolds, it may appear to the lawyer that the portents of abuse are strong or weak, clear or ambiguous, firm or wavering. When are these portents sufficiently certain so that the lawyer "knows" that the client intends an illegal objective and is bent on its accomplishment?

It is sometimes suggested that the dilemma is false, because surely a lawyer cannot "know" what a client intends. This suggestion is either disingenuous or absurd. Of course, speaking in terms of radical epistemology, it is true that a lawyer cannot "know" what a client—or anyone else—intends. In these terms it is impossible for a lawyer to "know" anything. Yet the practice of law is based on practical knowledge, that is, practical assessments leading to empirical conclusions which form the basis for irrevocable action. Lawyers certainly possess such practical knowledge. If a lawyer can have practical knowledge of how the purposes of others may affect his client, he can have the same knowledge of how his client's purposes may affect others. It is in that sense that the lawyer can "know" when a client's purpose is illegal. . . .

The general category embraced by the term "illegality" also includes, beyond the criminal law, various torts. Certain kinds of torts are readily subsumed under the rubric of "illegality." These torts include the civil counterparts of criminal offenses that are *mala in se:* wrongful death by willful unexcused act, physically harmful battery, knowing conversion, and some forms of abuse of process. Other intentional torts, such as piracy of trade secrets or invasion of privacy, can also be included.

On the other hand, it is less apparent why negligence should be regarded as "illegal" conduct even if it results in tort liability. Yet negligence is a violation of the legal standard of reasonable care and is in this sense a violation of law. Suppose, for example, a client asks his lawyer whether compliance with old safety regulations is sufficient, and the lawyer indicates that such compliance would be sufficient because a tenuous argument can be made that new and stricter safety regulations are constitutionally invalid. If someone is injured as a result of the client's noncompliance with the new regulations, is the lawyer chargeable with having materially assisted the client in "illegal conduct"? How would the outcome be affected if that violation also entails criminal sanctions?

. . . We may feel confident about including crimes that are *mala in se,* but as we move away from this core meaning, the boundaries become increasingly doubtful.

We can also approach the question from a different direction. There is a wide range of client conduct that gives rise to civil liability, but which we would not readily call "illegal" in the present context. Consider, for example, the deliberate default in performance of a contract obligation, the deliberate exercise of dominion and control over property of which another person claims ownership, or the deliberate decision to make a search and seizure of doubtful legality. Should any of these forms of conduct be categorized as "illegal" for the purpose of limiting the client endeavors that a lawyer may further?

The term "illegality" in ordinary legal parlance does not embrace breach of contract or invasion of a property interest. Yet there are breaches of contract and invasions of personal and property interests that are more flagrant and more harmful than many torts, and indeed more harmful than many regulatory offenses.

. . .

The law of legal ethics, for example, specially presupposes the law of torts and of agency. A lawyer in the service of a client is typically an agent. But legal representation is a special kind of agency, involving legally conferred special powers that provide the lawyer with some autonomy from the client in carrying out the agency. . . .

In general, the law of agency imposes limits on what an agent may, with legal impunity, do for a principal. Section 343 of the Restatement (Second) of Agency states: "An agent who does an act otherwise a tort is not relieved from liability by the fact that he acted . . . on account of the principal, except where he is exercising . . . a privilege held by him for the protection of the principal's interests. . . ." [15] As explained in Comment b to this section, an agent's act is privileged if "a reasonable belief in the existence of facts causes an act to be privileged, and a command by the principal gives the agent reason to believe in the existence of such facts." [16] Thus, if a client directs his lawyer to

---

15. Restatement (Second) of Agency § 343 (1957).

16. Id. Comment b. Comment b states that:

An agent who . . . defames or arrests another, or does any similar act, is not excused by the mere fact that he is acting as an agent. If, however, a reasonable belief in the existence of facts causes an act to be privileged, and a command by the principal gives the agent reason to believe in the existence of such facts, such command gives him a privilege to do the act. Thus, if a principal directs an agent to institute criminal proceedings against another, . . . if from the command the agent has reasonable

commence criminal proceedings against another, and if the lawyer "has reasonable grounds for believing the other guilty of the crime, the [lawyer] is not guilty of malicious prosecution."

Section 348 of the Restatement is also pertinent to the kinds of transactions in which lawyers can be involved. That section provides that "[a]n agent who fraudulently makes representations, uses duress, or knowingly assists in the commission of tortious fraud or duress by his principal or by others is subject to liability in tort to the injured person. . . ." The comments following section 348 make it clear that if a lawyer acts for a client in a transaction that the lawyer knows is founded on misrepresentations, the lawyer acts tortiously.[19]

. . .

The vital circumstance under the law of agency is therefore not the fact that the actor is an agent, but the existence of facts that render his actions privileged. Applying the law of agency to lawyers, the vital question is what the lawyer knows about the client's endeavor. Using defamation and false arrest as illustrations, Comment b to section 343 of the Restatement (Second) of Agency observes that *if* "a reasonable belief in the existence of facts causes an act to be privileged," and *if* what the agent (lawyer) is told by the principal (client) "gives the agent reason to believe in the existence of such facts," then the agent (lawyer) has the privilege that is conferred on innocent actors.

But what if the client's endeavor is *not* one that a "reasonable belief in the existence of facts" will cause to be privileged? For example, in the tort of conversion it is not a defense that the agent reasonably believes that the property was his principal's. This problem is explicitly addressed in section 349 of the Restatement (Second) of Agency: An agent whose acts "would otherwise constitute trespass to

grounds for believing the other guilty of the crime, the agent is not guilty of malicious prosecution.

The reference to "privilege" in this provision does not refer to a privilege of the agent. It refers to a privilege of the principal, that is, the client. This is clear from Restatement (Second) of Agency §§ 345, 346 (Tent. Draft No. 6, 1979):

§ 345. Agent Exercising Privileges of Principal.

An agent is privileged to do what otherwise would constitute a tort if his principal is privileged to have an agent do it and has authorized the agent to do it.

§ 346. Privilege to Protect Principal's Interests.

An agent is privileged to give such protection to the person or property of his principal as is authorized by the principal to the same extent as the principal is privileged to act in the protection of himself or his property.

19. Comment a, for example, states: "[A]n agent who enters into transactions with a buyer knowing that the buyer is relying upon the previous misrepresentations by the principal or other agent is liable to the same extent as if he had made the previous misrepresentations." Id. Comment a. Comment c adds:

[I]f an agent who has been given misinformation by a principal, on the strength of which he makes statements to a third person, later discovers the untruth and refrains from taking steps to inform the other party, the agent is subject to liability if subsequently the other party completes the transaction with the principal or another agent, relying in part upon the statements of the first agent.

Id. at Comment c.

or conversion of a chattel is not relieved from liability by the fact that he acts on account of his principal and reasonably, although mistakenly, believes that the principal is entitled to possession of the chattels." Under this rule, what is the situation of a lawyer who advises a client to seize property in possession of a debtor? [24]

The lawyer's knowledge is again the vital question in cases involving misrepresentations in a contract transaction. Under section 348 of the Restatement (Second) of Agency, for example, a lawyer faces liability if he "knowingly assists in the commission of tortious fraud" by his client. If the lawyer proceeds "knowing that the buyer is relying upon the previous misrepresentations by the [client]," then the laywer is "liable to the same extent as if he had made the previous misrepresentations." [26] Moreover, if the lawyer "has been given misinformation by a [client], on the strength of which he makes statements to a third person, [and] later discovers the untruth and refrains from taking steps to inform the other party, the [lawyer] is subject to liability if subsequently the other party completes the transaction . . . relying in part upon the statements of the [lawyer]." [27] Under these rules, then, a lawyer would be liable if he discovered on the eve of a closing that the other party had relied on statements by the client that the lawyer knew were false or fraudulently misleading.[28] Such conduct also would seem to be "illegal" within the meaning of DR 7–102(A)(7).

The rules of tort law are similar to the rules of agency, but are cast in terms of "persons acting in concert." That agents and principals act "in concert" is clear as a matter of ordinary usage. Section 343, Comment d of the Restatement (Second) of Agency expressly refers to section 876 of the Restatement (Second) of Torts, which is entitled "Persons Acting in Concert." Section 876 provides:

> For harm resulting to a third person from the tortious conduct of another, one is subject to liability if he
>
> > (a) does a tortious act in concert with the other or pursuant to a common design with him, or
> >
> > (b) knows that the other's conduct constitutes a breach of duty and gives substantial assistance or encouragement to the other so to conduct himself. . . .[30]

24. Flagg Bros., Inc. v. Brooks, 436 U.S. 149 (1978) addresses the situation of a lawyer who advises a client about seizing property in the possession of a debtor. It would seem that if the lawyer "assists" the client, and if the seizure turns out not to be legally privileged, then the lawyer, as well as the client, is prima facie legally responsible. Restatement (Second) of Agency § 343, Comment d, says that "[T]he act of the agent may play too small a part to render him legally responsible for the result, or the agent's innocence and purpose may create a privilege for him to act." It is hard to see how the lawyer's role in such a situation is "too small" to count. The comment does not indicate the scope of the privilege that could result in immunity.

26. [§ 348] Comment a.

27. Id. Comment c.

28. . . . [See] SEC v. National Student Marketing Corp., 457 F.Supp. 682 (D.D.C.1978) [reprinted below at p. 108.] . . .

30. Restatement (Second) of Torts § 876 (1977).

Advice to a tortfeasor is equivalent to active participation in the tort if the advisor knows that the contemplated act is tortious, and if the advice is a "substantial factor in causing the resulting tort." [31]

. . .

Finally, one can look to the principles of complicity expressed in the criminal law for guidance. Section 2.06(1) of the Model Penal Code provides that "[a] person is guilty of an offense if it is committed by his own conduct or by the conduct of another person for which he is legally accountable. . . ." [36] Section 2.06(2)(c) of the Code provides that a person is legally accountable for the conduct of another person if he is an "accomplice of such other person." And section 2.06(3)(a)(ii) provides that an accomplice is one who "aids . . . in planning or committing" the offense "with the purpose of promoting or facilitating the commission of the offense." Restating these provisions, a lawyer is guilty of an offense if he aids a client in facilitating conduct that is an offense.[39]

31. The full text of comment d to § 876 states that:

Advice or encouragement to act operates as a moral support to a tortfeasor and if the act encouraged is known to be tortious it has the same effect upon the liability of the adviser as participation or physical assistance. If the encouragement or assistance is a substantial factor in causing the resulting tort, the one giving it is himself a tortfeasor and is responsible for the consequences of the other's act.

Id. Comment d.

The Restatement (Second) of Torts, like the Restatement (Second) of Agency, recognizes that the involvement of an agent in the principal's purposes must rise above some minimum. Comment d to Restatement (Second) of Torts § 876 also provides:

The assistance of or participation by the defendant may be so slight that he is not liable for the act of the other. In determining this, the nature of the act encouraged, the amount of assistance given by the defendant, his presence or absence at the time of the tort, his relation to the other and his state of mind are all considered. (See Illustration 9).

Id.

Illustration 9 is as follows:

A is employed by B to carry messages to B's workmen. B directs A to tell B's workmen to tear down a fence that B believes to be on his own land but that in fact, as A knows, is on the land of C. A delivers the message and the workmen tear down the fence. Since A was a servant used merely as a means of communication, his assistance is so slight that he is not liable to C.

Id. Illustration 9.

In the Restatements, the Illustrations generally are clear cases—the ones that the members of the Institute can agree on—and not borderline cases. If Illustration 9 is a clear case of noninvolvement, the implication is that when a person acts as considerably more than a messenger he is rendering "assistance." Lawyers rarely act merely as messengers. Cf. In re Sears, 71 N.J. 175, 364 A.2d 777 (1976) (attorney suspended from the practice of law for attempting, on behalf of his client, to influence a Federal Securities and Exchange Commission investigation).

. . .

36. Model Penal Code § 2.06(1) (Proposed Official Draft, 1962).

39. There is very little authority on the degree of lawyer involvement in a client's criminal endeavor that would constitute "aiding." See Johnson v. Youden, [1950] 1 K.B. 544, involving a criminal prosecution against a solicitor who effected the conveyance of real property at a price in excess of that permitted by applicable price control regulations. The action was dismissed because there was no showing that the solicitor knew about the

The case law on the question is sparse, . . . In most of the cases, the lawyer has overtly assisted his client in accomplishing manifestly illegal purposes. Thus, courts have held that it is improper for a lawyer to give advice as to how to commit a crime or fraud [41] or how to conceal criminal or fraudulent acts.[42] These cases beget law that is not hard to formulate. There is less guidance when the conduct is less blatant, but there is enough to point the way. One case, for example, states the test . . . as whether "the lawyer conveyed to the client the idea that by adopting a particular course of action [the client] may successfully [accomplish the illegal purpose]?" [43] As to the mode of assistance, courts have held that it is unlawful for a lawyer to negotiate for his client in pursuance of an illegal purpose [44] or to prepare documents to effectuate it.[45] As to the extent of knowledge that will result in complicity, the cases say not only that liability results from actual knowledge of the client's illegal purpose, but also that it results from knowledge of facts that reasonably should excite suspicion.[46]

This analysis indicates the dimensions of the lawyer's duty under criminal and civil law to refrain from "assisting" a client in conduct that is "illegal." A lawyer violates that duty if:

(1) The client is engaged in a course of conduct that violates the criminal law or is an intentional violation of a civil obligation, other than failure to perform a contract or failure to sustain a good faith claim to property;

(2) The lawyer has knowledge of the facts sufficient to reasonably discern that the client's course of conduct is such a violation; and

(3) The lawyer facilitates the client's course of conduct either by giving advice that encourages the client to pursue the conduct or indicates how to reduce the risks of detection, or by performing an act that substantially furthers the course of conduct.

. . .

calculation of the price such that, given his assumed knowledge of the law, he knew that the price violated the law.

41. E.g., In re Feltman, 51 N.J. 27, 237 A.2d 473 (1968).

42. E.g., Townsend v. State Bar, 32 Cal.2d 592, 197 P.2d 326 (1948); In re Giordano, 49 N.J. 210, 229 A.2d 524 (1967).

43. In re Bullowa, 223 A.D. 593, 602, 229 N.Y.S. 145, 154 (1928). See also Attorney Grievance Comm'n v. Kerpelman, 288 Md. 241, 420 A.2d 940 (1980).

44. E.g., In re La Duca, 62 N.J. 133, 299 A.2d 405 (1973).

45. E.g., Galbraith v. State Bar, 218 Cal. 329, 23 P.2d 291 (1933).

46. E.g., In re Wines, 370 S.W.2d 328 (Mo.1963); State ex rel. Nebraska State Bar v. Holscher, 193 Neb. 729, 230 N.W.2d 75 (1975); In re Blatt, 65 N.J. 539, 324 A.2d 15 (1974).

JAMES J. FULD, "LAWYERS' STANDARDS AND RESPONSIBILITIES IN RENDERING OPINIONS"

33 Business Lawyer 1295 (1978).*

Sometimes the practical aspects of standards are as important, if not more important, than the theoretical standards. This is particularly true in the field of legal opinions where there are so few standards to begin with.

. . .

. . . [C]onscientious lawyers are deeply concerned today when delivering opinions. It is probably true that the more conscientious the lawyer, the more frequently and the more deeply he is concerned. There is a cumulative effect: opinions are being requested in increasing types of transactions, the requested opinions are being increasingly broadened as to scope, the class of persons who may rely on lawyers' opinions may be expanding, and lawyers are being increasingly sued on expanding theories.

Nor are these concerns limited to formal written opinions—the concerns also apply to informal opinions, and even to "implied" or "silent" opinions, which I will discuss later.

The absence of decisions and generally established principles in this area heightens the concerns. The mere fact of a publicly-known claim by a plaintiff or an administrative agency is embarrassing to a lawyer's reputation, even if the lawyer subsequently proves he used due care or otherwise prevails. A lawyer and his law firm are proud of their professional endeavors, their reputations are on the line and they do not want to be on the defensive. Nor is it sufficient for the opinion to have been correct in itself: a correct opinion can be alleged to have been used in furtherance of a client's illegal or fraudulent plan, and the lawyer is likely to find himself as a co-defendant.

. . .

Thus, we see today the importance of generally established principles in the field of opinions so that the responsibilities of lawyers are clearer—not only to defend a lawsuit against himself if that should be necessary, but, much more important, to avoid the lawsuit in the first place, all within the framework of the lawyer fully performing his duties to his client, any addressee of his opinion and, where appropriate, others.

. . .

. . . [M]any of the practical problems relating to opinions are "lawyer-made". Some opinions are required by the government; others are requested by one's own client. But generally the most time-consuming opinions are requested by, and have to be negotiated with, the receiving lawyer—what I refer to as "lawyer-made." The lawyer

---

for the buyer of a business asks the lawyer for the seller for opinions covering a great many areas. In negotiated transactions, opinions requested today are frequently broader in scope than opinions many years ago.

Perhaps a "zero-base budgeting" approach should be adopted: is any opinion really necessary in this matter? Or is the *entire* requested opinion really necessary?

Subject to considerations mentioned later, it is proper to ask for an opinion on a matter to "smoke out" legal problems. But the law is frequently not clear, and one should not ask for unascertainable certainty. To the extent that a lawyer is unable to give the other side an unqualified favorable opinion, it is a warning to the recipient of certain legal risks which the recipient should evaluate. If a lawyer says he is uncomfortable in giving a particular opinion because of a disclosed problem, no attempt should ordinarily be made by the receiving lawyer to force the giving of such an opinion; the giving lawyer should not be asked to assume the risks of a disclosed problem—that risk should properly be evaluated and assumed by the recipient of the opinion. If the public is involved, an unqualified opinion where the law is not clear would create a false sense of certainty.

The problem is frequently compounded by the unequal negotiating strengths of the two parties. A client in poor financial condition that needs a loan from a bank has little bargaining power. It is fair for the bank to exact concessions from the borrower; it is not fair or responsible for bank counsel to attempt to force an unreasonable opinion from borrower's counsel.

Nor is it responsible for receiving lawyer to offer to withdraw a request for a particular opinion in exchange for a business point—or for giving lawyer to offer a business point in exchange for not having to opine on a particular matter.

Should a receiving lawyer ask for an opinion which he would be unwilling to give? Are legal opinions excluded from the Golden Rule? Some lawyers seem to have "two files of opinions" covering the same type of transaction—one file of opinions to be received from the other lawyer, and one file of opinions to be given to the other lawyer. I have heard the "two files of opinions" approach defended on the ground that each lawyer is entitled to try to obtain the best possible advantages for his client. I disagree. An opinion is not the same as a lease, which may be drafted either from the landlord's point of view or from the tenant's point of view. While the business provisions of a lease may vary widely, a professional opinion should not depend upon which side one represents.

Some opinions, I believe, cannot as a practical matter be given responsibly, and if given, might injure both the giving party and the receiving party. For example, I do not see how a law firm can, as a practical matter, responsibly give an opinion that its client has complied with all federal, state and local laws. Particularly if the law firm has represented the client for a lengthy time, and if the client has freely discussed its tax, antitrust, labor, pension, discrimination and other day-to-day problems with its counsel, it is not realistic for such counsel to give such an opinion. . . .

If pressed to give such a broad opinion, the law firm might prepare a list of possible tax, labor, discrimination, antitrust and other legal problems. If such list is, with the client's consent, delivered to the other side, in either draft or final form, the client will have waived its attorney-client privilege with respect to those matters. But the transaction may not close, and the government or a third party can require the client, its lawyers and recipients to testify under oath about the disclosed matters and to submit related papers to examination.

. . .

There is a further important aspect to requesting such a broad opinion, namely, Canon 4, which provides that a lawyer should preserve the confidences and secrets of his client. . . . There is a major public interest served in encouraging a client to speak freely with his lawyer.

Where the client is entering into a once-in-a-lifetime transaction, such as a sale of a business, it may be appropriate for the buyer to require the seller to waive the privilege and cause his lawyer to disclose to the buyer all secrets relating to the seller's business. (Although, as indicated above, the buyer may be ill-advised to have the privilege waived.)

But where the requested waiver would be recurrent, such as the lawyer's annual letter to the auditors, the client's confidences must not be disclosed, or else a client will not speak freely with his lawyer. Similarly, if all lenders in a city require, as a condition to their loans, that lawyers disclose clients' confidences, the public interest served in encouraging a client to speak freely with his lawyer will be defeated. Since loans are made frequently, it seems contrary to the purpose of Canon 4 for lenders' lawyers to generally request the borrowers' lawyers to reveal confidences, . . .

. . .

Opinions about mixed factual-legal matters require great care. For example, a lawyer may be asked to give an opinion whether his client is in default under one or more specified agreements, or has complied with one or all statutes. The facts are crucial to such opinions, and a lawyer should be cautious.

Nor are the duties of the receiving lawyer clear. May he accept the offered opinion if it appears reasonable on its face? Or should he investigate before advising his client that the client may "rely" on the offered opinion? Can he do a "little" investigation, and stop there?

What should the receiving lawyer do about an opinion which is perfect as to language but which he believes the giving lawyer has delivered without sufficient investigation? May the receiving lawyer advise his client that he may "rely" on such an opinion?

Suppose the opining lawyer states that he relies on an officer's certificate—should the receiving lawyer examine the officer's certificate? Is it better for him to see the certificate or not? . . .

Independence of counsel, . . ., either vis-à-vis the client or another party to the transaction, should be disclosed in the opinion, and in any summary of, or reference to, the opinion. A stockholder, director or close family relationship to the client should be disclosed. But there are other situations where it is difficult to decide whether there is such a lack of independence that there should be disclosure. For example, would material unpaid legal fees and disbursements from prior transactions constitute a creditor interest in the client which should be disclosed? Suppose the fee for this transaction, or the amount or collectibility of the fee, is as a practical matter largely dependent on the consummation of the transaction? Suppose this client accounts for a large percentage of the lawyer's practice? Or suppose the lawyer and one of the principals of the client have been making investments in unrelated business ventures?

Questions frequently exist when counsel is requested to give an opinion on the law of a foreign state or country. Counsel in every state is expected to be able to give an opinion on federal law. And most corporate lawyers feel comfortable in giving simple opinions regarding Delaware law, a sort of "federal corporate law." Where counsel himself has supervised the incorporation of a foreign corporation, it is hard to justify to the client why he must now engage local counsel to opine on due incorporation. In other instances, the matter may be so obvious that engaging local counsel is unnecessary.

However, in most instances, I believe counsel is well advised to engage local counsel where a question of law involving another state or country is involved. While counsel who gives an erroneous opinion on domestic law is generally liable only for negligence, at least one New York case may indicate that counsel who does not consult local counsel and gives an erroneous opinion on foreign law may be liable as an insurer.[2] Putting it slightly differently, one could say that a lawyer may not be exercising due care in certain circumstances if he gives an opinion on the law of another state without having first consulted local counsel. Whereas counsel who uses due care in the selection of local counsel is not liable for the negligence of local counsel not known to retaining counsel.

. . .

One of the most difficult practical problems to deal with in opinions relates to qualified opinions. One's own client usually understands the need for, and does not object to receiving, a qualified opinion, or an opinion that reveals doubts as to conclusions or refers to contrary views. The qualified opinion may well be oral. The client probably would not have requested the opinion if the matter were problem-free.

2. Degen v. Steinbrink, 202 App.Div. 477, 195 N.Y.S. 810 (1st Dept. 1922), aff'd mem. 236 N.Y. 669, 142 N.E. 328 (1923).

But when the opinion is to be delivered to another party, receiving counsel is frequently reluctant to receive such a qualified opinion. The problems raised in the qualified opinion may have to be publicly disclosed—for instance, in a proxy statement describing a merger of two publicly-owned corporations. The opinion may alert the government or third parties to tax or anti-trust claims that have not been asserted. . . .

On the other hand, if a lawyer has substantial doubt about his legal conclusion, he should state so in his opinion. He may commence his opinion by saying that the law is not clear on the particular facts, or that an administrative agency has, or may have, contrary views, but that in his view a court would ultimately reach a specified conclusion. The recipient of the opinion has been warned and then proceeds at his own risk. Nor do I think it generally desirable for the lawyer to deliver a "clean" written conclusion, but to set forth his doubts, or the possible contrary views of others, in a memorandum to the file. While the lawyer may have orally communicated the uncertainties to the recipient, the written opinion may be seen, summarized or referred to by others who do not know of the uncertainties. And, if reliance on an opinion may be a protection to the client, a client on the defensive may abuse the situation by producing only the clean opinion; the lawyer could be properly criticized for making possible such an abuse.

. . .

Frequently, the resolution of this problem takes the form of no written opinion at all. I have learned of instances of a sale of a business in exchange for stock of the purchaser—after many hours of discussions regarding their respective opinions, it was agreed, with relief, that neither firm would deliver an opinion. Or, when asked whether his client is in compliance with all laws (the "smoking-out" inquiry), a lawyer drafts such a long list of possible tax, labor, pension, discrimination, antitrust and other horrors—all open to examination by third parties and no longer protected by privilege, the receiving lawyer decides these are "normal business risks" and withdraws the request.

I do not claim that no opinion is the best solution. I am not sure where it leaves the two clients. I am not even sure where it leaves the two law firms.

There are some situations where opinions have become so customary that it would, I think, be impossible as a practical matter to omit them. For example, in a public offering, I have never heard of the underwriters failing to receive, as part of their due diligence, an opinion from counsel to the seller.

But in all sorts of business transactions, although the requested opinions may be broad, I find an increasing trend toward the omission, or an extreme narrowing, of opinions, particularly where there are experienced counsel on both sides. Written opinions, if given, have been limited, for example, to such "safe" subjects as due incorporation of the corporation and due authorization of the agreement.[3]

But the failure to give a written opinion, or the giving of only a limited, safe opinion, does not really mean that the lawyer is not representing his client and legally blessing the transaction from his client's standpoint. In a real sense, the lawyer is giving an "implied" or "silent" opinion that it is legally reasonable for his client to proceed with the transaction. But the danger of the "implied opinion" is that it is undefined, both from the standpoint of the client and from the standpoint of the lawyer. The client may have one understanding of his legal risks (small); and the lawyer may have another understanding of the legal risks (substantial) he has, by shrugs, intonation or orally, communicated to the client. In many situations, cost-conscious clients frequently specify that there be no, or limited, research, but nevertheless ask for an informal or silent opinion.

.   .   .

In a real sense, informal opinions, oral and written, and "implied" opinions are as frequently requested by clients, are as important to clients, and relate to equally weighty matters, as formal written opinions. They create as much or more exposure for the lawyer. . . .

To whom does the opining lawyer owe duties? It is clear that he has an obligation to his client, and if the lawyer addresses his opinion to a third party, he has duties to the third party. I believe, however, that the duties may not be exactly the same. To his client the lawyer owes a duty to deliver an opinion which is appropriate for the client and which the client can understand and act upon; there is no one else who can help the client to understand the opinion and if necessary obtain a different opinion. But a third-party recipient is usually represented by his own lawyer, who is uniquely familiar with the third-party's particular legal and tax problems, and the opining lawyer's duties are therefore merely to give his careful opinion on the matters requested.

The more difficult question, of course, is the extent to which an opining lawyer has a duty, and liability, to persons other than those to whom his opinion is addressed. . . .

Recent cases . . ., involving both lawyers and accountants, indicate that an opining lawyer will probably be held to owe a duty of competence and care to specific persons or limited classes of persons to which the lawyer intended, or knew, the opinion would be provided and who could reasonably be expected to rely on the opinion. This is particularly likely if such use of the opinion was the principal "end and aim" of the lawyer's opinion.

In the hope of avoiding liability to a class of persons, a lawyer may state that he is limiting his opinion to the addressee and that only the

---

3. One would also hope that bank lawyers who set policy by suggesting forms of opinions to be received by the banks would give flexibility to younger attorneys who represent the banks.

addressee may rely on the opinion. While I would urge counsel to include such a statement in his opinion where appropriate, I suspect that, as the law develops in the future, a limitation which is contrary to realistic expectations would not be upheld.

· · ·

Whatever the law may ultimately be held to be, I would recommend that a lawyer assume that his opinion, or a summary of, or reference to, it, will be seen by persons other than the original recipient, and that the lawyer may be charged with legal responsibility for their reliance. Such an opinion should, therefore, not only attempt to limit the class of persons who may rely on the opinion, but perhaps more importantly, include all qualifications, conditions, assumptions and references to other documents in order to alert subsequent users of the opinion regarding any uncertainties involved. Anyone other than the intended recipient should be told to consult his own advisor. And, if this is understood in advance with the client, the opinion should further state that no summary of, or reference to, the opinion is to be made without the lawyer's written consent. Even all these steps may not be sufficient, but I cannot think of anything else.

· · ·

In addition to the general principles mentioned above, I would make the following practical general suggestions, none of which is intended to reduce the lawyer's obligations to clients or others but which may help to protect lawyers giving opinions as well as protecting clients and the public:

1. Negotiate the text of the opinion as early as possible. If there is a contract prior to closing, the opinion should be negotiated at the time the contract is negotiated—not later when the closing papers are being prepared. The exact text of the opinion, with all of its qualifications, conditions, assumptions and references to other documents should be included, if possible, in the contract or as a separately initialed paper.

Avoid, if possible, having the client sign an agreement by which the lawyer must give at the closing a favorable opinion on certain specified matters "and on such other legal matters as receiving counsel's client may reasonably request." . . .

2. Have the text of a proposed opinion reviewed by two lawyers, preferably two partners, and preferably one having no relationship to the matter. If the text is to be included in the contract, the time for the review is before the contract is signed. If the opinion refers to contracts, the reviewing lawyer should also examine these contracts.

3. Have the opinion signed by a partner.

4. Where there is substantial doubt, the opinion should generally set forth the qualifications, such as absence of clear authority, contrary decisions, possible contrary views of regulatory agencies,

any substantial question as to independence of counsel, limitations as to persons who may rely on the opinion, assumptions of facts, reliance on other counsel, reliance on officers' certificates, etc.

5. Avoid being an additional warranter of facts.

One common exception to the foregoing is for company counsel to give an opinion to underwriters that such counsel has no reason to believe that the prospectus contains any untrue statement of a material fact or omits to state a material fact.

6. Avoid giving a favorable opinion on a matter which businessmen and lawyers know may be uncertain—for example, that a corporation complies with all federal, state and local laws and requirements; . . .

7. Make sure that the adjectives and phrases used to describe agreements are appropriate. For example, according to the dictionaries, the word "binding" means under "definite legal obligation." An opinion that "an agreement is legally binding" probably indicates a judgment that the entire agreement is lawful. But suppose the lawyer believes that an acquisition agreement may violate the antitrust laws? . . .

8. Avoid a prediction as to the outcome of litigation, or the amount of client liability, . . .

9. Do not over-opine. For example, the only usually applicable SEC requirement for an opinion under the basic Form S–1 is an opinion of counsel to the Company as to the legality of the securities being offered; for stock, this means whether the shares will, when sold, "be legally issued, fully paid and non-assessable." No opinion is required by the SEC regarding the legality of the offering. Therefore, the relevant part of the prospectus should read: "Legal Opinion. The legality of the *securities* being offered hereby will be passed on by A"; not: "Legal Matters. Legal matters in connection with this *offering* of stock are being passed upon by B." . . .

Opinion Letters and M.R. 2.3

Other articles on rendering opinions for third parties include: Redlich, Lawyers' Standards and Responsibilities in Rendering Opinions, 33 Bus.Law. 1317 (1978); and Note, Attorney Liability to Third Parties for Corporate Opinion Letters, 64 B.U.L.Rev. 415 (1984). See also ABA Statement of Policy Regarding Auditors' Requests for Information, 31 Bus.Law. 1709 (1976). For a bibliography, see Joint Committee of the Real Property Sections of the State Bar of California and the Los Angeles County Bar Assn., Report: Legal Opinions in California Real Estate Transactions, 42 Bus.Law. 1139, 1203–05 (1987).

The Code did not address evaluations of the client's affairs for use by third parties. M.R. 2.3 provides that a lawyer may undertake such an evaluation as long as: (1) it is reasonable to believe that making the evaluation is compatible with the lawyer's other duties to the client; and (2) the client consents after consultation. As to the confidentiality of information learned in the course of making the evaluation, M.R. 2.3(b) states:

> Except as disclosure is required in connection with a report of an evaluation, information relating to the evaluation is otherwise protected by Rule 1.6 [—the rule on confidentiality].

The Comment to 2.3 states:

> The quality of an evaluation depends on the freedom and extent of the investigation upon which it is based. Ordinarily a lawyer should have whatever latitude of investigation seems necessary as a matter of professional judgment. Under some circumstances, however, the terms of the evaluation may be limited. For example, certain issues or sources may be categorically excluded, or the scope of search may be limited by the time constraints of the noncooperation of persons having relevant information. Any such limitations which are material to the evaluation should be described in the report. If after a lawyer has commenced an evaluation, the client refuses to comply with the terms upon which it was understood the evaluation was to have been made, the lawyer's obligations are determined by law, having reference to the terms of the client's agreement and the surrounding circumstances.

Notice that the Comment refers to law outside the Rules in determining whether disclosure of adverse information may be necessary. Whether the lawyer may withdraw and whether disclosure is necessary to avoid assisting a fraud also are answered by reference to criminal, tort and relevant statutory law.

Read Model Rule 4.1. How is it related to M.R. 2.3? M.R. 4.1 uses the word "knowingly." Read the definition of "knowingly" in the Terminology section of the Model Rules. Should a different word or phrase have been substituted for "knowingly" in M.R. 4.1? What would M.R. 2.3 and 4.1 have required of the lawyer doing the lien search in *Greycas*?

We will come back to M.R. 4.1 when we discuss confidentiality and disclosure of client fraud in Chapter 4.

C. SECURITIES LAW

SECURITIES AND EXCHANGE COMMISSION v. NATIONAL STUDENT MARKETING CORP.

United States District Court for the District of Columbia, 1978.
457 F.Supp. 682.

[National Student Marketing Corporation (NSMC), which marketed products for high school and college students, was a prosperous company in 1969, or so the financial community thought. In that year NSMC expressed an interest in acquiring Interstate National Corporation, an insurance holding company.

On June 10, 1969, NSMC's president and one of its senior vice-presidents made a presentation to the Interstate directors concerning the proposed merger. They provided the Interstate directors with NSMC's 1968 annual report, its financial report for the first half of 1969, and financial projections of earnings for the fiscal year ending on August 31, 1969. They sweetened their initial offer (1) from one share of NSMC common stock for every two shares of Interstate to two shares of NSMC stock for every three shares of Interstate; and (2) by promising the Interstate directors that they would be permitted to sell up to 25% of the NSMC shares they would acquire in a registered public offering planned for the fall of 1969.

This resulted in an agreement in principle for the merger. NSMC and Interstate issued press releases, which included information about NSMC's earnings for the first half of fiscal year 1969.

On August 12, 1969, the Interstate directors met to review the final version of the merger agreement. The agreement provided: (1) that both corporations warranted that the information in their Proxy statements would "be accurate and correct and [would] not omit to state a material fact necessary to make such information not misleading"; and (2) that the financial statements included "are true and correct and have been prepared in accordance with generally accepted accounting principles". It also included NSMC's specific assurance that its 1968 year-end and May 31, 1969, nine-month financial statements:

> fairly present the results of the operation of NSMC . . . for the periods indicated, subject in the case of the nine-month statements to year-end audit adjustments.

The agreement also provided that the merger was conditioned on the prior receipt by each corporation of (1) an opinion letter from the other corporation's lawyers that all transactions in connection with the merger had been taken in full compliance with applicable law; and (2) a satisfactory "comfort letter" from the other corporation's independent public accountants. Each comfort letter was to state that the accountants had no reason to believe that any material adjustments in the interim financials were required in order fairly to present the results of the operations of the company. The agreement could be terminated by mutual consent of the two corporations' boards of directors at any time prior to completion of the merger. It also gave each party the right to waive any of the conditions to that party's obligations. Finally, the agreement specified that the merger be consummated on or before November 28, 1969.

Both corporations used proxy statements and notices of special stockholder meetings to secure stockholder approval of the proposed merger. The material sent by Interstate to its shareholders included a copy of the merger agreement, NSMC's proxy statement and NSMC's financial statement for August 31, 1968 and the nine-month interim financial statement, ending on May 31, 1969. The nine-month interim statement showed an NSMC profit of approximately $700,000. The shareholders of both companies seemed enthusiastic about the merger, approving it by large majorities.

In mid-October Peat Marwick—the independent accountant as it happened for both Interstate and NSMC—began working on the comfort letter on NSMC's financial condition. It soon determined that NSMC's nine-month interim financials had to be adjusted so that, instead of showing a $700,000 profit for these nine months, NSMC would show a loss of almost $200,000. Peat Marwick discussed the proposed adjustments with representatives of NSMC, but neither the accountants nor NSMC told Interstate of the proposed change. Peat Marwick completed a draft of the comfort letter on the morning of the closing.

The closing was scheduled for 2:00 p.m. on Friday, October 31, at the New York offices of the law firm of White & Case. White & Case represented NSMC, with Epley as the partner in charge of the firm's representation. Epley and other White & Case associates were at the meeting in behalf of NSMC, along with NSMC's president, Randell, and senior vice-president Joy. The law firm of Lord Bissel & Brook, through its partners Meyer and Schauer, represented Interstate. Meyer was also a director and shareholder of Interstate. Interstate's president, Brown, and three other members of the Interstate board of directors and executive committee were also at the meeting in Interstate's behalf.]

* * *

Although Schauer had had an opportunity to review most of the merger documents at White & Case on the previous day, the comfort letter had not been delivered. When he arrived at White & Case on the morning of the merger, the letter was still not available, but he was informed by a representative of the firm that it was expected to arrive at any moment.

The meeting proceeded. When the letter had not arrived by approximately 2:15 p.m., Epley telephoned Peat Marwick's Washington office to inquire about it. Anthony M. Natelli, the partner in charge, thereupon dictated to Epley's secretary a letter which provided in part:

[N]othing has come to our attention which caused us to believe that:

1. The National Student Marketing Corporation's unaudited consolidated financial statements as of and for the nine months ended May 31, 1969:

   a. Were not prepared in accordance with accounting principles . . . followed in the preparation [of previous financial statements];

   b. Would require any material adjustments for a fair and reasonable presentation of the information shown except with respect to [NSMC's nine month interim financial statement covering the period ending on] . . . May 31, 1969 . . . our examination . . . disclosed the following significant adjustments which in our opinion should be reflected retroactive to May 31, 1969:

1. In adjusting the amortization of deferred costs at May 31, 1969 . . . an adjustment of $500,000 was required. . . .

2. In August 1969 management wrote off receivables in amounts of $300,000. It appears that the uncollectibility of these receivables could have been determined at May 31, 1969 and such charge off should have been reflected as of that date.

3. Acquisition costs in the amount of $84,000 for proposed acquisitions which the Company decided not to pursue were transferred from additional paid-in capital to general and administrative expenses. In our opinion, these should have been so transferred as of May 31, 1969.

· · ·

Epley delivered one copy of the typed letter to the conference room where the closing was taking place. Epley then returned to his office.

Schauer was the first to read the unsigned letter. He then handed it to Cameron Brown, advising him to read it. . . . [Meyer also read it.] They asked Randell and Joy a number of questions relating to the nature and effect of the adjustments. The NSMC officers gave assurances that the adjustments would have no significant effect on the predicted year-end earnings of NSMC and that a substantial portion of the $500,000 adjustments to deferred costs would be recovered. Moreover, they indicated that NSMC's year-end audit for fiscal 1969 had been completed by Peat Marwick, would be published in a couple of weeks, and would demonstrate that NSMC itself had made each of the adjustments for its fourth quarter. The comfort letter, they explained, simply determined that those adjustments should be reflected in the third quarter ended May 31, 1969, rather than the final quarter of NSMC's fiscal year. Randell and Joy indicated that while NSMC disagreed with what they felt was a tightening up of its accounting practices, everything requested by Peat Marwick to "clean up" its books had been undertaken.

At the conclusion of this discussion, certain of the Interstate representatives, including at least Brown, Schauer and Meyer, conferred privately to consider their alternatives in light of the apparent nonconformity of the comfort letter with the requirements of the Merger Agreement. Although they considered the letter a serious matter and the adjustments as significant and important, they were nonetheless under some pressure to determine a course of action promptly since there was a 4 p.m. filing deadline if the closing were to be consummated as scheduled on October 31.[20] Among the alternatives considered were: (1) delaying or postponing the closing, either to secure

20. The pressure to close on October 31 derived from a public announcement to that effect; it was therefore likely that any delay would have had an adverse impact on the stock of both companies. The 4 p.m. deadline was the closing time of the District of Columbia office where the merger documents were to be filed.

more information or to resolicit the shareholders with corrected financials; (2) closing the merger; or (3) calling it off completely.

The consensus of the directors was that there was no need to delay the closing. The comfort letter contained all relevant information and in light of the explanations given by Randell and Joy, they already had sufficient information upon which to make a decision. Any delay for the purpose of resoliciting the shareholders was considered impractical because it would require the use of year-end figures instead of the stale nine-month interim financials. Such a requirement would make it impossible to resolicit shareholder approval before the merger upset date of November 28, 1969, and would cause either the complete abandonment of the merger or its renegotiation on terms possibly far less favorable to Interstate. The directors also recognized that delay or abandonment of the merger would result in a decline in the stock of both companies, thereby harming the shareholders and possibly subjecting the directors to lawsuits based on their failure to close the merger. The Interstate representatives decided to proceed with the closing. They did, however, solicit and receive further assurances from the NSMC representatives that the stated adjustments were the only ones to be made to the company's financial statements and that 1969 earnings would be as predicted. When asked by Brown whether the closing could proceed on the basis of an unsigned comfort letter, Meyer responded that if a White & Case partner assured them that this was in fact the comfort letter and that a signed copy would be forthcoming from Peat Marwick, they could close. Epley gave this assurance. Meyer then announced that Interstate was prepared to proceed, the closing was consummated, and a previously arranged telephone call was made which resulted in the filing of the Articles of Merger at the Office of the Recorder of Deeds of the District of Columbia. Large packets of merger documents, including the required counsel opinion letters, were exchanged.[22] The closing was solemnized with a toast of warm champagne.

22. The LBB opinion letter, delivered to NSMC at the closing, reads in pertinent part:
Gentlemen:

We have acted as counsel to Interstate in connection with the merger of Interstate into NSMC pursuant to the Plan. In such capacity, we have examined the Plan together with Exhibits A, B and C thereto; the charters, by-laws in minutes of Interstate and its Subsidiaries (as defined in the Plan), corporate records, certificates of public officials and of officers and representatives of Interstate and such other documents deemed necessary to enable us to give the opinion hereinafter expressed.

Based on the foregoing and having due regard to legal considerations we deem relevant, we are of the opinion that:
. . .

7. The Plan has been duly executed and delivered by Interstate and is a valid and binding obligation in accordance with its terms and any corporate action by Interstate required in order to authorize the transactions therein contemplated has been taken.

8. To our knowledge, neither Interstate nor any Subsidiary is engaged in or threatened with any legal action or other proceeding, or has incurred or been charged with any presently pending violation of any Federal, state or local law or administrative regulation, which would materially adversely affect or impair the financial condition, business, operations, prospects, properties or assets of Interstate.

Unknown to the Interstate group, several telephone conversations relating to the substance of the comfort letter occurred on the afternoon of the closing between Peat Marwick representatives and Epley. . . . Epley was told that an additional paragraph would be added in order to characterize the adjustments. The paragraph recited that with the noted adjustments properly made, NSMC's unaudited consolidated statement for the nine-month period would not reflect a profit as had been indicated but rather a net loss, and the consolidated operations of NSMC as they existed on May 31, 1969, would show a break-even as to net earnings for the year ended August 31, 1969. Epley had the additional paragraph typed out, but failed to inform or disclose this change to Interstate. In a second conversation, after the closing was completed and the Interstate representatives had departed, Epley was informed of still another proposed addition, namely, a paragraph urging resolicitation of both companies' shareholders and disclosure of NSMC's corrected nine-month financials prior to closing. To this, he responded that the deal was closed and the letter was not needed. Peat Marwick nonetheless advised Epley that the letter would be delivered and that its counsel was considering whether further action should be taken by the firm.

The final written draft of the comfort letter arrived at White & Case late that afternoon. Peat Marwick believed that Interstate had been informed and was aware of the conversations between its representatives and Epley and of its concern about the adjustments. Because of this belief and especially since the merger had been closed without benefit of the completed letter, Peat Marwick's counsel perceived no obligation to do anything further about the merger. Nonetheless, a signed copy of the final letter was sent to each board member of the two companies, presumably in an effort to underline the accountants' concern about consummation of the merger without shareholder resolicitation.

The signed comfort letter was delivered to the Interstate offices on Monday, November 3. It was first seen and read by Donald Jeffers, Interstate's chief financial officer. He had not been present at the October 31 closing or informed of the adjustments to the interim financials. Concerned, he contacted Brown immediately and read the letter to him. Since a meeting with other Interstate principals was scheduled for the next morning the letter was added to the other matters to be discussed.

The signed letter was virtually identical to the unsigned version delivered at the closing, except for the addition of the following two paragraphs:

. . .

10. All other action and proceedings required by law or the Plan to be taken by Interstate at or prior to the Effective Date in connection with the Plan and the transactions provided for therein have been duly and validly taken.

. . .

Your attention is called, however, to the fact that if the aforementioned adjustments had been made at May 31, 1969 the unaudited consolidated statement of earnings of National Student Marketing Corporation would have shown a net loss of approximately $80,000. It is presently estimated that the consolidated operations of the company as it existed at May 31, 1969 will be approximately a break-even as to net earnings for the year ended August 31, 1969.

In view of the above mentioned facts, we believe the companies should consider submitting corrected interim unaudited financial information to the shareholders prior to proceeding with the closing.

The only other change was the reduction in the write-off to receivables from $300,000 to $200,000, making total negative adjustments to NSMC's nine-month financials in the amount of $784,000.

At the meeting the following day, the matter was fully discussed by the former Interstate principals. Of particular concern were the additional "break-even" and "resolicitation" paragraphs.[25] Brown explained what had occurred at the closing and the reasons for the decision to consummate the merger. He called Meyer at LBB, who by that time was also aware of the letter. After some discussion, it was decided that more information was needed. Brown and Jeffers agreed to contact Peat Marwick and Meyer agreed that his firm would contact Epley at White & Case.

On that afternoon, Schauer contacted Epley by telephone. Epley stated that he had not known of the additional paragraphs until after the closing. He added that in any case the additions did not expand upon the contents of the earlier unsigned letter; the "break-even" paragraph simply reflected the results of an arithmetic computation of the effects of the adjustments, and the "resolicitation" paragraph was gratuitous and a matter for lawyers, not accountants. While Schauer disagreed, Epley again responded that the additional paragraphs made no difference and that NSMC regarded the deal as closed.

. . . Meanwhile, the market value of NSMC stock continued to increase, and the directors noted that any action on their part to undo the merger would most likely adversely affect its price. By the end of the week, the decision was made to abstain from any action. Thereafter, Brown issued a memorandum to all Interstate employees announcing completion of the merger. No effort was ever made by any of the defendants to disclose the contents of the comfort letter to the former shareholders of Interstate, the SEC or to the public in general.

25. A significant cause of their concern was a statement contained in a copy of a letter from Peat Marwick to Epley which accompanied the signed comfort letter; that letter suggested that Epley was aware of the additional paragraphs on the day of the closing. SEC Exhibit 57, Letter dated October 31, 1969, from Peat Marwick to Mr. Eplee (sic). Jeffers, however, was concerned with the adjustments in general, stating that it was very unusual for them to be included in a comfort letter, that he was surprised the Interstate representatives had closed without a signed comfort letter, and that the deferred cost adjustment of $500,000 was "a hell of a big adjustment,".

D. *The Stock Sales*

Early in the negotiations the principal Interstate shareholders understood that they would be able to sell a portion of the NSMC stock received in the merger through a public offering planned for the fall of 1969. Various shareholders, including Brown, Tate, Allison, Bach and Meyer, intended to profit by this opportunity and sell up to 25 percent of their newly acquired stock. . . .

White Weld began processing the sales on the afternoon of October 31. It subsequently sold a total of 59,500 shares of NSMC stock. The gross received was slightly less than $3 million. Brown received approximately $500,000 for his shares and Meyer received approximately $86,000 for the shares he held . . . White Weld was never informed of the comfort letter adjustments before it undertook the sale as agents for the Interstate principals.

. . .

E. *Subsequent Events*

Following the acquisition of Interstate and several other companies NSMC stock rose steadily in price, reaching a peak in mid-December. However, in early 1970, after several newspaper and magazine articles appeared questioning NSMC's financial health, the value of the stock decreased drastically. Several private lawsuits were filed and the SEC initiated a wide-ranging investigation which led to the filing of this action.

II. THE PRESENT ACTION

[This was a civil proceeding brought by the Securities and Exchange Commission, seeking injunctive sanctions against NSMC, the NSMC representatives and the Interstate representatives for their participation in alleged securities law violations in the merger of the two companies. While the suit was in the discovery stage, NSMC and its representatives, including Peat Marwick, the Peat Marwick partner who dictated the "comfort letter" and Epley, consented to the entry of judgments of permanent injunctions against them. White & Case, also a defendant, entered into a settlement with the SEC. Thus, the only defendants that remained before the court in this case were those who had represented Interstate: the law firm of Lord, Bissel & Brook; Meyer and Schauer, the partners in charge of the Interstate representation; and Brown, the former president of Interstate, and at the time of this decision, a consultant to NSMC.] *

. . . [T]he Commission alleges that the defendants, both as principals and as aiders and abettors, violated § 10(b) of the 1934 Act,[37] Rule

---

* Editor's note: Before reading on think about what, if anything, the lawyers for Interstate did wrong. What, if anything, should they have done differently before the closing meeting? At the closing meeting? After the closing meeting?

37. Section 10(b), 15 U.S.C. § 78j(b), reads as follows:

10b–5 promulgated thereunder,[38] and § 17(a) of the 1933 Act,[39] through their participation in the Interstate/NSMC merger and subsequent stock sales by Interstate principals, in each instance without disclosing the material information revealed by the Peat Marwick comfort letter.

Numerous charges, all of which appear to allege secondary liability, are leveled against the attorney defendants. Schauer is charged with "participating in the merger between Interstate and NSMC," apparently referring to his failure to interfere with the closing of the merger after receipt of the comfort letter. Such inaction, when alleged to facilitate a transaction, falls under the rubric of aiding and abetting. See Kerbs v. Fall River Industries, Inc., 502 F.2d 731, 739–40 (10th Cir. 1974). Both Schauer and Meyer are charged with issuing false opinions in connection with the merger and stock sales, thereby facilitating each transaction, and with acquiescence in the merger after learning the contents of the signed comfort letter. The Commission contends that the attorneys should have refused to issue the opinions in view of the adjustments revealed by the unsigned comfort letter, and after receipt of the signed version, they should have withdrawn their opinion with regard to the merger and demanded resolicitation of the Interstate shareholders. If the Interstate directors refused, the attorneys should have withdrawn from the representation and informed the shareholders or the Commission. . . .

> It shall be unlawful for any person, directly or indirectly, by the use of any means or instrumentality of interstate commerce or of the mails, or of any facility of any national securities exchange—
>
> . . .
>
> (b) To use or employ, in connection with the purchase or sale of any security registered on a national securities exchange or any security not so registered, any manipulative or deceptive device or contrivance in contravention of such rules and regulations as the Commission may prescribe as necessary or appropriate in the public interest or for the protection of investors.

38. Rule 10b–5, 17 C.F.R. § 240.10b–5, provides:

> It shall be unlawful for any person, directly or indirectly, by the use of any means or instrumentality of interstate commerce, or of the mails or of any facility of any national securities exchange,
>
> (a) To employ any device, scheme, or artifice to defraud,
>
> (b) To make any untrue statement of a material fact or to omit to state a material fact necessary in order to make the statements made, in the light of the circumstances under which they were made, not misleading, or
>
> (c) To engage in any act, practice, or course of business which operates or would operate as a fraud or deceit upon any person, in connection with the purchase or sale of any security.

39. Section 17(a), 15 U.S.C. § 77q(a), provides:

> It shall be unlawful for any person in the offer or sale of any securities by the use of any means or instruments of transportation or communication in interstate commerce or by the use of the mails, directly or indirectly—
>
> (1) to employ any device, scheme, or artifice to defraud, or
>
> (2) to obtain money or property by means of any untrue statement of a material fact or any omission to state a material fact necessary in order to make the statements made, in the light of the circumstances under which they were made, not misleading, or
>
> (3) to engage in any transaction, practice, or course of business which operates or would operate as a fraud or deceit upon the purchaser.

Since any liability of the alleged aiders and abettors depends on a finding of a primary violation of the antifraud provisions, the Court will first address the issues relating to the Commission's charges against the principals. . . .

A. *Nexus with a Sale*

For the SEC to prove a violation of the antifraud provisions, it must demonstrate that the alleged misconduct was "in the offer or sale" of a security under § 17(a) or "in connection with the purchase or sale" of a security under § 10(b) and Rule 10b–5. The Commission has made the requisite showing for each of the provisions with respect to the defendants' activities leading to the closing of the merger. . . .

B. *Materiality*

Also essential to an alleged violation of the antifraud provisions is that the omission or misstatement be material. . . .

Initially, the sheer magnitude of the adjustments supports a finding that they were material. The interim financials issued by NSMC reflected a profit of $702,270 for the nine-month period end[ing] May 31, 1969. . . . The aggregate adjustments amounted to $884,000, thereby reducing the reported profit by 125 percent and resulting in a net loss for the nine-month period of approximately $180,000. Viewing these figures alone, it is difficult to imagine how the adjustments could not be material.

. . .

C. *Scienter*

Finally, there must be proof that Brown and Meyer acted with the requisite degree of culpability. Unfortunately, the level of culpability required in an SEC injunctive action is far from certain. . . .

Though these are important issues, the resolution of which would be welcome to the securities bar, the Court concludes that they need not be decided at this time, because the conduct of Brown and Meyer in this case meets the prevailing standard for scienter.

After receiving the unsigned comfort letter at the closing, the Interstate representatives immediately expressed concern over the new information; they caucused privately and sought and received various oral assurances from the NSMC representatives. Moreover, the new information included adjustments which were far from insubstantial; they reduced the reported profit of NSMC by several hundreds of thousands of dollars and converted what had been a sizable profit into a net loss. Despite the obvious materiality of this information, especially as demonstrated by their conduct, they made a conscious decision not to disclose it. Such conduct has been found sufficient to meet the scienter requirement. McLean v. Alexander, 420 F.Supp. 1057, 1080–82 (D.Del. 1976); see Nassar & Co., Inc. v. SEC, 185 U.S.App.D.C. 125, 130 n. 3,

566 F.2d 790, 795 n. 3 (1977) (Leventhal, J., concurring); Lanza v. Drexel & Co., 479 F.2d 1277, 1305 (2d Cir.1973).

· · ·

. . . Brown and Meyer expected to profit handsomely from the merger and the subsequent stock sales. They were in no haste to disseminate the comfort letter information, and in fact they never revealed the adjustments, even after NSMC's year-end audit had been released . . .

In any event, to the extent an inference of *actual* intent to deceive, manipulate, or defraud may be inappropriate, the defendants' actions here clearly constitute "the kind of recklessness that is equivalent to wilful fraud," SEC v. Texas Gulf Sulphur Co., 401 F.2d at 868 (concurring opinion), and which also satisfies the scienter requirement. . . .

IV. AIDING AND ABETTING

The Court must now turn to the Commission's charges that the defendants aided and abetted these two violations of the antifraud provisions. The violations themselves establish the first element of aiding and abetting liability, namely that another person has committed a securities law violation. . . . The remaining elements, though not set forth with any uniformity, are essentially that the alleged aider and abettor had a "general awareness that his role was part of an overall activity that is improper, and [that he] knowingly and substantially assisted the violation." SEC v. Coffey [493 F.2d 1304, 1316 (6th Cir.1974) cert. denied, 420 U.S. 908 (1975)].

The Commission's allegations of aiding and abetting by the defendants, seem to fall into four basic categories: (1) the failure of the attorney defendants to take any action to interfere in the consummation of the merger; (2) the issuance by the attorneys of an opinion with respect to the merger; (3) the attorneys' subsequent failure to withdraw that opinion and inform the Interstate shareholders or the SEC of the inaccuracy of the nine-month financials; and (4) the issuance by the attorneys and Brown of an opinion and letter, respectively, concerning the validity of the stock sales under Rule 133.* The SEC's position is that the defendants acted or failed to act with an awareness of the fraudulent conduct by the principals, and thereby substantially assisted the two violations. The Court concurs with regard to the attorneys' failure to interfere with the closing, but must conclude that the remaining actions or inaction alleged to constitute aiding and abetting did not substantially facilitate either the merger or the stock sales.

As noted, the first element of aiding and abetting liability has been established by the finding that Brown and Meyer committed primary violations of the securities laws. Support for the second element, that the defendants were generally aware of the fraudulent activity, is provided by the previous discussion concerning scienter. . . . De-

---

* Editor's note: This refers to the legality under SEC Rule 133 of sales of stock by the Interstate principals as "insiders," following the merger.

spite the obvious materiality of the information, see section III–B supra, each knew that it had not been disclosed prior to the merger and stock sale transactions. Thus, this is not a situation where the aider and abettor merely failed to discover the fraud, see Rolf v. Blyth, Eastman Dillon & Co., 570 F.2d at 52 (Mansfield, J., dissenting), or reasonably believed that the victims were already aware of the withheld information, Hirsch v. du Pont, 553 F.2d 750, 759 (2d Cir.1977). . . .

The final requirement for aiding and abetting liability is that the conduct provide knowing, substantial assistance to the violation. In addressing this issue, the Court will consider each of the SEC's allegations separately. The major problem arising with regard to the Commission's contention that the attorneys failed to interfere in the closing of the merger is whether inaction or silence constitutes substantial assistance. While there is no definitive answer to this question, courts have been willing to consider inaction as a form of substantial assistance when the accused aider and abettor had a duty to disclose. . . .

Upon receipt of the unsigned comfort letter, it became clear that the merger had been approved by the Interstate shareholders on the basis of materially misleading information. In view of the obvious materiality of the information, especially to attorneys learned in securities law, the attorneys' responsibilities to their corporate client required them to take steps to ensure that the information would be disclosed to the shareholders. However, it is unnecessary to determine the precise extent of their obligations here, since it is undisputed that they took no steps whatsoever to delay the closing pending disclosure to and resolicitation of the Interstate shareholders. But, at the very least, they were required to speak out at the closing concerning the obvious materiality of the information and the concomitant requirement that the merger not be closed until the adjustments were disclosed and approval of the merger was again obtained from the Interstate shareholders. Their silence was not only a breach of this duty to speak, but in addition lent the appearance of legitimacy to the closing, . . . Contrary to the attorney defendants' contention, imposition of such a duty will not require lawyers to go beyond their accepted role in securities transactions, nor will it compel them to "err on the side of conservatism, . . . thereby inhibiting clients' business judgments and candid attorney-client communications." Courts will not lightly overrule an attorney's determination of materiality and the need for disclosure. However, where, as here, the significance of the information clearly removes any doubt concerning the materiality of the information, attorneys cannot rest on asserted "business judgments" as justification for their failure to make a legal decision pursuant to their fiduciary responsibilities to client shareholders.

The Commission also asserts that the attorneys substantially assisted the merger violation through the issuance of an opinion that was false and misleading due to its omission of the receipt of the comfort letter and of the completion of the merger on the basis of the false and misleading nine-month financials. The defendants contend that a technical reading of the opinion demonstrates that it is not false and misleading, and that it provides accurate opinions as to Interstate's compliance with certain corporate formalities. Of concern to the Court, however, is not the truth or falsity of the opinion, but whether it substantially assisted the violation. Upon consideration of all the circumstances . . ., the Court concludes that it did not.

Contrary to the implication made by the SEC, the opinion issued by the attorneys at the closing did not play a large part in the consummation of the merger. Instead, it was simply one of many conditions to the obligation of NSMC to complete the merger. It addressed a number of corporate formalities required of Interstate by the Merger Agreement, only a few of which could possibly involve compliance with the antifraud provisions of the securities laws. Moreover, the opinion was explicitly for the benefit of NSMC, which was already well aware of the adjustments contained in the comfort letter. Thus, this is not a case where an opinion of counsel addresses a specific issue and is undeniably relied on in completing the transaction. Compare SEC v. Coven, 581 F.2d 1020, at 1028; SEC v. Spectrum, Ltd., 489 F.2d 535 (2d Cir.1973). Under these circumstances, it is unreasonable to suggest that the opinion provided substantial assistance to the merger.

The SEC's contention with regard to counsel's alleged acquiescence in the merger transaction raises significant questions concerning the responsibility of counsel. The basis for the charge appears to be counsel's failure, after the merger, to withdraw their opinion, to demand resolicitation of the shareholders, to advise their clients concerning rights of rescission of the merger, and ultimately, to inform the Interstate shareholders or the SEC of the completion of the merger based on materially false and misleading financial statements. The defendants counter with the argument that their actions following the merger are not subject to the coverage of the securities laws.

The filing of the complaint in this proceeding generated significant interest and an almost overwhelming amount of comment within the legal profession on the scope of a securities lawyer's obligations to his client and to the investing public. The very initiation of this action, therefore, has provided a necessary and worthwhile impetus for the profession's recognition and assessment of its responsibilities in this area. The Court's examination, however, must be more limited. Although the complaint alleges varying instances of misconduct on the part of several attorneys and firms, the Court must narrow its focus to the present defendants and the charges against them.

Meyer, Schauer and Lord, Bissell & Brook are, in essence, here charged with failing to take any action to "undo" the merger. The Court has already concluded that counsel had a duty to the Interstate shareholders to delay the closing of the merger pending disclosure and resolicitation with corrected financials, and that the breach of that duty constituted a violation of the antifraud provisions through aiding and abetting the merger transaction. The Commission's charge, however, concerns the period following that transaction. Even if the attorneys' fiduciary responsibilities to the Interstate shareholders continued beyond the merger, the breach of such a duty would not have the requisite relationship to a securities transaction, since the merger had already been completed. It is equally obvious that such subsequent action or inaction by the attorneys could not substantially assist the merger.

The final contention of the SEC concerns the issuance by the attorneys and Brown of the Rule 133 opinion and letter, respectively. [These documents asserted that the Interstate directors could sell their shares without violating Rule 133.] Little discussion is necessary with respect to this charge, for the Commission has clearly failed to show that these documents substantially assisted the stock sales. Neither of the documents were required by the Merger Agreement, but were requested by NSMC at the closing of the merger. The documents were not intended for the investing public, but for the sole use of NSMC and its counsel in preparing a formal, independent opinion concerning the validity of the sales under Rule 133. Further, the documents were limited to primarily factual issues relevant to the requirements of the Rule, and in no way indicated that they could be relied upon with regard to compliance with the antifraud provisions. Under the circumstances, the Court concludes that the Rule 133 documents issued by the attorneys and Brown did not substantially assist the stock sales by Interstate principals, specifically Brown and Meyer.

Thus, the Court finds that the attorney defendants aided and abetted the violation of § 10(b), Rule 10b–5, and § 17(a) through their participation in the closing of the merger.

V. APPROPRIATENESS OF INJUNCTIVE RELIEF

Although the Commission has proved past violations by the defendants, that does not end the Court's inquiry. Proof of a past violation is not a prerequisite to the grant of injunctive relief . . . but it may, in combination with other factors, warrant an inference of future misconduct by the charged party, SEC v. Manor Nursing Centers, Inc., 458 F.2d 1082, 1100 (2d Cir.1972). The crucial question, though, remains not whether a violation has occurred, but whether there exists a reasonable likelihood of future illegal conduct by the defendant, . . .

. . .

The Commission has not demonstrated that the defendants engaged in the type of repeated and persistent misconduct which usually justifies the issuance of injunctive relief . . . Instead, it has shown violations which principally occurred within a period of a few hours at the closing of the merger in 1969. The Commission has not charged, or even suggested, that the defendants were involved in similar misconduct either before or after the events involved in this proceeding. Thus, the violations proved by the SEC appear to be part of an isolated incident, unlikely to recur and insufficient to warrant an injunction. . . .

Finally, the Commission asserts that an injunction is necessary because the professional occupations of the defendants provide significant opportunities for further involvement in securities transactions. It notes that . . . Meyer, Schauer and LBB continue to be involved in various corporate activities, including securities transactions, as part of their legal practice. . . . [T]hat fact is countered somewhat by their professional responsibilities as attorneys and officers of the court to conform their conduct to the dictates of the law. The Court is confident that they will take appropriate steps to ensure that their professional conduct in the future comports with the law.

· · ·

Questions and Comments

The court sets forth three elements necessary to establish aiding and abetting a violation of § 10(b), Rule 10b–5, and § 17(a): (1) a violation of the securities law by the principal (client); (2) the defendant knew that her role was part of illegal activity; and (3) the defendant substantially assisted in the violation.

Did the officers of Interstate violate the securities laws? Did Interstate's lawyers assist the violation?

What, if anything, should the lawyers for NSMC and Interstate have done differently during the merger negotiations? Before the closing meeting? At the meeting?

The opinion letters exchanged by the lawyers were held not to be a basis of their liability. Why not?

Read Model Rule 1.13(b) and the Comment thereto. Would it have helped the lawyers in *National Student Marketing* avoid liability?

BARKER v. HENDERSON
United States Court of Appeals, Seventh Circuit, 1986.
797 F.2d 490.

EASTERBROOK, CIRCUIT JUDGE.

For several years Michigan Baptist Foundation, Inc., built and operated a retirement village in Florida. It sold lifetime leases to the apartments in Estero Woods Village (the Project). In order to finance the Project until it could receive revenue from the leases, the Foundation issued bonds secured by its interest in the land and ongoing construction. Many of the bonds were sold in small amounts to people who, we assume, were unsophisticated and unable to afford losing their investments. In October 1976 Lee County Bank, the Trustee for the bonds, refused to participate in further issues. The Foundation then sold unsecured notes for another 17 months, until, at the request of state officials, a state court enjoined the sale of further instruments. The total sales exceed $7 million in principal. None of the bonds or notes were registered under the Securities Act of 1933, 15 U.S.C. §§ 77a–77aa. We shall assume that the materials used to sell the bonds and notes omitted essential information about the risks involved in the Project.

The purchasers of bonds between January 1974 and October 1976, and of notes between November 1976 and March 1978, are the plaintiffs in this suit under § 10(b) of the Securities Exchange Act of 1934, 15 U.S.C. § 78j(b), and the SEC's Rule 10b–5, 17 C.F.R. § 240.10b–5. . . .

Henderson, Franklin, Starnes & Holt (the Law Firm) furnished legal advice to the Foundation and its predecessors in interest (collectively the Foundation) from 1971 through 1976. Taylor, Edenfield, Gilliam & Wiltshire (the Accounting Firm) furnished accounting services during the same period. . . .

William Graddy, a partner of the Law Firm, gave advice to the Foundation at the inception of the project. Julian Clarkson, another partner of the Law Firm, was a director of the Trustee and chairman of its Trust Committee. Fred Edenfield, a partner of the Accounting Firm, gave advice to the Foundation at the outset of the project. Edenfield and Graddy were good friends. The plaintiffs' case against the two Firms is essentially that (a) the Firms sent the Foundation down the wrong path, failing at the outset to insist that it register the securities and disclose the risks involved; (b) the Firms knew of the Foundation's continued solicitation of funds but did not "blow the whistle"; (c) the Firms induced the Trustee to lend implied support to the securities through October 1976 by acting as Trustee.

Graddy and other attorneys at the Law Firm assisted the Foundation in organizing the Project under state law, drawing up its bylaws, and negotiating the purchase of the land. The purchase was complex, with the seller financing much of the sale and releasing the mortgage in strips as the Foundation paid installments. Graddy and Edenfield were among the incorporating directors of the Foundation, although they were immediately replaced by the permanent directors. Graddy knew of the plan to finance the Project through bonds, and he asked the Trustee to serve in that role. Graddy prepared the trust indenture. The indenture, although legally sufficient, did not contain controls sufficient to prevent the losses that ensued.

The Foundation raised its first money in 1972. Graddy and Edenfield reviewed a draft of the proposed selling document in 1971. Edenfield reviewed a draft projection in 1973, the same year Graddy reviewed a draft letter of solicitation. Neither asked the Foundation to make substantial changes. We assume that both men should have realized that there were substantial risks—that the Project was thinly capitalized, and that the repayment of the bonds would require sales of further bonds, leases, or both, and that even a small problem could scuttle the Project. Both Graddy and Edenfield knew that other retirement villages had run into trouble—both financial difficulties and problems under the securities laws. Graddy knew that some of the directors of the Foundation had purchased an option on land in which the Foundation was interested and later sold their interest to the Foundation in exchange for some of the Foundation's bonds. Self-dealing could imperil the Foundation's exemption from the requirement of registration. See § 3(a)(4) of the '33 Act, 15 U.S.C. § 77c(a)(4). (It is uncontested, however, that these bonds were cancelled and that the Foundation never lost its status as a tax-exempt religious or charitable organization, and that no court has held that the securities should have been registered under the '33 Act.)

In September 1973 Graddy prepared the papers to increase the maximum amount of bonds the Foundation could sell. Edenfield received a pro forma balance sheet prepared by the Foundation. In 1976 Graddy participated in meetings at which an officer of the Trustee explored doubts about the Project. After these meetings, and other exchanges, the Trustee remained on the job until October. Graddy was aware of the possibility that the Foundation's failure to secure timely releases of the seller's interest in the land could imperil the security for the bonds. (As it turned out, the releases were late in coming, but the bonds still ended up with liens superior to those of the life-lease holders, the potentially competing claimants.)

The Law Firm and the Accounting Firm received the Foundation's selling documents during 1974–78 but did nothing to stop the sale of the securities and facilitated their sale by answering the Trustee's inquiries in a fashion that led the Trustee not to drop out until October 1976. We will assume that some of the answers to the Trustee's questions concealed legal difficulties. For example, the Law Firm allowed the Trustee to conclude that there were "[n]o known defaults" under the indenture, meaning that the Foundation had not "defaulted" in the payment of principal or interest; but a jury might conclude that the Law Firm should have known that the Trustee was interested in whether any legal problems, such as potential liability under the securities law, had arisen.

The following is also undisputed:

— Neither Firm reviewed or approved any of the materials used to sell the securities between 1974 and 1978. None of the drafts that the Firms saw in 1971 and 1973 was used to sell securities during 1974–78.

— Neither Firm received any of the proceeds of the sales. Neither Firm had a representative on the Foundation's board.

— Neither Firm's name appeared on any document used to sell the securities at any time.

— At Graddy's request, the Foundation retained two other law firms to review the promotional materials and give advice about the securities laws. One or both of these firms reviewed the materials used during 1974–78. Graddy told the Foundation that he had no expertise in securities matters.

— During 1974–75 the Law Firm billed the Foundation a total of $125. It ceased representing the Foundation in any way before the first note was sold.

— The Accounting Firm prepared the Foundation's financial statements through 1975, but none of these statements was used in any promotional material. The Foundation requested Edenfield to sign a pro forma balance sheet in 1973 for use in the promotional materials; he refused. During the audit for 1975 the Accounting Firm found that officers of the Foundation had drawn unauthorized sums and qualified its opinion of the financial statement. The Foundation then fired the Accounting Firm.

The district court held, and we agree, that these undisputed facts require summary judgment for the two Firms, even taking other inferences in the light most favorable to the plaintiffs.

I

The Securities Act of 1933 has an intricate set of rules establishing who is liable when securities are sold by the use of false or misleading documents. Section 11, 15 U.S.C. § 77k, creates presumptive liability for the issuer, all members of its board, and all who sign the prospectus or are named as preparing it. Members of the board and other signers can use a series of "due diligence" and "reliance on expertise" defenses. . . .

Neither the Law Firm nor the Accounting Firm is an issuer, director, signatory of a prospectus, offeror, or seller of securities. Neither can be liable under § 11 or § 12 of the '33 Act. Although the plaintiffs briefly argue that the Firms are "control persons" under § 20(a) of the '34 Act, 15 U.S.C. § 78t, the provision parallel to § 15, this gets them nowhere. This provision is applicable only to people who actually exercised control over the issuers, sellers, and other people directly liable. E.g., Metge v. Baehler, 762 F.2d 621, 630–31 (8th Cir.1985), cert. denied, [474] U.S. [1057], 106 S.Ct. 798, 88 L.Ed.2d 774 (1986); Lanza v. Drexel & Co., 479 F.2d 1277, 1299 (2d Cir.1973) (en banc). The Firms had no ability to control the Foundation. Their ability to persuade and give counsel is not the same thing as "control," which almost always means the practical ability to *direct* the actions of the people who issue or sell the securities. The Firms had no such authority; they received the selling materials for 1974–78 through the mails, after they had been issued. This is not sufficient for "control" under § 15 or § 20.

The plaintiffs principally rely on § 10(b) of the '34 Act and Rule 10b–5. See Herman & MacLean v. Huddleston, 459 U.S. 375, 103 S.Ct. 683, 74 L.Ed.2d 548 (1983), holding that these provisions support implied private rights of action even when they overlap with the express rights of action under §§ 11, 12, 15, and 20. Section 10(b) forbids the use of "any manipulative or deceptive device or contrivance". Rule

10b–5 makes it unlawful, in the connection with the purchase or sale of a security:

(1) to employ any device, scheme, or artifice to defraud,

(2) to make any untrue statement of a material fact or to omit to state a material fact necessary in order to make the statements made, in the light of the circumstances under which they were made, not misleading, or

(3) to engage in any act, practice, or course of business which operates or would operate as a fraud or deceit upon any person.

Neither the statute nor the rule identifies the addressees of these commands. A natural reading of their language is that the commands apply to the same people otherwise covered by the '33 and '34 Acts—issuers, directors, signatories and identified drafters of documents, offerors, sellers, and those who control them. In common with the other courts of appeals, however, this court has held that § 10(b) and Rule 10b–5 establish liability for aiders, abetters, and conspirators with those primarily liable, even if the aiders, abetters, and conspirators could not be called "control persons" under § 15 or § 20. . . . These principles of implied secondary liability have been criticized, see Daniel R. Fischel, Secondary Liability Under Section 10(b) of the Securities Act of 1934, 69 Calif.L.Rev. 80 (1981), and the Supreme Court has twice reserved decision on them, see Herman & MacLean, 459 U.S. at 379 n. 5, 103 S.Ct. at 685 n. 5; Ernst & Ernst v. Hochfelder, 425 U.S. 185, 191–92 n. 7, 96 S.Ct. 1375, 1380 n. 7, 47 L.Ed.2d 668 (1976). The Firms do not ask us to reconsider . . . [the rule of secondary implied liability]. . . . They argue only that secondary liability does not sweep up all people who can be characterized as participants in or contributors to the success of the firm that issues the securities. We agree. A court must take care lest the implied right of action under Rule 10b–5 unravel the presumptions and defenses created by Congress.

Ernst & Ernst, like this case, was a suit seeking to hold an accounting firm liable for misstatements in connection with the sale of securities. The plaintiffs contended that had Ernst & Ernst been more careful in doing its audits, it would have discovered the fraud. This court held that an accountant has a duty of inquiry and due care, a duty owed to investors as well as to issuers of securities, and that the accountant's negligent failure to carry out its duty had caused the investors' injury. The Supreme Court held, to the contrary, that people may be liable under § 10(b) and Rule 10b–5 only if they act with intent to deceive. (We have since concluded that recklessness meets the standard of wrongful intent. See Sundstrand Corp. v. Sun Chemical Corp., 553 F.2d 1033, 1040 (7th Cir.), cert. denied, 434 U.S. 875, 98 S.Ct. 224, 54 L.Ed.2d 155 (1977). The Court pointed out that both statute and rule refer to manipulative and deceptive conduct, which at common law meant conduct with bad intent. *Herman & MacLean* then concluded that because of the scienter requirement under § 10(b) and Rule 10b–5, an overlap in remedies will not undo the structure of §§ 11, 12,

15, and 20. These statutes establish liability without fault for a limited group of people, and grant defenses; implied rights of action may cover a larger group, but there must be proof of fault and intent. . . .

· · ·

There is no direct evidence that either Firm acted with intent to deceive any purchaser of the Foundation's securities. There is indeed no evidence that either Firm saw any of the Foundation's selling documents during the period 1974–78 until after the document had been placed in use. There is no serious claim that either Firm intentionally or recklessly gave bad advice to the Foundation. The Accounting Firm was fired after catching a problem in the Foundation's internal affairs. A jury might conclude that the Law Firm was negligent in drafting a "loose" indenture and in obtaining belated releases of the mortgage on the land, but negligence does not establish the necessary scienter, and neither of these errors (if they were errors) was the subject of a scheme to defraud. The securities laws do not impose liability for ordinary malpractice, even though that malpractice may diminish the value of the issuer and thus of the issuer's securities. (We do not say whether there was malpractice here.)

The plaintiffs insist that the Firms *must* have known that the Foundation's selling documents were inaccurate and, because they did not do anything to stop the sales and answered queries from the Trustee, they *must* have had the necessary mental state. If this were enough to establish scienter, however, the scienter doctrine would not do anything to distinguish liability under § 10(b) and Rule 10b–5 from the presumptive or absolute liability under §§ 11, 12, 15, and 20. A plaintiff's case against an aider, abetter, or conspirator may not rest on a bare inference that the defendant "must have had" knowledge of the facts. The plaintiff must support the inference with some reason to conclude that the defendant has thrown in his lot with the primary violators.

Law firms and accountants may act or remain silent for good reasons as well as bad ones, and allowing scienter or conspiracy to defraud to be inferred from the silence of a professional firm may expand the scope of liability far beyond that authorized in *Ernst & Ernst* and *Herman & MacLean*. If the plaintiff does not have direct evidence of scienter, the court should ask whether the fraud (or cover-up) was in the interest of the defendants. Did they gain by bilking the buyers of the securities? Cf. *Dirks*, 463 U.S. at 662–64, 103 S.Ct. at 3265–66. In this case the Firms did not gain. They received none of the proceeds from the sales. They did not receive fees for rendering advice in connection with the sales to the plaintiffs. Both Firms billed so little time to the Foundation between 1974 and 1976 (and none after October 1976) that it is inconceivable that they joined a venture to feather their nests by defrauding investors. They had nothing to gain and everything to lose. There is no sound basis, therefore, on which a jury could infer that the Firms joined common cause with other offenders or aided and abetted a scheme with the necessary state of mind.

The district court also held that the Firms had not committed any forbidden act, had not participated in a scheme to defraud by remaining silent when there was a duty to speak. This, too, is a correct conclusion. Neither lawyers nor accountants are required to tattle on their clients in the absence of some duty to disclose. ITT v. Cornfeld, 619 F.2d at 925; SEC v. Spectrum, Ltd., 489 F.2d 535 (2d Cir.1973). Cf. United States v. Matthews, 787 F.2d 38 (2d Cir.1986). To the contrary, attorneys have privileges not to disclose. See Upjohn Corp. v. United States, 449 U.S. 383, 101 S.Ct. 677, 66 L.Ed.2d 584 (1981).

The extent to which lawyers and accountants should reveal their clients' wrongdoing—and to whom they should reveal—is a question of great moment. There are proposals to change the rules of legal ethics and the SEC's regulations governing accountants. The professions and the regulatory agencies will debate questions raised by cases such as this one for years to come. We express no opinion on whether the Firms did what they should, whether there was malpractice under state law, or whether the rules of ethics (or other fiduciary doctrines) ought to require lawyers and accountants to blow the whistle in equivalent circumstances. We are satisfied, however, that an award of damages under the securities laws is not the way to blaze the trail toward improved ethical standards in the legal and accounting professions. Liability depends on an *existing* duty to disclose. The securities law therefore must lag behind changes in ethical and fiduciary standards. The plaintiffs have not pointed to any rule imposing on either Firm a duty to blow the whistle.

Questions and Comments

The court in *Barker* did not use the three-part test for aiding and abetting violations used in *National Student Marketing* and, which is used by most other courts. Analyze the *Barker* facts under the three-part test. What result?

Both *Barker* and *National Student Marketing* hold that intent to deceive must be established but that recklessness meets that standard. In *National Student Marketing,* how did the court establish the wrongful intent of the lawyers for Interstate? Did the lawyers for Interstate intend to deceive in a way that the lawyers for the Foundation did not?

Where there is no direct evidence that the lawyers knew that the documents were false or misleading, how can the plaintiffs nevertheless make out a case of wrongful intent according to the court in *Barker?* Compare *Benjamin,* printed earlier in this chapter, and *Barker* on the question of inferring wrongful intent. Are they inconsistent?

Is the problem in *Barker* absence of both direct evidence of wrongful intent and positive activity to facilitate the fraud? Was silence or a failure to act the only role of the lawyers for the Foundation? What did the lawyers for Interstate do other than remain silent?

The court in *Barker* says, "an award of damages under the securities laws is not the way to blaze the trail toward improved ethical standards in the legal . . . profession. . . . The securities law . . . must lag behind changes in ethical and fiduciary standards." Should ethical rules dictate who is liable under the securities laws?

The Foundation's Other Lawyers

How important is it that Graddy told his client he was not an expert in securities law and advised getting other counsel?

As the court in *Barker* notes, the Foundation did get other counsel, presumably experts in securities matters. These lawyers, the firm of Dykema, Gossett, were also sued by the plaintiffs in *Barker* for aiding and abetting violations of the securities law. The plaintiffs claimed that Dykema knowingly participated in the securities fraud. The complaint alleged that:

> [s]hortly after being retained by [the Foundation], Dykema Gossett was made aware of the grave financial . . . situation of the Foundation, of the Foundation's unlawful sale of its Note Certificates . . . and of the fact that the legally required disclosures had not been made by the Foundation in connection with such sales. . . .
>
> . . . [I]t was [also] alleged that . . . [a partner in Dykema] "as late as the spring of 1978, when the Foundation's future was hopeless . . . urged and advised that the sale of the Note Certificates be continued."
>
> American Home Assurance Company v. Dykema, Gossett . . ., 811 F.2d 1077, 1079 (7th Cir.1987).

Dykema settled the case, paying the plaintiffs $612,500.

Liability for Aiding and Abetting Under § 10b and Rule 10b–5

In Roberts v. Peat, Marwick, 857 F.2d 646 (9th Cir.1988), the court held that the plaintiffs had stated a cause of action against Peat, Marwick for aiding and abetting a violation of § 10(b).

> The . . . investors have alleged that Peat, Marwick knew of the alleged violation but allowed the use of its name in offering memoranda despite that knowledge. These facts may be sufficient to create a duty to disclose in Peat, Marwick. Investors can reasonably be expected to assume that an accounting firm would not consent to the use of its name on reports and offering memoranda it knew were fraudulent. Thus, it may be reasonable to expect an accountant to disclose fraud in this type of situation, where the accountant's information is superior and the cost to the accountant of disclosure is minimal.
>
> Id. at 653.

The court distinguished *Barker* on a number of grounds, including: that *Barker* involved a motion for summary judgment not a motion to dismiss; that in *Barker* there was no evidence that the lawyers had seen the selling documents during the relevant period, and no evidence that they had intentionally or recklessly given the sellers bad advice; and that the lawyers names were not on the prospectus. In contrast, the court concluded that in this case, there were sufficient allegations of Peat, Marwick's knowledge of the fraud "to create a possible duty to disclose information concerning the alleged fraud." Id.

In determining whether there is a duty to disclose under § 10(b) the Ninth Circuit looks at five "non-exclusive" factors:

1. the relationship of the defendant to the plaintiff;

2. the defendant's access to information as compared with the plaintiff's access;

3. the benefit that the defendant derives from the relationship with the plaintiff;

4. the defendant's awareness of plaintiff's reliance; and

5. the defendant's activity in initiating the securities transaction.

Roberts, 857 F.2d at 653–54, citing White v. Abrams, 495 F.2d 724, 735–6 (9th Cir.1974).

These factors were discussed in holding that plaintiffs had failed to state a claim against the fraud doer's lawyers. The lawyers had prepared accurate title opinions for the offering but had omitted information about a conflict of interest about which the purchasers claimed they were entitled to know.

In Abell v. Potomac Insurance Co., 858 F.2d 1104 (5th Cir.1988), the firm conceded that it substantially assisted the scheme by preparing the bond offering. The court proceeded to examine whether the firm was:

"generally aware" of its role in furthering the fraudulent scheme, and whether its assistance was "knowing."

In Woodward [v. Metro Bank, 522 F.2d 84 (5th Cir.1975),] we explained what these scienter requirements mean. . . .

When it is impossible to find any duty of disclosure, an alleged aider-abettor should be found liable only if scienter of the high "conscious intent" variety can be proved. Where some special duty of disclosure exists, then liability should be possible with a lesser degree of scienter. . . . In a case combining silence/inaction with affirmative assistance, the degree of knowledge required should depend on how ordinary the assisting activity is in the business involved. If the evidence shows no more than transactions constituting the daily grist of the mill, we would be loathe to find 10b–5 liability without clear proof of intent to violate the securities law. Conversely, if the method or transaction is atypical or lacks business justification, it may be possible to infer the knowledge necessary for aiding and abetting liability. In any case, the assistance must be substantial before liability can be imposed under 10b–5.

Id. at 97 (citations and footnotes omitted).

Liability of Lawyers as Principals, Sellers, Offerers or Control Persons

Lawyers as entrepreneur investors, directors, officers or signatories of prospectuses may be liable as principals under the securities laws provisions that impose liability without proof of wrongful intent. See, e.g., *Benjamin* supra; S.E.C. v. Manor Nursing Centers, Inc., 458 F.2d 1082 (2d Cir.1972); S.E.C. v. Coven, 581 F.2d 1020 (2d Cir.1978), cert. denied, 440 U.S. 950 (1979).

Assuming the lawyer does not sign the prospectus, the question is when, if ever, are the lawyers for offerers of securities sufficiently involved in the offering to impose liability under the "strict liability" provisions of the securities laws.

In Pinter v. Dahl, 486 U.S. 622, 108 S.Ct. 2063 (1988), the Supreme Court, interpreting § 12(1) of the '33 Act, held that while privity was not essential, "the language of [the section] contemplates a buyer-seller relationship not unlike traditional contractual privity." 108 S.Ct. at 2076. Aiding and abetting liability under this section was thus rejected, but so was the narrow reading suggested in *Barker*. The section's reach is broader than traditional privity in that it includes those who "successfully solicit the purchase, motivated at least in part by a desire to serve [their] own financial interests *or those of the securities owner.*" 108 S.Ct. at 2079 (emphasis added). Thus, the court concluded that § 12(1) extended to brokers but not to those "whose motivation [in soliciting the sale is] solely to benefit the buyer." 108 S.Ct. at 2078.

One can easily see how lawyers representing offerers are more analogous to brokers than the latter type of person. However, the court emphasized that brokers were people from whom one "purchased" securities in some sense. In contrast, lawyers and accountants "whose involvement is only the performance of their professional services" are not people from whom the "buyer . . . in any meaningful sense, 'purchase[s] the security . . .'" 108 S.Ct. at 2081. The court thus disapproved of extending § 12(1) to cover securities lawyers acting qua securities lawyers. See Wilson v. Saintine Exploration and Drilling Corp., 872 F.2d 1124 (2d Cir.1989) (holding that the Supreme Court's analysis in *Pinter* applied equally to § 12(2); and that a law firm that prepared and distributed private placement memorandum to purchasers was not a "seller" subject to strict liability).

Lawyers as Control Persons

In *Seidel v. Public Service Company of New Hampshire*, 616 F.Supp. 1342 (D.C.N.H.1985), the court held that lawyers could be "control persons."

> Attorneys fall within the ambit of 'controlling persons' when they are in some sense culpable participants in the acts perpetrated by the controlled person. . . . It is difficult to perceive that a corporation and its board of directors would not follow the advice of counsel in situations concerning documents to be issued for examination by prospective investors, particularly where such documents bear the imprimatur of expertise on the part of such counsel.

Id. at 1362.

Compare *Westlake v. Abrams*, 565 F.Supp. 1330, 1350 (N.D.Ga.1983):

> [A]n attorney cannot be held to be a controlling person under the federal securities laws for vigorously performing legitimate litigation activities for his client. Unless the plaintiff shows that an attorney participated in fraud or a similarly culpable act or . . . the plaintiff shows that the attorney pursued legal representation in blatant violation of . . . Canon 7 [of the Code of Professional Responsibility, the lawyer] cannot be held to be a controlling person merely because he renders advice in pursuing litigation on behalf of his client.

D. TAX LAW

ABA FORMAL OPINION 85–352

American Bar Association, Standing Committee on Professional Ethics.
July 7, 1985.

Tax Return Advice; Reconsideration of Formal Opinion 314

The Committee has been requested by the Section of Taxation of the American Bar Association to reconsider the "reasonable basis" standard in the Committee's Formal Opinion 314 governing the position a lawyer may advise a client to take on a tax return.

Opinion 314 (April 27, 1965) was issued in response to a number of specific inquiries regarding the ethical relationship between the Internal Revenue Service and lawyers practicing before it. The opinion formulated general principles governing this relationship, including the following: "[A] lawyer who is asked to advise his client in the course of the preparation of the client's tax returns may freely urge the statement of positions most favorable to the client just as long as there is a reasonable basis for this position." (Emphasis supplied).

The Committee is informed that the standard of "reasonable basis" has been construed by many lawyers to support the use of any colorable claim on a tax return to justify exploitation of the lottery of the tax return audit selection process. (This criticism has been expressed by the Section of Taxation and also by the U.S. Department of the Treasury and some legal writers. See, e.g., Robert H. Mundheim, Speech as General Counsel to Treasury Department, reprinted in How to Prepare and Defend Tax Shelter Opinions: Risks and Realities for Lawyers and Accountants (Law and Business, Inc. 1981); Rowen, When May a Lawyer Advise a Client That He May Take a Position on a Tax Return?, 29 Tax Lawyer 237 (1976).) This view is not universally held, and the Committee does not believe that the reasonable basis standard, properly interpreted and applied, permits this construction.

However, the Committee is persuaded that as a result of serious controversy over this standard and its persistent criticism by distinguished members of the tax bar, IRS officials and members of Congress, sufficient doubt has been created regarding the validity of the standard so as to erode its effectiveness as an ethical guideline. For this reason, the Committee has concluded that it should be restated. Another reason for restating the standard is that since publication of Opinion 314, the ABA has adopted in succession the Model Code of Professional Responsibility (1969; revised 1980) and the Model Rules of Professional Conduct (1983). Both the Model Code and the Model Rules directly address the duty of a lawyer in presenting or arguing positions for a client in language that does not refer to "reasonable basis." It is therefore appropriate to conform the standard of Opinion 314 to the language of the new rules.

This opinion reconsiders and revises only that part of Opinion 314 that relates to the lawyer's duty in advising a client of positions that can be taken on a tax return. It does not deal with a lawyer's opinion on tax shelter investment offering, which is specifically addressed by this Committee's Formal Opinion 346 (Revised), and which involves very different considerations, including third party reliance.

The ethical standards governing the conduct of a lawyer in advising a client on positions that can be taken in a tax return are no different from those governing a lawyer's conduct in advising or taking positions for a client in other civil matters. Although the Model Rules distinguish between the roles of advisor and advocate, (See, for example, Model Rules 2.1 and 3.1) both roles are involved here, and the ethical standards applicable to them provide relevant guidance. In many cases a lawyer must realistically anticipate that the filing of the tax return may be the first step in a process that may result in an adversary relationship between the client and the IRS. This normally occurs in situations when a lawyer advises an aggressive position on a tax return, not when the position taken is a safe or conservative one that is unlikely to be challenged by the IRS.

Rule 3.1 of the Model Rules . . . is in essence a restatement of DR 7–102(A)(2) of the Model Code . . . [DR 7–102(A)(2) states: "In his representation of a client, a lawyer shall not: . . . (2) Knowingly advance a claim or defense that is unwarranted under existing law, except that he may advance such claim or defense if it can be supported by good faith argument for an extension, modification or reversal of existing law." Rule 3.1] states in pertinent part: "A lawyer shall not bring or defend a proceeding, or assert or controvert an issue therein, unless there is a basis for doing so that is not frivolous, which includes a good faith argument for an extension, modification or reversal of existing law." Rule 1.2(d), which applies to representation generally, states: "A lawyer shall not counsel a client to engage, or assist a client, in conduct that the lawyer knows is criminal or fraudulent, but a lawyer may discuss the legal consequences of any proposed course of conduct with a client and may counsel or assist a client to make a good faith effort to determine the validity, scope, meaning or application of the law."

On the basis of these rules and analogous provisions of the Model Code, a lawyer, in representing a client in the course of the preparation of the client's tax return, may advise the statement of positions most favorable to the client if the lawyer has a good faith belief that those positions are warranted in existing law or can be supported by a good faith argument for an extension, modification or reversal of existing law. A lawyer can have a good faith belief in this context even if the lawyer believes the client's position probably will not prevail. (Comment to Rule 3.1; see also Model Code EC 7–4.) However, good faith requires that there be some realistic possibility of success if the matter is litigated.

This formulation of the lawyer's duty in the situation addressed by this opinion is consistent with the basic duty of the lawyer to a client, recognized in ethical standards since the ABA Canons of Professional Ethics, and in the opinions of this Committee: zealously and loyally to represent the interests of the client within the bounds of the law.

Thus, where a lawyer has a good faith belief in the validity of a position in accordance with the standard stated above that a particular transaction does not result in taxable income or that certain expenditures are properly deductible as expenses, the lawyer has no duty to require as a condition of his or her continued representation that riders be attached to the client's tax return explaining the circumstances surrounding the transaction or the expenditures.

In the role of advisor, the lawyer should counsel the client as to whether the position is likely to be sustained by a court if challenged by the IRS, as well as of the potential penalty consequences to the client if the position is taken on the tax return without disclosure. Section 6661 of the Internal Revenue Code imposes a penalty for substantial understatement of tax liability which can be avoided if the facts are adequately disclosed or if there is or was substantial authority for the position taken by the taxpayer. Competent representation of the client would require the lawyer to advise the client fully as to whether there is or was substantial authority for the position taken in the tax return. If the lawyer is unable to conclude that the position is supported by substantial authority, the lawyer should advise the client of the penalty the client may suffer and of the opportunity to avoid such penalty by adequately disclosing the facts in the return or in a statement attached to the return. If after receiving such advice the client decides to risk the penalty by making no disclosure and to take the position initially advised by the lawyer in accordance with the standard stated above, the lawyer has met his or her ethical responsibility with respect to the advice.

In all cases, however, with regard both to the preparation of returns and negotiating administrative settlements, the lawyer is under a duty not to mislead the Internal Revenue Service deliberately, either by misstatements or by silence or by permitting the client to mislead. Rules 4.1 and 8.4(c); DRs 1–102(A)(4), 7–102(A)(3) and (5).

In summary, a lawyer may advise reporting a position on a return even where the lawyer believes the position probably will not prevail, there is no "substantial authority" in support of the position, and there will be no disclosure of the position in the return. However, the position to be asserted must be one which the lawyer in good faith believes is warranted in existing law or can be supported by a good faith argument for an extension, modification or reversal of existing law. This requires that there is some realistic possibility of success if the matter is litigated. In addition, in his role as advisor, the lawyer should refer to potential penalties and other legal consequences should the client take the position advised.

Note on Tax Law

The conflict over the lawyer's duty in tax return preparation has been going on for at least 40 years. See Paul, The Responsibilities of the Tax Adviser, 63 Harv.L.Rev. 377 (1950). The underlying conflict concerns how far the lawyer is required to indicate on the return that claims for exemptions of income from tax, or for deductions from otherwise taxable income, are legally debatable. If the return must indicate that a claim of exemption or deduction is legally debatable, that indication can "flag" the return for special attention of the Internal Revenue Service. Such special attention in turn can result in disallowance that otherwise would not have been imposed, and consequently higher tax for the client. Behind this scenario is the fact that the IRS does not audit all returns, but only a small fraction of them. Hence, to the extent the lawyer, or other professional assisting the taxpayer, puts a "flag" on the client's return, the client may be worse off than if he had no professional assistance.

There is no debate over the extremes of the lawyer's responsibility. On one hand, the client may not be assisted in tax evasion, such as failing to report income that is clearly reportable or claiming deductions based on fictitious events or transactions. Such behavior is the crime of aiding and abetting tax evasion, see, e.g., United States v. Feaster, 843 F.2d 1392 (6th Cir.), cert. denied, 109 S.Ct. 244 (1988) (unreported opinion, text available on WESTLAW) and is a violation of the ethical rule that a lawyer may not assist a client in crime or fraud. On the other hand, the client is entitled to claim every "legitimate" exemption and deduction. It is certainly legitimate to claim an exemption or deduction notwithstanding that a plausible legal argument could be made against it. The area of controversy lies between these boundaries.

The conflict is conducted in two rhetorical media. One is the verbal formula to define the lawyer's responsibility, i.e., whether the claimed exemption or deduction has a "reasonable basis," rests on "substantial authority," or some other formulation. The other is that of proper analogy between filing a tax return and some other legal transaction. ABA Formal Opinion 85–352 adopts the analogy to a pleading in litigation, wherein the assertions may be predicated on interpretation of law and fact most favorable to the proponent, short of frivolousness. Critics point out that pleadings are filed between parties with a ripened legal dispute, whereas a tax return is a submission of information which, in principle, is not in dispute. Another analogy could be a securities disclosure document, such as was involved in *National Student Marketing*. That is, the tax return would have to disclose any fact or circumstance that a reasonable tax collector would think material in determining the amount of tax due under the return. Needless to say, the bar has not encouraged this analogy. But this analogy does suggest how broad is the area of disagreement as to what standard should govern the lawyer who is advising a client in preparing a return.

Still more deeply, the problem of the lawyer's role in advising a client as to tax liability turns on the client's reporting responsibility under the tax law. Present tax law does not require that a tax return conform to the standards of disclosure that apply under the securities law. The tax penalty rules, imposing surcharges for under-reporting, indeed reflect profound ambivalence on the part of Congress, generally imposing a penalty only where there is no "substantial authority" for the taxpayer's position.

In an illuminating survey, Durst, The Tax Lawyer's Professional Responsibility, 39 U.Fla.L.Rev. 1027 (1987), Professor Durst shows the anomaly in trying to require the lawyer to advise the taxpayer to adhere to a higher standard of reporting than is required by the penalty provisions of the tax law. Put differently, if tax lawyers are expected to give advice that is "down the middle of the fairway" so far as taxpayer liability is concerned, the way to do this is to impose that standard directly on the taxpayer.

Did the ABA Opinion take adequate account of the standards of candor and disclosure that govern pleadings and representations to a court? See DR 7–102(A)(2), (3), and (6); M.R. 3.1 and 3.3. A tax return could be regarded as an ex parte submission, couldn't it? M.R. 3.3(d) provides: "In an ex parte proceeding, a lawyer shall inform the tribunal of all material facts known to the lawyer which will enable the tribunal to make an informed decision, whether or not the facts are adverse." See also generally B. Wolfman & J. Holden, Ethical Problems in Modern Tax Practice (2d ed. 1985).

E. PROCEDURAL LAW

Of the bodies of law external to the rules of professional conduct that are important for lawyers, none is more significant than the law of procedure. For the lawyer, the law of procedure is a set of legal empowerments accompanied by limitations and obligations. The very term "attorney" denotes one who is an agent in legal matters, particularly litigation. Agency is itself a relationship involving powers, limitations, and obligations. See generally Restatement Second of Agency. Agency law governs lawyers in many contexts in which the rules of professional conduct are silent or incomplete. Moreover, legal regulation allows only lawyers to undertake agent relationships that involve "practice of law." See, e.g., Florida Bar v. Brumbaugh, 355 So.2d 1186 (Fla.1978), reprinted in Chapter 10. The term "practice of law" is indeterminate at the margin of meaning but certainly includes advocacy in criminal and civil litigation. Hence, the law of procedure has special significance for lawyers because only they may be employed as advocates.

The function of advocacy is governed by and takes its form from the law of criminal and civil procedure. The rules of procedure, although they generally address the "parties," contemplate that litigation ordinarily will be conducted by lawyers.

Empowerments in the Law of Procedure

The law of procedure is largely a set of legal empowerments. For example, Rule 4(a) of the Federal Rules of Civil Procedure begins as follows:

Upon the filing of the complaint the clerk shall forthwith issue a summons to the plaintiff or the plaintiff's attorney . . .

Rule 4(a) does not say so, but rather presupposes that the complaint being filed will have been drafted by the attorney for the plaintiff in conformity with the pleading rules stated in Fed.R.Civ.P. 8–12 and other provisions of the Federal Rules. Rule 4(a) similarly presupposes that the summons itself will have been prepared by the plaintiff's attorney, in contemplation that the clerk will simply stamp the document, record that fact, and then hand the summons back to the lawyer, who will take care of getting it served. Similarly, Fed.R.Civ.P. 26(a) provides that "parties may obtain discovery . . . upon oral examination or written questions . . .," but contemplates that the discovery will be conducted by attorneys on behalf of parties.

Criminal procedure has similar presuppositions. For example 18 U.S.C. § 3041 provides:

> For any offense against the United States, the offender may, by any
> . . . judge of the United States . . . be arrested and imprisoned
> or released as provided in chapter 207 of this title . . .

Section 3041 does not say so, but it presupposes that ordinarily a judge will order such arrest only on application of the United States District Attorney, a Justice Department lawyer, or some other lawyer for the Government.

Thus commencing criminal or civil litigation, with potentially momentous effect on the lives of the parties involved, for most practical purposes is exclusively within the authority of people who are lawyers. The same holds for all subsequent stages of litigation. Litigation is an exercise of the power of the state over which lawyers have important control.

Limitations

The powers that lawyers exercise in conducting litigation are subject to all kinds of limitations. These limits are the focus of Chapter 5 below. For example, Fed.R.Civ.P. 11 provides:

> The signature of an attorney . . . constitutes a certificate by the signer that the signer has read the pleading, motion, or other paper; that to the best of the signer's knowledge, information, and belief formed after reasonable inquiry it is well grounded in fact and is warranted by existing law or a good faith argument for the extension, modification, or reversal of existing law, and that it is not interposed for any improper purpose, such as to harass or to cause unnecessary delay or needless increase in the cost of litigation.

Another set of explicit sanctions is in Rule 37, governing discovery.

Cutting across all activities directly involving the courts is the sanction of contempt of court. The contempt power is founded both in common law and in statute, e.g., 18 U.S.C. § 1401, which provides as regards criminal contempt:

> A court of the United States shall have power to punish by fine or imprisonment . . . such contempt of its authority . . . as . . . misbehavior of any person in its presence or so near thereto as to obstruct the administration of justice . . .

Pervasive in the law of procedure is another set of limitations, the requirement that procedural options be exercised in timely fashion or otherwise be forfeited. The most obvious is the statute of limitations itself, governing the time within which litigation must be commenced following the occurrence of a legal grievance. (The failure of a lawyer to bring suit within the limitations period is the most obvious form of legal malpractice. See Mallen & Smith, Legal Malpractice, § 24.13 (3d ed. 1989).) But virtually every procedural empowerment carries with it a limitation on the time within which it can be invoked. See, e.g.,

Fed.R.Civ.P. 6, "Time"; Rule 60(b) (limitations on a motion to set aside a judgment on the ground of its procurement by mistake or fraud).

Another kind of limitation on lawyer powers is found in requirements of court permission for procedural steps to be taken. An example is Rule 23, which permits an action to proceed as a class action only upon the court's authorization. Rule 23(c)(1) provides:

> As soon as practicable after the commencement of an action brought as a class action, the *court* shall determine by order *whether* it is to be so maintained. (emphasis supplied)

Another example is the broad power conferred on the court by Fed.R.Civ.P. 26(c) to regulate discovery, including power to direct that "discovery not be had." Fed.R.Civ.P. 26(c)(1). More generally is the scope of a court's "inherent power," often expressed in capacious terms, e.g., Millholen v. Riley, 211 Cal. 29, 33, 293 P. 69, 71 (1930):

> A court set up by the Constitution has within it the power of self-preservation, indeed, the power to remove all obstructions to its successful and convenient operation.

Obligations

A power conferred on a lawyer by the law of procedure also carries with it obligations concerning how the power is exercised. Broadly speaking, the lawyer has an obligation to the client to employ powers of litigation to maximize the client's interest. Model Rules 1.1 and 1.2(a). At the same time, the lawyer has an obligation not to employ those powers in a way that is illegal, fraudulent, or merely for harassment. See Fed.R.Civ.P. 11, quoted above; Rule 16 (governing pretrial conferences and giving the court authority for "discouraging wasteful pretrial activities"); and Rule 37, referred to above. A more general obligation to conduct litigation within the limits of accepted conventions is implied in the concept that a lawyer is an "officer of the court." As stated in Cohen v. Hurley, 366 U.S. 117, 122, 81 S.Ct. 954, 959 (1961):

> It is no less true than trite that lawyers must operate in a three-fold capacity, as self-employed businessmen as it were, as trusted agents of their clients, and as assistants to the court in search of a just solution of disputes.

The lawyer's obligations to the court and to opposing parties in connection with litigation are codified in M.R. 3.1 through 3.8. See also M.R. 3.9 dealing with obligations in nonadjudicative proceedings. These Rules refer to the law of procedure both expressly and impliedly. For example, a key formula in M.R. 3.1 corresponds to that in Fed.R. Civ.P. 11, quoted above. M.R. 3.1 provides:

> A lawyer shall not bring or defend a proceeding, or assert or controvert an issue therein, unless there is a basis for doing so that is not frivolous, which includes a good faith argument for an extension, modification or reversal of existing law . . .

Another example of reference to the law of procedure in the Rules of Professional Conduct is M.R. 3.4(a), which provides:

A lawyer shall not *unlawfully* obstruct another party's access to evidence or *unlawfully* alter, destroy or conceal a document or other material having potential evidentiary value . . . (emphasis supplied)

More generally, M.R. 3.4(c) provides:

A lawyer shall not knowingly disobey an obligation under the *rules of a tribunal* except for an open refusal based on an assertion that no valid obligation exists . . . (emphasis supplied)

A question of proper professional conduct in litigation therefore usually depends, wholly or in part, on the law of procedure. However, the law of procedure is itself a distillate of professional practice. After all, the modern codified version of procedural law had its origin in common law, which in turn reflects the historic practice of law. See generally, e.g., James & Hazard, Civil Procedure, § 1.3 et seq. (3d ed. 1984). Moreover, the law of procedure connotes the understandings of the community of practicing lawyers, i.e., procedure is understood in terms of the bar's concepts, norms, and expectations about appropriate behavior in conducting litigation. Since the community of practicing lawyers is not homogenous in experience, interest, political position, and ethical concepts, there are inevitably controversies over what the law of procedure permits and requires of lawyers. See generally Chapter 1 above.

This takes us back to *Commonwealth v. Stenhach*, see p. 35 above, doesn't it?

Chapter III

COMPETENCE

Introductory Notes

I find no pleasure in saying to you that the majority of lawyers who appear in court are so poorly trained that they are not properly performing their job . . .

From more than twenty years of active practice . . . and from more than ten years on the bench, I think I have gained a fairly reasonable . . . view of what goes on in courtrooms . . . [M]y appraisal of courtroom performance was so low that I began to check it with lawyers and judges in various parts of the country to see whether I misjudged . . .

On the most favorable view expressed, seventy-five percent of the lawyers appearing in the courtroom were deficient by reason of poor preparation, lack of ability to conduct a proper cross-examination, lack of ability to present expert testimony, . . . lack of ability to frame objections . . ., [and] lack of basic analytic ability in the framing of issues . . .

Burger, A Sick Profession?, 5 Tulsa L.J. 1 (1968). [Chief Justice Warren Burger, then a judge on the United States Court of Appeals, first delivered these remarks at the Winter Convention of the American College of Trial Lawyers, April 11, 1967. In a later article, Chief Justice Burger continued to assert that 75% might be an accurate figure, but accepted as a "working hypothesis that from one-third to one-half of the lawyers who appear in serious cases are not really qualified to render fully adequate representation." Burger, The Special Skills of Advocacy: Are Specialized Training and Certification of Advocates Essential to Our System of Justice?, 42 Fordham L.Rev. 227, 234 (1978).]

How Widespread is Incompetence?

Documenting the level of competence in the practice of law is virtually impossible. The concern and the suspicion that incompetence is widespread has been criticized as unscientific, anecdotal and overstated. For example, Cramton and Jensen, The State of Trial Advocacy and Legal Education: Three New Studies, 30 J.Leg.Ed. 253 (1979–80), argues that Chief Justice Burger's estimates are not supported by the available evidence. But see Lawpoll, 64 A.B.A.J. 832 (1978) (nationwide survey of lawyers showing that 41% of those responding, and 72% of the litigators, agreed with Chief Justice Burger's "working hypothesis" of one-third to one-half incompetent). Also see Maddi, Trial Advocacy Competence: The Judicial Perspective, 1978 Am.B.Found.Res.J. 105 (survey of 40 judges in the Second Circuit: these judges thought 10 to

12% of the lawyers they observed in civil and criminal cases to be incompetent; national survey of more than one thousand federal and state trial judges: their estimate was 20% incompetent, but that dropped to 13% when they were asked about the lawyers in the last five trials over which they had presided). Cramton and Jensen point out that another study (Partridge and Bermont) shows that when asked to rate actual trial "performance" rather than to give a general impression of incompetence, the judges said only 8.6% were incompetent—although they said another 16.8% were barely adequate. Cramton and Jensen, supra at 257. Cramton and Jensen urge caution in considering proposals to amend the law school curriculum as a means of addressing incompetent trial performance given how sketchy our understanding is of the relationship between competence and law school study. See also Blair, Trial Lawyer Incompetence: What the Studies Suggest About the Problem, the Causes and the Cure, 11 Cap. U.L.Rev. 419 (1982); and Cort & Sammons, The Search for "Good Lawyering": A Concept and Model of Lawyering Competencies, 29 Clev.St.L.Rev. 397 (1980). Are lawyers less competent today than in the past? What evidence would be sufficient to answer this question?

Read M.R. 1.1, the Comment thereto, and DR 6–101.

A. MALPRACTICE

Introductory Note

In 1978 the American Bar Association established the National Legal Malpractice Data Center to collect information on malpractice claims against lawyers. The Center's figures are based on data submitted by participating insurance companies. The Center's figures do not include claims against uninsured lawyers, about whom no statistics are available.

As of January 1985, the Center's data showed that almost 50 percent of all reported claims are in real estate and personal injury matters. Forty four percent of the claims involve allegations that the lawyer's knowledge of the law was faulty or inadequate; 26% involve poor office administration; 16% involve errors in client relations (e.g., conflicts of interest); 12% involve intentional error; the remaining 2% involve miscellaneous causes.

Sole practitioners and lawyers from firms of two to five lawyers accounted for almost 80% of the claims. Sixty-seven percent of all lawyers in 1985 practiced alone or in firms of five or fewer lawyers. About 20% of the claims involved lawyers in firms with six to thirty lawyers, a percentage about equal to the number of lawyers in firms of this size. About 2% of the claims involved lawyers in practice with more than 30 lawyers; 11.2% of all lawyers were in firms of 51 or more lawyers. See also Mallen, "Malpractice at a Glance" July 1985 California Lawyer.

The low percentage of claims against lawyers in large firms may be misleading. Large firms often have malpractice liability insurance policies with sizeable deductibles and thus may not report small claims. On the other hand, more sole and small firm practitioners may be uninsured.

LUCAS v. HAMM

Supreme Court of California, 1961.

56 Cal.2d 583, 15 Cal.Rptr. 821, 364 P.2d 685, cert. denied, 368 U.S. 987 (1962).

GIBSON, CHIEF JUSTICE.

Plaintiffs, who are some of the beneficiaries under the will of Eugene H. Emmick, deceased, brought this action for damages against defendant L.S. Hamm, an attorney at law who had been engaged by the testator to prepare the will. They have appealed from a judgment of dismissal entered after an order sustaining a general demurrer to the second amended complaint without leave to amend.

The allegations of the first and second causes of action are summarized as follows: Defendant agreed with the testator, for a consideration, to prepare a will and codicils thereto for him by which plaintiffs were to be designated as beneficiaries of a trust provided for by paragraph Eighth of the will and were to receive 15% of the residue as specified in that paragraph. Defendant, in violation of instructions and in breach of his contract, negligently prepared testamentary instruments containing phraseology that was invalid by virtue of section 715.2 and former sections 715.1 and 716 of the Civil Code relating to restraints on alienation and the rule against perpetuities.[1] Paragraph Eighth of these instruments "transmitted" the residual estate in trust and provided that the "trust shall cease and terminate at 12 o'clock noon on a day five years after the date upon which the order distribut-

1. Former section 715.1 of the Civil Code, as it read at the times involved here, provided: "The absolute power of alienation cannot be suspended, by any limitation or condition whatever, for a period longer than 21 years after some life in being at the creation of the interest and any period of gestation involved in the situation to which the limitation applies. The lives selected to govern the time of suspension must not be so numerous or so situated that evidence of their deaths is likely to be unreasonably difficult to obtain."

Section 715.2 reads as follows: "No interest in real or personal property shall be good unless it must vest, if at all, not later than 21 years after some life in being at the creation of the interest and any period of gestation involved in the situation to which the limitation applies. The lives selected to govern the time of vesting must not be so numerous or so situated that evidence of their deaths is likely to be unreasonably difficult to obtain. It is intended by the enactment of this section to make effective in this State the American common-law rule against perpetuities."

Former section 716, as it read at the times involved here, provided: "Every future interest is void in its creation which, by any possibility, may suspend the absolute power of alienation for a longer period than is prescribed in this chapter. Such power of alienation is suspended when there are no persons in being by whom an absolute interest in possession can be conveyed. The period of time during which an interest is destructible pursuant to the uncontrolled volition and for the exclusive personal benefit of the person having such a power of destruction is not to be included in determining the existence of a suspension of the absolute power of alienation or the permissible period for the vesting of an interest within the rule against perpetuities."

ing the trust property to the trustee is made by the Court having jurisdiction over the probation of this will." After the death of the testator the instruments were admitted to probate. Subsequently defendant, as draftsman of the instruments and as counsel of record for the executors, advised plaintiffs in writing that the residual trust provision was invalid and that plaintiffs would be deprived of the entire amount to which they would have been entitled if the provision had been valid unless they made a settlement with the blood relatives of the testator under which plaintiffs would receive a lesser amount than that provided for them by the testator. As the direct and proximate result of the negligence of defendant and his breach of contract in preparing the testamentary instruments and the written advice referred to above, plaintiffs were compelled to enter into a settlement under which they received a share of the estate amounting to $75,000 less than the sum which they would have received pursuant to testamentary instruments drafted in accordance with the directions of the testator.

. . .

. . . We are of the view that the extension of his liability to beneficiaries injured by a negligently drawn will does not place an undue burden on the profession, particularly when we take into consideration that a contrary conclusion would cause the innocent beneficiary to bear the loss. . . .

It follows that the lack of privity between plaintiffs and defendant does not preclude plaintiffs from maintaining an action in tort against defendant.

. . .

The general rule with respect to the liability of an attorney for failure to properly perform his duties to his client is that the attorney, by accepting employment to give legal advice or to render other legal services, impliedly agrees to use such skill, prudence, and diligence as lawyers of ordinary skill and capacity commonly possess and exercise in the performance of the tasks which they undertake. [Citations omitted] The attorney is not liable for every mistake he may make in his practice; he is not, in the absence of an express agreement, an insurer of the soundness of his opinions or of the validity of an instrument that he is engaged to draft; and he is not liable for being in error as to a question of law on which reasonable doubt may be entertained by well-informed lawyers. See Lally v. Kuster, 177 Cal. 783, 786, 171 P. 961; Savings Bank v. Ward, 100 U.S. 195, 198, [(1880) . . .] These principles are equally applicable whether the plaintiff's claim is based on tort or breach of contract.

The complaint, as we have seen, alleges that defendant drafted the will in such a manner that the trust was invalid because it violated the rules relating to perpetuities and restraints on alienation. These closely akin subjects have long perplexed the courts and the bar. Professor Gray, a leading authority in the field, stated: "There is something in the subject which seems to facilitate error. Perhaps it is because the mode of reasoning is unlike that with which lawyers are most familiar. . . . A long list might be formed of the demonstrable blunders with regard to its questions made by eminent men, blunders which they themselves have been sometimes the first to acknowledge; and there are few lawyers of any practice in drawing wills and settlements who have not at some time either fallen into the net which the Rule spreads for the unwary, or at least shuddered to think how narrowly they have escaped it." Gray, The Rule Against Perpetuities (4th ed. 1942) p. xi; see also Leach, Perpetuities Legislation (1954) 67 Harv.L.Rev. 1349 (describing the rule as a "technicality-ridden legal nightmare" and a "dangerous instrumentality in the hands of most members of the bar"). Of the California law on perpetuities and restraints it has been said that few, if any, areas of the law have been fraught with more confusion or concealed more traps for the unwary draftsman; that members of the bar, probate courts, and title insurance companies make errors in these matters; that the code provisions adopted in 1872 created a situation worse than if the matter had been left to the common law, and that the legislation adopted in 1951 (under which the will involved here was drawn), despite the best of intentions, added further complexities. (See 38 Cal.Jur.2d 443; Coil, Perpetuities and Restraints; A Needed Reform (1955) 30 State Bar J. 87, 88–90.)

In view of the state of the law relating to perpetuities and restraints on alienation and the nature of the error, if any, assertedly made by defendant in preparing the instrument, it would not be proper to hold that defendant failed to use such skill, prudence, and diligence as lawyers of ordinary skill and capacity commonly exercise. The provision of the will quoted in the complaint, namely, that the trust was to terminate five years after the order of the probate court distributing the property to the trustee, could cause the trust to be invalid only because of the remote possibility that the order of distribution would be delayed for a period longer than a life in being at the creation of the interest plus 16 years (the 21–year statutory period less the five years specified in the will). Although it has been held that a possibility of this type could result in invalidity of a bequest (Estate of Johnston, 47 Cal.2d 265, 269–270, 303 P.2d 1; Estate of Campbell, 28 Cal.App.2d 102, 103 et seq., 82 P.2d 22), the possible occurrence of such a delay was so remote and unlikely that an attorney of ordinary skill acting under the same circumstances might well have "fallen into the net which the Rule spreads for the unwary" and failed to recognize the danger. . . .

The third cause of action contains additional allegations as follows: After admission of the will and codicils to probate, Harold Houghton Emmick, Walton Russell Emmick, Clelta Inez Spelman, and Retha Newell, hereinafter called the contestants, instituted a will contest. The executors, defendant, and the contestants tentatively reached a settlement agreement, subject to court approval, under which $10,000 would be paid to the contestants from the assets of the estate in return for which each contestant would sign an "appropriate release." Defendant was negligent in the performance of his duties in that he caused to be executed on behalf of the estate and those interested therein, including plaintiffs, releases which did not preclude the contestants from a subsequent attack upon the validity of the testamentary instruments. After complete execution of the releases and their transmittal to escrow but before approval of the compromise by the court, defendant was advised by competent counsel that the residual clause of the will and codicils was invalid as a violation of the rule against perpetuities and that as a consequence the phraseology of the releases was inadequate to protect the estate and persons interested therein, and defendant was requested by competent counsel to modify the releases and insert appropriate language suggested by counsel under which the contestants would release the estate and persons interested in it from any claims of whatsoever kind or nature. Defendant refused to do so and also refused to call the court's attention to the recommendations. As a consequence of the failure to direct the matter to the attention of the court, the order approving the compromise was made on the assumption that the releases would give adequate protection. The sum of $10,000 was paid to the contestants from the assets of the estate, and the releases were filed in the proceedings. Subsequently the contestants joined in a legal attack upon the validity of the residual clause of the will and codicils and by virtue of the invalidity of the clause participated in the settlement referred to above concerning paragraph Eighth of the will. If the releases had been prepared in accord with good legal practice they would have precluded such participation, with the result that plaintiffs would have received an additional sum of $15,000 from the estate.

This cause of action, unlike the first two, does not concern defendant's conduct as attorney for the testator, but, rather, asserted negligence by him when acting as attorney for the executors with respect to the execution of releases in the settlement of a will contest based on lack of testamentary capacity. It is undisputed that the releases were adequate to preclude any further litigation of that contest, but plaintiffs assert that defendant had a duty to obtain releases which, in addition, would waive all other claims of the contestants against the estate and prevent them from subsequently attacking the validity of the trust provisions.

There are no allegations that the contestants, either at the time of the negotiations for the settlement or at the time of the signing of the releases, were willing to waive their rights to make other attacks upon the will after the settlement of that contest. In the absence of additional allegations we must assume that the agreed sum of $10,000 was intended solely for the settlement of the contest and the ground on which it was based, i.e., lack of testamentary capacity, and it would ordinarily be expected that the contestants would have demanded an additional sum for a more extensive waiver terminating their rights to attack the validity of the various provisions of the will. The written releases, of course, were required to conform to the settlement agreement. Under these circumstances it could well be argued that the attorneys for the contestants would have been derelict in their duty to their clients if they had approved broader releases. At most, under the allegations, defendant had a duty to request that the contestants sign broader releases, but there is no allegation that he failed to ask them to do so. The third count does not state a cause of action for negligence.

Although defendant pointed out in both the trial court and this court that there is no allegation that he could have secured releases different from the ones given, plaintiffs make no claim that they can amend their complaint so as to cure the deficiency, and we cannot properly hold that the trial court abused its discretion in denying leave to amend.

The judgment is affirmed.

TRAYNOR, SCHAUER, MCCOMB, PETERS, WHITE and DOOLING, JJ., concur.

Liability to Third Parties for Malpractice

The traditional rule is that absent fraud, collusion, or privity of contract, an attorney is not liable to a third party for professional malpractice. National Savings Bank v. Ward, 100 U.S. 195 (1880). But a growing number of jurisdictions have abandoned the requirement of privity of contract, either by using a balancing of factors approach or by employing a third party beneficiary theory. See *Greycas, Inc. v. Proud,* and the notes that follow it in Chapter 2 above.

Intended Beneficiaries of a Will

A number of state courts follow the holding in *Lucas v. Hamm,* allowing a claim for malpractice by the intended beneficiaries of a will. See, e.g., Schreiner v. Scoville, 410 N.W.2d 679 (Iowa 1987); Auric v. Continental Cas. Co., 111 Wis.2d 507, 331 N.W.2d 325 (1983); and Lorraine v. Grover, 467 So.2d 315 (Fla.1985).

In *Lorraine,* the Florida court reaffirmed the traditional rule that privity was required but recognized an exception for the beneficiaries of a will to whom lawyers have a "direct duty." For a similar approach see Needham v. Hamilton, 459 A.2d 1060 (D.C.App.1983). Pennsylvania reached the same result but refused to do so under tort law. Guy v. Liederbach, 501 Pa. 47, 459 A.2d 744 (1983). Rejecting California's balancing of factors as unworkable, the Pennsylvania Supreme Court settled instead on liability to the intended beneficiary under Restatement (Second) Contract § 302(1) (1981) (intended beneficiaries of a contract may recover on the contract when necessary to effectuate the intention of the parties to the contract). See also Hale v. Groce, 304 Or. 281, 744 P.2d 1289 (1987) (intended beneficiary's tort action barred by statute of limitations but may proceed under contract theory); and Stowe v. Smith, 184 Conn. 194, 441 A.2d 81 (1981); but see Krawczyk v. Stingle, 208 Conn. 239, 543 A.2d 733 (1988) (intended beneficiaries had no claim when they had been disinherited because the lawyer failed to arrange for timely execution of the estate planning documents and the testator died before the documents were executed).

New York, however, has rejected negligence claims against lawyers brought by the intended beneficiaries of wills, see, e.g., Victor v. Goldman, 74 Misc.2d 685, 344 N.Y.S.2d 672 (1973), aff'd, 43 A.D.2d 1021, 351 N.Y.S.2d 956 (2d Dept.1974), as well as negligence claims by other third parties. In 1983 a New York court summarized the current law on third party liability in that state: "It is thus evident that New York has not retreated from the requirement of privity in legal malpractice cases." Calamari v. Grace, 98 A.D.2d 74, 469 N.Y.S.2d 942 (1983). But see Crossland Saving FSB v. Rockwood Insurance Co., 700 F.Supp. 1274 (S.D.N.Y.1988) (holding that New York recognizes a lawyer's liability to third parties for negligent misrepresentation in some circumstances). Crossland is discussed in the notes following *Greycas* in Chapter 2 above.

In Metzker v. Slocum, 272 Or. 313, 537 P.2d 74 (1975), a lawyer had been hired 10 years earlier to carry out an adoption. As a result of his negligence the adoption was never perfected. The parents subsequently divorced and the minor child was left without support. The child sued the lawyer for negligence. The Oregon court held that the lawyer was not liable to the child, a third party to the original transaction. The court said that even applying the liberal California test for third party liability (balancing various factors) there would be no liability because the relationship between the negligence and the harm was too tenuous and the foreseeability of harm to the child was minimal. The latter proposition seems absurd, doesn't it?

Overview of the Tort of Malpractice

The elements of a legal malpractice claim are:

1. an attorney-client relationship or, in those jurisdictions that have rejected privity, some other showing that there was a duty to the plaintiff, i.e., that the primary purpose of the attorney-client relationship was to directly benefit or influence the plaintiff;

2. a failure by the lawyer to exercise the care, skill or diligence that reasonably competent lawyers exercise under similar circumstances;

3. proximate cause, i.e., the lawyer's failure has to be shown to have been the proximate cause of the plaintiff's injury;

4. damages, i.e., a showing that but for the lawyer's conduct the plaintiff would have achieved a different and more advantageous result in the transaction or litigation.

See Togstad v. Vesely, Otto, Miller & Keefe, 291 N.W.2d 686 (Minn. 1980), printed in Chapter 6 below and the notes following it for a discussion of when, for purposes of a legal malpractice claim, an attorney-client relationship will be found to exist.

The law of malpractice is a subject in itself. In the notes that follow, we touch on only a few of the many questions in this area. For more general treatment of this subject see Mallen and Smith, Legal Malpractice (3d ed. 1989); Wolfram, Modern Legal Ethics § 5.6 et seq. (1986); Prosser and Keeton on Torts pp. 185 et seq. (5th ed. 1984). There is a literature on subsidiary problems such as use of expert testimony, e.g., Liebson, Legal Malpractice Cases: Special Problems in Identifying Issues of Law and Fact and in the Use of Expert Testimony, 75 Ky.L.J. 1 (1986–87); accrual of the cause of action and tolling of the statute of limitations through continuation of the lawyer-client relationship, Koffler, Legal Malpractice Statutes of Limitations: A Critical Analysis of a Burgeoning Crisis, 20 Akron L.Rev. 209 (1986); liability for particular types of mistakes, e.g., Note, Liability of Attorneys for Legal Opinions Under the Federal Securities Laws, 27 B.C.L.Rev. 325 (1986).

Note on the Standard of Care

The decision in *Lucas* suggests that judges as well as lawyers have trouble understanding the rule against perpetuities. If a reasonably competent lawyer could not be expected to understand the rule against perpetuities, is it equitable that courts apply it to disinherit people? What about complicated tax and securities problems? Complicated problems of criminal procedure?

In Smith v. Lewis, 13 Cal.3d 349, 530 P.2d 589 (1975), the California Supreme Court held a lawyer liable for failing to assert his client's community interest in the retirement benefits of the client's spouse. The lawyer argued that the law on retirement benefits was so unclear at the time he represented the plaintiff that he could not be liable for making a mistake as to it. Apparently at the time of the representation, the California Supreme Court had not ruled on the status of retirement benefits, but appellate court authority existed for treating the spouse's state retirement benefits as community property. The court cited the standard of care articulated in *Lucas* and said that under this standard it was necessary for the court to examine the "indicia of the law . . . readily available" to the lawyer at the time of the representation. The court reviewed "the major authoritative reference works which attorneys routinely consult for a brief and reliable exposition of the law" and found that they all indicated that vested state retirement benefits were generally treated as community property. The works examined by the court included A.L.R.; Am.Jur.2d; Cal. Jur.2d; and a hornbook on California law. The court noted that the status of *federal* retirement benefits was more questionable in 1967, but that the lawyer failed to conduct reasonable research into their proper characterization.

In holding the lawyer liable for failing to assert his client's interest in the state and federal retirement benefits, the court said:

If the law on a particular subject is doubtful or debatable, an attorney will not be held responsible for failing to anticipate the manner in which the uncertainty will be resolved. . . . But even with respect to an unsettled area of the law, we believe an attorney assumes an obligation to his client to undertake reasonable research in an effort to ascertain relevant legal principles and to make an informed decision as to a course of conduct based upon an intelligent assessment of the problem. . . .

Smith, 530 P.2d at 595.

The duty to conduct a reasonable investigation of applicable law set forth in *Smith* holds lawyers to a higher standard than suggested by *Lucas*. Nevertheless, the court in *Smith* did not retreat from the position on the rule against perpetuities stated in *Lucas*:

[N]o lawyer would suggest the property characterization of . . . retirement benefits to be so esoteric an issue that defendant could not reasonably have been expected to be aware of it or its probable resolution. (*Lucas v. Hamm* [cite omitted]). In *Lucas* we held that the rule against perpetuities poses such complex and difficult problems for the draftsman that even careful and competent attorneys occasionally fall prey to its traps. The situation before us is not analogous.

Id. at 596.

Also see Aloy v. Mash, 38 Cal.3d 413, 696 P.2d 656 (1985) (employing the reasonable investigation standard of *Smith* and repeating in dicta the distinction between less difficult areas of law and the rule against perpetuities).

In The T.J. Hooper, 60 F.2d 737, 740 (2d Cir.1932), Judge Learned Hand wrote:

[I]n most cases reasonable prudence is in fact common prudence; but strictly it is never its measure; a whole calling may have unduly lagged in the adoption of new and available devices. It never may set its own tests, however persuasive be its usages. Courts must in the end say what is required; there are precautions so imperative that even their universal disregard will not excuse their omission.

In *The T.J. Hooper* the court found the defendant negligent for not having a working radio set aboard its tug boat. It is interesting to note that, contrary to what Hand's language suggests, most tugs did have radios. See The T.J. Hooper, 53 F.2d 107, 111 (S.D.N.Y.1931). [The authors thank Professor Roger C. Cramton of Cornell, who after reading an earlier draft of this book, suggested that we check the facts in *The T.J. Hooper*. This shows how helpful consulting with others can be and how important it is to read carefully the original case, no matter how sure one is about what it says.]

Although professions are shown considerable deference, there are examples of a profession's practice being held to be negligent. For example, it is the general practice of surgeons to delegate to a nurse the job of keeping track of the sponges during an operation. Nevertheless, this practice has been found to be negligent. See, e.g., Truhitte v. French Hospital, 128 Cal.App.3d 332, 180 Cal.Rptr. 152 (1982).

In Gleason v. Title Guarantee Co., 300 F.2d 813 (5th Cir.1962) a lawyer, instead of checking titles, relied on telephone conversations with the title company, which was the customary practice of lawyers in that area of Florida. The court, citing *The T.J. Hooper,* said that what is customary is no defense if the custom is negligent itself. Even if most lawyers misunderstand the rule against perpetuities, should it be negligent for a lawyer to draft a will with future interest provisions if she does not understand the rule?

National Standard or That of the Local Legal Community

Kellos v. Sawilowsky, 172 Ga.App. 263, 322 S.E.2d 897 (1985) held that the standard to be applied was that of lawyers practicing in the state of Georgia but noted that in practice it would make little difference whether one applied a national or local standard.

Walker v. Bangs, 92 Wash.2d 854, 601 P.2d 1279 (1979), held that if a lawyer holds himself out as specializing in a particular field, he "will be held to the standard of performance of those who hold themselves out as specialists in the area". Compare Mayo v. Engel, 733 F.2d 807 (11th Cir.1984), which held that a lawyer was not liable for professional negligence in a trademark search where the firm never held itself out to be expert in trademark work. Should the firm be liable for accepting the representation?

In Horne v. Peckham, 97 Cal.App.3d 404, 158 Cal.Rptr. 714 (1979), the lawyer, after consulting "the client's accountant . . ., a two volume set of American Jurisprudence" and a tax "expert" who, unknown to the lawyer, had been admitted to the bar only one year earlier, drew up a trust to shelter the client's money from federal taxes. Not surprisingly, the lawyer botched it and the trust failed to accomplish its purpose. The lawyer testified that he told the client he had "no expertise in tax matters." The court affirmed the jury verdict against the lawyer for malpractice and approved a jury instruction that it "is the duty of an attorney who is a general practitioner to refer his client to a specialist or recommend the assistance of a specialist if under the circumstances a reasonably careful and skillful practitioner would do so." 158 Cal.Rptr. at 720. If no expert is consulted, the lawyer will be held to the standard of a specialist in the field.

Expert Testimony in Malpractice Cases

The plaintiff in a malpractice action generally must produce expert testimony to establish both the level of care owed by the attorney under the circumstances and the failure to conform to that level of care. See Wagenmann v. Adams, 829 F.2d 196, 218 (1st Cir.1987); Progressive Sales v. Williams, Willeford, Boger, Grady & Davis, 86 N.C.App. 51, 356

S.E.2d 372 (1987). A somewhat ironic example of the use of expert testimony is provided by Waldman v. Levine, 544 A.2d 683 (D.C.App. 1988). In *Waldman,* the lawyers advised the client to settle a medical malpractice claim for little over $2,000 without consulting a medical expert in OB/GYN matters; the client's claim was that her daughter's death after childbirth was due to obstetric malpractice. The expert in the malpractice case against the lawyers testified that failing to consult an OB/GYN expert in such a case was "conduct . . . below the minimum standard of care for attorneys in medical malpractice cases." 544 A.2d at 687. The court affirmed the jury's verdict against the lawyers and the award of $600,000 in damages.

Expert testimony is generally unnecessary "when the attorney's lack of care and skill is so obvious that the trier of fact can find negligence as a matter of common knowledge." O'Neil v. Bergan, 452 A.2d 337, 341 (D.C.App.1982). See also, e.g., *Wagenmann,* supra, at 220, holding expert testimony was unnecessary to establish that a lawyer committed malpractice against a client, who had been arrested for disturbing the peace, by telling the client that his only alternatives were to leave town immediately or commit himself to a mental hospital and by taking no action to secure the client's release when the client was involuntarily committed. Examples of other cases where expert testimony was held to be unnecessary include: Sorenson v. Fio Rito, 90 Ill.App.3d 368, 413 N.E.2d 47, 53 (1980) (failure to take any action with regard to estate matters); Olfe v. Gordon, 93 Wis.2d 173, 286 N.W.2d 573, 578 (1980) (client insisted that his divorce be kept out of the newpapers; lawyer promised to do so, but the law required that the divorce be published and lawyer arranged for publication without notifying client); George v. Caton, 93 N.M. 370, 600 P.2d 822, 829 (1979) (failure to sue before expiration of limitations period). Georgia requires that an expert's affidavit be filed in order to maintain an action for malpractice. Ga.Code Ann. 9–11–9.1. This provision was upheld against a challenge that it was unconstitutional in Patterson v. Atlanta Bar Assn., 373 S.E.2d 514 (Ga.1988), cert. denied, 109 S.Ct. 1135 (1989).

Not long ago it was extremely difficult to get one lawyer to testify against another in a malpractice action. Today, it is much easier, although in some areas of the country it is more difficult than in others and in all communities with relatively few lawyers, the need for expert testimony may still present a nearly insurmountable barrier to successful suit. In *Patterson,* supra, the plaintiffs claimed, *inter alia,* that individual members of the bar and various bar associations were engaged in a conspiracy to prevent lawyers from testifying as expert witnesses in malpractice cases. The court found that no evidence of conspiracy had been presented. Nevertheless, the filing of such a suit lends some support to the proposition that finding a lawyer to testify against another lawyer is still not a simple matter.

The Obligation to Report Professional Misconduct of Other Lawyers

Connected to the question of the unwillingness of lawyers to testify against other lawyers is the widely ignored obligation under both the Code and Rules to report the professional misconduct of other lawyers. DR 1–103(A) and M.R. 8.3. On the widespread neglect of these rules, see Wolfram, Modern Legal Ethics § 12.10.1 n. 17 at 683 (1986). The Model Rules narrow the scope of the obligation to report misconduct from that in the Code in two respects: (1) M.R. 8.3(a) requires a lawyer to report only those violations that raise "a substantial question as to the lawyer's honesty, trustworthiness or fitness as a lawyer in other respects"; (2) the Rules do not require a lawyer to report if knowledge of the violation is based on client confidences, M.R. 8.3(c). In contrast, the Code requires a lawyer to report all violations, with an exception only for information based on "privileged" communications. Presumably this covers only information protected by the attorney-client privilege and not, for example, information learned from a third party in the course of representing a client. See Chapter 4 below on the difference between confidential information and privileged communications. There are few instances of lawyers being disciplined for violating the reporting requirements, but one recent instance demonstrates that serious consequences may result.

In In re Himmel, 125 Ill.2d 531, 533 N.E.2d 790 (1988), the client's first lawyer, Casey, stole the client's settlement money. The client retained Himmel to get her money back, agreeing to pay him one-third of anything she recovered. Himmel negotiated a settlement and drafted an agreement that provided for Casey to pay the client slightly over three times the amount he misappropriated. The agreement included a promise by the client not to initiate criminal, civil or disciplinary action against Casey. Casey did not honor the agreement and Himmel ultimately filed suit against Casey on behalf of the client, who was awarded $100,000 in damages.

Himmel never informed the Disciplinary Commission of Casey's misconduct and based on this failure Himmel was charged with violating DR 1–103(A). The court rejected Himmel's argument that he had no duty to report a violation that the client had already reported, stating that the actions of a client cannot relieve a lawyer of duties under the Code. The court also rejected his argument that the client requested that he not report the matter, stating that as an officer of the court a lawyer could not avoid his ethical responsibilities based on a client's request. It also found that Himmel's knowledge of the violation was not based on privileged information and that therefore the exception to the reporting duty did not apply. The information was held to be outside the attorney-client privilege because the client had communicated the information to the lawyer while in the presence of unnecessary third parties. This normally destroys any claim of attorney-client privilege, see Chapter 4 below at p. 200, but it has no effect on the lawyer's duty to keep confidences. On this point, the broader exception in the Rules would dictate a different result.

The court suspended Himmel from the practice of law for one year. Particularly troublesome to the court was that both Himmel and his client "ran afoul" of the criminal code's prohibition against compounding a crime, which prohibits receiving consideration in exchange for agreeing not to prosecute or report a crime, here the original theft of the client's money.

Compare Wisconsin State Bar Committee on Professional Discipline, Formal Opinion E–89–1Z, May 24, 1989, ABA/BNA Lawyer's Manual, p. 236, interpreting the Wisconsin version of the Model Rules, and holding that a lawyer has no duty to report if the client instructs the lawyer not to, which of course the client will do if the lawyer so advises.

Limiting Liability to the Client for Malpractice

DR 6–102 prohibits a lawyer from contracting with the client to limit the lawyer's malpractice liability. M.R. 1.8(h) relaxes the absolute ban by providing that a lawyer may prospectively limit her malpractice liability to the client but only if permitted under applicable state law *and* the client is independently represented. Further, M.R. 1.8(h) prohibits a lawyer from settling a malpractice claim with a client or former client who is not represented by independent counsel unless the lawyer first advises the client in writing that independent representation would be appropriate. There is no similar provision in the Code. In In re Tallon, 86 A.D.2d 897, 447 N.Y.S.2d 50 (1982), the court disciplined a lawyer for having his client sign a general release of all malpractice claims against him without first notifying her of the nature of her potential claims, withdrawing from the representation and advising her of her right to retain independent representation in the matter. See also In re Weiblen, 439 N.W.2d 7 (Minn.1989) (lawyer attempted to obtain complete release from liability for any malpractice); Committee on Legal Ethics v. Hazlett, 367 S.E.2d 772 (W.Va.1988) (request for malpractice release as a condition of turning over client's files). Generally see Gross, Contractual Limitations on Attorney Malpractice Liability: An Economic Approach, 75 Kentucky L.J. 793 (1986–87).

Malpractice Insurance

The cost of maintaining legal malpractice insurance has risen dramatically in the last ten years. In California, one commentator reported, insurance premiums in 1986 had "more than quadrupled from $65,000 to $300,000 for each lawyer." Uninsured and Insecure, California Lawyer 59, June 1987. More lawyers and firms now forego insurance altogether—"go bare." Should lawyers be required to carry malpractice insurance as a condition of practice? See Schneyer, Mandatory Malpractice Insurance for Lawyers in Wisconsin and Elsewhere, 1979 Wis.L.Rev. 1019 (presenting a study on the need for mandatory insurance); and Wolfram, Modern Legal Ethics § 5.6.8 (1986) (arguing that mandatory insurance may not be efficient). Or. Rev.Stat. § 9.080 requires that lawyers have insurance. In Hass v. Oregon State Bar, 883 F.2d 1453 (9th Cir.1989), the court upheld Oregon's requirement that all Oregon-based lawyers purchase primary malpractice insurance from the state bar against a challenge that it violated the antitrust laws and the Commerce Clause of the Constitution.

Policies for legal malpractice insurance typically exclude from coverage: (1) claims arising out of criminal acts of the lawyer; (2) claims arising out of "any dishonest, fraudulent or malicious act, error or omission" of the lawyer; and (3) "punitive or exemplary damages, fines, sanctions or penalties." In Perl v. St. Paul Fire & Marine Insurance Co., 345 N.W.2d 209 (Minn.1984), the lawyers had failed to disclose to the client that the insurance adjuster with whom the firm negotiated on the client's behalf worked for the law firm as an investigator. The client was awarded as damages a full refund of the fees she had paid the lawyers. The lawyer's insurance company refused to pay, claiming that such damages were excluded by the policy's terms and if not excluded, the policy was void as against public policy. The court held there was coverage: (1) the exclusion for fraudulent acts did not exclude breach of a fiduciary duty, which is "constructive" not "actual" fraud; and (2) reimbursement of attorney's fees was not the equivalent of "exemplary or punitive damages," which the policy excluded from coverage. However, the court held that a policy that insures lawyers against loss of attorney's fees upon breach of their fiduciary duties is void as against public policy. The force of this opinion, however, is vitiated by the court's final holding that the policy was not void to the extent that it insured the firm as opposed to the individual lawyer who committed the breach. Which of the court's conflicting messages is the right one?

Violation of Ethical Rules as a Basis for Malpractice

The Preliminary Statement to the Model Code of Professional Responsibility states that the Code "does not undertake to define standards for civil liability of lawyers for professional conduct." The Scope Section of Model Rule states: "Violation of a Rule should not give rise to a cause of action nor should it create any presumption that a legal duty has been breached."

Why not? Does this mean that reasonably careful lawyers breach the Rules on occasion?

Compare Lipton v. Boesky, 110 Mich.App. 589, 313 N.W.2d 163, 166–67 (1981): "The Code of Professional Responsibility is a standard of practice for attorneys which expresses in general terms the standards of professional conduct expected of lawyers in their relationships with the public, the legal system and the profession. Holding a specific client unable to rely on the same standards in his professional relations with his own attorney would be patently unfair. We hold that, as with statutes, a violation of the Code is rebuttable evidence of malpractice." See also Wolfram, Modern Legal Ethics § 2.6.1 (1986); Miami International Realty Co. v. Paynter, 841 F.2d 348, 352 (10th Cir.1988) ("Colorado courts have not decided how its Code of Professional Responsibility is to be treated as an element of proof in a malpractice case," although it appears clear that under Colorado case law the Code does not create a private cause of action.).

B. EFFECTIVE ASSISTANCE OF COUNSEL UNDER THE SIXTH AMENDMENT

STRICKLAND v. WASHINGTON

Supreme Court of the United States, 1984.
466 U.S. 668, 104 S.Ct. 2052, 80 L.Ed.2d 674.

JUSTICE O'CONNOR delivered the opinion of the Court.

This case requires us to consider the proper standards for judging a criminal defendant's contention that the Constitution requires a conviction or death sentence to be set aside because counsel's assistance at the trial or sentencing was ineffective.

I

A

During a 10–day period in September 1976, respondent planned and committed three groups of crimes, which included three brutal stabbing murders, torture, kidnapping, severe assaults, attempted murders, attempted extortion, and theft. After his two accomplices were arrested, respondent surrendered to police and voluntarily gave a lengthy statement confessing to the third of the criminal episodes. The State of Florida indicted respondent for kidnaping and murder and appointed an experienced criminal lawyer to represent him.

Counsel actively pursued pretrial motions and discovery. He cut his efforts short, however, and he experienced a sense of hopelessness about the case, when he learned that, against his specific advice, respondent had also confessed to the first two murders. By the date set for trial, respondent was subject to indictment for three counts of first-degree murder and multiple counts of robbery, kidnaping for ransom, breaking and entering and assault, attempted murder, and conspiracy to commit robbery. Respondent waived his right to a jury trial, again acting against counsel's advice, and pleaded guilty to all charges, including the three capital murder charges.

In the plea colloquy, respondent told the trial judge that, although he had committed a string of burglaries, he had no significant prior criminal record and that at the time of his criminal spree he was under extreme stress caused by his inability to support his family. . . . He also stated, however, that he accepted responsibility for the crimes. . . . The trial judge told respondent that he had "a great deal of respect for people who are willing to step forward and admit their responsibility" but that he was making no statement at all about his likely sentencing decision.

Counsel advised respondent to invoke his right under Florida law to an advisory jury at his capital sentencing hearing. Respondent rejected the advice and waived the right. He chose instead to be sentenced by the trial judge without a jury recommendation.

In preparing for the sentencing hearing, counsel spoke with respondent about his background. He also spoke on the telephone with respondent's wife and mother, though he did not follow up on the one unsuccessful effort to meet with them. He did not otherwise seek out character witnesses for respondent. . . . Nor did he request a psychiatric examination, since his conversations with his client gave no indication that respondent had psychological problems. . . .

Counsel decided not to present and hence not to look further for evidence concerning respondent's character and emotional state. That decision reflected trial counsel's sense of hopelessness about overcoming the evidentiary effect of respondent's confessions to the gruesome crimes. It also reflected the judgment that it was advisable to rely on the plea colloquy for evidence about respondent's background and about his claim of emotional stress: the plea colloquy communicated sufficient information about these subjects, and by forgoing the opportunity to present new evidence on these subjects, counsel prevented the State from cross-examining respondent on his claim and from putting on psychiatric evidence of its own. . . .

Counsel also excluded from the sentencing hearing other evidence he thought was potentially damaging. He successfully moved to exclude respondent's "rap sheet." . . . Because he judged that a presentence report might prove more detrimental than helpful, as it would have included respondent's criminal history and thereby would have undermined the claim of no significant history of criminal activity, he did not request that one be prepared. . . .

At the sentencing hearing, counsel's strategy was based primarily on the trial judge's remarks at the plea colloquy as well as on his reputation as a sentencing judge who thought it important for a convicted defendant to own up to his crime. Counsel argued that respondent's remorse and acceptance of responsibility justified sparing him from the death penalty. . . . Counsel also argued that respondent had no history of criminal activity and that respondent committed the crimes under extreme mental or emotional disturbance, thus coming within the statutory list of mitigating circumstances. He further argued that respondent should be spared death because he had surrendered, confessed, and offered to testify against a codefendant and because respondent was fundamentally a good person who had briefly gone badly wrong in extremely stressful circumstances. The State put on evidence and witnesses largely for the purpose of describing the details of the crimes. Counsel did not cross-examine the medical experts who testified about the manner of death of respondent's victims.

The trial judge found several aggravating circumstances with respect to each of the three murders. He found that all three murders were especially heinous, atrocious, and cruel, all involving repeated stabbings. All three murders were committed in the course of at least one other dangerous and violent felony, and since all involved robbery, the murders were for pecuniary gain. All three murders were committed to avoid arrest for the accompanying crimes and to hinder law enforcement. In the course of one of the murders, respondent knowingly subjected numerous persons to a grave risk of death by deliberately stabbing and shooting the murder victim's sisters-in-law, who sustained severe—in one case, ultimately fatal—injuries.

With respect to mitigating circumstances, the trial judge made the same findings for all three capital murders. First, although there was no admitted evidence of prior convictions, respondent had stated that he had engaged in a course of stealing. In any case, even if respondent had no significant history of criminal activity, the aggravating circumstances "would still clearly far outweigh" that mitigating factor. Second, the judge found that, during all three crimes, respondent was not suffering from extreme mental or emotional disturbance and could appreciate the criminality of his acts. Third, none of the victims was a participant in, or consented to, respondent's conduct. Fourth, respondent's participation in the crimes was neither minor nor the result of duress or domination by an accomplice. Finally, respondent's age (26) could not be considered a factor in mitigation, especially when viewed in light of respondent's planning of the crimes and disposition of the proceeds of the various accompanying thefts.

In short, the trial judge found numerous aggravating circumstances and no (or a single comparatively insignificant) mitigating circumstance. With respect to each of the three convictions for capital murder, the trial judge concluded: "A careful consideration of all matters presented to the court impels the conclusion that there are insufficient mitigating circumstances . . . to outweigh the aggravating circumstances." See Washington v. State, 362 So.2d 658, 663–664 (Fla. 1978), (quoting trial court findings), cert. denied, 441 U.S. 937, 99 S.Ct. 2063, 60 L.Ed.2d 666 (1979). He therefore sentenced respondent to death on each of the three counts of murder and to prison terms for the other crimes. The Florida Supreme Court upheld the convictions and sentences on direct appeal.

B

Respondent subsequently sought collateral relief in state court on numerous grounds, among them that counsel had rendered ineffective assistance at the sentencing proceeding. Respondent challenged counsel's assistance in six respects. He asserted that counsel was ineffective because he failed to move for a continuance to prepare for sentencing, to request a psychiatric report, to investigate and present character witnesses, to seek a presentence investigation report, to present meaningful arguments to the sentencing judge, and to investigate the medical examiner's reports or cross-examine the medical experts. In support of the claim, respondent submitted 14 affidavits from friends, neighbors, and relatives stating that they would have testified if asked to do so. He also submitted one psychiatric report and one psychological report stating that respondent, though not under the influence of extreme mental or emotional disturbance, was "chronically frustrated and depressed because of his economic dilemma" at the time of his crimes. . . .

The trial court denied relief without an evidentiary hearing, finding that the record evidence conclusively showed that the ineffectiveness claim was meritless. . . . Four of the assertedly prejudicial errors required little discussion. [The trial court dealt with two of the asserted errors at greater length: the failure to investigate and present character witnesses. As to both of these grounds, the court concluded under] the standard for ineffectiveness claims articulated by the Florida Supreme Court in Knight v. State, 394 So.2d 997 (1981), that respondent had not shown that counsel's assistance reflected any substantial and serious deficiency measurably below that of competent counsel that was likely to have affected the outcome of the sentencing proceeding. The court specifically found: "[A]s a matter of law, the record affirmatively demonstrates beyond any doubt that even if [counsel] had done each of the . . . things [that respondent alleged counsel had failed to do] at the time of sentencing, there is not even the remotest chance that the outcome would have been any different. The plain fact is that the aggravating circumstances proved in this case were completely *overwhelming*. . . ."

. . .

C

Respondent next filed a petition for a writ of habeas corpus in the United States District Court for the Southern District of Florida. . . .

. . . On the legal issue of ineffectiveness, the District Court concluded that, although trial counsel made errors in judgment in failing to investigate nonstatutory mitigating evidence further than he did, no prejudice to respondent's sentence resulted from any such error in judgment. . . .

On appeal, a panel of the United States Court of Appeals for the Fifth Circuit affirmed in part, vacated in part, and remanded with instructions to apply to the particular facts the framework for analyzing ineffectiveness claims that it developed in its opinion. . . . The panel decision was itself vacated when . . . the Eleventh Circuit, decided to rehear the case en banc. The full Court of Appeals developed its own framework for analyzing ineffective assistance claims and reversed the judgment of the District Court and remanded the case for new factfinding under the newly announced standards.

. . .

Turning to the merits, the Court of Appeals stated that the Sixth Amendment right to assistance of counsel accorded criminal defendants a right to "counsel reasonably likely to render and rendering reasonably effective assistance given the totality of the circumstances." The court remarked in passing that no special standard applies in capital cases such as the one before it: the punishment that a defendant faces is merely one of the circumstances to be considered in determining whether counsel was reasonably effective. . . .

[W]e granted certiorari to consider the standards by which to judge a contention that the Constitution requires that a criminal judgment be overturned because of the actual ineffective assistance of counsel.

II

In a long line of cases . . . this Court has recognized that the Sixth Amendment right to counsel exists, and is needed, in order to protect the fundamental right to a fair trial. . . .

. . .

For that reason, the Court has recognized that "the right to counsel is the right to the effective assistance of counsel." . . .

The Court has not elaborated on the meaning of the constitutional requirement of effective assistance in cases—presenting claims of "actual ineffectiveness." In giving meaning to the requirement, however, we must take its purpose—to ensure a fair trial—as the guide. The benchmark for judging any claim of ineffectiveness must be whether counsel's conduct so undermined the proper functioning of the adversarial process that the trial cannot be relied on as having produced a just result.

The same principle applies to a capital sentencing proceeding such as that provided by Florida law. . . .

III

A convicted defendant's claim that counsel's assistance was so defective as to require reversal of a conviction or death sentence has two components. First, the defendant must show that counsel's performance was deficient. This requires showing that counsel made errors so serious that counsel was not functioning as the "counsel" guaranteed the defendant by the Sixth Amendment. Second, the defendant must show that the deficient performance prejudiced the defense. This requires showing that counsel's errors were so serious as to deprive the defendant of a fair trial, a trial whose result is reliable. Unless a defendant makes both showings, it cannot be said that the conviction or death sentence resulted from a breakdown in the adversary process that renders the result unreliable.

A

As all the Federal Courts of Appeals have now held, the proper standard for attorney performance is that of reasonably effective assistance. . . . The Court indirectly recognized as much when it stated in McMann v. Richardson, 397 U.S. [759], 770, 771, that a guilty plea cannot be attacked as based on inadequate legal advice unless counsel was not "a reasonably competent attorney" and the advice was not "within the range of competence demanded of attorneys in criminal cases." See also Cuyler v. Sullivan, 446 U.S. [335], 344. When a convicted defendant complains of the ineffectiveness of counsel's assistance, the defendant must show that counsel's representation fell below an objective standard of reasonableness.

More specific guidelines are not appropriate. The Sixth Amendment refers simply to "counsel," not specifying particular requirements of effective assistance. It relies instead on the legal profession's maintenance of standards sufficient to justify the law's presumption that counsel will fulfill the role in the adversary process that the Amendment envisions. . . . The proper measure of attorney performance remains simply reasonableness under prevailing professional norms.

Representation of a criminal defendant entails certain basic duties. Counsel's function is to assist the defendant, and hence counsel owes the client a duty of loyalty, a duty to avoid conflicts of interest. . . . From counsel's function as assistant to the defendant derive the overarching duty to advocate the defendant's cause and the more particular duties to consult with the defendant on important decisions and to keep the defendant informed of important developments in the course of the prosecution. Counsel also has a duty to bring to bear such skill and knowledge as will render the trial a reliable adversarial testing process. . . .

These basic duties neither exhaustively define the obligations of counsel nor form a checklist for judicial evaluation of attorney performance. In any case presenting an ineffectiveness claim, the performance inquiry must be whether counsel's assistance was reasonable considering all the circumstances. Prevailing norms of practice as reflected in American Bar Association standards and the like . . ., are guides to determining what is reasonable, but they are only guides. No particular set of detailed rules for counsel's conduct can satisfactorily take account of the variety of circumstances faced by defense counsel or the range of legitimate decisions regarding how best to represent a criminal defendant. Any such set of rules would interfere with the constitutionally protected independence of counsel and restrict the wide latitude counsel must have in making tactical decisions. . . . Indeed, the existence of detailed guidelines for representation could distract counsel from the overriding mission of vigorous advocacy of the defendant's cause. Moreover, the purpose of the effective assistance guarantee of the Sixth Amendment is not to improve the quality of legal representation, although that is a goal of considerable importance to the legal system. The purpose is simply to ensure that criminal defendants receive a fair trial.

Judicial scrutiny of counsel's performance must be highly deferential. It is all too tempting for a defendant to second-guess counsel's assistance after conviction or adverse sentence, and it is all too easy for a court, examining counsel's defense after it has proved unsuccessful, to conclude that a particular act or omission of counsel was unreasonable. . . . A fair assessment of attorney performance requires that every effort be made to eliminate the distorting effects of hindsight, to reconstruct the circumstances of counsel's challenged conduct, and to evaluate the conduct from counsel's perspective at the time. Because of the difficulties inherent in making the evaluation, a court must indulge a strong presumption that counsel's conduct falls within the wide range of reasonable professional assistance; that is, the defendant must overcome the presumption that, under the circumstances, the challenged action "might be considered sound trial strategy." See Michel v. Louisiana, 350 U.S. [91], 101. There are countless ways to provide effective assistance in any given case. Even the best criminal defense attorneys would not defend a particular client in the same way. . . .

The availability of intrusive post-trial inquiry into attorney performance or of detailed guidelines for its evaluation would encourage the proliferation of ineffectiveness challenges. Criminal trials resolved unfavorably to the defendant would increasingly come to be followed by a second trial, this one of counsel's unsuccessful defense. Counsel's performance and even willingness to serve could be adversely affected. Intensive scrutiny of counsel and rigid requirements for acceptable assistance could dampen the ardor and impair the independence of defense counsel, discourage the acceptance of assigned cases, and undermine the trust between attorney and client.

Thus, a court deciding an actual ineffectiveness claim must judge the reasonableness of counsel's challenged conduct on the facts of the particular case, viewed as of the time of counsel's conduct. A convicted defendant making a claim of ineffective assistance must identify the acts or omissions of counsel that are alleged not to have been the result of reasonable professional judgment. The court must then determine whether, in light of all the circumstances, the identified acts or omissions were outside the wide range of professionally competent assistance. In making that determination, the court should keep in mind that counsel's function, as elaborated in prevailing professional norms, is to make the adversarial testing process work in the particular case. At the same time, the court should recognize that counsel is strongly presumed to have rendered adequate assistance and made all significant decisions in the exercise of reasonable professional judgment.

These standards require no special amplification in order to define counsel's duty to investigate, the duty at issue in this case. As the

Court of Appeals concluded, strategic choices made after thorough investigation of law and facts relevant to plausible options are virtually unchallengeable; and strategic choices made after less than complete investigation are reasonable precisely to the extent that reasonable professional judgments support the limitations on investigation. In other words, counsel has a duty to make reasonable investigations or to make a reasonable decision that makes particular investigations unnecessary. In any ineffectiveness case, a particular decision not to investigate must be directly assessed for reasonableness in all the circumstances, applying a heavy measure of deference to counsel's judgments.

The reasonableness of counsel's actions may be determined or substantially influenced by the defendant's own statements or actions. Counsel's actions are usually based, quite properly, on informed strategic choices made by the defendant and on information supplied by the defendant. In particular, what investigation decisions are reasonable depends critically on such information. For example, when the facts that support a certain potential line of defense are generally known to counsel because of what the defendant has said, the need for further investigation may be considerably diminished or eliminated altogether. And when a defendant has given counsel reason to believe that pursuing certain investigations would be fruitless or even harmful, counsel's failure to pursue those investigations may not later be challenged as unreasonable. In short, inquiry into counsel's conversations with the defendant may be critical to a proper assessment of counsel's investigation decisions, just as it may be critical to a proper assessment of counsel's other litigation decisions. . . .

B

An error by counsel, even if professionally unreasonable, does not warrant setting aside the judgment of a criminal proceeding if the error had no effect on the judgment. . . . The purpose of the Sixth Amendment guarantee of counsel is to ensure that a defendant has the assistance necessary to justify reliance on the outcome of the proceeding. Accordingly, any deficiencies in counsel's performance must be prejudicial to the defense in order to constitute ineffective assistance under the Constitution.

In certain Sixth Amendment contexts, prejudice is presumed. Actual or constructive denial of the assistance of counsel altogether is legally presumed to result in prejudice. So are various kinds of state interference with counsel's assistance. . . . Prejudice in these circumstances is so likely that case-by-case inquiry into prejudice is not worth the cost. . . . Moreover, such circumstances involve impairments of the Sixth Amendment right that are easy to identify and, for that reason and because the prosecution is directly responsible, easy for the government to prevent.

One type of actual ineffectiveness claim warrants a similar, though more limited, presumption of prejudice. In Cuyler v. Sullivan, 446

U.S., at 345–350, the Court held that prejudice is presumed when counsel is burdened by an actual conflict of interest. In those circumstances, counsel breaches the duty of loyalty, perhaps the most basic of counsel's duties. Moreover, it is difficult to measure the precise effect on the defense of representation corrupted by conflicting interests. Given the obligation of counsel to avoid conflicts of interest and the ability of trial courts to make early inquiry in certain situations likely to give rise to conflicts, see, e.g., Fed.Rule Crim.Proc. 44(c), it is reasonable for the criminal justice system to maintain a fairly rigid rule of presumed prejudice for conflicts of interest. Even so, the rule is not quite the *per se* rule of prejudice that exists for the Sixth Amendment claims mentioned above. Prejudice is presumed only if the defendant demonstrates that counsel "actively represented conflicting interests" and that "an actual conflict of interest adversely affected his lawyer's performance." Cuyler v. Sullivan, *supra,* 446 U.S., at 350, 348.

Conflict of interest claims aside, actual ineffectiveness claims alleging a deficiency in attorney performance are subject to a general requirement that the defendant affirmatively prove prejudice. The government is not responsible for, and hence not able to prevent, attorney errors that will result in reversal of a conviction or sentence. Attorney errors come in an infinite variety and are as likely to be utterly harmless in a particular case as they are to be prejudicial. They cannot be classified according to likelihood of causing prejudice. Nor can they be defined with sufficient precision to inform defense attorneys correctly just what conduct to avoid. Representation is an art, and an act or omission that is unprofessional in one case may be sound or even brilliant in another. Even if a defendant shows that particular errors of counsel were unreasonable, therefore, the defendant must show that they actually had an adverse effect on the defense.

It is not enough for the defendant to show that the errors had some conceivable effect on the outcome of the proceeding. Virtually every act or omission of counsel would meet that test, . . . and not every error that conceivably could have influenced the outcome undermines the reliability of the result of the proceeding. Respondent suggests requiring a showing that the errors "impaired the presentation of the defense." That standard, however, provides no workable principle. Since any error, if it is indeed an error, "impairs" the presentation of the defense, the proposed standard is inadequate because it provides no way of deciding what impairments are sufficiently serious to warrant setting aside the outcome of the proceeding.

On the other hand, we believe that a defendant need not show that counsel's deficient conduct more likely than not altered the outcome in the case. This outcome-determinative standard has several strengths. It defines the relevant inquiry in a way familiar to courts, though the inquiry, as is inevitable, is anything but precise. The standard also reflects the profound importance of finality in criminal proceedings. Moreover, it comports with the widely used standard for assessing motions for new trial based on newly discovered evidence. . . . Nevertheless, the standard is not quite appropriate.

. . . The high standard for newly discovered evidence claims presupposes that all the essential elements of a presumptively accurate and fair proceeding were present in the proceeding whose result is challenged. . . . An ineffective assistance claim asserts the absence of one of the crucial assurances that the result of the proceeding is reliable, so finality concerns are somewhat weaker and the appropriate standard of prejudice should be somewhat lower. The result of a proceeding can be rendered unreliable, and hence the proceeding itself unfair, even if the errors of counsel cannot be shown by a preponderance of the evidence to have determined the outcome.

Accordingly, the appropriate test for prejudice finds its roots in the test for materiality of exculpatory information not disclosed to the defense by the prosecution, . . . and in the test for materiality of testimony made unavailable to the defense by Government deportation of a witness. . . . The defendant must show that there is a reasonable probability that, but for counsel's unprofessional errors, the result of the proceeding would have been different. A reasonable probability is a probability sufficient to undermine confidence in the outcome.

In making the determination whether the specified errors resulted in the required prejudice, a court should presume, absent challenge to the judgment on grounds of evidentiary insufficiency, that the judge or jury acted according to law. An assessment of the likelihood of a result more favorable to the defendant must exclude the possibility of arbitrariness, whimsy, caprice, "nullification," and the like. A defendant has no entitlement to the luck of a lawless decisionmaker, even if a lawless decision cannot be reviewed. The assessment of prejudice should proceed on the assumption that the decisionmaker is reasonably, conscientiously, and impartially applying the standards that govern the decision. It should not depend on the idiosyncracies of the particular decisionmaker, such as unusual propensities toward harshness or leniency. Although these factors may actually have entered into counsel's selection of strategies and, to that limited extent, may thus affect the performance inquiry, they are irrelevant to the prejudice inquiry. Thus, evidence about the actual process of decision, if not part of the record of the proceeding under review, and evidence about, for example, a particular judge's sentencing practices, should not be considered in the prejudice determination.

The governing legal standard plays a critical role in defining the question to be asked in assessing the prejudice from counsel's errors. When a defendant challenges a conviction, the question is whether there is a reasonable probability that, absent the errors, the factfinder would have had a reasonable doubt respecting guilt. When a defendant challenges a death sentence such as the one at issue in this case, the question is whether there is a reasonable probability that, absent the errors, the sentencer—including an appellate court, to the extent it independently reweighs the evidence—would have concluded that the balance of aggravating and mitigating circumstances did not warrant death.

In making this determination, a court hearing an ineffectiveness claim must consider the totality of the evidence before the judge or jury. Some of the factual findings will have been unaffected by the errors, and factual findings that were affected will have been affected in different ways. Some errors will have had a pervasive effect on the inferences to be drawn from the evidence, altering the entire evidentiary picture, and some will have had an isolated, trivial effect. Moreover, a verdict or conclusion only weakly supported by the record is more likely to have been affected by errors than one with overwhelming record support. Taking the unaffected findings as a given, and taking due account of the effect of the errors on the remaining findings, a court making the prejudice inquiry must ask if the defendant has met the burden of showing that the decision reached would reasonably likely have been different absent the errors.

IV

A number of practical considerations are important for the application of the standards we have outlined. Most important, in adjudicating a claim of actual ineffectiveness of counsel, a court should keep in mind that the principles we have stated do not establish mechanical rules. Although those principles should guide the process of decision, the ultimate focus of inquiry must be on the fundamental fairness of the proceeding whose result is being challenged. In every case the court should be concerned with whether, despite the strong presumption of reliability, the result of the particular proceeding is unreliable because of a breakdown in the adversarial process that our system counts on to produce just results.

To the extent that this has already been the guiding inquiry in the lower courts, the standards articulated today do not require reconsideration of ineffectiveness claims rejected under different standards. . . . In particular, the minor differences in the lower courts' precise formulations of the performance standard are insignificant: the different formulations are mere variations of the overarching reasonableness standard. With regard to the prejudice inquiry, only the strict outcome-determinative test, among the standards articulated in the lower courts, imposes a heavier burden on defendants than the tests laid down today. The difference, however, should alter the merit of an ineffectiveness claim only in the rarest case.

Although we have discussed the performance component of an ineffectiveness claim prior to the prejudice component, there is no reason for a court deciding an ineffective assistance claim to approach the inquiry in the same order or even to address both components of the inquiry if the defendant makes an insufficient showing on one. In particular, a court need not determine whether counsel's performance was deficient before examining the prejudice suffered by the defendant as a result of the alleged deficiencies. The object of an ineffectiveness claim is not to grade counsel's performance. If it is easier to dispose of an ineffectiveness claim on the ground of lack of sufficient prejudice, which we expect will often be so, that course should be followed. Courts should strive to ensure that ineffectiveness claims not become so burdensome to defense counsel that the entire criminal justice system suffers as a result.

The principles governing ineffectiveness claims should apply in federal collateral proceedings as they do on direct appeal or in motions for a new trial. . . . Since fundamental fairness is the central concern of the writ of habeas corpus, . . . no special standards ought to apply to ineffectiveness claims made in habeas proceedings.

Finally, in a federal habeas challenge to a state criminal judgment, a state court conclusion that counsel rendered effective assistance is not a finding of fact binding on the federal court to the extent stated by 28 U.S.C. § 2254(d). . . . Although state court findings of fact made in the course of deciding an ineffectiveness claim are subject to the deference requirement of § 2254(d), and although district court findings are subject to the clearly erroneous standard of Federal Rule of Civil Procedure 52(a), both the performance and prejudice components of the ineffectiveness inquiry are mixed questions of law and fact.

V

Having articulated general standards for judging ineffectiveness claims, we think it useful to apply those standards to the facts of this case in order to illustrate the meaning of the general principles. The record makes it possible to do so. There are no conflicts between the state and federal courts over findings of fact, and the principles we have articulated are sufficiently close to the principles applied both in the Florida courts and in the District Court that it is clear that the factfinding was not affected by erroneous legal principles. . . .

Application of the governing principles is not difficult in this case. The facts as described above, make clear that the conduct of respondent's counsel at and before respondent's sentencing proceeding cannot be found unreasonable. They also make clear that, even assuming the challenged conduct of counsel was unreasonable, respondent suffered insufficient prejudice to warrant setting aside his death sentence.

With respect to the performance component, the record shows that respondent's counsel made a strategic choice to argue for the extreme emotional distress mitigating circumstance and to rely as fully as possible on respondent's acceptance of responsibility for his crimes. Although counsel understandably felt hopeless about respondent's prospects, nothing in the record indicates, as one possible reading of the District Court's opinion suggests, that counsel's sense of hopelessness distorted his professional judgment. Counsel's strategy choice was well within the range of professionally reasonable judgments, and the decision not to seek more character or psychological evidence than was already in hand was likewise reasonable.

The trial judge's views on the importance of owning up to one's crimes were well known to counsel. The aggravating circumstances were utterly overwhelming. Trial counsel could reasonably surmise from his conversations with respondent that character and psychological evidence would be of little help. Respondent had already been able to mention at the plea colloquy the substance of what there was to know about his financial and emotional troubles. Restricting testimony on respondent's character to what had come in at the plea colloquy ensured that contrary character and psychological evidence and respondent's criminal history, which counsel had successfully moved to exclude, would not come in. On these facts, there can be little question, even without application of the presumption of adequate performance, that trial counsel's defense, though unsuccessful, was the result of reasonable professional judgment.

With respect to the prejudice component, the lack of merit of respondent's claim is even more stark. The evidence that respondent says his trial counsel should have offered at the sentencing hearing would barely have altered the sentencing profile presented to the sentencing judge. As the state courts and District Court found, at most this evidence shows that numerous people who knew respondent thought he was generally a good person and that a psychiatrist and a psychologist believed he was under considerable emotional stress that did not rise to the level of extreme disturbance. Given the overwhelming aggravating factors, there is no reasonable probability that the omitted evidence would have changed the conclusion that the aggravating circumstances outweighed the mitigating circumstances and, hence, the sentence imposed. Indeed, admission of the evidence respondent now offers might even have been harmful to his case: his "rap sheet" would probably have been admitted into evidence, and the psychological reports would have directly contradicted respondent's claim that the mitigating circumstance of extreme emotional disturbance applied to his case.

Our conclusions on both the prejudice and performance components of the ineffectiveness inquiry do not depend on the trial judge's testimony at the District Court hearing. We therefore need not consider the general admissibility of that testimony, although, that testimony is irrelevant to the prejudice inquiry. Moreover, the prejudice question is resolvable, and hence the ineffectiveness claim can be rejected, without regard to the evidence presented at the District Court hearing. The state courts properly concluded that the ineffectiveness claim was meritless without holding an evidentiary hearing.

Failure to make the required showing of either deficient performance or sufficient prejudice defeats the ineffectiveness claim. Here there is a double failure. More generally, respondent has made no showing that the justice of his sentence was rendered unreliable by a breakdown in the adversary process caused by deficiencies in counsel's assistance. Respondent's sentencing proceeding was not fundamentally unfair.

We conclude, therefore, that the District Court properly declined to issue a writ of habeas corpus. The judgment of the Court of Appeals is accordingly

Reversed.

Questions and Comments

In *Strickland*, Justice Brennan filed an opinion concurring in the opinion of the Court, but dissenting from its judgment because the case involved the death penalty. Should the courts hold counsel to a higher standard in death penalty cases? See State v. Davis, 116 N.J. 341, 561 A.2d 1082, 1089 (1989) (refusing to interpret the state constitution as requiring a more stringent test of competency in death penalty cases than the test in *Strickland*).

Justice Marshall dissented in *Strickland*. He argued, first, that to tell the lower courts that counsel in a criminal case must act like " 'a reasonably competent attorney' is to tell them nothing", and that the Supreme Court should not have disapproved of the admirable job that lower courts had been doing in creating workable objective standards of reasonableness. Second, he expressed strong disagreement with the "prejudice" standard adopted by the Court. He argued that it was often very difficult to tell whether a convicted defendant would have done better with competent counsel. A more fundamental problem with the prejudice standard, he argued, was that it treated the Sixth Amendment's guarantee of effective assistance of counsel as if its only purpose was to ensure that the innocent were not convicted:

> . . . In my view, the guarantee also functions to ensure that convictions are obtained only through fundamentally fair procedures. The majority contends that the Sixth Amendment is not violated when a manifestly guilty defendant is convicted after a trial in which he was represented by a manifestly ineffective attorney. I cannot agree. Every defendant is entitled to a trial in which his interests are vigorously and conscientiously advocated by an able lawyer. A proceeding in which the defendant does not receive meaningful assistance in meeting the forces of the State does not, in my opinion, constitute due process.

Strickland, MARSHALL, J., dissenting, 466 U.S. 711. Justice Marshall also criticized the majority's repeated emphasis on the heavy presumption in favor of competence that the lower courts were admonished to apply.

In United States v. Cronic, 466 U.S. 648, 104 S.Ct. 2039 (1984), decided the same day as *Strickland*, the Court held that it is not enough to show that the lawyer was not a criminal lawyer, the defendant must show specific errors. The lawyer who defended Cronic was a real estate specialist. See also People v. Perez, 24 Cal.3d 133, 594 P.2d 1 (1979) (en banc) (upholding the representation of indigent defendants with their consent by "certified" law students supervised by an attorney).

GENEGO, "THE FUTURE OF EFFECTIVE ASSISTANCE OF COUNSEL: PERFORMANCE STANDARDS AND COMPETENT REPRESENTATION"

22 American Criminal Law Review 181 (1984).*

I. INTRODUCTION

In recent years, significant effort has been devoted to improving the quality of the legal representation afforded criminal defendants. Perhaps the most visible part of that effort has been the work of scholars and litigators who have sought to convince courts that individuals accused of crimes are entitled, under the United States Constitution, to representation by attorneys who perform in a reasonably competent manner. In the 1960s, most courts only reversed convictions on grounds that counsel gave "ineffective assistance" when an attorney's performance made a "farce and mockery" of a trial or a plea of guilty. Gradually, however, the federal courts altered that approach as they adopted a standard requiring representation that was "reasonably competent." Last term, the United States Supreme Court finally addressed the issue of what kind of representation the Constitution requires. In Strickland v. Washington, the Court held that a defendant in a criminal case is entitled to legal representation that accords with "reasonableness under prevailing professional norms."

In making this long awaited and hard won pronouncement, however, the Court expressed the view that its adoption of a standard of reasonable competence will have little practical impact. In light of the significant burdens that the *Strickland* opinion has placed upon defendants who challenge the adequacy of counsel, the Court is probably right.

. . .

1. *The Court's Application Of The Test In* Strickland v. Washington

. . .

A psychiatric examination of Washington could have been relevant to the sentencing proceeding in two respects. First, an examination might have established the existence of a mental disturbance that could have supported a finding of a mitigating factor under the Florida death penalty statute. Second, even if a report did not establish the actual existence of a mental disturbance, a report might have substantiated Washington's claim that he was acting under extreme mental stress.

While such stress is not a statutory mitigating factor, such evidence would have presented Washington in a more sympathetic light.

. . .

2. *Application Of The* Strickland *Test Generally*

The *Strickland* Court's instructions to lower courts about how to apply the tests for ineffectiveness claims further illustrate the Court's efforts to undercut the test it has announced. The Court's opinion repeatedly stresses that, when reviewing claims of ineffective assistance of counsel, courts must apply a "presumption" of competency. According to the Court, "counsel is strongly presumed to have rendered adequate assistance and made all significant decisions in the exercise of reasonable professional judgment." A court must apply a "heavy measure of deference" to the decisions of an attorney not to investigate.

The Court's repeated invocation of a presumption of adequate defense is not supported by any data indicating that defense counsel are, in fact, generally competent. In fact, available evidence suggests that defense counsel, particularly those for indigent defendants, are often overworked, undercompensated, and frequently inexperienced.[140] Even where the attorneys are competent professionals, economic and caseload burdens often seriously impair their ability to provide adequate representation to all their clients.[141]

In addition to the burden of overcoming a strong presumption of reasonably competent representation, the Court stated it would attribute a "strong presumption of reliability" to all trial *results*. Thus, the Court placed upon defendants alleging sixth amendment ineffectiveness claims a second burden: that of establishing prejudice. This burden further ensures that the Court's standard will rarely result in the reversal of any convictions. Even if defendants are able to overcome the strong presumption of competency and establish that their attorneys failed to provide adequate representation, they are not automatically entitled to relief. Defendants must prove prejudice, defined by the Court as "a reasonable probability that, but for counsel's unprofessional errors, the result of the proceeding would have been different." One need not be a lawyer to appreciate the difficulty of meeting the prejudice requirement established by the Court. Given the inherent subjectivity of determining whether past results would probably have

140. See, e.g., N. Lefstein, Criminal Defense Services for the Poor (1982) (study examining state systems of defense services for the poor; noting various problems resulting from "woeful funding" of such systems); Law Enforcement Assistance Administration, U.S. Department of Justice, The National Manpower Survey of the Criminal Justice System, Vol. IV: Courts 51 (1978) (forty percent of public defenders surveyed reported insufficient training for job); Note, Providing Counsel for the Indigent Accused: The Criminal Justice Act, 12 Am.Crim.L.Rev. 789 (1975) (survey concluding plan established by Criminal Justice Act of 1964 to expand sixth amendment protection resulted in under-funded system tolerating inexperienced and ineffective attorneys).

141. See National Legal Aid & Defender Assoc., The Other Face of Justice (1973) (in depth statistical study of indigent defense systems concluding that inadequate funding and manpower have hindered ability to provide effective representation) . . .

been different, defendants will successfully prove clear cases of prejudice only where there is evidence that they should not have been convicted.

. . .

The Court's opinion suffers from an even more fundamental defect. The Court fails to distinguish between the purposes of the sixth amendment guarantee of counsel and the actual job of defense attorneys in criminal prosecutions. The purpose of the sixth amendment right to counsel provision is to ensure a fair trial and produce a result society may comfortably call just. The Court assumes that this is also the role of defense counsel. Thus, in the Court's equation, an attorney provides inadequate representation only when society cannot rely on the result as just.

The role of an attorney for a defendant facing criminal prosecution is not, however, to see that his or her client received a fair trial and that a just outcome resulted. The attorney's role is to do everything ethically proper to see that the client receives the most favorable outcome possible—whether or not it produces an outcome which society considers just.[152] Society relies on the adversary system to produce just results from partisan advocacy. The guiding principle in determining whether an attorney has provided effective representation must then be whether he or she discharged the role of partisan advocate faithfully and zealously, not whether the performance yielded what a court views as a just result.

In addition to limiting the substantive impact of the reasonably competent standard, the Court's decision also has significant procedural implications. *Strickland* will reduce the time courts must devote to disposing of ineffective assistance claims and will discourage defendants from raising such challenges. The Court speaks of ineffectiveness claims as entailing an "intrusive post-trial inquiry," the availability of which needs to be restricted so as not to "encourage the proliferation of ineffectiveness challenges." . . .

. . .

It may perhaps have been naive to have hoped that this, or any other, Supreme Court would have established an exacting test for assistance of counsel claims and a method of implementation that would have required critical examination of the quality of representation received by defendants in criminal cases. Inadequate representation is a major institutional problem. By all accounts there are far too many defendants who are represented by inadequate counsel; the courts cannot, in the limited context of granting postconviction relief, adequately respond to the problem. When confronted with such fundamental issues in the criminal justice system, courts have tended to

---

152. Model Code of Professional Responsibility Canon 7 (1979). Ethical Consideration 7–1 states: "The duty of a lawyer, both to his client and the legal system, is to represent his client zealously within the bounds of the law. . . ." Id. at EC 7–1. For an in depth discussion of the lawyer's role within the adversary system, see M.H. Freedman, Lawyers Ethics In An Adversary System 9–26 (1975).

respond by legitimating "necessary evils," such as when the Supreme Court upheld the constitutionality of plea bargaining. Perhaps, then, it was inevitable that the Court, even while adopting the new language of ineffective assistance law, would ensure that the substance of the old "farce and mockery" test remained to shore up the walls of the criminal justice system.

．　．　．

B. THE ROLE OF PERFORMANCE STANDARDS

1. *The Development of Standards*

Standards are not new to the criminal justice system or to the practice of criminal defense.[166] The most well-known example of standards is the American Bar Association Project on Standards for Criminal Justice.[167] The ABA Standards address nearly every aspect of the criminal justice system. The Standards for the Defense Function, first approved in 1968 and revised in 1979, specifically address the role of the defense attorney.

Many people in the legal profession believe that it is simply not possible to develop specific performance standards. These critics maintain that the work of the criminal defense attorney must vary with the facts of each particular case and that no general list of specific duties can possibly take account of the vagaries of individual, fact-specific cases. . . .

．　．　．

The need to make individualized strategic decisions, however, does not preclude the development of effective performance standards. . . .

There are, for example, some obligatory actions which should be taken in all cases, while in other cases, the attorney would be expected to take specific actions unless he or she had sound strategic reasons for not doing so. Further, there are certain decisions and possible actions which will always turn on the facts and circumstances of the individual case. In the latter category, performance standards would not dictate that the attorney take a particular action or make a specific decision. Standards would, however, identify the factors to be considered in deciding upon a course of action and would also identify the information the attorney should obtain and evaluate in deciding how to proceed.

---

166. See, e.g., Resnik & Shaw, Prisoners of Their Sex: Health Problems of Incarcerated Women, in Prisoners' Rights Sourcebook 319, 340–62 (I. Robbins ed. 1980) (discussing development of standards of health care for women's correctional institutions); United States Department of Justice, Federal Standards for Prisons and Jails (1980) (standards intended to aid correctional administrators as guidelines in operation and administration of prisons and jails); Model Code of Pre–Arraignment Procedure (1975) (model statute governing police powers and practice in law enforcement and related pretrial procedures).

167. Standards for Criminal Justice (2d ed. 1980) [hereinafter cited as ABA Standards].

A specific context will illustrate how performance standards might work, and the sentencing context can provide such an example. One of the basic obligations of an attorney representing a defendant at sentencing is to advocate the least restrictive and least burdensome sentencing alternative that is realistic, given the facts and circumstances of the case. While standards could not dictate the specific kind of sentence the attorney should propose, standards could delineate what an attorney should know to make a competent decision about what to advocate. First, there are obvious factors: penalties, the applicable fines, restitution and forfeiture provisions and the discretion the sentencing court has in deciding what sanctions to impose. Second, when the client faces imprisonment, the attorney will also need to know the applicability and operation of relevant parole statutes and regulations, the possible location and conditions of a client's confinement,[187] the availability of correctional programs and services, the effect of the sentence on deportation, the opportunities for the client to surrender directly to the place of confinement and the impact of committed fines or restitution obligations.

Thus, the attorney should know the procedures of the sentencing court, including whether presentence reports are prepared for the court by a probation officer or by other court officials, the methods available for having input into such reports and for correcting errors in the reports, and what opportunities exist for submitting a defense sentencing memorandum. Further, defense counsel should be aware of whether the prosecution or any victims will have an opportunity to provide input into the sentencing decision. Finally, defense counsel should be familiar with the procedures to be followed by the court at the sentencing hearing, including the methods for the presentation of evidence or information on behalf of the defendant. To choose and execute a sentencing strategy in an effective manner, an attorney should know and take into account all these factors. In sum, performance standards walk the line between overarching and ultimately vague generalities and instruction for how to proceed in a specific case. Standards *inform*, rather than make decisions for lawyers.

Note

For an example of a pre-*Strickland* effort to develop objective standards see Judge Bazelon's article, The Realities of *Gideon* and *Argersinger,* 64 Geo.L.J. 811, 837–838 (1976). See Berger, The Supreme Court and Defense Counsel: Old Roads, New Paths—A Dead End?, 86

---

187. The location and conditions of correctional facilities can vary greatly and significantly affect the defendant's experience while imprisoned. Such information may persuade a judge to recommend or designate commitment to a particular institution or may even affect the length or type of sentence imposed. See, e.g., United States v. Dragna, No. 83–5275 (9th Cir. May 29, 1984); see also 18 U.S.C. § 4208 (1982) (provisions for residential treatment centers, extension of limits of confinement, work furlough); 28 C.F.R. § 503 (1983) (provisions for Bureau of Prisons, central office, regional offices, institutions, and staff training centers).

Colum.L.Rev. 9 (1986), for a thoughtful and thorough review of the Supreme Court cases on ineffective assistance of counsel.

The Effect of Strickland

A recent survey of the case law, Note, How to Thread the Needle: Toward a Checklist–Based Standard for Evaluating Ineffective Assistance of Counsel Claims, 77 Geo.L.J. 413, 458–461 (1988), reported that as of May 30, 1988, the United States Courts of Appeals had heard 702 cases alleging ineffective assistance of counsel since the decision in *Strickland.* The ineffectiveness claim was sustained in only 30 cases, 4.27%. In one-half of the 12 circuits, accounting for 165 of the 702 cases, no defendant had prevailed in a claim of ineffective assistance of counsel. In the other six circuits, four to six percent of the defendants were successful in making out the claim with the exception of the Seventh Circuit in which nearly 10% of the defendants were successful. Justice Burger's "working hypothesis" that at least one-third to one-half of trial lawyers are incompetent, see p. 141 above, may be an overstatement. But even assuming that the more modest estimates provided by the judges in the Maddi or Partridge and Bermont studies are correct (see p. 142 above), only the Seventh Circuit seems to be ensuring that criminal defendants receive competent representation. The other circuits may, however, be following the dictates of *Strickland* more faithfully.

Perhaps the most troubling statistic provided by the author of the Georgetown note is that, of the 672 cases rejecting the defendant's claim, 291 (43.3%) did so on the ground that prejudice had not been shown. In other words, in almost half of the cases, the defendant's allegations of bungling were "relegated to [the] 'guilty anyway' category." Note, supra at 433. In the 291 "no prejudice" cases the courts rarely addressed the performance of counsel. Nevertheless, in 37 "no prejudice" cases (5.27%) the court indicated that counsel's performance was less than adequate. In 227 cases the courts found that counsel's performance was adequate; and in 154 cases the courts found neither inadequate performance nor prejudice.

Examples of "Competent" Representation After Strickland

In Mitchell v. Kemp, 762 F.2d 886 (11th Cir.1985), the District Court had concluded that the "tactical decisions" of Mitchell's counsel were reasonable under *Strickland.* The Court of Appeals stated that the lawyer's conduct raised a "difficult question," but affirmed on the ground that it was the result of strategic choices. The Supreme Court denied cert., 483 U.S. 1026 (1987). The following is from Justice Marshall's dissent from the Court's denial of certiorari, in which Justices Brennan and Blackmun joined:

> Lest we permit the lower courts to conclude that the Sixth Amendment guarantees no more than that "a person who happens to be a lawyer is present at trial alongside the accused"—a notion expressly disavowed in *Strickland* . . . .—the Court should now

give life to the *Strickland* standard. Accordingly, I would grant certiorari . . .

. . . [P]etitioner pleaded guilty to the murder of a 14–year old boy in the course of a convenience-store robbery. At the sentencing proceeding . . . the State called five witnesses and introduced documentary evidence to support its contention that petitioner should receive the death penalty. Defense counsel called no witnesses and presented no mitigating evidence. The court sentenced petitioner to die. . . .

. . . [P]etitioner's appointed attorney made *no* attempt to interview *any* potential mitigating witnesses. . . .

Nor did counsel pursue a vigorous defense with respect to the circumstances of the crime. He did not interview the police officer who witnessed the petitioner's confession which the state used to establish . . . certain aggravating circumstances in support of the death sentence, even though petitioner had told him that the officer—the cousin of the victim—had held a gun to petitioner's head to extract the confession. Counsel's reason for not speaking to the officer was that "I personally don't like the man." Counsel did not interview the sole witness to the crime, who provided the key testimony for the prosecution at sentencing. He filed *no pretrial* motions. . . .

Counsel's failure to investigate mitigating circumstances left him ignorant of the abundant information that was available to an attorney exercising minimal diligence in fighting for Billy Mitchell's life. The affidavits of individuals who would have testified on petitioner's behalf fill 170 pages of the record in the District Court. . . .

Had defense counsel tapped these resources, he would have been able to present the sentencing judge with a picture of a youth who, despite growing up in "the most poverty-stricken and crime-ridden section of Jacksonville, Florida," had impressed his community as a person of exceptional character. He had been captain of the football team; leader of the prayer before each game; an above-average student; an active member of the student council, school choir, church choir, glee club, math club, and track team; a boy scout; captain of the patrol boys; and an attendant to the junior high school queen.

. . . .

An account of what happened to this well-adjusted young person was also readily available to anyone who took the time to ask. When petitioner was 16 years old, his parents were divorced, and soon thereafter petitioner . . . and two friends were arrested for attempted robbery. Petitioner professed his innocence, but was persuaded by his father to plead guilty, because "things would go easier for him." The charges against the two friends were dropped. Petitioner was sentenced to six months in prison, where he was subjected to repeated homosexual attacks, experienced severe depression, and lost 30 pounds. When he was released, he continued to be highly depressed, and eventually committed the crime for which he received a sentence of death.

Counsel's explanation for his total lack of preparation for the sentencing hearing is that he carried an "ace in the hole." His sole strategy for representing his client's interest rested on his belief that, under Georgia law, the State would not be permitted to introduce any evidence of aggravating circumstances of which the defense had not been notified in writing. Prior to sentencing, the prosecution had provided petitioner's counsel with oral notice . . ., but had not furnished written notice. Although the state statute upon which counsel's theory relied did not mention written notice, and no court decision had ever required that such notice be in writing, counsel was content to rest his entire defense, and the fate of his client, on an untried legal theory. At sentencing, counsel took the first opportunity to object to the admission of aggravating evidence of which he had not received prior written notice; the court promptly overruled his objection, and the "ace in the hole" was gone. Even if counsel had been correct in his interpretation of state law, of course, the State could have provided the requisite written notice at any time before the hearing, which would have left petitioner equally defenseless.

. . . [P]etitioner's attorney also claimed that he had not wished to present any mitigating character evidence because that would have opened the door to the State's introduction of petitioner's prior conviction. . . . In this case, [such a decision] was patently unreasonable. . . . Moreover, under state law, the prior conviction would have been admissible even though the defense put on no evidence. If counsel made any decisions at all, they were barren of even minimal supporting information or knowledge.

. . .

As a result of counsel's nonfeasance, no one argued to the sentencing judge that petitioner should not die. The judge heard only a technical argument regarding the admissibility of aggravating circumstances without prior written notice, which he consistently rejected, in addition to a reference to petitioner's youth. . . . Prejudice to the defendant's case is obvious when not even a suggestion that petitioner's life had some value, that his crime was aberrational, or that he was suffering from severe depression reached the ears and the conscience of the sentencing judge. . . . The judge heard not even a plea for mercy.

107 S.Ct. at 3249–3252.

Can a failure to investigate ever suffice to establish ineffective assistance of counsel? In Kimmelman v. Morrison, 477 U.S. 365, 366, 106 S.Ct. 2574, 2578 (1986), the Supreme Court held counsel ineffective when his failure to conduct pretrial discovery resulted in a failure to raise an objection under the Fourth Amendment to illegally seized evidence. See also Sullivan v. Fairman, 819 F.2d 1382, 1391–3 (7th Cir. 1987) (failure to contact witnesses whose testimony contradicted that of government's witnesses was ineffective and prejudicial). Nonetheless, in the vast majority of cases even a complete failure to investigate does not lead to reversal. See, e.g., Burger v. Kemp, 483 U.S. 776, 107 S.Ct. 3114 (1987) (no investigation of mitigating evidence for presentation at defendant's capital sentencing hearing); Ballou v. Booker, 777 F.2d 910, 914 (4th Cir.1985) (failure to interview rape victim or examining physicians not unreasonable when counsel already "knew" what happened); Aldrich v. Wainwright, 777 F.2d 630, 633 (11th Cir.1985) (failure to interview state's witnesses or otherwise investigate along with counsel's admission that he was "totally unprepared" demonstrated unreasonable performance, but not prejudicial); Hoots v. Allsbrook, 785 F.2d 1214, 1221 (4th Cir.1986) (failure to investigate unreasonable but not prejudicial).

What Constitutes Prejudice

In *Strickland* the Court states that prejudice will be presumed in certain limited circumstances: when there has been an "actual or constructive denial of the assistance of counsel altogether," or when the government interferes with counsel's assistance in such a way that "prejudice . . . is so likely that case-by-case inquiry into prejudice is not worth the cost."

In *Strickland,* the court made it clear that a defendant need not show prejudice when her trial was conducted without counsel despite her desire for representation and when counsel in a criminal case was under an actual conflict of interest, see *Cuyler v. Sullivan,* reprinted in Chapter 7 below. Since *Strickland,* the Court has affirmed that prejudice is not required in the following two situations. The first is failure to file an *Anders* brief. Anders v. California, 386 U.S. 738, 87 S.Ct. 1396 (1967), requires appellate counsel in criminal cases who seek leave to withdraw based on their judgment that an appeal is meritless to file a brief referring to anything in the record that might arguably support the appeal. Such a brief is called an *Anders* brief. In Penson v. Ohio, 109 S.Ct. 346 (1988), the Court held that failure to file an *Anders* brief requires reversal; no showing of prejudice is required, nor may such conduct be labeled harmless error. The second situation is when the defendant is prevented from conferring with her counsel for any significant period of time. See Geders v. United States, 425 U.S. 80, 96 S.Ct. 1330 (1976) (defendant not allowed to confer with counsel during overnight trial recess). In Perry v. Leeke, 109 S.Ct. 594 (1989), the Court reaffirmed that a violation of *Geders* was not subject to the requirement that prejudice be shown, but held that *Geders* was not violated when the defendant was prevented from conferring with counsel during a 15–minute trial recess, that prejudice therefore had to be shown and that it was not.

Apart from these situations, there are relatively few instances in which the courts have dispensed with the requirement of demonstrating prejudice. The category of "actual or constructive denial" is interpreted quite narrowly. For example, in Smith v. Ylst, 826 F.2d 872 (9th Cir.1987), psychiatric reports showed that the defendant's lawyer suffered "paranoid psychotic reactions" during the trial, but the court upheld the conviction because the defendant failed to show prejudice. Also see Berry v. King, 765 F.2d 451, 454 (5th Cir.1985), cert. denied, 476 U.S. 1164 (1986) (no presumption of prejudice on showing that defense counsel was addicted to drugs, and prejudice not shown by his stipulation to virtually all elements of the crime when state could easily have proved the elements). Where an "actual or constructive" denial has been found, the courts have sometimes used the doctrine of harmless error to avoid reversal, see, e.g., Thomas v. Kemp, 796 F.2d 1322, 1326–27 (11th Cir.), cert. denied 479 U.S. 996 (1986) (defendant, facing capital charge, was denied presence of a lawyer at preliminary hearing; no reversal because harmless error); Siverson v. O'Leary, 764 F.2d 1208 (7th Cir.1985) (defense counsel's absence during jury deliberations and when jury returned verdict presumed prejudicial but error harmless).

Government interference with the right to counsel must be egregious before prejudice will be presumed. "Not all government interference triggers the per se [prejudice] rule. The common thread in cases where the government's conduct was found to be 'egregious' is conduct which jeopardizes the integrity of the legal process." United States v. Perry, 857 F.2d 1346, 1349 (9th Cir.1988) (giving examples).

Are there specific blunders by counsel so blatantly incompetent that no separate showing of prejudice should be required? What about failing to remove for cause an obviously biased juror? Compare Presley v. State, 750 S.W.2d 602 (Mo.App.), cert. denied, 109 S.Ct. 514 (1988) (holding that prejudice is presumed in this situation), with Wicker v. McCotter, 783 F.2d 487 (5th Cir.), cert. denied, 478 U.S. 1010 (1986) (holding such conduct was a strategic choice).

Effective Assistance of Counsel Under State Constitutions

The state courts—the laboratories of our federal judicial system—are free to develop more rigorous standards for judging effective assistance of counsel under state constitutional provisions. However, almost all follow *Strickland.* See, e.g., State v. Nash, 143 Ariz. 392, 694 P.2d 222 (1985); People v. Ledesma, 43 Cal.3d 171, 729 P.2d 839 (1987); People v. Albanese, 104 Ill.2d 504, 473 N.E.2d 1246 (1984); State v. Davis, 116 N.J. 341, 561 A.2d 1082 (1989).

Compare Commonwealth v. Buehl, 510 Pa. 363, 508 A.2d 1167, 1174 (1986), holding that the Pennsylvania Constitution requires the same showing of prejudice as in *Strickland,* but a different inquiry as to counsel's performance: the court asks whether the course the defendant suggests counsel should have pursued is frivolous; if not, then the court asks whether the course counsel chose "had some reasonable basis designed to serve the best interests of [the] client." It is unclear whether this formulation makes any difference. Also see Gibson v. State, 110 Idaho 631, 718 P.2d 283, 287 (1986) (reserving the question of whether the Idaho Constitution demands a different standard than *Strickland*).

Malpractice Claims Against Criminal Defense Lawyers

In Ferri v. Ackerman, 444 U.S. 193, 100 S.Ct. 402 (1979) the Supreme Court held that counsel appointed in federal criminal cases under the criminal Justice Act of 1964 enjoy no inherent immunity from malpractice claims.

Several courts have held that when a criminal defendant's ineffective assistance of counsel claim has been fully heard and denied, the doctrine of collateral estoppel bars a subsequent civil malpractice suit against the lawyer. Zeidwig v. Ward, 548 So.2d 209 (Fla.1989); Knoblauch v. Kenyon, 163 Mich.App. 712, 415 N.W.2d 286 (1987); Johnson v. Raban, 702 S.W.2d 134 (Mo.App.1985). In *Zeidwig* the court reasoned:

> If we were to allow a claim in this instance, we would be approving a policy that would approve the imprisonment of a defendant for a criminal offense . . . but which would allow the same defendant to collect from his counsel damages . . . because he was improperly imprisoned.

Does this result in criminal defense lawyers being held to a lesser standard in malpractice cases than civil lawyers? For a recent case awarding malpractice damages, after the defendant's criminal conviction had been overturned, see Holliday v. Jones, 216 Cal.App.3d 102, 264 Cal.Rptr. 448 (1989).

In Polk County v. Dodson, 454 U.S. 312, 323, 102 S.Ct. 445, 453 (1981), the Supreme Court held that a public defender "when performing a lawyer's traditional functions as counsel to a defendant in a criminal proceeding" does not act "under color of state law" within the meaning of 42 U.S.C. § 1983. The plaintiff had sued under § 1983, claiming that his rights to counsel and to due process were violated when his counsel moved to withdraw on the ground that he thought plaintiff's appeal was frivolous. In Tower v. Glover, 467 U.S. 914, 104 S.Ct. 2820 (1984), the Court held that § 1983 applies when a plaintiff alleges that the public defender conspired with state officials to ensure the plaintiff's conviction.

Refusing to Proceed to Trial

United States v. Wendy, 575 F.2d 1025 (2d Cir.1978), held it improper to hold appointed counsel in contempt of court for refusing to proceed to trial because he was a tax lawyer who had never tried a case before. See also State v. Gasen, 48 Ohio App.2d 191, 356 N.E.2d 505 (1976) (reversing a contempt citation of a public defender who refused to proceed with a preliminary hearing because the court had not given him time to read the file on the case or consult with the defendants); and Easley v. State, 334 So.2d 630 (Fla.App.1976) (lawyer not in contempt because he had an obligation to tell defendant that he lacked competence to proceed).

C. OTHER CHECKS ON INCOMPETENCE

The Ethics Rules on Competence

The Canons of Ethics did not contain a provision on competence. Canon 6 of the Model Code recognized the importance of competence: "A Lawyer Should Represent a Client Competently." Despite grandiloquent language in the ECs under Canon 6, the disciplinary rule on competence is not stringent. DR 6–101(A)(1) states that a lawyer shall not "handle a legal matter which he knows or should know that he is not competent to handle, without associating with . . . a lawyer who is competent to handle it." EC 6–3 explains that this does not prevent a novice in an area of law from accepting employment in that area, "if in good faith he expects to become qualified through study and investigation, as long as such preparation would not result in unreasonable delay or expense to the client." Once the representation has been accepted, DR 6–102(A)(2) provides that a lawyer shall not "handle a matter without preparation adequate in the circumstances" and DR 6–102(A)(3) prohibits the lawyer from "neglect[ing] a legal matter entrusted to him."

M.R. 1.1 provides:

A lawyer shall provide competent representation to a client. Competent representation requires the legal knowledge, skill, thoroughness and preparation reasonably necessary for the representation.

The Comment to M.R. 1.1 states that while "[i]n many instances, the required proficiency is that of the general practitioner", "[e]xpertise in a particular field of law may be required in some circumstances." However, the Comment also contains language similar to EC 6–5 to the effect that a novice can provide adequate representation if she engages in necessary study or associates with someone of established competence in the field.

M.R. 1.3 requires that a lawyer act with reasonable diligence; and M.R. 1.4(a) requires that a lawyer "keep a client reasonably informed of the status of the representation and promptly comply with reasonable requests for information."

Discipline for incompetence has been relatively rare. See Martyn, Lawyer Competence and Lawyer Discipline: Beyond the Bar? 71 Geo. L.J. 705 (1981). Most cases involve either egregious and often repeated instances of incompetence or incompetence combined with other misconduct. See, e.g., Attorney Grievance Committee v. Werner, 315 Md. 172, 553 A.2d 722 (1989) (gross neglect, multiple misrepresentations and failure to cooperate with bar authorities); Office of Disciplinary Counsel v. Henry, 664 S.W.2d 62 (Tenn.1983) (gross incompetence in four cases, including filing an answer and amended answer to a criminal indictment "setting forth in detail [the defendant's] version of the homicide"); People ex rel. Goldberg v. Gordon, 199 Colo. 296, 607 P.2d 995 (1980) (unnecessary probate); In re Albert, 390 Mich. 234, 212 N.W.2d 17 (1973) (neglect of the claims of a number of clients and failure to keep clients informed of the status of their cases); In re Kennedy, 254 S.C. 463, 176 S.E.2d 125 (1970) (repeated instances of incompetence).

Court opinions often state that it is inappropriate to impose discipline for conduct that amounts "only" to negligent malpractice. See, e.g., Florida Bar v. Neale, 384 So.2d 1264, 1265 (Fla.1980); Committee on Legal Ethics v. Mullins, 159 W.Va. 647, 226 S.E.2d 427 (1976). Also see ABA Informal Op. 1273 (1973). Is this position justified?

Some states have adopted a standard of competence different from that in the Code or Rules. For example, California Rule of Prof. Conduct 3–110 provides:

(A) A member shall not intentionally, or with reckless disregard, or repeatedly fail to perform legal services competently.

(B) To perform legal services competently means diligently to apply the learning and skill necessary to perform the member's duties arising from employment or representation. If the member does not have sufficient learning and skills when the employment or representation is undertaken, or during the course of the employment or representation, the member may nonetheless perform such duties competently by associating or, where appropriate, professionally consulting another member reasonably believed to be competent, or by acquiring sufficient learning and skill before performance is required, if the member has sufficient time, resources, and ability to do so.

(C) As used in this rule, the term "ability" means a quality or state of having sufficient learning and skill and being mentally, emotionally, and physically able to perform legal services.

Is this an improvement over M.R. 1.1?

Continuing Legal Education

Voluntary continuing legal education (CLE) is a major part of a modern lawyer's professional life. Providing CLE is a large and highly competitive industry. Virtually all bar associations, national, state, and local, provide various kinds of CLE programs: lectures, panels, video and audio, pamphlets, checklists, books, and articles. Many private publishers and other entrepreneurs also provide offerings. Some lawyers take a heavy load of courses; others never or rarely attend. It is the latter group that is suspected of needing such training most. Because of fear that those who need it most take it least, CLE has been made mandatory in some states. Apart from mandatory requirements, how much CLE training is sufficient? How does a lawyer gauge whether her level of knowledge of a subject is at least average except by going to courses to hear what other lawyers know on the subject? Is conveying such awareness itself a sufficient justification for mandatory CLE?

A growing number of states require a lawyer to receive specified hours of continuing legal education each year. Lawyers have challenged "mandatory CLE," as it is called, but these challenges have failed. See, e.g., Verner v. Colorado, 716 F.2d 1352 (10th Cir.1983) (mandatory CLE does not violate lawyers' constitutional rights to due process, free speech or assembly, equal protection of the law, the 8th Amendment's prohibition against cruel and unusual punishment, or the 13th Amendment's prohibition against involuntary servitude; the state may require lawyers to take CLE courses as a condition of maintaining their licenses); see also Brown v. McGarr, 774 F.2d 777 (7th Cir.1985) (practice requirements for federal "trial bar" do not deprive lawyers of property without due process of law).

Peer Review

For over a decade the American Bar Association and the American Law Institute, through their joint CLE enterprise ALI–ABA, have experimented with "peer review." The concept of peer review is that lawyers can maintain and improve their competence by submitting their practice methods to the scrutiny of knowledgeable colleagues for comment and constructive criticism. See ALI–ABA Committee on Continuing Professional Education, A Model Peer Review System (Discussion Draft, April 15, 1980). ALI–ABA has since supported experimental peer review programs in several localities, including Maryland and North Dakota. However, peer review has had difficulty gaining acceptance. The procedure contemplates that lawyers shall be subject to peer review if their practice is found substandard, for example in connection with a grievance inquiry. For obvious reasons, lawyers do not wish to be so designated. Also, the psychology of education is such that it is not easy to teach someone after having called her incompetent. On the other hand, making peer review universally compulsory would be an expensive form of mandatory CLE.

Informal peer review of course goes on all the time. Weren't Chief Justice Burger's remarks about the competence of trial lawyers, quoted at the beginning of this chapter, essentially peer review? Isn't peer review involved in evaluating an associate in a law firm for partnership and establishing the shares of partners in the profits of a firm's practice? It seems plausible that the reason law firms experience lower rates of malpractice claims than sole practitioners is that the members of a firm undergo continuous peer review in the ordinary course of the firm's practice.

Reputation and the Market

Classically, a lawyer's proficiency was reflected in his reputation. Reputation is established partly through the opinion of clients, but at least equally through the opinion of other lawyers. To this extent, a lawyer's reputation is the distillate of peer review. Reputation still is very important within the circle of a lawyer's professional acquaintance. A nonspecialist practitioner located in a metropolitan area rather than a face-to-face community, however, has a very disconnected circle of acquaintance. In part that is what is meant by the "impersonal nature" of modern law practice. It seems clear that the informal peer review expressed in professional reputation is relatively weak in the metropolis, outside well developed legal specializations. Are there formal systems that can assure maintenance of professional competence?

Why not trust the market to differentiate between competent and incompetent lawyers? The market probably operates pretty well as regards specialized types of legal services provided to sophisticated clients such as business corporations. For example, consider the search made for the lawyer in the *Brobeck* case, Chapter 6 below. However, available evidence indicates that ordinary people use a lawyer's services on only two or three occasions in a lifetime. See Curran and Spalding, *The Legal Needs of the Public* (1974). Such limited experience as a client is not much of a basis for making market comparisons. Should individual clients and prospective clients be able to pool their experience by joining together to purchase legal services? That is what prepaid and legal services plans involve, do they not? See Chapter 10 below.

Admission standards for law school and requirements for admission to the bar are two other possible means of ensuring competence. These are discussed in Chapter 10 below on Regulation of the Practice of Law.

Chapter IV

CONFIDENTIALITY: THE RULES

Introductory Note

The law governing client confidences has two sources: agency law and the law of evidence. Lawyers like all agents have a duty to treat information from and about their principals as confidential to the extent that it is intended to be so by the principal, and a duty not to use information about the principal against the principal or for the personal gain of the agent. This duty continues even after the agency is terminated. The duty of confidentiality is broader than the attorney-client privilege: The duty of confidentiality extends to information about the client that the lawyer learns from third parties; the privilege extends only to information transmitted between client and lawyer directly. An agent's duty of confidentiality, however, does not allow the agent to refuse to testify or produce evidence about confidential matters in court or before other government bodies that have the power to compel testimony, such as administrative agencies or legislative committees. This is where the attorney-client privilege comes into play.

The attorney-client privilege is a rule of evidence. The law of evidence excludes some evidence because it is presumptively unreliable, e.g., evidence that violates the hearsay rule. It excludes other evidence to protect an interest or relationship (e.g., the marital relationship) deemed of sufficient importance that the law tolerates the loss of reliable evidence to protect the interest. Exclusionary rules of the latter type are known as privileges. Because recognizing a privilege entails a loss to the truth-seeking function, privileges are interpreted narrowly, and the burden is on the proponent of the privilege to prove that its elements have been met.

The modern rationale for the attorney-client privilege is that the privilege encourages open communication between clients and their lawyers, which in turn serves the interests of clients who need effective legal representation and society's interests in having clients advised about the legality of proposed actions and effectively represented in the adversary process.

The attorney-client privilege is recognized in every jurisdiction either by statute or common law. In federal courts the contours of the privilege are determined by federal law when the case involves a federal question and by state law in diversity cases. See Federal Rule of Evidence 501.

The privilege was recognized at English common law as early as the 16th Century, although it was applied sporadically and not fully accepted until after 1800. Hazard, An Historical Perspective on the Attorney–Client Privilege, 66 Calif.L.Rev. 1061, 1070 (1978). Its development in American law has been through common law and statute and not as a matter of constitutional right. Federal and state constitutions recognize rights supported by the attorney-client privilege, namely the right to counsel and the privilege against self-incrimination. The connection between the Fifth Amendment privilege against incrimination and the attorney-client privilege is considered in the *Fisher* case below. As to the Sixth Amendment's right to counsel, the connection between the privilege and the Constitution remains uncertain. See Marano v. Holland, 366 S.E.2d 117 (W.Va.1988) (citing cases suggesting but not holding that the Sixth Amendment right to counsel includes some form of attorney-client privilege). The federal circuit courts agree, however, that *state use* of information protected by the attorney-client privilege may infringe the defendant's right to counsel, although they differ on what is material infringement. See United States v. Mastroianni, 749 F.2d 900 (1st Cir.1984) (describing the differences among the circuit courts). These cases assume the existence of a state privilege and implicitly acknowledge its importance to the Sixth Amendment's right to counsel in criminal trials. They strongly suggest that should a state legislature abolish the attorney-client privilege, the courts would hold the statute unconstitutional. This point will likely remain theoretical because no state is likely to abolish the privilege. Whether the courts would hold that at some point a narrowing of the privilege was unconstitutional is the more important and more difficult question. Thus far the courts have shown no inclination to require any particular scope for the privilege under the Sixth Amendment. It is also true that no state has sought to restrict the privilege significantly.

On the history of the privilege see Hazard, An Historical Perspective on the Attorney–Client Privilege, 66 Calif.L.Rev. 1061 (1978); Radin, The Privilege of Confidential Communication Between Lawyer and Client, 16 Calif.L.Rev. 487 (1928). On the connection between the Sixth Amendment and the privilege, see Seidelson, The Attorney–Client Privilege and Clients' Constitutional Rights, 6 Hofstra L.Rev. 693 (1978).

A. ATTORNEY–CLIENT PRIVILEGE

The scope of the attorney-client privilege is a complicated subject in its own. The materials which follow give an overview. Generally see Cleary et al., McCormick's Evidence c. 10 (3rd ed. 1984); C. Wolfram, Modern Legal Ethics § 6.3 et seq. (1986); 8 J. Wigmore, Evidence § 2291 (J. McNaughton rev. ed. 1961); and Developments in the Law— Privileged Communication: III. Attorney–Client Privilege, 98 Harv.L. Rev. 1501 (1985).

The precise formulation of the attorney-client privilege varies from jurisdiction to jurisdiction. Proposed Federal Rule of Evidence 503, although not enacted by Congress, is often referred to by courts as a modern statement of the rule:

PROPOSED FEDERAL RULE OF EVIDENCE 503 LAWYER–CLIENT PRIVILEGE

[Not enacted]

(a) **Definitions.** As used in this rule:

(1) A "client" is a person, public officer, or corporation, association, or other organization or entity, either public or private, who is rendered professional legal services by a lawyer, or who consults a lawyer with a view to obtaining professional legal services from him.

(2) A "lawyer" is a person authorized, or reasonably believed by the client to be authorized, to practice law in any state or nation.

(3) A "representative of the lawyer" is one employed to assist the lawyer in the rendition of professional legal services.

(4) A communication is "confidential" if not intended to be disclosed to third persons other than those to whom disclosure is in furtherance of the rendition of professional legal services to the client or those reasonably necessary for the transmission of the communication.

(b) **General rule of privilege.** A client has a privilege to refuse to disclose and to prevent any other person from disclosing confidential communications made for the purpose of facilitating the rendition of professional legal services to the client, (1) between himself or his representative and his lawyer or his lawyer's representative, or (2) between his lawyer and the lawyer's representative, or (3) by him or his lawyer to a lawyer representing another in a matter of common interest, or (4) between representatives of the client or between the client and a representative of the client, or (5) between lawyers representing the client.

(c) **Who may claim the privilege.** The privilege may be claimed by the client, his guardian or conservator, the personal representative of a deceased client, or the successor, trustee, or similar representative of a corporation, association, or other organization, whether or not in existence. The person who was the lawyer at the time of the communication may claim the privilege but only on behalf of the client. His authority to do so is presumed in the absence of evidence to the contrary.

(d) **Exceptions.** There is no privilege under this rule:

(1) *Furtherance of crime or fraud.* If the services of the lawyer were sought or obtained to enable or aid anyone to commit or plan to commit what the client knew or reasonably should have known to be a crime or fraud; or

(2) *Claimants through same deceased client.* As to a communication relevant to an issue between parties who claim through the same

deceased client, regardless of whether the claims are by testate or intestate succession or by *inter vivos* transaction; or

(3) Breach of duty by lawyer or client. As to a communication relevant to an issue of breach of duty by the lawyer to his client or by the client to his lawyer; or

(4) Document attested by lawyer. As to a communication relevant to an issue concerning an attested document to which the lawyer is an attesting witness; or

(5) Joint clients. As to a communication relevant to a matter of common interest between two or more clients if the communication was made by any of them to a lawyer retained or consulted in common, when offered in an action between any of the clients.

Advisory Committee's Note

Subdivision (a). (1) The definition of "client" includes governmental bodies, . . . and corporations, ... The definition also extends the status of client to one consulting a lawyer preliminarily with a view to retaining him, even though actual employment does not result. . . . The client need not be involved in litigation; the rendition of legal service or advice under any circumstances suffices. . . . The services must be professional legal services; purely business or personal matters do not qualify. . . .

. . .

(2) A "lawyer" is a person licensed to practice law in any state or nation. . . . "Lawyer" also includes a person reasonably believed to be a lawyer. . . .

(3) The definition of "representative of the lawyer" recognizes that the lawyer may, in rendering legal services, utilize the services of assistants in addition to those employed in the process of communicating. Thus the definition includes an expert employed to assist in rendering legal advice. . . . It also includes an expert employed to assist in the planning and conduct of litigation, though not one employed to testify as a witness. . . . The definition does not, however, limit "representative of the lawyer" to experts. . . .

(4) The requisite confidentiality of communication is defined in terms of intent. A communication made in public or meant to be relayed to outsiders or which is divulged by the client to third persons can scarcely be considered confidential. . . . The intent is inferable from the circumstances. Unless intent to disclose is apparent, the attorney-client communication is confidential. Taking or failing to take precautions may be considered as bearing on intent.

Practicality requires that some disclosure be allowed beyond the immediate circle of lawyer-client and their representatives without impairing confidentiality. Hence the definition allows disclosure to persons "to whom disclosure is in furtherance of the rendition of professional legal services to the client," contemplating those in such relation to the client as "spouse, parent, business associate, or joint client." Comment, California Evidence Code § 952.

Disclosure may also be made to persons "reasonably necessary for the transmission of the communication," without loss of confidentiality.

Subdivision (b) sets forth the privilege, using the previously defined terms: client, lawyer, representative of the lawyer, and confidential communication.

Substantial authority has in the past allowed the eavesdropper to testify to overheard privileged conversations and has admitted intercepted privileged letters. Today, the evolution of more sophisticated techniques of eavesdropping and interception calls for abandonment of this position. The rule accordingly adopts a policy of protection against these kinds of invasion of the privilege.

The privilege extends to communications (1) between client or his representative and lawyer or his representative, (2) between lawyer and lawyer's representative, (3) by client or his lawyer to a lawyer representing another in a matter of common interest, (4) between representatives of the client or the client and a representative of the client, and (5) between lawyers representing the client. All these communications must be specifically for the purpose of obtaining legal services for the client; otherwise the privilege does not attach.

The third type of communication occurs in the "joint defense" or "pooled information" situation, where different lawyers represent clients who have some interests in common. In Chahoon v. Commonwealth, 62 Va. 822 (1871), the court said that the various clients might have retained one attorney to represent all; hence everything said at a joint conference was privileged, and one of the clients could prevent another from disclosing what the other had himself said. The result seems to be incorrect in overlooking a frequent reason for retaining different attorneys by the various clients, namely actually or potentially conflicting interests in addition to the common interest which brings them together. The needs of these cases seem better to be met by allowing each client a privilege as to his own statements. Thus if all resist disclosure, none will occur. . . . But, if for reasons of his own, a client wishes to disclose his own statements made at the joint conference, he should be permitted to do so, and the rule is to that effect. The rule does not apply to situations where there is no common interest to be promoted by a joint consultation, and the parties meet on a purely adversary basis. . . .

Subdivision (c). The privilege is, of course, that of the client, to be claimed by him or by his personal representative. The successor of a dissolved corporate client may claim the privilege. . . .

The lawyer may not claim the privilege on his own behalf. However, he may claim it on behalf of the client. It is assumed that the ethics of the profession will require him to do so except under most unusual circumstances. American Bar Association, Canons of Professional Ethics, Canon 37. His authority to make the claim is presumed unless there is evidence to the contrary, as would be the case if the client were now a party to litigation in which the question arose and were represented by other counsel. . . .

Subdivision (d) in general incorporates well established exceptions.

(1) The privilege does not extend to advice in aid of future wrongdoing. . . . The wrongdoing need not be that of the client. The provision that the client knew or reasonably should have known of the criminal or fraudulent nature of the act is designed to protect the client who is erroneously advised that the proposed action is within the law.

(2) Normally the privilege survives the death of the client and may be asserted by his representative. Subdivision (c), supra. When, however, the identity of the person who steps into the client's shoes is in issue, as in a will contest, the identity of the person entitled to claim the privilege remains undetermined until the conclusion of the litigation. The choice is thus between allowing both sides or neither to assert the privilege, with authority and reason favoring the latter view. . . .

(3) The exception is required by considerations of fairness and policy when questions arise out of dealings between attorney and client, as in cases of controversy over attorney's fees, claims of inadequacy of representation, or charges of professional misconduct. . . .

(4) When the lawyer acts as attesting witness, the approval of the client to his so doing may safely be assumed, and waiver of the privilege as to any relevant lawyer-client communications is a proper result. . . .

(5) . . . The situation with which this provision deals is to be distinguished from the case of clients with a common interest who retain different lawyers. See subdivision (b)(3) of this rule, supra.

Wigmore's Test

The most concise formulation of the rule is Wigmore's, which sets out eight elements:

(1) Where legal advice is sought

(2) from a professional legal advisor in his capacity as such

(3) the communications relating to that purpose

(4) made in confidence

(5) by the client

(6) are at the client's instance permanently protected

(7) from disclosure by himself or the lawyer

(8) except if the privilege is waived.

UPJOHN v. UNITED STATES

Supreme Court of the United States, 1981.
449 U.S. 383, 101 S.Ct. 677, 66 L.Ed.2d 584.

JUSTICE REHNQUIST delivered the opinion of the Court.

We granted certiorari in this case to address important questions concerning the scope of the attorney-client privilege in the corporate context and the applicability of the work-product doctrine in proceedings to enforce tax summonses. . . .

I

Petitioner Upjohn Co. manufactures and sells pharmaceuticals here and abroad. In January 1976 independent accountants conducting an audit of one of Upjohn's foreign subsidiaries discovered that the subsidiary made payments to or for the benefit of foreign government officials in order to secure government business. The accountants so informed petitioner, Mr. Gerard Thomas, Upjohn's Vice President, Secretary, and General Counsel. Thomas is a member of the Michigan and New York Bars, and has been Upjohn's General Counsel for 20 years. He consulted with outside counsel and R.T. Parfet, Jr., Upjohn's Chairman of the Board. It was decided that the company would conduct an internal investigation of what were termed "questionable payments." As part of this investigation the attorneys prepared a letter containing a questionnaire which was sent to "All Foreign General and Area Managers" over the Chairman's signature. The letter began by noting recent disclosures that several American companies made "possibly illegal" payments to foreign government officials and emphasized that the management needed full information concerning any such payments made by Upjohn. The letter indicated that the Chairman had asked Thomas, identified as "the company's General Counsel," "to conduct an investigation for the purpose of determining the nature and magnitude of any payments made by the Upjohn Company or any of its subsidiaries to any employee or official of a foreign government." The questionnaire sought detailed information concerning such payments. Managers were instructed to treat the investigation as "highly confidential" and not to discuss it with anyone other than Upjohn employees who might be helpful in providing the requested information. Responses were to be sent directly to Thomas. Thomas and outside counsel also interviewed the recipients of the questionnaire and some 33 other Upjohn officers or employees as part of the investigation.

On March 26, 1976, the company voluntarily submitted a preliminary report to the Securities and Exchange Commission on Form 8–K disclosing certain questionable payments. A copy of the report was simultaneously submitted to the Internal Revenue Service, which immediately began an investigation to determine the tax consequences of the payments. Special agents conducting the investigation were given lists by Upjohn of all those interviewed and all who had responded to the questionnaire.   On November 23, 1976, the Service issued a summons pursuant to 26 U.S.C. § 7602 demanding production of:

"All files relative to the investigation conducted under the supervision of Gerard Thomas to identify payments to employees of foreign governments and any political contributions made by the Upjohn Company or any of its affiliates since January 1, 1971 and to determine whether any funds of the Upjohn Company had been improperly accounted for on the corporate books during the same period.

"The records should include but not be limited to written questionnaires sent to managers of the Upjohn Company's foreign affiliates, and memorandums or notes of the interviews conducted in the United States and abroad with officers and employees of the Upjohn Company and its subsidiaries."

The company declined to produce the documents specified in the second paragraph on the grounds that they were protected from disclosure by the attorney-client privilege and constituted the work product of attorneys prepared in anticipation of litigation.   On August 31, 1977, the United States filed a petition seeking enforcement of the summons under 26 U.S.C. §§ 7402(b) and 7604(a) in the United States District Court for the Western District of Michigan. . . .

II

Federal Rule of Evidence 501 provides that "the privilege of a witness . . . shall be governed by the principles of the common law as they may be interpreted by the courts of the United States in light of reason and experience."   The attorney-client privilege is the oldest of the privileges for confidential communications known to the common law.   8 J. Wigmore, Evidence § 2290 (McNaughton rev. 1961).   Its purpose is to encourage full and frank communication between attorneys and their clients and thereby promote broader public interests in the observance of law and administration of justice.   The privilege recognizes that sound legal advice or advocacy serves public ends and that such advice or advocacy depends upon the lawyer's being fully informed by the client.   As we stated last Term in Trammel v. United States, 445 U.S. 40, 51, 100 S.Ct. 906, 913, 63 L.Ed.2d 186 (1980): "The lawyer-client privilege rests on the need for the advocate and counselor to know all that relates to the client's reasons for seeking representation if the professional mission is to be carried out."   And in Fisher v. United States, 425 U.S. 391, 403, 96 S.Ct. 1569, 1577, 48 L.Ed.2d 39 (1976), we recognized the purpose of the privilege to be "to encourage clients to make full disclosure to their attorneys."   This rationale for the privilege has long been recognized by the Court, see Hunt v. Blackburn, 128 U.S. 464, 470, 9 S.Ct. 125, 127, 32 L.Ed. 488 (1888) . . . Admittedly complications in the application of the privilege arise when the client is a corporation, which in theory is an artificial creature of the law, and not an individual; but this Court has assumed that the privilege applies when the client is a corporation. United States v. Louisville & Nashville R. Co., 236 U.S. 318, 336, 35 S.Ct. 363, 369, 59 L.Ed. 598 (1915), and the Government does not contest the general proposition.

The Court of Appeals, however, considered the application of the privilege in the corporate context to present a "different problem," since the client was an inanimate entity and "only the senior management, guiding and integrating the several operations, . . . can be said to possess an identity analogous to the corporation as a whole." The first case to articulate the so-called "control group test" adopted by the court below, Philadelphia v. Westinghouse Electric Corp., 210 F.Supp. 483, 485 (ED Pa.), petition for mandamus and prohibition denied sub nom. General Electric Co. v. Kirkpatrick, 312 F.2d 742 (CA3 1962), cert. denied, 372 U.S. 943 . . . (1963), reflected a similar conceptual approach:

> "Keeping in mind that the question is, Is it the corporation which is seeking the lawyer's advice when the asserted privileged communication is made?, the most satisfactory solution, I think, is that if the employee making the communication, of whatever rank he may be, is in a position to control or even to take a substantial part in a decision about any action which the corporation may take upon the advice of the attorney, . . . then, in effect, *he is (or personifies) the corporation* when he makes his disclosure to the lawyer and the privilege would apply." (Emphasis supplied.)

Such a view, we think, overlooks the fact that the privilege exists to protect not only the giving of professional advice to those who can act on it but also the giving of information to the lawyer to enable him to give sound and informed advice. . . . The first step in the resolution of any legal problem is ascertaining the factual background and sifting through the facts with an eye to the legally relevant. See ABA Code of Professional Responsibility, Ethical Consideration 4–1:

> "A lawyer should be fully informed of all the facts of the matter he is handling in order for his client to obtain the full advantage of our legal system. It is for the lawyer in the exercise of his independent professional judgment to separate the relevant and important from the irrelevant and unimportant. The observance of the ethical obligation of a lawyer to hold inviolate the confidences and secrets of his client not only facilitates the full development of facts essential to proper representation of the client but also encourages laymen to seek early legal assistance."

See also Hickman v. Taylor, 329 U.S. 495, 511, 67 S.Ct. 385, 393–394, 91 L.Ed. 451 (1947).

In the case of the individual client the provider of information and the person who acts on the lawyer's advice are one and the same. In the corporate context, however, it will frequently be employees beyond the control group as defined by the court below—"officers and agents

. . . responsible for directing [the company's] actions in response to legal advice"—who will possess the information needed by the corporation's lawyers. Middle-level—and indeed lower-level—employees can, by actions within the scope of their employment, embroil the corporation in serious legal difficulties, and it is only natural that these employees would have the relevant information needed by corporate counsel if he is adequately to advise the client with respect to such actual or potential difficulties. This fact was noted in Diversified Industries, Inc. v. Meredith, 572 F.2d 596 (CA8 1978) (en banc):

"In a corporation, it may be necessary to glean information relevant to a legal problem from middle management or non-management personnel as well as from top executives. The attorney dealing with a complex legal problem 'is thus faced with a "Hobson's choice". If he interviews employees not having "the very highest authority", their communications to him will not be privileged. If, on the other hand, he interviews *only* those employees with the "very highest authority", he may find it extremely difficult, if not impossible, to determine what happened.'" Id., at 608–609 (quoting Weinschel Corporate Employee Interviews and the Attorney–Client Privilege, 12 B.C.Ind. & Com.L.Rev. 873, 876 (1971)).

The control group test adopted by the court below thus frustrates the very purpose of the privilege by discouraging the communication of relevant information by employees of the client to attorneys seeking to render legal advice to the client corporation. The attorney's advice will also frequently be more significant to noncontrol group members than to those who officially sanction the advice, and the control group test makes it more difficult to convey full and frank legal advice to the employees who will put into effect the client corporation's policy. See, e.g., Duplan Corp. v. Deering Milliken, Inc., 397 F.Supp. 1146, 1164 (DSC 1974) ("After the lawyer forms his or her opinion, it is of no immediate benefit to the Chairman of the Board or the President. It must be given to the corporate personnel who will apply it").

The narrow scope given the attorney-client privilege by the court below not only makes it difficult for corporate attorneys to formulate sound advice when their client is faced with a specific legal problem but also threatens to limit the valuable efforts of corporate counsel to ensure their client's compliance with the law. In light of the vast and complicated array of regulatory legislation confronting the modern corporation, corporations, unlike most individuals, "constantly go to lawyers to find out how to obey the law," Burnham, The Attorney–Client Privilege in the Corporate Arena, 24 Bus.Law. 901, 913 (1969), particularly since compliance with the law in this area is hardly an instinctive matter, see, e.g., United States v. United States Gypsum Co., 438 U.S. 422, 440–441, 98 S.Ct. 2864, 2875–2876, 57 L.Ed.2d 854 (1978) ("the behavior proscribed by the [Sherman] Act is often difficult to distinguish from the gray zone of socially acceptable and economically justifiable business conduct"). The test adopted by the court below is difficult to apply in practice, though no abstractly formulated and unvarying "test" will necessarily enable courts to decide questions such as this with mathematical precision. But if the purpose of the attorney-client privilege is to be served, the attorney and client must be able to predict with some degree of certainty whether particular discussions will be protected. An uncertain privilege, or one which purports to be certain but results in widely varying applications by the courts, is little better than no privilege at all. The very terms of the test adopted by the court below suggest the unpredictability of its application. The test restricts the availability of the privilege to those officers who play a "substantial role" in deciding and directing a corporation's legal response. Disparate decisions in cases applying this test illustrate its unpredictability. Compare, e.g., Hogan v. Zletz, 43 F.R.D. 308, 315–316 (ND Okl.1967), aff'd in part sub nom. Natta v. Hogan, 392 F.2d 686 (CA10 1968) (control group includes managers and assistant managers of patent division and research and development department), with Congoleum Industries, Inc. v. GAF Corp., 49 F.R.D. 82, 83–85 (ED Pa. 1969), aff'd, 478 F.2d 1398 (CA3 1973) (control group includes only division and corporate vice presidents, and not two directors of research and vice president for production and research).

The communications at issue were made by Upjohn employees to counsel for Upjohn acting as such, at the direction of corporate superiors in order to secure legal advice from counsel. As the Magistrate found, "Mr. Thomas consulted with the Chairman of the Board and outside counsel and thereafter conducted a factual investigation to determine the nature and extent of the questionable payments *and to be in a position to give legal advice to the company with respect to the payments*." (Emphasis supplied.) Information, not available from upperchelon management, was needed to supply a basis for legal advice concerning compliance with securities and tax laws, foreign laws, currency regulations, duties to shareholders, and potential litigation in each of these areas. The communications concerned matters within the scope of the employees' corporate duties, and the employees themselves were sufficiently aware that they were being questioned in order that the corporation could obtain legal advice. The questionnaire identified Thomas as "the company's General Counsel" and referred in its opening sentence to the possible illegality of payments such as the ones on which information was sought. App. 40a. A statement of policy accompanying the questionnaire clearly indicated the legal implications of the investigation. The policy statement was issued "in order that there be no uncertainty in the future as to the policy with respect to the practices which are the subject of this investigation." It began "Upjohn will comply with all laws and regulations," and stated that commissions or payments "will not be used as a subterfuge for bribes or illegal payments" and that all payments must be "proper and legal." Any future agreements with foreign distributors or agents were to be approved "by a company attorney" and any questions concerning the policy were to be referred "to the company's General Counsel." This statement was issued to Upjohn employees worldwide, so that even those interviewees not receiving a questionnaire were aware of the legal implications of the interviews. Pursuant to explicit instructions from the Chairman of the Board, the communications were considered "highly confidential" when made, and have been kept confidential by the company. Consistent with the underlying purposes of the attorney-client privilege, these communications must be protected against compelled disclosure.

The Court of Appeals declined to extend the attorney-client privilege beyond the limits of the control group test for fear that doing so would entail severe burdens on discovery and create a broad "zone of silence" over corporate affairs. Application of the attorney-client privilege to communications such as those involved here, however, puts the adversary in no worse position than if the communications had never taken place. The privilege only protects disclosure of communications; it does not protect disclosure of the underlying facts by those who communicated with the attorney:

"[T]he protection of the privilege extends only to *communications* and not to facts. A fact is one thing and a communication concerning that fact is an entirely different thing. The client cannot be compelled to answer the question, 'What did you say or write to the attorney?' but may not refuse to disclose any relevant fact within his knowledge merely because he incorporated a statement of such fact into his communication to his attorney." Philadelphia v. Westinghouse Electric Corp., 205 F.Supp. 830, 831 (ED Pa.1962).

See also Diversified Industries, 572 F.2d, at 611; State ex rel. Dudek v. Circuit Court, 34 Wis.2d 559, 580, 150 N.W.2d 387, 399 (1967) ("the courts have noted that a party cannot conceal a fact merely by revealing it to his lawyer"). Here the Government was free to question the employees who communicated with Thomas and outside counsel. Upjohn has provided the IRS with a list of such employees, and the IRS has already interviewed some 25 of them. While it would probably be more convenient for the Government to secure the results of petitioner's internal investigation by simply subpoenaing the questionnaires and notes taken by petitioner's attorneys, such considerations of convenience do not overcome the policies served by the attorney-client privilege. As Justice Jackson noted in his concurring opinion in Hickman v. Taylor, 329 U.S., at 516, 67 S.Ct., at 396: "Discovery was hardly intended to enable a learned profession to perform its functions . . . on wits borrowed from the adversary."

Needless to say, we decide only the case before us, and do not undertake to draft a set of rules which should govern challenges to investigatory subpoenas. Any such approach would violate the spirit of Federal Rule of Evidence 501. . . . While such a "case-by-case" basis may to some slight extent undermine desirable certainty in the boundaries of the attorney-client privilege, it obeys the spirit of the Rules. At the same time we conclude that the narrow "control group test" sanctioned by the Court of Appeals, in this case cannot, consistent with "the principles of the common law as . . . interpreted . . . in the light of reason and experience," Fed.Rule Evid. 501, govern the development of the law in this area.

III

Our decision that the communications by Upjohn employees to counsel are covered by the attorney-client privilege disposes of the case so far as the responses to the questionnaires and any notes reflecting responses to interview questions are concerned. The summons reaches further, however, and Thomas has testified that his notes and memoranda of interviews go beyond recording responses to his questions. To the extent that the material subject to the summons is not protected by the attorney-client privilege as disclosing communications between an employee and counsel, we must reach the ruling by the Court of Appeals that the work-product doctrine does not apply to summonses issued under 26 U.S.C. § 7602.[6]

The Government concedes, wisely, that the Court of Appeals erred and that the work-product doctrine does apply to IRS summonses. . . .

As we stated last Term, the obligation imposed by a tax summons remains "subject to the traditional privileges and limitations." United States v. Euge, 444 U.S. 707, 714, 100 S.Ct. 874, 879–880, 63 L.Ed.2d 741 (1980). Nothing in the language of the IRS summons provisions or their legislative history suggests an intent on the part of Congress to preclude application of the work-product doctrine. Rule 26(b)(3) codifies the work-product doctrine, and the Federal Rules of Civil Procedure are made applicable to summons enforcement proceedings by Rule 81(a)(3). . . . While conceding the applicability of the work-product doctrine, the Government asserts that it has made a sufficient showing of necessity to overcome its protections. The Magistrate apparently so found. The Government relies on the following language in *Hickman:*

> "We do not mean to say that all written materials obtained or prepared by an adversary's counsel with an eye toward litigation are necessarily free from discovery in all cases. Where relevant and nonprivileged facts remain hidden in an attorney's file and where production of those facts is essential to the preparation of one's case, discovery may properly be had. . . . And production might be justified where the witnesses are no longer available or can be reached only with difficulty." 329 U.S., at 511, 67 S.Ct., at 394.

The Government stresses that interviewees are scattered across the globe and that Upjohn has forbidden its employees to answer questions

---

6. The following discussion will also be relevant to counsel's notes and memoranda of interviews with the seven former employees should it be determined that the attorney-client privilege does not apply to them.

it considers irrelevant. The above-quoted language from *Hickman,* however, did not apply to "oral statements made by witnesses . . . whether presently in the form of [the attorney's] mental impressions or memoranda." Id., at 512, 67 S.Ct., at 394. As to such material the Court did "not believe that any showing of necessity can be made under the circumstances of this case so as to justify production. . . . If there should be a rare situation justifying production of these matters petitioner's case is not of that type." Id., at 512–513, 67 S.Ct., at 394–395. . . . Forcing an attorney to disclose notes and memoranda of witnesses' oral statements is particularly disfavored because it tends to reveal the attorney's mental processes, 329 U.S., at 513, 67 S.Ct., at 394–395 ("what he saw fit to write down regarding witnesses' remarks"); id., at 516–517, 67 S.Ct., at 396 ("the statement would be his [the attorney's] language, permeated with his inferences") (Jackson, J., concurring).[8]

Rule 26 accords special protection to work product revealing the attorney's mental processes. The Rule permits disclosure of documents and tangible things constituting attorney work product upon a showing of substantial need and inability to obtain the equivalent without undue hardship. This was the standard applied by the Magistrate. Rule 26 goes on, however, to state that "[i]n ordering discovery of such materials when the required showing has been made, the court shall protect against disclosure of the mental impressions, conclusions, opinions or legal theories of an attorney or other representative of a party concerning the litigation." Although this language does not specifically refer to memoranda based on oral statements of witnesses, the *Hickman* court stressed the danger that compelled disclosure of such memoranda would reveal the attorney's mental processes. It is clear that this is the sort of material the draftsmen of the Rule had in mind as deserving special protection. See Notes of Advisory Committee on 1970 Amendment to Rules, 28 U.S.C.App., p. 442.

Based on the foregoing, some courts have concluded that *no* showing of necessity can overcome protection of work product which is based on oral statements from witnesses. See, e.g., In re Grand Jury Proceedings, 473 F.2d 840, 848 (CA8 1973) (personal recollections, notes, and memoranda pertaining to conversation with witnesses); In re Grand Jury Investigation, 412 F.Supp. 943, 949 (ED Pa.1976) (notes of conversation with witness "are so much a product of the lawyer's thinking and so little probative of the witness's actual words that they are absolutely protected from disclosure"). Those courts declining to adopt an absolute rule have nonetheless recognized that such material is entitled to special protection. See, e.g., In re Grand Jury Investigation, 599 F.2d 1224, 1231 (CA3 1979)

8. Thomas described his notes of the interviews as containing "what I considered to be the important questions, the substance of the responses to them, my beliefs as to the importance of these, my beliefs as to how they related to the inquiry, my thoughts as to how they related to other questions. In some instances they might even suggest other questions that I would have to ask or things that I needed to find elsewhere."

("special considerations . . . must shape any ruling on the discoverability of interview memoranda . . .; such documents will be discoverable only in a 'rare situation' "); Cf. In re Grand Jury Subpoena, 599 F.2d 504, 511–512 (CA2 1979).

We do not decide the issue at this time. It is clear that the Magistrate applied the wrong standard when he concluded that the Government had made a sufficient showing of necessity to overcome the protections of the work-product doctrine. The Magistrate applied the "substantial need" and "without undue hardship" standard articulated in the first part of Rule 26(b)(3). The notes and memoranda sought by the Government here, however, are work product based on oral statements. If they reveal communications, they are, in this case, protected by the attorney-client privilege. To the extent they do not reveal communications, they reveal the attorneys' mental processes in evaluating the communications. As Rule 26 and *Hickman* make clear, such work product cannot be disclosed simply on a showing of substantial need and inability to obtain the equivalent without undue hardship.

While we are not prepared at this juncture to say that such material is always protected by the work-product rule, we think a far stronger showing of necessity and unavailability by other means than was made by the Government or applied by the Magistrate in this case would be necessary to compel disclosure. . . .

The Holding in Upjohn and Other Tests for the Corporate Privilege

Defining the "client" when the lawyer represents an organization is critical. Communications from nonclients about the client's affairs are not protected by the privilege. See, e.g., In re Fischel, 557 F.2d 209 (9th Cir.1977).

The strongest argument for the "control group" test is that it prevents too broad a "zone of silence" over corporate affairs. After *Upjohn* could a corporation route all corporate documents through its general counsel's office ostensibly to keep its lawyer informed but actually to set up a later claim of privilege? Would such a plan work?

See Sexton, A Post–Upjohn Consideration of the Attorney–Client Privilege, 57 N.Y.U.L.Rev. 443 (1982); Note, The Attorney–Client Privilege and the Corporate Client: Where Do We Go After Upjohn?, 81 Mich.L.Rev. 665 (1983).

The Corporate Privilege Under State Law

It is important to remember that *Upjohn* is not controlling in state courts or in federal diversity cases. See, e.g., Consolidated Coal Co. v. Bucyrus–Erie Co., 89 Ill.2d 103, 59 Ill.Dec. 666, 432 N.E.2d 250 (1982) (*Upjohn* rejected; control group test applied). However, most states reach the same result as *Upjohn*. See, e.g., Leer v. Chicago, Milwaukee, S.P. & Pac. Ry., 308 N.W.2d 305 (Minn.1981); and Marriott Corp. v.

American Academy of Psychotherapists, Inc., 157 Ga.App. 497, 277 S.E.2d 785 (1981). Also see Rossi v. Blue Cross and Blue Shield, 73 N.Y. 2d 588, 540 N.E.2d 703 (1989) (discussing limits of the privilege for in-house counsel).

The Requirement that the Communication be Made in Confidence

No privilege attaches to communications made in the presence of a third party unless that person's presence is necessary to protect the client's interests. See, e.g., In re Himmel, 125 Ill.2d 531, 533 N.E.2d 790 (1988) (communication in front of mother and fiancée not privileged unless they were agents of the client); Bolyea v. First Presbyterian Church of Wilton, 196 N.W.2d 149 (N.D.1972) (communication in front of others not necessary to the preparation of a deed—no privilege). See also United States v. Pipkins, 528 F.2d 559 (5th Cir.1976).

Who May Claim the Privilege on Behalf of the Corporation?

The current management of the corporation controls the privilege on behalf of the corporation. When management is replaced, the successor controls the privilege. This can result in decisions to waive the privilege that may be very embarrassing to members of the prior management. See Commodity Futures Trading Commission v. Weintraub, 471 U.S. 343 (1985) (court appointed successor may waive the corporation's privilege).

Moreover, shareholders may successfully challenge management's decision to invoke the privilege and thereby gain access to otherwise confidential corporate communications. See Garner v. Wolfinbarger, 430 F.2d 1093 (5th Cir.1970) (setting out factors to be considered in whether to grant shareholders access to otherwise privileged information). This case and its progeny are discussed in Chapter 9 below at pp. 753–756.

Advising Corporate Employees not to Speak with Opposing Counsel

In *Upjohn* corporate employees were "forbidden . . . to answer questions" posed by government lawyers that the company considered irrelevant. M.R. 3.4(f) provides that: "A lawyer shall not . . . request a person other than a client to refrain from voluntarily giving relevant information to another party unless: (1) the person is a relative or an employee or other agent of a client; and (2) the lawyer reasonably believes that the person's interests will not be adversely affected by refraining from giving such information." Whether the opposing party may contact employees of the organization directly without notifying the organization's lawyer is covered in Chapter 9 below at pp. 851–861. Generally see Rule 4.2 and its Comment.

Are Communications from the Lawyer to the Client Protected by the Privilege?

Wigmore's formulation of the privilege limits it to communications made by the client to the lawyer. What about what the lawyer says to the client? Some courts hold that all communications from lawyer to client are privileged, even when initiated by the lawyer. This approach relies in part on the lawyer's duty to keep the client informed and assumes that any statement by the lawyer would reveal a confidence entrusted to her by the client. See, e.g., In re LTV Securities Litigation, 89 F.R.D. 595, 602 (N.D.Tex.1981); Hercules, Inc. v. Exxon Corp., 434 F.Supp. 136, 144–145 (D.Del.1977); Jack Winter, Inc. v. Koratron Company, Inc., 54 F.R.D. 44, 46 (N.D.Cal.1971).

The other approach extends the privilege to lawyer statements only when the court finds that the statements in fact contain the substance of a client confidence. See, e.g., American Standard Inc. v. Pfizer, Inc., 828 F.2d 734 (Fed.Cir.1987); United States v. Amerada Hess Corp., 619 F.2d 980, 986 (3d Cir.1980).

The Work–Product Doctrine

Introductory Note

The work product doctrine is connected to, but different from, the attorney-client privilege. As *Upjohn* demonstrates, documents prepared by the lawyers in anticipation of litigation that did not include communications protected by the privilege were governed by the work product rule.

The leading case on the work product doctrine is Hickman v. Taylor, 329 U.S. 495, 67 S.Ct. 385 (1947). In *Hickman* the Court recognized a qualified immunity for the work product of lawyers, holding that such material was discoverable only upon a substantial showing of "necessity or justification." *Hickman* has been codified in Federal Rule of Civil Procedure 26(b)(3), which provides in part:

> [A] party may obtain discovery of [material] . . . otherwise discoverable under . . . this rule and prepared in anticipation of litigation . . . only upon showing that the party seeking discovery has substantial need of the materials in the preparation of his case and that he is unable without undue hardship to obtain the substantial equivalent of the materials by other means. In ordering discovery of such materials when the required showing has been made, the court shall protect against disclosure of the mental impressions, conclusions, opinions, or legal theories of an attorney . . . concerning the litigation.

Material other than lawyer mental impressions, theories and opinions is called "fact work product," and can be obtained only upon a showing of need. For example, work product has been held discoverable for impeachment purposes, Brennan v. Engineered Products, 506 F.2d 299 (8th Cir.1974); Dingler v. Halcyon, 50 F.R.D. 211 (E.D.Pa.1970); because a witness is unavailable, Xerox v. IBM, 64 F.R.D. 367 (S.D.N.Y. 1974) (witness lost memory); Fidelity & Deposit Co. v. Strauss, 52 F.R.D. 536 (E.D.Pa.1971) (witness employee of adversary); Almaguer v. Chicago, R.I.R.R., 55 F.R.D. 147 (E.D.Neb.1972) (witness hostile); because of the delay or expense that would be incurred if the opposing party were not given access to the material, Arney v. Hormel Co., 53 F.R.D. 179 (D.Minn.1971); and where the passage of time makes the material otherwise inaccessible, Hamilton v. Canal Barge Co., 395 F.Supp. 975 (E.D.La.1974). *Upjohn* appears to raise the level of hardship required to obtain fact work product.

The Lawyer's Mental Impressions and Theories

The language in Rule 26(b)(3) and in corresponding state formulations of the work product doctrine accords the mental impressions, opinions and theories of the lawyer special protection. Whether mental impressions, etc. are absolutely protected from discovery is left open in *Upjohn.* What showing of need did the Government make in *Upjohn?*

Most state courts follow the lead in *Upjohn,* holding that absent some extreme necessity the mental impressions of lawyers are not discoverable. See, e.g., Klaiber v. Orzel, 148 Ariz. 320, 714 P.2d 813 (1986); Consolidation Coal Co. v. Bucyrus–Erie Co., 89 Ill.2d 103, 59 Ill. Dec. 666, 432 N.E.2d 250 (1982); and Parks v. United States, 451 A.2d 591 (D.C.App.1982). Others hold that under no circumstances are mental impressions discoverable. See, e.g., Broussard v. State Farm Mutual, 519 So.2d 136 (La.1988); Dennie v. Metropolitan Medical Center, 387 N.W.2d 401 (Minn.1986).

Material Prepared in Anticipation of Litigation

As formulated, the work product rule protects only material prepared in "anticipation of litigation." As *Upjohn* demonstrates, this can include reports prepared prior to the filing of a complaint. On the other hand, "the work product rule does not come into play merely because there is a remote prospect of future litigation." Diversified Industries, Inc. v. Meredith, 572 F.2d 596, 604 (8th Cir.1977). See also Sims v. Knollwood Park Hospital, 511 So.2d 154 (Ala.1987) (fact that litigation eventually ensues is not, by itself, enough to designate materials prepared by a lawyer as work product prepared in anticipation of litigation). The scope of the phrase "prepared in anticipation of litigation" is uncertain:

Courts have attempted to explain exactly what anticipation of litigation means, but such efforts have not helped to resolve the issue. For example, some courts indicate that a party . . . anticipates litigation where there is a "substantial probability" of "imminent" litigation or when there is a "prospect" of litigation. Another requirement is that there be "some possibility" of litigation; however, a "mere possibility" of litigation is not enough. Other courts have stated that there must be an "eye" towards litigation or that litigation need only be a reasonable "contingency." These methods for redefining the word anticipation do little more than say that litigation is anticipated when litigation is anticipated.

Note, Work Product Discovery: A Multifactor Approach to the Anticipation of Litigation Requirement in Federal Rule of Civil Procedure 26(b)(3), 66 Iowa L.Rev. 1277, 1277–78 (1981) (footnotes omitted). . . .

Whether material was prepared in anticipation of litigation, is an important question for insurance companies. Are all claims investigations "in anticipation of litigation?" Two positions have emerged. Most courts say that litigation is not "anticipated" until an attorney has become involved and has prepared the documents herself or has requested their preparation. See McDougall v. Dunn, 468 F.2d 468, 474–75 (4th Cir.1972); State Farm Fire & Casualty v. Perrigan, 102 F.R.D. 235, 237–38 (W.D.Va.1984); American Banker's Insurance v. Colorado Flying Academy, 97 F.R.D. 515, 517–18 (D.Colo.1983). See generally Woodward, Insurance Companies and Work Product Immunity Under Indiana Trial Rule 26(b)(3): Indiana Adopts a Fact–Sensitive Approach, 19 Ind.L.Rev. 139, 141–42 (1986). Under this rule, unless the insurer's investigation has been performed at the request or under the direction of an attorney, the materials resulting from the investigation are "conclusively presumed to have been made in the ordinary course of business and not in anticipation of litigation." Henry Enterprises v. Smith, 225 Kan. 615, 592 P.2d 915, 920 (1979). The court in Hawkins v. District Court, 638 P.2d 1372, 1378 (Colo.1982) (en banc), stated the rationale for this rule as follows:

> Because a substantial part of an insurance company's business is to investigate claims made by an insured against the company or by some other party against an insured, it must be presumed that such investigations are part of the normal business activity of the company and that reports and witness' statements compiled by or on behalf of the insurer in the course of such investigations are ordinary business records as distinguished from trial preparation materials.

Id. (quoting Thomas Organ Co., 54 F.R.D. 367, 373 (N.D.Ill.1972)).

A second position is that virtually all insurance investigations are made in anticipation of litigation. See Ashmead v. Harris, 336 N.W.2d 197, 201 (Iowa 1983); Firemen's Fund Insurance v. McAlpine, 120 R.I. 744, 391 A.2d 84, 89–90 (1978).

Should attorney involvement in a claims investigation be sufficient to satisfy the "anticipation of litigation" requirement? See National Farmers Union Property and Casualty Co. v. District Court, 718 P.2d 1044 (Colo.1986) (memoranda prepared by lawyers for insurance company not protected by work product rule because lawyers were performing same function as claims adjustor and the resulting report is an ordinary business record of the company, which is discoverable); Longs Drug Store v. Howe, 134 Ariz. 424, 657 P.2d 412 (1983). Compare Shelton v. American Motors Corp., 805 F.2d 1323, 1329 (8th Cir.1986) ("selection and compilation of documents [by lawyer] . . . reflects legal theories and thought processes which are protected as work product").

Material prepared as part of an ongoing crime or fraud, whether or not in anticipation of litigation, is not covered by the work product rule. See, e.g., In re Doe, 662 F.2d 1073, 1079–1080 (4th Cir.1981), cert. denied, 455 U.S. 1000 (1982); In re Antitrust Grand Jury, 805 F.2d 155 (6th Cir.1986). See also the discussion below at p. 225 of the crime-fraud exception to the attorney-client privilege.

Who May Invoke the Attorney–Client and Work Product Protection

It is settled law that the client, not the lawyer, "owns" the attorney-client privilege, which means that the lawyer cannot success-fully invoke the privilege if the client has waived it. See the discussion of waiver in the *von Bulow* case printed below and the notes following it. As to the work-product doctrine, there is conflict whether the lawyer or the client owns it. There is authority that the lawyer as well as the client must consent to disclosure, e.g., In re Special September 1978 Grand Jury, 640 F.2d 49 (7th Cir.1980). In Lasky, Haas, Cohler & Munter v. Superior Court, 172 Cal.App.3d 264, 218 Cal.Rptr. 205 (1985), the court interpreted a work product statute formulated differently from Rule 26(b)(3) to mean that the lawyer could resist disclosure of work product in the face of a client's request for it. The conclusion in that case may have been affected by the fact that the client's request apparently was under legal coercion from a third party. The court observed that its holding would not preclude a client from obtaining material relevant to a legal malpractice case. Hence, the point may be that work product is protected against third party discovery except with the consent of both lawyer and client.

The attorney-client privilege continues after the lawyer-client rela-tionship is terminated. However, courts are split whether work prod-uct protection terminates at the end of the litigation for which the material was prepared or continues thereafter. See United States v. IBM Corp., 66 F.R.D. 154, 178 (S.D.N.Y.1974) (terminates with the end of litigation); In re Murphy, 560 F.2d 326, 334 (8th Cir.1977) (protection extends to all future litigation). What, if anything, in the rationale for the work product rule suggests that its duration be limited?

On the work product doctrine see generally Special Project: The Work Product Doctrine, 68 Cornell L.Rev. 760 (1983).

FISHER v. UNITED STATES

Supreme Court of the United States, 1976.
425 U.S. 391, 96 S.Ct. 1569, 48 L.Ed.2d 39.

Mr. Justice White delivered the opinion of the Court.

In these two cases we are called upon to decide whether a summons directing an attorney to produce documents delivered to him by his client in connection with the attorney-client relationship is enforceable over claims that the documents were constitutionally immune from summons in the hands of the client and retained that immunity in the hands of the attorney.

I

In each case, an Internal Revenue agent visited the taxpayer or taxpayers [1] and interviewed them in connection with an investigation of possible civil or criminal liability under the federal income tax laws. Shortly after the interviews—one day later in No. 74–611 and a week or two later in No. 74–18—the taxpayers obtained from their respective accountants certain documents relating to the preparation by the accountants of their tax returns. Shortly after obtaining the documents—later the same day in No. 74–611 and a few weeks later in No. 74–18—the taxpayers transferred the documents to their lawyers— respondent Kasmir and petitioner Fisher, respectively—each of whom was retained to assist the taxpayer in connection with the investigation. Upon learning of the whereabouts of the documents, the Internal Revenue Service served summonses on the attorneys directing them to produce documents listed therein. In No. 74–611, the documents were described as "the following records of Tannebaum Bindler & Lewis [the accounting firm].

> "1. Accountant's workpapers pertaining to Dr. E.J. Mason's books and records of 1969, 1970 and 1971.[2]

> "2. Retained copies of E.J. Mason's income tax returns for 1969, 1970 and 1971.

> "3. Retained copies of reports and other correspondence between Tannenbaum Bindler & Lewis and Dr. E.J. Mason during 1969, 1970 and 1971."

In No. 74–18, the documents demanded were analyses by the accountant of the taxpayers' income and expenses which had been copied by the accountant from the taxpayers' canceled checks and deposit receipts.[3] In No. 74–611, a summons was also served on the accountant directing him to appear and testify concerning the documents to be produced by the lawyer. In each case, the lawyer declined to comply with the summons directing production of the documents, and enforcement actions were commenced by the Government under 26 U.S.C. §§ 7402(b) and 7604(a). In No. 74–611, the attorney raised in defense of the enforcement action the taxpayer's accountant-client privilege, his attorney-client privilege, and his Fourth and Fifth Amendment rights. In No. 74–18, the attorney claimed that enforcement would involve compulsory self-incrimination of the taxpayers in violation of their Fifth Amendment privilege, would involve a seizure of the papers without necessary compliance with the Fourth Amendment, and would

---

1. In No. 74–18, the taxpayers are husband and wife who filed a joint return. In No. 74–611, the taxpayer filed an individual return.

2. The "books and records" concerned the taxpayer's large medical practice.

3. The husband taxpayer's checks and deposit receipts related to his textile waste business. The wife's related to her women's wear shop.

violate the taxpayers' right to communicate in confidence with their attorney. In No. 74–18 the taxpayers intervened and made similar claims.

. . .

. . . In our view the documents were not privileged either in the hands of the lawyers or of their clients . . .

II

All of the parties in these cases and the Court of Appeals for the Fifth Circuit have concurred in the proposition that if the Fifth Amendment would have excused a *taxpayer* from turning over the accountant's papers had he possessed them, the *attorney* to whom they are delivered for the purpose of obtaining legal advice should also be immune from subpoena. Although we agree with this proposition for the reasons set forth in Part III, infra, we are convinced that, under our decision in Couch v. United States, 409 U.S. 322, 93 S.Ct. 611, 34 L.Ed. 2d 548 (1973), it is not the taxpayer's Fifth Amendment privilege that would excuse the *attorney* from production.

The relevant part of that Amendment provides:

"No person . . . shall be *compelled* in any criminal case to be a *witness against himself.*" (Emphasis added.)

The taxpayer's privilege under this Amendment is not violated by enforcement of the summonses involved in these cases because enforcement against a taxpayer's lawyer would not "compel" the taxpayer to do anything—and certainly would not compel him to be a "witness" against himself. The Court has held repeatedly that the Fifth Amendment is limited to prohibiting the use of "physical or moral compulsion" exerted on the person asserting the privilege . . . In *Couch v. United States,* supra, we recently ruled that the Fifth Amendment rights of a taxpayer were not violated by the enforcement of a documentary summons directed to her accountant and requiring production of the taxpayer's own records in the possession of the accountant. We did so on the ground that in such a case "the ingredient of personal compulsion against an accused is lacking." 409 U.S., at 329, 93 S.Ct., at 616. . . .

Here, the taxpayers are compelled to do no more than was the taxpayer in *Couch.* The taxpayers' Fifth Amendment privilege is therefore not violated by enforcement of the summonses directed toward their attorneys. This is true whether or not the Amendment would have barred a subpoena directing the taxpayer to produce the documents while they were in his hands.

The fact that the attorneys are agents of the taxpayers does not change this result. *Couch* held as much, since the accountant there was also the taxpayer's agent, and in this respect reflected a longstanding view. In Hale v. Henkel, 201 U.S. 43, 69–70, 26 S.Ct. 370, 377, 50 L.Ed. 652, 663 (1906), the Court said that the privilege "was never intended to permit [a person] to plead the fact that some third person might be incriminated by his testimony, even though he were the agent of such person. . . . [T]he Amendment is limited to a person who shall be compelled in any criminal case to be a witness against *himself*." (Emphasis in original.) "It is extortion of information from the accused himself that offends our sense of justice." Couch v. United States, supra, 409 U.S., at 328, 93 S.Ct., at 616 . . . Agent or no, the lawyer is not the taxpayer. The taxpayer is the "accused," and nothing is being extorted from him.

Nor is this one of those situations, which *Couch* suggested might exist, where constructive possession is so clear or relinquishment of possession so temporary and insignificant as to leave the personal compulsion upon the taxpayer substantially intact. 409 U.S., at 333, 93 S.Ct., at 618 . . . In this respect we see no difference between the delivery to the attorneys in these cases and delivery to the accountant in the *Couch* case. As was true in *Couch,* the documents sought were obtainable without personal compulsion on the accused.

. . . Here, the taxpayers retained any privilege they ever had not to be compelled to testify against themselves and not to be compelled themselves to produce private papers in their possession. *This* personal privilege was in no way decreased by the transfer. It is simply that by reason of the transfer of the documents to the attorneys, those papers may be subpoenaed without compulsion on the taxpayer. The protection of the Fifth Amendment is therefore not available. "A party is privileged from producing evidence but not from its production." Johnson v. United States, supra, 228 U.S., at 458, 33 S.Ct., at 572. . . .

The Court of Appeals for the Fifth Circuit suggested that because legally and ethically the attorney was required to respect the confidences of his client, the latter had a reasonable expectation of privacy for the records in the hands of the attorney and therefore did not forfeit his Fifth Amendment privilege with respect to the records by transferring them in order to obtain legal advice. It is true that the Court has often stated that one of the several purposes served by the constitutional privilege against compelled testimonial self-incrimination is that of protecting personal privacy. But the Court has never suggested that every invasion of privacy violates the privilege. Within the limits imposed by the language of the Fifth Amendment, which we necessarily observe, the privilege truly serves privacy interests; but the Court has never on any ground, personal privacy included, applied the Fifth Amendment to prevent the otherwise proper acquisition or use of evidence which, in the Court's view, did not involve compelled testimonial self-incrimination of some sort.[5]

5. There is a line of cases in which the Court stated that the Fifth Amendment was offended by the use in evidence of documents or property seized in violation of the Fourth Amendment. Gouled v. United States, 255 U.S. 298, 306, 41 S.Ct. 261, 264, 65 L.Ed. 647, 651 (1921); Agnello v. United States, 269 U.S. 20, 33–34, 46 S.Ct. 4, 6–7, 70 L.Ed. 145, 149–150 (1925); United States v. Lefkowitz, 285 U.S. 452, 466–467, 52 S.Ct. 420, 424, 76 L.Ed. 877, 883 (1932); Mapp v. Ohio, 367 U.S. 643, 661, 81 S.Ct. 1684, 1694, 6 L.Ed.2d 1081, 1093 (1961) (Black, J., concurring). But the Court purported to find elements of compulsion in

The proposition that the Fifth Amendment protects private information obtained without compelling self-incriminating testimony is contrary to the clear statements of this Court that under appropriate safeguards private incriminating statements of an accused may be overheard and used in evidence, if they are not compelled at the time they were uttered, Katz v. United States, 389 U.S. 347, 354, 88 S.Ct. 507, 512, 19 L.Ed.2d 576, 583 (1967); Osborn v. United States, 385 U.S. 323, 329–330, 87 S.Ct. 429, 432–433, 17 L.Ed.2d 394, 399–400 (1966); and Berger v. New York, 388 U.S. 41, 57, 87 S.Ct. 1873, 1882, 18 L.Ed.2d 1040, 1051 (1967); cf. Hoffa v. United States, 385 U.S. 293, 304, 87 S.Ct. 408, 414, 17 L.Ed.2d 374, 383 (1966); and that disclosure of private information may be compelled if immunity removes the risk of incrimination. Kastigar v. United States, 406 U.S. 441, 92 S.Ct. 1653, 32 L.Ed. 2d 212 (1972). If the Fifth Amendment protected generally against the obtaining of private information from a man's mouth or pen or house, its protections would presumably not be lifted by probable cause and a warrant or by immunity. The privacy invasion is not mitigated by immunity; and the Fifth Amendment's strictures, unlike the Fourth's, are not removed by showing reasonableness. The Framers addressed the subject of personal privacy directly in the Fourth Amendment. They struck a balance so that when the State's reason to believe incriminating evidence will be found becomes sufficiently great, the invasion of privacy becomes justified and a warrant to search and seize will issue. They did not seek in still another Amendment—the Fifth— to achieve a general protection of privacy but to deal with the more specific issue of compelled self-incrimination.

We cannot cut the Fifth Amendment completely loose from the moorings of its language, and make it serve as a general protector of privacy—a word not mentioned in its text and a concept directly addressed in the Fourth Amendment. We adhere to the view that the Fifth Amendment protects against "compelled self-incrimination, not [the disclosure of] private information." United States v. Nobles, 422 U.S. 225, 233 n. 7, 95 S.Ct. 2160, 2167, 45 L.Ed.2d 141 (1975).

Insofar as private information not obtained through compelled self-incriminating testimony is legally protected, its protection stems from other sources [6]—the Fourth Amendment's protection against seizures without warrant or probable cause and against subpoenas which suffer

such situations. "In either case he is the unwilling source of the evidence, and the Fifth Amendment forbids that he shall be compelled to be a witness against himself in a criminal case." Gouled v. United States, supra, 255 U.S., at 306, 41 S.Ct., at 264 . . . In any event the predicate for those cases, lacking here, was a violation of the Fourth Amendment. Cf. Burdeau v. McDowell, supra, 256 U.S. 465, 475–476, 41 S.Ct. 574, 576, 65 L.Ed. 1048, 1050–1051 (1921).

6. In Couch v. United States, 409 U.S. 322, 93 S.Ct. 611, 34 L.Ed.2d 548 (1973), on which taxpayers rely for their claim that the Fifth Amendment protects their "legitimate expectation of privacy," the Court differentiated between the things protected by the Fourth and Fifth Amendments. "We hold today that no Fourth or Fifth Amendment claim can prevail where, as in this case, there exists no legitimate expectation of privacy and no semblance of governmental compulsion against the person of the accused." Id., 409 U.S., at 336, 93 S.Ct., at 620 . . .

from "too much indefiniteness or breadth in the things required to be 'particularly described,'" Oklahoma Press Pub. Co. v. Walling, 327 U.S. 186, 208, 66 S.Ct. 494, 505, 90 L.Ed. 614, 629 (1946); In re Horowitz, 482 F.2d 72, 75–80 (CA2 1973) (Friendly, J.); the First Amendment, see NAACP v. Alabama, 357 U.S. 449, 462, 78 S.Ct. 1163, 1171, 2 L.Ed.2d 1488, 1499 (1958); or evidentiary privileges such as the attorney-client privilege.[7]

III

. . . The taxpayers in these cases, however, have from the outset consistently urged that they should not be forced to expose otherwise protected documents to summons simply because they have sought legal advice and turned the papers over to their attorneys. . . .

Confidential disclosures by a client to an attorney made in order to obtain legal assistance are privileged. 8 J. Wigmore, Evidence, § 2292 (McNaughton rev. 1961) (hereinafter Wigmore); McCormick § 87, p. 175. The purpose of the privilege is to encourage clients to make full disclosure to their attorneys. 8 Wigmore § 2291, and § 2306, p. 590; McCormick § 87, p. 175, § 92, p. 192 . . . As a practical matter, if the client knows that damaging information could more readily be obtained from the attorney following disclosure than from himself in the absence of disclosure, the client would be reluctant to confide in his lawyer and it would be difficult to obtain fully informed legal advice. However, since the privilege has the effect of withholding relevant information from the factfinder, it applies only where necessary to achieve its purpose. Accordingly it protects only those disclosures—necessary to obtain informed legal advice—which might not have been made absent the privilege. In re Horowitz, supra, 482 F.2d 72, at 81 (Friendly, J.); United States v. Goldfarb, supra, 328 F.2d 280; 8 Wigmore, § 2291, p. 554; McCormick, § 89, p. 185. This Court and the lower courts have thus uniformly held that pre-existing documents which could have been obtained by court process from the client when he was in possession may also be obtained from the attorney by similar process following transfer by the client in order to obtain more informed legal advice. Grant v. United States, 227 U.S. 74, 79–80, 33 S.Ct. 190, 192, 57 L.Ed. 423, 426 (1913); 8 Wigmore § 2307 and cases there cited; McCormick § 90, p. 185; Falsone v. United States, 205 F.2d 734 (CA5 1953); Sovereign Camp, W.O.W. v. Reed, 208 Ala. 457, 94 So. 910 (1922); Andrews v. Mississippi R. Co., 14 Ind. 169, 98 N.E. 49 (1860); Palatini v. Sarian, 15 N.J.Super. 34, 83 A.2d 24 (1951); Pearson v. Yoder, 39 Okl. 105, 134 P. 421 (1913); State ex rel. Sowers v. Olwell, 64 Wash.2d 828,

7. The taxpayers and their attorneys have not raised arguments of a Fourth Amendment nature before this Court and could not be successful if they had. The summonses are narrowly drawn and seek only documents of unquestionable relevance to the tax investigation. Special problems of privacy which might be presented by subpoena of a personal diary, United States v. Bennett, 409 F.2d 888, 897 (CA2 1969) (Friendly, J.), are not involved here.

First Amendment values are also plainly not implicated in these cases.

394 P.2d 681 (1964). The purpose of the privilege requires no broader
rule. Pre-existing documents obtainable from the client are not appreciably easier to obtain from the attorney after transfer to him. Thus,
even absent the attorney-client privilege, clients will not be discouraged
from disclosing the documents to the attorney, and their ability to
obtain informed legal advice will remain unfettered. It is otherwise if
the documents are not obtainable by subpoena *duces tecum* or summons
while in the exclusive possession of the client, for the client will then be
reluctant to transfer possession to the lawyer unless the documents are
also privileged in the latter's hands. . . . We accordingly proceed to
the question whether the documents could have been obtained by
summons addressed to the taxpayer while the documents were in his
possession. The only bar to enforcement of such summons asserted by
the parties or the courts below is the Fifth Amendment's privilege
against self-incrimination. . . .

IV

The proposition that the Fifth Amendment prevents compelled
production of documents over objection that such production might
incriminate stems from Boyd v. United States, 116 U.S. 616, 68 S.Ct.
524, 29 L.Ed. 746 (1886). *Boyd* involved a civil forfeiture proceeding
brought by the Government against two partners for fraudulently
attempting to import 35 cases of glass without paying the prescribed
duty. The partnership had contracted with the Government to furnish
the glass needed in the construction of a Government building. The
glass specified was foreign glass, it being understood that if part or all
of the glass was furnished from the partnership's existing duty-paid
inventory, it could be replaced by duty-free imports. Pursuant to this
arrangement, 29 cases of glass were imported by the partnership duty
free. The partners then represented that they were entitled to duty-
free entry of an additional 35 cases which were soon to arrive. The
forfeiture action concerned these 35 cases. The Government's position
was that the partnership had replaced all of the glass used in construction of the Government building when it imported the 29 cases. At
trial, the Government obtained a court order directing the partners to
produce an invoice the partnership had received from the shipper
covering the previous 29–case shipment. The invoice was disclosed,
offered in evidence, and used, over the Fifth Amendment objection of
the partners, to establish that the partners were fraudulently claiming
a greater exemption from duty than they were entitled to under the
contract. This Court held that the invoice was inadmissible and
reversed the judgment in favor of the Government. The Court ruled
that the Fourth Amendment applied to court orders in the nature of
subpoenas *duces tecum* in the same manner in which it applies to
search warrants, id., at 622, 6 S.Ct., at 528 . . . and that the Government may not, consistent with the Fourth Amendment, seize a person's
documents or other property as evidence unless it can claim a proprietary interest in the property superior to that of the person from whom

the property is obtained. Id., at 623–624, 6 S.Ct., at 528–529. . . . The invoice in question was thus held to have been obtained in violation of the Fourth Amendment. The Court went on to hold that the accused in a criminal case or the defendant in a forfeiture action could not be forced to produce evidentiary items without violating the Fifth Amendment as well as the Fourth. More specifically, the Court declared, "a compulsory production of the private books and papers of the owner of goods sought to be forfeited . . . is compelling him to be a witness against himself, within the meaning of the Fifth Amendment to the Constitution." Id., at 634–635, 6 S.Ct., at 534. . . . Admitting the partnership invoice into evidence had violated both the Fifth and Fourth Amendments.

Among its several pronouncements, *Boyd* was understood to declare that the seizure, under warrant or otherwise, of any purely evidentiary materials violated the Fourth Amendment and that the Fifth Amendment rendered these seized materials inadmissible. Gouled v. United States, 255 U.S. 298, 41 S.Ct. 261, 65 L.Ed. 647 (1921); Agnello v. United States, 269 U.S. 20, 46 S.Ct. 4, 70 L.Ed. 145 (1925); United States v. Lefkowitz, 285 U.S. 452, 52 S.Ct. 420, 76 L.Ed. 877 (1932). That rule applied to documents as well as to other evidentiary items—"[t]here is no special sanctity in papers, as distinguished from other forms of property, to render them immune from search and seizure, if only they fall within the scope of the principles of the cases in which other property may be seized. . . ." Gouled v. United States, supra, 255 U.S., at 309, 41 S.Ct., at 265 . . . . Private papers taken from the taxpayer, like other "mere evidence," could not be used against the accused over his Fourth and Fifth Amendment objections.

Several of Boyd's express or implicit declarations have not stood the test of time. . . .

[T]he Fifth Amendment does not independently proscribe the compelled production of every sort of incriminating evidence but applies only when the accused is compelled to make a *testimonial* communication that is incriminating. We have, accordingly, declined to extend the protection of the privilege to the giving of blood samples, Schmerber v. California, 384 U.S. 757, 763–764, 86 S.Ct. 1826, 1831–1832, 16 L.Ed. 2d 908, 915–916 (1966); to the giving of handwriting exemplars, Gilbert v. California, 388 U.S. 263, 265–267, 87 S.Ct. 1951, 1952–1954, 18 L.Ed. 2d 1178, 1181–1183 (1967); voice exemplars, United States v. Wade, 388 U.S. 218, 222–223, 87 S.Ct. 1926, 1929–1930, 18 L.Ed.2d 1149, 1154–1155 (1967); or the donning of a blouse worn by the perpetrator, Holt v. United States, 218 U.S. 245, 31 S.Ct. 2, 54 L.Ed. 1021 (1910). Furthermore, despite *Boyd,* neither a partnership nor the individual partners are shielded from compelled production of partnership records on self-incrimination grounds. Bellis v. United States, 417 U.S. 85, 94 S.Ct. 2179, 40 L.Ed.2d 678 (1974). It would appear that under that case the precise claim sustained in *Boyd* would now be rejected for reasons not there considered.

. . .

A subpoena served on a taxpayer requiring him to produce an accountant's workpapers in his possession without doubt involves substantial compulsion. But it does not compel oral testimony; nor would it ordinarily compel the taxpayer to restate, repeat, or affirm the truth of the contents of the documents sought. Therefore, the Fifth Amendment would not be violated by the fact alone that the papers on their face might incriminate the taxpayer, for the privilege protects a person only against being incriminated by his own compelled testimonial communications. Schmerber v. California, supra; United States v. Wade, supra, and Gilbert v. California, supra. The accountant's workpapers are not the taxpayer's. They were not prepared by the taxpayer, and they contain no testimonial declarations by him. Furthermore, as far as this record demonstrates, the preparation of all of the papers sought in these cases was wholly voluntary, and they cannot be said to contain compelled testimonial evidence, either of the taxpayers or of anyone else.[11] The taxpayer cannot avoid compliance with the subpoena merely by asserting that the item of evidence which he is required to produce contains incriminating writing, whether his own or that of someone else.

The act of producing evidence in response to a subpoena nevertheless has communicative aspects of its own, wholly aside from the contents of the papers produced. Compliance with the subpoena tacitly concedes the existence of the papers demanded and their possession or control by the taxpayer. It also would indicate the taxpayer's belief that the papers are those described in the subpoena. Curcio v. United States, 354 U.S. 118, 125, 77 S.Ct. 1145, 1150, 1 L.Ed.2d 1225, 1231 (1957). The elements of compulsion are clearly present, but the more difficult issues are whether the tacit averments of the taxpayer are both "testimonial" and "incriminating" for purposes of applying the Fifth Amendment. These questions perhaps do not lend themselves to categorical answers; their resolution may instead depend on the facts and circumstances of particular cases or classes thereof. In light of the records now before us, we are confident that however incriminating the contents of the accountant's workpapers might be, the act of producing them—the only thing which the taxpayer is compelled to do—would not itself involve testimonial self-incrimination.

11. The fact that the documents may have been written by the person asserting the privilege is insufficient to trigger the privilege, Wilson v. United States, 221 U.S. 361, 378, 31 S.Ct. 538, 543, 55 L.Ed. 771, 778 (1911). And, unless the Government has compelled the subpoenaed person to write the document, cf. Marchetti v. United States, 390 U.S. 39, 88 S.Ct. 697, 19 L.Ed.2d 889 (1968); Grosso v. United States, 390 U.S. 62, 88 S.Ct. 709, 19 L.Ed.2d 906 (1968), the fact that it was written by him is not controlling with respect to the Fifth Amendment issue. Conversations may be seized and introduced in evidence under proper safeguards, Katz v. United States, 389 U.S. 347, 88 S.Ct. 507, 19 L.Ed.2d 576 (1967); Osborn v. United States, 385 U.S. 323, 87 S.Ct. 429, 439, 17 L.Ed.2d 394 (1966); Berger v. New York, 388 U.S. 41, 87 S.Ct. 1873, 18 L.Ed.2d 1040 (1967); United States v. Bennett, 409 F.2d, at 897 n. 9, if not compelled. In the case of a documentary subpoena the only thing compelled is the act of producing the document and the compelled act is the same as the one performed when a chattel or document not authored by the producer is demanded. McCormick § 128, p. 261.

It is doubtful that implicitly admitting the existence and possession of the papers rises to the level of testimony within the protection of the Fifth Amendment. The papers belong to the accountant, were prepared by him, and are the kind usually prepared by an accountant working on the tax returns of his client. Surely the Government is in no way relying on the "truth-telling" of the taxpayer to prove the existence of or his access to the documents. 8 Wigmore § 2264, p. 380. The existence and location of the papers are a foregone conclusion and the taxpayer adds little or nothing to the sum total of the Government's information by conceding that he in fact has the papers. Under these circumstances by enforcement of the summons "no constitutional rights are touched. The question is not of testimony but of surrender." In re Harris, 221 U.S. 274, 279, 31 S.Ct. 557, 558, 55 L.Ed. 732, 735 (1911).

When an accused is required to submit a handwriting exemplar he admits his ability to write and impliedly asserts that the exemplar is his writing. But in common experience, the first would be a near truism and the latter self-evident. In any event, although the exemplar may be incriminating to the accused and although he is compelled to furnish it, his Fifth Amendment privilege is not violated because nothing he has said or done is deemed to be sufficiently testimonial for purposes of the privilege. This Court has also time and again allowed subpoenas against the custodian of corporate documents or those belonging to other collective entities such as unions and partnerships and those of bankrupt businesses over claims that the documents will incriminate the custodian despite the fact that producing the documents tacitly admits their existence and their location in the hands of their possessor. E.g., Wilson v. United States, 221 U.S. 361, 31 S.Ct. 538, 55 L.Ed. 771 (1911); Dreier v. United States, 221 U.S. 394, 31 S.Ct. 550, 55 L.Ed. 784 (1911); United States v. White, 322 U.S. 694, 64 S.Ct. 1248, 88 L.Ed. 1542 (1944); Bellis v. United States, 417 U.S. 85, 94 S.Ct. 2179, 40 L.Ed.2d 678 (1974); *In re Harris,* supra. The existence and possession or control of the subpoenaed documents being no more in issue here than in the above cases, the summons is equally enforceable.

Moreover, assuming that these aspects of producing the accountant's papers have some minimal testimonial significance, surely it is not illegal to seek accounting help in connection with one's tax returns or for the accountant to prepare workpapers and deliver them to the taxpayer. At this juncture, we are quite unprepared to hold that either the fact of existence of the papers or of their possession by the taxpayer poses any realistic threat of incrimination to the taxpayer.

As for the possibility that responding to the subpoena would authenticate [12] the workpapers, production would express nothing more

---

12. The "implicit authentication" rationale appears to be the prevailing justification for the Fifth Amendment's application to documentary subpoenas. Schmerber v. California, 384 U.S., at 763–764, 86 S.Ct., at 1832 . . . ("the privilege reaches . . . the compulsion of responses which are also communications, for example, compliance with a subpoena to produce one's papers. Boyd v. United States, 116 U.S. 616, 6 S.Ct. 524, 29 L.Ed. 746"); Couch v. United States, 409 U.S., at 344, 346, 93 S.Ct., at 611, 625 . . . (Marshall, J., dissenting) (the person complying with the subpoena "implicitly testifies

than the taxpayer's belief that the papers are those described in the subpoena. The taxpayer would be no more competent to authenticate the accountant's workpapers or reports [13] by producing them than he would be to authenticate them if testifying orally. The taxpayer did not prepare the papers and could not vouch for their accuracy. The documents would not be admissible in evidence against the taxpayer without authenticating testimony. Without more, responding to the subpoena in the circumstances before us would not appear to represent a substantial threat of self-incrimination. Moreover, in *Wilson v. United States,* supra; *Dreier v. United States,* supra; *United States v. White,* supra; *Bellis v. United States,* supra; and *In re Harris,* supra, the custodian of corporate, union, or partnership books or those of a bankrupt business was ordered to respond to a subpoena for the business' books even though doing so involved a "representation that the documents produced are those demanded by the subpoena," Curcio v. United States, 354 U.S., at 125, 77 S.Ct., at 1150 . . . .[14]

Whether the Fifth Amendment would shield the taxpayer from producing his own tax records in his possession is a question not involved here; for the papers demanded here are not his "private papers," see Boyd v. United States, supra, 116 U.S., at 634–635, 6 S.Ct., at 534 . . . . We do hold that compliance with a summons directing the taxpayer to produce the accountant's documents involved in these cases would involve no incriminating testimony within the protection of the Fifth Amendment.

. . .

MR. JUSTICE STEVENS took no part in the consideration or disposition of these cases.

MR. JUSTICE BRENNAN, concurring in the judgment.

I concur in the judgment. Given the prior access by accountants retained by the taxpayers to the papers involved in these cases and the

that the evidence he brings forth is in fact the evidence demanded"); United States v. Beattie, 522 F.2d 267, 270 (CA2 1975) (Friendly, J.) ("[a] subpoena demanding that an accused produce his own records is . . . the equivalent of requiring him to take the stand and admit their genuineness"), cert. pending, Nos. 75–407, 75–700; 8 Wigmore § 2264, p. 380 (the testimonial component involved in compliance with an order for production of documents or chattels "is the witness' assurance, compelled as an incident of the process, that the articles produced are the ones demanded"); McCormick § 126, p. 268 ("[t]his rule [applying the Fifth Amendment privilege to documentary subpoenas] is defended on the theory that one who produces documents (or other matter) described in the subpoena *duces tecum* represents, by his production, that the documents produced are in fact the documents described in the subpoena"); People v. Defore, 242 N.Y. 13, 27, 150 N.E. 585, 590 (1926) (Cardozo, J.) ("A defendant is 'protected from producing his documents in response to a *subpoena duces tecum,* for his production of them in court would be his voucher of their genuineness.' There would then be 'testimonial compulsion' ").

13. In seeking the accountant's "retained copies" of correspondence with the taxpayer in No. 74–611, we assume that the summons sought only "copies" of original letters sent from the accountant to the taxpayer—the truth of the contents of which could be testified to only by the accountant.

14. In these cases compliance with the subpoena is required even though the books have been kept by the person subpoenaed and his producing them would itself be sufficient authentication to permit their introduction against him.

wholly business rather than personal nature of the papers, I agree that the privilege against compelled self-incrimination did not in either of these cases protect the papers from production in response to the summonses. See Couch v. United States, 409 U.S. 322, 335–336, 93 S.Ct. 611, 619–620, 34 L.Ed.2d 548, 557–558 (1973); id., at 337, 93 S.Ct., at 620, 34 L.Ed.2d, at 559 (Brennan, J., concurring). I do not join the Court's opinion, however, because of the portent of much of what is said of a serious crippling of the protection secured by the privilege against compelled production of one's private books and papers. . . .

Documents Given to Lawyer by Client

If the subpoenaed documents had been created by the client solely to assist the lawyer in preparing a defense would the result in *Fisher* have been different? What if the documents were prepared by the lawyer in anticipation of the IRS bringing suit against Fisher?

The Court holds that under the attorney-client privilege, pre-existing documents in the hands of the lawyer are exempt from subpoena only if the documents would be exempt from subpoena under the Fifth Amendment in the hands of the client. The question then becomes whether the Fifth Amendment would protect the client from having to produce these documents. On this question the Court holds that compelled production does not violate the Fifth Amendment unless the compulsion is both "testimonial" and "incriminating." The documents here apparently were incriminating. Why were they not considered testimonial?

In United States v. Doe, 465 U.S. 605, 104 S.Ct. 1237 (1984), the Government subpoenaed business records from an individual. The Court held that the documents were not themselves privileged under the Fifth Amendment, clearing up any doubt remaining after *Fisher* as to whether an individual's business records enjoyed some special Fifth Amendment privilege not accorded to the records of a partnership or corporation. The Court went on to hold, however, that the act of producing the documents was sufficiently "testimonial" to give the defendant a Fifth Amendment right to refuse absent use immunity.

Whither Boyd?

The argument, rejected in *Doe*, that some special protection under the Fifth Amendment should be accorded an individual's business records comes from Boyd v. United States, 116 U.S. 616, 6 S.Ct. 524 (1886), one of the earliest Fourth and Fifth Amendment cases to be decided by the Supreme Court. In sweeping language, *Boyd* suggested that the Fifth and Fourth Amendments protected the private papers of an individual, "his dearest property." *Boyd*, 116 U.S. at 628. After *Doe*, the only vestige of such special protection for papers may be for non-business papers of an individual. Compare In re Three Grand Jury Subpoenas, dated January 5, 1988, 847 F.2d 1024 (2d Cir.1988) (issue of personal papers undecided by *Doe*), with Butcher v. Bailey, 753 F.2d 465 (6th Cir.1985) (there may be protection for personal private papers); and In re Grand Jury Proceedings on February 4, 1982, 759 F.2d 1418 (9th Cir.1985) (no protection for personal papers).

On the issues raised by *Fisher* and *Doe,* see Heidt, The Fifth Amendment Privilege and Documents—Cutting Fisher's Tangled Line, 49 Mo.L.Rev. 439 (1984); Mosteller, Simplifying Subpoena Law: Taking the Fifth Amendment Seriously, 73 Va.L.Rev. 1 (1987); and Note, Fifth Amendment Privilege for Producing Corporate Documents, 84 Mich.L. Rev. 1544 (1986).

Searches of Law Offices

Fisher deals with a subpoena and not a search warrant. Even where the defendant has a Fifth Amendment right to refuse to *produce* documents in compliance with a subpoena, she has no Fifth Amendment right to refuse to allow the police to conduct a search pursuant to a valid search warrant or a search otherwise constitutional under the Fourth Amendment. Therefore, if the government seeks to search the lawyer's office for incriminating documents the lawyer's objections must be grounded in the Fourth Amendment or the attorney-client privilege. If the search is constitutional under the Fourth Amendment and the documents are not covered by the attorney-client privilege (because, for example, they are pre-existing), the search will be upheld.

The cases on law office searches generally involve lawyers who themselves are the target of the search. See, e.g., Andresen v. Maryland, 427 U.S. 463, 96 S.Ct. 2737 (1976); In re Impounded Case (Law Firm), [Impounded I], 840 F.2d 196 (3d Cir.1988). In the latter case, the affidavit supporting the search warrant asserted probable cause to believe that the law firm and some of its lawyers were engaged in tax evasion and mail fraud. The alleged scheme involved the firm's failure to report accurately its share of personal injury awards. The government seized approximately 420 complete files from the office and documents from other closed personal injury files. The District Court had held that the search was unconstitutional because the warrant was overbroad inasmuch as it allowed the search and seizure of client files without particular allegations that settlements in those particular cases were underreported. The Court of Appeals upheld the search. It noted that searches of law offices were not per se unreasonable under the Fourth Amendment and that the proper role of the court was "to 'scrutinize carefully the particularity and breadth of the warrant authorizing the search, the nature and scope of the search, and any resulting seizure.'" 840 F.2d 196, at 200, quoting Klitzman & Gallagher v. Krut, 744 F.2d 955, 959 (3d Cir.1984). In *Klitzman* the court held the search overbroad because the warrant authorized a wholesale search and seizure of the firm's business records although only one lawyer was the target of the grand jury's suspicion. Unlike *Klitzman, Impounded I* involved charges of a regular and ongoing scheme by the firm and many of its lawyers and employees to defraud the government; the search was therefore not overbroad. As to the likelihood that the files contained client privileged information, the court found the procedure established by the magistrate sufficient to protect any privileged material; this procedure required that the government obtain leave of the court before examining any of the seized items. This controversy came before the Third Circuit again in In re Impounded Case (Law Firm), [Impounded II], 879 F.2d 1211 (3d Cir.1989). This time the question before the court was which of the seized but sealed documents the government could inspect. *Impounded II* involved the scope of the crime-fraud exception to the attorney-client privilege and is discussed in the note below at p. 226.

See also 42 U.S.C.A. §§ 2000aa–11, which requires the Attorney General to issue guidelines for searches of lawyer's offices and the offices of other professionals whose relationships with their clients are protected by privileges, e.g., doctors and clergy. The guidelines for searches of lawyer's offices appear at 37 Cri.L.Rep. (BNA) 2479.

UNITED STATES v. HODGE AND ZWEIG

United States Court of Appeals, Ninth Circuit, 1977.
548 F.2d 1347.

KENNEDY, CIRCUIT JUDGE:

The principal issues on this appeal are whether information demanded by an Internal Revenue Service subpoena is protected by the attorney-client privilege, by the fifth amendment privilege against self-incrimination, or by the rule which prohibits issuance of an IRS summons for an improper purpose.

Messrs. Richard A. Hodge and Robert M. Zweig, appellants here, are both members of the State Bar of California and are partners in the practice of law. From all indications in the record, they acted ethically and professionally throughout this matter. This decision may provide further guidance for the proper discharge of their professional responsibilities.

In November 1973, Special Agent Christopher of the IRS issued a summons pursuant to 26 U.S.C. § 7602 directed to appellants, individually and as a law partnership. The summons directed the attorneys to produce various business records pertaining to a client, one Joseph Ernest Sandino, Jr., for the calendar years 1970, 1971, and 1972. The requested information pertains to: (1) payments received by the attorneys from Sandino for legal services rendered to him; (2) payments received from Sandino for services rendered to Rena Sandino Joseph, Cindy Purdy, and Stephen Purdy; (3) payments received from Sandino on behalf of any other person; (4) payments received from any other person on behalf of Sandino. The attorneys refused to comply with the summons. The United States thereupon petitioned the district court for enforcement. The court directed compliance, and the attorneys appeal.[1]

About the same time as the IRS inquiry into Sandino's financial affairs, a protracted grand jury investigation centering around alleged drug activities of Sandino and some of his confederates was in progress. In order that we may properly consider appellants' claims in this case, it is useful to summarize the chronology of these two investigations.

In 1971, a federal grand jury in Nevada began an inquiry into an alleged conspiracy to import drugs by a group that government prosecutors sometimes called "the Sandino Gang." Hodge and Zweig represented several witnesses and suspects called before the grand jury, including Joe Sandino, Rena Joseph, Cindy Purdy, Bernard See, and Robert Gordon. The record before us does not indicate whether Stephen Purdy was a target of the drug investigation. In January 1972, Hodge was called before the grand jury and was asked to disclose information pertaining to fee arrangements and retainer agreements with clients who were being investigated by the grand jury. Zweig was subpoenaed by the grand jury in April 1972 and was asked similar questions. On each occasion, the attorneys refused to answer, invoking both the attorney-client privilege and the fifth amendment privilege against self-incrimination on behalf of themselves and their clients. See and Gordon were subsequently tried for various drug related offenses, including conspiracy to import marijuana, and were found guilty. We affirmed their convictions on appeal. United States v. See, 505 F.2d 845 (9th Cir.1974).

In March 1974, Sandino and several of his associates were charged with conspiracy to import marijuana. In the indictment, the Government alleged that as part of the conspiracy, the conspirators had agreed to provide bail and legal services for participants who were apprehended by law enforcement officials in the course of the criminal activities. Sandino, Rena Joseph, Cindy Purdy, and others eventually pleaded guilty to conspiracy charges and were sentenced.[2]

While the above criminal prosecution was pending, the IRS was continuing its tax investigation. Appellants failed to comply with the IRS summons of November 1973, and in August 1974, the district court ordered that the summons be enforced. This appeal followed. In light of this background, we turn to the contentions of the parties.

Appellants raise three grounds for reversing the district court's order enforcing the IRS summons. They first argue that the summons

1. The California Attorneys for Criminal Justice and the American Civil Liberties Union jointly filed a brief as amici curiae.

2. These persons pleaded guilty to a superseding information that charged that the conspiracy began on or about June 1, 1971 and continued until November 21, 1974. It also charged that as part of the conspiracy, defendants would provide money to be used for bail and legal services for the members of the conspiracy apprehended in the course of the unlawful activity. In addition, Sandino alone pleaded guilty to a second count in the information, charging him with interstate travel to aid an unlawful enterprise, in violation of 18 U.S.C. §§ 1952, 2.

was issued solely to gather information in aid of the pending criminal prosecution, and as such was issued for an improper purpose. Second, appellants assert that the fifth amendment bars enforcement of the summons, since compelled disclosure of the requested information would violate their own privilege against self-incrimination and that of their clients. Finally, they claim that the requested information is protected by the attorney-client privilege. We consider these contentions in order.*

. . .

Self–Incrimination.

Appellants, asserting their own rights and the rights of Sandino, argue that disclosure of the requested records would violate the fifth amendment privilege against self-incrimination.[7] They contend that disclosure would subject them and Sandino to prosecution for various drug violations that were being investigated at the time the summons was issued.

As to appellants' assertion of the privilege on their own behalf, the trial court, citing Zicarelli v. New Jersey State Commission of Investigation, 406 U.S. 472, 478, 92 S.Ct. 1670, 32 L.Ed.2d 234 (1972), concluded that appellants had "not demonstrated such a real danger of prosecution as would justify quashing the summons on the ground of fifth amendment protection." We cannot say that the court's determination is clearly erroneous. See United States v. Hart, 546 F.2d at 801–02.

Neither is disclosure of the information at issue precluded by assertion of the fifth amendment on behalf of Sandino. Sandino entered a plea of guilty to the first count of the drug-related criminal conspiracy charge and has been sentenced. It does not appear that any further charge is pending against Sandino at this time, nor do appellants contend that additional charges are anticipated. We conclude that Sandino is no longer in danger of incriminating himself and thus may not raise the fifth amendment as a bar to compelled testimony. It follows that appellants may not raise the fifth amendment on Sandino's behalf.[8]

Attorney–Client Privilege.

Appellants next contend that the attorney-client privilege precludes enforcement of the IRS summons. They assert the privilege on behalf of Sandino and other named clients, and on behalf of unnamed clients whose identity would necessarily be disclosed if the summons were enforced.

* Editor's note: On the first issue the court holds that the summons was properly issued.

7. Whether disclosure of these records would violate the fifth amendment rights of appellants' unnamed clients was neither considered by the trial court nor pressed on appeal. We do not reach that issue here.

8. We do not understand appellants to argue that disclosure is barred because it would incriminate Sandino in income tax violations, nor do we think that appellants could successfully make such an argument. See Couch v. United States, 409 U.S. 322, 93 S.Ct. 611, 34 L.Ed.2d 548 (1973); United States v. Cromer, 483 F.2d 99 (9th Cir.1973).

Before the effective date of the Federal Rules of Evidence, this circuit applied the law of the state in which the attorney-client relationship arose to determine whether or not a communication was privileged. Baird v. Koerner, 279 F.2d 623, 632 (9th Cir.1960). . . . We . . . hold that [now] the Federal Rules of Evidence govern our determination.

Fed.R.Evid. 501 provides in relevant part:

> Except as otherwise required by the Constitution of the United States or provided by Act of Congress or in rules prescribed by the Supreme Court pursuant to statutory authority, the privilege of a witness, person, government, State, or political subdivision thereof shall be governed by the principles of the common law as they may be interpreted by the courts of the United States in the light of reason and experience.

Accordingly, we turn to an examination of federal common law in order to rule on appellants' claim that the information requested in the IRS summons is protected by the attorney-client privilege.

As a general rule, where a party demonstrates that there is a legitimate need for a court to require disclosure of such matters, the identity of an attorney's clients and the nature of his fee arrangements with his clients are not confidential communications protected by the attorney-client privilege. In re Michaelson, 511 F.2d 882, 889 (9th Cir. 1975); Baird v. Koerner, 279 F.2d at 630; accord, United States v. Jeffers, 532 F.2d 1101, 1115 (7th Cir.1976); 8 J. Wigmore, Evidence § 2313 (McNaughton rev. 1961). The IRS has demonstrated that the information at issue is sought for a legitimate purpose—the collection of tax revenues. As a threshold matter, therefore, the information is not privileged.

The general rule, however, is qualified by an important exception: A client's identity and the nature of that client's fee arrangements may be privileged where the person invoking the privilege can show that a strong probability exists that disclosure of such information would implicate that client in the very criminal activity for which legal advice was sought. Baird v. Koerner, 279 F.2d at 630. While in Baird we enunciated this rule as a matter of California law, the rule also reflects federal law. See In re Grand Jury Proceedings, 517 F.2d 666, 671 (5th Cir.1975); Tillotson v. Boughner, 350 F.2d 663, 666 (7th Cir.1965). Appellants contend that the *Baird* exception applies to this case.

The *Baird* exception is entirely consonant with the principal policy behind the attorney-client privilege. "In order to promote freedom of consultation of legal advisors by clients, the apprehension of compelled disclosure from the legal advisors must be removed; hence the law must prohibit such disclosure except on the client's consent." 8 J. Wigmore, supra, § 2291, at 545. In furtherance of this policy, the client's identity and the nature of his fee arrangements are, in exceptional cases, protected as confidential communications.

As noted at the outset, the summons directs appellants to supply information pertaining to four types of transactions. The summons first requests information pertaining to legal fees paid by Sandino on his own behalf. There is no doubt that Sandino played an active role in the drug conspiracy; indeed, he pleaded guilty to that offense. Disclosure of this first category of information could in no way further implicate Sandino in criminal activity connected to the drug conspiracy, nor could it identify a suspect heretofore unknown to the Government. We do not understand appellants to argue otherwise. The *Baird* rule therefore does not apply to this request. The trial court did not err in ordering appellants to disclose information pertaining to legal fees paid by Sandino on his own behalf.

The second demand in the summons seeks information concerning payments made by Sandino to the attorneys on behalf of Rena Joseph and Cindy Purdy. The *Baird* rule is similarly inapplicable to that information. Those two persons, along with Sandino, pleaded guilty to the drug conspiracy; there is no indication that further charges are anticipated. Disclosure of this information would therefore not implicate these persons in the very criminal activity for which they sought legal advice. The trial court was correct in ordering disclosure of this information.

The summons also seeks information concerning payments made by Sandino on behalf of Stephen Purdy and unnamed clients, and by unnamed clients on behalf of Sandino. The record gives no indication whether Stephen Purdy was under investigation as a participant in the drug conspiracy; nor is there any evidence before us that he has been indicted or convicted of offenses arising out of the drug investigation. Likewise, we cannot know of the extent of involvement, if any, of possible unnamed clients. The question whether this information is protected by lawyer-client privilege is therefore considerably more troublesome.

Once a party seeking disclosure has met the initial burden of showing that it has a legitimate interest in the information requested, the individual asserting the privilege must demonstrate that the conditions of the *Baird* rule are satisfied. Appellants in this case have met that initial burden as to Stephen Purdy and the unnamed clients. The conspiracy indictment charged that the conspirators agreed to furnish bail and legal fees for those individuals apprehended in the course of the criminal enterprise. If appellants are required to divulge information that would show that the principal conspirator paid Stephen Purdy's legal fees, Stephen Purdy would no doubt be linked to the criminal enterprise by that disclosure. Similarly, disclosure of information pertaining to payments made by or on behalf of unnamed clients could implicate these unnamed clients in the drug conspiracy.

Consequently, as a threshold matter, the information appears to be covered by the attorney-client privilege under the *Baird* rationale.[10]

Our inquiry is not at an end, however. Because the attorney-client privilege is not to be used as a cloak for illegal or fraudulent behavior, it is well established that the privilege does not apply where legal representation was secured in furtherance of intended, or present, continuing illegality. United States v. Friedman, 445 F.2d 1076, 1086 (9th Cir.1971); see Clark v. United States, 289 U.S. 1, 15, 53 S.Ct. 465, 77 L.Ed. 993 (1933) . . . . The crime or fraud exception applies even where the attorney is completely unaware that his advice is sought in furtherance of such an improper purpose. United States v. Friedman, 445 F.2d at 1086; see Clark v. United States, 289 U.S. at 15, 53 S.Ct. 465.

To invoke the exception successfully, the party seeking disclosure (here the Government) must make out a prima facie case that the attorney was retained in order to promote intended or continuing criminal or fraudulent activity. United States v. Friedman, 445 F.2d at 1086; see Clark v. United States, 289 U.S. at 15, 53 S.Ct. 465, O'Rourke v. Darbishire, [1920] A.C. at 604. The record on appeal and the supplemental briefs and documents establish such a prima facie case. The information sought by the IRS concerns transactions with the appellants during 1970, 1971, and 1972. The superseding information to which Joe Sandino, Rena Joseph, and Cindy Purdy pleaded guilty charged that the conspiracy began at least as early as June 1971 and ended on November 21, 1974. In fact, there is strong evidence that the conspiracy began earlier, in 1970. The guilty pleas further demonstrate that as an integral part of the conspiracy the participants agreed to furnish bail and legal expenses for conspirators who might be apprehended by law enforcement officials. Presumably, such an agreement was designed to hinder any criminal drug prosecution arising out of the conspiracy; as such, the agreement constituted part of the consideration for engaging in the conspiratorial activity.[11]

In light of the above, we conclude that a prima facie case exists that payments to appellants, if any, made during the years 1970, 1971, and 1972 by and on behalf of Sandino were made pursuant to the conspiratorial agreement and thus in furtherance of the continuing drug conspiracy. We therefore hold that disclosure of the information requested in the IRS summons is required.

The IRS summons in this case was issued to accomplish a legitimate governmental purpose, viz. the collection of revenues. As noted in our consideration of Donaldson v. United States, [400 U.S. 517, 91 S.Ct. 534 (1971)] the summons was not intended to gather information in aid of the drug investigation. The allegation in the conspiracy

10. Our analysis assumes, of course, that appellants could show that Stephen Purdy and the various unnamed individuals whose identity they seek to protect are clients. If not, the attorney-client privilege is inapplicable in any event.

11. This is manifestly not a case where the attorneys were retained in order that the clients could ascertain whether or not some future course of action was lawful.

indictment charging that the conspirators agreed to furnish each others' legal fees was not a device to circumvent the attorney-client privilege, and the pleas of guilty to the drug offenses by various conspirators establish the existence of such an agreement.

In our legal system the client should make full disclosure to the attorney so that the advice given is sound, so that the attorney can give all appropriate protection to the client's interest, and so that proper defenses are raised if litigation results. The attorney-client privilege promotes such disclosure by promising that communications revealed for these legitimate purposes will be held in strict confidence. The privilege encourages persons to seek advice as to future conduct. But so important is full disclosure that the law recognizes the privilege even if the advice is sought by one who has already committed a bad act. Thus, the attorney-client privilege is central to the legal system and the adversary process. For these reasons, the privilege may deserve unique protection in the courts.

But a *quid pro quo* is exacted for the attorney-client confidence: the client must not abuse the confidential relation by using it to further a fraudulent or criminal scheme, and as a condition to continued representation, the lawyer is required to advise the client to cease any unlawful activities that the lawyer perceives are occurring. Law and society consent to the attorney-client privilege on these preconditions. By insisting on their observance, we safeguard the privilege itself and protect the integrity of the professional relation.

Because neither the client's identity nor the nature of his fee arrangements are generally privileged, the intrusive effect of our ruling in this case is minimal. And to the extent that appellants' clients had an expectation of confidentiality, that expectation was ill-founded; it has been sufficiently shown that the attorneys were retained in further-ance of a continuing conspiracy. There was a failure of one of the essential preconditions of the privilege. While this is a difficult case, we are convinced that disclosure is required.

Affirmed.

Fees and Identity of the Client

Why are fee arrangements and client identity considered non-privileged matters as a general rule?

In *Baird* the client had substantially underreported his income to the IRS and feared the imposition of penalties. His lawyer sent a check to the IRS, explaining why it was necessary to withhold the client's name. The Ninth Circuit upheld the lawyer's refusal to reveal his client's name, stating "it may well be the link that could form a chain of testimony necessary to convict an individual of a federal crime." 279 F.2d at 633.

While *Baird* is frequently cited as an exception to the general rule, it is rarely applied. See, e.g., In re Slaughter, 694 F.2d 1258 (11th Cir. 1982) and In re Grand Jury Proceedings, 680 F.2d 1026 (5th Cir.1982) (en banc) (both holding the exception is limited and narrow). See also In re Grand Jury Subpoena (Wine), 841 F.2d 230 (8th Cir.1988) (finding *Baird* inapplicable and noting the Ninth Circuit's limitation of *Baird* to its facts). In In re Grand Jury Subpoenas (Hirsch), 803 F.2d 493 (1986), the Ninth Circuit explicitly disapproved the oft-cited description of *Baird* in *Hodge and Zweig,* stating, "it is not the law that the requisites of the attorney-client privilege are met whenever evidence regarding the fees paid the attorney would implicate the client in a criminal offense regarding which the client sought legal advice." *Baird,* the court continued, involved "a unique factual situation" . . . "under the facts of that case, the client's identity was in substance [itself] a confidential communication." Id. at 497. In other words, the court read *Baird* as protecting fee and identity information which would implicate the client in criminal activity only when that information was communicated to the lawyer as part of the seeking of legal advice and not merely as a necessary corollary to seeking advice. Is this a sensible distinction? When the court calls *Baird's* facts unique does it refer to the fact that the lawyer and client were acting to rectify the fraud?

Fees and client identity generally are held not privileged. See United States v. Haddad, 527 F.2d 537 (6th Cir.1975); Colton v. United States, 306 F.2d 633 (2d Cir.1962); McCormick's Evidence § 9 (3d ed. 1984). See also In re Michaelson, 511 F.2d 882 (9th Cir.1975) (general rule that fees not privileged also applies to identity of person who paid the clients fees); In re Grand Jury Subpoena (Wine), 841 F.2d 230 (8th Cir.1988) (same). But see, United States v. Sims, 845 F.2d 1564 (11th Cir.1988) (fee information privileged when it would give the identity of a previously undisclosed client/suspect). Also see Corry v. Meggs, 498 So.2d 508 (Fla.Dist.Ct.App.1986) (state statutory privilege includes fees and identity).

Communications about a client's whereabouts generally are not privileged. See, e.g., In re Walsh, 623 F.2d 489 (7th Cir.1980), cert. denied, 449 U.S. 994 (1980); Burden v. Church of Scientology, 526 F.Supp. 44 (M.D.Fla.1981) (information on whereabouts needed to serve complaint); Commonwealth v. Maguigan, 511 Pa. 112, 511 A.2d 1327 (1986) (whereabouts of fugitive client not privileged); In re Doe, 117 Misc.2d 197, 456 N.Y.S.2d 312 (Cty.Ct.1982) (same). Compare In re Grand Jury Subpoena (Field), 408 F.Supp. 1169 (S.D.N.Y.1976) (client's new address privileged, despite general rule, because it was communicated to lawyer as part of obtaining legal advice about moving). But see In the Matter of Nackson, 221 N.J.Super. 187, 534 A.2d 65 (1987) (where other means available for obtaining information on fugitive client lawyer could not be compelled to disclose); Mercado v. Parent, 421 So.2d 740 (Fla.App.1982) (where no compelling ground to require lawyer to disclose client's whereabouts to execute judgment, whereabouts privileged).

A case that attracted substantial media attention is Baltes v. Doe I (Fla.Cir.Ct. 15th Jud.Cir. 10/13/88), reported at 57 U.S.L.W. 2268 (11/1/88). The client showed up at lawyer Krischer's office, stated his name and said that he was involved in a hit and run auto accident. He asked Krischer to negotiate a resolution of the matter with the authorities but not to reveal his identity. Without identifying the client, Krischer asked another lawyer, Richardson, to negotiate with the state's attorney. Baltes, the plaintiff in this civil suit against the nameless client, sought to compel Krischer to divulge the client's identity. The court held that identity was protected under the Florida statutory attorney-client privilege. Against the plaintiff's claim that the lawyer had a duty to divulge the client's identity to avoid assisting the client's criminal act, the court held that leaving the scene of an accident, without providing statutorily required information to the police or others involved in the accident, was not an ongoing crime and that the lawyers thus did not have a duty to disclose to avoid assisting in unlawful activity. The court held that the crime ended when the driver left the scene. Is this persuasive? The court in *Baltes* not only protected the client's identity, it held that neither the lawyer nor the client could be compelled to allow the plaintiff to examine the client's car or photographs of it as this might reveal his identity. How does this square with the holding in *Fisher?*

For a discussion of whether the lawyer is permitted to disclose voluntarily the client's whereabouts under the confidentiality rules, see the notes preceding the *Hawkins* case below.

As Wigmore's test highlights, only "communications" that are intended to be "confidential" are privileged. Thus, the physical characteristics of the client, such as complexion, demeanor, and dress are not generally considered privileged because they are neither "communications," nor matters which in the usual case a client considers confidential. United States v. Kendrick, 331 F.2d 110 (4th Cir.1964). Should a lawyer be permitted to testify over the client's objection on observations of the client's demeanor that speak to the client's competence? See *Kendrick* (yes); Gunther v. United States, 230 F.2d 222 (D.C.Cir.1956) (no).

The Crime/Fraud Exception

> The privilege takes flight if the relation is abused. A client who consults an attorney for advice that will serve him in the commission of a fraud will have no help from the law.

Justice Cardozo, writing in Clark v. United States, 289 U.S. 1, 15, 53 S.Ct. 465, 469 (1936).

The crime/fraud exception is a corollary to the prohibition against assisting a client to commit a fraud or crime, as noted in the next to the last paragraph in *Hodge and Zweig*. See also Ohio–Sealy Mattress Mfg.

Co. v. Kaplan, 90 F.R.D. 21 (N.D.Ill.1980) (the crime/fraud rule obliges the lawyer to advise the client to stop any unlawful activity in which the lawyer discovers the client is engaged).

The crime/fraud exception applies to ongoing criminal activity as well as to future criminal activity, but does not apply to past crimes about which the law seeks to encourage the seeking of legal counsel. The distinction between past crimes and ongoing ones is in principle clear. However, an all too common mistake is to treat fraud as a past crime while the fraud is still ongoing. See the *OPM* case reprinted below. An undiscovered, unrectified fraud is ongoing, not past.

The court in *Hodge and Zweig* notes that the "exception applies even where the attorney is completely unaware that his advice is sought in furtherance of . . . an illegal purpose." Why? Should the exception apply when the client is unaware that the intended purpose is illegal? How does proposed Rule 503, which is printed above, answer this question? In In re Impounded Case (Law Firm), [Impounded II], 879 F.2d 1211 (3d Cir.1989), the law firm, asserting the privilege on behalf of its innocent clients, claimed that the crime/fraud exception did not apply when the alleged criminality was solely that of the law firm. The court rejected this argument, holding that the privilege would have to yield to the societal interest of bringing to justice lawyers engaged in criminal activities. In *Ohio–Sealy,* the court held that a lawyer's efforts to restructure a restrictive trade agreement, to achieve the same effect without running afoul of Supreme Court precedent, did not demonstrate the lack of good faith on the clients' part that triggers the crime/fraud exception—despite documents revealing the clients' belief that their activities would ultimately be found illegal. The clients' belief was read as an evaluation of the weakness of their position, not as an awareness of wrongdoing. Also see State v. Green, 493 So.2d 1178, 1182 (La.1986) (lawyer's criminal intent of which client was unaware will not trigger crime/fraud exception).

In United States v. Zolin, 109 S.Ct. 2619 (1989), the Court addressed the following questions: (1) whether the trial court, at the request of the party seeking access to allegedly privileged material, may review the material *in camera* to determine whether the crime/fraud exception applies; and (2) what evidentiary showing must be made before such a review can be made. The Court held that the trial court may order an *in camera* review upon " 'a showing of a factual basis adequate to support a good faith belief by a reasonable person,' . . . that *in camera* review . . . may reveal evidence to establish the claim that the crime-fraud exception applies." Id. at 2631, quoting Caldwell v. District Court, 644 P.2d 26, 33 (Colo.1982). The Court also held that the content of the communication revealed in the *in camera* inspection could be used in determining whether a crime or fraud was involved. State law may differ from *Zolin.* For example, under Cal.Evid.Code § 915(a), the content of the communication may not be used to determine whether an exception to the privilege applies.

Once the judge has examined the evidence how is she to determine whether the exception applies? What opportunity should be afforded the asserter of the privilege to rebut the evidence that the exception applies? See Company X v. United States, 857 F.2d 710 (10th Cir.1988), cert. denied, 109 S.Ct. 3214 (1989) (determination that exception applies may be made upon *ex parte* showing and judge need not first examine all documents *in camera*).

For an article arguing that the crime/fraud exception is interpreted too broadly, see Fried, Too High a Price for Truth: The Exception to the Attorney–Client Privilege for Contemplated Crimes and Frauds, 64 N.C.L.Rev. 443 (1986).

While most civil frauds are criminal as well, the exception applies whether or not the fraud involves criminal liability. See In re Burlington Northern, Inc., 822 F.2d 518 (5th Cir.1987) (civil violation of the antitrust laws is a "fraud" sufficient to trigger the exception to the attorney-client privilege); Natta v. Zletz, 418 F.2d 633 (7th Cir.1969) (fraud upon the Patent and Trademark Office triggers the exception). Should the crime/fraud exception extend to the client's intent to commit any intentional tort? In *Modern Legal Ethics,* Wolfram suggests that "fraud" is and should be read as a catchall phrase to include any intentional wrong "involving a client acting with bad faith . . ." Id. § 6.4.10.

For an interesting discussion of the relationship between the *Noerr–Pennington* doctrine and the attorney-client privilege see In re Burlington Northern, Inc., 822 F.2d 518 (5th Cir.1987). The *Noerr–Pennington* doctrine is that petitioning of the government, which includes suing and in some cases defending a suit, is exempt from the antitrust laws unless the petitioning is a mere sham to cover violation of the antitrust laws. Eastern Railroad Presidents Conference v. Noerr Motor Freight, Inc., 365 U.S. 127, 81 S.Ct. 523 (1961); United Mine Workers v. Pennington, 381 U.S. 657, 85 S.Ct. 1585 (1965). *In re Burlington Northern* involved a claim of sham litigation. The plaintiffs sought access to conversations between the defendants and their lawyers to prove their claim of a sham defense.

On the crime/fraud exception and its relation to confidentiality, see Hazard, An Historical Perspective on the Attorney–Client Privilege, 66 Calif.L.Rev. 1061 (1978), with which compare Fried, Too High a Price for the Truth: The Exception to the Attorney–Client Privilege for Contemplated Crimes and Frauds, 64 N.C.L.Rev. 443 (1986), and Silbert, The Crime Fraud Exception to the Attorney–Client Privilege and Work–Product Doctrine, 23 Am.Crim.L.Rev. 351 (1986).

For a discussion of the controversy over subpoenaing lawyers before grand juries see Chapter 2 above.

Procedures for Invoking the Privilege

To assert the privilege, most courts hold that the witness must appear, testify and invoke the privilege in response to a particular question. In re Certain Complaints Under Investigation, 783 F.2d 1488, 1518 (11th Cir.1986) (collecting cases). The burden is then on the witness to prove that all the elements of the privilege are present. In re Grand Jury Empanelled February 14, 1978 (Markowitz), 603 F.2d 469 (3d Cir.1979). In determining whether the lawyer has asserted a valid claim of privilege, the district court may use an *in camera* proceeding to prevent the release of information which the assertion of privilege is designed to prevent. See *United States v. Zolin,* supra on the review of allegedly privileged material *in camera.*

The lawyer has a duty to invoke the privilege when called to testify about privileged matters; the client need not specially request that the lawyer do so. EC 4–4; Comment to Model Rule 1.6. See also United States v. Hodgson, 492 F.2d 1175, 1177 (10th Cir.1974). If the court finds that the matter is not privileged, the lawyer is not obliged to continue to refuse to testify in order to appeal the ruling. The lawyer may do so, however. Maness v. Meyers, 419 U.S. 449, 458–459, 95 S.Ct. 584, 591–592 (1975). But care must be exercised since the punishment for contempt could be immediate imprisonment and continuing sanctions. For an extreme case see Dike v. Dike, 75 Wash.2d 1, 448 P.2d 490 (1968) (trial judge had lawyer booked and held in jail until bail was paid; the court upheld the trial court's ruling on the privilege, but vacated its contempt order).

The Privilege Between Joint Clients or Cooperating Parties

If two or more people jointly retain a lawyer to represent them in a matter, communications by any of the clients to the lawyer on the subject of the joint representation are not privileged against use by one joint client against another. The issue comes up most often when one of the co-clients feels her interests have been inadequately represented and sues another or the lawyer. See, e.g., Brennan's, Inc. v. Brennan's Restaurants, Inc., 590 F.2d 168 (5th Cir.1979), reprinted in Chapter 8 below.

The theory is that the joint clients intended their communications to be secret from the rest of the world but not from one another. But see Ogden v. Groves, 241 So.2d 756 (Fla.App.1970) (attorney could testify only to statements by joint clients made in one another's presence and not to private statements by any of the joint clients to the lawyer). Courts generally do not allow one joint client to waive the privilege for use against (or by) a third party except that a joint client may waive the privilege as to her own statements. See, e.g., American Mut. Liab. Ins. Co. v. Superior Court, 38 Cal.App.3d 579, 113 Cal.Rptr. 561, 573 (1974); Western Fuels Ass'n v. Burlington No. R.R., 102 F.R.D. 201, 203 (D.Wyo.1984). But see Tunick v. Day, Berry & Howard, 40 Conn.Supp. 216, 486 A.2d 1147, 1149 (1984) (in suit against shared lawyer for malpractice, one of the joint clients could waive the privilege of other joint clients who were not parties to the suit).

The limited scope of the privilege in joint client relationships is a matter that the lawyer should consider and discuss with clients before entering into a representation of multiple clients. See M.R. 2.2(a)(1) (lawyer who acts as an intermediary between clients must consult with each client on, inter alia, "the effect on the attorney-client privilege").

While information received from one joint client about the subject matter of the joint representation is not *privileged* from disclosure against the other client, it may be a *confidence* that the lawyer has a duty not to disclose to the other client. See *Brennan's,* supra. If one client insists on confidentiality about matters involving the other client about which the other client should know to make informed decisions, the lawyer may not continue the joint representation on these terms.

Communications between co-parties and their lawyers for the purpose of conducting a joint strategy or furthering their common interests are considered privileged against third-parties but not against each other. See, e.g., United States v. McPartlin, 595 F.2d 1321 (7th Cir. 1979); Eisenberg v. Gagnon, 766 F.2d 770 (3d Cir.1985). But see Government of the Virgin Islands v. Joseph, 685 F.2d 857 (3d Cir.1982) (defendant gave statement to lawyer for co-defendant which implicated himself and exonerated the other; court held that privilege did not apply because statement was not given as part of common strategy).

The work product doctrine similarly extends to material shared between co-parties in furtherance of a common strategy. See, e.g., *McPartlin* supra.

IN RE CLAUS VON BULOW

United States Court of Appeals, Second Circuit, 1987.
828 F.2d 94.

Before LUMBARD, OAKES and CARDAMONE, CIRCUIT JUDGES.

CARDAMONE, CIRCUIT JUDGE:

Petitioner Claus von Bulow seeks a writ of mandamus directing the United States District Court for the Southern District of New York . . . to vacate its discovery order . . . granting plaintiff the right to discover certain conversations between petitioner and his attorneys. . . .

FACTS

On July 6, 1981 petitioner was indicted by a Newport County, Rhode Island, grand jury on two counts of assault with intent to murder for allegedly injecting his wife Martha von Bulow with insulin causing her to lapse into an irreversible coma. After a widely publicized jury trial, von Bulow was convicted on both counts on March 16, 1982. In April 1982 petitioner retained Harvard law professor Alan M. Dershowitz to represent him on appeal. In May 1982 von Bulow was sentenced to 30–years imprisonment, but granted bail pending appeal. On April 27, 1984 the Rhode Island Supreme Court reversed both convictions, State v. von Bulow, 475 A.2d 995 (R.I.), cert. denied, 469 U.S. 875 . . . (1984), and upon retrial, he was acquitted on June 10, 1985.

Shortly after the acquittal, petitioner's wife, by her next friends, Alexander Auersperg and Annie Laurie Auersperg–Kneissal, Martha von Bulow's children from a prior marriage (plaintiff), commenced this civil action in federal court against petitioner alleging common law assault, negligence, fraud, and RICO violations. These claims arose out of the same facts and circumstances as the Rhode Island criminal prosecution.

In May 1986 Random House published a book entitled *Reversal of Fortune—Inside the von Bulow Case,* authored by attorney Dershowitz, which chronicles the events surrounding the first criminal trial, the successful appeal, and von Bulow's ultimate acquittal. After obtaining an advance copy of the book, plaintiff's counsel notified petitioner on April 23, 1986 that it would view publication as a waiver of the attorney-client privilege. Von Bulow's counsel responded that no waiver had occurred and that, accordingly, he would not act to stop the book's publication. After the book was released, von Bulow and attorney Dershowitz appeared on several television and radio shows to promote it.

Plaintiff then moved to compel discovery of certain discussions between petitioner and his attorneys based on the alleged waiver of the attorney-client privilege with respect to those communications related in the book. In order to avoid piecemeal rulings on each communication, counsel stipulated in July 1986 as to those controversial subjects appearing in *Reversal of Fortune.* On February 12, 1987 the . . . District Court . . . found a waiver of the attorney-client privilege and ordered von Bulow and his attorneys to comply with discovery requested by plaintiff. Von Bulow By Auersperg v. von Bulow, 114 F.R.D. 71 (S.D.N.Y.1987).

Von Bulow now petitions this Court for a writ of mandamus directing the district court to vacate its discovery order. Because the relief sought is an extraordinary writ, we consider whether mandamus is an appropriate remedy and, if so, whether it should issue in this case.

.   .   .

I. *The Availability of the Writ*

A. *Novel Question of Law Raised*

First and foremost the petition raises significant novel questions of law justifying the issuance of a writ of mandamus. The district court held that the publication by an attorney of a book chronicling his client's case waives the attorney-client privilege—not just as to information actually disclosed in the book—but with respect to all communications underlying the subjects raised in it. . . . . [T]he district court's holding in extending the "fairness doctrine" to extrajudicial disclosures raises an issue which, so far as discernible, has not been previously litigated in this Circuit.

In our view, mandamus properly lies to review these issues of first impression. . . .

B. *The Importance of Granting Mandamus*

In addition to raising novel issues, this petition also presents two important reasons justifying the issuance of the writ in this case. Without mandamus, petitioner has no other remedy adequate to preserve his confidence. And because the district court's holding raises a legal issue of general applicability, its resolution will aid in this Circuit's effective administration of justice.

. . .

II. *The Propriety of the Discovery Order*

A. *The Waiver of the Attorney–Client Privilege*

By allowing publication of confidential communications in his attorney's book *Reversal of Fortune,* petitioner was held to have waived his attorney-client privilege. In reaching that conclusion, the district court considered the following facts. First, petitioner knew of, consented to, and actually encouraged attorney Dershowitz's plans to write a book providing an "insider look" into his case. Second, petitioner was warned before publication that such an act might trigger a waiver and, yet, took no active measures to preserve his confidences. Third, after publication, petitioner joined his attorney in enthusiastically promoting the book on television and radio shows. Based on these key facts, the district court determined that von Bulow had waived his attorney-client privilege.

Petitioner argues that this holding is erroneous because only the client—and not his attorney—may waive the privilege. Of course, the privilege belongs solely to the client and may only be waived by him. An attorney may not waive the privilege without his client's consent. Republic Gear Co. v. Borg–Warner Corp., 381 F.2d 551, 556 (2d Cir. 1967). Hence, absent a client's consent or waiver, the publication of confidential communications by an attorney does not constitute a relinquishment of the privilege by the client. See, e.g., Schnell v. Schnall, 550 F.Supp. 650, 653 (S.D.N.Y.1982) (no waiver of attorney-client privilege where attorney testified at SEC hearing without presence or authorization of client). See also *Wigmore,* supra, § 2325, at 633 (attorney's voluntary disclosures remain privileged unless impliedly authorized by client).

A client may nonetheless by his actions impliedly waive the privilege or consent to disclosure. See Drimmer v. Appleton, 628 F.Supp. 1249, 1252 (S.D.N.Y.1986) (implied consent); *Wigmore,* supra, § 2327. And an attorney may, in appropriate circumstances, possess "an implied authority to waive the privilege on behalf of his client." *Drim-*

mer, 628 F.Supp. at 1251; *Wigmore,* supra, § 2325. Moreover, it is the client's responsibility to insure continued confidentiality of his communications. In In re Horowitz, 482 F.2d 72 (2d Cir.), cert. denied, 414 U.S. 867 . . . (1973), Judge Friendly, speaking for the Court, warned: "[i]t is not asking too much to insist that if a client wishes to preserve the privilege under such circumstances, he must take some affirmative action to preserve confidentiality." Id. at 82.

Applying these principles, it is quite clear that in finding that von Bulow waived his privilege the district court did not abuse its discretion. In light of petitioner's acquiescence in and encouragement of *Reversal of Fortune's* publication, Judge Walker properly concluded that von Bulow consented to his attorney's disclosure of his confidences and effectively waived his attorney-client privilege. Our discussion now turns to examine the breadth of that waiver.

B. *The Scope of the Waiver*

1. *The Contents of the Published Conversations*

The district court held that plaintiffs were entitled to discover "the entire contents of all conversations from which Dershowitz published extracts in *Reversal of Fortune.*" . . . The four relevant conversations between von Bulow and his attorneys were their initial one, and the ones regarding the bail hearing, appellate strategy, and von Bulow's decision to testify on his own behalf. . . . Under that ruling, plaintiff is permitted to discover those parts of the four identified conversations not made public in the book. Petitioner argues that the district court's holding improperly broadened the fairness doctrine to include extrajudicial disclosures and that, accordingly, the discovery order cannot stand. We agree.

Relying on United States v. Tellier, 255 F.2d 441 (2d Cir.), cert. denied, 358 U.S. 821 . . . (1958) and Teachers Insurance & Annuity Association of America v. Shamrock Broadcasting Co., 521 F.Supp. 638 (S.D.N.Y.1981), the district judge based his decision on an extension of "[t]he principle that disclosure of a portion of a privileged conversation entitles an adversary to discovery of the matters discussed in the remainder of the conversation. . . ." . . . . The court reasoned that where reputation is at stake in a major case, it is tried today before the bar of public opinion, as well as in a courtroom. . . . Judge Walker believed it unfair to permit a party to make use of privileged information as a sword with the public, and then as a shield in the courtroom. . . . Thus, the trial judge found what is generally called a "waiver by implication" . . . based on fairness considerations.

These considerations—which underlie "the fairness doctrine"—aim to prevent prejudice to a party and distortion of the judicial process that may be caused by the privilege-holder's selective disclosure during litigation of otherwise privileged information. Under the doctrine the client alone controls the privilege and may or may not choose to divulge his own secrets. But it has been established law for a hundred years that when the client waives the privilege by testifying about what transpired between her and her attorney, she cannot thereafter insist that the mouth of the attorney be shut. Hunt v. Blackburn, 128 U.S. 464, 470–71, 9 S.Ct. 125, 127, 32 L.Ed. 488 (1888). From that has grown the rule that testimony as to part of a privileged communication, in fairness, requires production of the remainder. McCormick On Evidence § 93, at 194–95 (2d ed. 1972).

Yet this rule protecting the party, the factfinder, and the judicial process from selectively disclosed and potentially misleading evidence does not come into play when, as here, the privilege-holder or his attorney has made extrajudicial disclosures, and those disclosures have not subsequently been placed at issue during litigation. In fact, the cases finding, as the district court did here, implied waivers on account of fairness involved material issues raised by a client's assertions during the course of a judicial proceeding. See, e.g., Hunt v. Blackburn, 128 U.S. at 470–71, 9 S.Ct. at 127; . . . Smith v. Alyeska Pipeline Serv. Co., 538 F.Supp. 977, 979 (D.Del.1982) ("A client . . . may waive the privilege by *deliberately injecting into the case* the advice which he received from his attorney.") (emphasis added), aff'd, 758 F.2d 668 (Fed.Cir.1984), cert. denied, 471 U.S. 1066 . . . (1985); . . . International Tel. & Tel. Corp. v. United Tel. Co. of Fla., 60 F.R.D. 177, 185–86 (M.D.Fla.1973) ("[I]f the client or his attorney at his instance takes the stand and testifies to privileged communications in part this is a waiver as to the remainder . . . about the same subject"); . . .

Neither of the cases relied upon by the district court compel an opposite result. In *Tellier,* 255 F.2d 441, the government had called the defendant's attorney as its chief witness. The attorney testified to a conversation he had with defendant over the latter's objection. We held the conversation was not privileged because it was not intended to be confidential, but was meant to be passed on to third parties. This is quite different from the case at bar where von Bulow's conversations with attorney Dershowitz were originally intended to be confidential, and were therefore privileged, at least prior to disclosure. *Teachers Insurance,* 521 F.Supp. 638, is also unsupportive of the district court's conclusion. In that case a party had *voluntarily* disclosed documents to the SEC that would otherwise have been privileged, and this was held to have waived the privilege. These disclosures made in a trial setting have no application to disclosures in a book made outside a litigation context.

Applying the fairness doctrine, we hold therefore that the extrajudicial disclosure of an attorney-client communication—one not subsequently used by the client in a judicial proceeding to his adversary's prejudice—does not waive the privilege as to the undisclosed portions of the communication. Hence, though the district court correctly found a waiver by von Bulow as to the particular matters *actually disclosed* in the book, it was an abuse of discretion to broaden that waiver to include those portions of the four identified conversations which, because they were not published, remain secret.[1]

2. *Related Conversations With Dershowitz*

The district court next ruled that von Bulow's waiver extended to subject matter areas related to the published conversations with Dershowitz.[2] 114 F.R.D. at 79. This "subject matter waiver", which allows the attacking party to reach all privileged conversations regarding a particular subject once one privileged conversation on that topic has been disclosed, is simply another form of the waiver by implication rule discussed above. Like the "implied waiver", the subject matter waiver also rests on the fairness considerations at work in the context of litigation. See *Smith,* 538 F.Supp. at 979 ("It would be unfair to allow a client to assert the attorney-client privilege and prevent disclosure of damaging communications while allowing the client to disclose other selected communications solely for self-serving purposes.")

For this reason, it too has been invoked most often where the privilege-holder has attempted to use the privilege as both "a sword" and "a shield" or where the attacking party has been prejudiced at trial. See In Re Sealed Case, 676 F.2d 793, 809 n. 54 (D.C.Cir.1982) (Courts retain discretion "not to impose full waiver as to all communications on the same subject matter where the client has merely disclosed a communication to a third party, as opposed to making some use of it."); . . .

For example, in Weil v. Investment/Indicators, Research & Management, Inc., 647 F.2d 18 (9th Cir.1981), the Ninth Circuit held that the client had waived its attorney-client privilege "only as to communications about the matter actually disclosed" because the disclosure occurred early in the proceedings, was made to opposing counsel rather than to the court, and was not demonstrably prejudicial to other party. Professor Wigmore's formulation of the subject matter waiver rule also contemplates the testimonial use of privileged information in the courtroom:

1. Of course, it is conceivable that assertions before trial may mislead or prejudice an adversary at trial and thereby impede the proper functioning of the judicial system. For that reason plaintiff is entitled to attempt to demonstrate in subsequent proceedings that von Bulow's assertion of his attorney-client privilege is misleading or otherwise prejudicial. At such time, the district court may, in its discretion, reevaluate the scope of petitioner's waiver.

2. It held that the waiver encompassed the following subject matter areas: (1) the initial meeting between von Bulow and his attorney Dershowitz; (2) the development of new evidence leads; (3) the potential drug use by von Bulow's family members; (4) von Bulow's bail application; (5) appellate strategy; (6) the acceptance of the prosecution's lab results at the first trial; (7) the weaknesses in the prosecution's case; (8) scientific and other investigations undertaken by the defense; (9) whether von Bulow should testify on his own behalf; (10) defendant's life story; (11) defendant's ability to refute the testimony of Maria and Alexander; (12) whether von Bulow placed insulin in the black bag or needle; and (13) likely questions, answers, and jury responses should von Bulow take the stand. 114 F.R.D. at 80–83.

The client's offer of his own or the attorney's *testimony* as to a *specific communication* to the attorney is a waiver as to all other communications to the attorney on the same matter.

Wigmore, § 2327, at 638.

But where, as here, disclosures of privileged information are made extrajudicially and without prejudice to the opposing party, there exists no reason in logic or equity to broaden the waiver beyond those matters actually revealed. Matters actually disclosed in public lose their privileged status because they obviously are no longer confidential. The cat is let out of the bag, so to speak. But related matters not so disclosed remain confidential. Although it is true that disclosures in the public arena may be "one-sided" or "misleading", so long as such disclosures are and remain extrajudicial, there is no *legal* prejudice that warrants a broad court-imposed subject matter waiver. The reason is that disclosures made in public rather than in court—even if selective—create no risk of *legal* prejudice until put at issue in the litigation by the privilege-holder. Therefore, insofar as the district court broadened petitioner's waiver to include related conversations on the same subject it was in error.

3. *Related Conversations With Other Defense Attorneys*

Again invoking the fairness doctrine, the district court found that von Bulow's waiver extended to his conversations with all other defense attorneys which relate to the subject matter disclosed in the book. Since we have already found that the publication of *Reversal of Fortune* did not result in a sweeping subject matter waiver, that waiver *a fortiori* cannot extend to von Bulow's other attorneys.

CONCLUSION

In sum, mandamus lies in this case because the discovery issue involved is one of first impression and important to the administration of justice. The error asserted concerns a misapprehension of the basic purpose of the fairness doctrine, and its correction will provide direction in developing standards requisite to finding an implied waiver of the attorney-client privilege. Thus, the petition for a writ of mandamus is granted and the district court is directed to vacate its discovery order of February 12, 1987.

Writ of mandamus granted.

The Scope of the Waiver: Application of the Fairness Doctrine

The general rule is that client disclosure to third parties (or lawyer disclosure authorized by the client) destroys the privilege. See, e.g., Clady v. County of Los Angeles, 770 F.2d 1421 (9th Cir.1985) (general rule); United States ex rel. Edney v. Smith, 425 F.Supp. 1038 (E.D.N.Y. 1976), aff'd, 556 F.2d 556 (2d Cir.) (table), cert. denied, 431 U.S. 958 (1977) (implied waiver by own testimony); Weil v. Investment/Indicators, Research & Management, Inc., 647 F.2d 18, 23–25 (9th Cir.1981) (extrajudicial waiver); and United States v. American Tel. & Tel. Co., 642 F.2d 1285, 1299 (D.C.Cir.1980) (same). The court in *von Bulow* adheres to this general rule, but does so through a reference to the "fairness doctrine" that seems irrelevant and confusing. The fairness doctrine is a forensic rule derived from the principle of trial evidence law that when one part of a topic is opened, the whole topic is opened. A familiar application of this principle is that a criminal defendant who takes the stand waives the privilege against self-incrimination, and hence must respond to cross-examination, on all relevant matters, not merely those covered in his direct testimony. See *United States ex rel. Edney v. Smith,* supra.

This concept makes no sense as applied to *extrajudicial* disclosures, as were involved in *von Bulow.* The doctrine of waiver in extrajudicial disclosures is one of forfeiture of secrecy by the act of disclosure. The key issue is the scope of forfeiture. There seems no reason why von Bulow's disclosure of some secret information should carry with it forfeiture of other secret information.

Should the purpose of the extrajudicial disclosures make a difference? For example, should disclosures in a book intended to establish the innocence of a defendant, whether or not intended to mislead or prejudice, trigger a broader forfeiture than disclosures made to a government agency for purposes of assisting an ongoing investigation? Read footnote 1 of the court opinion. Should the party seeking disclosure have to show that the disclosure was actually misleading or should it be enough that the disclosure was intended to prejudice the proceedings?

Ironically, in 1984 von Bulow himself benefited from application of the fairness doctrine to extrajudicial waivers. In State v. von Bulow, 475 A.2d 995 (R.I.), cert. denied, 469 U.S. 875 (1984), von Bulow claimed, inter alia, that the trial court had erred in denying him access to communications between his wife's son and the son's lawyer. Von Bulow claimed that the son had shared (or at least authorized his lawyer to share) client confidences with the police to assist them in their investigation of Martha von Bulow's injury and that this amounted to a waiver of the son's attorney-client privilege, not only as to the communications that were shared but as to *related communications* between the son and his lawyer. The Rhode Island Supreme Court agreed with von Bulow, stating:

> . . . In the present case, Alex [the son] instructed Kuh [his lawyer] to contact the authorities. . . . Kuh turned over [to the authorities] a typewritten summary prepared by him detailing incidents that had led him and the family to conclude that defendant had attempted to kill his wife. . . .

> The state argues that in reporting to the authorities, Kuh never disclosed any of the actual confidential communications or documents reflecting these communications. . . .

. . . It is not necessary that actual privileged communications or documents reflecting such communications be disclosed to effect a waiver of the privilege. "[A] disclosure of, or even merely an assertion about, the communication may effect a waiver of privilege not only as to that communication, but also as to other communications made during the same consultation and communications made at other times about the same subject." United States v. Aronoff, 466 F.Supp. [855, 862 (S.D.N.Y.1979)] . . .

The facts of the present case are a classic example of the impermissible selective use of privileged information. While maintaining that communications were intended to be confidential, Alex and his attorney, at Alex's direction, disclosed information sufficient to trigger an investigation by the state and an indictment. These same parties later refused to disclose other evidence of the same communications. . . .

How does this analysis compare with that of the Second Circuit? Generally see Note, Fairness and the Doctrine of Subject Matter Waiver of the Attorney-Client Privilege in Extrajudicial Disclosure Situations, 1988 U.Ill.L.Rev. 999.

The Lawyer's Authority to Waive the Privilege on the Client's Behalf

Lawyers " 'possess an implied authority to waive the privilege on behalf of the client.' " *von Bulow,* quoting Drimmer v. Appleton, 628 F.Supp. 1249, 1252 (S.D.N.Y.1986). Whether the lawyer has authority to waive the privilege is a question of agency law, which looks to whether the disclosure was within the course of representation and not to whether the disclosure was prudent.

Privileged Disclosures

If the disclosure is itself privileged, it does not waive the privilege. For example, disclosure to other lawyers who are assisting with the case. See, e.g., Transmirra Prods. Corp. v. Monsanto Chemical Co., 26 F.R.D. 572, 576–77 (S.D.N.Y.1960); and the note above on the privilege between joint clients and cooperating parties. Generally see Proposed Federal Rule of Evidence 511 and Revised Uniform Rule of Evidence 510. Statements made in the course of settlement negotiations or plea bargaining are inadmissible to prove liability in subsequent litigation between the negotiating parties, see, e.g., Fed.R.Evid. 408 (statements in settlement negotiations); and Fed.R.Evid. 410(4) (statements in plea bargaining cannot later be used as admissions, if case goes to trial). Despite these rules, many lawyers as an added precaution preface any damaging disclosure by stating that the statement is made "without prejudice" or make the admission in hypothetical conditional form.

To encourage voluntary cooperation with the government, some courts have held that such disclosures do not waive the privilege as against other parties. See, e.g., Diversified Industries, Inc. v. Meredith,

572 F.2d 596, 611 (8th Cir.1977) (en banc); Byrnes v. IDS Realty Trust, 85 F.R.D. 679, 685 (S.D.N.Y.1980). Most courts, however, hold that disclosure to a potential adversary, including the government, constitutes a waiver as to others. In In re Subpoenas Duces Tecum, 738 F.2d 1367 (D.C.Cir.1984), Tesoro Petroleum provided the Securities and Exchange Commission with information on illegal foreign bribes in exchange for more lenient treatment from the SEC. Shareholders brought a derivative suit against the corporation and in discovery sought the documents Tesoro had provided to the SEC. The court held that the privilege was waived as to these documents, rejecting the argument that the waiver doctrine should yield to the public policy in favor of encouraging voluntary cooperation with the government. See also In re Martin Marietta, 856 F.2d 619 (4th Cir.1988).

Concerning the work product doctrine as to documents voluntarily disclosed to the government, see In re Sunrise Securities Litigation, 1989 WL 59605 (E.D.Pa.1989) (Unpublished Case) (not reported in F.Supp.); Chubb Integrated Systems v. National Bank of Washington, 103 F.R.D. 52, 67 (D.D.C.1984).

Inadvertent Disclosure

The traditional rule has been that inadvertent disclosure waives the privilege just as effectively as intentional disclosure. For cases adhering to this rule see, e.g., Underwater Storage, Inc. v. United States Rubber Co., 314 F.Supp. 546, 549 (D.D.C.1970); Chubb Integrated Systems, Ltd. v. National Bank of Washington, 103 F.R.D. 52 (D.D.C.1984). See also 8 Wigmore, Evidence § 2325 at 633 (McNaughton rev. 1961). The apparent justification is that inadvertent disclosure is inconsistent with an intention to preserve confidentiality.

The reality of modern discovery has made the inadvertent disclosure of privileged documents an increasing problem. See Transamerica Computer Co. v. IBM Corp., 573 F.2d 646 (9th Cir.1978). The case law on this subject is changing. One modern approach considers several factors in deciding whether the inadvertent disclosure waived the privilege: "(1) the reasonableness of the precautions to prevent inadvertent disclosure; (2) the time taken to rectify the error; (3) the scope of the discovery; (4) the extent of the disclosure; and (5) the 'overriding issue of fairness'." Hartford Fire Insurance Co. v. Garvey, 109 F.R.D. 323, 332 (N.D.Cal.1985), citing Lois Sportswear, U.S.A., Inc. v. Levi Strauss & Co., 104 F.R.D. 103 (S.D.N.Y.1985). See also Molly Warner Lien v. Wilson & McIlvaine, 1988 WL 130025 (N.D.Ill.1988) (Unpublished Case) (not reported in F.Supp.) (applying these factors court found no waiver where among 500 documents produced one contained privileged material, reasonable precautions had been taken to prevent disclosure, and the lawyer immediately withdrew the document from production when the error was discovered).

Some courts seem to have abandoned the traditional rule, holding that an inadvertent disclosure does not result in waiver. See Mendenhall v. Barber–Greene Co., 531 F.Supp. 951, 954–55 (N.D.Ill.1982). Also see Kansas–Nebraska Natural Gas v. Marathon Oil Co., 109 F.R.D. 12, 21 (D.Neb.1983). Other courts adhere to the traditional rule. International Digital Systems Corp. v. Digital Equipment Corp., 120 F.R.D. 445, 450 (D.Mass.1988) (stating that the strict rule "would probably do more than anything else to instill in attorneys the need for effective precautions against such disclosure").

Does this suggest that the fairness doctrine was irrelevant in both the von Bulow cases?

Client Waiver by Putting in Issue the Lawyer–Client Relationship

By challenging a conviction based on ineffective assistance of counsel, a petitioner waives the attorney-client privilege to the extent necessary to resolve the claim. See, e.g., United States v. Woodall, 438 F.2d 1317 (5th Cir.1970) (en banc); Evans v. Raines, 800 F.2d 884 (9th Cir.1986). Also see Smith v. Estelle, 527 F.2d 430, 434 n. 9 (5th Cir. 1976) (defendant's claim that he would have testified but for admission of unconstitutionally obtained confession waives the privilege as to communications relevant to determine the question); United States v. Miller, 600 F.2d 498, 501–02 (5th Cir.1979) (defendant waived privilege by raising defense of good faith reliance on attorney's advice).

Should raising an issue as to which privileged communications might be relevant be sufficient of itself to destroy the privilege? See Hearn v. Rhay, 68 F.R.D. 574 (E.D.Wash.1975) (waiver only if maintaining the privilege would result in "manifest injustice" to the opposing party and the information sought is "necessary"). Accord: Zenith Radio Corp. v. United States, 764 F.2d 1577 (Fed.Cir.1985); Greater Newburyport Clamshell Alliance v. Public Service Co. of New Hampshire, 838 F.2d 13 (1st Cir.1988).

See generally Davidson & Voth, Waiver of the Attorney–Client Privilege, 64 Or.L.Rev. 637 (1986); Marcus, The Perils of Privilege: Waiver and the Litigator, 84 Mich.L.Rev. 1605 (1986).

For a discussion of the "self-defense" exception to the attorney-client privilege, which allows lawyers to reveal privileged information when their actions are at issue, see the notes to *Meyerhofer* below.

B. CONFIDENTIALITY

Introductory Note

"Client confidences" is a broad category including all information about the client that the lawyer has a duty to keep secret. It includes information about the client learned from other sources. See Restatement (Second) of Agency §§ 395–96 (1958) (§ 395 provides that "an agent [has] a duty to the principal not to use or to communicate information confidentially given him by the principal or acquired by him during the course of or on account of his agency"). See also 2 F. Meechem, Treatise on the Law of Agency § 2150 (2d ed. 1914).

In addition to evidence and agency law, every state ethical code prescribes a duty of confidentiality, usually based on the provisions in the ABA Model Code or Model Rules. These provisions, while reflecting evidence and agency law, have not fully corresponded in breadth and limits to the rules of confidentiality under agency and evidence law. They might better be described as codifications of the profession's lore of confidentiality. The breadth of the exceptions to confidentiality acknowledged by the law of agency conflicts with the profession's understanding of its duty to preserve confidences. Under agency law, for example, the agent's duty of confidentiality is qualified by the agent's power to reveal confidences when necessary to protect a third party with a superior interest to the principal's interest in confidentiality. See § 395, comment (f); 2 F. Meechem, A Treatise on the Law of Agency § 2404 (2d ed. 1914). Contrast the exceptions in M.R. 1.6(b).

We first consider the scope of confidentiality under the Canons of Professional Ethics, the Code of Professional Responsibility and the Model Rules of Professional Conduct. Next, we examine the exceptions.

In examining the exceptions to confidentiality, there are two pervasive themes:

(1) What relationship do the confidentiality rules envision between a lawyer and a client who is engaged in criminal or fraudulent conduct?

(a) Do the rules allow sufficient room for a lawyer to protect herself from civil and criminal liability for the client's illegal conduct?

(b) Do the confidentiality rules adequately reinforce the prohibition against assisting a client in illegal conduct?

(2) Do the confidentiality rules properly balance the interests of clients and other societal and individual interests, such as protecting innocent third parties from harm?

The justification for the principle of client confidentiality is encouragement of clients to communicate fully with the lawyer and to seek early legal assistance even about embarrassing matters. See the Comment to M.R. 1.6 and EC 4-1. Is the exception in the law of agency, allowing disclosure to protect a "superior interest" of a third party, inadequate to serve the purposes of lawyer-client confidentiality?

Another interest served by confidentiality is more closely aligned with the law of agency. To encourage people to rely on others, they must be able to trust those in whose hands they place their affairs. The duty of confidentiality is a corollary of the more general duty of loyalty. This suggests a greater duty of loyalty, and a correspondingly greater duty of confidentiality, from those in whom a greater degree of trust is placed than in ordinary agents. Lawyers are not ordinary agents. However, lawyers are not the only professionals who are entrusted with matters of great importance and yet they receive greater protection for client confidences than that afforded other professionals, for example doctors. Compare the *Hawkins* case printed below with *Tarasoff,* which is discussed in the notes to *Hawkins.* In any case, why should this duty of loyalty extend to confidences about contemplated and ongoing illegal activity?

See Zacharias, Rethinking Confidentiality, 74 Iowa L.Rev. 351 (1989) for a review of the law of confidentiality and an empirical study of client and lawyer impressions of the confidentiality rule. Also see, Moore, Limits to Attorney–Client Confidentiality: A "Philosophically Informed" and Comparative Approach to Legal and Medical Ethics; and Nahstoll, The Lawyer's Allegience: Priorities Regarding Confidentiality, 41 Wash. & Lee L.Rev. 421, 433 (1984).

The Scope of the Duty of Confidentiality

The Canons of Professional Ethics

Canon 37 of the ABA's Canons of Professional Ethics, "Confidences of a Client," had two paragraphs: the first stated the duty; the second described exceptions. Canon 41, "Discovery of Imposition and Deception", contained another important exception to the duty. Paragraph one of Canon 37 provided:

It is the duty of a lawyer to preserve his client's confidences. This duty outlasts the lawyer's employment, and extends as well to his employees; and neither of them should accept employment which involves or may involve the disclosure or use of these confidences, either for the private advantage of the lawyer or his employees or to the disadvantage of the client, without his knowledge and consent, and even though there are other available sources of such information. A lawyer should not continue employment when he discovers that this obligation prevents the performance of his full duty to his former or to his new client.

Canon 37 proceeds as if the term "confidences" were self-explanatory and concerns itself with the scope of the duty. Also compare: M.R. 1.8(b), which implicitly allows the lawyer to *use* confidential information for the lawyer's own benefit as long as it does not disadvantage the client; and 1.9(c)(1), which allows the lawyer to use "generally known" information to disadvantage a former client. These provisions are discussed below.

Canon 37 incorporates a conflict of interest prohibition. Prohibiting the use as well as the disclosure also reflects concern with conflicts of interest and tracks the formulation of the agent's duty of confidentiality. See Restatement of Agency § 395 above. Under the Model Code and Rules these "conflict" issues are dealt with under separate headings. See DR 5–105 and M.R. 1.7 and 1.9. We too take up the conflicts question separately, see Chapters 7 and 8 below.

The Model Code of Professional Responsibility

DR 4–101 of the Code of Professional Responsibility is the Code's principal confidentiality provision. DR 4–101(A) defines the information to be protected. DR 4–101(B) defines the scope of the duty. DR 4–101(C) sets out exceptions. As in the Canons the question of client fraud is treated separately, DR 7–102(B)(1). DR 4–101(D) deals with disclosure and use of confidential information by the lawyer's agents.

DR 4–101(A) defines two types of confidential information, "confidences" and "secrets." All subsequent provisions of the Code apply to both categories. DR 4–101(A) provides that: "Confidence" refers to information protected by the attorney-client privilege under applicable law, and "secret" refers to other information gained in the professional relationship that the client has requested be held inviolate or the disclosure of which would be embarrassing or would be likely to be detrimental to the client.

The definition of "confidence" thus is a source external to the code; it is defined by the law of evidence. The definition of "secret" covers non-privileged information gained in the relationship; it does not cover information gained before or after the relationship. Should it? The attorney-client privilege is limited to information received from the client *during* the representation, but the agent's duty is broader, covering information ". . . acquired . . . on account of [the] agency." Recall that the law of agency applies to lawyers. Is this definition better than that in the Code provision? Is the agency definition broad enough?

"Secrets" does not cover all information gained in the course of the representation, only that which the client requests be secret or which would harm or embarrass the client if disclosed. Should the lawyer be left to decide whether information would harm or embarrass the client?

The distinction between "confidence" and "secret" became a source of controversy in interpreting an ABA amendment to DR 7–102(B)(1). See Hazard article below, describing the controversy and the ABA's resolution in Formal Opinion 341. The distinction has never assumed practical importance in determining whether there is a duty of confidentiality and was abandoned in the Model Rules, see M.R. 1.6.

DR 4–101(B) provides:

Except when permitted under DR 4–101(C), a lawyer shall not knowingly:

  (1) Reveal a confidence or secret of his client.

  (2) Use a confidence or secret of his client to the disadvantage of the client.

  (3) Use a confidence or secret of his client for the advantage of himself or of a third person, unless the client consents after full disclosure.

The Code specifies that "knowing" use or disclosure is the violation, apparently excluding inadvertent non-negligent disclosure. However DR 4–101(D) requires exercise of reasonable care in supervising agents who possess confidential client information, suggesting that negligent disclosure by the lawyer would violate DR 4–101(B).

Unlike Canon 37, the Model Code does specify that the duty of confidentiality continues after the lawyer-client relationship is ended, although this point is made in EC 4–6.

The Model Rules of Professional Conduct

General Description

M.R. 1.6 is the key provision on confidentiality. It was the most hotly debated of the rules during the drafting process of the Kutak Commission and on the floor of the ABA House of Delegates. In the process of being adopted by the states, it has also been more significantly redrafted than any of the other model rules. The heart of the controversy involves the scope of the exceptions, discussed later on.

Model Rule 1.6(a) is broader than DR 4–101. First, it protects all information "relating to the representation" whether the lawyer learned the information before, during or after the representation. Second, it applies whether or not disclosure would harm or embarrass the client. It also eliminates the word "knowingly" from its prohibition, stating flatly "a lawyer shall not."

Using as Opposed to Revealing Client Information

Use of confidential information is governed by the rules on conflict of interest. M.R. 1.8(b) prohibits using confidential information of a present client to the disadvantage of the client without the client's consent given after consultation except as M.R. 1.6 or 3.3 permit; and M.R. 1.9(c)(1) prohibits using confidential information of a former client to that client's disadvantage except as M.R. 1.6 and 3.3 permit *or* until the information has become generally known. Neither M.R. 1.6, 1.8(b) nor 1.9(c)(1) prohibit the use of confidential information to benefit the lawyer when the client will not be harmed by the use. Should a lawyer be prohibited from benefitting from a client confidence in a way that does not harm the client?

Such self-dealing is prohibited by the law of agency, see § 395 supra and the comment to § 388. Under some circumstances it may also constitute mail fraud, see Carpenter v. United States, 484 U.S. 19, 108 S.Ct. 316 (1987), discussed at greater length in Chapter 2 above at pp. 67–68. In *Carpenter* the court affirmed the conviction of a Wall Street Journal reporter who had traded in securities that he then mentioned in his market gossip column. The Court found that the information collected for the column was confidential information belonging to the Journal until published. The Court said: "Confidential business information has long been recognized as property. . . . The confidential information was generated from the business and the business had a right to decide how to use it prior to disclosing it to the public." 484 U.S. at 26, 108 S.Ct. at 321.

Use of confidential information to benefit the lawyer may also violate federal or state laws prohibiting insider trading.

Publicly Available Information as Confidential Information

Under the Rules as under the Code and Canons, the lawyer's obligation not to *reveal* confidential information applies whether or not the information is publicly known. See M.R. 1.9(c)(2). However, M.R. 1.9(c)(1), unlike the Canons or the Code, allows the *use* of generally known information against a *former* client. For cases on whether public information is confidential, see, e.g., City of Wichita v. Chapman, 214 Kan. 575, 521 P.2d 589, 596 (1974) (public information not a confidence); NCK Org. Ltd. v. Bregman, 542 F.2d 128, 133 (2d Cir.1976) (public information a confidence).

What interests are sacrificed by allowing a lawyer to use generally known information to the detriment of a former client? Why does Model Rule 1.8(b) not have an exception for generally known information similar to the one in M.R. 1.9(c)(1)? The law of agency allows agents to use confidential information to the disadvantage of a former principal when that information is available from public sources. See Restatement (Second) of Agency § 395 (1958). M.R. 1.9(c)(1)'s exception seems narrower than that of agency law in that the information must be "generally known."

Client Consent and Implied Authority to Reveal

Canon 37, DR 4–101(C)(1) and M.R. 1.6(a) all allow for disclosure of any client confidence if the client consents after consultation with the lawyer as to the consequences of such a decision. See also M.R. 1.8(b).

Lawyers, however, would be unable to do their job, which is to *represent* people, if they had to have express consent before speaking about anything that involves a confidence. The Comment to M.R. 1.6 explains:

> A lawyer is impliedly authorized to make disclosures about a client when appropriate in carrying out the representation, except to the extent that the client's instructions or special circumstances limit that authority. In litigation, for example, a lawyer may disclose information by admitting a fact that cannot properly be disputed, or in negotiation by making a disclosure that facilitates a satisfactory conclusion.

The Code has no similar provision on implied authority. However, the definition of "secrets" as information that would embarrass or harm the client if revealed yields a similar result.

Exceptions to Confidentiality

Introductory Note

Exceptions to the principle of confidentiality may be classified into three broad areas: the self-defense exception for the protection of lawyers threatened by their clients' actions; exceptions for the protection of innocent third parties who are being or may be victimized by the client; and the exception for fraud on the tribunal. The first two of these areas, self-defense and the defense of third parties, are covered in this chapter. The third category, fraud on the court, is the focus of Chapter 5.

Self–Defense

MEYERHOFER v. EMPIRE FIRE AND MARINE INS. CO.

United States Court of Appeals, Second Circuit, 1974.
497 F.2d 1190, cert. denied, 419 U.S. 998.

. . .

The full import of the problems and issues presented on this appeal cannot be appreciated and analyzed without an initial statement of the facts out of which they arise.

Empire Fire and Marine Insurance Company on May 31, 1972, made a public offering of 500,000 shares of its stock, pursuant to a registration statement filed with the Securities and Exchange Commission (SEC) on March 28, 1972. The stock was offered at $16 a share. Empire's attorney on the issue was the firm of Sitomer, Sitomer & Porges. Stuart Charles Goldberg was an attorney in the firm and had done some work on the issue.

Plaintiff Meyerhofer, on or about January 11, 1973, purchased 100 shares of Empire stock at $17 a share. He alleges that as of June 5, 1973, the market price of his stock was only $7 a share—hence, he has sustained an unrealized loss of $1,000. . . . Plaintiff Federman, on or about May 31, 1972, purchased 200 shares at $16 a share, 100 of which he sold for $1,363, sustaining a loss of some $237 on the stock sold and an unrealized loss of $900 on the stock retained.

On May 2, 1973, plaintiffs, represented by the firm of Bernson, Hoeniger, Freitag & Abbey (the Bernson firm), on behalf of themselves and all other purchasers of Empire common stock, brought this action alleging that the registration statement and the prospectus under which the Empire stock had been issued were materially false and misleading. Thereafter, an amended complaint, dated June 5, 1973, was served. The legal theories in both were identical, namely, violations of various sections of the Securities Exchange Act of 1933, the Securities Exchange Act of 1934, Rule 10b–5, and common law negligence, fraud and deceit. Damages for all members of the class or rescission were alternatively sought.

The lawsuit was apparently inspired by a Form 10–K which Empire filed with the SEC on or about April 12, 1973. This Form revealed that "The Registration Statement under the Securities Act of 1933 with respect to the public offering of the 500,000 shares of Common Stock did not disclose the proposed $200,000 payment to the law firm as well as certain other features of the compensation arrangements between the Company [Empire] and such law firm [defendant Sitomer, Sitomer and Porges]." Later that month Empire disseminated to its shareholders a proxy statement and annual report making similar disclosures.

The defendants named were Empire, officers and directors of Empire, the Sitomer firm and its three partners, A.L. Sitomer, S.J. Sitomer and R.E. Porges, Faulkner, Dawkins & Sullivan Securities Corp., the managing underwriter, Stuart Charles Goldberg, originally alleged to have been a partner of the Sitomer firm, and certain selling stockholders of Empire shares.

On May 2, 1973, the complaint was served on the Sitomer defendants and Faulkner. No service was made on Goldberg who was then no longer associated with the Sitomer firm. However, he was advised by telephone that he had been made a defendant. Goldberg inquired of the Bernson firm as to the nature of the charges against him and was informed generally as to the substance of the complaint and in particular the lack of disclosure of the finder's fee arrangement. Thus informed, Goldberg requested an opportunity to prove his non-involvement in any such arrangement and his lack of knowledge thereof. At this stage there was unfolded the series of events which ultimately resulted in the motion and order thereon now before us on appeal.

Goldberg, after his graduation from Law School in 1966, had rather specialized experience in the securities field and had published various books and treatises on related subjects. He became associated with the Sitomer firm in November 1971. While there Goldberg worked on phases of various registration statements including Empire, although another associate was responsible for the Empire registration statement and prospectus. However, Goldberg expressed concern over what he regarded as excessive fees, the nondisclosure or inadequate disclosure thereof, and the extent to which they might include a "finder's fee," both as to Empire and other issues.

The Empire registration became effective on May 31, 1972. The excessive fee question had not been put to rest in Goldberg's mind because in middle January 1973 it arose in connection with another registration (referred to as "Glacier"). Goldberg had worked on Glacier. Little purpose will be served by detailing the events during the critical period January 18 to 22, 1973, in which Goldberg and the Sitomer partners were debating the fee disclosure problem. In summary Goldberg insisted on a full and complete disclosure of fees in the Empire and Glacier offerings. The Sitomer partners apparently disagreed and Goldberg resigned from the firm on January 22, 1973.

On January 22, 1973, Goldberg appeared before the SEC and placed before it information subsequently embodied in his affidavit dated January 26, 1973, which becomes crucial to the issues now to be considered.

Some three months later, upon being informed that he was to be included as a defendant in the impending action, Goldberg asked the Bernson firm for an opportunity to demonstrate that he had been unaware of the finder's fee arrangement which, he said, Empire and the Sitomer firm had concealed from him all along. Goldberg met with members of the Bernson firm on at least two occasions. After consulting his own attorney, as well as William P. Sullivan, Special Counsel with the Securities and Exchange Commission, Division of Enforcement, Goldberg gave plaintiffs' counsel a copy of the January 26th affidavit which he had authored more than three months earlier. He hoped that it would verify his nonparticipation in the finder's fee omission and convince the Bernson firm that he should not be a defendant. The Bernson firm was satisfied with Goldberg's explanations and, upon their motion, granted by the court, he was dropped as a defendant. After receiving Goldberg's affidavit, the Bernson firm amended plaintiff's complaint. The amendments added more specific facts but did not change the theory or substance of the original complaint.

By motion dated June 7, 1973, the remaining defendants moved "pursuant to Canons 4 and 9 of the Code of Professional Responsibility, the Disciplinary Rules and Ethical Considerations applicable thereto, and the supervisory power of this Court" for the order of disqualification now on appeal.

By memorandum decision and order, the District Court ordered that the Bernson firm and Goldberg be barred from acting as counsel or participating with counsel for plaintiffs in this or any future action against Empire involving the transactions placed in issue in this lawsuit and from disclosing confidential information to others.

The complaint was dismissed without prejudice. The basis for the Court's decision is the premise that Goldberg had obtained confidential information from his client Empire which, in breach of relevant ethical canons, he revealed to plaintiffs' attorneys in their suit against Empire. The Court said its decision was compelled by "the broader obligations of Canons 4 and 9." *

There is no proof—not even a suggestion—that Goldberg had revealed any information, confidential or otherwise, that might have caused the instigation of the suit. To the contrary, it was not until after the suit was commenced that Goldberg learned that he was in jeopardy. The District Court recognized that the complaint had been based on Empire's—not Goldberg's—disclosures, but concluded because of this that Goldberg was under no further obligation "to reveal the information or to discuss the matter with plaintiffs' counsel."

Despite the breadth of paragraphs EC 4–4 and DR 4–101(B), DR 4–101(C) recognizes that a lawyer may reveal confidences or secrets necessary to defend himself against "an accusation of wrongful conduct." This is exactly what Goldberg had to face when, in their original complaint, plaintiffs named him as a defendant who wilfully violated the securities laws.

* Editor's note: In a footnote here the court quoted: EC 4–1; 4–4 through 4–6; DR 4–101; EC 9–1; and 9–6.

The charge, of knowing participation in the filing of a false and misleading registration statement, was a serious one. The complaint alleged violation of criminal statutes and civil liability computable at over four million dollars. The cost in money of simply defending such an action might be very substantial. The damage to his professional reputation which might be occasioned by the mere pendency of such a charge was an even greater cause for concern.

Under these circumstances Goldberg had the right to make an appropriate disclosure with respect to his role in the public offering. Concomitantly, he had the right to support his version of the facts with suitable evidence.

The problem arises from the fact that the method Goldberg used to accomplish this was to deliver to Mr. Abbey, a member of the Bernson firm, the thirty page affidavit, accompanied by sixteen exhibits, which he had submitted to the SEC. This document not only went into extensive detail concerning Goldberg's efforts to cause the Sitomer firm to rectify the nondisclosure with respect to Empire but even more extensive detail concerning how these efforts had been precipitated by counsel for the underwriters having come upon evidence showing that a similar nondisclosure was contemplated with respect to Glacier and their insistence that full corrective measures should be taken. Although Goldberg's description reflected seriously on his employer, the Sitomer firm and, also, in at least some degree, on Glacier, he was clearly in a situation of some urgency. Moreover, before he turned over the affidavit, he consulted both his own attorney and a distinguished practitioner of securities law, and he and Abbey made a joint telephone call to Mr. Sullivan of the SEC. Moreover, it is not clear that, in the context of this case, Canon 4 applies to anything except information gained from Empire. Finally, because of Goldberg's apparent intimacy with the offering, the most effective way for him to substantiate his story was for him to disclose the SEC affidavit. It was the fact that he had written such an affidavit at an earlier date which demonstrated that his story was not simply fabricated in response to plaintiff's complaint.

The District Court held: "All that need be shown . . . is that during the attorney-client relationship Goldberg had access to his client's information relevant to the issues here." See Emle Industries, Inc. v. Patentex, Inc., 478 F.2d 562 (2d Cir.1973). However, the irrebutable presumption of *Emle Industries* has no application to the instant circumstances because Goldberg never sought to "prosecute litigation," either as a party, compare Richardson v. Hamilton International Corp., 62 F.R.D. 413 (E.D.Pa.1974), or as counsel for a plaintiff party. Compare T.C. Theatre Corporation v. Warner Brothers Pictures, 113 F.Supp. 265 (S.D.N.Y.1953). At most the record discloses that Goldberg might be called as a witness for the plaintiffs but that role does not invest him with the intimacy with the prosecution of the litigation which must exist for the *Emle* presumption to attach.

In addition to finding that Goldberg had violated Canon 4, the District Court found that the relationship between Goldberg and the Bernson firm violated Canon 9 of the Code of Professional Responsibility which provides that:

EC 9–6 Every lawyer [must] strive to avoid not only professional impropriety but also the appearance of impropriety.

The District Court reasoned that even though there was no evidence of bad faith on the part of either Goldberg or the Bernson firm, a shallow reading of the facts might lead a casual observer to conclude that there was an aura of complicity about their relationship. However, this provision should not be read so broadly as to eviscerate the right of self-defense conferred by DR 4–101(C)(4).

Nevertheless, *Emle Industries, Inc. v. Patentex, Inc.*, supra, requires that a strict prophylactic rule be applied in these cases to ensure that a lawyer avoids representation of a party in a suit against a former client where there may be the appearance of a possible violation of confidence. To the extent that the District Court's order prohibits Goldberg from *representing* the interests of these or any other plaintiffs in this or similar actions, we affirm that order. We also affirm so much of the District Court's order as enjoins Goldberg from disclosing material information except on discovery or at trial.

The burden of the District Court's order did not fall most harshly on Goldberg; rather its greatest impact has been felt by Bernson, Hoeniger, Freitag & Abbey, plaintiffs' counsel, which was disqualified from participation in the case. The District Court based its holding, not on the fact that the Bernson firm showed bad faith when it received Goldberg's affidavit, but rather on the fact that it was involved in a tainted association with Goldberg because his disclosures to them inadvertently violated Canons 4 and 9 of the Code of Professional Responsibility. Because there are no violations of either of these Canons in this case, we can find no basis to hold that the relationship between Goldberg and the Bernson firm was tainted. The District Court was apparently unpersuaded by appellees' salvo of innuendo to the effect that Goldberg "struck a deal" with the Bernson firm or tried to do more than prove his innocence to them. Since its relationship with Goldberg was not tainted by violations of the Code of Professional Responsibility, there appears to be no warrant for its disqualification from participation in either this or similar actions. *A fortiori* there was no sound basis for disqualifying plaintiffs or dismissing the complaint.

Order dismissing action without prejudice and enjoining Bernson, Hoeniger, Freitag & Abbey from acting as counsel for plaintiffs herein reversed. . . . To the extent that the orders appealed from prohibit Goldberg from acting as a party or as an attorney for a party in any action arising out of the facts herein alleged, or from disclosing material information except on discovery or at trial, they are affirmed.

Questions

While the court's opinion concentrates on Goldberg's disclosure to the plaintiffs, the earlier disclosure to the SEC raises serious questions.

Is it possible that Empire did not know of the obligation to disclose the fee arrangement in the prospectus? Could the fraud have been the firm's and not the client's?

M.R. 1.13 speaks of the lawyer's duties to an organizational client. It prescribes a course of conduct to be followed when the lawyer knows that an agent of the organizational client is violating a legal obligation to the client or violating the law in a manner that might be imputed to the organization. See the note on M.R. 1.13, pp. 758–759 below. Under M.R. 1.13, should Goldberg have discussed the matter directly with Empire before going to the SEC? Would he have a duty to do so before disclosing to protect himself? See the Comment to Model Rule 1.6(b)(2), the self-defense exception to confidentiality, which states: "Where practicable and not prejudicial to the lawyer's ability to establish the defense, the lawyer should advise the client of the third party's assertions and request that the client respond appropriately." See also Canon 41 and DR 7–102(B), provisions dealing with client fraud, which require the lawyer to ask the client to rectify before the lawyer discloses the fraud.

If the Bernson firm had had access to and had used Goldberg's affidavit to file suit against Empire, what result? In Beiny v. Wynyard, 129 A.D.2d 126, 517 N.Y.S.2d 474 (1987), a law firm procured attorney-client privileged documents through deception. It was held that the evidence so procured should be suppressed and the firm disqualified. See also American Protection Ins. Co. v. MGM Grand Hotel–Las Vegas, Inc., (D.Nev.1984 unreported), app. dismissed, 765 F.2d 925 (9th Cir. 1985) (disqualification of lawyer for ex parte interrogation of other party's primary expert witness); cf. Goldenberg v. Corporate Air, Inc., 189 Conn. 504, 457 A.2d 296 (1983), overruled on other grounds in Burger & Burger, Inc. v. Murren, 202 Conn. 660, 522 A.2d 812 (1987) (disqualification for inadvertent access to opposing party's confidential information).

The Scope of the Self–Defense Exception

Almost without objection the bar has accepted that the principle of confidentiality must yield to a self-defense exception for lawyers. Even the American Trial Lawyer's draft of a Lawyer's Code of Conduct, which was in large part a response to the perceived attack on confidentiality embodied in the Kutak Commission draft of the Model Rules (see the Preface to the American Lawyer's Code of Conduct (ALCC)), contains a fairly broad self-defense exception to confidentiality. See ALCC Rule 1.5. For a general discussion and critique of the self-defense exception, see Levine, Self–Interest or Self–Defense: Lawyer Disregard of the Attorney–Client Privilege for Profit and Protection, 5 Hofstra L.Rev. 783 (1977).

Canon 37 provided that a lawyer could reveal "the truth" when an accusation was made by a client, but made no provision for self-defense when the accusation was made by a third party. This may be accounted for by the requirement in the Canons that the lawyer disclose client fraud, see Canon 41 and the discussion below.

Should the lawyer's ability to disclose in self-defense depend on whether the accusation is made by the client or by a third party? The Model Code and Rules reject such a distinction, see DR 4–101(C)(4) and M.R. 1.6(b)(2). But see ALCC Rule 1.5 (allowing disclosure of client confidences only *after charges are formally instituted* when the charge is by a third party, but allowing disclosures prior to formal charges when the accusation is by a client). Does an exception for charges made by third parties encourage third parties to sue lawyers in an attempt to gain access to confidential information? See the discussion of *First Federal* below at p. 253.

Canon 37 made no provision for disclosure in suits instituted by lawyers against their clients. The most common examples of which are suits by lawyers to collect their fees.

The Code of Professional Responsibility makes no distinction between accusations against the lawyer made by a third party and those made by the client. DR 4–101(C)(4) permits the lawyer to disclose: "Confidences or secrets necessary to establish or collect his fee or to defend himself or his employees, or associates against an accusation of wrongful conduct."

M.R. 1.6(b)(2) provides:

A lawyer may reveal [confidential] information to the extent the lawyer reasonably believes necessary . . . to establish a claim or defense on behalf of the lawyer in a controversy between the lawyer and the client, to establish a defense to a criminal charge or civil claim against the lawyer based upon conduct in which the client was involved, or to respond to allegations in any proceeding concerning the lawyer's representation of the client.

The Comment to M.R. 1.6 emphasizes a broad reading of this exception:

The lawyer's right to respond arises when an assertion of such complicity has been made. Paragraph (b)(2) does not require the lawyer to await the commencement of an action or proceeding that charges such complicity, so that a defense may be established by responding directly to a third party who has made such an assertion.

Several bar ethics opinions take the position that the lawyer may be forthcoming with the prosecutor when she learns that she has been accused by someone, even though the prosecutor has not yet threatened prosecution. See Ass'n Bar City of New York, Op. No. 1986–7; Mich. Op. CI–900 (1983); Maine Op. 55 (1985).

Should the exception be stretched even further to allow the lawyer to disclose prior to an "assertion" when the lawyer believes an assertion may be forthcoming? Is this what Goldberg did when he went to the SEC? Assuming Goldberg had gone to Empire and it had refused to disclose the false statements in the prospectus, would Goldberg then have been justified in going to the SEC prior to an "assertion" of wrongdoing? Even if so, was what he did "self-defense" given the proactive nature of his conduct. The more natural classification is disclosure to stop ongoing fraud rather than disclosure in self-defense, but the Model Rules treatment of client fraud disclosures makes resort to the self-defense exception necessary. See Model Rule 1.6(b)(1) (making no provision for disclosure of ongoing client fraud). This issue will be more fully explored when we take up client fraud below.

The breadth of M.R. 1.6(b)(2) is limited by the requirement that the lawyer reasonably believe the disclosures are necessary. The Comment adds: "disclosure should be no greater than the lawyer reasonably believes is necessary to vindicate innocence, the disclosure should be made in a manner which limits access to the information to the tribunal or other persons having a need to know it, and appropriate protective orders or other arrangements should be made by the lawyer to the fullest extent practicable." How do Goldberg's actions match up against these standards?

See also the Comment's statement that the lawyer should, where practicable, inform the client and request that the client itself respond to the charges. For a case where a lawyer was disciplined for using client confidences ostensibly in self-defense, see Dixon v. California State Bar, 187 Cal.Rptr. 30, 653 P.2d 321 (1982) (discipline imposed for using confidences in a suit brought by client to enjoin the lawyer from harassing client). See also Florida Bar v. Ball, 406 So.2d 459 (Fla.1981) (lawyer suspended for disclosing to adoption agency that clients did not pay the lawyer's fee and therefore might be a financial risk).

The Self–Defense Exception to the Attorney–Client Privilege

In an action to collect a fee, the lawyer may disclose otherwise privileged communications to establish the claim. See, e.g., Cannon v. U.S. Acoustics Corp., 532 F.2d 1118 (7th Cir.1976). The privilege also yields to the lawyer's need to defend herself in a malpractice suit brought against her by the client. See, e.g., Nave v. Baird, 12 Ind. 318, 319 (1859). If the client attacks the lawyer's work in a proceeding to which the lawyer is not a party, the privilege also yields. See, e.g., Flood v. Commissioner, 468 F.2d 904, 905 (9th Cir. 1972) (lawyer could testify to establish that settlement of former client's case was within lawyer's authority). A common example is a habeas corpus proceeding brought by a convicted person in which the claim is ineffective assistance of counsel. See the cases cited above in the note on p. 239.

Statutory definitions of the privilege include a self-defense exception. See, e.g., Proposed Federal Rule of Evidence 503(d)(3) (allowing disclosure of "communication[s] relevant to an issue of breach of duty by the lawyer to his client or by the client to his lawyer"); and West's Ann.Cal.Evid.Code § 958 (1966) ("no privilege . . . as to a communication relevant to an issue of breach, by the lawyer or by the client, of a duty arising out of the lawyer-client relationship"). These statutes, however, arguably provide no exception where the lawyer is accused of wrongdoing in complicity with the client, such as charged against Goldberg in the *Meyerhofer* case.

While the court in *Meyerhofer* deals only with confidentiality and not the attorney-client privilege, that case has been read as supporting an exception to the *privilege* where lawyers are accused of wrongdoing in complicity with a client. See In re National Mortgage Equity Corp., 120 F.R.D. 687 (C.D.Cal.), appeal dismissed, 849 F.2d 1166 (9th Cir. 1988), recognizing a self-defense exception to the attorney-client privilege, essentially parallel to *Meyerhofer*. In *National Mortgage Equity*, the law firm had provided advice and documentation in a private-placement securities issue in which, it later turned out, the issuer made fraudulent omissions but deceived the firm into believing that the disclosures had been made. Both the issuer and the firm were sued by the investors. At pre-trial, the firm sought to lift the attorney-client privilege enough to show that it had been deceived and had not been a party to the nondisclosure. The court ruled that the firm could offer such evidence.

In First Federal Savings & Loan Ass'n of Pittsburgh v. Oppenheim, Appel, Dixon & Co., 110 F.R.D. 557 (S.D.N.Y.1986), the court read *Meyerhofer* as implicitly accepting the proposition that in cases where the lawyer is accused of wrongdoing by a third party, "the attorney's interest in disclosure—at least to the extent necessary to defend himself—will usually outweigh the more general interest of the client in preserving confidences." Id. at 565.

In *Meyerhofer*, the court expressed concern that Goldberg had revealed more information than necessary to absolve himself. The court noted that Goldberg was "in a situation of some urgency . . ." and had consulted with his own lawyers and the SEC before making the disclosures to the opposing party. Nonetheless, it ordered that any subsequent disclosures be supervised by the district court. Based on this part of *Meyerhofer*, the court in *First Federal* ordered the lawyer to submit all proposed disclosures to the court for review *in camera* along with an affidavit explaining the necessity for each proposed disclosure. The client was then given the opportunity to respond to the lawyer's showing.

In deciding what disclosures to allow, the court used the "reasonable necessity" standard of M.R. 1.6.

The procedural safeguards adopted by the court in *First Federal* are in sharp contrast to the broad authorization of disclosure on a mere assertion by a third party which is sanctioned by the Model Rules and apparently the Model Code. Should the lawyer have to wait for formal charges to be instituted before invoking the self-defense exception to confidentiality? Should judicial approval be required before the lawyer reveals confidences? At least one commentator, Levine, Self–Interest or Self–Defense: Lawyer Disregard of the Attorney–Client Privilege for Profit and Protection, 5 Hofstra L.Rev. 783, 825–26 (1977), proposes the latter suggestion.

Client Fraud

The Perpetuation of Ambiguity

Perhaps no other subject in professional ethics has generated more heated debate than the lawyer's proper course of action upon discovery of client fraud. An historical review of the rules and ethics opinions on the subject reveals a morass of conflicting precepts. The continuity of ambiguity is striking: rules affirming a duty to disclose coexist with ethics opinions interpreting those rules as requiring non-disclosure. Compare Canon 41 with ABA Opinion 287, and DR 7–102(B)(1) with ABA Opinion 341. A rule appearing to require non-disclosure, M.R. 1.6, has a commentary that allows disclosure as long as it is done through signals instead of words. Most states adopting M.R. 1.6 have amended the ABA's proposal to allow (and in a few instances to require) disclosure of client fraud. See the chart of state variations on Model Rule 1.6 from Hazard & Hodes, The Law of Lawyering Appendix 4 reprinted below at p. 292. In any case, rules adopted by state courts provide for disclosure of client fraud, while the bar's interpretations move toward non-disclosure.

A Case Study: OPM

In OPM, the client was engaged in ongoing fraud and using the lawyers' services to perpetrate it. At some point the lawyers become aware of the problem. Their knowledge was gained in the professional relationship, based wholly on the confidences of the client. To reveal the fraud would constitute disclosure of client confidences. And yet, to withdraw without revealing would leave the firm open to civil and criminal charges.

The OPM lawyers eventually withdrew, but following the advice of their ethics consultants they refrained from disclosing the fraud to the victims or to the law firm which then took over and unwittingly continued the fraud. The trustee wrote:

> One thing seems clear; the firm could have followed other courses, consistent with their ethical responsibilities, that would have stopped the fraud. Instead, after receiving notice that it was dealing with a crook, it acted in a way that helped [OPM] continue the fraud for eight additional months during which financial institutions were bilked out of more than $85 million. After [the first law firm] resigned, OPM's in-house legal staff and [successor coun-

sel] closed fraudulent . . . lease financings totaling approximately $15 million.

In reading the OPM story, consider, at each stage of the unfolding events, what the lawyers should have done differently. Keep in mind that scams similar to OPM have been repeated over and over in other contexts, including the S & L scandals of the 1980's, Southwest oil industry investments in the 1970's and shaky smaller businesses every day. You may have such a business for a client.

Also consider whether the ethics "experts" could have been charged with aiding and abetting the fraud.

IN RE OPM LEASING SERVICES, INC.

Report of the Trustee Concerning Fraud and Other Misconduct in the Management of the Affairs of the Debtor

II. OPM: The Story in Brief

Mordecai Weissman founded his own leasing company in July 1970 at the age of twenty-three in hopes of prospering with a minimum investment of his own capital and effort. He called the new enterprise O.P.M. Leasing Services, Inc. . . .

OPM's principals often told customers and others in the business and financial communities that "O.P.M." stood for "other people's machines." To the outside world that watched OPM grow into one of the nation's largest computer leasing companies, this explanation seemed to fit OPM's role as intermediary between computer manufacturers and computer users.

But the truth was that the initials stood for "other people's money." The name connoted the plan of Weissman and Myron S. Goodman, his brother-in-law and partner, to rely almost exclusively on funds advanced by others to run the business. . . . Seen from the inside, their business relied on corruption and deception from the start to create an illusion of success. Meanwhile OPM actually lost money at ever increasing rates. By the end Weissman and Goodman were able to continue operating only with other people's money they obtained by fraud of record proportions.

The fraud relied heavily on a factor identified in yet another explanation offered for the OPM initials—"other people's mistakes." Numerous financiers, businessmen, and professionals acted through ignorance, carelessness, poor judgment, or self-interest in ways that permitted the fraud to continue for years. . . .

A. *"Other People's Machines": The Myth of OPM*

. . .

Mordecai Weissman founded OPM in his native Brooklyn with about $11,000 borrowed from relatives. His brother-in-law and boyhood acquaintance, Myron S. Goodman, joined OPM several months later. Weissman and Goodman thereafter jointly owned and operated

OPM, with Weissman as President and Goodman as Executive Vice President. At first OPM leased everything from office copiers to chicken fryers. It purchased the equipment it needed with funds advanced by financing institutions on the credit of the equipment users; OPM then repaid the financing institutions with rentals from the users.

In 1972 OPM began to focus its new business efforts on the growing field of minicomputers. Weissman and Goodman moved OPM's headquarters to Wall Street in hopes that the mystique associated with that nationally known address would give OPM an image of business and financial stature. Two years later OPM broke into the business of leasing mainframe computers, which cost several million dollars apiece. Thereafter Weissman and Goodman concentrated increasingly on mainframe leasing because it offered more cash per transaction and larger, more creditworthy lessees. OPM had entered the "big time."

Unlike some companies active in computer leasing that limited themselves to a brokerage capacity, OPM undertook certain continuing responsibilities (and therefore risks as well) for transactions it arranged. OPM's profit, at least in theory, included any excess of the debt financing proceeds above the cost of the equipment and any "residual value" in the equipment at the expiration of the lease. OPM often obtained additional funds by selling "equity participations" in the equipment to investors who could use tax benefits generated by the transactions. Other leasing companies found it hard to imagine how OPM made money because the deals it offered seemed too good to be true. But to lessees, OPM's rock-bottom rates and other appealing lease terms were hard to resist. As a result, OPM's business expanded dramatically.

Between 1975 and 1977 OPM's lease related assets quintupled to over $250 million. OPM seemed well on its way to realizing Goodman's dream of an "empire" with assets exceeding $1 billion. In 1978 OPM moved its staff by then numbering more than one hundred, into new, expensively furnished headquarters in the former United States Steel Corporation building at 71 Broadway. Weissman and Goodman had begun to mingle among the blue-chip mainstays of the business and financial communities. Household names—AT & T, American Express, the Bank of New York, General Motors, Merrill Lynch, Revlon, Rockwell—studded OPM's customer list. Prestigious Wall Street investment bankers—first Goldman Sachs and then Lehman Brothers Kuhn Loeb—arranged financing on OPM's lease transactions with some of the nation's largest financial institutions, including Chase Manhattan Bank, Chemical Bank, Manufacturers Hanover Trust Company, Metropolitan Life, and the Philadelphia Saving Fund Society. By year-end 1978 OPM's financial statements, certified by the large, well-known accounting firm of Fox & Company, reported total assets of over $412 million and healthy profits. And in December 1979 *Fortune* magazine lauded OPM's rapid ascent in the computer leasing business.

As their business grew, Weissman and Goodman assumed the lifestyle of successful entrepreneurs. Leaving behind their modest Brooklyn residences, they purchased lavish homes in exclusive Lawrence, Long Island, . . . They purchased a controlling interest in the First National Bank of Jefferson Parish, a large bank located in the New Orleans suburbs. They contributed over $3 million to charity . . .

. . .

Then, in February 1981 with abruptness that startled many in the business and financial worlds, the OPM bubble burst. The United States Attorney's Office in New York caused grand jury subpoenas to be served on OPM and several of its officers and employees. Within weeks OPM filed for bankruptcy. Newspaper reports indicated that Goodman and perhaps others had conducted a massive fraud amid all the trappings of success and integrity at OPM. Almost everything about OPM suddenly seemed a mystery: What had really been going on? . . .

Contrary to appearances, OPM in fact lost money in every year of its existence. OPM was insolvent virtually from inception, although Weissman and Goodman may not have been astute enough to know it.

Weissman and Goodman used OPM as a vehicle for pursuing their divergent personal goals. Weissman, who dreamed of retirement by age thirty-five to a life of leisure, minimized the time he spent at OPM. Goodman, on the other hand, wanted a billion dollar empire and managed OPM in ways that suited his egocentric and mercurial personality. He directed OPM's day-to-day operations in a degree of detail that sometimes became absurd. He surrounded himself with an entourage of aides-de-camp, whose principal function was to tote the twelve or more large document bags Goodman took with him everywhere. And he dealt so abusively with OPM's staff that he more than once threatened to remove the head or "another part of [the] anatomy" from one employee or another. At the same time, many OPM employees felt loyal to Goodman because of his boyish charm, chronic health problems, commitment to the company, and apparently sincere devotion to Orthodox Judaism. Weissman and Goodman also shared a fondness for installing relatives, many of whom lacked business skills, in highly paid positions at OPM.

Amid back-office chaos, Weissman and Goodman managed to keep OPM afloat for ten years only by improvising a series of fraudulent and dishonest responses to its business needs and constant cash flow problems.

1. *Payoffs, Dipsy–Doodles, and Phantoms*

Weissman first turned to corrupt practices as a way to obtain new business. With Goodman's assistance, he routinely made payments of sizable "commissions" to salesmen of equipment vendors to induce them to steer customers to OPM. As a result, OPM gained a virtual monopoly on leases of equipment of Basic Four Information Systems, a growing vendor of minicomputers.

But questionable payments to vendor employees did not lead to profits for OPM in the early years. Defaults by OPM's small customers forced OPM to assume their obligations in order to maintain goodwill with financing institutions. The opening of four branch offices in 1972 increased OPM's overhead without generating appreciable income.

. . . As a result, by November 1972 OPM faced severe cash shortages, suffered a net loss of over $124,000 for the fiscal year, and had a negative net worth of nearly $140,000.

Weissman and Goodman initially responded to OPM's cash plight by using the "slow pay" method common to many financially strapped businesses. When this method proved insufficient, Weissman and Goodman turned to lease fraud.

OPM's first fraudulent financing, in mid–1972, was triggered by the refusal of a lessee to sign an "equipment acceptance form" for equipment it had agreed to lease. Because OPM desperately needed the cash the financing of the lease would provide, Weissman and Goodman decided to forge the lessee's signature on the form and present it to the financing institution. As they would do in many subsequent transactions, Goodman crouched under a glass table and held a flashlight to assist Weissman trace the lessee's genuine signature from the lease onto the equipment acceptance form. The financing, supplied by Chase Manhattan, went off without a hitch, and Weissman and Goodman had entered the lease fraud business. . . . As OPM's cash problems continued unabated, Weissman and Goodman invented many variations on the lease fraud theme.

The first variation was double and triple discounting—obtaining financing from two or three financing institutions on the security of a single lease without disclosing the other encumbrance or encumbrances.

. . . Often using the glass table method, the pair then forged documents to be presented to Chase and OPM's two other primary financing sources—Chemical Bank and Tilden Commercial Alliance. Weissman and Goodman engaged in double and triple discounting to the tune of at least $4.2 million through 1976. One of OPM's outside accountants reportedly referred to double and triple discounts as "dispy–doodles."

Between 1975 and 1977, Weissman and Goodman phased out double and triple discounting and employed other forms of lease fraud. They financed entirely fictitious ("phantom") leases covering equipment that did not exist. They also financed fraudulent "piggyback" transactions in which one user had purportedly committed to lease equipment immediately after expiration of another user's lease of the same equipment. Documentation for the second, phantom lease was forged.

Weissman and Goodman also financed leases in which they had altered the lease documents after execution by the lessee. For example, they typed in a "6" before a "3" to turn a genuine three month lease into a fake sixty-three month lease. In another instance, they replaced pages in a lease for $146.75 per month and financed the new version as a lease for $58,000 per month.

The early lease frauds, the largest of which related to leases or purported leases with American Express Company and the Bank of New York, involved at least thirty-seven transactions and grossed over $40 million. To ensure that certain procedures employed by financing institutions did not uncover the fraud, Weissman (and occasionally Goodman) resorted to such ploys as retrieving documents from lessees and equipment vendors, maintaining phony payment records, and mailing checks to vendors at nonexistent addresses.

Far from solving OPM's cash problems, the early lease frauds ultimately exacerbated them because the fraudulent leases underlying the financings did not yield rental streams to repay the debt. Goodman managed to attract additional funds in part by supplying bogus financial statements to equity participants in genuine OPM lease transactions. But even these funds were insufficient to satisfy OPM's need for cash, which grew as the company's financial condition worsened. By November 1975, despite impressive growth in lease related assets (from $1.4 million in 1971 to $51.4 million in 1975), OPM's annual losses had grown to almost $278,000 and its negative net worth had reached almost $652,000.

2. *The Mainframe Gambit*

Weissman and Goodman thought they saw the solution to their problems in OPM's growing mainframe leasing business. Weissman had gained a toehold for OPM with mainframe users by making approximately $50,000 in cash payoffs to an IBM salesman in return for lists of IBM customers who had 360 Series mainframes on their premises or 370 Series mainframes on order. To make sure that prestigious companies like American Express and Fireman's Fund Insurance Company leased from OPM instead of its competitors, Weissman and Goodman made at least $600,000 in payoffs to at least twelve employees of lessees.

To wrest even more mainframe business from other leasing companies, OPM offered lower monthly rentals coupled with a longer lease term. Because the longer stream of rental payments generally supported a greater amount of debt financing (which was based on the present value of the rental stream), the proceeds of the debt financing and the equity participation transaction together sometimes exceeded by up to $1 million the amount necessary for OPM to purchase a $3 million mainframe. Weissman hoped the excess would allow OPM to buy out the existing fraudulent financings and ultimately turn the corner to profitability.

To overcome the reluctance of computer users to enter into a long term lease of equipment that could become obsolete rapidly, Weissman and Goodman offered an "early termination" option, under which the lessee could return equipment to OPM well before the full term of its lease expired.

. . .

Early termination options enabled OPM to expand dramatically but exposed it to disaster if the market value of leased equipment dropped and substantial numbers of lessees exercised their early termination rights. . . .

Lessees gobbled up the early termination deals so fast that from year-end 1975 to year-end 1978 OPM's stated lease related assets increased by an average of about $100 million per year. Cash-rich for the short term as a result of these deals, Weissman and Goodman managed to buy out all but one of the early fraudulent financings.

But it was just a matter of time before early termination commitments—the key to OPM's spectacular growth—would come back to haunt the company. In March 1977 IBM announced it was drastically reducing prices on the 370 Series of mainframe computers and introducing a more efficient 303X Series. The announcement was so devastating to OPM that Goodman almost passed out when he learned of it within minutes after it appeared on the New York Stock Exchange tape.

As the price cuts went into effect and the 303X Series later hit the market, OPM's customers began to exercise early termination options on the 370 Series equipment that by then constituted the bulk of OPM's lease portfolio.

. . .

As a result, OPM's cash shortages became more severe than ever.

Using a new kind of deception, Goodman succeeded in hiding the effects of the announcement for over three years. In May 1977 OPM issued year-end 1976 financial statements certified by its new auditors, Fox & Company. The financials reported profits ($1.7 million) and positive net worth (over $724,000) for the first time in OPM's history. The apparent positive trend reported on financials certified by Fox continued for the next two years. But the reported profits were possible only because Goodman had browbeaten Fox into inventing a method to permit OPM to recognize income from equity transactions prematurely. According to Price Waterhouse Co., the Trustee's accountants, the method of equity income recognition approved by Fox departed from generally accepted accounting principles, use of which would have resulted in continuing losses and a negative net worth of over $31 million by year-end 1978.

3. *Turning to Massive Fraud*

Procuring false and misleading certified financial statements did nothing, of course, to suppress OPM's appetite for cash. By late 1978 increasing early terminations, . . . [and other ventures . . . made] OPM's financial condition desperate.

Weissman and Goodman first resorted to another quick fix. Between December 1978 and February 1979 Goodman used OPM's accounts at the New Orleans bank and banks in New York and St. Paul to kite over $5 million in checks. But it became clear that check kiting was not an adequate solution. Not only did it fail to produce sufficient cash; it led to a federal criminal investigation culminating in a guilty plea by OPM in March 1980 to twenty-two counts of making false statements to banks.

In search of a more reliable source of cash, Goodman turned back to lease fraud and chose Rockwell International Corporation as the vehicle. Rockwell regularly leased large amounts of equipment from OPM, and Goodman personally handled the account through a close relationship with Sidney L. Hasin, the Rockwell employee most active in computer acquisitions. Rockwell's internal computer acquisition procedures did not appear likely to discover fraud, and Goodman correctly believed Rockwell's stature in the financial community would reduce the likelihood that financing institutions would contact Rockwell concerning any particular transaction.

In July and December 1978, Goodman fraudulently obtained financing on leases that Rockwell had executed but did not intend to take effect. Goodman was able to obtain genuine Rockwell signatures on documents needed for financing these leases.

Beginning in early 1979, Goodman recruited a team of accomplices. He appealed to their personal loyalty and promised—as he would time and again—promptly to buy out the fraudulent deals and cease the fraud. Goodman induced Weissman to prepare phony documents for two transactions, but Weissman played no further active role in the Rockwell fraud. Weissman acknowledges, however, that he intentionally closed his eyes to the continuation of the fraud. Moreover, Weissman willingly accepted his high salary and other benefits that he knew or should have known flowed directly or indirectly from fraud proceeds.

Goodman was able to coax several OPM employees into providing extensive assistance in handling the mechanics of the Rockwell fraud. Stephen M. Lichtman, Goodman's assistant, helped control the flow of documents to and from Rockwell's computer headquarters near Los Angeles. Allen Ganz, brother-in-law of Goodman and Weissman, created phony documents and helped make arrangements for the fraudulent leases to be financed. . . . Several other OPM employees had knowledge of or provided limited assistance in the Rockwell fraud at various times.

The second phase of the Rockwell fraud consisted of financing phantom leases. At first Goodman and his accomplices simply forged Rockwell signatures on leases and financing documents. Later they began creating leases and financing documents by removing signature pages from surplus counterparts of documentation for legitimate transactions and attaching them to fictitious documents they had prepared. They also fabricated title documents purporting to evidence OPM's ownership of the fictitious equipment listed on phony leases. To keep Rockwell from discovering the financing of phantom leases, Goodman instructed OPM's counsel, the New York law firm of Singer Hutner Levine & Seeman, to channel lease and financing documents destined for Rockwell through OPM. Goodman also took precautions to discourage financing institutions and Lehman, which arranged most of the financings, from contacting Rockwell concerning terms of the leases.

In late 1979 the Rockwell fraud entered a third phase. Instead of fabricating phantom leases, the fraud team began altering the terms of genuine Rockwell leases to make them appear to cover vastly more expensive equipment renting for much higher monthly amounts for longer periods of time. In one transaction, for example, Rockwell agreed to pay $6,000 per month on a thirty-six month lease, while the OPM fraud team financed a version of the lease purporting to obligate Rockwell to pay $64,365 per month over an eighty-four month lease term. Although the lease financing documentation required Rockwell to pay rent directly to the institution that financed the lease, Goodman arranged for Rockwell to make the relatively small payments on its version of altered leases to OPM which, in turn, used its own funds (obtained through additional fraudulent financings, naturally) to make the inflated payments on the financed version of the leases to the financing institutions.

When occasional "glitches" threatened to expose the scheme, the fraud team always stood ready to improvise a response to the crisis. They intercepted documents bound for Rockwell, retrieved them from under the noses of Rockwell employees, . . .

To ensure OPM's continued leasing relationship with Rockwell, Goodman created wildly inflated Cali/OPM * financial statements and presented them to Rockwell representatives.

The three phases of the Rockwell fraud together grossed over $188.3 million. But even that amount, much of which went to repay earlier fraudulent financings in a classic Ponzi scheme sequence, could not pull OPM out of the downward spiral caused by ever increasing early terminations. Notwithstanding premature recognition of income from equity participation transactions, a draft 1979 Cali "compilation report" prepared by Fox in the fall of 1980 showed a net loss of over $28 million and a negative net worth of approximately $21 million.

4. *Getting Caught*

The end of the fraud at OPM began in the fall of 1980 with an inquiry—not unlike several others before and after—concerning Rockwell's obligation to make rental payments directly to financing institutions. The lawyer who made the inquiry had no suspicion of fraud but simply regarded the matter as a technicality that he proposed

---

* Editor's note: Cali was the parent of OPM.

correcting by revising financing documents to permit Rockwell to pay OPM.

Rockwell investigated the matter for several months but could not locate any documentation for two of the leases at issue, which in fact were "phantoms." Eventually, Rockwell asked the financing institution that acted as paying agent on the leases to send copies. They arrived on February 10, 1981, the day before [OPM employees] were due for a meeting at Rockwell . . . concerning the mysterious leases. When [the employees] arrived on February 11, they presented [phony documents and a story] that the fraud team had fabricated [in] preparation for the meeting. When Rockwell confronted them with the wholly fictitious [leases] it had obtained from the paying agent, [one of the OPM employees,] Friedman, called Goodman, who instructed him to stall and call back every fifteen minutes until Goodman could think of a cover story. Four calls later, Goodman finally gave Friedman a far-fetched tale. The story initially pacified Rockwell, but nagging doubts soon led one of its employees to notice that the Rockwell signatures on the version of the leases received from the paying agent appeared forged.

After a flurry of meetings, on February 18 representatives of Rockwell and certain financing institutions presented their evidence of fraud to the United States Attorney's Office in New York. When grand jury subpoenas were served on OPM and several employees the next day, Weissman and Goodman hurried back from California while other fraud team members hastened to destroy documents that could link them to the fraud. Goodman planned to accept all blame for the fraud and claim everyone else blindly followed orders. Weissman even attempted to remain OPM's chief executive for a short time.

OPM filed a voluntary petition for reorganization on March 11, 1981; on March 27 appointment of the Trustee was approved by the Bankruptcy Court. For the next several months most of the fraud participants maintained strict silence in response to all inquiries from both the United States Attorney's Office and the Trustee. The only two who submitted to examination by the Trustee perjured themselves by denying participation in the fraud.

The complexion of both the civil and the criminal inquires began to change in June 1981, when Allen Ganz learned that a document marked as an exhibit in the Trustee's investigation tied him to the fraud. He resolved to confess and informed [two other OPM employees] of his change of heart. A short while later all three agreed to cooperate with the criminal investigation. Similar agreements were forthcoming later from the other fraud participants. On December 17, 1981, Weissman, Goodman, Allen Ganz, Lichtman, Friedman, Shulman, and Jeffry Resnick (a minor participant) all pleaded guilty to charges arising from the fraud. A year later they received sentences ranging up to twelve years in prison for Goodman and ten years for Weissman. All but Resnick are now incarcerated.

5. *What Happened to the Take?*

Goodman, Weissman, and other fraud participants maintain that, despite conducting one of the largest frauds in history, they never stashed away significant fraud proceeds. Weissman and Goodman assert that the overwhelming bulk of the fraud proceeds went to meet OPM's enormous cash obligations. Although limited by available resources and OPM's chaotic and incomplete records, the Trustee's investigation tended to confirm their story.

C. *"Other People's Mistakes": The Outsiders*

No less noteworthy than the remarkable saga of OPM from the inside is the combination of actions and inactions by various outsiders that permitted the fraud to occur and, in some instances, actively contributed to its success. Accountants, management consultants, lawyers, investment bankers, lessee representatives, bankers, and other businessmen all worked intimately with Goodman and Weissman in ways that exposed them to transactions used for the fraud. In the misguided belief that someone else was checking the bona fides of OPM's transactions or was acting to stop the fraud, all stood by while the fraud continued at an ever increasing pace.

1. *Accountants*

Accountants played a key role in permitting the frauds at OPM to continue for almost a decade. In OPM's first five years Goodman searched for an accounting firm sufficiently flexible to certify financial statements showing profits and positive net worth and to overlook signs of lease fraud on OPM's books. Goodman initially turned to "big eight" firms—Peat Marwick and Touche Ross—in the hope OPM would benefit from their prestige. But neither Peat Marwick nor Touche Ross proved willing to accept accounting techniques proposed by Goodman that would have reduced OPM's reported losses and net worth deficit.

For the 1973 audit Goodman thought he had found the flexibility he desired in Rashba & Pokart, a small New York accounting firm. Rashba & Pokart quickly became dependent on OPM for much of its billings. In addition, the partner responsible for the OPM account, Marvin Weissman, was a first cousin of Mordecai Weissman. Marvin Weissman remained Goodman's closest accounting consultant and confidant through April 1980.

Despite its small size and the family connection, Rashba & Pokart did not fulfill Goodman's expectations. When Rashba & Pokart presented draft 1973 financials showing OPM's largest losses and negative net worth ever, Goodman became so enraged he fired the firm. But Rashba & Pokart did not bend under Goodman's pressure. . . .

. . . Rashba & Pokart was reluctant to devote increased resources to the OPM engagement and was unwilling to certify financials with fraudulent financings still on the books. After considering other firms, Goodman sensed he had found the flexibility for which he had long been searching in Fox & Company, . . . the nation's eleventh or twelfth largest accounting firm. Goodman believed that Fox had sufficient size and respectability to lend legitimacy to OPM's financial statements but that it would be sufficiently dependent on OPM, which became one of the largest clients of Fox's New York office, to show the flexibility Goodman desired.

This time Goodman was not to be disappointed. Like Rashba & Pokart, Fox initially presented draft 1976 financials showing the largest losses and negative net worth ever. Enraged, Goodman directed Stephen S. Kutz, the Fox audit partner responsible for the OPM engagement, to "get back to the grindstone and try to figure out a way to show a profit." Unlike Rashba & Pokart, under Goodman's constant prodding Kutz developed a series of questionable accounting techniques that accomplished a "swing to positive" in 1976 for the first time in OPM's history and continued the trend through 1978.

Chief among these techniques was the "Kutz Method" of equity income recognition, which permitted OPM to record the cash received from sales of equity participations as income in the year those sales occurred rather than over a period of years and ignored the contingency that exercise of early termination options could turn the booked profits into disastrous losses. Use of the Kutz Method allowed OPM to recognize prematurely over $13.6 million of "income from equity participants" in 1977 and over $20.5 million in 1978.

As a result of the Kutz Method and other "creative" accounting techniques developed under pressure from Goodman, the Fox certified financials for 1976, 1977, and 1978 were materially false and misleading. . . .

. . .

While Fox never discovered the Rockwell fraud, Goodman confessed to Marvin Weissman in the spring of 1980 that he was engaged in massive lease fraud. Rashba & Pokart washed its hands of the matter by severing its relationship with OPM and forcing Goodman to tell Singer Hutner [OPM's law firm] that he had engaged in major wrongdoing.

At the same time, John A. Clifton, the head of OPM's in-house Accounting Department, was piecing together a picture of the Rockwell fraud . . .

Like Rashba & Pokart, Clifton resigned, but only after detailing what he knew in a letter that he had hand-delivered on June 12, 1980, to Andrew B. Reinhard, the Singer Hutner partner Clifton viewed as responsible for the OPM representation. The next day Clifton discovered that Goodman had somehow retrieved his letter, apparently unopened, from Reinhard. On advice of [his own personal] counsel, Clifton determined not to take further action because Singer Hutner was in "constructive receipt" of the letter.

Even after it became reasonably clear that for some reason Singer Hutner had not stopped the fraud, Rashba & Pokart and Clifton never reported Goodman to government authorities and misled Fox, Lehman, and other third parties about the real reasons for their resignations. Although Rashba & Pokart and Clifton may have had no legal duty to "blow the whistle" on Goodman, basic moral precepts should have led them to make disclosure, especially since they were more than mere bystanders to Goodman's crimes.

3. *Lawyers*

Lawyers played a critical role in the massive Rockwell lease fraud. Without their witting or unwitting assistance, the fraud simply could not have occurred.

The law firm of Singer Hutner Levine & Seeman (and its predecessor and successor firms) served as OPM's outside general counsel from 1971 to September 1980 and did not fully sever its relationship with OPM until December 1980. Singer Hutner closed all but seven of the fifty-four financings of fraudulent Rockwell leases.

Singer Hutner acquired OPM as a client in 1971 through Andrew B. Reinhard, the older brother of a close boyhood friend of Goodman. Reinhard was then a Singer Hutner associate and later became a partner. In 1972 Weissman and Goodman elected Reinhard the third director of OPM. As OPM's business expanded, Singer Hutner followed along, more than doubling in size to twenty-seven lawyers in 1980. By 1975 Singer Hutner participated in virtually every facet of OPM's business. Goodman likened the close relationship between OPM and Singer Hutner to a "bondage of the bookends."

From 1976 through 1980 Singer Hutner received legal fees of almost $7.9 million—sixty to seventy percent of its revenues—from OPM. Singer Hutner also received almost $2 million in reimbursement of expenses. . . .

One of the most difficult questions encountered during the Trustee's investigation was whether Reinhard knowingly participated in any of the fraudulent activities at OPM. Although the United States Attorney's Office determined not to seek a grand jury indictment against him, the decision not to prosecute is not dispositive.

The principal witness against Reinhard is Goodman. Goodman testified that, having previously told Reinhard about the early frauds at OPM, he informed Reinhard in early 1979 of his intention to finance three phantom Rockwell leases and successfully enlisted Reinhard's assistance in the fraud. . . . According to Goodman, Reinhard resisted but eventually agreed to help. Goodman testified that Reinhard reluctantly assisted in several subsequent fraudulent financings.

Through his lawyers Reinhard denies he had any knowledge of fraud at OPM apart from information obtained by his firm in June and September 1980. On advice of counsel, Reinhard invoked his Fifth Amendment privilege and refused personally to respond to any questioning by the Trustee concerning the fraud. . . .

Apart from Reinhard's probable complicity in the fraud from the outset, Singer Hutner's conduct as OPM's counsel in closing fraudulent Rockwell financings cannot be justified. By early 1979 Singer Hutner had received indications that Goodman and Weissman were capable of serious illegality. Some lawyers were aware that Weissman and Goodman had engaged in lease fraud and commercial bribery, and the firm knew that Goodman had recently perpetrated a $5 million check kiting scheme. Singer Hutner also had knowledge of facts showing that OPM was suffering severe cash shortages that provided a motive for further fraud.

In the sixteen months between the first financing of phantom Rockwell leases in February 1979 and Goodman's first confession to Singer Hutner of serious wrongdoing in June 1980, numerous facts came to Singer Hutner's attention that should have raised suspicions about the bona fides of OPM–Rockwell leases. The closings of Rockwell transactions in 1979 and 1980 differed from other OPM closings in several significant respects. Among other things, Goodman and his accomplices directed Singer Hutner to send Rockwell's copies of financing documents to OPM after the closings and instructed the lawyers not to contact Rockwell without Goodman's prior permission. No equity participations were sold in the expensive equipment shown on numerous Rockwell leases. IBM mass storage units began to appear on purported leases to Rockwell in numbers far greater than Rockwell could possibly need. Insurance for Rockwell equipment came from OPM's insurer, despite Rockwell's contractual obligation to maintain the insurance. A number of inconsistencies and peculiarities appeared in title documents presented by the fraud team for Rockwell closings. Singer Hutner was also aware that, on certain leases, OPM made rental payments to financing institutions in the lessee's place. With all these red flags, Singer Hutner should have exercised extreme caution in closing OPM–Rockwell lease financings. Instead, until June 1980 the firm closed these transactions on a business as usual basis.

On June 12, 1980, Goodman met with Joseph L. Hutner, a Singer Hutner partner, and confessed that he had engaged in past "wrongful transactions" in an amount exceeding $5 million. During a break in the meeting, Goodman somehow retrieved the letter Clifton had sent to Reinhard describing the details of the Rockwell fraud. Goodman refused to return the letter or provide additional details of his acknowledged wrongdoing, citing his desire for assurances that Singer Hutner would keep the information secret under the attorney-client privilege.

Singer Hutner promptly retained Joseph M. McLaughlin, then dean of Fordham Law School, and Henry Putzel, III, formerly an associate professor of professional responsibility at Fordham, to advise the firm on its ethical responsibilities in dealing with Goodman's disclosure. Whether or not Singer Hutner's conduct based on their advice was "ethical" (a legal question the Trustee does not address), it was woefully inadequate to prevent further fraud. After June 1980

Singer Hutner closed fifteen additional fraudulent Rockwell transactions totaling $70 million.

Singer Hutner kept Goodman's misdeeds secret and continued closing OPM transactions on the basis of certificates from Goodman attesting to the legitimacy of the transactions. The Trustee believes Singer Hutner was wrong in relying on Goodman's representations that the fraud had stopped and ignoring substantial evidence that it had not. Just after Goodman's confession, Clifton's lawyer had informed Hutner and another Singer Hutner partner of Clifton's belief that OPM could not survive without continued wrongdoing. In addition, on two occasions in June and July Singer Hutner lawyers noticed peculiarities in title documents used in fraudulent Rockwell lease financings that should have led them to seek to confirm their authenticity with third parties.

For months Goodman resisted pressure to make full disclosure of the fraud to Singer Hutner by a series of gambits including a threat to jump out of a window in OPM's ninth story offices if pressed further. In September 1980 Goodman finally came clean, or so he claimed. At a meeting with the Singer Hutner partners, Goodman described the mechanics of the Rockwell fraud and quantified it at $30 million—only about $100 million short of the truth. Notwithstanding Goodman's continued insistence that the fraud had stopped by June 1980, and Goodman's hysterical threat to "bring down this firm," on September 23 Singer Hutner voted to resign as OPM's counsel.

With Putzel's approval, Singer Hutner agreed to characterize its resignation misleadingly as a "mutual determination of our firm and [OPM] to terminate our relationship as general counsel." Singer Hutner also agreed to continue rendering legal services over a two and one-half month transition period to avoid unnecessary injury to OPM.

In late September or early October Goodman dropped the bombshell that the fraud had in fact continued throughout the summer of 1980. Despite this shocking acknowledgement by Goodman that he had continued to use Singer Hutner as an instrument of fraud even after his initial confession of wrongdoing, Putzel advised Singer Hutner that it could not ethically warn successor counsel of the danger that Goodman would use them to help finance additional fraudulent transactions.

Singer Hutner, of course, relies on the advice it received from McLaughlin and Putzel to justify its conduct during the summer and fall of 1980. While the Trustee does not attempt to resolve the question whether that advice was consistent with the legal profession's code of ethics, it is clear that McLaughlin and Putzel could have advised other courses, consistent with Singer Hutner's ethical responsibilities, that would have stopped the fraud. Although McLaughlin and Putzel in good faith considered their advice appropriate in the circumstances, the Trustee believes it was in fact the worst possible advice from the point of view of OPM, the third parties with whom it dealt, Singer Hutner's successor counsel, and Singer Hutner itself. Accordingly, McLaughlin and Putzel must shoulder significant responsibility for their client's conduct.

But Singer Hutner cannot properly shift all blame for its actions after Goodman's first confession of wrongdoing to McLaughlin and Putzel. While Singer Hutner relied on McLaughlin and Putzel for advice on its ethical obligations, McLaughlin and Putzel relied on the firm for the central factual predicate for their advice—whether the fraud was continuing. On issues like the significance of irregularities in title documents and the weight to be accorded Clifton's prediction that OPM could not continue in business without further fraud, Singer Hutner was the expert.

Viewed as a whole, the Trustee finds Singer Hutner's conduct nothing short of shocking, given the warnings it received before June 1980 and the remarkable events of the summer and early fall. Although Singer Hutner cites its ethical obligation not to injure its client unnecessarily, the most questionable aspects of Singer Hutner's conduct raise issues beyond professional ethics. Even after learning that Goodman had engaged in major wrongdoing, Singer Hutner continued to close OPM debt financings without obtaining prior disclosure of the nature of the wrongdoing and without independently verifying transaction facts. No rule of professional ethics can or should exempt lawyers from the general legal proscriptions against willful blindness to their clients' crimes or reckless participation in them.[4]

4. *Investment Bankers*

From late 1975 until October 1980, OPM relied on two of Wall Street's oldest and most prestigious investment banking firms—Goldman Sachs (from 1975 to March 1978) and Lehman (from March 1978 to October 1980)—to arrange debt financing on its lease transactions. The presence of these firms as OPM's investment bankers carried a reassuring implication of sponsorship to virtually everyone who dealt with OPM.

. . .

Goldman Sachs and Lehman did not discover that Goodman, Weissman, and their accomplices were forging and altering lease documents because they did not contact lessees or vendors to verify basic transaction facts. But neither Goldman Sachs nor Lehman represented to institutions that it was verifying transaction facts, and Lehman's private placement memoranda expressly stated that the information they contained came from OPM and that Lehman did not vouch for its accuracy. Lehman made this disclaimer with good reason. Among other things, it did not know enough about computers to recognize as fraudulent OPM's purported leases to Rockwell of over twenty percent

---

4. After Singer Hutner's withdrawal, OPM's young in-house lawyers and the law firm of Kaye, Scholer, Fierman, Hays & Handler represented OPM in its lease transactions. Kept in the dark by Goodman and Singer Hutner about the real reasons for the departure of Singer Hutner, OPM's in-house staff unwittingly closed six fraudulent financings of Rockwell leases and Kaye Scholer unwittingly closed one.

of the world's supply of IBM mass storage units on transactions for which Lehman arranged financing.

A number of facts came to Lehman's attention during its work for OPM that raised questions about the integrity of Weissman and Goodman and OPM's viability. In March 1979 Lehman learned that OPM had repeatedly kited checks . . . . By May 1979 Lehman learned from its review of Cali's 1978 financial statements that over the next five years OPM faced a $76 million shortfall. . . . Between January and August 1980 Lehman gradually learned . . . that OPM's accounting systems were chaotic, that cash flow difficulties were increasing, that an audit for 1979 was unlikely, and that Goodman and Weissman had withdrawn over $1.5 million from OPM for personal purposes at a time when OPM was probably insolvent. But Lehman continued to serve OPM until October 1980 and did not disclose any of these problems to the institutions from which it solicited permanent financing for OPM.

. . .

5. *Tax Shelter Promoters*

OPM relied principally on two sophisticated New York tax lawyers—Kent M. Klineman and Joel Mallin—to whom it paid over $18 million in commissions to solicit investors in OPM's equity participation transactions.

Goodman regularly supplied Klineman with bogus OPM financial statements, which Klineman then transmitted to equity investors. Goodman also claims he twice presented Klineman's lawyers with phony title documentation for equipment covered by transactions. In addition, Goodman claims Klineman arranged for an equipment appraiser, whom Goodman called "Klineman's boy," to provide inflated "valuations" that Klineman derived by working backward from the amount of capital available from investors. Although Klineman and the appraiser deny knowledge of these improprieties, it is clear Klineman undertook virtually no investigation of the accuracy of OPM's financial statements despite his acknowledged "due diligence" obligation. And because an inflated appraisal would provide more cash to OPM, greater tax benefits to investors, and higher fees for Klineman, no party to the transactions had much immediate interest in checking into possibly false valuations.

. . .

6. *Lessees*

The lease frauds at OPM were possible in part because lessees, who were mainly concerned with the amount of their monthly rentals and their early termination rights, viewed financings as necessary annoyances. Lessees generally did not maintain procedures to protect against fraud and did not attend closings of financings, where they could have seen that financing institutions were receiving very different documents from those the lessees had executed. In addition, some employees of lessees were corrupt, willfully blind, or reckless in their disregard of OPM's misconduct.

. . .

7. *Financing Institutions*

The "other people" whose money kept OPM in business included some of the nation's largest financial institutions—commercial banks, savings institutions, insurance companies, investment trusts, pension funds, and others. There is no evidence that employees at any defrauded institution acted in complicity with Weissman and Goodman. The success of the fraud instead depended on the failure of institutions or their counsel to verify basic transaction facts with vendors or lessees and the institutions' willingness to accept lease payments from OPM rather than from lessees directly.

. . .

During the period of the Rockwell fraud, an integral part of OPM's leasing business was "bridge financing." In a bridge financing transaction, a financing institution would advance funds required for OPM to purchase and install equipment and would be repaid with the proceeds of a subsequent "permanent financing." Beginning in August 1978, OPM's virtually exclusive source of bridge financing was the First National Bank of Saint Paul, which Lehman had introduced to OPM. St. Paul never sought to verify transaction facts with lessees or vendors and did not even send a representative to attend closings. St. Paul instead relied on Lehman, with whom it had a long term prior relationship, as its "eyes and ears" in New York. Although Lehman informed St. Paul of OPM's check kiting and financial problems, St. Paul continued doing business with OPM until Lehman's resignation in October 1980 and ultimately financed almost $60 million in fraudulent OPM–Rockwell lease transactions, over $10 million of which were outstanding at the time of OPM's bankruptcy.

Eighteen other institutions, . . . extended over $125 million in permanent financing on fraudulent OPM–Rockwell transactions. With one exception, the institutions undertook no efforts to verify transaction facts with lessees or equipment vendors, even though a single telephone call before each closing probably would have been sufficient to prevent or uncover the fraud. Without specific basis, the institutions believed that Lehman's arrangement of the transactions assured their bona fides. The institutions also drew comfort from their representation by some of the nation's most respected law firms as closing counsel. But while the lawyers for financing institutions generally attended closings, they focused exclusively on assuring that the closing documentation gave their clients what they bargained for and did not seek to verify the underlying transaction facts. As one lawyer who closed numerous OPM lease financings explained: "If there were any concern about protecting against fraud, we wouldn't be at the closing in the first place."

Questions and Comments

Notice that the witness against the lawyer Reinhard was the client, Goodman. While Singer Hunter was not criminally prosecuted, it reportedly paid out millions of dollars to the fraud victims in settlement of the civil claims against it for having aided the fraud. All the institutions in the OPM tale had lawyers. What did those lawyers do wrong?

GEOFFREY C. HAZARD, Jr., "RECTIFICATION OF CLIENT FRAUD: DEATH AND REVIVAL OF A PROFESSIONAL NORM"

33 Emory Law Journal 271 (1984).*

. . .

II. The Client Fraud Problem

To begin with, the client fraud problem should be clearly stated, so that there is common ground as to the matter to be addressed. The problem arises when a lawyer undertakes representation in a transaction that he assumes is nonfraudulent but then, having done substantial professional work to carry out the transaction, discovers that the transaction involves fraud against the other party to the transaction or against some other party. What is the lawyer required or permitted to do at that point?

. . .

III. What the Problem is Not

My experience in discussions of the client fraud problems resigns me to realization of how easily the problem becomes confused, sometimes perhaps deliberately. The tangents go in several directions. They will be briefly explored in the interest of focusing attention on the specific problem under consideration.

A. *The Problem is Not One of Initial Lawyer Complicity*

The statement of the client fraud problem often evokes from lawyers a protest that the lawyer did not know about the client's fraud. That is true only if the transaction is considered at the initial stage, at which the lawyer was by hypothesis ignorant of the fraudulent element. After that, he did know.

The distinction becomes clear if we suppose that the lawyer *did* know about the fraudulent element at the outset of the transaction, before having taken any steps that affect another party to the proposed transaction. If the lawyer knows of the fraudulent element at this stage, the law is clear that he may not proceed to implement the transaction. By the same token, the legal consequences to the lawyer if he does implement the transaction are also clear. Such acts

* Copyright © 1984 by the Emory Law Journal.

as preparing documents or engaging in their transmission constitute substantial assistance to a fraudulent scheme. The legal consequences of giving such assistance are: first, that the lawyer is a joint tortfeasor in the tort of fraud; [11] second, if the conduct is criminally proscribed as well as being a tort (as generally will be the case, given the operation of the mail fraud laws), that the lawyer is guilty as an accessory to the crime of fraud; [12] and, third, that the lawyer is guilty of professional misconduct that can be the basis of censure, suspension, or disbarment.[13]

B. *The Problem Is Not One of A Lawyer's Being Innocently Exploited by a Fraud–Doing Client*

The statement of the client fraud problem often evokes another response, this time the protest that a lawyer who was unaware of fraud in a transaction is not guilty of professional misconduct, or of a civil or criminal wrong. That proposition is quite true. A lawyer is not legally guilty of assisting a fraudulent project unless he knows that the project is fraudulent. But that proposition also does not address the problem at hand.

In the first place, the lawyer's ignorance of the client's fraudulent purpose precludes his being charged with complicity only so long as the ignorance continues. When the lawyer's ignorance ceases—that is, when he acquires knowledge of the fraud—he then has the mental state of an accessory. Having that mental state is not alone sufficient to constitute being an accessory, for being an accessory requires the additional element of giving assistance to the project. But once the requisite mental state has been acquired, an act in furtherance of the project entails the combination of assistance and guilty knowledge, and that combination constitutes the offense of assisting fraud.[16] Thus, the fact that the lawyer may have innocently begun the representation does not obviate the fact that the representation ceases to be innocent once the lawyer becomes aware of the fraudulent basis of the transaction.

It is also true that if, upon discovering the fraud, the lawyer wholly terminates further assistance to the project, he is not guilty of being an accessory. In principle, this is the same situation as if the lawyer had never learned of the fraud at all—he has simply been the ignorant instrument of the client's fraudulent purpose. But the lawyer must have ceased his assistance in the transaction immediately upon learning of its fraudulent character. If, for example, the lawyer became

---

11. See, e.g., Roberts v. Ball, Hunt, Hart, Brown & Baerwitz, 57 Cal.App.3d 104, 128 Cal.Rptr. 901 (1976); see Hazard, How Far May a Lawyer Go in Assisting a Client in Legally Wrongful Conduct?, 35 U. Miami L.Rev. 669 (1981).

12. E.g., United States v. Benjamin, 328 F.2d 854 (2d Cir.1964); see also Hazard, supra note 11; cf. Beckler & Epner, Principal White Collar Crimes, Business Crimes: A Guide for Corporate and Defense Counsel (1982) (J. Glekel ed.).

13. E.g., In re Blatt, 65 N.J. 539, 324 A.2d 15 (1974). [See Rule 1.2(d) and DR7–102(A) (7)].

16. Cf., e.g., United States v. Alvarez, 625 F.2d 1196 (5th Cir.1980).

aware of the fraud before the closing of the transaction, the participation in the closing would surely constitute "assisting" accomplishment of the client's fraudulent purpose.[17]

We will presently come back to the question of terminating assistance. The point here is simply that the lawyer will be legally innocent only if it is found that his awareness of the fraud did not precede any act on his part that substantially furthered the transaction. . . . However, the problem of "midpoint discovery" raises the question of what it means for a lawyer to discover or "know" what his client is up to. This question requires exploration because it runs through all variations of the client fraud problem.

C. The Problem Is Not that the Lawyer Cannot "Know" of a Client's Fraud

There are several intricacies in the question of a lawyer's knowledge of a client's fraud. The first intricacy is that of determining when a lawyer has come to "know" about the fraud being committed by his client. The criteria for determining whether a lawyer "knows" of a client's fraudulent purposes are more exacting than many lawyers seem to suppose.

Some lawyers, for example, at least profess that they cannot "know" anything—that facts exist only when a jury has found them in a verdict. This incapacity to "know" is a form of cognitive dissonance useful and legitimate for trial advocates, particularly those who represent criminal defendants. A lawyer's representation of a criminal defendant is easier if the lawyer does not "know" the accused is guilty.[18] A criminal defense lawyer therefore wants to believe that he does not "know" anything about his client, at least until a jury "knows" it for him, as it were. The same cognitive incapacity can help sustain the civil advocate. . . .

The special encapsulation of knowledge that is permitted in the advocate's mind, however, is not ordinarily sanctioned where the lawyer's representation of the client entails a function *other* than that of trial advocate. This point can be demonstrated by considering the situation of a lawyer who is consulted by a client concerning a proposed transaction that the lawyer realizes will be fraudulent if carried out.

Suppose, first, that the lawyer's service to the client consists solely of listening to the proposal, then advising the client that the project would be fraudulent if carried out, and thereupon refusing to provide any further service with regard to the matter. It is clear that this activity does not make the lawyer an accessory if the client thereafter carries out the project. Under general principles of accessorial liabili-

---

17. E.g., SEC v. National Student Mktg. Corp., 457 F.Supp. 682 (D.D.C.1978).

18. Cf. Lord Brougham's famous dictum: "An advocate, in the discharge of his duty, knows but one person in all the world, and that is his client." 2 Trial of Queen Caroline 8 (1821). Compare the clear-eyed analysis in Freedman, Professional Responsibility of the Criminal Defense Lawyer: The Three Hardest Questions, 64 Mich.L.Rev. 1469, 1472 (1966).

ty, mere knowledge of another's fraudulent purposes does not make the auditor an accomplice. However, the lawyer's innocence of complicity flows not from his lack of "knowledge" of the client's purpose, but from his failure to lend aid to that purpose.

 . . . However, if the office lawyer goes beyond listening and advising that fraud is fraud, his state of knowledge is not given special legal protection. The rule that governs beyond the point of honest advice is that a lawyer may not "counsel or assist" the client in a crime or fraud.[23] "Counsel," according to the definition applicable in this context, means "instruction or recommendation" and "interchange of opinion especially on possible procedure." [24] . . . The offense of "counselling" a crime or fraud, like the offense of "assisting," involves a combination of elements. One of the elements is the act of "encouraging" the client in the fraudulent project, that is, saying things and giving signs that tend to resolve the client's ambivalence or to allay his anxiety concerning a wrongful course of action. The second element is the lawyer's knowledge that the clients' projected course is a "crime or fraud." The rule against "counselling" a client in a crime or fraud thus incorporates the proposition that a lawyer can "know" what his client is up to. The office lawyer, unlike the advocate, has no legal immunity in giving assistance on the basis that he does not "know" what he knows.

Indeed, when it comes to determining what an office lawyer can be found to "know" about his client's purposes, the cases go further. The decisions say that a lawyer cannot "close his eyes" to facts that are readily apparent.[26] The lawyer will be taken as having seen such facts. They also say that a lawyer must apprehend the significance, considered as a whole, of facts that may be innocuous when considered in isolation.[27] The cases also say that a lawyer must gauge the significance of a fact, or set of facts, with the comprehension of one familiar with the type of transaction involved.[28] Thus, far from having the advocate's license to pretend ignorance of the truth about his client, the legal counsellor, for the purposes of the crime/fraud rule, may be taken as knowing what an alert lawyer would know upon looking with a professional eye at the totality of circumstances there to be seen.

D. *The Problem Is Not That an Innocent Lawyer Can "Take Care of Himself"*

Another response to the client fraud problem is one that might be called "white-collar macho." It is expressed in the retort that a lawyer who cannot take care of himself regarding client fraud is "not worth his

23. Model Rules of Professional Conduct 1.2(d) (1983); Model Code of Professional Responsibility DR–7–102(A)(7) (1981); cf. Model Penal Code § 2.04 (proposed official draft 1962).

24. Webster's Third New International Dictionary 518 (1971).

26. E.g., In re Blatt, 65 N.J. 539, 324 A.2d 15 (1974).

27. E.g., United States v. Benjamin, 328 F.2d 854 (2d Cir.1964).

28. E.g., SEC v. National Student Mktg. Corp., 457 F.Supp. 682 (D.D.C.1978).

salt." Implicit in this retort is the proposition that the concern over the crime/fraud rule is academic nattering beneath the notice of tough-minded professionals. Hence, the argument implicitly continues, we should have a blanket confidentiality rule, and stop worrying about it.[29]

The fact is, however, that some clients are at least as tough and clever as their lawyers. As a result, an innocent lawyer—however competent and however watchful—is inevitably at risk in any transaction where the client could commit fraud.

That the innocent lawyer is at risk becomes obvious if we take account of certain additional facts in the transactions we are talking about. These facts are: (1) the client is engaged in fraud and does not want the lawyer to know about it; (2) the client generally has as good or better access to the material facts as the lawyer; (3) the client often can take initiatives to exploit these facts that the lawyer will have difficulty in discovering; (4) the client may be able to destroy evidence that would exonerate the lawyer; (5) the question of the lawyer's complicity will be determined by circumstantial evidence and not solely on the lawyer's protestation that he is innocent; (6) by the time the lawyer's complicity is an issue, the client may be out of the picture, for example in jail or in the Bahamas; (7) if the client is still in the picture, he may contend that he was the innocent in the transaction; (8) the lawyer's complicity under civil or criminal law, as distinct from the law of professional discipline, may be determined by lay jurors, who may not have much sympathy for lawyers.

Moreover, the client may know a good deal of law, some of it possibly acquired in earlier fraud litigation. The client's knowledge of law may extend to the law of client-lawyer confidentiality. If the client had that legal knowledge, and if the rule of confidentiality fully protected proposed fraud, then the client, having gotten all the service he could out of the lawyer, could lawfully demand that the lawyer keep his mouth shut, at least until the lawyer is interrogated by a grand jury or named as a defendant in a disciplinary or civil fraud proceeding.

I do not see how in such circumstances a lawyer, no matter how tough and how clever, could avoid being the subject of a criminal investigation or a defendant in a civil fraud suit. The lawyer of course might succeed in establishing his innocence. . . . Surviving that experience is a way of "taking care" of one's self, but it is not very tender care.

III. SOME COROLLARIES

It may further clarify the central question if we also resolve some preliminary issues that do not seem seriously in dispute.

---

29. The lawyers holding this view generally are advocates, who don't handle transactions in which they can be implicated in client fraud, rather than securities lawyers, who do handle such transactions.

A. The Lawyer Must Have a Reasonable Basis for Supposing that Fraud Is Involved

The information suggesting that a client's project is fraudulent should be substantial before it can be given significance so far as the lawyer's course of action is concerned. A lawyer should not intercept a client on mere suspicion or rumor. There seems no great need to worry that lawyers will be trigger-happy about apparent client fraud, although there have been cases in which such predisposition might have been manifested.[30] A lawyer has very strong incentives not to interpret a client's project as fraudulent or to intercept the project if he does make that interpretation. If he acts on a mistaken premise that fraud is involved, the certain results will be acrimony and possible litigation with the client, damage to the lawyer's reputation for being untrustworthy with client confidences, risk of disciplinary proceedings for having unjustifiably betrayed a client confidence, and peer disapproval. This array of deterrents is so formidable that rule-makers should be careful not to add legal deterrents that would reduce the lawyer's ambit of action to the vanishing point. It is therefore enough to say that the lawyer should have a reasonable basis for concluding that fraud is involved before acting. Obviously, a more stringent requirement, such as that there should be a provable case against the client, would virtually preclude the possibility of the lawyer's action except in most egregious situations.

B. As Little Damage as Possible Should Be Done to the Client

If the lawyer decides to act, he should proceed in such a way as to damage the client as little as reasonably possible. This is a general principle regarding action that may harm others. The principle is especially applicable to action affecting a person to whom the actor has some sort of protective responsibility, as a lawyer has to a client.

In the client fraud situation, this principle has several implications. The lawyer should if possible try to prevent the fraud, rather than rectifying it after the scheme is under way. Prevention if successful will leave the fraud unconsummated, and probably undiscovered and hence unpunished; the intended fraud will simply be an ugly secret between client and lawyer. Interception after the fraud is under way, on the other hand, is more likely not only to result in the client's suffering sanctions but also in the lawyer's having to give evidence in the imposition of such sanctions.

It must be noted, however, that there is unavoidable tension between the proposition that the lawyer should act early, to prevent the fraud, and the requirement that he should act only on the basis of solid information. The longer the wait, the more solid the information, but also the greater the likelihood of the client's deeper inculpation.

---

30. Cf. Meyerhofer v. Empire Fire & Marine Ins. Co., 497 F.2d 1190 (2d Cir.), cert. denied, 419 U.S. 998 (1974).

A corollary of the principle of doing the least possible damage to the client is that, in addressing the client upon discovering the fraud, the lawyer should warn the client about the lawyer's responsibilities if the fraudulent project materializes. Giving such a warning to a client is of course a most difficult, delicate task. But unless the client is given such a warning, the client may persist when otherwise he might have been deflected in his purpose. The client should also be made to realize that if the project goes forward, the lawyer will not only have to withdraw but also may wind up being an adverse witness.

The confrontation in giving such a warning is so odious that many lawyers evidently wish there were some escape from having to do so. The only escape within the boundaries of the lawyer's own obligations to the law, however, is by the route of silent withdrawal. In some situations, that may be sufficient warning to deflect the client from his purpose, but in others it may not. If it is not, and the project goes forward, the lawyer may find himself being diversely involved, possibly as a witness, in a client fraud that he and the client both know might have been prevented by a warning from the lawyer.

The principle of least damage to the client obviously cannot have much practical scope in situations where the project is so far advanced that third parties have acted in reliance. Anything the lawyer does at that stage is almost certainly bound to hurt the client. This is the excruciating difficulty of the "midpoint discovery" situation, where the fraud has gone so far forward that its injurious consequences have begun to unfold. But again the lawyer's only alternative to withdrawing after a warning, aside from now becoming an accomplice in the fraud, would be to withdraw silently.

As a practical matter, it may be doubted how "silent" a withdrawal can be at this stage. What are the other parties to make of the fact that the lawyer fails to show up for the closing? It is also doubtful that such a withdrawal will adequately protect the lawyer against being drawn into litigation over the fraud. In any case, the lawyer has no lawful course of action that guarantees no serious consequences to the client. This fact simply has to be accepted.

C. *The Lawyer Must Be Allowed a "Self Defense" Exception to the Confidentiality Rule*

Another proposition undisputed in the bar's debate over the client fraud problem is that the lawyer should be allowed to defend himself against charges of complicity in the client's fraud. Needless to say, the bar itself has accepted the "self defense" provision without much debate. That is, although vehemently opposed to "whistle blowing" on clients as a general proposition, lawyers accept the necessity for doing so as a matter of self defense. This attitude is readily intelligible as a matter of crude self interest on the part of lawyers. This does not mean, however, that such a provision is inappropriate. The point of difficulty is not that a self defense provision illegitimately protects lawyers, but that it protects *only* lawyers.

Unless there is a self defense exception, the result of the confidentiality rule would be that a lawyer could be held liable for assisting client fraud on the basis of evidence that he would be legally prohibited from rebutting. Neither the law of confidentiality nor the attorney-client privilege has ever been construed to have that effect. The "self defense" proviso is nevertheless troubling not because as such it protects lawyers, but because, if it stands alone, in its usual operation it gives lawyers preferred treatment among victims of the client's fraud.

The preferred treatment accorded lawyers results from the fact that in its ordinary application, the self defense proviso is operative only when a third party is actually victimized. The self defense exception by its terms applies only when the lawyer is accused of complicity. But such an accusation requires an accuser, which presupposes a victim. The lawyer's being unjustly accused is simply a secondary consequence of the original fraud. Thus, if the "self defense" provision stands alone, in the ordinary course of events it gives protection to innocent victims who are lawyers but not to other victims.

On general legal principles such a preference for lawyers, as compared with third party victims, seems very difficult to justify, to put it mildly. As compared with other victims, the lawyer is likely to be in a superior position to prevent the wrong. As compared with other victims, he probably runs a lesser risk of suffering actual injury if the fraud is consummated. Moreover, the client-lawyer relationship between the lawyer and the fraud-doer justifies no special protection for the *lawyer*. Both the lawyer and the third party are simply "arms length" contractors with the client. Indeed, situations can be imagined where the relationship between the fraud-doer and the third party gives rise to a higher measure of legal protection to the third party than to the lawyer.[33] Thus, aside from purely invidious self protection in the legal profession's composing its own rules of the game, there seems to be no explanation for allowing lawyers to breach client confidences to protect themselves but not to protect others.

At least three aspects of the "self defense" exception to the confidentiality rule merit attention, however, in considering the interests of third-party victims. The first is that the self defense exception comes into play, except under extraordinary circumstances, only after the client-lawyer relationship has terminated. Conceivably, of course, a dispute over a lawyer's complicity in client fraud could proceed while the client-lawyer relationship endured. But such a situation is hardly a practical possibility; the parties will surely have dissolved their "relationship of trust and confidence." Thus, the "self defense" excep-

---

33. Specifically, when the client is a fiduciary in relation to the third party.

tion to the confidentiality rule, for practical purposes, allows disclosure of confidences only as against a *former* client. There is an intelligible distinction between disclosure as regards a present client and disclosure as regards a former client. Assuming such a distinction is intelligible, the "self defense" exception is consistent with that distinction.

A second aspect of the "self defense" exception is that it is likely to come into play only where the lawyer's services in some way facilitated the fraud on the third party. If the lawyer's services were unrelated to the fraud, and his learning of the fraud was only incidental to the representation, the lawyer probably would not face a charge of complicity, which is the trigger for the self defense exception.

The distinction has been illuminated by Professor Bernard Wolfman, who gave me an example that could easily arise in the practice of a tax lawyer or other specialist.[34] Suppose that a tax lawyer is retained by the client to resist a deficiency claim asserted by the Internal Revenue Service. The tax lawyer becomes satisfied that the deductions, or whatever, are nonfraudulent but also discovers in the course of working on the case that the client's earnings, correctly reported, had been derived from fraud practiced on a third party—for example, embezzlement from his employer. Suppose, further, that the embezzlement evidently was continuing.

In such a situation the lawyer knows of past client fraud that the lawyer could help rectify, and also of intended fraud that the lawyer could prevent. On one hand, there is a moral basis for saying that the lawyer should be permitted to take action to either effect, and indeed a basis for saying that morally he is required to take such action. But, on the other hand, there is also a moral basis for saying that he should remain silent, that protecting the confidentiality of confidential advisers is a value more weighty than that of protecting innocent victims, at least where the offense does not involve physical injury of person. The latter moral proposition provides a basis for a legal distinction that would permit disclosure when the lawyer is the instrument of fraud, but could not permit disclosure when the lawyer discovers the fraud as an incident to representation in another subject matter.

The third aspect of the self defense exception concerns the distinction in protective action between preventing a fraud before it occurs and rectifying a fraud after it has occurred. The self defense exception operates only when the fraud has occurred, or at least is well on its way to occurring, and thus applies only to rectification.

Several moral differences between prevention and rectification could be considered significant, but they more or less offset one another. The lawyer is likely to have a unique opportunity of prevention, compared with other possible intervenors, by reason of access to the facts while the transaction is in the making. Prevention involves the

34. See also B. Wolfman & J. Holden, Ethical Problems in Federal Tax Practice (1981).

lawyer's moral initiative, whereas after the fact rectification may simply be a byproduct of the lawyer's saving himself. Preventive action by definition shapes the future, making it better, whereas rectification deals with the past and mitigates but does not undo the course of events. A consummated fraud has irreparable aspects—the pollution of society's moral climate, the destruction of a trust relationship. Prevention therefore is an opportunity for achieving a greater good than is rectification.

On the other hand, preventive action by definition involves prediction of events, and hence uncertainty as to whether the fraud will actually be consummated, whereas rectification is predicated on brute historical fact. Preventive action therefore involves the risk of betraying a client who, even absent the lawyer's intervention, would recede from the fraudulent purpose. Rectification is an opportunity for doing lesser good but at much less risk of unnecessary wrong.

All of this goes to the point that, while the "self defense" exception may be invidious standing alone, it has both independent justification and dimensions that are relevant in considering whether, when, or how far a lawyer might be allowed to protect a third party.

D. *The Problem Restated*

With the false and collateral issues put aside, the problem of client fraud can be restated in the following way: What should a lawyer be permitted or required to do when he learns that the client's project is fraudulent at a point when it is simply too late for innocuous withdrawal?

One solution available *a priori,* of course, is that the lawyer could help the client complete the project, and indeed help conceal the fraud. James Gould Couzzens reminds us in *By Love Possessed* that this option is not unthinkable, and indeed that it is morally intelligible.[35] Assisting the fraud or covering it up, however, is foreclosed as a matter of law as distinct from morals. A "lawyer" by definition exists and functions in a legal system. A legal system necessarily claims that its norms in general are supreme normative commands as against other normative imperatives such as morals or personal conscience. The law cannot license some of its subjects, least of all "lawyers," to assist in the commission or concealment of transactions that it defines as serious wrongs, such as fraud. To do so would license lawyers to be instruments for subverting the structure of law itself.

Assuming that possibility is foreclosed, the legal lines have to be drawn somewhere around two nodal points. One is protection of the lawyer, the other protection of third party victims or prospective victims. We have already indicated that a self defense exception to the confidentiality rule is justified, at least if it does not give preferential

---

35. J. Cozzens, By Love Possessed (1957).

treatment to lawyers. The focus thus is on protection of third party victims.

The problematic variables, in addition to whether there ought to be any exception for protection of third parties, are: (1) Whether the lawyer may act only when he has been an instrument of the fraud; (2) Whether the authority should cover prevention or rectification, or both; (3) Whether there must be a warning to the client where possible; and (4) Whether the authority to take action should be discretionary or mandatory.

· · · ·

The Canons of Professional Ethics and the Model Code of Professional Responsibility on Client Fraud

Canon 37, which stated the duty to keep confidences and included a self-defense exception, also provided: "The announced intention of a client to commit a crime is not included within the confidences which [the lawyer] is bound to respect." . . .

Canon 41 directly dealt with the lawyer's obligations upon discovery of a fraud perpetrated by the client. Canon 41 provided:

When a lawyer discovers that some fraud or deception has been practiced, which has unjustly imposed upon the court or a party, he should endeavor to rectify it; at first by advising his client, and if his client refuses to forego the advantage thus unjustly gained, he should promptly inform the injured person or his counsel, so that they may take appropriate steps.

Canon 41 imposed a mandatory duty to disclose both past and ongoing fraud, whether or not the lawyer's services had been used to perpetrate the fraud. For example, disclosure would be required of a lawyer drawing a will who discovers that the client has fraudulently been collecting disability compensation while working full-time.

The apparent clarity of the Canons was confounded by the ethics opinions that interpreted them. ABA Formal Opinion 268 (1945) stated that a lawyer, who learns that his client intends to commit perjury and consequently withdraws has no discretion to reveal the intended perjury to successor counsel employed to present it. Whither Canon 37? ABA Formal Opinion 287 (1953) stated that a lawyer who discovered his client had committed perjury in a civil case could not disclose it because that would violate the duty to keep confidences. Whither Canon 41?

There was hence already some considerable confusion about the lawyer's duty upon discovery of client fraud when the Model Code was adopted in 1969. As initially written and as adopted in the vast majority of states, the Code appeared to reaffirm the explicit provisions of the Canons and overturn the contrary interpretations of the ethics opinions. DR 4–101(C)(3) provided: "A lawyer may reveal . . . [t]he intention of his client to commit a crime and the information necessary to prevent the crime."

Like Canon 37, DR 4–101(C)(3) applied to all future crimes and was discretionary.

Again like the Canons, the Code dealt with the discovery of past fraud in a separate provision. DR 7–102(B)(1) as originally adopted provided:

> A lawyer who receives information clearly establishing that [h]is client has, in the course of the representation, perpetrated a fraud upon a person or tribunal shall promptly call upon his client to rectify the same, and if his client refuses or is unable to do so, he shall reveal the fraud to the affected person or tribunal.

This provision is ambiguous as to whether the lawyer's services must have been employed in the fraud. The better interpretation is that it does entail such a requirement, since the phrase "in the course of the representation" modifies "perpetrated a fraud" rather than "receives information."

DR 7–102(B)(1) as originally promulgated did not expressly indicate whether the duty to disclose fraud was an exception to the confidentiality rule. It must have been an exception, however. That is, it is difficult to see how a lawyer could "reveal fraud to the affected person," as required by DR 7–102(B)(1), while at the same time obeying the injunction of DR 4–101(B) that "a lawyer shall not reveal a confidence or secret of his client," where "secret" is defined by in DR 4–101(A) as "information gained in the professional relationship . . . the disclosure of which would be embarrassing or would be likely to be detrimental to the client." Also a footnote to DR 7–102(B)(1) refers the lawyer to DR 4–101(C)(2) allowing disclosure "when permitted under Disciplinary Rules . . ."

In most Code states today, DR 7–102(B)(1) stands in the form stated above.

The ambiguity in the bar's attitude toward the lawyer's obligations upon discovery of client fraud is evidenced by the 1974 amendment to DR 7–102(B)(1) and the ethics opinion that interpreted it, ABA Opinion 341. The 1974 ABA amendment to the Model Code altered DR 7–102(B)(1) to read as follows, the amendment being in emphasis:

> A lawyer who receives information clearly establishing that:

> (1) His client has, in the course of the representation, perpetrated a fraud upon a person or tribunal shall promptly call upon his client to rectify the same, and if his client refuses or is unable to do so, he shall reveal the fraud to the affected person or tribunal, *except when the information is protected as a privileged communication.*

The amendment was probably intended to cancel the duty to reveal fraud when doing so would require revealing information that would be prejudicial to the client. In other words, the term "privileged communications" probably meant "confidence or secret" and not just information protected by the attorney-client privilege ("confidences" under the Code). But this would be to cancel the duty in DR 7–102(B)(1) in virtually all circumstances in which the duty could arise: Can anyone imagine a situation in which the lawyer could reveal a client's fraud, the client having refused to do so, without prejudicial effect on the client? On this interpretation, the amendment operatively repeals the duty to disclose fraud, while nominally preserving it, which is surely disingenuous.

The ABA Committee on Ethics and Professional Responsibility in 1975 issued Formal Opinion 341, which officially interpreted the amendment as referring to both "confidences" and "secrets." Opinion 341 states:

> [s]uch an interpretation does not wipe out DR 7–102(B)(1), because DR 7–102(B)(1) applies to information received from any source, and it is not limited to information gained in the professional relationship as is DR 4–101. Under the suggested interpretation, the duty imposed by DR 7–102(B) would remain in force if the information clearly establishing a fraud on a person or tribunal and committed by a client in the course of representation were obtained by the lawyer from a third party (but not in connection with [the lawyer's] professional relationship with the client), because it would not be a confidence or secret of a client entitled to confidentiality.

In other words, the lawyer has a duty to disclose client fraud when fortuitously informed by a person, who is unaware that the lawyer is representing the client implicated, that the client committed fraud in the course of the representation.

Opinion 341 also requires a tortured reading of the 1974 amendment. Specifically, it requires that the term "privileged communication" be read to refer *not* to the rule of evidentiary privilege, which applies only when the lawyer is under *compulsion to testify,* but to the rule of confidentiality, which applies to autonomous disclosures on the part of the lawyer.

The 1974 amendment to DR 7–102(B)(1) was accepted only in fourteen states. With or without the amendment, however, the Code position on client fraud is almost totally incoherent on the subject of client fraud.

The Model Rules of Professional Conduct on Client Fraud

Hazard, "Rectification of Client Fraud . . ." 33 Emory Law Journal 271 (1984) (continued)

B. *The Rejected Kutak Proposal*

It was the Code's incomprehensibility that induced the Kutak Commission to undertake a reformulation. The Kutak Commission proposal concerning client fraud, proposed Rule 1.6(b), was as follows:

A lawyer may reveal [confidential] information to the extent the lawyer reasonably believes necessary:

(1) to prevent the client from committing a criminal or fraudulent act that the lawyer reasonably believes is likely to result in . . . substantial injury to the financial interests or property of another; [or] (2) to rectify the consequences of a client's criminal or fraudulent act in the furtherance of which the lawyer's services had been used. . . .[43]

This provision covered prevention of a fraud, whether or not the lawyer's services had been involved, and rectification of a fraud where the lawyer's services had been used, both courses of action being discretionary and neither requiring a warning to the client. . . .

These were the proposals that evoked the outcry that the Kutak Commission proposed "whistle blowing" and "making the lawyer into a policeman."

The principal criticism concerned . . . the very idea of permitting disclosure of client fraud—whether for prevention or rectification, whether with warning or not, whether discretionary or mandatory. The argument was that permitting disclosure would constitute a "radical" change from the Code of Professional Responsibility. As we have seen, however, the Code gives the lawyer broad discretion to reveal client confidences and secrets to prevent any client behavior, including fraud, that would be a crime. And, as the Code stood in well over half the states, it *required* a lawyer to take action regarding client fraud, whether or not a crime. These legal facts were of little moment to the critics. They persuaded the bar that the Kutak proposal would have opened wide new exceptions to confidentiality, whereas in fact the Kutak proposal would have narrowed these exceptions.

This factual aspect of the argument against the Kutak proposal is now largely of historical and sociological interest. Suffice it to say that the Kutak proposal was essentially consistent with the law as it stood, soberly considered. The more significant aspect of the argument against the Kutak proposal was the flat proposition that disclosure of client confidences to protect third-party victims should not be permitted

---

43. Model Rules of Professional Conduct Rule 1.6(b) (Proposed Final Draft 1981).

at all. This thesis is important because it is the key to understanding Model Rule 1.6 as adopted by the ABA.

C. *ABA Model Rule 1.6*

In adopting the Model Rules of Professional Responsibility, the ABA House of Delegates eliminated the Kutak Commission's proposals as to both preventing and rectifying client fraud. However, it enlarged the "self defense" exception in modest but significant ways. As adopted by the ABA, Rule 1.6 . . .

. . . makes no provision at all for client fraud. It is a comprehensive and unqualified prohibition of disclosure, subject only to the homicide/bodily injury exception, the "self defense" exception, and the uncontroversial exception regarding disclosures "impliedly authorized" to carry out the representation. It leaves unanswered the question: What does a lawyer do to protect himself in a situation where he has unwittingly been made the instrument of client fraud, but has not yet been charged with complicity (which would activate the "self defense" exception)? And what can he do to protect a third-party victim in such circumstances?

Members and friends of the Kutak Commission put these questions to the proponents of the amendment. The first order answer, given in the debates in the ABA House of Delegates, was that the lawyer should withdraw from the representation. This looks like a nice solution. There are client fraud situations in which the lawyer's withdrawal from the representation will adequately protect him and the third-party victim. Thus, withdrawal itself would signal the lawyer's innocence and also tip off the opposing party if: (1) the transaction had not yet been consummated, so that the fraud could be prevented rather than having to be rectified; and (2) the lawyer's act of withdrawing would be understood by the opposing party to mean that the transaction should be aborted rather than completed through substitute counsel. That is, the opposing party would have to smell something fishy.

This solution preserves intact the rule of confidentiality in broadly comprehensive form. It has great rhetorical appeal, and obviously did so for the House of Delegates. It also covers some variations of the fraud problem in a way that would be entirely satisfactory to a morally conscientious lawyer. But it has two serious limitations for the morally conscientious lawyer or for a lawyer merely interested in protecting his own skin. First, the remedy of withdrawal is too late if the transaction has already been closed—what if the third party discovers the fraud thereafter? Second, what if the third party does not comprehend the significance of the withdrawal?

The lawyer's withdrawal would signal that something was wrong to most lawyers, brokers, and legally sophisticated principals. The scenario would go something like this, all carefully avoiding a "disclosure":

Scene 1:

Opposing Party's Lawyer (OPL) to Withdrawing Lawyer (WL): "Can you tell me the basis of your withdrawal?"

WL: "No. You must ask my client."

OPL to Fraud–Doing Client (FDC): "Why did your lawyer withdraw?"

FDC to OPL: "Because of a conflict of interest he suddenly discovered. Now I have to pay for a second lawyer. You guys always look out for number one."

Scene 2:

OPL, being very knowledgeable about the rules of confidentiality and very wary, to WL: "Your former client says you withdrew on account of conflict of interest. Is that true?"

WL, remembering that if he answers affirmatively he will in effect assist his client in committing the fraud, and that he may tell the truth in order to avoid doing that, to OPL: "That is not why I withdrew."

Scene 3:

OPL to FDC: "Your former lawyer says that his withdrawal was not on account of conflict of interest. I insist that you authorize him to tell me the circumstances, or the deal is off."

This scenario, if properly performed by the third party's counsel or by the third party himself, will do the job of protecting both the withdrawing lawyer and the third party. It is consistent with Rule 1.6 as adopted by the ABA, and with the debate upon which the vote was based. But, to return to the tough questions, what if the lawyer discovers the fraud after he has completed the representation, too late to "withdraw," and, in any event, what if the third party is a small country bank, or a rich "poor widow," who does not understand the signal?

D. *The Parliamentary Denouement*

At this point it is useful to describe the parliamentary sequence in which the Model Rules and the Comment were adopted by the ABA House of Delegates.

. . . [T]he Preamble, Model Rules, and Comment were . . . presented to the House of Delegates in August 1982 for general debate and deliberation. [I]t was decided to consider *only* the black letter in the first round of deliberations. The Comment would be considered after the black letter was adopted, in the interest of conserving time and attention. In the interest of rationing time, it was further decided to commence with the more important and controversial Rules.

Accordingly, discussion in the August 1982 session began with the black letter of Rule 1.5 (fees) and then went on to Rule 1.6. . . .

. . . In February the House addressed the black letter of Rule 1.6 . . . .. [T]he House rejected the Kutak proposal and adopted the formulation that eliminated the client fraud exception. The House then proceeded with the rest of the black letter Rules, adopting them all with various amendments.

. . . Deliberations on the black letter had consumed all the time available at the February meeting. Hence, consideration of the Comment was deferred to the next meeting of the House, in August 1983.

Since many of the black letter provisions had been amended in the February deliberations, it was obvious that much of the Comment required corresponding amendment. Also, since the debate had been both exhaustive and indicative of House sentiment, it made sense to both the Kutak proponents and the interested opponents to work out an agreed revision of the Comment. Negotiations to this end were conducted.

In the course of the negotiations directed to Rule 1.6, it was pointed out that withdrawal would not serve to extricate the lawyer unless the other side understood that withdrawal could be a "signal." It was also pointed out that withdrawal as such would not work at all where the transaction had been consummated before the lawyer discovered the fraud, because there would be no extant representation from which to withdraw.

It was in this context that the opponents of the Kutak Commission fully explicated their solution to the conundrum. The basic proposition, which is now embedded in Rule 1.6, is this: *An act or statement of the lawyer that does not reveal the content of client confidential information does not constitute a disclosure of such information.*

From this it follows that the lawyer may give a sufficient signal that the transaction is smelly, so long as he does not reveal the information upon which he reached the conclusion that he should give such a signal. . . . [T]he proposition permits the lawyer to do any of the following, depending on what is needed to get across the message:

1. Announce that he is withdrawing.

2. Withdraw any work product over which he still has control, such as closing documents.

3. Withdraw any work product that had been used in a completed transaction, by announcing: "The [closing statement] which I prepared is hereby withdrawn."

4. Withdraw any *implication* that might be drawn from his participation in the transaction, by announcing: "I withdraw my participation in the transaction, and any implication that might be drawn therefrom."

5. And, according to one exponent of the adopted version, advising a hopelessly naive opposite party, such as a rich "poor widow," as

follows: "I must tell you that you should not buy the [property], for reasons I cannot disclose."

All of these measures, it will be observed, do not as such contain the information from which the lawyer deduced that the transaction was fraudulent. Therefore, so the argument goes, they are consistent with the duty prescribed in Rule 1.6 not to "reveal information relating to the representation."

The foregoing analysis is the premise of the revised Comment to Rule 1.6 adopted by the House of Delegates. The Comment implements the analysis and permits signals such as those described above. The Comment states:

> Neither this Rule nor Rule 1.8(b) nor Rule 1.16(d) prevents the lawyer from giving notice of the fact of withdrawal, and the lawyer may also withdraw or disaffirm any opinion, document, affirmation or the like.

V. The Revival of Disclosure

A. *The ABA's Formula*

To one of only ordinary sophistication, the ABA's resolution of the client problem in substance permits disclosure. Giving a signal—going through a ritual that is intended to be a signal and is understood as a signal—is surely to "reveal" the information that the signal denotes. If that were not the purpose, why give the signal? And if that is the purpose, why not frankly call it a disclosure? What the ABA has done is loudly to proclaim that a lawyer may not blow the whistle, but quietly to affirm that he may wave a flag.

· · ·

[Another] explanation is that the ABA wanted a statutory rule of confidentiality "up front," but also some kind of common law or common lore exception for cases of fraud or other urgent necessity. . . .

. . . Thus, as so often occurs in legislation these days, the parliamentary body can take the high ground of general principle and leave it to the courts to do the dirty work of interpolating the necessary qualifications. That may be exemplary legislating by contemporary standards but it is not serious law-making.

The trouble with the solution in Rule 1.6 and the Comment as adopted is that some fools may not understand that Rule 1.6 does not mean what it seems to mean. There is reason to be concerned with this possibility. For example, I am told on good authority that, immediately after the House of Delegates' action on Rule 1.6, one of the lawyers in the *OPM* case received several congratulatory calls from fellow lawyers, celebrating the ABA's vindication of his decision not to blow the whistle on the scams his firm had been helping.

More fundamentally, the formula that "a signal is not a disclosure" formula seriously compromises the definition of confidentiality in cases where confidentiality obviously *should not* be compromised. Consider this hypothetical:

A married couple, Kim and Stacy, have known a lawyer socially for some time, but on a casual basis involving infrequent encounters. Without Stacy's knowledge, Kim consults the lawyer on the implications of getting a divorce, wanting simply to think about it for the time being. A few days later, the lawyer sees Stacy on the street and says, "It was good to see Kim the other day."

The lawyer's remark does not reveal the *content* of anything communicated by Kim. Hence, it is not a violation of the concept of confidentiality enacted in Rule 1.6. Needless to say, however, the remark is certainly a breach of confidence as that concept has always been understood in the profession.

. . .

It will of course be protested that "this is not what was meant" by Rule 1.6 and the Comment, as adopted. What was *meant* in the adopted formula was that a lawyer may give a signal, by withdrawal, etc., only in circumstances where doing so is a justified exception to the general principle of confidentiality. However, this leaves open the essential question: What should be the definition of this justified exception? The lawyer's course of action in the justified exception can be described disparagingly or euphemistically: blowing the whistle, waving the flag, making noisy withdrawal, making a disclosure, call it what one will. The hard problem, unanswered in the ABA's resolution of Rule 1.6, is to define the circumstances in which the lawyer may or should act.

State Variations of Model Rule 1.6

Because of the inadequacy of M.R. 1.6 to deal with the problems of client fraud, many states have substantially changed it as they have adopted the Rules of Professional Conduct. Pennsylvania's version, printed below, represents a common variant. After the Pennsylvania rule, there is a chart summarizing the changes in M.R. 1.6 made by various states.

The proposed Restatement of the Law Governing Lawyers § 117B, Tentative Draft No. 2 (4/7/89), also abandons the approach of M.R. 1.6 in favor of discretionary disclosure to prevent substantial financial loss threatened by the client's criminal or fraudulent act. The controversy over the appropriate course of action when faced with client fraud, however, continues. Two versions of § 117B were included for discussion, one by the Reporters and one by the Director of the ALI, an author of this book. While both allow for discretionary disclosure to prevent substantial financial harm, the Director's Proposal gives that discretion only when, "[t]he lawyer's services were employed in the client's course of conduct and the loss is likely to occur if the lawyer takes no action." Both proposals deal only with prevention. The lawyer who discovers that her services were used to perpetrate a fraud after the loss has occurred should look to the self-defense exception in § 116 for the scope of her right to disclose.

Pennsylvania Rules of Professional Conduct

RULE 1.6 Confidentiality of Information

(a) A lawyer shall not reveal information relating to representation of a client unless the client consents after consultation, except for disclosures that are impliedly authorized in order to carry out the representation, and except as stated in paragraphs (b) and (c).

(b) A lawyer shall reveal such information if necessary to comply with the duties stated in Rule 3.3.

(c) A lawyer may reveal such information to the extent that the lawyer reasonably believes necessary:

(1) to prevent the client from committing a criminal act that the lawyer believes is likely to result in death or substantial bodily harm or substantial injury to the financial interests or property of another;

(2) to prevent or to rectify the consequences of a client's criminal or fraudulent act in the commission of which the lawyer's services are being or had been used; or

(3) to establish a claim or defense on behalf of the lawyer in a controversy between the lawyer and the client, to establish a defense to a criminal charge or civil claim or disciplinary proceeding against the lawyer based upon conduct in which the client was involved, or to respond to allegations in any proceeding concerning the lawyer's representation of the client.

(d) The duty not to reveal information relating to representation of a client continues after the client-lawyer relationship has terminated.

STATE VARIATIONS OF MODEL RULE 1.6

A lawyer may [should] [shall] reveal confidential information to:

| Model Rule 1.6 | Prevent Future Crime | | | Prevent Future Fraud | Rectify Past Crime or Fraud |
	Death or Bodily Harm	Any Crime	Financial or Property Injury		
Arizona	Shall	May			
Arkansas		May			
Connecticut	Shall		May		May
Delaware	May				
Florida	Shall	Shall			
Idaho		May			
Indiana		May			
Kansas		May			
Louisiana	May				
Maryland	May		May	May	May
Minnesota		May			
Mississippi		May			
Missouri	May				
Montana	May				
Nevada	Shall	May		May	May
New Hampshire	May		May		
New Jersey	Shall		Shall	Shall	May
New Mexico	Should		May		
North Carolina		May			
North Dakota	Shall		May	May	May
Oregon		May			
Pennsylvania	May		May		May
South Dakota	May				May
Utah	May		May	May	May
Virginia		Shall			May
Washington		May			
Wisconsin	Shall		Shall		May
Wyoming		May			
Proposed Texas:	Shall	May	Shall	Shall	Shall
Kutak Proposal:	May		May	May	May

2 Hazard and Hodes, The Law of Lawyering, App. 4 (1987).

Sources: ABA–BNA Lawyer's Manual on Professional Conduct (through Feb. 17, 1988).

Questions and Comments

Should the rules on client fraud mandate disclosure by the lawyer instead of merely permitting it?

The Scope section of the Model Rules states that "[v]iolation of a Rule should not give rise to a cause of action nor should it create any presumption that a legal duty has been breached." The Model Code contained a similar statement. See the Preliminary Statement to the Model Code. These statements have, however, been to little avail. Courts have freely used the standards in lawyer codes to judge the behavior of lawyers in tort actions and other legal contexts where the lawyer's conduct is in issue. See, e.g., Woodruff v. Tomlin, 616 F.2d 924, 936 (6th Cir.), cert. denied, 449 U.S. 888 (1980) (Code's rules are evidence of standard in legal malpractice case involving impermissible conflict of interest); Lipton v. Boesky, 110 Mich.App. 589, 313 N.W.2d 163 (1981) (evidence of Code violation creates rebuttable presumption of malpractice); and United States v. DeLucca, 630 F.2d 294, 301 (5th Cir. 1980), cert. denied, 450 U.S. 983 (1981) (in determining lawyer's criminal liability for participation in conspiracy with client, it is appropriate to consider Code provisions). One reason, therefore, for avoiding a mandatory duty to disclose client fraud in the ethics rules is that it might increase the lawyer's exposure to civil suit. In those cases, where the lawyer made timely withdrawal so as to avoid any act that might substantially assist the fraud, a mandatory disclosure rule might impose civil liability for failing to disclose. See Rotunda, The Notice of Withdrawal and the New Model Rules of Professional Conduct: Blowing the Whistle and Waving the Flag, 63 Ore.L.Rev. 455, 482 (1984).

Note that while the Canons and Model Code dealt with client fraud on the tribunal in the same manner that they dealt with client fraud on private parties, the Model Rules takes a sharply different approach to the two problems. While the Model Rules as adopted made no provision for disclosure of client fraud on third parties, it *mandated* disclosure of client fraud on the court. See M.R. 3.3. The question of fraud on the tribunal is covered in Chapter 5 below.

Model Rule 4.1

Model Rule 4.1, Truthfulness in Statements to Others, provides:

In the course of representing a client a lawyer shall not knowingly:

(a) make a false statement of material fact or law to a third person; or

(b) fail to disclose a material fact to a third person when disclosure is necessary to avoid assisting a criminal or fraudulent act by a client, unless disclosure is prohibited by Rule 1.6.

Read the definition of "knowingly" in the Terminology section of the Model Rules. Should the Rule say "knowingly or recklessly"?

The reference to M.R. 1.6 invites lawyers to keep silent about a client's material omissions even when disclosure "is necessary to avoid assisting a criminal or fraudulent act by the client." Lawyers who read M.R. 4.1(b) this way must believe either that the ethics rules require them to risk imprisonment and civil penalties when the only alternative is to "turn in" their fraud-doing clients; or that the Rules provide some sort of defense to conduct that would otherwise be criminal or civil fraud.

One possible reconciliation of M.R. 4.1(b) and the law of fraud is that the ABA decided against discipline for lawyers who tacitly assist fraud, returning the problem to the civil and criminal law. But this reading assumes lawyers will understand that civil and criminal law "trumps" the surface meaning of M.R. 1.6 and 4.1—a questionable and risky assumption.

Confidentiality When Bodily Harm or Death May Result

Introductory Note

The ultimate test of one's commitment to principle comes in those situations when life is threatened. Are we willing to go to war to protect the interest: are we willing to kill or be killed? To sacrifice others? Constitutional law students are familiar with the question of whether the press should be enjoined from printing troop movements if publication would threaten the lives of the soldiers. In the area of client confidentiality, decisions where life hangs in the balance are extremely rare—in contrast to the frequency in which substantial economic harm is threatened by client fraud. Nevertheless, examining confidentiality in these extreme situations illuminates the principle at stake, our commitment to it, and our compassion for the suffering of others.

In this light, it is interesting to note that the strongest proponent of confidentiality, Professor Monroe Freedman, holds that confidentiality should yield to the duty to protect life. See the court's reference to Freedman's position in *Fentress*, printed below. See also ALCC Proposed Rule 1.6, printed below (Professor Friedman was one of two Reporters for the ALCC).

To begin we quote from Cover, *Justice Accused* 108 (1975), a brilliant examination of the response of judges, particularly antislavery judges, to cases involving enforcement of the slave laws. Professor Cover is discussing the few cases that directly raised the question of the right of slaves to revolt:

> Moralists have often sought to strip ethical issues of the complicating layers of fact and competing interests that seem to always characterize choice in society. Indeed the common association of natural right with a preexisting state of nature is itself an example of such an attempt. The tendency remains strong today as it was thousands of years ago. We have the relatively recent attempt of Professor Fuller to plumb the depths of the scope of responsibility

for the taking of human life, the famous case of the speluncean explorers, [L. Fuller, The Case of the Speluncean Explorers, 62 Harv.L.Rev. 616 (1949),] which itself is but an elaboration of the hypothetical of Rabbi Akiva, now two millennia old, of two men lost in the desert with enough water for one. [Babylonian Talmud, *Tractate Baba Mezia, 62a.*] What is of interest to us is not only that philosophers should create such hypotheticals, but that where life imitated art, where events have occurred that seem in part to mirror the choices presented by these hypotheticals, jurists have seized on the cases as presenting fundamental problems about the nature of law. Thus, cases like *United States v. Holmes* and *Regina v. Dudley and Stephens* have received extended attention from jurists. [Regina v. Dudley and Stephens, 14 Q.B.D. 273 (1884) involved the killing of a boy by ship-wrecked sailors in the good-faith belief that without cannibalism all would die. The boy was not consulted. In United States v. Holmes, 26 F.Cas. 360 (No. 15, 383) (C.C.D.Pa.1842), a mate directed seamen to throw passengers overboard from a lifeboat after shipwreck. It was reasonable to believe that if all stayed aboard, the boat would have gone down.]

The same inclination to seize on dramatic and rare instances of stark moral choice and to analyze them stripped of context can be discerned in the field of legal ethics. A favorite example of law professors is the client who confesses to her lawyer that she has committed a crime for which another is scheduled to be executed on the morrow. See, e.g., A. Kaufman, Problems in Professional Responsibility 212–14, 216–218 (2d Ed.1984). Professor Kaufman, who also makes the point that such examples are rare in practice and "are designed to test the limits of our belief in the principle of confidentiality", provides a real occurrence of the "electrocution" problem from the infamous Leo Frank case. See Frank v. Mangum, 237 U.S. 309 (1915).

After the conviction of Frank had been affirmed, a client told [Judge Arthur] Powell, then a practicing attorney, that he, not Frank, had committed the murder. Powell reports that his decision not to reveal the confidential communication was eased by the commutation of Frank's sentence to life imprisonment. Shortly thereafter, Frank was lynched by a mob. See Powell, *I Can Go Home Again* 287–292 (2d printing 1943) and Powell, Privilege of Counsel and Confidential Communications, 6 Ga.Bar J. 333 (1944). The case has returned to the newspapers again. An eyewitness to the crime broke 69 years of silence to state he had seen the state's chief witness carrying the unconscious or dead body of the victim. Obeying threats from the "murderer" and the injunction of his mother, he kept quiet. New York Times, Mar. 8, 1982, p. A12 col. 1. The Georgia Board of Pardons, however, denied a posthumous pardon to Mr. Frank because it was not possible "to decide conclusively his guilt or innocence." Id., Dec. 10, 1983, p. A10 col. 1.

On the other hand, such examples may focus our attention where the ball is not; may reassure us that in extreme situations we would do the heroic—cheap reassurance; may train us to see moral choice only when it is presented in stark terms; and may help us ignore the important lesson that in searching for an "ethical" or "moral" course of action, the choices are apparent only after examining the context. See the Gilligan excerpt reprinted in Chapter 1. The hard ethical questions in life arise not in those rare instances that mirror the moralist's stark hypotheticals, but in the vaguer, infinitely more complex arena of ordinary life.

The Professional Rules

As explained above, both the Canons of Professional Ethics and the Model Code of Professional Responsibility permit disclosure of any crime that the client intends to commit regardless of how trivial it is. See Canon 37 and DR 4–101(C)(3). The Model Rules tightened up this permission. M.R. 1.6(b)(1) provides: "A lawyer *may* reveal [confidential] information to the extent the lawyer *reasonably believes* necessary: (1) to prevent the client from committing a *criminal* act that the lawyer *believes* is likely to result in *imminent death or serious bodily injury* (emphasis added)."

Disclosure is permissive as opposed to mandatory under this provision. The scope of disclosure is judged by an objective standard: "to the extent the lawyer *reasonably believes* necessary." But the lawyer's honest, even if unreasonable, belief that imminent death or serious bodily injury will result suffices. The word "imminent" was added to the Rule on the floor of the ABA House of Delegates. Why? Should any bodily injury suffice to trigger permissive disclosure? Why the word "serious"?

To illuminate the restrictions in M.R. 1.6(b)(1) consider the electrocution hypothetical described above. If the client had committed fraud (unrectified and therefore ongoing/future criminal conduct) to secure the conviction of the innocent person who was to be executed, then the lawyer could disclose. But what if the client had not participated in fraud to secure the conviction?

Recall *Spaulding v. Zimmerman,* printed in Chapter I. Would Model Rule 1.6 have permitted disclosure to David Spaulding that he had an aneurysm? Compare proposed ALCC Rule 1.6: "A lawyer may reveal a client's confidence when and to the extent that the lawyer reasonably believes that divulgence is necessary to prevent imminent danger to human life. The lawyer shall use all reasonable means to protect the client's interests that are consistent with preventing loss of life." This proposal was not approved by the Commission on Professional Responsibility of the American Trial Lawyer's Association, which put forth the ALCC. The ALCC as approved proposed no exception to the duty of confidentiality for disclosure of either client fraud on third parties or the threat of death or bodily harm.

Suppose the client had committed fraud to secure the conviction of an innocent person for a crime that was the client's, but the punishment was 2 years imprisonment. Could the lawyer disclose under M.R. 1.6? Does imprisonment amount to serious bodily harm? Does M.R. 3.3 help?

Earlier drafts of the Model Rules imposed a mandatory duty to disclose information necessary "to prevent the client from committing an act that would seriously endanger the life or safety of a person, result in wrongful detention or incarceration of a person . . ." Unofficial Drafts of Aug. 20, 1979 and Sept. 21, 1979, Rule 1.5(b)(1). Putting aside for the moment the change from mandatory to permissive disclosure, what is to be made of the elimination of the right to disclose noncriminal acts of the client that would result in death or wrongful imprisonment and the elimination of any explicit mention of wrongful imprisonment as a ground for disclosure? Do you think the bar's position reflects the fact that most lawyers would not disclose to prevent wrongful imprisonment or execution?

PEOPLE v. FENTRESS

Dutchess County Court, 1980.
103 Misc.2d 179, 425 N.Y.S.2d 485.

· · ·

ALBERT M. ROSENBLATT, JUDGE.

· · ·

The defendant stands indicted for intentional murder [Penal Law 125.25[1]]. While the facts adduced before the grand jury are sufficient to establish the crime, the defendant avers that the indictment must be dismissed because it is the product of tainted and inadmissible evidence, presented in violation of the attorney-client privilege, as codified in CPLR 4503. . . .

CPLR Section 4503 reads as follows:

§ 4503.　Attorney

(a) Confidential communication privileged; non-judicial proceedings. Unless the client waives the privilege, an attorney or his employee, or any person who obtains without the knowledge of the client evidence of a confidential communication made between the attorney or his employee and the client in the course of professional employment, shall not disclose, or be allowed to disclose such communication, nor shall the client be compelled to disclose such communication, in any action, disciplinary trial or hearing, or administrative action, proceeding or hearing conducted by or on behalf of any state, municipal or local governmental agency or by the legislature or any committee or body thereof. Evidence of any such communication obtained by any such person, and evidence resulting therefrom, shall not be disclosed by any state, municipal or local governmental agency or by the legislature or any committee or body thereof. . . .

Upon the underscored language, the defendant bases his contention that the indictment rests on proof "resulting" from the breach, but for which there would have been no arrest, discovery of evidence, or indictment. . . .

The defendant . . . expressed grave concern about negotiating the mine field through which he could present proof of an alleged breach by the former attorney, Wallace Schwartz, without waiving the very confidentiality of the communications themselves. . . .

. . . To resolve the quandary, both sides expressly consented to a prohibition against any use by the prosecution, on its case-in-chief at trial, of any allegedly confidential statements adduced at the hearing. In that manner, the defendant would surrender nothing in the exercise of his right (and burden) to attempt to prove the violation of CPLR 4503, while the People would be permitted, at the trial, to use testimony adduced at the hearing, for impeachment or rebuttal purposes only, analogous to the rule in Harris v. New York, 401 U.S. 222, 91 S.Ct. 643, 28 L.Ed.2d 1. . . .

FINDINGS OF FACT

Albert Fentress was a schoolteacher in the City of Poughkeepsie School System.

Among his colleagues there for more than a decade was Enid Schwartz, a fellow teacher and personal friend, whom Fentress visited at her home once or twice yearly. Her friendship with Fentress was substantial, and was based on his having taught two of her children, as well as on the independent basis of their relationships as colleagues over the years.

One of these sons, Wallace, had been taught by Fentress in the ninth grade, and through the years had developed an independent personal friendship with him. After graduating, Wallace Schwartz and Fentress visited at each others' homes and had engaged in sports together.

After Wallace graduated from law school, and joined a civil firm in New York City, he gave Fentress his card and told him that he could call him at any time. On August 20, 1979, the Court finds the following to have occurred:

2:12 a.m.

Fentress, from his home at 216 Grand Avenue in Poughkeepsie, called Wallace Schwartz at the latter's home in Hartsdale, Westchester County. The first thing that Fentress said was that he was about to kill himself. Fentress spoke in a low monotone, and was distraught, but coherent. He told Schwartz that he had just killed someone, that a terrible thing had happened, which he could not square with God, and that he was going to kill himself.

Incredulous, Wallace Schwartz said it must have been an accident, but was told it was not, and that there had been a sexual mutilation as well.

In continuing attempts to dissuade his valued friend from suicide, Wallace Schwartz told Fentress that suicide would not square anything with God, and that whatever had happened, Fentress could get help. Wallace Schwartz invited Fentress to his house, and offered to go to Fentress' house, but Fentress refused.

Wallace Schwartz then suggested various persons who might be able to call and stay with Fentress, all of whom were rejected. However, later in the conversation Fentress said he would like the local rabbi, Rabbi Zimet, to come to his house and asked Wallace Schwartz to call the rabbi for him, which Wallace Schwartz agreed to do immediately. Fentress said he would leave the door open, and wait for the rabbi. It was also agreed that the police be summoned. . . .

Schwartz testified that it was his "legal" advice to Fentress that the police be called.

Fentress agreed, and stated that he would like to have both *Wallace Schwartz and the rabbi* present when the police arrived. . . .

At this point, of course, Schwartz did not have firsthand knowledge of the facts, but, recognizing the urgent need for immediate action (he could not fully conclude that any victim was actually dead) and because he was some fifty miles away, he immediately attempted to arrange to contact the rabbi.[1]

2:40 a.m.

Wallace Schwartz called his mother, Enid Schwartz, who lived in Poughkeepsie, to enlist her aid in calling the rabbi and arranging for him to go to Fentress' house.

Wallace Schwartz told Enid of the call he had just received, and of his extreme anxiety about Fentress having said that there had been a killing, or that he had killed someone, and that he was going to kill himself, and wanted Rabbi Zimet to come to see him. Enid, herself a close friend of Fentress, agreed to call the rabbi but said she was going to call Albert Fentress first to verify that there was a real problem there.

2:45 a.m.

As soon as Enid hung up, she called and asked Fentress *what had happened.* He told her either that he had killed someone, or that there had been a killing.

Notably, she never told Fentress that Wallace Schwartz had revealed to her any of the substance of the conversation between Fentress and Wallace Schwartz.

---

1. It should be noted, at this point, that Fentress was not and is not Jewish. While there was some peripheral discussion at the hearing about the possible clergyman-penitent relationship, the court finds it lacking. Rabbi Zimet, as it turned out, could not be reached, and through no one's fault never appeared at defendant's house or spoke to the defendant. The only connection between the defendant and the rabbi is that they both were at Wallace Schwartz' wedding where, one may speculate, they may have met.

When Enid telephoned Fentress she did not state or imply, nor could she have concluded, that Fentress had committed a crime. She knew, from Wallace, that Fentress may have killed *someone*, but she could not have concluded whether it was self-defense or the justifiable killing of an intruder, or willful murder. Her overriding concern was for the preservation of the life of her friend, Albert Fentress. When she began the conversation by asking Fentress what happened, Fentress stated that there had been a killing.

During the 2:45 a.m. conversation, Enid told Fentress that the police must be called, saying either "You must call the police" or "I am going to call the police." Fentress' response was that he would like Rabbi Zimet there waiting until the police came. She got the understanding that Albert Fentress acknowledged that it was proper for the police to come. . . .

Notably, Fentress did not state that he wanted his attorney there, only the rabbi. This is important, in that Fentress recognized that the presence of an attorney in the case would not (or should not) stem the arrival of the police. The Court thus finds that Fentress agreed that the police be called, and further, that he did not attempt to place any condition, as to the presence of an attorney, on their being called. His wish for a rabbi, while understandable for purposes of spiritual comfort, has no legal implications whatever.

2:50 a.m.

After Enid spoke to Fentress, she immediately called Rabbi Zimet but there was no answer.

While Fentress had asked her to let him know if she reached the rabbi, she was fearful that if she informed him of her failure, he might carry out his suicide threat.

It was because she could not reach the rabbi that she decided to call the police, to protect Fentress from harming himself.

2:59 a.m.

Enid Schwartz called her son Wallace, to tell him of her unsuccessful attempts to reach the rabbi, and her intention to call the police. The Court finds that the decision to call the police was made by Enid alone, although Wallace Schwartz concurred in it, principally because they both wished to prevent the defendant's suicide. Because of Wallace Schwartz' concern for Fentress' (legal) position, he cautioned his mother to be discreet in what she told the police, and to limit her remarks to the effect that there may have been a shooting at Fentress's house, and that there was fear that Fentress might commit suicide.

3:05 a.m.

Enid called the police and told Officer Thomas Ghee that it was reported to her by her son, and then by Fentress, that there had been a shooting or killing at his home. She warned the police that because of

Fentress' alleged suicidal intentions, it would be unwise to approach with sirens.

3:15 a.m.

The police, dispatched by Sgt. Krauer, arrived at defendant's house. The lights were on and the door open. Fentress was seated next to an open window, and beckoned: "Officer, please come in and take the gun."

3:19 a.m.

The defendant was given his *Miranda* warnings, according to Officer Perkins. The defendant declined to speak, stating that he was "waiting for his attorney," whom "he had already contacted," and whom he was expecting shortly. The police desisted questioning.

3:30 a.m.

Fentress was driven to the police station, and told the police that his attorney was Wallace Schwartz. After arriving at the police station, Fentress, on three or four occasions, asked for "his attorney, Wallace Schwartz."

5:09 a.m.

Wallace Schwartz arrived in Poughkeepsie, and advised the police that he was not a criminal lawyer and would not be able to properly represent the defendant. By that time Wallace Schwartz had decided to recommend Peter L. Maroulis to the defendant.

Peter L. Maroulis telephoned the police, and instructed them not to question the defendant. They had not; they did not.

As additional findings of facts, the Court further concludes that:

At no time before the arrest did Wallace Schwartz ever tell Fentress that he was representing him or that he was not representing him in the matter. The conversation, understandably, dealt with more immediate affairs.

Wallace Schwartz never told the police how he wanted them to deal with Fentress regarding questioning, procedures, or the like.

Although Wallace Schwartz never for a moment envisioned himself as being Fentress' attorney of record in this case, Fentress, in speaking to Wallace Schwartz during the 2:10 a.m. phone call, spoke to him as a friend and as an attorney, and the disclosures to Wallace Schwartz are within the attorney-client privilege.

When Enid made the decision to call Fentress at 2:45 a.m., she did so on her own, independently, and, in calling, did not act as the agent of Wallace Schwartz.

Fentress' disclosures to Enid during the 2:45 a.m. conversation, were voluntarily and independently made, without duress, pressure, or exploitation of any kind. Fentress made those disclosures without any knowledge that Enid already knew (through her conversation with Wallace Schwartz) what had occurred, and absent any subjective thoughts that disclosure to Enid was on constraint of or a necessary concomitant of his earlier statements to Wallace Schwartz. These disclosures to Enid were totally attenuated from those earlier disclosures to Wallace Schwartz. Wallace Schwartz never told Fentress that he was going to communicate with Enid. This is a significant omission, supportive of the factual conclusion that Fentress, when responding to Enid's inquiry as to "what happened," removed the conversation from the ambit of any pre-existing attorney-client confidentiality which had been formed at his 2:12 a.m. conversation with Wallace Schwartz. The omission, among other things, eviscerates defendant's claim that for purposes of the attorney-client relationship, Enid was Wallace's agent.

The disclosures by Fentress to Enid Schwartz were not within the scope of the attorney-client privilege.

During the 2:45 a.m. conversation with Enid, Fentress voluntarily consented that the police be called.

CONCLUSIONS OF LAW

. . .

The primary issues to be decided are, therefore, whether the requisites for confidentiality were established, and if so, whether they were waived by Fentress.

Wigmore, as usual, is an apt starting place, and provides the most orderly formulation of the rule (8 Wigmore on Evidence, Sec. 2292, McNaughton Rev.1961):

[1] Where legal advice of any kind is sought

[2] from a professional legal adviser in his capacity as such,

[3] the communications relating to that purpose,

[4] made in confidence

[5] by the client,

[6] are at his instance permanently protected

[7] from disclosure by himself or by the legal adviser,

[8] except the protection be waived.

II

WALLACE SCHWARTZ' PROFESSIONAL CAPACITY

If Wallace Schwartz was not being consulted in a professional capacity for legal advice, the inquiry is at an end. . . . The district attorney argues that Wallace Schwartz was predominantly a friend, who never handled a criminal case, and was neither retained nor gave any appreciable amount of legal advice to the defendant. To be sure, he "withdrew" in favor of Mr. Maroulis at the earliest time, and made no secret of his discomfort in the unfamiliar surroundings of the criminal law.

It is well settled, however, that the professional relationship may exist in a financial vacuum, and that the absence of a fee or retainer does not alone destroy it (People v. Arroyave, 49 N.Y.2d 264, 425 N.Y.S.2d 282, 401 N.E.2d 393, January 10, 1980; Bacon v. Frisbie, 80 N.Y. 394; Gage v. Gage, 13 App.Div. 565, 43 N.Y.S. 810).

Under any view, the defendant and Wallace Schwartz were friends. And while there would be no privilege if Wallace Schwartz was acting solely as a friend, abjuring professional involvement (Kitz v. Buckmaster, 45 App.Div. 283, 61 N.Y.S. 64, mot. for lv. to app. den. 47 App.Div. 633, 62 N.Y.S. 1140), it may be inferred that the defendant communicated with Wallace Schwartz because he was not only a friend but an attorney, from whom he was seeking support, advice, and guidance. That Wallace Schwartz was in effect called upon to serve as psychologist, therapist, counselor, and friend, does not derogate from his role as lawyer (Privileged Communications, 71 Yale L.J. 1226 at 1252).

Fentress told the police on several occasions that he had an attorney, Wallace Schwartz, and was eagerly awaiting his arrival. It is indicative of his own subjective and articulated belief that he contacted his friend, Wallace Schwartz, *qua attorney* (Nichols v. Village Voice, Inc., 99 Misc.2d 822, 417 N.Y.S.2d 415), but did not, and could not, have concluded that their conversation was to be kept confidential in all respects.

III

THE LEGAL ADVICE

Fentress urges, as he must to fit within Section 4503, that his call was for "legal advice." Ironically, the only "legal advice" which he can identify—and the Court adopts it as such—is the advice that the police must be called, the very advice which Fentress is now trying to disown. He cannot have it both ways.

Wallace Schwartz's advice was not the least bit unprofessional. Even the most seasoned criminal lawyers often "legally advise" their clients to turn themselves in for reasons which are strategic, if not moral. An experienced criminal practitioner might, of course, refrain from making that suggestion and still be on arguably stable grounds (both legally and ethically, despite the existence of an undetected body),[3] but he would have to weigh the risk of its ultimate discovery, and the disdain of a jury for any defense interposed by someone who had the cunning to suppress the corpus delicti. Duplicity is not tactically sound "legal advice." What other "legal advice" could Wallace Schwartz have given?

---

3. People v. Belge, 83 Misc.2d 186, 372 N.Y.S.2d 798, aff'd 50 A.D.2d 1088, 376 N.Y.S.2d 771, aff'd 41 N.Y.2d 60, 390 N.Y.S.2d 867, 359 N.E.2d 377; N.Y.State Bar op. # 479 (1978). Editor's note: See the discussion of Belge (The Buried Bodies Case) in Chapter 1 at p. 50.

Had Schwartz affirmatively advised Fentress to conceal or dispose of the body, he would have been counselling the commission of a crime (Penal Law 215.40(2), impeding the discovery of evidence; People v. DeFelice, 282 App.Div. 514, 125 N.Y.S.2d 80) which involves professional actions beyond those found endurable in *Belge.* They are violative of Code of Professional Responsibility DR 1–102A(4)(5), and may thus demolish the attorney-client privilege itself.[4] According to the Code of Professional Responsibility EC 7–5, "A lawyer should never encourage or aid his client to commit criminal acts or counsel his client on how to violate the law and avoid punishment therefor."

IV

NONCONFIDENTIALITY

Not every communication made to a lawyer in his professional capacity is confidential or intended to be so. As a general rule the question of privileged confidentiality depends on the circumstances. . . . Fentress' intentions and his reasonable expectations of confidentiality or disclosure, as expressed and inferred from his conversations are of critical importance. (See 24 Ohio State L.J., supra, at 26) Fentress, when he spoke to Wallace Schwartz at 2:12 a.m., imparted the killing, and his suicidal intentions. Wallace Schwartz told him, and he agreed, that the police would have to be called. According to testimony of Wallace Schwartz:

> "Al (Fentress) indicated that he would leave the door open for the rabbi, that the rabbi can come over, and that he would wait for the rabbi, and that at that time I, meaning me, could call the police. . . . *I wanted to make sure that Al understood what I intended to do.*"

> "Towards the end of the conversation the police were (again) mentioned in relation to his waiting for me with the rabbi. I believe at that time it was Al that mentioned that I could call the police at that time."

4. The privilege may not be asserted when the communication relates to the commission of a future crime, or to advise the client to suppress or destroy evidence (United States v. Gordon–Nikkar, 5th Cir., 518 F.2d 972, 975; United States v. Goldenstein, 8th Cir., 456 F.2d 1006, 1011, cert. denied 416 U.S. 943, 94 S.Ct. 1951, 40 L.Ed.2d 295; Note, The Future Crime or Tort Exception to Communications Privileges, 77 Harv.L.Rev. 730 [1964]), or to conceal wrong doing (Tierney v. Flower, 32 A.D.2d 392, 302 N.Y.S.2d 640; People ex rel. Vogelstein v. Warden of County Jail, 150 Misc. 714, 270 N.Y.S. 362, aff'd 242 App.Div. 611, 271 N.Y.S. 1059; See, Tarlow, Witness For The Prosecution, A New Role for Defense Lawyer, J. of Crim.Def., Vol. 1, p. 365, n. 114; Clark v. State, 159 Tex.Cr. R. 187, 261 S.W.2d 339, cert. denied 346 U.S. 855, 74 S.Ct. 69, 98 L.Ed. 369, rehearing denied 346 U.S. 905, 74 S.Ct. 217, 98 L.Ed. 404.) The same result would follow, of course, if the attorney were to aid in impeding discovery of evidence (United States v. Weinberg, 3 Civ., 226 F.2d 161, cert. denied 350 U.S. 933, 76 S.Ct. 305, 100 L.Ed. 815; See, R.A. Sedler and J.J. Simeone, The Realities of Attorney–Client Confidences, 24 Ohio State L.J., No. 1, p. 41). Lastly, there is the actual entrustment of evidence to the lawyer. See, The Right of a Criminal Defense Attorney to Withhold Physical Evidence Received From His Client, 38 U.Chi.L.Rev. 211, 213.

The conclusion is inescapable, and the Court has found as a fact, that Fentress did not intend to keep the corpus of the crime from the police. His renunciation of confidentiality (as to the fact of the homicide) appeared again when Enid suggested that the police be called, and Fentress again specifically disavowed any expectation of keeping the fact of the homicide from the police. Enid's testimony confirms it, and the Court has adopted as a fact, the defendant's expectations of non-confidentiality regarding the corpus:

Q: He expected the police to come?

A: I don't know what he expected. That's what he *said* to me. . . .

When Fentress concurred in the decision to call the police, he waived confidentiality of the *corpus*. Both to Wallace Schwartz and Enid Schwartz, he knew that disclosure to the police was inevitable both from his viewpoint and from the advice he received from his attorney, and later, from his friend, Enid Schwartz. His express eschewal of confidentiality is controlling (Rosseau v. Bleau, 131 N.Y. 177, 183, 30 N.E. 52, 53). "If the communication is made to an attorney with the knowledge and intent that it be disclosed to a third person it is fairly clear that it was not meant to be kept confidential and it is therefore not privileged." . . .

V

AGENCY AND WAIVER

After the 2:12 a.m. conversation between Fentress and Wallace Schwartz, and the 2:40 a.m. conversation between Wallace Schwartz and Enid, Fentress received a telephone call from Enid at 2:45 a.m. She did not tell Fentress that Wallace Schwartz had related to her any admissions that Fentress made to Wallace Schwartz. She began immediately by asking Fentress what happened, and he then told her that there had been a killing. They both then agreed that the police would have to be summoned . . . with Fentress stating that he wanted her to call Rabbi Zimet.

At this point, for reasons which are expanded upon below, the Court finds that the conversation between Fentress and Enid, in which he divulged the killing, was a communication made independently freely by Fentress to Enid, a friend and teaching colleague whom he had known for ten years. He did not make the disclosure on the belief or expectation that Enid was an extension of Wallace Schwartz, qua attorney, or under the impression that she was Wallace Schwartz' agent for *purposes of any attorney-client* confidentiality.

The Court has found as a fact that Fentress's disclosure to her was not prompted on *constraint* of any previous disclosure that he made to Wallace Schwartz, but was independent of it, causally disconnected, and in response to a question by a friend who did not intimate to him that she was privy to any actual facts regarding his actions (United States v. Bayer, 331 U.S. 532, 540, 67 S.Ct. 1394, 1398, 91 L.Ed. 1654; People v.

Tanner, 30 N.Y.2d 102, 106, 331 N.Y.S.2d 1, 4, 282 N.E.2d 98, 99; People v. Jennings, 33 N.Y.2d 880, 352 N.Y.S.2d 444, 307 N.E.2d 561). The little that Enid knew—of a highly ambiguous nature—she did not disclose to Fentress and he could not have reasonably believed that she was privy to any *incriminating* facts merely from her inquiry, apprehensive though it was, as to "what happened." When Fentress replied, and told her that he killed someone, no confidentiality existed or was intended by him, and any previous attorney-client privilege which may have been created by the (2:12 a.m.) call between Fentress and Wallace Schwartz had been broken and attenuated. Thus, the evidence before the grand jury was not the "result" of any breach of attorney-client confidentiality within the meaning of CPLR 4503 even if, arguendo, complete confidentiality between Fentress and Wallace Schwartz was intended. This conclusion is confirmed by Fentress's repeated recognition and statements to Enid that the police were to be summoned. Hence, Enid was under no legal or ethical duty to refrain from calling the police. She had not only the defendant's express approval to do so, but her own unilateral and unfettered choice in the matter, just as any person is free to call the police when a friend has confided that he has killed someone and is about to kill himself.

. . .

The advice later given by Wallace Schwartz to his mother, Enid, at 2:59 a.m., that she should be discreet in what she tells the police because there "may" be an attorney-client privilege, did not and does not alter the relationship between Fentress and Enid. To the extent that there was an attorney-client relationship between Fentress and Wallace Schwartz, Enid was no part of it, nor was she in any manner acting as her son's agent, qua attorney. After her conversation with Fentress at 2:40 a.m., she was entirely free to call the police on her own for the reasons given. It is hard to conceive of anyone doing otherwise.

The defendant recognizes that the *presence* of an unnecessary third party will destroy confidentiality. . . . The waiver doctrine, however, is applied not only when a third non-indispensible person is present, but when such a person is let in on the secret before (Workman v. Boylan Buick, Inc., 36 A.D.2d 978, 321 N.Y.S.2d 983), during or after the attorney-client consultation. Thus, when the client, *after consultation,* reveals the contents of the consultation to someone else a waiver is effectuated (People v. Hitchman, 70 A.D.2d 695, 416 N.Y.S.2d 374). This is not new, and represents the unswerving application of the waiver doctrine on the basis of voluntary disclosures made by clients to third persons after the initial consultation. . . .

Enid was not a person whose participation was necessary for furtherance of the professional relationship. Had she been present during the 2:12 a.m. conversation, her role as a friend could not be transmuted into that of an attorney's agent [7] or be perceived as essen-

7. Naturally, the mere fact that Enid and Wallace Schwartz were related does not itself create agency, (Anno. 96 A.L.R.2d 125, Persons Other Than Client or Attorney

tial to or in furtherance of the attorney-client conference (Baumann v. Steingester, 213 N.Y. 328, 332, 107 N.E. 578, 579).

. . .

VI

SUICIDE

The defendant's announced suicidal intentions pervade the case. Wallace Schwartz was burdened with a trilemma. He had just been told of a frightful homicide and an undiscovered victim. Secondly, Fentress said he was about to take a second life, his own. Given the desperation of the call, it would not have been possible for Wallace Schwartz, or anyone else, to determine whether the victim was still alive or beyond all hope. Fentress had mentioned drinking and a sexual mutilation as well. Schwartz could not possibly travel quickly enough to save anyone's life, but he knew that lives were in serious jeopardy at the very least. The implication of Fentress' motion is that Wallace Schwartz somehow broke a confidence by telephoning his parents, who lived moments away from Fentress, who was their friend as well, for the express purpose of complying with Fentress' request that Rabbi Zimet be summoned to the scene, and to avert a suicide.

The ethical oath of secrecy must be measured by common sense. . . .

To exalt the oath of silence, in the face of imminent death, would, under these circumstances, be not only morally reprehensible, but ethically unsound. As Professor Monroe Freedman reminds us, "At one extreme, it seems clear that the lawyer should reveal information necessary to save a life." (10 Crim.L.Bull., No. 10, p. 987). If the ethical duty exists primarily to protect the client's interests, what interest can there be superior to the client's life itself?

The issue was addressed in N.Y.State Bar op. 486 (1978) (New York State Bar Journal, August 1978). Posing the question "May a lawyer disclose his client's expressed intention to commit suicide?" the New York State Bar Association, in interpreting EC 4-2 and DR 4-101(C)(3) answered in the affirmative, despite the repeal of suicide as a crime (See, L.1919, ch. 414; Former Penal Law Sec. 2301; Meacham v. NYSMBA, 120 N.Y. 237, 242, 24 N.E. 283, 284).

Thus, even if the defendant flatly forbade Wallace Schwartz from calling the police, the ethical duty of silence would be of dubious operability. We need not decide the legal consequences of such an interdiction, having rejected the defendant's contention that he did not acquiesce in the call to the police, and having found waiver by repetition to Enid Schwartz.

. . .

Affected by, or Included Within, Attorney–Client Privilege, § 5) and the Court finds no other evidence to justify any finding of agency.

Questions and Comments

Does the New York statute cover material protected by the attorney-client privilege only or does it also cover material protected by the duty of client confidentiality?

When does talking to a friend, who happens to be a lawyer, become a privileged communication? Do you agree with the court's characterization of Schwartz's advice as legal advice?

The court says that Fentress renounced confidentiality as to the homicide. Do you agree? Why did the court find that Enid was not acting as the lawyer's agent? Is this reasoning persuasive?

Was the discussion of suicide necessary to this opinion? The court relies on the N.Y. State Bar opinion approving of disclosure to prevent the client's suicide and states, "If the ethical duty exists primarily to protect the client's interests, what interest can there be superior to the client's life itself?" Had Fentress not threatened suicide would the court have approved of the lawyer's disclosure? Would this court have approved disclosure in *Spaulding v. Zimmerman?*

Would the Model Rules permit disclosure in a case like *Fentress?* In ABA Informal Opinion 83–1500 (1983), the ABA Committee on Ethics and Professional Responsibility decided that under *both* the Model Code and the Model Rules a lawyer could disclose his client's intent to commit suicide in a jurisdiction where suicide was no longer a crime. The Committee cited with approval the New York State Bar Association opinion cited in *Fentress* and a similar opinion in Massachusetts, Mass.Bar Assoc. Opinion 79–61 (1979). It also relied on EC 7–12 and Model Rule 1.14, which provide that a lawyer has special responsibilities when the client is suffering from a disability.

In New Jersey Opinion 280, 97 N.J.L.J. 361 (1974), the New Jersey Advisory Committee on Professional Ethics concluded "that where an attorney for a parent has facts that demonstrate a propensity of that parent to engage in child abuse and hence the continuing unfitness of that parent to raise its [sic] child, . . . the information *must* be provided to the [state] Children's Bureau." (emphasis added). The Committee emphasized that the state's interest in child welfare makes this crime *sui generis,* thus justifying the obligation to report a "propensity" to commit it. Is this opinion wise?

"LAWYER REFUSES TO REVEAL NAME OF CHILD MOLESTER"

Washington Post, January 13, 1980, Page D3.
By Athelia Knight and Joseph Bouchard.*

On Dec. 16, two boys were sexually molested by a middle-aged man in the basement of Lisner auditorium on the campus of George Washington University.

---

* Copyright © 1980 by the Washington Post.

Five days later, an attorney in a downtown law firm contacted District of Columbia police. The lawyer said he represented the man who had committed the acts on the two boys, ages 10 and 11. The attorney, who refused to identify his client but said he comes from a prominent family, wanted to make a plea bargaining agreement. The attorney was referred to the U.S. attorney's office, which refused to agree to the plea bargain. The attorney left, refusing to name his client.

Thus far, there has been no arrest in the case and city police are furious.

"As far as we are concerned, it's obstruction of justice," said one police investigator.

D.C. police on Friday released a composite drawing of the suspect. The suspect is a white male in his 40s, about 6 feet tall with a stocky build. He has a ruddy complexion. On the day of the incident, he was wearing a blue ski jacket, grey pants and brown shoes.

According to an investigator, the drawing was done a day after the incident, but was only released two days ago because of printing problems.

The incident occurred about 6:30 p.m., on Sunday, Dec. 16, according to police. The boys were in the basement of Lisner during a break in a performance to get sodas.

While at the soda machine, the man sexually molested them.

The boys, who live in the Washington suburbs, were frightened and told the man they had to return upstairs and fled.

"If they had not been as cool as they were, there is no telling what would have happened," said the mother of one of the boys.

Five days later, police sources said, a detective in the department's sex investigation squad received a telephone call from James Michael Bailey, a lawyer who said he represented the man police were seeking in connection with the case. Bailey said his client was frightened by the experience, and had never done anything like that before, the sources reported. They said Bailey told police that the man came from a prominent family and that he would turn himself in if he could be promised that he would be released.

Bailey declined yesterday to comment on the account by police sources.

The attorney then followed up the call with a visit to police headquarters at 300 Indiana Ave. NW, where he talked with the investigator a second time.

At one point during the conversation, the lawyer said if police tried to find out who the suspect was efforts would be made to get him out of town, police sources reported.

Bailey and another attorney in his firm were taken to the U.S. Attorney's office, where a plea bargain agreement was turned down.

Questions and Comments

Courts usually hold that the whereabouts of a client is not privileged, see cases cited in the note on pp. 224–225 above. But is the information confidential? In other words, may the lawyer disclose absent a court order? Would the lawyer in the Washington Post article be permitted to disclose the name and whereabouts of his client under the Model Code? Under the Model Rules?

ABA Informal Opinion 1141 (1970) involved a lawyer contacted by a deserter from the military. The opinion turns on the deserter's purpose in consulting the lawyer. If the deserter contacts the lawyer to discuss his rights, the lawyer should treat the client's whereabouts as privileged. If the deserter wants advice on how best to evade capture, the lawyer must: advise him to turn himself in; refuse to represent him if he declines to do so; and advise him that the lawyer will reveal his whereabouts if the client, continuing in his intention to evade capture, contacts the lawyer a second time. (Is the client likely to call back?)

The committee also tried to reconcile the ABA's previous opinions on what the lawyer with a fugitive client should do, no mean feat.

Should bail-jumping and eluding arrest under an outstanding warrant be treated differently from the circumstances in the Washington Post article?

Compare Dike v. Dike, 75 Wash.2d 1, 448 P.2d 490 (1968), where the court held that a lawyer, whose client had taken her child from the child's custodian in contempt of a court order, had a duty to answer the court's questions about the client's whereabouts, with Brennan v. Brennan, 281 Pa.Super. 362, 422 A.2d 510 (1980), where the court held the lawyer did not have to disclose the client's whereabouts in a child custody case in which the trial court had not yet decided whether it had jurisdiction.

HAWKINS v. KING COUNTY
Court of Appeals of Washington, Division 1, 1979.
24 Wn.App. 338, 602 P.2d 361.

· · ·

SWANSON, ACTING CHIEF JUDGE.

Michael Hawkins, acting through his guardian ad litem, and his mother Frances M. Hawkins, appeal from a summary judgment dismissing attorney Richard Sanders from an action sounding in tort. Appellants contend Sanders, court-appointed defense attorney for Michael Hawkins, was negligent and committed malpractice by failing to divulge information regarding his client's mental state at a bail hearing. We find no error and affirm.

On July 1, 1975, Michael Hawkins was booked for possession of marijuana. Following his court appointment as Hawkins' defense counsel on July 3, 1975, Richard Sanders conferred with Hawkins for about 45 minutes, at which time Hawkins expressed the desire to be released from jail.

Also on July 3, 1975, Sanders talked with Palmer Smith, an attorney employed by Hawkins' mother Frances Hawkins, to assist in having Hawkins either hospitalized or civilly committed. Smith told Sanders then, and reiterated by letter, that Hawkins was mentally ill and dangerous. On July 8, 1975, Dr. Elwood Jones, a psychiatrist, telephoned and wrote Sanders and averred Hawkins was mentally ill and of danger to himself and others and should not be released from custody. Sanders represented that he intended to comply with his client's request for freedom.

On July 9, 1975, a district judge released Hawkins on a personal surety bond. At the bail hearing, Sanders did not volunteer any information regarding Hawkins' alleged illness or dangerousness, nor were any questions in that vein directed to him either by the judge or the prosecutor. Smith, Jones, and Mrs. Hawkins were informed of Hawkins' release, and all parties later met on two occasions in a counseling environment.

On July 17, 1975, about 8 days after his release, Michael Hawkins assaulted his mother and attempted suicide by jumping off a bridge, causing injuries resulting in the amputation of both legs. The Hawkinses commenced an action for damages against King County, the State of Washington, Community Psychiatric Clinic, Inc., and one of its employees on August 16, 1976, and amended the suit on November 30, 1977, to name Sanders a party defendant. Sanders filed a motion to dismiss for failure to state a claim. . . .

On appeal, the Hawkinses essentially present two arguments: First, that by his failure at the bail hearing to disclose the information he possessed regarding Michael Hawkins' mental state, defense counsel Sanders subjected himself to liability for malpractice, as court rules and the Code of Professional Responsibility mandate such disclosure on ethical and legal grounds. Second, that by the same omission Sanders negligently violated a common law duty to warn foreseeable victims of an individual he knew to be potentially dangerous to himself and others. See Tarasoff v. Regents of University of California, 17 Cal.3d 425, 131 Cal.Rptr. 14, 551 P.2d 334 (1976).

Sanders asserts the Hawkinses have failed to demonstrate that he breached any duty owed to them and, as an attorney appointed by the court to represent an indigent defendant, that he was a quasi-judicial officer, immune from civil liability.

We defined the elements of a legal malpractice action in Hansen v. Wightman, 14 Wash.App. 78, 88, 538 P.2d 1238, 1246 (1975), as

the existence of an attorney-client relationship, *the existence of a duty on the part of a lawyer,* failure to perform the duty, and the negligence of the lawyer must have been a proximate cause of damage to the client.

(Footnote omitted. Citations omitted. Italics ours.) The Court, in Cook, Flanagan & Berst v. Clausing, 73 Wash.2d 393, 395, 438 P.2d 865, 867 (1968) defined the standard care for Washington lawyers:

> [T]he correct standard to which the plaintiff is held in the performance of his professional services is that degree of care, skill, diligence and knowledge commonly possessed and exercised by a reasonable, careful and prudent lawyer in the practice of law in this jurisdiction.

We further note that the Code of Professional Responsibility sets standards of ethics for all members of the Bar of this state.

In considering appellants' argument that Hawkins' defense counsel breached an ethical and legal duty to disclose information to the court, we observe that a lawyer is ethically bound to advocate zealously his client's interests to the fullest extent permitted by law and the disciplinary rules. CPR 7, DR 7–101(A)(1).

Appellants argue that the information Sanders received was particularly relevant to the issues the bail-hearing judge is required to resolve on pretrial release pursuant to CrR 3.2.[2] In support of this contention, appellants cite DR 7–102(A)(3), which states:

> (A) In his representation of a client, a lawyer shall not:
>
>   .   .   .
>
> (3) Conceal or knowingly fail to disclose that which he is required by law to reveal.

Assuming without deciding that the information received by Sanders from Dr. Jones and Mrs. Hawkins' attorney did not constitute a "confidence or secret" which a lawyer generally may not reveal, neither CrR 3.2 nor JCrR 2.09 specifies who has the duty to provide facts for the court's consideration. The quoted rules state only that "the court shall, on the available information, consider the relevant facts . . ." JCrR 2.09(b); CrR 3.2(b).[3] Further, the Hawkinses ignore an ethical

---

2. The pretrial release hearing was conducted in justice court; therefore, JCrR 2.09 governs; however the provisions of JCrR 2.09 and CrR 3.2 are identical. Both rules identify the relevant factors as follows:

> the length and character of the defendant's residence in the community; his employment status and history and financial condition; his family ties and relationships; his reputation, character and mental condition; his history of response to legal process; his prior criminal record; the willingness of responsible members of the community to vouch for the defendant's reliability and assist him in appearing in court; the nature of the charge; and any other factors indicating the defendant's ties to the community.

3. The American Bar Association's standards relating to pretrial release include this commentary: "The basic criticism of the administration of bail has been that magistrates were required to make decisions without having sufficient facts. . . . No agency charged with the specific duty of ascertaining facts relevant to release other than the defendant's criminal record and the nature of the present charge ordinarily exists. Unfortunately counsel, who is present in only a limited number of cases at this stage, seldom makes a special effort to supply the judicial officer with background facts. . . .

standard of paramount importance: that an attorney must advocate zealously his client's interests to the fullest extent permissible by law and the disciplinary rules. CPR 7 DR 7–101(A)(1).

While it can be argued that the draftsmen of JCrR 2.09 assumed defense counsel would participate in furnishing information for the court, there is no indication as to the length to which defense counsel should go in revealing information damaging to his client's stated interests. Manifestly, defense counsel has an ethical duty to disclose that which he is required by law to reveal. Appellants, however, have not cited any clear provision of the law which *requires* defense counsel to volunteer information damaging to his client's expressed desire to be released from custody.

We believe that the duty of counsel to be loyal to his client and to represent zealously his client's interest overrides the nebulous and unsupported theory that our rules and ethical code mandate disclosure of information which counsel considers detrimental to his client's stated interest. Because disclosure is not "required by law," appellants' theory of liability on the basis of ethical or court rule violations fails for lack of substance.

Turning then to the Hawkinses' theory of a common law duty to warn or disclose, we note common law support for the precept that attorneys must, upon learning that a client plans an assault or other violent crime, warn foreseeable victims. See Tarasoff v. Regents, supra; State ex rel. Sowers v. Olwell, 64 Wash.2d 828, 394 P.2d 681 (1964); Dike v. Dike, 75 Wash.2d 1, 448 P.2d 490 (1968). *Olwell* and *Dike* make clear our Supreme Court's willingness to limit the attorney's duty of confidentiality when the values protected by that duty are outweighed by other interests necessary to the administration of justice. The difficulty lies in framing a rule that will balance properly "the public interest in safety from violent attack" against the public interest in securing proper resolution of legal disputes without compromising a defendant's right to a loyal and zealous defense. We are persuaded by the position advanced by amicus "that the obligation to warn, when confidentiality would be compromised to the client's detriment, must be permissive at most, unless it appears beyond a reasonable doubt that the client has formed a firm intention to inflict serious personal injuries on an unknowing third person."

Because appellants rely to a great extent upon *Tarasoff* in arguing a common law duty to disclose, we will demonstrate that the *Tarasoff* decision is inapposite even though the facts are equally atypical and tragic. Tatiana Tarasoff was killed by one Prosenjit Poddar. The victim's parents alleged that 2 months earlier Poddar confided his

---

Where public defender and other assigned lawyers provide representation on an institutional basis, they are frequently too pressed for time to make a special point of such an inquiry and, most important, to verify the information they may receive in an interview.

"The ideal system would involve the creation of an independent agency answerable directly to the court." (Citations omitted.) ABA Standards Relating to Pretrial Release § 4.5 (Approved Draft 1968) commentary at 50.

intention to kill Tatiana to a defendant, Dr. Moore, a psychologist employed by the University of California. After a brief detention of Poddar by the police at Moore's request, Poddar was released pursuant to order of Dr. Moore's superior. No one warned Tatiana of her peril. The plaintiffs claimed the defendant psychologists had a duty to warn foreseeable victims. Defendants denied owing any duty of reasonable care to Tatiana. The trial court sustained a demurrer to the complaint which was reversed on appeal. The Supreme Court of California concluded that the complaint could be amended to state a cause of action against the psychologists by asserting that they had or should have determined Poddar presented a serious danger to Tatiana, pursuant to the standards of their profession, but had failed to exercise reasonable care for her safety.

In *Tarasoff*, the defendant psychologists had first-hand knowledge of Poddar's homicidal intention and knew it to be directed towards Tatiana Tarasoff, who was wholly unaware of her danger. The knowledge of the defendants in *Tarasoff* was gained from statements made to them in the course of treatment and not from statements transmitted by others. Further, the California court in *Tarasoff* did not establish a new duty to warn, but only held that psychologists must exercise such reasonable skill, knowledge, and care possessed and exercised by members of their profession under similar circumstances.

In the instant case Michael Hawkins' potential victims, his mother and sister, knew he might be dangerous and that he had been released from confinement, contrary to Tatiana Tarasoff's ignorance of any risk of harm. Thus, no duty befell Sanders to warn Frances Hawkins of a risk of which she was already fully cognizant. Further, it must not be overlooked that Sanders received no information that Hawkins planned to assault anyone, only that he was mentally ill and likely to be dangerous to himself and others. That Sanders received no information directly from Michael Hawkins is the final distinction between the two cases.

The common law duty to volunteer information about a client to a court considering pretrial release must be limited to situations where information gained convinces counsel that his client intends to commit a crime or inflict injury upon unknowing third persons. Such a duty cannot be extended to the facts before us.

In view of our disposition of this case, we do not reach the question of respondent Sanders' claimed immunity from civil liability.

The decision of the superior court granting summary judgment dismissing the respondents as party defendants is affirmed.

DORE and RINGOLD, JJ., concur.

Questions and Comments

The Malpractice Claim

Under the Model Code or Model Rules could the lawyer have disclosed Hawkins' state of mind? Does M.R. 1.14 or EC 7–12 help resolve this question?

The court points out that no questions on Hawkins' mental state were posed to Sanders in the bail hearing. Would Sanders have had a duty to answer such questions honestly? See M.R. 3.3. If Sanders had lied or "fudged" in response to questions in court, would the result on the malpractice claim have been different?

A Tarasoff Duty for Lawyers?

Should the law impose civil liability on lawyers who fail to warn of their clients' intent to endanger others? If so, what should be the scope of such a duty?

While finding no duty the *Hawkins* court states that it would require lawyers to "volunteer information . . . to the court considering pretrial release where information gained convinces counsel that his client intends to commit a crime or inflict injury upon *unknowing* third persons." The duty apparently would be limited to cases of threatened physical injury. Should there be a similar duty to warn victims of the client's intended fraudulent schemes? Is physical injury of such a different order?

Tarasoff v. Regents of University of California, 17 Cal.3d at 431, 131 Cal.Rptr. 14, 551 P.2d at 340 (1976) (*Tarasoff II*), is the seminal case on the psychiatrist's duty to warn or otherwise protect others from patients who the doctor knew or should have known were dangerous. While *Tarasoff* is often referred to as the case establishing a duty to "warn," the duty described therein was not limited to warning.

> The discharge of this duty may require the therapist to take one or more of various steps, depending upon the nature of the case. Thus it may call for him to warn the intended victim or others likely to apprise the victim of the danger, to notify the police, or to take whatever other steps are reasonably necessary under the circumstances.

> *Tarasoff II,* 131 Cal.Rptr. at 20.

Does *Hawkins* intimate a duty on the lawyer's part other than to volunteer information?

Recall the facts of *Spaulding v. Zimmerman,* printed in Chapter 1 above. If David Spaulding had died a year after the settlement, would it have been appropriate to hold Zimmerman civilly liable for having failed to disclose the aneurysm to David or the court? Should Zimmerman's lawyers be jointly liable?

In many of the cases following *Tarasoff* an important factor has been whether the victims were readily identifiable, the theory being that the scope of potential liability for professionals would be too broad if not limited to identifiable victims.

On the requirement that the victim be identifiable, see Lipari v. Sears, Roebuck & Co., 497 F.Supp. 185, 194 (D.Neb.1980) ("Although the *Tarasoff* decision did not emphasize the identifiability of the victim in its analysis, subsequent California decisions have limited the scope of the therapist's duty to identifiable victims."). The California case limiting *Tarasoff* in this manner is Thompson v. County of Alameda, 27 Cal.3d 741, 167 Cal.Rptr. 70, 614 P.2d 728 (1980). Also see Brady v. Hopper, 751 F.2d 329 (10th Cir.1984) (suit by James Brady, President Reagan's press secretary, against John Hinckley's psychiatrist); Leedy v. Hartnett, 510 F.Supp. 1125 (M.D.Pa.1981), aff'd, 676 F.2d 686 (3d Cir. 1982); Cooke v. Berlin, 153 Ariz. 220, 735 P.2d 830 (App.1987). But see Schuster v. Altenberg, 144 Wis.2d 223, 424 N.W.2d 159 (1988) (under Wisconsin tort law, psychiatrists' duty to warn or protect third parties not limited to cases where victim is readily identifiable); and Jablonski by Pahls v. United States, 712 F.2d 391 (9th Cir.1983) (psychological profile indicating violence against women close to patient sufficiently "targeted").

What should be the standard of information that triggers the duty? Subjective or objective? If objective, should it be that the lawyer was in possession of information that would "convince a reasonable lawyer . . ."? That would "cause a reasonable lawyer to believe . . ."? Does it matter?

As of the summer of 1989, our research has not discovered a case imposing liability on a lawyer for failing to warn of a client's intended dangerous conduct. At the same time, there have been numerous cases since *Tarasoff* recognizing the liability of psychiatrists and psychologists for failure to warn of their client's intent to harm others or to take other appropriate steps. See, e.g., Naidu v. Laird, 539 A.2d 1064 (Sup. Ct.Del.1988); Evans v. Morehead Clinic, 749 S.W.2d 696 (Ky.App.1988); Davis v. Lhim, 124 Mich.App. 291, 335 N.W.2d 481 (1983); McIntosh v. Milano, 168 N.J.Super. 466, 403 A.2d 500 (1979) and cases cited in the notes above. The new battleground in this area is the liability of the state for releasing dangerous parolees or improperly supervising probationers. See, e.g., Division of Corrections v. Neakok, 721 P.2d 1121 (Alaska 1986); Sterling v. Bloom, 111 Idaho 211, 723 P.2d 755 (1986).

Why Impose a Duty on Psychotherapists and Not Others?

Is there a reason for imposing liability on therapists for failing to warn others about their dangerous clients and not on lawyers or other people in a special relationship with the dangerous person that would give them special access to the client's intent? The proposition that therapists are better able to predict dangerousness than other people is questionable. See Task Force Report, Clinical Aspects of the Violent

Individual (American Psychiatric Assn. 1974) at 28 (claiming that psychiatrists are no better than anyone else at predicting dangerousness); *Sterling v. Bloom,* supra. But see Givelber, Bowers & Blitch, Tarasoff, Myth and Reality: An Empirical Study of Private Law in Action, 1984 Wis.L.Rev. 443, 456–67 ("The task of assessing dangerousness is not viewed [by those therapists surveyed] as being beyond the competence of individual therapists or as a matter upon which therapists cannot agree.").

Does the fact that psychiatrists (and probation boards) routinely make judgments about dangerousness, e.g., in civil commitment hearings, provide a reason for acting as if they were capable of predicting dangerousness for purposes of tort liability?

Unlike probation boards and psychiatrists, lawyers are not in the business of predicting dangerousness. But to the extent that liability of psychiatrists and state authorities does not turn on special ability to judge dangerousness, different tort treatment for lawyers cannot be justified. Another basis for distinguishing lawyers from state correction authorities is that the latter may be in a better position to control the conduct of the tort-feasor. See *Davis v. Lhim,* supra, which makes control over the patient a key to the psychiatrist's tort liability for subsequent harmful acts.

The principle that an affirmative duty to act to protect others may be imposed on a person when there is a special relationship between that person and the dangerous person, or between that person and the victim, is a generally accepted albeit vaguely justified principle of tort law. Ordinarily, tort law does not impose upon one person a duty to control the conduct of another person to prevent the latter from harming a third party. Restatement Second of Torts § 314. The special relationship principle is an exception to this general statement. "Special relationship" is not defined in the Restatement; instead Section 314A of the Restatement sets out illustrations of such special relationships. The doctor-patient relationship, as evidenced by *Tarasoff,* is one such relationship.

In A Perspective on Client Confidentiality, 131 Am.J.Psych. 1021, 1022 (1974), Dr. Eric A. Plaut argues that psychiatrist-patient confidentiality is subject to more exceptions than that between priest and penitent because "psychiatrists have extensive civil authority, e.g., in circumstances involving abortions, personal injury suits, commitment procedures, and not-guilty-by-reason-of-insanity pleas." He concludes: "So long as we retain civil authority, our claim to confidentiality will always be subject to compromise." What implications does this have for lawyer confidentiality? Interestingly, this language was quoted with approval by the New Jersey Superior Court in *McIntosh* supra, 403 A.2d at 513. For a critique of the special relationship doctrine in tort law see, e.g., Note, Affirmative Duty After Tarasoff, 11 Hofstra L.Rev. 1013 (1983) (arguing that it is time that tort law recognize a more general affirmative duty to act to protect others instead of one limited to special relationships); Note, Professional Obligation and the Duty to Rescue: When Must a Psychiatrist Protect His Patient's Intended Victim, 91 Yale L.J. 1430 (1982) (criticizing courts for failing to articulate components of the relationship that create affirmative duties).

The Confidentiality Obligations of Physicians

As quoted by the court in *McIntosh* supra, 403 A.2d at 512:

[Section] 9 of the Principles of Medical Ethics (1957), . . . reads:

A physician may not reveal the confidences entrusted to him in the course of medical attendance, or the deficiencies he may observe in the character of patients, unless he is required to do so by law or unless it becomes necessary in order to protect the welfare of the individual or of the community.

How does this compare with the lawyer rules?

Two studies following *Tarasoff* have found that psychotherapists regard a duty to protect third parties from violent patients as consistent with their ethical obligations. See Givelber et al. supra, 1984 Wis. L.Rev. at 473–76, 486; and Mills, Sullivan & Eth, Protecting Third Parties: A Decade After Tarasoff, 144 Am.J.Psych. 68, 69–70 (Jan. 1987).

Much of the debate on the proper scope of lawyer-client confidentiality turns on speculation about impairment of the lawyer-client relationship. The Givelber et al., article cited above, found that, contrary to predictions, *Tarasoff* has neither discouraged therapists from treating dangerous patients nor apparently increased the use of involuntary commitment for those patients viewed as dangerous.

In 1988, the American Medical Association amended its ethics rules to deal with the physician's responsibility to sexual partners of a patient carrying the AIDS virus:

Ideally, a physician should attempt to persuade the infected party to cease endangering the third party; if persuasion fails, the authorities should be notified; and if the authorities take no action, the physician should notify and counsel the endangered third party.

The AMA also urged that any state laws protecting doctor-patient confidences that would prevent such disclosure be amended to allow compliance with the amendment. New York Times, 7/1/88, p. A11.

For a thoroughgoing analysis of the implications of *Tarasoff* for lawyers, see Merton, Confidentiality and the "Dangerous" Patient: Implications of Tarasoff for Psychiatrists and Lawyers, 31 Emory L.J. 263 (1982).

SISSELA BOK *SECRETS* (1982)

Chapter II: Secrecy and Moral Choice
pp. 15–28.*

Secrecy and Moral Choice

> *"Tell me your secrets."*
> *I say not a word, for this is under my control.*
> *"But I will fetter you."*
> *What is that you say, man? Fetter me?*
> *My legs you will fetter, but my deliberate*
> *choice not even Zeus has the power to overcome.*
>
> EPICTETUS, *Discourses*

A Thought–Experiment

Imagine four different societies: two of them familiar from religious and mythological thinking, the other two closer to science fiction. To the extent that each reflects aspects of our own world, it will arouse the ambivalence and unease characteristic of conflicts over secrecy.

— In the first of the four imaginary societies, you and I cannot keep anything secret; but others, or at least someone, perhaps a deity, can. We are transparent to them, either because we are incapable of concealment or because they have means of penetrating all our defenses.

— In the second society, all is reversed. You and I can pierce all secrets. A magic ring and a coat of invisibility give us access to these secrets, unbeknownst to those on whom we focus our attention.

— In the third society, no one can keep secrets from anyone who desires to know them. Plans, actions, fears, and hopes are all transparent. Surprise and concealment are out of the question.

— In the fourth society, finally, everyone can keep secrets impenetrable at will. All can conceal innocuous as well as lethal plans, the noblest as well as the most shameful acts, and hatreds and conspiracies as much as generosity and self-sacrifice. Faces reveal nothing out of turn; secret codes remain unbroken.

Abstract, for now, from possible supernatural influences that might render these societies either more or less benign, and consider how it

---

* Copyright © 1982 by Sissela Bok. Reprinted by permission of Pantheon Books, a division of Random House, Inc.

would be to live in each one. Would these societies not all turn out to be less desirable than our own, with all its conflicts over secrecy and openness, all its unpredictability and imperfection? Despite its inadequate protection of personal liberties, its difficulties in preserving either the secrecy or the openness on which human beings thrive, and its many abuses, our own world nevertheless differs from each of the four above in ways for which we must be grateful.

It is precisely those elements of our own experience which bring us closest to one or another of the four that are most troubling. Thus the first society—in which you and I can keep no secrets—might appeal to saints who seek to live with few shelters, few secrets, and to the publicity-hungry who want the spotlight for theirs. But life for most of us would be too exposed, too vulnerable, without a measure of secrecy. We might wish for the transparency of this imagined world at chosen moments, with close friends; but we are also aware of its resemblance to the experience of persons subjected to the modern methods of interrogation, surveillance, and thought-control now employed in so many countries. . . .

The second world, in which you and I can penetrate all secrets, echoes the perennial desire to satisfy all one's curiosity by moving unseen among others while learning their most closely held secrets. Yet as we reflect on the power that would be ours in this second world, we might hestitate to accept it. We would have to recognize not only its intrusiveness but its dangers to us, the unseen intruders and manipulators. The experience of this imagined society is brought closer for those who employ the new techniques of surveillance and of surreptitious probing—the one-way mirrors, the electronic eavesdropping, the elaborate undercover investigations. That even many who avail themselves of such techniques are uneasy about them is clear from the debates over their use among social scientists or reporters or police agents.

Some might argue that these new techniques of probing, along with refined versions of very old ones, are becoming so common that we are approaching, rather, the third imaginary society, in which no one can keep secrets from anyone intent on knowing them. . . .   [W]hat would the world be like if methods making secrecy impossible were generally available?

Might there be benefits in such universal transparency, as long as all could avail themselves of it? It would not only rule out secrecy but the very possibility of deceit and hypocrisy. Would such a state of openness among human beings not be nobler than the concealment we live with, and all the dissimulation it makes possible? Openness and sincerity, after all, are qualities we prize. As Meister Eckhart said, we call him a good man who reveals himself to others and, in so doing, is of use to them.

On reflection, even those most in favor of openness among human beings might nevertheless reject the loss of all secrecy; or else advocate it only for certain exceptional persons who choose it for themselves and are able to tolerate it. Advocates of *universal* transparency have usually envisioned it for some future society free of the conflicts and contradictions of our own. Thus Sartre held that "transparency must substitute itself at all times for secrecy," but that this will be possible only when material want has been suppressed. At such a time, he argued, the relationship between men will no longer be antagonistic:

> I can imagine rather easily the day when two men will have no more secrets from one another because they will keep secrets from no one, since the subjective life, just as much as the objective life, will be totally offered, given.

Yet the desire for such mutual transparency, even when relegated to a future, idealized world, should give pause. We must consider the drawbacks of too much information as well as those of being kept in the dark. And we must take into account our responses to all that we might learn about one another in such a world. Would we be able to cope with not only the quantity but also the impact upon us of the information thus within reach? And if secrecy were no longer possible, would brute force turn out to be the only means of self-defense and of gaining the upper hand? It is not inconceivable that the end result of a shift to the third imagined society would be chaos.

Aspects of the fourth society, finally, might develop precisely in response to the felt threat from increased transparency. They are foreshadowed in the governmental and commercial use of the "unbreakable codes" that cryptographers are currently designing, and in mechanisms to foil electronic eavesdropping. If such methods became available to everyone, and were capable of protecting all that people might wish to hide, how would our lives change? It is not certain that society as we now know it could survive such changes, for it depends in part on the possibility of predicting and forestalling or preparing for danger. Given a state in which no one could penetrate the secrets of others, nor know what harm they threatened, would those with the most far-reaching plans for aggression or crime win out? Or would so many fear such plans, and try to forestall them with violence of their own, that all would end in one great pre-emptive conflagration?

. . .

. . . [B]ecause secrecy is so often negatively defined and viewed as primarily immature, guilty, conspiratorial, or downright pathological, I shall first discuss the need for the protection it affords.

Consider how, in George Orwell's *Nineteen Eighty-four*, Winston Smith tried to preserve one last expression of independence from the Thought-police. He had decided to begin a diary, even though he knew he thereby risked death or at least twenty-five years in a forced-labor camp. He placed himself in an alcove in his living room where the telescreen could not see him, and began to write. When he found himself writing DOWN WITH BIG BROTHER over and over, he panicked and was tempted to give up.

He did not do so, however, because he knew that it was useless. Whether he wrote DOWN WITH BIG BROTHER, or whether he refrained from writing it, made no difference. Whether he went on with the diary, or whether he did not go on with it, made no difference. The Thought-police would get him just the same. . . .

Subjected to near-complete surveillance, Winston Smith was willing to risk death rather than to forgo the chance to set down his thoughts in secret. To the extent that he retained some secrecy for his views, he had a chance to elude the Thought-police. Though aware that "sooner or later they were bound to get to you," he did not know that he was under surreptitious observation even as he prepared to write—that his most secret undertaking was itself secretly spied upon.

Conflicts over secrecy—between state and citizen, as in this case, or parent and child, or in journalism or business or law—are conflicts over power: the power that comes through controlling the flow of information. To be able to hold back some information about oneself or to channel it and thus influence how one is seen by others gives power; so does the capacity to penetrate similar defenses and strategies when used by others. True, power requires not only knowledge but the capacity to put knowledge to use; but without the knowledge, there is no chance to exercise power. To have no capacity for secrecy is to be out of control over how others see one; it leaves one open to coercion. To have no insight into what others conceal is to lack power as well. Those who are unable or unwilling ever to look beneath the surface, to question motives, to doubt what is spoken, are condemned to live their lives in ignorance, just as those who are unable to keep secrets of their own must live theirs defenseless.

. . . .

In seeking some control over secrecy and openness, and the power it makes possible, human beings attempt to guard and to promote not only their autonomy but ultimately their sanity and survival itself. The claims in defense of this control, however, are not always articulated. Some take them to be so self-evident as to need no articulation; others subsume them under more general arguments about liberty or privacy. But it is important for the purposes of considering the ethics of secrecy to set forth these claims. . . .

The claims in defense of some control over secrecy and openness invoke four different, though in practice inseparable, elements of human autonomy: identity, plans, action, and property. They concern protection of what we are, what we intend, what we do, and what we own.

The first of these claims holds that some control over secrecy and openness is needed in order to protect identity: the sense of what we identify ourselves as, through, and with. Such control may be needed to guard solitude, privacy, intimacy, and friendship. It protects vulnerable beliefs or feelings, inwardness, and the sense of being set apart: of having or belonging to regions not fully penetrable to scrutiny, including those of memory and dream; of being someone who is more, has become more, has more possibilities for the future than can ever meet the eyes of observers. Secrecy guards, therefore, not merely isolated secrets about the self but access to the underlying experience *of* secrecy.

Human beings can be subjected to every scrutiny, and reveal much about themselves; but they can never be entirely understood, simultaneously exposed from every perspective, completely transparent either to themselves or to other persons. They are not only unique but unfathomable.* The experience of such uniqueness and depth underlies self-respect and what social theorists have called the sense of "the sacredness of the self." This sense also draws on group, familial, and societal experience of intimacy and sacredness, and may attach to individual as well as to collective identity. The growing stress in the last centuries on human dignity and on rights such as the right to privacy echoes it in secular and individualized language.

· · ·

Not only does control over secrecy and openness preserve central aspects of identity; it also guards their *changes,* their growth or decay, their progress or backsliding, their sharing and transformation of every kind.† Here as elsewhere, while secrecy can be destructive, some of it is indispensable in human lives. Birth, sexual intimacy, death, mourning, experiences of conversion or of efforts to transcend the purely personal are often surrounded by special protections, and with rituals that combine secrecy and openness in set proportions.

· · ·

The second and third claims to control over secrecy presuppose the first. Given the need to guard identity, they invoke, in addition, the need for such control in order to protect certain plans and actions.

Choice is future-oriented, and never fully expressed in present action. It requires what is most distinctive about human reasoning: intention—the capacity to envisage and to compare future possibilities, to make estimates, sometimes to take indirect routes to a goal or to wait. What is fragile, unpopular, perhaps threatened, such as Winston

---

* Many have written about individuals as worlds, universes, or networks, unfathomable in practice if not in principle. And the death of an individual has been likened to the burning down of a great library or to a universe going extinct, as the inwardness and focus and connections of a life are lost, along with the sense of what William Blake called "the holiness of minute particulars."

† Identities and boundaries may themselves be transformed by the revelation or the penetration of certain secrets. And revealing, penetrating, and guarding secrets, in turn, often make use of transformations:

—Some ways of revealing secrets require a transformation, such as an initiation, on the part of those who are to share the secret. Their oath of secrecy, too, transforms their obligations. Their identity may undergo a metamorphosis of growth or destruction.

—Some secrets are transformed so as to be more easily guarded, through codes, miniaturization, or oracular sayings that only initiates will understand.

—Certain transformations allow the penetration of secrets. Becoming a "fly on the wall," or wearing the invisibility ring of myth or folk tale; all kinds of disguise; the bugging of rooms and electronic surveillance from afar: these changes allow probing of secrets otherwise carefully guarded.

Smith's plan to express his views freely in his diary, seeks additional layers of secrecy. To the extent that it is possible to strip people of their capacity for secrecy about their intentions and their actions, their lives become more transparent and predictable; they can then the more easily be subjected to pressure and defeated.

Secrecy for plans is needed, not only to protect their formulation but also to develop them, perhaps to change them, at times to execute them, even to give them up. Imagine, for example, the pointlessness of the game of chess without secrecy on the part of the players. Secrecy guards projects that require creativity and prolonged work: the tentative and the fragile, unfinished tasks, probes and bargaining of all kinds. An elopement or a peace initiative may be foiled if prematurely suspected; a symphony, a scientific experiment, or an invention falters if exposed too soon. In speaking of creativity, Carlyle stressed the need for silence and secrecy, calling them "the element in which great things fashion themselves together."

Joint undertakings as well as personal ones may require secrecy for the sharing and working out of certain plans and for cooperative action. Lack of secrecy would, for instance, thwart many negotiations, in which all plans cannot easily be revealed from the outset. Once projects are safely under way, however, large portions of secrecy are often given up voluntarily, or dispelled with a flourish. Surprises are sprung and jokes explained. The result of the jury trial can be announced, the statue unveiled, the secretly negotiated treaty submitted for ratification, the desire to marry proclaimed. Here again, what is at issue is not secrecy alone, but rather the control over secrecy and openness. Many projects need both gestation and emergence, both confinement and publicity. Still others, such as certain fantasies and daydreams and hopes, may be too ephemeral or intimate, at times too discreditable, ever to see the light of day.

Secrecy about plans and their execution, therefore, allows unpredictability and surprise. These are often feared; yet without them human existence would not only be unfree but also monotonous and stifling. . . .

The fourth claim to control over secrecy concerns property. At its root, it is closely linked to identity, in that people take some secrets, such as hidden love letters, to *belong* to them more than to others, to be *proper to* them. We link such secrets with our identity, and resist intrusions into them. But the claim to own secrets about oneself is often far-fetched. Thus the school-bus driver who has a severe heart condition cannot rightfully claim to *own* this medical information, even though it concerns him intimately. Even when outsiders have less need to share the information than in such a case, the question who owns a secret may be hard to answer. Should one include only those "about whom" it is a secret, those who claim a right to decide whether or not to disclose it, or all who know it?

In addition to such questions of owning secrets, secrecy is invoked to protect what one owns. We take for granted the legitimacy of hiding silver from burglars and personal documents from snoopers and busybodies. Here, too, the link to identity is close, as is that to plans and their execution. For had we no belongings whatsoever, our identity and our capacity to plan would themselves be threatened, and in turn survival itself. . . .

The four claims to control over secrecy and openness to protect identity, plans, action, and property are not always persuasive. They may be stretched much too far, or abused in many ways. No matter how often these claims fail to convince, however, I shall assume that they do hold for certain fundamental human needs. Some capacity for keeping secrets and for choosing when to reveal them, and some access to the underlying experience of secrecy and depth, are indispensable for an enduring sense of identity, for the ability to plan and to act, and for essential belongings. With no control over secrecy and openness, human beings could not remain either sane or free.

The Dangers of Secrecy

Against every claim to secrecy stands, however, the awareness of its dangers. It is the experience of these dangers that has led so many to view secrecy negatively, and that underlies statements such as that by Lord Acton, that "every thing secret degenerates." Such categorical dismissals are too sweeping, but they do point to the harm that secrets can do both to those who keep them and to those from whom they are kept—harm that often thwarts and debilitates the very needs for which I have argued that control over secrecy is indispensable.

Secrecy can harm those who make use of it in several ways. It can debilitate judgment, first of all, whenever it shuts out criticism and feedback, leading people to become mired down in stereotyped, unexamined, often erroneous beliefs and ways of thinking. Neither their perception of a problem nor their reasoning about it then receives the benefit of challenge and exposure. Scientists working under conditions of intense secrecy have testified to its stifling effect on their judgment and creativity. And those who have written about their undercover work as journalists, police agents, and spies, or about living incognito for political reasons, have described similar effects of prolonged concealment on their capacity to plan and to choose, at times on their sense of identity.

Secrecy can affect character and moral choice in similar ways. It allows people to maintain façades that conceal traits such as callousness or vindictiveness—traits which can, in the absence of criticism or challenge from without, prove debilitating. And guilty or deeply embarrassing secrets can corrode from within before outsiders have a chance to respond or to be of help. This deterioration from within is the danger Acton referred to in his statement, and is at the root of the common view that secrecy, like other exercises of power, can corrupt.

These risks of secrecy multiply because of its tendency to spread. Aware of the importance of exercising control over secrecy and openness, people seek more control whenever they can, and rarely give up portions of it voluntarily. In imitation and in self-protection, others then seek more as well. The control shifts in the direction of secrecy whenever there is negligence or abuse to cover up; as a result, as Weber pointed out, bureaucracies and other organizations surround themselves with ever greater secrecy to the extent that circumstances permit.

As secrecy debilitates character and judgment, it can also lower resistance to the irrational and the pathological. It then poses great difficulties for individuals whose controls go awry. We know all the stifling rigidity that hampers those who become obsessed with secrecy. For them, secrecy no longer serves sanity and free choice. It shuts off the safety valve between the inner and the shared worlds. We know, too, the pathologies of prying into the private spheres of others, and of losing all protection for one's own: voyeurism and the corresponding hunger for self-exposure that destroy the capacity to discriminate and to choose.

The danger of secrecy, however, obviously goes far beyond risks to those who *keep* secrets. If they alone were at risk, we would have fewer reasons to try to learn about, and sometimes interfere with, their secret practices. Our attitude changes radically as soon as we suspect that these practices also hurt others. And because secrecy can debilitate judgment and choice, spread, and become obsessive, it often affects others even when it is not intended to. This helps explain why, in the absence of clear criteria for when secrecy is and is not injurious, many people have chosen to regard all secrecy as potentially harmful.

When the freedom of choice that secrecy gives one person limits or destroys that of others, it affects not only his own claims to respect for identity, plans, action, and property, but theirs. The power of such secrecy can be immense. Because it bypasses inspection and eludes interference, secrecy is central to the planning of every form of injury to human beings. It cloaks the execution of these plans and wipes out all traces afterward. It enters into all prying and intrusion that cannot be carried out openly. While not all that is secret is meant to deceive— as jury deliberations, for instance, are not—all deceit does rely on keeping something secret. And while not all secrets are discreditable, all that is discreditable and all wrongdoing seek out secrecy (unless they can be carried out openly without interference, as when they are pursued by coercive means).

Such secrecy can hamper the exercise of rational choice at every step: by preventing people from adequately understanding a threatening situation, from seeing the relevant alternatives clearly, from assessing the consequences of each, and from arriving at preferences with respect to them. Those who have been hurt in such a way by the secrecy of others may in turn seek greater control over secrecy, and thus in turn experience its impairment of choice, its tendency to spread, its capacity to corrupt and to invite abuse.

Moral Considerations

Given both the legitimacy of some control over secrecy and openness, and the dangers this control carries for all involved, there can be no presumption either for or against secrecy in general. Secrecy differs in this respect from lying, promise-breaking, violence, and other practices for which the burden of proof rests on those who would defend them. Conversely, secrecy differs from truthfulness, friendship, and other practices carrying a favorable presumption.

The resulting challenge for ethical inquiry into the aims and methods of secrecy is great. Not only must we reject definitions of secrecy that invite approval or disapproval; we cannot even begin with a moral presumption in either direction. This is not to say, however, that there can be none for particular practices, nor that these practices are usually morally neutral. But it means that it is especially important to look at them separately, and to examine the moral arguments made for and against each one.

. . .

. . . [S]ecrecy both promotes and endangers what we think beneficial, even necessary for survival. It may prevent harm, but it follows maleficence like a shadow. Every misdeed cloaks itself in secrecy unless accompanied by such power that it can be performed openly. And while secrecy may heighten a sense of equality and brotherhood among persons sharing the secret, it can fuel gross intolerance and hatred toward outsiders. At the heart of secrecy lies discrimination of some form, since its essence is sifting, setting apart, drawing lines. Secrecy, moreover, preserves liberty, yet this very liberty allows the invasion of that of others.

Chapter V

DUTY TO THE COURT

This chapter examines the advocate's special responsibilities to the court and how the legal norms governing the advocate differ from those governing the office lawyer. When a lawyer acts as an advocate rather than as a facilitator of transactions should she have different obligations when confronted with client fraud? Is there a difference in this respect between a criminal defense lawyer and a civil advocate?

A. A SUMMARY AND REVIEW OF THE LAWYER'S LIABILITY FOR FRAUD IN TRANSACTIONS NOT DIRECTLY CONNECTED TO COURT PROCEEDINGS

As demonstrated in Chapter 2, when acting as a facilitator of client transactions a lawyer who lies to a third party may be liable under civil or criminal law for fraud. A lawyer may "lie" by making a false statement with the intent to deceive (or to aid a client in deceiving) another; or by omitting material facts in circumstances where there is a duty to disclose those facts; or by failing to correct the false statements or material omissions of a client while acting in a transaction based on those statements or omissions. While a lawyer ordinarily is not guilty of *criminal* fraud unless she acted with the intent to deceive, acting with reckless disregard as to whether statements or omissions are false or misleading may be enough to satisfy the requirement of intent. See, e.g., *United States v. Benjamin* in Chapter 2 above. The lawyer who acts *recklessly* may also be liable for *civil* fraud. A lawyer may also be liable for negligent misrepresentation. See, e.g., *Greycas* in Chapter 2.

A lawyer who acts with indifference as to whether or not the client is committing fraud in a transaction, or as if incapable of discerning the truthfulness of the client's statements, therefore risks liability as an aider and abettor of the client's criminal and civil wrongs. The assertion that the lawyer must never be the judge of her client's cause is simply incorrect for out-of-court transactions.

B. PERJURY

Deliberate Corruption of Court Processes

A lawyer who deliberately corrupts court processes is subject to criminal prosecution and severe disciplinary sanctions. Advising another to testify falsely is a crime. United States v. Vesich, 724 F.2d 451 (5th Cir.1984) (lawyer convicted of obstruction of justice, 18 U.S.C. § 1503, for advising a client to testify falsely before a grand jury). The offense of subornation of perjury, see, e.g., 18 U.S.C. § 1621, requires that perjury actually have been committed, but a lawyer may be convicted of obstructing justice for advising a client or witness to lie even if perjury does not result. See United States v. Silverman, 745 F.2d 1386 n. 7 at 1394 (11th Cir.1984) (citing cases).

A lawyer may be held criminally liable for submitting false documents on behalf of a client. For example, in United States v. Lopez, 728 F.2d 1359 (11th Cir.1984) a lawyer was convicted under 18 U.S.C. § 1001 for falsifying the dates on his client's application for permanent resident status. See also United States v. Vaughn, 797 F.2d 1485 (9th Cir.1986). A lawyer may also be liable for conspiracy to suborn perjury or obstruct justice. See 18 U.S.C. § 371. Knowingly presenting false evidence or destroying or concealing evidence may be punished as contempt. See, e.g., United States v. Temple, 349 F.2d 116, 117 (4th Cir.1965) ("Lying to a judge is certainly misbehavior . . . and therefore punishable [as contempt].").

Monetary sanctions, including payment of the opposing side's attorneys' fees, may be imposed on lawyers who deliberately mislead the court or the opposing party. See Fed.R.Civ.P. 26 and 37 (governing discovery); Fed.R.Civ.P. 11 (lies or misstatements in papers filed with the court); 28 U.S.C. § 1927 (monetary sanctions against lawyers who unreasonably and vexatiously multiply the proceedings). See, e.g., Carlucci v. Piper Aircraft, 775 F.2d 1440 (11th Cir.1985) (discussing the applicability of Rule 37 and § 1927 to deliberate misconduct). [The provisions discussed in this paragraph also apply to negligent misstatements or negligent omissions of material information. See the notes following *Golden Eagle,* below.]

A court also has inherent power to award attorneys fees for "bad faith" or frivolous conduct of a case. See, e.g., *Carlucci,* supra, citing, inter alia, Roadway Express v. Piper, 447 U.S. 752, 765–67, 100 S.Ct. 2455, (1980).

Knowingly presenting or creating false evidence is also a violation of ethical rules. DR 7–102(A)(6), M.R. 3.4(a), M.R. 3.4(b) (creating false evidence); DR 7–102(A)(4), M.R. 3.3(a)(4) (using/offering false evidence). See also DR 7–102(A)(3), DR 7–109(A), M.R. 3.4(a) (concealing or failing to reveal evidence required to be revealed by law). See, e.g., In the Matter of Benson, 431 N.W.2d 120 (Minn.1988) (disbarment for, among other violations, alteration of documents and conspiracy to present perjured testimony); Louisiana State Bar Ass'n v. Stewart, 500 So.2d 360 (La.1987) ("The appropriate penalty for . . . suborning perjury is generally disbarment . . . ."); In re Sandground, 542 A.2d 1242 (D.C. App.1987) (assisting client to conceal information about funds in response to discovery requests); In the Matter of Ireland, 146 Ariz. 340, 706 P.2d 352 (1985) (misrepresenting client's assets to court and instructing client to testify falsely); Davis v. California, 33 Cal.3d 231, 188 Cal.Rptr. 441, 655 P.2d 1276 (1983) (wilful deception of the court).

However, the line between impermissible and permissible activity is not always clear. The metaphor of battle for the adversary concept of a trial suggests that the trial lawyer is not expected to act as a "civilian." A trial would not be a trial—at least not as we know it—if the parties were expected merely to disclose the truth rather than to contest it. But the trial lawyer is no more privileged to engage in fraud than a soldier is privileged to engage in torture. When does the advocate cross the line?

Client Perjury

If the lawyer has advised and encouraged her client to testify truthfully and the client still insists upon lying what should the lawyer do? The ethics rules require the lawyer to withdraw if necessary to avoid violating the rules or other law. DR 2–110(B)(2); M.R. 1.16(a)(1). Does withdrawal, assuming the trial has not begun and the court grants permission, end the problem?

What steps, if any, should the lawyer take before seeking to withdraw? What should the lawyer tell the court when asking permission to withdraw? Does it matter whether the case is civil or criminal? What should the lawyer do if the court denies permission to withdraw? Is it proper to seek withdrawal in the midst of a trial, if that is when the contemplated perjury is discovered? How certain should the lawyer be that the testimony will be perjurious before taking other action? What if the lawyer discovers the perjury after it has been offered?

NIX v. WHITESIDE

Supreme Court of the United States, 1986.
475 U.S. 157, 106 S.Ct. 988, 89 L.Ed.2d 123.

CHIEF JUSTICE BURGER delivered the opinion of the Court.

We granted certiorari to decide whether the Sixth Amendment right of a criminal defendant to assistance of counsel is violated when an attorney refuses to cooperate with the defendant in presenting perjured testimony at his trial.[1]

I

A

Whiteside was convicted of second degree murder by a jury verdict which was affirmed by the Iowa courts. The killing took place on February 8, 1977 in Cedar Rapids, Iowa. Whiteside and two others

---

1. Although courts universally condemn an attorney's assisting in presenting perjury, Courts of Appeals have taken varying approaches on how to deal with a client's insistence on presenting perjured testimony. The Seventh Circuit, for example, has held that an attorney's refusal to call the defendant as a witness did not render the conviction constitutionally infirm where the refusal to call the defendant was based on the attorney's belief that the defendant would commit perjury. United States v. Curtis, 742 F.2d 1070 (CA7 1984). The Third Circuit found a violation of the Sixth Amendment where the attorney could not state any basis for her belief that defendant's proposed alibi testimony was perjured. United States ex rel. Wilcox v. Johnson, 555 F.2d 115 (CA3 1977). See also Lowery v. Cardwell, 575 F.2d 727 (CA9 1978) (withdrawal request in the middle of a bench trial, immediately following defendant's testimony).

went to one Calvin Love's apartment late that night, seeking marihuana. Love was in bed when Whiteside and his companions arrived; an argument between Whiteside and Love over the marihuana ensued. At one point, Love directed his girlfriend to get his "piece," and at another point got up, then returned to his bed. According to Whiteside's testimony, Love then started to reach under his pillow and moved toward Whiteside. Whiteside stabbed Love in the chest, inflicting a fatal wound.

Whiteside was charged with murder, and when counsel was appointed he objected to the lawyer initially appointed, claiming that he felt uncomfortable with a lawyer who had formerly been a prosecutor. Gary L. Robinson was then appointed and immediately began investigation. Whiteside gave him a statement that he had stabbed Love as the latter "was pulling a pistol from underneath the pillow on the bed." Upon questioning by Robinson, however, Whiteside indicated that he had not actually seen a gun, but that he was convinced that Love had a gun. No pistol was found on the premises; shortly after the police search following the stabbing, which had revealed no weapon, the victim's family had removed all of the victim's possessions from the apartment. Robinson interviewed Whiteside's companions who were present during the stabbing and none had seen a gun during the incident. Robinson advised Whiteside that the existence of a gun was not necessary to establish the claim of self defense, and that only a reasonable belief that the victim had a gun nearby was necessary even though no gun was actually present.

Until shortly before trial, Whiteside consistently stated to Robinson that he had not actually seen a gun, but that he was convinced that Love had a gun in his hand. About a week before trial, during preparation for direct examination, Whiteside for the first time told Robinson and his associate Donna Paulsen that he had seen something "metallic" in Love's hand. When asked about this, Whiteside responded that

"in Howard Cook's case there was a gun. If I don't say I saw a gun I'm dead."

Robinson told Whiteside that such testimony would be perjury and repeated that it was not necessary to prove that a gun was available but only that Whiteside reasonably believed that he was in danger. On Whiteside's insisting that he would testify that he saw "something-metallic" Robinson told him, according to Robinson's testimony,

"we could not allow him to [testify falsely] because that would be perjury, and as officers of the court we would be suborning perjury if we allowed him to do it; . . . I advised him that if he did do that it would be my duty to advise the Court of what he was doing and that I felt he was committing perjury; also, that I probably would be allowed to attempt to impeach that particular testimony."

Robinson also indicated he would seek to withdraw from the representation if Whiteside insisted on committing perjury.[2]

Whiteside testified in his own defense at trial and stated that he "knew" that Love had a gun and that he believed Love was reaching for a gun and he had acted swiftly in self defense. On cross examination, he admitted that he had not actually seen a gun in Love's hand. Robinson presented evidence that Love had been seen with a sawed-off shotgun on other occasions, that the police search of the apartment may have been careless, and that the victim's family had removed everything from the apartment shortly after the crime. Robinson presented this evidence to show a basis for Whiteside's asserted fear that Love had a gun.

The jury returned a verdict of second-degree murder and Whiteside moved for a new trial, claiming that he had been deprived of a fair trial by Robinson's admonitions not to state that he saw a gun or "something metallic." The trial court held a hearing, heard testimony by Whiteside and Robinson, and denied the motion. The trial court made specific findings that the facts were as related by Robinson.

The Supreme Court of Iowa affirmed respondent's conviction. State v. Whiteside, 272 N.W.2d 468 (1978). That court held that the right to have counsel present all appropriate defenses does not extend to using perjury, and that an attorney's duty to a client does not extend to assisting a client in committing perjury. Relying on DR 7–102(A)(4) of the Iowa Code of Professional Responsibility for Lawyers, which expressly prohibits an attorney from using perjured testimony, and Iowa Code § 721.2 (now Iowa Code § 720.3 (1985)), which criminalizes subornation of perjury, the Iowa court concluded that not only were Robinson's actions permissible, but were required. The court commended "both Mr. Robinson and Ms. Paulsen for the high ethical manner in which this matter was handled."

B

Whiteside then petitioned for a writ of habeas corpus in the United States District Court for the Southern District of Iowa. In that petition Whiteside alleged that he had been denied effective assistance of counsel and of his right to present a defense by Robinson's refusal to allow him to testify as he had proposed. The District Court denied the writ. Accepting the State trial court's factual finding that Whiteside's intended testimony would have been perjurious, it concluded that there could be no grounds for habeas relief since there is no constitutional right to present a perjured defense.

2. Whiteside's version of the events at this pretrial meeting is considerably more cryptic:

"Q. And as you went over the questions, did the two of you come into conflict with regard to whether or not there was a weapon?

"A. I couldn't—I couldn't say a conflict. But I got the impression at one time that maybe if I didn't go along with—with what was happening, that it was no gun being involved, maybe that he will pull out of my trial."

The United States Court of Appeals for the Eighth Circuit reversed and directed that the writ of habeas corpus be granted. *Whiteside v. Scurr,* 744 F.2d 1323 (CA8 1984). The Court of Appeals accepted the findings of the trial judge, affirmed by the Iowa Supreme Court, that trial counsel believed with good cause that Whiteside would testify falsely and acknowledged that under *Harris v. New York,* 401 U.S. 222, 91 S.Ct. 643, 28 L.Ed.2d 1 (1971), a criminal defendant's privilege to testify in his own behalf does not include a right to commit perjury. Nevertheless, the court reasoned that an intent to commit perjury, communicated to counsel, does not alter a defendant's right to effective assistance of counsel and that Robinson's admonition to Whiteside that he would inform the court of Whiteside's perjury constituted a threat to violate the attorney's duty to preserve client confidences. According to the Court of Appeals, this threatened violation of client confidences breached the standards of effective representation set down in *Strickland v. Washington,* 466 U.S. 668, 104 S.Ct. 2052, 80 L.Ed.2d 674 (1984). The court also concluded that *Strickland*'s prejudice requirement was satisfied by an implication of prejudice from the conflict between Robinson's duty of loyalty to his client and his ethical duties. A petition for rehearing en banc was denied. . . . We granted certiorari . . . and we reverse.

II

A

The right of an accused to testify in his defense is of relatively recent origin. Until the latter part of the preceding century, criminal defendants in this country, as at common law, were considered to be disqualified from giving sworn testimony at their own trial by reason of their interest as a party to the case. . . .

By the end of the nineteenth century, however, the disqualification was finally abolished by statute in most states and in the federal courts. . . . Although this Court has never explicitly held that a criminal defendant has a due process right to testify in his own behalf, cases in several Circuits have so held and the right has long been assumed. . . .

B

In *Strickland v. Washington,* we held that to obtain relief by way of federal habeas corpus on a claim of a deprivation of effective assistance of counsel under the Sixth Amendment, the movant must establish both serious attorney error and prejudice. . . .

In *Strickland,* we acknowledged that the Sixth Amendment does not require any particular response by counsel to a problem that may arise. Rather, the Sixth Amendment inquiry is into whether the attorney's conduct was "reasonably effective." A court reviewing a claim of ineffective assistance must "indulge a strong presumption that counsel's conduct falls within the wide range of reasonable professional assistance." In giving shape to the perimeters of this range of reasonable professional assistance, *Strickland* mandates that

"Prevailing norms of practice as reflected in American Bar Association Standards and the like, . . . are guides to determining what is reasonable, but they are only guides."

Under the *Strickland* standard, breach of an ethical standard does not necessarily make out a denial of the Sixth Amendment guarantee of assistance of counsel. When examining attorney conduct, a court must be careful not to narrow the wide range of conduct acceptable under the Sixth Amendment so restrictively as to constitutionalize particular standards of professional conduct and thereby intrude into the State's proper authority to define and apply the standards of professional conduct applicable to those it admits to practice in its courts. In some future case challenging attorney conduct in the course of a state court trial, we may need to define with greater precision the weight to be given to recognized canons of ethics, the standards established by the State in statutes or professional codes, and the Sixth Amendment, in defining the proper scope and limits on that conduct. Here we need not face that question, since virtually all of the sources speak with one voice.

C

We turn next to the question presented: the definition of the range of "reasonable professional" responses to a criminal defendant client who informs counsel that he will perjure himself on the stand. We must determine whether, in this setting, Robinson's conduct fell within the wide range of professional responses to threatened client perjury acceptable under the Sixth Amendment.

In *Strickland,* we recognized counsel's duty of loyalty and his "overarching duty to advocate the defendant's cause," Plainly, that duty is limited to legitimate, lawful conduct compatible with the very nature of a trial as a search for truth. Although counsel must take all reasonable lawful means to attain the objectives of the client, counsel is precluded from taking steps or in any way assisting the client in presenting false evidence or otherwise violating the law. This principle has consistently been recognized in most unequivocal terms by expositors of the norms of professional conduct since the first Canons of Professional Ethics were adopted by the American Bar Association in 1908. The 1908 Canon 32 provided that

"No client, corporate or individual, however powerful, nor any cause, civil or political, however important, is entitled to receive nor should any lawyer render any service or advice involving disloyalty to the law whose ministers we are, or disrespect of the judicial office, which we are bound to uphold, or corruption of any person or persons exercising a public office or private trust, or deception or betrayal of the public. . . . He must . . . observe and advise his client to observe the statute law. . . ."

Of course, this Canon did no more than articulate centuries of accepted standards of conduct. Similarly, Canon 37, adopted in 1928, explicitly acknowledges as an exception to the attorney's duty of confidentiality a client's announced attention to commit a crime:

"The announced intention of a client to commit a crime is not included within the confidences which [the attorney] is bound to respect."

These principles have been carried through to contemporary codifications of an attorney's professional responsibility. Disciplinary Rule 7–102 of the Model Code of Professional Responsibility (1980), entitled "Representing a Client Within the Bounds of the Law," provides that

"(A) In his representation of a client, a lawyer shall not:

. . .

"(4) Knowingly use perjured testimony or false evidence.

. . .

"(7) Counsel or assist his client in conduct that the lawyer knows to be illegal or fraudulent."

This provision has been adopted by Iowa, and is binding on all lawyers who appear in its courts. See Iowa Code of Professional Responsibility for Lawyers (1985). The more recent Model Rules of Professional Conduct (1983) similarly admonish attorneys to obey all laws in the course of representing a client:

"*RULE 1.2* Scope of Representation

. . .

"(d) A lawyer shall not counsel a client to engage, or assist a client, in conduct that the lawyer knows is criminal or fraudulent. . . ."

Both the Model Code of Professional Conduct [sic] and the Model Rules of Professional Conduct also adopt the specific exception from the attorney-client privilege for disclosure of perjury that his client intends to commit or has committed. DR 4–101(C)(3) (intention of client to commit a crime); Rule 3.3 (lawyer has duty to disclose falsity of evidence even if disclosure compromises client confidences). Indeed, both the Model Code and the Model Rules do not merely *authorize* disclosure by counsel of client perjury; they *require* such disclosure. See Rule 3.3(a)(4); DR 7–102(B)(1); Committee on Professional Ethics and Conduct of Iowa State Bar Association v. Crary, 245 N.W.2d 298 (Iowa 1976).

These standards confirm that the legal profession has accepted that an attorney's ethical duty to advance the interests of his client is limited by an equally solemn duty to comply with the law and standards of professional conduct; it specifically ensures that the client may not use false evidence. This special duty of an attorney to prevent and disclose frauds upon the court derives from the recognition that perjury is as much a crime as tampering with witnesses or jurors by way of promises and threats, and undermines the administration of justice.

The offense of perjury was a crime recognized at common law, and has been made a felony in most states by statute, including Iowa. An attorney who aids false testimony by questioning a witness when perjurious responses can be anticipated, risks prosecution for subornation of perjury under Iowa Code § 720.3 (1985).

It is universally agreed that at a minimum the attorney's first duty when confronted with a proposal for perjurious testimony is to attempt to dissuade the client from the unlawful course of conduct. Model Rules of Professional Conduct, Rule 3.3, Comment; Wolfram, Client Perjury, 50 S.Cal.L.Rev. 809, 846 (1977). A statement directly in point is found in the Commentary to the Model Rules of Professional Conduct under the heading "False Evidence":

> "When false evidence is offered by the client, however, a conflict may arise between the lawyer's duty to keep the client's revelations confidential and the duty of candor to the court. Upon ascertaining that material evidence is false, the lawyer *should seek to persuade the client that the evidence should not be offered* or, if it has been offered, that its false character should immediately be disclosed." (emphasis added).

The Commentary thus also suggests that an attorney's revelation of his client's perjury to the court is a professionally responsible and acceptable response to the conduct of a client who has actually given perjured testimony. Similarly, the Model Rules and the commentary, as well as the Code of Professional Responsibility adopted in Iowa expressly permit withdrawal from representation as an appropriate response of an attorney when the client threatens to commit perjury. Model Rules of Professional Conduct, Rule 1.16(a)(1), Rule 1.6, Comment (1983); Code of Professional Responsibility, DR 2–110(B), (C) (1980). Withdrawal of counsel when this situation arises at trial gives rise to many difficult questions including possible mistrial and claims of double jeopardy.[6]

---

6. In the evolution of the contemporary standards promulgated by the American Bar Association, an early draft reflects a compromise suggesting that when the disclosure of intended perjury is made during the course of trial, when withdrawal of counsel would raise difficult questions of a mistrial holding, counsel had the option to let the defendant take the stand but decline to affirmatively assist the presentation of perjury by traditional direct examination. Instead, counsel would stand mute while the defendant undertook to present the false version in narrative form in his own words unaided by any direct examination. This conduct was thought to be a signal at least to the presiding judge that the attorney considered the testimony to be false and was seeking to disassociate himself from that course. Additionally, counsel would not be permitted to discuss the known false testimony in closing arguments. See ABA Standards for Criminal Justice, 4–7.7 (2d ed. 1980). Most courts treating the subject rejected this approach and insisted on a more rigorous standard, see, e.g., United States v. Curtis, 742 F.2d 1070 (CA7 1984); McKissick v. United States, 379 F.2d 754 (CA5 1967), aff'd after remand, 398 F.2d 342 (CA5 1968); Dodd v. Florida Bar, 118 So.2d 17, 19 (Fla.1960). The Eighth Circuit in this case and the Ninth Circuit have expressed approval of the "free narrative" standards. Whiteside v. Scurr, 744 F.2d 1323, 1331 (CA8 1984); Lowery v. Cardwell, 575 F.2d 727 (CA9 1978).

The essence of the brief *amicus* of the American Bar Association reviewing practices long accepted by ethical lawyers, is that under no circumstance may a lawyer either advocate or passively tolerate a client's giving false testimony. This, of course, is consistent with the governance of trial conduct in what we have long called "a search for truth." The suggestion sometimes made that "a lawyer must believe his client not judge him" in no sense means a lawyer can honorably be a party to or in any way give aid to presenting known perjury.

D

Considering Robinson's representation of respondent in light of these accepted norms of professional conduct, we discern no failure to adhere to reasonable professional standards that would in any sense make out a deprivation of the Sixth Amendment right to counsel. Whether Robinson's conduct is seen as a successful attempt to dissuade his client from committing the crime of perjury, or whether seen as a "threat" to withdraw from representation and disclose the illegal scheme, Robinson's representation of Whiteside falls well within accepted standards of professional conduct and the range of reasonable professional conduct acceptable under *Strickland*.

. . .

The Court of Appeals' holding that Robinson's "action deprived [Whiteside] of due process and effective assistance of counsel" is not supported by the record since Robinson's action, at most, deprived Whiteside of his contemplated perjury. Nothing counsel did in any way undermined Whiteside's claim that he believed the victim was reaching for a gun. Similarly, the record gives no support for holding that Robinson's action "also impermissibly compromised [Whiteside's] right to testify in his own defense by conditioning continued representation . . . and confidentiality upon [Whiteside's] *restricted* testimony." The record in fact shows the contrary: (a) that Whiteside did testify, and (b) he was "restricted" or restrained only from testifying falsely and was aided by Robinson in developing the basis for the fear that Love was reaching for a gun. Robinson divulged no client communications until he was compelled to do so in response to Whiteside's post-trial challenge to the quality of his performance. We see this as a case in which the attorney successfully dissuaded the client from committing the crime of perjury.

Paradoxically, even while accepting the conclusion of the Iowa trial court that Whiteside's proposed testimony would have been a criminal act, the Court of Appeals held that Robinson's efforts to persuade Whiteside not to commit that crime were improper, *first*, as forcing an impermissible choice between the right to counsel and the right to

The Rule finally promulgated in the current Model Rules of Professional Conduct rejects any participation or passive role whatever by counsel in allowing perjury to be presented without challenge.

testify; and *second,* as compromising client confidences because of Robinson's threat to disclose the contemplated perjury.

. . .

Whatever the scope of a constitutional right to testify, it is elementary that such a right does not extend to testifying *falsely.* In *Harris v. New York*, we assumed the right of an accused to testify "in his own defense, or to refuse to do so" and went on to hold that

"that privilege cannot be construed to include the right to commit perjury. See United States v. Knox, 396 U.S. 77 [90 S.Ct. 363, 24 L.Ed.2d 275] (1969); cf. Dennis v. United States, 384 U.S. 855 [86 S.Ct. 1840, 16 L.Ed.2d 973] (1966). Having voluntarily taken the stand, petitioner was under an obligation to speak truthfully. . . ." 401 U.S., at 225, 91 S.Ct., at 645.

In *Harris* we held the defendant could be impeached by prior contrary statements which had been ruled inadmissible under Miranda v. Arizona, 384 U.S. 436, 86 S.Ct. 1602, 16 L.Ed.2d 694 (1966). *Harris* and other cases make it crystal clear that there is no right whatever—constitutional or otherwise—for a defendant to use false evidence. See also United States v. Havens, 446 U.S. 620, 626–627, 100 S.Ct. 1912, 1916–1917, 64 L.Ed.2d 559 (1980).

The paucity of authority on the subject of any such "right" may be explained by the fact that such a notion has never been responsibly advanced; the right to counsel includes no right to have a lawyer who will cooperate with planned perjury. A lawyer who would so cooperate would be at risk of prosecution for suborning perjury, and disciplinary proceedings, including suspension or disbarment.

Robinson's admonitions to his client can in no sense be said to have forced respondent into an *impermissible* choice between his right to counsel and his right to testify as he proposed for there was no *permissible* choice to testify falsely. For defense counsel to take steps to persuade a criminal defendant to testify truthfully, or to withdraw, deprives the defendant of neither his right to counsel nor the right to testify truthfully. . . .

On this record, the accused enjoyed continued representation within the bounds of reasonable professional conduct and did in fact exercise his right to testify; at most he was denied the right to have the assistance of counsel in the presentation of false testimony. Similarly, we can discern no breach of professional duty in Robinson's admonition to respondent that he would disclose respondent's perjury to the court. The crime of perjury in this setting is indistinguishable in substance from the crime of threatening or tampering with a witness or a juror. A defendant who informed his counsel that he was arranging to bribe or threaten witnesses or members of the jury would have no "right" to insist on counsel's assistance or silence. Counsel would not be limited to advising against that conduct. An attorney's duty of confidentiality, which totally covers the client's admission of guilt, does not extend to a client's announced plans to engage in future criminal conduct. . . .

In short, the responsibility of an ethical lawyer, as an officer of the court and a key component of a system of justice, dedicated to a search for truth, is essentially the same whether the client announces an intention to bribe or threaten witnesses or jurors or to commit or procure perjury. No system of justice worthy of the name can tolerate a lesser standard.

The rule adopted by the Court of Appeals, which seemingly would require an attorney to remain silent while his client committed perjury, is wholly incompatible with the established standards of ethical conduct and the laws of Iowa and contrary to professional standards promulgated by that State. The position advocated by petitioner, on the contrary, is wholly consistent with the Iowa standards of professional conduct and law, with the overwhelming majority of courts,[8] and with codes of professional ethics. Since there has been no breach of any recognized professional duty, it follows that there can be no deprivation of the right to assistance of counsel under the *Strickland* standard.

E

We hold that, as a matter of law, counsel's conduct complained of here cannot establish the prejudice required for relief under the second strand of the *Strickland* inquiry. . . .

Whether he was persuaded or compelled to desist from perjury, Whiteside has no valid claim that confidence in the result of his trial has been diminished by his desisting from the contemplated perjury. Even if we were to assume that the jury might have believed his perjury, it does not follow that Whiteside was prejudiced.

In his attempt to evade the prejudice requirement of *Strickland,* Whiteside relies on cases involving conflicting loyalties of counsel. In Cuyler v. Sullivan, 446 U.S. 335, 100 S.Ct. 1708, 64 L.Ed.2d 333 (1980), we held that a defendant could obtain relief without pointing to a specific prejudicial default on the part of his counsel, provided it is established that the attorney was "actively represent[ing] conflicting interests."

Here, there was indeed a "conflict," but of a quite different kind; it was one imposed on the attorney by the client's proposal to commit the crime of fabricating testimony without which, as he put it, "I'm dead." This is not remotely the kind of conflict of interests dealt with in *Cuyler v. Sullivan.* Even in that case we did not suggest that all multiple representations necessarily resulted in an active conflict rendering the representation constitutionally infirm. If a "conflict" between a client's proposal and counsel's ethical obligation gives rise to a presump-

8. See United States v. Curtis, 742 F.2d 1070 (CA7 1984); Committee on Professional Ethics v. Crary, 245 N.W.2d 298 (Iowa 1976); State v. Robinson, 290 N.C. 56, 224 S.E.2d 174 (1976); Thornton v. United States, 357 A.2d 429 (D.C.1976); State v. Henderson, 205 Kan. 231, 468 P.2d 136 (1970); McKissick v. United States, 379 F.2d 754 (CA5 1967); In re King, 7 Utah 2d 258, 322 P.2d 1095 (1958); In re Carroll, 244 S.W.2d 474 (Ky.1951); Hinds v. State Bar, 19 Cal.2d 87, 119 P.2d 134 (1941). Contra, Whiteside v. Scurr, 744 F.2d 1323 (CA8 1984); Lowery v. Cardwell, 575 F.2d 727 (CA9 1978).

tion that counsel's assistance was prejudicially ineffective, every guilty criminal's conviction would be suspect if the defendant had sought to obtain an acquittal by illegal means. Can anyone doubt what practices and problems would be spawned by such a rule and what volumes of litigation it would generate?

Whiteside's attorney treated Whiteside's proposed perjury in accord with professional standards, and since Whiteside's truthful testimony could not have prejudiced the result of his trial, the Court of Appeals was in error to direct the issuance of a writ of habeas corpus and must be reversed.

Reversed.

JUSTICE BRENNAN, concurring in the judgment.

This Court has no constitutional authority to establish rules of ethical conduct for lawyers practicing in the state courts. Nor does the Court enjoy any statutory grant of jurisdiction over legal ethics.

Accordingly, it is not surprising that the Court emphasizes that it "must be careful not to narrow the wide range of professional conduct acceptable under the Sixth Amendment so restrictively as to constitutionalize particular standards of professional conduct and thereby intrude into the State's proper authority to define and apply the standards of professional conduct applicable to those it admits to practice in its courts." I read this as saying in another way that the Court *cannot* tell the states or the lawyers in the states how to behave in their courts, unless and until federal rights are violated.

Unfortunately, the Court seems unable to resist the temptation of sharing with the legal community its vision of ethical conduct. But let there be no mistake: the Court's essay regarding what constitutes the correct response to a criminal client's suggestion that he will perjure himself is pure discourse without force of law. As Justice Blackmun observes, *that* issue is a thorny one, but it is not an issue presented by this case. Lawyers, judges, bar associations, students and others should understand that the problem has not now been "decided."

I join Justice Blackmun's concurrence because I agree that respondent has failed to prove the kind of prejudice necessary to make out a claim under *Strickland*.

JUSTICE BLACKMUN, with whom JUSTICE BRENNAN, JUSTICE MARSHALL, and JUSTICE STEVENS join, concurring in the judgment.

How a defense attorney ought to act when faced with a client who intends to commit perjury at trial has long been a controversial issue.[1]

1. See, e.g., Callan and David, Professional Responsibility and the Duty of Confidentiality: Disclosure of Client Misconduct in an Adversary System, 29 Rutgers L.Rev. 332 (1976); Rieger, Client Perjury: A Proposed Resolution of the Constitutional and Ethical Issues, 70 Minn.L.Rev. 121 (1985); compare, e.g., Freedman, Professional Responsibility of the Criminal Defense Lawyer: The Three Hardest Questions, 64 Mich.L.Rev. 1469 (1966), and ABA Standards for Criminal Justice, Proposed Standard 4–7.7 (2d ed. 1980) (approved by the Standing Committing on Association Standards for Criminal Justice, but not yet submitted to the House of Delegates), with Noonan, The Purposes of Advocacy and the

But I do not believe that a federal habeas corpus case challenging a state criminal conviction is an appropriate vehicle for attempting to resolve this thorny problem. When a defendant argues that he was denied effective assistance of counsel because his lawyer dissuaded him from committing perjury, the only question properly presented to this Court is whether the lawyer's actions deprived the defendant of the fair trial which the Sixth Amendment is meant to guarantee. Since I believe that the respondent in this case suffered no injury justifying federal habeas relief, I concur in the Court's judgment.

. . .

B

The Court approaches this case as if the performance and prejudice standard requires us in every case to determine "the perimeters of [the] range of reasonable professional assistance," but *Strickland v. Washington* explicitly contemplates a different course:

> "Although we have discussed the performance component of an ineffectiveness claim prior to the prejudice component, there is no reason for a court deciding an ineffective assistance claim to approach the inquiry in the same order. . . . In particular, a court need not determine whether counsel's performance was deficient before examining the prejudice suffered by the defendant as a result of the alleged deficiencies. . . .

. . . In this case, respondent has failed to show any legally cognizable prejudice. Nor, as is discussed below, is this a case in which prejudice should be presumed.

The touchstone of a claim of prejudice is an allegation that counsel's behavior did something "to deprive the defendant of a fair trial, a trial whose result is reliable." *Strickland*. . . . The only effect Robinson's threat had on Whiteside's trial is that Whiteside did not testify, falsely, that he saw a gun in Love's hand.[4] Thus, this Court must ask whether its confidence in the outcome of Whiteside's trial is in any way undermined by the knowledge that he refrained from presenting false testimony.

This Court long ago noted: "All perjured relevant testimony is at war with justice, since it may produce a judgment not resting on truth. Therefore it cannot be denied that it tends to defeat the sole ultimate objective of a trial." In re Michael, 326 U.S. 224, 227, 66 S.Ct. 78, 79, 90 L.Ed. 30 (1945). When the Court has been faced with a claim by a defendant concerning prosecutorial use of such evidence, it has "consistently held that a conviction obtained by the knowing use of perjured

---

Limits of Confidentiality, 64 Mich.L.Rev. 1485 (1966), and ABA Model Rules of Professional Conduct, Rule 3.3 and comment, at 66–67 (1983).

4. This is not to say that a lawyer's threat to reveal his client's confidences may never have other effects on a defendant's trial. Cf. United States ex rel. Wilcox v. Johnson, 555 F.2d 115 (CA3 1977) (finding a violation of Sixth Amendment when an attorney's threat to reveal client's purported perjury caused defendant not to take the stand at all).

testimony is fundamentally unfair, and must be set aside if there is any reasonable likelihood that the false testimony could have affected the judgment of the jury" (footnote omitted). United States v. Agurs, 427 U.S. 97, 103, 96 S.Ct. 2392, 2397, 49 L.Ed.2d 342 (1976). See also, e.g., Napue v. Illinois, 360 U.S. 264, 269, 79 S.Ct. 1173, 1177, 3 L.Ed.2d 1217 (1959); Pyle v. Kansas, 317 U.S. 213, 216, 63 S.Ct. 177, 178, 87 L.Ed. 214 (1942); Mooney v. Holohan, 294 U.S. 103, 112, 55 S.Ct. 340, 341, 79 L.Ed. 791 (1935). Similarly, the Court has viewed a defendant's use of such testimony as so antithetical to our system of justice that it has permitted the prosecution to introduce otherwise inadmissible evidence to combat it. [citations omitted]. The proposition that presenting false evidence could contribute to (or that withholding such evidence could detract from) the reliability of a criminal trial is simply untenable.

It is no doubt true that juries sometimes have acquitted defendants who should have been convicted, and sometimes have based their decisions to acquit on the testimony of defendants who lied on the witness stand. It is also true that the Double Jeopardy Clause bars the reprosecution of such acquitted defendants, although on occasion they can be prosecuted for perjury. See, e.g., United States v. Williams, 341 U.S. 58, 63–65, 71 S.Ct. 595, 598–599, 95 L.Ed. 747 (1951). But the privilege every criminal defendant has to testify in his own defense "cannot be construed to include the right to commit perjury." Harris v. New York, 401 U.S., at 225, 91 S.Ct., at 645. To the extent that Whiteside's claim rests on the assertion that he would have been acquitted had he been able to testify falsely, Whiteside claims a right the law simply does not recognize. "A defendant has no entitlement to the luck of a lawless decisionmaker, even if a lawless decision cannot be reviewed." *Strickland*. . . . Since Whiteside was deprived of neither a fair trial nor any of the specific constitutional rights designed to guarantee a fair trial, he has suffered no prejudice.

The Court of Appeals erred in concluding that prejudice should have been presumed. *Strickland v. Washington* found such a presumption appropriate in a case where an attorney labored under " 'an actual conflict of interest [that] adversely affected his . . . performance,' " . . . . In this case, however, no actual conflict existed. I have already discussed why Whiteside had no right to Robinson's help in presenting perjured testimony. Moreover, Whiteside has identified no right to insist that Robinson keep confidential a plan to commit perjury. . . . Here, Whiteside had no legitimate interest that conflicted with Robinson's obligations not to suborn perjury and to adhere to the Iowa Code of Professional Responsibility.

In addition, the lawyer's interest in not presenting perjured testimony was entirely consistent with Whiteside's best interest. If Whiteside had lied on the stand, he would have risked a future perjury prosecution. Moreover, his testimony would have been contradicted by the testimony of other eyewitnesses and by the fact that no gun was ever found. In light of that impeachment, the jury might have concluded that Whiteside lied as well about his lack of premeditation and thus might have convicted him of first-degree murder. And if the judge believed that Whiteside had lied, he could have taken Whiteside's perjury into account in setting the sentence. United States v. Grayson, 438 U.S. 41, 52–54, 98 S.Ct. 2610, 2616–2618, 57 L.Ed.2d 582 (1978). In the face of these dangers, an attorney could reasonably conclude that dissuading his client from committing perjury was in the client's best interest and comported with standards of professional responsibility.[7] In short, Whiteside failed to show the kind of conflict that poses a danger to the values of zealous and loyal representation embodied in the Sixth Amendment. A presumption of prejudice is therefore unwarranted.

C

In light of respondent's failure to show any cognizable prejudice, I see no need to "grade counsel's performance." *Strickland*. . . . The only federal issue in this case is whether Robinson's behavior deprived Whiteside of the effective assistance of counsel; it is not whether Robinson's behavior conformed to any particular code of legal ethics.

Whether an attorney's response to what he sees as a client's plan to commit perjury violates a defendant's Sixth Amendment rights may depend on many factors: how certain the attorney is that the proposed testimony is false, the stage of the proceedings at which the attorney discovers the plan, or the ways in which the attorney may be able to dissuade his client, to name just three. The complex interaction of factors, which is likely to vary from case to case, makes inappropriate a blanket rule that defense attorneys must reveal, or threaten to reveal, a client's anticipated perjury to the court. Except in the rarest of cases, attorneys who adopt "the role of the judge or jury to determine the facts," United States ex rel. Wilcox v. Johnson, 555 F.2d 115, 122 (CA3 1977), pose a danger of depriving their clients of the zealous and loyal advocacy required by the Sixth Amendment.[8]

I therefore am troubled by the Court's implicit adoption of a set of standards of professional responsibility for attorneys in state crim-

---

7. This is not to say that an attorney's ethical obligations will never conflict with a defendant's right to effective assistance. For example, an attorney who has previously represented one of the State's witnesses has a continuing obligation to that former client not to reveal confidential information received during the course of the prior representation. That continuing duty could conflict with his obligation to his present client, the defendant, to cross-examine the State's witnesses zealously. See Lowenthal, Successive Representation by Criminal Lawyers, 93 Yale L.J. 1 (1983).

8. A comparison of this case with *Wilcox* is illustrative. Here, Robinson testified in detail to the factors that led him to conclude that respondent's assertion he had seen a gun was false. The Iowa Supreme Court found "good cause" and "strong support" for Robinson's conclusion. State v. Whiteside, 272 N.W.2d at 471. Moreover, Robinson gave credence to those parts of Whiteside's account which, although he found them implausible and unsubstantiated, were not clearly false. By contrast, in *Wilcox*, where defense counsel actually informed the judge that she believed her client intended to lie and where her threat to withdraw in the middle of the trial led the defendant not to take the stand at all, the Court of Appeals found "no evidence on the record of this case indicating that Mr. Wilcox intended to perjure himself," and characterized counsel's beliefs as "private conjectures about the guilt or innocence of [her] client." 522 F.2d at 122.

inal proceedings. The States, of course, do have a compelling interest in the integrity of their criminal trials that can justify regulating
the length to which an attorney may go in seeking his client's
acquittal. But the American Bar Association's implicit suggestion in
its brief *amicus curiae* that the Court find that the Association's
Model Rules of Professional Conduct should govern an attorney's
responsibilities is addressed to the wrong audience. It is for the
States to decide how attorneys should conduct themselves in state
criminal proceedings, and this Court's responsibility extends only to
ensuring that the restrictions a State enacts do not infringe a defendant's federal constitutional rights. Thus, I would follow the suggestion made in the joint brief *amici curiae* filed by 37 States at the
certiorari stage that we allow the States to maintain their "differing
approaches" to a complex ethical question. The signal merit of
asking first whether a defendant has shown any adverse prejudicial
effect before inquiring into his attorney's performance is that it
avoids unnecessary federal interference in a State's regulation of its
bar. Because I conclude that the respondent in this case failed to
show such an effect, I join the Court's judgment that he is not
entitled to federal habeas relief.

JUSTICE STEVENS, concurring in the judgment.

Justice Holmes taught us that a word is but the skin of a living
thought. A "fact" may also have a life of its own. From the perspective of an appellate judge, after a case has been tried and the evidence
has been sifted by another judge, a particular fact may be as clear and
certain as a piece of crystal or a small diamond. A trial lawyer,
however, must often deal with mixtures of sand and clay. Even a
pebble that seems clear enough at first glance may take on a different
hue in a handful of gravel.

As we view this case, it appears perfectly clear that respondent
intended to commit perjury, that his lawyer knew it, and that the
lawyer had a duty—both to the court and to his client, for perjured
testimony can ruin an otherwise meritorious case—to take extreme
measures to prevent the perjury from occurring. The lawyer was
successful and, from our unanimous and remote perspective, it is now
pellucidly clear that the client suffered no "legally cognizable
prejudice."

Nevertheless, beneath the surface of this case there are areas of
uncertainty that cannot be resolved today. A lawyer's certainty that a
change in his client's recollection is a harbinger of intended perjury—as
well as judicial review of such apparent certainty—should be tempered
by the realization that, after reflection, the most honest witness may
recall (or sincerely believe he recalls) details that he previously overlooked. Similarly, the post-trial review of a lawyer's pre-trial threat to
expose perjury that had not yet been committed—and, indeed, may
have been prevented by the threat—is by no means the same as review
of the way in which such a threat may actually have been carried out.

Thus, one can be convinced—as I am—that this lawyer's actions were a proper way to provide his client with effective representation without confronting the much more difficult questions of what a lawyer must, should, or may do after his client has given testimony that the lawyer does not believe. The answer to such questions may well be colored by the particular circumstances attending the actual event and its aftermath.

Because Justice Blackmun has preserved such questions for another day, and because I do not understand him to imply any adverse criticism of this lawyer's representation of his client, I join his opinion concurring in the judgment.

Questions *Whiteside* Did Not Resolve

Although there were questions from the bench in *Whiteside* on how a lawyer is to "know" that the client intends to commit perjury, the opinions did not resolve the question of how certain a lawyer must be before acting on her judgment that the client will perjure herself. See Freedman, Client Confidences and Client Perjury: Some Unanswered Questions, 136 U.Pa.L. Rev. 1939 (1988); and Appel, The Limited Impact of *Nix v. Whiteside* on Attorney–Client Relations, 136 U.Pa.L.Rev. 1913 (1988) (both describing the oral argument in *Whiteside*). The court in *Doe,* the next principal case, addresses this issue and we leave our exploration of when a lawyer "knows" that the client will commit perjury to the notes following *Doe.* For those of you who wish to consider this issue now, see the questions on pp. 357–358 below on how Robinson knew Whiteside's story was a lie, and the notes on pp. 359–361.

Whiteside itself does not say what a lawyer *must* do when faced with client perjury in a criminal case. It merely states what a lawyer may do, in conformity with the state's ethical standards, without unconstitutionally violating the defendant's rights. What action by the lawyer would run afoul of the defendant's constitutional rights?

Dealing With Perjurious Testimony Discovered During a Criminal Trial

In *Whiteside,* all steps occurred before the trial itself and within the attorney-client relationship (no third party was informed of the client's plans). If the client had continued to insist on testifying that he saw a gun or metallic object, what should the lawyer have done?

Prior to *Whiteside,* two decisions United States ex rel. Wilcox v. Johnson, 555 F.2d 115 (3d Cir.1977), and Lowery v. Cardwell, 575 F.2d 727 (9th Cir.1978), suggested that any action to prevent client perjury by a criminal defense lawyer, apart from confidentially trying to persuade the defendant to testify truthfully, would violate the defendant's constitutional rights.

In *Wilcox* the lawyer believed that the defendant's proposed alibi testimony would be perjurious. She told the client she did not want to put him on the stand, but he insisted. The lawyer informed the trial judge in a side bar conference that her client insisted on testifying over her objection and that, if the judge permitted, she would make a motion to withdraw based on her belief that the testimony would be perjury and her obligation not to present false evidence. The court ruled that if the client insisted on testifying, he would permit counsel to withdraw and the defendant would have to proceed without counsel for the remainder of the trial. The defendant then agreed not to testify. The Third Circuit held that the trial judge's ruling, threatening a loss of counsel, violated the defendant's right to counsel and his right to testify. The lawyer's behavior was criticized on two grounds. First, the lawyer requested to withdraw only if the defendant insisted on testifying. If there was an obligation to withdraw because of suspected future perjury, it applied whether or not the defendant continued to insist on testifying. Second, without a "firm factual basis" for her belief that the client intended to perjure himself, it was improper to disclose the intended perjury to the court.

The Third Circuit did not say whether the lawyer's seeking to withdraw is tantamount to informing the court of the lawyer's suspicions. Is it? May defense counsel in a criminal case seek to withdraw (or threaten to withdraw) only upon a "firm factual basis" for her belief that the client will commit perjury? See M.R. 1.16(a) requiring withdrawal if a violation of the rules *will* result; and M.R. 1.16(b)(1) permitting withdrawal if the lawyer *reasonably believes* the client's proposed course of action is criminal or fraudulent. Also see M.R. 3.3(a)(4), prohibiting the lawyer from offering evidence she *knows* to be false; and M.R. 3.3(c) giving the lawyer discretion to refuse to offer evidence she *reasonably believes* to be false.

In *Lowery v. Cardwell*, during his client's testimony the defense lawyer was surprised by what he was convinced was perjury. The case was being tried to a judge without a jury. The lawyer immediately requested permission to withdraw. The lawyer offered no reason for his request and the judge sought none, but refused the request. The Ninth Circuit held that the lawyer's motion to withdraw was tantamount to an announcement to the judge that his client had lied and thereby deprived the client of a fair trial. The court suggested that the lawyer could fulfill his obligation not to offer false evidence by letting the defendant testify in a narrative style without questioning from counsel.

> While a knowledgeable judge or juror, alert to the ethical problems faced by attorneys . . . might infer perjury from [this procedure], counsel's belief [that the testimony was perjury] would not appear in the clear and unequivocal manner presented by the facts here. . . .
>
> The distinction we draw is between a passive refusal to lend aid to perjury and such direct action as we find here—the addressing of the court in pursuit of court order granting leave to withdraw.

Lowery, 575 F.2d at 731.

Is this a realistic distinction?

Whiteside suggests that disclosure to the court in some circumstances is appropriate, but in that case the court was not the factfinder. Compare Butler v. United States, 414 A.2d 844 (D.C.App.1980) (recusal of judge required where trial judge, sitting as trier of fact, learns from defense counsel that defendant plans to commit perjury).

The Narrative Approach

The narrative solution endorsed in *Lowery* was proposed by the ABA's Criminal Justice Section in its draft of the ABA Standards of Criminal Justice. Defense Function Standard 4–7.7 provides that a defense lawyer should attempt to persuade the defendant to testify truthfully; if this attempt fails, the lawyer should seek to withdraw where feasible; if this fails, the lawyer should have the defendant tell her story in a narrative without further questioning (assistance) by counsel. Before the defendant takes the stand, the lawyer should make a private record of the fact that the defendant is taking the stand against the lawyer's advice, presumably including a statement of why this advice was given. The lawyer may not argue the defendant's false version of the facts to the jury. Standard 4–7.7 was omitted from the second edition of the Standards in 1979. The "narrative" solution was rejected by the Model Rules, as explained in the Comment to M.R. 3.3. But see the D.C. Bar's version of M.R. 3.3, which is similar to 4–7.7. What are the virtues of the narrative approach? The problems?

The narrative approach has received some endorsement from the Supreme Court of California, which held that, at least where ordered by the judge, it was neither inconsistent with the defendant's rights nor apparently a violation of the lawyer's duty to refrain from offering false evidence. People v. Guzman, 45 Cal.3d 915, 755 P.2d 917 (1988). Accord: State v. Fosnight, 235 Kan. 52, 679 P.2d 174 (1984); Coleman v. State, 621 P.2d 869 (Alaska 1980). Cf. ABA Formal Op. 353 (1988), specifically rejecting the approach of 4–7.7 and stating: "[T]he lawyer can no longer rely on the narrative approach to insulate the lawyer from a charge of assisting the client's perjury."

In *Guzman,* supra, prior to the defendant's testimony defense counsel informed the court, outside the jury's presence, that the defendant would testify against his advice and would use the narrative approach. The court advised the defendant to follow the lawyer's advice and not testify, and that the rules of evidence would apply and the defendant was ill-equipped to handle objections. The defendant insisted and did testify in narrative format. In closing argument, the defendant's lead counsel made no mention of this testimony, although second counsel did refer to it. The court found no violation of defendant's constitutional rights.

After *Whiteside,* the Supreme Court in Rock v. Arkansas, 483 U.S. 44, 107 S.Ct. 2704 (1987) recognized the constitutional right of a criminal defendant to testify, but noted that this does not include the right to testify falsely, as *Whiteside* makes clear. Given the defendant's right to testify, what else can the trial court do, when informed by the defense counsel that she believes the defendant will lie, except let the defendant testify after proper warnings? The only question then would be whether the court should permit a narrative statement or order defense counsel to question the witness in the regular fashion. See United States v. Henkel, 799 F.2d 369 (7th Cir.1986) (lawyer moved to withdraw just before defendant's testimony; trial judge correctly understood this to mean counsel believed the defendant would commit perjury; the court offered the defendant the chance to testify through a narrative statement without assistance of counsel, which the client declined; held: no violation of defendant's rights because no right to have counsel's assistance to testify falsely).

The Duty to Remonstrate with the Client Before Taking Other Action

When a client proposes perjury, the lawyer should point out the dangers of being prosecuted for perjury. In a criminal case, the lawyer should also point out the defendant's sentence may be increased if the court believes the defendant has perjured herself. See United States v. Grayson, 438 U.S. 41, 98 S.Ct. 2610 (1978) (legitimate sentencing consideration as it bears on the likelihood of the defendant being rehabilitated). When the lawyer discovers that the testimony was perjurious only after it has been offered, the lawyer should point out that recantation is a defense to perjury. To make out a complete defense of recantation, however, the recantation must be (1) made before the prior false testimony has substantially affected the relevant proceeding, and (2) made before it has become manifest that the falsity of the prior testimony will be exposed. See, e.g., United States v. Scivola, 766 F.2d 37 (1st Cir.1985). Also see the note on *United States v. Long,* below at p. 359, which describes the court's discussion of the duty to remonstrate.

Other Case Law

In *Wilcox* and *Lowery,* the lawyer was at least initially unsuccessful in convincing the client not to testify falsely and some form of disclosure to the judge ensued. On the other hand, when the client accedes to the lawyer's decision, the courts have had little difficulty rejecting claims of interference with the right to counsel or to testify. For example, in United States v. Rantz, 862 F.2d 808 (10th Cir.1988), cert. denied, 109 S.Ct. 1554 (1989), the court found that the lawyer's belief that the testimony would be false and ultimately detrimental to the defense was an adequate basis for the lawyer's refusal to call the defendant. The lawyer's belief was based on the overwhelming evidence offered by the prosecution, showing that the defendant was the initiator of the conspiracy. See also Williams v. Kemp, 846 F.2d 1276 (11th Cir.1988); and Commonwealth v. Blystone, 519 Pa. 450, 549 A.2d 81 (1988), aff'd on other grounds, 110 S.Ct. 1078 (1990); State v. Fleck, 49 Wash.App. 584, 744 P.2d 628 (1987).

If the lawyer is obligated not to present false testimony, is the defendant denied effective assistance of counsel when the lawyer presents a defense based on perjury? In North Dakota v. Skjonsby, 417 N.W.2d 818 (N.D.1987), the defendant claimed that he was denied effective assistance of counsel because his trial lawyer *failed* to stop him from offering a perjurious defense. The defendant had told significantly different versions of his story at various points, as had the witness who corroborated the defendant's fabricated story at trial. The court held that the evidence available to the trial lawyer was not sufficient to find that he knew or should have known that the fabricated defense was a lie. See also People v. Avery, 129 A.D.2d 852, 513 N.Y.S.2d 883, 887 (1987) ("Having knowingly and willingly participated in an attempt to obstruct justice through perjured testimony, he is not in a position to ask this court to undo the consequences of his own conscious wrongdoing on the ground that he was encouraged in this attempt by his defense attorney.") But see State v. Lee, 142 Ariz. 210, 689 P.2d 153 (1984): After being unable to convince his client not to rely on perjurious witnesses, the lawyer acceded to the clients' demand that they be called. The lawyer had them testify by narrative statement. After their testimony the lawyer told the judge in chambers why he had called the witnesses and that he believed they had perjured themselves. He also told the judge that he might waive closing argument because he did not know if he could "get up in front of the jury and make an argument based on what I am positive in my own mind is perjured testimony." He did not make a closing argument. The Arizona Supreme Court held that the calling of perjurious witnesses' on the client's demand fell below the standard of minimally competent representation.

The Government's Use of Perjured Testimony to Obtain a Conviction

If the government knowingly uses perjured testimony to secure a conviction, the defendant is entitled to a new trial if "the false testimony could . . . in any reasonable likelihood have affected the judgment of the jury. . . ." Giglio v. United States, 405 U.S. 150, 154 (1972) (quoting Napue v. Illinois, 360 U.S. 264, 271 (1959)). Also see Avery v. Procunier, 750 F.2d 444 (5th Cir.1985); United States v. Jones, 730 F.2d 593 (10th Cir.1984).

Sanders v. Sullivan, 863 F.2d 218 (2d Cir.1988), held that the government's *unwitting* use of perjured testimony violates due process if truthful testimony would "most likely change the outcome of the trial."

In Re GRIEVANCE COMMITTEE OF THE UNITED STATES DISTRICT COURT, DISTRICT OF CONNECTICUT

JOHN DOE, ESQUIRE v. THE FEDERAL GRIEVANCE COMMITTEE

United States Court of Appeals, Second Circuit, 1988.
847 F.2d 57.

Before VAN GRAAFEILAND, WINTER and ALTIMARI, CIRCUIT JUDGES.

ALTIMARI, CIRCUIT JUDGE:

Appellant John Doe, an attorney . . . appeals from an order of
the United States District Court for the District of Connecticut . . .
which suspended Doe from practicing before any court in the District
for a period of six months after finding that Doe violated Disciplinary
Rule 7–102(B)(2) of the Code of Professional Responsibility (the "Code").
The district court's conclusion, that Doe violated the Code, was based
upon evidence that Doe suspected that a witness lied at a deposition
and Doe did not disclose the witness's alleged perjury to the court.
Because we conclude that Doe lacked information clearly establishing
the existence of a fraud on the court, we reverse.

FACTS and BACKGROUND

The conduct which formed the basis for the district court's disciplinary decision arose during the discovery phase of an action pending
before Judge Zampano in the District of Connecticut. On two occasions, Doe had conversations with his client, the plaintiff in the underlying action ("client"), concerning possible perjury by a deposition
witness and subornation of perjury by attorneys representing the defendant. These conversations occurred immediately before and some time
after the witness, who was an employee of defendant, testified at a
deposition taken by Doe. During the first conversation between Doe
and client ("conversation one") which occurred just prior to the deposition, client related to Doe a conversation client had with the deposition
witness. According to client, the witness told him that defendant's
attorneys had instructed him "to change his story when responding to
certain questions at (his) deposition." A few months after the deposition, Doe had a subsequent conversation with client ("conversation
two") where client related another conversation he engaged in with
witness. During this second conversation, witness told client that he
had "followed the instructions (of defendant's attorneys) and had lied in
response to (those) questions (at the deposition)." Witness also told
client that he nevertheless would testify truthfully at trial.

Approximately one year after witness's deposition, the substance of
Doe's conversations with client was brought to the attention of Judge
Zampano. After this information was received, Judge Zampano indicated to the parties that he would hold a hearing to investigate possible
misconduct during discovery in the action in connection with the Doe/

client conversations as well as other matters.[2] Pending resolution of the misconduct allegations, Judge Zampano stayed further proceedings in the underlying action. On December 18, 1984, a closed hearing was held during which client, witness and Doe testified. Client testified that he did in fact have two conversations with witness (as summarized above) and that he had reported those conversations to Doe during conversations one and two. Witness's testimony at the hearing completely contradicted client's. He stated that he never had any conversations with client regarding his deposition testimony. He also denied that he had been instructed to lie or had in fact lied at his deposition.

Finally, Doe testified at the hearing that client related his conversations with witness (in substantially the manner set forth above) and that he believed that client had those conversations with witness. With respect to the first conversation, Doe explained, however, that he gave little credence to witness's suggestion that defendant's attorneys had instructed him to lie at the deposition, primarily because he doubted that defendant's attorneys would engage in subornation of perjury and also because he felt that witness's statements to client reflected nothing more than a "layperson's [mis]interpretation of deposition preparation." With respect to conversation two, Doe stated that he had personally suspected that witness had not told the truth at his deposition, but he explained that it did not occur to him that he had an ethical obligation to report to the court this information. In fact, he believed just the opposite. Doe thought that he was ethically obligated *not to reveal* the information since it constituted privileged client confidences and/or secrets. Doe explained, however, that he would disclose the information regarding witness's possible perjury at trial, presumably to impeach witness's testimony.

Judge Zampano subsequently issued an opinion in September 1985 in which he found, *inter alia,* that, as between client and witness, "one of the two is a perjurer." Judge Zampano concluded, however, that "the special hearing was not the appropriate forum in which to resolve the conflict." Rather, he decided that "[j]udgment on the credibility of these witnesses must be left to the usual and customary processes available to test the truthfulness of individuals' pretrial and trial statements given under oath." Thus, Judge Zampano left the question of whether perjury has been committed and by whom for determination at trial.

2. Apparently during discovery, plaintiff had access to confidential documents of defendants. Suspecting that someone in their organization was turning over these confidential documents to plaintiff, defendant sought to discover the identity of the "mole" in their organization. Defendant's investigation was carried on to such a point that even Doe and client were questioned during their depositions regarding their knowledge concerning the existence of the mole. Both denied having knowledge of the mole's existence and stated that they had not engaged in conversations with defendant's employees outside the course of ordinary business. With this information also available to Judge Zampano, he decided to investigate possible misconduct regarding the plaintiff's use of defendant's confidential documents and whether Doe and client answered truthfully at their depositions when asked about the identity of the mole. None of these allegations of misconduct, however, is the subject of this appeal.

Despite the fact that Judge Zampano decided that the special hearing was not the "appropriate forum" for determining whether witness, or client, had engaged in perjury, he nevertheless ordered that questions regarding Doe's involvement in this matter be referred to a Grievance Committee for an investigation and recommendation as to appropriate action concerning possible ethical misconduct. Judge Zampano observed that Doe may have violated his duty under DR 7–102(B)(2) when he did not disclose to the court the information he possessed concerning witness's potential perjury and defendant's attorneys' alleged subornation of perjury.

In January 1986, a hearing was held before the Grievance Committee which was comprised of practitioners from the District of Connecticut. According to the reference from Judge Zampano, the Grievance Committee was to determine whether Doe violated DR 7–102(B)(2). Thus, the Committee necessarily had to determine whether Doe had "information clearly establishing . . . a fraud on the tribunal" as a result of 1) his conversations with client and 2) his own independent information regarding evidence in the underlying action. The Grievance Committee also had to determine whether, since most of the information Doe had concerning witness's alleged perjury came from client, Doe was obligated under the Code *not* to reveal that information since it constituted privileged client confidences and/or secrets. See DR 4–101(B).

During Doe's testimony before the Grievance Committee, he again explained that, after he had conversation one with client, he doubted that any wrongdoing had occurred. He stated, however, that after conversation two (which occurred after Doe had taken witness's deposition), he believed that witness had lied at the deposition. Doe explained, however, that the basis for this belief did not originate from his conversations with client, but rather was the product of his own independent conclusions drawn from his knowledge of the case:

> Well, it didn't really relate to the message that (client) related to me. I mean, as I was taking (witness's) deposition, based on other evidence in the case, either documents or testimony of dealers or (defendant's other) witnesses, there were inconsistencies. There were situations in which there was evidence that (witness) was involved in something which he was denying that he was involved—a meeting or a course of action in which (others) had testified or other (defendant's) employees testified that he was involved in which he was either not recalling or denying. So, I didn't think he was telling the truth.

Doe also stated that he felt that most of defendant's other witnesses were not telling the truth during discovery.

Also testifying before the Grievance Committee was an ethics professor from New York University. In relevant part, the professor explained that an attorney's duty to maintain his client's confidences and secrets under DR 4–101(B) overrides his obligation under DR 7–102(B) to reveal information regarding a potential fraud on the court. The professor testified further that, in order to trigger an attorney's obligation under DR 7–102(B) to disclose "information clearly establishing . . . a fraud on the tribunal," he must have actual knowledge of the alleged fraud. Finally, the professor opined that nothing in the present record would have triggered Doe's duty to disclose the information regarding the potential perjury or subornation of perjury since he lacked actual knowledge.

In an opinion issued on July 2, 1986, the Grievance Committee recommended that no disciplinary action be taken against Doe and that the complaint lodged against him be dismissed. In pertinent part, the Grievance Committee concluded, first, that

> (b)ecause (Doe's) knowledge of the alleged subornation of perjury by (defendant's attorneys) and his knowledge of (witness's) alleged deposition perjury were based upon client confidences clearly protected from disclosure by the attorney-client privilege and, therefore, by DR 4–101(B), he had no ethical obligation under DR 7–102(B)(2) or any other disciplinary rule to reveal these alleged frauds to . . . Judge Zampano(,)

and, second, that

> (e)ven if Conversations One and Two do not fall with (sic) the attorney-client privilege, (Doe) had no obligation under DR 7–102(B)(2) to reveal either conversation to the court because he did not have *knowledge clearly establishing* that (defendant's attorneys) had attempted to suborn (witness's) perjury or that (witness) in fact had failed to tell the truth at this deposition. Instead, (Doe) testified that he believed Conversation One reflected a layman's (witness's) misinterpretation of deposition preparation. With respect to Conversation Two, (Doe) *merely suspected* from his own assessment of the facts of the underlying lawsuits that (witness) and other (of defendant's) witnesses were not truthful during their deposition testimony. . . . Without *knowledge clearly establishing* either alleged fraud, it would have been extremely detrimental to his clients' interests in hotly contested litigation and to his attorney-client relationship for (Doe) to have attempted to prevail upon (client) to permit him to reveal his privileged communications in Conversations One and Two to the court.

After the Grievance Committee issued its unanimous decision exonerating Doe, its recommendation to dismiss the complaint came before the district court. After reviewing the transcripts of the proceedings before Judge Zampano and the Grievance Committee, the district court concluded that Doe violated DR 7–102(B)(2) and ordered that he be suspended from practice before any court in the District for six months.

DISCUSSION

. . .

B.   *DR 7–102(B) and the "information clearly establishing" requirement.*

Disciplinary Rule 7–102(B)(2) provides that, when a "lawyer . . .
receives information clearly establishing that . . . (a) person other
than his client has perpetrated a fraud upon a tribunal(, he) shall
promptly reveal the fraud to the tribunal." Under this rule, an
attorney's ethical duty to report a fraud on the court is triggered once
he receives "information clearly establishing" the existence of a fraud
on the court. The district court interpreted the term "information
clearly establishing" to mean that the lawyer must have "clear and
convincing evidence" that a fraud on the court has occurred before the
obligation to disclose the fraud arises. Applying this standard, the
district court found that, based upon conversations one and two, Doe
did not have clear and convincing evidence that defendant's attorneys
engaged in subornation of perjury and, thus, the court concluded that
he was not obligated to disclose this information. The court also
recognized that conversations one and two did not provide Doe with
clear and convincing evidence of witness's alleged perjury. Nevertheless, the court concluded that Doe's subjective beliefs concerning witness's veracity coupled with the information he received from client
provided him with clear and convincing evidence of witness's perjury.
Accordingly, the district court found that he violated the disciplinary
rule by failing to disclose the information concerning witness's alleged
perjury. We disagree.

Determining whether an attorney has received "information clearly establishing" a fraud on the court—and thus triggering his duty to
disclose that information to the affected tribunal—is a "difficult task."
ABA Comm. on Ethics and Professional Responsibility, Formal Op. 341
(1975). Our inquiry into the term's meaning is made even more
difficult because it is not used in any other Code provision and was not
included in any provision of the Code's predecessor, the Canons of
Professional Ethics (1908). Nor is the term included in any provision of
the Code's successor, the Model Rules of Professional Conduct (1983),
and our exhaustive research has uncovered no court or professional
ethics committee decision that has definitively interpreted what the
term means. Thus, we are left to examining the Code to determine the
drafter's intent,[3] reviewing the context in which the term has been

---

3.   The Committee which drafted the Code "intentionally compiled no record of its
discussions and deliberations" because of a concern for potentially inhibiting the discussion of participants. See American Bar Foundation, Annotated Code of Professional
Responsibility, xi (1979) ("Annotated Code"). Therefore, no comprehensive legislative
history of the Code exists. Id.

In addition, discerning the meaning of DR 7–102(B)(2) is further complicated by the fact
that that provision was not included in the preliminary draft of the Code circulated for
comment. See Annotated Code at 306–07. Because the preliminary draft was criticized

applied, and searching out definitions of the term adopted in other jurisdictions. We do, however, have the benefit of the ethics professor's expert opinion on this subject.

After examining the Code, we observe that in most Code provisions that obligate an attorney to take affirmative measures to preserve the integrity of the judicial system, knowledge is required before the disclosure duty arises. See, e.g., DR 1–103(A) (requires that "(a) lawyer possessing unprivileged *knowledge* of a violation of DR 1–102 [(governing attorney misconduct)] shall report such *knowledge* to a tribunal or other authority empowered to investigate or act upon such violation") (emphasis added); DR 1–103(B) (requires that "(a) lawyer possessing unprivileged *knowledge* or evidence concerning another lawyer or judge shall reveal fully such *knowledge* or evidence upon proper request of a tribunal or other authority empowered to investigate or act upon the conduct of lawyers or judges") (emphasis added). It therefore seems reasonable that the Code's drafters would have intended that a knowledge standard be included in DR 7–102(B)(2) before triggering its affirmative disclosure obligations.

When the ethics professor testified at the hearings before the Grievance Committee, he opined that the term "information clearly establishing" requires that the attorney have actual knowledge of the alleged fraud. When questioned on this issue, a member of the Committee pointed out that if the drafters of the Code had intended that a knowledge standard govern DR 7–102(B), they would have used the term "knowledge" or "actual knowledge" in the rule, as was the case in other Code provisions. The professor responded, however, that the drafter's failure to use the actual term "knowledge" in the rule reflected nothing more than poor draftsmanship rather than an intent to adopt some standard less than actual knowledge. The Grievance Committee apparently was satisfied with the professor's analysis because it agreed with his conclusions and adopted a knowledge standard for the purposes of the rule. So do we.

We note that at least one jurisdiction has endeavored to provide its attorneys with some guidance in this area. In Virginia, an attorney is required to reveal "[i]nformation which *clearly establishes* that his client has, in the course of the representation, perpetrated a fraud related to the subject matter of the representation upon a tribunal." DR 4–101(D)(1), Revised Virginia Code of Professional Responsibility (1983) (emphasis added). Included in this rule is a definition for the term "information clearly establishing" which provides that "[i]nformation is *clearly established* when the client *acknowledges* to the attorney that he has perpetrated a fraud upon a tribunal." Id. (emphasis added). Thus, Virginia has adopted an actual knowledge standard for determining when an attorney has received sufficient information to "clearly establish" that his client has committed a fraud.

for "not requiring a lawyer to reveal misconduct of others," when the Code came out in final form, it included the obligations contained in DR 7–102(B). Id. Thus, it was included in the Code without being subject to public scrutiny.

Consistent with Virginia's approach are decisions from other jurisdictions arising in the context where an attorney suspects that his client intends to commit perjury. Those cases permit the attorney to attempt to rectify or reveal the client's perjury only if the attorney has information establishing a "firm factual basis" that the client will commit perjury. See, e.g., Whiteside v. Scurr, 744 F.2d 1323, 1328 (8th Cir.1984), rev'd on other grounds, 475 U.S. 157, 106 S.Ct. 988, 89 L.Ed. 2d 123 (1986); United States ex. rel. Wilcox v. Johnson, 555 F.2d 115, 122 (3d Cir.1977). As explained in *Whiteside*, "[m]ere suspicion or inconsistent statements . . . are insufficient to establish that the defendant's testimony would have been false." 744 F.2d at 1328.

Our experience indicates that if any standard less than actual knowledge was adopted in this context, serious consequences might follow. If attorneys were bound as part of their ethical duties to report to the court each time they strongly suspected that a witness lied, courts would be inundated with such reports. Court dockets would quickly become overburdened with conducting these collateral proceedings which would necessarily hold up the ultimate disposition of the underlying action. We do not believe that the Code's drafters intended to throw the court system into such a morass. Instead, it seems that the only reasonable conclusion is that the drafters intended disclosure of only that information which the attorney reasonably knows to be a fact and which, when combined with other facts in his knowledge, would clearly establish the existence of a fraud on the tribunal.

To interpret the rule to mean otherwise would be to require attorneys to disclose mere suspicions of fraud which are based upon incomplete information or information which may fall short of clearly establishing the existence of a fraud. We do not suggest, however, that by requiring that the attorney have actual knowledge of a fraud before he is bound to disclose it, he must wait until he has proof beyond a moral certainty that fraud has been committed. Rather, we simply conclude that he must clearly know, rather than suspect, that a fraud on the court has been committed before he brings this knowledge to the court's attention.

Applying the above to the instant appeal, it becomes clear that Doe did not violate his ethical duties when he did not report to the court the information he possessed concerning witness's potential perjury. Neither the information Doe received from conversations one and two, nor his independent information concerning the facts of the case, provided him with knowledge that a fraud on the court had taken place. Although Doe's subjective beliefs may have caused him to suspect strongly that witness lied, they did not amount to actual knowledge that witness committed a fraud on the court.

CONCLUSION

We must always be mindful that the perspective of a judge differs greatly than that of the practicing attorney. "From the perspective of (a)

. . . judge, . . . a particular fact may be as clear and certain as a piece of crystal or a small diamond. A trial lawyer, however, must often deal with mixtures of sand and clay. Even a pebble that seems clear enough at first glance may take on a different hue in a handful of gravel." Nix v. Whiteside (Stevens, J., concurring in the judgment). Here, an attorney's reputation was put in question because he failed to report his suspicion that an adverse witness lied. As Judge Zampano recognized after he conducted the special hearing, the proper forum for resolving that question is not a collateral proceeding, but is the trial itself. Determining credibility is unquestionably the hallmark of the adversarial system. By awaiting trial, armed with his beliefs concerning witness's veracity and ready to impeach witness's credibility, Doe acted in a manner consistent with the traditional role of a trial lawyer. We therefore conclude that Doe violated no ethical duty by not reporting his suspicions to the court.

In view of the foregoing, we reverse the district court's order suspending Doe from practice.

VAN GRAAFEILAND, CIRCUIT JUDGE, concurring:

Although I concur fully in Judge Altimari's well-reasoned opinion, I write separately because I would put the case even more strongly than he did.

Untruthful testimony by a witness, which has not been suborned by his lawyer, does not, standing alone, constitute fraud upon the court. Serzysko v. Chase Manhattan Bank, 461 F.2d 699, 702 (2d Cir.), cert. denied, 409 U.S. 883, 93 S.Ct. 173, 34 L.Ed.2d 139 (1972); Bulloch v. United States, 721 F.2d 713, 718–19 (10th Cir.1983); Great Coastal Express, Inc. v. International Brotherhood of Teamsters, 675 F.2d 1349 (4th Cir.1982), cert. denied, 459 U.S. 1128, 103 S.Ct. 764, 74 L.Ed.2d 978 (1983). This is particularly true where, as here, the testimony is given during a pre-trial deposition. Until the deposition is placed in evidence, it does not become part of the case before the court. See Miles v. Ryan, 484 F.2d 1255, 1261 n. 4 (3d Cir.1973); Demara v. Employers Liability Assurance Corp., 250 F.2d 799, 800 (5th Cir.), cert. denied, 358 U.S. 845, 79 S.Ct. 69, 3 L.Ed.2d 79 (1958); United States v. Brookhaven, 134 F.2d 442, 447 (5th Cir.1943).

Accordingly, even if appellant was convinced that an opposing witness had testified falsely during his deposition, DR 7–102(B)(2) did not require appellant to disclose this to the court. The drafters of the Rule must have realized that it is one thing to be convinced of something; it is another thing to prove it. I can think of no better way for a lawyer to damage his client's case than by making a pretrial accusation of perjury that he is unable to prove.

Actual Knowledge

Consider *Nix v. Whiteside* again: How did Robinson, Whiteside's lawyer, know that his client intended to perjure himself? How does the court in *Whiteside* conclude that the testimony would have been perjurious? Are you convinced that Whiteside did not see a knife or metallic-looking object? Justice Stevens' concurrence concentrates on the difficulty of being sure that a client intends to commit perjury. How can Justice Stevens be sure that Whiteside did not "after reflection . . . sincerely believe" that he saw a metallic object?

The court in *Doe* holds that "clearly establishing" means "actual knowledge . . . he must clearly know, rather than suspect . . . ."

What made Doe's basis of knowledge inadequate to meet the standard set out by the court?

EC 7–26, which was not cited in *Doe,* states:

"The law and Disciplinary Rules prohibit the use of fraudulent, false, or perjured testimony or evidence. A lawyer who knowingly participates in introduction of such testimony or evidence is subject to discipline. A lawyer should, however, present any admissible evidence his client desires to have presented unless he knows, *or from facts within his knowledge should know,* that such testimony or evidence is false, fraudulent, or perjured."

Does the "actual knowledge" standard in *Doe* include things the lawyer "should have known"? In *United States v. Benjamin,* printed in Chapter II above, the Second Circuit imposed criminal liability when a professional "deliberately closes his eyes to facts he has a duty to see." Is this standard inapplicable to client perjury?

Judge Frankel has written that "[T]he sharp eye of the cynical lawyer becomes at strategic moments a demurely averted and filmy gaze," leaving him "unfettered by clear prohibitions that actual 'knowledge of the truth' might expose." Frankel, The Search for Truth: An Umpireal View," 123 U.Pa.L.Rev. 1031, 1039 (1975).

M.R. 3.3(a)(4) provides:

A lawyer shall not *knowingly*: . . . (4) offer evidence that the lawyer *knows* to be false. If a lawyer has offered material evidence and comes to *know* of its falsity, the lawyer shall take reasonable remedial measures. (emphasis added).

The Terminology Section states that "Knowingly . . . or Knows denotes actual knowledge," but adds that "a person's knowledge may be inferred from circumstances." Does this resolve the problem of the unusually credulous or deliberately blind lawyer?

Consider ABA Formal Op. 353 n. 9 (1988), which states:

The Committee notes that some trial lawyers report that they have avoided the ethical dilemma posed by Rule 3.3 because they follow a practice of not questioning the client about the facts in the case and, therefore, never "know" that a client has given false testimony. Lawyers who engage in such practice may be violating their duties under Rule 3.3 and their obligation to provide competent representation under Rule 1.1. ABA Defense Function Standards 4–3.2(a) and (b) are also applicable.

Model Rule 3.3(c) gives the lawyer discretion to refuse to offer evidence that she *reasonably believes* is false. In exercising this discretion, the lawyer is not permitted to reveal client confidences. Only when the lawyer "knows" that the evidence is false does the duty in 3.3(a)(4) override the obligations of confidentiality, see M.R. 3.3(b). ABA Formal Op. 353 (1987) emphasizes that M.R. 3.3's obligation to disclose client perjury "is strictly limited" to situations when the lawyer "knows" the testimony offered was false. "[O]rdinarily [this knowledge will be] based on admissions the client has made to the lawyer. The lawyer's suspicions are not enough." The opinion cites *Wilcox* for the last proposition.

Note on *United States v. Long*

After being reversed in *Whiteside*, the Eighth Circuit spoke again on the issue of client perjury in criminal trials, United States v. Long, 857 F.2d 436 (8th Cir.1988). In *Long*, the lawyer told the trial judge, out of the presence of the jury, that his client Jackson wanted to testify but that the lawyer was "concerned about his testimony." The judge excused everyone from the court except Jackson, his lawyer and a United States Marshal. The lawyer then said,

> "I'm not sure if it wouldn't be appropriate for me to move for a withdrawal . . . based upon what I think may be elicited on the stand. . . . I'm concerned about the testimony that may come out and I'm under an obligation to the Court."

After the trial judge made sure that the defendant understood both that he had a right to testify and that his lawyer had an obligation not to place evidence "which he believed to be untrue" before the court, the judge stated that the defendant could take the stand and offer a narrative statement without questioning from his lawyer. The judge further stated that if the lawyer found things in the testimony that he believed were false "he may have other obligations at that point." The client did not testify.

The Eighth Circuit distinguished *Long* from *Whiteside* in three respects. First, in *Whiteside* there had been a finding that had the defendant testified he would have perjured himself, but here the basis for the lawyer's belief that his client would perjure himself was unknown and an evidentiary hearing was needed to determine that basis. Second, Whiteside did testify whereas Jackson did not. Without an evidentiary hearing the court said it could not determine whether the lawyer's actions prevented Jackson from testifying *truthfully*. Third, in *Whiteside* the lawyer "did not reveal his belief about his client's anticipated testimony to the trial court." In contrast, the court found the disclosure in *Long* to be "quite explicit." Before such disclosure is made, the lawyer must remonstrate with the client and after the disclosure the trial judge must take steps to minimize the resulting prejudice to the defendant. These steps would include: ensuring that the defendant understood his right to testify and that any waiver was voluntary; telling the defendant that he would be permitted to proceed in a narrative fashion and that counsel would not refer in argument to testimony which counsel had a firm factual basis for believing false; and warning the defendant of the penalties for perjury.

The Eighth Circuit addressed how certain a lawyer should be before disclosing the defendant's intent to commit perjury.

> "Counsel must act if, but only if, he or she has 'a firm factual basis' for believing that the defendant intends to testify falsely or has testified falsely. . . . It will be a rare case in which this factual requirement is met. Counsel must remember that they are not triers of fact, but advocates. In most cases a client's credibility will be a question for the jury."

> . . . In discussing the attorney's duty to report possible client perjury, the [Supreme Court's] majority [opinion in *Whiteside*] states that it extends to "a client's *announced* plans to engage in future conduct." (emphasis added). Thus, a clear expression of intent to commit perjury is required before an attorney can reveal client confidences.

> . . .

> . . . Moreover, even a statement of an intention to lie on the stand does not necessarily mean the client will indeed lie once on the stand. Once a client hears the testimony of other witnesses, takes an oath, faces a judge and jury, and contemplates the prospect of cross-examination by opposing counsel, she may well change her mind and decide to testify truthfully.

> As Justice Blackmun observes, an attorney who acts on belief of possible client perjury takes on the role of the fact finder, a role which perverts the structure of our adversary system. A lawyer who judges a client's truthfulness does so without the many safeguards inherent in our adversary system. He likely makes his decision alone, without the assistance of fellow fact finders. He may consider too much evidence, including that which is untrustworthy. Moreover, a jury's determination on credibility is always tempered by the requirement of proof beyond a reasonable doubt. A lawyer, finding facts on his own, is not necessarily guided by such a high standard.

Long, 875 F.2d at 445.

Does this mean that "a firm factual basis" can only be an explicit announcement by the defendant that she intends to perjure herself? Is this consistent with *Whiteside*? Even where the client announces such an intention, the Eighth Circuit suggests that a firm factual basis for disclosing the contemplated perjury may not be present. Is the Eighth Circuit unsure whether a lawyer can ever "know" that her client intends to commit perjury?

In a footnote, the Eighth Circuit discussed two procedures. One is that when defense counsel believes the defendant will commit perjury, a recess be called before the testimony proceeds. A hearing would then be held by a judge other than the one presiding at trial to determine whether the proposed testimony would be perjurious. The standard would be proof beyond a reasonable doubt. See Rieger, Client Perjury: A Proposed Resolution of the Constitutional and Ethical Issues, 70 Minn.L.Rev. 121, 153 (1985). The other suggestion is for a board of attorneys to decide the issue. See Erickson, The Perjurious Defendant: A Proposed Solution to Defense Lawyer's Conflicting Ethical Obligations to the Court and to His Client, 59 Den.L.J. 75, 88 (1981). Commenting on these suggestions, the Eighth Circuit said: "Either of these procedures would assist attorneys in determining whether there is a firm factual basis for believing a client is about to commit perjury, although we do not say, at this point, that the Constitution necessarily requires their implementation." *Long* n. 10 at 447. Are there problems with implementing either of these solutions?

Can Trial Lawyers Ever "Know"? Radical Epistemology Revisited

St. Thomas Aquinas said concerning a confession to a priest:

Whatever the priest knows through confession he, in a sense, does not know, because he possesses this knowledge not as man, but as the representative of God. He may, therefore, without qualms of conscience, swear to his ignorance in court, because the obligation of a witness extends only to his human knowledge.

Kurtscheid, A History of the Seal of Confession transl. by F.A. Marks (1927), pp. 194–195.

At trial a lawyer acts, and is expected to act, as if she were incapable of knowing that her client is guilty. Should this expectation of wilful blindness be extended to whether testimony offered is perjurious? Is the lawyer's ability to know things different once inside the courtroom than it is outside? Is the criminal defense lawyer "incapable" of "knowing" only when in the process of conducting the trial, but capable of knowing at side bar conferences or other exchanges outside the presence of the jury? What about the testimony of other defense witnesses? The authenticity of documents or other physical evidence? If we treat criminal defense lawyers as incapable of knowing whether evidence is false or not, should civil lawyers be treated the same in the interest of protecting their clients' due process rights?

Perjury in Civil Cases

The underlying matter in *Doe* was civil. The criminal cases requiring a high degree of certainty regarding client perjury are based on the constitutional rights of the accused. How does the court in *Doe* justify its standard?

Fed.R.Civ.P. 11, discussed below, and similar rules in the states require a lawyer to conduct a reasonable investigation so that any paper filed with the court is "well grounded in fact . . .". See, e.g., Coburn

Optical v. Cilco, 610 F.Supp. 656, 659 (M.D.N.C.1985) ("If all the attorney has is his client's assurance that facts exist or do not exist, when a reasonable inquiry would reveal otherwise, he has not satisfied his obligation [under Rule 11]."); and Kendrick v. Zanides, 609 F.Supp. 1162, 1172 (N.D.Cal.1985) (when the lawyer has a document refuting the client's allegations, she must investigate). Contrast In re Grand Jury Subpoena, 615 F.Supp. 958, 969 (D.Mass.1985) ("So long as the attorney does not have obvious indications of the client's fraud or perjury, the attorney is not obligated to undertake an independent investigation before advancing his client's position."). See also M.R. 3.1.

False Evidence Offered by the Opposing Party

How important was it in *Doe* that the apparent fraud was perpetrated by a witness for the other side?

The Code provision at issue in *Doe,* DR 7–102(B)(2), covers fraud committed by anyone other than the client, which the court reads to include fraud by the opposing party. The court could have held that DR 7–102(B)(2) did not cover fraud committed by the opposing party; and that the only provision requiring a lawyer to report such conduct was DR 1–103(A), which imposes a duty to report professional misconduct only if this knowledge is "unprivileged."

Note that Model Rule 8.3, on reporting professional misconduct, applies only to non-confidential information, whereas M.R. 3.3(b) makes it clear that the obligation not to offer false evidence applies "even if compliance requires disclosure of information otherwise protected by Rule 1.6." Should a lawyer have a greater or lesser obligation to report fraud on the court committed by her own witnesses?

Rule 60(b) and Fraud on the Court

"Fraud on the court" as used in DR 7–102(B) traditionally has been interpreted to include the introduction of false evidence. See, e.g., Attorney Grievance Committee v. Sperling, 296 Md. 558, 463 A.2d 868 (1983) (rejecting a narrow reading of "fraud on the court" and holding that "fraud" under DR 7–102(B) includes false swearing); *Nix v. Whiteside,* supra; ABA Formal Op. 341 (1975); Informal Op. 1314 (1975); and Formal Op. 287 (1953) (interpreting similar language in the Canons of Professional Ethics). See also ABA Formal Opinion 353 (1987) (interpreting the words "criminal or fraudulent act by the client" in M.R. 3.3(a)(2) as including perjury and the introduction of false evidence because any other reading would be "irrational").

Judge Graafeiland's concurrence cites cases for the proposition that "untruthful testimony, which has not been suborned by [a] lawyer, does not, standing alone, constitute fraud upon the court." The cases cited do not involve DR 7–102(B) or any counterpart, however; they all involve motions under Fed.R.Civ.P. 60(b) to set aside a judgment because of fraud on the court.

Fed.R.Civ.P. 60(b)(3) allows setting aside a judgment procured on the basis of "fraud . . ., misrepresentation, or other misconduct of an adverse party." Courts refer to Rule 60(b)(3) fraud as "fraud between the parties" to distinguish it from "fraud on the court" covered by Rule 60(b)(6). The introduction of false evidence without the attorney's knowing involvement in the fraud is not considered "fraud on the court" under 60(b)(6), see, e.g., Bulloch v. United States, 721 F.2d 713, 718 (10th Cir.1983), aff'd on rehearing, 763 F.2d 1115 (1985); Amstar Corp. v. Envirotech Corp., 823 F.2d 1538 (Fed.Cir.1987), but it may constitute "fraud between the parties" under 60(b)(3), see, e.g., Great Coastal v. International Brotherhood of Teamsters, 675 F.2d 1349 (4th Cir.1982). A motion for relief under 60(b)(3) must be filed within a reasonable time and in any case no later than one year after judgment. On the other hand, Fed.R.Civ.P. 60(b)(6), allowing the court to set aside a judgment "for any other reason justifying relief" and primarily used to set aside judgments for "fraud on the court," has no time limit. See, e.g., Hazel-Atlas Glass Co. v. Hartford-Empire Co., 322 U.S. 238, 64 S.Ct. 997 (1944). For this reason the courts construe "fraud on the court" "very narrowly" for purposes of Rule 60(b), see, e.g., *Great Coastal*, at 1356 ("The principal concern motivating narrow construction is that the otherwise nebulous concept of "fraud on the court" could easily overwhelm the specific provision of 60(b)(3) and its time limitation and thereby subvert the balance of equities contained in the Rule.").

The court in *Great Coastal,* 675 F.2d at 1357, further justified its refusal to grant relief from the judgment by saying: "[P]erjury and fabricated evidence are evils that can and should be exposed at trial, and the legal system encourages and expects litigants to root them out as early as possible. In addition, the legal system contains other sanctions against perjury." Is this reasoning equally applicable to DR 7–102(B)(2)? To DR 7–102(B)(1)?

When the lawyer is *knowingly* involved in the introduction of false evidence, it *is* "fraud on the court" under Rule 60(b)(6), and courts will entertain a motion to vacate without regard to the one year limit, see, e.g., *Great Coastal,* at 1357; Hazel-Atlas Glass Co. v. Hartford-Empire Co., 322 U.S. 238, 64 S.Ct. 997 (1944) (tampering by attorney with administration of justice requires vacation of judgment, whether or not behavior actually influenced the trial); Virgin Islands Housing Authority v. David, 823 F.2d 764 (3d Cir.1987) (reversal of judgment for lawyer's misrepresentation of territorial court's decision in argument before district court); Synanon Foundation v. Bernstein, 503 A.2d 1254 (D.C.App.1986) (attorneys subornation of perjury and their own false statements).

Lying at a Deposition

Judge Graafeiland's statement that depositions are not part of the case until they are placed in evidence is wrong or irrelevant. Testifying falsely in a sworn deposition is perjury, see, e.g., 18 U.S.C. § 1623 ("Whoever under oath in any proceeding before or *ancillary* to any court . . . knowingly makes any false material declaration . . .);

United States v. Moreno, 815 F.2d 725 (1st Cir.1987) (prosecution for false deposition testimony in a civil action). Also see In Matter of Application of Charles M., 313 Md. 168, 545 A.2d 7 (1988) (denying admission to the bar to a person who as a layman had lied in a deposition).

In Committee on Professional Ethics v. Crary, 245 N.W.2d 298 (Iowa 1976), cited in *Whiteside,* the lawyer was held guilty of professional misconduct when he sat silently by while his client lied during a deposition; the court treated this as tantamount to assisting a client to lie at trial. There was no question that Crary knew his client, Mrs. Curtis, was lying because her lie was that she was in Chicago with a woman friend when the truth was that she was with Crary, her lawyer, with whom she was having an affair. The deposition was taken in a divorce action between Mrs. Curtis and her husband.

. . . Assuming respondent did not know in advance that Mrs. Curtis was going to lie, his guilt was in failing to stop her or otherwise to call a halt when she started to lie. . . .

The attorney functions at the heart of the fact-finding process, both in trial and in pre- and post-trial proceedings. If he knowingly suffers a witness to lie, he undermines the integrity of the fact-finding system of which he himself is an integral part. . . .

. . . We do not place the decision on [his] failure to inform opposing counsel or the court of the truth. In the present case no need really existed for this. Opposing counsel was not misled. His subsequent questions revealed he knew [where Mrs. Curtis had actually been]; he made [her] perjury patent. The vice . . . was not in failing to reveal the truth but in participating in the corruption of the fact-finding system by knowingly permitting Mrs. Curtis to lie. . . . Contrast with respondent's conduct the acts of [his partner] Mr. Gray. When that attorney suspected on Friday that Mrs. Curtis was lying he confronted respondent and upon learning the truth said, "She can't sit there and tell this story." He thereupon recessed the deposition.

Id. at 305–06.

The court also rejected Crary's contention that disclosure would have violated his duty to protect his client's confidences.

Accord: Attorney Grievance Committee v. Sperling, 296 Md. 558, 463 A.2d 868 (1983).

What Should the Rules on Client Perjury Be?

Introductory Note

Case law and ethics rules and opinions notwithstanding, at least in the case of a criminal defendant who intends to commit perjury, a substantial segment of the practicing bar believes the lawyer must present such testimony if the client insists. In Kenneth Mann's revealing book, *Defending White Collar Criminals* 121 (1985), a lawyer tells Mann:

> It's my mission and obligation to defend the client, not to sit in moral, ethical or legal judgment of him. I cannot join him in transgressing the law, but whatever he does of his own impetus, whatever way he conducts himself in attempting to protect himself, is a decision he has to make independent of what I do. I must inform him of the consequences and significance of his action, but not punish him or sanction him or in other ways initiate law enforcement actions against him. My role in the adversary system is to protect him.

Another lawyer admonishes an associate who believed that a client had lied to a government agency:

> "What you are telling me is that the client is not telling the truth. What I am saying is that the response is credible. We are not law enforcement agents." Id. at 110.

The following contributions in the debate are noteworthy: Curtis, The Ethics of Advocacy, 4 Stan.L.Rev. 3 (1951); Drinker, Some Remarks on Mr. Curtis' "The Ethics of Advocacy," 4 Stan.L.Rev. 349 (1952); Noonan, The Purpose of Advocacy and the Limits of Confidentiality, 64 Mich.L.Rev. 1485 (1966); Frankel, The Search for Truth: An Umpireal View, 123 U.Pa.L.Rev. 1031 (1975); Uviller, The Advocate, The Truth, and Judicial Hackles: A Reaction to Judge Frankel's Idea, 123 U.Pa.L. Rev. 1067 (1975); M. Freedman, Lawyers' Ethics in an Adversary System (1975); Lefstein, The Criminal Defendant Who Proposes Perjury: Rethinking the Defense Lawyer's Dilemma, 6 Hofstra L.Rev. 665 (1978).

Before exploring what the rules should be, we provide a brief overview of what the rules now say.

What the Rules Are Now

The Supreme Court in *Whiteside* read both the Model Code and Model Rules as not merely authorizing disclosure of client perjury but requiring it. The ethics professor testifying in *Doe* seems to say, to the contrary, that the attorney's duty to keep client confidences, DR 4–101(B), overrides her obligation to reveal fraud on the court, DR 7–102(B). The Code provision on client fraud on the court is DR 7–102(B)(1), which also covers client fraud on third parties. Cf. DR 7–102(B)(2) covering fraud on the court committed by non-clients. In Chapter 4, we discussed the ambiguity of DR 7–102(B)(1) as it applies to client fraud on third parties, see pp. 282–284 above, and that discussion is equally applicable to DR 7–102(B)(1)'s treatment of client fraud on the court.

The ABA ethics opinions on fraud on the court, like the ethics opinions on fraud on third parties, have added to the confusion. Despite the language of DR 7–102(B)(1), i.e., "lawyer . . . shall reveal . . .", ABA ethics opinions took the position that when the lawyer learns of the client's false testimony after the fact, the lawyer may not disclose, see Informal Op. 1314 (1975) and Formal Op. 341 (1975), but may have a duty to cease further representation of the client, see Formal Op. 287 (1953) (interpreting the Canons). When the lawyer learns of the client's *intent* to commit perjury, the lawyer must advise the client that the lawyer is bound to take one of two courses of action: withdraw prior to submission of the false testimony, or, if the client persists in her plan, report the client's intent to the tribunal, see ABA Informal Op. 1314 (1975). The perpetuation of ambiguity continues. See the note in Chapter 4 at p. 254.

Commentators have argued extensively about what the Code requires of the lawyer faced with client perjury. See, e.g., the articles cited above. The courts, in contrast, have been clear that a lawyer has to take some action when she *knows* that a client or witness intends to lie. The cases are unanimous in requiring the lawyer at least to remonstrate with the client and to withdraw if the client insists on perjuring herself. See, e.g., *Crary* and *Long,* supra. We have found no court opinion suggesting that it is proper for a lawyer to act as if testimony that she knows to be false is true. Not only the Supreme Court in *Whiteside* but the majority of courts state that at some point the lawyer has a duty to disclose client perjury so as to avoid assisting fraud on the tribunal. See, e.g., *Doe,* printed above; *Crary,* supra. The cases discussed in the notes to *Whiteside,* with the exception of *Lowery* (bench trial), all seem to take this position. The decisions base the duty to disclose on the lawyer's duty not to assist criminal activity and not to offer false evidence. See DR 7–102(A)(7) and DR 7–102(A)(4).

Compare State v. Lee, 142 Ariz. 210, 689 P.2d 153 (1984) (en banc) (criminal case: lawyer should move to withdraw but should not inform the court of the specific basis for the request; lawyer should state only that an "irreconcilable conflict" makes continued representation extremely difficult); In re A., 276 Or. 225, 554 P.2d 479, 486 (1976) (civil case: lawyer should encourage the client to permit the lawyer to disclose the fraud on the court, inform the client that the lawyer will have to withdraw if there is no disclosure, and then withdraw if the client refuses to disclose). Cf. Lefstein, Reflections on the Client Perjury Dilemma and *Nix v. Whiteside,* Crim.Just., Summer 1986, at 27, 28 (accusing the majority opinion in *Whiteside* of "a shocking misstatement of the law pertaining to client perjury").

Read M.R. 3.3 and its Comment.

Paragraph (a) of 3.3 specifies several situations in which the lawyer's duty of candor to the tribunal overrides the duty of confidentiality; M.R. 3.3(b) makes this hierarchy of duties explicit.

Notice that the duty to take "remedial" measures, when one discovers after the fact that false evidence has been offered, extends only to evidence that is "material."

The lawyer's duty to disclose that evidence she offered was false applies to any material evidence she learns is false while the proceeding is ongoing, see M.R. 3.3(b) and the Comment to 3.3. Should the rule also apply after the proceedings are over? How does the Comment justify the time limit? (How is any statute of limitations justified?)

Does a lawyer have discretion to disclose fraud she learns about after the proceedings are over? Clearly so if disclosure is necessary to establish a defense against a possible charge that the lawyer participated in the fraud, M.R. 1.6(b)(2). The Comment to M.R. 1.6 also provides that nothing in 1.6 prevents a lawyer from withdrawing or disaffirming "any opinion, document, affirmation, or the like." Would this apply to a judgment or settlement procured by fraud?

M.R. 3.3(c) gives the lawyer discretion to refuse to offer evidence that the lawyer "reasonably believes is false." M.R. 3.3(d) requires the lawyer in an ex parte proceeding to inform the judge of "all material facts known to the lawyer" that, as the Comment explains, "the lawyer reasonably believes are necessary" for the judge to reach "an informed decision,", "whether or not the facts are adverse."

In ABA Formal Op. 353 (1987), the ABA committee on Professional Ethics stated its understanding of the lawyer's duties under M.R. 3.3:

> If, prior to the conclusion of the proceedings, a lawyer learns that the client has given testimony the lawyer knows is false, and the lawyer cannot persuade the client to rectify the perjury, the lawyer must disclose the client's perjury to the tribunal, notwithstanding the fact that the information to be disclosed is information relating to the representation.

> If the lawyer learns that the client intends to testify falsely before a tribunal, the lawyer must advise the client against such course of action, informing the client of the consequences of giving false testimony including the lawyer's duty of disclosure to the tribunal. Ordinarily, the lawyer can reasonably believe that such advice will dissuade the client from giving false testimony and, therefore, may examine the client in the normal manner. However, if the lawyer knows, from the client's clearly stated intention, that the client will testify falsely, and the lawyer cannot effectively withdraw from the representation, the lawyer must either limit the examination of the client to subjects on which the lawyer believes the client will testify truthfully; or, if there are none, not permit the client to testify; or, if this is not feasible, disclose the client's intention to testify falsely to the tribunal.

MONROE H. FREEDMAN, "PERJURY: THE LAWYER'S TRILEMMA"

1 Litigation 26 (No. 1, Winter 1975).*

. . .

If we recognize that professional responsibility requires that an advocate have full knowledge of every pertinent fact, then the lawyer must seek the truth from the client, not shun it. That means that the attorney will have to dig and pry and cajole, and, even then, the lawyer will not be successful without convincing the client that full disclosure to the lawyer will never result in prejudice to the client by any word or action of the attorney. That is particularly true in the case of the indigent criminal defendant, who meets the lawyer for the first time in the cell block or the rotunda of the jail. . . .

However, the inclination to mislead one's lawyer is not restricted to the indigent or even to the criminal defendant. Randolph Paul has observed a similar phenomenon among a wealthier class in a far more congenial atmosphere. The tax adviser, notes Mr. Paul, will sometimes have to "dynamite the facts of his case out of the unwilling witnesses on his own side—witnesses who are nervous, witnesses who are confused about their own interest, witnesses who try to be too smart for their own good, and witnesses who subconsciously do not want to understand what has happened despite the fact that they must if they are to testify coherently." Mr. Paul goes on to explain that the truth can be obtained only by persuading the client that it would be a violation of a sacred obligation for the lawyer ever to reveal a client's confidence. Of course, once the lawyer has thus persuaded the client of the obligation of confidentiality, that obligation must be respected scrupulously.

· · ·

. . . The Canadian Bar Association, for example, takes an extremely hard line against the presentation of perjury by the client, but it also explicitly requires that the client be put on notice of that fact. Obviously, any other course would be a gross betrayal of the client's trust, since everything else said by the attorney in attempting to obtain complete information about the case would indicate to the client that no information thus obtained would be used to the client's disadvantage.

On the other hand, the inevitable result of the position taken by the Canadian Bar Association would be to caution the client not to be completely candid with the attorney. That, of course, returns us to resolving the trilemma by maintaining confidentiality and candor, but sacrificing complete knowledge. . . .

· · ·

. . . I continue to stand with those lawyers who hold that the lawyer's obligation of confidentiality does not permit him to disclose the facts he has learned from his client which form the basis for his conclusion that the client intends to perjure himself. What that means—necessarily, it seems to me—is that, at least the criminal defense attorney, however unwillingly in terms of personal morality, has a professional responsibility as an advocate in an adversary system

Ethics in an Adversary System (1975); see also "Personal Responsibility in a Professional System," 27 Cath.U.L.Rev. 191 (1978), and "Legal Ethics and the Suffering Client," 36 Cath.U.L.Rev. 331 (1987)).

to examine the perjurious client in the ordinary way and to argue to the jury, as evidence in the case, the testimony presented by the defendant.

Questions and Comments

Professor Freedman's argument is in part dependent on positing three duties—knowing all the facts, keeping confidences, and candor to the court. What about the lawyer's responsibility (under the criminal law and under the ethics rules) to refrain from assisting criminal activity?

Professor Freedman argues that "it is simply too much to expect of a human being . . . facing loss of liberty and the horrors of imprisonment not to attempt to lie. . . ." Are there different considerations for civil lawyers?

If Professor Freedman's central concern is the criminal defendant's right to tell her story, why is his argument not one for freeing the criminal defendant from the penalties of perjury or from the requirement of an oath?

At common law until the 19th century, a party, including a criminal accused, was disqualified from testifying, on the ground that the temptation to falsify would put his soul in jeopardy. In some states a criminal defendant came to be accorded a right to testify but only unsworn. In Ferguson v. Georgia, 365 U.S. 570, 81 S.Ct. 756 (1961), the Supreme Court struck down a Georgia law that limited a criminal defendant to *unsworn* testimony at trial. Justice Frankfurter, concurring in *Ferguson,* noted, however, that giving a defendant the option of testifying under oath or making an unsworn statement works to the defendant's benefit and is not a violation of constitutional rights. Id. at 599–600, 81 S.Ct. at 772 (Frankfurter, J., concurring). Courts that have reconsidered this question agree with Justice Frankfurter. See, e.g., Bontempo v. Fenton, 692 F.2d 954, 959–61 (3d Cir.1982) and United States v. Robinson, 783 F.2d 64, 66 (7th Cir.1986). For a discussion of the historical transition from a rule of defendant's incompetency to testify to a rule of competency, see *Ferguson,* 365 U.S. 573–582, 81 S.Ct. 758–763.

If the defendant presented unsworn testimony, should the jury be told that the defendant's testimony is given without threat of penalty if found to be false?

———

Is Assisting Perjury Like Assisting Other Crimes?

Professor Freedman's argument implicitly rests on the proposition that perjury is unlike other crimes that corrupt court processes. The American Lawyer's Code of Conduct adopts this distinction. The Comment to ALCC Chapter 1 explains:

The corruption cases [i.e., cases where a judge or juror has been bribed or subject to extortion, see ALCC Rule 1.4] are an appropriate exception [to the confidentiality rule] because the corruption of the impartial judge, or jury vitiates the adversary system itself. Since cases of corruption are infrequent, the exception should not have significant impact on the lawyer-client relationship. By contrast, cases of false testimony are more frequent, and the adversary system anticipates and is specifically designed to cope with false testimony through cross-examination, rebuttal, and observation of demeanor during testimony.

See also the District of Columbia Rules of Professional Conduct, specifically D.C. Rules 1.6(c)(2); 3.3(b); 3.3(d) (giving the lawyer discretion to reveal a client's intent to bribe or intimidate judges, witnesses or jurors, but prohibiting disclosure of intended client perjury of a criminal defendant or past fraud on the court when disclosure would reveal client confidences).

In *Nix v. Whiteside*, supra, the Court rejects the distinction:

The crime of perjury in this setting is indistinguishable in substance from the crime of threatening or tampering with a witness or juror. A defendant who informed his counsel that he was arranging to bribe or threaten witnesses or members of the jury would have no "right" to insist on counsel's assistance or silence. Counsel would not be limited to advising against that conduct. An attorney's duty of confidentiality, which totally covers the client's admission of guilt, does not extend to a client's announced plans to engage in future criminal conduct. . . .

Whiteside, 475 U.S. at 174.

All commentators assert that perjury is pervasive and underprosecuted. See, e.g., Arkin and Bogatin, Perjury in Civil Litigation—The Unpunished Crime, N.Y.L.J. 25 May 1984 at 1; Comment, Perjury: The Forgotten Offense, 65 J.Crim.L. & Criminology 361 (1974); Whitman, A Proposed Solution to the Problem of Perjury in Our Courts, 39 Dickinson L.Rev. 127 (1955); McClintock, What Happens to Perjurers, 24 Minn.L.Rev. 727 (1940).

Other evidence suggests that when the crime of perjury is prosecuted it is taken very seriously by the courts. Courts are more likely to imprison a convicted perjurer than a defendant convicted of other white collar crimes, see Sourcebook of Criminal Justice Statistics (1982), Tables 5.18 and 5.19, at 461 and 466. Judges often express the view that perjury is a most serious crime because it thwarts and potentially destroys the search for truth. See, e.g., United States v. Otto, 54 F.2d 277, 279 (2d Cir.1931); Edwards v. State, 577 P.2d 1380 (Wyo.1978).

The failure to devote prosecutorial resources to prosecutions for perjury may, in part, reflect that prosecutors share Professor Freedman's expectation that people charged with crimes will lie and that prosecutors have doubts, like his, about punishing defendants for doing so. Perjury is a difficult crime to prove. Many courts require that corroborating evidence be nearly indisputable. See, e.g., United States v. Neff, 212 F.2d 297 (3d Cir.1954); United States v. Thompson, 379 F.2d 625 (6th Cir.1967). Also, judge's alternatives to prosecutions for perjury are seen as viable. One is to increase the sentence of a defendant who has perjured herself during trial. In United States v. Grayson, 438 U.S. 41, 98 S.Ct. 2610 (1978), the Supreme Court held that a judge's belief that the defendant had perjured herself is a valid sentencing consideration because it is seen as relevant to how likely the defendant is to be rehabilitated. See also Eagle, Civil Remedies for Perjury: A Proposal for a Tort Action, 19 Ariz.L.Rev. 349, 369–72 (1977); and the note on Perjury as a Tort below, p. 429.*

In a more recent article, Professor Freedman has returned to the question of how perjury can be distinguished from other crimes that corrupt court processes:

. . . bribery is clandestine, usually not suspected when committed, and difficult to detect. Perjury, by contrast, takes place in the goldfish bowl of the courtroom, before a skeptical judge and jury, and is subject to immediate impeachment. Also, when perjury is detected by the court, the defendant faces the likelihood of an increased sentence.

Further, as *Whiteside* illustrates, the lawyer ordinarily learns about the defendant's intended perjury as a result of a series of interviews with the client about the very offense that has been charged. That is, the lawyer's knowledge of the client's perjury is usually the direct outcome of lawyer-client communications about the crime that has been charged. Thus, knowledge of the "future crime" of perjury is inextricably interwoven with the crime that is the subject of the representation. A client's announcement of an intent to kill a witness, on the other hand, is a fact that stands separate and apart from communications about the crime that is the subject of the representation, such as what Whiteside did or did not see in the victim's hand just before he stabbed him.

Freedman, Client Confidences and Client Perjury: Some Unanswered Questions, 136 U.Pa.L.Rev. 1939 (1988).

Is There a Significant Difference Between the Defendant Lying and the Lawyer Assisting or Acquiescing to the Defendant's Lie?

To illustrate the "trilemma" Professor Freedman posits a defendant falsely accused of robbery whose truthful testimony about his whereabouts (i.e., that he was near the scene at the time of the crime) might lead the jury to convict him. By positing this case, Professor Freedman presents us with a scenario in which lying seems not only reasonable but, perhaps more important, not a clear moral wrong.

---

* The authors acknowledge the contribution of J.F.O. McAllister of Yale Law School, whose paper, Perjury: Scope, Reasons, Solutions, May 1986, under the supervision of Professor Stephen Wizner of the Yale Law School and on file with the authors, provided many useful insights.

How is it "known" in Professor Freedman's case, except hypothetically, that the client has been *falsely* accused? Would it indeed be reasonable for a defendant in this situation to lie? What dangers are there for the innocent defendant who lies and is thought by the fact-finder to have lied?

Assuming there are some circumstances in which it is reasonable for an innocent defendant to lie, a number of questions remain. First, does the moral justification for the defendant's lying extend to the lawyer, giving lawyers who represent defendants in these circumstances a moral justification for assisting the lie? Second, if some defendants are morally justified in lying, must the lawyer assist all defendants to lie because any other stance would distinguish between clients according to whether the lawyer believed them to be truly innocent? Third, if the lawyer is morally justified in assisting at least some defendants to lie, does that mean that the ethics rules should leave it to the lawyer's discretion when to assist perjury and when not? Does it mean that the rules should *require* lawyers to assist perjury?

These questions are posed and insightfully discussed by Professor Carl M. Selinger in his article, The Perry Mason Perspective and Others: A Critique of Reductionist Thinking about the Ethics of Untruthful Practices by Lawyers for "Innocent" Defendants, 6 Hofstra L.Rev. 631 (1978).

Professor Selinger concludes that an innocent defendant is morally justified in perjuring herself to avoid the greater wrong of unjustified imprisonment. Do you agree with Professor Selinger's resolution of his first question? Should a lawyer advise the client that lying in court is unlawful but not immoral if she is innocent? Would that be counseling (assisting, encouraging) the client to commit criminal conduct? See M.R. 1.2(d).

Professor Selinger argues that a lawyer's oath to uphold the law places her under a special obligation not to break the rules for adjudicating disputes; and that by voluntarily participating in the criminal justice system the lawyer assumes two special obligations (1) to conduct herself in accordance with the rules for finding the facts; and (2) to accept the judgments reached by the system when reached in accordance with the system's own rules. Do you agree?

Professor Selinger rejects a rule that would allow lawyers to assist "good" lying as opposed to "bad" lying because it would be difficult to administer such a rule in an evenhanded manner, and it would provide little guidance to lawyers trying to figure out what was prohibited.

Shifting Perspectives: The View From the Outside

SISSELA BOK, LYING (1979)
Chapter XI, Lies Protecting Peers and Clients.
pp. 154–173.*

[. . .] it is obviously a most effective protection for legitimate secrets that it should be universally understood and expected that those who ask questions which they have no right to ask will have lies told to them;

—H. Sidgwick, *The Methods of Ethics*

It is only the cynic who claims "to speak the truth" at all times and in all places to all men in the same way but who, in fact, develops nothing but a lifeless image of the truth. He dons the halo of the fanatical devotee of truth who can make no allowance for human weaknesses; but, in fact, he is destroying the living truth between men. He wounds shame, desecrates mystery, breaks confidence, betrays the community in which he lives.

—Dietrich Bonhoeffer, "What is Meant by "Telling the Truth"?"

I don't see why we should not come out roundly and say that one of the functions of the lawyer is to lie for his client; and on rare occasions, as I think I have shown, I believe it is.

—Charles Curtis, "The Ethics of Advocacy"

Confidentiality

Here is a crime contemplated but not yet consummated, without malice, it is true, but nonetheless wilful, and from the basest and most sordid motives. The prospective victim is most often a pure young woman, confiding in the love and honor of the man who is about to do her this unspeakable wrong. [. . .] A single word [. . .] would save her from this terrible fate, yet the physician is fettered hand and foot by his cast-iron code, his tongue is silenced, he cannot lift a finger or utter a word to prevent this catastrophe.

So wrote a physician in 1904, to whom a syphilitic patient had announced his plan to marry without letting his fiancée know of his condition. At a time when venereal disease could almost never be cured and was a subject so sensitive that prospective spouses could not discuss it, many a physician was confronted by an agonizing choice: whether to uphold his duty of honoring the confidences of patients, or to help an innocent future victim, whose health might otherwise be destroyed, and whose children could be born malformed or retarded. Physicians still face similar conflicts: Should they reveal the recurring mental illness of patients soon to be married? Severe sexual problems? Progressively incapacitating genetic disease? One doctor recently wrote that he had seen many "impossible marriages" contracted because he could not violate his oath of professional secrecy. To keep silent regarding a patient's confidences is to honor one of the oldest obligations in medicine. Lawyers do the same for their clients, as do priests in hearing confessions.

Silence is often sufficient to uphold this obligation. But sometimes the silence is so interpreted that the secret stands revealed thereby. What if the parents of the young girl became suspicious and asked the physician if there was anything to prevent their daughter's marriage to the young man? For the doctor merely to stammer that he cannot reveal confidences is to confirm their suspicions. A lie is the simplest way to protect the secret, though some have worked out subtle forms of evasion in answering unauthorized questions regarding a professional secret, such as: "I know nothing about it" (with the mental reservation "to communicate to others").

Difficult choices arise for all those who have promised to keep secret what they have learned from a client, a patient, or a penitent. How to deflect irate fathers asking whether their daughters are pregnant and by whom; how to answer an employer inquiring about the psychiatric record of someone on his staff; how to cope with questions from the press about the health of a congressional candidate: such predicaments grow more common than ever. The line between appropriate and inappropriate requests for information may shift from one society to another and be revised over time; but wherever the line is drawn, those charged with secrets have to decide how best to protect them.

A similar loyalty also shields colleagues. Politicians, for instance, or doctors or lawyers are reluctant to divulge the incompetence or dishonesty of their fellows. Once again, when silence would give the game away, lying is one alternative. Some choose it even when they know that innocent persons will thereby be injured—mutilated through a clumsy operation, or embroiled in a law suit that never should have begun.

Are there limits to this duty of secrecy? Was it ever meant to stretch so as to require lying? Where does it come from and why is it so binding that it can protect those who have no right to impose their incompetence, their disease, their malevolence on ignorant victims?

At stake is fidelity, keeping faith with those who have confided their secrets on condition that they not be revealed. Fidelity to clients and peers is rooted in the most primeval tribal emotions: the loyalty to self, kin, clansmen, guild members as against the more diffusely perceived rest of humanity—the unrelated, the outsiders, the barbarians. Defending one's own is the rule long before justice becomes an issue. It precedes law and morality itself. Allied to the drive for self-preservation, it helps assure collective survival in a hostile environment. To reveal the truth about a friend can then come to mean that one is a "false friend." And to be "true" to kin and clan can mean confronting the world on their behalf with every weapon at one's disposal, including every form of deceit.

This drive to protect self and kin, friends and associates, persists even where moral rules and laws are recognized. Certain limits are then established: fraud and assault come to be circumscribed. But the limits are uncertain where these strong personal and professional bonds are present. And so lies to protect confidentiality come to be pitted against the restrictions on harming innocent persons. Practices, some legitimate, others shoddy, persist and grow behind the shield of confidentiality.

In order to distinguish between them, we have to ask: How is confidentiality itself defended? On what principles does it rest? And when, if ever, can those principles be stretched to justify lies in the protection of confidences?

Three separate claims are advanced in support of keeping secrets confidential. First, that we have a right to protect ourselves and those close to us from the harm that might flow from disclosure; second, that fairness requires respect for privacy; and third, that added respect is due for that which one has *promised* to keep secret.

The first claim appeals to the principle of avoiding harm. The lie to cover up for a friend, a client, a colleague may prevent injuries to their lives, even their liberty. The pilot whose heart condition is revealed may lose his job; the syphilitic fiancé may be jilted; the physician accused of malpractice may be convicted. Yet this appeal to principle obviously has its limits. To lie to avoid harm to the pilot or the fiancé can bring on greater harm, or more undeserved harm, to the passengers or the young woman about to marry. It is here that the perspective *within* a profession can be limiting; the bond of confidentiality can dim the perception of the suffering imposed on outsiders. This is especially true when it is not certain that any one person will be harmed—if a surgeon's addiction, say, means that one out of ten patients who would otherwise have lived die during operations.

The second claim invokes the right to privacy. Many requests for information are unwarranted and inherently unjust. To respond to them with silence or to turn them down is, then, to provide no more than what is due; but many are so perplexed or so frightened that they lie instead. Bonhoeffer relates such a case:

[. . .] a teacher asks a child in front of the class whether it is true, that his father often comes home drunk. It is true, but the child denies it.

In this category fall also all the illegitimate inquiries regarding political beliefs, sexual practices, or religious faith. In times of persecution, honest answers to such inquiries rob people of their freedom, their employment, respect in their communities. Refusing to give information that could blacklist a friend is then justified; and in cases where refusal is difficult or dangerous, lying may fall into the category of response to a crisis. One has a right to protect oneself and others from illegitimate inquiries, whether they come from intruders, from an oppressive government, or from an inquisitorial religious institution. A large area of each person's life is clearly his to keep as secret as he wishes. This is the region of *privacy,* of personal concerns and liberty not to be tampered with.

The delineation of this region of private concerns is today in considerable disarray. Should contraceptive choices, for example, or choices to abort, be protected? Should employers be able to give job seekers lie-detector tests? How can privacy be secured against unwarranted inroads? Each year, ever more records are kept by schools, psychiatrists, employers, probation officers, and by vast government and insurance computer systems. Investigators collect derogatory (or what happens to be thought derogatory at any one time) information, which is then sought by many more groups—prospective employers, the government, scholars doing research, and the press. Personal privacy is under constant pressure; and the lines between legitimate and illegitimate inquiries need continuous vigilance.

But is the young fiancé's syphilis properly in this region of his private concerns? Surely his future wife has a stake in learning about it. And surely a physician's drug addiction or alcoholism is more than his private affair, just as the guilt of the client on whose behalf the lawyer cooperates in perjury is not a matter of privacy alone.

The third claim in defense of confidentiality allows disclosure of secrets to prevent harm and to guard privacy, unless a promise has been made not to reveal the information in question. Even when confidentiality is not otherwise fair or beneficial, the argument runs, a promise can make it so. And even when ordinary promises might well be broken, professional ones to clients, to patients, or to those coming for confession, remain inviolate. When a confessor protects a secret, he may do what he would not do for those to whom he has made no promise of secrecy. This promise may exert such a strong pull as to override not only veracity alone and not only the desire to allow no harm to be done, but both together.

What is it, then, about promises, that endows them with such power? In the first place, in making a promise, I set up expectations, an equilibrium; should I break my promise, I upset that equilibrium and fail to live up to those expectations; I am unfair, given what I had promised and what I now owe to another. Second, in breaking faith, I am failing to make my promise *come true.** If I make a promise, knowing I shall break it, I am lying. Third, professional promises to clients are granted special inviolability so that those who most need help will feel free to seek it. Without a social policy allowing the protection of such secrets, people might not confide in lawyers or clergy. In this way, many would fail to benefit from legitimate means to help them.

But even this appeal to the sanctity of promises must surely have its limits. We can properly promise only what is ours to give or what it is right for us to do in the first place. Having made a promise adds no justification at all to an undertaking to do something that is in itself wrong. Here again, the question which must be asked of the deceptive practices shielded by confidentiality is what, exactly, *can* be thought of as rightly having been promised to clients and peers. The three claims made for confidentiality must be kept separate, then, as we look at practices of professional confidentiality to clients and to colleagues.

---

* Many philosophers have regarded promise-keeping as revealing the truth about what one promised. This would make promises one part of veracity. Others, such as Ross, have looked at veracity as part of promise-keeping: as a "general undertaking to tell the truth"—a promise of a kind. But all see the two as closely connected.

When they are not seen clearly, their limits grow dim; the rhetoric of loyalty may then take over, expanding those limits to include what was never meant to be protected by confidentiality. Or else the reverse may happen, so that the region of privacy shrinks in the face of unwarranted inquiries.

. . .

Fidelity to Clients

The relationship between a lawyer and his client is one of the intimate relations. You would lie for your wife. You would lie for your child. There are others with whom you are intimate enough, close enough, to lie for them when you would not lie for yourself. At what point do you stop lying for them? I don't know and you are not sure.

This statement by Charles Curtis, a well-known Boston lawyer, has stirred up much discussion and some censure. Are there persons for whom one would lie when one would not lie for oneself? And why should there be such a difference? The same questions have arisen for clergymen and physicians who protect the secrets of their parishioners or patients. At stake here is not the protection of colleagues; it is the defense, thought more legitimate, of information given by clients to professionals in strictest confidence.

Most would agree with Curtis that the relationship between professional and client, like that between husband and wife, requires that certain secrets be protected. But few have come out in public to stretch that privilege so far as to include lying. Curtis himself drew the line at lying in court. More recently, however, Monroe Freedman, Dean of Hofstra Law School and author of a well-known book on legal ethics, has advocated some forms of deception even in the courtroom:

. . . the criminal defense attorney, however unwillingly in terms of personal morality, has a professional responsibility as an advocate in an adversary system to examine the perjurious client in the ordinary way and to argue to the jury, as evidence in the case, the testimony presented by the defendant.

If, that is, a lawyer has a client who lies to the court and thus commits perjury, Professor Freedman holds that this defense lawyer has the professional responsibility to ask questions which do not contest this testimony and even to use the false testimony in making the best case for the client to the court officers and the jury. That this can involve lying is beyond doubt. Nor is there serious doubt that such instances are not rare in actual practice. Yet perjury has traditionally been more abhorred than other lying. How is it, then, that it has come to be thus defended, albeit by a minority of commentators? Defended, moreover, not just as a regrettable practice at times excusable, but actually as a *professional responsibility*.

One reason, once again, lies in the tribal ethic of avoiding harm to oneself and one's own. But it is often supported by an argument upholding the overriding strength of the privilege of confidentiality whenever a client gives information in confidence. Such a privilege is often thought to need no justification. Lawyers see it as so manifestly different from the shadier privileges claimed through the ages, ranging from the feudal sexual privilege to the excesses of "executive privilege," as to require no defense.

And yet, if we are to understand whether it *should* absolve lying in court, we must ask: What underlies the special claim of this privilege of confidentiality? Lawyers advance three arguments to support it. They argue, first, that even the most hardened criminal has a right to advice, help, and skilled advocacy; the right to a person loyal to him in particular. Fairness demands that his concerns be given a hearing; but he can convey his predicament honestly only if he is assured that his confidence will not be betrayed.

We can accept this argument and still not see why it should be stretched to justify lies. The assumption that the privilege can be thus stretched goes counter to the long tradition barring false witness, and the very special proscription of perjury. In the Jewish and Christian traditions, for example, false witness and perjury are the most serious forms of deception, inviting the most dire punishment. And a number of distinctions relevant to the dilemmas for contemporary lawyers have been worked out in some detail. Look, for example, at the ninth-century Penitential of Cummean:

> 8. He who makes a false oath shall do penance for four years.

> 9. But he who leads another in ignorance to commit perjury shall do penance for seven years.

> 10. He who is led in ignorance to commit perjury and afterward finds it out, one year.

> 11. He who suspects that he is being led into perjury and nevertheless swears, shall do penance for two years, on account of his consent.

A second argument for confidentiality goes beyond the individual client's rights. It holds that not only should we all be able to expect discretion from our lawyers, but that the social system as a whole will benefit if confidences can be kept. Otherwise, clients may not dare to reveal their secrets to their lawyers, who, in turn, will not be able to present their cases adequately. Even though injustice may result in individual cases when a zealous lawyer succeeds in concealing a client's misdeeds in court, the general level of justice will be raised, it is claimed, if clients can trust their lawyers to keep their secrets. For some, this argument stretches, once again, all the way to lying in court. And, once more, they adduce no further argument for so enlarging the principle.

Such arguments are often cemented, finally, by an appeal to the principle of veracity. Veracity itself will be advanced, many argue, if each side pushes as hard as it can to defeat the other. In the "adversary system of justice," truth is held to be more likely to emerge as a result of the contest between opposing forces if the accused is both defended and prosecuted "zealously within the bounds of the law." The adversary system is often contrasted by its supporters to the "inquisitorial system of law," wherein the state itself inquires into all the facts before bringing a trial. In a sense, those who advocate building on perjurious testimony in court then claim that lies can be a mechanism for producing truth. Yet this claim has never, to my knowledge, been empirically established. There is no reason why it could not be experimentally tested, in simulated court situations, for example. In the meantime, it seems self-contradictory to press it to the point of saying that truth will be advanced if we loosen the restrictions on perjury in court.

How, then, can these claims be evaluated? The strain on lawyers within the adversary system becomes evident precisely at this point—where the principle of confidentiality collides with the necessity to stay "within the bounds of the law."

The task of evaluating these claims is hampered by the fact that they have received little genuine inquiry recently within the legal profession, and even less outside it. Those who take up the question, in courses and textbooks on professional responsibility, of what lawyers in today's courts should do give no references to the debates on such issues in moral philosophy and in theology; nor do they refer students and practitioners to authors within the legal profession itself who have confronted these questions, such as Grotius and Pufendorf. This, in turn, is perhaps not to be wondered at, since philosophers themselves have paid little attention to such issues in the last few centuries.

But historical and professional insularity has dangers. It impoverishes; it leads to a vacuum of genuine analysis. Thus, one recent textbook on the professional responsibility of lawyers holds merely:

> There is simply no consensus, for example, as to the lawyer's duty to the court if he knows his client is lying. In that and other situations a lawyer can only be sensitive to the issues involved and resolve these difficult cases as responsibly as he or she is able.

Closer to throwing up one's hands one cannot get. To leave such choice open to the sensitive and the responsible without giving them criteria for choice is to leave it open as well to the insensitive and the corrupt. References to responsibility and sensitivity are made to take the place of analysis and broader inquiry.

The problem here, as with many other deceptive professional practices, is that the questions are too often left up to the professionals themselves, whereas the issues obviously touch the *public* welfare intimately. There is, then, a great need for a wider debate and analysis of these issues. When does the privilege of confidentiality exceed the boundaries of the law? When does the promise on which confidentiality is based turn out to be itself illegitimate? Do we want a society where lawyers can implicitly promise to guard their clients' secrets through perjury and lies? Such a debate would have to go far beyond the confines of the American Bar Association and the teaching of professional responsibility in law schools.

If the public were to enter such a debate, it is much more likely that we should see the concerns central to this book come to the foreground: concerns for the consequences of a professional *practice* and on those engaging in it, their peers, the system of justice and society at large; concerns for the ways in which such practices spread, and for the added institutional damage which then results.

The slope here is very slippery indeed. For if some lies in court to protect a client's confidences are all right, why not others? If the lawyer is sole judge of what is a tolerable lie, what criteria will he use? Will there not be pressure to include other lies, ostensibly also to protect the client's confidence? And if lawyers become *used* to accepting certain lies, how will this affect their integrity in other areas?

One effect of a public debate of these questions would inevitably be increased knowledge about deceptive professional practices in the law. And it can be argued that this knowledge ought then to be shared with all who participate in trials—most especially judges and juries. Should juries perhaps then be instructed to take into account the fact that a number of lawyers believe it their right to build upon perjured testimony?

It is clear that even those lawyers willing to support such a right for themselves would not wish juries to be thus instructed. But if they ask themselves why, they may come to see their own behavior in a different perspective. The most important reasons they might advance showing why juries should not have such knowledge are that it should remain easy to mislead them, that their trust in the legal profession and in courtroom procedures should remain whole. More than that, once forewarned, any juror with even minimal sense would then have to be quite suspicious about every *other* possible form of deception on the part of lawyers.

Imagining such instructions to the jury shows, I believe, that those who wish to tell lies in court, even for the best of motives, cannot expose these motives to the light of publicity. They want to participate in a practice but not have it generally known that they do.

Can it be argued that such lies are so common by now that they form an accepted practice that everyone knows about—much like a game or bargaining in a bazaar? But in that case, why should lawyers feel so uncomfortable at the prospect of instructing the jury about the practice? The fact is that, even though lawyers may know about such a practice, it is not publicly known, especially to jurors, much less consented to.

I believe, therefore, that a public inquiry into the appropriateness of lying in court on behalf of perjurious clients would lead to a perception that there are limits to acceptable advocacy in court. And these limits, moreover, are not different because of the lawyer-client relationship. That relationship, with its privilege of confidentiality, does not in itself justify lying for clients. At the very least, the limits set would have to exclude actual presentation of perjury by lawyers as well as the more circuitous ways of building upon a client's perjury. Lawyers themselves might well be grateful for the standards to be publicly discussed and openly established. They could then more easily resist pressure from clients and resolve to their own satisfaction what might otherwise seem to present them with a confusing conflict of personal and professional principle.

Once again, what is needed is the ability to shift perspectives and to see not only the needs that press for perjury and lying, but the effect that such practices have upon the deceived and social trust. Judge Marvin E. Frankel describes thus such a shift:

> [. . .] our adversary system rates truth too low among the values that institutions of justice are meant to serve. [. . .] [O]ur more or less typical lawyer selected as a trial judge experiences a dramatic change in perspective as he moves to the other side of the bench.

C. RULE 11

Introductory Note

In actual effect on the practice of law, the single most important development in the law of professional responsibility in recent years has been the 1983 amendment to Rule 11 of the Federal Rules of Civil Procedure. The amended rule provides that the lawyer's signature on any paper filed in federal court represents the lawyer's warranty:

1. that the lawyer has read the paper
2. that the lawyer has undertaken a reasonable inquiry as to the law and facts contained therein
3. that the lawyer believes, after such inquiry, that the paper is:
   a. well-grounded in fact and
   b. warranted by existing law or a good faith argument for the extension, modification or reversal of existing law

and

4. that the paper is not interposed for any improper purpose, such as to harass or to cause unnecessary delay or needless increase in the cost of litigation.

Unlike the old rule, the new rule

(1) requires that the lawyer conduct a reasonable inquiry before making a factual assertion *or* legal argument;

(2) is violated whenever a reasonable lawyer would not have believed what the lawyer believed when submitting the paper, i.e., the new rule requires an *objective* basis; and

(3) requires that sanctions be imposed whenever the rule is violated instead of leaving it to the court's discretion.

Rule 11 sanctions are now commonplace. Before the 1983 amendments Rule 11 motions had been filed in only nineteen reported cases; in the first two years after the rule was amended, there were 200 reported cases involving Rule 11 sanctions. Thomas v. Capital Security Services, Inc., 836 F.2d 866 n. 14 (5th Cir.1988) (en banc) (citing statistics from Kassin, An Empirical Study of Rule 11 Sanctions 2 (Fed.Jud.Center 1985); and Nelken, Sanctions Under Amended Federal Rule 11—Some "Chilling" Problems in the Struggle Between Compensation and Punishment, 74 Geo.L.J. 1313, 1326 (1986)). See also Schwarzer, Rule 11 Revisited, 101 Harv.L.Rev. 1013 (1988); Vairo, Report to the Advisory Committee on Amended Rule 11 of the Federal Rules of Civil Procedure 5 (unpublished, Sept. 1987).

The changes in Rule 11 and the resulting increase in the frequency of sanctions have been widely criticized particularly by the plaintiffs and civil rights bar, as well as by many legal academics. Critics contend that Rule 11 stunts the growth of new legal interpretations because it can be (and is, they argue) used to penalize lawyers who persist in challenging existing doctrine. See, e.g., Nelkin, supra; Cochran, Recent Developments in Response to Rule 11 Problems, 9 Cornerstone 1 (November/December 1987) (memorandum prepared to support The Center for Constitutional Rights's national study on the use of Rule 11 and its negative effect on the rights of litigants). But see Parness, More Stringent Sanctions Under Federal Civil Rule 11: A Reply to Professor Nelken, 75 Geo.L.J. 1937 (1987). See also Symposium: Amended Rule 11 of the Federal Rules of Civil Procedure: How Go the Best Laid Plans?, 54 Fordham L.Rev. 1 (1985); Note, A Uniform Approach to Rule 11 Sanctions, 97 Yale L.J. 901 (1988); Note, Plausible Pleadings Developing Standards for Rule 11 Sanctions, 100 Harv.L.Rev. 630 (1987); Note, The Dynamics of Rule 11: Preventing Frivolous Litigation by Demanding Professional Responsibility, 61 N.Y.U.L. Rev. 300 (1986).

Many states have adopted rules modeled on Federal Rule 11 as amended in 1983. See, e.g., 110 Ill.Rev.Stat. 2–611 (1987); Kansas Stat. Ann. § 60–211 (1987); Ky.Rules Civ.Proc.R. 11 (1984); Mich.Civ.Rule 2.114; 20 Mont.Code Ann.Rule 11 (1988); N.C.Gen.Stat. § 1A–1, Rule 11 (1986); Okl.Stat. tit. 12, § 2011 (1987); and Wyo.Stat. § 1–14–128. Virginia's rule mirrors the federal rule but also covers oral motions. Va.Code § 8.01–271.1 (1988).

Does Rule 11 go too far? Not far enough? Should the Rule be amended to address more specifically the concerns about chilling legitimate advocacy? When, if ever, does advocacy go too far? Are there other deterrents that would be effective but less "chilling"?

GOLDEN EAGLE DISTRIBUTING CORPORATION v. BURROUGHS CORPORATION

United States Court of Appeals, Ninth Circuit, 1986.
801 F.2d 1531.

SCHROEDER, CIRCUIT JUDGE.

I. INTRODUCTION

This is an appeal from the imposition of sanctions under Rule 11 of the Federal Rules of Civil Procedure as amended in 1983. The appellant, a major national law firm, raises significant questions of first impression.

The relevant portions of the amended Rule provide:

Every pleading, motion, and other paper of a party represented by an attorney shall be signed by at least one attorney of record in his individual name, whose address shall be stated. A party who is not represented by an attorney shall sign his pleading, motion, or other paper and state his address. . . . The signature of an attorney or party constitutes a certificate by him that he has read the pleading, motion, or other paper; that to the best of his knowledge, information, and belief formed after reasonable inquiry it is well grounded in fact and is warranted by existing law or a good faith argument for the extension, modification, or reversal of existing law, and that it is not interposed for any improper purpose, such as to harass or to cause unnecessary delay or needless increase in the cost of litigation. If a pleading, motion, or other paper is not signed, it shall be stricken unless it is signed promptly after the omission is called to the attention of the pleader or movant. If a pleading, motion, or other paper is signed in violation of this rule, the court, upon motion or upon its own initiative, shall impose upon the person who signed it, a represented party, or both, an appropriate sanction, which may include an order to pay to the other party or parties the amount of the reasonable expenses incurred because of the filing of the pleading, motion, or other paper, including a reasonable attorney's fee.

The appellant Kirkland & Ellis is the law firm that represented the defendant Burroughs in the underlying litigation. The sanctions which we review here stemmed from an unsuccessful motion for summary judgment filed by appellant on Burroughs' behalf. . . .

. . .

The district court held that the positions taken by the appellant in its motions papers were supportable, both legally and factually. The district court concluded, however, . . . that the appellant should have stated that a position it was taking was grounded in a "good faith argument for the extension, modification, or reversal of existing law" rather than implying that its position was "warranted by existing law." Second, the court held that the appellant's moving papers had failed to cite contrary authority in violation of the ABA's Model Rules of Professional Conduct, and that this breach constituted a violation of Rule 11.

. . .

II. PROCEDURAL BACKGROUND OF THIS DISPUTE

Golden Eagle Distributing Corporation filed the underlying action in Minnesota state court for fraud, negligence, and breach of contract against Burroughs, because of an allegedly defective computer system. Burroughs removed the action to the federal district court in Minnesota. Burroughs then moved pursuant to 28 U.S.C. § 1404(a) to transfer the action to the Northern District of California. The district court granted the motion, noting that all of the sources of proof, including the relevant documents and the computer system at issue, and almost all of the witnesses, were located in California.

Burroughs next filed the motion for summary judgment which gave rise to the sanctions at issue here. It argued that the California, rather than the Minnesota, statute of limitations applied. . . .

. . . .

A. The Statute of Limitations Argument

Kirkland & Ellis's opening memorandum argued that Golden Eagle's claims were barred by California's three-year statute of limitations. The question was whether the change of venue from Minnesota to California affected which law applied. Kirkland & Ellis essentially argued that under Van Dusen v. Barrack, 376 U.S. 612, 84 S.Ct. 805, 11 L.Ed.2d 945 (1964), California's law applied because a Minnesota court would have dismissed the action on *forum non conveniens* grounds. . . .

. . .

In imposing sanctions, the district court held that Kirkland & Ellis's argument was "misleading" because it suggested that there already exists a *forum non conveniens* exception to the general rule that the transferor's law applies. *Golden Eagle,* 103 F.R.D. at 126–28. *Van Dusen* raised the issue but did not decide it. 376 U.S. at 640, 84 S.Ct. at 821.

Kirkland & Ellis's corollary argument, that a Minnesota court would have dismissed the case on *forum non conveniens* grounds, was found to be "misleading" because it failed to note that one prerequisite to such a dismissal is that an alternative forum be available. See Bongards' Creameries v. Alfa–Laval, Inc., 339 N.W.2d 561, 562 (Minn. 1983). Burroughs had pointed out in its Rule 11 memorandum, however, that the meaning of the term "available forum" is not settled. Compare Wasche v. Wasche, 268 N.W.2d 721, 723 (Minn.1978) (statute of limitations bar may affect dismissal) with Hill v. Upper Mississippi

Towing Corp., 252 Minn. 165, 89 N.W.2d 654 (1958) (suggesting available forum is where defendant is amenable to process).

. . .

B. The Economic Damages Argument

Kirkland & Ellis also argued that Golden Eagle's claim for negligent manufacture lacked merit because Golden Eagle sought damages for economic loss, and such damages are not recoverable under California law. Kirkland & Ellis relied on Seely v. White Motor Co., 63 Cal.2d 9, 403 P.2d 145, 45 Cal.Rptr. 17 (1965). In *Seely,* the California Supreme Court limited recovery in negligence and strict liability tort actions to damages for personal injuries and harm to physical property.

The district court sanctioned Kirkland & Ellis for not citing three cases whose holdings it concluded were adverse to *Seely:* the California Supreme Court's opinion in J'Aire Corp. v. Gregory, 24 Cal.3d 799, 598 P.2d 60, 157 Cal.Rptr. 407 (1979), and two intermediate appellate court decisions interpreting *J'Aire's* effect on *Seely*, Pisano v. American Leasing, 146 Cal.App.3d 194, 194 Cal.Rptr. 77 (1983), and Huang v. Garner, 157 Cal.App.3d 404, 203 Cal.Rptr. 800 (1984).[1] The district court held that these omissions violated counsel's duty to disclose adverse authority, embodied in Model Rule 3.3, . . . which the court viewed as a "necessary corollary to Rule 11." *Golden Eagle,* 103 F.R.D. at 127.

Kirkland & Ellis continues to maintain vigorously that the cases are not directly adverse authority and that they are distinguishable. In this appeal we assume that they are directly contrary in order to reach the larger question of whether Kirkland & Ellis's failure to cite them was a violation of Rule 11.

III. THE BACKGROUND OF THE 1983 AMENDMENTS TO RULE 11 AND THEIR INTERPRETATION IN THE COURTS

Under the 1983 amendments to Rule 11, an attorney signing any motion in federal court warrants that the motion is well-grounded in fact, that it is warranted by existing law or a good faith argument for an extension, modification or reversal of existing law, and that it is not filed for an improper purpose. . . .

The Advisory Committee Note to the amendments comments at length on their purpose. The members of the Advisory Committee, as well as its reporter, also commented extensively as individuals. All the comments make it clear that the amendments' major purposes were the deterrence of dilatory or abusive pretrial tactics and the streamlining of litigation. The Advisory Committee Note on the amendments to Rule 11, for example, states that the amended Rule will accomplish these purposes "by lessening frivolous claims or defenses." 97 F.R.D. 165, 198 (1983). . . .

---

1. Kirkland & Ellis did cite and discuss *J'Aire* in its reply brief after the case was called to its attention in plaintiff's response.

. . .

Th[e] expansion [of Rule 11] gave rise to concerns that the new Rule might have unfortunate results in at least two respects. The first was that the amended Rule might tend to chill creativity in advocacy and impede the traditional ability of the common law to adjust to changing situations. The Advisory Committee responded . . ..

The rule is not intended to chill an attorney's enthusiasm or creativity in pursuing factual or legal theories. The court is expected to avoid using the wisdom of hindsight and should test the signer's conduct by inquiring what was reasonable to believe at the time the pleading, motion, or other paper was submitted.

Id. at 199.

Another major concern was that the broadened availability of sanctions might lead to protracted and expensive satellite litigation over the appropriateness of sanctions. . . .

. . . The leading decision in this circuit has identified the two major problems to which the amendments were directed as the problem of "frivolous filings" and the problem of "misusing judicial procedures as a weapon for personal or economic harassment." Zaldivar v. City of Los Angeles, 780 F.2d 823, 830 (9th Cir.1986). Along the same lines, the leading decision of the Second Circuit announced tests for the mandatory imposition of sanctions under both parts of the Rule. Sanctions should be imposed if (1) "after reasonable inquiry, a competent attorney could not form a reasonable belief that the pleading (or other paper) is well grounded in fact and is warranted by existing law or a good faith argument for the extension, modification or reversal of existing law" or if (2) "a pleading (or other paper) has been interposed for any improper purpose." Eastway [Construction Corp. v. City of New York] 762 F.2d [243] at 25 [(2d Cir.1985)]; see also McLaughlin v. Western Casualty & Surety Co., 603 F.Supp. 978, 981 (S.D.Ala.1985).

Courts have sanctioned attorneys for violating the first part of the Rule in a variety of circumstances. A legal position which is superficially plausible has been held sanctionable where it has no basis in the law and ignores relevant United States Supreme Court authority contrary to the position asserted. Rodgers v. Lincoln Towing Service, Inc., 771 F.2d 194, 205 (7th Cir.1985). A factually baseless contention that exigent circumstances justified a warrantless entry led to sanctions in Frazier v. Cast, 771 F.2d 259 (7th Cir. 1985). A leading example of imposition of sanctions for violation of the second part of Rule 11 is Chevron, USA, Inc. v. Hand, 763 F.2d 1184 (10th Cir.1985), in which sanctions were upheld because the defendant had agreed to a stipulated settlement to dismiss the case and hired another attorney solely to delay the entry of the stipulated dismissal.

There is general agreement that whether the first of the two Rule 11 requirements has been satisfied is to be determined by use of an objective standard. . . .

As to the second, "not for improper purposes," part of Rule 11, we emphasized in *Zaldivar* the objective nature of the standard. We stated that a complaint which complies with the "well-grounded in fact and warranted by . . . law" clause cannot be sanctioned as harassment under Rule 11, regardless of the subjective intent of the attorney or litigant. *Zaldivar,* 780 F.2d at 832.

. . .

IV. STANDARD OF REVIEW

The courts of appeals have given some consideration to standards of review in sanction cases. Because Rule 11 mandates sanctions when it is violated, the prevailing view of the courts of appeals is that whether specific conduct violated the Rule is a legal question which must be reviewed de novo. *Zaldivar,* 780 F.2d at 828; *Eastway,* 762 F.2d at 254 n. 7. If there is any dispute as to factual determinations concerning the conduct, the determinations would be reviewed under a clearly erroneous standard. *Zaldivar,* 780 F.2d at 828. Since the district court has wide discretion in determining what sanctions should be imposed for violation of the Rule, however, the appropriateness of the sanctions must be reviewed under an abuse of discretion standard. Id.; Westmoreland v. CBS, Inc., 770 F.2d 1168, 1175 (D.C.Cir.1985); *Eastway,* 762 F.2d at 254 n. 7.

V. THE APPLICATION OF RULE 11 IN THIS CASE

The district court's application of Rule 11 in this case strikes a chord not otherwise heard in discussion of this Rule. The district court did not focus on whether a sound basis in law and in fact existed for the defendant's motion for summary judgment. Indeed it indicated that the motion itself was nonfrivolous. 103 F.R.D. at 126. Rather, the district court looked to the manner in which the motion was presented. The district court in this case held that Rule 11 imposes upon counsel an ethical "duty of candor." *Golden Eagle,* 103 F.R.D. at 127. The court drew its principles from Rule 3.3 of the ABA's Model Rules and the accompanying comment. It said:

> The duty of candor is a necessary corollary of the certification required by Rule 11. A court has a right to expect that counsel will state the controlling law fairly and fully; indeed, unless that is done the court cannot perform its task properly. A lawyer must not misstate the law, fail to disclose adverse authority (not disclosed by his opponent), or omit facts critical to the application of the rule of law relied on.

Golden Eagle, 103 F.R.D. at 127.

. . .

We need not here definitively resolve the problems of the proper role of the courts in enforcing the ethical obligations of lawyers.[3] We must consider only whether Rule 11 requires the courts to enforce ethical standards of advocacy beyond the terms of the Rule itself.

The district court's invocation of Rule 11 has two aspects. The first, which we term "argument identification" is the holding that counsel should differentiate between an argument "warranted by existing law" and an argument for the "extension, modification, or reversal of existing law." The second is the conclusion that Rule 11 is violated when counsel fails to cite what the district court views to be directly contrary authority. We deal with each in turn, noting at the outset that many of our observations are applicable to both aspects of the court's interpretation of Rule 11.

A. "Argument Identification"

. . .

The text of the Rule does not require that counsel differentiate between a position which is supported by existing law and one that would extend it. The Rule on its face requires that the motion be either one or the other. . . . It is not always easy to decide whether an argument is based on established law or is an argument for the extension of existing law. Whether the case being litigated is or is not materially the same as earlier precedent is frequently the very issue which prompted the litigation in the first place. Such questions can be close.

Sanctions under Rule 11 are mandatory. See, e.g., *Eastway,* 762 F.2d at 254 n. 7. In even a close case, we think it extremely unlikely that a judge, who has already decided that the law is not as a lawyer argued it, will also decide that the loser's position was warranted by existing law. Attorneys who adopt an aggressive posture risk more than the loss of the motion if the district court decides that their argument is for an extension of the law which it declines to make. What is at stake is often not merely the monetary sanction but the lawyer's reputation.

The "argument identification" requirement adopted by the district court therefore tends to create a conflict between the lawyer's duty zealously to represent his client, Model Code of Professional Responsibility Canon 7, and the lawyer's own interest in avoiding rebuke. The concern on the part of the bar that this type of requirement will chill advocacy is understandable.[4] . . .

3. Our judicial system reserves at least some role. See Roadway Express, Inc. v. Piper, 447 U.S. 752, 766–67, 100 S.Ct. 2455, 2464, 65 L.Ed.2d 488 (1980); Eash v. Riggins Trucking Inc., 757 F.2d 557, 564–65 (3d Cir.1985) (en banc).

4. The ABA's litigation section has commented, for example, that the *Golden Eagle* decision "caused complete consternation in the practicing bar which sees vigorous advocacy, seemingly without regard to its possible misrepresentations to the court, as the hallmark of aggressive and justified representation of the client."

Moreover, Rule 11 does not apply to the mere making of a frivolous argument. The Rule permits the imposition of sanctions only when the "pleading, motion, or other paper" itself is frivolous, not when one of the arguments in support of a pleading or motion is frivolous. Nothing in the language of the Rule or the Advisory Committee Notes supports the view that the Rule empowers the district court to impose sanctions on lawyers simply because a particular argument or ground for relief contained in a non-frivolous motion is found by the district court to be unjustified. . . .

· · ·

There is another risk when mandatory sanctions ride upon close judicial decisions. The danger of arbitrariness increases and the probability of uniform enforcement declines. The Federal Judicial Center recently studied the application of Rule 11 in fairly routine cases involving issues far less sophisticated than those involved in this case. The conclusion was as follows:

> Overall, we found that although the 1983 amendments appear to have increased judges' readiness to enforce the new certification requirements, their success thus far has been limited. Of specific concern are the findings that there is a good deal of interjudge disagreement over what actions constitute a violation of the rule, only partial compliance with the desired objective standard, inaccurate and systematically biased normative assumptions about other judges' reactions to frivolous actions, and a continued neglect of alternative, nonmonetary means of response.

· · ·

B. The Failure to Cite Adverse Authority

· · ·

Were the scope of the rule to be expanded as the district court suggests, mandatory sanctions would ride on close decisions concerning whether or not one case is or is not the same as another. We think Rule 11 should not impose the risk of sanctions in the event that the court later decides that the lawyer was wrong. The burdens of research and briefing by a diligent lawyer anxious to avoid any possible rebuke would be great. And the burdens would not be merely on the lawyer. If the mandatory provisions of the Rule are to be interpreted literally, the court would have a duty to research authority beyond that provided by the parties to make sure that they have not omitted something.

· · ·

In rejecting the district court's broad interpretation of Rule 11, we do not suggest that the court is powerless to sanction lawyers who take positions which cannot be supported. A lawyer should not be able to proceed with impunity in real or feigned ignorance of authorities which render his argument meritless. See, e.g., Rodgers v. Lincoln Towing Service, Inc., 771 F.2d 194, 205 (7th Cir.1985). In addition, Rule 11 is not the only tool available to judges in imposing sanctions on lawyers. However, neither Rule 11 nor any other rule imposes a requirement that the lawyer, in addition to advocating the cause of his client, step first into the shoes of opposing counsel to find all potentially contrary authority, and finally into the robes of the judge to decide whether the authority is indeed contrary or whether it is distinguishable. It is not in the nature of our adversary system to require lawyers to demonstrate to the court that they have exhausted every theory, both for and against their client. Nor does that requirement further the interests of the court. It blurs the role of judge and advocate. The role of judges is not merely to

> match the colors of the case at hand against the colors of many sample cases spread out upon their desk. . . . It is when the colors do not match, when the references in the index fail, when there is no decisive precedent, that the serious business of the judge begins.

B. Cardozo, The Nature of the Judicial Process 21 (1922). In conducting this "serious business," the judge relies on each party to present his side of the dispute as forcefully as possible. The lawyers cannot adequately perform their role if they are required to make predeterminations of the kind the district court's approach to Rule 11 would necessitate.

· · ·

The Ninth Circuit denied a sua sponte request for an en banc hearing in *Golden Eagle.* Judge Noonan's dissent from that denial, joined by four other judges, follows:

GOLDEN EAGLE DISTRIBUTING CORPORATION v. BURROUGHS CORPORATION

United States Court of Appeals, Ninth Circuit, 1987.
809 F.2d 584.

NOONAN, CIRCUIT JUDGE, with whom SNEED, ANDERSON, HALL, and KOZINSKI, CIRCUIT JUDGES, join dissenting from the denial of a sua sponte request for en banc hearing:

· · ·

. . . The district judge had in front of him a brief which did three things. The brief flatly misrepresented Minnesota law as having definitively decided the issue of *forum non conveniens* in a way favorable to the defendant. The brief insinuated that federal law on the same issue was definitively established the way the defendant would have liked. The brief set out California law without qualification and without mention of later authority which for purposes of the present opinion is assumed to have been "directly contrary." The court sanctioned Kirkland, Ellis for these three statements of law, each of which was not "warranted." The truth or falsity of a statement is not merely a matter of "the manner" in which a position is presented. A false statement presented as a true statement is simply a misstatement. It is not warranted. It should be sanctionable.

. . . The opinion substitutes extreme hypotheticals for the case at hand. It imagines close cases where a judge might sanction a lawyer because the judge disagrees with his argument. But close cases exist that test the workability of any rule, civil or criminal. They are not a reason for repealing the rule. Here, on the opinion's own admission, the case was not close. Kirkland, Ellis failed to cite "directly contrary" authority.

. . .

How can a brief be warranted by existing law if its argument goes in the face of "directly contrary" authority from the highest court of the jurisdiction whose law is being argued? How can a brief be warranted to be "a good faith argument for the extension, modification, or reversal of existing law" when there is not the slightest indication that the brief is arguing for extension, modification or reversal?

. . .

The opinion puts the question as one of "argument identification," treating Kirkland, Ellis' failure as a failure to identify correctly its argument as one for extension of existing law. But Kirkland, Ellis' failure was far greater. Kirkland, Ellis made no argument at all for extending existing law. It simply misrepresented the law it cited.

. . .

. . . The Rule mandates sanctions for any legal papers filed in federal court with *any* improper purpose. The opinion reads "any" out of the Rule.

. . .

. . . The opinion says that the signatory attorney "warrants." "Warrants" is a verb meaning "to assure a person of the truth of what is said." *Webster's,* Meaning 2b.

How can a lawyer offer testimony to the truth of what he has filed, how can he assure a person of its truth, if it is a misrepresentation?

. . .

. . . The opinion goes on to cite with apparent approval the view of the American Bar Association's Litigation Section that "the practicing bar" sees vigorous advocacy "seemingly without regard to its possible misrepresentations to the court" as the mark of "justified representation of the client."

This vision of vigorous advocacy "seemingly" indifferent to misrepresentations is cited by the opinion as "understandable" concern by the bar that vigorous advocacy not be chilled. Identification of vigorous advocacy with indifference to misrepresentation reflects a one-sided view. It is a view that has been repudiated by modern legal ethics. There is no reason to revive the old, discredited view, much less to incorporate the old view into an interpretation of Rule 11. Vigorous advocacy is, necessarily, truthful advocacy.

A distinct shift from the old view was made in a report by the Joint Conference on Professional Responsibility established by the American Bar Association and the Association of American Law Schools. "Confronted by the layman's charge" that the lawyer is "nothing but a hired brain and voice," this committee undertook to set out the duties of lawyers in terms of social functions that made the lawyer's role understandable, acceptable, and even necessary. See Introductory Statement of Co-chairmen Lon L. Fuller and John D. Randall, "Professional Responsibility: Report of the Joint Conference," 44 *ABA Journal* 1159 (1958). The report, in large measure, reflected the jurisprudence, the insights, and the wisdom of Professor Fuller. The report stressed that "the integrity of the adjudicative process itself" depends upon the participation of the advocate in order to hold in suspense the mind of the judge, prevent premature closure of the judge's mind, and make a wise decision possible. The function of the advocate defined his responsibilities and the limits of advocacy. The report concluded that a lawyer whose "desire to win leads him to muddy the headwaters of decision" and who "distorts and obscures" the true nature of a case "trespasses against the obligations of professional responsibility." Id. at 1161.

Modern codes of ethics have followed this line of thought. The American Bar Association's *Model Code of Professional Responsibility* invoked the report of the Joint Conference in stating that a lawyer today "stands in special need of a clear understanding of his obligations and of the vital connection between these obligations and the role his profession plays in society." Preamble, fn. 3, ABA Model Code of Professional Responsibility (1974). The first disciplinary rule of the Code is that "a lawyer shall not . . . engage in conduct involving dishonesty, fraud, deceit or misrepresentation." DR 1–102(A)(4). The Disciplinary Rule does not distinguish misrepresentation of fact and misrepresentation of law.

More specifically, under the general heading, "Representing a Client Zealously", the Model Code provides that a lawyer "shall not . . . knowingly advance a claim or defense that is unwarranted under existing law, except that he may advance such claim or defense if it can be supported by good faith argument for an extension, modification, or reversal of existing law." DR 7–102(A)(2). Ethical Consideration 7–23 in the same Code declares, "Where a lawyer knows of legal authority in the controlling jurisdiction directly adverse to the position of his client, he should inform the tribunal of its existence unless his adversary has done so . . ." EC 7–23.

The standards of the Model Code are substantially followed in the Model Rules of Professional Conduct of the American Bar Association. Rule 3.3 under the heading, "Candor Toward the Tribunal" makes it a black letter rule that a lawyer should not knowingly "fail to disclose to the tribunal legal authority in the controlling jurisdiction known to the lawyer to be directly diverse to the position of the client and not disclosed by opposing counsel." Model Rules 3.3(a)(3). The note on this

Rule goes on to say, "Legal argument based on a knowingly false representation of law constitutes dishonesty toward the tribunal . . . The underlying concept is that legal argument is a discussion seeking to determine the legal premises properly applicable to the case."

In black letters the Model Rules also provide, "A lawyer shall not bring or defend a proceeding, or assert or controvert an issue therein unless there is a basis for doing so that is not frivolous, which includes a good faith argument for an extension, modification, or reversal of existing law." Model Rule 3.1. Commentary on this Rule explicitly links it to DR 7–102(A)(2) of the Model Code.

Amazingly, the opinion of the court fails to acknowledge the source for the language of Rule 11 that a paper should be "warranted by existing law or a good faith argument for the extension, modification or reversal of existing law." Both the ABA's Model Rules, adopted on August 2, 1983, and Rule 11, which became effective August 1, 1983, are properly seen as based on DR 7–102(A)(2) of the Model Code in their treatment of what a lawyer should not do. If the objective standard of Rule 11 is higher than the subjective standard of Model Rule 3.3, that is no reason for the court to ignore the link between Rule 11 and the ethical standards of the bar.

It is equally surprising that the opinion of the court does not acknowledge that in the ABA's Model Rules, frivolousness is specifically defined by the absence of "a good faith argument for an extension, modification or reversal of existing law." Frivolousness does not only consist, as the court appears to assume, in making a baseless claim. Frivolousness also consists in making a legal argument without a good faith foundation.

. . . Not only does the opinion suggest a view of unrestrained advocacy repudiated by modern authorities, it favors a type of analysis sponsored by the Eighth Circuit and overruled by the Supreme Court [in *Whiteside*]. The opinion takes the position that a requirement of truthful argumentation "tends to create a conflict between the lawyer's duty zealously to represent his client" and "the lawyer's own interest in avoiding rebuke."

Precisely such an analysis was offered by the Eighth Circuit in relieving the lawyer of an obligation not to present perjury. That court found "a conflict of interest" between the lawyer's duty to represent his client zealously and the lawyer's ethical duty not to present perjury. Whiteside v. Scurr, 744 F.2d 1323 (8th Cir.1984); rehearing en banc denied, 750 F.2d 713 (8th Cir.1984). Reversing the Eighth Circuit, the Supreme Court noted that there was no conflict of duties when the lawyer was asked by his client to assist "in the presentation of false testimony." . . .

A client has as little right to the presentation of false arguments as he has to the presentation of false testimony. No conflict exists when a lawyer confines his advocacy by his duty to the court. The opinion is insensitive and unresponsive to the teaching of the Supreme Court that a restraint on the freedom of a lawyer to present falsity as truth does not create any true conflict. The lawyer has a duty to work within the boundaries of professional responsibility. He is not free to suborn testimony, to perjure himself, to offer perjured testimony, or to misrepresent facts or law. . . .

III. Alternative Avenues

The opinion, in its penultimate phase concedes that a lawyer "should not be able to proceed with impunity in real or feigned ignorance of authorities which render his argument meritless," and the opinion acknowledges that "Rule 11 is not the only tool available to judges in imposing sanctions on lawyers." . . .

The General Rules of the United States District Court for the Northern District of California, Rule 110–3, prescribe:

> Every member of the bar of this court and any attorney permitted to practice in this court under Local rule 110–2 shall be familiar with and comply with the standards of professional conduct required of members of the State Bar of California and contained in the State Bar Act, the Rules of Professional Conduct of the State Bar of California, and decisions of any court applicable thereto; maintain the respect due courts of justice and judicial officers; perform with the honesty, care, and decorum required for the fair and efficient administration of justice; discharge the obligations owed to his clients and to the judges of the court.

A lawyer who misrepresents the law has failed to discharge the obligations owed to the judges of the court. He is subject to sanctions under General Rules 110–6 and 110–7. The difference between those sanctions and the sanctions now made inapplicable by the court is that under Rule 11 the sanctions are mandatory; under the rules of the district court, the sanctions are to be imposed in the sound discretion of the district judge. . . .

. . .

Where a court has applied sanctions on a basis which is subsequently held to be mistaken, and the case is remanded, the court retains the power to award sanctions on a proper basis, such as the inherent power of the court to sanction the bad faith of counsel. Roadway Express, Inc. v. Piper, 447 U.S. at 767, 100 S.Ct. at 2464.

Questions

What, if anything, was wrong with Kirkland & Ellis' argument about *Van Dusen*? Its argument that the Minnesota court would have dismissed the case on *forum non conveniens* grounds? Its failure to cite *J'Aire*?

Do any of these arguments violate M.R. 3.3? Did Kirkland & Ellis' motion violate M.R. 3.1?

How are Model Rules 3.3 and 3.1 or their Code counterparts, DR 7–102(A)(1)(2)(3)(5) and DR 7–106(B)(1), related to Rule 11 according to the panel in *Golden Eagle*? According to Judge Noonan?

Is the reference to the bar's view of "vigorous advocacy", see footnote 4 of the panel decision, cited with approval as Judge Noonan claims? For what purpose is it cited? How do the two opinions envision the role of the advocate?

The panel suggests that Rule 11 sanctions are never appropriate unless the entire paper is frivolous. But see Community Electric Service v. National Electrical Contractors, 869 F.2d 1235 (9th Cir.1989) discussed in the note below at p. 397.

Papers Not Well Grounded in Fact

Many Rule 11 cases involve positively false factual assertions or assertions not supported by the underlying facts. The falsity need not be deliberate or even reckless. Under Rule 11 it is enough that the lawyer failed to make a reasonable pre-filing inquiry to ascertain what the facts were. See, e.g., King v. Idaho Funeral Service Association, 862 F.2d 744 (9th Cir.1988).

To determine whether an attorney or party made a reasonable inquiry into the facts, the trial court considers: how much time the signer had for the investigation; the extent to which the attorney had to rely on the client for factual foundation; whether the case was accepted from another attorney; the complexity of the facts; and the need for discovery to develop the claim. Thomas v. Capital Security Services, Inc., 836 F.2d 866, 988 (5th Cir.1988); Brown v. Federation of State Medical Bds., 830 F.2d 1429 (7th Cir.1987).

The Fifth Circuit stated: "Blind reliance on the client is seldom a sufficient inquiry . . ." Southern Leasing Partners Ltd. v. McMullan, 801 F.2d 783, 788 (5th Cir.1986); see Coburn Optical Industries v. Cilco, Inc., 610 F.Supp. 656, 659 (M.D.N.C.1985) (lawyer sanctioned for not verifying his client's claim that it did not do business in the jurisdiction). The easier it is to verify the facts, the greater the obligation to do so. See, e.g., Continental Air Lines, Inc. v. Group Systems International Far East, Ltd., 109 F.R.D. 594, 597 (C.D.Cal.1986) (when the information is publicly available, the lawyer must verify her client's version of the facts). In Calloway v. Marvel Entertainment Group, 854 F.2d 1452, 1470 (2d Cir.1988), rev'd on other grounds sub nom. Pavelic & LeFlore v. Marvel Entertainment Group, 110 S.Ct. 456 (1989), the court said that although a lawyer is entitled to rely on client statements that are "objectively reasonable," relying on client statements without other pre-filing inquiry may be sanctionable conduct.

When there is no reasonable way to verify the client's statements through independent sources, the lawyer should question the client thoroughly, not simply accept the client's version on faith alone. See

Nassau–Suffolk Ice Cream v. Integrated Resources, Inc., 118 F.R.D. 45 (S.D.N.Y.1987).

A Duty to Disclose Adverse Facts Under Rule 11?

Judge Schwarzer has argued that "[i]t would . . . defeat the purpose of the prefiling investigation requirement if attorneys were left free to conceal or misrepresent critical adverse information." Schwarzer, Rule 11 Revisited, 101 Harv.L.Rev. 1013, 1023 (1988). The ethical rules require some degree of candor to the court, see M.R. 3.3, but the scope of the "duty of candor" under Rule 11 is unclear.

The majority view is that Rule 11 does not impose a continuing duty to update or withdraw papers. See, e.g., Oliveri v. Thompson, 803 F.2d 1265 (2d Cir.1986); Gaiardo v. Ethyl Corp., 835 F.2d 479 (3d Cir. 1987); Thomas v. Capital Sec. Services, Inc., 836 F.2d 866 (5th Cir.1988) (en banc) (reversing panel decision holding there was a continuing duty). But see Herron v. Jupiter Transp. Co., 858 F.2d 332, 335–36 (6th Cir.1988) (Rule 11 imposes a continuing obligation to review papers already submitted to ensure that they are still in compliance with the rule); Collins v. Walden, 834 F.2d 961 (11th Cir.1987) (suggesting a continuing duty exists under Rule 11). The Supreme Court has thus far managed to avoid ruling on the many important questions raised by Rule 11, including the continuing duty question. However, in Pavelic & LeFlore v. Marvel Entertainment Group, 110 S.Ct. 456 (1989), the one important Rule 11 case decided by the Court (discussed in the note on Type of Sanction below at p. 402), the Court stuck closely to the language of the Rule, which suggests that the Court would not find that it imposes a continuing duty. But even if there is no continuing duty to update papers,

> parties [are not] entitled to continuing immunity if they acquire or should acquire knowledge under the Rule's standard before a later filing. Subsequent papers must be judged by information available when they are filed. For example, a defendant's answer may be in the spirit of the Rule at the time of filing, but a motion for summary judgment founded on the same theory may violate the Rule if investigation or research shows that the initial information was incorrect. Liability would be based on circumstances present when the motion is filed, not when the answer was filed.

Gaiardo v. Ethyl Corporation, 835 F.2d 479, 484 (3d Cir.1987), citing Pantry Queen Foods, Inc. v. Lifschultz Fast Freight, 809 F.2d 451, 454 (7th Cir.1987).

See also National Association of Radiation Survivors v. Turnage, 115 F.R.D. 543, 548 (N.D.Cal.1987) (Rule 11 sanctions appropriate where statements in papers were contradicted by discovery material wrongfully withheld).

Partly Frivolous Papers

The position in *Golden Eagle* that Rule 11 sanctions apply only if the *entire* paper is frivolous was rejected in Szabo Food Service, Inc. v. Canteen Corp., 823 F.2d 1073, 1077 (7th Cir.1987) (each claim should be evaluated separately); and Frantz v. U.S. Powerlifting Federation, 836 F.2d 1063 (7th Cir.1987) (Rule 11 applies to every statement in every paper).

The majority approach is somewhere between. For example, in Calloway v. Marvel Entertainment Group, 854 F.2d 1452 (2d Cir.1988), rev'd on other grounds sub nom. Pavelic & LeFlore v. Marvel Entertainment Group, 110 S.Ct. 456 (1989), the Second Circuit noted that the claim in question was not a "minor sub-claim" but the primary basis for opposing summary judgment and involved a serious charge against the defendant, i.e., forgery. See also Mary Ann Pensiero, Inc. v. Lingle, 847 F.2d 90, 97 (3d Cir.1988) (no sanctions for one dubious count among other reasonable ones, but "the practice of 'throwing in the kitchen sink' at times may be so abusive as to merit Rule 11 [sanctions]"). Recent Ninth Circuit cases sustain sanctions for improperly naming a party in a suit even though the pleading as a whole was not frivolous. See Community Electric Service v. National Electrical Contractors, 869 F.2d 1235 (9th Cir.1989). See also Aetna Life Insurance Co. v. Alla Medical Services, Inc., 855 F.2d 1470 (9th Cir.1988) (motions and papers, other than complaints, may be sanctioned under the improper purpose part of Rule 11, even if not all the arguments therein are frivolous, when they demonstrate a persistent pattern of clearly abusive litigation activity).

The Supreme Court has yet to speak on the degree of candor required by Rule 11. Neitzke v. Williams, 109 S.Ct. 1827 (1989), however, makes it clear that not every complaint that fails to state a claim under Fed.R.Civ.P. 12(b)(6) can be considered meritless. In *Neitzke* the issue was whether a complaint filed in forma pauperis that failed to state a claim under Rule 12(b)(6) is automatically frivolous under 28 U.S.C. § 1915(d), which provides that a court may dismiss a claim filed in forma pauperis ". . . . if satisfied that the action is frivolous or malicious."

In holding that failure to state a claim under Rule 12(b)(6) could not be equated with "frivolousness" under § 1915(d), the court noted that:

> Close questions of federal law, including claims filed pursuant to 42 U.S.C. § 1983, have on a number of occasions arisen on motions to dismiss for failure to state a claim, and have been substantial enough to warrant this Court's granting review, under its certiorari jurisdiction, to resolve them. See, e.g., . . . Bivens v. Six Unknown Fed. Narcotics Agents, 403 U.S. 388 (1971); [and] Jones v. Alfred Mayer Co., 392 U.S. 409 (1968). It can hardly be said that the substantial legal claims raised in these cases were so defective that they should never have been brought at the outset. To term

these claims frivolous is to distort measurably the meaning of frivolousness both in common and legal parlance. Indeed, we recently reviewed the dismissal under Rule 12(b)(6) of a complaint based on 42 U.S.C. § 1983 and found by a 9–0 vote that it had, in fact, stated a cognizable claim—a powerful illustration that a finding of a failure to state a claim does not invariably mean that the claim is without arguable merit.

109 S.Ct. at 1833.

As to the standard for judging a frivolous complaint under § 1915(d) the court stated: "[A] complaint . . . is frivolous where it lacks an arguable basis in law or in fact." Whether this standard will be applied by the Court in Rule 11 cases (Rule 11 does not contain the word "frivolous") and what the Court will find violates Rule 11 are questions that await answers.

Meritless Legal Arguments

The law, as interpreted by courts, changes and must change. At the same time, it needs considerable stability, without which it ceases to be the "rule of law" and becomes rule by fiat. This tension is reflected in the arguments over Rule 11. The question is whether courts can distinguish between legal arguments not well-grounded in law or "a good faith argument for the extension, modification or reversal of existing law," on the one hand, and, on the other hand, innovative and creative lawyering that ensures that law can "adjust to changing situations," *Golden Eagle,* supra.

Contrast the excerpt below from Szabo Food Service, Inc. v. Canteen Corp., 823 F.2d 1073, 1080–82 (7th Cir.1987), with the panel decision in *Golden Eagle.* First we provide a brief statement of the facts. Szabo–Digby bid on a contract to provide food at the Cook County Jail in Chicago. The contract was awarded to Canteen, the low bidder. Szabo–Digby filed suit in federal court alleging that it was the victim of racial discrimination, that the procedures used to award the contract deprived it of property in violation of the due process clause of the Fourteenth Amendment, and that the state in awarding the contract had violated state law; the complaint invoked pendent jurisdiction to support the last claim. The District Court granted Szabo–Digby's request for expedition, ordering Canteen to file its responding papers within 72 hours. "As Canteen tells the tale, there followed round-the-clock preparation of the background materials and briefs necessary to oppose Szabo–Digby's request for emergency relief." Three hours before Canteen's papers were due Szabo–Digby served a notice of voluntary dismissal and filed suit in state court based solely on the state law claim. After discovery in that suit, the state court granted judgment in favor of Canteen. At the time of the Seventh Circuit's opinion in *Szabo* the state case was on appeal. The Seventh Circuit said, in part:

. . . Szabo–Digby does not argue for the modification of existing law, and its brief in this court contends that the complaint is adequately supported by fact and law. The due process branch of the complaint is not. Szabo–Digby's theory of due process is wacky, sanctionably so.

. . .

Szabo–Digby tries to get around its lack of a property interest—as well as the fact that it got oodles of process and is getting more in the state courts—by insisting that it did not get all the process to which it is entitled under state law. . . . The Supreme Court has held, in cases Szabo–Digby does not cite, that the due process clause does not require states to follow their own procedures, if there is no underlying property interest. Olim v. Wakinekona, 461 U.S. 238, 248–51 (1983) . . . Perhaps Szabo–Digby means by "arbitrary and capricious" that the County Board was wrong on the merits: that it "deserved" the contract. But then it runs smack into Bishop v. Wood, 426 U.S. 341, 349–50 (1976), which holds that when there is no substantive property interest there is no review of "the merits" under the due process clause. . . .

If Szabo–Digby were trying to get the Supreme Court to reconsider *Olim* or *Bishop* we would not be keen to impose sanctions; a party is free to ask for reconsideration even when the court is unlikely to respond favorably. But this was not Szabo–Digby's strategy. It ignored *Bishop, Olim,* and the wealth of cases in this circuit holding that the Constitution does not guarantee that states will follow their own law. It ignored the language of the Board's invitation to bid [—language the Supreme Court of Illinois held did not create an entitlement to receive the contract. Polyvend, Inc. v. Puckorius, 77 Ill.2d 287, 294–96, 395 N.E.2d 1376, 1379 (1979), appeal dismissed for want of a substantial federal question, 444 U.S. 1062 (1980)]. It ignored *Polyvend.* It relied almost entirely on a pre-*Olim* opinion of a district court in Pennsylvania and on a more recent decision of the Eighth Circuit that assumed a position like Szabo–Digby's arguendo on the way to deciding the case for defendants on the merits. L & H Sanitation, Inc. v. Lake City Sanitation, Inc., 769 F.2d 517, 523–24 (8th Cir.1985); Three Rivers Cablevision, Inc. v. City of Pittsburgh, 502 F.Supp. 1118 (W.D.Pa. 1980). Szabo–Digby's ability to find obscure cases such as *Three Rivers* suggests that its presentation of the due process issue does not suffer from want of time to track down citations. What it does suffer from is "[t]he ostrich-like tactic of pretending that potentially dispositive authority against a litigant's contention does not exist." Hill v. Norfolk & Western Ry., 814 F.2d 1192, 1198 (7th Cir. 1987); see also Bonds v. Coca–Cola Co., 806 F.2d 1324, 1328 (7th Cir.1986).

We have paid close attention to the argument in Szabo–Digby's brief not because Rule 11 requires scholarly exposition or exhaustive research—it does not—but because a court must take care not to penalize arguments for legal evolution. . . . Rule 11 creates difficulties by simultaneously requiring courts to penalize frivolous suits and protecting complaints that, although not supported by existing law, are bona fide efforts to change the law. The only way to find out whether a complaint is an effort to change the law is to examine with care the arguments counsel later adduce. When counsel represent that something cleanly rejected by the Supreme Court is governing law, then it is appropriate to conclude that counsel are not engaged in trying to change the law; counsel either are trying to buffalo the court or have not done their homework. Either way, Rule 11 requires the court to impose a sanction . . .

In dissent JUDGE CUDAHY wrote:

. . .

. . . The majority's "wackiness" conclusion requires an analysis consuming five dense paragraphs and citing more than twenty cases—a possible indicator that the result is not so blindingly obvious as to bring it reasonably within the ambit of Rule 11. A similar indicator is the fact that one of the "obscure cases" on which this "frivolous" due process claim was based—Three Rivers Cablevision, Inc. v. City of Pittsburgh, 502 F.Supp. 1118 (W.D.Pa. 1980)—has been explicitly approved by an Illinois court for its approach to due process. Northwest Disposal Co. v. Village of Fox Lake, 119 Ill.App.3d 546, 551, 456 N.E.2d 691, 695 (1983) ("We recognize the very limited due process right for unsuccessful bidders as established under the rationale of Three Rivers."). (footnote omitted)

In addition, there are real problems with imposing Rule 11 sanctions for a pleading—as not "warranted by existing law or a good faith argument for the extension, modification, or reversal of existing law"—on the basis of the sophistication of the legal arguments presented to defend the pleading and the erudition displayed by the responsible counsel. Here both counsel are sophisticated. And Szabo–Digby has cited relevant state and federal authority to support its due process claim. But I sense that, in general, with the majority's approach to what might be "objectively frivolous," ingenious and sophisticated (read expensive) rhetoric can salvage almost any position and avoid sanctions. But beware counsel, whose research (or resources) is not unlimited or whose skills in argumentation fall short of the most finely honed.

Due process, unfortunately, is an area where creativity and frivolity sometimes threaten to merge; I would be more restrained than my brethren in handing out sanctions for civil rights claims.

For the chilling effect of today's decision will reach as tellingly to the most meritorious such claim as to the least.

823 F.2d at 1085–86 (Cudahy, J., dissenting).

Should Certain Types of Claims be Judged More Leniently?

Judge Cudahy suggests that courts should be more reluctant to sanction legal arguments in civil rights cases than in some other areas of law. What justification is there for giving civil rights cases lenient treatment under Rule 11? Cf. Christiansburg Garment Co. v. EEOC, 434 U.S. 412, 422, 98 S.Ct. 694, 700 (1978) (attorney's fees may not be assessed against a plaintiff who fails to state a claim under 42 U.S.C. § 1988 or under Title VII of the Civil Rights Act of 1964 unless the complaint is frivolous).

Courts have shown reluctance to impose sanctions under Rule 11 for frivolous habeas corpus petitions. Rule 11 does not apply to criminal proceedings, but habeas corpus proceedings are civil. We have found only one habeas case approving the imposition of sanctions against the defendant (or defense counsel) under Rule 11, United States v. Quin, 836 F.2d 654, 657 (1st Cir.1988) (sanctions appropriate when writ was used for "purely civil effect, the prevention of deportation"). Compare United States ex rel. Potts v. Chrans, 700 F.Supp. 1505, 1525 (N.D.Ill.1988):

> The habeas statutes and rules provide the federal courts with ample power to cut these petitions off at the pass by dismissing them either immediately or after the government has filed an answer. To add Rule 11 to these powers would present a barrier to the ability of individuals to obtain the special relief only habeas provides—a barrier that, though not inconsistent with the express provisions of the Habeas Rules, is certainly inconsistent with their spirit.

Cf. Taylor v. Commonwealth of Pennsylvania, 686 F.Supp. 492 (M.D.Pa. 1988), in which the district court imposed Rule 11 sanctions on *government counsel* for filing a frivolous motion to dismiss a habeas petition. Generally on whether Rule 11 applies against government lawyers, see Adamson v. Bowen, 855 F.2d 668 (10th Cir.1988) (holding that the Equal Access to Justice Act, 28 U.S.C. § 2412 (1981) waives the government's sovereign immunity as to Rule 11).

Read M.R. 3.1 and its comment. Should it have addressed the responsibilities of a lawyer representing a convicted person in a habeas proceeding? What should the standard be?

Papers Filed for Improper Purpose

The "improper purpose" part of Rule 11 has been held to cover a variety of abusive litigation practices. See, e.g., Deere & Co. v. Deutsche Lufthansa, 855 F.2d 385 (7th Cir.1988) (filing repetitive papers that refuse to accept judge's ruling on an issue and fail to address remaining issues in the litigation); Hudson v. Business Forms, Inc., 836

F.2d 1156 (9th Cir.1987) (counterclaim brought for purpose of harassing plaintiff into dropping the case and deterring others from bringing suit); Perkinson v. Gilbert/Robinson Inc., 821 F.2d 686 (D.C.Cir.1987) (misstatements in papers as part of a persistent pattern of discovery abuse). Despite the word "purpose," courts have held that this part of the Rule like the rest of the rule requires an objective determination of whether a reasonable lawyer acting as the lawyer did in this case would have been acting for improper purpose.

Type of Sanction

The courts agree that deterrence, not compensation, is the principal goal of Rule 11 and that therefore courts should impose the least severe sanction that is likely to deter. See Jackson v. The Law Firm of O'Hara, Ruberg et al., 875 F.2d 1224, 1229 (6th Cir.1989) (noting agreement among the circuits). See also Brown v. Federation of State Medical Bds., 830 F.2d 1429 (7th Cir.1987).

> A party who seeks attorney's fees as a Rule 11 sanction must mitigate damages by acting promptly and avoiding any unnecessary expenses in responding to papers that violate the rule. . . . It is an abuse of discretion to award all fees claimed when a party has expended a great deal of time and effort defending patently frivolous claims that could have been dismissed on motion or request for a pretrial conference at an early stage in the proceedings. Oliveri v. Thompson, 803 F.2d 1265, 1280 (2d Cir.1986); United Food & Commercial Workers v. Armour & Co., 106 F.R.D. 345, 349–50 (N.D.Cal.1985). Such fees are not "reasonable."

Jackson, supra at 1230.

Rule 11 provides for penalties against the lawyer, the client or both. Generally, courts seek to allocate sanctions between lawyer and client according to the relative responsibility of each for the Rule 11 violation. See, e.g., Chevron, U.S.A., Inc. v. Hand, 763 F.2d 1184, 1187 (10th Cir. 1985); In re Ruben, 825 F.2d 977, 986 (6th Cir.1987) (court reversed sanctions imposed on plaintiff for her bad faith in filing a suit, explaining that if any fault existed, it lay with the attorneys).

In Pavelic & LeFlore v. Marvel Entertainment Group, 110 S.Ct. 456 (1989), the Supreme Court held that a court cannot impose sanctions under Rule 11 against the attorney's law firm; sanctions are only authorized against the lawyer(s) who actually sign the paper or the represented party. Note, however, that this decision relied on the particular language of Rule 11. Firmly established principles of agency and partnership would have dictated a different result, but the Court explained that the text of the Rule showed an intent to depart from these common law principles. Sanctions could, therefore, continue to be imposed on the law firm as long as the sanctions were based on authority other than Rule 11, e.g., 28 U.S.C. § 1927 or the court's inherent power.

D. 28 U.S.C. § 1927: UNREASONABLY AND VEXATIOUSLY MULTIPLYING THE PROCEEDINGS

Section 1927 provides:

Any attorney or other person admitted to conduct cases in any court of the United States or any Territory thereof who so multiplies the proceedings in any case unreasonably and vexatiously may be required by the court to satisfy personally the excess costs, expenses, and attorneys' fees reasonably incurred because of such conduct.

The decisions are in conflict whether § 1927 requires subjective bad faith on the part of counsel. Compare, e.g., Haynie v. Ross Gear Div. of TRW, Inc., 799 F.2d 237, 243 (6th Cir.1986) (subjective bad faith not required) with e.g., Oliveri v. Thompson, 803 F.2d 1265, 1273 (2d Cir. 1986) ("an award under § 1927 must be supported by a finding of bad faith . . .").

But subjective bad faith exists, for example, when a lawyer " 'knowingly *or* recklessly raises a frivolous argument *or* argues a meritorious claim for the purpose of harassing an opponent' . . . [or undertakes t]actics . . . with the intent to increase expenses. . . . Even if an attorney's arguments are meritorious, his conduct may be sanctionable if in bad faith." New Alaska Development Corp. v. Guetschow, 869 F.2d 1298, 1306 (9th Cir.1989).

E. SANCTIONS FOR DISCOVERY ABUSE

National Hockey League v. Metropolitan Hockey Club Inc., 427 U.S. 639, 96 S.Ct. 2778 (1976), upheld a dismissal of an action under Fed.R.Civ.P. 37 upon a finding of failure in bad faith to comply with discovery. This policy was reenforced by amendments to Rules 26 and 37 in 1980 and 1983. Rule 26(g) and Rule 37(b) provide that sanctions may include the award of attorneys fees. In addition, Rule 37(b) provides that negative inferences may be drawn from a party's refusal to comply with discovery, that the party may be prevented from contesting certain matters, and that the court may dismiss the claim or enter a default judgment for noncompliance. See Apex Oil Co. v. Belcher Co., 855 F.2d 1009 (2d Cir.1988), discussing the relationship between Rule 11 and Rule 26(g), Rule 37(c) and § 1927. Also see Carlucci v. Piper Aircraft Corp., Inc., 775 F.2d 1440 (11th Cir.1985) (discussing statutes and rules authorizing sanctions for discovery abuse, including the court's inherent power).

F. SANCTIONS AT THE APPELLATE LEVEL

Sanctions for frivolous legal arguments at the appellate level are most often levied under Fed.R.App.P. 38:

If a court of appeals shall determine that an appeal is frivolous, it may award just damages and single or double costs.

Rule 38 does not make the imposition of sanctions mandatory upon a finding that the appeal is frivolous. In Mays v. Chicago Sun-Times, 865 F.2d 134 (7th Cir.1989), the court stated that Rule 38 involves two questions: (1) is the appeal frivolous? (2) is this an appropriate case for sanctions? Subjective bad faith is not required. See, e.g., Sparks v. NLRB, 835 F.2d 705, 707 (7th Cir.1987). An argument with merit enough to escape Rule 11 sanctions at the trial level may be sanctionable under Rule 38 if pressed on appeal. See, e.g., Coghlan v. Starkey, 852 F.2d 806, 817 (5th Cir.1988) ("the unreasonableness of litigating [these] unsupported and meritless legal positions rose to a level appropriate for sanctions only after the opinion below elaborated why current law could not support the contention advanced"). On the other hand, appealing a Rule 11 sanction may result in additional sanctions under Rule 38. See, e.g., Hale v. Harney, 786 F.2d 688, 692 (5th Cir. 1986) (after Rule 11 sanctions were imposed counsel persisted by appealing a claim clearly barred by Supreme Court decisions). Blatantly mischaracterizing a court opinion in an appellate brief may also lead to sanctions. See, e.g., *Mays,* supra at 140 ("We can think of no better example of a pleading not well grounded in fact or law than a brief that falsely imputes a particular position to this court."). Courts have also imposed sanctions against lawyers who file frivolous motions for Rule 38 sanctions. See, e.g., Meeks v. Jewel Cos., 845 F.2d 1421 (7th Cir. 1988).

Rule 38 is not the only vehicle for sanctioning frivolous conduct on appeal. See, e.g., Limerick v. Greenwald, 749 F.2d 97 (1st Cir.1984) (sanctions under 28 U.S.C. § 1927 and 42 U.S.C. § 1988); In re Disciplinary Action Curl, 803 F.2d 1004 (9th Cir.1986) (Rule 11 applies on appeal through Rule 5 of the Ninth Circuit rules). But see Braley v. Campbell, 832 F.2d 1504, 1510 n. 4 (10th Cir.1987) (en banc) (Rule 11 not applicable on appeal). Sanctions on appeal may be imposed under the court's inherent power. Trohimovich v. Commissioner, 776 F.2d 873, 876 (9th Cir.1985). See also 28 U.S.C. § 1912, which provides: "Where a judgment is affirmed by the Supreme Court or a court of appeals, the court in its discretion may adjudge to the prevailing party just damages for his delay, and single or double costs." See Natasha, Inc. v. Evita Marine Charters, Inc., 763 F.2d 468, 472 (1st Cir.1985).

Counsel should withdraw rather than pursue a frivolous appeal. But what about a court appointed lawyer representing an indigent criminal defendant on appeal? In Anders v. California, 386 U.S. 738, 744, 87 S.Ct. 1396, 1400 (1967), the Court held that counsel must accompany her request to withdraw with a brief setting forth "anything in the record that might arguably support the appeal." This brief is commonly referred to as an *Anders* brief. In McCoy v. Court of Appeal of Wisconsin, 486 U.S. 429, 108 S.Ct. 1895 (1988), the Court considered a Wisconsin Supreme Court rule that required that the *Anders* brief include "a discussion of why the issue lacks merit." The defendant claimed that requiring his counsel to present the weaknesses in his cause deprived him of his Sixth Amendment right to effective assistance of counsel. The Court upheld the Wisconsin rule, stating that it furthered the interest underlying *Anders,* i.e., protecting the defendant from counsel's mistaken conclusion that the appeal lacked merit by assisting the court to make an independent determination. In dissent, Justice Brennan, joined by Justices Marshall and Blackmun, argued that the Wisconsin rule violated the lawyer's duty to advocate "the undivided interests of his client." The dissenters found this particularly troublesome because only indigent defendants would be affected by the rule.

In In re Becraft, 885 F.2d 547 (9th Cir.1989), the court sanctioned defense counsel in a criminal case under Rule 38 for filing a frivolous petition for rehearing after the Ninth Circuit had affirmed the conviction, stating that counsel's argument that the federal tax laws did not apply to resident U.S. citizens had no basis in law. For pressing this argument in the petition for rehearing counsel was sanctioned $2,500. The court noted that it could find no precedent for imposing Rule 38 sanctions upon counsel in a criminal case and expressed concern that sanctioning a criminal defendant's counsel would chill counsel's willingness to advance novel legal positions. Nevertheless, the court awarded sanctions in this case, emphasizing that Becraft had raised the same frivolous argument in other circuits and other cases in the Ninth Circuit and that the sanctions here were imposed not for arguments on direct appeal but for arguments already rejected on appeal and pressed in a petition for rehearing.

For more on the lawyer's responsibilities on appeal in a criminal case, see the note on Jones v. Barnes, 463 U.S. 745, 103 S.Ct. 3308 (1983) in Chapter 6 below and the discussion following it. Chapter 6 also addresses the allocation of authority between the defendant and the lawyer in the conduct of a criminal case. Improper trial tactics by criminal defense lawyers are discussed later in this chapter.

G. INTERPRETATIONS OF COUNSEL'S DUTY TO ADVANCE ARGUMENTS

In In re Solerwitz, 848 F.2d 1573 (Fed.Cir.1988), the court rejected the opinion of three ethics experts, who testified that a lawyer has an "ethical" duty to press an appeal, if the client so desires, apparently without regard to any objective assessment about the merits. According to the court's summary,

> Professor [Monroe] Freedman, [one of the ethics experts,] stated that "as long as counsel in good faith believes that his case is not frivolous, . . . it is his duty to proceed with it notwithstanding any instructions to the contrary from the court" and that "the court is required to bend over backwards to defer to counsel's judgment with regard to what is filed and what is argued . . ." . . . [The trial judge] found Professor Freedman "regards as frivolous only a paper that is fallacious on its face as distinguished from sham pleading in which the argument is plausible but the

lawyer knows or should know that the underlying facts are not
there to support it." . . . Professor Hellerstein [a second ethics
expert in the case, expressed the] opinion that "a lawyer has an
obligation to persist in making and remaking the same argument
to an intermediate court at least until the Supreme Court foreclosed that court on the merits." . . . [He] testified that in his
entire practice he never once turned down a client's request to
bring an appeal because he believed it was frivolous, if [he] felt
there was anything that could be argued . . .

Id. at 1576–77.

Mr. Solerwitz, the lawyer whose conduct was in issue, had continued to
press appeals in 154 cases—stemming from the firing of the air traffic
controllers by President Reagan—after the court had decided twelve
cases that it believed presented all the issues and the Supreme Court
had denied certiorari in all those lead cases. Mr. Solerwitz was
suspended from the practice of law before the court for one year.

H. TORT REMEDIES AGAINST LAWYERS FOR CONDUCT IN LITIGATION?

FRIEDMAN v. DOZORC

Supreme Court of Michigan, 1981.
412 Mich. 1, 312 N.W.2d 585.

LEVIN, JUSTICE.

The plaintiff is a physician who, after successfully defending in a
medical malpractice action, brought this action against the attorneys
who had represented the plaintiffs in the former action. Dr. Friedman
sought under a number of theories to recover damages for being
compelled to defend against an allegedly groundless medical malpractice action. The trial court granted the defendants' motions for summary and accelerated judgment.

The Court of Appeals affirmed in part and reversed in part. We
granted leave to appeal to consider what remedies may be available to a
physician who brings such a "countersuit".

We hold that:

(1) The plaintiff has failed to state an actionable claim on a theory
of negligence because an attorney owes no duty of care to an adverse
party in litigation;

(2) The plaintiff has failed to state an actionable claim on a theory of
abuse of process because there is no allegation that defendants committed
an irregular act in the use of the process issued in the prior case;

(3) The plaintiff has failed to state an actionable claim on a theory
of malicious prosecution because his complaint did not allege interference with his person or property sufficient to constitute special injury
under Michigan law.

. . . .

I

Leona Serafin entered Outer Drive Hospital in May, 1970, for treatment of gynecological problems. A dilation and curettage was performed by her physician, Dr. Harold Krevsky. While in the hospital, Mrs. Serafin was referred to the present plaintiff, Dr. Friedman, for urological consultation. Dr. Friedman recommended surgical removal of a kidney stone which was too large to pass, and the operation was performed on May 20, 1970. During the surgery, the patient began to ooze blood uncontrollably. Although other physicians were consulted, Mrs. Serafin's condition continued to worsen and she died five days after the surgery. An autopsy was performed the next day; the report identified the cause of death as thrombotic thrombocytopenic purpura, a rare and uniformly fatal blood disease, the cause and cure of which are unknown.

On January 11, 1972, attorneys Dozorc and Golden, the defendants in this action, filed a malpractice action on behalf of Anthony Serafin, Jr., for himself and as administrator of the estate of Leona Serafin, against Peoples Community Hospital Authority, Outer Drive Hospital, Dr. Krevsky and Dr. Friedman, as well as another physician who was dismissed as a defendant before trial. In December, 1974, the case went to trial in Wayne Circuit Court. No expert testimony tending to show that any of the defendants had breached accepted professional standards in making the decision to perform the elective surgery or in the manner of its performance was presented as part of the plaintiff's case. The judge entered a directed verdict of no cause of action in favor of Dr. Friedman and the other defendants at the close of the plaintiff's proofs. The judge subsequently denied a motion for costs brought by codefendant Peoples Community Hospital Authority, pursuant to GCR 1963, 111.6. The Court of Appeals affirmed and this Court denied leave to appeal.

Dr. Friedman commenced the present action on March 17, 1976 in Oakland Circuit Court. The following excerpt from his complaint summarizes his theories of recovery and the injuries he allegedly sustained as a result of the initiation and prosecution of the malpractice action:

"13. That as a direct and proximate result of the negligence, malicious prosecution and abuse of process of these Defendants, the Plaintiff, SEYMOUR FRIEDMAN, M.D., has endured grievous damages, including, but not limited to, the following: the cost of defending the aforesaid cause and the appeal, an increase in his annual malpractice insurance premiums for so long as he practices medicine, the loss of two young associates from his office who could no longer afford to pay the increased malpractice insurance premiums thereby requiring him to work excessive hours without relief, damages to his reputation as a physician and surgeon, embarrassment and continued mental anguish."

The defendants moved for summary . . . and . . . accelerated judgment. . . . The judge granted both motions in November, 1976, concluding that (1) plaintiff had failed to state a cause of action for negligence because there was "no relationship other than that of adversaries" between the defendants and plaintiff and hence there was "no duty owing"; and (2) the refusal of the trial judge in the prior action to find that the claims advanced by the defendants on behalf of their client were unreasonable and should render them responsible under GCR 1963, 111.6 for litigation expenses of their opponents established that the prior action was brought with probable cause and therefore precluded a subsequent action for malicious prosecution or abuse of process.

The Court of Appeals affirmed the dismissal insofar as it was based on failure to state a claim on the theories of negligence and abuse of process. However, it reversed the dismissal of the cause of action sounding in malicious prosecution and remanded this cause to the trial court, declaring that an adverse ruling on a defendant's motion under GCR 111.6 did not bar a subsequent malicious prosecution action and that the facts surrounding the filing and continuation of the prior action were in dispute.

. . . .

II

A

Plaintiff and amici in support urge this Court to hold that an attorney owes a present or prospective adverse party a duty of care, breach of which will give rise to a cause of action for negligence. We agree with the circuit judge and the Court of Appeals that an attorney owes no actionable duty to an adverse party.

Plaintiff and amici argue that an attorney who initiates a civil action owes a duty to his client's adversary and all other foreseeable third parties who may be affected by such an action to conduct a reasonable investigation and re-examination of the facts and law so that the attorney will have an adequate basis for a good-faith belief that the client has a tenable claim. Plaintiff contends that this duty is created by the Code of Professional Responsibility and by the Michigan General Court Rules.[6]

Plaintiff further argues that an attorney's separate duty under the Code of Professional Responsibility to zealously represent a client is limited by the requirement that the attorney perform within the bounds of the law.* Acting within the bounds of the law is said to encompass refraining from asserting frivolous claims; this charge upon

---

6. Plaintiff's brief refers to Code of Professional Responsibility and Canons, Canon 1, DR 1–102(A), Canon 6, DR 6–101(A), Canon 7, DR 7–102(A), and various Ethical Considerations associated with Canon 7, especially EC 7–4 and EC 7–10, as well as to GCR 1963, 111.6 and 114.

* Editor's note: Here the court quoted DR 7–102(A)(1); (A)(2); EC 7–4; and EC 7–10.

the profession imposes upon counsel a duty to the public, the courts and the adverse party to conduct a reasonable investigation. Plaintiff contends that since the duty to investigate already arises from the attorney-client relationship under the code and court rules, recognition of a cause of action for negligence will impose no new obligation on the attorney.

Defendants counter that an attorney cannot be liable to third parties for acts that result from client representation in the absence of fraud or collusion. An attorney's only actionable legal duty is owed to his or her client. An attorney cannot owe a duty to the client's legal opponent because of the very duty that is owed to the client. An attorney owing one duty to a client and another duty to the client's adversary, each of whom have adverse interests, would be faced with an irreconcilable conflict of interest.

B

In a negligence action the question whether the defendant owes an actionable legal duty to the plaintiff is one of law which the court decides after assessing the competing policy considerations for and against recognizing the asserted duty.

. . .

Assuming that an attorney has an obligation to his client to conduct a reasonable investigation prior to bringing an action, that obligation is not the functional equivalent of a duty of care owed to the client's adversary. We decline to so transform the attorney's obligation because we view such a duty as inconsistent with basic precepts of the adversary system.

The duties, professional and actionable, owed to the client by the attorney acting as advocate and adviser are broader than the obligation of reasonable investigation. Those duties concern decisions which the attorney makes on behalf of, and often in consultation with, the client, regarding the manner of proceeding with the client's cause. A decision to proceed with a future course of action that involves litigation will necessarily adversely affect a legal opponent. If an attorney were held to owe a duty of due care to both the client and the client's adversary, the obligation owing to the adversary would extend beyond undertaking an investigation and would permeate all facets of the litigation. The attorney's decision-making and future conduct on behalf of both parties would be shaped by the attorney's obligation to exercise due care as to both parties. Under such a rule an attorney is likely to be faced with a situation in which it would be in the client's best interest to proceed in one fashion and in the adversary's best interest to proceed contrariwise. However he chooses to proceed, the attorney could be accused of failing to exercise due care for the benefit of one of the parties.

. . .

In short, creation of a duty in favor of an adversary of the attorney's client would create an unacceptable conflict of interest [10] which would seriously hamper an attorney's effectiveness as counsel for his client. Not only would the adversary's interests interfere with the client's interests, the attorney's justifiable concern with being sued for negligence would detrimentally interfere with the attorney-client relationship. As the California Supreme Court observed in Goodman v. Kennedy, 18 Cal.3d 335, 344, 556 P.2d 737, 743, 134 Cal.Rptr. 375 (1976):

> "The attorney's preoccupation or concern with the possibility of claims based on mere negligence (as distinct from fraud or malice) by any with whom his client might deal 'would prevent him from devoting his entire energies to his client's interests' (Anderson v. Eaton, 211 Cal. 113, 116, 293 P. 788, 790 [1930]). The result would be both 'an undue burden on the profession' (Lucas v. Hamm, 56 Cal.2d 583, 589 [15 Cal.Rptr. 821, 824, 364 P.2d 685, 688 (1961)]) and a diminution in the quality of the legal services received by the client." (Footnote omitted.)

. . .

. . . We reiterate what this Court said in State Bar Grievance Administrator v. Corace, 390 Mich. 419, 434–435, 213 N.W.2d 124 (1973):

> "[O]ur adversary system 'intends, and expects, lawyers to probe the outer limits of the bounds of the law, ever searching for a more efficacious remedy, or a more successful defense'."

We agree with those courts in other jurisdictions which have relied on the policy of encouraging free access to the courts as a reason for declining to recognize a negligence cause of action in physician counter-suits.[12] No appellate court has yet approved such a cause of action.

. . .

10. Under a section entitled Conflicts in Litigation, the comments to the Discussion Draft of ABA Model Rules of Professional Conduct, 48 USLW, No. 32, Supplement, p. 8 (February 19, 1980), most aptly identify the type of conflict of interest presented under the instant facts:

> "Most if not all questions of conflict of interest are questions of degree. As noted above, minor and inevitable conflicts inherent in client-lawyer relationships necessarily must be tolerated. On the other hand, a conflict of interest may be so sharp as to preclude the lawyer from representing a particular client. For example, under no circumstances could a lawyer properly represent both the plaintiff and the defendant in contested litigation, or represent parties to a negotiation whose interests are fundamentally antagonistic to each other. When it is plain that prejudice to the client's interests is likely to result, the lawyer should not undertake the representation even with the consent of the client. A client's consent does not legitimate a lawyer's abuse of professional office."

12. Weaver v. Superior Court of Orange County, 95 Cal.App.3d 166, 156 Cal.Rptr. 745 (1979); Berlin v. Nathan, 64 Ill.App.3d 940, 21 Ill.Dec. 682, 381 N.E.2d 1367 (1978); Lyddon v. Shaw, 56 Ill.App.3d 815, 14 Ill.Dec. 489, 372 N.E.2d 685 (1978); Brody v. Ruby, 267 N.W.2d 902 (Iowa, 1978); Spencer v. Burglass, 337 So.2d 596 (La.App., 1976); Hill v. Willmott, 561 S.W.2d 331 (Ky.App., 1978).

III

To recover upon a theory of abuse of process, a plaintiff must plead and prove (1) an ulterior purpose and (2) an act in the use of process which is improper in the regular prosecution of the proceeding. Spear v. Pendill, 164 Mich. 620, 623, 130 N.W. 343 (1911).[18]

Plaintiff contends he has pleaded that defendants' ulterior purpose in filing the former malpractice action was to coerce payments of large sums of money from plaintiff for defendants' financial gain by means of their contingent-fee arrangement with the former plaintiff. In addition, plaintiff alleges that irregular use of process was shown by defendants' filing of the complaint without adequate investigation.

Defendants counter that plaintiff's pleadings are deficient in failing to allege an act by the defendants beyond mere initiation of a lawsuit and an ulterior purpose other than settlement of a lawsuit.

We need not decide whether plaintiff's pleadings sufficiently allege that the defendants had an ulterior purpose in causing process to issue, since it is clear that the plaintiff has failed to allege that defendants committed some irregular act in the use of process. The only act in the use of process that plaintiff alleges is the issuance of a summons and complaint in the former malpractice action. However, a summons and complaint are properly employed when used to institute a civil action, and thus plaintiff has failed to satisfy the second element required in *Spear,* supra, 623, 130 N.W. 343, where the Court observed " '[t]his action for abuse of process lies for the improper use of process after it has been issued, not for maliciously causing it to issue.' "

. . .

IV

Plaintiff relies upon the same allegations respecting defendants' conduct and their failure to meet professional standards which assertedly constitute negligence in contending that he has pled a cause of action for malicious prosecution. He argues that the question of probable cause in a malicious prosecution action against the attorney for an opposing party turns on whether the attorney fulfilled his duty to reasonably investigate the facts and law before initiating and continuing a lawsuit. If the attorney's investigation discloses that the claim is not tenable, then it is his obligation to discontinue the action.

---

18. The Restatement Torts, 2d, explains the tort of abuse of process as follows:

"The gravamen of the misconduct for which the liability stated in this section is imposed is not the wrongful procurement of legal process or the wrongful initiation of criminal or civil proceedings; it is the misuse of process, no matter how properly obtained, for any purpose other than that which it was designed to accomplish. Therefore, it is immaterial that the process was properly issued, that it was obtained in the course of proceedings that were brought with probable cause and for a proper purpose, or even that the proceedings terminated in favor of the person instituting or initiating them. The subsequent misuse of the process, though properly obtained, constitutes the misconduct for which the liability is imposed under the rule stated in this section." 3 Restatement Torts, 2d, § 682, comment a, p. 474.

Defendants respond that Michigan is among those jurisdictions that have not abandoned the special injury requirement in actions for the malicious prosecution of civil proceedings. They urge, in addition, that this Court adopt a rule that a successful motion pursuant to GCR 1963, 111.6 in the former lawsuit is a necessary condition precedent to institution of a subsequent malicious prosecution action by the former defendant.

We agree with defendants that under Michigan law special injury remains an essential element of the tort cause of action for malicious prosecution of civil proceedings. Although the circuit judge did not rest [his] decision on the plaintiff's failure to plead special injury, summary judgment . . . for failure to state a claim could be appropriately entered on that basis; the factual disputes asserted by plaintiff are immaterial.

A

The recognition of an action for malicious prosecution developed as an adjunct to the English practice of awarding costs to the prevailing party [20] in certain aggravated cases where the costs remedy was thought to be inadequate and the defendant had suffered damages beyond the expense and travail normally incident to defending a lawsuit. In 1698 three categories of damage which would support an action for malicious prosecution were identified: injury to one's fame (as by a scandalous allegation), injury to one's person or liberty, and injury to one's property.[21] To this day the English courts do not

---

20. The early common law required any complainant who lost his suit to pay his opponent *wer,* a monetary penalty which varied with the complainant's status. After the Norman conquest, *wer* gave way to *amercement,* a more flexible sanction paid to the court. Although every unsuccessful initiator of legal proceedings was subject to *amercement,* the amount, at least in theory, varied according to the wrongfulness of the complainant's conduct. Note, Groundless Litigation and the Malicious Prosecution Debate: A Historical Analysis, 88 Yale L.J. 1218, 1221–1223 (1979).

Amercement lost its effectiveness over time as the amounts assessed were subjected to limits and diminished by inflation. Id., 1226, fn. 63. Parliament eventually sought to revive a system of internal sanctions through a number of statutes which allowed prevailing defendants—and plaintiffs (see Goodhart, Costs, 38 Yale L.J. 849, 852–853 [1929])—to recover all or part of their costs of litigation. Id., p. 853, and Note, supra, p. 1226, fn. 64, both citing 23 Hen. 8, c. 15, § 1 (1531) (allowing costs at the discretion of the court to a prevailing defendant in actions of trespass, case, debt or covenant, detinue, account, and contract, or on any statute); 8 Eliz. 1, c. 2 (1565) (allowing costs and damages to the defendant where the plaintiff had caused arrest or attachment by invoking summary process and had delayed or discontinued prosecution of the claim on the merits); and 4 Jac. 1, c. 3 (1607) (allowing the defendant to recover costs whenever the plaintiff might have recovered them had he prevailed).

The Statute of Marlbridge (also Marleberge, Marlborough), 52 Hen. 3, c. 6 (1267), has been described as a watershed which signaled the replacement of a previously recognized right to bring a subsequent action for false suit with a sweeping system for allowing prevailing defendants in civil cases to recover costs, including attorney fees, in the original action. See, e.g., 52 Am.Jur.2d, Malicious Prosecution, § 9, pp. 191–192. But other sources state that the asserted pre-statute right of action is "mythical," Note, supra, p. 1225, n. 59, and that the statute "was an isolated instance" of the unsuccessful plaintiff being subject to liability to the defendant as well as *amercement.* Goodhart, supra, p. 853.

21. Savile v. Roberts, 1 Ld.Raym. 374, 378, 91 Eng.Rep. 1147, 1149–1150 (1698).

recognize actions for malicious prosecution of either criminal or civil proceedings unless one of these types of injury, as narrowly defined by the cases, is present.[22]

A substantial number of American jurisdictions today follow some form of "English rule" to the effect that "in the absence of an arrest, seizure, or special damage, the successful civil defendant has no remedy, despite the fact that his antagonist proceeded against him maliciously and without probable cause." [23] A larger number of jurisdictions, some say a majority, follow an "American rule" permitting actions for malicious prosecution of civil proceedings without requiring the plaintiff to show special injury.[24]

B

The plaintiff's complaint does not allege special injury. We are satisfied that Michigan has not significantly departed from the English rule and we decline to do so today.

This Court heretofore has neither recognized the unrestricted availability of a tort cause of action, analogous to malicious prosecution, for the wrongful initiation or continuation of civil proceedings, nor abrogated the traditional requirement that a plaintiff alleging wrongful institution of civil proceedings have suffered special injury in the nature of an interference with person or property. . . .

. . .

In the foregoing cases . . . the plaintiff suffered some special injury equivalent to a seizure of property as a result of the defendant's institution of civil proceedings. . . .

. . . We are persuaded that the special injury requirement should be retained to limit the circumstances in which an action for the malicious prosecution of civil proceedings can be maintained.

Most commentators appear to favor abrogation of the special injury requirement to make the action more available and less difficult to maintain.[34] Their counsel should, however, be evaluated skeptically.

22. For discussion of what will constitute the requisite injury, see Quartz Hill Consolidated Gold Mining Co. v. Eyre, L.R. 11 QBD 674, 689–693, 52 LJQB (NS) 488 (1883) (opinion of Bowen, L.J.); and Wiffen v. Bailey & Romford Urban Dist. Council, [1915] 1 KB 600.

23. 52 Am.Jur.2d, supra, § 10, p. 192. The Reporter's Note at 5 Restatement Torts, 2d, Appendix, § 674, p. 438, identifies 16 states which require some form of special injury in order to support an action for wrongful civil proceedings. O'Toole v. Franklin, 279 Or. 513, 518, fn. 3, 569 P.2d 561 (1977), lists the same 16 states and adds Kentucky.

24. 52 Am.Jur.2d, supra, § 10, p. 193; Prosser, Torts (4th ed.), § 120, p. 853. The Reporter's Note, supra, lists 30 states which purportedly follow this majority rule. O'Toole v. Franklin, supra, pp. 518–519, fn. 4, 569 P.2d 561, identifies 23 states.

Since the Reporter's Note and *O'Toole* differ over the categorization of Kentucky (see fn. 23, supra), and both include Michigan (see part IVB of this opinion) as a "majority rule" state, the classification of the states does not appear to be entirely reliable.

34. Prosser, supra, § 120, p. 851; Note, Promoting Recovery by Claimants in Iowa Malicious Prosecution Actions, 64 Iowa L.Rev. 408 (1979); Note, Malicious Prosecution: An Effective Attack on Spurious Medical Malpractice Claims?, 26 Case Western Reserve

The lawyer's remedy for a grievance is a lawsuit, and a law student or tort professor may be particularly predisposed by experience and training to see the preferred remedy for a wrongful tort action as another tort action. In seeking a remedy for the excessive litigiousness of our society, we would do well to cast off the limitations of a perspective which ascribes curative power only to lawsuits.

We turn to a consideration of Dean Prosser's criticisms of the three reasons commonly advanced by courts for adhering to the English rule. First, to the assertion that the costs awarded to the prevailing party are intended as the exclusive remedy for the damages incurred by virtue of the wrongful litigation, Prosser responds that "in the United States, where the costs are set by statute at trivial amounts, and no attorney's fees are allowed, there can be no pretense at compensation even for the expenses of the litigation itself." [35] This argument is compelling, but it does not necessarily justify an award of compensation absent the hardship of special injury or dictate that an award of compensation be assessed in a separate lawsuit. Second, to the arguments that an unrestricted tort of wrongful civil proceedings will deter honest litigants and that an innocent party must bear the costs of litigation as the price of a system which permits free access to the courts, Prosser answers that "there is no policy in favor of vexatious suits known to be groundless, which are a real and often a serious injury." [36] But a tort action is not the only means of deterring groundless litigation, and other devices may be less intimidating to good-faith litigants. Finally, in response to the claim that recognition of the tort action will produce interminable litigation, Prosser argues that the heavy burden of proof which the plaintiff bears in such actions will safeguard bona fide litigants and prevent an endless chain of countersuits. But if few plaintiffs will recover in the subsequent action, one may wonder whether there is any point in recognizing the expanded cause of action. If the subsequent action does not succeed, both parties are left to bear the expenses of two futile lawsuits, and court time has been wasted as well.

Although this case arises upon the plaintiff doctor's assertions that the defendant attorneys wrongfully prosecuted a medical malpractice action against him, if we were to eliminate the special injury requirement that expansion of the tort of malicious prosecution would not be limited to countersuits against attorneys by aggrieved physicians. An action for malicious prosecution of civil proceedings could be brought by *any* former defendant—person, firm or corporation, private or public— in whose favor a prior civil suit terminated, against the former plaintiff or the plaintiff's attorney or both. In expanding the availability of such an action the Court would not merely provide a remedy for those required to defend groundless medical malpractice actions, but would

L.Rev. 653, 657–662 (1976); Birnbaum, Physicians Counterattack: Liability of Lawyers for Instituting Unjustified Medical Malpractice Actions, 45 Fordham L.Rev. 1003, 1090 (1977).

35. Prosser, supra, § 120, p. 851.

36. Id.

arm all prevailing defendants with an instrument of retaliation, whether the prior action sounded in tort, contract or an altogether different area of law.

This is strong medicine—too strong for the affliction it is intended to cure. To be sure, successful defense of the former action is no assurance of recovery in a subsequent tort action, but the unrestricted availability of such an action introduces a new strategic weapon into the arsenal of defense litigators, particularly those whose clients can afford to devote extensive resources to prophylactic intimidation.

. . .

V

Apart from special injury, elements of a tort action for malicious prosecution of civil proceedings are (1) prior proceedings terminated in favor of the present plaintiff, (2) absence of probable cause for those proceedings, and (3) "malice," more informatively described by the Restatement as "a purpose other than that of securing the proper adjudication of the claim in which the proceedings are based." [43]

The following discussion addresses the chief concern of this case: the conditions under which the attorney for an unsuccessful plaintiff may be held liable.

A

The absence of probable cause in bringing a civil action may not be established merely by showing that the action was successfully defended.[44] To require an attorney to advance only those claims that will ultimately be successful would place an intolerable burden on the right of access to the courts.

The Court of Appeals adopted, and plaintiff endorses, the standard for determining whether an attorney had probable cause to initiate and continue a lawsuit articulated in Tool Research & Engineering Corp. v. Henigson, 46 Cal.App.3d 675, 683–684, 120 Cal.Rptr. 291 (1975):

> "The attorney is not an insurer to his client's adversary that his client will win in litigation. Rather, he has a duty 'to represent his client zealously . . . [seeking] any lawful objective through legally permissible means . . . [and presenting] for adjudication any lawful claim, issue, or defense.' (ABA, Code of Professional Responsibility, EC 7–1, DR 7–101[A][1], ...) So long as the attorney does not abuse that duty by prosecuting a claim which a reasonable lawyer would not regard as tenable or by unreasonably neglecting to investigate the facts and law in making his determination to proceed, his client's adversary has no right to assert

43. See, generally, Prosser, supra, § 120, pp. 850–856, and 3 Restatement Torts, 2d, §§ 674–681B, pp. 452–473. Propriety of purpose is discussed in § 676.

44. See Prosser, supra, § 120, p. 855. Cf. Drobczyk v. Great Lakes Steel Corp., 367 Mich. 318, 322, 116 N.W.2d 736 (1962).

malicious prosecution against the attorney if the lawyer's efforts prove unsuccessful.

. . .

"The attorney's obligation is to represent his client honorably and ethically, and he may, without being guilty of malicious prosecution, vigorously pursue litigation in which he is unsure of whether his client or the client's adversary is truthful, so long as that issue is genuinely in doubt."

The *Henigson* court also said: "An attorney has probable cause to represent a client in litigation when, after a reasonable investigation and industrious search of legal authority, he has an honest belief that his client's claim is tenable in the forum in which it is to be tried."

In our view, this standard, while well-intentioned, is inconsistent with the role of the attorney in an adversary system.

Our legal system favors the representation of litigants by counsel. Yet the foregoing standard appears skewed in favor of non-representation; the lawyer risks being penalized for undertaking to present the client's claim to a court unless satisfied, after a potentially substantial investment in investigation and research, that the claim is tenable.

A lawyer may be confronted with the choice between allowing the statute of limitation to run upon a claim with which the client has only recently come forward, or promptly filing a lawsuit based on the information in hand. Such dilemmas are particularly likely to arise in connection with medical malpractice claims because a statute provides a six-month limitation period for bringing an action based on a belatedly discovered claim as an alternative to the normal two-year limitation period for malpractice actions. Time will not always permit "a reasonable investigation and industrious search of legal authority" before the lawyer must file a complaint to preserve the client's claim—and thus, perhaps, avoid an action by the client for legal malpractice.

In medical malpractice actions the facts relevant to an informed assessment of the defendant's liability may not emerge until well into the discovery process. Sometimes the relevant facts are not readily ascertainable. In the instant case, for example, defendants maintain that their efforts to acquire Mrs. Serafin's medical records were rebuffed until they commenced suit and thereupon became able to invoke established discovery procedures and the implicit power of the court to compel disclosure; it may be the practice of some doctors or hospitals to refuse to release medical records until a lawsuit has been commenced.

Moreover, the *Henigson* standard suggests rather ominously that every time a lawyer representing, say, a medical malpractice plaintiff encounters a fact adverse to the client's position or an expert opinion that there was no malpractice, he must immediately question whether to persevere in the action. An attorney's evaluation of the client's case should not be inhibited by the knowledge that perseverance may place the attorney personally at risk; the next fact or the next medical opinion may be the one that makes the case, and such developments may occur even on the eve of trial.

Indeed, a jury-submissible claim of medical malpractice may sometimes be presented even without specific testimony that the defendant physician violated the applicable standard of care. Thus, a lawyer may proceed in the good-faith belief that his proofs will establish a prima facie case of medical malpractice without expert testimony, only to find that the court disagrees. Such conduct is not the equivalent of proceeding without probable cause.

Indeed, whether an attorney acted without probable cause in initiating, defending or continuing proceedings on behalf of a client should not normally depend upon the extent of the investigation conducted. The Code of Professional Responsibility does not expressly impose any duty upon a lawyer to conduct an independent investigation of the merits of a client's claim. DR 7–102(A), upon which plaintiffs in the instant action rely, states only that a lawyer shall not:

"(1) File a suit, assert a position, conduct a defense, delay a trial, or take other action on behalf of his client *when he knows or when it is obvious that such action would serve merely to harass or maliciously injure another.*

"(2) *Knowingly* advance a claim or defense that is unwarranted under existing law, except that he may advance such claim or defense if it can be supported by good faith argument for an extension, modification, or reversal of existing law." (Emphasis supplied.)

DR 7–102(A) and the other professional standards to which plaintiff refers consistently incorporate a requirement of *scienter* as to groundlessness or vexatiousness, not a requirement that the lawyer take affirmative measures to verify the factual basis of his client's position. A lawyer is entitled to accept his client's version of the facts and to proceed on the assumption that they are true absent compelling evidence to the contrary.[53] The only general limitation on the lawyer's acceptance of employment is found in DR 2–109(A),[54] the language of which parallels DR 7–102(A). And, although DR 6–101(A)(2) states that

53. Cf. Murdock v. Gerth, 65 Cal.App.2d 170, 179, 150 P.2d 489, 493 (1944):

"It would be inimical to the administration of justice if an attorney were to be held liable to a malicious prosecution action where, after an honest, industrious search of the authorities, upon facts stated to him by his client, he advises the latter that he has a good cause of action, although the courts upon a trial of such action decide that the attorney's judgment was erroneous. If the issue which the attorney is called upon to decide is fairly debatable, then under his oath of office, he is not only authorized but obligated to present and urge his client's claim upon the court. And if it subsequently is determined that the position honestly taken by the attorney was erroneous he should be relieved from responsibility."

54. "A lawyer shall not accept employment on behalf of a person if he knows or it is obvious that such a person wishes to:

"(1) Bring a legal action, conduct a defense, or assert a position in litigation, or otherwise have steps taken for him, merely for the purpose of harassing or maliciously injuring any person.

a lawyer shall not "[h]andle a legal matter without preparation adequate in the circumstances," that preparation need not entail verification of the facts related by the client.

Framed as it is in terms of "reasonableness", the *Henigson* standard is difficult to reconcile with the lawyer's obligation to represent his client's interests zealously.[55] "Zealous representation" contemplates that the lawyer will go to the limits for his client, representing him loyally, tenaciously and single-mindedly. The question of whether a lawyer "abused that duty" is not a matter of what a hypothetical reasonable practitioner would have done in the same circumstances, but of whether the lawyer's conduct was beyond the limits of reason or the bounds of the law [56] although another "reasonable" lawyer, or many such lawyers, might not have acted similarly.

The Restatement's definition of probable cause provides ample guidance whether damages are sought from a lawyer, his client or both:

"One who takes an active part in the initiation, continuation or procurement of civil proceedings against another has probable cause for doing so if he reasonably believes in the existence of the facts upon which the claim is based, and either

"(a) correctly or reasonably believes that under those facts the claim *may* be valid under the applicable law, or

"(b) believes to this effect in reliance upon the advice of counsel, sought in good faith and given after full disclosure of all relevant facts within his knowledge and information." [57] (Emphasis supplied.)

As applied to a plaintiff's lawyer, this standard would allow lack of probable cause to be found where the lawyer proceeded with knowledge that the claim had no factual or legal basis, but would impose no obligation to investigate if the lawyer could reasonably believe the facts to be as the client alleged.

"(2) Present a claim or defense in litigation that is not warranted under existing law, unless it can be supported by good faith argument for an extension, modification, or reversal of existing law." DR 2–109(A), Acceptance of Employment.

55. "A lawyer should represent a client zealously within the bounds of the law." Canon 7.

56. See EC 7–3:

"Where the bounds of law are uncertain, the action of a lawyer may depend on whether he is serving as advocate or adviser. A lawyer may serve simultaneously as both advocate and adviser, but the two roles are essentially different. In asserting a position on behalf of his client, an advocate for the most part deals with past conduct and must take the facts as he finds them. By contrast, a lawyer serving as adviser primarily assists his client in determining the course of future conduct and relationships. While serving as advocate, a lawyer should resolve in favor of his client doubts as to the bounds of the law. In serving a client as adviser, a lawyer in appropriate circumstances should give his professional opinion as to what the ultimate decisions of the courts would likely be as to the applicable law."

57. 3 Restatement Torts, 2d, § 675, pp. 457–458.

B

This Court has said, in opinions addressed to the tort of malicious prosecution, that malice may be inferred from the facts that establish want of probable cause, although the jury is not required to draw that inference.[58] This rule, developed in cases where damages were sought from a lay person who initiated proceedings, fails to make sufficient allowance for the lawyer's role as advocate and should not be applied in determining whether a lawyer acted for an improper purpose.

A client's total lack of belief that the action he initiates or continues can succeed is persuasive evidence of intent to harass or injure the defendant by bringing the action. But a lawyer who is unaware of such a client's improper purpose may, despite a personal lack of belief in any possible success of the action, see the client and the claim through to an appropriate conclusion without risking liability. Restatement 2d, Torts, § 674, comment *d,* states:

> "An attorney who initiates a civil proceeding on behalf of his client or one who takes any steps in the proceeding is not liable if he has probable cause for his action (see § 675); *and even if he has no probable cause and is convinced that his client's claim is unfounded, he is still not liable if he acts primarily for the purpose of aiding his client in obtaining a proper adjudication of his claim.* (See § 676). An attorney is not required or expected to prejudge his client's claim, and although he is fully aware that its chances of success are comparatively slight, it is his responsibility to present it to the court for adjudication if his client so insists after he has explained to the client the nature of the chances." (Emphasis supplied.)

While a client's decision to proceed with litigation although he knows that the facts are not as alleged, or that a proper application to the facts of existing law (or any modification thereof which can be advanced in good faith) will not support the claim, is indicative of the client's ulterior, malicious motive, that inference cannot so easily be drawn from conduct of a lawyer who owes his client a duty of representation and is unaware of the client's improper purpose. The lawyer who "acts primarily for the purpose of aiding his client in obtaining a proper adjudication of his claim," albeit with knowledge that the claim is not tenable, should not be subject to liability on the thesis that an inference of an improper purpose may be drawn from the lawyer's continuing to advance a claim which he knew to be untenable.[60]

---

58. Hamilton v. Smith, 39 Mich. 222 (1878); Drobczyk v. Great Lakes Steel Corp., supra; Renda v. International Union, UAW, 366 Mich. 58, 100–101, 114 N.W.2d 343 (1962).

60. In, most if not, all attorney-client relationships, decision-making authority ultimately rests with the client. A client may, in apparent good faith, insist upon pressing the claim although the attorney has explained that it has no chance of succeeding. An attorney's ability to withdraw from representation is limited if the client objects.

The Restatement defines the mental element of the tort of wrongful civil proceedings as "a purpose other than that of securing the proper adjudication of the claim in which the proceedings are based." A finding of an improper purpose on the part of the unsuccessful attorney must be supported by evidence independent of the evidence establishing that the action was brought without probable cause.[61]

We affirm that portion of the Court of Appeals decision which upheld summary judgment in favor of defendants on plaintiff's claims sounding in negligence and abuse of process. With respect to plaintiff's claim for malicious prosecution, we reverse the decision of the Court of Appeals and affirm the trial court's grant of summary judgment; we do so on the ground that an action for malicious prosecution of a civil action may not be brought absent special injury and the plaintiff failed to plead special injury.

KAVANAGH, WILLIAMS and RYAN, JJ., concur.

LEVIN, JUSTICE (concurring).

Much of the discussion of the problem of unjustified litigation suffers from an undue focus upon the need to compensate the injury suffered by the defendant subjected to a groundless and malicious action. Groundless civil litigation is, however, more than an affliction visited upon a few scattered individuals; it besets the judicial system as a whole. It is, therefore, appropriate to think of it as a systemic problem and to fashion a remedy which preserves and strengthens the integrity of the civil litigation system rather than randomly providing a fortuitous amount of compensation in a handful of isolated cases.

In England, the losing party in a civil action is ordinarily required to reimburse the prevailing party for that portion of the latter's litigation costs which is determined by the judge or an officer of the court to have been "necessary."[1] The recovery thus obtained is usually incomplete, but greater costs can be awarded if the litigation was vexatious or groundless.[2]

The English system has been criticized because the risk of responsibility for a portion of the opponent's actual costs may deter debatable, good-faith claims.[3]

Commentators have also been skeptical of the potential of court-administered sanctions within the original lawsuit as a remedy for groundless litigation because in this country the costs awarded to the prevailing party in a civil action are typically fixed by statute at

---

61. A contingent fee arrangement or the expectation of the attorney that he will ultimately receive a fee for his services is not evidence of an improper purpose. In contrast, a purpose to secure an improper adjudication of the client's claim, as by coercing a settlement unrelated to the merits from an opponent who wishes to avoid the harassment, expense or delay of letting the lawsuit run its course, is an improper purpose. See 3 Restatement Torts, 2d, § 674, comment *d,* p. 453.

1. Goodhart, Costs, 38 Yale L.J. 849, 854–862 (1929).

2. Id., 861–862.

3. Ackerman v. Kaufman, 41 Ariz. 110, 114, 15 P.2d 966 (1932). But see Goodhart, supra, pp. 874–876.

amounts which pale beside the actual costs incurred in litigation, and American courts have generally been inclined to leave revision of costs schemes to the legislatures.[4]

I am of the opinion, however, that this Court can appropriately devise an approach to wrongful litigation which is capable of providing both an appropriate measure of deterrence and reasonable compensation for wronged litigants without imperiling the right of free access to the courts. The remedy, quite simply, is to recognize the inadequacy of existing provisions for the taxation of costs and to adopt a new and distinct court rule authorizing the judge to whom a civil action is assigned to order payment of the prevailing party's actual expenses, including reasonable attorneys' fees and limited consequential damages, where the action was wrongfully initiated, defended or continued.[5] Depending upon the circumstances, payment might be required of the attorney, the client or both. The factual questions implicit in such an evaluation of the losing side's conduct would be resolved by the judge after a prompt post-termination hearing at which the parties could call witnesses and they and their attorneys could testify.

The foundation for developing such a comprehensive structure for controlling vexatious litigation is already in place. GCR 1963, 111.6, provides:

> "Unwarranted Allegations and Denials. If it appears at the trial that any fact alleged or denied by a pleading ought not to have been so alleged or denied and such fact if alleged is not proved or if denied is proved or admitted, the court may, if the allegation or denial is unreasonable, require the party making such allegation or denial to pay to the adverse party the reasonable expenses incurred in proving or preparing to prove or disprove such fact as the case may be, including reasonable attorney fees."

The principles of GCR 1963, 111.6, can readily be extended to wrongful litigation and defense as well as wrongful pleading and can be made applicable regardless of the stage at which the prior litigation terminates; the award of fees and expenses should be limited to those incurred after the point at which the action should have been discontinued or liability admitted.

The sum recoverable should include all fees and administrative charges incurred because of the litigation as well as reasonable attorney's fees. The judge could award a prevailing defendant in a professional malpractice case an additional sum for loss of income-producing time and injury to professional reputation or business resulting from

---

4. Note, Groundless Litigation and the Malicious Prosecution Debate: A Historical Analysis, 88 Yale L.J. 1218, 1232–1233 (1979). See, also, McCormick, Damages, ch. 8, pp. 234–259.

5. Adoption of such a rule appears to be an appropriate exercise of this Court's plenary power over practice and procedure in Michigan courts. See Perin v. Peuler (On Rehearing), 373 Mich. 531, 540–541, 130 N.W.2d 4 (1964). . . .

the wrongful action if the amount is capable of being calculated with reasonable certainty.[6]

The rule could provide that the standard to be applied by the judge in determining whether such an award should be made is whether the losing party or his attorney had proceeded without probable cause and for an improper purpose.[7] So defining the inquiry, in terms of the traditional elements of a cause of action for malicious prosecution of civil proceedings, allows the judge to consult existing precedent for guidance.

Having such a determination made by the judge to whom the original proceeding was assigned would have a number of advantages over assessment of these questions by judge and jury in a separate tort action:

First, a strategy for evaluating the propriety of litigation which is administered exclusively by judges is more susceptible of consistent application and careful supervision than a strategy which relies on a group of laymen chosen at random, often for one day and one trial. Confiding the question solely to the judge avoids the bifurcation of function associated with jury trial on the critical issue of probable cause in an action for malicious prosecution of civil proceedings. Limiting

6. The proposed procedure would not appear to violate a constitutional right of jury trial. U.S. Const., Am. VII, preserving the right of jury trial in common-law suits where the amount in controversy exceeds twenty dollars, does not apply to the states through the Fourteenth Amendment. Melancon v. McKeithen, 345 F.Supp. 1025 (E.D.La., 1972), aff'd per curiam sub nom. Mayes v. Ellis, 409 U.S. 943, 93 S.Ct. 289, 34 L.Ed.2d 214 (1972).

Const.1963, art. I, § 14, preserves the right of jury trial only in causes of action which were part of the common law prior to its adoption. See Conservation Dep't v. Brown, 335 Mich. 343, 346, 55 N.W.2d 859 (1952).

The procedure suggested here would not involve a cause of action in the usual sense of that term, and certainly not one predating the Michigan Constitution. See, generally, Curtis v. Loether, 415 U.S. 189, 194–195, 94 S.Ct. 1005, 1008–1009, 39 L.Ed.2d 260 (1974); Atlas Roofing Co. v. Occupational Safety & Health Review Comm., 430 U.S. 442, 97 S.Ct. 1261, 51 L.Ed.2d 464 (1977).

7. The rule could incorporate the basic concepts of an action for wrongful civil proceedings—absence of probable cause and malice (improper purpose)—as expressed in the Restatement Torts, 2d, §§ 674, 675, 676, 681 and 681A, but differ in the following respects:

(i) an award could be made to a plaintiff as well as to a defendant who prevails in the underlying cause where the requisite elements (absence of probable cause and malice in maintaining or defending the cause and damages) are established;

(ii) an award could be restricted to damages for specific pecuniary loss, including actual attorney fees and other expense reasonably incurred in maintaining or defending the proceedings and any harm to professional or business reputation; recovery for defamation not affecting professional or business reputation or for emotional distress need not be provided for;

(iii) the judge who presided in the underlying cause claimed to have been wrongfully brought or defended could decide the matter without a jury following a hearing which would be required to be concluded within a specified time which parallels the time for a motion for a new trial or judgment notwithstanding the verdict; a motion seeking such an award could be required to be filed by the prevailing party within a limited time after entry of judgment in the underlying cause; hearing on probable cause, malice and damages could be required to be concluded promptly after filing of the motion; findings of fact and conclusions of law could be required to be filed by the judge soon thereafter; any appeal could be consolidated with an appeal on the merits of the underlying cause.

recovery to actual pecuniary loss, thereby eliminating recovery for emotional distress, and relying on a judge to assess damages, combined with the greater control that appellate courts exercise over a judge's findings as compared to a jury's verdict, should tend to avoid awards which might intimidate good-faith litigants.

Second, the judge would usually be familiar with the history of the case; the necessary evidence could be adduced and the relevant findings made in far more efficient fashion than if a new action and a separate trial before a different judge were required.

Third, parties who might be reluctant to initiate further litigation although they felt themselves wronged would be more likely to avail themselves of internal sanctions than of the opportunity to start a separate action which would take its place on the crowded docket and which the defendants would be likely to resist with all available means.

. . . By adopting a court rule this Court would address the problem directly and in a manner compatible with its responsibility to exercise close control and supervision.

This is unmistakably a test case, brought primarily to secure a change in the law. If a court rule responsive to the problem of wrongful litigation is ultimately adopted, the plaintiff and others who have rallied to his cause may win the war even if they have lost this battle.

In pursuing this case, the plaintiff and his supporters have taken a leading role in directing our attention to a widely held concern that today the courts are burdened and innocent parties harassed by an epidemic of frivolous lawsuits. The measure proposed here will put the validity of that perception to the test. All those who feel that they have been made the victims of wrongful litigation would be able to seek a prompt remedy without facing the difficulties and delay inherent in a subsequent tort action.

The effectiveness of such a rule would depend upon the vigilance of the judges who would apply it. The opinion of the Court in the instant case describes certain instances in which sanctions should not be imposed against an attorney. Nothing in the opinion of the Court should, however, be understood as indicating that the Court is unwilling to commit itself to the imposition of sanctions against an attorney where it is appropriate.

WILLIAMS, J., concurs.

COLEMAN, CHIEF JUSTICE (concurring in part, dissenting in part).

. . .

Central to this case is the judicial process of weighing two different potential harms caused by two different types of groundless litigation, only one of which has been given much consideration by the majority. On the one hand, there is the potential harm which could be caused by groundless malicious prosecution suits. On the other hand, there is the harm caused by all other types of groundless litigation. In upholding the special injury requirement, the majority has engaged in much speculation as to what the effects of groundless malicious prosecution suits might be. Little, if any, consideration is given to the harmful effects of other groundless litigation. The retention of the special injury requirement leaves lawyers, in most cases, free from the concern of defending one type of potentially groundless litigation, but at the expense of subjecting the rest of society to the threat of suffering many kinds of groundless litigation without recompense.

The one-sided treatment is especially apparent with respect to the argument regarding the possible increase of legal malpractice insurance premiums. The other side of the coin is that physician plaintiffs and amici obviously conclude, whether correctly or incorrectly, that their defense of groundless litigation has contributed to the high cost of medical malpractice insurance policies with resultant higher costs to patients. Redress for frivolous litigation, they believe, might provide some relief. The majority, when suggesting that the defense of groundless malicious prosecution cases might have some effect on legal malpractice insurance, seems unaware or unconcerned that a different type of groundless litigation may already be having an effect on medical malpractice insurance.

Prediction of how malicious prosecution suits might affect one type of insurance or another is speculative at best. However, one would not expect that the adverse effects of groundless litigation would affect attorneys, or the bringing of lawsuits, to a greater extent than the threat of groundless lawsuits presently affects the rest of our society.

On balance, the effect which malicious prosecution cases without the special injury requirement would have on access to the courts would be less than the effect which other types of groundless litigation has on society. Importantly, the elements of such a malicious prosecution case (lack of probable cause and improper motive) are narrow in scope and not easily met. This narrowness would likely mean that frivolous malicious prosecution cases would more clearly show their frivolous nature than groundless litigation of other varieties. Also, unlike in other cases, attorneys are the ones who must consider what threat, if any, a groundless malicious prosecution suit presents. Certainly, attorneys are in a better position than other members of society to recognize groundless litigation for what it is. Thus, they are in a better position to limit the extent to which the fear of a frivolous malicious prosecution action will affect their conduct.

. . . .

The Negligence Claim

Courts have uniformly rejected negligence claims brought against lawyers by people those lawyers had sued on behalf of a client. In addition to *Dozorc* see: Morowitz v. Marvel, 423 A.2d 196 (D.C.App. 1980); Drago v. Buonagurio, 46 N.Y.2d 778, 778–779, 413 N.Y.S.2d 910,

386 N.E.2d 821 (1978); Spencer v. Burglass, 337 So.2d 596, 600–601 (La. App.1976). The courts have likewise rejected the argument that the ethics rules, in particular the rules against maintaining frivolous suits, create a legal duty that extends to the opposing party. Accord: Mozzochi v. Beck, 204 Conn. 490, 529 A.2d 171 (1987). For a persuasive presentation of the contrary position see Wolfram, The Code of Professional Responsibility as a Measure of Attorney Liability in Civil Litigation, 30 S.C.L.Rev. 281, 310–314 (1979).

Do the reasons given in *Dozorc* for rejecting the negligence claim apply with equal force to the type of claim allowed in *Greycas,* printed in Chapter 2 above? Why allow broader liability to third parties when the lawyer is acting as a facilitator of transactions than when the lawyer is acting as an advocate?

In Garcia v. Rodey et al., 106 N.M. 757, 750 P.2d 118 (1988), the plaintiffs dropped claims against individual school board members, relying, they alleged, on opposing counsel's assertion made in chambers to the judge that the school board would not claim sovereign immunity on the claim against the board as a corporate entity. After judgment for the plaintiffs, the school board invoked sovereign immunity in a post-trial motion and that position was sustained by the courts on appeal. The plaintiffs then instituted this action for, inter alia, negligent misrepresentation against the lawyers for the school board. The New Mexico Supreme Court affirmed the dismissal of the plaintiffs' complaint for failure to state a cause of action, holding that lawyers owe no duty of due care to their clients' adversaries. As for the specific claim of negligent misrepresentation, the court stated: "The very nature of the adversary process precludes justifiable reliance by an opposing party." Id. at 123. Is this statement too broad?

Abuse of Process

Why does the court in *Dozorc* reject the abuse of process claim?

The Restatement 3d of Torts § 682 states that a party is liable for abuse of process when it uses legal process primarily to accomplish a purpose for which it is not designed. Comment *b* to § 682 explains that the word "primarily" was added to exclude liability "when the process is used for the purpose for which it was intended, but there is an incidental motive of spite or an ulterior purpose of benefit to the defendant." As explained in *Dozorc,* the tort has two elements: 1) an ulterior purpose; and 2) a willful act that is improper in the regular conduct of the proceeding. See Prosser and Keeton, Torts (5th Ed.1984) § 121.

Mozzochi v. Beck, 204 Conn. 490, 529 A.2d 171 (1987), involved an abuse of process claim against lawyers. The plaintiff alleged that the lawyers had maintained suit despite learning that the allegations were untrue and that the suit therefore was wholly without merit. The court concluded:

> [A]lthough attorneys have a duty to their clients and to the judicial
> system not to pursue litigation that is utterly groundless, that duty
> does not give rise to a third party action for abuse of process unless
> the third party can point to specific misconduct intended to cause
> specific injury outside of the normal contemplation of private
> litigation. Any other rule would ineluctably interfere with the
> attorney's primary duty of robust representation of the interests of
> his or her client.
>
> 529 A.2d at 174.

Implicitly, this says that factually baseless claims are within the
"normal contemplation of private litigation." Given M.R. 3.1, Fed.R.
Civ.P. 11 and state counterparts to these rules, how can maintaining a
factually baseless claim be regarded as "normal"? Do M.R. 3.1 and
Rule 11 "ineluctably" interfere with the attorney's primary duty of
"robust" representation?

Compare Raine v. Drasin, 621 S.W.2d 895 (Ky.1981) (verdict against
lawyer, including punitive damages, for filing complaint against two
doctors when the lawyer had in his possession medical records showing
the claim lacked substance).

Malicious Prosecution

Absence of Probable Cause

In *Dozorc,* the court rejects the standard for judging probable cause
articulated by the California court in *Henigson.* Why?

One reason given is that "[t]ime will not always permit 'a reasonable investigation and industrious search of legal authority.'" Reread
the note on p. 395 above on what constitutes a reasonable investigation
under Rule 11. Do Rule 11 cases recognize that availability of time is a
factor in the reasonableness of investigation?

In a recent opinion the California Supreme Court partially disapproved of the standard articulated in *Henigson.* Sheldon Appel Co. v.
Albert & Oliker, 47 Cal.3d 863, 765 P.2d 498 (1989). *Henigson* said that
probable cause had an objective component (reasonable investigation
and industrious legal research) and a subjective component (honest
belief). In *Sheldon Appel,* the court (1) rejected the subjective component, holding that it was irrelevant to the issue of probable cause
whether the lawyer actually believed the suit was tenable; (2) held that
probable cause was ordinarily for the court to decide as a matter of law
and not for the jury; and (3) held that if there was such probable cause,
it is immaterial that the attorney may not have made an adequate
investigation.

How is a court to judge whether the prior action was instituted
with probable cause? The standard, according to *Sheldon Appel,* is
whether, on the facts as known to the lawyer at the time she instituted
suit, the suit was objectively tenable. Expert testimony on this question is not permitted. 765 P.2d at 510.

How does the *Sheldon Appel* position on probable cause differ from that of the court in *Dozorc?*

Malice

When does an attorney act with malice according to *Dozorc?*

In *Sheldon Appel,* the court held that once the judge finds that the prior action was *not* objectively tenable, then the fact that the lawyer never thought it tenable and the fact that she failed to do any research before filing become relevant to whether the suit was instituted with malice.

Note that when a *party* is sued for malicious prosecution, reliance on counsel's advice may serve to negate the element of malice. See, e.g., Noell v. Angle, 217 Va. 656, 231 S.E.2d 330 (1977). However, reliance on counsel will not serve to negate malice when the client withholds facts from the lawyer. See, e.g., Derby v. Jenkins, 32 Md. App. 386, 363 A.2d 967, 971 (1976).

Is Court Rule Better than Tort Rule?

Courts have kept tight rein on tort suits to redress frivolous litigation while enlarging the scope of court sanctions against lawyers who bring frivolous suits. Justice Levin, concurring in *Dozorc,* argues for court rule instead of tort rule. Why is a court rule preferable?

Some states have created medical malpractice screening panels, designed to reduce the number of frivolous suits and encourage pretrial settlements. Typically, a panel is composed of a judge, lawyer and physician. After filing a complaint, the parties to the suit are required to participate in an evidentiary hearing conducted by the panel to determine whether there is enough evidence to support a claim against the defendant. See, e.g., Ariz.Rev.Stat. § 12–567 (1988). These panels have been criticized for adding time and expense to the settlement process, being generally biased toward the defendant and having lax standards for panel members and administration. See, e.g., Bedlin and Nejelski, Unsettling Issues About Settling Civil Litigation, 68 Judicature 9, 11 (1984) (which also cites at n. 5, state cases finding the panel system unconstitutional).

After *Dozorc* Michigan changed its rule on sanctions for frivolous litigation. M.C.R. 2.114 is substantially similar to Fed.R.Civ.P. 11 and is considerably more stringent than Michigan's old rule.

For a discussion of tort liability and court sanctions, see Wade, On Frivolous Litigation: A Study of Tort Liability and Procedural Sanctions, 14 Hofstra L.Rev. 433 (1986).

Discipline for Filing Frivolous Suits

Read DR 7–102(A)(1) and (A)(2). Does the word "merely" make DR 7–102(A)(1) too lenient? DR 7–102(A)(1) prohibits vexatious suits only "when the lawyer knows or when it is obvious . . . ." Should this test be more objective, i.e., "when a reasonable lawyer would know"? Compare M.R. 3.1. Note that M.R. 3.1 tracks the language of DR 7–

102(A)(2). What about colorable claims brought "merely to harass
. . ."? See the Preamble to the Model Rules: "A lawyer should use
the law's procedures only for legitimate purposes and not to harass or
intimidate others." Also note that M.R. 8.4(d) prohibits "conduct
prejudicial to the administration of justice." Unlike DR 7–102(A)(1),
the standard under M.R. 3.1 is objective.

Whatever the rules, disciplinary action is rarely taken against a
lawyer for frivolous litigation. Of the relatively few cases that do
impose discipline, most involve multiple instances of frivolous filings,
see, e.g., In re Solerwitz, 848 F.2d 1573 (Fed.Cir.1988) (lawyer suspended
for one year from practice before the court for continuing to press over
one hundred frivolous appeals); People v. Kane, 655 P.2d 390 (Colo.
1982) (lawyer suspended for 3 years for filing frivolous appeals); In re
Jafree, 93 Ill.2d 450, 444 N.E.2d 143 (1982) (lawyer disbarred for filing
numerous frivolous suits to harass defendants). But see In re Paauwe,
294 Or. 171, 654 P.2d 1117 (1982) (30 day suspension for filing frivolous
appeal); In re Lauer, 108 Wis.2d 746, 324 N.W.2d 432 (1982) (lawyer
reprimanded for frivolous claim).

In Committee on Legal Ethics of the West Virginia State Bar v.
Douglas, 370 S.E.2d 325 (W.Va.1988), the court sent a strong message to
the state's disciplinary committee that the filing of frivolous litigation
should be taken more seriously. Whether this will have a salutary
effect remains to be seen. In addition to the chronic problems of
disciplinary bodies, i.e., overworked, underpaid and sometimes less than
fully competent professional staffs, there is a question of evenhanded-
ness in enforcement. As a practical (or political) matter it is more
likely that discipline for filing frivolous suits will be visited upon sole
and small firm practitioners than lawyers in large and prestigious
firms or government attorneys.

Tortious Spoliation of Evidence

A few states have imposed tort liability for the intentional or
negligent destruction or loss of evidence. In cases involving the negligent destruction of evidence, the claim is usually that the defendant
interfered with the plaintiff's efforts to sue some third party by negligently destroying or losing potential evidence. The plaintiff must show
that the defendant had a special relationship to the plaintiff that
entailed a duty to preserve the evidence, see, e.g., Bondu v. Gurvich,
473 So.2d 1307 (Fla.Dist.App.1984) (hospital failed to preserve certain
medical records of the plaintiff; as a result plaintiff lost a medical
malpractice lawsuit against doctors). See also Pirrocchi v. Liberty
Mutual Insurance Co., 365 F.Supp. 277 (E.D.Pa.1973) (action against
claims adjustor for losing the chair that allegedly caused plaintiff's
injuries, making it impossible for plaintiff to sue the chair's manufacturer). Compare, e.g., Parker v. Thyssen Min. Constr., Inc., 428 So.2d
615 (Ala.1983) (employer had no duty to preserve evidence for employee's potential civil action against third parties); Coley v. Arnot Ogden
Mem. Hospital, 107 A.D.2d 67, 485 N.Y.S.2d 876 (1985) (same).

Cases alleging intentional spoliation of evidence have involved parties that the plaintiff would have sued had the evidence not been destroyed. In Koplin v. Rosel Well Perforators, Inc., 241 Kan. 206, 734 P.2d 1177 (1987), the court said the facts did not justify recognizing this new tort, but described the cases in two jurisdictions, California and Alaska, that did recognize it:

> . . . In Smith v. Superior Court, 151 Cal.App.3d 491, 198 Cal. Rptr. 829 (1984), the plaintiff was injured when the rear wheel and tire flew off a van and crashed into plaintiff's windshield. Immediately after the accident, the van was towed to Abbott Ford, Inc., the dealer that had customized the van with "deep dish mag wheels". . . . Within a few days following the accident, Abbott Ford agreed with Smith's counsel to preserve the physical evidence, consisting of certain automotive parts, for later use in a possible action against Abbott Ford and/or others. The evidence was subsequently lost or destroyed making it impossible for Smith to pursue her claim. She then sued alleging a cause of action against Abbott Ford for "tortious interference with [a] prospective civil action by spoliation of evidence,". . . . The court . . . found [this tort] to be analogous to the tort of intentional interference with a prospective business advantage. . . .

> . . . In Hazen v. Municipality of Anchorage, 718 P.2d 456 (Alaska 1986), a tape recording was taken of the plaintiff by an undercover police officer immediately prior to her arrest for prostitution at her massage parlor. The plaintiff claimed, in an action against the arresting officers, the city, and the city attorney, that the tape contained exculpatory statements and on the tape she denied sex was available at her parlor. Later, however, the tape somehow became inaudible and the plaintiff asserted it had been intentionally altered. The Alaska Supreme Court . . . held plaintiff had a cause of action for intentional interference with a prospective civil action by spoliation of evidence. . . .

Id. at 1180–81.

Cases rejecting this tort include: LaRaia v. Superior Court, 150 Ariz. 118, 722 P.2d 286 (1986); and Miller v. Montgomery County, 64 Md. App. 202, 494 A.2d 761 (1985) (emphasizing that because destruction was by opposing party, plaintiff had other remedies available, i.e., negative inferences would be drawn about what the material would have shown).

Perjury as a Tort

The common law rule followed in most jurisdictions is that, in the absence of a statute, it is not a tort to commit perjury or suborn perjury. See Prosser & Keeton, Torts (5th Ed.1984) § 114; Harper & James, Torts § 5.22. There are a number of justifications given for this rule: (1) it protects society's interest in finality of judgments; (2) it prevents multiplication of litigation; and (3) it prevents the intimidation of witnesses and parties. Shepherd v. Epps, 179 Ga.App. 685, 347 S.E.2d 289 (1986). However, if the plaintiff otherwise states a cause of action, e.g., for malicious prosecution or conspiracy to defraud the plaintiff of property, proof of the use of perjury may establish other elements of the plaintiff's case. See, e.g., Snyder v. Faget, 295 Ala. 197, 326 So.2d 113 (1976) (perjury may be demonstrated to prove an overt act in furtherance of conspiracy to defraud). In conspiracy cases, the courts usually require that the perjury be part of a larger scheme or plan to injure the plaintiff. See Stolte v. Blackstone, 213 Neb. 113, 328 N.W.2d 462 (1982) (collecting and discussing cases).

Liability for perjury or suborning perjury may be predicated upon a statute. For example, N.Y. Jud. Law § 487 authorizes an injured person to recover treble damages in a civil action from an attorney "guilty of any deceit or collusion with intent to deceive the court or any party."

There is a dispute over whether perjury constitutes a predicate act for purposes of a civil RICO claim. Compare Rand v. Anaconda–Ericsson, Inc., 623 F.Supp. 176, 182 (E.D.N.Y.1985), aff'd, 794 F.2d 843, 849 (2d Cir.1986) (perjury not a predicate act), with C & W Construction Co. v. Brotherhood of Carpenters and Joiners, 687 F.Supp. 1453 (D.Hawaii 1988) (perjury may be a predicate act).

Immunity from Suit for Defamation

Lawyers and other participants in judicial proceedings are absolutely immune from suit for defamation based on statements made in the course of those proceedings or "reasonably related" thereto. See Restatement 2d of Torts, § 586; Prosser & Keeton on Torts § 114 (5th Ed.1984). Some courts recognize only a qualified privilege for comments "preliminary to a proposed judicial proceeding." See, e.g., Pinkston v. Lovell, 296 Ark. 543, 759 S.W.2d 20 (1988) (comments by lawyer in conversation with clients on advisability of malpractice action are privileged if the initiation of proceedings in good faith is being seriously considered). Others recognize an absolute privilege for these comments. See Arneja v. Gildar, 541 A.2d 621 (D.C.App.1988) (ethnic slurs).

The broad reach of the privilege has been criticized:

> In the hands of some courts, the privilege has been reshaped into something very much like a privilege for a lawyer to be bumptious and unrestrained in all matters vaguely related to litigation and regardless of whether the communication is calculated to advance or to retard justice or the proceeding. . . . Courts have employed the privilege beyond defamation and have held that suits are barred by the same immunity if they are based on negligent misrepresentation, invasion of privacy, or intentional infliction of emotional distress.

Wolfram, Modern Legal Ethics (1986) at 231.

I. TRIAL TACTICS

Communicating With Opposing Parties and Witnesses

When the Other Person Has a Lawyer

DR 7–104(A)(1) and M.R. 4.2 require that lawyers communicate with other represented parties through those parties' lawyers and not by speaking to the parties directly. Both rules allow for direct communication where the other party's lawyer has consented or the law otherwise authorizes direct communication. An example of the latter situation is when the other party is the government; the First Amendment's right to petition for grievances allows some direct communication with the government itself. Vega v. Bloomsburgh, 427 F.Supp. 593 (D.Mass.1977).

The rules do not, and indeed could not, prevent one client from communicating with another, but a lawyer may not circumvent these rules by getting a nonlawyer to communicate with the party in the lawyer's stead. M.R. 8.4(a); People v. Hobson, 39 N.Y.2d 479, 348 N.E. 2d 894 (1976); Schantz v. Eyman, 418 F.2d 11 (9th Cir.1969).

Writing on problems in tax ethics in the Federal Bar Association's Newsletter, Attorney Margaret M. Richardson analyzed the following question:

> A District Counsel attorney makes a settlement offer in a pending Tax Court case, but suspects that taxpayer's lawyer has not communicated the offer to his client—possibly to prolong the proceedings and enlarge the fees. How may District counsel ensure that the settlement offer is communicated to taxpayer?

> Taxpayer's counsel has an ethical duty to inform his client of the settlement offer. Model Rules 1.2(a), 1.4. Despite an ethical breach by taxpayer's attorney ethical rules prohibit the District Counsel attorney from communicating the settlement offer directly to the taxpayer. Model Rules 4.2 and 8.4(a).

Ms. Richardson offers the following options open to District Counsel attorney:

> a. Urge the lawyer to have taxpayer present at the next settlement conference

> b. Seek the lawyer's consent to directly contact the taxpayer

> c. Discuss the settlement at the pretrial conference when taxpayer is present

> d. Initiate disciplinary proceedings against the lawyer either with the state disciplinary agency or the Director of Practice of the Internal Revenue Service, see 32 C.F.R. 10.50–10.75 (1983)

Compare Leubsdorf, Communicating with Another Lawyer's Client: The Lawyer's Veto and the Client's Interest, 127 U.Pa.L.Rev. 683 (1979) (proposing that a lawyer be allowed to communicate with any person by letter with a simultaneous copy to the person's lawyer or directly as long as the person's lawyer is informed prior to the contact).

In criminal matters should the rule on direct communication be stronger? Weaker?

It is not a violation of the accused's Sixth Amendment right to counsel for government counsel to question the accused without defense counsel being present or being informed, so long as the accused knowingly and intelligently waives his right to have defense counsel there. Patterson v. Illinois, 487 U.S. 285, 108 S.Ct. 2389 (1988). Justice Stevens writing in a dissent joined by Justices Brennan and Marshall argued that the Constitution should require no less protection for the fairness of criminal proceedings than of civil proceedings. As Justice Robertson of the Mississippi Supreme Court put it, dissenting in Minnick v. Mississippi, 1988 WL 139185 (Miss.1988) (not reported in So.2d):

> Or, suppose [in a civil case] the [defendant's] investigator [talked directly to the plaintiff and] obtained a[n oral] statement that compromises plaintiff's case. We know well what would happen, the only point of mystery being whether defense counsel would be shot or flogged.

> We regard this rule as a fair one. Its genesis lies in our concern with fairness. That the third party has a lawyer is taken as an expression of his wish to be dealt with only through counsel. There is substantial probability of the party being overreached when his lawyer is not there. The integrity of the lawyer-client relationship is at stake.

> I know of no basis for assuming that a prosecuting attorney is exempt from these rules. Indeed, the district attorney has a special responsibility for assuring that the accused has counsel and is not taken unfair advantage of. . . .

> If the efficacy of our criminal justice system depends upon the accused not asserting or enjoying his claims and protections regarding access to counsel, then there is something very wrong with that system.

In Mills Land & Water Co. v. Golden West Refining Co., 186 Cal.App.3d 116, 230 Cal.Rptr. 461 (1986), the court disqualified a lawyer who had violated DR 7–104(A)(1) by communicating directly with a member of the board of directors of the opposing party, a corporation. The court refused to suppress any information gained in the improper conversation that was otherwise discoverable, stating that the exclusionary rule was inappropriate in *civil* litigation. In criminal prosecutions evidence obtained through direct communication with the accused would not be discoverable. Should this make a difference in fashioning a remedy?

Prosecutors who bypass defense counsel are rarely subjected to discipline. See In re Burrows, 291 Or. 135, 629 P.2d 820 (1981). For imposition of discipline for direct communication in civil litigation, see, e.g., Toledo Bar Ass'n v. Westmeyer, 35 Ohio St.3d 261, 520 N.E.2d 223 (1988); Florida Bar v. Shapiro, 413 So.2d 1184 (Fla.1982).

In United States v. Hammad, 858 F.2d 834 (2d Cir.1988), the prosecutor furnished an informant with a false subpoena and a hidden tape recorder whereby the informant recorded conversations with the defendant. The prosecutor knew the defendant was represented by counsel in the matter under investigation. The Sixth Amendment was not at issue because the incident took place as part of an investigation, not after criminal proceedings had been instituted. The court held that the ethics rule on communicating with represented persons applies to prosecutors, but that the legitimate use of informants in an investigation was within the "authorized by law" exception to the rule. Here, however, the use of the informant was held not legitimate because the prosecutor engaged in "egregious misconduct" in using a "specious and contrived subpoena" and hence violated DR 7–104(A)(1). The court further held that exclusion of the evidence would be an appropriate remedy. Other cases approving of exclusion of the evidence as a remedy for violating DR 7–104(A)(1) include United States v. Killian, 639 F.2d 206 (5th Cir.1981); People v. Hobson, 39 N.Y.2d 479, 348 N.E.2d 894 (1976). Contra: Gentry v. Texas, 770 S.W.2d 780, 791 (Tex. Crim.App.1988) (en banc) (disciplinary action against the prosecution, not exclusion of evidence, is the appropriate remedy); Suarez v. Florida, 481 So.2d 1201 (Fla.1985) (same).

Mills Land, supra, involved a corporation as the opposing party. When the opposing party is an entity, as distinct from an individual, determining who may be contacted directly and who not is more complicated. This question is discussed in *Wright v. Group Health Hospital,* printed in Chapter 9 below, and in the notes following that case.

Communicating With People Not Represented by Counsel

DR 7–104(A)(2) provides that a lawyer shall not give advice to someone not represented by counsel "other than the advice to seek a lawyer". M.R. 4.3 provides that when the other person is not represented, "the lawyer shall not state or imply that the lawyer is disinterested." Further, if the lawyer "knows or reasonably should know that the unrepresented person misunderstands the lawyer's role in the matter, the lawyer shall make reasonable efforts to correct the misunderstanding." Note too that DR 1–102(A)(4) and M.R. 8.4(d) prohibit "conduct involving dishonesty, fraud, deceit or misrepresentation."

See also ABA Informal Opinion 908 (1966) (before interviewing a potential defendant, a lawyer must advise her that the lawyer is counsel for the plaintiff); ABA Formal Opinion 117 (1934) (a lawyer who interviews an employee of an opposing party or a nonparty witness must disclose the lawyer-client relationship).

Is handing the unrepresented person a legal document to sign a violation of the rule? See W.T. Grant v. Haines, 531 F.2d 671 (2d Cir.

1976) (interviewing adverse party, who was not represented by a lawyer, permitted, but suggesting that seeking to examine confidential personal papers would violate the rule). But see ABA Formal Op. 84–350 (1984) (withdrawing two previous ABA Informal Opinions, 1140 (1970) and 1255 (1940), which had prohibited lawyers from presenting documents to adverse parties who were not represented by counsel).

M.R. 3.8(c) prohibits a prosecutor from seeking "to obtain from an unrepresented accused a waiver of important pretrial rights, such as the right to a preliminary hearing." Should this rule be limited to prosecutors?

M.R. 3.4(f) provides that a lawyer shall not request a person, other than the client, "to refrain from voluntarily giving relevant information to another party." However, the lawyer can so advise a person who is a relative, employee or agent of the client, *if* "the lawyer reasonably believes that the person's interests will not be adversely affected by refraining from giving such information." A lawyer may not advise another to refrain from cooperating if that advice is in furtherance of the client's illegal activity. See In re Blatt, 65 N.J. 539, 324 A.2d 15 (1971) (lawyer urged witnesses not to cooperate with federal investigation); In re Russell, 59 N.J. 315, 282 A.2d 42 (1971) (lawyer advised witnesses, who were represented by another lawyer, to plead the Fifth to help client).

Other Limits on Gathering Evidence

A lawyer may not use illegal means to gather evidence. There are no exceptions for lawyers under the law of fraud, burglary, theft, illegal use of the mail or the wiretapping statutes. See ABA, Standards Relating to the Prosecution Function and the Defense Function, Standard 4–4.2 ("It is unprofessional conduct for a lawyer knowingly to use illegal means to obtain evidence or information or to employ, instruct, or encourage others to do so."); Markham v. Markham, 272 So.2d 813 (Fla.1973); Lucas v. Ludwig, 313 So.2d 12 (La.App.1975); and Tennessee Bar Association v. Freemon, 50 Tenn.App. 567, 362 S.W.2d 828 (1961).

In addition, the ethics rules prohibiting "dishonesty, fraud, deceit or misrepresentation" may place more stringent limits on the ways in which lawyers may gather evidence. See, e.g., ABA Formal Opinion 337 (1974) (lawyers should record conversations only with the consent or prior knowledge of all the parties to the conversation); ABA Informal Opinion 1407 (1978) (in accord with 337). But see ABA Informal Opinion 1357 (1975) (statements made at a public meeting may be recorded).

United States v. Ofshe, 817 F.2d 1508 (11th Cir.1987), involved evidence improperly gathered by a prosecutor. Assistant United States Attorney Turow (later the author of Presumed Innocent) had the defendant's lawyer tape conversations with the defendant. The government argued that Ofshe's lawyer was "keen on diminishing his [own] criminal responsibility by acting as an informant." The lawyer/informer did not withdraw from representing the defendant before "bugging" him. The court refused the defendant's motion to dismiss the indictment, stating that the appropriate remedy was suppression of the evidence thus garnered. Nevertheless, the court called the conduct "reprehensible" and suggested referral to the state's disciplinary commission. Turow defended his conduct in an article, Law School vs. Reality, New York Times Magazine, 9/18/88 p. 52: "I believed—and continue to believe—that neither clients nor lawyers have the right to plan crimes secure from government law enforcement efforts."

On aiding and abetting the destruction or concealment of evidence see the *Stenhach* case in Chapter 1 and the notes following it.

Special Responsibilities of Prosecutors

M.R. 3.8 outlines the Special Responsibilities of a prosecutor. See also ABA Standards on the Administration of Criminal Justice (The Prosecution Function), particularly 3–3.9, Discretion in the Charging Decision.

In Brady v. Maryland, 373 U.S. 83, 83 S.Ct. 1194 (1963), the Supreme Court held that the prosecutor must reveal to the defense, upon request, exculpatory evidence "material either to guilt or to punishment." See also Moore v. Illinois, 408 U.S. 786, 92 S.Ct. 2562 (1972) (elaborating on the *Brady* rule). In United States v. Agurs, 427 U.S. 97, 96 S.Ct. 2392 (1976), the Supreme Court held that when the exculpatory evidence creates a reasonable doubt, the prosecution must disclose the evidence to the defense even if there is no request. But see United States v. Bagley, 473 U.S. 667, 105 S.Ct. 3375 (1985) (prosecution's failure to disclose evidence that could have effectively impeached government witnesses does not require automatic reversal; reversal required only if nondisclosure might have affected outcome).

DR 7–103(B) requires the prosecutor to disclose to the defense, whether or not the defense makes a request, evidence "that tends to negate the guilt of the accused, mitigate the degree of the offense, or reduce the punishment." See also M.R. 3.8(d), which adopts the same standard as DR 7–103(B), except that in connection with sentencing the rule allows a prosecutor to withhold mitigating information that is privileged or is protected by order of a tribunal.

In People v. Jones, 44 N.Y.2d 76, 404 N.Y.S.2d 85, 375 N.E.2d 41 (1978), the court held that the prosecutor did not violate the defendant's due process rights by failing to reveal during plea negotiations that the state's key witness had died. The court held that the prosecutor had neither a constitutional nor an ethical duty to reveal this information, as long as the prosecutor made no affirmative misrepresentation. The information was held to be outside the *Brady* rule because it was not exculpatory; the death of the witness merely made it difficult for the state to prove its case.

In Fambo v. Smith, 433 F.Supp. 590 (W.D.N.Y.1977), aff'd, 565 F.2d 233 (2d Cir.1977), the court held that while the prosecutor did have a duty to disclose to the defendant that physical evidence critical to one of the counts of the indictment had been destroyed, the failure to do so did not affect the fairness of defendant's plea bargain.

Are these cases consistent with *Brady* and *Agurs*? With *Bagley*? With EC 7–13, which sets forth the justifications for the special responsibilities of a prosecutor? With ABA Standard Relating to the Prosecution Function 3–4.1, which says "[i]t is unprofessional conduct for a prosecutor knowingly to make false statements or representations in the course of plea discussion . . . ."

The prosecution also has a duty to preserve evidence, California v. Trombetta, 467 U.S. 479, 104 S.Ct. 2528 (1984). In *Trombetta,* the Supreme Court held that the loss or destruction of evidence does not violate the due process clause of the Constitution absent "official animus" or a "conscious effort to suppress exculpatory evidence." 467 U.S. at 488, 104 S.Ct. at 2533. In addition, the destroyed evidence must be "material" to the suspect's defense under a two part test. First, the exculpatory value of the evidence has to have been apparent prior to the destruction of the evidence; and second, the evidence has to be such that the defendant would be unable to obtain comparable evidence by other reasonably available means.

For a revealing look at the ethics of white collar criminal defense lawyers, see Mann, Defending White Collar Crime (1985). For reflections on the ethics of prosecutors, see Fisher, In Search of the Virtuous Prosecutor, 15 Am.J. of Criminal Law 197 (1988). Misconduct of criminal defense lawyers is taken up in the notes following the Underwood excerpt below.

Secret Agreements to Settle

Secret agreements to settle in a civil case are often referred to as Mary Carter agreements, from Booth v. Mary Carter Paint Co., 202 So. 2d 8 (Fla.App.1967), overruled in part by Ward v. Ochoa, 284 So.2d 385, 388 (Fla.1973). *Mary Carter* upheld the validity and nondisclosure of a secret agreement between the plaintiff and two of the three defendants that limited the maximum liability of those two defendants. Mary Carter agreements come in many forms, but the classic features are: (1) the liability of the agreeing defendant is limited, although it remains a party to the action; (2) the existence of the agreement is withheld from the nonsettling parties to the suit and/or the judge and/or the jury; (3) the plaintiff is guaranteed a minimum recovery, whether or not the verdict amount is less or indeed whether there is judgment for the plaintiff.

There is a lively debate over the legitimacy of Mary Carter agreements. See, e.g., Entmann, Mary Carter Agreements: An Assessment of Attempted Solutions, 38 U.Fla.L.Rev. 521 (1986); R. Eubanks & A. Cocchiarella, In Defense of "Mary Carter," 26 For The Defense 14 (1984).

The two greatest dangers with these agreements are: (1) collusion between the settling defendants and the plaintiff to manage the trial in such a way that leaves the nonsettling defendant holding the bag; and (2) deceiving or misleading the court and/or jury by keeping from them the existence of the agreement, which might lead them to weigh the credibility of the settling defendants' evidence differently.

The current trend in the courts is to validate Mary Carter agreements as long as they are fully disclosed to the court and the other parties to the action. See, e.g., Slusher v. Ospital, 777 P.2d 437 (Utah 1989); Riggle v. Allied Chemical Corp., 378 S.E.2d 282 (W.Va.1989). Courts will, however, invalidate an agreement whose provisions are for one reason or another deemed to be void as against public policy. See Lum v. Stinnett, 87 Nev. 402, 488 P.2d 347 (1971) (agreement called for counsel to engage in unethical conduct). Generally see Abbott Ford v. Superior Court of Los Angeles County, 43 Cal.3d 858, 741 P.2d 124 (1987) (adopting a case by case approach to the validity of "sliding scale" agreements and discussing the various forms such agreements take).

Some courts require the agreement to be disclosed to the jury unless it would confuse the issues. See Ratterree v. Bartlett, 238 Kan. 11, 707 P.2d 1063 (1985).

A California statute requires that the existence and terms of the agreement be disclosed to the jury. West's Ann. Cal.Code Civ.Proc. § 877.5.

The Advocate–Witness Rules

When, if ever, may the trial lawyer act as a witness in the case she is trying? Many firms offer wide-ranging services to their clients, e.g., negotiating contracts, establishing pension funds, handling tax matters and defending or prosecuting litigation. The lawyer who negotiated the contract or set up the tax plan may have relevant testimony to offer in later litigation on these matters. Should the lawyer be allowed to serve as trial counsel? In many firms, that lawyer would not handle litigation matters, although in some small shops one lawyer may do all these things. In firms with litigation departments, may the lawyers in that department continue as trial counsel when a lawyer in the same firm should be called as a witness on matters at issue in the litigation?

Read EC 5–9. Compare the Comment to M.R. 3.7. Does the Comment understate the problems in acting as advocate and witness?

The Model Code provides that a lawyer shall not accept employment, or if employment has already begun shall withdraw from the representation, if the lawyer knows or it is obvious that the lawyer *or any member of the lawyer's firm* "ought to be called as a witness." See DR 5–101(B) (accepting employment); and DR 5–102 (withdrawing from employment). There are exceptions. DR 5–101(B) and DR 5–102(A). A lawyer may serve as advocate and witness *on the client's behalf,* if she or a member of her firm ought to testify *and* any of the following conditions are met:

> (1) the testimony will be solely on an uncontested matter;

> (2) the testimony will be solely on "a matter of formality" and there is no reason to believe testimony in opposition will be offered;

> (3) the testimony will be solely on the "nature and value of legal services rendered in the case";

> or

> (4) refusing to represent (or to continue to represent) the client "would work a substantial hardship on the client because of the distinctive value of the lawyer or his firm as counsel in the particular case."

What happens when the opposing party proposes to call the lawyer as witness? The Code allows the lawyer to continue the representation unless the testimony will prejudice the client. DR 5–102(B). The broader exception for testifying when called by opposing counsel is apparently an attempt to forestall opposing counsel from calling lawyers as witnesses in order to disqualify them. Is the exception in this situation too broad?

Is DR 5–102(B) consistent with the statements in EC 5–9?

M.R. 3.7(a) provides: "A lawyer shall not act as advocate at a trial in which the lawyer is likely to be a necessary witness except where . . . ." The exceptions are based on the Code. M.R. 3.7(b) addresses whether other lawyers in the firm are disqualified from acting as trial counsel. It states: "A lawyer may act as an advocate in a trial in which another lawyer in the lawyer's firm is likely to be called as a witness unless precluded from doing so by Rule 1.7 or Rule 1.9." M.R. 1.7 and 1.9 prescribe when a lawyer must withdraw or decline to take a case because of a conflict of interest. Generally see Chapters 7 and 8 below. Here, it will suffice to note that the Code provisions automatically impute disqualification to other members of the lawyer/witness' firm, whereas M.R. 3.7(b) provides that, unless disqualified by a conflict of interest between the advocate and the client, the advocate from the same firm may proceed. Consider the following example, which you may wish to consider again after studying Chapter 7 on conflicts of interest.

> Lawyer Davis from the firm of Davis and Michael represents IMT Corp. Lawyer Michael handled contract negotiations for IMT and would be a necessary witness to establish some basic facts about the negotiation. If there is any likelihood that Michael's testimony (elicited on direct or cross) will contradict testimony of IMT employees or otherwise be adverse to IMT interests, Davis should not act as lawyer because to continue would create a conflict between her obligations to client IMT and to her firm and partner Michael. She would be less likely to impeach Michael's adverse testimony because of her relationship to him and their firm. If the testimony

might be adverse to IMT, it does not matter whether IMT calls Michael to the stand or whether the opposing party plans to call him.

Imagine a scenario where Davis could proceed. Aside, from the question of imputed disqualification, how else does M.R. 3.7 differ from the Code? See Cannon Airways v. Franklin Holdings Corp., 669 F.Supp. 96, 99 (D.Del.1987) (holding that "likely to be a necessary witness" covers fewer situations than the Code formulation, "ought to be called . . ."); and Culebràs Enterprises v. Rivera–Ross, 846 F.2d 94, 98 (1st Cir.1988) (noting the Code's prohibition against accepting employment is broader than the M.R. 3.7's prohibition against acting as advocate at trial; and holding that 3.7 does not prevent a lawyer from performing case-related pretrial work as long as the lawyer did not take an active role at trial).

As to use of the advocate-witness rule as a tactic to disqualify counsel, see Borman v. Borman, 378 Mass. 775, 393 N.E.2d 847 (1979) (court should order disqualification only if "continued participation taints the legal system or the trial" itself); J.D. Pflaumer, Inc. v. Department of Justice, 465 F.Supp. 746 (E.D.Pa.1979) (similar). Also see S & S Hotel Ventures L.P. v. 777 S.H. Corp., 69 N.Y.2d 437, 515 N.Y.S.2d 735, 508 N.E.2d 647 (1987) (great deference to trial lawyer's decision to stay in the case); and Pulliam v. Pulliam, 738 S.W.2d 846 (Ky.App.1987). But see, e.g., MacArthur v. Bank of New York, 524 F.Supp. 1205 (S.D.N.Y.1981) (discussing the importance of the rule and the need for strict interpretation).

Should the client be able to waive the rule's prohibition by foregoing counsel's testimony? *MacArthur*, supra, says the client may not do so. Contra: Pain Prevention Lab, Inc. v. Electronic Waveform Labs, Inc., 657 F.Supp. 1486, 1498 (N.D.Ill.1987).

When the lawyer/witness is a prosecutor should the same rules apply or should the government's need to proceed as "the only game in town" override the advocate-witness ban? Neither the Code nor M.R. 3.7 makes an exception for prosecutors. See American Bar Association Standards Relating to the Prosecution and Defense Function 3–3.1(f): "Unless a prosecutor is prepared to forgo impeachment of a witness by the prosecutor's own testimony as to what the witness stated in an interview or to seek leave to withdraw from the case in order to present the impeaching testimony, a prosecutor should avoid interviewing a prospective witness except in the presence of a third person." The Standard seems to be in conflict with the preference in both the Rules and the Code for testimony over representation when there is a choice to be made.

However reluctant some courts are to disqualify private counsel based on the advocate-witness rule, they are more reluctant to disqualify prosecuting attorneys for violating the rule. See, e.g., State v. Johnson, 702 S.W.2d 65 (Mo.1985); and Scherrer v. State, 294 Ark. 227, 742 S.W.2d 877 (1988). But see Pease v. District Court, 708 P.2d 800

(Colo.1985) (disqualifying a prosecuting attorney because two former prosecutors were to testify against the defendant and requiring that a special prosecutor be appointed to try the case); and United States v. Prantil, 764 F.2d 548 (9th Cir.1985) (remanded for new trial because prosecuting attorney should have been disqualified and available for defense to call as witness). In United States v. Johnston, 690 F.2d 638 (7th Cir.1982) (en banc), the court held that DR 5–101(B) applies to prosecutors and extends to testimony offered in a suppression hearing before a judge. Should the rule be dispensed with when the case, civil or criminal, is being tried to a judge? Reread EC 5–9 and the Comment to M.R. 3.7.

Articles on the advocate-witness rule include: Wydick, Trial Counsel as Witness: The Code and the Model Rules, 15 U.C. Davis L.Rev. 651 (1982); Enker, The Rationale of the Rule that Forbids a Lawyer to be Advocate and Witness in the Same Case, 1977 Am.Bar.Found.Res.J. 455; and Note, The Advocate–Witness Rule: If Z, Then X, But Why?, 52 N.Y.U.L.Rev. 1365 (1977).

Dirty Tricks in Court

RICHARD H. UNDERWOOD, "ADVERSARY ETHICS: MORE DIRTY TRICKS"

6 Am.J. of Trial Advocacy 265 (1982).*

. . .

III.   Presenting the Case–In–Chief

A.   *The Deliberate Injection of Inadmissible Evidence*

In spite of the clear dictates of the Code of Professional Responsibility that counsel may not "state or allude to any matter that he has no reasonable basis to believe is relevant to the case or that will not be supported by admissible evidence," [51] many lawyers cannot resist the temptation to elicit objectionable and prejudicial evidence, and then move forward without a pause to preclude objection or a motion to strike. In fact, there is an attitude prevalent in the trial bar that:

> [an] improper question should be asked unless it is of such prejudicial character that the refusal of the trial court to declare a mistrial would be reversible error. This practice is sometimes used for the very purpose of confronting adverse counsel with the

---

51. See also ABA Model Code of Professional Responsibility DR7–106(c)(1) (Final Draft 1981). See also Model Rules of Professional Conduct, Rule 3.4(e) (Proposed Final Draft 1981):

[A lawyer shall not] in trial, allude to any matter that the lawyer does not reasonably believe is relevant or that will not be supported by admissible evidence. . . .

. . .

A lawyer should not propose a stipulation in the jury's presence unless he knows or has reason to believe the opposing lawyer will accept it.

difficult choice of waiving objection by failing to make it, or else make an objection that may lead the jury to conclude that he is attempting to withhold information from them.[53]

Unless trial judges deal sternly with such unfair tactics the aggrieved party will have little recourse. Some examples of improper questioning on direct and cross-examination illustrate the nature of such gamesmanship.

A classic example of the injection of inadmissible evidence occurred in Fike v. Grant,[56] in which a "general question" became the vehicle for a discussion of liability insurance. The daughter of a personal injury plaintiff testified that on the morning following the accident she went alone to defendant's place of business, and then was asked by plaintiff's counsel whether she talked about the accident:

A. Would you like to know what I asked them?

Q. You may tell all that was said.

A. I went for the purpose of asking Mr. and Mrs. Fike—

Q. Just a minute. Speak a little slower and talk to the jury.

A. I went to the Fike's place of business to inquire about the insurance on their car and Mr. and Mrs. Fike—

Q. Was that all you asked them?

A. No.

Similar misconduct, clearly calculated, occurred in County of Maricopa v. Maberry.[57] During that trial an expert medical witness testified on behalf of the medical malpractice defendant that the decedent's death was the result of voluntary ingestion of a massive dose of amphetamines. At the close of cross-examination plaintiff's lawyer proceeded:

53. [Keeton, Trial Tactics, 2d ed. 1973] at 59. Compare Curtis v. Greenstein Trucking Co., 397 F.2d 483 (7th Cir.1968) (trial court did not abuse its discretion in determining that plaintiff's asking of objectionable questions, thereby forcing defendants' counsel to make 60 objections, only 7 of which were overruled, did not have a prejudicial effect on the jury).

Of course, the Code does not prohibit counsel from asking questions merely because there is some doubt about admissibility, although the better practice is for counsel to seek a ruling on admissibility before trial, thereby insuring that expected testimony may properly be incorporated into the opening statement. Cf. County of Maricopa v. Maberry, 555 F.2d 207, 222 n. 18 (9th Cir.1977). There are many examples of similar misconduct in the presentation of opening statements. Compare United States v. Schindler, 614 F.2d 227 (9th Cir.1980) (reference, in opening statement in mail fraud prosecution, to a witness' concern for her life, and question on direct examination, "Did you ever have a conversation with Mr. Schindler during which the subject of contracts to kill someone arose?"); Smith v. Covell, 100 Cal.App.3d 947, 161 Cal.Rptr. 377 (1980) (reference in opening statement to purported diagnoses that plaintiff's pain was "in her mind, that she has an antagonism toward her husband and this is her way of punishing her husband," the statements being without factual support in the record). See also Note, The Scope of Permissible Comment In A Civil Action In Kentucky, 58 Ky.L.J. 512, 520–25 (1970).

56. 39 Ariz. 549, 8 P.2d 242 (1932).

57. 555 F.2d 207 (9th Cir.1977).

Q. Doctor, at the time that your deposition was taken, I will ask you this, sir, isn't it a fact that at one point you interrupted and said: "Off the record. Come on, Ken—"

[Counsel for defendant]: Your Honor, I object.

Q. "Come on, Ken. You've got a damned good case and you know it." You said that, didn't you, Doctor?

A. I don't recall.[58]

. . . .

B. On Leading Questions

Closely related to the immediately preceding tactics is the practice of coaching witnesses while they are on the stand by means of leading questions.

Since the Code of Professional Responsibility does not explicitly condemn the practice of coaching a witness with leading questions [61] the problems of abuse of this tactic are ever present. Concerning this problem Judge Keeton notes:

The vice of the question is telling the witness what the lawyer wants him to say. Having received the message, the witness can then answer a non-leading question in the desired way, even though the leading question is stricken. Consequently you may sometimes be tempted to ask a leading question deliberately, realizing that an objection to it will be sustained.[62]

Consider the following line of questioning from a reported case:

[During direct examination of a witness]

Q. Directing your attention back to July, 1966, did you buy some virgin metal, virgin nickel from anyone in July, 1966?

A. Yes, sir, I did.

Q. Did you buy approximately eleven hundred ninety-nine pounds of metal back at that time?

A. I did.

58. The statement referred to was not, in fact, in the deposition. Citing counsel for violation of DR 7–106(C) the Court observed at 555 F.2d 207, 217 that:

The lawyer did not pause after the objection of his opposing counsel to permit a statement of grounds for his objection, or permit the judge to rule, before the witness answered. There could be little doubt in any experienced trial lawyer's mind hearing this question, in the manner and sequence in which it was propounded, why it was asked. . . .

61. Keeton, supra note [53] at 49, suggests that the following provisions apply: DR 7–106(C): In appearing in his professional capacity before a tribunal, a lawyer shall not:

. . .

(7) Intentionally or habitually violate any established rule of procedure or of evidence.

. . .

EC 7–25: . . . a lawyer should not by subterfuge put before a jury matters which it cannot properly consider.

62. Keeton, supra note [53] at 49.

[Defense counsel]: I object to leading. He should know how much he bought.

The Court: I sustain the objection.

[Defense counsel]: I ask that the jury be instructed.

The Court: The jury is instructed they are not to consider the question for any purpose. I sustained the objection.

Q. Do you recall how much of this virgin nickel you bought back in July of 1966?

A. I bought eleven hundred ninety-nine pounds.

[Defense counsel]: I objected after the leading question was asked of him and he turned around and asked how much. As important as that is to this case, I object to that being brought into evidence. He put words in his mouth and then asked him again.

The Court: That's overruled.[63]

In this example, the court's cautionary instruction was completely ineffectual, and the jury, in effect, heard the "testimony" twice.

Experienced trial lawyers will use objections to leading questions cautiously, fearing that little will be gained by repeated objections and that such objections might cause resentment on the part of the jury.[64] All too often the result of this is that the proponent of testimony will be tempted to cross the line between occasional and unconscionable coaching. For example, in Straub v. Reading Co.,[65] an FELA case tried in the Eastern District of Pennsylvania, the appellate court observed:

Regarding leading questions, appellee [plaintiff below] asserts that this problem is within the control of the trial court. . . . But where that control is lost or at least palpably ignored and the conduct is a set pace running the length of the trial which produces a warped version of the issues as received by the jury, then that body never did have the opportunity to pass upon the whole case and judgment based on that kind of twisted trial must be set aside.

· · ·

[In the case at bar] little seems to have been left to a spontaneous explanatory answer. At times the witnesses seemed relatively unnecessary except as sounding boards.[66]

---

63. Lawrence v. Texas, 457 S.W.2d 561 (Tex.App.1970) (the appellate court stated the conventional rule that a case will not be reversed in the absence of a showing that the trial judge abused his discretion in allowing leading questions).

64. Compare F. Lane, 2 Goldstein Trial Techniques § 13.01 (1969).

65. 220 F.2d 177 (3d Cir.1955).

66. Id. at 179, 182. But see Gardner v. Meyers, 491 F.2d 1184 (8th Cir.1974) (leading questions used 81 times, but in the absence of objection at trial issue could not be heard on appeal).

C. *Dumb Shows, Improper Displays and Other Dirty Tricks*

The most notorious "dirty tricks" on record consist of ingenious efforts to distract or mislead the jury by means of "dumb shows." [67] Arguably not all "dumb shows" are unethical, however many are. Fortunately, few attorneys would attempt the more outlandish exhibitions, but that is not to say that such tricks will not turn up in tomorrow's reporters.

. . .

Another recent instance of gross misconduct was reported in Richardson v. Employers Liability Assurance Corp., Ltd.,[70] a suit for Employer's alleged failure to settle claims in good faith under the uninsured motorist provisions of an insurance policy. During the second day of trial, defense counsel moved for a mistrial on the ground that plaintiff's counsel had placed a photo-copy of a legal newspaper on counsel table, in full view of the jurors, which bore the headline:

DIDN'T SETTLE IN POLICY LIMITS; OK MENTAL SUFFERING AWARD

Plaintiff's counsel's transparently lame explanation was that the newspaper article was reference material, although the case reported was three years old, and available in the official reports. By obtaining the cooperation of the trial judge, defense counsel were able to note the position of the "exhibit" and take photographs from several points in the courtroom to preserve the record for appeal. . . .

D. *Some Objections to Objections*

Not all trial judges take care to preclude counsel from making argumentative comments in the course of making objections. As a result "objections for jury purposes" are not uncommon in American courtrooms.[73] Such "speaking objections" should be viewed as a violation of EC 7–25 of the Code of Professional Responsibility, that "a

---

67. The terminology is from [G.] Vetter, [successful Civil Litigation: How to Win Your Case Before You Enter the Courtroom (1977)] at 225. A few examples related by a variety of commentators should illustrate the nature of such "non-verbal persuaders."

An artifice often attributed to Clarence Darrow . . . a nearly invisible wire is inserted into a cigar so that when the cigar is smoked everyone's attention will be focused on the ash, which magically does not fall. . . .

. . .

If the kid's a crawler, the best time to let him loose is during final argument. Imagine that little tyke crawling right up to you (make sure he comes to you and not the DA, or worse yet, the judge; a smear of Gerber's peaches around the cuff worked for me) while you're saying, "Don't strike down this good man, father to little Jimmy. Why, Jimmy!" Pick the child up and give him to Daddy. If the DA objects and gets them separated, so much the better. Moses himself couldn't part a father and son without earning disfavor in the eyes of the jury. Babies are truly miracles of life; they've saved many a father years of long-distance parenting. If your client's childless, rent a kid for trial.

. . .

70. 25 Cal.App.3d 232, 102 Cal.Rptr. 547 (1972).

73. Compare M. Belli, Modern Trials 616 (Student ed. 1963):

An exception to the rule of objecting only when counsel is prepared to sustain the objection is "objection for jury purposes." Every trial lawyer is familiar with this procedure. It is not unethical if its purpose is further to emphasize, for example, the limited purpose of the introduction of certain testimony.

lawyer should not by subterfuge put before a jury matters which it cannot properly consider." [74] However it is often difficult to distinguish a legitimate objection accompanied by an explanation of grounds from a frivolous objection used solely for argument.

. . .

IV. Cross–Examination

Pity the witness:

Of all unfortunate people in this world, none are more entitled to sympathy and commiseration than those whom circumstances oblige to appear upon the witness stand in court. You are called to the stand and place your hand upon a copy of the Scriptures in sheepskin binding, with a cross on the one side and none on the other, to accommodate either variety of the Christian faith. You are then arraigned before two legal gentlemen, one of whom smiles at you blandly because you are on his side, the other eying you savagely for the opposite reason. The gentleman who smiles, proceeds to pump you of all you know; and having squeezed all he wants out of you, hands you over to the other, who proceeds to show you that you are entirely mistaken in all your supposition; that you never saw anything you have sworn to; that you never saw the defendant in your life; in short, that you have committed direct perjury. He wants to know if you have ever been in state prison, and takes your denial with the air of a man who thinks you ought to have been there, asking all the questions over again in different ways; and tells you with an awe inspiring severity, to be very careful what you say. He wants to know if he understood you to say so and so, and also wants to know whether you meant something else. Having bullied and scared you out of your wits, and convicted you in the eyes of the jury of prevarication, he lets you go. By and by everybody you have fallen out with is put on the stand to swear that you are the biggest scoundrel they ever knew, and not to be believed under oath. Then the opposing counsel, in summing up, paints your moral photograph to the jury as a character fit to be handed down to time as the typification of infamy—as a man who has conspired against innocence and virtue, and stands convicted of the attempt. The judge in his charge tells the jury if they believe your testimony, etc., indicating that there is even a judicial doubt of your veracity; and you go home to your wife and family, neighbors and acquaintances, a suspected man— all because of your accidental presence on an unfortunate occasion! [81]

. . .

---

74. McElhaney, Making and Meeting Objections, 2 Litigation 43 (1975).

81. F. Wellman, The Art of Cross–Examination 194–95 (1936). Compare Commonwealth v. Rooney, 365 Mass. 484, 313 N.E.2d 105, 112–13 (1974):

[The judicial function] will not long succeed if a witness innocent of everything except his coincidental presence at a time and place where something relative to a crime

The following provisions of the Code of Professional Responsibility are frequently ignored during the cross-examination of witnesses, as is illustrated in many judicial opinions:

DR 7–106 Trial Conduct. . . .

(C) In appearing in his professional capacity before a tribunal, a lawyer shall not:

(1) State or allude to any matter that he has no reasonable basis to believe is relevant to the case or that will not be supported by admissible evidence.

(2) Ask any question that he has no reasonable basis to believe is relevant to the case and that is intended to degrade a witness or other person.

(3) Assert his personal knowledge of the facts in issue, except when testifying as a witness.

(4) Assert his personal opinion . . . as to the credibility of a witness, as to the culpability of a civil litigant, or as to the guilt or innocence of an accused; . . . .

. . .

(6) Engage in undignified or discourteous conduct which is degrading to a tribunal.

A. Outright Harassment

In each of the following examples counsel's cross-examination served no legitimate purpose, and was intended to humiliate or degrade the witness.

Counsel for plaintiff approached the defendant, and after addressing him by name gratuitously added:

Q. The last time I saw you, you had a plastic bag on your head— [84]

In another case, counsel, having been admonished not to interject his personal comments into the examination of witnesses, approached a

---

occurred is to be subjected to a bruising, grueling and abrasive cross-examination in which questions are loaded with unsupported insinuations of improper motives, negligence, incompetence, perjury or, worse, suspicion of guilt of the crime for which the defendant is on trial. The doctor who sutured the defendant's knife wounds at the hospital emergency room was cross-examined as though he were a defendant in a malpractice case. The cross-examination of some of the Commonwealth's witnesses at the trial of this case violated their right to fair and reasonable treatment, and evidenced an unwarranted assumption that only the defendant had rights to be protected. The proper discharge of counsel's duty to his client does not require such an assumption. Equally important, the integrity and continued efficacy of the judicial process cannot permit it. The judge presiding over the trial of a case has the power to keep the examination of witnesses within the limits of common decency and fairness, and he has the duty to exercise that power promptly and firmly when it becomes necessary to do so.

84. International Ass'n of Bridge, Structural & Ornamental Iron workers, Local 387 v. Moore, 149 Ga.App. 431, 254 S.E.2d 438, (1979) (the court offered counsel a mistrial).

prosecution witness who had manifested some inability to determine directions on an exhibit at trial:

Q. Have you ever done any flying?

A. No.

Q. I recommend that you don't.[85]

. . .

B. *Cross–Examination By Innuendo*

One of the most common abuses of cross-examination takes the form of a question implying a serious charge against the witness, for which counsel has little or no proof. All too often, trial attorneys ask such questions for the sole purpose of "waft[ing] an unwarranted innuendo into the jury box." [87]

. . .

The trial judge has considerable discretion to limit cross-examination which is not directed to the real issues of the case, and which suggests misconduct on the part of the witness.[89] Moreover, the trial judge may caution counsel or demand a showing of "good faith" as a prerequisite to such cross-examination.[90] Authority may even be found sustaining the right of the opposing party to call the cross-examiner to the stand and inquire into the "good faith basis" for a line of questions.[91]

. . .

Kiefel v. Las Vegas Hacienda, Inc.[94] not only provides an illustration of improper cross-examination, but also suggests a meaningful remedy for such abuses. Plaintiff had brought suit against a motel chain to recover damages from an assault inflicted by an intruder who gained entry to her room. During his cross-examinations of plaintiff and her husband defense counsel propounded questions insinuating that plaintiff and her husband had had an altercation the previous evening, that her husband had made numerous calls to plaintiff's room prior to the assault, and that she recognized the intruder as her husband. When such questions elicited denials, counsel intended that impeachment would follow, when in fact no impeachment would follow. The trial judge found that such tactics, coupled with a variety of other abuses, not only justified a new trial, but also an assessment of costs and attorney fees against the defendant and defense counsel. . . .

85. Hawk v. Superior Court, 42 Cal.App.3d 108, 116 Cal.Rptr. 713, 724 (1974) (counsel held in contempt).

87. Michelson v. United States, 335 U.S. 469, 481, 69 S.Ct. 213, 221, 93 L.Ed. 168, 176, (1948). . . .

89. See, e.g., State v. Crawford, 202 N.W.2d 99 (Iowa 1972) (collecting cases).

90. Cf. United States v. Greer, 643 F.2d 280 (5th Cir.1981).

91. United States v. Pugliese, 153 F.2d 497, 499 (2d Cir.1945). Cf. United States v. Cardarella, 570 F.2d 264, 268 (8th Cir.1978).

94. 39 F.R.D. 592 (N.D.Ill.1966), aff'd, 404 F.2d 1163 (7th Cir.1988).

V. Summation

In an earlier day, charges of misconduct during closing argument were likely to receive short shrift. . . .

Notwithstanding counsel's traditional right to a certain rhetorical license in "summing-up," today's trial attorney must take care to observe his ethical obligations to the tribunal, to the opposing party, counsel, and witnesses, and to his own client.

. . .

A. Greasy Kid Stuff

Any attorney who has undertaken the defense of a large corporation or an insurance company has suffered it—the tactic that is somewhat charitably referred to as "dehumanizing the defendant." For example, in spite of the well established and salutary rule that the relative wealth or poverty of a party is ordinarily inadmissible, and that arguments regarding the wealth of the defendant are improper (unless about a legitimate claim for punitive or exemplary damages), deliberate incitement of bias along such lines continues to generate a surprising number of reported appellate opinions. Consider the following examples.

. . .

(I)n Draper v. Airco, Inc.[114] a wrongful death action brought against United States Steel Corporation, Airco, Inc., and W.V. Pangbourne & Co., arising from the electrocution of a lineman who was installing a switch on an energized line on premises owned by U.S. Steel, counsel for the plaintiff made repeated references to the wealth of defendants and then carried on "somewhat incoherently:"

> I am going to make the equalizer between the multimillion dollar there for [Plaintiff] and her kids, it's right here. On that side of the room are bills of dollars and on this side of the room is the equalizer. . . . [I]n this case I brought you the giants, the giants of the industrial world . . . I am going to ask you to tumble the magnificent big companies here with all their engineers.[115]

A jury verdict for $585,789.55 was gained, and then lost.

. . .

Comments

Compare these quotes from Keeton, Trial Tactics and Methods 2d Ed. (Boston: Little Brown & Co., © 1973), with the foregoing excerpt from Underwood:

> Probably you will be at your best as an advocate when you cause the judge and jury to believe that the decision you are urging them to reach is a decision you would reach yourself. Yet the Code

114. 580 F.2d 91 (3d Cir.1978).
115. Id. at 95.

of Professional Responsibility, in one of its Disciplinary Rules, prohibits any direct statement of belief in your cause. . . . It seems more consistent with the apparent objectives of the rule, as well as the prevailing practice, to treat it as a regulation of the form and manner of your conduct . . . rather than a regulation requiring that you not display, even indirectly, any appearance of commitment to your cause. Indeed, if interpreted as precluding even an indirect display of commitment to your cause, the rule could hardly be reconciled with your acknowledged duty as an advocate to bring "zeal" to your representation of your cause.

Id. at 2–3.

In some exceptional instances, asking questions that are clearly improper and prejudicial is regarded as misconduct of counsel sufficient to warrant a mistrial or new trial . . . If you believe that the evidence of doubtful admissibility is likely to have a strong influence on the findings of the jury in the case, you may conclude that the chance of reversal is worth taking: the decision is based upon weighing the probable value of the evidence to you in its influence on the jury against the disadvantage of possible reversal of a favorable verdict and judgment.

Id. at 58–60.

Most articles on courtroom ethics focus on the criminal defense lawyer, see, e.g., Freedman, Professional Responsibility of the Criminal Defense Lawyer: The Three Hardest Questions, 64 Mich.L.Rev. 1469 (1966); Subin, The Criminal Lawyer's "Different Mission": Reflections on the "Right" to Present a False Case, 1 Geo. J. Legal Ethics 125 (1987) (proposing that it be considered improper for a criminal defense lawyer to refute a fact that she knows is true beyond a reasonable doubt); Mitchell, Reasonable Doubts Are Where you Find Them: A Response to Professor Subin . . ., 1 Geo J. Leg.Ethics 339 (1987).

The special latitude accorded a criminal defense lawyer, see, e.g., M.R. 3.1, is not a carte blanche. It is the "obligation of defense counsel to defend his client within the rules of the game; he has neither duty nor right to break the rules." United States v. Lowery, 733 F.2d 441, 446 (7th Cir.1984). See United States v. Thoreen, 653 F.2d 1332 (9th Cir.1981) (lawyer held in contempt of court for substituting someone else for the defendant at the defense table to test a witness' identification of the defendant); People v. Lewis, 75 Ill.App.3d 560, 393 N.E.2d 1380 (1979) (defense lawyer properly informed court that his client was feigning inability to communicate in effort to be found incompetent to stand trial).

In Taylor v. Illinois, 484 U.S. 400, 108 S.Ct. 646 (1988), defense counsel omitted a witness from the list of defense witnesses given to the prosecution. The Supreme Court upheld exclusion of this witness' testimony.

To ameliorate hardball litigation techniques in civil cases "courtesy codes" have been proposed. See, e.g., Proposed Code of Litigation

Conduct (1988), disapproving of such practices as: taking advantage of an opponent's known absence from the office to serve papers; writing letters that ascribe to one's adversary a position she has not taken; making *ad hominem* arguments in legal papers; and falsely holding out the possibility of settlement as a means of delaying discovery or trial. Proliferation of these codes demonstrates the bar's concern with incivility in its ranks. Also see Commission on Professionalism, ABA, . . . A Blueprint for the Rekindling of Lawyer Professionalism, reprinted in 112 F.R.D. 243 (1987); and Rotunda, Lawyers and Professionalism: A Commentary on the Report of the . . . Commission on Professionalism, 18 Loy.U.Chi.L.Rev. 1149 (1987). However, without a community capable of imposing informal sanctions, such as ostracism, there is little hope for real improvement. Moreover, however lofty their purpose, "courtesy codes" may increase ambiguity about what is actually prohibited.

KENNEY HEGLAND, "MORAL DILEMMAS IN TEACHING TRIAL ADVOCACY"
32 Journal of Legal Education 69 (1982).*

. . .

A. *The Search for Victory, as Opposed to Truth*

Of necessity, litigation presented in a simulation cannot be treated as a search for what "really happened" since nothing did. The exercise becomes a game in which the role of the lawyer is to manipulate the few given facts into any pattern or theory which will prevail. Once adopted, this attitude may carry over to the handling of real clients.

It is sometimes legitimate to sacrifice truth for another important interest, such as to protect individual constitutional rights, but that is not my concern here. What I am concerned about is the process of factual emphasis, shaving, and fudging that turns the negligent drunk driver, for example, into the personification of carefulness. Advocacy courses which utilize simulations can teach that factual distortion is the obligation of effective counsel.

A hearing regarding revocation of a liquor license, from the files of NITA, provides a vivid example. The clerk of the defendant store is alleged to have "knowingly sold Harold Watkins, an intoxicated person, liquor." On direct examination the liquor control agent testifies that he was sitting in his car across the street from the store and that he observed Watkins stagger into the store, approach the counter, and purchase a bottle which appeared to be wine. Watkins then left the store and was stopped by the agent, who determined that he was indeed drunk. In Watkins's hand was a bottle of cheap wine.

After the direct examination, a student will be asked to cross-examine on behalf of the liquor store. A typical cross-examination will

* Copyright © 1988 by Kenney Hegland. Reprinted with permission.

focus on the agent's ability to see Watkins actually purchase the wine in the store. The student will argue that perhaps Watkins stole the wine. This is a good theory; the student sits down. "Why did you assume," asks a member of the teaching team, "that Watkins was drunk? If he was not drunk, the store has a good defense. Even if he was drunk, can the arresting officer prove that the clerk knew so?"

At one level, such critique serves educational goals. Lawyers, like other people, assume too much. In the *Rosenberg* case, for example, the defense assumed that the secret to the atomic bomb had been stolen, arguing only that the Rosenbergs were not guilty of the crime. Perhaps a better defense would have been that the secret had never been stolen at all.[6] The constant reminder that we tend to close too quickly on problems and take too much for granted is invaluable.[7]

At another level, however, the critique becomes destructive. The student infers that all avenues of attack are open to him and that the only criterion for selection is effectiveness with the jury. Which of the possible theories is the most convincing: that Watkins was really sober, or that Watkins, although drunk, stole the bottle in the store or had it with him when he entered? Because the problem is hypothetical, because there is no clerk to tell the lawyer his version of what happened, the lawyer is free to manufacture possibilities and to attack any of the adversary's vulnerabilities. Litigation becomes, not a process of truth seeking, but a forum for clever argument.

. . .

Even if we can never really know what did happen in a given situation, there are many instances in which we can be sure of what did not occur. That there is no truth does not imply that there are no lies. Assume, for example, that the clerk admits to his lawyer that he sold the wine to Watkins but denies that he knew Watkins was drunk. Perhaps we will never be absolutely sure as to one aspect of what happened, whether the clerk knew or not. Here the lawyer's art is needed to sharpen the dispute, to test theories, to challenge recollections and to point out competing interests. The trier of fact relies on the lawyer's art to assist him in reaching the best possible judgment as to what really happened. However, to employ the same technique to suggest that Watkins stole the wine is to use one's lawyering skills to lie. Watkins did not steal the bottle, and we know it.[8]

6. For the literary account of the case, see E.L. Doctorow, The Book of Daniel (New York: Bantam, 1971).

7. A major block to creativity is early closure on a problem. I have attempted to apply some of the insights of writers in the field of creativity to legal problem solving. See Kenney Hegland, Trial and Practice Skills in a Nutshell 167–91 (St. Paul, Minn.: West Publishing Co., 1978).

8. That "no truth" does not equal "no lies" is so obvious that I hate to admit it took a book to bring it to my attention. See Sissela Bok, Lying (New York: Pantheon Books, 1978). Professor Bok, in discussing various professional lies, makes a very interesting proposal concerning lawyers' techniques. She urges that the jury be instructed as to what they are. To use my example:

B. Law as a Game

There is no question that NITA-type programs are a great deal of fun. Those playing the parts of witnesses—often law students—are usually bright and contentious. Excitement fills the air when they cross swords with the student-lawyer in cross-examination. Because there is no oath taken, because there are so few given facts, the witness is at a considerable advantage—one slip, one loose question, and the student-lawyer is impaled. The spectators are delighted. Their laughter, however, reinforces a moral bankruptcy—the belief that there is nothing inherently important or meaningful about the lawyering process. The purpose of the process is to win and to avoid embarrassment. One learns techniques, not to accomplish justice, not to resolve human problems, but rather to avoid getting egg on one's face.

It is certainly true that the practice of law, particularly trial work, is in many ways gamelike. There is no need to apologize. A great deal of personal satisfaction comes from playing well and winning. This satisfaction is inherent in the process; it is not dependent on any external goal, such as "doing justice" or "helping solve human problems." As with all games, one approaches the practice of law with a desire to play well and win. We should not lament this aspect of lawyering or feel guilty about our enjoyment of it. Indeed, we should share our students' joy when they "do it right." [9]

What we must not do, however, is forget that lawyering is more than just a game to all the players, even to law teachers and students. For teaching purposes it is often necessary to assign students arbitrarily to one side or the other in a fabricated dispute in which there are no clients, injuries, or crimes. We should be aware, however, that the lesson actually taught may be that *it doesn't matter*. To compensate for this distortion and the cynicism to which it often leads, the law teacher must encourage discussion of the normative side of lawyering and why *it does matter very much*.

C. The Problem of Imputing Ends to Clients

Because there is no client, the student-lawyer cannot discuss with a real person the ends and means of the litigation. He must therefore

Ladies and Gentlemen of the jury, in considering the testimony of the witnesses and the closing argument of the lawyers, please keep in mind that the lawyers have attended trial advocacy workshops where they practiced cutting off witnesses and other techniques of controlling them. These lawyers were told that the worst sin a lawyer can make is to allow a witness to explain a statement he makes. These lawyers were told not to let on that an adverse witness has made a mistake on the stand until time of closing argument when the witness has gone home and hence can't explain the error. Finally, in considering the impassioned pleas you just heard, just remember that each attorney would have gladly represented the other side.

If we really believe in the propriety of technique, why not?

9. For a delightful and insightful look at the "game" of litigation, see Arthur Leff, Law and . . ., 87 Yale L.J. 989 (1978).

impute a goal to the client, and that goal is, of course, to win by any lawful means.

Is it true that clients want to win by any lawful means? There is a growing recognition in legal literature that the "hired gun" debate, wherein the client makes some immoral and outrageous demand upon the lawyer, is somewhat beside the point.[10] In practice the far more common problem arises when the lawyer *assumes* that the client wants him to do something immoral and outrageous and, with a shrug, goes about doing it. That is, lawyers generally assume that their clients are interested only in their short term financial gain or, in the case of both civil and criminal defendants, in escaping all responsibility. William Simon notes the clearest example.[11] When a criminal suspect confesses to police, lawyers are apt to believe that the confession occurred because he was not warned properly. No rational person would confess to a crime. Never mind the basic human needs to communicate and make atonement.

In the context of the trial advocacy course, students may come to the conclusion that all is justified by a favorable verdict because that favorable verdict is the client's only concern. One NITA case, for example, involves a criminal prosecution in which the state's star witness, Laura Hobson, is the ex-girlfriend of the defendant. Laura, the file explains, has a very mixed background. One component of the NITA program is the expert demonstration of lawyering skills. After watching a very polished, aggressive, and experienced litigator virtually destroy Laura, I spoke with a student I knew to be both sensible and sensitive. "NITA is just a great program," he beamed. "Man, what that lawyer did to Laura Hobson—made her into a dope-crazed whore."

Arguments and style are analyzed only from the perspective of technique: "In terms of jury impact, should you go after the dope before the sleeping around?" "In this day of women's lib, maybe you shouldn't get into the sleeping around at all." Teachers making such a critique may not be as Machiavellian as they sound. Perhaps we mean "I think it stinks" but fear that such assertions make us vulnerable to criticism. We thus attempt to transfer our subjective, emotional reaction by saying "The jury won't like it." When we fail to voice our inner reservations, however, we *appear* Machiavellian in saying or implying that jury impact is the only proper consideration.

Is it all that clear that Laura's ex-boyfriend would have her turned into a "dope-crazed whore" for the sake of a favorable verdict? Perhaps he still has warm feelings for her. Perhaps he is simply unwilling to see another human attacked viciously as a condition of his own freedom. A client's life does not end when the jury returns, except, of course, in NITA.

10. See, e.g., Warren Lehman, The Pursuit of a Client's Interest, 77 Mich.L.Rev. 1078 (1979).

11. William Simon, The Ideology of Advocacy, 1978 Wisc.L.Rev. 29.

It has struck me, in discussing with students the cases they are handling in clinical placements, that there are certain parallels between the practice of law and the early medical practice of "bleeding." The doctors who utilized that technique believed, as they had been taught to believe, that bleeding was in the best interests of their patients. They had no idea that they would be held up for ridicule and scorn in the twentieth century.

Many clients seem worse off for having sought legal help, not because their cases were handled improperly, but because they were handled properly. The movie *Kramer v. Kramer* takes the easy shot. Lawyers in custody cases often assume that their clients' only interest is winning custody and do immeasureable damage to the parent-child relationship. Even people involved in business do not always find legal preventive medicine conducive to economic health.[12] Lawyers who plan for disaster and assume that their clients will want to escape all liability when disaster strikes may destroy budding business relationships by substituting adversity and suspicion for cooperation and trust. With all due apologies to Professor Fried, with a lawyer for a friend, perhaps a client doesn't need enemies.[13]

In Laura Hobson's case, the lawyer *assumes* that his client wants, indeed, insists upon, the devastating cross-examination. In conducting it, the lawyer is *not* responsible for the harm inflicted upon Laura because he is only doing his job, only pursuing the lawful goals of his client. And, of course, the client is *not* responsible for Laura's injury; he was simply sitting there. This is the result of imputing ends to clients: injury without responsibility, injury without anyone ever saying "It is worth it to me to inflict this pain." [14]

These, then, are the problems inherent in the NITA approach: the lessening of the lawyer's obligation to the truth, the reinforcement of the game theory of law, and the problem of imputing ends to clients. Some of their negative thrust can be diverted by warning the students of the dangers inherent in all simulation courses and discussing the issues these dangers raise. Discussions of this sort, however, will never make the same impression on a student as would the experience of representing real clients in real cases. We give up meaningful inquiry into central lawyering questions if we retreat totally into the classroom.

12.   See, e.g., Stewart Macaulay, Non–Contractual Relations in Business: A Preliminary Study, 28 Am.Soc.Rev. 55 (1963).

13.   Charles Fried, Lawyer as Friend, 85 Yale L.J. 1060 (1975).

14.   Beyond the problem of imputed ends, i.e., cases in which the lawyer assumes the client wants him to do something immoral and outrageous, there are also, to be sure, situations in which the client expressly requests something immoral and outrageous. Should the lawyer turn Laura into "a dope-crazed whore" if his client insists? The usual debate views it as a matter of power: either the lawyer does what he thinks proper, or he capitulates to the client and becomes the "hired gun." Thomas Shaffer, in a very provocative article, views this situation as a matter of communication in which neither side wins, but in which both reason and feel their way towards a mutually acceptable solution in which "conscience is offered, not asserted." Thomas Shaffer, The Practice of Law as Moral Discourse, 55 Notre Dame Law, 231, 241 (1979).

Simulated skills courses can, however, meaningfully address other issues, and it is to these issues that I now turn.[15]

II

This is an exciting time in legal education. Whole new areas of scholarship and insight open up as we investigate not only what judges do all day but also what the lawyer's day involves. The excitement of discovery, however, will not be captured if we stay at the superficial level of technique. There are richer mines to be explored—the philosophical and psychological underpinnings of technique. I do not have a map of how to reach these deeper mines; in my own classes I am tentative. I simply present some relevant lines of inquiry here.

One of the black-letter rules of trial advocacy programs is "Never ask 'why?' on cross!" There is general agreement that during cross-examination the questioning lawyer must be in tight control of the witness. Irving Younger, that masterful teacher whose magical touch transforms the quagmires of murky doctrine into light and playful meadows, refers to this rule as a commandment. The supposed necessity of tight witness control in cross-examination is supported by war stories. One classic tale involves a witness who testifies that the defendant bit off the victim's nose. The first part of the cross-examination establishes beyond all doubt that the witness, due to position and lighting conditions, could not have seen the defendant bite the victim's nose. The lawyer is not satisfied, however, and he asks the dreaded One–Question–Too–Many:

Q: You admit that you didn't see the defendant bite off the victim's nose. In fact, when the victim screamed, you admit you were looking the other way. How can you sit there and tell this jury that the defendant bit off his nose?

A: Because I saw him spit it out.

15. I have two specific suggestions that I think would curb some of the otherwise distorting aspects of the use of simulated problems. The first is to put some truth into the problems. The second is to have students sit as jurors.

Truth would be added to the hypothetical problems if the instructor, for example, told the defendant whether she was guilty or not and told the witness whether he got that good look or whether his close relationship with the plaintiff colors his testimony. The witnesses should be encouraged to visualize the incidents to which they are to testify. If they saw an "intersection" accident, they should visualize a particular intersection. The witness still can lie on the stand about the physical characteristics of the intersection, but because the witness has a particular intersection in mind, the testimony will be perjury rather than poetry.

Another device to bring technique down to the level of reality is to have students play the parts of jurors. Under the NITA model, each student caps off his experience with one or two jury trials with lay jurors. Students are unanimous as to the educational value of talking to the jurors after the trial. They learn a lot about technique: "Oh, we jurors saw what you were up to and we thought you were real clever. Of course, we weren't taken in." It is difficult to assess techniques of influencing decision-makers without ever having made a decision oneself. I would have the students, at the first session, sit through a short trial as jurors and then decide the case. This is particularly important in law schools. Many law students have never sat through a trial and hence have no sense of the whole of it.

In teaching commandments, one need not convince the novice of their basic moral, philosophic, or psychological truth: all one must do is convince him that all hell will break loose if they are not obeyed. Far too often, in advocacy programs I have attended or taught, that is the prevailing pedagogy. Tacit assumptions should be opened to inquiry. Why should a lawyer never ask "why?" on cross-examination? What dictates this controlling, fearful, and ultimately hostile view of lawyering?

Maybe one shouldn't ask "why?" because the witness has been lying all along, and once he realizes the bind he is in, he will make something up to get out of it: "Oh yes, now I see your point. I saw him spit it out." The assumption implicit in this argument is that human nature is such that all people will perjure themselves or at least that so many will that we, as lawyers, must treat them all as perjurers. This is an interesting and debatable proposition. Perhaps the commandment rests, not on a view of human nature, but on a view of human memory. Although witnesses will not generally perjure themselves, many will unconsciously invent facts or explanations that are consistent with their interests. Memory may be such that inconvenient facts are quickly forgotten and convenient ones quickly manufactured. Again, this is an interesting and debatable proposition.[16] Or perhaps one should not allow explanations on cross because the lawyer knows that the witness is telling the truth. Even though the defendant's lawyer knows the defendant bit off the nose, his task may be to mislead the jury into believing otherwise. If the rule against asking "why?" rests on the game theory of law, then surely that is also an interesting and debatable position.

What are the psychological effects of the commandment on the lawyers who accept it? What happens to a person who comes to believe that this is a world of self-interest and perjury, or an even scarier world where there is no reality but only points of view? How will lawyers with these world views treat their clients? For what purposes will they use the law? In short, what are the consequences of the technique? Does its acceptance advance justice?

. . .

Politics and the Courtroom

The act of sentencing a convicted defendant is among [the] most routine of acts performed by judges. Yet it is immensely revealing of the way in which [legal] interpretation is shaped by violence. First, examine the event from the perspective of the defendant. The defendant's world is threatened. But he sits,

16. A highly interesting book on the relationship between objective reality and human subjective account of it is Thomas S. Kuhn, The Structure of Scientific Revolutions (Chicago: University of Chicago Press, 1962). Kuhn's basic point is that theory precedes fact, even in scientific endeavors.

usually quietly, as if engaged in a civil discourse. If convicted, the defendant customarily walks—escorted—to prolonged confinement, usually without significant disturbance to the civil appearance of the event. It is, of course, grotesque to assume that the civil facade is "voluntary" except in the sense that it represents the defendant's autonomous recognition of the overwhelming array of violence ranged against him, and of the hopelessness of resistance or outcry. . . . [A few defendants who have reached their own understandings of the legal order have overtly attempted to deny the fiction that the trial is a joint or communal civil event where interpretations of facts and legal concepts are tested and refined. The playing out of such an overt course of action ends with the defendant physically bound and gagged. Bobby Seale taught those of us who lived through the 1960's that the court's physical control over the defendant's body lies at the heart of the criminal process. The defendant's "civil conduct," therefore can never signify a shared understanding of the event; it may signify his fear that any public display of his interpretation of the event as "bullshit" will end in violence perpetrated against him, pain inflicted upon him. Our constitutional law, quite naturally enough, provides for the calibrated use of ascending degrees of overt violence to maintain the "order" of the criminal trial. See, e.g., Illinois v. Allen, 397 U.S. 337 (1970); Tigar, The Supreme Court, 1969 Term—Foreward: Waiver of Constitutional Rights; Disquiet in the Citadel, 84 Harv. L.Rev. 1 (1970) . . .] *

There are societies in which contrition or shame control defendants' behavior to a greater extent than does violence. . . . But I think it is unquestionably the case in the United States that most prisoners walk into prison because they know they will be dragged or beaten into prison if they do not walk. They do not organize force against being dragged because they know that if they wage this kind of battle they will lose—very possibly their lives.

If I have exhibited some sense of sympathy for the victims of this violence it is misleading. Very often the balance of terror in this regard is just as I would want it. But I do not wish us to pretend that we talk our prisoners into jail. The "interpretations" or "conversations" that are the preconditions for violent incarceration are themselves implements of violence.

Cover, Violence and the Word, 95 Yale L.J. 1601, 1608–09 (1986).

What then is the criminal defense lawyer's role—or for that matter, the role of a lawyer in a civil proceeding that threatens to divest a client of her child, her property, or something else held dear—when the client decides to respond by breaking the rules of the proceeding as a protest, as a challenge, as a statement that what is going on will not be calmly accepted?

* Editor's note: The bracketed material appeared originally as a footnote.

NORMAN DORSEN AND LEON FRIEDMAN, *DISORDER IN THE COURT* (1973)
pp. 56–64, 272, 276–277.*

The Chicago Conspiracy Trial

The most notorious disorderly trial in recent years was the Chicago conspiracy trial of 1969–70. In that case, eight leading members of the Vietnam antiwar movement were indicted under the federal anti-riot statute of 1968 for conspiring, organizing, and inciting riots during the 1968 Democratic National Convention in Chicago. It appears from the evidence introduced at the trial that seven of the eight defendants— David Dellinger, Abbie Hoffman, Jerry Rubin, Rennie Davis, Tom Hayden, Lee Weiner, and John Froines—had planned to hold massive demonstrations in the streets and parks of Chicago at the time of the 1968 convention to protest the continuation of the Vietnam war. After extensive negotiations with city officials, permits for large-scale demonstrations were refused. Nevertheless, rallies were held, which led to violent confrontations between the demonstrators and the Chicago police.

Subsequent investigations by a special committee of the National Violence Commission concluded that the disturbances that ensued were the result of a "police riot" . . .

The trial drew considerable public notice because of the notoriety of the defendants and because this was the first use of a statute which was of doubtful constitutionality. From its inception numerous incidents occurred which attracted even more attention. In the week before the trial began, four of the attorneys who had appeared earlier in the case for specific pretrial motions telegrammed that they were withdrawing from further participation. On the motion of the United States attorney, Judge Julius Hoffman took the unusual step of issuing bench warrants to have all four arrested and brought before him. Five days later, after a storm of protest from lawyers and law professors, he vacated the order.

Additional contention arose because of the judge's refusal to postpone the trial until Charles Garry of California, who was engaged to act as Bobby Seale's lawyer, had recovered from a gall bladder operation. Seale insisted from the first days of the trial that he was unrepresented until Garry appeared. On September 26, he said to the court:

> If I am consistently denied this right of legal defense counsel of my choice who is effective by the judge of this Court, then I can only see the judge as a blatant racist of the United States Court.

On the same day the court reprimanded Tom Hayden for giving a clenched fist salute to the jury and Abbie Hoffman for blowing them kisses. On September 30, the court discharged one juror after reading to her the contents of a threatening letter signed "The Black Panther," which had been sent to her home. On October 15, the defendants asked to celebrate Vietnam Moratorium Day and tried to drape the counsel table with American and N.L.F. flags. On October 22 the defendants tried to bring a birthday cake into the courtroom for Bobby Seale.

The . . . particular incidents that gave rise to the greatest number of contempt citations were as follows:

Gagging and Binding of Bobby Seale

The most serious disorders occurred over the problem of representation for Bobby Seale. After Charles Garry became unavailable, William Kunstler filed an appearance for Seale ostensibly in order to see him at the county jail. On the first day of the trial, he also filed a general appearance for four of the defendants, including Seale. On September 26 Seale rejected Kunstler as his lawyer and thereafter insisted on his right to defend himself. The court and Seale argued about this issue at almost every opportunity. On October 14, the following colloquy occurred:

> *Mr. Seale:* I don't have counsel, Judge, I don't stand up because—
>
> *The Court:* Mr. Kunstler filed his appearance for Mr. Seale. The record shows it orally and in writing, sir. . . .
>
> *Mr. Seale:* Hey, you don't speak for me. I would like to speak on behalf of my own self and have my counsel handle my case in behalf of myself.
>
> How come I can't speak in behalf of myself? I am my own legal counsel. I don't want these lawyers to represent me.
>
> *The Court:* You have a lawyer of record and he has been of record here since the 24th.
>
> *Mr. Seale:* I have been arguing that before the jury heard one shred of evidence. I don't want these lawyers because I can take my own legal defense and my lawyer is Charles Garry.
>
> *The Court:* I direct you, sir, to remain quiet.
>
> *Mr. Seale:* And just be railroaded?
>
> *The Court:* Will you remain quiet?
>
> *Mr. Seale:* I want to defend myself, do you mind, please?

On October 20 Bobby Seale made a motion to act as his own lawyer. The U.S. attorney opposed the motion and Judge Hoffman ruled that Seale was represented by Kunstler and could not discharge him. The court of appeals later ruled that Judge Hoffman acted improperly in not inquiring whether Seale wanted Kunstler to represent him.

The conflict escalated on October 28, when Seale again insisted on his right to represent himself.

> *Mr. Seale:* . . . You are in contempt of people's constitutional rights. You are in contempt of the constitutional rights of the

mass of the people of the United States. You are the one in contempt of people's constitutional rights. I am not in contempt of nothing. You are the one who is in contempt. The people of America need to admonish you and the whole Nixon administration.

Mr. Hayden: Let the record show the judge was laughing.

Mr. Seale: Yes, he is laughing.

The Court: Who made that remark?

Mr. Foran [prosecutor]: The defendant Hayden, your Honor, made the remark. . . .

The Court: You are not doing very well for yourself.

Mr. Seale: Yes, that's because you violated my constitutional rights, Judge Hoffman. That's because you violated them overtly, deliberately, in a very racist manner. Somebody ought to point out the law to you. . . .

On the next day, October 29, Seale addressed a group of his followers in the courtroom before the judge appeared. As soon as the court was called into session, Richard Schultz, the assistant United States attorney, spoke:

Mr. Schultz: If the Court please, before you came into this courtroom, if the Court please, Bobby Seale stood up and addressed this group.

Mr. Seale: That's right, brother. I spoke on behalf of my constitutional rights. I have a right to speak on behalf of my constitutional rights. That's right.

Mr. Schultz: And he told those people in the audience, if the Court please—and I want this on the record. It happened this morning— that if he's attacked, they know what to do. He was talking to these people about an attack by them.

Mr. Seale: You're lying. Dirty liar. I told them to defend themselves. You are a rotten racist pig, fascist liar, that's what you are. You're a rotten liar. You are a fascist pig liar.

I said they had a right to defend themselves if they are attacked, and I hope that the record carries that, and I hope the record shows that tricky Dick Schultz, working for Richard Nixon and [his] administration all understand that tricky Dick Schultz is a liar, and we have a right to defend ourselves, and if you attack me I will defend myself.

Seale was forcibly put into his chair by the marshals. After he again insisted on his right to represent himself, the court took a brief recess. Seale was then taken out of the courtroom by the marshals and returned bound and gagged in his chair. The gag was not secure, and he could still speak through it. Kunstler described the scene for the record:

Mr. Kunstler: I wanted to say the record should indicate that Mr. Seale is seated on a metal chair, each hand handcuffed to the leg of the chair on both the right and left sides so he cannot raise his hands, and a gag is tightly pressed into his mouth and tied at the rear, and that when he attempts to speak, a muffled sound comes out.

Mr. Seale (gagged): You don't represent me. Sit down, Kunstler.

The Court: Mr. Marshal, I don't think you have accomplished your purpose by that kind of a contrivance. We will have to take another recess.

On the next day, October 30, 1969, Seale was again bound and gagged.

Mr. Weinglass: If your Honor please, the buckles on the leather strap holding Mr. Seale's hand is digging into his hand and he appears to be trying to free his hand from that pressure. Could he be assisted?

The Court: If the marshal has concluded that he needs assistance, of course.

Mr. Kunstler: Your Honor, are we going to stop this medieval torture that is going on in this courtroom? I think this is a disgrace.

Mr. Rubin: This guy is putting his elbow in Bobby's mouth and it wasn't necessary at all.

Mr. Kunstler: This is no longer a court of order, your Honor; this is a medieval torture chamber. It is a disgrace. They are assaulting the other defendants also.

The three days from October 28 through October 30 produced the most serious crisis in the trial. Of the 137 citations for contempt against the defendants, 47 occurred then. Seale was cited six times for his actions and the remaining defendants for their support of Seale and their protest against what was happening to him. One week later, on November 5, 1969, Seale was held in contempt by Judge Hoffman and severed from the trial. He was sentenced to forty-eight months in jail—three months for each of sixteen acts of misconduct. The court of appeals later held that four of the sixteen specifications dealing with Seale's attempt to defend himself were insufficient to justify contempt charges. After the case was reversed and sent back by the court of appeals for retrial before a different judge, the government decided not to reprosecute the contempt charges because it did not wish to disclose information concerning wiretaps of Seale.

Ralph Abernathy Incident

Two other triggering events that led to numerous contempt citations were the refusal to allow Reverend Ralph Abernathy to testify and the revocation of the bail of David Dellinger. On Friday, January 31, the defense indicated it was prepared to rest its case on Monday, February

2, after submitting some television film. Over the weekend, another witness, Ralph Abernathy, became available. On Monday morning, Kunstler asked to reopen the case to allow Abernathy to testify. Judge Hoffman refused the request.

> *The Court:* There have been several witnesses called here during this trial . . . whose testimony the Court ruled could not even be presented to the jury—singers, performers, and former office holders. I think in the light of the representations made by you unequivocally, sir, with no reference to Dr. Abernathy, I will deny your motion that we hold—

> *Mr. Kunstler:* . . . Your Honor. . . . I think what you have just said is about the most outrageous statement I have ever heard from a bench, and I am going to say my piece right now, and you can hold me in contempt right now if you wish to. You have violated every principle of fair play when you excluded Ramsey Clark from that witness stand. The New York Times, among others, has called it the ultimate outrage in American justice.

> *Voices:* Right on.

> *Mr. Kunstler:* I am outraged to be in this court before you. Now because I made a statement on Friday that I had only a cameraman, and I discovered on Saturday that Ralph Abernathy, who is the chairman of the Mobilization, is in town, and he can be here. . . . I am trembling because I am so outraged, I haven't been able to get this out before, and I am saying it now, and then I want you to put me in jail if you want to. You can do anything you want with me. . . . because I feel disgraced to be here.

Kunstler was then ordered to make no reference to Abernathy before the jury.

> *Mr. Schultz:* Your Honor, may the defendants and their counsel then not make any reference in front of this jury that they wanted Dr. Abernathy to testify?

> *Mr. Kunstler:* No, no.

> *The Court:* I order you not to make such a statement.

> *Mr. Kunstler:* We are not going to abide by any such comment as that. Dr. Ralph Abernathy is going to come into this courtroom, and I am going to repeat my motion before that jury.

> *The Court:* I order you not to.

> *Mr. Kunstler:* Then you will have to send me to jail, I am sorry. We have a right to state our objection to resting before the jury.

> *The Court:* Don't do it.

After the jury was brought into the court, Abernathy arrived and Kunstler immediately asked that he be allowed to testify. The request was refused.

.   .   .

Lawyer Contempts

The contempt citations against the two lawyers in the case did not involve abusive language or obscene remarks. The government said in its appellate brief, "The attorneys present a far different case; they did not heap vituperation upon the judge as did their clients, but rather repeatedly contested rulings by the judge to the point of obstructing the trial." Thus Weinglass was cited for refusing to sit down immediately after being ordered to do so, for asking questions on cross-examination beyond the scope of the direct examination, for repeating citations of legal authorities, for continuing an argument after the judge had ruled on it, and for making disrespectful remarks about the prosecution. He also was cited for making "invidious comparisons" between the court's treatment of the government's case and of the defense's.

Kunstler was cited for similar transgressions, such as refusing to sit down or continuing to argue. The court also cited him for going into the substance of a document not introduced in evidence and for arguing about the time of recess. In addition he defied specific orders of the court not to mention before the jury certain matters which the court had ruled on. Kunstler was given the maximum sentence of six months for these transgressions and an additional six months for his intemperate remarks on the morning of the Abernathy affair. He also received four months for telling the court, "You brought this on [referring to fistfights between the marshals and spectators.] This is your fault," and four months for accusing the government of using violence in the courtroom and of liking to strike women. He was also cited for referring to the gagging of Bobby Seale as "medieval torture" and for expressing his approval of disapproving groans from the spectators.

Total Contempt Citations

Aside from the cluster of disruptions described above, the trial proceeded without significant interruption for four and a half months. There were individual incidents from time to time, produced in part by the unconventional life style and political activism of the defendants: Rubin was cited twice for wearing judicial robes in court; Hoffman, for blowing kisses to the jury and asking the court, "How is your war stock doing"; Dellinger, for requesting a moment of silence on Moratorium Day; and all of the defendants were cited for interrupting the court or making comments on political subjects or the proceedings. At the very end of the trial, immediately after the jury was charged, Judge Hoffman handed down a total of 159 citations for contempt, 121 against the defendants other than Seale and 38 against the two lawyers. The largest single category (36 citations) consisted of defendants refusing to rise at the beginning or close of a court session. In 27 cases they called the judge a name or accused him of prejudice or injustice or made sarcastic comments to him, mostly arising from the incidents described above. In 10 cases they interrupted or insulted the prosecution, and in 11 cases they applauded or laughed in the courtroom.

On May 11, 1972, all the contempt convictions of the defendants and the lawyers were reversed by the Seventh Circuit Court of Appeals. The appellate court held that the judge cannot wait until the end of the trial to punish the defendants and the lawyers.

> . . . the trial judge must disqualify himself if he waits to act until the conclusion of the trial. When the trial proceedings have terminated, the need for proceeding summarily is not present.

The court also determined that Bobby Seale could not be punished summarily by the judge.

The court of appeals sent the case back to the district court level for retrial of the contempt before a judge other than Judge Hoffman. . . .

Appendix A

. . .

In December 1970 a total of *4,687* questionnaires were mailed to all trial judges of general jurisdiction throughout the United States and to the criminal court judges in New York City and California. . . .

. . .

Question 19. How should a judge deal with passive insubordination by a defendant or his counsel, e.g., a refusal to stand at the start of proceedings or to address the court as "your Honor"?

Defendant

319	ignore
162	contempt of court
120	warning of contempt
96	explain proper procedure, lecture on bad manners
59	handled by conference in chambers (reprimand, explain rules of conduct)
26	treat each situation individually
23	removal of defendant until he agrees to follow rules
14	bailiff takes care of situation
9	no experience in matter
4	overlook during trial but keep in mind when sentencing
1	open court without jury so they will not be aware of defendant's insubordination
3	refuse to start court
2	publish court rules concerning courtroom etiquette
1	judge remains standing until everyone in courtroom stands
1	declare mistrial
1	warn jury to disregard these actions
1	open court prior to appearance of those who refuse to stand
214	no answer

Attorney

216	ignore
198	contempt of court

Attorney

131	warning of contempt
108	request conformance to norm
45	report conduct to bar association
68	conference in chambers
26	discipline by bar association
20	treat each situation individually
11	disbarment
11	suspension from practice in trial court
9	bailiff takes care of situation
9	no experience
4	remove attorney from case
3	refuse to start court
2	mistrial
2	revoke lawyer's right to practice in this courtroom in future
2	publish court rules concerning courtroom etiquette
1	do not recognize for comments
1	open court prior to appearance of those who refuse to stand
1	judge remains standing until everyone in courtroom stands
188	no answer

Question 20. How should a judge deal with subtle forms of obstruction, such as a lawyer knowingly asking improper questions, engaging in dilatory tactics beyond the norm, persisting in taking positions overruled by the court, and so on?

329	warn attorney he will be held in contempt
215	warn attorney in private
196	contempt of court
63	disciplinary action through bar association
50	use patience and firmness
39	warn attorney in public
23	mistrial
21	recess court and warn lawyer
16	exclude attorney, appoint substitute counsel
7	ignore it
6	no experience
3	maintain composure
88	no answer

GEOFFREY C. HAZARD Jr., "SECURING COURTROOM DECORUM"

80 Yale L.J. 433 (1970).*

The spectacle of *United States v. Dellinger,* has impelled two distinguished organizations of the legal profession to promulgate rules designed to secure courtroom decorum. In July, 1970, the American

College of Trial Lawyers, through a special Committee on Disruption of the Judicial Process, published its Report and Recommendations. In January, 1971, the American Bar Association received a report on Standards Relating to the Function of a Trial Judge from its Advisory Committee on the Judge's Function, a constituent of the ABA's Project on Standards for Criminal Justice.

. . .

I. The Control of Trial Participants

. . .

. . . [T]he two Reports cover overlapping but somewhat different subject matter.[28] On the aspects of forensic misconduct that are of greatest practical importance and difficulty, however, the Reports cover common ground. These are the intertwined problems of judicial intemperance and lawyer misconduct. These problems are difficult to solve simply because the possible remedies and sanctions by which to control them are so limited as compared to those which may be invoked against a litigant or spectator. A disruptive spectator may simply be excluded from the trial. Members of the news media can be excluded if their presence intrudes on calm and orderly procedure. A comparable principle applies to those whose right of attendance derives from their affinity with the defendant—spouse, relatives, priest, etc. As to litigants, Illinois v. Allen [32] has now made clear that a defendant's presence at trial is a right that can be denied if he refuses to conform to elemental requirements of courtroom decorum. Accordingly, where a litigant's disturbances obstruct fulfillment of his opportunity to participate, he may be excluded and his trial conducted in absentia. But while in special circumstances bystanders and even litigants can be dispensed with and a trial still be held, the same is not true of the judge nor, in an adversary system, of counsel. In the extraordinary case that would test our definition of a trial, they are the primary participants.[33]

28. The Trial Lawyers Report alludes to the fact that the advocate's courtroom representation of his client is a phase of a responsibility that has begun outside of court, while the ABA Report refers to the advocate's function only as of the beginning of trial. The Trial Lawyers Report requires the lawyer to exercise a restraining influence on his client, while the ABA Report proscribes misconduct of lawyer and litigant without reference to accessorial implications. The Trial Lawyers Report presupposes a trial in which the litigant is represented by counsel, while the ABA Report has provisions applicable to a defendant appearing pro se. On the basis of what may be a different attitude toward conservation of trial time, the Trial Lawyers Report admits of the possibility of a continuance as a remedy and a mistrial as a sanction for forensic misconduct, while the ABA Report omits explicit reference to either of these devices.

32. 397 U.S. 337 (1970).

33. The defendant who represents himself would still be subject to the *Allen* requirements of maintaining elementary decorum, and could be excluded if he, after proper warning, continued to disrupt the trial. In that case the court would presumably endeavor to appoint counsel, even over defendant's objection. *Cf.* Mayberry v. Pennsylvania, 91 S.Ct. 499, 506 (1971) (concurring opinion); ABA Report, Standards C.2, C.3, and C.4.

A. *Who Adjudicates?*

The central question at the stage of adjudicating a contempt is who shall preside. The ABA Report's proposal is equivocal. It says that the trial judge may ordinarily hear the contempt, but provides for referral where "his conduct was so integrated with the alleged contempt that he contributed to it or was otherwise involved, or his objectivity can for any reason plausibly be questioned." [34] As applied to misconduct by lawyers, the exception nearly swallows the rule. . . . [For example,] where a lawyer's trial conduct has been grossly disruptive, it may have been that the judge's efforts to control the trial were simply ineffectual, which is itself an involvement of a very disturbing kind, or were even provocative, which is also a form of involvement. Putting the matter differently, under the ABA proposal arguments suggest themselves that would render legally infirm any attempt by the trial judge to hear a contempt except in the most clear-cut instances. Those are not the cases that test a code.

The Trial Lawyers Report does not attempt considered analysis of the question of who should preside at the contempt hearing. The position taken is the traditional one that the trial judge should conduct the hearing. The Report recognizes that the trial judge may refer the matter to another judge but its commentary disaffirms and even disparages such a possibility.

The Trial Lawyers Report concedes that "some persons are troubled by the thought of a judge acting not only in that capacity [as judge] but also as accuser and prosecutor" and responds by saying that the trial judge has the responsibility to "keep a case moving" and to "keep it under control at all times." The response is true but irrelevant: the police have the duty to keep a crowd moving and to keep it under control, but we do not for that reason give them exclusive authority to punish misconduct at a police line. Perhaps recognizing the weakness of this response, the Trial Lawyers Report goes on to suggest that impartiality in adjudicating the contempt can be secured through appeal . . .

This must be one of the few occasions where an association of barristers has argued that a fair appeal procedure is a sufficient corrective for an apparently biased trial procedure. There are other paradoxes in the argument. The assumption that an appeal will be taken contradicts the assumption that summary determination is essen-

34. ABA Report, Standard F.5. The Supreme Court has recently given substantial support to this approach to hearing courtroom contempts. In Mayberry v. Pennsylvania, 91 S.Ct. 499 (1971), the Court reversed the contempt sentence of a defendant who represented himself, noting that "[w]here . . . [a judge] does not act the instant the contempt is committed, but waits until the end of the trial, on balance, it is generally wise where the marks of the unseemly conduct have left personal stings to ask a fellow judge to take his place." Id. at 504. At the end of its opinion, the Court also stated an apparently broader rule: "Our conclusion is that by reason of the Due Process Clause of the Fourteenth Amendment a defendant in criminal contempt proceedings should be given a public trial before a judge other than the one reviled by the contemnor." Id. at 505.

tial. Treating the trial court contempt conviction as in effect only an indictment returnable in the appellate court denigrates the tribunal whose stature is sought to be enhanced. And what is involved in the reversal of a contempt in such circumstances: that the trial judge was wrong in his instincts for issuing the citation and wrong also in his considered decision to convict at the contempt hearing? A procedural scheme that thus forces choice between a lawyer's career and a judge's reputation is surely more heroic than prudent.

Contemplation of these consequences leads one to reconsider the premises. Why shouldn't the traditional view be abandoned and instead the rule adopted that lawyer contempts shall be heard by another judge, if possible one from another locality? Administering such a rule would not entail much additional cost, unless it is supposed that a summary contempt conviction can rest solely on the trial judge's memory of the events at issue—a procedure which would be the ultimate form of trial *in camera*.[37] Requiring a contempt hearing to be held by another judge expresses the same principle as the rule which bars a judge from hearing a case in which he has a financial or familial interest, and recognizes that professional probity is at least as precious to a judge as money or kinship.

What would be lost? If the trial judge was fair and the lawyer intemperate, what clearer vindication of the judge? If the judge was not fair or the lawyer not intemperate, what surer vindication of the lawyer? The adversary method of eliciting facts can be employed before another trial judge but is unavailable in an appellate court—is the adversary method less useful when the complaining witness is a judge? Is the ugly spectacle of judging the judges more repugnant than refusing to subject them to searching judgment? One can almost hear the anxious rejoinder welling up only to be suppressed by awareness of its implication: what if most, or all, of these lawyer contempt citations were found to be unwarranted? What, indeed?

C. *Trial Procedures*

Neither the Trial Lawyers Report nor the ABA Report goes extensively into the matter of trial procedures in cases likely to engender conflicts between judge and lawyer. Both contain general precepts which are at the same time unexceptionable and only moderately illuminating. One could wish for much more concrete proposals, for example:

---

37. Both federal and state law require the presiding judge to support a summary contempt conviction with some record of the incidents in question. In federal courts, Rule 42(a) of the Federal Rules of Criminal Procedure provides that: "A criminal contempt may be punished summarily if the judge certifies that he saw or heard the conduct constituting the contempt and that it was committed in the actual presence of the court. The order of contempt shall recite the facts and shall be signed by the judge and entered of record." The general rule applicable in most states is that "the record must set out the proceedings of the lower court and the facts which support its jurisdiction and constitute the contempt." 17 C.J.S. *Contempt* § 122 (1963).

The use of daily or at least weekly conferences in chambers between court and counsel to smooth and restore working relationships and to anticipate evidentiary questions and rulings;

The definitive explication of "continuing objection" positions by counsel and "same ruling" decisions by the court to minimize the repetition of irreconcilable differences;

The requirement of written briefing of major substantive and evidentiary positions, with responsive rulings *in limine* by the court, so that positions are made as clear as possible.

Between them the reports have two proposals on trial procedure that surely merit general implementation. The ABA Report proposes that

the trial judge, whether before a criminal trial or at its beginning, should prescribe and make known the ground rules relating to conduct which the parties, the prosecutor, the defense counsel, the witnesses, and others will be expected to follow in the courtroom. . . .

The other proposal appears only in the Trial Lawyers Report and is that the lawyer has the obligation

to advise any client appearing in a courtroom of the kind of behavior expected and required of him there, and to prevent him, so far as lies within the lawyer's power, from creating disorder or disruption in the courtroom.

The reach of the duty is not elaborated. It is not stated, for example, what a lawyer is supposed to do if the client persistently misbehaves despite his advice to the contrary. The Manson case in Los Angeles Superior Court presents that problem and suggests that it is no real answer to say the lawyer should resign from the case, for what will his successor do? But if the outer limits of the duty are imprecise the same is not true of its initial form: the lawyer should tell his client to behave himself, and do so with sincerity or at least its verisimilitude.

Of late it has been argued otherwise—that his client's courtroom conduct is none of the lawyer's business. The contention is that the lawyer is but an agent, that the client as principal can have his case presented any way he wants to, and that the agent's responsibility ends with giving the principal advice. More fundamentally, it is suggested that there are cases where the defendant's style is itself on trial and in such cases the defendant has, as it were, a right of affirmative defense.

There is something to this. The client does have certain procedural initiatives which the advocate can neither waive nor exercise on the client's behalf: the right to speak before pronouncement of sentence, the right to advice on consequences before tendering a guilty plea, the right to be present and to confront witnesses, and perhaps the right to testify against his counsel's advice. Furthermore, the hippy or yippy defendant has a right to insist that the impartiality by which he is adjudged not depend on changing his life-style *pendente lite,* just as the poor man should not have to change his clothes nor the black man his skin. It is also no doubt true that judges and prosecutors often confuse *déshabillé* with disorder and perceive loud mannerisms as literally making noise.

When due allowance is made for all these considerations, however, the fact is that we have witnessed some trials in which the defendants have talked when they should have been silent, moved about when they should have been seated, gesticulated when they should have been in repose. The lawyer's duty to admonish his clients against such misbehavior is sometimes supported by the argument that he has special leverage on them and should use it to help his professional colleague on the bench in keeping order. There is truth in this but also odium, particularly to the members of a generation that is highly and understandably sensitive to manipulation. The lawyer's duty to admonish his clients surely rests on more substantial ground than that as an officer of the court he is also one of its bailiffs.

The duty, it may be suggested, is a component of the lawyer's own role as advocate. The role of advocate is that of speaking to questions of law and fact in a particular kind of forum in accordance with specified opportunities and sequences. It would be quite clear that the lawyer could not play his role if whenever he tried to speak he was ignored, or interrupted or drowned out by a bullhorn. The lawyer's part, however, is not soliloquy but—the pun is irresistible—a trialogue, a series of ordered exchanges with the judge and opposing counsel. If the judge and opposing counsel cannot speak without disruption or hindrance, then the lawyer's appearances and cues are lost or disordered and at some point his role and reason for being there simply collapse. If the advocate does not contribute to sustaining these forensic requirements, he has to that extent abdicated his role and literally has no place in the performance. And if he does not believe in his role and cannot live it, he should seek another calling, just as an atheist should leave the priesthood.

The same, of course, goes for the judge and the prosecutor. To some who observed the "Chicago Eight" trial, one of the appalling things was the noisome patter of witticism and jokes by Judge Hoffman. It is conceivable that if he had consistently avoided playing it like a minstrel show, the defendants might not have played it like a circus.

Courtroom Order in the Political Trial

The immediate inspiration of the recommendations by the Trial Lawyers and the ABA was a "political" trial. Their appositeness to that kind of dispute requires brief further analysis.

A political trial is one in which the defendants—they are usually plural—are tried for conduct that is interpreted by them and by the community at large as a challenge to the legitimacy of the political order. The conduct may be pure challenge, such as advocating overthrow of the government, or a challenge manifested in conduct that is independently unlawful, such as a riot or sit-in. When uttered, the challenge constitutes an appeal to some public or other for support. The subsequent trial is of itself conclusive evidence that the challenge failed, for if it succeeded the defendants would have been vindicated and not face prosecution.

From the viewpoint of the challenged authority, the issues in a political trial are defined by its positive law: whether the challenge enjoys the immunity afforded to free speech; whether all defendants were accomplices to the illegal elements of the enterprise; whether, regarding challenges expressed as action, there were excuses or justifications such as antecedent illegal action by officials; and so on. From the viewpoint of the defendants, however, these are only some of the issues. If the defendants desire exoneration, their surest recourse is not legal defense but public contrition, for in that event there would usually be no trial. A political case that goes to trial is one in which the defendants have counterclaims.

The counterclaims in a political trial are based on a maddening combination of transcendental political or ethical issues and procedural technicality. One counterclaim is that the regime—all of it or the part directly involved in the altercation—is illegitimate according to some theory of political justice so that the actions of its officials are not clothed with legal authority and therefore amount to naked coercion. A subsidiary count is that the court trying the case is part of the illegal system and that its proceeding is a juridical pretension and a farce, as indeed it is if the premise is accepted.

The second counterclaim is that the court will not try the case with proper observance of its own legal procedure. This claim depends on technical and sometimes hypertechnical interpretation of procedural law and may involve tactics which seek to make it a self-fulfilling prophecy. Like the first counterclaim, it asserts that the court is not really a court. But the second counterclaim is supported by an argument which is diametrically opposite to that supporting the first counterclaim. The argument is that according to the tribunal's own law, the tribunal is not functioning as one.

A political trial thus involves two and perhaps three concurrent proceedings. In the "straight" one, the prosecutor is the accuser, the defendants are the accused and the judge and jury are arbiters. In the trial of defendants' first counterclaim, the defendants are the accusers, the prosecutor and the judge (and sometimes the jury) are the accused, and the arbiter is indefinitely the jury (hence the struggles at voir dire), the defendants' circle of sympathizers, the world at large, or history. The alignment of the parties is the same in the defendants' second counterclaim except that the arbiter is the appellate courts.

The confusion over the participants' position is confounded by evidentiary problems. The evidence for the government in a political trial consists largely of the defendants' utterances—writings, speeches, discussions. These are what actuated the prosecution in the first place and what constitute the legal basis for regarding the defendants' conduct as peculiarly wrongful. Hence, in putting on its case the prosecution inevitably rebroadcasts the defendants' challenge of the regime and thus introduces evidence which defendants regard as relevant to their first counterclaim, that the tribunal is illegitimate. Defining the proper scope of these proofs involves continual rulings that are subject to the claim of prejudicial error. Sometimes the defendants seek to introduce even fuller accounts of their utterances. If this effort is successful, it buttresses their first counterclaim; if it is unsuccessful, it buttresses the contention that the court is not trying the case fairly.

The proceeding as a whole is thus suffused with ambiguity: proofs consisting of speeches, which bear simultaneously on issues that have been pleaded and others that have not been, which are punctuated by evidentiary and procedural issues laden with double or triple meaning, which are advanced by participants who are intermittently forgetful that the conflict encompasses the agenda and their respective roles. Rules that clarify the official roles and responsibilities in the hearing of such a case can help define the issues in the underlying struggle over whether the official version of the proceedings shall prevail. Reaffirmation of the contempt power confirms the consequences if the established order does prevail. The established order, however, by its own terms cannot win the struggle by the threatening mechanisms of legal prescription and penal sanction. It can win only through steadfast and unpretentious fulfillment of official roles, especially that of the judge. In the emphasis it tries to give this aspect of the problem, the ABA Report may have made a particularly important contribution. At the same time, it is well to recognize that the struggles represented in political trials will not disappear until fundamental political dissension also disappears. That day may be less welcome than many might think.

On the obligation to provide representation to "unpopular" clients, see EC 7–9; EC 7–17; M.R. 1.2(b); Green, The Other Government (1975), pp. 270–288; Krash, Professional Responsibility to Clients and the Public Interest: Is There a Conflict?, 55 Chicago Bar Record 31 (1974); Kaufmann, A Professional Agenda, 6 Hofstra L.Rev. 619 (1978) (describing how the ethics rules embody and have always embodied a tension between the obligation owed one's client and the obligation owed to the public at large).

Chapter VI

THE LAWYER–CLIENT RELATIONSHIP

A. FORMING THE RELATIONSHIP

TOGSTAD v. VESELY, OTTO, MILLER & KEEFE

Supreme Court of Minnesota, 1980.
291 N.W.2d 686.

PER CURIAM.

This is an appeal by the defendants from a judgment of the Hennepin County District Court involving an action for legal malpractice. The jury found that the defendant attorney Jerre Miller was negligent and that, as a direct result of such negligence, plaintiff John Togstad sustained damages in the amount of $610,500 and his wife, plaintiff Joan Togstad, in the amount of $39,000. Defendants (Miller and his law firm) appeal to this court from the denial of their motion for judgment notwithstanding the verdict or, alternatively, for a new trial. We affirm.

In August 1971, John Togstad began to experience severe headaches and on August 16, 1971, was admitted to Methodist Hospital where tests disclosed that the headaches were caused by a large aneurism [1] on the left internal carotid artery. [2] The attending physician, Dr. Paul Blake, a neurological surgeon, treated the problem by applying a Selverstone clamp to the left common carotid artery. The clamp was surgically implanted on August 27, 1971, in Togstad's neck to allow the gradual closure of the artery over a period of days.

In the early morning hours of August 29, 1971, a nurse observed that Togstad was unable to speak or move. At the time, the clamp was one-half (50%) closed. Upon discovering Togstad's condition, the nurse called a resident physician, who did not adjust the clamp. Dr. Blake was also immediately informed of Togstad's condition and arrived about an hour later, at which time he opened the clamp. Togstad is now severely paralyzed in his right arm and leg, and is unable to speak.

Plaintiffs' expert, Dr. Ward Woods, testified that Togstad's paralysis and loss of speech was due to a lack of blood supply to his brain. Dr. Woods stated that the inadequate blood flow resulted from the clamp being 50% closed and that the negligence of Dr. Blake and the hospital precluded the clamp's being opened in time to avoid permanent brain damage. . . .

1. An aneurism is a weakness or softening in an artery wall which expands and bulges out over a period of years.

2. The left internal carotid artery is one of the major vessels which supplies blood to the brain.

473

About 14 months after her husband's hospitalization began, plaintiff Joan Togstad met with attorney Jerre Miller regarding her husband's condition. Neither she nor her husband was personally acquainted with Miller or his law firm prior to that time. John Togstad's former work supervisor, Ted Bucholz, made the appointment and accompanied Mrs. Togstad to Miller's office. Bucholz was present when Mrs. Togstad and Miller discussed the case.[3]

Mrs. Togstad had become suspicious of the circumstances surrounding her husband's tragic condition due to the conduct and statements of the hospital nurses shortly after the paralysis occurred. One nurse told Mrs. Togstad that she had checked Mr. Togstad at 2 a.m. and he was fine; that when she returned at 3 a.m., by mistake, to give him someone else's medication, he was unable to move or speak; and that if she hadn't accidentally entered the room no one would have discovered his condition until morning. Mrs. Togstad also noticed that the other nurses were upset and crying, and that Mr. Togstad's condition was a topic of conversation.

Mrs. Togstad testified that she told Miller "everything that happened at the hospital," including the nurses' statements and conduct which had raised a question in her mind. She stated that she "believed" she had told Miller "about the procedure and what was undertaken, what was done, and what happened." She brought no records with her. Miller took notes and asked questions during the meeting, which lasted 45 minutes to an hour. At its conclusion, according to Mrs. Togstad, Miller said that "he did not think we had a legal case, however, he was going to discuss this with his partner." She understood that if Miller changed his mind after talking to his partner, he would call her. Mrs. Togstad "gave it" a few days and, since she did not hear from Miller, decided "that they had come to the conclusion that there wasn't a case." No fee arrangements were discussed, no medical authorizations were requested, nor was Mrs. Togstad billed for the interview.

Mrs. Togstad denied that Miller had told her his firm did not have expertise in the medical malpractice field, urged her to see another attorney, or related to her that the statute of limitations for medical malpractice actions was two years. She did not consult another attorney until one year after she talked to Miller. Mrs. Togstad indicated that she did not confer with another attorney earlier because of her reliance on Miller's "legal advice" that they "did not have a case."

On cross-examination, Mrs. Togstad was asked whether she went to Miller's office "to see if he would take the case of [her] husband. . . ." She replied, "Well, I guess it was to go for legal advice, what to do, where shall we go from here? That is what we went for." Again in response to defense counsel's questions, Mrs. Togstad testified as follows:

3. Bucholz, who knew Miller through a local luncheon club, died prior to the trial of the instant action.

Q　And it was clear to you, was it not, that what was taking place was a preliminary discussion between a prospective client and lawyer as to whether or not they wanted to enter into an attorney-client relationship?

A　I am not sure how to answer that. It was for legal advice as to what to do.

Q　And Mr. Miller was discussing with you your problem and indicating whether he, as a lawyer, wished to take the case, isn't that true?

A　Yes.

. . . Miller testified that "[t]he only thing I told her [Mrs. Togstad] after we had pretty much finished the conversation was that there was nothing related in her factual circumstances that told me that she had a case that our firm would be interested in undertaking."

Miller also claimed he related to Mrs. Togstad "that because of the grievous nature of the injuries sustained by her husband, that this was only my opinion and she was encouraged to ask another attorney if she wished for another opinion" and "she ought to do so promptly." He testified that he informed Mrs. Togstad that his firm "was not engaged as experts" in the area of medical malpractice, and that they associated with the Charles Hvass firm in cases of that nature. Miller stated that at the end of the conference he told Mrs. Togstad that he would consult with Charles Hvass and if Hvass's opinion differed from his, Miller would so inform her. Miller recollected that he called Hvass a "couple days" later and discussed the case with him. It was Miller's impression that Hvass thought there was no liability for malpractice in the case. Consequently, Miller did not communicate with Mrs. Togstad further.

. . .

Kenneth Green, a Minneapolis attorney, was called as an expert by plaintiffs. He stated that in rendering legal advice regarding a claim of medical malpractice, the "minimum" an attorney should do would be to request medical authorizations from the client, review the hospital records, and consult with an expert in the field. John McNulty, a Minneapolis attorney, and Charles Hvass testified as experts on behalf of the defendants. McNulty stated that when an attorney is consulted as to whether he will take a case, the lawyer's only responsibility in refusing it is to so inform the party. He testified, however, that when a lawyer is asked his legal opinion on the merits of a medical malpractice claim, community standards require that the attorney check hospital records and consult with an expert before rendering his opinion.

Hvass stated that he had no recollection of Miller's calling him in October 1972 relative to the Togstad matter. He testified that:

A　. . . when a person comes in to me about a medical malpractice action, based upon what the individual has told me, I have to make a decision as to whether or not there probably is or probably is not, based upon that information, medical malpractice. And if, in my judgment, based upon what the client has told me, there is not medical malpractice, I will so inform the client.

Hvass stated, however, that he would never render a "categorical" opinion. In addition, Hvass acknowledged that if he were consulted for a "legal opinion" regarding medical malpractice and 14 months had expired since the incident in question, "ordinary care and diligence" would require him to inform the party of the two-year statute of limitations applicable to that type of action.

This case was submitted to the jury by way of a special verdict form. The jury found that Dr. Blake and the hospital were negligent and that Dr. Blake's negligence (but not the hospital's) was a direct cause of the injuries sustained by John Togstad; that there was an attorney-client contractual relationship between Mrs. Togstad and Miller; that Miller was negligent in rendering advice regarding the possible claims of Mr. and Mrs. Togstad; that, but for Miller's negligence, plaintiffs would have been successful in the prosecution of a legal action against Dr. Blake; and that neither Mr. nor Mrs. Togstad was negligent in pursuing their claims against Dr. Blake. . . .

1. In a legal malpractice action of the type involved here, four elements must be shown: (1) that an attorney-client relationship existed; (2) that defendant acted negligently or in breach of contract; (3) that such acts were the proximate cause of the plaintiffs' damages; (4) that but for defendant's conduct the plaintiffs would have been successful in the prosecution of their medical malpractice claim. See, Christy v. Saliterman, 288 Minn. 144, 179 N.W.2d 288 (1970).

. . .

We believe it is unnecessary to decide whether a tort or contract theory is preferable for resolving the attorney-client relationship question raised by this appeal. The tort and contract analyses are very similar in a case such as the instant one,[4] and we conclude that under either theory the evidence shows that a lawyer-client relationship is present here. The thrust of Mrs. Togstad's testimony is that she went to Miller for legal advice, was told there wasn't a case, and relied upon this advice in failing to pursue the claim for medical malpractice. In addition, according to Mrs. Togstad, Miller did not qualify his legal opinion by urging her to seek advice from another attorney, nor did Miller inform her that he lacked expertise in the medical malpractice

---

4. Under a negligence approach it must essentially be shown that defendant rendered legal advice (not necessarily at someone's request) under circumstances which made it reasonably foreseeable to the attorney that if such advice was rendered negligently, the individual receiving the advice might be injured thereby. See, e.g., Palsgraf v. Long Island R. Co., 248 N.Y. 339, 162 N.E. 99, 59 A.L.R. 1253 (1928). Or, stated another way, under a tort theory, "[a]n attorney-client relationship is created whenever an individual seeks and receives legal advice from an attorney in circumstances in which a reasonable person would rely on such advice." 63 Minn.L.Rev. 751, 759 (1979). A contract analysis requires the rendering of legal advice pursuant to another's request and the reliance factor, in this case, where the advice was not paid for, need be shown in the form of promissory estoppel. See, 7 C.J.S., Attorney and Client, § 65; Restatement (Second) of Contracts, § 90.

area. Assuming this testimony is true, as this court must do, see, Cofran v. Swanman, 225 Minn. 40, 29 N.W.2d 448 (1947),[5] we believe a jury could properly find that Mrs. Togstad sought and received legal advice from Miller under circumstances which made it reasonably foreseeable to Miller that Mrs. Togstad would be injured if the advice were negligently given. Thus, under either a tort or contract analysis, there is sufficient evidence in the record to support the existence of an attorney-client relationship.

Defendants argue that even if an attorney-client relationship was established the evidence fails to show that Miller acted negligently in assessing the merits of the Togstads' case. They appear to contend that, at most, Miller was guilty of an error in judgment which does not give rise to legal malpractice. Meagher v. Kavli, 256 Minn. 54, 97 N.W. 2d 370 (1959). However, this case does not involve a mere error of judgment. The gist of plaintiffs' claim is that Miller failed to perform the minimal research that an ordinarily prudent attorney would do before rendering legal advice in a case of this nature. The record, through the testimony of Kenneth Green and John McNulty, contains sufficient evidence to support plaintiffs' position.

In a related contention, defendants assert that a new trial should be awarded on the ground that the trial court erred by refusing to instruct the jury that Miller's failure to inform Mrs. Togstad of the two-year statute of limitations for medical malpractice could not constitute negligence. The argument continues that since it is unclear from the record on what theory or theories of negligence the jury based its decision, a new trial must be granted. Namchek v. Tulley, 259 Minn. 469, 107 N.W.2d 856 (1961).

The defect in defendants' reasoning is that there is adequate evidence supporting the claim that Miller was also negligent in failing to advise Mrs. Togstad of the two-year medical malpractice limitations period and thus the trial court acted properly in refusing to instruct the jury in the manner urged by defendants. One of defendants' expert witnesses, Charles Hvass, testified:

Q Now, Mr. Hvass, where you are consulted for a legal opinion and advice concerning malpractice and 14 months have elapsed [since the incident in question], wouldn't—and you hold yourself out as competent to give a legal opinion and advice to these people concerning their rights, wouldn't ordinary care and diligence require that you inform them that there is a two-year statute of limitations within which they have to act or lose their rights?

A Yes. I believe I would have advised someone of the two-year period of limitation, yes.

5. As the *Cofran* court stated, in determining whether the jury's verdict is reasonably supported by the record a court must view the credibility of evidence and every inference which may fairly be drawn therefrom in a light most favorable to the prevailing party. 225 Minn. 42, 29 N.W.2d 450.

Consequently, based on the testimony of Mrs. Togstad, i.e., that she requested and received legal advice from Miller concerning the malpractice claim, and the above testimony of Hvass, we must reject the defendants' contention, as it was reasonable for a jury to determine that Miller acted negligently in failing to inform Mrs. Togstad of the applicable limitations period.

. . .

Questions and Comments

Could a lawyer require clients who come for initial interviews to sign a contract stating that in exchange for a free initial consultation the client waives the right to sue for malpractice occurring in the initial interview? What if the contract stated that the initial interview was merely exploratory and was not to create an attorney-client relationship? See DR 6–102(A) and M.R. 1.8(h), and the note on limiting one's liability for malpractice in Chapter 3 above at p. 155.

For a discussion of the factors that trigger an obligation to people or entities that lack formal client status, see Westinghouse Elec. Corp. v. Kerr–McGee Corp., 580 F.2d 1311 (7th Cir.1978) printed below in Chapter 7.

On whether an attorney-client relationship continues where the lawyer has intermittently handled several matters for a client, but failed to file an answer to a complaint that had been left at the lawyer's office, see North Carolina Bar v. Sheffield, 73 N.C.App. 349, 326 S.E.2d 320 (1985). See also Jacobson v. Pitman–Moore, 624 F.Supp. 937 (D.Minn.1985), aff'd, 786 F.2d F.2d 1172 (8th Cir.1986) (mix-up in transfer of case from one firm to another).

Limiting Liability Through Limiting the Scope of Employment

M.R. 1.2(c) allows a lawyer to limit the objectives of the representation with client consent. The Comment states: "The terms upon which the representation is undertaken may exclude specific objectives or means." But this "agreement . . . must accord with the Rules of Professional Conduct and other law. Thus the client may not be asked to agree to representation so limited in scope as to violate M.R. 1.1, requiring competent representation, or to surrender the right to terminate the lawyer's services, or the right to settle litigation that the lawyer might wish to continue."

The Rule and Comment thus preclude an agreement limiting the scope of representation to the lawyer's off-the-cuff opinion based on no research or investigation, such as the advice provided by attorney Miller in *Togstad*. But could the agreement specify that for a reduced fee the lawyer only promises limited research? See Wolfram, Modern Legal Ethics § 5.6.7 (arguing that such an agreement is proper under M.R. 1.2). Would such an agreement comport with M.R. 1.1?

B. FEES

The Amount of the Fee

Introductory Note

Systematic studies of legal fees and the basis of their calculation are rare. A valuable study is Kritzer, Sarat, Trubek, Bumiller and McNichol, Understanding the Costs of Litigation: The Case of the Hourly–Fee Lawyer, 1985 Am.Bar.Found.Res.J. 559, studying hourly fee charges. Other bases of fees include contingent fees (see section on contingent fees below) and those charged as a percentage of the amount in a transaction, for example, a percentage of the price in a sale of real property or the amount of an estate in probate. The fee resulting from an hourly fee is the product of the hourly rate times the number of hours. Generally, the hourly rate is standard and calibrated to the lawyer's experience, while the number of hours is the product of the adversariness of the matter, the stakes, and the relative legal technicality of the matter. However, as economic analysis would suggest, both the standard hourly rate and the number of hours committed are informed and constrained by the charges made by other lawyers in the same market.

For an economic analysis of a firm's basis for division of profits among partners, see Gilson and Mnookin, Sharing Among the Human Capitalists: An Economic Inquiry into the Corporate Law Firm and How Partners Split Profits, 37 Stan.L.Rev. 313 (1985).

Padding Bills

Law firm bills sometimes are padded. Many young lawyers report instances of recording more hours than were worked; recording lower echelon lawyers' hours as those of one with a higher hourly rate; billing personal time; etc. . . . Disbursements may similarly be inflated. Informal support for these practices includes: rationalizations (e.g., "this is not a regular client of the firm"; the client is itself rapacious); and, operating methods that elicit compliance with inflationary billing practices and prevent their disclosure. The latter include partner control of the time sheets and work assignments, signals concerning the effect of "loyalty" to the firm on pay increases, and promotion, etc.
. . .

Excessive Fees

The courts have the power to scrutinize lawyer fee contracts to ensure that the fee charged is not excessive. The authority to examine lawyers' fees with greater care than ordinary commercial contracts is based on the courts' inherent and statutory power to regulate the profession, see, e.g., Smitas v. Rickett, 102 A.D.2d 928, 477 N.Y.S.2d 752 (1984); Watson v. Cook, 427 So.2d 1312 (La.App.1983); In re LiVolsi, 85 N.J. 576, 428 A.2d 1268 (1981). In examining fee arrangements courts state that they are guided by the list of factors in DR 2–106 and M.R. 1.5(a). See discussion of the professional rules below.

DR 2–106 defines a "clearly excessive" fee in terms of whether the fee is "reasonable." This confusion over the standard is repeated in the cases. In addition, courts sometimes use words, such as "fair" and "equitable" when judging the fee. See, e.g., Ackermann v. Levine, 788 F.2d 830 (2d Cir.1986). M.R. 1.5(a) states: "A lawyer's fee shall be reasonable. . . ." Calif.Rule of Professional Conduct 4–200(A) prohibits "unconscionable" fees.

In McKenzie Construction, Inc. v. Maynard, 758 F.2d 97, 101 (3d Cir.1985), the court distinguished the standard for disciplining an attorney in a fee case from the standard for enforcing a fee contract:

> Under certain circumstances, it may be unfair to sanction or discipline an attorney for a fee that can be called objectively 'unreasonable,' but not 'clearly excessive,' especially if the unreasonableness is due to factors that occur after the fee arrangement is made.

> In contrast, when the matter is enforcement of a fee contract in an adversary proceeding between an attorney and his former client, we do not believe a judge's determination of unreasonableness should be based on as stringent a showing. In the latter case the court is not deciding whether a lawyer's conduct is unethical but whether, as against the client, it has resulted in such an enrichment at the expense of the client that it offends a court's sense of fundamental fairness and equity. See Dunn v. H.K. Porter Co., Inc., [602 F.2d 1105 (3rd Cir.1979)]; Allen v. United States, 606 F.2d 432, 435 (4th Cir.1979).

In a dispute between attorney and client over the fee, the attorney generally has the burden of justifying the fee; the client, even when she is suing to recover part of the fee charged, does not bear the burden of proving that the fee was too high. See, e.g., McKenzie Construction, supra at 100: "This allocation of the burden of proof is premised on the relationship of trust owed by a lawyer to his client . . . This approach is at the very heart of the special relationship between attorney and client."

In Brobeck, Phleger & Harrison v. Telex Corp., 602 F.2d 866 (9th Cir.1979), the court enforced an agreement under which a law firm was due $1 million for not much work. Telex had sued IBM and won a $259.5 million antitrust judgment but lost an $18 million counterclaim. On appeal, IBM obtained reversal of the judgment against it and affirmance of its counterclaim judgment against Telex. Telex's judgment thus went from $241 million positive to $18 million negative, enough to bankrupt the company. Telex's best chance of survival was to be heard in the Supreme Court, and for that "they decided to search for the best available lawyer . . .," eventually settling on Lasky, a partner at Brobeck. Lasky "would consent to an arrangement only if he would receive a sizable contingent fee in the event of success." The parties negotiated a complicated contract specifying different fees for various eventualities. After Lasky filed the petition for certiorari with the Supreme Court and the Supreme Court granted the petition, Telex and IBM reached a settlement in which they dropped their claims and called their dispute a wash. Lasky claimed the $1 million dollar fee due under the contract; Telex contended that such a fee was unconscionable given that Lasky's only service was filing the petition for certiorari. The court held the contract must be reviewed with "reference to the time it was made and cannot be resolved by hindsight." 602 F.2d at 875. At the time the contract was made, Telex was in deep trouble and needed a very high profile lawyer. Under the circumstances, the court found the contract between Telex and Brobeck was not such that "no man in his sense and not under a delusion would make on the one hand, and as no honest and fair man would accept on the other," id. at 875 quoting Swanson v. Hempstead, 64 Cal.App.2d 681, 688, 149 P.2d 404, 407 (1944).

After *Brobeck* there may be no fee that a court would consider excessive when the client is a sophisticated commercial player. See Ackermann v. Levine, 788 F.2d 830, 843 (2d Cir.1986) (". . . the American client was a sophisticated business person with competent American international legal counsel."). Reflecting the holding in *Brobeck,* Calif.R.Prof. Conduct 4–200(B)(2) provides that the client's "sophistication" is a factor to be considered in judging whether the fee is unconscionable.

Boston and Maine Corporation v. Sheehan, Phinney, Bass & Green, 778 F.2d 890 (1st Cir.1985), involved an eminent domain proceeding by the State of New Hampshire to take Boston & Maine's land. Although the usual fee in an eminent domain case was 50% of the difference between the state's offer and the final recovery, the attorneys agreed to take 15% of that difference. Having won a settlement of $2.3 million, they billed their clients for a $199,000 contingent fee, and other expenses as agreed. The railroad by then was in bankruptcy and the bankruptcy court reduced the firm's fee to $80,000. The Court of Appeals reversed, finding that "Sheehan brought to the task a high degree of both experience and expertise in what is considered a rather specialized legal undertaking. The outcome of this type of case may depend as much on the confidence which state officials and judges have in the retained attorneys as in the accuracy per se of their legal work." Id. at 899. (Did this language harken to the fact that Warren Rudman, a former attorney-general of New Hampshire and now of Gramm–Rudman fame, was a partner in the law firm?)

In practice, court intervention concerning lawyers' fees is limited to situations where the court believes that the client is in need of special protection. Thus, courts are quick to find fees excessive and reduce them in cases where the client is a minor, Hoffert v. General Motors Corp., 656 F.2d 161 (5th Cir.1981) (lawyer voluntarily reduced 40% contingency fee to 33%; court further reduced it to 20%); where the client is poor, United States v. Strawser, 800 F.2d 704 (7th Cir.1986) (criminal defense lawyer's fee so high that defendant rendered indigent and therefore unable to hire counsel to pursue appeal); or where the client is a class, Dunn v. H.K. Porter, 602 F.2d 1105 (3d Cir.1979).

Courts also protect middle-class clients who have had little or no prior experience with lawyers, for example, Jacobson v. Sassower, 66 N.Y.2d 991, 499 N.Y.S.2d 381, 489 N.E.2d 1283 (1985). The agreement between client and lawyer to handle a divorce provided for an hourly fee of $100 and: ". . . a non-refundable retainer of $2,500 (which is not to be affected by any possible reconciliation between myself and my wife). Said retainer is to be credited against your charges . . ."

After the lawyer had completed 10 hours of work on the matter, the client discharged her without cause. The client sued to recover the difference between the retainer of $2500 and the hourly fee charge of $1000. The court held for the client, stating:

> In cases of doubt or ambiguity, a contract must be construed most strongly against the party who prepared it, and favorably to a party who had no voice in the selection of its language. Additionally, and as a matter of public policy, courts pay particular attention to fee arrangements between attorneys and their clients. An attorney has the burden of showing that a fee contract is fair, reasonable, and fully known and understood by the client. . . .

> This retainer agreement was ambiguous because it did not state clearly that the "non-refundable retainer of $2,500" was intended to be a minimum fee and that the entire sum would be forfeited notwithstanding any event that terminated the attorney-client relationship prior to 25 hours of service. In the absence of such clear language, defendant was required to establish that plaintiff understood that those were the terms of the agreement and she failed to do so. Indeed, defendant does not claim that she explained the nature and consequences of the nonrefundable retainer clause to plaintiff before he executed the contract and the trial judge accepted plaintiff's evidence that he did not understand the payment to be a minimum fee.

489 N.E.2d at 1284.

Most courts assert that they have a special obligation to scrutinize contingent fee arrangements with unsophisticated clients. See, e.g., The Committee on Legal Ethics of the West Virginia Bar v. Tatterson, 352 S.E.2d 107, 113–114 (W.Va.1986) ("The requirement that the client be fully informed applies especially to a contingent-fee contract . . . Contracts for contingent fees, generally have a greater potential for overreaching of clients than fixed-fee contracts [and] are closely scrutinized by the courts where there is a question as to their reasonableness."); In re Teichner, 104 Ill.2d 150, 470 N.E.2d 972 (1984).

How the Question of Fees Comes Before the Court

Whether the lawyer's fee is excessive may come before the court in several ways. The court may be required to approve the fee in connection with a settlement on behalf of a minor or a class. See *Hoffert* and *Dunn,* supra. The lawyer may sue the client to recover a fee, as in *Brobeck,* or the client may sue to recover fees already paid, as in *Jacobson.* Fee questions may also be raised in disciplinary proceedings (see the note below); where one party is assessed the other's attorney's fee, for example under Fed.R.Civ.Proc. 11 (authorizing sanctions, including an award of attorneys' fees, for filing pleadings not supported by the facts or the law) or 42 U.S.C. § 1988 (giving courts discretion to award the prevailing party reasonable attorney's fees in federal civil rights actions); and in probate and bankruptcy proceedings where the court must approve the award of fees out of the estate or trust.

Beyond these situations, upon a client's complaint a court may review a lawyer's fee in a summary proceeding "without nice regard to jurisdictional, case or controversy, pleading, or other procedural requirements that normally govern suits." Wolfram, Modern Legal Ethics § 9.1 at 499 (1986). See, e.g., Coffelt v. Shell, 577 F.2d 30 (8th Cir. 1978) (trial judge acted on his own motion to reduce lawyer's fee). Compare United States v. Vague, 697 F.2d 805 (7th Cir.1983), where summary proceedings on the court's own motion were disapproved. In *Vague,* there was no complaint from the client and the district court judge learned the amount of the attorney's fee from the presentence report. Troubled by the amount, the judge held a hearing, found that the fee was excessive and ordered a partial refund. The Court of Appeals reversed, stating it was "a mistake to graft onto a lawsuit an issue that the judge is neither asked nor required to resolve." Id. at 808. The court held that in ordering restitution, the judge exceeded his power; he should have referred the matter to the appropriate bar committee or appointed an independent prosecutor under the procedures for disciplining lawyers prescribed by the rules of court. *Vague* was disapproved in Carlucci v. Piper Aircraft Corp., Inc., 775 F.2d 1440 (11th Cir.1985).

The Professional Rules on the Size of the Fee

DR 2–106(A) prohibits a lawyer from contracting, charging or collecting an "illegal or clearly excessive fee." M.R. 1.5(a) eliminates mention of "excessive" and simply states that "[a] lawyer's fee shall be reasonable." Both DR 2–106 and M.R. 1.5(a) list multiple factors relevant in determining the reasonableness of a fee. These factors include virtually every possibly relevant factor. Do these make the criterion of "reasonableness" or "excessiveness" any more definite? For an even more extensive list of factors see Calif.R.Prof. Conduct 4–200(B).

One of the factors to be considered is the customary fee in the locality for similar services. See M.R. 1.5(a)(3) and DR 2–106(B)(3). Minimum fee schedules were once common. See Note, A Critical Analysis of Bar Associations Minimum Fee Schedules, 85 Harv.L.Rev. 971 (1972). In Goldfarb v. Virginia State Bar, 421 U.S. 773, 95 S.Ct.

2004 (1975), the Supreme Court held these schedules illegal under the antitrust laws.

Discipline for charging an excessive fee is rare, but does occur. See, e.g., Florida State Bar v. Moriber, 314 So.2d 145 (Fla.1975) (lawyer suspended for 45 days for charging an unreasonable and excessive fee). When discipline is imposed, it is often in cases where the lawyer has engaged in some other misconduct as well, such as misleading the client on the difficulty of the legal matter involved.   See, e.g., Mississippi State Bar Association v. A Mississippi Attorney, 489 So.2d 1081 (Miss. 1986); Committee on Legal Ethics v. Tatterson, 352 S.E.2d 107 (W.Va. 1986).   See also Disciplinary Counsel v. Stinson, 25 Ohio St.3d 130, 495 N.E.2d 434 (1986) (lawyer charged excessive fee, neglected a matter, and created false evidence); Myers v. Virginia State Bar, 226 Va. 630, 312 S.E.2d 286 (1984) (lawyer charged excessive fee, misrepresented the amount to the court, and misled the client into believing that the court had approved the fee); In re Quillan, 1 Law.Man.Prof. Conduct 574 (Tenn.Supr.Ct. Board of Prof.Resp.1984) (lawyer charged excessive fee and led the client to believe that he was able to improperly influence a public official).   Generally see Annotation, Attorney's Charging Excessive Fee as Ground for Disciplinary Action, 11 A.L.R.4th 133 (1982).

The necessarily vague criteria in DR 2–106 and M.R. 1.5 raise questions about the fairness of disciplining lawyers for "unreasonable" fees.   For example, in Attorney Grievance Commission v. Wright, 306 Md. 93, 507 A.2d 618 (1986), three lawyers testified that the fee was reasonable and three that it was not.   The court described all six lawyers as meeting the standard of DR 2–106, i.e., they were all "lawyer[s] of ordinary prudence."   The court held that the disciplinary agency had failed to meet its burden of showing the fee was "clearly excessive."   The court did, however, find that the lawyer had violated DR 9–102(B)(4), by continuing to hold the clients' money in excess of the fee agreed upon.

Court Awarded Attorneys' Fees

Statutes Authorizing the Award of Attorneys' Fees

Many statutes now provide that the losing party may be required to pay the other side's attorney's fees.   For a list of more than 100 federal fee-shifting statutes see Marek v. Chesny, 473 U.S. 1, 42–51, 105 S.Ct. 3012, 3035–39 (1985) (Brennan, J., dissenting).

Calculation of a "reasonable fee" under such statutes has consumed enumerable hours at the trial court level, generated a formidable number of appellate court decisions and occasioned much comment in the journals.   See, e.g., Dobbs, Awarding Attorney Fees Against Adversaries: Introducing the Problem, 1986 Duke L.J. 435; Rowe, The Legal Theory of Attorney Fee Shifting: A Critical Overview, 1982 Duke L.J. 651; Leubsdorf, The Contingency Factor in Fee Awards, 90 Yale L.J. 473 (1981); Berger, Court Awarded Attorneys' Fees: What is "Reasonable?," 126 U.Pa.L.Rev. 281 (1977).   Lawyers seeking up-to-date information may subscribe to the Attorney Fee Awards Reporter, a journal devoted to this issue. Books include Larson, E., Federal Court Awards of Attorney's Fees (1981); and Speiser, S., Attorneys' Fees (1973).

Two major approaches to fee setting have developed. One method is outlined in Johnson v. Georgia Highway Express, Inc., 488 F.2d 714 (5th Cir.1974), a class action under Title VII of the Civil Rights Act of 1964. *Johnson* indicated that the trial court should consider: (1) the time and labor required; (2) the novelty and difficulty of the questions; (3) the skill requisite to perform the legal service properly; (4) the preclusion of other employment by the attorney due to acceptance of the case; (5) the customary fee; (6) whether the fee is fixed or contingent; (7) time limitations imposed by the client or the circumstances; (8) the amount involved and the results obtained; (9) the experience, reputation and ability of the attorneys; (10) the 'undesirability' of the case; (11) the nature and length of the professional relationship with the client; and (12) awards in similar cases. Id. at 717–719. The Senate Report on the Civil Rights Attorney's Fees Awards Act of 1976 approved the *Johnson* formula, S.Rep. No. 94–1011, 94th Cong., 2d Sess. 4, reprinted in 1976 U.S.Code Cong. & Admin.News 5908, 5912. Compare M.R. 1.5(a). The Supreme Court, while not quite adopting *Johnson,* has stated that the case "provides guidance to Congress' intent because both the House and Senate Reports [on 42 U.S.C. § 1988] refer to the 12 [*Johnson*] factors . . ." Blanchard v. Bergeron, 109 S.Ct. 939, 943 (1989) citing Hensley v. Eckerhart, 461 U.S. 424, 429–31 (1983). Many appellate courts endorse the *Johnson* factors. See, e.g., Parker v. Anderson, 667 F.2d 1204 (5th Cir.1982); Marion v. Barrier, 694 F.2d 229 (11th Cir.1982). However the *Johnson* approach has been criticized as imprecise, redundant, lacking an analytical framework, and giving undue weight to results achieved. Moore v. Jas. H. Matthews & Co., 682 F.2d 830 (9th Cir.1982); Copeland v. Marshall, 641 F.2d 880 (D.C.Cir.1980) (en banc). See also Justice Scalia's concurrence in *Blanchard,* supra at 946, criticizing the Court's acceptance of *Johnson.*

The second major method for setting attorney fees was developed by the Third Circuit in *Lindy I* and clarified in *Lindy II.* See, Lindy Bros. v. American Radiator & Stan. San. Corp., 487 F.2d 161 (3d Cir. 1973) (Lindy I), 540 F.2d 102 (3d Cir.1976) (Lindy II). Under this approach a basic figure or "lodestar" is derived by multiplying the number of hours reasonably expended by a reasonable hourly rate for the attorney's services. The "lodestar" sum may then be adjusted upward or downward to reflect the contingent nature of the case or the unusual quality (good or bad) of the legal service in the particular case.

In Pennsylvania v. Delaware Valley Citizens' Council for Clean Air, 478 U.S. 546, 563, 106 S.Ct. 3088, 3097 (1986) (Delaware Valley I), the Court noted the advantages of the *Lindy* -lodestar approach, stating that it "provided a more analytical framework . . . than the unguided 'factors' [in] *Johnson.*" But see, e.g., *Blanchard,* supra (*Johnson* factors are starting point for analysis). Other Supreme Court cases using the

Lindy formula are cited in the Report of the Third Circuit Task Force printed below.

In Pennsylvania v. Delaware Valley Citizens' Council for Clean Air, 483 U.S. 711, 107 S.Ct. 3078 (1987) (Delaware Valley II), the Supreme Court 5–4 recognized that the factor of contingency may be taken into account in determining a court-awarded fee; that the contingency factor should be based on the risk in the type of case and not the particular case; but that the factor of "novelty and difficulty" might itself reflect the same factors as are involved in the contingency factor.

REPORT OF THE THIRD CIRCUIT TASK FORCE ON COURT AWARDED ATTORNEY FEES

108 F.R.D. 237, 1985.

FOREWORD

Over ten years ago the Third Circuit devised the *Lindy* time/rate (lodestar) method for the determination of court-awarded attorneys' fees. Because a number of difficulties have been encountered in applying the *Lindy* formulation, Chief Judge Aldisert requested that a Task Force of judges and lawyers be formed to study the subject and to make recommendations on the criteria to be utilized in determining attorneys' fee awards.

· · ·

I.   *The Existing Lindy Time/Rate Regime*

A.   *Overview* . . .

· · ·

Since *Lindy I*, the Third Circuit has emphasized, both in fund-in-court cases * (like *Lindy* itself) and in a variety of statutory fee cases, that individual determinations of reasonable billing rates are required for the lodestar computation. Most circuits that have defined their fee-setting standards have followed the lead of the Third Circuit. The Fifth Circuit, however, in its well known decision in Johnson v. Georgia Highway Express, Inc.,[17] adopted a twelve-factor scale in lieu of *Lindy*. Soon thereafter, *Johnson* was adopted by the Ninth Circuit as well.

Yet, most commentators consider *Johnson* to be little different from *Lindy* because the first criterion of the *Johnson* test, and indeed the one most heavily weighted, is the time and labor factor. Similarly,

---

* Editor's footnote: "[The] common-fund doctrine . . . allows a person who maintains a law suit that results in the creation, preservation, or increase of a fund in which others have a common interest to be reimbursed from that fund for litigation expenses incurred. The doctrine is 'part of the historic equity jurisdiction of the federal courts,' and contemplates 'fair and just allowances for expenses and counsel fees,' to be paid by those who have benefited from the efforts expended on their behalf." Task Force 108 F.R.D. at 241. For the cites to the two *Lindy* decisions, see p. 485 above.

17.   488 F.2d 714 (5th Cir.1974).

many of the *Johnson* factors are subsumed within the initial calculation of hours reasonably expended at a customary hourly rate. . . .

. . . (T)he *Lindy* lodestar approach recently received the Supreme Court's imprimatur—at least in statutory fee cases—in Hensley v. Eckerhart.[24] . . . Even more recently, in Blum v. Stenson,[27] Justice Powell, for a unanimous Court, declared that the lodestar generally is "presumed to be the reasonable fee"; the base standard for fee determinations, even for cases litigated by not-for-profit law offices, was to be the prevailing market rate in the relevant community.

Despite this growth in acceptance in the last ten years, *Lindy* has come under increased criticism, with some observers asserting that its technique causes more problems than it solves.[28] This Task Force study of court-awarded attorneys' fees is an attempt to appraise the *Lindy* technique and to make suggestions for the future.

B. *Deficiencies of the Lindy Process*

Whatever the merits of the *Lindy* objectives and the degree to which they are being achieved, there is a widespread belief that the deficiencies of the current system either offset or exceed its benefits. . . . What follows is a list of accusations advanced against *Lindy*. . . .

1. Lindy *increases the workload of an already overtaxed judicial system.* As a result of *Lindy,* the fee-setting process has become more costly in terms of the time and effort expended on it. The increased documentation demanded by the *Lindy* approach, the practice of conducting fee hearings (including the use of "experts"), and the desire to avoid misfeasance have so magnified the process that the system's human and physical resources are being deflected from other, perhaps more important, duties.[30]

2. *The elements of the* Lindy *process are insufficiently objective and produce results that are far from homogenous.* Widespread variations in fees awarded lawyers, often in the same community, by different judges, and in different categories of cases, have led to a loss of predictability as to treatment, as well as a loss of confidence in the integrity of the fee-setting procedure.

3. *The* Lindy *process creates a sense of mathematical precision that is unwarranted in terms of the realities of the practice of law.* Per-

---

24. 461 U.S. 424, 103 S.Ct. 1933, 76 L.Ed.2d 40 (1983).

27. 465 U.S. 886, 104 S.Ct. 1541, 79 L.Ed.2d 891 (1984).

28. See, e.g., Lauter, When the Court Awards Fees, 7 Nat.L.J. 43 (July 8, 1985) pp. S1–S16; Lerach, Alternative Approaches for Awarding Attorneys' Fees in Federal Court Litigation: It's Time to Unload the Lodestar (1984) (unpublished report on fees presented to the Ninth Circuit; advocates abolishing *Lindy* and returning to percentage based fees) (William S. Lerach, Esq., Milberg Weiss Bershad Specthrie & Lerach, San Diego, California).

30. Questions pertaining to the use of expert testimony and the need for documentation were recently addressed by a divided panel of the Third Circuit in Ramco Indus. Prod. Corp. v. Dunlap, 776 F.2d 1136 (3d Cir.1985).

haps the most obvious illustration of this phenomenon is that *Lindy* requires a calculation based on the petitioning attorney's customary billing rates. But many plaintiffs' lawyers who seek fees usually work on the basis of contingent fee arrangements and do not have a "customary" or "normal" billing rate. Accordingly, they argue, the notion that their "customary" or "normal" billing rates are being used is highly misleading.[31] . . .

4. *Lindy is subject to manipulation by judges who prefer to calibrate fees in terms of percentages of the settlement fund or the amounts recovered by the plaintiffs or of an overall dollar amount.* Those who tend to doubt the objectivity of the *Lindy* process occasionally complain that some judges are too result-oriented. These judges, it is charged, first determine what they wish to award, either in percentage or dollar amount terms, and then massage the major variables in the *Lindy* fee-setting procedure—hours allowed, market rates, contingency, and quality—until the desired result is achieved.[32]

5. *Although designed to curb certain abuses,* Lindy *has led to others.* As was strongly suggested in a recent Third Circuit decision, In re Fine Paper Antitrust Litigation,[33] *Lindy* encourages lawyers to expend excessive hours, and, in the case of attorneys presenting fee petitions, engage in duplicative and unjustified work, inflate their "normal" billing rate, and include fictitious hours or hours already billed on other matters, perhaps in the hope of offsetting any hours the court may disallow.[34] These various forms of running the meter are accompanied in a number of cases by the presence of far too many law firms submitting fee petitions. The latter phenome-

31. This is made all the more difficult by the requirement recently prescribed by the Supreme Court in Blum v. Stenson, 465 U.S. 886, 895–96 n. 11, 104 S.Ct. 1541, 1547 n. 11, 79 L.Ed.2d 891, 900 n. 11 (1984) that to assist the court's determination of a reasonable hourly rate, in the statutory fee context, a fee applicant should produce "satisfactory evidence" in addition to the attorney's own affidavits that the requested rate is in line with prevailing rates.

32. This assertion appears to be supported by a study presented by United States District Judge Thomas A. Masterson at the 1977 Third Circuit Judicial Conference. Judge Masterson had tabulated the fees awarded by district courts within the Third Circuit under the *Lindy* lodestar regime from 1973 to the date of his presentation. In each case, the fee award was presented as a function of a percentage of the overall settlement amount. The statistics revealed that many of the judges systematically awarded fees in the range of twenty to twenty-five percent of the fund, regardless of type of case, benefits to the class, number of hours billed, size of fund, size of plaintiff class, or any other relevant factor. See, e.g., Baughman v. Wilson Freight Forwarding Co., 79 F.R.D. 520 (W.D.Pa.1977), reversed and remanded, 583 F.2d 1208 (3d Cir.1978) (fee award 26% of antitrust settlement); Coleco Indus. Inc. v. Berman, 423 F.Supp. 275 (E.D.Pa.1976) (contract indemnity: 20–25%); Entin v. Barg, 412 F.Supp. 508 (securities class action: 23.9%); Dorfman v. First Boston Corp., 70 F.R.D. 366 (E.D.Pa.1976) (securities class action: 23.5%); Lindy Bros. Builders, Inc. v. American Radiator & Standard Sanitary Corp., 382 F.Supp. 999 (E.D.Pa.1974) (antitrust class action settlement: 27.8% from unrepresented claimants; 53.8% from represented claimants); Bleznak v. C.G.S. Scientific Corp., 387 F.Supp. 1184 (E.D.Pa.1974) (securities class action: 30%).

33. 751 F.2d 562 (3d Cir.1984), affirming in part, reversing in part, 98 F.R.D. 48 (E.D. Pa.1983) (district court opinion emphasizes abuse by plaintiffs' lawyers).

34. Id.

non seems to be the inevitable by-product of a fee-setting scheme based on hours worked regardless of the number of lawyers involved, rather than a limited percentage of a fixed monetary recovery.[35]

6. Lindy *creates a disincentive for the early settlement of cases.* Because of *Lindy's* emphasis on hours worked, lawyers—including defense counsel who typically bill their clients on an hourly basis—have little or no incentive to settle cases at the earliest appropriate opportunity. To the contrary, there appears to be a conscious, or perhaps unconscious, desire to keep the litigation alive despite a reasonable prospect of settlement, to maximize the number of hours to be included in computing the lodestar.

7. Lindy *does not provide the district court with enough flexibility to reward or deter lawyers so that desirable objectives, such as early settlement, will be fostered.* Many believe that *Lindy's* preoccupation with the lodestar computation deprives the trial court of much needed discretion to take proper account of the variousness of litigation. On the other hand, greater discretion is likely to exacerbate the lack of uniformity described in item 2, above, and contribute to the concerns of the public interest bar discussed in item 8, below.

8. *The* Lindy *process works to the particular disadvantage of the public interest bar.* There is a strong feeling among public interest, particularly civil rights, lawyers that whatever *Lindy's* merits may be in other contexts, it has a decidedly negative impact on them and is undermining the efficacy of many of the fee statutes Congress has enacted. The claim is that lodestars in the so-called "money" cases, such as securities and antitrust actions, are set higher than they are in cases under statutes promoting nonmonetary social objectives, such as the Civil Rights Attorneys Fees Awards Act of 1976. It even has been suggested that this is true either because some judges are not disposed toward the policies reflected in these statutes and simply do not wish to encourage actions under them, or because in many cases the size of the fee requested seems disproportionate to the amount of economic recovery (or the value of the non-economic recovery) provided the claimants. . . . Several members of the Task Force expressed the view that fee awards in recent years in the social action context

---

35. Under the *Lindy* system every lawyer involved may petition for an award as long as the lawyer comports with the contemporaneous time-keeping requirements and can justify the hours spent to the court. Under the contingency system, however, the portion of the recovery pie to be devoted to attorneys' fees does not vary according to the number of attorneys involved in the case. Thus, under *Lindy*, in the large fund cases, there may be the unpleasant spectre of management committees or countless lawyers petitioning for a fee from a fund based on work, the value of which frequently seems marginal.

Another cause of this abuse may be the political maneuvering to obtain "votes" for a stipulated recommendation as to the appointment of lead counsel in multi-party cases. Candidates for lead counsel, it has been said, refer clients to other lawyers in order to get additional votes. In return for their votes, the new lawyers are compensated by the promise of additional *Lindy* hours.

have been so discouraging that few attorneys will accept a civil rights case.[38]

9. *Despite the apparent simplicity of the* Lindy *formulation, considerable confusion and lack of predictability remain in its administration.* This point, of course, is implicit in a number of the preceding paragraphs. But there are administrative difficulties beyond those already mentioned. For example, the *Lindy* requirement that community rates be applied only raises the question of rates in which community? Yet, in some complex cases affecting people on a nationwide scale, a national rate might be justified—a position adopted by Judge Jack B. Weinstein in In re "Agent Orange" Product Liability Litigation.[39] If however, a local rate is chosen, there is ambiguity as to whether it is the forum's rate or each petitioning attorney's local rate.

C.   *The Need to Distinguish Between Fund-in-Court Cases and Statutory Fee Cases*

The Task Force believes that a distinction must be drawn between fund-in-court cases and statutory fee cases since the policies behind the two categories differ greatly. The *Lindy* lodestar method, however, first developed and applied in the context of a fund-in-court case, has been transferred to the statutory fee environment with little attention to the differences between these two types of cases.

The purpose of the "equitable-fund," "common-fund," or "fund-in-court" doctrine, enunciated by the Supreme Court over a century ago in Trustees of the Internal Improvement Fund v. Greenough,[42] is to avoid the unjust enrichment of those who benefit from the fund that is created, protected, or increased by the litigation and who otherwise would bear none of the litigation costs. . . .

A key element of the fund case is that the fees are not assessed against the unsuccessful litigant (fee shifting), but rather are taken from the fund or damage recovery (fee spreading), thereby avoiding the unjust enrichment of those who otherwise would be benefited by the fund without sharing in the expenses incurred by the successful litigant.

In sharp contrast to the fund-in-court cases are the substantial number of statutory causes of action, such as those created by the federal securities, antitrust, civil rights, copyright, and patent acts, that include provisions for attorneys' fees—typically characterized as being "reasonable" in amount—to be awarded to the prevailing party. These

---

38. This may become all the more true in the wake of Marek v. Chesny, 473 U.S. 1, 105 S.Ct. 3012, 87 L.Ed.2d 1 (1985) in which the Supreme Court held that a prevailing civil rights litigant entitled to fees under 42 U.S.C. § 1988 may be barred from recovering any fees for work performed after rejecting a settlement offer under Federal Rule 68 when less ultimately is recovered than the amount proffered in settlement.

39. 611 F.Supp. 1296 (E.D.N.Y.1985) (memorandum and order on attorneys' fees and final judgment).

42. 105 U.S. 527 (1881).

are clearly of the "fee shifting" variety. Illustrative is the Civil Rights Attorney's Fees Awards Act of 1976, which gives federal courts the discretion to award attorneys' fees to the prevailing party in suits brought to enforce certain provisions of the civil rights acts.

Rather than being based on the equitable notion that those who have benefited from litigation should share its costs, the legislative history of these fee acts makes it clear that the intent of Congress was to encourage private enforcement of the statutory substantive rights, whether they be economic or noneconomic, through the judicial process. . . .

Another difference between fund-in-court and statutory fee cases is that in the former category there is a greater need for the judge to act as a fiduciary for the beneficiaries (who are paying the fee), particularly in the class action situation, because few, if any, of the action's beneficiaries actually are before the court at the time the fees are set. Judicial scrutiny is necessary inasmuch as the fee will be paid out of the fund established by the litigation, in which the defendant no longer has any interest, and the plaintiff's attorney's financial interests conflict with those of the fund beneficiaries. As a result, there is no adversary process that can be relied upon in the setting of a reasonable fee. In statutory fee cases, however, the losing party who will pay the fee is before the court, thus obviating any need for special judicial involvement. Arguably, all the judge need do is rule on the fee application based on the competing presentations of the adversaries.

Despite these differences between fund cases and statutory fee cases, the *Lindy* formulation was applied to both without any real analysis of the propriety of doing so or the impact it would have. . . .

. . .

III. *Fund-in-Court Cases*

. . . [T]he Task Force agreed that the fundamental differences between statutory fee and fund-in-court cases should be recognized in the fee-setting process. . . .

. . .

[T]he Task Force recommends that in the traditional common-fund situation and in those statutory fee cases that are likely to result in a settlement fund from which adequate counsel fees can be paid, the district court, on motion or its own initiative and at the earliest practicable moment,[62] should attempt to establish a percentage fee arrangement agreeable to the Bench and to plaintiff's counsel. In statutory fee cases the negotiated fee would be applied in the event of

62. It is assumed that the "earliest practicable moment" will be immediately after the pleadings are closed and before discovery is fully underway. However, the judicial members of the Task Force expressed differences as to when they would establish the percentage fee arrangement. Most likely, high management judges will want to settle the fee question at the outset of the case. Others may prefer not to become a participant so early in the proceedings and may wish to wait until the case is better formed. All lawyer members of the Task Force, however, desired early clarification of the fee issue.

settlement; in all fully litigated statutory fee cases the award would continue to be determined in an adversary manner under the basic *Lindy* approach, with the modifications suggested in the next section.

The negotiated fee, and the procedure for arriving at it, should be left to the court's discretion. In most instances, it will involve a sliding scale dependent upon the ultimate recovery, the expectation being that, absent unusual circumstances, the percentage will decrease as the size of the fund increases.* In order to promote early settlement, the negotiated fee also could provide a percentage or fixed premium incentive based on how quickly or efficiently the matter was resolved. Other possibilities for custom-tailoring a fee arrangement abound.

· · ·

This negotiated fee procedure has a number of potentially desirable effects. By establishing the fee agreement early in the litigation, any and all inducement or inclination to increase the number of *Lindy* hours will be reduced, since the amount of work performed will not be permitted to alter the contingent fee. In addition, another alleged *Lindy* evil will be minimized because there will be a substantial inducement for plaintiff's counsel to settle the matter quickly, since the fee scale will have been established and counsel's compensation will not be enhanced by a delay. The negotiated percentage scheme also will eliminate the cumbersome, enervating, and often surrealistic process of preparing and evaluating fee petitions that now plagues the Bench and Bar under *Lindy*. Finally, the proposal offers attorneys a degree of predictability that many believe currently is lacking.

Note, however, that the advantage of the negotiated fee procedure will be entirely undermined if, at the end of the litigation, counsel have the right to renegotiate depending upon the result accomplished, the time devoted, the number of lawyers involved, or other factors relating to the case. In other words, renegotiation should not be permitted and the agreement should be strictly adhered to by the court, unless at the end of the case matters are presented that were not within the reasonable contemplation of the parties at the time the fee arrangement was negotiated.

· · ·

IV. *Statutory Cases*

A. *Retention of Lindy in Statutory Fee Cases*

The Task Force concluded that the basic framework of the *Lindy* method should be retained in those statutory fee cases in which there is a risk that the economic rewards will not produce a fund from which a reasonable fee can be awarded. The following factors led the Task Force to this decision:

1) The years of experience under *Lindy* have provided some degree of objectivity and predictability to the fee-setting process. . . .

* Editor's note: See the Coffee article in Ch. 10 for a critique of this approach.

2)   *Blum v. Stenson* and *Hensley v. Eckerhart* may have placed the Supreme Court's imprimatur on the *Lindy* time/rate system—at least in civil rights cases under Section 1988 of Title 42, and quite possibly in all statutory fee cases. . . .

3)   Members of the Task Force felt that the potential for *Lindy* abuse was greater in fund-in-court cases than in statutory fee cases. . . .

4)   Finally, in the context of public interest and civil rights litigation, a fee-setting scheme based on time and market rates seems most consistent with the public policies embedded in the legislative provisions. . . .

Nonetheless, the Task Force believes many of the perceived deficiencies in the *Lindy* process are real; they must be ameliorated and its administration improved. The following recommendations were motivated by the goals of objectification and simplification of the fee-setting process in statutory fee cases.

B. *Recommendations*

1. *Standardization of Hourly Rates*

One of the more time-consuming aspects of the *Lindy* process is the necessity of determining the "customary" or "normal" billing rate for each petitioning lawyer based on the nature of the work performed and then multiplying this rate by the number of hours expended. . . .

If simplicity of administration were the only objective, a single rate, applicable to all lawyers submitting fee petitions within the district, might be employed. But, the Task Force recognized that a single rate was unrealistic and probably unfair, given the tremendous variations in fee-setting situations. . . . Therefore, in principle it seems certain general categories of attorneys, perhaps partners and associates, or perhaps those with less than 10 years' experience in practice and those with more than 10 years' experience, to avoid too wide a disparity between the standardized hourly rate and the individual lawyer's actual marketplace value. An even more finely tuned set of categories may be appropriate.[70] Regardless of what categories are

---

70. A highly developed standardized rate schedule might look something like that adopted by Community Legal Services, Inc., Philadelphia, Pennsylvania:

Category	Range of Hourly Rates
Law Students	$ 30.00– $50.00
Attorneys with post law school experience under two years	$ 60.00– $85.00
Attorneys with 2–5 years experience	$ 80.00–$120.00
Attorneys with 6–10 years experience	$100.00–$160.00
Attorneys with more than 10 years experience	$125.00–$180.00
Supervising Attorneys, Project Heads, Managing Attorneys, Deputy Director, Executive Director	$130.00–$200.00
Paralegals I and II	$ 30.00– $40.00
Senior and Supervisory Paralegals	$ 40.00– $60.00

chosen, the Task Force recommends that the schedule be uniformly applied to all lawyers and in all cases.

. . .

2. *Controlling Hours*

Perhaps the sharpest attack on the *Lindy* regime is the claim that its preoccupation with attorneys' time and market rates encourages the expenditure of excessive or unnecessary hours and, in some instances, attracts more lawyers to the plaintiffs' side of court-awarded fee cases than necessary. Quite understandably, district judges find it difficult, indeed, in most instances, impossible, to police these matters by looking over the shoulders of lawyers to monitor the way they handle their cases. To impose that obligation on the Bench is unrealistic, unduly time-consuming, and typically will amount to little more than an exercise in hindsight.

The Task Force believes that a significant improvement in the current situation can be achieved if counsel and the court discuss various fee matters at the scheduling and pretrial conferences provided for by Federal Rules of Civil Procedure 16 and 26. . . .[79]

. . . [T]he court might ask plaintiff's counsel to submit a proposed budget for the litigation, or require counsel to consider stipulating to a projected range of hours that will be consumed by a case. Defense counsel also might be requested to present estimates. Of course, as is true of all matters dealt with at a pretrial conference, the preliminary treatment of fee questions should not be cast in concrete. Nonetheless, the court should manifest sufficient control by estimating the maximum hours to be included in the lodestar, so that the attorneys understand that excessive discovery or any other lawyer hyperactivity will not be tolerated or compensated.

. . .

Despite the foregoing, should a judge believe that too many *Lindy* hours have been billed, "[t]he district court may attempt to identify specific hours that should be eliminated, or it may simply reduce the award to account for the limited success. The court necessarily has discretion in making this equitable judgment." [80]

79. By encouraging early judicial involvement, the Task Force does not mean in any way to chill independent and uninhibited advocacy. Some members of the Task Force thought that early judicial involvement in fee matters could make it more difficult to litigate vigorously because the district court's early impressions of the merits of a case possibly could influence the amount negotiated for the fee. For example, a district judge might favor early settlements for reasons of relief of court dockets or administrative convenience, irrespective of the merits of the action. Objective guidelines established by the local district Fee Advisory Committee could provide whatever protections thought needed.

80. Hensley v. Eckerhart, 461 U.S. 424, 436–37, 103 S.Ct. 1933, 1941, 76 L.Ed.2d 40, 52 (1983).

3. *Multipliers—Augmentation and Discount*

Since *Lindy,* Third Circuit fee determinations involving the contingency and quality factors have ranged between a negative multiplier, to multipliers of four or more. But this practice undoubtedly will be affected by Blum v. Stenson,[84] in which the Supreme Court limited upward adjustments to "those rare cases in which the success was 'exceptional.' "

The Task Force believes the Lindy multiplier practice should be revised in several respects. First, the quality factor should be eliminated from consideration. This factor is superfluous since it reflects the type of performance expected of all attorneys and theoretically already has been taken into account by the district court in setting standardized rates. . . .

In contrast to its views on the quality factor, the Task Force feels that the contingency factor, which it defines simply as "the risk of winning or losing," *should be considered in all cases.*[95] Plaintiffs' attorneys always face the prospect of receiving no compensation in statutory fee cases. Accordingly, even modest risks in cases in which liability is reasonably certain to be established should be recognized in the fee-setting process.[96]

Other factors that the Task Force thought should be considered in adjusting the basic fee are: (1) the result obtained in the action; (2) the petitioning attorney's contribution to a prompt or a delayed resolution of the action; and (3) the delay in receiving attorneys' fees. The second factor is designed to encourage early settlement by providing an incentive that neutralizes an attorney's possible predilection to increase the number of hours invested in a case for lodestar purposes. As to the third factor, which is designed to recognize the economic effects of a delay in receiving attorneys' fees, the court either may use a multiplier or may make an award to the attorney under the current scheduled hourly rate rather than the one in force when the work actually was done. An award of interest at an appropriate rate also could be employed to compensate for a delay in payment.

4. *The Special Problem of the Public Interest Bar*

As previously noted, there is a strong feeling among public interest and civil rights lawyers that the *Lindy* process has not always been applied to their advantage. The proposals for standardized fees and the elimination of the quality factor represent attempts to eliminate the possible sources of any adverse discriminatory treatment. The proposals should reaffirm the need for a neutral fee-setting process that does not relate fees in statutory cases to subjective judgments about

84. 465 U.S. 886, 104 S.Ct. 1541, 79 L.Ed.2d 891 (1984).

95. Of course, an upward multiplier may not be applied when forbidden by Congress. See Underwood v. Pierce, 761 F.2d 1342 (9th Cir.1985) (multiplier may not be applied to fees awarded under the Equal Access to Justice Act).

96. See, e.g., Leubsdorf, The Contingency Factor in Attorney Fee Awards, 90 Yale L.J. 473 (1981).

"benefit" and does not become mired in a concern about the dollars recovered and the dollars to be awarded in fees. It is hoped that the procedure outlined above will assure public interest and civil rights lawyers adequate compensation to enable them to pursue vindication of various public policies without regard to whether they produce economic or noneconomic benefits.

. . .

Comments

In Blum v. Stenson, 465 U.S. 886, 104 S.Ct. 1541 (1984), the Court held that the reasonable hourly rate for attorneys' fees is the prevailing rate in the community for the type of work performed, even where the attorneys are with a non-profit legal services organization. In Save Our Cumberland Mountains, Inc. v. Hodel, 857 F.2d 1516 (D.C.Cir.1988) (en banc), the court held that for-profit lawyers who customarily charge below the prevailing market rate to serve particular types of clients may nonetheless recover attorneys' fees based on the prevailing rate. Also see Missouri v. Jenkins, 109 S.Ct. 2463 (1989) (work of paralegals and law clerks may be compensated at market rates rather than actual cost to attorneys).

Should statutory awards of attorneys' fees be limited to the amount provided in the plaintiff's contingent fee arrangement with its lawyer? See Blanchard v. Bergeron, 109 S.Ct. 939 (1989) (no). What if the statutory award is less than the contingent fee agreement? May the lawyer seek recovery of the remainder from the client? See Venegas v. Skaggs, 867 F.2d 527 (9th Cir.1989), cert. granted sub nom. Venegas v. Mitchell, 110 S.Ct. 45 (1989), (yes).

The distinction between common fund cases and statutory fee cases emphasized in the Third Circuit Report has been used by other courts. For example, in Skelton v. General Motors Corp., 860 F.2d 250 (7th Cir. 1988), the court reasoned that it should be easier to qualify for an enhancement of the fee based on the risk of not prevailing in common fund cases than in statutory fee cases. Risk enhancement in statutory fee cases penalizes the defendant with a strong case, whereas this is not a problem in common fund cases because the fee is charged against the plaintiffs' recovery, not to the defendant.

For more on court awarded fees see *Evans v. Jeff D.*, printed later in this chapter, and the Coffee article and notes in Chapter 10 below.

Illegal Fees

Illegal fees are prohibited explicitly by DR 2–106(A) and implicitly by M.R. 1.5(a) and 8.4. Illegal fees include fees collected by a public official when a statute prohibits the private practice of law while in office, see State v. Stakes, 227 Kan. 711, 608 P.2d 997 (1980); fees above those awarded by the court in cases where the court has exclusive power to decide fees, see In re Crane, 96 Ill.2d 40, 449 N.E.2d 94 (1983); fees collected for an illegal purpose, In re Connaghan, 613 S.W.2d 626

(Mo.1981) (en banc) (lawyer collected fees to bribe state legislator); and fees above the maximum amount allowed by a statute. Fees that the lawyer knows have been paid with the proceeds of criminal activity have also been considered illegal fees. See In re Prescott, 271 N.W.2d 822 (Minn.1978). Whether a lawyer may be required to forfeit such funds under the federal forfeiture statutes is discussed above in Chapter 2.

Various federal and state statutes limit the fees a lawyer can charge in particular types of legal work. See, e.g., Federal Tort Claims Act, 28 U.S.C. § 2678; Social Security Act, 42 U.S.C. § 406; and Veterans Benefit Act, 38 U.S.C. § 3404(c). These limits have been upheld by the courts against contentions that they unconstitutionally interfere with the right to counsel and violate separation of powers by infringing upon the court's power to regulate the profession.

Walters v. National Association of Radiation Survivors, 473 U.S. 305, 105 S.Ct. 3180 (1985), upheld the $10 fee limit for representing a veteran seeking benefits from the Veterans Administration. The limit was adopted by Congress in 1864 to prevent lawyers from taking advantage of Civil War Veterans. The veterans claimed that the fee limit "denied them any realistic opportunity to obtain legal representation in presenting their claims to the VA and hence violated their rights under the Due Process Clause of the Fifth Amendment and under the First Amendment." The Court said the limit furthered Congress' goal of fostering an informal, nonadversarial process that would allow veterans to get their benefits without lawyers. It held that the veterans would have to show that the present lawyerless proceedings of the VA resulted in error in a significant number of cases and that lawyers would improve the process. On remand the plaintiffs undertook to offer proof of pervasive misconduct by the VA in passing upon certain types of veterans claims. See N.Y. Times, "Trial Begins on Letting Veterans Hire Lawyers to Press Disability Claims," Sept. 9, 1987 p. A16. On a number of occasions legislation has been introduced in Congress to increase the fees lawyers may collect in these cases. For example, one bill called for a limit of $750 for a losing claim and a contingency fee of no more than 25% for a successful claim. Thus far, all such legislation has been defeated in large part because of the powerful lobbying of the national veterans group which now provides volunteers to represent veterans before the Veterans Administration. It was in *Walters* that the Veterans Administration was heavily sanctioned under Rule 11 for lying about the existence of and destroying massive numbers of documents being sought in discovery. See National Association of Radiation Survivors v. Turnage, 115 F.R.D. 543 (N.D. Cal.1987), which is noted in Chapter 5 above at p. 396.

The Supreme Court of West Virginia has held that the attorney fee provisions of the Black Lung Benefits Act unconstitutionally deny claimants access to lawyers in violation of due process. Committee on Legal Ethics v. Triplett, 378 S.E.2d 82 (W.Va.1988), cert. granted, 110 S.Ct. 48 (1989). The lawyer was charged with engaging in conduct "involving dishonesty, fraud, deceit or misrepresentation," see DR 1–102(A)(4) and M.R. 8.4(c), for collecting a fee not authorized by the Act. Triplett's clients signed contingency fee contracts which provided that they would pay him 25% of any benefits collected. The Act requires lawyers to file a fee request with the Department of Labor and provides that no fee shall be paid until there has been a final decision on the claim.

State statutes placing limits on attorneys fees are also common, for example, worker's compensation laws, see Mack v. City of Minneapolis, 333 N.W.2d 744 (Minn.1983) (noting that almost all worker's compensation laws impose limits on attorney's fees). Discipline proceedings for violating such limits include Louisiana State Bar Association v. Thalheim, 504 So.2d 822 (La.1987); Hudock v. Virginia State Bar, 233 Va. 390, 355 S.E.2d 601 (1987). Many states have general limits on the percentage lawyers may charge as contingency fees: some states now set ceilings on the percent in all personal injury cases; others in medical malpractice cases only. See the note on p. 510 below. Exceeding these limits is charging an illegal fee.

Contracting With the Client for the Rights to the Client's Story

Another prohibited fee arrangement is a contract that gives the lawyer the literary or movie rights to the client's story. See DR 5–104(B) and M.R. 1.8(d). The reason for prohibiting such arrangements is that what makes "good copy" does not necessarily make a good defense. The movie rights, for example, may be more if the client gets the death penalty than if she gets 20 years. Another problem with such arrangements is the broad advance waiver of client confidences that they imply. See the *von Bulow* case printed above in Chapter 4.

The reasons for prohibiting these contracts apply with equal force when the lawyer contracts with a third party to produce a book, movie or other portrayal based on information relating to the representation, and M.R. 1.8(d) extends the prohibition to cover these third party contracts. Cases coming before the courts have involved convicted defendants seeking to have their convictions overturned. The claim is that the the contract created a conflict of interest for the lawyer that resulted in ineffective assistance of counsel. Courts usually respond by criticizing the contract but upholding the conviction. See, e.g., United States v. Marrera, 768 F.2d 201 (7th Cir.1985) (the contract alone is insufficient to show ineffective assistance of counsel); Dumond v. State, 294 Ark. 379, 743 S.W.2d 779 (1988). Cf. People v. Corona, 80 Cal.App. 3d 684, 145 Cal.Rptr. 894 (1978) (conviction reversed because of counsel's gross neglect of basic duties and failure to develop key defenses; an alternate ground for reversal was that the literary contract between lawyer and client created an impermissible conflict of interest).

In Maxwell v. Superior Ct. of Los Angeles, 30 Cal.3d 606, 639 P.2d 248 (1982), however, the California Supreme Court held that the defendant's constitutional right to counsel gave him the right to transfer the rights to his story to his lawyer in exchange for legal representation as long as he did so knowingly, voluntarily and after full disclosure by counsel of the risks and benefits involved in such a deal.

Many states have enacted laws that limit the extent to which a criminal defendant may profit from the story of her crime. These laws typically provide that—with the exception of a reasonable amount for attorneys fees—the proceeds from portrayals based on criminal activity are to be used to compensate the victims.

Division of Fees

M.R. 1.5(e) permits a "division of fees" among lawyers. See also DR 2–107(A). For enforcement of a contract between lawyers governing division of fee between them, see Stissi v. Interstate & Ocean Transp. Co., 814 F.2d 848 (2d Cir.1987). Compare In re "Agent Orange" Product Liability Litigation, 818 F.2d 210 (2d Cir.1987) (invalidating agreement among lawyers that provided disincentive to adequate representation of class).

Fee Arbitration

The Comment to M.R. 1.5 provides: "If a procedure has been established for resolution of fee disputes, such as an arbitration or mediation procedure established by the bar, the lawyer should conscientiously consider submitting to it."

No state requires a client to arbitrate a fee dispute, presumably because such a rule would violate the client's constitutional right to a jury trial. But some require the lawyer to arbitrate if the client requests it. Anderson v. Elliott, 555 A.2d 1042 (Me.1989), upheld a Maine bar rule requiring lawyers to arbitrate fee claims at the client's request. The court rejected the claim that the rule violated the lawyer's right to a jury trial:

> . . . [The] thesis that a suit to recover a [lawyer's] fee is just like any other suit for money damages for breach of contract . . . ignores the uniqueness of the attorney's relation to the court and to the client. . . .

> . . .

> The attorney stands in a relationship of trust and confidence, both to the client and to the court. The overriding responsibility and authority of the Supreme Judicial Court to superintend that professional relationship is a complete answer to the constitutional challenge to Maine's client-initiated [mandatory fee arbitration system].

Id. at 1047, 1050.

Also see In re LiVolsi, 85 N.J. 576, 428 A.2d 1268 (1981); and Kelley Drye & Warren v. Murray Indus., Inc., 623 F.Supp. 522 (D.N.J.1985) (both upholding New Jersey's client-initiated mandatory fee arbitration system).

Should the courts enforce a contract between lawyer and client that requires the client to submit to arbitration in the event of a fee dispute? Once a lawyer and client submit to arbitration should the result be binding? In California neither party is bound if either appeals the decision, unless there is a prior agreement to be bound. In New Jersey both parties are bound.

Consider Marino v. Tagaris, 395 Mass. 397, 480 N.E.2d 286 (1985). The lawyer, Marino, billed Tagaris $66,570.47 for representing her in a divorce proceeding. Tagaris questioned the bill and agreed to submit to arbitration:

> [T]he client signed the standard form petition for arbitration . . . in which she agreed to be legally bound by the decision of the arbitrators [who were lawyers in divorce practice]. [She] also received two documents from the board . . . "A Guide to the Fee Arbitration Board" (guide) and "Rules of the Legal Fee Arbitration Board of Massachusetts Bar Association" (rules).

> [At the hearing, t]he client appeared without counsel, relying on the representation in the guide that "these proceedings are informal," as well as oral representations made to her by the board's staff before the hearing that she would not need an attorney. The client claims that she and her father spoke for not more than two minutes, followed by a lengthy presentation by the attorney. After the attorney had presented his case, the client and her father sought to make additional statements, but were not permitted to do so, allegedly because the arbitrators were "running behind schedule."

> [The arbitrators decided that the lawyer was entitled to the full amount of the bill.] The client did not seek to vacate the arbitration award in court, allegedly because she did not realize that she had such a right. . . . [The client has thirty days to move to vacate.] After the . . . thirty day[s], the attorney brought an action to confirm the . . . award. [Judgment was entered for the lawyer] and the client appealed.

Id. at 288.

The court reversed the award on two grounds: that the information provided the client did not adequately inform her of her rights to appeal; and that the arbitration proceedings were not adequately described to her. In discussing the second of these grounds, the court said:

> . . . There is nothing inherently wrong with encouraging self-representation by clients. Nevertheless, a client who is unsophisticated in legal proceedings and is not given an adequate advance understanding of the hearing may well be intimidated by being virtually the only nonattorney present. Since such a person also lacks the legal background to know the factors relevant in mounting a successful challenge to the . . . fee, this might lead to a

perception by the client that she is on an unequal footing with the attorney. . . .

> . . . [I]n conversations with the board's staff prior to the hearing, it was stressed to her that she did not need an attorney to represent her, since the hearing was "informal." Similarly, the guide states that "these proceedings are informal." These broad statements do little to aid client's understanding of what is to take place. Moreover, the lay person's expectations probably differ substantially from the attorney's awareness that an "informal" hearing merely means that the strict rules of evidence will be relaxed.

Id. at 289–290. (emphasis added).

The court in *Marino* stated that these problems could be cured by fully informing the client in advance on the nature of the proceedings. What information could be provided? Does the client need to be told that bringing a lawyer would be helpful? If so, what is the advantage that arbitration has for the client over a lawsuit? Can the proceedings be made "informal" in a lay person's understanding of that word? Would non-lawyers on the panel cure the problem? Is the disparity of the parties' positions in the process described in *Marino* "a perception" problem or a reality? Some bar associations include lay persons on their arbitration panels. See Devine, Mandatory Arbitration of Attorney–Client Fee Dispute: A Concept Whose Time Has Come, 14 U.Tol.L. Rev. 1205 (1986) (summarizing the various state procedures and enforcement mechanisms).

Client Confidentiality in Fee Disputes

A lawyer may reveal client confidences to collect a fee or establish a defense in a dispute with the client over the fee. See DR 4–101(c)(4) and M.R. 1.6(b)(2) and the discussion of this issue in Chapter 4 below. The Comment to M.R. 1.6 explains:

> A lawyer entitled to a fee is permitted by paragraph (b)(2) to prove the services rendered in an action to collect it. This aspect of the rule expresses the principle that the beneficiary of a fiduciary relationship may not exploit it to the detriment of the fiduciary.
> . . . [T]he lawyer must make every effort practicable to avoid unnecessary disclosure of information relating to a representation, to limit disclosure to those having the need to know it, and to obtain protective orders or make other arrangements minimizing the risk of disclosure.

Should a lawyer advise a client that confidential information may be disclosed if the client proceeds to challenge the lawyer's fee? See Lindenbaum v. State Bar, 26 Cal.2d 565, 160 P.2d 9 (1945) (improper to threaten client with disclosure).

Contingent Fees

Generally

In a contingent fee arrangement the lawyer is compensated only if a positive result is obtained for the client—the fee is contingent on the result. A contingent fee is usually calculated as a percentage of the client's recovery, but a contract calling for the lawyer to receive a fixed amount if the client prevailed would also be a contingent fee contract. In most personal injury cases, the plaintiff's lawyer's fee is contingent, but contingent fees are not limited to personal injury work. See *Boston and Maine,* supra, 778 F.2d 890 (1st Cir.1985) (contingent fee in an eminent domain case). Contingent fees are common in tax refund practice, suits challenging wills, debt collection cases and class action suits for damages.

While contingent fee arrangements are common for a plaintiff, they are sometimes used in civil cases by the defendant. In *Brobeck,* supra, see note on p. 480, for example, Telex was in the position of a defendant with respect to the counterclaims against it. See also Dunham v. Bentley, 103 Iowa 136, 72 N.W. 437 (1897) (defendant agreed to pay thirty percent of her interest in any estate property that the lawyer successfully protected from creditor's claims). In Wunschel v. Clabaugh, 291 N.W.2d 331 (Iowa 1980), the court held invalid a contingent fee contract by a defendant in a tort damages case that calculated the defense lawyer's fee as a percentage of the difference between the amount of the plaintiff's prayer for relief and the amount actually recovered by the plaintiff. The court reasoned that a prayer is often exaggerated for strategic purposes; that it is misleading to suggest that the difference between the prayer and actual recovery is due to the defense lawyer's skills; and that a reasonable client adequately informed would not agree to a fee calculated on this basis.

Contingent fees in this country originally were considered illegal as a form of champerty. See Note, Lawyer's Tight Rope—Use and Abuse of Fees, 41 Cornell L.Q. 683, 685–6 (1956); and Radin, Maintenance by Champerty, 24 Calif.L.Rev. 48 (1935). They are still prohibited in Great Britain and many other countries, although in 1988 both the English Bar, constituted of Barristers, and the Law Society, constituted of Solicitors, in Great Britain were reconsidering whether to allow what they call "no win, no fee." See London Times, July 12, 1988. In the United States, they are now universally accepted; Maine, the last state to accept contingent fees, lifted its prohibition in 1965. At first, acceptance was grudging—contingency fees were disreputable although not illegal. See, e.g., Rooney v. Second Avenue R.R., 18 N.Y. 368 (1858). See generally F. MacKinnon, Contingent Fees (1964). The disrepute was based on two fears: that lawyers would be tempted to use illegal or unethical means to win judgments, for example, manufacturing evidence or bringing frivolous suits in the hopes of coercing a settlement; and that lawyers would put their own interests before those of the client, e.g., settling a case early, thereby guaranteeing the lawyer the greatest return for the smallest amount of work, when the client would be better served by pursuing the matter through trial.

There remain some types of cases in which they are prohibited, notably divorce and criminal work. See the notes below on pp. 507–509. Contingent fees are most often justified as a necessary means of broadening access to justice, allowing those otherwise unable to afford counsel to obtain representation in the courts. They are often referred to as "the poor man's door to the courthouse." See, e.g., Arnold v. The Northern Trust Co., 116 Ill. 157, 506 N.E.2d 1279, 1281 (1987); In the Matter of a Member of the State Bar of Arizona John F. Swartz, 141 Ariz. 266, 686 P.2d 1236, 1242 (1984). In countries that prohibit contingent fees, lawyers are paid by public funds to represent indigent civil litigants. What is wrong with that solution?

The courts generally will enforce a "usual" contingent fee agreement between parties who bargained and contracted. Unusual ones are scrutinized. If the court wishes to approve the contract, it says its review is based on the circumstances at the time the contract was signed. See, e.g., *Brobeck*, discussed on p. 480 above. If the court wishes to reject the contract, it says its review is based on all the circumstances, i.e., as events evolved. Compare *Brobeck* and *Boston & Maine*, discussed on p. 481 above, with McKenzie Const., Inc. v. Maynard, 758 F.2d 97 (3d Cir.1985), involving a contingent fee for recovery of money owed by the Government on a construction contract. The attorney agreed to take ⅓ of the recovery plus expenses, which ended up coming to $65,000 or $790 per hour. The trial court ordered the contract enforced, but the Court of Appeals ordered the contract reexamined in view of the situation as it evolved.

The courts are inclined to closer scrutiny when the client is unsophisticated, particularly if the contingent fee is substantial and the work legally elementary. See, e.g., Randolph v. Schuyler, 284 N.C. 496, 201 S.E.2d 833 (1974).

The court on its own motion may review a contingent fee arrangement, at least if the client is entitled to special protection of the court. See, e.g., Schlesinger v. Teitelbaum, 475 F.2d 137 (3d Cir.1973) (client was a seaman); Cappel v. Adams, 434 F.2d 1278 (5th Cir.1970) (clients were children); Dunn v. H.K. Porter Co., 602 F.2d 1105 (3d Cir.1979) (class action suits).

Continuing Criticism of Contingent Fees

Criticism of contingent fees continues. The argument that they encourage frivolous suits is still used. See, e.g., Roa v. Lodi, 37 Cal.3d 920, 211 Cal.Rptr. 77, 695 P.2d 164, 170–71 (1985): "The legislature may also have imposed limits on contingency fees in [medical malpractice cases] as a means of deterring attorneys from either instituting frivolous suits or encouraging their clients to hold out for unrealistically high settlements." The court in *Roa* found such a rationale reasonable and upheld the limits.

Another criticism is that contingency fees create inevitable conflicts between the interests of lawyer and client. The rationale for this criticism is laid out in the following excerpt.

DOUGLAS E. ROSENTHAL, LAWYER AND CLIENT: WHO'S IN CHARGE? (1974)
pp. 96–112.*

The single source of pressure upon the lawyer most likely to affect adversely the client's interest, and which can most easily be documented, is the strain of prolonged litigation and the economics of case preparation. Simply put, a quick settlement is often in the lawyer's financial interest, while waiting the insurer out is often in the client's financial interest. To understand how this can be, consider . . . how a plaintiff attorney's time might plausibly be spent on a single medium-value claim, raising no special problems, where the attorney is experienced and very conscientious in case preparation. Two competing pressures affect the lawyer's motivation to terminate the case: on the one hand, the sooner he settles, the less effort expended pursuing the claim; on the other hand, given the reluctance of most insurers to make generous early settlements the longer he holds out the greater the recovery he can anticipate. If attorneys billed their clients on an hourly basis, the lawyer's motive for early settlement would be canceled. This, however, is almost never done. Instead, the client pays a fee contingent upon the eventual recovery. If there is no recovery, there is no fee; with some recovery, a large percentage of it goes to the attorney as a fee. . . .

.   .   .

The widespread assumption that the contingent fee makes the lawyer a "partner" of the client in his claim with complete mutuality of interest in the ultimate case disposition is, in dollars and cents, simply not true. To see why, let us add some details to the hypothetical medium-sized claim, not unlike several made by the sampled clients. Let us value the attorney's work time at $40 an hour (a conservative figure since approximately $20 of this figure usually goes for office overhead) and assume that he is both efficient and hard working and puts in eight productive hours per work day. Assume further that the defendant's insurer's claims adjuster has formulated the following settlement policy: (1) to make an initial settlement offer of $2,000 during the first three months after the accident; (2) to raise it to $3,000 just prior to a scheduled examination before trial (about one year after the accident); and (3) to make a final offer of $4,000 during the final pretrial negotiation (about three years after the accident). Assume further that the plaintiff's lawyer is reasonably confident that he can get a jury verdict if the case goes to trial and that, if tried, the verdict would be for about $8,000. Finally, assume (as is frequently the situation) that the attorney charges the client the maximum fee permitted under the Appellate Division rules. Table 4.2 shows the relative returns that the attorney and his client will realize at each of the four termination stages. In the given case, the lawyer's financial interest lies in quick settlement at the discounted early offer of $2,000. The client's financial interest lies in going to trial. A lawyer who literally made his client's interest his own, in more than a few of these cases, would quickly be out of business.

Table 4.2: Relative Returns to Lawyer and Client at Each Recovery Stage

Time after Accident	Gross Recovery	Lawyer's Fee	Lawyer's Costs	Lawyer's Net	Client's Net
3 months	$2,000	$ 900	$ 160	$ 740	$1,100
1 year	3,000	1,300	1,120	180	1,700
3 years	4,000	1,650	2,400	—750	2,350
trial	8,000	3,050	4,480	—1,430	4,950

. . .

. . . Faced with an economic crunch, even after weeding out the thin cases and utilizing economies of specialization, the ethical and competent attorney has four realistic options for proceeding with the claim: (1) He can cut corners in preparing the case. (2) He can build his fee by charging disbursements to the client. (3) He can persuade the client that a discounted early settlement is in his best interest. (4) He can bring the existing interest conflict to the client's attention and negotiate a compromise claims strategy. Lawyers employ various combinations of these options in their work, although the fourth is not used frequently. The first three of these options for making the economics of representation feasible put the lawyer in direct conflict with his client's interest—without making the client aware of the fact.

. . .

When faced with an economic interest that competes with the client's, most attorneys employ the device of preparing the client to accept less than he anticipates and persuading him that it is in his best interest to do so—"cooling the client out." Cooling the client out is not per se good or bad. Most lawyers justify the practice because, they claim, most clients expect to become rich out of their claims. Where this unrealistic expectation is indeed held, the client must be disabused to forestall inevitable disappointment. However, interviews indicate that some clients have lost the "pot of gold" mentality by the time they reach the lawyer. For many of them, being cooled out by their attorney is less justifiable as a reality principle. Instead, it makes sense only as a way to make the case disposition economically feasible for the attorney. If the lawyer can convince the client that holding out for a trial or pretrial last-ditch settlement offer is dangerous, he can manage the client into an early discounted settlement. This may well be the main reason why a majority of clients receive a smaller recovery than the panel evaluation of their case worth.

. . .

. . . The inexorability of the economic conflict of interest between lawyer and client in so many cases, raises a serious question about the appropriateness of the traditional ideal that an ethical and competent lawyer can and will make the client's interest his own. Goffman puts the matter as follows:

> Performers often foster the impression that they have ideal motives . . . and ideal qualifications for the role and that it was not necessary for them to suffer any indignities, insults, and humiliations, or make any tacitly understood "deals" in order to acquire the role. . . . Reinforcing these ideal impressions there is a kind of "rhetoric of training" whereby . . . licensing bodies require practitioners to absorb a mystical range and period of training, in part to maintain a monopoly, but in part to foster the impression that the licensed practitioner is someone who has been reconstituted by his learning experience and is now set apart from other men.[27] . . .

Questions and Comments

Do the provisions of M.R. 1.7(b), which require consent after full disclosure, adequately deal with the problems raised by Rosenthal? What information should a lawyer provide under 1.7(b) before advising the client to accept an early settlement of a claim covered by a contingent fee contract?

Contingent fees are also criticized as a means to charge excessive fees to unwitting clients. The theory of a contingent fee is that a lawyer will agree to assume the risk of no fee in exchange for the chance to make more than in a fixed fee situation, assuming the client prevails. The problem is that lawyers have superior knowledge of the risks involved. Critics contend that many of the cases in which lawyers charge the customary one-third of recovery are cases where recovery is for all practical purposes assured. In The Committee on Legal Ethics of the West Virginia State Bar v. Tatterson, 352 S.E.2d 107, 113–14 (W.Va.1986), the court upheld discipline of a lawyer who had charged a thirty-three percent contingency fee for settling a claim to the life insurance proceeds due the client upon her husband's death:

> Courts have generally insisted that a contingent fee be truly contingent. . . . In the absence of any real risk, an attorney's purportedly contingent fee which is grossly disproportionate to the amount of work required is a "clearly excessive fee" within the meaning of [DR] 2–106(A). See Florida Bar v. Moriber, 314 So.2d 145, 146–49 (Fla.1975) (33⅓% of moneys due to client upon mother's death; layman could have performed same services as attor-

27. Goffman, The Presentation of Self in Everyday Life, p. 46.

ney; major funds passed to client by operation of law); In re Teichner, 104 Ill.2d 150, 153–54, 160–63, 470 N.E.2d 972, 973–74, 977–78 (1984) (25% of group life insurance; insurer paid proceeds routinely without question; attorney's claimed services were "artificial" and "exaggerated") . . .

See also Attorney Grievance Commission v. Kemp, 303 Md. 664, 496 A.2d 672 (1985) (contingent fee improper under a guaranteed health coverage plan or a no-fault automobile insurance plan); In re Kennedy, 472 A.2d 1317 (Del.1984) (50% of disability workers' compensation to which there was a clear entitlement); Harmon v. Pugh, 38 N.C.App. 438, 248 S.E.2d 421 (1978) (20% of life insurance is excessive when lawyer's service consisted of writing to get medical information and autopsy report).

The Professional Rules on Contingent Fees

Contingent fees are given little specific attention by the Model Code. DR 5–103(A)(2) allows them as an exception to the general prohibition to acquiring a propriety interest in litigation; DR 2–106(B) (8) says that whether a fee is contingent or fixed should be a factor in considering its reasonableness; and DR 2–106(C) prohibits them in criminal defense work. EC 2–20 states that they are "rarely justified" in domestic relation cases.

M.R. 1.5(c) specifically authorizes contingency fees where not prohibited by 1.5(d) or other law, but requires that all contingency fees be in writing. Under M.R. 1.5(c), the writing must include:

the method by which the fee is to be determined, including the percentage or percentages that shall accrue to the lawyer in the event of settlement, trial or appeal, litigation, and other expenses to be deducted from the recovery, and whether such expenses are to be deducted before or after the contingent fee is calculated.

M.R. 1.5(c) also requires the lawyer to provide the client with a written statement upon completion of the representation detailing the outcome, the client's share, the lawyer's share, and how the division of proceeds was calculated.

Should the rules require that all fee contracts be in writing? That the lawyer relate the proposed fee to the factors specified in M.R. 1.5(a)? As adopted in some states, Rule 1.5(b) provides: "When the lawyer has not regularly represented the client, the basis or rate of the fee shall be communicated to the client in writing, before or within a reasonable time after commencing the representation."

The ABA's version of 1.5(b) says such an agreement shall be "preferably in writing."

The Prohibition on Contingent Fees in Divorce Cases

The rationale for prohibiting contingent fees in divorce cases is that it contravenes the strong public interest in preserving marriages because such a fee makes it less likely that the lawyers will urge reconciliation. See, e.g., Florida Bar v. Winn, 208 So.2d 809 (Fla.1968); In re Fisher, 15 Ill.2d 139, 153 N.E.2d 832 (1958); Baskerville v. Baskerville, 246 Minn. 496, 75 N.W.2d 762 (1956); McCarthy v. Santangelo, 137 Conn. 410, 78 A.2d 240 (1951). Divorce itself used to be regarded as almost against public policy and in many states usually could be obtained only upon proof of criminal misconduct or adultery. A contingent fee was considered an unduly dangerous inducement to legal dissolution of marriage. The prohibition undoubtedly worked to the detriment of women, who in the typical marriage held little property or income-producing capacity and therefore lacked means to pay a fixed fee. In most marriages, this meant the male partner had greater freedom to dissolve the relationship and was at less financial risk in doing so than he would otherwise have been. On the other hand, a contingent fee deters the lawyer from facilitating reconciliation, for that would eliminate the division of property from which the fee could be paid. Moreover, in most jurisdictions today the impecunious spouse, still usually the wife, can require that the other party pay attorneys' fees, including a part payment at the beginning of the litigation. See C. Wolfram, Modern Legal Ethics § 9.4.4 (1986). Compare Marriage of Gonzales, 51 Cal.App.3d 340, 124 Cal.Rptr. 278 (1975). Is reconciliation always a good to be encouraged?

The interest in encouraging reconciliation does not explain cases that disallow contingent fees in actions to modify or enforce divorce agreements. See, e.g., Licciardi v. Collins, 180 Ill.App.3d 1051, 536 N.E.2d 840 (1989) (contingent fee unethical and therefore void in action to modify a divorce decree seven years after its entry).

If a lawyer takes a divorce case on a contingent basis, most states allow the lawyer to recover on the basis of *quantum meruit.* See *Baskerville* supra. But see *Licciardi,* supra (no *quantum meruit* recovery). For an argument that contingent fees should be allowed in divorce cases, see Comment, Professional Responsibility—Contingent Fees in Domestic Relations Actions: Equal Freedom to Contract for the Domestic Relations Bar, 62 N.C.L.Rev. 381 (1984).

The Prohibition of Contingent Fees in Criminal Defense Work

The rationale for prohibiting contingent fees for prosecuting a criminal case is based on the special obligations of the prosecutor to see justice done. See M.R. 3.8 on the Special Responsibilities of a Prosecutor and the Comment; and Rule 3–1.1, ABA Standards Relating to the Administration of Criminal Justice, The Prosecution Function. *Cf. People ex rel. Clancy v. Superior Court,* discussed below. Contingent fees encourage prosecutions based on the likelihood of conviction regardless of whether the conviction would be just. Can a similar argument be made to justify prohibiting contingent fees for defense lawyers?

All states prohibit contingent fees for the defense of a criminal case. However, the fact that the lawyer's fee was contingent is not enough to establish a claim for ineffective assistance of counsel in a postconviction proceeding for a new trial. See, e.g., People v. Winkler, 71 N.Y.2d 592, 523 N.E.2d 485 (1988); Downs v. Florida, 453 So.2d 1102 (Fla.1984); Schoonover v. Kansas, 218 Kan. 377, 543 P.2d 881 (1976). But see United States ex rel. Simon v. Murphy, 349 F.Supp. 818 (E.D. Pa.1972) (new trial granted where counsel represented defendant on contingent fee basis, which provided no fee if a guilty plea was entered, and counsel failed to communicate in a timely fashion to defendant the prosecutor's offer of a plea bargain to a lesser offense and persistently advised defendant not to plead guilty). In *Schoonover,* supra, while the trial judge refused the defendant a new trial, he referred the lawyer to the state bar, which imposed discipline. In re Complaint made against Myron S. Steere, 217 Kan. 276, 536 P.2d 54 (1975).

The prohibition against contingent fees in criminal cases may be a formalism. Private attorneys retained in criminal cases almost invariably demand prepayment of their anticipated fee.

Should contingent fees be prohibited for government lawyers prosecuting civil enforcement claims for the same reasons that they are disallowed in criminal cases? Government employment of lawyers on a contingent fee basis has generated few cases, typically involving part-time government lawyers or lawyers hired on a one-time basis to prosecute a single action. Full-time government lawyers are compensated on a salary basis so the issue of contingent fees does not arise.

In People ex rel. Clancy v. The Superior Court of Riverside County, 39 Cal.3d 740, 218 Cal.Rptr. 24, 705 P.2d 347, 352 (1985), the court held that a contingent fee is improper in certain kinds of government civil cases. "[T]here is a class of civil actions that demands the representative of the government be absolutely neutral. This requirement precludes the use in such cases of a contingent fee arrangement." The court held that such cases include: eminent domain actions where the government lawyer's duty is to conduct "a sober inquiry into values, designed to strike a just balance between the economic interests of the public and those of the landowner . . . ."; and actions to abate a public nuisance, where "on the one hand is the interest of the people in ridding their city of an obnoxious or dangerous condition; on the other hand is the interest of the landowner in using his property as he wishes." Id. Could the same point be made about "private attorney general" actions?

Prohibiting Contingent Fees in Other Cases

Some states prohibit contingent fees in situations such as lobbying, see Maggio, Lobbying—Multistate Statutory Scheme, 38 Notre Dame L.Rev. 79, 85–6 (1962); or serving as lawyer for an executor of an estate, see, e.g., Estate of Hastings, 108 Cal.App.2d 713, 239 P.2d 684 (1952). But see, e.g., Haverstock v. Wolf, 491 F.Supp. 447 (D.Minn.1980) (public policy does not bar contingent fees when client is contesting a will).

Should contingent fees be prohibited when the client is a minor? See M.R. 1.14 on Clients Under a Disability and the Comment.

In Arnold v. Northern Trust Co., Guardian, 116 Ill.2d 157, 506 N.E. 2d 1279, 1281 (1987), the court refused to require advance court approval of a contingent fee in personal injury cases where the plaintiff is a minor, holding such contracts would be enforced unless the terms were unreasonable: "A court can do nothing for a minor not before it, and injured minors are as likely as adults to require the key to the courthouse which contingent-fee provides. If [they] were uniformly unavailable [to] minors . . ., the likely result would be to deprive many minors of quality legal representation."

Contingent Fee Schedules

A number of states have enacted so-called "tort reform legislation" as a means of curbing tort suits. These statutes typically prescribe maximum fee schedules for lawyers. In some states, for example New Jersey and New York, the maximum fee schedules apply to all personal injury cases handled on a contingent basis; in others, the fee schedules are limited to a particular type of suit, most commonly medical malpractice.

The fee schedules vary in the particulars, but generally allow for a sliding scale. For example, under California's Medical Injury Compensation Reform Act of 1975 (MICRA), Calif.Bus. and Prof.Code § 6146, the plaintiff's lawyer in a medical malpractice case may charge no more than:

40 percent	of first $50,000 of client's recovery
33⅓ percent	of next $50,000
25 percent	of next $500,000
15 percent	of any amount exceeding $600,000

Compare Florida's system, which does not drop off to 30% until the client's recovery is between $1–2 million dollars, and allows the lawyer to collect 20% of any recovery in excess of $2 million dollars. See Florida Bar re Amendment to the Code of Professional Responsibility, 494 So.2d 960 (Fla.1986). Under Florida's rule if the defendant admits liability and requests a trial on damages only, the percentages for lawyers' fees are lower: 33⅓ of any recovery up to $1 million through trial; 20% of any recovery in excess of $1–2 million; 15% of any recovery in excess of $2 million.

Some federal laws specify a single maximum percentage fee no matter how large the client's recovery. For example, the Federal Tort Claims Act allows fees no greater than 25% of any recovery once a case has been filed and 20% of any recovery prior to filing. It is easy to see how the Federal Tort Claims Act would encourage lawyer's to file suit to gain a greater part of the recovery. What incentives do the California and Florida systems provide?

The courts have been almost unanimous in upholding these fee schedules. See, e.g., Bernier v. Burris, 113 Ill.2d 219, 497 N.E.2d 763

(1986); Roa v. Lodi Medical Group, Inc., 37 Cal.3d 920, 211 Cal.Rptr. 77, 695 P.2d 164 (1985); Johnson v. St. Vincent Hospital, Inc., 273 Ind. 374, 404 N.E.2d 585 (1980); American Trial Lawyers v. New Jersey Supreme Court, 66 N.J. 258, 330 A.2d 350 (1974); and Gair v. Peck, 6 N.Y.2d 97, 160 N.E.2d 43 (1959), whether they apply only to medical malpractice case as in *Bernier, Roa* and *Johnson* or more broadly. But see Carson v. Maurer, 120 N.H. 925, 424 A.2d 825 (1980), striking down a New Hampshire law that limited plaintiffs' rights in medical malpractice cases and imposed a fee schedule for such actions. Also see Heller v. Frankston, 504 Pa. 528, 475 A.2d 1291 (1984) (striking down statute requiring arbitration of medical malpractice claims and with it the provisions limiting attorneys fees in such cases). The latter two decisions have not been followed in other states.

In sustaining the maximum fee schedule, the Florida court in Florida Bar re Amendment, 494 So.2d 960, 964 (Fla.1986) also provided that the clients may cancel any contingent contract within three days of its execution and required lawyers to provide clients with an elaborate statement of their rights:

STATEMENT OF CLIENT'S RIGHTS

Before you, the prospective client, arrange a contingency fee agreement with a lawyer, you should understand this Statement of your rights as a client. This Statement is not part of the actual contract between you and your lawyer, but as a prospective client, you should be aware of these rights:

1. There is no legal requirement that a lawyer charge a client a set fee or percentage of money recovered in a case. You, the client, have the right to talk with the lawyer about the proposed fee and to bargain about the rate or percentage as in any other contract. If you do not reach an agreement with one lawyer you may talk with other lawyers. . . .

3. Before hiring a lawyer, you, the client, have the right to know about the lawyer's education, training and experience. If you ask, the lawyer should tell you specifically about his or her actual experience dealing with cases similar to yours. If you ask, the lawyer should provide information about special training or knowledge and give you this information in writing if you request it.

4. Before signing a contingency fee contract with you, a lawyer must advise you whether he or she intends to handle your case alone or whether other lawyers will be helping with the case. If your lawyer intends to refer the case to other lawyers he or she should tell you what kind of fee sharing arrangement will be made with the other lawyers. If lawyers from different law firms will represent you, at least one lawyer from each firm must sign the contingency fee contract. . . .

7. You, the client, have the right to be told by your lawyer about possible adverse consequences if you lose the case. Those

adverse consequences might include money which you might have to pay to your lawyer for costs, and liability you might have for attorney's fees to the other side. . . .

10. You, the client, have the right to make the final decision regarding settlement of a case. Your lawyer must notify you of all offers of settlement before and after the trial. Offers during the trial must be immediately communicated and you should consult with your lawyer regarding whether to accept a settlement. However, you must make the final decision to accept or reject a settlement. . . .

Why is such a statement required only in contingent fee cases? Compare M.R. 1.5. The Florida statement has 11 paragraphs. Would it be more understandable if it covered fewer eventualities and were a lot shorter? Does a client need a lawyer to deal with her lawyer? Why not?

Structured Settlements

Large personal injury claims may be resolved by a "structured settlement." Essentially, this is a plan of payments over time instead of full cash payment. Typically, the plan calls for substantial cash up front, in contemplation that this will be used to pay the lawyer's contingent fee share, and an annuity to provide periodic payments to the claimant over a term of years. A structured settlement involves a major investment decision and inherent conflict between the lawyer and the client. Questions can arise whether the lawyer adequately counselled the client about the investment aspects of the settlement and about the existence and implications of the conflict between them. For a case involving malpractice liability in mishandling a structured settlement, see Perez v. Pappas, 98 Wn.2d 835, 659 P.2d 475 (1983). See also Meyer, Settling in Your Client's Interest, Calif.Lawyer, July, 1988, p. 53.

C. Scope of the Lawyer's Authority

Introductory Note

M.R. 1.2(a) states:

A lawyer shall abide by a client's decision concerning the objectives of representation, subject to paragraphs (c), (d) and (e), and shall consult with the client as to the means by which they are to be pursued. A lawyer shall abide by the client's decision whether to accept an offer of settlement of a matter. In a criminal case, the lawyer shall abide by the client's decision, after consultation, with the lawyer, as to a plea to be entered, whether to waive jury trial and whether the client will testify.

M.R. 1.2(c) says a lawyer may limit the objectives of representation if the client consents after consultation; 1.2(d) prohibits the lawyer from counseling or otherwise assisting a client to commit a fraud or crime;

1.2(e) states that if a client expects assistance prohibited by the rules of professional conduct, the lawyer should explain the limits imposed by the rules. The Model Code of Professional Responsibility has no counterpart to M.R. 1.2. But see EC 7-7 (on the client's right to make decisions "affecting the merits of the cause or substantially prejudicing the rights of the client"); EC 7-8 (on the client's right to decide whether to forego legally available means or objectives because of nonlegal factors); and DR 7-101 (lawyer shall not fail to seek the lawful objectives of the client except that she may avoid offensive tactics without violating this rule). Also see the Comment to M.R. 1.2.

INTERNATIONAL TELEMETER CORP. v. TELEPROMPTER CORP.

United States Court of Appeals, Second Circuit, 1979.
592 F.2d 49.

LUMBARD, CIRCUIT JUDGE:

In this case, originally brought as a suit for patent infringement, defendant Teleprompter Corporation appeals from a judgment of the district court, Motley, J., filed on February 21, 1978 after a bench trial and amended March 7, 1978, insofar as it (1) directs Teleprompter to pay plaintiff International Telemeter Corporation (ITC) $245,000 plus interest and costs for Teleprompter's breach of an agreement settling patent litigation, and (2) dismisses without prejudice Teleprompter's counterclaim for a declaration of the patent's invalidity.

The parties agree that New York law governs the enforceability of the settlement agreement, which was negotiated, consummated, and to be performed in New York, and which was explicitly made subject to New York law. The issues are (1) whether there was a binding settlement agreement enforceable against Teleprompter, and (2) whether enforcement of the settlement agreement violates the public policy enunciated in Lear v. Adkins, 395 U.S. 653, 89 S.Ct. 1902, 23 L.Ed.2d 610 (1969). As Teleprompter has not persuaded us that the district court erred in finding that the parties had consummated a binding settlement agreement or that this agreement violates the policy of *Lear,* supra, we affirm.

I

The relevant facts are undisputed. The present action arises from a suit for patent infringement commenced by ITC on March 15, 1968 against several defendants in the District Court for the Western District of Washington. On September 1, 1970, Teleprompter intervened as a defendant and counterclaimant in the action, seeking, *inter alia,* declarations of patent invalidity and noninfringement. Following the dismissal of several claims and counterclaims, by 1973 the only parties remaining in the litigation were ITC, Teleprompter, and Philip D. Hamlin and Hamlin International Corporation (collectively, the "Hamlin defendants").

In February, 1973, William Bresnan, then President of Teleprompter, wrote to Arthur Groman, a Los Angeles attorney, asking if ITC wished to "discuss . . . a [negotiated] resolution of the patent litigation." On February 9, 1973, Groman responded by sending to Bresnan a draft license agreement proposed by ITC as a basis for settling the litigation. The draft agreement provided for minimum royalties of $75,000 for the first three years and damages for past infringement totalling $240,000. Bresnan turned down the proposed agreement but suggested that a meeting be arranged to discuss possible settlement.

The requested settlement meeting took place in New York City in April, 1973. Present on behalf of Teleprompter were William K. Kerr, Jules P. Kirsch, and Bresnan himself. Present on behalf of ITC were Morton Amster, Thomas Harrison, and Kenneth Merklen. All but Bresnan were acting as lawyers. The first meeting proved inconclusive.

In early July, 1973, after a further settlement proposal of Bresnan made on May 30 was found unacceptable by ITC, the parties met a second time. According to Amster, at this meeting the parties "negotiated the terms of the settlement." The parties assigned to Amster the task of preparing the initial drafts of the agreement, which included the following terms: an aggregate payment by Teleprompter of $245,000 in settlement of all claims against Teleprompter and the Hamlin defendants, the licensing of Teleprompter and the Hamlin defendants under the disputed patent, the dismissal of the pending litigation, and the issuance of a press release. These basic terms were never altered during the subsequent negotiations.

On July 26, 1973, Amster sent Kerr a copy of the draft agreements together with a proposed schedule for payments totalling $245,000.

There followed a series of minor revisions and exchanges of revised drafts. Amster, as attorney for ITC, and Kirsch, as attorney for Teleprompter, agreed to final changes at a meeting held on August 28 or September 7, 1973. Thereafter, on September 10, 1973, "clean drafts" were forwarded by Amster to Kirsch. On September 26, 1973, Amster sent to Kirsch copies of the Teleprompter and Hamlin license agreements and copies of the stipulation and order of dismissal to be filed in the patent lawsuit pending in the Western District of Washington. In his covering letter, Amster remarked, "Hopefully we have attended to all the minor changes and the documents are in condition for execution. . . . Perhaps upon a review of the papers, you would be willing to advise your local counsel [in the Washington litigation] that the case is settled so that he and [ITC's local counsel] can advise Judge Boldt that the case is settled and that a proposed stipulation and order will be filed shortly."

On October 3, 1973, Kirsch did so advise Teleprompter's Seattle counsel, Richard Williams. That same day, Williams wrote to Judge Boldt that "the final Settlement Agreement has been transmitted to all parties for the purpose of signature . . . we should be in a position to present a Stipulation and Order of Stipulation to the Court for its consideration and entry." Williams further advised the court that the pending trial date "may be vacated." A copy of this letter was sent to Amster. If Williams overstated the parties' proximity to settlement, as Kirsch later claimed at trial, Kirsch failed to correct the allegedly mistaken impression conveyed to the trial court.

Just as the parties were finishing their work on the settlement documents, a dispute arose between Teleprompter and the Hamlin defendants over the Hamlin defendants' obligation to pay amounts claimed by Teleprompter pursuant to its intervention agreement with the Hamlin defendants. Rather than allow the settlement agreement to founder on this last minute disagreement between the defendants, Kirsch acted to secure a separate peace between Teleprompter and ITC. On October 25 and October 26, 1973, he telephoned and wrote to Amster to advise him of the falling out between Teleprompter and the Hamlin defendants and attempted to secure a settlement as to ITC and Teleprompter on precisely the same terms as those already agreed upon. In his October 26 letter, Kirsch wrote as follows to Amster:

Dear Mort:

As I advised you in our telephone discussions on Thursday and Friday, October 25 and 26, 1973, Mr. Hamlin is unwilling to pay Teleprompter the amounts due Teleprompter pursuant to the August 3, 1970 Intervention Agreement. As a consequence, *Teleprompter now wishes to settle the litigation only with respect to Teleprompter on the terms which had been agreed upon with respect to Teleprompter in the Settlement Agreement and the License Agreement which accompanied your September 26, 1973 letter, and I understand that this is agreeable with ITC.* . . .

In our telephone conversation on October 26, 1973, you and I agreed that I would revise the Settlement Agreement to limit its terms to Teleprompter only, that Teleprompter will make the payments specified in Schedule 1 to the original Settlement Agreement, that Teleprompter will execute the original ITC–Teleprompter License Agreement, and that I would revise the Stipulation and Order of Dismissal to limit dismissal of the action to Teleprompter only. . . .

Sincerely,
Jules P. Kirsch

(Emphasis added.)

Thus Kirsch's letter committed Teleprompter to a settlement on the terms "which had been agreed upon" and which were already set forth in the draft settlement papers accompanying Amster's September 26, 1973 letter. At trial, Kirsch confirmed that he had Teleprompter's authorization to send this October 26, 1973 letter. In fact, Kirsch sent a copy of this letter to Teleprompter's general counsel, Barry Simon. If this letter inaccurately conveyed Teleprompter's intent to be bound,

Simon made no effort to set the matter straight. All that remained to be done before a formal signed agreement could be executed was to eliminate mechanically all reference to the Hamlin defendants in the draft agreement.

Several important events occurred on October 29, 1973. Kirsch duly revised the settlement papers to delete all references to the Hamlin defendants and forwarded the revised documents to Amster on the morning of October 29. These were listed as follows:

1. A revised settlement agreement.

2. An unrevised Schedule 1 to the revised settlement agreement.

3. A revised stipulation and order of dismissal as to Teleprompter only.

4. An unrevised ITC–Teleprompter license agreement.

5. A revised joint announcement of settlement and dismissal of the litigation as to Teleprompter only.

Kirsch also sent a separate letter to Amster asking him to call as soon as he had finished reviewing the settlement papers "so that if there are any changes you wish to have made, we can discuss them. If necessary I can arrange for them to be made before I leave for Los Angeles this afternoon. In that way the final papers can be delivered promptly to Teleprompter for execution and returned to you." No changes were suggested by Amster. All that remained was to obtain the requisite signatures and make delivery. Consequently, that afternoon Kirsch wrote another letter to Amster, enclosing three copies of the stipulation and order of dismissal as to Teleprompter which Kirsch had signed and dated October 29, 1973. Amster also signed the stipulation and order of dismissal that afternoon, as requested by Kirsch. Kirsch also requested that Amster send a ribbon copy of the stipulation and order to ITC's Seattle, Washington counsel and return a signed electrostatic copy to Kirsch. Kirsch advised Amster that he had called Williams, Teleprompter's Seattle counsel, and that Williams would sign the stipulation upon receiving it from ITC's Seattle counsel and would then file it with the court.

That afternoon, October 29, Kirsch sent to Peter A. Gross, the assistant general counsel of Teleprompter, copies of the settlement agreement. Gross was to have these documents executed by Teleprompter and returned to Amster together with a certified check in the amount of $26,250.00 pursuant to Schedule 1 of the settlement agreement. Kirsch advised Gross that Amster would then arrange to have the signed agreements and the check delivered to ITC; duplicate signed copies of the settlement and license agreements would then be returned to Gross. Finally, Kirsch advised Gross that he was arranging to have the stipulation and order of dismissal filed in court by Teleprompter's Seattle counsel.

The following day, October 30, 1973, Teleprompter's president, Bresnan, signed the settlement agreement. Although plaintiff had demanded production of this document before trial, its existence came to light for the first time at trial during the testimony of Bresnan, after Judge Motley had overruled objections to questions concerning communications between Bresnan and Teleprompter's counsel. When the settlement agreement was first brought to him by Gross, Bresnan refused to sign without the approval of Jack Kent Cooke, Chairman of the Board and Chief Executive Officer of Teleprompter. At Gross' insistence, however, Bresnan signed the document "subject to the proviso that it would not be delivered until it had been reviewed with Mr. Cooke and also with Mr. Greene [Teleprompter's treasurer]."

That same day, October 30, Kirsch arrived in California as planned. That afternoon, he received a telephone message at his hotel, which read as follows: "Mr. Gross called. The settlement is O.K. Papers and check will go out tomorrow."

In what was apparently yet another reference to Bresnan's signing of the final agreement, on October 31, 1973, Kirsch wrote to Hamlin, advising him that "Teleprompter has decided to settle with ITC . . . a revised Settlement Agreement as between ITC and Teleprompter only and a revised Stipulation of Dismissal of the Action as to Teleprompter only have been executed." Based on communications with Teleprompter, Kirsch believed these representations to be duly authorized and accurate when made. Indeed, Kirsch sent copies of this letter to Simon and to Gross, Teleprompter's in-house counsel, and to Amster and Harrison, ITC's counsel. If this letter inaccurately conveyed the impression that a settlement had been consummated, Teleprompter did not move to correct that impression.

Thereafter, new management at Teleprompter refused to proceed with the settlement agreement. Accordingly, on November 16, 1973, Kirsch called Amster to tell him that he had been mistaken in his earlier belief that Teleprompter had agreed to the settlement with ITC and had in fact executed the settlement. Kirsch confirmed the telephone conversation in a letter of the same date which reads as follows:

Dear Mort:

This letter will confirm that in my telephone conversation with you this afternoon I advised you that since I wrote a letter to Mr. Hamlin dated October 31, 1973, a copy of which was sent to you, in which I stated that the revised Settlement Agreement had been executed, I have learned that in fact the revised Settlement Agreement was not executed. . . .

Sincerely,
Jules P. Kirsch

Kirsch's statement in this letter that the settlement agreement had never been executed conflicted not only with his prior statements, but also with Bresnan's later admission at trial that he had in fact signed the agreement. In any event, after sending this letter, Kirsch withdrew as Teleprompter's counsel in this dispute.

On November 28, 1973, Amster wrote to Kirsch stating that he had received Kirsch's November 16 letter but had nevertheless advised ITC that it had a legally enforceable agreement with Teleprompter.

. . .

The district court found that the parties had reached a final agreement as to the terms of the settlement and that both had manifested objective indications of their intent to be bound by October 29, 1973. . . .

As the district court found, the record strongly suggests that both parties would have signed prior to October 26, 1973 but for the disagreement between Teleprompter and the Hamlin defendants. The October 26 letter clearly indicates that all that remained to be done regarding the written agreement was to eliminate the now superfluous references to the Hamlin defendants. Kirsch's October 26 letter to Amster contains both an unequivocal expression of Teleprompter's intention to settle and a listing by incorporation of all the essential terms of the settlement. Although asked for his comments, Amster had none.

If there remained any doubt as to the nature of the parties' intent as of October 26, that doubt was dispelled by the events of October 29. On that day Kirsch sent to Amster for signing a complete set of settlement papers. All that remained was to have Bresnan sign the settlement agreement, to have local counsel in Seattle sign the stipulation and order of dismissal, and to file the necessary papers in court. Particularly significant, in our view, was the signing and transmittal to opposing counsel of the stipulation and order of dismissal. Teleprompter could have requested that the signed stipulation be held in escrow pending the signing and delivery of the other documents. It did not. Accordingly, Amster acted as any other reasonable person would have when he concluded that there was a binding agreement as of October 29, if not before. As the district court concluded, "these two lawyers would not have signed the stipulation unless they understood that both parties intended to be bound at that juncture and that all that remained to be done was the formalization of what had been agreed."

Subsequent communications by Teleprompter to ITC further support the district court's finding that the parties believed that a binding agreement had been consummated. On October 31, Kirsch stated in a letter to Amster that "Teleprompter had decided to settle with ITC as to Teleprompter only . . . a revised Settlement Agreement . . . and . . . Stipulation of Dismissal . . . have been executed." Teleprompter officials who authorized this communication received copies of this letter and did not disavow its contents.

. . . Teleprompter argues that Kirsch had no authority to bind Teleprompter to a settlement. Kirsch, however, was acting within the ambit of his apparent authority and ITC was entitled to rely upon

Kirsch's authority so long as there was no reason to believe that he was exceeding it. Teleprompter knew that ITC believed that Kirsch had the requisite authority and did nothing to correct this impression. In fact, ITC had no reason to think that Kirsch was exceeding his authority and Teleprompter had no reason to correct any misimpression because, as the district court found, Kirsch had full authority to negotiate and consummate a settlement. That a lawyer should have such authority is not rare. In this case, moreover, Kirsch kept Teleprompter apprised at all times of what he was doing. Teleprompter officials were sent copies of all the correspondence which the district court relied upon in finding a binding agreement. Teleprompter officials failed to disavow Kirsch's actions even when Kirsch sent them copies of his October 31 letter announcing that the settlement was executed.

The district court's decision is consistent with New York case law dealing with similar situations. . . . See generally Restatement (Second) of Contracts § 26 (Tent.Draft # 1–7 1962) ("Manifestations of assent that are in themselves sufficient to conclude a contract will not be prevented from so operating by the fact that the parties also manifested an intention to prepare and adopt a written memorial thereof; but the circumstances may show that the agreements are preliminary negotiations").

. . . The cases relied upon by the appellant are distinguishable on their facts from the case at bar. In Scheck v. Francis, 26 N.Y.2d 466, 311 N.Y.S. 841, 260 N.E.2d 493 (1970) the Court of Appeals found that the parties did not intend to be bound before signing and delivery, and further, that there was no proof that the parties had ever reached an agreement on the terms of the disputed contract. Similarly, in Schwartz v. Greenberg, 304 N.Y. 250, 107 N.E.2d 65 (1952), the Court of Appeals held that the refusal to deliver a signed agreement defeated the contract because "the parties did not intend to be bound until a written agreement had been signed and delivered." Whether or not the parties have manifested an intent to be bound must depend in each case on all the circumstances. Here the district court specifically found an intent to be bound prior to signing and delivery of a written agreement.

. . .

FRIENDLY, CIRCUIT JUDGE, concurring:

The difficulty in deciding this case comes from the gap between the realities of the formation of complex business agreements and traditional contract formulation. The nature of the gap is well described in a passage in 2 Schlesinger (ed.), Formation of Contracts: A Study of the Common Core of Legal Systems 1584–86 (1968), reprinted in Farnsworth, Young and Jones, Cases and Materials on Contracts (2d ed. 1972) at 99–100, which is reproduced in the margin.[1] Under a view con-

---

1. "Especially when large deals are concluded among corporations and individuals of substance, the usual sequence of events is not that of offer and acceptance; on the

forming to the realities of business life, there would be no contract in such cases until the document is signed and delivered; until then either party would be free to bring up new points of form or substance, or even to withdraw altogether. However, I cannot conscientiously assert that the courts of New York or, to the extent they have not spoken, the Restatement of Contracts 2d § 26 and comment C (Tent.Drafts 1–7 Revised and Edited) have gone that far, nor can I find a fair basis for predicting that the New York Court of Appeals is yet prepared to do so.

On the other hand, it does seem to me that the New York cases cited by the majority can be read as holding, or at least as affording a fair basis for predicting a holding, that when the parties have manifested an intention that their relations should be embodied in an elaborate signed contract, clear and convincing proof is required to show that they meant to be bound before the contract is signed and delivered. Such a principle would accord with what I believe to be the intention of most such potential contractors; they view the signed written instrument that is in prospect as "the contract", not as a memorialization of an oral agreement previously reached. Also, from an instrumental standpoint, such a rule would save the courts from a certain amount of vexing litigation. The clear and convincing proof could consist in one party's allowing the other to begin performance, as in Viacom International, Inc. v. Tandem Productions, Inc., 526 F.2d 593 (2d Cir.1975) and V'Soske v. Barwick, 404 F.2d 495 (2 Cir.1968), cert. denied, 394 U.S. 921, 89 S.Ct. 1197, 22 L.Ed.2d 454 (1969), or in unequivocal statements by the principals or authorized agents that a complete agreement had been reached and the writing was considered to be of merely evidentiary significance.

The facts forcefully marshalled by Judge Lumbard make a strong case for finding that the latter condition has been satisfied here. What weighs especially with me is Kirsch's letter of October 26, not claimed to have been unauthorized, saying that "Teleprompter now wishes to settle the litigation only with respect to Teleprompter on the terms which had been agreed upon with respect to Teleprompter" in the earlier three-party settlement "and I understand that this is agreeable

contrary, the businessmen who originally conduct the negotiations, often will consciously refrain from ever making a binding offer, realizing as they do that a large deal tends to be complex and that its terms have to be formulated by lawyers before it can be permitted to become a legally enforceable transaction. Thus the original negotiators will merely attempt to ascertain whether they see eye to eye concerning those aspects of the deal which seem to be most important from a business point of view. Once they do, or think they do, the negotiation is then turned over to the lawyers, usually with instructions to produce a document which all participants will be willing to sign. . . . When the lawyers take over, again there is no sequence of offer and acceptance, but rather a sequence of successive drafts. These drafts usually will not be regarded as offers, for the reason, among others, that the lawyers acting as draftsmen have no authority to make offers on behalf of their clients. After a number of drafts have been exchanged and discussed, the lawyers may finally come up with a draft which meets the approval of all of them, and of their clients. It is only then that the parties will proceed to the actual formation of the contract, and often this will be done by way of a formal 'closing' . . . or in any event by simultaneous execution or delivery in the course of a more or less ceremonial meeting, of the document or documents prepared by the lawyers."

with ITC". From then on the job of transforming the three-party agreement into a two-party one was largely scrivener's work and Teleprompter manifested no dissatisfaction with Kirsch's performance of this. Upon the understanding that our decision rests on the unique facts here presented and that we are not entering a brave new world where lawyers can commit their clients simply by communicating boldly with each other, I concur in the judgment of affirmance.

The Lawyer's Authority to Settle in Civil Cases

The traditional rule has been summarized as follows:

> The law is settled that an attorney of record may not compromise, settle or consent to a final disposition of his client's case without express authority . . . However, this general principal must be considered in connection with the rule that an attorney of record is *presumed* to have authority to compromise and settle litigation of his client, and a judgment entered upon an agreement by the attorney of record will be set aside only upon affirmative proof of the party seeking to vacate the judgment that the attorney had no right to consent to its entry.

> St. Amand v. Marriott Hotel, Inc., 430 F.Supp. 488, 490 (E.D. La.1977), aff'd, 611 F.2d 881 (5th Cir.1980), cited with approval in Mid–South Towing Co. v. Har–Win, Inc., 733 F.2d 386, 390 (5th Cir. 1984) (interpreting federal law).

Accord: Morgan v. South Bend Community School Corp., 797 F.2d 471 (7th Cir.1986); Nehleber v. Anzalone, 345 So.2d 822 (Fla.App.1977); Harrop v. Western Airlines, Inc., 550 F.2d 1143 (9th Cir.1977) (applying California law); United States v. Beebe, 180 U.S. 343, 21 S.Ct. 371 (1901).

Courts want to encourage settlements and support their finality, so the burden of establishing that the lawyer lacked authority has been described as a "heavy" one. There is a strong presumption that the lawyer acted within the scope of authority. See Surety Insurance Co. of California v. Williams, 729 F.2d 581, 582–583 (8th Cir.1984). A lawyer's statement that she had authority is "highly probative" although not conclusive. An evidentiary hearing should be held. *Mid–South Towing*, supra, 733 F.2d at 391. The client's knowing failure to disapprove of the settlement within a reasonable time will be construed as a ratification. Cf. Capital Dredge and Dock Corp. v. Detroit, 800 F.2d 525 (6th Cir.1986) (no ratification when the client does not understand that the claim has been compromised).

Is a client's grant of a general power to settle without specifying specific limits or instructions enough to constitute "express authority" to settle? In Smedley v. Temple, 782 F.2d 1357, 1360 (5th Cir.1986), the court suggested that it was. Also see Mitchum v. Hudgens, 533 So.2d 194, 201 (Ala.1988) (lawyer hired by insurance company to represent insured not liable to insured for malpractice for settling case without insured's permission. Insurance policy language was *implicit* consent to any settlement insured and lawyer deemed proper). Cf. notes in Chapter 7 at p. 645, on lawyers hired by insurance companies to represent the insured. Does M.R. 1.2 or 1.4 require the lawyer to check with the client before entering into a settlement or may the lawyer proceed on the basis of the client's general direction "to settle it?"

As the *Telemeter* case suggests, many jurisdictions hold that a client will be bound when the attorney has "apparent authority" to enter a settlement, even if she lacks "express" or "actual" authority.

According to the Restatement Second of Agency, "actual authority" (express or implied) exists when the principal (the client) through words or deeds causes *the agent* reasonably to believe that she has the authority to act, § 26. "Apparent authority" exists when the principal through words or deeds causes *a third party* reasonably to believe that the agent has the principal's authority to act, § 27. For apparent authority, courts generally require a showing of reliance and good faith on the part of the third party. See Terrain Enterprises, Inc. v. The Western Casualty and Surety Co., 774 F.2d 1320 (5th Cir.1985) (applying Mississippi law).

In Edwards v. Born, Inc., 792 F.2d 387, 390 (3d Cir.1986), the court, while acknowledging that "[i]t is . . . well settled that an attorney does not possess the inherent authority to compromise [the client's claim] by virtue of his retention," noted the trend toward a rule that would bind clients when lawyers had "apparent authority" to settle their claims. The court rejected the argument that "apparent authority" was the minority rule and should be rejected, holding:

> [i]n the absence of a clear trend in either direction, the district court . . . may apply the "better rule." . . . We find that enforcing settlement agreements on the basis of apparent authority is consistent with the principles of agency law, the policies favoring settlements generally, and the notions of fairness to the parties in the adjudicatory process.

Id.

The trend is not, however, unanimous. See particularly *Morgan,* supra, where the Seventh Circuit sharply criticizes cases accepting apparent authority and states that "compromise judgments depend on the actual authority of the person purporting to compromise the claim." 797 F.2d at 478. Also see Blanton v. Womancare, 38 Cal.3d 396, 212 Cal.Rptr. 151, 696 P.2d 645 (1986) (lawyer by reason of employment has no apparent authority to bind the client to arbitrate).

In *Edwards,* the lower court had found that the lawyer had apparent authority based on the following facts: (1) the lawyer had represented Edwards since the suit was filed; (2) the lawyer transmitted all communications between Edwards and the opposing parties; (3) the pretrial order required that the lawyers appear with the authority to settle; and (4) the lawyer had been entrusted to select the examining physicians for trial. Is this sufficient to show apparent authority? The appellate court held it was not, but on remand ordered the district court to consider whether "actual authority could be implied from the totality of the relationship between [the lawyer] and Edwards . . ." Id. at 392. Compare Fennell v. TLB Kent Co., 865 F.2d 498 (2d Cir. 1989) (apparent authority is created only by the representations of the principal to the third party and cannot be created by the agent's own actions or representations; authority to represent a client and appear at conferences does not create apparent authority to settle).

In *Fennell,* supra, the client knew that his lawyers were engaged in settlement discussions with the opposing party, did not ask his lawyers to stop these discussions, would have accepted a higher settlement figure, and did not tell the opposing party's counsel that his lawyers' authority was limited in any way. The Second Circuit held that these facts could not create apparent authority.

The Sixth Circuit's opinion in Capital Dredge and Dock Corp. v. Detroit, 800 F.2d 525, 530–31 (6th Cir.1986), represents the opposite extreme:

> . . . Thus, a third party who reaches a settlement agreement with an attorney employed to represent his client in regard to the settled claim is generally entitled to enforcement of the . . . agreement even if the attorney was acting contrary to the client's express instructions. In such a situation, the client's remedy is to sue his attorney for professional malpractice. The third party may rely on the attorney's apparent authority unless he has reason to believe that the attorney has no authority to negotiate a settlement.
>
> But for this rule of law, prudent litigants could not rely on opposing counsel's representation of authorization to settle. Fear of a later claim that counsel lacked authority to settle would require litigants to go behind counsel to the opposing party in order to verify authorization for every settlement offer.

With this statement the court turns the traditional rule on its head. Compare the Sixth Circuit's concern about the power lawyers need to function in the real world of litigation with Judge Friendly's concurrence. Does the Sixth Circuit have a different type of lawyer in mind than Judge Friendly? A different type of client?

Did the lawyer in *Telemeter* possess apparent or actual authority? What could a lawyer do to ensure that the opposing party understood that there was no deal until a written settlement agreement was signed?

Authority to Settle on Behalf of the Government

In Delaware Valley Citizens' Counsel v. Pennsylvania, 755 F.2d 38 (3d Cir.), cert. denied, 474 U.S. 819 (1985), the Third Circuit affirmed the authority of lawyers for the state to enter a consent decree. The state lawyers had entered into a consent decree providing that Pennsylvania would seek state legislation to establish a franchise system for testing vehicle emissions. The decree provided that if such a law was not passed, the State Department of Transportation would establish a private inspection system on its own authority. The legislature did not act, and the Department of Transportation set up the system.

Members of the Pennsylvania legislature sued to annul the decree on the grounds that the lawyer representing the state had no authority to enter the consent decree. In Scanlon v. Commonwealth, Department of Transportation, 502 Pa. 577, 467 A.2d 1108, 1115 (1983), the Supreme Court of Pennsylvania sided with the legislators, holding that the lawyer had no authority to enter the consent decree which was therefore a "nullity." The Third Circuit, however, held that the federal courts determine the authority of litigants and their agents in federal courts. It then reaffirmed its earlier decision, 675 F.2d 470 (1982), that Pennsylvania was bound, noting that the "Pennsylvania Department of Justice, members of which were signatories of this decree, has the exclusive power to compromise and settle law suits against the Commonwealth." 755 F.2d at 41.

The Seventh Circuit expressed its disapproval of *Delaware Valley* in Morgan v. South Bend, 797 F.2d 471, 477 (7th Cir.1986), another case involving counsel for the government entering an agreement: "*Delaware Valley* held that the entry of the consent decree was conclusive on the question of authority. We doubt that the Third Circuit meant to allow any employee of a state to bind the entire state just by signing his name to a consent decree, though this would be the logical consequence of the decision." Also see Derrickson v. Danville, 845 F.2d 715 (7th Cir. 1988) (again criticizing *Delaware Valley*).

United States Department of Justice regulations provide that settlements over $750,000 can be entered only by the Deputy Attorney General on the Attorney General's behalf. In most other cases, the Assistant Attorney General is authorized to settle for amounts below this, and United States Attorneys are authorized to settle for $200,000 or less. See 28 C.F.R. §§ 0.160–0.161, Appendix to Subpart Y. In White v. United States, 639 F.Supp. 82, 90 (M.D.Pa.1986), aff'd, 815 F.2d 697 (3d Cir.1987), the District Court refused to enforce a settlement of $2 million entered into by a United States Attorney, holding that the lawyer had no apparent authority. "[P]arties who deal with a Government agent are charged with notice of the limits of the agent's authority. The government is not bound by agreements of agents beyond the scope of their authority in part because of this constructive knowledge."

Allocation of Decision-making Authority on Other Matters in Civil Cases

In Blanton v. Womancare, Inc., 38 Cal.3d 396, 212 Cal.Rptr. 151, 696 P.2d 645, 650 (1985), the court described the lawyer's authority to make decisions other than compromising or settling a client's claim:

Considerations of procedural efficiency require . . . that in the course of a trial there be but one captain per ship. An attorney must be able to make such tactical decisions as whether to call a particular witness, and the court and opposing counsel must be able to rely upon the decisions he makes, even when the client voices opposition in open court. . . . In such tactical matters, it may be said that the attorney's authority is implied in law, as a necessary incident to the function he is engaged to perform.

Is it essential that the lawyer have the right to decide which witnesses to call? What stipulations to enter into? What objections to make? Doctors know more than their clients, but we accept the principle that if there are alternate treatments available, the patient should decide after consultation (assuming she is conscious, sane and of legal age). Is the lawyer involved in litigation analogous to the surgeon in an operating room? Should it be assumed that the lawyer has not considered specific points of trial strategy until after the trial has actually begun? Is it possible to explain trial strategy choices to the client clearly enough that she can make the decision?

The Comment to M.R. 1.2 states: "A clear distinction between objectives and means sometimes cannot be drawn, and in many cases the client-lawyer relationship partakes of a joint undertaking. In questions of means, the lawyer should assume responsibility for technical and legal tactical issues, but should defer to the client regarding such questions as the expense to be incurred and concern for third persons who might be adversely affected." Is this helpful?

If clients had the right to decide on tactics, would increased ethical violations by lawyers be the result? In medicine this does not seem to have happened. It is understood that a patient's right to decide on treatment is bounded by the law—a doctor cannot prescribe an illegal drug. Would not a similar understanding work for lawyers and clients?

The analogy to medicine fails to capture that the lawyer, unlike the doctor, practices her craft through language and posture, i.e., means that appear intelligible to the client. The language of court (or of contract) resembles the language of the outside world. It is easy to imagine a client, armed with decision-making authority, who insists on speaking out for herself in court (or in negotiation). It is more difficult to imagine a patient wanting to give herself a blood test or any other medical procedure. Is it possible to explain how court-talk is different and thus convince the client that she is better off not interfering? Must legal institutions—through case law, court procedures and ethics rules—reinforce the client's subordinate role for her own good?

In Hunt v. Bankers Trust Co., 799 F.2d 1060 (5th Cir.1986), the court held that a lawyer had implied authority to consent to the issuance of a preliminary injunction prohibiting any party from filing bankruptcy until a final judgment was issued in the pending case. Is this a "compromise or settlement" of the client's case or a decision on tactics?

Does a lawyer have authority to waive the client's attorney-client privilege? The general rule is that a lawyer may not waive the privilege without the client's consent, but consent may be express or implied. See the Comment to M.R.Rule 1.6: "A lawyer is impliedly authorized to make disclosures about a client when appropriate in carrying out the representation, except to the extent that the client's instructions or special circumstances limit that authority." In In re von Bulow, 828 F.2d 94 (2d Cir.1987), printed above in Chapter 4, the court held that a client who actively encouraged the lawyer's publication of a book that he should have realized would reveal client confidences, waived the privilege. Was the publication of the book a disclosure "appropriate in carrying out the representation?"

Clients in civil cases generally are bound by the mistakes of their lawyers as well as by their intended acts. The leading case in this area is Link v. Wabash Railroad, 370 U.S. 626, 82 S.Ct. 1386 (1962) (dismissal of plaintiff's case upon failure of his lawyer to comply with court order governing procedure). For more on how the lawyer's errors can jeopardize a client's suit, see Chapter 5 above.

The courts usually treat the client as knowing what the lawyer knows; there is an almost irrebuttable presumption that the lawyer has communicated relevant information concerning the representation to the client. See *Link* supra. Knowledge the lawyer possesses that affects the client in some matter outside the scope of the relationship is not imputed to the client. See, e.g., Manale v. Lambert, 1987 WL 10863 (E.D.La.1987) (Unpublished Case) (not reported in F.Supp.).

The principle that lawyers should have broad authority has been criticized by commentators, who argue that this gives the client too small a role in deciding her fate. If one purpose of trial is to affirm the individual's dignity and autonomy, that goal is ill-served by giving lawyers control over the process. See, e.g., Martyn, Informed Consent in the Practice of Law, 48 Geo.Wash.L.Rev. 307 (1980); Spiegel, The New Model Rules of Professional Conduct: Lawyer–Client Decision-making and the Role of Rules in Structuring the Lawyer–Client Dialogue, 1980 Am.B.Found.Res.J. 1003; Berger, The Supreme Court and Defense Counsel: Old Roads, New Paths—A Dead End?, 86 Colum.L. Rev. 9 (1986); Strauss, Toward a Revised Model of Attorney–Client Relationship: The Argument for Autonomy, 65 N.C.L.Rev. 315 (1987). Cf. Simon, Ethical Discretion in Lawyering, 101 Harv.L.Rev. 1083 (1988) (arguing for lawyers to exercise more discretion in representing clients to avoid assisting the client in immoral acts; the lawyer should ask herself whether what the client wants the lawyer to do will further justice). See also Maute, Allocation of Decisionmaking Authority Under the Model Rules of Professional Conduct, 17 U.C.Davis L.Rev. 1049 (1984); and Andersen, Informed Decision-making in an Office Practice, 28 Bost.Coll.L.Rev. 225 (1987).

In Maute, supra, 17 U.C.Davis L.Rev. at 1050, the author observes that acting upon a paternalistic model lawyers may "disserve their clients when they pursue ends that they have imputed to their clients through means that they have not discussed with them."

It is said to be morally and legally important that the client fully participate in decisions involved in the representation. Nevertheless, there are considerations that are difficult to reconcile with an equal participatory model. First, typically the lawyer knows more about the legal aspects of the problem than the client, and more than the client practically can be told. Second, typically the lawyer is inured to the emotional distress of conflict and therefore can deal with it more steadily—this may be the other side of being "sensitive." Third, the decisions in carrying out a legal matter often require unabashed assertiveness—as where an impecunious widower should take bankruptcy to avoid paying back rent to a landlord who may need the money almost as much as he. Lawyers are used to taking such measures, while ordinary people are not. Also, some clients expect the lawyer to take responsibility for a difficult choice: "Tell me what I ought to do." Should such a wish be respected? These things said, lawyers often have strong inclinations and temptations to manipulate clients.

For empirical studies, see Neustader, When Lawyer and Client Meet, 35 Buffalo L.Rev. 177 (1986); Fleming, Client Games: Defense Attorney Perspectives on Their Relations with Criminal Clients, 1986 Am.Bar.Found.Res.J. 253. Clients also have strong temptations to manipulate their lawyers, for example, by presenting a favorable version of the facts. In a deeper sense, it is impossible for the relationship to be wholly free of manipulation. See Ellman, Lawyer and Client, 34 UCLA L.Rev. 717 (1987). Compare Strauss, Toward a Revised Model of Attorney–Client Relationship: The Argument for Autonomy, 65 N.C.L. Rev. 315 (1987). In any case, when the client has limited capacity, as in the case of a child, full participation of the client is impossible. See M.R. 1.14.

Allocation of Decision-making in Criminal Cases

Decisions that the Client has the Right to Make

The rule of thumb in criminal cases is similar to that in civil cases, i.e., questions on tactics and procedural matters are ones the lawyer may decide, questions on whether to compromise the client's cause are for the defendant. However, in criminal cases "procedural matters" are often matters of the defendant's fundamental rights, and it has long been recognized that at least four key matters should be decided by the defendant. "[T]he accused has the ultimate authority to make certain fundamental decisions regarding the case . . . [They are] whether to plead guilty, waive a jury trial, testify in his or her own behalf, or take an appeal." Jones v. Barnes, 643 U.S. 745, 751, 103 S.Ct. 3308, 3312 (1983).

If the lawyer makes any of the decisions mentioned above without the client's consent, a new trial will be ordered. The converse is also true: a defendant who makes the decision against counsel's advice is held to it. In People v. Robles, 2 Cal.3d 205, 85 Cal.Rptr. 166, 466 P.2d 710 (1970), the defendant insisted on taking the stand over his lawyer's objection. On appeal, the defendant argued that the trial court had erred in allowing his testimony because the decision was tactical and within the province of the lawyer. The court upheld the conviction, stating that "where . . . a defendant insists that he wants to testify, he cannot be deprived of that opportunity." 466 P.2d at 716. Generally see the notes following *Nix v. Whiteside* in Chapter 5 above.

Conduct by a lawyer that is the "practical equivalent" of entering a guilty plea over the client's objection has been considered ground for reversal. See Brookhart v. Janis, 384 U.S. 1, 86 S.Ct. 1245, 1248 (1966) (lawyer's agreeing, over client's objection, that the trial should be conducted as a "prima facie trial," in which the defense would neither present evidence nor cross-examine witnesses, was "the practical equivalent of a plea of guilty."). But see People v. Ratliff, 41 Cal.3d 675, 224 Cal.Rptr. 705, 715 P.2d 665 (1986) (at trial lawyer may decide to concede client's guilt to a lesser charge without client's consent; this is a trial tactic whose use is properly vested with the lawyer; it is not tantamount to pleading guilty). Does *Ratliff* make sense?

M.R. 1.2(a) and § 4–5.2 of the ABA Standards Relating to the Administration of Criminal Justice, The Defense Function, provide that the defendant has the ultimate authority to decide the first three of the decisions specified in *Jones;* Defense Function Standard 4–8.2(a) completes the list by reserving the decision on whether to appeal for the defendant.

Some jurisdictions add to the list of decisions that the defendant has a right to make. See Townsend v. Superior Court, 15 Cal.3d 774, 126 Cal.Rptr. 251, 543 P.2d 619 (1975) (whether to waive the right to a speedy trial); People v. Gauze, 15 Cal.3d 709, 125 Cal.Rptr. 773, 542 P.2d 1365 (1975) (whether competent defendant will enter a plea of insanity).

In People v. Frierson, 39 Cal.3d 803, 218 Cal.Rptr. 73, 705 P.2d 396 (1985), the defendant was charged with first degree murder with special circumstances, a capital charge. The only affirmative defense available to him was that of diminished capacity, which he wanted his counsel to present. Counsel refused, making the "tactical" decision to reserve evidence of diminished capacity for presentation to the jury during the penalty phase of the trial. Counsel reasoned that the evidence was unlikely to produce a conviction for a lesser offense at the guilt phase of trial and was more likely to persuade the jury not to impose the death penalty at the penalty phase, if they were hearing the evidence at that stage for the first time.

The conflict between the lawyer's strategy and the defendant's wishes was made known to the trial court, which ruled that the decision whether to present a defense was for counsel, not the defendant. After the prosecution's case, the defense rested without presenting any evidence. The defense counsel, in an in-chambers conference immediately thereafter, informed the court that the decision not to present a defense had been his and that the client had strongly disagreed. "I took the precaution of advising the court informally a couple of days ago about this problem . . . [My client is] still of a strong, very strong position—state of mind that he would like to present a diminished capacity defense." 705 P.2d at 400. The trial judge confirmed that the lawyer had brought this problem to his attention earlier, but that he had not wished to hear specifics then for fear of infringing the defendant's right against self-incrimination. The court then ruled that the lawyer acted appropriately in overriding his client's wishes. The defendant was convicted.

The lawyer then followed through on his strategy and presented evidence of diminished capacity to the jury at the penalty phase. The prosecutor countered in his closing argument: "It's very interesting that the defense should offer evidence bearing on the defendant's mental state . . . at this phase of the trial . . . [P]remeditation and deliberation was [sic] an important element in the guilt phase . . . Now, why wasn't it offered at the first phase of the trial? . . . I submit to you that it's a matter of clever trial tactics. . . . because [defense counsel] knew that [this] evidence wasn't going to convince anybody at the guilt phase . . . [and that if he then used the evidence] at the penalty phase . . ., [it] would have no impact." Id. at 398–399. The jury sentenced the defendant to death.

The California Supreme Court reversed the death penalty and ordered a new trial on the issue of whether there were "special circumstances." The court described its holding in narrow terms: the decision to withhold the presentation of any defense in the guilt phase of a capital case, when the defendant desires that a defense be presented and when there is some credible evidence to support it, is not one the lawyer may properly make. Id. at 403.

Was *Frierson* merely a case where a trial strategy went wrong? Should the decision on whether to present a defense be one a criminal defendant always has a right to make? What if there is no credible evidence? Who decides what is credible?

The Decision to Reject a Plea Bargain Offer

A guilty plea will be set aside if entered without client consent. Boykin v. Alabama, 395 U.S. 238, 89 S.Ct. 1709 (1969). The Supreme Court has not decided what remedy, if any, will be provided to a defendant whose lawyer *rejects* a plea bargain without client consent. Several courts have noted the difference between accepting a plea and rejecting one. See, e.g., Iowa v. Kraus, 397 N.W.2d 671 (Iowa 1986); Johnson v. Duckworth, 793 F.2d 898 (7th Cir.1986). These courts point out that when a defense lawyer pleads the client guilty without consent, the defendant loses her right to a fair trial and all the other protections afforded by that process. But when a defense lawyer rejects a plea without informing the client or without the client's consent, the defendant proceeds to trial. Would reversing that trial and ordering a new one be a sensible remedy? As the Iowa court said in *Kraus:* "One more fair trial, or even a series of them, would not necessarily revive the lost chance [for a plea bargain]." Is the answer to provide no remedy?

Courts have had difficulty with this dilemma. See, e.g., *Johnson v. Duckworth,* supra, holding that a lawyer who rejects a plea bargain without client consent ordinarily violates the defendant's Sixth Amendment right to effective counsel, but that in this case it was reasonable because the defendant was 17, confused and the lawyer talked to the client's parents before deciding. The court also noted that the defendant had made no showing that he would have accepted the proffered plea, which would ordinarily be required before relief was granted. Also see Lloyd v. State, 258 Ga. 645, 373 S.E.2d 1 (1988) (failure to communicate plea unreasonable but no prejudice where no evidence that defendant would have accepted the offer).

Other courts have ordered new trials, perhaps to put the defendant once again in the position where she can attempt to bargain with the prosecutor. E.g., State v. Simmons, 65 N.C.App. 294, 309 S.E.2d 493 (1983). Of course, there is no guarantee that the prosecutor will repeat the offer given that one trial already resulted in a conviction for a greater charge.

In *Kraus,* supra, the Iowa court remanded the case, directing that the accused again be allowed to enter a plea on the terms rejected by his lawyer (a plea to a lesser offense). "If a guilty plea is entered judgment shall be pronounced accordingly and defendant's conviction of second-degree murder shall stand as reversed. If the defendant fails or refuses to enter such a plea his conviction . . . shall stand affirmed." 397 N.W.2d at 676. Also see Turner v. Tennessee, 858 F.2d 1201 (6th Cir.1988) (state may not withdraw plea offer unless it can show no vindictiveness in doing so). But see Commonwealth v. Copeland, 381 Pa.Super. 382, 554 A.2d 54, 60 (1988) (court may only order "imperfect relief" of new trial and cannot order the state to reinstate its plea offer).

See Alschuler, The Defense Attorney's Role in Plea Bargaining, 84 Yale L.J. 1179, 1306–7 (1975) (the client's right to decide whether to plead guilty is only realized in a technical sense; many defense lawyers believe their judgment on the plea should prevail: if the client resists, she should find a new lawyer).

Decisions the Lawyer May Make

ABA Defense Function Standard 4–5.2(b) and (c) provide:

(b) The decisions on what witnesses to call, whether and how to conduct cross-examination, what jurors to accept or strike, what trial motions should be made, and all other strategic and tactical decisions are the exclusive province of the lawyer after consultation with the client.

(c) If a disagreement on significant matters of tactics or strategy arises between the lawyer and the client, the lawyer should make a record of the circumstances, the lawyer's advice and reasons, and the conclusion reached. The record should be made in a manner which protects the confidentiality of the lawyer-client relationship.

Outside the four areas entrusted to the client's control, courts have upheld the lawyer's right to decide strategic matters in a criminal case, notwithstanding that the client has objected, that fundamental rights were waived, or that the lawyer had ample opportunity to consult with the client but did not. See People v. Ratliff, 41 Cal.3d 675, 224 Cal. Rptr. 705, 715 P.2d 665 (1986).

How would courts monitor a requirement that counsel obtain the client's consent prior to waiving any constitutional rights? Are the practical difficulties insurmountable? How do courts monitor whether a defendant has freely agreed to waive the right to trial by jury, to testify, or to plead guilty?

Decisions the lawyer may make without client consent include: which witnesses to call, Connecticut v. Davis, 199 Conn. 88, 506 A.2d 86 (1986); whether to agree to a mistrial, People v. Ferguson, 67 N.Y.2d 383, 494 N.E.2d 77 (1986); whether a defense is plausible, Moreno v. Estelle, 717 F.2d 171 (5th Cir.1983); the nature of closing argument, United States v. Mayo, 646 F.2d 369 (9th Cir.1981); whether to waive objection to the racial composition of the grand jury, Winters v. Cook, 489 F.2d 174 (5th Cir.1973); and whether to seek a change of venue after extensive pretrial publicity, Curry v. Slansky, 637 F.Supp. 947 (D.Nev.1986).

Consider the following exchange from the trial record in Connecticut v. Davis, 506 A.2d at 87:

[Defense Counsel]: . . . [B]efore the jury comes in, I'd like to make a statement for the record. My client . . . has asked me to call one witness, who in my judgment, I do not think it would be wise to call, and under those circumstances, I have declined to follow [my client's] instructions . . .

The Court: Well, I have to assume that the decision not to call this particular witness is a tactical decision that experienced trial counsel has made. He's the one who's lived with the case. He's been in attendance throughout and I respect this judgment. I have no basis or reason to make an independent judgment.

JONES V. BARNES

Supreme Court of the United States, 1983.
463 U.S. 745, 746, 103 S.Ct. 3308, 77 L.Ed.2d 987.

CHIEF JUSTICE BURGER delivered the opinion of the Court.

We granted certiorari to consider whether defense counsel assigned to prosecute an appeal from a criminal conviction has a constitutional duty to raise every non-frivolous issue requested by the defendants. . . . This Court in holding that a State must provide counsel for an indigent appellant on his first appeal of right, recognized the superior ability of trained counsel in the "examination of the record, research of the law, and marshalling of the arguments . . ." Douglas v. California [372 U.S. 353, 83 S.Ct. 814 (1963)] . . . Yet by promulgating a per se rule that the client, not the professional advocate, must be allowed to decide what issues are to be pressed, the Court of Appeals [in this case] seriously undermines the ability of counsel to present the client's case in accord with counsel's professional evaluation.

Experienced advocates since time beyond memory have emphasized the importance of winnowing out weaker arguments on appeal and focusing on one central issue if possible, or at most on a few key issues . . .

An authoritative work on appellate practice observes:

Most cases present only one, two, or three significant questions. . . . Usually . . . if you cannot win on a few major points, the others are not likely to help, and to attempt to deal with a great many in the limited number of pages allowed for briefs will mean that none may receive adequate attention. The effect of adding weak arguments will be to dilute the force of the stronger ones. R. Stern, Appellate Practice in the United States, 266 (1981).

There can hardly be any question about the importance of having the appellate advocate examine the record with a view to selecting the most promising issues for review. This has assumed a greater importance in an era when oral argument is strictly limited in most courts—often to as little as 15 minutes—and when page limits on briefs are widely imposed. . . . Even in a court that imposes no time or page limits, however, the new per se rule laid down by the Court of Appeals is contrary to all experience and logic. A brief that raises every colorable issue runs the risk of burying good arguments—those that, in the words of the great advocate John W. Davis, "go for the jugular." Davis, The Argument of an Appeal, 26 A.B.A.J. 895, 897 (1940)—in a verbal mound made up of strong and weak contentions.

. . .

JUSTICE BRENNAN with whom JUSTICE MARSHALL joins, dissenting.

The Sixth Amendment provides that "[i]n all criminal prosecutions, the accused shall enjoy the right . . . to have the *Assistance of Counsel*" (emphasis added). I find myself in fundamental disagreement with the Court over what a right to "the assistance of counsel" means. The import of words like "assistance" and "counsel" seem inconsistent with a regime under which counsel appointed by the State to represent a criminal defendant can refuse to raise issues with arguable merit on appeal when the client, after hearing his assessment of the case and his advice, has directed him to raise them . . .

. . .

. . . [I]n Faretta v. California, 422 U.S. 806, 95 S.Ct. 2525, 45 L.Ed. 2d 562 (1975), [holding a criminal defendant has a right to proceed without counsel] . . . we observed:

> . . . To force a lawyer on a defendant can only lead him to believe that the law contrives against him. . . . The right to defend is personal. The defendant, and not his lawyer or the State, will bear the personal consequences of a conviction. It is the defendant, therefore, who must be free personally to decide whether in his particular case counsel is to his advantage. And although he may conduct his own defense ultimately to his own detriment his choice must be honored out of that respect for the individual which is the lifeblood of the law. *Illinois v. Allen* (Brennan, J., concurring).

. . .

. . . [T]he Court argues that good appellate advocacy demands selectivity among arguments. That is certainly true—the Court's advice is good. It ought to be taken to heart by every lawyer called upon to argue an appeal . . . and by his client. It should take little or no persuasion to get a wise client to understand that, if staying out of prison is what he values most, he should encourage his lawyer to raise only his two or three best arguments on appeal, and he should defer to his lawyer's advice as to which are the best arguments. The Constitution, however, does not require clients to be wise, and other policies should be weighed in the balance as well.

It is no secret that indigent clients often mistrust the lawyers appointed to represent them. There are many reasons for this, some perhaps unavoidable even under perfect conditions—differences in education, disposition, and socioeconomic class—and some that should (but may not always) be zealously avoided. A lawyer and his client do not always have the same interests. Even with paying clients, a lawyer may have a strong interest in having judges and prosecutors think well of him, and, if he is working for a flat fee—a common arrangement for criminal defense attorneys—or if his fees for court appointments are lower than he would receive for other work, he has an obvious financial incentive to conclude cases on his criminal docket swiftly. Good lawyers undoubtedly recognize these temptations and resist them, and they endeavor to convince their clients that they will. It would be naive, however, to suggest that they always succeed in either task. A constitutional rule that encourages lawyers to disregard their clients "wishes without compelling need can only exacerbate the clients" suspicions of their lawyers . . .

. . .

. . . In many ways, having a lawyer becomes one of the many indignities visited upon someone who has the ill fortune to run afoul of the criminal justice system.

I cannot accept the notion that lawyers are one of the punishments a person receives merely for being accused of a crime. Clients, if they wish are capable of making informed judgments about which issues to appeal, and when they exercise that prerogative their choices should be respected unless they would require lawyers to violate their consciences, the law or their duties to the court.

Comments

In People v. Vasquez, 70 N.Y.2d 1, 509 N.E.2d 934 (1987), the defendant had asked his appointed counsel to raise ten points on appeal; the lawyer decided to raise only one. In the brief the lawyer wrote: "As shall be indicated this is the fifth point out of a total of ten points the defendant-appellant wishes his appellate counsel to address. It has substantial merit in light of two recent decisions of the United States Supreme Court in appellate counsel's opinion; whereas the other points the defendant-appellant seeks to raise do not." The brief, after developing the lawyer's argument, proceeded: "The remaining nine points the defendant-appellant requested his counsel to review have been carefully reviewed by his counsel, and in light of the record, the applicable statutory and case law, they have been found to be without merit." The court ruled that counsel's gratuitous disparagement of his client's nine other arguments denied him effective assistance of counsel:

> The procedure to be followed by appellate counsel when a client requests that several points be presented to the court, some with merit and some with none, is to argue the claim found meritorious and make no comment about claims considered frivolous. As to them, counsel should instruct his client why he believes the points frivolous and advise him that if he still thinks they should be addressed, defendant may file a pro se brief with the court. If the client chooses to do so, counsel should protect his client's opportunity to submit written argument on the points by notifying the court of his intentions.

509 N.E.2d at 922.

But see McCoy v. Wisconsin Court of Appeals, 108 S.Ct. 1895 (1988) (Wisconsin rule requiring the lawyer to include an explanation of why the lawyer believes the appeal is frivolous in any brief filed pursuant to Anders v. California, 386 U.S. 738, 87 S.Ct. 1396 (1967)—see the discussion of this case in Chapter 5 above at p. 404—does not deprive the defendant of effective assistance of counsel).

Autonomy to Opt for Death

If the defendant has the right to insist that a defense of diminished capacity be presented, People v. Frierson, supra, does he have the right to insist that such a defense not be presented. In the penalty phase of capital cases at least, the California Supreme Court has held he does not, People v. Deere, 41 Cal.3d 353, 710 P.2d 925 (1985). The court described the penalty phase of Deere's trial as follows:

Counsel first permitted his client to make a brief statement to the court . . . "I know what I done was wrong" . . . "I always believed [in] an eye for an eye. I feel I should die for the crimes I done." . . .

. . . [T]he defense attorney's honest but mistaken belief that he had "no right whatsoever to infringe upon his [client's] decisions about his own life" operated to deny defendant his right to the effective assistance of counsel. While counsel should of course endeavor to comply with his client's wishes to the maximum extent consistent with his legal and ethical responsibilities, he is not— contrary to a popular misconception—a mere "mouthpiece." As we recently found it necessary to reiterate, "Once an attorney is appointed to represent a client, he assumes the authority and duty to control the proceedings. The scope of this authority extends to matters such as deciding what witnesses to call, whether and how to conduct cross-examination, what jurors to accept or reject, what motions to make, and most other strategic and tactical determinations."

The rule clearly applies to the issue before us. . . .
710 P.2d at 929, 931.

The court stressed the state's interest in the reliable and fair administration of penalty decisions in capital cases, reasoning that a penalty trial at which available mitigating evidence is not presented is "no penalty trial at all." Id. at 934. See also People v. Burgener, 41 Cal.3d 505, 714 P.2d 1251 (1986) (at penalty phase defense lawyer at client's request asked jury to return the death penalty; held: ineffective assistance of counsel). But see In re Guzman, 45 Cal.3d 915, 755 P.2d 917 (1988) (defense counsel's acquiescence in client's desire not to present mitigating evidence is not ineffective assistance of counsel); Trimble v. State, 693 S.W.2d 267 (Mo.App.1985) (at client's insistence in a capital case no evidence tending to show he might be guilty only of a lesser offense was introduced; death sentence upheld).

Was the client's (or the lawyer's) decision in *Deere* a "strategic or tactical" one? On representing mentally impaired criminal defendants, see Uphoff, The Role of the Criminal Defense Lawyer in Representing The Mentally Impaired Defendant: Zealous Advocate or Officer of the Court?, 1988 Wis.L.Rev. 65. See also the discussion in the note on disabled clients at p. 558 below.

In Gilmore v. Utah, 429 U.S. 1012, 97 S.Ct. 436 (1976), the Supreme Court affirmed the right of a person to refuse to appeal a death sentence. The court had previously granted the petition for a stay filed by Bessie Gilmore, the defendant's mother, which it now vacated, dismissing the action brought by his mother as "next friend" to stop the execution. In Lenhard v. Wolff, 603 F.2d 91 (9th Cir.1979), the defendant's lawyers sought a writ of habeas corpus and a stay of their former client's execution, which the client refused to fight. They argued that in this case, unlike *Gilmore,* there had never been a showing that their client was competent to waive his rights. The Ninth Circuit refused to stay the execution because there was no evidence in the record that raised a doubt about the client's competence.

Does the autonomy argument made by Justice Brennan in his dissent in *Jones* justify allowing a client to decide to forego legal tactics that might save her from the death penalty?

D. CONFLICTS BETWEEN LAWYER AND CLIENT

EVANS v. JEFF D.

Supreme Court of the United States, 1986.
475 U.S. 717, 106 S.Ct. 1531, 89 L.Ed.2d 747.

JUSTICE STEVENS delivered the opinion of the Court.

The Civil Rights Attorney's Fees Awards Act of 1976 (Fees Act) provides that "the court, in its discretion, may allow the prevailing party . . . a reasonable attorney's fee" in enumerated civil rights actions. 90 Stat. 2641, 42 U.S.C. § 1988. In Maher v. Gagne, 448 U.S. 122, 100 S.Ct. 2570, 65 L.Ed.2d 653 (1980), we held that fees *may* be assessed against state officials after a case has been settled by the entry of a consent decree. In this case, we consider the question whether attorney's fees *must* be assessed when the case has been settled by a consent decree granting prospective relief to the plaintiff class but providing that the defendants shall not pay any part of the prevailing party's fees or costs. We hold that the District Court has the power, in its sound discretion, to refuse to award fees.

I

The petitioners are the Governor and other public officials of the State of Idaho responsible for the education and treatment of children who suffer from emotional and mental handicaps. Respondents are a class of such children who have been or will be placed in petitioners' care.[1]

On August 4, 1980, respondents commenced this action by filing a complaint against petitioners in the United States District Court for the District of Idaho. The factual allegations in the complaint described deficiencies in both the educational programs and the health care services provided respondents. These deficiencies allegedly violated the United States Constitution, the Idaho Constitution, four federal statutes, and certain provisions of the Idaho Code. The complaint prayed for injunctive relief and for an award of costs and attorney's fees, but it did not seek damages.

On the day the complaint was filed, the District Court entered two orders, one granting the respondents leave to proceed *in forma pauper-*

---

1. The number of children in petitioners' custody, as well as the duration of that custody, fluctuates to a certain degree. Although it appears that only 40 or 50 children are in custody at any one moment, the membership in respondents' class is apparently well over 2,000.

is, and a second appointing Charles Johnson as their next friend for the sole purpose of instituting and prosecuting the action. At that time Johnson was employed by the Idaho Legal Aid Society, Inc., a private, nonprofit corporation that provides free legal services to qualified low-income persons.[2] Because the Idaho Legal Aid Society is prohibited from representing clients who are capable of paying their own fees,[3] it made no agreement requiring any of the respondents to pay for the costs of litigation or the legal services it provided through Johnson. Moreover, the special character of both the class and its attorney-client relationship with Johnson explains why it did not enter into any agreement covering the various contingencies that might arise during the course of settlement negotiations of a class action of this kind.

Shortly after petitioners filed their answer, and before substantial work had been done on the case, the parties entered into settlement negotiations. They were able to reach agreement concerning that part of the complaint relating to educational services with relative ease and, on October 14, 1981, entered into a stipulation disposing of that part of the case. The stipulation provided that each party would bear its "own attorney's fees and costs thus far incurred." The District Court promptly entered an order approving the partial settlement.

Negotiations concerning the treatment claims broke down, however, and the parties filed cross-motions for summary judgment. Although the District Court dismissed several of respondents' claims, it held that the federal constitutional claims raised genuine issues of fact to be resolved at trial. Thereafter, the parties stipulated to the entry of a class certification order, engaged in discovery, and otherwise prepared to try the case in the spring of 1983.

In March 1983, one week before trial, petitioners presented respondents with a new settlement proposal. As respondents themselves characterize it, the proposal "offered virtually all of the injunctive relief [they] had sought in their complaint." The Court of Appeals agreed with this characterization, and further noted that the proposed relief was "more than the district court in earlier hearings had indicated it was willing to grant." 743 F.2d 648, 650 (CA9 1984). As was true of the earlier partial settlement, however, petitioners' offer included a provision for a waiver by respondents of any claim to fees or costs.[4] Originally, this waiver was unacceptable to the Idaho Legal Aid Society, which had instructed Johnson to reject any settlement offer conditioned upon a waiver of fees, but Johnson ultimately determined that

2. Although Johnson subsequently entered private practice and apparently bore some of the financial burden of the litigation himself, any award of costs or fees would inure to the benefit of Idaho Legal Aid.

3. Idaho Legal Aid receives grants under the Legal Services Corporation Act, 42 U.S.C. §§ 2996–2996*l*, and is not allowed to represent clients who are capable of paying their own legal fees, see § 2996f(b)(1); 45 CFR § 1609 (1984).

4. Petitioners append to their brief on the merits the parties' correspondence setting forth their respective positions on settlement. Without embarking on a letter-by-letter discussion of the status of the fee waiver in the bargaining, it is clear that petitioners' proposals uniformly included fee waivers while respondents' almost always did not.

his ethical obligation to his clients mandated acceptance of the proposal. The parties conditioned the waiver on approval by the District Court.[5]

After the stipulation was signed, Johnson filed a written motion requesting the District Court to approve the settlement "except for the provision on costs and attorney's fees," and to allow respondents to present a bill of costs and fees for consideration by the court. At the oral argument on that motion, Johnson contended that petitioners' offer had exploited his ethical duty to his clients—that he was "forced," by an offer giving his clients "the best result [they] could have gotten in this court or any other court," to waive his attorney's fees.[6] The District Court, however, evaluated the waiver in the context of the entire settlement and rejected the ethical underpinnings of Johnson's argument. Explaining that although petitioners were "not willing to concede that they were obligated to [make the changes in their practices required by the stipulation], . . . they were willing to do them as long as their costs were outlined and they didn't face additional costs," it concluded that "it doesn't violate any ethical considerations for an attorney to give up his attorney fees in the interest of getting a better bargain for his client[s]." Accordingly, the District Court approved the settlement and denied the motion to submit a costs bill.

When respondents appealed from the order denying attorney's fees and costs, petitioners filed a motion requesting the District Court to suspend or stay their obligation to comply with the substantive terms of the settlement. Because the District Court regarded the fee waiver as a material term of the complete settlement, it granted the motion. The Court of Appeals, however, granted two emergency motions for stays requiring enforcement of the substantive terms of the consent decree pending the appeal. More dramatically, after ordering preliminary relief, it invalidated the fee waiver and left standing the remainder of the settlement; it then instructed the District Court to "make its own determination of the fees that are reasonable" and remanded for that limited purpose. 743 F.2d, at 652.

5. Paragraph 25 of the settlement agreement provides:

"Plaintiffs and defendants shall each bear their own costs and attorney's fees thus far incurred, if so approved by the Court."

In addition, the entire settlement agreement was conditioned on the District Court's approval of the waiver provision under Federal Rule of Civil Procedure 23(e).

6. Johnson's oral presentation to the District Court reads in full as follows:

"In other words, an attorney like myself can be put in the position of either negotiating for his client or negotiating for his attorney's fees, and I think that that is pretty much the situation that occurred in this instance.

"I was forced, because of what I perceived to be a result favorable to the plaintiff class, a result that I didn't want to see jeopardized by a trial or by any other possible problems that might have occurred. And the result is the best result I could have gotten in this court or any other court and it is really a fair and just result in any instance and what should have occurred years earlier and which in fact should have been the case all along. That result I didn't want to see disturbed on the basis that my attorney's fees would cause a problem and cause that result to be jeopardized."

In explaining its holding, the Court of Appeals emphasized that Rule 23(e) of the Federal Rules of Civil Procedure gives the court the power to approve the terms of all settlements of class actions,[8] and that the strong federal policy embodied in the Fees Act normally requires an award of fees to prevailing plaintiffs in civil rights actions, including those who have prevailed through settlement. The court added that "[w]hen attorney's fees are negotiated as part of a class action settlement, a conflict frequently exists between the class lawyers' interest in compensation and the class members' interest in relief." 743 F.2d, at 651–652. "To avoid this conflict," the Court of Appeals relied on Circuit precedent which had "disapproved simultaneous negotiation of settlements and attorney's fees" absent a showing of "unusual circumstances." Id., at 652.[10] In this case, the Court of Appeals found no such "unusual circumstances" and therefore held that an agreement on fees "should not have been a part of the settlement of the claims of the class." Ibid. It concluded:

> "The historical background of both Rule 23 and section 1988, as well as our experience since their enactment, compel the conclusion that a stipulated waiver of all attorney's fees obtained solely as a condition for obtaining relief for the class should not be accepted by the court." Ibid.

The importance of the question decided by the Court of Appeals, together with the conflict between its decision and the decisions of other Courts of Appeals, led us to grant certiorari. We now reverse.

II

The disagreement between the parties and *amici* as to what exactly is at issue in this case makes it appropriate to put certain aspects of the case to one side in order to state precisely the question that the case does present.

To begin with, the Court of Appeals' decision rested on an erroneous view of the District Court's power to approve settlements in class actions. Rule 23(e) wisely requires court approval of the terms of any settlement of a class action, but the power to approve or reject a settlement negotiated by the parties before trial does not authorize the court to require the parties to accept a settlement to which they have

---

8. "Dismissal or Compromise. A class action shall not be dismissed or compromised without the approval of the court, and notice of the proposed dismissal or compromise shall be given to all members of the class in such manner as the court directs." Fed. Rules Civ.Proc. 23(e).

10. That precedent, Mendoza v. United States, 623 F.2d 1338 (CA9 1980), like the Third Circuit decision in Prandini v. National Tea Co., 557 F.2d 1015 (1977), which both the *Mendoza* court and the panel below cited approvingly, instituted a ban on simultaneous negotiations of merits and attorney's fees issues to prevent attorneys from trading relief benefiting the class for a more generous fee for themselves. See Mendoza v. United States, supra, at 1352–1353; Prandini v. National Tea Co., 557 F.2d, at 1020–1021. In neither of those cases had the court rejected a part of the settlement and enforced the remainder.

not agreed. . . . [12] The options available to the District Court were essentially the same as those available to respondents: it could have accepted the proposed settlement; it could have rejected the proposal and postponed the trial to see if a different settlement could be achieved; or it could have decided to try the case. The District Court could not enforce the settlement on the merits and award attorney's fees anymore than it could, in a situation in which the attorney had negotiated a large fee at the expense of the plaintiff class, preserve the fee award and order greater relief on the merits. The question we must decide, therefore, is whether the District Court had a duty to reject the proposed settlement because it included a waiver of statutorily authorized attorney's fees.

That duty, whether it takes the form of a general prophylactic rule or arises out of the special circumstances of this case, derives ultimately from the Fees Act rather than from the strictures of professional ethics. Although respondents contend that Johnson, as counsel for the class, was faced with an "ethical dilemma" when petitioners offered him relief greater than that which he could reasonably have expected to obtain for his clients at trial (if only he would stipulate to a waiver of the statutory fee award), and although we recognize Johnson's conflicting interests between pursuing relief for the class and a fee for the Idaho Legal Aid Society, we do not believe that the "dilemma" was an "ethical" one in the sense that Johnson had to choose between conflicting duties under the prevailing norms of professional conduct. Plainly, Johnson had no *ethical* obligation to seek a statutory fee award. His ethical duty was to serve his clients loyally and competently.[14] Since the proposal to settle the merits was more favorable than the probable outcome of the trial, Johnson's decision to recommend acceptance was consistent with the highest standards of our profession. The District Court, therefore, correctly concluded that approval of the settlement involved no breach of ethics in this case.

The defect, if any, in the negotiated fee waiver must be traced not to the rules of ethics but to the Fees Act.[15] Following this tack,

12. See Pasadena City Board of Education v. Spangler, 427 U.S. 424, 437, 96 S.Ct. 2697, 2705, 49 L.Ed.2d 599 (1976); United States v. United Shoe Machinery Corp., 391 U.S. 244, 251, 88 S.Ct. 1496, 1500, 20 L.Ed.2d 562 (1968); Railway Employees v. Wright, 364 U.S. 642, 651, 81 S.Ct. 368, 373, 5 L.Ed.2d 349 (1961); United States v. Swift & Co., 286 U.S. 106, 114, 52 S.Ct. 460, 462, 76 L.Ed. 999 (1932).

14. Generally speaking, a lawyer is under an ethical obligation to exercise independent professional judgment on behalf of his client; he must not allow his own interests, financial or otherwise, to influence his professional advice. ABA, Model Code of Professional Responsibility EC 5-1, 5-2 (as amended 1980); ABA, Model Rules of Professional Conduct 1.7(b), 2.1 (as amended 1984). Accordingly, it is argued that an attorney is required to evaluate a settlement offer on the basis of his client's interest, without considering his own interest in obtaining a fee; upon recommending settlement, he must abide by the client's decision whether or not to accept the offer, see Model Code of Professional Responsibility EC 7-7 to EC 7-9; Model Rules of Professional Conduct 1.2(a).

15. Even state bar opinions holding it unethical for defendants to request fee waivers in exchange for relief on the merits of plaintiffs' claims are bottomed ultimately on § 1988. See District of Columbia Bar Legal Ethics Committee, Op. No. 147, reprinted in 113 Daily Wash.L.Rep. 389, 394–395 (1985); Committee on Professional and Judicial

respondents argue that the statute must be construed to forbid a fee waiver that is the product of "coercion." They submit that a "coercive waiver" results when the defendant in a civil rights action (1) offers a settlement on the merits of equal or greater value than that which plaintiffs could reasonably expect to achieve at trial but (2) conditions the offer on a waiver of plaintiffs' statutory eligibility for attorney's fees. Such an offer, they claim, exploits the ethical obligation of plaintiffs' counsel to recommend settlement in order to avoid defendant's statutory liability for its opponents' fees and costs.[16]

The question this case presents, then, is whether the Fees Act requires a district court to disapprove a stipulation seeking to settle a civil rights class action under Rule 23 when the offered relief equals or exceeds the probable outcome at trial but is expressly conditioned on waiver of statutory eligibility for attorney's fees. For reasons set out below, we are not persuaded that Congress has commanded that all such settlements must be rejected by the District Court. Moreover, on the facts of record in this case, we are satisfied that the District Court did not abuse its discretion by approving the fee waiver.

III

The text of the Fees Act provides no support for the proposition that Congress intended to ban all fee waivers offered in connection with substantial relief on the merits.[17] On the contrary, the language of the

Ethics of the New York City Bar Association, Op. No. 82–80, p. 1 (1985); id., at 4–5 (dissenting opinion); Committee on Professional and Judicial Ethics of the New York City Bar Association, Op. No. 80–94, reprinted in 36 Record of N.Y.C.B.A. 507, 508–511 (1981); Grievance Commission of Board of Overseers of the Bar of Maine, Op. No. 17, reprinted in Advisory Opinions of the Grievance Commission of the Board of Overseers of the Bar 69–70 (1983). For the sake of completeness, it should be mentioned that the bar is not of one mind on this ethical judgment. See Final Subcommittee Report of the Committee on Attorney's Fees of the Judicial Conference of the United States Court of Appeals for the District of Columbia Circuit, reprinted in 13 Bar Rep. 4, 6 (1984) (declining to adopt flat rule forbidding waivers of statutory fees). Cf. State Bar of Georgia, Op. No. 39, reprinted in 10 Ga.St.Bar News No. 2, p. 5 (1984) (rejecting the reasoning of the Committee on Professional and Judicial Ethics of the New York City Bar Association in the context of lump-sum settlement offers for the reason, among others, that "[t]o force a defendant into proposing a settlement offer wherein plaintiffs['] statutory attorney fees are not negotiated . . . [means that] meaningful settlement proposals might never be made. Such a situation undeniably . . . is inimical to the resolution of disputes between parties").

16. See Committee on Professional and Judicial Ethics of the New York City Bar Association, Op. No. 80–94, reprinted in 36 Record of N.Y.C.B.A., at 508 ("Defense counsel thus are in a uniquely favorable position when they condition settlement on the waiver of the statutory fee: they make a demand for a benefit which the plaintiff's lawyer cannot resist as a matter of ethics and which the plaintiff will not resist due to lack of interest"). Accord, District of Columbia Bar Legal Ethics Committee, Op. No. 147, reprinted in 113 Daily Wash.L.Rep., at 394.

17. The operative language of the Fees Act provides, in its entirety:

"In any action or proceeding to enforce a provision of sections 1977, 1978, 1979, 1980, and 1981 of the Revised Statutes, title IX of Public Law 92–318, or in any civil action or proceeding, by or on behalf of the United States of America, to enforce, or charging a violation of, a provision of the United States Internal Revenue Code, or title VI of the Civil Rights Act of 1964, the court, in its discretion, may allow the prevailing party, other than the United States, a reasonable attorney's fee as part of the costs." 90 Stat. 2641, 42 U.S.C. § 1988.

Act, as well as its legislative history, indicates that Congress bestowed on the "prevailing *party*" (generally plaintiffs) a statutory eligibility for a discretionary award of attorney's fees in specified civil rights actions.[19] It did not prevent the party from waiving this eligibility anymore than it legislated against assignment of this right to an attorney, such as effectively occurred here. Instead, Congress enacted the fee-shifting provision as "an integral part of the remedies necessary to obtain" compliance with civil rights laws, S.Rep. No. 94–1011, p. 5 (1976), U.S.Code Cong. & Admin.News 1976, p. 5912, to further the same general purpose—promotion of respect for civil rights—that led it to provide damages and injunctive relief. The statute and its legislative history nowhere suggest that Congress intended to forbid *all* waivers of attorney's fees—even those insisted upon by a civil rights plaintiff in exchange for some other relief to which he is indisputably not entitled [20]—anymore than it intended to bar a concession on damages to secure broader injunctive relief. Thus, while it is undoubtedly true that Congress expected fee shifting to attract competent counsel to represent citizens deprived of their civil rights, it neither bestowed fee awards upon attorneys nor rendered them nonwaivable or nonnegotiable; instead, it added them to the arsenal of remedies available to combat violations of civil rights, a goal not invariably inconsistent with conditioning settlement on the merits on a waiver of statutory attorney's fees.[22]

19. This straightforward reading of § 1988 accords with the view held by the majority of the Courts of Appeals. See, e.g., Jonas v. Stack, 758 F.2d 567, 570, n. 7 (CA11 1985) ("Strict conformity to the language of [§ 1988] would require that the [fee] application be made by the attorney in the name of his client, the prevailing party. We consider this to be the procedure of choice, since it ensures that awards made under the Act compensate their intended beneficiaries"); Brown v. General Motors Corp., 722 F.2d 1009, 1011 (CA2 1983) ("Under [42 U.S.C. § 1988] it is the prevailing party rather than the lawyer who is entitled to attorney's fees"); Cooper v. Singer, 719 F.2d 1496, 1506–1507 (CA10 1983) (distinguishing between client's and counsel's entitlement to fees in the course of holding that "if the *client's* section 1988 fee award . . . is less than the amount owed to the attorney under the contingent fee agreement, then the lawyer will be expected to reduce his fee to the amount awarded by the courts" (emphasis added)); White v. New Hampshire Dept. of Employment Security, 629 F.2d 697, 703 (CA1 1980) ("[A]ward of attorney's fees goes to 'prevailing party,' rather than attorney"), rev'd on other grounds, 455 U.S. 445, 102 S.Ct. 1162, 71 L.Ed.2d 325 (1982). But cf. James v. Home Construction Co. of Mobil Inc., 689 F.2d 1357, 1358–1359 (CA11 1982) (disagreeing with Smith v. South Side Loan Co., 567 F.2d 306, 307 (CA5 1978) ("[A]n award [of attorney's fees] is the right of the party suing not the attorney representing him"), and construing Truth in Lending Act's mandatory award of attorney's fees as "creat[ing] a right of action for attorneys to seek fee awards after settlement of the plaintiff's claim." 689 F.2d, at 1359).

20. Judge Wald has described the use of attorney's fees as a "bargaining chip" useful to plaintiffs as well as defendants. In her opinion concurring in the judgment in Moore v. National Assn. of Security Dealers, Inc., she wrote:

"On the other hand, the *Jeff D.* approach probably means that a defendant who is willing to grant immediate prospective relief to a plaintiff case, but would rather gamble on the outcome at trial than pay attorneys' fees and costs up front, will never settle. In short, removing attorneys' fees as a 'bargaining chip' cuts both ways. It prevents defendants, who in Title VII cases are likely to have greater economic power than plaintiffs, from exploiting that power in a particularly objectionable way; but it also deprives plaintiffs of the use of that chip, even when without it settlement may be impossible and the prospect of winning at trial may be very doubtful." 246 U.S.App. D.C., at 133, 762 F.2d at 1112.

22. Indeed, Congress specifically rejected a mandatory fee-shifting provision, see H.R. Rep. No. 94–1558, supra, at 3, 5, 8; 122 Cong.Rec. 35123 (1976) (remarks of Rep. Drinan),

In fact, we believe that a general proscription against negotiated waiver of attorney's fees in exchange for a settlement on the merits would itself impede vindication of civil rights, at least in some cases, by reducing the attractiveness of settlement. . . .

Most defendants are unlikely to settle unless the cost of the predicted judgment, discounted by its probability, plus the transaction costs of further litigation, are greater than the cost of the settlement package. If fee waivers cannot be negotiated, the settlement package must either contain an attorney's fee component of potentially large and typically uncertain magnitude, or else the parties must agree to have the fee fixed by the court. Although either of these alternatives may well be acceptable in many cases, there surely is a significant number in which neither alternative will be as satisfactory as a decision to try the entire case.[23]

The adverse impact of removing attorney's fees and costs from bargaining might be tolerable if the uncertainty introduced into settlement negotiations were small. But it is not. The defendants' potential liability for fees in this kind of litigation can be as significant as, and sometimes even more significant than, their potential liability on the merits. This proposition is most dramatically illustrated by the fee awards of district courts in actions seeking only monetary relief.[24] Although it is more difficult to compare fee awards with the cost of

a proposal which the dissent would virtually reinstate under the guise of carrying out the legislative will. Even proponents of nonwaivable fee awards under § 1988 concede that "one would have to strain principles of statutory interpretation to conclude that Congress intended to utilize fee non-negotiability to achieve the purposes of section 1988." Calhoun, Attorney–Client Conflicts of Interest and the Concept of Non–Negotiable Fee Awards under 42 U.S.C. § 1988, 55 U.Colo.L.Rev. 341, 385 (1984). This conclusion is buttressed by Congress' decision to emulate the "over fifty" fee-shifting provisions that had been successful in enlisting the aid of "private attorneys general" in the prosecution of other federal statutes that had been on the books for decades. H.R.Rep. No. 94–1558, supra, at 3, 5. Accord, S.Rep. No. 94–1011, supra, at 3. See also 122 Cong.Rec., supra, at 35123 (appendix to remarks of Rep. Drinan) (listing more than 50 fee-shifting statutes). No one has suggested that the purpose of any of those fee-shifting provisions has been frustrated by the absence of a prohibition against fee waivers.

23. It is unrealistic to assume that the defendant's offer on the merits would be unchanged by redaction of the provision waiving fees. If it were, the defendant's incentive to settle would be diminished because of the risk that attorney's fees, when added to the original merits offer, will exceed the discounted value of the expected judgment plus litigation costs. If, as is more likely, the defendant lowered the value of its offer on the merits to provide a cushion against the possibility of a large fee award, the defendant's offer on the merits will in many cases be less than the amount to which the plaintiff feels himself entitled, thereby inclining him to reject the settlement. Of course, to the extent that the merits offer is somewhere between these two extremes the incentive of both sides to settle is dampened, albeit to a lesser degree with respect to each party.

24. See, e.g., Rivera v. Riverside, 763 F.2d 1580, 1581–1583 (CA9 1985) (city ordered to pay victorious civil rights plaintiffs $245,456.25 following a trial in which they recovered a total of $33,350 in damages), cert. granted, 474 U.S. 917, 106 S.Ct. 244, 88 L.Ed.2d 253 (1985); Cunningham v. City of McKeesport, 753 F.2d 262, 269 (CA3 1985) (city ordered to pay some $35,000 in attorney's fees in a case in which judgment for the plaintiff was entered in the amount of $17,000); 205 U.S.App.D.C. 390, 401, Copeland v. Marshall, 641 F.2d 880, 891 (1980) (en banc) ($160,000 attorney's fees awarded for obtaining $33,000 judgment); Skoda v. Fontani, 646 F.2d 1193, 1194 (CA7), on remand, 519 F.Supp. 309, 310 (ND Ill.1981) ($6,086.12 attorney's fees awarded to obtain $1 recovery). Cf. Marek v. Chesny, 473 U.S. [1] at 7, 105 S.Ct. [3012] at 3015 ($171,692.47 in claimed attorney's fees and costs to obtain $60,000 damages judgment).

injunctive relief, in part because the cost of such relief is seldom reported in written opinions, here too attorney's fees awarded by district courts have "frequently outrun the economic benefits ultimately obtained by successful litigants." 122 Cong.Rec. 31472 (1976) (remarks of Sen. Kennedy).[25] Indeed, in this very case "[c]ounsel for defendants view[ed] the risk of an attorney's fees award as the most significant liability in the case." Brief for Defendants in Support of Approval of Compromise in Jeff D. v. Evans, No. 80–4091 (D.Idaho), p. 5. Undoubtedly there are many other civil rights actions in which potential liability for attorney's fees may overshadow the potential cost of relief on the merits and darken prospects for settlement if fees cannot be negotiated.

The unpredictability of attorney's fees may be just as important as their magnitude when a defendant is striving to fix its liability. Unlike a determination of costs, which ordinarily involve smaller outlays and are more susceptible of calculation, see Marek v. Chesny, 473 U.S. [1] at 7, 105 S.Ct. [3012] at 3015 (1985), "[t]here is no precise rule or formula" for determining attorney's fees, Hensley v. Eckerhart, 461 U.S. 424, 436, 103 S.Ct. 1933, 1941, 76 L.Ed.2d 40 (1983).[26] Among other considerations, the district court must determine what hours were reasonably expended on what claims, whether that expenditure was reasonable in light of the success obtained, see id., at 436, 440, 103 S.Ct., at 1941, 1943, and what is an appropriate hourly rate for the services rendered. Some District Courts have also considered whether a "multiplier" or other adjustment is appropriate. The consequence of this succession of necessarily judgmental decisions for the ultimate fee award is inescapable: a defendant's liability for his opponent's attorney's fees in a civil rights action cannot be fixed with a sufficient degree of confidence to make defendants indifferent to their exclusion from negotiation.[27] It is therefore not implausible to anticipate that parties to a significant

25. See, e.g., Grendel's Den, Inc. v. Larkin, 749 F.2d 945, 960 (CA1 1984) (awarding $113,640.85 in fees and expenses for successful challenge to law zoning liquor establishments in Larkin v. Grendel's Den, 459 U.S. 116, 103 S.Ct. 505, 74 L.Ed.2d 297 (1982)).

26. While this Court has identified "the number of hours reasonably expended on the litigation multiplied by a reasonable hourly rate" as "[t]he most useful starting point for determining the amount of a reasonable fee," Hensley v. Eckerhart, 461 U.S., at 433, 103 S.Ct., at 1939, the "product of reasonable hours times a reasonable rate does not end the inquiry," id., at 434, 103 S.Ct., at 1940, for "there may be circumstances in which the basic standard of reasonable rates multiplied by reasonably expended hours results in a fee that is either unreasonably low or unreasonably high." Blum v. Stenson, 465 U.S. 886, 897, 104 S.Ct. 1541, 1548, 79 L.Ed.2d 891 (1984). "A district court is expressly empowered to exercise discretion in determining whether an award is to be made and if so its reasonableness." Id., at 902, n. 19, 104 S.Ct., at 1550, n. 19. See Hensley v. Eckerhart, 461 U.S., at 437, 103 S.Ct., at 1941. The district court's calculation is thus anything but an arithmetical exercise.

27. The variability in fee awards is discussed in, for example, Berger, Court Awarded Attorneys' Fees: What is "Reasonable"?, 126 U.Pa.L.Rev. 281, 283–284 (1977); Diamond, The Firestorm over Attorney Fee Awards, 69 A.B.A.J. 1420, 1420 (1983); and National Association of Attorneys General, Report to Congress: Civil Rights Attorney's Fees Awards Act of 1976 (Feb. 3, 1984), reprinted in Hearing on The Legal Fee Equity Act (S. 2802) before the Subcommittee on the Constitution of the Senate Committee on the Judiciary, 98th Cong., 2d Sess., 280–293 (1984).

number of civil rights cases will refuse to settle if liability for attorney's fees remains open,[28] thereby forcing more cases to trial, unnecessarily burdening the judicial system, and disserving civil rights litigants. Respondents' own waiver of attorney's fees and costs to obtain settlement of their educational claims is eloquent testimony to the utility of fee waivers in vindicating civil rights claims.[29] We conclude, therefore, that it is not necessary to construe the Fees Act as embodying a general rule prohibiting settlements conditioned on the waiver of fees in order to be faithful to the purposes of that Act.[30]

IV

The question remains whether the District Court abused its discretion in this case by approving a settlement which included a complete fee waiver. As noted earlier, Rule 23(e) wisely requires court approval of the terms of any settlement of a class action. The potential conflict among members of the class—in this case, for example, the possible

28. This is the experience of every judge and a majority of the members of a Third Circuit Task Force which concluded that that Circuit's ban on fee negotiations "tends to discourage settlement in some cases and, on occasion, makes it impossible." Report of the Third Circuit Task Force: Court Awarded Fees 38 (1985) . . .

29. Respondents implicitly acknowledge a defendant's need to fix his total liability when they suggest that the parties to a civil rights action should "exchange information" regarding plaintiff's attorney's fees. See, e.g., Committee on Professional and Judicial Ethics of the New York City Bar Association, Op. No. 82–80, p. 2 (1985); Grievance Commission of Board of Overseers of the Bar of Maine, Op. No. 17, Advisory Opinions of the Grievance Commission of the Board of Overseers of the Bar 70 (1983). If this exchange is confined to time records and customary billing rates, the information provides an insufficient basis for forecasting the fee award for the reasons stated above. If the "exchange" is more in the nature of an "assurance" that attorney's fees will not exceed a specified amount, the rule against waiving fees to obtain a favorable settlement on the merits is to that extent breached. Apparently, some parties have circumvented the rule against simultaneous negotiation in one Circuit by means of tacit agreements of this kind. See El Club Del Barrio, Inc. v. United Community Corps., 735 F.2d, at 101, n. 3 (defendants' counsel suggest that the Third Circuit's ban on simultaneous negotiations is "'more honored in the breach'"); . . .

30. The Court is unanimous in concluding that the Fees Act should not be interpreted to prohibit all simultaneous negotiations of a defendant's liability on the merits and his liability for his opponent's attorney's fees. See opinion of Brennan, J., dissenting, post, at 1555–1556, 1556–1557. We agree that when the parties find such negotiations conducive to settlement, the public interest, as well as that of the parties, is served by simultaneous negotiations. Cf. supra, at pp. 1540–1542. This reasoning applies not only to individual civil rights actions, but to civil rights class actions as well.

Although the dissent would allow simultaneous negotiations, it would require that "whatever fee the parties agree to" be "found by the court to be a 'reasonable' one under the Fees Act." Post, at 1551. See post, at 1551, n. 6. The dissent's proposal is imaginative, but not very practical. Of the 10,757 "other civil rights" cases filed in federal court last year—most of which were 42 U.S.C. § 1983 actions for which § 1988 authorizes an award of fees—only 111 sought class relief. See Annual Report of the Director of the Administrative Office of the United States Courts, An Analysis of the Workload of the Federal Courts for the Twelve Month Period Ended June 30, 1985 pp. 281, 555 (1985). Assuming that of the approximately 99% of these civil rights actions that are not class actions, a further 90% would settle rather than go to trial, the dissent's proposal would require district courts to evaluate the reasonableness of fee agreements in several thousand civil rights cases annually while they make that determination in slightly over 100 civil rights class actions now. Moreover, if this novel procedure really is necessary to carry out the purposes of the Fees Act, presumably it should be applied to all cases arising under federal statutes that provide for fee shifting. But see n. 22, supra.

conflict between children primarily interested in better educational programs and those primarily interested in improved health care—fully justifies the requirement of court approval.

The Court of Appeals, respondents, and various *amici* supporting their position, however, suggest that the court's authority to pass on settlements, typically invoked to ensure fair treatment of class members, must be exercised in accordance with the Fees Act to promote the availability of attorneys in civil rights cases. Specifically, respondents assert that the State of Idaho could not pass a valid statute precluding the payment of attorney's fees in settlements of civil rights cases to which the Fees Act applies. From this they reason that the Fees Act must equally preclude the adoption of a uniform state-wide policy that serves the same end, and accordingly contend that a consistent practice of insisting on a fee waiver as a condition of settlement in civil rights litigation is in conflict with the federal statute authorizing fees for prevailing parties, including those who prevail by way of settlement.[31] Remarkably, there seems little disagreement on these points. Petitioners and the *amici* who support them never suggest that the district court is obligated to place its stamp of approval on every settlement in which the plaintiffs' attorneys have agreed to a fee waiver. The Solicitor General, for example, has suggested that a fee waiver need not be approved when the defendant had "no realistic defense on the merits," Brief for United States as *Amicus Curiae* Supporting Reversal 23, n. 9; see id., at 26–27, or if the waiver was part of a "vindictive effort . . . to teach counsel that they had better not bring such cases,".

We find it unnecessary to evaluate this argument, however, because the record in this case does not indicate that Idaho has adopted such a statute, policy, or practice. Nor does the record support the narrower proposition that petitioners' request to waive fees was a vindictive effort to deter attorneys from representing plaintiffs in civil rights suits against Idaho. It is true that a fee waiver was requested and obtained as a part of the early settlement of the education claims, but we do not understand respondents to be challenging that waiver, and they have not offered to prove that petitioners' tactics in this case merely implemented a routine state policy designed to frustrate the objectives of the Fees Act. Our own examination of the record reveals no such policy.

In light of the record, respondents must—to sustain the judgment in their favor—confront the District Court's finding that the extensive structural relief they obtained constituted an adequate *quid pro quo* for

31. See Committee on Professional and Judicial Ethics of the New York City Bar Association, Op. No. 80–94, reprinted in 36 Record of N.Y.C.B.A., 507, 510 (1981) ("[T]he long term effect of persistent demands for the waiver of statutory fees is to . . . undermine efforts to make counsel available to those who cannot afford it"). Accord, District of Columbia Bar Legal Ethics Committee, Op. No. 147, reprinted in 113 Daily Wash.L.Rep. 389, 394 (1985). National staff counsel for the American Civil Liberties Union estimates that requests for fee waivers are made in more than half of all civil rights cases litigated. See Winter, Fee Waiver Requests Unethical: Bar Opinion, 68 A.B. A.J. 23 (1982).

their waiver of attorney's fees.[33] The Court of Appeals did not overturn this finding. . . .

What the outcome of this settlement illustrates is that the Fees Act has given the victims of civil rights violations a powerful weapon that improves their ability to employ counsel, to obtain access to the courts, and thereafter to vindicate their rights by means of settlement or trial. For aught that appears, it was the "coercive" effect of respondents' statutory right to seek a fee award that motivated petitioners' exceptionally generous offer. Whether this weapon might be even more powerful if fee waivers were prohibited in cases like this is another question,[34] but it is in any event a question that Congress is best equipped to answer. Thus far, the Legislature has not commanded that fees be paid whenever a case is settled. Unless it issues such a command, we shall rely primarily on the sound discretion of the district courts to appraise the reasonableness of particular class-action settlements on a case-by-case basis, in the light of all the relevant circumstances. In this case, the District Court did not abuse its discretion in upholding a fee waiver which secured broad injunctive relief, relief greater than that which plaintiffs could reasonably have expected to achieve at trial.

The judgment of the Court of Appeals is reversed.

It is so ordered.

JUSTICE BRENNAN, with whom JUSTICE MARSHALL and JUSTICE BLACKMUN join, dissenting.

Ultimately, enforcement of the laws is what really counts. It was with this in mind that Congress enacted the Civil Rights Attorney's Fees Awards Act of 1976, 42 U.S.C. § 1988 (Act or Fees Act). Congress authorized fee shifting to improve enforcement of civil rights legislation by making it easier for victims of civil rights violations to find lawyers willing to take their cases. Because today's decision will make it more difficult for civil rights plaintiffs to obtain legal assistance, a result plainly contrary to Congress' purpose, I dissent.

33. From the declarations of respondents' counsel in the lower courts, as well as those of the District Court and the Court of Appeals, all of which are quoted in Part I, supra, we understand the District Court's approval of the stipulation settling the health services claims to have rested on the determination that the provision waiving attorney's fees and costs was fair to the class—i.e., the fee waiver was exchanged for injunctive relief of equivalent value.

34. We are cognizant of the possibility that decisions by individual clients to bargain away fee awards may, in the aggregate and in the long run, diminish lawyers' expectations of statutory fees in civil rights cases. If this occurred, the pool of lawyers willing to represent plaintiffs in such cases might shrink, constricting the "effective access to the judicial process" for persons with civil rights grievances which the Fees Act was intended to provide. H.R.Rep. No. 94–1558, p. 1 (1976). That the "tyranny of small decisions" may operate in this fashion is not to say that there is any reason or documentation to support such a concern at the present time. Comment on this issue is therefore premature at this juncture. We believe, however, that as a practical matter the likelihood of this circumstance arising is remote. See Moore v. National Assn. of Securities Dealers, Inc., 246 U.S.App.D.C., at 133, n. 1, 762 F.2d, at 1112, n. 1 (Wald, J., concurring in judgment).

I

The Court begins its analysis by emphasizing that neither the language nor the legislative history of the Fees Act supports "the proposition that Congress intended to ban all fee waivers offered in connection with substantial relief on the merits." I agree. There is no evidence that Congress gave the question of fee waivers any thought at all. However, the Court mistakenly assumes that this omission somehow supports the conclusion that fee waivers are permissible. On the contrary, that Congress did not specifically consider the issue of fee waivers tells us absolutely nothing about whether such waivers ought to be permitted. It is black-letter law that "[i]n the absence of specific evidence of Congressional intent, it becomes necessary to resort to a broader consideration of the legislative policy behind th[e] provision. . . ."

II

The Court asserts that Congress authorized fee awards "to further the same general purpose—promotion of respect for civil rights—that led it to provide damages and injunctive relief." . . .

Obviously, the Fees Act is intended to "promote respect for civil rights." Congress would hardly have authorized fee awards in civil rights cases to promote respect for the securities laws. But discourse at such a level of generality is deceptive. The question is *how* did Congress envision that awarding attorney's fees would promote respect for civil rights? . . . In theory, Congress might have awarded attorney's fees as simply an additional form of make-whole relief, the threat of which would "promote respect for civil rights" by deterring potential civil rights violators. If this were the case, the Court's equation of attorney's fees with damages would not be wholly inaccurate. However, the legislative history of the Fees Act discloses that this is not the case. Rather, Congress provided fee awards to ensure that there would be lawyers available to plaintiffs who could not otherwise afford counsel, so that these plaintiffs could fulfill their role in the federal enforcement scheme as "private attorneys general," vindicating the public interest.[1]

. . . In May 1975, this Court in Alyeska Pipeline Service Co. v. Wilderness Society, 421 U.S. 240, 95 S.Ct. 1612, 44 L.Ed.2d 141, ruled that the equitable powers of the federal courts did not authorize fee awards on the ground that a case served the public interest. Although

1. This is not to deny that the threat of liability for attorney's fees contributes to compliance with civil rights laws and that this is a desirable effect. . . . My point is simply that this effect was not what led Congress to enact the Fees Act. Significantly, the Court cites nothing from the legislative history—or anywhere else for that matter—to support its argument that, in awarding attorney's fees to prevailing parties, Congress thought it was merely adding one more remedy to the plaintiff's existing "arsenal." As the discussion which follows clearly establishes, this is because Congress viewed attorney's fees as a special kind of remedy designed to serve a specific purpose.

recognizing that "Congress has opted to rely heavily on private enforcement to implement public policy and to allow counsel fees so as to encourage private litigation," the Court held that "congressional utilization of the private-attorney-general concept can in no sense be construed as a grant of authority to the Judiciary . . . to award attorneys' fees whenever the courts deem the public policy furthered by a particular statute important enough to warrant the award." Id., at 263, 95 S.Ct., at 1624. Instead, the Court ruled, only Congress could authorize awarding fees as a means of encouraging private actions in the name of public policy. Id., at 269–271, 95 S.Ct., at 1627–1629.

In the wake of *Alyeska,* Congress acted to correct "anomalous gaps" in the availability of attorney's fees to enforce civil rights laws, S.Rep. No. 94–1011, p. 1 (1976) (hereafter S.Rep.).[2] See H.R.Rep. No. 94–1558, p. 2 (1976) (hereafter H.R.Rep.); 122 Cong.Rec. 31472 (1976) (remarks of Sen. Kennedy). Testimony at hearings on the proposed legislation disclosed that civil rights plaintiffs, "a vast majority of [whom] cannot afford legal counsel," H.R.Rep. at 1, were suffering "very severe hardships because of the *Alyeska* decision," id., at 2. The unavailability of fee shifting made it impossible for legal aid services, "already short of resources," to bring many lawsuits, and, without much possibility of compensation, private attorneys were refusing to take civil rights cases. Id., at 3. . . . Congress found that *Alyeska* had a "devastating" impact on civil rights litigation, and it concluded that the need for corrective legislation was "compelling." . . .

Accepting this Court's invitation, see *Alyeska,* supra, 421 U.S., at 269–271, 95 S.Ct., at 1627–1629, Congress passed the Fees Act in order to reestablish the *Newman* regime under which attorney's fees were awarded as a means of securing enforcement of civil rights laws by ensuring that lawyers would be willing to take civil rights cases. The legislative history manifests this purpose with monotonous clarity.
. . .

III

As this review of the legislative history makes clear, then, by awarding attorney's fees Congress sought to attract competent counsel to represent victims of civil rights violations.[3] Congress' primary purpose was to enable "private attorneys general" to protect the public interest by creating economic incentives for lawyers to represent them. The Court's assertion that the Fees Act was intended to do nothing more than give individual victims of civil rights violations another remedy is thus at odds with the whole thrust of the legislation. Congress determined that the public as a whole has an interest in the

2. *Alyeska* was decided on May 12, 1975. Senator Tunney introduced S. 2278 on July 31, 1975. The bill was signed by the President and became effective on October 19, 1976.

3. Even the Court acknowledges that "it is undoubtedly true that Congress expected fee shifting to attract competent counsel to represent citizens deprived of their civil rights. . . ." Ante, at 1539 (footnote omitted). Ironically, the only authority the Court cites from the legislative history is in support of this statement.

vindication of the rights conferred by the civil rights statutes over and above the value of a civil rights remedy to a particular plaintiff.[4]

I have gone to great lengths to show how the Court mischaracterizes the purpose of the Fees Act because the Court's error leads it to ask the wrong question. Having concluded that the Fees Act merely creates another remedy to vindicate the rights of individual plaintiffs, the Court asks whether negotiated waivers of statutory attorney's fees are "invariably inconsistent" with the availability of such fees as a remedy for individual plaintiffs. Not surprisingly, the Court has little difficulty knocking down this frail straw man. But the *proper* question is whether permitting negotiated fee waivers is consistent with Congress' goal of attracting competent counsel. It is therefore necessary to consider the effect on *this* goal of allowing individual plaintiffs to negotiate fee waivers.

A

Permitting plaintiffs to negotiate fee waivers in exchange for relief on the merits actually raises two related but distinct questions. First, is it permissible under the Fees Act to negotiate a settlement of attorney's fees simultaneously with the merits? Second, can the "reasonable attorney's fee" guaranteed in the Act be waived? As a matter of logic, either of these practices may be permitted without also permitting the other. For instance, one could require bifurcated settlement negotiations of merits and fees but allow plaintiffs to waive their fee claims during that phase of the negotiations. Alternatively, one could permit simultaneous negotiation of fees and merits but prohibit the plaintiff from waiving statutory fees. This latter possibility exists because there is a *range* of "reasonable attorney's fees" consistent with the Fees Act in any given case. [Cites omitted] . . .[6] [T]he Court's discussion conflates the different effects of these practices, and its opinion is of little use in coming to a fair resolution of this case. An independent examination leads me to conclude: (1) that plaintiffs should not be permitted to waive the "reasonable fee" provided by the Fees Act; but (2) that parties may undertake to negotiate their fee

---

4. The Court seems to view the options as limited to two: either the Fees Act confers a benefit on attorneys, a conclusion which is contrary to both the language and the legislative history of the Act, ante, at 1538–1539; or the Fees Act confers a benefit on individual plaintiffs, who may freely exploit the statutory fee award to their own best advantage. It apparently has not occurred to the Court that Congress might have made a remedy available to individual plaintiffs primarily for the benefit of the *public*. . . . As long as the interests of individual plaintiffs coincide with those of the public, it does not matter whether Congress intended primarily to benefit the individual or primarily to benefit the public. However, when individual and public interests diverge, as they may in particular situations, we must interpret the legislation so as not to frustrate Congress' intentions. See Brooklyn Savings Bank v. O'Neil, 324 U.S. 697, 704, 65 S.Ct. 895, 900, 89 L.Ed. 1296 (1945).

6. Thus, even if statutory fees cannot be waived, the parties may still want to agree on a fee (or a range of acceptable fees) that they believe to be within the range of fees authorized by the Act. The parties may then, if they choose to do so, make their settlement on the merits contingent upon the district court's approval of their negotiated fee as within the range of "reasonable" fees contemplated by the Fees Act.

claims simultaneously with the merits so long as whatever fee the parties agree to is found by the court to be a "reasonable" one under the Fees Act.

B

1

It seems obvious that allowing defendants in civil rights cases to condition settlement of the merits on a waiver of statutory attorney's fees will diminish lawyers' expectations of receiving fees and decrease the willingness of lawyers to accept civil rights cases. Even the Court acknowledges this possibility. . . . The Court tells us, however, that "[c]omment on this issue" is "premature at this juncture" because there is not yet supporting "documentation." The Court then goes on anyway to observe that "as a practical matter the likelihood of this circumstance arising is remote."

I must say that I find the Court's assertions somewhat difficult to understand. . . .[7] [C]ommentators have recognized that permitting fee waivers creates disincentives for lawyers to take civil rights cases and thus makes it more difficult for civil rights plaintiffs to obtain legal assistance. See, e.g., Moore v. National Assn. of Securities Dealers, Inc., 246 U.S.App.D.C. 114, 133–134, 762 F.2d 1093, 1112–1113 (Wald, J., concurring in judgment) id., at 138, 762 F.2d, at 1117 (Wright, J., dissenting) (1985); Shadis v. Beal, 685 F.2d 824, 830–831 (CA3), cert. denied sub nom. O'Bannon v. Shadis, 459 U.S. 970, 103 S.Ct. 300, 74 L.Ed.2d 282 (1982); Kraus, [supra, n. 7,] 29 Vill.L.Rev., at 625, 633–638; Comment, Settlement Offers Conditioned Upon Waiver of Attorneys' Fees: Policy, Legal, and Ethical Considerations, 131 U.Pa.L.Rev. 793, 814–816 (1983); Committee on Professional and Judicial Ethics of the New York City Bar Association, Op. No. 80–94, reprinted in 36 Record of N.Y.C.B.A. 507, 508–509 (1981).

. . . [I]t does not require a sociological study to see that permitting fee waivers will make it more difficult for civil rights plaintiffs to obtain legal assistance. It requires only common sense. Assume that a civil rights defendant makes a settlement offer that includes a demand for waiver of statutory attorney's fees. The decision whether to accept or reject the offer is the plaintiff's alone, and the lawyer must abide by

---

7. It is especially important to keep in mind the fragile nature of the civil rights bar. Even when attorney's fees are awarded, they do not approach the large sums which can be earned in ordinary commercial litigation. See Berger, Court Awarded Attorneys' Fees: What is "Reasonable"?, 126 U.Pa.L.Rev. 281, 310–315 (1977). It is therefore cost inefficient for private practitioners to devote much time to civil rights cases. Consequently, there are very few civil rights practitioners, and most of these devote only a small part of their time to such cases. Kraus, [Ethical and Legal Concerns in Compelling the Waiver of Attorney's Fees . . .,] 29 Vill.L.Rev., [597] at 633–634 (citing studies indicating that less than 1% of lawyers engage in public interest practice). Instead, civil rights plaintiffs must depend largely on legal aid organizations for assistance. These organizations, however, are short of resources and also depend heavily on statutory fees. H.R. Rep. 3; Kraus, supra, at 634; see also, Blum v. Stenson, 465 U.S. 886, 894–895, 104 S.Ct. 1541, 1546–1547, 79 L.Ed.2d 891 (1984).

the plaintiff's decision. See, e.g., ABA, Model Rules of Professional Conduct 1.2(a) (1984); ABA, Model Code of Professional Responsibility EC 7–7 to EC 7–9 (1982).[8] As a formal matter, of course, the statutory fee belongs to the plaintiff, and thus technically the decision to waive entails a sacrifice only by the plaintiff. As a practical matter, however, waiver affects only the lawyer. Because "a vast majority of the victims of civil rights violations" have no resources to pay attorney's fees, H.R. Rep. 1,[9] lawyers cannot hope to recover fees from the plaintiff and must depend entirely on the Fees Act for compensation.[10] The plaintiff thus has no real stake in the statutory fee and is unaffected by its waiver. See Lipscomb v. Wise, 643 F.2d 319, 320 (CA5 1981) (*per curiam*). Consequently, plaintiffs will readily agree to waive fees if this will help them to obtain other relief they desire.[11] As summed up by the Legal Ethics Committee of the District of Columbia Bar:

> "Defense counsel . . . are in a uniquely favorable position when they condition settlement on the waiver of the statutory fee: They make a demand for a benefit that the plaintiff's lawyer cannot resist as a matter of ethics and one in which the plaintiff has no

8. The attorney is, in fact, obliged to advise the plaintiff whether to accept or reject the settlement offer based on his independent professional judgment, and the lawyer's duty of undivided loyalty requires that he render such advice free from the influence of his or his organization's interest in a fee. See, e.g., ABA, Model Code of Professional Responsibility EC 5–1, EC 5–2, DR 5–101(A) (1982); ABA, Model Rules of Professional Conduct 1.7(b), 2.1 (1984). Thus, counsel must advise a client to accept an offer which includes waiver of the plaintiff's right to recover attorney's fees if, on the whole, the offer is an advantageous one. See, e.g., Commission Op. No. 17 (1981), Advisory Opinions of the Grievance Commission of the Board of Overseers of the Bar of Maine 69, 70 (1983); District of Columbia Bar, Legal Ethics Committee, Op. No. 147, reprinted in 113 Daily Washington Law Reporter 389, 394 (1985). . . .

9. . . . Indeed, legal aid organizations receiving funds under the Legal Services Corporation Act, 42 U.S.C. §§ 2996–2996*l*, are prohibited from representing individuals who are capable of paying their own legal fees. See § 2996f(b)(1); 45 CFR § 1609 (1985).

10. Nor can attorneys protect themselves by requiring plaintiffs to sign contingency agreements or retainers at the outset of the representation. *Amici* legal aid societies inform us that they are prohibited by statute, court rule, or Internal Revenue Service regulation from entering into fee agreements with their clients. Brief for NAACP Legal Defense and Educational Fund, Inc., et al. as *Amici Curiae* 10–11; Brief for Committee on Legal Assistance of the Association of the Bar of the City of New York as *Amicus Curiae* 12–13. Moreover, even if such agreements could be negotiated, the possibility of obtaining protection through contingency fee arrangements is unavailable in the very large proportion of civil rights cases which, like this case, seek only injunctive relief. In addition, the Court's misconceived doctrine of state sovereign immunity, see Atascadero State Hospital v. Scanlon, 473 U.S. 234, 247, 105 S.Ct. 3142, 3150, 87 L.Ed.2d 171 (1985) (Brennan, J., dissenting), precludes damages suits against governmental bodies, the most frequent civil rights defendants. Finally, even when a suit is for damages, many civil rights actions concern amounts that are too small to provide real compensation through a contingency fee arrangement. Of course, none of the parties has seriously suggested that civil rights attorneys can protect themselves through private arrangements. After all, Congress enacted the Fees Act because, after *Alyeska*, it found such arrangements wholly inadequate.

11. This result is virtually inevitable in class actions where, even if the class representative feels sympathy for the lawyer's plight, the obligation to represent the interests of absent class members precludes altruistic sacrifice. In class actions on behalf of incompetents, like this one, it is the lawyer himself who must agree to sacrifice his own interests for those of the class he represents. See, e.g., ABA, Model Code of Professional Responsibility EC 7–12 (1982).

interest and therefore will not resist." Op. No. 147, reprinted in 113 Daily Washington Reporter, supra n. 8, at 394.

Of course, from the lawyer's standpoint, things could scarcely have turned out worse. He or she invested considerable time and effort in the case, won, and has exactly nothing to show for it. Is the Court really serious in suggesting that it takes a study to prove that this lawyer will be reluctant when, the following week, another civil rights plaintiff enters his office and asks for representation? Does it truly require that somebody conduct a test to see that legal aid services, having invested scarce resources on a case, will feel the pinch when they do not recover a statutory fee?

And, of course, once fee waivers are permitted, defendants will seek them as a matter of course, since this is a logical way to minimize liability. Indeed, defense counsel would be remiss *not* to demand that the plaintiff waive statutory attorney's fees. A lawyer who proposes to have his client pay more than is necessary to end litigation has failed to fulfill his fundamental duty zealously to represent the best interests of his client. Because waiver of fees does not affect the plaintiff, a settlement offer is not made less attractive to the plaintiff if it includes a demand that statutory fees be waived. Thus, in the future, we must expect settlement offers routinely to contain demands for waivers of statutory fees.[12]

The cumulative effect this practice will have on the civil rights bar is evident. It does not denigrate the high ideals that motivate many civil rights practitioners to recognize that lawyers are in the business of practicing law, and that, like other business people, they are and must be concerned with earning a living. The conclusion that permitting fee waivers will seriously impair the ability of civil rights plaintiffs to obtain legal assistance is embarrassingly obvious.

Because making it more difficult for civil rights plaintiffs to obtain legal assistance is precisely the opposite of what Congress sought to achieve by enacting the Fees Act, fee waivers should be prohibited. We have on numerous prior occasions held that "a statutory right conferred on a private party, but affecting the public interest, may not be waived or released if such waiver or release contravenes the statutory policy." [Cites omitted]. This is simply straightforward application of the well-established principle that an agreement which is contrary to public policy is void and unenforceable. See Restatement (Second) of Contracts § 178 . . . [Cites omitted].[14]

---

12. The Solicitor General's suggestion that we can prohibit waivers sought as part of a "vindictive effort" to teach lawyers not to bring civil rights cases, Tr. of Oral Arg. 22, a point that the Court finds unnecessary to consider, is thus irrelevant. Defendants will seek such waivers in every case simply as a matter of sound bargaining. Indeed, the Solicitor General's brief suggests that this will be the bargaining posture of the United States in the future.

14. To be sure, prohibiting fee waivers will require federal courts to make a determination they would not have to make if fees could be waived. However, this additional chore will not impose a significant burden. In assessing the impact of making statutory fees nonwaivable on the business of the federal courts, it is important not to overlook the

This all seems so obvious that it is puzzling that the Court reaches a different result. The Court's rationale is that, unless fee waivers are permitted, "parties to a significant number of civil rights cases will refuse to settle. . . ." This is a wholly inadequate justification for the Court's result.

．．．

In an attempt to justify its decision to elevate settlement concerns, the Court argues that settlement "provides benefits for civil rights plaintiffs as well as defendants and is consistent with the purposes of the Fees Act" because " '[s]ome plaintiffs will receive compensation in settlement where, on trial, they might not have recovered, or would have recovered less than what was offered.' "   ．．．

. . . The fact that fee waivers may produce some settlement offers that are beneficial to a few individual plaintiffs is hardly "consistent with the purposes of the Fees Act," if permitting fee waivers fundamentally undermines what Congress sought to achieve. Each individual plaintiff who waives his right to statutory fees in order to obtain additional relief for himself makes it that much more difficult for the next victim of a civil rights violation to find a lawyer willing or able to bring *his* case. As obtaining legal assistance becomes more difficult, the "benefit" the Court so magnanimously preserves for civil rights plaintiffs becomes available to fewer and fewer individuals, exactly the opposite result from that intended by Congress. ．．．

．．．

Second, even assuming that settlement practices are relevant, the Court greatly exaggerates the effect that prohibiting fee waivers will have on defendants' willingness to make settlement offers. This is largely due to the Court's failure to distinguish the fee waiver issue from the issue of simultaneous negotiation of fees and merits claims. The Court's discussion mixes concerns over a defendant's reluctance to settle because total liability remains uncertain with reluctance to settle because the cost of settling is too high. However, it is a prohibition on simultaneous negotiation, not a prohibition on fee waivers, that makes it difficult for the defendant to ascertain his total liability at the time he agrees to settle the merits. Thus, while prohibiting fee waivers may deter settlement offers simply because requiring the defendant to pay a "reasonable attorney's fee" increases the total cost of settlement, this is a separate issue altogether, and the Court's numerous arguments about

context in which the fee determination is made. Unlike in the adversarial context, if the parties have agreed to a fee (or a range of acceptable fees) as part of a settlement, the court will not be required to hear testimony or engage in judicial factfinding in order to resolve disputes over hours reasonably spent, hourly rates, and the like. Similarly, the court will not have to decide whether to enhance the lodestar to reflect high-quality representation or risk of nonsuccess, or to prepare an opinion in anticipation of appellate review. The court's simple task will be to review the parties' raw billing data in order to determine whether the court itself *could* reasonably have made a fee award of the amount agreed to by the parties. Such calculations will, in the vast majority of cases, require little time or effort.

why defendants will not settle unless they can determine their total liability at the time of settlement, are simply beside the point.[17]   . . .

. . .

C

I would, on the other hand, permit simultaneous negotiation of fees and merits claims, since this would not contravene the purposes of the Fees Act. Congress determined that awarding prevailing parties a "reasonable" fee would create necessary—and sufficient—incentives for attorneys to work on civil rights cases. Prohibiting plaintiffs from waiving statutory fees ensures that lawyers will receive this "reasonable" statutory fee. Thus, if fee waivers are prohibited, permitting simultaneous fees and merits negotiations will not interfere with the Act; the lawyer will still be entitled to and will still receive a reasonable attorney's fee.   . . .

IV

Although today's decision will undoubtedly impair the effectiveness of the private enforcement scheme Congress established for civil rights legislation, I do not believe that it will bring about the total disappearance of "private attorneys general." It is to be hoped that Congress will repair this Court's mistake. In the meantime, other avenues of relief are available. The Court's decision in no way limits the power of state and local bar associations to regulate the ethical conduct of lawyers. Indeed, several Bar Associations have already declared it unethical for defense counsel to seek fee waivers. See Committee on Professional Ethics of the Association of the Bar of the City of New York, Op. No. 82–80 (1985); District of Columbia Legal Ethics Committee, Op. No. 147, supra n. 8, 113 Daily Washington Law Reporter, at 389. Such efforts are to be commended and, it is to be hoped, will be followed by other state and local organizations concerned with respecting the intent of Congress and with protecting civil rights.

In addition, it may be that civil rights attorneys can obtain agreements from their clients not to waive attorney's fees.[20] Such agreements simply replicate the private market for legal services (in which attorneys are not ordinarily required to contribute to their client's recovery[21]), and thus will enable civil rights practitioners to make it

17. For the reasons stated in Part III–C, I would permit simultaneous negotiation of fees and merits. The parties could agree upon a reasonable fee which would be subject to judicial approval under the Fees Act. Any settlement on the merits could be made contingent upon such approval. By permitting defendants to ascertain their total liability prior to settling, this approach fully alleviates the Court's concerns in this regard.

20. Since Congress has not sought to regulate ethical concerns either in the Fees Act or elsewhere, the legality of such arguments is purely a matter of local law. See Nix v. Whiteside, 475 U.S. 157, 176, 106 S.Ct. 988, 999, 89 L.Ed.2d 123 (1986) (Brennan, J., concurring in judgment).

21. One of the more peculiar aspects of the Court's interpretation of the Fees Act is that it permits defendants to require plaintiff's counsel to contribute his compensation to

economically feasible—as Congress hoped—to expend time and effort litigating civil rights claims.

. . .

Questions and Comments

What is a lawyer's proper course when offered a more-than-generous settlement for her client on the condition that she waive her attorney's fee? Was part of the problem in *Evans v. Jeff D.* that the lawyer had not anticipated such an offer from the defendant and reached an understanding with the client as to what the response should be? Given the nature of the client in *Jeff D.*, with whom would such an understanding have been made?

As both the opinions in *Jeff. D.* note, several bar associations had issued opinions holding it to be unethical for defendants to request fee waivers in exchange for relief on the merits. The majority emphasizes that these opinions were based on interpretations of the Fees Act and its purposes. In large measure that is true. Are these opinions vitiated by the decision in *Jeff. D.?* See Comment, *Evans v. Jeff D.* and the Proper Scope of State Ethics Decisions, 73 Va.L.Rev. 783 (1987), arguing that *Jeff. D.* should be taken as superseding state ethics decisions on this matter.

The New York City Bar Association's Committee on Professional and Judicial Ethics withdrew N.Y.Opinion 80–94 (1984), which is cited in *Jeff. D.*, in N.Y.Opinion 87–4 (1987). Opinion 87–4 says that whether a defendant may offer settlement conditioned on waiver of attorneys' fees is to be determined on a case-by-case basis, and lists nine factors to be considered in determining whether such an offer is ethical. It further states that plaintiffs' counsel is not ethically bound to accept a waiver of attorneys' fees. Why not?

Is *Jeff. D.* consistent with the purposes of the Fees Act as described by the Court? See The Supreme Court, 1985 Term: Leading Case: III. Federal Statutes and Regulations, 100 Harv.L.Rev. 258 (1986) (arguing that *Jeff. D.* undermines the Fees Act).

In most personal injury cases, the plaintiff's lawyer has a contingent fee arrangement. If the defendant offers the plaintiff $50,000 on the condition that plaintiff not pay the lawyer, presumably the plaintiff would have no incentive to accept because the lawyer could later sue for the fee due under the contract. In suits based on fee-shifting statutes, a lawyer could likewise sue her client to recover any agreed upon fee, but there are two problems with this remedy: (1) as in *Jeff. D.*, the plaintiff may have no monetary award from which to pay counsel, having sued or

---

satisfying the plaintiff's claims. In ordinary civil litigation, no defendant would make— or sell to his adversary—a settlement offer conditioned upon the plaintiff's convincing his attorney to contribute to the plaintiff's recovery. Yet today's decision creates a situation in which plaintiff's attorneys in civil rights cases are required to do just that. Thus, rather than treating civil rights claims no differently than other civil litigation, ante, at 1540 (quoting Marek v. Chesny, 473 U.S. 1, 10, 105 S.Ct. 3012, 3017, 87 L.Ed.2d 1 (1985)), the Court places such litigation in a quite unique—and unfavorable—category.

settled for injunctive relief; and (2) the governing bodies and granting agencies that control and support public interest law firms may prohibit or strongly protest the firm (or agency) bringing suit against the disadvantaged clients, whom it is dedicated to serve.

Could a plaintiff's lawyer serving on a contingent fee basis sue the defense counsel for tortious interference with contract? See, e.g., State Farm Mutual Insurance Co. v. St. Joseph's Hospital, 107 Ariz. 498, 489 P.2d 837 (1971) (holding that a lawyer may bring an action for tortious interference with contract against a third party who, for her own benefit, interferes with the lawyer-client relationship). Accord: Sharrow, Chartered v. State Farm Mutual Automobile Insurance Co., 306 Md. 754, 511 A.2d 492 (1986); Edwards v. Travelers Insurance of Hartford, Conn., 563 F.2d 105 (6th Cir.1977) (applying Tennessee law); Weiss v. Marcus, 51 Cal.App.3d 590, 124 Cal.Rptr. 297 (1975).

Why shouldn't civil rights lawyers have a similar cause of action? If they had contracts with their clients requiring the client to pay a contingent fee whether or not the court awarded fees, they could sue for tortious interference with contract. However, there is usually no such contract. Could a lawyer sue for tortious interference with a contract in which the client promises not to accept any settlement that was conditioned on a fee waiver? Should courts uphold such contracts?

Contracts Purporting to Restrict the Client's Right to Settle

Justice Brennan's dissent suggests that civil rights lawyers might find a way to live with *Jeff. D.* by asking their clients to agree not to accept any settlement conditioned on a fee waiver or that would result in the lawyer's receiving less than a "reasonable fee," noting that it is a matter of local law whether such agreements would be allowed.

The comment to M.R. 1.2 states, "[T]he client may not be asked to agree . . . to surrender . . . the right to settle litigation that the lawyer might wish to continue." See Lewis v. S.S. Baune, 534 F.2d 1115, rehearing denied, 545 F.2d 1299 (5th Cir.1976) (clauses in contract between lawyer and client prohibiting a settlement without lawyer's consent are void as against public policy). But see La.Rev.Stat.Ann. § 37–218 (Supp.1976) (permits a lawyer by contract to prohibit the client from settling without the lawyer's written consent).

What is wrong with agreements that limit the client's right to settle? For a discussion of this question see Calhoun, Attorney–Client Conflicts of Interest and the Concept of Non–Negotiable Fee Awards under 42 U.S.C. § 1988, 55 U.Colo.L.Rev. 341 (1984).

Negotiating Attorneys' Fees

In *Jeff. D.* the Supreme Court rejected the ban on simultaneous negotiations articulated in Prandini v. National Tea Co., 557 F.2d 1015 (3d Cir.1977) (lawyers' fees may not be negotiated until the parties have reached settlement on the damage award of the underlying claim). The

Court emphasized the need for the defendant to know what its ultimate liability would be before settling. Can this need be satisfied without permitting simultaneous negotiation of fees? The defendant's need for certainty on its maximum exposure might be satisfied by having the plaintiff's lawyer supply information on the firm's hourly charge and the number of hours worked, as the dissent in *Jeff. D.* argues. However, this approach neglects the possibility of the court awarding a multiplier to the basic "lodestar" calculation (lodestar is hours times hourly rate). Plaintiff could promise that no multiplier would be sought, but wouldn't that be negotiating the fee?

Disabled Clients

In *Jeff. D.*, the client was a class of mentally disabled youngsters. Does that affect what the lawyer should do? See M.R. 1.14, Client Under a Disability. We leave for Chapter 9 the question of the responsibility of the lawyer who represents a class, but what of the responsibility of the lawyer who directly represents a minor or disabled person?

The Model Code has no rule on representing a client under a disability, although EC 7–12 does deal with this issue. The thrust of M.R. 1.14 is similar to EC 7–12, although read with its Comment the Rule provides more detail. Rule 1.14 provides:

> (a) When the client's ability to make adequately considered decisions in connection with the representation is impaired, whether because of minority, mentally disability or for some other reason, the lawyer shall, as far as possible, maintain a normal client-lawyer relationship with the client.

> (b) A lawyer may seek the appointment of a guardian or take other protective action with respect to a client, only when the lawyer reasonably believes that the client cannot adequately act in the client's own interest.

Paragraph (a) of the rule and the corresponding Comment remind the lawyer that a client under a disability may still be capable of participating in the representation, even if the client is unable to participate as fully as other clients. As the Comment states:

> . . . [A]n incapacitated person may have no power to make legally binding decisions. Nevertheless, a client lacking legal competence often has the ability to understand, deliberate upon, and reach conclusions about matters affecting the client's own well-being. . . . The fact that the client suffers a disability does not diminish the lawyer's obligation to treat the client with attention and respect.

It has been held that the lawyer must ordinarily respect the client's decision to contest a civil commitment proceeding or to refrain from asserting an incompetency defense in a criminal case. See, e.g., In re Link, 713 S.W.2d 487 (Mo.1986) (in civil incompetency proceedings, where lawyer concludes that the client is capable of understanding the matter, the lawyer must abide by the client's decisions on whether to waive or exercise a right). See also Frendak v. United States, 408 A.2d 364 (D.C.App.1979) (defendant's decision to waive insanity defense should be respected). But see In re the Marriage of Beverly C. Rolfe, 216 Mont. 39, 699 P.2d 79 (1985) (while lawyer representing disabled client ordinarily should be guided by client, in custody proceedings lawyer should advocate child's best interests even where they are at odds with child's wishes); Thompson v. Wainwright, 787 F.2d 1447 (11th Cir.1986) (lawyer who believed that his client had mental problems should not have relied on his client's request that he forego the *investigation* of mitigating evidence).

When a legally incompetent client is adjudged unable to make a decision such as whether to dispose of property, the lawyer cannot act unless the lawyer has been legally appointed as guardian. If a guardian already exists, the lawyer "should ordinarily look to the representative for decisions on behalf of the client." Comment to M.R. 1.14. See EC 7–12 to the same effect. Why does the Comment qualify this statement with the word "ordinarily"? See Neely, Handicapped Advocacy: Inherent Barriers and Partial Solutions in the Representation of Disabled Children, 33 Hastings L.J. 1359 (1982) (arguing that lawyers for a disabled client should not accept without critical examination the decisions made by a guardian on behalf of the client). For a general analysis of the lawyer's relationship with the guardian of a disabled client or the fiduciary for any dependent client see Hazard, Triangular Lawyer Relationships, reprinted in Chapter 9 below. The presence of a guardian does not relieve the lawyer of the obligation to treat the disabled client as a client to the extent possible, particularly in maintaining communication. See the Comment to M.R. 1.14.

When there is no guardian M.R. 1.14(b) cautions that the lawyer should seek the appointment of a guardian "only when the lawyer reasonably believes that the client cannot adequately act in the client's own interests." But as the Comment suggests, even where the lawyer believes the standard of 1.14(b) has been met, seeking a guardian and thereby raising the question of incompetency may on balance do more harm to the client than good. The Comment says: "The lawyer's position in such cases is an unavoidably difficult one." It advises that the lawyer might seek guidance from a mental health professional.

When the lawyer decides that on balance a guardian should not be sought, the lawyer acts as de facto guardian, making certain decisions for the client and sometimes deciding to act against the client's express wishes. In State v. Aumann, 265 N.W.2d 316 (Iowa 1978), for example, the court held it proper, given the extent of the client's disability, for the lawyer to have decided against the client's wishes to take an appeal.

In Paternalism and the Legal Profession, 1981 Wis.L.Rev. 454, 455, Professor Luban gives the following two hypotheticals, arguing that in the first the lawyer would be justified in overriding the client's decision, but not in the second where the client is able to articulate values for the decision:

> You are the court-appointed attorney representing the interests of a thirteen-year-old boy in a custody case. You must make a report to the court about who should get custody . . . Your client, an inarticulate and unhappy looking boy in a faded jean jacket, is sullen and suspicious. He says he would rather live with his father, but falls silent when you try to find out why. The father is a glad-handing, sporadically employed alcoholic; the mother is a hard-working disciplinarian who lives with her mother in a tidy row-house. Both women appear concerned for your client's welfare. In your opinion, the boy prefers his father because his father lets him get away with more; the social worker on the case tells you that the boy is part of a drinking and doping crowd.

. . .

> Your client is a teen-ager who was involved in a car accident in which his date was killed. He is charged with driving while intoxicated and vehicular homicide, but some of the circumstances are unclear, and the prosecutor offers to let him plead guilty to reckless operation of a vehicle. Client, however, insists that he will plead guilty to the greater charges, and in an emotional scene tells you that he cannot live with himself unless he publicly confesses what he knows to be his crime and expiates the guilt by going to jail.

See also Tremblay, On Persuasion and Paternalism: Lawyer Decision-making and the Questionably Competent Client, 1987 Utah L.Rev. 515. Professor Tremblay identifies six options available to the lawyer and finds that each one entails its own ethical problems: (1) follow the client's expressed wishes whatever the consequences; (2) seek a guardian; (3) allow the family of the disabled client to make the decisions usually reserved for the client; (4) act as a de facto guardian; (5) try to persuade the client to accept the lawyer's judgment on the appropriate course to follow; and (6) withdraw. He concludes that lawyer supersession of the client's right to make decisions is only warranted in emergencies; that only in extreme cases should the lawyer seek a guardian; that relying in part on the family is justifiable; and that non-coercive persuasion is the appropriate course in moderate cases of disability. Id. at 584. See also Uphoff, The Role of the Criminal Defense Lawyer in Representing The Mentally Impaired Defendant: Zealous Advocate or Officer of the Court?, 1988 Wis.L.Rev. 65 (exploring alternatives to raising competency for the lawyer representing a mentally impaired criminal defendant).

On representing children, see Wizner and Berkman, Being a Lawyer for a Child Too Young to be a Client: A Clinical Study, 68 Neb.L.Rev. 330 (1989); Mnookin, Burt, Chambers, Wald, Sugarman, Zimring and Solomon, In the Interest of Children: Advocacy, Law Reform and Public Policy (1985); Guggenheim, The Right to be Represented But Not Heard: Reflections on Legal Representation of Children, 59 N.Y.U.L.Rev. 76 (1984) (concluding that "mature" children—the author suggests children over seven might be considered in this category—should be allowed to direct their lawyers' conduct; but that for children too young to direct the lawyer's conduct none of the existing models for the lawyer are adequate).

Transactions Between Lawyer and Client

Trust Accounts

The Prohibition Against Commingling Funds

> I will on no occasion blend with my own my client's money. If kept *distinctly as his,* it will be less liable to be considered *as my own.*

> From David Hoffman's Fifty Resolutions on the professional responsibility of lawyers published in 1836, reprinted in J. Ram, A Treatise on Facts as Subjects of Inquiry by a Jury 386–399 (3d ed. 1982).

Although this simple rule has been recognized as fundamental for as long as lawyers have had written ethics codes, it is still one of the most frequent bases for disciplinary action against lawyers. See Matter of Hessler, 549 A.2d 700 n. 1 (D.C.App.1988), citing Annotation, Attorney's Commingling of Client's Funds with His Own as Grounds for Disciplinary Action—Modern Status, 94 A.L.R.3d 846, 850 (1979).

The Code provision on safeguarding client property is DR 9–102. Brickman, The Advance Fee Payment Dilemma, 10 Cardozo L.Rev. 647, 656 (1989) provides a summary of the provisions of this rule:

> . . . [Its] design . . . can be best gleaned if the protections are listed in the chronological order in which they come to apply to client property. The birth of fiduciary concern occurs when the attorney comes into possession of client property in any of its various forms; for example securities or funds. At that point, if it did not come directly from the client he is to notify the client of its receipt. The attorney must initiate careful record keeping procedures for all client property in his possession regardless of whether it came to him directly from the client or was paid or delivered by a third party, and is to render an accounting to the client whenever appropriate. If the property is in the form of securities or other valuable items, it is to be safeguarded by placement in a safe deposit box (or other safe place) as quickly as possible. If the property is in the form of "funds of clients paid to a lawyer" including "funds belonging in part to a client and in part presently or potentially to the lawyer," it is to be safeguarded by segregating it from the lawyer's personal funds and depositing it to a client security account.

M.R. 1.15, Safekeeping Property, is substantially similar to DR 9–102, but it applies also to property of a third person that is in the lawyer's possession in connection with the representation.

As to funds partly or potentially belonging to the lawyer, the lawyer may withdraw funds from the trust account when payment from the client is due *unless* the client disputes the lawyer's claim, in which case the disputed portion "shall not be withdrawn, until the dispute is finally resolved." DR 9–102(A)(2). M.R. 1.15(c) is to the same effect. A fair reading of these provisions requires the lawyer to deposit money received as a general retainer in a trust account and allows withdrawal only as the fee is earned. The majority of jurisdictions require such segregation. See, e.g., In re Aronson, 352 N.W.2d 17 (Minn.1984); and Miele v. Commissioner, 72 T.C. 284 (1979) (interpreting Pennsylvania code to require segregation of retainer fees). For a more complete list see Brickman, The Advance Fee Dilemma, supra, n. 47 at 655. (Professor Brickman argues that the majority rule is correct). A minority of jurisdictions permit the lawyer to deposit advance fee payments in the general office account. See, e.g., N.Y. State Bar Assn. Comm. on Professional Ethics, Op. 570 (1985); and D.C. Bar, Op. 113 (1982).

The prohibition against commingling is violated whether the lawyer deposits the client's money in the lawyer's account or the lawyer's money is deposited in the client's trust account. A violation occurs even if the lawyer was merely negligent. "[I]t is essentially a per se offense." In re Hessler, 549 A.2d 700 n. 3 (D.C.App.1988); Fitzsimmons v. State Bar, 34 Cal.3d 327, 667 P.2d 700, 702 (1983). Courts treat violations of the ban against commingling of funds very seriously. See, e.g., In re Pierson, 280 Or. 513, 571 P.2d 907, 908–09 (1977) (a single conversion of client funds will result in disbarment); Akron Bar Ass'n v. Hughes, 46 Ohio St.2d 369, 348 N.E.2d 712, 715 (1976) (penalty for commingling of funds is either indefinite suspension or disbarment). In Matter of Wilson, 81 N.J. 451, 409 A.2d 1153, 1154–55 (1979), the court held that in cases of intentional commingling the court would not consider a lawyer's inexperience, an otherwise outstanding career or the lawyer's restitution of the funds as mitigating factors:

> [The lawyer] knowingly used his client's money as if it were his own. We hold that disbarment is the only appropriate discipline [and] . . . use this occasion to state that generally all such cases shall result in disbarment.

Like many rules governing the behavior of lawyers, this one has its roots in the confidence and trust which clients place in their attorneys. Having sought his advice and relying on his expertise, the client entrusts the lawyer with the transaction—including the handling of the client's funds. . . .

It is a trust built on centuries of honesty and faithfulness. Sometimes it is reinforced by personal knowledge of a particular lawyer's integrity or a firm's reputation. The underlying faith, however, is in the legal profession, the bar as an institution. No other explanation can account for clients' customary willingness to entrust their funds to relative strangers simply because they are lawyers.

· · ·

> What are the merits of these cases? The attorney has stolen the client's money. No clearer wrong suffered by a client at the hands of one he had every reason to trust can be imagined. The public is entitled, not as a matter of satisfying unjustifiable expectations, but as a simple matter of maintaining confidence, to know that never again will that person be a lawyer. . . .

In discussing whether restitution should matter in determining the appropriate discipline, the court said:

> When restitution is used to support the contention that the lawyer intended to "borrow" rather than steal, it simply cloaks the mistaken premise that unauthorized use of clients' funds is excusable when accompanied by an intent to return them. The act is no less a crime. . . . Banks do not rehire tellers who "borrow" depositors' funds. Our professional standards, if anything, should be higher. . . .

Id. at 1156.

Record Keeping

Both the Code and the Rules require that the lawyer maintain complete records of all funds and property maintained by the lawyer for another. M.R. 1.15(a) specifies that the records be kept for five years following the termination of the representation. New Jersey, which generally has stricter regulations for the legal profession than most other jurisdictions, has detailed requirements for law office bookkeeping, including provisions on recording the flow of all entrusted funds, billing the client, paying others on behalf of the client, and reconciling ledger and bank statements. The records must be kept "in accordance with generally accepted accounting practice" and retained for seven years, along with "copies of those portions of each client's case file reasonably necessary for a complete understanding of the financial transactions pertaining thereto." N.J.Court Rules 1:21–6. Some other states have adopted requirements above those in the Code and Rules, e.g., N.H. Rule 37 § 7 (specifying accounting system, including separate ledger pages for each client and an index to all trust accounts).

The American Bar Association has been considering an amendment to the Model Rules that would require a lawyer's financial accounts to be subject to random inspection by the bar regulatory agency. Several jurisdictions, in addition to New Jersey, have adopted audit procedures, e.g., Iowa Code Ann. § 61–610, Court Rule 121.4 (1975); Wash. Rules for Lawyer Discipline, Rule 13.1(a) (1985). See generally Hecht, Audit Procedures for Lawyers' Trust Accounts: Their Use and Benefit, ABA Standing Committee on Lawyer's Responsibility for Client Protection (1985).

Client Security Funds

Many jurisdictions have set up client security funds to provide some reimbursement for clients whose assets have been misappropriated by a lawyer admitted to the state bar. These funds are often maintained by mandatory contributions from lawyers in the state or by state bar dues money. They are woefully inadequate as a means of providing restitution for victims of lawyer dishonesty. The amount maintained in such accounts is far below the amount lawyers actually misappropriate each year. To qualify for funds, the client must show that all avenues of relief against the lawyer have been exhausted to no avail. Further, there are usually other demanding showings that the client must make to obtain compensation. Assuming the client makes it over those hurdles, there are generally ceilings on the amount each client may recover; the amount paid out per lawyer who violates the rule no matter how many clients are injured; and/or the amount per transaction.

Why shouldn't lawyers be required to obtain a fidelity bond against defalcation with client funds?

Keeping the Money of Multiple Clients in One Account

The rules allow a lawyer to use one trust account to deposit the funds of multiple clients. This is necessary because for many clients the lawyer may hold amounts too small or too briefly to justify the maintenance of a separate trust account. If, on the other hand, the client's funds are great enough and the time the lawyer is to hold those funds is long enough, the lawyer should put the money in a separate interest bearing account. See, e.g., In re Petition of Minn. State Bar Ass'n, 332 N.W.2d 151, 157 (Minn.1982). The Comment to M.R. 1.15 states that "[s]eparate trust accounts may be warranted when administering estate monies or acting in similar fiduciary capacities." A state statute or case law may require the maintenance of a separate account in certain situations. See, e.g., Attorney Grievance Commission v. Boehm, 293 Md. 476, 446 A.2d 52 (1982) (separate account necessary when administering an estate).

IOLTA Funds

IOLTA stands for Interest on Lawyers Trust Accounts. Trust accounts containing the funds of multiple clients were traditionally non-interest bearing accounts because the lawyer has no right to the interest, and calculating and distributing the interest to each client was not administratively feasible. Today, almost all states have IOLTA plans. Under these plans the funds of multiple clients are kept in interest bearing "IOLTA accounts." The state either requires the lawyer to maintain the money of multiple clients in these accounts or allows the lawyer to do so. When an IOLTA account has been established, the bank pays the aggregate interest on the account to the state bar's IOLTA program. The money is used primarily to fund legal services for the poor, but other uses include funding of client security accounts or projects relating to the administration of justice.

Where lawyers are required to participate, the funds raised by IOLTA programs are substantial. Florida, the state where IOLTA began, raised almost $1 million in the first year that its mandatory plan was in operation. In less than five years, California's mandatory program raised $40 million. Where the plans are voluntary, lawyer participation is generally low perhaps due to the fact that lawyers who keep their money in non-interest bearing accounts are favored customers of banks. Is it ethical to accept benefits from a bank in exchange for keeping a non-interest bearing account?

After the Federal Government cutbacks in funding for legal services programs for the poor in the early 1980's (see Chapter 10), IOLTA programs were expected to help make up the shortfall. Revenue has, however, been far below expectations where IOLTA programs are voluntary. In 1988, responding to the great difference in effectiveness between mandatory and voluntary programs, the ABA House of Delegates adopted a resolution urging states to make their voluntary IOLTA programs mandatory.

In Cone v. State Bar of Florida, 819 F.2d 1002 (11th Cir.1987), Florida's mandatory IOLTA program was upheld against a challenge that it constituted an unconstitutional taking of property without just compensation. See also Carroll v. State Bar of California, 166 Cal.App. 3d 1193, 213 Cal.Rptr. 305 (1985) (upholding the California mandatory program against various constitutional challenges).

The biggest threat to the continued vitality of IOLTA plans is technological innovation. Banks are developing software that makes it cost effective to keep track of the interest earned by relatively small amounts of money deposited within larger accounts. A few banks have already made these subaccounting services available to lawyers. If the interest can be returned to the client, can IOLTA plans be justified?

Business Transactions With Clients

Lawyer-client business dealings are addressed by DR 5–104(A) of the Code and M.R. 1.8(a).

Rule 1.8(a) provides that:

A lawyer shall not enter into a business transaction with a client . . . unless:

(1) the transaction and terms . . . are fair and reasonable to the client and are fully disclosed and transmitted in writing to the client . . .;

(2) the client is given reasonable opportunity to seek the advice of independent counsel in the transaction; and

(3) the client consents in writing thereto.

The rules governing business transactions with a client apply whether or not the lawyer is "actually" representing the client in the transaction. The focus is whether an ordinary person in the circumstances would look to the lawyer as a protector rather than an adversary or a person dealing at arms length. Sexton v. Arkansas Supreme Court Committee on Professional Conduct, 299 Ark. 439, 774 S.W.2d 114 (1989); Matter of Spear, 160 Ariz. 545, 774 P.2d 1335 (1989). A violation may be established whether or not the client suffers economic loss. Committee on Professional Ethics and Conduct v. Baker, 269 N.W.2d 463, 466 (Iowa 1978). Even where the terms of the transaction are reasonable, failure to make full disclosure of the potential conflict of interest is a violation. See In re Appeal of Panel's Affirmance, 425 N.W.2d 824 (Minn.1988). On the requirement that a client be given a reasonable opportunity to seek the advice of independent counsel, see Matter of Smyzer, 108 N.J. 47, 527 A.2d 857, 862 (1987) (interpreting Rule 1.8(a)(2), the court stated that a "passing suggestion" that a client consult a second attorney does not discharge the lawyer's duty to carefully explain to the client the need for independent legal advice upon entry into business transactions in which the lawyer and client have different interests).

Under common law, a lawyer in a transaction with a client is treated as a fiduciary. As such the lawyer has the burden of proving that the transaction is "fair and equitable" to the client. In some jurisdictions this requirement is augmented by a "presumption" that such a transaction is tainted by fraud. It is not always clear whether the presumption means more than imposing on the lawyer the burden of proof.

Most of the reported cases appear to involve one of the following situations: (1) lawyer buying estate property from estate beneficiaries; (2) lawyer investing funds awarded in settlement of personal injury or wrongful death action; (3) loan from client to lawyer; (4) secured loan from lawyer to client. In most cases the client was not an experienced business person. Little wonder the cases make hard law.

For illustrative cases, see Matter of Smyzer, supra (lawyer convinced client to invest proceeds from the sale of her home in a holding company without disclosing his interest in the company); Sexton, supra, (client loan to lawyer; terms usurious; failure to disclose risks of nonpayment); Matter of Wolk, 82 N.J. 326, 413 A.2d 317 (1980) (lawyer advised widow to invest $10,000 of her inheritance in a second mortgage on property worth half that amount which was owned by a company in which the lawyer owned a 25 percent interest, concealing from her the recent purchase price of the property, its real value, and that the taxes on it were unpaid).

In light of this sad experience, it would be defensible to prohibit any business transaction with a client except transactions in the client's ordinary course of business, such as buying a car from a client in the automobile business. Such a prohibition may be the practical effect of some court decisions, for example, Matter of Neville, 147 Ariz. 106, 708 P.2d 1297 (1985). In Neville the client was an experienced real estate trader who had been represented by the lawyer in various real estate deals over a period of ten years. Dispute arose concerning certain deals in which the lawyer participated. The court said:

> The policy expressed by DR 5–104 is based on the realization that those who consider themselves clients come to depend upon the confidentiality and fairness arising from their relationships with their attorneys. They do not take a transactional approach to these relationships, turning their confidence on and off at the end of each transaction . . .

> We hold . . . that . . . DR 5–104(A) . . . applies . . . to transactions in which . . . an ordinary person would look to the lawyer as a protector rather than as an adversary . . .

> The lawyer must give the client that information which he would have been obliged to give if he had been counsel rather than interested party . . .

If this statement of the law applies to a client who had long experience in the very type of transaction, would any substantial transaction between lawyer and client in effect be voidable at the client's option? Should a lawyer deal with a client on that assumption? Should a lawyer deal with a client at all?

For statements suggesting that the only safe course is for a lawyer to avoid all business transactions with a client, see, e.g., Matter of Spear, 160 Ariz. 545, 774 P.2d 1335, 1344 (1989) ("The better rule may be to prohibit entirely lawyer-client business dealings . . . As a general rule . . . no lawyer should allow a client to invest or otherwise participate in the lawyer's business ventures unless the client obtains independent legal advice. Nothing else will protect our profession's integrity and the public interest."); Committee on Professional Ethics v. Postma, 430 N.W.2d 387, 391–92 (Iowa 1988) ("[W]e have done our best to discourage business ventures between attorneys and their clients . . . [The lawyer has] three alternatives when [the client proposes a deal]. The safest and perhaps best course [is] to refuse to participate . . . Alternatively, he [can] recommend . . . the client obtain independent advice. Finally . . . he [can make] the least desirable choice . . . he [can] attempt . . . to meet the high standard of disclosure . . ."); Matter of Pascoe, 113 N.J. 229, 549 A.2d 1247, 1248 (1988) ("As a general rule, an attorney should refrain from engaging in transactions with a client or former client who has not obtained independent legal advice on the matter"; client's long experience in transactions of this type does not exonerate the lawyer who otherwise violates the rule). Cf. Alala v. Peachtree Plantations, Inc., 292 S.C. 160, 355 S.E.2d 286 (1987) (after carefully scrutinizing lawyer/client transaction court found that it was acceptable given that the clients were three experienced land developers and the terms of the contract were fair).

On the risks of participating in a business venture with a client, see Merton, The Evils of Lawyer–Client Deals, California Lawyer, December 1987, p. 53; and Benevino, Attorney–Client Business Transactions: An Analysis of the Ethical Problems, 6 J.Law & Com. 443 (1986).

Acquiring an Interest in Litigation and Advancing Funds to the Client

Both the Model Code and the Model Rules prohibit the lawyer from acquiring a propriety interest in litigation. DR 5–103(A) and M.R. 1.8(j). There are, however, exceptions. The lawyer may acquire a lien against the client's property to secure the lawyer's fee or expenses when other law so provides. The lawyer may advance litigation costs when and to the extent that the rules allow. See DR 5–103(B) and M.R. 1.8(e).

An attorney's retaining lien allows a lawyer to keep possession of the client's property, but not to sell it, until the client pays what is owed to the lawyer. A charging lien attaches to the proceeds of litigation and allows the lawyer to recover expenses and fees incurred in that litigation. For guidelines on whether to invoke a retaining lien, see ABA Inf.Op. 1461 (1980). See also Rubel v. Brimacombe & Schlecte, P.C., 86 B.R. 81 (E.D.Mich.1988) (using the guidelines to decide whether to allow an attorney's charging lien). Lawyers may be disciplined for asserting charging liens that are the equivalent of illegal contingent fees. See, e.g., State ex rel. Nebraska Bar Ass'n v. Jensen, 171 Neb. 1, 105 N.W.2d 459 (1960) (attorney's lien upon 15% of wife's alimony, in effect a contingent fee contract). On attorneys' liens generally, see Wolfram, Modern Legal Ethics § 9.6.3, pp. 558–562 (1986).

As for advancing costs of litigation to the client, DR 5–103(B) provides:

> While representing a client in connection with contemplated or pending litigation, a lawyer shall not advance or guarantee financial assistance to his client, except that a lawyer may advance or guarantee the expenses of litigation, including court costs, expenses of investigation, expenses of medical examination, and costs of obtaining and presenting evidence, provided that the client remains ultimately liable for such expenses.

M.R. 1.8(e) is somewhat different. It provides:

> A lawyer shall not provide financial assistance to a client in connection with pending or contemplated litigation, except that:
>
> (1) A lawyer may advance court costs and expenses of litigation, the repayment of which may be contingent on the outcome of the matter; and
>
> (2) A lawyer representing an indigent client may pay court costs and expenses of litigation on behalf of the client.

Both rules implicitly prohibit the lawyer from advancing the client money for anything other than litigation expenses, i.e., for living expenses or doctor bills while litigation is pending. Why?

What are the differences between the above two provisions? Given that contingent fees are allowed in some cases, why not allow other means of acquiring an interest in litigation? What purposes are served by these rules?

In Louisiana State Bar Ass'n v. Edwins, 329 So.2d 437 (La.1976), the court held that a lawyer could provide financial assistance to a client under certain circumstances, provided that the advances were not used to solicit clients. The problems engendered by this approach are discussed in Sims v. Selvage, 499 So.2d 325 (La.App.1986). In *Sims,* the client discharged his lawyer, testifying that he did so because the lawyer refused to provide money to pay his medical fees. The court said of the *Edwins* rule:

> The obviously well intended interpretation of [DR] 5–103(B) in [*Edwins*] . . ., to allow "a lawyer's guarantee of necessary medical treatment for his client, even for a non-litigation related illness . . . if the lawyer for reasons of humanity can afford to do so", and to authorize as expenses of litigation, "the advance or guarantee by a lawyer to a client (who has already retained him) of minimal living expenses, of minor sums necessary to prevent foreclosures, or of necessary medical treatment" . . . has created problems within the profession that override any benefit to the client. *Edwins,* in conjunction with [case law] allowing the client to withdraw from the contingency fee contract with relative impunity, pretty well guarantees that clients will not remain with the attorney who does not gear his practice to providing this type of service. No attorney solicitation is necessary. The reputation of providing these services is enough to draw the client. . . . The profession is demeaned [by this situation]. Surely, it is time to reconsider this whole area.

> Id. at 329.

A few other states allow lawyers to advance funds in situations prohibited under the Model Code and Model Rules. See, e.g., California Rule of Court 4–210. Also see M.R. 1.8(e) as amended in Minnesota and North Dakota.

For a critical view of the prohibition against acquiring an interest in litigation as it applies to plaintiffs' lawyers in class action suits, see Coffee, Understanding the Plaintiff's Attorney . . . reprinted in Chapter 9 below.

Gifts from Clients

Courts have always looked at gifts from clients with a highly skeptical eye and have invalidated them on a theory of presumptive fraud unless the lawyer has clearly demonstrated that the gift was not the result of undue influence or overreaching. See, e.g., Matter of Putnam's Will, 257 N.Y. 140, 177 N.E. 399 (1931); McDonald v. Hewlett, 102 Cal.App.2d 680, 228 P.2d 83 (1951); Laspy v. Anderson, 361 S.W.2d 680 (Mo.1962). For more recent cases to the same effect, see, e.g., Klaskin v. Klepak, 126 Ill. 376, 534 N.E.2d 971 (1989); In re Mapes, 738 S.W.2d 853 (Mo.1987).

While the Code lacks a disciplinary rule on the subject, EC 5–5 provides that: "[a] lawyer should not suggest to his client that a gift be made" to the lawyer; and that before accepting any gift from the client the lawyer should urge the client to obtain advice from an independent person. EC 5–5 concludes: "Other than in exceptional circumstances, a lawyer should insist that an instrument in which [the client names the lawyer as a beneficiary] be prepared by another lawyer selected by the client." The lack of a specific disciplinary rule has not deterred courts from disciplining lawyers for conduct not in conformity with EC 5–5. Discipline has been imposed under DR 5–101(A), the general conflict of interest provision, and under DR 1–102(A)(4) and (A)(6), prohibiting conduct that adversely reflects on the lawyer's fitness to practice. See, e.g., Matter of Rentiers, 297 S.C. 33, 374 S.E.2d 672 (1988) (public reprimand under DR 5–101(A) for drafting a will in which the lawyer/draftsman was named as executor, trustee of a testamentary trust and given a one year option to purchase two pieces of real estate at half their market value; the court found that the lawyer failed to disclose that the will would be vulnerable to attack upon grounds of undue influence and that other problems would attend any challenge); Mahoning County Bar Association v. Theofilos, 36 Ohio St.3d 43, 521 N.E.2d 797 (1988) (lawyer disciplined under DR 1–102(A)(6) for drafting a will that provided a $200,000 bequest for lawyer and his son and provided nothing for the client's relatives; lawyer failed to insist that independent counsel draft the will); Matter of Sherbunt, 134 A.D.2d 723, 520 N.Y.S.2d 885 (1987) (disciplined under DR 1–102(A)(6) for accepting $45,000 gift from an elderly client without urging that the client seek disinterested advice); and In re Vogel, 92 Ill.2d 55, 440 N.E.2d 885 (1982) (disciplined for failing to make full disclosure before writing himself into the will).

M.R. 1.8(c) states:

A lawyer shall not prepare an instrument giving the lawyer or a person related to the lawyer as parent, child, sibling, or spouse any substantial gift from a client including a testamentary gift, except where the client is related to the donee.

This absolute prohibition goes beyond pre-Rules case law, which permitted a lawyer to draft such an instrument, if the lawyer has urged the client to seek independent legal assistance, provided full disclosure and the client continued to insist that the lawyer do so. See the cases cited above. The Rule is, however, narrower than the cases in that the Rule only applies to substantial gifts transferred by instruments drafted by the lawyer/beneficiary. What about gifts transferred without papers?

The Comment to M.R. 1.8 assumes that any substantial gift will require the preparation of documents and thus will fall under 1.8(c). As for smaller gifts, the Comment states that these may be accepted as long as "the transaction meets general standards of fairness." Even if another lawyer drafts the instrument of transfer, remember that the gift is still a transaction between the lawyer/beneficiary and the client and thus must meet the standard of fairness imposed by M.R. 1.8(a).

Model Rule 1.8(c) provides an exception for instruments drafted by a lawyer for people to whom the lawyer is related. This exception does not, however, apply to friends of the lawyer. Lawyers must insist that friends who wish to make a gift to the lawyer retain other counsel to draft the documents of transfer. Even relatives of the lawyer (and the lawyer herself) are well advised to have independent counsel draft any documents of tranfer whenever possible, the exception in 1.8(c) notwithstanding. If the relative wishes to make a substantial gift to the lawyer or there is any chance that the gift will be challenged, independent counsel should be obtained.

Note that when a lawyer is disqualified under M.R. 1.8(c), those in practice with the lawyer are likewise disqualified. See M.R. 1.10, discussed in Chapter 8 below.

For a thorough examination of the legality and propriety of an estate lawyer writing a will that names the lawyer as a beneficiary or as executor or as attorney for the estate, see Johnston, An Ethical Analysis of Common Estate Planning Practices—Is Good Business Bad Ethics?, 45 Ohio State L.J. 57 (1984).

E.   TERMINATING THE LAWYER–CLIENT RELATIONSHIP

PLAZA SHOE STORE V. HERMEL
Supreme Court of Missouri, en banc, 1982.
636 S.W.2d 53.

MORGAN, JUDGE.

The appellants, Plaza Shoe Store, et al., brought the underlying suit against Hermel, Inc., apparently for alleged negligence in the design and construction of a building which appellants leased. This action was eventually settled with appellants receiving approximately $58,000, which was placed in escrow by the court. Greene, Cassity, Carnahan, Freemont & Greene, respondents, had been employed originally by appellants under a contingent fee contract to handle the action against Hermel, Inc., but they had been discharged prior to any judgment or settlement. Respondents filed their Notice of Attorneys' Lien, and then moved the court to distribute a certain amount of the funds in connection therewith. The case at bar involves the trial, held without a jury, on the attorneys' lien issue.

The facts necessary for resolution of this case were ably set out in a detailed "findings of fact" by the Hon. J. Powell. The findings, without benefit of quotation marks, are:

1.   Plaintiffs and movants entered into a contingent fee contract whereby plaintiffs were to pay movants one-third (⅓) of any and all

amounts received by way of settlement in the above-captioned law suit, plus all out-of-pocket expenses.

2.   At the time movants received this case, it had minimal settlement value for the following reasons:

a.   The named plaintiff was neither the occupant nor the tenant of the premise and had sustained no damages.

b.   The Statute of Limitations was about to lapse as to the Plaza Mall, Inc., the proper party of this action, and defendant was aware the wrong party was named as plaintiff.

c.   Plaintiff had withheld rents without placing same into escrow, and a Motion for Summary Judgment was pending wherein defendants allege breach of the lease and sought termination of same.

d.   The lease in question specifically prohibited recovery for damaged merchandise due to negligence on the part of defendant Hermel, Inc.

e.   No offers of settlement or compromise had been made prior to movants' entry into this case.

3.   The time expended and charges assessed by the various attorneys for movants in this case were as follows:

Attorney	Time (Hours)	In Office Charges Per Hour	Out Office Charges Per Hour
Douglas W. Greene	115–¾ (per stipulation)	$50.00	$60.00
J. Douglas Cassity	40	40.00	50.00
James P. Ferguson	158–¾	40.00	40.00
Robert W. Freeman	2	40.00	40.00
Douglas W. Greene III	10–¾	40.00	40.00
John M. Carnaham III	¼	40.00	40.00
William D. Shepard	6	40.00	40.00

4.   This case was a very complex case involving numerous issues, and expenditures of time and charges as set out above were reasonable.

5.   Movants provided excellent representation to plaintiffs and obtained good results in the following respects:

a.   Movants took a three-year-old case with no settlement offers and a total prayer for damages of $43,441.40 and obtained an offer of settlement of $50,000.00 cash, plus the possibility of a reduction of rent for the remaining fifteen years on plaintiffs' lease with defendant.

b.   Movants amended the original petition to add the proper plaintiffs who actually suffered the damages set out in the original petition.

c.   Movants conducted extensive discovery which disclosed knowledge on the part of the architect and builder of the Battlefield Mall that a dangerous condition existed, but that said architect and builder failed to take steps to correct same.

d. Movants added as defendants the architect and builder of said Battlefield Mall and obtained contributions from them to the final settlement in this case.

6. Movants received and conveyed to plaintiffs offers of $25,000.00, $32,500.00, and $47,500.00, but in each instance advised plaintiffs to refuse same.

7. Movants received an offer of settlement from defendants for a $50,000.00 cash payment plus a possibility of a reduction of rent in the remaining fifteen years on plaintiffs' lease with defendant Hermel, Inc.

8. Movants relayed that offer of $50,000.00 cash plus a possibility of a reduction of rent payments to plaintiffs and recommended the same be accepted.

9. Plaintiffs, upon being advised of said offer, accused movants of being crooks and selling them out to defendants. Said allegations by plaintiffs were unfounded and without merit.

10. Upon being accused by plaintiffs of being crooks and selling plaintiffs out to defendants, movants could no longer adequately represent plaintiffs and terminated their employment contract with plaintiffs.

11. Movants duly filed notice of attorneys' lien and subsequently entered into a stipulation with plaintiffs agreeing movants would release all papers to plaintiffs and no waiver of attorneys' lien would be construed or raised by plaintiffs.

12. On October 22, 1976, movants submitted a bill to plaintiffs seeking a fee of $16,470.00, plus costs. The Memorandum of Agreement, which is movants' Exhibit 13, and the lien filed in this cause, was based upon a fee of $16,470.00, plus costs. Said amount does not represent one-third of $50,000.00, and movants now seek $16,666.66, plus out-of-pocket expense. The court finds that movants are committed to the original amount claimed as a fee, i.e., $16,470.00.

13. The court finds that movants charged plaintiffs for costs and expenses in the amount of $1,258.07. The court further finds that movants did not credit plaintiffs with two payments of $116.55 as shown by plaintiff's evidence. The court further finds that one of the out-of-pocket expenses is investigator fees totaling $252.12. Movants were unable to produce the name of such investigator, nor did they produce any time slips of such investigator. The court concludes that such expense is not supported by the evidence.

14. The court finds that movants are entitled to a fee of $16,470.00, plus out-of-pocket expense of $772.85, or a total of $17,242.85.

15. In the event it shall be determined that this court erred in upholding the contingency fee contract, the court finds from the evidence that the reasonable value of the services rendered by the attorneys is: Ferguson, $6,390.00; Greene, $5,787.50; Cassity, $1,600.00; Others, $640.00; or $14,417.50.

All hours other than the hours of attorney Greene have been computed at $40.00 per hour. Attorney Greene's 115¾ hours has been figured at $50.00 per hour. Therefore, a judgment based upon reasonable value of services rendered would be $15,190.35, which includes the out-of-pocket expenses heretofore found to be proper.

This case comes before us upon transfer from the Court of Appeals, Southern District, with an opportunity to consider again the proper recovery to be made available to an attorney discharged without cause by a client after legal services have been rendered pursuant to a contingent fee contract but before judgment or settlement has been reached. Prior decisions in this state have held that an attorney may treat the contract as rescinded and sue for the reasonable value of services rendered until the time of discharge; or, at his or her option treat the cause of action as liquidated by reduction to judgment (or settlement) and proceed upon the contingent fee contract. . . . Appellants invite this court to review the above holdings, taking into account the modern trend toward limiting the discharged attorney's recovery to the reasonable value of services rendered up to the time of discharge.

Before examining the "limitation of recovery" question, we first attend to appellants' first point of error, i.e., . . . that the only manner by which an attorney may enforce his lien, when discharged prior to judgment or settlement, is by an independent proceeding.

. . .

> . . . The remedy for enforcing the lien is not only left to the court, but in the final analysis it is up to the court to determine whether the method selected by the attorney is appropriate under all the facts and circumstances. . . . And an attorney is not restricted to any particular remedy for the foreclosing of his lien. He may proceed by an independent suit against the party who was the defendant in the original case. . . . Or he may proceed against the same party by motion in the original case. (Citations omitted).

[Satterfield v. Southern Railway Co., 287 S.W.2d 395, 397 (Mo.App. 1956).]

As movants-respondents point out in their brief, it would make little sense to permit an attorney to proceed directly against the defendants in the original case, yet decline to allow him to proceed against a fund paid into court by the same defendants. For this reason, and because of the wide latitude given to the trial court to determine the appropriateness of the method selected to enforce an attorney's lien, we find this point lacks merit.

A more interesting but difficult issue is the remedy to be allowed an attorney, employed under a contingent fee contract, discharged without cause before settlement or judgment, yet after rendering valuable legal services. Missouri has been among those states that adhere to the so-called "contract rule" with the employment agreement between attorney and client being treated as any other employment contract. However, there are persuasive reasons why the contract between attorney and client should not be lumped together with those of ordinary trades. . . .

The Florida Supreme Court recently found need to reevaluate its policy with reference to the recovery an attorney employed under a contingent fee contract may have, after discharge without cause, in Rosenberg v. Levin, 409 So.2d 1016 (Fla.1982). After recognizing the differing theories, discussed later herein, with respect to alternative means of recovery available to the discharged attorney, the court enunciated the public policy which must guide the Court throughout any discussion: "The attorney-client relationship is one of special trust and confidence. The client must rely entirely on the good faith efforts of the attorney in representing his interests. This reliance requires that the client have complete confidence in the integrity and ability of the attorney and that absolute fairness and candor characterize all dealings between them." 409 So.2d at 1021. From this premise, the Court logically reasoned that the unique aspects of the attorney-client relationship dictate that the client be given greater freedom to change legal representation than might be tolerated in other employment relationships. With this, the court overruled prior holdings which followed the majority or "contract rule," and adheres now to the growing minority or "modern rule", which limits the discharged attorney's recovery to the reasonable value of services rendered (quantum meruit). Id. at 1022. See the annotation in 92 ALR 3rd at 690, captioned: "Limitation To Quantum Meruit Recovery, Where Attorney Employed Under Contingent Fee Contract Is Discharged Without Cause."

The so-called modern rule is built upon the foundation of the special confidence and trust which should set the attorney-client relationship apart from other employment relationships. As stated in Martin v. Camp, 219 N.Y. 170, 114 N.E. 46 (1916), at p. 47, "the peculiar relation of trust and confidence that such a relationship implies injects into the contract certain special and unique features." Taking into account this special relationship, and the greater freedom to change legal representation mandated thereby, the courts which observe the modern rule allow a client to discharge his attorney, with or without cause, at any time.[1] . . . To quote again from the *Martin* case:

> The discharge of the attorney by his client does not constitute a breach of the contract, because it is a term of such contract, implied from the peculiar relationship which the contract calls into existence, that the client may terminate the contract at any time with or without cause.

114 N.E. at 48.

1. E.g., Martin v. Camp, 219 N.Y. 170, 114 N.E. 46, 47 (1916); Rosenberg v. Levin, slip op. June 11, 1981; Fracasse v. Brent, 6 Cal.3d 784, 494 P.2d 9, 100 Cal.Rptr. 385 (1972).

Besides being in the best interests of both the clients and the legal profession as a whole, *Rosenberg,* supra, at 1021, it can be said that the modern rule strikes a better balance between the client's power to discharge his attorney without undue restrictions and the attorney's right to fair compensation for services rendered. The majority-contract rule, which contemplates requiring payment of the contracted contingent fee regardless of the posture of the case at the time of discharge, was and continues to be patently unfair to clients, particularly where the client truly has lost faith in the attorney. See 41 Cincinnati Law Review 1003 (1972). As the Florida court correctly observed, the contract rule can "have a chilling effect on the client's power to discharge his attorney." *Rosenberg,* supra, at 1021. The economics of paying a discharged attorney the full contract price, and then hiring another attorney to continue his work, may be prohibitive. This danger is especially apparent in contingency fee situations, where "each" attorney may receive a large percentage of the client's final recovery. The consequences of the contract rule, in practical terms, may be that clients are forced to continue in their service attorneys in whose integrity, judgment or capacity they have lost confidence. See Salopek v. Schoemann, 20 Cal.2d 150, 124 P.2d 21 (1942) (Gibson, C.J., concurring).

Notwithstanding the logic and public policy which support the more modern view, there remain several problems under either theory. . . .

. . . [See] Note, Attorney's Right To Compensation When Discharged Without Cause From A Contingent Fee Contract, 15 Wake Forrest L.Rev. 677, 686 (1979).

[One] problem arises within the issue of "how much" the discharged attorney may recover. . . .

The better rule, undoubtedly, would be to use the contract price as an upper limit or ceiling on the amount the discharged attorney could recover. . . .

Our adoption of the modern rule limiting the recovery of the attorney to the reasonable value of services rendered, not to exceed the contracted fee, and payable only upon the occurrence of the contingency, makes the case at bar easily disposed of. Paragraph 15 of the trial court's findings of fact anticipated that the contingency fee contract approach could be overruled, and, in the alternative, found from the evidence that the reasonable value of the services rendered by the attorneys, including proper out-of-pocket expenses, equaled $15,190.35. . . .

. . .

Questions and Comments

In other "employment-at-will" situations, public policy concerns have been held to limit the employer's discretion to dismiss an employee for unjust cause, for example, dismissals for refusing to break the

law. Should a client be allowed to fire its in-house lawyer for refusing
to assist in illegal conduct? See Herbster v. North American Co., 150
Ill.App.3d 21, 501 N.E.2d 343 (1986), printed in Chapter 10 below.

The "modern rule"—as it is called in *Plaza Shoe*—is now the
majority rule. All recent cases have agreed that recovery in *quantum
meruit* should replace recovery on the contract. See, e.g., Fox &
Associates Co. v. Purdon, 44 Ohio St.3d 69, 541 N.E.2d 448 (1989)
(adopting quantum meruit rule when client discharges lawyer retained
on a contingent fee). Should retainer agreements be subject to the
quantum meruit theory? Should a contract making a retainer agreement nonrefundable be honored? See, e.g., Jacobson v. Sassower, 66
N.Y.2d 991, 489 N.E.2d 1283 (1985) (where retainer clause ambiguous
on whether retainer is refundable, it is construed against lawyer, who is
thus only entitled to compensation in *quantum meruit*).

Under DR 2–110(B)(4) and M.R. 1.16(a)(3) the lawyer is required to
withdraw when the client dismisses her. If, however, the case is before
a court, court permission is necessary before withdrawing and the court
may withhold its permission. Courts are reluctant to allow indigent
defendants to switch appointed counsel because judges suspect that this
is merely a tactic to delay the proceedings. When the request is made
after the trial has begun, the defendant "must show good cause, such as
an actual conflict of interest, a complete breakdown in communication
or an irreconcilable conflict with his attorney." Wilson v. Mintzes, 761
F.2d 275, 280 (6th Cir.1985). In Ogala Sioux Tribe v. United States, 862
F.2d 275 (Fed.Cir.1988), cert. denied, 109 S.Ct. 2087 (1989) the tribe
sought to fire lawyers who had handled this complex case for 30 years.
The court had awarded the tribe over $40 million dollars for land ceded
under an 1868 treaty and the sole remaining issue was the amount of
government offsets. The court upheld the trial court's refusal to
terminate the authority of the lawyers to stipulate to this amount,
emphasizing that the tribe had not found substitute counsel who could
handle the case without significant delay.

Mandatory Withdrawal

DR 2–110 and M.R. 1.16 cover withdrawal, mandatory and permissive. The Code provision differs from the Rules in that it seems not to
require withdrawal except in a case before a tribunal. See DR 2–110(B).
The better and common reading is that withdrawal is required under
the Code in any of the situations listed in DR 2–110(B) whether or not
the lawyer is before a tribunal.

As noted above, both the Code and the Rules require withdrawal
when the client discharges the lawyer. Also withdrawal is required if
the lawyer is too ill to continue the representation. DR 2–110(B)(3) and
M.R. 1.16(a)(2). See also DR 6–101(A)(3) and M.R. 1.1 and 1.3 (dealing
with lawyer competence and diligence). Finally and perhaps most
important, withdrawal is required when the continuing representation
will result in a violation of the ethics rules or other law. DR 2–110(B)

(2) and M.R. 1.16(a)(1). Note that while DR 2–110(B)(2) does not mention "other law," it is a violation of the Code to violate other law in the course of the representation, DR 7–102(B)(7), and thus withdrawal is required under DR 2–110(B)(2).

How sure must the lawyer be that the representation will result in a violation of other law or the rules before withdrawal is mandatory? Do DR 2–110(C)(2) and M.R. 1.16(b)(2) help answer the question? Also see DR 2–110(C)(1)(a), (b) and (c).

The provisions on withdrawal are part of the "package" of ethical rules dealing with client crime or fraud. They should be read in conjunction with DR 7–102(A)(7) and M.R. 1.2(d) (prohibiting lawyer participation in criminal or fraudulent conduct); DR 4–101(C)(3); DR 7–102(B)(1); M.R. 1.6(b); and the Comment to 1.6(b) on giving notice of withdrawal (regulating the disclosure of client confidences to prevent or rectify criminal or fraudulent conduct); DR 7–102(B)(1) and M.R. 3.3 (on disclosing fraud on the court); M.R. 2.3 (evaluations conducted for third parties); and M.R. 4.1 (honesty in dealing with nonclients).

M.R. 1.16 covers declining to undertake representation as well as withdrawal. Therefore, the provisions in M.R. 1.16(a) would require a lawyer not to accept employment in any of the situations outlined in that section. The Code deals with the decision to accept employment in a separate provision, DR 2–109.

Permissive Withdrawal

DR 2–110(C) and M.R. 1.16(b) state the circumstances under which a lawyer *may* withdraw from representation—"fire" the client. Lawyers do not have the same freedom as clients to withdraw from the relationship. If the matter is before a tribunal, withdrawal must be with the court's permission.

M.R. 1.16(b) is clearer in differentiating between withdrawal for cause and withdrawal without cause. A lawyer may withdraw (or decline to undertake representation) for any reason or no reason as long as withdrawal can be accomplished without "material adverse effect" on the client. A lawyer may withdraw even if there is harm to the client if the withdrawal is for any of the six reasons listed in 1.16(b). DR 2–110(C), permissive withdrawal before a tribunal, also list six reasons, but the reasons listed in the Code and Rules differ. Compare DR 2–110(C) and M.R. 1.16(b). In some sense, all of the items in the Code's list deal with client misconduct. M.R. 1.16(b)(5) and (6) do not necessarily involve client conduct at all. Do they give the lawyer too much latitude? Is M.R. 1.16(b)(6) so broad that it swallows the rest of 1.16(b)?

In Picker Int'l v. Varian Associates, 869 F.2d 578 (Fed.Cir.1989), the court held that a lawyer could not withdraw from representation, regardless of actual prejudice, if the purpose was to take on representation in a matter hostile to the client but nonrelated to the prior matter.

Does this extend the duty of loyalty or merely state a corollary? Compare M.R. 1.7 and 1.9. See Chapter 7 generally.

General Considerations

Under the Code, whether a lawyer is required to withdraw or permitted to withdraw, it must be accomplished in accordance with DR 2–110(A). Compare M.R. 1.16(c) and (d). In addition to M.R. 1.16, other Model Rules regulate a lawyer's actions after withdrawal. For example, the Comment to M.R. 1.6 on giving notice of withdrawal, see Chapter 4 above; and M.R. 1.9, prohibiting future representations that are materially adverse to a former client unless the former client consents, see Chapter 8 below, and requiring the lawyer to keep in confidence the former client's secrets.

Chapter VII

CONFLICTS OF INTEREST I: INTRODUCTION AND CONFLICTS IN CONCURRENT REPRESENTATION

A. INTRODUCTION TO CONFLICTS OF INTEREST

The Underlying Concerns in Conflict Cases

An attorney is bound to disclose to his client every adverse retainer, and even every prior retainer, which may affect the discretion of the latter. No man can be supposed to be indifferent to the knowledge of facts, which work directly on his interests, or bear on the freedom of his choice of counsel. When a client employs an attorney, he has a right to presume, if the latter be silent on the point, that he has no engagements, which interfere, in any degree, with his exclusive devotion to the cause confided to him; that he has no interest, which may betray his judgment, or endanger his fidelity.

—Justice Storey, Williams v. Reed, 3 Mason 405, 418, Fed. Case No. 17,733 (C.C. Maine 1824).

The rules on conflict of interest do not aim at elimination of all possible conflicts; this is impossible. Even if we envisioned lawyers as ascetics, renouncing all self interest, devoted only to their calling—and we have no such vision—even if our notion of a lawyer was someone who served one client for the entirety of her career—and, of course, it is not—conflicting interests would be present: the client's interest would still sometimes conflict with the interests of third parties or with the law itself. Dealing with conflicting interests is inherent in the lawyer's life.

Conflicts of interest problems are not unique to the lawyer-client relationship. The practice of law is a social relationship comparable to partnership, a joint venture or friendship. Any such relationship between two people carries the potential for a conflict of interest: each party has her own interests, which may conflict with the interests of the other.

Thus, the conflict questions faced by lawyers may be greater in number and intensity than those faced by most other people, but everyone faces similar questions. This is not to say that conflicts rules in non-lawyer relationships (e.g., a business partnership) are a sure guide in analyzing lawyer conflicts of interest. The lawyer-client relationship is unique by definition, i.e., it is a relationship whose object is the rendering of legal advice and counsel. The most striking implication of this fact is that the rendering of illegal aid is, by definition, outside the bounds of the relationship. This is not true in the same

580

sense for any of the other relationships. In addition, a lawyer has a special legal duty of confidentiality to the client, recognized in importance by a corresponding attorney-client privilege protecting client confidences in court.

All voluntary social relations are based on some measure of loyalty (commitment) and trust. Loyalty stands in opposition to betrayal. The measure of loyalty required to sustain the relation depends on the purpose of the relation itself and the stakes: less might be required to have a viable or satisfactory employer/employee relationship than a satisfactory marriage. It is therefore necessary to speak of loyalty and trust specifically between lawyer and client. We are not here addressing the general question of whether clients ever "really" trust their lawyers or should: about mistrust engendered by stereotypes (true or false) about the profession; about mistrust that might arise from difference between the lawyer's class, economic status or race and that of the client. These are important issues. Here we are talking only about mistrust created when a lawyer acts as the client's agent in the face of serious conflicting interests. Ideal lawyer-client relationships in this respect may be impossible, but "reasonable loyalty" is not.

Questions of loyalty and trust speak both to the quality of the lawyer-client *relationship* and to the quality of the *representation*. If the client does not see the conflict as a betrayal, i.e., fails to appreciate the conflict or chooses to disregard it, the representation might nevertheless suffer. That is, there is a good chance that the lawyer with a serious conflict will shortchange her client, even if inadvertently. This aspect of conflict of interest rules reinforces competency in representation.

The Several Faces of Conflicts

There are two primary categories of conflicts to which the lawyer is exposed: conflicts between clients; and conflicts between the lawyer and the client. The latter was dealt with in Chapter 6 above.

"Conflicts between clients" generally are analyzed in two major aspects: concurrent and successive representation. Conflict in concurrent representation involves conflict between two present or two prospective clients or between one present and one prospective client. Conflict in successive representation involves conflict between a former client and a present or prospective client. Concurrent representation is the focus of this chapter, and successive representation is the focus of Chapter 8.

The Matter of "Matter" and the Question of "Adversity"

A client seeks representation but her interests are adverse to those of an existing client or a former client. A key question is whether the "matter" involved is the "same or substantially related to" the matter in which the other client is being represented or was represented.

Suppose persons with adverse or potentially adverse interests seek representation by the same lawyer or law firm in matters totally unrelated to the matter in which their interests differ. May the lawyer undertake both representations? In the case of *concurrent* representation, if the matters are related, and if there is any degree of potential adversity of interest—as there always is—a conflict problem necessarily is presented. If the matters are *unrelated,* the key question is whether this adversity amounts to antagonism. Both "relatedness" and degree of "adversity" are questions of degree.

In *successive* representation, when matters are unrelated the lawyer ordinarily can proceed without the former client's permission. When the two matters in the successive representations are "the same or substantially related," a conflict may be presented. Most successive representation cases turn on whether two matters are substantially related. The rules give the former client priority over a potential client if an impermissible conflict could arise from the new representation. There is also a continuing duty of confidentiality concerning a former client's affairs. See M.R. 1.9(c).

A lawyer is allowed to sue a former client on behalf of a new client where the matter of the lawsuit is unrelated to the matter in which the former client was represented. A lawyer cannot directly oppose a present client even in a totally unrelated matter. Does this distinction make sense?

The established answer is that the lawyer owes her former client a duty of confidentiality that continues after the termination of the relationship, but the lawyer does not owe the former client a duty of eternal loyalty. Hence if matters are unrelated, a lawyer likely will be able to represent a new client against a former client without exploiting her former client's confidences. In contrast, if the matters are related, the risk of exploiting the former client's confidences is always present. And since the duty of confidentiality is a continuing one, this risk must be avoided.

If there is little risk of disclosing confidences when matters are totally unrelated, why not permit concurrent representation of adverse interests in unrelated matters?

The answer has been that a present client is entitled not only to protection of confidences but to the kind of relationship that makes confiding possible.

What if two or more clients seek joint representation. Should they be barred from making this choice in all situations where their interests are adverse? Potentially adverse?

The more adverse the clients' interests are, the more likely it becomes that one of them will be shortchanged in the loyalty she commands and the protection her confidences are given. Determining when interests are so adverse that the concurrent representation should not be permitted is often a difficult question.

Conflicts Between Clients and Others to Whom a Lawyer Owes a Duty

Akin to conflicts in concurrent representation are conflicts between a client's interests and some third party who is not a client but to whom the lawyer owes some duty nevertheless. These include: the officers of a corporation where, as is usually the case, the lawyer represents the corporation as such and not the officers; an insurance company or other third party who is paying for the lawyer's services to the client; and the person for whom a lawyer prepares an evaluation of the client's affairs with the understanding that that person can rely on the lawyer's evaluation, e.g., the person who receives the lawyer's opinion letter on the legality of the client's securities registration. Some of these problems are dealt with at the end of this chapter; others are considered in Chapter 9 below. Preparing an evaluation for a third party was discussed in Chapter 2.

Imputed Disqualification

A further question is whether lawyers in the same firm with a lawyer who is disqualified because of a conflict are themselves also disqualified.

Can one lawyer with a conflict taint a whole firm? If you are disqualified because you are in a firm with a disqualified lawyer, do you stay disqualified when you move to a new firm? If you go to a new firm, is everyone there now disqualified too? If you are disqualified because one of your partners is disqualified, when that partner leaves the firm are you still disqualified? These questions are dealt with in Chapter 8.

Who is the Client?

In conflicts between clients (concurrent and successive), as well as in conflicts between the lawyer and the client, the problem may turn on who it is, among various candidates, that the lawyer represents. This is particularly true when a group or organization is involved.

This question of client identity arises as well in contexts other than conflicts. For example, when the client is an organization, to whom does the lawyer owe the duty of communication? From whom shall she take instruction on settlement? To whom does she owe the duty to keep confidences? The question of client identity where the lawyer represents an organization will be examined in the context of conflicts in Chapter 9.

B. CONCURRENT REPRESENTATION

Diverging Vectors and Antagonism

The rules governing conflicts of interest in concurrent representation address two problems: 1) the problem of diverging vectors; how can a lawyer adequately represent two clients, interested in the same matter, whose interests diverge; and 2) the problem of antagonism; how can a client trust her lawyer, if that lawyer represents the client's opponent?

When a lawyer seeks to represent two clients in matters that are related, the lawyer confronts both diverging vectors and the potential for antagonism. When the two matters are unrelated, there is no problem of diverging vectors. For example, a lawyer is representing Bob in an eviction suit against Mark and then is asked by Hector to sue Bob for defamation. The lawyer could present each cause without deflection of effort in deference to the other cause.

But the problem of antagonism would remain. From Bob's perspective, what counts is that his lawyer is aligned with his adversary. The breach of loyalty and the concomitant loss of trust will be hardly less than if the two matters were related. For an example of such a case, see Bodily v. Intermountain Health Care Corp., 649 F.Supp. 468 (D.Utah 1986). In *Bodily,* "Bob" fired the firm when he learned that it was suing him on behalf of "Hector" in an unrelated matter. "Bob" then moved to disqualify the firm from representing "Hector." The court held that the firm had violated DR 5–105, see discussion of this provision below, but refused to disqualify the firm because its ethical misconduct had not prejudiced "Bob" in the litigation brought by "Hector". Notice that the standard in judging whether to disqualify a lawyer in ongoing litigation may differ from the standard for judging whether the lawyer has violated the ethics rules. We return to this point later in this Chapter.

The degree to which vectors diverge and the level of antagonism depend on the degree of adversity between client A and B. If one is suing the other, the vectors are directly opposed and the antagonism between A and B is at its legal maximum. In a joint venture they can entirely share common goals or see themselves as allies in a common fight; if so, the vectors coincide and there may be little or no antagonism between them.

The Canons and the Code of Professional Responsibility

Canon 6 of Canons of Professional Ethics:

It is unprofessional to represent conflicting interests, except by express consent of all concerned given after a full disclosure of the facts. Within the meaning of this canon, a lawyer represents conflicting interests when in behalf of one client, it is his duty to contend for that which duty to another client requires him to oppose.

While Canon 6 seemed to say that consent would permit a lawyer to proceed no matter what the conflict, the courts did not interpret it this way. See, e.g., Kelly v. Greason, 23 N.Y.2d 368, 244 N.E.2d 456 (1968); In re A. and B., 44 N.J. 331, 209 A.2d 101 (1965). However, consent allowed a lawyer to proceed in the face of a conflict that would have precluded dual representation in the absence of consent. See, e.g.,

Arden v. State Bar of California, 52 Cal.2d 310, 341 P.2d 6 (1959). This distinction between "consentable" and "unconsentable" conflicts remains a basic conflicts concept.

The key conflicts provision of the Code of Professional Responsibility is DR 5–105. DR 5–105(C) provides that a lawyer may not concurrently represent clients with "differing interests," unless 1) the lawyer obtains consent after full disclosure and 2) it is "obvious" that the lawyer can "adequately represent" both clients.

The term "obvious" implies an objective standard. Hence, it is not enough that the client actually consents. The circumstances must satisfy an independent authority, such as a court or a disciplinary board, that the lawyer properly proceeded with the multiple representation.

When is it "obvious" that a lawyer can "adequately represent" both clients? In Unified Sewerage Agency v. Jelco, Inc., 646 F.2d 1339 (9th Cir.1981), the court specified several factors in deciding whether two clients can be adequately represented: the nature of the litigation or other matter; the information to which the lawyer has access; the client's ability to recognize her vulnerability and protect her interests; and the questions in dispute.

Many cases avoid the difficulties of "obvious" by concentrating on consent and the client's "right" to choose her own counsel. But the client's right to choose her own counsel is not unqualifiedly paramount. In serious conflicts, the client may have only the right to get another lawyer. See, e.g., Rice v. Baron, 456 F.Supp. 1361, 1374 (S.D.N.Y.1978) (even with consent the representation might not have been proper—lawyer represented plaintiffs with possible counterclaims against one another); also Sapienza v. New York News, 481 F.Supp. 676 (S.D.N.Y. 1979).

Model Rules of Professional Conduct

Case law on conflicts issues filled the gaps left by the Canons and the Code. To a large extent, M.R. 1.7 through 1.15, and 2.2 and 2.3 codify that case law. One could also include M.R. 1.16, Declining and Terminating the Representation, and 2.1, Advisor, in the list of rules relevant to conflicts problems. Whenever a lawyer wants to withdraw and her client wants her to continue or would be harmed by her withdrawal, there is a conflict of interest. Similarly, M.R. 2.1 speaks of professional judgment, not affected by conflicting interests. But the list of rules potentially relevant to conflicts problems does not end even there. For example, concerning confidentiality under M.R. 1.6, a lawyer wants to communicate a client's confidence but the client does not agree: what "interests" are allowed to outweigh those of the client?

M.R. 1.7(a) prohibits the representation of a client whose interests are directly adverse to another client's interests, unless:

1) the lawyer reasonably believes that the representation will not adversely affect the *relationship* with the other client; and

2) each client consents after consultation. (emphasis added).

When can a lawyer "reasonably believe" that the relationship will not be adversely affected? The use of the word "relationship" here instead of "representation" is significant. It is difficult to represent interests directly adverse to an individual client without the *relationship* with that client being "adversely affected", even if the matters are wholly unrelated. Is the client consent proviso empty?

As the Comment to M.R. 1.7 points out, there are times when the proviso applies, particularly where the clients are organizations. For example, a lawyer represents Corporation X in all its securities matters; company Y, a bakery, is one of 30 subsidiaries of Corporation X; the lawyer is hired by Z who wants to sue company Y for breaching a delivery contract. The lawyer may reasonably believe that this suit will not have any adverse effect on the relationship with Corporation X. The lawyer would then be able to proceed, *if* after explaining the potential problems (consultation), Corporation X gave its consent. That is, the lawyer would be able to proceed assuming that it is reasonable to believe that neither the relationship with X nor that with Z would be adversely affected and consent is obtained from *both* clients after consultation.

Another example of when the proviso to M.R. 1.7(a) might apply is as follows: A lawyer working for the Securities and Exchange Commission wants to represent a pro bono client whose welfare benefits are about to be revoked. The adverse party in the welfare case is the Department of Health and Human Services, a part of the federal government. Would it not be reasonable for the SEC lawyer to believe that her relationship with the SEC (the federal government) will not be adversely affected by her representing the welfare recipient before HHS? This example assumes that there is no other law prohibiting the lawyer from representing the pro bono client. However, there is other law on this issue. 18 U.S.C. § 205 prohibits an employee of the Government from representing anyone before any department, agency or court in any matter in which the Government is a party or has a direct and substantial interest. The ABA proposed that § 205 be amended to allow pro bono representation in situations as in the example; the Government actively opposed this proposal, which failed to pass. For a case allowing lawyers representing the state government to proceed against the state in an unrelated matter, see Aerojet Properties, Inc. v. New York, 138 A.D.2d 39, 530 N.Y.S.2d 624 (App.Div.1988).

Interests "Directly Adverse"

The paradigm of direct adversity is one client suing another: the lawyer may not, without consent, represent her client's opponent in any matter, no matter how unrelated to the client's suit. Apart from litigation, it seems clear that when two clients are involved in a hostile negotiation their interests are also directly adverse. Further along the continuum situations become more difficult to assess: how adverse are the interests of two parties in friendly negotiations? The parties always have some divergent aims, for example, one wants to buy for the least amount of money and the other wants to sell for the greatest. The interests here do not seem directly adverse, but are they nevertheless adverse enough to preclude one lawyer representing both parties? Consider M.R. 1.7(b).

M.R. 1.7(b) provides that a lawyer shall not represent a client if the representation may be "materially limited" by the lawyer's responsibilities to another client or to a third person, or by the lawyer's own interests.

The lawyer may, however, proceed in such situations if: 1) she reasonably believes the *representation* will not be affected; and 2) the client consents after consultation.

Under M.R. 1.7(b) the emphasis is on the quality of the representation to be provided. The rule does not use the term "adverse" to describe the other interests that might trigger the rule. This is because responsibilities of the lawyer to another client might interfere with a concurrent representation even where the clients' interests are not so opposed as to be called "adverse." Thus, the duty of loyalty might cause the lawyer to be less committed to a client with a different interest in the matter; the duty of confidentiality might result in hesitancy to discuss related issues with a second client; and the duty of due diligence might cause the lawyer to neglect one matter in favor of another that is more demanding of her time or more lucrative, etc.

Imagine a contract renewal negotiation between a ballet dancer and the New York City Ballet. The ballet company hires Law Firm Y to represent it in the negotiation with the dancer and you represent the dancer. Should you simultaneously represent the ballet company in a real estate negotiation with the City of New York? Does M.R. 1.7(b) apply? 1.7(a)? What more would you like to know before deciding?

What if the New York City Ballet, whom you have helped with real estate deals, wants you to represent it in the negotiation with the dancer, and the dancer wants you to represent him too. Should you undertake to represent both the ballet dancer and the company in working out the best contract for both?

What if instead of an employment contract, it is two people who want to start up a business? Or two people who want amicably to work out a divorce settlement? Should the clients' desire to use one lawyer, either to save money or to keep the negotiation friendly, be decisive? M.R. 2.2 may be helpful in an analysis of these questions. Also see the Multiparty Hypotheticals at the end of this chapter.

Finally, what about so-called "positional" conflicts—arguing for one client that law A is valid, while at the same time arguing for another that law A is invalid? From the Comment to M.R. 1.7:

A lawyer may represent parties having antagonistic positions on a legal question that has arisen in different cases, unless representation of either client would be adversely affected. Thus, it is ordinarily not improper to assert such positions in cases pending in different trial courts, but it may be improper to do so in cases pending at the same time in an appellate court.

Does this mean that you should not assert contrary legal positions in unrelated cases in the same trial court? Be clear that the conflict is not cured by foregoing a particular argument on behalf of one client so as not to end up asserting contrary positions before the same court. The decision to forego the argument is tainted because it is influenced by obligations to another client. See *Fiandaca v. Cunningham*, printed later in this chapter.

Model Rule 2.2

M.R. 2.2 covers the lawyer who acts as an intermediary between two clients who have adverse interests, but who share a common purpose that may transcend their differences. M.R. 2.2 may be considered a specific application of 1.7(b). It gives the lawyer who contemplates acting as an intermediary between two clients more specific guidance than 1.7 alone provides.

Note on Per Se Bans on Concurrent Representation

While courts are quick to disapprove "unconsented" concurrent representation, they are reluctant to overrule client consent to the representation of conflicting interests. This recognizes the importance of the client's right to select counsel of her own choosing and, within limits, to select the kind of representation as between full-blown partisanship and intermediation.

The Supreme Court of New Jersey refused to approve a New Jersey ethics committee opinion that would have imposed an absolute ban on the joint representation of a government entity and individual government officials as defendants in § 1983 actions. The ethics committee was concerned that a case-by-case approach was too uncertain. The court thought the absolute ban was overinclusive, i.e., that there are some situations where the dual representation does not present an actual conflict:

> Only in the most sensitive circumstances have we imposed a per se rule of disqualification. In the past we have by administrative directive prohibited the joint representation of driver and passenger in automobile negligence cases (other than those involving husband and wife or parent and child).

In the Matter of Petition for Review of Opinion 552 of the Advisory Committee on Professional Ethics, 102 N.J. 194, 507 A.2d 233, 239 n. 3 (1986).

Why is the driver-passenger situation "sensitive" enough to adopt a per se rule and not the § 1983 situation?

See also Fleming v. State, 246 Ga. 90, 270 S.E.2d 185 (1980) (absolute ban on representing more than one defendant in death penalty cases).

WESTINGHOUSE ELEC. CORP. v. KERR–MCGEE CORP.

United States Court of Appeals, Seventh Circuit, 1978.
580 F.2d 1311.

SPRECHER, CIRCUIT JUDGE.

. . .

The four separate appellants are some of the defendants in this antitrust case who were each denied their motions to disqualify the law firm of Kirkland and Ellis ("Kirkland") from further representing the plaintiff Westinghouse Electric Corporation ("Westinghouse"). Whether fortuitously or by design, on the same day, October 15, 1976, Kirkland, while representing the American Petroleum Institute ("API"), of which three of the appellants, Gulf Oil Corporation ("Gulf"),[1] Kerr–McGee Corporation ("Kerr–McGee") and Getty Oil Company ("Getty"), were members, released a report which took an affirmative position on the subject of competition in the uranium industry, while simultaneously filing this lawsuit, representing Westinghouse, seeking to establish an illegal conspiracy in restraint of trade in the uranium industry.

The fourth appellant, Noranda Mines Limited ("Noranda"), asserts a different conflict of interest in Kirkland resulting from its prior representation of Noranda from 1965 to 1967 in several matters. . . .

I

On September 8, 1975, Westinghouse, a major manufacturer of nuclear reactors, notified utility companies that 17 of its long-term uranium supply contracts had become "commercially impracticable" under § 2–615 of the Uniform Commercial Code. In response, the affected utilities filed 13 federal actions, one state action, and three foreign actions against Westinghouse, alleging breach of contract and challenging Westinghouse's invocation of § 2–615. The federal actions were consolidated for trial in the Eastern District of Virginia at Richmond. . . .

As an outgrowth of its defense of these contract actions, Westinghouse on October 15, 1976, filed the present antitrust action against 12 foreign and 17 domestic corporations engaged in various aspects of the uranium industry.

Kirkland's representation of Westinghouse's uranium litigation has required the efforts of 8 to 14 of its attorneys and has generated some $2.5 million in legal fees.

---

1. Gulf Minerals Canada Limited is also a defendant but for convenience hereafter is included with Gulf Oil Corporation as "Gulf."

Contemporaneously with its Westinghouse representation in the uranium cases, Kirkland represented API, using six of its lawyers in that project.

In October, 1975, Congress was presented with legislative proposals to break up the oil companies, both vertically by separating their control over production, transportation, refining and marketing entities, and horizontally by prohibiting cross-ownership of alternative energy resources in addition to oil and gas. Since this proposed legislation threatened oil companies with a potential divestiture of millions of dollars of assets, in November, 1975, the API launched a Committee on Industrial Organization to lobby against the proposals. On December 10, 1975, API's president requested that each company designate one of its senior executives to facilitate coordination of the Committee's activities with the individual companies.

The Committee was organized into five task forces. The Legal Task Force was headed by L. Bates Lea, General Counsel of Standard Oil of Indiana, assisted by Stark Ritchie, API's General Counsel.

On February 25, 1976, Ritchie wrote to Frederick M. Rowe, a partner in Kirkland's Washington office, retaining the firm to review the divestiture hearings and "prepare arguments for use in opposition to this type of legislation." On May 4, 1976, Ritchie added that the Kirkland firm's work for API "should include the preparation of possible testimony, analyzing the probable legal consequences and antitrust considerations of the proposed legislation" and "you should make an objective survey and study of the probable effects of the pending legislation, specifically including probable effects on oil companies that would have to divest assets." Ritchie noted that "[a]s a part of this study, we will arrange for interviews by your firm with a cross-section of industry personnel." The May 4 letter to Rowe concluded with:

> Your firm will, of course, act as an independent expert counsel and hold any company information learned through these interviews in strict confidence, not to be disclosed to any other company, or even to API, except in aggregated or such other form as will preclude identifying the source company with its data.

On May 25, 1976, Ritchie sent to 59 API member companies a survey questionnaire seeking data to be used by Kirkland in connection with its engagement by API. In the introductory memorandum to the questionnaire, Ritchie advised the 59 companies that Kirkland had "ascertained that certain types of data pertinent to the pending anti-diversification legislation are not now publicly available" and the API "would appreciate your help in providing this information to Kirkland. . . ." The memorandum included the following:

> Kirkland, Ellis & Rowe is acting as an independent special counsel for API, and will hold any company information in strict confidence, *not to be disclosed to any other company, or even to API,*

except in aggregated or such other form as will preclude identifying the source company with its data.

(Emphasis in original). The data sought was to assist Kirkland "in preparing positions, arguments and testimony in opposition to this type of legislative [divestiture]" and was not to be sent to API but rather to Kirkland.

Pursuant to the provision in Ritchie's May 4, 1976 letter to Rowe that interviews would be arranged with a cross-section of industry personnel, Nolan Clark, a Kirkland partner, interviewed representatives of eight oil companies between April 29 and June 15, 1976.

After going through several drafts, the final Kirkland report to API was released on October 15, 1976. The final report contains 230 pages of text and 82 pages of exhibits. References to uranium appear throughout the report and uranium is the primary subject of about 25 pages of text and 11 pages of exhibits. The report marshalls a large number of facts and arguments to show that oil company diversification does not threaten overall energy competition. In particular the report asserts that the relatively high concentration ratios in the uranium industry can be expected to decline, that current increases in uranium prices are a result of increasing demand, that oil company entry into uranium production has stimulated competition and diminished concentration, that oil companies have no incentive to act in concert to restrict coal or uranium production and that the historical record refutes any charge that oil companies have restricted uranium output. The report concludes that "the energy industries, both individually and collectively, are competitive today and are likely to remain so." 448 F.Supp. at 1296.

As noted at the outset of this opinion, the API report was issued on the same day as the present antitrust suit was filed against several defendants, including Gulf, Kerr–McGee and Getty.

The district court concluded that "[a] comparison of the two documents reveals a rather basic conflict in their contentions and underlying theories." 448 F.Supp. at 1295. The court also observed that "[p]erhaps in recognition of the diametrically opposing theories of the API report and the Westinghouse complaint, Kirkland does not attempt to rebut the oil companies' charges that it has simultaneously taken inconsistent positions on competition in the uranium industry." 448 F.Supp. at 1296.

Gulf, Kerr–McGee and Getty are substantial dues-paying members of API. Kerr–McGee and Getty are also represented on API's board of directors.

At Ritchie's request, the cross-section interviews were mainly arranged by Gerald Thurmond, Washington Counsel of Gulf Oil Company and a member of API's Antitrust Strategy Group. On May 11, 1976, Thurmond advised Gulf officials that Nolan Clark of Kirkland planned to visit them. Attached to Thurmond's letter were the questions "which will be covered" in the meeting.[2]

The meeting was held on May 28, 1976 in Denver. Nolan Clark represented Kirkland. In attendance for Gulf were six vice presidents, a comptroller and a regional attorney. Also present was a Harvard professor who "also is working with API on the same subject." The meeting lasted more than two hours followed by lunch, during which discussions continued. After the meeting and in three letters from Gulf vice president Mingee to Clark dated August 10, 11 and 13, Gulf submitted specific information sought by Clark through the questionnaire and other written questions and in each letter Mingee stressed the confidential basis upon which the information was supplied.

Nolan Clark's interview with two Kerr–McGee vice presidents took place in Oklahoma City on June 9, 1976 and lasted about three hours. Clark was given considerable background information on Kerr–McGee's uranium industry, including mining locations, uranium conversion process, and pellet fabrication. On the subject of uranium marketing and pricing, one of the Kerr–McGee vice presidents described the escalating prices and tightening supplies in the current market, and the reasons behind the trends. Kerr–McGee sent its completed questionnaire to Clark on August 25, 1976.

Kirkland did not interview any Getty personnel. However, Getty received the confidential API questionnaire which requested it to estimate the value of its assets subject to proposed divestiture and its research and development outlays in alternative energy fields. Getty completed the questionnaire and mailed its data sheets to Nolan Clark on June 4, 1976, with the understanding that the data would be held in confidence.

II

The crux of the district court's determination was based upon its view that an "attorney-client relationship is one of agency to which the general rules of agency apply" and "arises *only* when the parties have given their consent, either express or implied, to its formation." 448 F.Supp. at 1300 (emphasis supplied). Although some courts have stated that the attorney-client relation is one of agency and that the general rules of law applicable to agencies apply, in none of those cases was an

2. The questions were prepared by Nolan Clark as "the kinds of questions I might want to ask":

In which alternative energy businesses is your company engaged? How, when, and why did your company enter these businesses?

What assets would your company have to divest in order to get out of alternate energy businesses?

Of the affected assets, could some be divested in the form of independent operating entities? Which? Could other affected assets be sold to other presently existing entities? Which? Are you in some alternate energy businesses which could not be sold, but rather would have to be liquidated? If so, what would your estimate losses be?
. . .

agency principle applied to assist an attorney to avoid what would otherwise be an obligation to his client. . . .

· ·

The district court first determined that there existed no explicit or express attorney-client relationship in that no oil company representative requested Kirkland to act as its attorney orally or in writing and Kirkland did not accept such employment orally or in writing. The district court found that "Kirkland sent its legal bills to the API, and was compensated only by the API." 448 F.Supp. at 1301. A professional relationship is not dependent upon the payment of fees [6] nor, as we have noted, upon the execution of a formal contract.[7]

The court then purported to determine whether the professional relationship "may be implied from the conduct of the parties." First, it found no "indicia" such as "the preparation of a legally-binding document like a contract or a will, or the attorney's appearance in a judicial or quasi-judicial proceeding." 448 F.Supp. at 1301. Second, the court searched for evidence of three fundamental characteristics of an agency relationship: the power to affect the legal relations of the principal and others; a fiduciary who works on behalf of his principal and primarily for his benefit; and a principal who has the right to control the conduct of the agent. 448 F.Supp. at 1301–03. Using these tests, the court concluded that "[v]iewed in its totality, we believe that the evidence shows that no attorney-client relationship has existed between Kirkland and the oil companies." As we have indicated, to apply only the agency tests is too narrow an approach for determining whether a lawyer's fiduciary obligation has arisen.

The district court also erroneously permitted itself to be influenced by the size of the law firm involved. In addition to identifying Kirkland as one of the largest law firms in Chicago with a two-city operation including 130 lawyers in the Chicago office and 40 lawyers in the Washington, D.C. office, the court observed that "[w]ith the modern-day proliferation of large law firms representing multi-billion dollar corporations in all segments of the economy and the governmental process, it is becoming increasingly difficult to insist upon absolute fidelity to rules prohibiting attorneys from representing overlapping legal interests." 448 F.Supp. at 1287–88.

6. Allman v. Winkelman, 106 F.2d 663, 665 (9th Cir.1939), cert. denied, 309 U.S. 668, 60 S.Ct. 608, 84 L.Ed. 1014 (1940) ("lawyer's advice to his client establishes a professional relationship though it be gratis"); Fort Meyers Seafood Packers, Inc. v. Steptoe and Johnson, 127 U.S.App.D.C. 93, 94, 381 F.2d 261, 262 (1967), cert. denied, 390 U.S. 946, 88 S.Ct. 1033, 19 L.Ed.2d 1135 (1968) (attorney's fees paid by third party "If appellant is not obligated to pay appellees for their services, it does not follow that there was no attorney-and-client relation"); Dresden v. Willock, 518 F.2d 281, 286 (3d Cir.1975) ("The fact that Dresden was to be paid by receiving stock in the enterprise did not change the nature of the [attorney-client] relationship"); E.F. Hutton & Co. v. Brown, 305 F.Supp. 371, 388 (S.D.Tex.1969) (Relation of attorney and client "is not dependent on the payment of a fee").

7. Udall v. Littell, 25 U.S.App.D.C. 89, 97, 366 F.2d 668, 676 (1966), cert. denied, 385 U.S. 1007 (1967); E.F. Hutton & Co. v. Brown, supra note 6, at 388.

Although the court recognized that "where courts have found a disclosure of client information to one member of a law firm, such knowledge has traditionally been imputed to all members of his firm," it opted in this case to reject "this rigid approach, in recognition of the changing realities of modern legal practice." 448 F.Supp. at 1304.

The district court abused its discretion in applying a narrow, formal agency approach to determining the attorney-client relation and in applying a different imputation of knowledge principle in the case of a large law firm than that "traditionally" and recently applied by this circuit to sole practitioners and smaller firms. Schloetter v. Railoc of Indiana, Inc., 456 F.2d 706, 710 (7th Cir.1976).

III

. . .

Three district courts have held that each individual member of an *unincorporated* association is a client of the association's lawyer. In Halverson v. Convenient Food Mart, Inc., 458 F.2d 927, 930 (7th Cir. 1972), we held that a lawyer who had represented an informal group of 75 franchisees "[b]ecause . . . [he] in effect had represented and benefited every franchisee, ... could reasonably believe that each one of them was his client."

Here we are faced with neither an ordinary commercial corporation nor with an informal or unincorporated association, but instead with a nation-wide trade association with 350 corporate and 7,500 individual members (448 F.Supp. at 1290) and doing business as a non-profit corporation.

We need not make any generalized pronouncements of whether an attorney for such an organization represents every member because this case can and should be decided on a much more narrow ground.

There are several fairly common situations where, although there is no express attorney-client relationship, there exists nevertheless a fiduciary obligation or an implied professional relation:

(1) The fiduciary relationship existing between lawyer and client extends to preliminary consultation by a prospective client with a view to retention of the lawyer, although actual employment does not result.[12]

(2) When information is exchanged between co-defendants and their attorneys in a criminal case, an attorney who is the recipient of such information breaches his fiduciary duty if he later, in his representation of another client, is able to use this information to the

---

12. ABA Code of Professional Responsibility, EC 4 1: "Both the fiduciary relationship existing between lawyer and client and the proper functioning of the legal system require the presentation by the lawyer of confidences and secrets of one who has employed or sought to employ him." Cf. McCormick on Evidence (2d ed. 1972), § 88, p. 179: "Communications in the course of preliminary discussion with a view to employing the lawyer are privileged though the employment is in the upshot not accepted." See also, Taylor v. Sheldon, 172 Ohio St. 118, 173 N.E.2d 892, 895 (1961).

detriment of one of the co-defendants, even though that co-defendant is not the one which he represented in the criminal case. Wilson P. Abraham Const. Corp. v. Armco Steel Corp., 559 F.2d 250 (5th Cir.1977) (disqualification case).

(3) When an insurer retains an attorney to investigate the circumstances of a claim and the insured, pursuant to a cooperation clause in the policy, cooperates with the attorney, the attorney may not thereafter represent a third party suing the insured nor indeed continue to represent the insurer once a conflict of interest surfaces.[13]

(4) In a recent case, where an auditor's regional counsel was instrumental in hiring a second law firm to represent some plaintiffs suing the auditor and where the second firm through such relationship was in a position to receive privileged information, the second law firm, although having no direct attorney-client relationship with the auditor, was disqualified from representing the plaintiffs. Fund of Funds, Ltd. v. Arthur Andersen & Co., 567 F.2d 225 (2d Cir.1977).

(5) In a recent case in this circuit, a law firm who represented for many years both the plaintiff in an action and also a corporation which owned 20% of the outstanding stock of the defendant corporation, was permitted to continue its representation of the plaintiff but was directed to disassociate itself from representing or advising the corporation owning 20% of defendant's stock. Whiting Corp. v. White Machinery Corp., 567 F.2d 713 (7th Cir.1977).

In none of the above categories or situations did the disqualified or disadvantaged lawyer or law firm actually represent the "client" in the sense of a formal or even express attorney-client relation. In each of those categories either an implied relation was found or at least the lawyer was found to owe a fiduciary obligation to the laymen.

The professional relationship for purposes of the privilege for attorney-client communications "hinges upon the client's belief that he is consulting a lawyer in that capacity and his manifested intention to seek professional legal advice."[14] The affidavits before the district court established that: the Washington counsel for Gulf "was given to believe that the Kirkland firm was representing both API and Gulf;" Kerr–McGee's vice president understood a Kirkland partner to explain that Kirkland was working on behalf of API and also its members such as Kerr–McGee; and Getty's vice president stated that in submitting data to Kirkland he "acted upon the belief and expectation that such submission was made in order to enable [Kirkland] to render legal service to Getty in furtherance of Getty's interests."

---

13. ABA, Opinions of the Committee on Professional Ethics (1967 ed.), Formal Op. 247 (1942). See also, State Farm Mutual Automobile Ins. Co. v. Walker, 382 F.2d 548 (7th Cir. 1967), cert. denied, 389 U.S. 1045, 88 S.Ct. 789, 19 L.Ed.2d 837 (1968). For general discussion of conflicts inherent in insurance matters, see H. Drinker, Legal Ethics (1953) 114–18; L. Patterson and F. Cheatham, The Profession of the Law (1971) 237–40.

14. McCormick on Evidence (2d ed. 1972), § 88, p. 179. See also R. Wise, Legal Ethics (1970) 284: "The deciding factor is what the prospective client thought when he made the disclosure, not what the lawyer thought."

A fiduciary relationship may result because of the nature of the work performed and the circumstances under which confidential information is divulged.[18] The Supreme Court approved and transmitted to Congress in 1972 the Federal Rules of Evidence,[19] which included among the lawyer-client privilege rules eventually eliminated by Congress, the following definition: [20]

> A "client" is a person, public officer, or corporation, association, or other organization or entity, either public or private, who is rendered professional legal services by a lawyer, or who consults a lawyer with a view to obtaining professional legal services from him.

. . .

Although Kirkland asserted, and the district court agreed, that it constructed a "Chinese wall" between the 8 to 14 Chicago-based attorneys working for Westinghouse and the 6 D.C.-based attorneys working for API, both conceded that William Jentes, one of Kirkland's lead attorneys working on the Westinghouse antitrust complaint, in August 1976 agreed with API task force head Lea, to prepare a legal memorandum analyzing arguments which had been advanced to broaden the scope of existing antitrust laws to outlaw interlocking directorates. Lea forwarded the Kirkland memorandum to the API, which mailed it to its member-company contact officers on September 23, 1976. Despite this breach of the "wall," we do not recognize the wall theory as modifying the presumption that actual knowledge of one or more lawyers in a firm is imputed to each member of that firm.[27] Here there exists a very reasonable possibility of improper professional conduct despite all efforts to segregate the two sizeable groups of lawyers.[28]

Kirkland has argued that the oil companies were aware that Kirkland was representing Westinghouse while it was also representing API, inasmuch as Kirkland sought discovery from Kerr–McGee, Getty and abortively from Gulf, relating to the Richmond litigation, in the way of voluntary interviews, depositions and the production of documents. The point, however, is not that the oil companies were aware that Kirkland represented Westinghouse but whether the oil companies were aware that such representation would lead to Kirkland represent-

---

18. Note Attorney's Conflict of Interests: Representation of Interest Adverse to That of Former Client, 55 Bost.U.L.Rev. 61, 66 (1975).

19. Supreme Court Order, November 20, 1972.

20. Rules of Evidence for the United States Courts and Magistrates as approved by Supreme Court (West Pub. Co. 1972). Rule 503(a)(1).

27. Schloetter v. Railoc of Indiana, Inc., 546 F.2d 706, 710 (7th Cir.1976). See also, Fund of Funds, Ltd. v. Arthur Andersen & Co., 435 F.Supp. 84, 96 (S.D.N.Y.), rev'd in part and aff'd in part, 567 F.2d 225, 229, n. 10 (2d Cir.1977).

28. Judge Fairchild notes that he has a different view on this point. It is his understanding that on appeal, Kirkland does not rely on a Chinese wall theory. In his opinion, if it had been established that there was real insulation in all relevant particulars between the lawyers working in the Washington office on the API Report and those working in the Chicago office on the antitrust action, imputation of knowledge to all partners would be eliminated from consideration and a different result may have been appropriate.

ing Westinghouse in a lawsuit in which the oil companies would be defendants. As the district court noted, "none of the [Kirkland] Washington attorneys working on the API divestiture assignment knew of the separate Westinghouse antitrust complaint until it was filed in court on October 15 [1976], after the stock exchanges closed on that day." 448 F.Supp. at 1296. If some of Kirkland's own partners were not aware of the Westinghouse antitrust complaint until it was filed, the oil companies can scarcely be presumed to have greater knowledge that it was impending with themselves as some of the defendants. It was Kirkland's duty to keep the oil companies advised of actual or potential conflicts of interest, not the oil companies' burden to divine those conflicts.

Gulf, Kerr–McGee and Getty each entertained a reasonable belief that it was submitting confidential information regarding its involvement in the uranium industry to a law firm which had solicited the information upon a representation that the firm was acting in the undivided interest of each company . . .

The fact that the two contrary undertakings by Kirkland occurred contemporaneously, with each involving substantial stakes and substantially related to the other, outbalances the client's interest in continuing with its chosen attorney. However, we believe that Westinghouse should have the option and choice of dismissing Gulf, Kerr–McGee and Getty from the antitrust case or discharging Kirkland as its attorney in the case. Substitute counsel has represented Westinghouse in the case since February 17, 1978, so that the impact of any change-over has been somewhat eased.

IV

The Noranda motion to disqualify Kirkland was based on an entirely different set of circumstances.

Noranda is a Canadian corporation organized under the laws of the Province of Ontario, having its principal place of business in Toronto. In 1965, Kirkland represented Noranda in the formation of a joint venture with Central Farmers Fertilizer Company, a domestic corporation centered in Chicago, Illinois. By that agreement, Noranda and Central formed a Canadian corporation to mine potash in Canada. The only possible nexus between the Central transaction and the present litigation is Noranda's belief that Kirkland may have learned the name of one of its executives, D.E.G. Schmitt, whose deposition was scheduled. The district court, finding that "[e]ven Noranda admits that Kirkland has alternate public sources of information for Schmitt's identity," found no substantial relationship between the character of a potash joint venture and a uranium price-fixing conspiracy, 448 F.Supp. at 1308.

In 1967, Kirkland, working in conjunction with Noranda's general counsel in Toronto, advised Noranda on the impact of United States' antitrust, corporation, securities and tax laws on a proposed exchange offer involved in Noranda's abortive effort to acquire control of Essex Wire Corporation. The mechanics of the exchange required the formation of a Delaware subsidiary of the Canadian parent corporation. Kirkland organized the American subsidiary, which included the naming of three Kirkland attorneys as incorporators, the holding of the first meeting, and the election of directors. Three Kirkland attorneys studied the antitrust issues which culminated in the preparation of a "Fact Book," which analyzed the competitive impact of the prospective acquisition. Both Noranda and Essex sold copper cable and wire in the United States and Noranda was to become the supplier of Essex's considerable copper requirements.

The tender offer was aborted and on August 1, 1967, Kirkland returned to Noranda all of its personal material. Kirkland simultaneously destroyed the longhand notes of its attorneys who viewed corporate data. Kirkland has not represented Noranda on any matter since 1967.

Noranda contended that Kirkland gained access in 1965–1967 to its relationship to Noranda Sales Corporation, Ltd. and Kerr–Addison Mines Limited, the first of which tied Noranda into doing business in Illinois and the second of which is involved in the uranium industry. After an exhaustive study of the affidavits and material submitted, 448 F.Supp. at 1306–10, the district court found no substantial relationship between Kirkland's earlier representation relating to the copper industry and the presently-alleged uranium price-fixing conspiracy which did not begin until 1972. The court concluded that "the Westinghouse complaint concerns a completely different industry and a completely different time." Noranda's relation to Noranda Sales and Kerr–Addison appears in publicly-available documents, such as Noranda's annual reports and Dun and Bradstreet reports.

. . . .

When is a Client a "Client"?

In IBM v. Levin, 579 F.2d 271 (3d Cir.1978) the court held that IBM was a present client of the firm, despite the fact that the firm "had no specific assignment from IBM on hand on the day that [the firm filed suit against IBM] and even though [the firm] performed services for IBM on a fee for services basis rather than pursuant to a retainer agreement . . ." Id. at 281. The court found that "the pattern of repeated retainers, both before and after the filing of the complaint, supports the finding of a continuous relationship." Id.

See also Fund of Funds Ltd. v. Arthur Andersen & Co., 435 F.Supp. 84, 95 (S.D.N.Y.), aff'd in part, rev'd in part on other grounds, 567 F.2d 225 (2d Cir.1977) (representation should be treated as concurrent even if the firm—in an effort to avoid the conflict—ceases representation of one of the clients before the motion to disqualify is filed).

Is initial contact with a person seeking representation enough to establish an attorney-client relationship for purposes of the conflicts rules? Can a person "taint" a lawyer by interviewing her?

In Hughes v. Paine, Webber, Jackson and Curtis, Inc., 565 F.Supp. 663 (N.D.Ill.1983), one of the defendants met with a partner in the law firm that was representing the plaintiffs. The defendant talked with the lawyer about the possibility of his representing him in an SEC investigation arising out of the acts at the heart of the plaintiff's case against the defendant. But the defendant did not then seek to hire the firm; instead, he sought other counsel. The court refused to disqualify the firm from continuing to represent the plaintiffs. At the time the defendant consulted the plaintiffs' law firm, he had every reason to know that the firm was handling the case against him, having received a letter about the case written on behalf of the plaintiffs by the law firm on its stationery.

The court, citing *Westinghouse,* found that there had been an attorney-client relationship between the lawyer consulted and the defendant and that consequently an irrebuttable presumption arose that confidential information had been passed to that lawyer. But the court also held, contrary to *Westinghouse,* that the defendant had never been a client of the "firm", only of the lawyer consulted. Since the client had never been a "firm" client, the court held that the presumption that the lawyer passed information on to his partners could be rebutted.

Is *Hughes* the best analysis of the "taint shopping" problem? The Scope section of the Model Rules states that the client-lawyer relationship does not exist until the client has asked the lawyer to render service and the lawyer has agreed, but that "some duties, such as the duty of confidentiality . . . may attach when the lawyer agrees to consider whether a client-lawyer relationship shall be established." Does this help? See B.F. Goodrich v. Formosa Plastics Corp., 638 F.Supp. 1050, 1052–53 (S.D.Tex.1986) (attorney-client relationship not established in preliminary interview when firm was but one of five interviewed, demonstrating client did not intend attorney-client relationship; firm would only be disqualified if confidences were actually communicated).

Could firms draft waiver agreements providing that anything told to them in an initial interview was not confidential? What about provisions that waive, not the right to confidentiality, but the right to complain of future conflicts? See the discussion of these provisions in the note on Advance Waiver of Conflicts, p. 600 below.

Adversity in Unrelated Matters

In *Westinghouse,* the court points to the substantial relationship between the two matters as a factor justifying disqualification. Why? Would the firm have been disqualified if it had been representing the two clients in totally unrelated matters?

In Cinema 5, Ltd. v. Cinerama, Inc., 528 F.2d 1384 (2d Cir.1976), a leading case on concurrent representation, the firm argued that it should be allowed to proceed against a present client because the matter in which it represented the client bore no "substantial relationship" to that in which it was suing the client. The Court said:

> Putting it as mildly as we can, we think it would be questionable conduct for an attorney to participate in any lawsuit against his own client without the knowledge and consent of all concerned . . .
>
> Whether such adverse representation, without more, requires disqualification in every case, is a matter we need not now decide. We do hold, however, that the 'substantial relationship' test does not set a sufficiently high standard by which the necessity for disqualification should be determined. That test may properly be applied only where the representation of a former client has been terminated . . . Where the relationship is a continuing one, adverse representation is prima facie improper . . . and the attorney must be prepared to show, at the very least, that there will be no actual or *apparent* conflict in loyalties or diminution in the vigor of his representation.

Id. at 1386–1387.

The court in *Westinghouse* may have found the relationship between the two matters important because it was balancing the rights of one client against the right of another to continue with counsel of its choice. Should a different standard be used in deciding whether to discipline a lawyer for a conflict, as distinct from the standard in disqualification cases? See, e.g., Bodily v. Intermountain Health Care Corp., 649 F.Supp. 468 (D.Utah 1986), described on p. 584 above.

The law codified in M.R. 1.7 and 1.9 by and large developed not in disciplinary cases but in court cases on motions to disqualify. Is this portion of the Model Rules then uniquely applicable to conflicts questions arising outside the disciplinary process?

Advance Waiver of Conflicts

To avoid disqualifications, firms increasingly employ provisions in retainer agreements whereby the client agrees to waive certain future conflicts should they arise. These provisions usually relate to successive conflicts, i.e., conflicts that might occur after the firm has concluded representing the client who signs the waiver. But the provisions sometimes apply to concurrent representation.

An early case dealing with such a provision, In re Boone, 83 Fed. 944, 957 (N.D.Cal.1897), refused to enforce a release permitting the lawyer subsequently to represent his client's opponent in the same matter. The court said, "[the] client may waive a privilege which the relation of attorney and client confers upon him, but he cannot enter into an agreement whereby he consents that the attorney may be released from all the duties, burdens, obligations and privileges pertaining to the duty of attorney and client . . . Courts owe a duty to themselves, to the public, and to the profession which the temerity or improvidence of clients cannot supersede."

In Westinghouse Elec. Corp. v. Gulf Oil Corp., 588 F.2d 221 (7th Cir.1978), the client had agreed that the firm could continue to represent another client even if a conflict developed between the two clients' interests. The Court, citing *In re Boone*, disqualified the firm despite the agreement, holding that the agreement could not give the firm permission to use the client's confidences against its own interests in favor of another client. See also Kennecott Copper Corp. v. Curtiss–Wright Corp., 584 F.2d 1195 (2d Cir.1978). What if the consent agreement provided for an "insulation wall" within the firm?

Procedures to Discover Conflicts

The court in Hughes v. Paine, Webber, supra, 565 F.Supp. at 673, criticized the law firm's procedures for discovering conflicts. The procedure involved a clerk's survey of the current matter file titles to determine clients and matters represented by the firm. The court said that "it should be noted that a files check may not reveal even the most obvious conflict, e.g., a new client seeks to sue a person who, it later turns out, is the chief executive officer of a corporate client."

The court recommended that in addition to a files check, a "new cases" memorandum be circulated within the firm "briefly describing the subject matter and the parties" before finally accepting any new case. Would this be adequate? What about affiliated corporations? Recall that Gulf Oil was not an immediate client of the firm in the *Westinghouse* case but was a member of the trade association, the American Petroleum Institute, which was the client. What about adverse parties in non-litigation matters, such as contentious negotiations? What about the addition of new parties in litigation? See the Comment to M.R. 1.7 (calling on lawyers to adopt "reasonable procedures, appropriate for the size and type of firm and practice" to discover conflicts).

Definition of "Firm"

The law generally has treated lawyers in the same firm as a single lawyer for purposes of conflict of interest questions. Is this fiction too far from the reality as applied to large firms with offices in many cities? How much information is really shared? Would an office in one city be any less vigorous in presenting a case against a client represented in an unrelated matter by a branch office in another city than against the client of a firm two floors above it in an office complex? Would client confidentiality be less respected?

The rule of *Westinghouse* effectively limits the size of firms. At some point, expansion does not pay if it excessively multiplies the number of cases in which the firm will be disqualified. Can firms avoid this problem by forming relationships with "corresponding firms" in

different cities rather than opening branch offices? See ABA Formal
Opinion 84–351 (1984) ("affiliated" firms are treated as one firm for
conflicts purposes). How close a relationship between one firm and
another would signify that they are de facto the same firm for purposes
of the conflicts rules?

With respect to lawyers who share office space but not fees, the
Comment to M.R. 1.10 says:

> Whether two or more lawyers constitute a firm [for purposes of the
> conflicts rules] can depend on the specific facts. For example, two
> practitioners who share office space and occasionally consult or
> assist each other ordinarily would not be regarded as constituting a
> firm. However, if they present themselves to the public in a way
> suggesting that they are a firm or conduct themselves as a firm,
> they should be regarded as a firm for the purposes of the Rules
> . . .

See Shelton v. Shelton, 151 A.D.2d 659, 542 N.Y.S.2d 719 (1989)
(lawyer who sublet office space within a firm not member of the firm
for purposes of conflicts rules). Cf. United States v. Cheshire, 707
F.Supp. 235 (M.D.La.1989) (lawyers who maintained separate practice
but shared office space and letterhead, which described them as an
"Association of Attorneys," treated as one firm under conflicts rules).
See also ABA Informal Opinion 1486 (1982) (lawyers who share office
space may represent conflicting interests if they "exercise reasonable
care" to protect their clients' confidences).

Lawyers Related to Other Lawyers

M.R. 1.8(i) states:

> A lawyer related to another lawyer as parent, child, sibling or
> spouse shall not represent a client in a representation directly
> adverse to a person who the lawyer knows is represented by the
> other lawyer except upon consent by the client after consultation
> regarding the relationship.

Under the Model Rules, a lawyer disqualified under M.R. 1.8(i) does
not taint the rest of his firm.

There is no counterpart to M.R. 1.8(i) in the Code. DR 5–101(A)
and DR 5–105(D), the general provisions on conflicts and imputed
disqualification give no specific guidance in this situation and would
seem to require the disqualification of the entire firm whenever a
lawyer in it is disqualified because married or otherwise closely related
to an opposing lawyer. This was not, however, the reading given by
ABA Formal Op. 340 (1975). In that opinion the ethics committee
rejected a per se rule of imputed disqualification, but emphasized the
need for the related lawyers to take special precautions to preserve
client confidences.

There are few cases, most of them dealing with opposing lawyers
who are married to each other. For a case involving a father and son

representing opposing interests, see Peek v. Harvey, 599 S.W.2d 674 (Tex.Civ.App.1980) (disqualification would have been proper but reversal not required because no showing of harm).

The cases on spouses generally accord with the Model Rules approach of requiring disqualification when interests are directly adverse but not insisting on imputed disqualification. In Jones v. Jones, 258 Ga. 353, 369 S.E.2d 478 (1988), the court refused to find impropriety even though the married lawyers represented clients whose interests were directly adverse. The court suggested it would adopt a rule based on 1.8(i) to govern future cases and invited comments from the bar.

M.R. 1.8(i) does not apply by its terms to people who are dating on a regular basis, but M.R. 1.7(a) would apply and would yield the same result as 1.8(i). As for imputed disqualification of dating lawyers disqualified under 1.7(a), the more sensible reading of M.R. 1.10 would be to treat those lawyers in the same way that 1.8(i) treats related lawyers, i.e., not requiring that the whole firm be disqualified. In People v. Jackson, 167 Cal.App.3d 829, 213 Cal.Rptr. 521 (1985), the question was whether the defendant was denied effective assistance of counsel because his lawyer was involved in an ongoing romantic relationship with the prosecutor that she did not disclose to the defendant. The court reversed the conviction. See also Gregori v. Bank of America, 207 Cal.App.3d 291, 254 Cal.Rptr. 853 (1989) (disqualification of firm not warranted when lawyer in firm dated secretary in opponent's firm unless confidences were likely disclosed).

Generally see: Cross, Ethical Issues Facing Lawyer–Spouses and Their Employers, 34 Vand.L.Rev. 1435 (1981); and Word, Risk and Knowledge in Interspousal Conflicts of Interest, 7 Whittier L.Rev. 943 (1985).

Lawyers for the Government

The rules of professional conduct, Model Code and Model Rules, apply to government and private lawyers alike. Government attorneys are, in general, bound to follow the rules in the bar with jurisdiction over their conduct. Federal preemption may, however, abrogate a state standard inconsistent with federal law. Cf. United States v. Klubock, 832 F.2d 664 (1st Cir.1987) (en banc), discussed in Chapter 2 above at p. 74.

In addition various ethics codes have been promulgated by various federal, state and local agencies, and agencies may also provide that their lawyers should be guided by the Model Code or Model Rules. See, e.g., the regulations for the Department of Justice Lawyers, 28 C.F.R. § 45.735–1(b) (to be guided by Model Code).

The Model Rules provide that government lawyers are bound by the conflicts rules that bind other lawyers including 1.7, see the Comment to M.R. 1.10, with the following exception: when one government lawyer is disqualified because of a former representation in private practice, whether those working in the government with that lawyer are disqualified is controlled by M.R. 1.11, not 1.10. When a lawyer is disqualified because of prior representation of the government, whether those in private practice with that lawyer are likewise disqualified is again governed by M.R. 1.11 and not 1.10. These matters, as well as the other provisions of 1.11, will be explored in Chapter 8 below. The point here is that 1.11 provides some special rules for the government lawyer, but those rules primarily deal with conflicts caused by successive representation. (The one exception is M.R. 1.11(c)(2), covering negotiating for private employment while working for the government.)

In Young v. United States ex rel. Vuitton et Fils, S.A., 481 U.S. 787, 107 S.Ct. 2124 (1987), the defendants violated a settlement order enjoining them from further infringing on the Vuitton's trademark. The judge appointed Vuitton's lawyers as special prosecutors to prosecute the defendants for contempt. The Supreme Court upheld the court's power to appoint private lawyers to prosecute contempt charges. However, it held that appointing Vuitton's lawyers was improper because of their interest in the matter. Citing Berger v. United States, 295 U.S. 78, 88, 55 S.Ct. 629 (1935), and EC 7–13, to the effect that a prosecutor's job is not merely to convict but to seek justice, Justice Brennan's opinion for the Court said:

> Because of this unique responsibility, federal prosecutors are prohibited from representing the government in any matter in which they, their family, or their business associates have any interest, 18 U.S.C. § 208(a). . . .
>
>   . . .
>
> If a Justice Department attorney pursued a contempt prosecution for violation of an injunction benefitting any client of that attorney involved in the underlying civil litigation, that attorney would be open to a charge of committing a felony under § 208(a).
>
> Furthermore that conduct would violate the ABA ethical provisions, since the attorney could not discharge the obligation of undivided loyalty to both clients where both have a direct interest. The government's interest [in a contempt prosecution] is in dispassionate assessment of the propriety of criminal charges for affronts to the judiciary. The private party's interest is in obtaining the benefits of the court's order. While these concerns sometimes may be congruent, sometimes they may not. A prosecutor may be tempted to bring a tenuously supported prosecution if such a course promises financial or legal rewards for the private client. Conversely, a prosecutor may be tempted to abandon a meritorious prosecution if a settlement providing benefits to the private client is conditioned on a recommendation against criminal charges.

481 U.S. 803, 805.

Also see People ex rel. Clancy v. Superior Court, 39 Cal.3d 740, 218 Cal. Rptr. 24, 705 P.2d 347 (1985) (impermissible conflict created by government hiring of private lawyer on a contingent basis in civil abatement proceedings because of the affinity between such proceedings and criminal prosecutions and the incompatibility of the prosecution function and payment based on whether a conviction is obtained).

In Federal Trade Commission v. American National Cellular, 868 F.2d 315 (9th Cir.1989), the question was whether full-time government lawyers involved in civil litigation against a party on behalf of the government could be involved in prosecuting the party for criminal contempt arising out of the civil litigation. The court distinguished *Vuitton* based on the contrast between private attorneys' obligations to their clients and the functions of a disinterested prosecutor. Nevertheless, the court held that a second concern in *Vuitton,* the need for prosecutors to appear impartial would require disqualification where the lawyers handling the criminal case were closely involved with the civil litigation. Was the court right to dismiss the possibility of actual conflict arising from the government's desire to win the civil suit? The special conflicts problems faced by present and former government lawyers are taken up in more depth in Chapters 8 and 9 below.

Lawyers Supplied by the Government

The government not only employs lawyers to represent itself (whoever or whatever that is), it also pays lawyers to represent others, e.g., public defenders. These lawyers face many of the problems of vicarious conflicts encountered by lawyers in firms. For example, are all public defenders members of a single firm, no matter how many different offices the public defender "firm" has, perhaps even in different cities? See ABA Informal Opinion 1418 (1978) (a public defender office in one city cannot represent a defendant whose interests conflict with a defendant represented by a public defender office in another city where both offices are under the control of the state's chief public defender). See also Commonwealth v. Westbrook, 484 Pa. 534, 400 A.2d 160 (1979) (lawyers working for public defender are members of the same firm).

Compare New Jersey v. Bell, 90 N.J. 163, 447 A.2d 525 (1982): multiple representation by a public defender office does not in itself give rise to a presumption of prejudice. The court stated that there were three reasons for presuming prejudice when a private law firm was involved: (1) that all firm members usually have access to confidential information; (2) that the entire firm shares an economic interest in the clients of each attorney; and (3) that public confidence in the integrity of the bar would be eroded if a lawyer's partner were allowed to do what the lawyer herself could not. It held that these considerations did not apply to public defender's offices. Do you agree? Is the court merely trying to facilitate economical representation of indigent people? In accord: People v. Free, 112 Ill.2d 154, 492 N.E.2d 1269 (1986).

As to lawyers in the military assigned to represent service people in court martials, see ABA Informal Opinion 1474 (1982).

In Flores v. Flores, 598 P.2d 893 (Alaska 1979) the court said that the state's legal services office, Alaska Legal Services Corporation (ALSC), need not be treated as a private law firm for purposes of conflict questions. The court encouraged ALSC to develop regulations on "recordkeeping, access to files, supervision and physical separation of offices which would be sufficient to ensure that two attorneys employed by ALSC could represent conflicting positions in litigation, each having undivided loyalty to his client and fully able to exercise . . . independent professional judgment." Id. at 896–897. Compare the case printed below.

FIANDACA v. CUNNINGHAM
United States Court of Appeals, First Circuit, 1987.
827 F.2d 825.

COFFIN, CIRCUIT JUDGE.

This opinion discusses two consolidated appeals related to a class action brought by twenty-three female prison inmates sentenced to the custody of the warden of the New Hampshire State Prison. The suit challenges the state of New Hampshire's failure to establish a facility for the incarceration of female inmates with programs and services equivalent to those provided to male inmates at the state prison. After a bench trial on the merits, the district court held that the state had violated plaintiffs' right to equal protection of the laws and ordered the construction of a permanent in-state facility for plaintiffs no later than July 1, 1989. It also required the state to provide a temporary facility for plaintiffs on or before November 1, 1987, but prohibited the state from establishing this facility on the grounds of the Laconia State School and Training Center ("Laconia State School" or "LSS"), New Hampshire's lone institution for the care and treatment of mentally retarded citizens.

One set of appellants consists of Michael Cunningham, warden of the New Hampshire State Prison, and various executive branch officials responsible for the operation of the New Hampshire Department of Corrections ("state"). They challenge the district court's refusal to disqualify plaintiffs' class counsel, New Hampshire Legal Assistance ("NHLA"), due to an unresolvable conflict of interest. See N.H.Rules of Professional Conduct, Rule 1.7(b). They also seek to overturn that portion of the district court's decision barring the establishment of an interim facility for female inmates at LSS, arguing that this prohibition is unsupported either by relevant factual findings, see Fed.R.Civ.P. 52(a), or by evidence contained in the record.

The other group of appellants is comprised of the plaintiffs in a separate class action challenging the conditions and practices at the Laconia State School, Garrity v. Sununu, No. 78–116–D (D.N.H. filed April 12, 1978), including the New Hampshire Association for Retarded Citizens ("NHARC") and the mentally retarded citizens who currently reside at LSS (the "*Garrity* class"). This group sought unsuccessfully to intervene in the relief phase of the instant litigation after the conclusion of the trial, but prior to the issuance of the court's final memorandum order. See Fed.R.Civ.P. 24. On appeal, these prospective intervenors argue that the district court abused its discretion in denying their motion.

We begin by presenting the relevant facts and then turn to our analysis of the legal issues raised by each of these appeals.

I. *Factual Setting.*

This case began in June, 1983, when plaintiffs' appellate counsel, Bertram Astles, filed a complaint on behalf of several female inmates sentenced to the custody of the state prison warden and incarcerated at the Rockingham County House of Corrections. NHLA subsequently became co-counsel for plaintiffs and filed an amended complaint expanding the plaintiff class to include all female inmates who are or will be incarcerated in the custody of the warden. In the years that followed, NHLA assumed the role of lead counsel for the class, engaging in extensive discovery and performing all other legal tasks through the completion of the trial before the district court. Among other things, NHLA attorneys and their trial expert, Dr. Edyth Flynn, twice toured and examined potential facilities at which to house plaintiffs, including buildings at the Laconia State School, the New Hampshire Hospital in Concord, and the Youth Development Center in Manchester.

Pursuant to Fed.R.Civ.P. 68, the state offered to settle the litigation on August 1, 1986, in exchange for the establishment of a facility for female inmates at the current Hillsborough County House of Corrections in Goffstown. The state had already negotiated an agreement with Hillsborough County to lease this facility and expected to have it ready for use by the end of 1989. Plaintiffs rejected this offer, however, primarily because the relief would not be available for over three years and because the plan was contingent on Hillsborough County's ability to complete construction of a new facility for the relocation of its prisoners. Plaintiffs desired an in-state facility within six to nine months at the latest and apparently would not settle for less.

The state extended a second offer of judgment to plaintiffs on October 21, 1986. This offer proposed to establish an in-state facility for the incarceration of female inmates at an existing state building by June 1, 1987. Although the formal offer of judgment did not specify a particular location for this facility, the state informed NHLA that it planned to use the Speare Cottage at the Laconia State School. NHLA, which also represented the plaintiff class in the ongoing *Garrity* litigation, rejected the offer on November 10, stating in part that "plaintiffs do not want to agree to an offer which is against the stated interests of the plaintiffs in the *Garrity* class." The state countered by moving immediately for the disqualification of NHLA as class counsel in the case at bar due to the unresolvable conflict of interest inherent in NHLA's representation of two classes with directly adverse interests.

The court, despite recognizing that a conflict of interest probably existed, denied the state's motion on November 20 because NHLA's disqualification would further delay the trial of an important matter that had been pending for over three years. It began to try the case four days later.

The *Garrity* class filed its motion to intervene on December 11, ten days after the conclusion of the trial on the merits. The group alleged that it had only recently learned of the state's proposal to develop a correctional facility for women at the Laconia State School. The members of the class were concerned that the establishment of this facility at the school's Speare Cottage, which they understood to be the primary building under consideration, would displace 28 residents of the school and violate the remedial orders issued by Chief Judge Devine in *Garrity,* 522 F.Supp. at 239–44, as well as N.H.Rev.Stat.Ann. ch. 171–A. The district court denied the motion to intervene on December 23, assuring the applicant-intervenors that it would "never approve a settlement which in any way disenfranchises patients of LSS or contravenes the letter or intent of [Chief Judge] Devine's order in *Garrity.*"

Meanwhile, the court agreed to hold up its decision on the merits pending the conclusion of ongoing settlement negotiations, permitting the principal parties to spend the month of December, 1986, engaged in further efforts to settle the case. Within approximately one week after the conclusion of the trial, the parties reached an understanding with regard to a settlement agreement which called for the establishment of a "fully operational facility at the present site of the Laconia State School for the incarceration of female inmates by November 1, 1987." The agreement also provided that all affected residents of LSS would receive appropriate placements at least two months prior to the opening of the correctional facility. After negotiating this agreement, NHLA moved to withdraw as class co-counsel on December 11 and attorney Astles signed the settlement agreement on plaintiffs' behalf. The state, however, refused to sign the agreement.

This collapse of the post-trial settlement efforts prompted Judge Loughlin, the district judge in the instant case, and Chief Judge Devine, the *Garrity* trial judge, to convene a joint settlement conference on December 22, 1986. At this conference, plaintiffs formally withdrew their consent to the original settlement agreement in light of the state's refusal to abide by the agreement. Both parties agreed, nevertheless, to try once again to settle the matter in a manner acceptable to all concerned and to report to the en banc court by January 12, 1987. Judge Loughlin, apparently believing that NHLA's conflict of interest prevented its effective performance as plaintiffs' class counsel, granted NHLA's pending motion to withdraw the day after the joint settlement conference. NHLA, however, had reconsidered its withdrawal from the case in light of the state's failure to sign the settlement agreement and it immediately petitioned the court to be reinstated as class counsel. The court denied the motion for reinstatement, reasoning that the "doctrine of necessity," its purported justification for denying the state's earlier disqualification motion in the face of NHLA's conflict of interest, no longer had force because the case had been tried to a conclusion.

The district court finally announced its decision on the merits on January 13, 1987. Finding that the conditions of confinement, programs, and services available to New Hampshire female prisoners are not on par with the conditions, programs, and services afforded male inmates at the New Hampshire State Prison, the court held that such gender-based, inferior treatment violates the Equal Protection clause of the Fourteenth Amendment. As a primary remedy, it ordered the state to establish "a permanent facility comparable to all of the facilities encompassed at the New Hampshire State Prison . . . to be inhabited no later than July 1, 1989." In crafting a temporary remedy, it reiterated that "there shall not be a scintilla of infringement upon the rights and privileges of the *Garrity* class," and proceeded to rule that the state had to provide plaintiffs with "a building comparable to the Speare Building," but that such facility "shall not be located at the Laconia State School or its environs." This appeal resulted.

II. *Appeal of State Department of Corrections.*

. . .

. . .

A. *Refusal to Disqualify for Conflict of Interest.*

The state's first argument is that the district court erred in permitting NHLA to represent the plaintiff class at trial after its conflict of interest had become apparent. As we recognized in Kevlik v. Goldstein, 724 F.2d 844 (1st Cir.1984), a district court is vested with broad power and responsibility to supervise the professional conduct of the attorneys appearing before it. Id. at 847. It follows from this premise that "[w]e will not disturb the district court['s] finding unless there is no reasonable basis for the court's determination." Id. We must determine, therefore, whether the court's denial of the state's disqualification motion amounts to an abuse of discretion in this instance.

The state's theory is that NHLA faced an unresolvable conflict because the interests of two of its clients were directly adverse after the state extended its second offer of judgment on October 21, 1986. The relevant portion of New Hampshire's Rules of Professional Conduct states:

A lawyer shall not represent a client if the representation of that client may be materially limited by the lawyer's responsibilities to another client . . . unless:

(1) the lawyer reasonably believes the representation will not be adversely affected; and

(2) the client consents after consultation and with knowledge of the consequences.

. . .

N.H.Rules of Professional Conduct, Rule 1.7(b). The comment to Rule 1.7 prepared by the ABA goes on to state:

Loyalty to a client is also impaired when a lawyer cannot consider, recommend or carry out an appropriate course of action for the client because of the lawyer's other responsibilities or interests. The conflict in effect forecloses alternatives that would otherwise be available to the client.

N.H.Rules of Professional Conduct, Rule 1.7, comment. In this case, it is the state's contention that the court should have disqualified NHLA as class counsel pursuant to Rule 1.7 because, at least with respect to the state's second offer of judgment, NHLA's representation of the plaintiff class in this litigation was materially limited by its responsibilities to the *Garrity* class.

We find considerable merit in this argument. The state's offer to establish a facility for the incarceration of female inmates at the Laconia State School, and to use its "best efforts" to make such a facility available for occupancy by June 1, 1987, presented plaintiffs with a legitimate opportunity to settle a protracted legal dispute on highly favorable terms. As class counsel, NHLA owed plaintiffs a duty of undivided loyalty: it was obligated to present the offer to plaintiffs, to explain its costs and benefits, and to ensure that the offer received full and fair consideration by the members of the class. Beyond all else, NHLA had an ethical duty to prevent its loyalties to other clients from coloring its representation of the plaintiffs in this action and from infringing upon the exercise of its professional judgment and responsibilities.[4]

NHLA, however, also represents the residents of the Laconia State School who are members of the plaintiff class in *Garrity*. Quite understandably, this group vehemently opposes the idea of establishing a correctional facility for female inmates anywhere on the grounds of LSS. As counsel for the *Garrity* class, NHLA had an ethical duty to advance the interests of the class to the fullest possible extent and to oppose any settlement of the instant case that would compromise those interests. In short, the combination of clients and circumstances placed NHLA in the untenable position of being simultaneously obligated to represent vigorously the interests of two conflicting clients. It is inconceivable that NHLA, or any other counsel, could have properly performed the role of "advocate" for both plaintiffs and the *Garrity*

---

4. The fact that the conflict arose due to the nature of the state's settlement offer, rather than due to the subject matter of the litigation or the parties involved, does not render the ethical implications of NHLA's multiple representation any less troublesome. Among other things, courts have a duty to "ensur[e] that at all stages of litigation . . . counsel are as a general rule available to advise each client as to the particular, individualized benefits or costs of a proposed settlement." Smith v. City of New York, 611 F.Supp. 1080, 1090 (S.D.N.Y.1985).

class, regardless of its good faith or high intentions. Indeed, this is precisely the sort of situation that Rule 1.7 is designed to prevent.

Plaintiffs argue on appeal that there really was no conflict of interest for NHLA because the state's second offer of judgment was unlikely to lead to a completed settlement for reasons other than NHLA's loyalties to the *Garrity* class. We acknowledge that the record contains strong indications that settlement would not have occurred even if plaintiffs had been represented by another counsel. For instance, in ruling on the intervention motion, the district court stated that, pursuant to its duties under Fed.R.Civ.P. 23(e), it would not approve a settlement that infringed in any way on the rights of the LSS residents. Furthermore, as plaintiffs contend, the second offer of judgment was unattractive because it was phrased in "best efforts" language and did not set a firm date for establishment of the facility. The question, however, is not whether the state's second offer of judgment would have resulted in a settlement had plaintiffs' counsel not been encumbered by a conflict of interest. Rather, the inquiry we must make is whether plaintiffs' counsel was able to represent the plaintiff class unaffected by divided loyalties, or as stated in Rule 1.7(b), whether NHLA could have reasonably believed that its representation would not be adversely affected by the conflict. Our review of the record and the history of this litigation—especially NHLA's response to the state's second offer, in which it stated that "plaintiffs do not want to agree to an offer which is against the stated interests of plaintiffs in the *Garrity* case"—persuade us that NHLA's representation of plaintiffs could not escape the adverse effects of NHLA's loyalties to the *Garrity* class.

Both the district court and plaintiffs on appeal have also advanced the belief that "necessity" outweighed the adverse effects of NHLA's conflict of interest in this instance and justified the denial of the state's pre-trial disqualification motion. See United States v. Will, 449 U.S. 200, 213–17, 101 S.Ct. 471, 480–82, 66 L.Ed.2d 392 (1980). . . .

While it is surely laudable that the court was anxious to resolve a lingering dispute concerning an unfortunate state of affairs, we fail to see how the doctrine of *necessity* is implicated in a case such as this. As plaintiffs' counsel admitted at oral argument, there was no particular emergency at the time of the court's decision to ignore the conflict of interest and proceed to trial. Plaintiffs simply continued to suffer the effects of the same inequitable treatment that had persisted for many years. While it would have been desirable to avoid delaying the trial for up to a year or more, it certainly was not "necessary" in the sense of limiting the court to but one potential course of action. We realize that other courts occasionally consider the possible effects of delay in ruling on disqualification motions, see, e.g., Laker Airways Ltd. v. Pan American World Airways, 103 F.R.D. 22, 27–28 (D.D.C.1984) ("Were the motion to disqualify to be granted, the resulting additional delay might well be crippling."), but in this circuit, arguments premised on delay have been less availing. As we held in *Kevlik*, 724 F.2d at 844, "we cannot, in the face of a breach of professional duty, ignore the wrong because appellees' counsel neglected to discern the conflict earlier, *or even opted to delay litigation by raising the motion. . . .*" Id. at 848 (emphasis supplied).

Absent some evidence of *true* necessity, we will not permit a meritorious disqualification motion to be denied in the interest of expediency unless it can be shown that the movant strategically sought disqualification in an effort to advance some improper purpose. Thus, the state's motivation in bringing the motion is not irrelevant; as we recognized in *Kevlik*, "disqualification motions can be tactical in nature, designed to harass opposing counsel." Id. However, the mere fact that the state moved for NHLA's disqualification just prior to the commencement of the trial is not, without more, cause for denying its motion. See id. There is simply no evidence to support plaintiffs' suggestion that the state "created" the conflict by intentionally offering plaintiffs a building at LSS in an effort "to dodge the bullet again" with regard to its "failure to provide instate housing for the plaintiff class." We do not believe, therefore, that the state's second offer of judgment and subsequent disqualification motion were intended to harass plaintiffs. Rather, our reading of the record indicates that a more benign scenario is more probable: the state made a good faith attempt to accommodate plaintiffs by offering to establish a correctional facility in an existing building at the Laconia State School and, once NHLA's conflict of interest with regard to this offer became apparent, the state moved for NHLA's disqualification to preserve this settlement option.

. . .

B. *Proper Remedy.*

In light of the district court's error in ignoring NHLA's conflict of interest, we believe it necessary to remand the case for further proceedings. We must consider a further question, however: must the district court now start from scratch in resolving this dispute? The state argues that the court's failure to disqualify NHLA is plain reversible error, and therefore requires the court to try the matter anew. We subscribe to the view, however, that merely "conducting [a] trial with counsel that should have been disqualified does not 'indelibl[y] stamp or taint' the proceedings." Warpar Manufacturing Corp. v. Ashland Oil, Inc., 606 F.Supp. 866, 867 (N.D.Ohio, E.D.1985) (quoting Firestone Tire & Rubber Co. v. Risjord, 449 U.S. 368, 376, 101 S.Ct. 669, 674, 66 L.Ed. 2d 571 (1981)). With this in mind, we look to the actual adverse effects caused by the court's error in refusing to disqualify NHLA as class counsel to determine the nature of the proceedings on remand. Cf. Board of Education of New York v. Nyquist, 590 F.2d 1241, 1246 (2d Cir.1979) (courts should be hesitant to disqualify an attorney unless trial will be tainted); Smith v. City of New York, 611 F.Supp. at 1091–92 (same); SMI Industries Canada Ltd. v. Caelter Industries, Inc., 586 F.Supp. 808, 814 (N.D.N.Y.1984) (same).

We do not doubt that NHLA's conflict of interest potentially influenced the course of the proceedings in at least one regard: NHLA could not fairly advocate the remedial option—namely, the alternative of settling for a site at the Laconia State School—offered by the state prior to trial. The conflict, therefore, had the potential to ensure that the case would go to trial, a route the state likely wished to avoid by achieving an acceptable settlement. Nevertheless, we do not see how a trial on the merits could have been avoided given the manner in which the case developed below. Judge Loughlin stated on the record that he would not approve a settlement infringing on the rights of LSS residents, and under Rule 23(e), any settlement of this class action required his approval to be effective. It seems to us, therefore, that even if some other counsel had advised plaintiffs to accept the state's offer for a building at LSS, a trial on the merits would have been inevitable.

With respect to the merits of the equal protection issue, the state has been unable to identify any way in which the court's error adversely affected its substantial rights at trial. The state admits that it had long recognized the need to establish an in-state facility for female inmates comparable to the state prison and that it had already taken steps in this direction by negotiating an agreement for the use of the present Hillsborough County House of Correction beginning in 1989. The evidence adduced at trial confirmed what both parties had known all along—that female state inmates do not enjoy services, programs, and conditions of confinement similar to those afforded the male inmates at the state prison—and this evidence led the court to conclude that the state had violated plaintiffs' right to equal protection of the laws.

The state has not directly challenged any of the district court's findings, which were based on the overwhelming evidence of inequitable treatment, and there has been no suggestion that the proceedings on the merits and the court's holding on the issue of liability were tarnished in any way by NHLA's participation. Indeed, as the state had to concede at oral argument, if the trial had been bifurcated into liability and remedy phases, NHLA's conflict of interest would have tainted its representation of plaintiffs—and required disqualification—only in the second, remedial phase of the trial. It seems plain to us, therefore, that at least with regard to the court's determination on the merits of the equal protection issue, the error in refusing to disqualify NHLA as class counsel is not inconsistent with substantial justice and should not require retrial of this issue. For these reasons, we hold that, with regard to the merits of the case, the district court's failure to disqualify NHLA constitutes harmless error at most, Fed.R.Civ.P. 61, and we affirm the district court's holding that the state violated plaintiffs' rights to equal protection of the laws.

The situation is different, however, with respect to the remedy designed by the district court. We believe that it would be inappropriate to permit the court's remedial order—which includes a specific prohibition on the use of LSS—to stand in light of the court's refusal to disqualify NHLA. The ban on the use of buildings located on the grounds of LSS is exactly the sort of remedy preferred by NHLA's *other* clients, the members of the *Garrity* class, and therefore has at least the appearance of having been tainted by NHLA's conflict of interest. Consequently, we hold that the district court's remedial order must be vacated and the case remanded for a new trial on the issue of the proper remedy for this constitutional deprivation. This determination leads us to the question of which parties should be permitted to participate in this new trial, an issue that forms the heart of the appeal brought by NHARC and the other members of the *Garrity* class as prospective intervenors. [The court allowed the intervention].

Questions

Should the prisoners have been permitted to waive the conflict? In deciding on the validity of any such waiver should the court be concerned that the prisoners might have seen the legal services program as counsel of last resort? Assuming a valid waiver on the part of the prisoners, would it also be necessary to get a waiver from the LSS residents? Who has the power to consent to the conflict on behalf of the LSS residents? Does M.R. 1.14 help answer this question?

Should the court have paid more attention to the fact that a legal services program represented both classes? To the fact that alternate counsel might not have been available to either class? Should this be a factor in judging "true necessity?"

Does the court too lightly dismiss the harm to the prisoners caused by delay?

What about the state's motives in proposing the LSS site? Why would the state have persisted in offering the LSS site given the judge's statement that he would not approve this site? Why did the state refuse to sign the settlement agreement? What other evidence could plaintiffs have offered to show the state's improper motives?

What about the remedy? Is it too harsh? How important should deterring lawyer misconduct be in fashioning a conflicts remedy? Discipline for violating the conflicts rules is rare unless there are other ethical violations, such as self-dealing or dishonesty. See, e.g., Lake County Bar Assn. v. Gargiuolo, 62 Ohio St.2d 239, 404 N.E.2d 1343 (1980) (simultaneous conflict and self-dealing); Codiga v. State Bar, 20 Cal.3d 788, 144 Cal.Rptr. 404, 575 P.2d 1186 (1978) (lying to conceal conflict).

Should the court have held the state lacked standing to raise the conflict? The majority of courts do not require any special showing of standing before entertaining a motion to disqualify based on a conflict of interest. See, e.g., Kevlik v. Goldstein, 724 F.2d 844, 847–48 (1st Cir. 1984) (standing to raise a disqualification motion based on ethical responsibility of all lawyers to bring to the court's attention possible ethical violations); United States v. Clarkson, 567 F.2d 270, 271 n. 1 (4th Cir.1977) (attorney is obligated to call to court's attention "facts justifying a disqualification of counsel"); Brown v. Williamson Tobacco Corp. v. Daniel Int'l Corp., 563 F.2d 671, 673 (5th Cir.1977) (same); Shadid v. Jackson, 521 F.Supp. 87, 89 (E.D.Tex.1981) (party has standing because of interest in avoiding delay that might result should conflict later require disqualification). But see In re Yarn Processing Patent Validity Litigation, 530 F.2d 83, 88 (5th Cir.1976) (party lacked standing to challenge opposing lawyer's conflict of interest). Generally see Greene, Everybody's Doing It—But Who Should Be?: Standing to Make a Motion Based on Attorney's Representation of a Client with Interests Adverse to Those of a Former Client, 6 U.Puget Sound L.Rev. 205 (1983).

Estoppel or Previous Consent

It has been said to be that "mere delay or laches" is not a defense to a motion to disqualify. Emle Industries, Inc. v. Patentex, Inc., 478 F.2d 562, 574 (2d Cir.1973). In *Emle,* the court confronted a three year delay in the filing of the motion, but nonetheless said, "Since . . . disqualification is in the public interest, the court cannot act contrary to that interest by permitting a party's delay in moving for disqualification to justify the continuance of a breach of the Code of Professional Responsibility." Id. at 573. See also EZ Paintr Corp. v. Padco, Inc., 746 F.2d 1459, 1463 (Fed.Cir.1984).

But this position has now been rejected by most courts. See, e.g., Cox v. American Cast Iron Pipe Co., 847 F.2d 725, 729 (11th Cir.1988); Trust Corp. of Montana v. Piper Aircraft Corp., 701 F.2d 85, 87 (9th Cir. 1983); MacArthur v. Bank of New York, 524 F.Supp. 1205, 1209 (S.D. N.Y.1981) ("the burden on the party seeking disqualification may be greater as a result of his undue delay"); Glover v. Libman, 578 F.Supp. 748, 760 (N.D.Ga.1983) (failure to file timely motion estops party from moving to disqualify later). Note that *Emle* was decided before disqualification motions became widely used.

In United Sewerage Authority v. Jelco, Inc., 646 F.2d 1339 (9th Cir. 1981) disqualification was denied on the basis of client consent, coupled with delay and the finding that it was "obvious" that the firm could adequately conduct the present representation despite the fact that the two disputes involved the same contract, since different contract provisions were in issue.

See also City of Cleveland v. Cleveland Electric Illuminating Co., 440 F.Supp. 193 (N.D.Ohio 1976), aff'd without published opinion, 573 F.2d 1310 (6th Cir.1977) (city retained firm as counsel in one matter while the firm was in heated struggle with city on behalf of another client; held: the firm may continue).

Appealability of Disqualification Motions

In 1985, the Supreme Court held that orders granting the disqualification of lawyers in civil cases are not appealable prior to judgment on the merits under 28 U.S.C. § 1291, Richardson–Merrell Inc. v. Koller, 472 U.S. 424, 105 S.Ct. 2757 (1985). The Court had previously held that *denials* of disqualification motions in civil cases were not appealable under § 1291, Firestone Tire & Rubber Co. v. Risjord, 449 U.S. 368, 101 S.Ct. 669 (1981), and in Flanagan v. United States, 465 U.S. 259, 104 S.Ct. 1051 (1984), the Court held that in a criminal case the granting of a disqualification motion is not immediately appealable.

The courts' impatience with disqualification motions underlies these holdings. In discussing the potential for frivolous appeals of motions to disqualify, the Supreme Court said, "Given an attorney's personal and financial interest in the disqualification decision, orders disqualifying counsel may be more likely to lead to an interlocutory appeal than other pretrial rulings, whether those rulings are correct or otherwise." Richardson–Merrell, 472 U.S. at 434, 105 S.Ct. at 2763. And the Court rejected the argument that the disqualified lawyer's desire for vindication was a valid ground for interlocutory appeal. "As a matter of professional ethics . . . the appeal should turn entirely on the client's interest." Id. at 435, 105 S.Ct. at 2763.

The rule is different in many state courts. See, e.g., Maddocks v. Ricker, 403 Mass. 592, 531 N.E.2d 583 (1988); Russell v. Mercy Hospital, 15 Ohio St.3d 37, 472 N.E.2d 695 (1984) (both holding grant of motion to disqualify appealable); Gregori v. Bank of America, 207 Cal. App.3d 291, 254 Cal.Rptr. 853 (Ct.App.1989) (denial of motion to disqualify appealable). Also see Hoggard v. Snodgrass, 770 S.W.2d 577 (Tex.App.1989) (mandamus available to review denial of motion to disqualify).

The consequence of *Richardson–Merrell* is that disqualification orders will not be reviewed before judgment on the merits. However, for some clients, although not for many, there may be some relief available before final judgment. In footnote 13 of the *Firestone* case, the Court said:

> In the proper circumstances, the moving party may seek sanctions short of disqualification, such as a protective order limiting counsel's ability to disclose or to act on purportedly confidential information. If additional facts in support of the motion develop in the course of litigation, the moving party might ask the trial court to reconsider its decision. Ultimately, if dissatisfied with the result in the District Court and absolutely determined that it will be harmed irreparably, a party may seek to have the question certified for interlocutory appellate review pursuant to 28 U.S.C. § 1292(b) . . . . and in exceptional circumstances for which it was designed, a writ of mandamus from the court of appeals might be available . . .

449 U.S. at 337 n. 13.

In *Richardson–Merrell* the court cited this footnote, adding that another remedy may exist for disqualified lawyers whose reputations are "egregiously injured" by the disqualification order but whose clients are satisfied by substitute counsel. Those lawyers "might be able to obtain relief from the Circuit Judicial Council pursuant to 28 U.S.C. § 332(d) (1)." 472 U.S. at 435, 105 S.Ct. at 2763.

In Grand Jury Subpoena of Rochon, 873 F.2d 170 (7th Cir.1989), the court recognized another exception to the rule in Richardson–Merrell, holding that an order disqualifying the Attorney General of the United States from participating in a criminal investigation was immediately appealable. Rochon, a former FBI agent, had filed a civil action against the FBI, the Attorney General (then Edwin Meese III) and other federal officials, alleging racial harassment by the FBI and that the Justice Department had conducted a criminal investigation in bad faith to delay resolution of Rochin's EEO complaints. The Justice Department empaneled a grand jury, which then subpoenaed Rochon and his wife to testify. Rochon moved to disqualify the Attorney General and the entire Civil Rights Division staff from participating in the grand jury investigation; the district court granted the motion. In holding that this order was immediately appealable, the court distinguished Flanagan, supra and Richardson–Merrell, supra:

> An order disqualifying government counsel in a criminal case, however, is a different matter, for if it is not immediately appealable, it is effectively unreviewable. For example, in this case, if the grand jury declines to issue any indictments, the government could not appeal because the case would be over. If the grand jury does issue indictments and any defendants subsequently are found guilty, the government, of course, would not seek review. If, on the other hand, any defendants were found not guilty, appellate review of the district court's disqualification order would be precluded by the double jeopardy clause. . . . Thus, in the only instance in which the government would want to press an appeal, the district court's decision preventing the Attorney General from participating in the grand jury investigation is unreviewable. An order disqualifying government counsel in a criminal case, therefore, is a final collateral order immediately appealable under section 1291. It conclusively determines the disputed question—whether challenged counsel will be permitted to continue his representation. . . . It also resolves an important issue completely separate from the merits of the underlying action. The grand jury, of course, is considering whether Rochon's treatment at the Chicago field office should lead to the prosecution of any individual for a violation of federal law. The disqualification issue, on the other hand, focuses on the question whether the filing of a civil suit against the Attorney General alleging that the investigation into the Chicago field office incidents has been conducted in bad faith requires his disqualification from the investigation. Answering the latter does not require consideration of the former. Finally, as noted above, an order disqualifying government counsel in a criminal case is effectively unreviewable. . . .

Id. at 173.

Does this effectively distinguish *Flanagan* and *Richardson–Merrell?*

When a client appeals after final judgment, claiming that the grant or denial of a disqualification motion was reversible error, what is the standard by which this claim should be judged? Must the client show prejudice resulted? How can a client show that it was prejudiced when substitute counsel tried the case? The Supreme Court in *Firestone* and *Richardson–Merrell* expressly reserved the question of whether a client in a civil case would have to show prejudice resulting from the disqualification order when appealing after judgment on the merits. For discussion of what a criminal defendant must show on appeal, see the notes following *Cuyler v. Sullivan,* printed below.

Moving to disqualify counsel for strategic purposes is a misuse of the ethical provisions, as is frivolously resisting a motion to disqualify. While disciplinary action for such behavior is extremely rare, Rule 11 sanctions may be imposed against a lawyer who files a frivolous motion to disqualify or defends against a motion to disqualify when there is no legal or factual basis for doing so. See, e.g., Optyl Eyeware Fashion Intn'l Corp. v. Style Companies, Ltd., 760 F.2d 1045 (9th Cir.1985) (sanctions for filing frivolous motion to disqualify); Original Appalachian Artworks, Inc. v. May Dept. Stores Co., 640 F.Supp. 751 (N.D.Ill. 1986) (same); Analytica v. NPD Research, Inc., 708 F.2d 1263 (7th Cir. 1983) (sanctions for defending against a motion to disqualify). The court may also sanction a lawyer under 28 U.S.C. § 1927 for vexatiously multiplying the proceedings by bringing a groundless motion to disqualify. See Wold v. Minerals Eng'g Co., 575 F.Supp. 166 (D.Colo. 1983); and North American Foreign Trading Corp. v. Zale Corp., 83 F.R.D. 293 (S.D.N.Y.1979).

The state courts are also concerned about the increased use of disqualification motions for strategic purposes. See, e.g., Gorovitz v. Planning Board of Nantucket, 394 Mass. 246, 475 N.E.2d 377, 380 n. 7 (1985) ("Court resources are sorely taxed by the increasing use of disqualification motions as harassment or dilatory tactics"). See also Alexander v. Superior Court, 141 Ariz. 157, 685 P.2d 1309, 1317 (1984).

Curing a Simultaneous Conflict

EC 5–19 suggests that a lawyer who represents multiple clients with potentially differing interests may cure the problem by deferring to the judgment of the client who objects to the multiple representation and withdrawing from representing that client. Courts have recognized that the ex ante prohibitions on conflicts should not always be imposed ex post to disqualify. See, e.g., Bodily v. Intermountain Health Care Corp., 649 F.Supp. 468 (D.Utah 1986), discussed above at p. 584; and Pennwalt Corp. v. Plough, Inc., 85 F.R.D. 264 (D.Del.1980) (both involving simultaneous representation in unrelated matters). But see Picker International Inc. v. Varian Associates, Inc., 869 F.2d 578 (Fed. Cir.1989). In *Picker,* a newly merged law firm found itself representing clients directly adverse in unrelated matters. The court held that the conflict could not be cured by dropping one client. Note that had the lawyers successfully withdrawn from the litigation prior to the merger, the case would be analyzed as one of successive representation: since opposing *former* clients in matters *unrelated* to the previous representation is not a problem under the ethics rules, see Chapter 8 below, the newly merged firm would have been allowed to proceed. For another case involving conflicts created by law firm merger, see Harte Biltmore Ltd. v. First Pennsylvania Bank, N.A., 655 F.Supp. 419, 421 (S.D.Fla.1987). For articles on the ethical problems encountered when firms merge, see p. 967 below in Chapter 10.

The question of whether successor counsel may use the work product of disqualified counsel is taken up in *First Wisconsin Mortgage Trust v. First Wisconsin Corp.,* reprinted in Chapter 8 below.

CUYLER v. SULLIVAN

Supreme Court of the United States, 1980.
446 U.S. 335, 64, 100 S.Ct. 1708, 64 L.Ed.2d 333.

MR. JUSTICE POWELL delivered the opinion of the Court.

The question presented is whether a state prisoner may obtain a federal writ of habeas corpus by showing that his retained defense counsel represented potentially conflicting interests.

I

Respondent John Sullivan was indicted with Gregory Carchidi and Anthony DiPasquale for the first-degree murders of John Gorey and Rita Janda. The victims, a labor official and his companion, were shot to death in Gorey's second-story office at the Philadelphia headquarters of Teamsters' Local 107. Francis McGrath, a janitor, saw the three defendants in the building just before the shooting. They appeared to be awaiting someone, and they encouraged McGrath to do his work on another day. McGrath ignored their suggestions. Shortly afterward, Gorey arrived and went to his office. McGrath then heard what sounded like firecrackers exploding in rapid succession. Carchidi, who was in the room where McGrath was working, abruptly directed McGrath to leave the building and to say nothing. McGrath hastily complied. When he returned to the building about 15 minutes later, the defendants were gone. The victims' bodies were discovered the next morning.

Two privately retained lawyers, G. Fred DiBona and A. Charles Peruto, represented all three defendants throughout the state proceedings that followed the indictment. Sullivan had different counsel at the medical examiner's inquest, but he thereafter accepted representation from the two lawyers retained by his codefendants because he could not afford to pay his own lawyer.[1] At no time did Sullivan or his lawyers object to the multiple representation. Sullivan was the first

---

1. DiBona and Peruto were paid in part with funds raised by friends of the three defendants. The record does not disclose the source of the balance of their fee, but no

defendant to come to trial. The evidence against him was entirely circumstantial, consisting primarily of McGrath's testimony. At the close of the Commonwealth's case, the defense rested without presenting any evidence. The jury found Sullivan guilty and fixed his penalty at life imprisonment. Sullivan's post-trial motions failed, and the Pennsylvania Supreme Court affirmed his conviction by an equally divided vote. Commonwealth v. Sullivan, 446 Pa. 419, 286 A.2d 898 (1971).[2] Sullivan's codefendants, Carchidi and DiPasquale, were acquitted at separate trials.

Sullivan then petitioned for collateral relief under the Pennsylvania Post Conviction Hearing Act, Pa.Stat.Ann., Tit. 19, § 1180–1 *et seq.* (Purdon Supp.1979–1980). He alleged, among other claims, that he had been denied effective assistance of counsel because his defense lawyers represented conflicting interests. In five days of hearings, the Court of Common Pleas heard evidence from Sullivan, Carchidi, Sullivan's lawyers, and the judge who presided at Sullivan's trial.

DiBona and Peruto had different recollections of their roles at the trials of the three defendants. DiBona testified that he and Peruto had been "associate counsel" at each trial. Peruto recalled that he had been chief counsel for Carchidi and DePasquale, but that he merely had assisted DiBona in Sullivan's trial. DiBona and Peruto also gave conflicting accounts of the decision to rest Sullivan's defense. DiBona said he had encouraged Sullivan to testify even though the Commonwealth had presented a very weak case. Peruto remembered that he had not "want[ed] the defense to go on because I thought we would only be exposing the [defense] witnesses for the other two trials that were coming up." Sullivan testified that he had deferred to his lawyers' decision not to present evidence for the defense. But other testimony suggested that Sullivan preferred not to take the stand because cross-examination might have disclosed an extramarital affair. Finally, Carchidi claimed he would have appeared at Sullivan's trial to rebut McGrath's testimony about Carchidi's statement at the time of the murders.

. . .

The Pennsylvania Supreme Court affirmed both Sullivan's original conviction and the denial of collateral relief. Commonwealth v. Sullivan, 472 Pa. 129, 371 A.2d 468 (1977). The court saw no basis for Sullivan's claim that he had been denied effective assistance of counsel at trial. It found that Peruto merely assisted DiBona in the Sullivan trial and that DiBona merely assisted Peruto in the trials of the other two defendants. Thus, the court concluded, there was "no dual repre-

part of the money came from either Sullivan or his family. See United States ex rel. Sullivan v. Cuyler, 593 F.2d 512, 518, and n. 7 (CA3 1979).

2. The Pennsylvania Supreme Court denied two petitions for reargument. See Commonwealth v. Sullivan, 472 Pa. 129, 180, 371 A.2d 468, 492 (1977) (Pomeroy, J., concurring and dissenting). Meanwhile, Sullivan's *pro se* petitions for federal habeas corpus relief were dismissed for failure to exhaust state remedies. See United States ex rel. Sullivan v. Cuyler, supra, at 515, and n. 4.

sentation in the true sense of the term." Id., at 161, 371 A.2d, at 483. The court also found that resting the defense was a reasonable tactic which had not denied Sullivan the effective assistance of counsel. Id., at 162, 371 A.2d, at 483–484.

Having exhausted his state remedies, Sullivan sought habeas corpus relief in the United States District Court for the Eastern District of Pennsylvania. . . . Peruto in the trials of Sullivan and his codefendants established, as a matter of law, that both lawyers had represented all three defendants. The court recognized that multiple representation " 'is not tantamount to the denial of effective assistance of counsel. . . .' " But it held that a criminal defendant is entitled to reversal of his conviction whenever he makes " 'some showing of a possible conflict of interest or prejudice, however remote. . . .' " . . . The court acknowledged that resting at the close of the prosecutor's case "would have been a legitimate tactical decision if made by independent counsel." Nevertheless, the court thought that action alone raised a possibility of conflict sufficient to prove a violation of Sullivan's Sixth Amendment rights. The court found support for its conclusion in Peruto's admission that concern for Sullivan's codefendants had affected his judgment that Sullivan should not present a defense. To give weight to DiBona's contrary testimony, the court held, "would be to . . . require a showing of actual prejudice." 593 F.2d at 522.

. . .

IV

We come [now] to Sullivan's claim that he was denied the effective assistance of counsel guaranteed by the Sixth Amendment because his lawyers had a conflict of interest. The claim raises two issues expressly reserved in Holloway v. Arkansas, 435 U.S. [475] at 483–484, 98 S.Ct. [1173] at 1178 [(1978)]. The first is whether a state trial judge must inquire into the propriety of multiple representation even though no party lodges an objection. The second is whether the mere possibility of a conflict of interest warrants the conclusion that the defendant was deprived of his right to counsel.

A

In *Holloway,* a single public defender represented three defendants at the same trial. The trial court refused to consider the appointment of separate counsel despite the defense lawyer's timely and repeated assertions that the interests of his clients conflicted. This Court recognized that a lawyer forced to represent codefendants whose interests conflict cannot provide the adequate legal assistance required by the Sixth Amendment. Id., at 481–482, 98 S.Ct., at 1177. Given the trial court's failure to respond to timely objections, however, the Court did not consider whether the alleged conflict actually existed. It simply held that the trial court's error unconstitutionally endangered the right to counsel. Id., at 483–487, 98 S.Ct., at 1178–1180.

Holloway requires state trial courts to investigate timely objections to multiple representation. But nothing in our precedents suggests that the Sixth Amendment requires state courts themselves to initiate inquiries into the propriety of multiple representation in every case.[10] Defense counsel have an ethical obligation to avoid conflicting representations and to advise the court promptly when a conflict of interest arises during the course of trial.[11] Absent special circumstances, therefore, trial courts may assume either that multiple representation entails no conflict or that the lawyer and his clients knowingly accept such risk of conflict as may exist.[12] Indeed, as the Court noted in *Holloway,* supra, at 485–486, 98 S.Ct., at 1179, trial courts necessarily rely in large measure upon the good faith and good judgment of defense counsel. "An 'attorney representing two defendants in a criminal matter is in the best position professionally and ethically to determine when a conflict of interest exists or will probably develop in the course of a trial.' " 435 U.S., at 485, 98 S.Ct., at 1179, quoting State v. Davis, 110 Ariz. 29, 31, 514 P.2d 1025, 1027 (1973). Unless the trial court knows or reasonably should know that a particular conflict exists, the court need not initiate an inquiry.

10. In certain cases, proposed Federal Rule of Criminal Procedure 44(c) provides that the federal district courts "shall promptly inquire with respect to . . . joint representation and shall personally advise each defendant of his right to the effective assistance of counsel, including separate representation." See also ABA Project on Standards for Criminal Justice, Function of the Trial Judge § 3.4(b) (App.Draft 1972).

Several Courts of Appeals already invoke their supervisory power to require similar inquiries. See United States v. Waldman, 579 F.2d 649, 651–652 (CA1 1978); United States v. DeBerry, 487 F.2d 448, 452–454 (CA2 1973); United States v. Cox, 580 F.2d 317, 321 (CA8 1978), cert. denied, 439 U.S. 1075, 99 S.Ct. 851, 59 L.Ed.2d 43 (1979); United States v. Lawriw, 568 F.2d 98 (CA8 1977), cert. denied, 435 U.S. 969, 98 S.Ct. 1607, 56 L.Ed.2d 60 (1978); cf. Ford v. United States, 126 U.S.App.D.C. 346, 348–349, 379 F.2d 123, 125–126 (1967). As our promulgation of Rule 44(c) suggests, we view such an exercise of the supervisory power as a desirable practice. See generally Schwarzer, Dealing with Incompetent Counsel—The Trial Judge's Role, 93 Harv.L.Rev. 633, 653–654 (1980).

Although some Circuits have said explicitly that the Sixth Amendment does not require an inquiry into the possibility of conflicts. United States v. Steele, 576 F.2d 111 (CA6) (per curiam), cert. denied, 439 U.S. 928, 99 S.Ct. 313, 58 L.Ed.2d 321 (1978); United States v. Mavrick, 601 F.2d 921, 929 (CA7 1979), a recent opinion in the Second Circuit held otherwise, Colon v. Fogg, 603 F.2d 403, 407 (1979).

11. ABA Code of Professional Responsibility, DR 5–105, EC 5–15 (1976); ABA Project on Standards for Criminal Justice, Defense Function § 3.5(b) (App.Draft 1971).

Seventy percent of the public defender offices responding to a recent survey reported a strong policy against undertaking multiple representation in criminal cases. Forty-nine percent of the offices responding never undertake such representation. Lowenthal, Joint Representation in Criminal Cases: A Critical Appraisal, 64 Va.L.Rev. 939, 950, and n. 40 (1978). The private bar may be less alert to the importance of avoiding multiple representation in criminal cases. See Geer, Representation of Multiple Criminal Defendants: Conflicts of Interest and the Professional Responsibilities of the Defense Attorney, 62 Minn.L.Rev. 119, 152–157 (1978); Lowenthal, supra, at 961–963.

12. See United States v. Kidding, 560 F.2d 1303, 1310 (CA7), cert. denied, 434 U.S. 872, 98 S.Ct. 217, 54 L.Ed.2d 151 (1977); United States v. Mandell, 525 F.2d 671, 675–677 (CA7 1975), cert. denied, 423 U.S. 1049, 96 S.Ct. 774, 46 L.Ed.2d 637 (1976); Geer, supra n. 11, at 145–146.

Nothing in the circumstances of this case indicates that the trial court had a duty to inquire whether there was a conflict of interest. The provision of separate trials for Sullivan and his codefendants significantly reduced the potential for a divergence in their interests. No participant in Sullivan's trial ever objected to the multiple representation. DiBona's opening argument for Sullivan outlined a defense compatible with the view that none of the defendants was connected with the murders. The opening argument also suggested that counsel was not afraid to call witnesses whose testimony might be needed at the trials of Sullivan's codefendants. Finally, as the Court of Appeals noted, counsel's critical decision to rest Sullivan's defense was on its face a reasonable tactical response to the weakness of the circumstantial evidence presented by the prosecutor. 593 F.2d, at 521, and n. 10. On these facts, we conclude that the Sixth Amendment imposed upon the trial court no affirmative duty to inquire into the propriety of multiple representation.

B

Holloway reaffirmed that multiple representation does not violate the Sixth Amendment unless it gives rise to a conflict of interest. See 435 U.S., at 482, 98 S.Ct., at 1177. Since a possible conflict inheres in almost every instance of multiple representation, a defendant who objects to multiple representation must have the opportunity to show that potential conflicts impermissibly imperil his right to a fair trial. But unless the trial court fails to afford such an opportunity, a reviewing court cannot presume that the possibility for conflict has resulted in ineffective assistance of counsel. Such a presumption would preclude multiple representation even in cases where " '[a] common defense . . . gives strength against a common attack.' " Id., at 482–483, 98 S.Ct., at 1178, quoting Glasser v. United States, 315 U.S. 60, 92, 62 S.Ct. 457, 475, 86 L.Ed. 680 (1942) (Frankfurter, J., dissenting).

In order to establish a violation of the Sixth Amendment, a defendant who raised no objection at trial must demonstrate that an actual conflict of interest adversely affected his lawyer's performance. In Glasser v. United States, for example, the record showed that defense counsel failed to cross-examine a prosecution witness whose testimony linked Glasser with the crime and failed to resist the presentation of arguably inadmissible evidence. Id., at 72–75, 62 S.Ct. at 465–467. The Court found that both omissions resulted from counsel's desire to diminish the jury's perception of a codefendant's guilt. Indeed, the evidence of counsel's "struggle to serve two masters [could not] seriously be doubted." Id., at 75, 62 S.Ct., at 467. Since this actual conflict of interest impaired Glasser's defense, the Court reversed his conviction.

Dukes v. Warden, 406 U.S. 250, 92 S.Ct. 1551, 32 L.Ed.2d 45 (1972), presented a contrasting situation. Dukes pleaded guilty on the advice of two lawyers, one of whom also represented Dukes' codefendants on an unrelated charge. Dukes later learned that this lawyer had sought leniency for the codefendants by arguing that their cooperation with the police induced Dukes to plead guilty. Dukes argued in this Court that his lawyer's conflict of interest had infected his plea. We found " 'nothing in the record . . . which would indicate that the alleged conflict resulted in ineffective assistance of counsel and did in fact render the plea in question involuntary and unintelligent.' " Id., at 256, 92 S.Ct., at 1554, quoting Dukes v. Warden, 161 Conn. 337, 344, 288 A.2d 58, 62 (1971). Since Dukes did not identify an actual lapse in representation, we affirmed the denial of the habeas corpus relief.

Glasser established that unconstitutional multiple representation is never harmless error. Once the Court concluded that Glasser's lawyer had an actual conflict of interest, it refused "to indulge in nice calculations as to the amount of prejudice" attributable to the conflict. The conflict itself demonstrated a denial of the "right to have the effective assistance of counsel." 315 U.S., at 76, 62 S.Ct., at 467. Thus, a defendant who shows that a conflict of interest actually affected the adequacy of his representation need not demonstrate prejudice in order to obtain relief. See Holloway, supra, 435 U.S., at 487–491, 98 S.Ct., at 1180–1182. But until a defendant shows that his counsel actively represented conflicting interests, he has not established the constitutional predicate for his claim of ineffective assistance. See Glasser, supra, 315 U.S., at 72–75, 62 S.Ct., at 465–467.[15]

C

The Court of Appeals granted Sullivan relief because he had shown that the multiple representation in this case involved a possible conflict of interest. We hold that the possibility of conflict is insufficient to impugn a criminal conviction. In order to demonstrate a violation of his Sixth Amendment rights, a defendant must establish that an actual conflict of interest adversely affected his lawyer's performance. Sullivan believes he should prevail even under this standard. He emphasizes Peruto's admission that the decision to rest Sullivan's defense reflected a reluctance to expose witnesses who later might have testified for the other defendants. The petitioner, on the other hand, points to DiBona's contrary testimony and to evidence that Sullivan himself wished to avoid taking the stand. Since the Court of Appeals did not weigh these conflicting contentions under the proper legal standard, its judgment is vacated and the case is remanded for further proceedings consistent with this opinion.

So ordered.

MR. JUSTICE BRENNAN, concurring in Part III of the opinion of the Court and in the result.

· · ·

15. See Comment, Conflict of Interests in Multiple Representation of Criminal Co-Defendants, 68 J.Crim.L. & C. 226, 231–232 (1977).

Holloway v. Arkansas, 435 U.S. 475, 98 S.Ct. 1173, 55 L.Ed.2d 426 (1978), settled that the Sixth Amendment right to effective assistance of counsel encompasses the right to representation by an attorney who does not owe conflicting duties to other defendants. While *Holloway* also established that defendants usually have the right to share a lawyer if they so choose, that choice must always be knowing and intelligent. The trial judge, therefore, must play a positive role in ensuring that the choice was made intelligently. The court cannot delay until a defendant or an attorney raises a problem, for the Constitution also protects defendants whose attorneys fail to consider, or choose to ignore potential conflict problems. . . .

The Conflict Standards in Criminal Cases

Cuyler requires a defendant to show both that counsel actively represented conflicting interests, and that the conflict "adversely affected" counsel's performance. The defendant need not show "prejudice," i.e., that the result would have been different but for the conflict. Contrast this to the rule in *Strickland v. Washington* discussed in Chapter 3 above. What is the difference between "adversely affected" and "prejudice"? Contrast *Cuyler* with the standard in civil cases. *Westinghouse,* for example, did not require proof of adverse effect from the conflict.

The Third Circuit on remand in *Cuyler* held that the representation was adversely affected in that the lawyer did not call the codefendant to testify because doing so would have been against that defendant's interest.

What does it take to show an "actual conflict" and conduct "adversely affected"? Should a showing that defense counsel simultaneously represents an important prosecution witness suffice? See, e.g., Castillo v. Estelle, 504 F.2d 1243 (5th Cir.1974) (conviction reversed). But see Wycoff v. Nix, 869 F.2d 1111 (8th Cir.1989) (concurrent representation of defendant and potential prosecution witness not an actual conflict because witness was not called and matters in representation were unrelated); and United States v. Gambino, 864 F.2d 1064 (3d Cir. 1988) (no reversal under *Cuyler* despite the fact that defense counsel, without defendant's knowledge, was representing a third party and failed to advance argument for defendant that the third party and not the defendant was the source of the heroin).

Given the above cases, it is not surprising that when a prosecution witness is a former client of the defense counsel, courts are unlikely to find an actual conflict. See, e.g., United States v. Friedman, 854 F.2d 535 (2d Cir.1988); and United States v. Cunningham, 672 F.2d 1064 (2d Cir.1982). Also see Nance v. Benson, 794 F.2d 1325 (8th Cir.1986) (no actual conflict where defense counsel had previously represented intended victim of defendant's fraud).

For examples of cases finding an "actual conflict" with an "adverse effect", see Mannhalt v. Reed, 847 F.2d 576 (9th Cir.1988), cert. denied, 109 S.Ct. 260 (1989) (at trial prosecution witness accused defense counsel of involvement in defendant's crime); and United States ex rel. Duncan v. O'Leary, 806 F.2d 1307 (7th Cir.1986) (collusion between defense attorney and prosecutor). How much more protection is actually afforded the defendant under *Cuyler* than under *Strickland?*

Some courts do not require a showing of adverse effect, reasoning that such an effect is likely to consist of an omission by the lawyer— options passed by, strategies neglected, etc. Proving a negative is difficult and should be unnecessary if the defendant can show an actual conflict existed. On this basis the Massachusetts Supreme Judicial Court, interpreting its state constitution's guarantee of effective assistance of counsel, held that adverse effect will be presumed even if the defendant knew of the potential conflict before the trial began. Commonwealth v. Hodge, 386 Mass. 165, 434 N.E.2d 1246 (1982). In that case, one of the prosecution's witnesses was being represented by the defendant's lawyer in an unrelated civil case. The court held that the possibility that the lawyer might go easy when cross-examining this witness warranted reversal without a showing of actual adverse effect. Also see People v. Spreitzer, 123 Ill.2d 1, 525 N.E.2d 30, 34 (1988) (describing the kinds of cases in which the Illinois courts will presume adverse effect).

Disfavoring Multiple Representation in Criminal Cases

Multiple representation in criminal cases is strongly discouraged by the ethical rules and the case law. See the Comment to M.R. 1.7; ABA Standards for Criminal Justice, The Defense Function 3.5(b); Fed. Rule Crim.Proc. 44(c). The cases hold that any doubts as to potential conflict should be resolved in favor of separate counsel. See, e.g., Lollar v. United States, 376 F.2d 243 (D.C.Cir.1967); State v. Bush, 108 Ariz. 148, 493 P.2d 1205 (1972).

Several commentators urge a complete ban on dual representation in criminal cases: Geer, Representation of Multiple Criminal Defendants, 62 Minn.L.Rev. 119 (1978); Lowenthal, Joint Representation in Criminal Cases, 64 Va.L.Rev. 939 (1978); Tague, Multiple Representation and Conflicts of Interest in Criminal Cases, 67 Geo.L.J. 1075 (1979). Also see Fleming v. State, 246 Ga. 90, 270 S.E.2d 185 (1980) (imposing an absolute ban on a lawyer representing more than one defendant in death penalty cases).

Why is the predisposition against dual representation so strong? First, of course, there is a significant possibility that a conflict in a criminal case will result in a defendant being convicted who should be acquitted. A co-defendant with more money (a higher-up in the hierarchy, for example) may pay the lawyer's fee and call the shots. Whenever a third person pays the lawyer's fee there is a potential conflict between that person's interests and the client's. For rules on third parties paying for the lawyer see DR 5–107(A) and (B); M.R. 1.7(b); 1.8(f); and 5.4(c).

Second, is the Prisoner's Dilemma problem. Assume two prisoners (co-defendants). Each can either inform on the other to the prosecutor or keep quiet. The prosecutor promises each that if either informs she will be sentenced to no more than one year, but if one informs and the other remains silent, the one who keeps quiet will receive between 5 and 10 years. The best choice for each individual, acting alone, is to inform on the other. An even better result is, however, imaginable. If they could cooperate with each other they would both likely go free for lack of evidence. But cooperation may as a practical matter be impossible.

Prosecutors in fact use divide and conquer tactics in plea-bargaining. A common defense strategy by a single defense lawyer can counter this tactic. But co-defendants in the real world are never in equal positions; the degree of their culpability and the penalties each faces are different. The lawyer who tries to counsel co-defendants in the real world, given their unequal position, cannot counsel the same course for both. Yet the choices made by one—particularly, whether to accept the prosecutor's offer—are crucial to the fate of the other.

For example, in United States v. Sutton, 794 F.2d 1415 (9th Cir. 1986), the prosecutor offered Sutton the chance to plead guilty to one of nine counts against him in exchange for the prosecutor's promise to drop the other eight charges against him and to drop all charges against Sutton's co-defendants, one of whom, Lynn Ann Morgan, was Sutton's longtime female companion and the mother of his children, and the other of whom was Morgan's sister. Sutton and Lynn Ann Morgan were represented by the same lawyer; the lawyer advised Sutton to accept the deal. On appeal, the court refused to allow him to withdraw his guilty plea based on his counsel's conflict of interest. But see, Thomas v. Foltz, 818 F.2d 476 (6th Cir.), cert. denied, 484 U.S. 870 (1987) (one lawyer represented three co-defendants; the prosecutor offered to reduce the charges to second degree murder if all three would plead guilty; defendant Thomas was quite resistant but eventually decided to plead guilty; held: counsel was operating under an actual conflict of interest that adversely affected his representation of Thomas).

Finally, the courts may also be worried about the possibility of cooperative perjury. Should that be a factor in considering the legitimacy of joint representation?

Disqualifying Defense Counsel

When a criminal defendant is denied counsel of her choice, the defendant's Sixth Amendment right to counsel is implicated. United States v. Curcio, 680 F.2d 881 (2d Cir.1982) (government's interest in disqualifying defendant's counsel does not override defendant's choice of counsel where defendant's waiver of the right to separate representation was knowing and voluntary). Nevertheless, Flanagan v. United

States, 465 U.S. 259, 104 S.Ct. 1051 (1984), held that an order disqualifying defense counsel for a conflict of interest is not immediately appealable under 28 U.S.C. § 1291. The defendant must await appeal upon final judgment to pursue the claim that she was denied counsel of her choice. Contrast Grand Jury Subpoena of Rochon, 873 F.2d 170 (7th Cir.1989), discussed above at p. 617.

Flanagan left undecided whether prejudice must be shown when a defendant is wrongly denied counsel of her choice, i.e., where the trial judge's order of disqualification was erroneous. In United States v. Rankin, 779 F.2d 956 (3d Cir.1986), the defendant's counsel had been disqualified and the defendant was convicted. On appeal the government argued that the defendant had been represented by competent substitute counsel. The court rejected this argument, stating "A defendant who is arbitrarily deprived of the right to select his own counsel need not demonstrate prejudice." Id. at 960. In accord: Anaya v. Colorado, 764 P.2d 779 (Colo.1988).

This leaves the question of when it is wrong to disqualify counsel over defendant's protest, because of a conflict. The Supreme Court addressed that question in Wheat v. United States, 486 U.S. 153, 108 S.Ct. 1692 (1988). In *Wheat,* the district court denied Wheat's request to be represented by the same lawyer who was representing two other people charged with involvement in the drug distribution conspiracy that formed the basis for the charges against Wheat. Wheat expressed his willingness to waive the conflict, as the other defendants had done, and asserted that the Sixth Amendment gave him the right to counsel of his choice. Wheat was to be tried separately from the other parties. Nevertheless, the district court, citing the likelihood that these people would be witnesses at one another's trials, held that counsel would be operating with an irreconcilable conflict and thus refused to allow counsel to represent Wheat. At trial, Wheat was convicted and he appealed claiming that the court's rejection of his counsel of choice violated his Sixth Amendment rights. The Supreme Court upheld the conviction:

> Unfortunately for all concerned, a district court must pass on the issue of whether or not to allow a waiver of a conflict of interest by a criminal defendant not with the wisdom of hindsight after the trial has taken place, but in the murkier pre-trial context when relationships between parties are seen through a glass, darkly. The likelihood and dimensions of nascent conflicts of interest are notoriously hard to predict, even for those thoroughly familiar with criminal trials. It is a rare attorney who will be fortunate enough to learn the entire truth from his own client, much less be fully apprised before trial of what each of the Government's witnesses will say on the stand. A few bits of unforeseen testimony or a single previously unknown or unnoticed document may significantly shift the relationship between multiple defendants. These imponderables are difficult enough for a lawyer to assess, and even more difficult to convey by way of explanation to a criminal

defendant untutored in the niceties of legal ethics. Nor is it amiss to observe that the willingness of an attorney to obtain such waivers from his clients may bear an inverse relation to the care with which he conveys all the necessary information to them.

For these reasons we think the District Court must be allowed substantial latitude in refusing waivers of conflicts of interest not only in those rare cases where an actual conflict may be demonstrated before trial, but in the more common cases where a potential for conflict exists which may or may not burgeon into an actual conflict as the trial progresses.

108 S.Ct. at 1699.

In Fuller v. Diesslin, 868 F.2d 604 (3d Cir.1989), the court reaffirmed its holding in *Rankin,* see notes above, that prejudice is presumed when choice of counsel is wrongfully denied, rejecting the argument that *Wheat* overruled *Rankin.*

Compare the concern in *Wheat* for potential conflicts of interest with the showing the defendant has to make under *Cuyler.* Justice Marshall, dissenting in *Wheat,* joined by Justice Brennan, criticized the majority for its unwarranted deference to the district court's decision, given the importance of the Sixth Amendment right involved. Justice Stevens in dissent, joined by Justice Blackmun, emphasized the voluntary nature of defendant's waiver of the conflict.

Should the defendant be allowed to waive any conflict, no matter how serious? If she makes the waiver for strategic purposes? See United States v. Bradshaw, 719 F.2d 907 (7th Cir.1983) (co-defendants had strategic purposes in presenting a common defense). Should voluntary waiver bar any future claim of ineffective counsel based on the conflict? How would courts determine whether a waiver is voluntary or informed? See Duncan v. Alabama, 881 F.2d 1013 (11th Cir.1989) (one of the defendant's court appointed lawyers had represented the murder victim in her efforts to stop the defendant from harassing her; the other of his lawyers had represented the district attorney in a divorce action and could foresee continuing to represent him; held: the defendant's waiver of these conflicts barred him from raising them after conviction).

In *Wheat,* the Court states: "Nor does a waiver by the defendant necessarily solve the problem, for we note, without passing judgment on, the apparent willingness of Courts of Appeals to entertain ineffective assistance claims from defendants who have specifically waived the right to conflict-free counsel." 108 S.Ct. at 1698. This statement does not sound particularly approving of the practice described, does it? Is the Court suggesting that waiver should cure all conflicts for post-conviction purposes?

Contrast United States ex rel. Tineo v. Kelly, 870 F.2d 854 (2d Cir. 1989), holding that disqualification of counsel before trial based on prior representation of a government witness is not a denial of the defendant's right to counsel of her choice.

In Alcocer v. Superior Court, 206 Cal.App.3d 951, 254 Cal.Rptr. 72 (1988), the court held that under the California Constitution, trial courts do not have the same wide latitude to disqualify defendant's counsel of choice that the federal courts have under *Wheat.* "A court abridges a defendant's right to counsel when it removes retained defense counsel in the face of a defendant's willingness to make an informed and intelligent waiver of his right to . . . conflict-free counsel." 254 Cal.Rptr. at 75. The court rejected any other rule as "paternalistic", quoting from John Stuart Mill's famous book *On Liberty* and writing itself that "[a] right that is imposed, as compared to a right that is chosen, is an impoverished right." Id. at 74. Is the line between what is "chosen" and what "imposed" easy to discern in this context?

Inquiring to Determine Whether a Conflict Exists

In federal cases when one lawyer proposes to represent multiple defendants, the judge must hold a hearing to advise each defendant of her right to separate counsel. Fed.R.Crim.P. 44(c). Rule 44(c) further states that "[u]nless there is good cause to believe no conflict of interest is likely to arise, the court shall take such measures as may be appropriate to protect each defendant's right to counsel." The presumption is clearly against the dual representation.

How can a court adequately satisfy itself that the defendant's waiver is voluntary and appropriate without breaching client confidences? See In re Paradyne Corp., 803 F.2d 604 (11th Cir.1986) (granting mandamus against a proposed in camera inquiry by the trial court). Also see United States v. Roth, 860 F.2d 1382 (7th Cir.1988) (trial court's failure to probe possible conflicts does not invalidate defendant's waiver).

When one counsel represents multiple defendants, should a failure to conduct a Rule 44(c) inquiry constitute per se reversible error? See United States v. Colonia, 870 F.2d 1319 (7th Cir.1989) (no reversal in absence of showing of actual conflict).

State courts are not bound to follow the procedure specified in Rule 44(c). However, when a defendant objects to representation on the basis of a conflict, the court must inquire into it and appoint independent counsel if there is a potential conflict.

STATE v. CALLAHAN

Supreme Court of Kansas, 1982.
232 Kan. 136, 652 P.2d 708.

PER CURIAM:

This is an original proceeding in discipline. The proceeding is the result of a complaint filed on behalf of Mrs. Ruth Fulton.

Ruth Fulton, an elderly lady, owned 320 acres of land in Butler County which she had inherited from her father. Although she was born in Kansas, she has been a resident of California for over 60 years, and the land had been leased to a neighboring landowner for a number of years.

In 1974, Mrs. Fulton decided to sell her land. She first offered it to her tenant who declined the offer. He advised, however, that a Lowell Lygrisse was in the market for such property and offered to contact him.

Subsequently, Lygrisse called Mrs. Fulton by phone and a tentative agreement was reached. During this conversation, Lygrisse suggested that the respondent, John Callahan, handle the transaction for both of them. Mrs. Fulton agreed, and later called respondent and retained his services.

The interpretation of the parties as to respondent's scope of employment differed. Mrs. Fulton stated that she believed respondent would act as a California escrow officer would and protect the interests of both parties. Respondent testified that he believed that he represented both parties as a scrivener to draw the papers and close the sale only after the terms of the purchase agreement had been negotiated between the parties.

Respondent prepared two contracts controlling the sale in accordance with the terms provided by Lygrisse and without consulting Mrs. Fulton. The first contract was entitled "Real Estate Purchase Contract." It provided for a sale price of $96,000.00, to be paid $24,000.00 at the time of closing and the balance in three annual installments of $24,000.00 each. The first annual installment was to be secured by a certificate of deposit.

The contract was unusual, however, in that it provided that the seller would execute and deliver a deed to the buyer at closing, and that the land would be included with other land in a mortgage to the Federal Land Bank. Although Mrs. Fulton did not fully understand the transaction, she signed the contract on November 14, 1974, in reliance upon respondent.

On December 11, 1974, respondent wrote to Mrs. Fulton enclosing a deed for her to sign and informed her that he would hold the deed until the first $24,000.00 was paid. He also informed her that when Lygrisse secured his loan from the Federal Land Bank, respondent would purchase a certificate of deposit in the amount of $24,000.00 and pledge it as security for the second payment, and that he would then formalize the agreement on the balance owing. Mrs. Fulton signed the deed and returned it to respondent.

Thereafter, respondent filed and conducted the necessary legal action to quiet title to the land and obtained inheritance tax clearance. He also advised Mrs. Fulton as to certain tax consequences of the sale. He billed Mrs. Fulton on March 14, 1975, for his services in clearing the title and was paid.

The second contract was entitled "Pledge, Escrow and Agreement." It recited the schedule of payments on the unpaid balance and set up an escrow of the certificate of deposit securing the first annual payment due April 1, 1976.

It differed from the first contract of sale in that Paragraph 7 provided for acceleration of the unpaid balance upon default and provided:

> "In the event of default and nonpayment of any judgment therefore the Fulton's shall have a specific lien on the real estate covered hereby subject only to the Federal Land Bank first mortgage of record."

Mrs. Fulton signed the agreement on May 21, 1975, in reliance on respondent's request as her attorney, without independent legal advice, believing that the provisions of paragraph 7 would effectively place her in the position of a second mortgagee. She further assumed respondent would record anything necessary to perfect her "specific lien." No such other documents were prepared or recorded by respondent.

For several years before and after 1974, respondent was Lygrisse's personal attorney, and they were each owners of 50% of the common stock of L–C Farm Co., Inc., a corporation engaged in buying and selling farms and other real estate. Respondent was required to and did personally guarantee some or all of the debts of the corporation which at times exceeded $500,000.00. The Fulton farm was not purchased for the account of L–C Farms Co., Inc., however, and no claim is made that respondent personally acquired any interest therein. Respondent admits that he did not disclose to Mrs. Fulton his business relationship with Lygrisse.

No problems arose until Lygrisse defaulted on the final payment due April 1, 1978. Mrs. Fulton called respondent several times for advice. He told her that Lygrisse had suffered some business reversals but that he was sure Lygrisse would make the final payment. Sometime in late 1978, she contacted respondent again and asked how long she had to file for foreclosure. Respondent advised her that she had five years from the date of default, but suggested again that she didn't need to foreclose, that he was sure Lygrisse would pay.

In May of 1979, Mrs. Fulton and her husband traveled to Wichita and met with respondent for the first time in person. They asked respondent to file a foreclosure action on what they perceived to be their second mortgage. Respondent declined, citing as his reason a conflict of interest, but he agreed to refer them to another attorney. He did not advise them at that time that they did not have a secured interest in the real estate.

The Fultons then went to see Lygrisse who promised to pay them within a few weeks. When the payment was not forthcoming, Mrs. Fulton again phoned respondent who again assured them that he believed Lygrisse would pay and advised them not to foreclose.

Finally, on March 1, 1980, Mr. Fulton called respondent and again asked for the name of an attorney to file foreclosure proceedings.

During this conversation, respondent for the first time advised the Fultons that they had no mortgage and that all they had was a promissory note.

The Fultons were subsequently referred to Jim Lawing of Wichita who prepared and filed a malpractice action against respondent. Shortly thereafter respondent filed a voluntary petition in bankruptcy and was ultimately discharged.

In the spring of 1980, the Federal Land Bank foreclosed its mortgage against the Fulton farm. Mrs. Fulton was not a party to the action and learned of the action through independent inquiry. Included in the action was a second mortgage given to an El Dorado bank by Lygrisse around the time the down payment to Mrs. Fulton was made. She has never received the final payment of $24,000.00.

Following a letter of complaint from Jim Lawing to the disciplinary administrator, a formal complaint with Lawing's letter attached was filed by the disciplinary administrator before the Board for Discipline of Attorneys. A hearing was held on November 18, 1981, and the hearing panel found that respondent had violated disciplinary rules DR 5–105(B), DR 6–101(A)(3), and DR 1–102(A)(4). It recommended indefinite suspension of respondent. Respondent has taken exception to the report.

The hearing panel found that respondent had violated DR 5–105(B) in that he represented both the sellers and the buyer when a conflict of interest existed by failing to warn the sellers that they did not have a perfected second mortgage or security interest.

Disciplinary rule DR 5–105(B) and (C) reads as follows:

"*Refusing to Accept or Continue Employment if the Interests of Another Client May Impair the Independent Professional Judgment of the Lawyer.*

. . .

"(B) A lawyer shall not continue multiple employment if the exercise of his independent professional judgment in behalf of a client will be or is likely to be adversely affected by his representation of another client, except to the extent permitted under DR 5–105(C).

"(C) In the situations covered by DR 5–105(A) and (B), a lawyer may represent multiple clients if it is obvious that he can adequately represent the interest of each and if each consents to the representation after a full disclosure of the possible effect of such representation on the exercise of his independent professional judgment on behalf of each."

It is respondent's contention that the terms of the sale were agreed upon between the parties before he was employed and that he only represented the parties, insofar as the contract of sale was concerned, as a scrivener to write up the contract and close the sale in accordance with the prior agreement of the parties. He asserts further that he was under no duty to suggest "better terms" for the seller or to make and record a second mortgage not called for by the terms of the contract.

Under the circumstances here, however, we fail to see how respondent could have been unaware that he was not exercising his independent professional judgment in behalf of the Fultons in preparing the contract solely on the terms dictated by Lygrisse without consulting the Fultons, or at least advising them of the risk inherent in not taking a second mortgage to secure the balance of the purchase price.

Furthermore, respondent did not make a full disclosure to the Fultons of his close business and professional associations with the buyer.

This court, in State v. Hilton, 217 Kan. 694, 698, 538 P.2d 977 (1975), stated:

"The unmistakable intent of DR 5–105(C) is exemplified in 'Ethical Considerations' [EC] 5–15 (ABA Standards, Code of Professional Responsibility). It reads in pertinent part:

" 'If a lawyer is requested to undertake or to continue representation of multiple clients having potentially differing interests, he must weigh carefully the possibility that his judgment may be impaired or his loyalty divided if he accepts or continues the employment. He should resolve all doubts against the propriety of the representation. . . . ' "

The panel also found respondent guilty of violating DR 1–102(A)(4) in that he misrepresented to the sellers that they had a specific lien on the property sold, subject only to a first mortgage to the Federal Land Bank, when in fact they had no such lien.

DR 1–102(A)(4) provides:

"*Misconduct.*

"(A) A lawyer shall not:

. . . .

"(4) Engage in conduct involving dishonesty, fraud, deceit, or misrepresentation."

Respondent contends that nothing in the pledge agreement provides for a second mortgage. Paragraph 7, he argues, refers only to a lien given to a judgment under K.S.A. 60–2202 (Corrick), and when considered with other provisions of the contract amounts to no more than a warranty that Lygrisse would not allow a subsequent lien or mortgage to attach.

Again, under the circumstances here, we fail to see how the Fultons could reasonably have given such an interpretation to this provision. They believed that they had a "specific lien," and on several occasions when the Fultons inquired of respondent about foreclosure proceedings, he failed to disclose to them that there was no valid foreclosable interest and advised them not to foreclose. He finally offered to give them the name of another attorney to handle such an action. They were not advised that they had no security interest to foreclose until almost two years after the final payment was due.

The duty of good faith imposed upon an attorney does not always cease immediately upon termination of his employment. It continues as long as the influence created by the relationship continues. Alexander v. Russo, 1 Kan.App.2d 546, 571 P.2d 350, rev. denied 222 Kan. 749 (1977). The Fultons still looked to respondent for aid, and his conduct in failing to disclose to them that they had no lien on the property to secure the balance due them clearly rises to the level of deceit and dishonesty.

.   .   .

"Full Disclosure" as Predicate of Consent

In Financial General Bankshares v. Metzger, 523 F.Supp. 744, 771 (D.D.C.1981), rev'd on other grounds, 680 F.2d 768 (D.C.Cir.1982), discussed further in Chapter 9 below at p. 766, the court said full disclosure means "[an] affirmative revelation by the attorney of all the facts, legal implications, possible effects, and other circumstances relating to the proposed representation." The fact that the client knows the lawyer represents another client whose interests are adverse does not constitute full disclosure.

California Rule 3–310 requires the *written* consent of the parties before a lawyer may proceed to represent conflicting interests. In practice this is interpreted not to require that the predicate disclosure also be in writing.

Providing full disclosure is not easy.

Uncertainty about the facts: The lawyer is supposed to detail the facts relating to the proposed representation(s). However, there is often much uncertainty about the facts, e.g., what the lawyer has been retained to do on behalf of either client initially may be uncertain; at the outset there are many as yet undiscovered facts, etc.

The rules on confidentiality: How is a lawyer to make full disclosure without breaching the other client's confidences?

Change of facts: Facts change as transactions move forward. Disclosure in this sense must be an ongoing process.

Must a client get another lawyer's advice before consenting to representation by a lawyer with a conflict? In Aetna Cas. & Sur. Co. v. United States, 570 F.2d 1197 (4th Cir.1978), the lower court had ruled, 438 F.Supp. 886 (W.D.N.C.1977), that consent given without the advice of independent counsel cannot be presumed to be informed. The court of appeals reversed.

See also Moore, Conflicts of Interest in the Simultaneous Representation of Multiple Clients, 61 Tex.L.Rev. 211 (1982).

The Lawyer as Intermediary

The Code and the Rules

The Code of Professional Responsibility observes that "[a] lawyer is often asked to serve as an impartial arbitrator or mediator in matters which involve present or former clients." EC 5–20. Not much specific guidance is given for performing such a role, however. EC 5–20 says the lawyer "may serve in either capacity if he first discloses such present or former relationships." Hence, under the Code the lawyer must look to DR 5–105, the general rule on conflicts of interest.

M.R. 2.2 has a complex set of provisions on the lawyer as intermediary. Subparagraph (a)(1) specifies issues the lawyer should discuss with the clients before obtaining their consent. Subparagraphs (a)(2) and (a)(3) require that the lawyer reasonably believe: that the matter can be resolved on terms compatible with the clients' best interests; that each client will be able to make informed decisions; that there is little risk of material prejudice to either client's interests should the contemplated resolution fail; and that the common representation can be undertaken impartially and without improper effect on the responsibilities the lawyer has to either client.

M.R. 2.2(b) prescribes how the lawyer should proceed while acting as an intermediary. M.R. 2.2(c) requires the lawyer to withdraw if either client requests or if the lawyer can no longer meet the requirements of paragraph (a). After withdrawing, the lawyer may not represent any of the clients in the matter that was the subject of the intermediation.

Wouldn't a lawyer seeking to adjust a matter between clients be better off to call it "adjustment" and be governed by M.R. 1.7?

A lawyer who decides to act as an intermediary faces serious risks. In Klemm v. Superior Court, 75 Cal.App.3d 893, 142 Cal.Rptr. 509, 514 (1977), the court identified at least some of these risks:

- if the lawyer fails fully to inform the clients of the facts, risks, and potential disadvantages of the joint representation, the lawyer may be civilly liable to those clients for any loss suffered

- the lawyer lays himself open to charges, whether well founded or not, of unethical and unprofessional conduct

- the validity of any agreement negotiated without independent representation of each of the parties is vulnerable to easy attack as having been procured by misrepresentation, fraud and overreaching.

The court concluded that "[i]t thus behooves counsel to cogitate carefully and proceed cautiously before placing himself/herself in such a position." 142 Cal.Rptr. at 514.

Representing Buyer and Seller

In re Kamp, 40 N.J. 588, 194 A.2d 236 (1963), holds that a lawyer seeking to represent both the seller and buyer in a real estate or similar transaction must disclose to each his relationship to the other, the pitfalls of dual representation which might make it desirable for each party to have separate counsel, and "[t]he full significance of the representation of conflicting interests . . . If the attorney cannot properly represent the buyer in all aspects of the transaction because of his relationship to the seller, full disclosure requires that he inform the buyer of the limited scope of his intended representation of the buyer's interests and point out the advantages of the buyer's retaining independent counsel." 199 A.2d at 240. Can a lawyer be sure this formula has been fulfilled?

While concurrent representation of buyers and sellers has been conventional in many localities, it is risky and should not be undertaken without carefully examining the circumstances surrounding the proposed representation, including the lawyer's past relationships with both clients and the attitude of both clients towards the proposed representation and each other. In Matter of Banta, 412 N.E.2d 221 (Ind.1980) a lawyer was reprimanded for having relayed to the buyer inaccurate facts given to the lawyer by the seller.

It is proper in some circumstances for a lawyer to bring two clients together to facilitate a deal between them, see, e.g., Atlantic Richfield Co. v. Sybert, 295 Md. 347, 456 A.2d 20 (1983). But when the lawyer has a longstanding relationship with one party and a new relationship with the other, it can be unreasonable to believe that she can be impartial between them. See Comment to M.R. 2.2; Attorney Grievance Commission v. Collins, 298 Md. 532, 457 A.2d 1134 (1983); In re Lanza, 65 N.J. 347, 322 A.2d 445 (1974); In re Nelson, 112 Wis.2d 292, 332 N.W.2d 811 (1983). For a case where despite the differences in relationships the court found the dual representation acceptable see Dillard v. Broyles, 633 S.W.2d 636 (Tex.Ct.App.1982).

OPINION NO. 80–23, 1980

(Divorce Mediation)

Association of the Bar of the City of New York,
Committee on Professional Ethics.

We have been asked whether lawyers may ethically participate in a divorce mediation program organized by a non-profit organization. The organization has a staff of licensed mental health professionals who provide marital and family therapy. It now proposes to offer what is known as "structured mediation" in marital cases. Such mediation involves a trained therapist consulting with separating or divorcing couples to aid them in working out various aspects of the separation or divorce, including issues of property division, and child custody, visitation and support. We have been asked whether a lawyer could (a) become part of the mediating team, (b) give impartial legal advice to the parties, such as advice on the tax consequences of proposed separation or divorce agreements, or (c) draft a divorce or settlement agreement after the terms of such agreement have been approved by the parties. We have also been asked whether a participating lawyer could be paid, either by the parties to the mediation or by the organization.

This inquiry raises important and difficult questions concerning the participation of lawyers in non-adversarial roles in dispute resolution. The Code of Professional Responsibility provides comparatively detailed guides for the lawyer representing clients in the adversarial role of zealous advocate or confidential adviser. The Code also recognizes that lawyers may serve as "impartial arbitrators or mediators" (EC 5–20). However, the Code nowhere defines these latter roles and their responsibilities or expressly considers the role of lawyers asked to provide impartial legal assistance to parties with differing interests, in an effort to compose their differences without resort to adversary negotiation or litigation. The Committee nevertheless believes that the principles of the Code permit the extrapolation of certain guidelines for lawyers asked to participate in such non-adversarial activities.

We conclude, first, that the Code does not impose a *per se* bar to lawyer participation in divorce mediation activities, or to the provision of impartial legal assistance to parties engaged in divorce mediation. At the same time, we believe that particularly in the sensitive area of divorce, the application of labels such as "mediation" or "impartial" advice does not satisfy the Code's concerns for the administration of justice, the dangers inherent in the reliance of laymen with differing interests on the legal advice of a single lawyer, and the appearance of impropriety attendant on such situations. Rather, we conclude that a lawyer asked to participate in divorce mediation and to provide impartial legal advice or assistance in drawing up an agreement must take certain precautions, specified hereafter . . . We also conclude that there are some situations, also discussed below, where these dangers and the potential harm to the interests of the parties are so great that it is entirely inappropriate for a lawyer to participate in mediation or to attempt to give impartial legal assistance. . . .

I.

The issues raised here require the harmonization of differing policies reflected in the Code of Professional Responsibility. On the one hand, the Code provides that a lawyer may represent multiple clients only "if it is *obvious* that he can adequately represent the interest of each and if each consents to the representation after full disclosure of the possible effect of such representation on the exercise of his independent professional judgment on behalf of each." DR 5–105(C) (emphasis supplied). Applying this principle, it has been repeatedly held that the conflicts inherent in a matrimonial proceeding are such, that it is never appropriate to represent both spouses. Thus, New York State Opinion 258 (1972) states:

> It would be improper for a lawyer to represent both husband and wife at any stage of a marital problem, even with full disclosure and informed consent of both parties. The likelihood of prejudice is so great in this type of matter as to make impossible adequate representation of both spouses, even where the separation is "friendly" and the divorce uncontested.

This opinion further cites with approval the view that such representation is improper even if the parties consent and merely are seeking to have the lawyer reduce to writing an agreement that the parties independently arrived at.

On the other hand, EC 5–20 states that a lawyer may serve in the capacity of an "impartial arbitrator or mediator" even for present or former clients provided the lawyer makes appropriate disclosures and thereafter declines to represent any of the parties in the dispute. Accordingly, New York State Opinion 258 also acknowledges that a lawyer can serve as a "mediator" in a matrimonial dispute.

The difficulty arises because the Code nowhere explains what activities constitute "mediation", what responsibilities a lawyer has when acting as a mediator, when a lawyer is "representing" parties or whether it is possible for a lawyer to give legal guidance to all parties to a dispute—to "represent the situation"—without representing any of them or being involved in the conflicts which representing them would involve. See Hazard, Ethics in the Practice of Law 58–68 (1978).

Mediation, particularly in the context of divorce disputes, could have a number of meanings. It could mean acting as an intermediary between the parties to find common ground between them on such matters as who gets what piece of property or who gets custody of a child. Such activity may or may not involve the exercise of professional legal judgments.*

On the other hand, mediation could mean attempting to resolve matters that involve complicated tax or other legal ramifications. As professor Hazard has pointed out, the word "mediator" can:

> "imply that the lawyer is a spokesman for the position of each of the parties, as well as one who listens to the parties express their positions for themselves. It can imply that the lawyer is actively involved, indeed aggressively involved, in exploring alternative arrangements by which the positions of the parties can be accommodated in a comprehensive resolution of the matter at hand." Hazard, *supra* at 63.

---

* The American Arbitration Association has a program for divorce mediation in which the family mediator is not permitted to give legal advice; once the mediator produces a resolution, the parties are referred to their own attorneys. See generally Spencer and Zammit, Mediation–Arbitration: Proposal for Private Resolution of Disputes Between Divorced or Separated Parents, 1976 Duke L.J. 911, notes 34–42 and accompanying text.

Two other Bar Associations, to our knowledge, have rendered opinions in circumstances similar to those involved here. They have concluded that lawyer participation in divorce mediation—including the rendering of impartial legal advice and the preparation of a written agreement—is permissible because the Code permits mediation and because the lawyer is not "representing" either party and hence does not come within the strictures of DR 5–105 on the representation of clients with differing interests. Oregon State Bar Proposed Opinion 79–46 (1980); Boston Bar Opinion 78–1 (1978). Both opinions recognize the dangers in such situations of inequalities in the bargaining power of the parties and the potential for misunderstandings and later recrimination against the lawyer. They nevertheless conclude, with considerable reluctance, that the lawyer may undertake divorce mediation activities including the provision of impartial legal assistance, provided the lawyer makes it clear that the lawyer represents neither party, and obtains the parties' consent. . . .

II.

This Committee recognizes that there are circumstances where it is desirable that parties to a matrimonial dispute be afforded an alternative to the adversarial process, with its legal and emotional costs. . . .

At the same time, the Committee also recognizes that in some circumstances, the complex and conflicting interests involved in a particular matrimonial dispute, the difficult legal issues involved, the subtle legal ramifications of particular resolutions, and the inequality in bargaining power resulting from differences in the personalities or sophistication of the parties make it virtually impossible to achieve a just result free from later recriminations of bias or malpractice, unless both parties are represented by separate counsel. In the latter circumstances, informing the parties that the lawyer "represents" neither party and obtaining their consent, even after a full explanation of the risks, may not be meaningful; the distinction between representing both parties and not representing either, in such circumstances, may be illusory. . . . Further, the "impartial" lawyer may in fact be making difficult choices between the interests of the parties in giving legal advice or in drafting provisions of a written agreement which purports merely to embody the parties' prior agreement. Although the parties may consent to the procedure, one or both may not be capable of giving truly informed consent due to the difficulty of the issues involved. In such circumstances, a party who is later advised that its interests were prejudiced in mediation or that the impartial advice offered or written agreement drawn, by the lawyer-mediator, favored the other spouse is likely to believe that it was misled into reliance on the impartiality of the lawyer-mediator. . . .

On the other hand, there are clearly circumstances where these difficulties are not involved and where the parties can truly understand, and the lawyer can plainly carry out, a representation that the lawyer represents neither party.

This seems likely, for example, where the lawyer is not being asked to exercise any professional legal judgment—for example where the lawyer is seeking to bring about a compromise or find a common ground for the division of articles of personal property. Such typical mediation activities can be performed by non-lawyers and we cannot conclude that the Code (which permits lawyers to serve as mediators) intended to bar lawyers from performing the same activities.

It also seems true that the lawyer can meaningfully state that he or she represents neither of the parties where the parties simply ask the lawyer to describe the legal consequences of a particular agreement they have reached. Performing such activities would not involve the lawyer in making choices between the interests of the parties.

Nevertheless, even with regard to such activities, there are likely to be situations of such complexity and difficulty that the lawyer must make the judgment that one or both of the parties' consent cannot be considered fully informed. This may be true even where the lawyer merely is asked to provide services that lay mediators may perform or where the legal question he is asked does not require him to choose between the parties' interests. For example, what may appear to be simply a resolution of a dispute about the division of property, may in fact have complicated and subtle tax consequences about which the parties are unaware. The divorce process has always been considered of special concern to the state and as such, an integral part of the administration of justice. Where the lawyer recognizes that the issues raised by a particular divorce dispute are so difficult or complex that they cannot be fairly or justly resolved unless each party is guided by its own separate counsel, the lawyer's participation in a mediation of the dispute may be prejudicial to the administration of justice. See DR 1–102(A)(5).

Accordingly, to harmonize these various considerations, we have concluded that lawyers may participate in the divorce mediation procedure proposed in the inquiry here, only on the following conditions.

To begin with, the lawyer may *not* participate in the divorce mediation process where it appears that the issues between the parties are of such complexity or difficulty that the parties cannot prudently reach a resolution without the advice of separate and independent legal counsel.

If the lawyer is satisfied that the situation is one in which the parties can intelligently and prudently consent to mediation and the use of an impartial legal adviser, then the lawyer may undertake these roles provided the lawyer observes the following rules:

First, the lawyer must clearly and fully advise the parties of the limitations on his or her role and specifically, of the fact that the lawyer represents neither party and that accordingly, they should not look to the lawyer to protect their individual interests or to keep confidences of one party from the other.

Second, the lawyer must fully and clearly explain the risks of proceeding without separate legal counsel and thereafter proceed only with the consent of the parties and only if the lawyer is satisfied that the parties understand the risks and understand the significance of the fact that the lawyer represents neither party.

Third, a lawyer may participate with mental health professionals in those aspects of mediation which do not require the exercise of professional legal judgment and involve the same kind of mediation activities permissible to lay mediators.

Fourth, lawyers may provide impartial legal advice and assist in reducing the parties' agreement to writing only where the lawyer fully explains all pertinent considerations and alternatives and the consequences to each party of choosing the resolution agreed upon.

Fifth, the lawyer may give legal advice only to both parties in the presence of the other.

Sixth, the lawyer must advise the parties of the advantages of seeking independent legal counsel before executing any agreement drafted by the lawyer.

Seventh, the lawyer may not represent either of the parties in any subsequent legal proceedings relating to the divorce.

Underlying these guidelines is the requirement that the lawyers' participation in the mediation process be conditioned on *informed* consent by the parties. The February 6, 1981 working draft of the American Bar Association's proposed Model Rules of Professional Conduct would set specific guidelines for a lawyer acting as an "intermediary" between clients in an effort to compose their differences. Among other things, the proposal would require the lawyer to satisfy himself or herself that "each client will be able to make adequately informed decisions in the matter." The guidelines provided here would require the lawyer to make a similar judgment, and to decide that certain situations are too complex for a parties' consent to the process to be considered "informed." We recognize that such a standard does not provide a bright-line test, but it is essential if the interests of the parties are to be protected and the parties' consents are to be meaningful.

III.

Inasmuch as the divorce mediation program will be operated by laymen and involve the participation of non-lawyer mental health professionals, certain additional considerations are warranted. New York Judiciary Law § 476, *et seq.* prohibits the practice of law by law persons. New York Judiciary Law § 495 prohibits the practice of law by corporations or voluntary associations. If the activities of the non-lawyer staff of the divorce mediation program constitute the unauthorized practice of law, it would be improper for lawyers to assist them in such activities. DR 3–101.

Questions and Comments

One spouse's undue influence over the other is a serious impediment to representing both husband and wife in domestic relations cases. Divorce, custody or prenuptial agreements can all be challenged on the ground of overreaching. Representation of both spouses by one lawyer is a perfect invitation to such a challenge.

In Blum v. Blum, 59 Md.App. 584, 477 A.2d 289 (App.1984), the court cited with approval the Maryland State Bar Association Committee on Ethics opinion Docket 78–25, April 11, 1978. That opinion said that since divorce actions are inherently adversarial and involve great potential of opposing interests on such issues as support, child custody, visitation, ownership and division of property, one attorney should not represent both the husband and the wife. Compare Klemm v. Superior Court, 75 Cal.App.3d 893, 142 Cal.Rptr. 509 (1977).

In *Klemm,* one factor that may have led the court to sustain the dual representation was that the challenge to the support agreement was brought not by either spouse but by the County of Fresno, which wanted the husband to pay child support to offset the AFDC payments being made to the mother. The wife asserted that she was content with the agreement for no support.

For a useful review of the bar association opinions on the problem addressed in M.R. 2.2 and the hostility to mediatory representation in divorce proceedings, see Note, Model Rule 2.2 and Divorce Mediation: Ethics Guideline or Ethics Gap?, 65 Wash.U.L.Q. 223 (1987).

A lawyer represents a closely held corporation or a partnership whose members are friends or siblings. Trouble erupts between the partners. They have sharp differences about the course that the business should take, or one accuses the other of bad faith or malfeasance in her performance for the business. They come to the lawyer and ask her to work out a fair dissolution. What are the risks to the lawyer? To the clients? How is this case different from the case of a marriage that is in serious difficulty? Under the standards stated in ABCNY Inq. Ref. No. 80–23, supra, should the lawyer insist that the parties obtain separate representation? For more on representing partnerships and closely held corporations, see Chapter 10 below.

Consider the following hypotheticals.

————

Multi–Party Representation: Hypothetical Problems

a. Mr. X and Ms. Y are referred to our office by their insurance advisor. We have never dealt with Mr. X and Ms. Y before although their insurance advisor is a good referral source. Mr. X and Ms. Y are about to be married and want to enter into a prenuptial agreement. Both Mr. X and Ms. Y have considerable personal estates.

b. Same as example (a) except that we have represented Mr. X for many years with respect to his first marriage.

c. Same as example (b) except that Ms. Y has no personal assets.

d. Mr. C, Mr. L and Ms. A come into our office to form a limited partnership. Mr. C has been a client of the firm for many years and plans on entering the partnership as a general partner. Mr. L is a landowner who will contribute land and Ms. A is an architect who will contribute architectural drawings and specifications. Mr. L and Ms. A plan to be limited partners. At the first meeting, it is discovered that the only agreement thus far is that cash distributions will be shared 50% to Mr. C and 25% each to Mr. L and Ms. A. The parties want us to put together the partnership. The parties have not discussed nor are they even aware of the many substantive points at which their interests can vary from one another.

e. Dr. A and Dr. B have an established partnership and have come to us for an incorporation and the design of a pension plan.

f. Dr. A is a one-woman professional corporation who is a long-standing client of our firm. Dr. A comes to us and asks that we represent her and Dr. B in forming a new A–B professional corporation.

g. We formed the A–B corporation many years ago. Upon formation, Dr. A was our primary contact, but over the years Dr. A and Dr. B have been equal in their communication with our firm. Dr. A is approaching retirement age and is trying to negotiate a better buy-out agreement with Dr. B than the agreement which we designed and both doctors signed. Dr. A and Dr. B are still communicating but are not getting along.

Representing Insurance Companies and the Insured

In General

For many years the ABA waffled on the lawyer's responsibility in representing an insured through retainer by an insurer. ABA Formal Opinion 247 (1942) declined to say whether information given by the insured to the lawyer is confidential as against the insurer. The opinion stated that this "is a question of law and not of ethics," a question on which the courts were divided. See Annot. 108 A.L.R. 505 for court decisions on this issue contemporaneous with Opinion 247.

ABA Formal Opinion 282 (1950), however, took the position that "The essential point of ethics involved is that the lawyer so employed shall represent the insured as his client with undivided fidelity . . ." This is the accepted rule today. See, e.g., Parsons v. Continental National American Group, 112 Ariz. 223, 550 P.2d 94, 99 (1976) ("When an attorney who is an insurance company's agent uses the confidential relationship between an attorney and a client to gather information so as to deny the insured coverage under the policy in the garnishment proceeding, we hold that such conduct constitutes a waiver of any policy defense, and is so contrary to public policy that the insurance company is estopped as a matter of law from disclaiming liability under an exclusionary clause in the policy."). Accord: State Farm Mutual Automobile Ins. Co. v. Walker, 382 F.2d 548 (7th Cir.1967) (en banc) (lawyer cannot disclose the information and must withdraw from representing both the insurer and the insured).

DR 5–107(B) provides that "A lawyer shall not permit a person who recommends, employs, or pays him to render legal services for another to direct or regulate his professional judgment in rendering such legal services."

M.R. 1.8(f) provides a lawyer shall not accept payment from another for legal services to a client unless: (1) the client consents after consultation; (2) there is no interference with the lawyer's independence or professional judgment or with the client-lawyer relationship; and (3) information relating to representation of the client is protected as required by M.R. 1.6 (the rule on confidentiality).

In addition, M.R. 1.8(b) provides that "[a] lawyer shall not use information relating to representation of a client to the disadvantage of the client unless the client consents after consultation." Observe that "use" of information may be made without disclosure of such information.

Settling an Insurance Claim

In Crisci v. Security Insurance Co., 66 Cal.2d 425, 429, 58 Cal.Rptr. 13, 16, 426 P.2d 173, 176 (1967), the court said: "When there is a great risk of a recovery beyond the policy limits so that the most reasonable manner of disposing of the claim is a settlement which can be made within those limits, a consideration in good faith of the insured's interest requires the insurer to settle the claim." In *Crisci*, it was the insurance company that was being sued, not the lawyer. In Purdy v. Pacific Automobile Ins. Co., 157 Cal.App.3d 59, 203 Cal.Rptr. 524 (1984), the insured sued the lawyer (hired by the insurance company) for failing to settle within the policy limits when the insured was obviously liable. The court found that the lawyer's actions were not the proximate cause of the insured's injury: the insurance company's refusal to settle was an intervening cause.

May the insurer settle without the insured's consent? See Rogers v. Robson, Masters, Ryan, Brumund & Belom, 81 Ill.2d 201, 407 N.E.2d 47 (1980) (although insurance policy authorized the insurer to settle without the insured's consent, the insured had a cause of action against the lawyer who settled against his instructions and without fully disclosing to him the intent to settle. The lawyer's duty concerning settlement without the client's consent stemmed from the attorney-client relationship, not the policy). Accord: L & S Roofing Supply Co. v. St. Paul Fire & Marine Ins. Co., 521 So.2d 1298 (Ala.1987); Lieberman v. Employers Insurance of Wausau, 84 N.J. 325, 419 A.2d 417

(1980). See DR 5–106, M.R. 1.8(g), M.R. 1.2(a). But see Mitchum v. Hudgens, 533 So.2d 194 (Ala.1988) (lawyer not liable to insured for malpractice for settling without insured's consent when policy gave insurer exclusive power to handle settlement matters; the court distinguished *L & S Roofing,* supra, by noting that here the insurer had not reserved rights against the insured, who therefore had no financial stake in the settlement).

For an examination of the appropriate course of conduct for a lawyer representing insurer and insured during settlement negotiations, see Hartford Accident & Indemnity Co. v. Foster, 528 So.2d 255, 270–273 (Miss.1988) (concluding that "the ethical dilemma . . . would tax Socrates, and no decision or authority we have studied furnishes a completely satisfactory answer."). On Feb. 7, 1972, the ABA House of Delegates adopted ABA National Conference of Lawyers and Liability Insurers, Guiding Principles, reprinted in 20 Fed.Ins.Couns.Q. 95. (1972). These principles had already been accepted by the major casualty and liability insurance companies. The principles were rescinded by the ABA in August 1980, apparently to avoid antitrust implications arising from such a trade agreement, but presumably they are still accepted by the insurance companies.

While most court decisions have held that the lawyer retained by the insurer to represent an insured must treat the insured as the client when a conflict arises, the guiding principles take a different view in several important respects.

One section provides that if the lawyer discovers a question of coverage he must notify both the company and the insured, and the insured should be invited to retain her own counsel at her own expense to represent her separate interest, Paragraph IV.

Another principle, however, provides that if the insured tells the lawyer something that would indicate a lack of coverage, and if this communication is made "under circumstances indicating the insured's belief that such disclosure would not be revealed to the insurance company but would be treated as a confidential communication to the attorney," the lawyer should not tell the company, but neither should she "discuss with the insured the legal significance of the disclosure or the nature of the coverage question." Paragraph VI. Finally, Paragraph IX provides that if the lawyer decides to withdraw, "the insured should be fully advised of such decision and the reasons therefor . . ."

It is difficult to reconcile Paragraph IX's call for full disclosure to the insured before withdrawal and Paragraph's VI's admonition not to inform the insured of the legal significance of the coverage question. More important, it seems impossible to reconcile Paragraph VI's requirement that the lawyer not inform the insured of the legal significance or the nature of the coverage question with the duties of a lawyer to advise her client. See M.R. 1.4.

See also Moritz v. The Medical Protective Co. of Fort Wayne, Indiana, 428 F.Supp. 865 (W.D.Wis.1977); Hamilton v. State Farm Insurance Co., 83 Wash.2d 787, 523 P.2d 193 (1974); A. Windt, Insurance Claims and Disputes; Representation of Insurance Companies and Insureds (1982); and Wunnicke, The Eternal Triangle: Standards of Ethical Representation by the Insurance Defense Lawyer, For the Defense, February 1989, p. 7.

Chapter VIII

CONFLICT OF INTEREST II: SUCCESSIVE REPRESENTATION AND IMPUTED DISQUALIFICATION

A. SUCCESSIVE REPRESENTATION

The Substantial Relationship Test

The substantial relationship test, important in concurrent representation cases, is central in successive representation cases. In successive representation, if the matters are not the "same or substantially related," the lawyer may proceed without even consulting the former client. If the matters are substantially related, the former client's consent must be obtained before going forward.

Oddly enough, the Model Code has no provision specifying whether, and if so when, it is proper for a lawyer to oppose a former client on behalf of a present client. The courts filled the gap, relying on pre-Code common law principles. The case law on this subject has been multiplying in recent years, largely in connection with motions to disqualify. See Chapter 7 above at p. 618, on the misuse of motions to disqualify counsel.

Lacking a specific Code provision on conflicts with former clients, courts relied on Canon 4 (preserving client confidences), Canon 5 (exercising independent judgment) and Canon 9 (avoiding the appearance of impropriety) in fashioning the law on this subject. The basic test antedated the Code, being first enunciated by Judge Weinfeld in T.C. Theatre Corp. v. Warner Brothers Pictures, Inc., 113 F.Supp. 265, 268–269 (S.D.N.Y.1953):

> I hold that the former client need show no more than that matters embraced within the pending suit wherein his former attorney appears on behalf of his adversary are substantially related to the matters or cause of action wherein the attorney previously represented him, the former client. The Court will assume that during the course of the former representation confidences were disclosed to the attorney bearing on the subject matter of the representation. It will not inquire into their nature and extent. Only in this manner can the lawyer's duty of absolute fidelity be enforced and the spirit of the rule relating to privileged communications be maintained.

Model Rule 1.9

The Model Rules, unlike the Model Code, specifically deal with the question of successive representation. M.R. 1.9(a) provides that a lawyer shall not: "represent another person in the same or a substantially related matter in which that person's interests are materially adverse to the interests of the former client unless the former client consents after consultation."

Notice that the rule uses the substantial relationship test. Also notice that it only applies when the new client's interests are *materially adverse* to those of the former client. It is in this sense a rule against "switching sides." Third, notice that the former client's consent (after consultation) is enough to cure the conflict. This is not a "consent plus" rule like M.R. 1.7, which requires that the representation be objectively reasonable.

M.R. 1.9(c) (originally adopted by the ABA and adopted in many states as M.R. 1.9(b)) is a reminder that the lawyer also has a continuing duty of confidentiality to a former client. Even if the former client consents under M.R. 1.9(a) to the new representation, that consent does not obviate the lawyer's continuing duty of confidentiality. M.R. 1.9(b), as amended, is concerned with imputed disqualification and will be addressed later in this chapter.

M.R. 1.9 applies to all lawyers, including those whose former client was the government. Note, however, that lawyers who formerly worked for the government are bound by M.R. 1.11 *in addition* to M.R. 1.9. As we will see later in this chapter, M.R. 1.11 restricts a lawyer's representation of new clients in the same or substantially related matters, even when the new client's interests are in harmony with that of the former government client.

Was this Person Previously a Client?

Under the rule limiting representation adverse to a former client, it first must be shown that an attorney-client relationship previously existed between the objecting party and the lawyer.

Whether a person previously was a client involves essentially the same issues as determining whether a person presently has become a client. See the *Togstad* case printed in Chapter 6 above at p. 473, and the *Westinghouse* case printed in Chapter 7 above at p. 589. The alleged relationship can be considered "objectively," i.e., whether a reasonable observer would conclude that a lawyer-client relationship had existed. It can also be considered "subjectively," i.e., whether the alleged erstwhile client supposed that the lawyer was representing her. The court in *Westinghouse* adopted a combined standard: If the *client reasonably believed* that the relationship existed then the client had a right to believe the information communicated was confidential, and an attorney-client relationship will be held to have existed for purposes of conflict questions.

The distinction among the tests may be purely conceptual, even for a client who "taint shops," i.e., tries to create objective manifestations of consulting the lawyer with no real intention of retaining him. The tactic of "taint shopping" has been recognized as a problem by the courts. See, e.g., Hughes v. Paine, Webber . . . 565 F.Supp. 663 (N.D.

Ill.1983) (discussed in the notes to Westinghouse at p. 599). See also Levin v. Ripple Twist Mills, Inc., 416 F.Supp. 876 (E.D.Pa.1976), appeal dismissed, 549 F.2d 795 (3d Cir.1977).

What are the "Matters"?

Assuming there was an attorney-client relationship, is the present "matter" substantially related to the "matter" in which the lawyer represented the former client? This requires specification of the two things to be compared. Where both representations were of private clients, each "matter" usually is a lawsuit or a negotiation, in either case with more or less discernible identity. Where the prior or present client is a government agency, the definition of "matter" is much more amorphous. In that context the debate centers on whether tasks like drafting legislation or regulations are to be considered "matters" for purposes of the conflicts rules. For example, can a lawyer who drafts legislation later challenge it?

Are the Matters Substantially Related?

The courts have employed difficult formulas for "substantially related." Some decisions adopt what seems a broad definition. For example, the Fifth Circuit in Kraft Inc. v. Alton Box Board Co., 659 F.2d 1341, 1346 (5th Cir.1981), held that the prior representation "need only be akin to the present action in a way reasonable persons would understand as important to the issues involved."

While *Kraft* used the broad term "akin," it also used an objective standard, "reasonable persons," and required the matters be related in a manner "*important* to the *issues*." What makes the relationship "important" is a combination of at least two factors: how divergent are the vectors—the interests—of the two clients—in the two matters; and how relevant the information the lawyer would have received in the former representation is to the present matter—how potentially harmful that information might be.

Perhaps the broadest formula was suggested in Chugach Electric Association v. United States District Court, 370 F.2d 441 (9th Cir.1966). The case involved a former corporate general counsel, hence a lawyer who probably knew everything about the client's legal affairs. But the court said of the lawyer's former association with the opposing party that it "would provide him with greater insight and understanding of the significance of subsequent events . . . . and offer a promising source of discovery." 370 F.2d at 443.

A narrower formula has been adopted by the Second Circuit. In Government of India v. Cook Industries, Inc., 569 F.2d 737, 739–740 (2d Cir.1978) the court said that the relationship between the two matters must be "patently clear," the issues "identical" or "essentially the same". Also see Federal Deposit Insurance Corp. v. Amundson, 682 F.Supp. 981, 988 (D.Minn.1988). But see Anchor Packing v. Pro–Seal, 688 F.Supp. 1215, 1220 (E.D.Mich.1988) (Sixth Circuit rejects this narrow view, citing General Electric Co. v. Valeron, 608 F.2d 265, 267 (6th Cir.1979)).

The broad interpretation of "substantially related" in *Chugach Electric,* supra, has not been followed by other circuits and the Ninth Circuit appears to have abandoned it. See United Sewerage Agency v. Jelco, Inc., 646 F.2d 1339, 1351 (9th Cir.1981); Merle Norman Cosmetics, Inc. v. United States District Court, 856 F.2d 98, 100–101 (9th Cir. 1988). But it stands on the opposite end of the spectrum from the Second Circuit's view of "identity of issues." *Chugach* could be said to stand for a "till death do us part" approach, while the Second Circuit cases adopt a "here today, gone tomorrow" attitude. It should make a difference, shouldn't it, whether the first representation concerned an isolated transaction, as distinct from long-term general counseling? Few cases have involved the latter, which unmistakably would implicate disloyalty. Is that what the court in *Chugach* had in mind?

Notwithstanding the confusion over how loyalty should figure into the analysis, it seems clear that the central concern in the "substantial relation" test is the likelihood that confidential information relevant to the present case is possessed by the lawyer by virtue of her former relationship with the objecting party.

The risk to confidences must be assessed without revealing the confidences that the test seeks to protect. The problem is one of drawing inferences from the circumstances. This in turn involves a heavy interjection of the judges' experience in practice and her attitude toward loyalty to clients. A judge whose practice had been general counseling is likely, other things being equal, to have a different attitude from one whose practice was litigation or other "here today, gone tomorrow" transactions.

Another source of uncertainty is that the test seeks to protect competing interests. While the former client must be reasonably protected, the present client has a right to the counsel of its choice.

The Presumption That Confidential Information Was Received

If the court finds that the two matters are substantially related, it will presume that the lawyer possesses confidential information and that the information will be used, even if inadvertently, to the detriment of the former client. The presumption is ordinarily irrebuttable. See, e.g., Fred Weber Inc. v. Shell Oil Co., 566 F.2d 602, 608 (8th Cir. 1977), cert. denied, 436 U.S. 905 (1978); Schloetter v. Railoc, Inc., 546 F.2d 706, 710 (7th Cir.1976).

We return to the function of the substantial relationship test in the notes following *Brennan's.* A comprehensive review of the test is in U.S. Football League v. National Football League, 605 F.Supp. 1448 (S.D.N.Y.1985). Compare Satellite Financial Planning Corp. v. First Nat. Bank of Wilmington, 652 F.Supp. 1281 (D.Del.1987).

BRENNAN'S INC. V. BRENNAN'S RESTAURANTS, INC.

United States Court of Appeals, Fifth Circuit, 1979.
590 F.2d 168.

TJOFLAT, CIRCUIT JUDGE:

This is an action for trademark infringement and unfair competition. This appeal, however, concerns the disqualification of attorneys. The district court barred the appellants' attorneys from further representing them on grounds of conflict of interest. The correctness of this order is the only issue before us.

I

The underlying dispute in this case arises out of the business affairs of the Brennan family of New Orleans, Louisiana, who have been in the restaurant business for many years. All of the corporate parties are owned and closely held by various members of the Brennan family. Appellee Brennan's, Inc., the plaintiff below, owns and operates Brennan's restaurant at 417 Royal Street in New Orleans. The corporate appellants own and operate other restaurants in Louisiana, Texas, and Georgia. . . .

Prior to 1974, all the members of the Brennan family were stockholders and directors of plaintiff, and some of them were stockholders and directors of the corporate defendants. All the corporations were independent legal entities in the sense that none held any of the stock of another, but they were all owned by members of the Brennan family and had interlocking boards of directors. In 1971, Edward F. Wegmann became general counsel for the family businesses, and his retainer was paid pro rata by all the corporations. He continued this joint representation until November 1973.

As part of his services, Mr. Wegmann, in close cooperation with trademark counsel in Washington, D.C., prosecuted applications for the federal registration of three service marks: "Brennan's," "Breakfast at Brennan's," and a distinctive rooster design. A registration for the rooster design was issued in February 1972, but the applications for the other two marks were initially denied on the ground that they were primarily a surname. On the advice of Washington trademark counsel, Mr. Wegmann collected data supporting a demonstration that the marks had acquired a secondary meaning,[2] and the applications were amended to include this material. Registrations were subsequently issued in plaintiff's name in March 1973. These registered service marks are the subject of this lawsuit.

Later in 1973 a dispute developed within the Brennan family over the operation and management of the family businesses. This dispute was resolved in November 1974 by dividing the corporations' stock

---

2. This supporting data included numerous local and national advertisements, articles from several publications and letters commending the quality of Brennan's, and statements of the dollar volume of sales and advertising.

between the two opposing family groups. Plaintiff became 100% owned by one group and the corporate defendants became 100% owned by the second group, composed of the individual defendants. Mr. Wegmann elected to continue to represent defendants and severed his connections with plaintiff and its shareholders.

At no time during the negotiations which culminated in the November 1974 settlement was there any discussion of who would have the right to use the registered service marks. Both sides claimed ownership of the marks and continued to use them after the settlement. Attempts to negotiate a license or concurrent registration were unsuccessful. Plaintiff filed this suit for trademark infringement and unfair competition on May 21, 1976. In their answer and counterclaim defendants alleged that the marks were registered in plaintiff's name for convenience only, and, "in truth and actuality, the applications were filed and the registrations issued for the benefit and ownership of all of the Brennan family restaurants, including the corporate defendants." Defendants also alleged that the marks and registrations are invalid.

Upon the filing of this suit, Mr. Wegmann, on behalf of the defendants, retained the services of Arnold Sprung, a New York patent and trademark attorney, to assist him in the defense of the case. On October 22, 1976, plaintiff moved for the disqualification of both attorneys: Mr. Wegmann on the ground that his present representation was at odds with the interests of plaintiff, his former client, and Mr. Sprung by imputation of Mr. Wegmann's conflict. After a hearing, the district court granted the motion. It found that the subject matter of the present suit is substantially related to matters in which Mr. Wegmann formerly represented plaintiff, and to allow him now to represent an interest adverse to his former client creates the appearance of impropriety. It also found that "the close working relationship which has been shown to exist between Mr. Wegmann and Mr. Sprung creates a significant likelihood that Mr. Sprung would have had access to or been informed of confidential disclosures made to Mr. Wegmann by his former client."

II

. . .

Defendants argue that the district court failed to consider that in his prior representation of plaintiff, Mr. Wegmann also represented defendants. This fact of joint representation is crucial, they assert, since no confidences can arise as between joint clients. Hence, the argument goes, Mr. Wegmann violates no ethical duty in his present representation.

We have not addressed this precise question before. In Wilson P. Abraham Construction Corp. v. Armco Steel Corp., [559 F.2d 250 (5th Cir.1977)] we reaffirmed the standard that "a former client seeking to disqualify an attorney who appears on behalf of his adversary, need only to show that the matters embraced within the pending suit are *substantially related* to the matters or cause of action wherein the attorney previously represented him," 559 F.2d at 252 (emphasis in original),[4] but we acknowledged that "[t]his rule rests upon the presumption that confidences potentially damaging to the client have been disclosed to the attorney during the former period of representation," id. Defendants contend that this presumption cannot apply in this case. This argument, in our view, interprets too narrowly an attorney's duty to "preserve the confidences and secrets of a client." ABA Code of Professional Responsibility, Canon 4 (1970).[5] The fundamental flaw in defendants' position is a confusion of the attorney-client evidentiary privilege with the ethical duty to preserve a client's confidences. Assuming the prior representation was joint, defendants are quite correct that neither of the parties to this suit can assert the attorney-client privilege against the other as to matters comprehended by that joint representation. Garner v. Wolfinbarger, 430 F.2d 1093, 1103 (5th Cir. 1970), cert. denied, 401 U.S. 974, 91 S.Ct. 1191, 28 L.Ed.2d 323 (1971). But the ethical duty is broader than the evidentiary privilege: "This ethical precept, unlike the evidentiary privilege, exists without regard to the nature or source of information or the fact that others share the knowledge." ABA Code of Professional Responsibility, EC 4–4 (1970). "A lawyer should not use information acquired in the course of the representation of a client to the disadvantage of the client. . . ." Id. EC 4–5. The use of the word "information" in these Ethical Considerations as opposed to "confidence" or "secret" is particularly revealing of the drafters' intent to protect all knowledge acquired from a client, since the latter two are defined terms. See id., DR 4–101(A).[6] Information so acquired is sheltered from use by the attorney against his client by virtue of the existence of the attorney-client relationship. This is true without regard to whether someone else may be privy to it. NCK Organization v. Bregman, 542 F.2d 128, 133 (2d Cir.1976). The obligation of an attorney not to misuse information acquired in the course of representation serves to vindicate the trust and reliance that clients place in their attorneys. A client would feel wronged if an opponent prevailed against him with the aid of an attorney who formerly represented the client in the same matter. As the court recognized in E.F.

4. Accord, Celanese Corp. v. Leesona Corp. (In re Yarn Processing Patent Validity Litigation), 530 F.2d 83, 89 (5th Cir.1976); American Can Co. v. Citrus Feed Co., 436 F.2d 1125, 1128 (5th Cir.1971); T.C. Theater Corp. v. Warner Bros. Pictures, 113 F.Supp. 265, 268 (S.D.N.Y.1953).

5. As the profession's own expression of its ethical standards, the Code of Professional Responsibility, Ethical Considerations, and Disciplinary Rules provide substantial guidance to federal courts in evaluating the conduct of attorneys appearing before them. See NCK Organization v. Bregman, 542 F.2d 128, 129 (2d Cir.1976); Woods v. Covington County Bank, 537 F.2d 804, 810 (5th Cir.1976).

6. *DR 4–101 Preservation of Confidences and Secrets of a Client.*

(A) "Confidence" refers to information protected by the attorney-client privilege under applicable law, and "secret" refers to other information gained in the professional relationship that the client has requested be held inviolate or the disclosure of which would be embarrassing or would be likely to be detrimental to the client.

Hutton & Co. v. Brown, 305 F.Supp. 371, 395 (S.D.Tex.1969), this would undermine public confidence in the legal system as a means for adjudicating disputes. We recognize that this concern implicates the principle embodied in Canon 9 that attorneys "should avoid even the appearance of professional impropriety." ABA Code of Professional Responsibility, Canon 9 (1970). We have said that under this canon there must be a showing of a reasonable possibility that some specifically identifiable impropriety in fact occurred and that the likelihood of public suspicion must be weighed against the interest in retaining counsel of one's choice. Woods v. Covington County Bank, 537 F.2d 804, 812–13 (5th Cir.1976). The conflict of interest is readily apparent here, however, and we think that the balance weighs in favor of disqualification. See Zylstra v. Safeway Stores, Inc., 578 F.2d 102 (5th Cir.1978) (adopting per se rule of disqualification in class action cases for attorneys who are members of the class or partners or spouses of named plaintiffs). The need to safeguard the attorney-client relationship is not diminished by the fact that the prior representation was joint with the attorney's present client. Accordingly, we find the rule of *Wilson P. Abraham Construction Corp. v. Armco Steel Corp.* fully applicable to this case. Since the district court's findings of prior representation and substantial relationship are not disputed, we affirm the disqualification of Mr. Wegmann.

III

Whether Mr. Sprung should be disqualified presents a more difficult case. He has never had an attorney-client relationship with plaintiff; the district court disqualified him by imputation of Mr. Wegmann's conflict. Up to this point we have accepted, for the sake of argument, defendants' assertion that they were formerly joint clients with plaintiff of Mr. Wegmann. There is no dispute that plaintiff and defendants were previously represented by Mr. Wegmann simultaneously, but plaintiff maintains that, at least with respect to the registration of the service marks, Mr. Wegmann was representing plaintiff alone. The district court made no findings on the issue. Because we think that the disqualification of Mr. Sprung may turn on this fact and others not found by the court below, we vacate that part of the court's order relating to Mr. Sprung and remand the cause for further proceedings. For the guidance of the court on remand, we set forth our view of the applicable ethical standards.

If the court finds that Mr. Wegmann previously represented plaintiff and defendants jointly, we can see no reason why Mr. Sprung should be disqualified. As between joint clients there can be no "confidences" or "secrets" unless one client manifests a contrary intent. See Garner v. Wolfinbarger, 430 F.2d 1093, 1103 (5th Cir.1970), cert. denied, sub nom. Garner v. First American Life Insurance Co., 401 U.S. 974, 91 S.Ct. 1191, 28 L.Ed.2d 323 (1971); ABA Code of Professional Responsibility, DR 4–101 (1970). Thus, Mr. Sprung could not have learned anything from Mr. Wegmann that defendants did not already know or have a right to know. Plaintiff argues that this permits the defendants indirectly to gain the benefit of Mr. Wegmann's services when they could not do so directly. If the representation was joint, however, defendants possess no information as to which plaintiff could have had any expectation of privacy in relation to the defendants. The only remaining ground for disqualification then would be an appearance of impropriety. In Part II of this opinion, we decided there is such an appearance when an attorney represents an interest adverse to that of a former client in a matter substantially related to the subject of the prior representation. Mr. Sprung has never been plaintiff's counsel, however; he is only the co-counsel of one who was. We are enjoined not to give Canon 9 an overly broad application and to maintain "a reasonable balance between the need to ensure ethical conduct on the part of lawyers . . . and other social interests, which include the litigant's right to freely chosen counsel." Woods v. Covington County Bank, 537 F.2d 804, 810 (5th Cir.1976). In the case of Mr. Sprung, we think the balance weighs against disqualification. . . .[7]

If the district court finds that Mr. Wegmann did not previously represent these parties jointly, it does not necessarily follow that Mr. Sprung should be disqualified. The courts have abjured a per se approach to the disqualification of co-counsel of disqualified counsel. Akerly v. Red Barn System, Inc., 551 F.2d 539 (3rd Cir.1977); American Can Co. v. Citrus Feed Co., 436 F.2d 1125 (5th Cir.1971). In the absence of an attorney-client relationship between Mr. Sprung and plaintiff, a presumption of disclosure of confidences is inappropriate. Wilson P. Abraham Construction Corp. v. Armco Steel Corp., 559 F.2d 250, 253 (5th Cir.1977). Mr. Sprung should not be disqualified unless he has learned from Mr. Wegmann information the plaintiff had intended not be disclosed to the defendants. See id.

. . . .

Successive Representation of Joint Clients

A few cases recognize a distinction between primary and secondary clients, and hold that when a joint representation terminates, the lawyer may continue representing the primary client against the secondary one. The genesis of the "primary client" analysis is Allegaert v. Perot, 565 F.2d 246 (2d Cir.1977). In *Allegaert,* the court said "before the substantial relationship test is even implicated, it must be shown that the attorney was in a position where he could have received

---

7. It is very likely that Mr. Wegmann will be a witness in this case. He handled the registrations for the service marks which are the subject of this suit. Moreover, he prepared and notarized two affidavits that were executed at the time the registrations were issued. Defendants rely on these affidavits in support of their claim of ownership of the marks. The circumstances of their execution and the facts to which these affidavits purport to attest will undoubtedly be a subject of dispute at trial and Mr. Wegmann's knowledge may be relevant. If he represented all the family corporations at the time, however, none of his knowledge is privileged and his testimony could freely be sought by either side.

information which his former client might reasonably have assumed the attorney would withhold from his present client." Id. at 250. The court held that because the moving party "necessarily knew that information given to [the law firm] would certainly be conveyed to [its] primary clients . . ., the substantial relationship test is inapposite," and the law firm need not now be disqualified. Id.

While the language of *Allegaert* would seem to contradict *Brennan's*, the facts of *Allegaert* suggest an important distinction.

In *Allegaert* the law firm representing Perot had represented it for some time. Perot and Walston entered into an agreement for joint operation of a business. The firm represented both Walston and Perot's interests in a substantially related matter affecting that business—a stockholder derivative action which involved challenges to the business. Thereafter, Walston went into bankruptcy and asserted a claim against Perot. With the exception of the stockholder derivative suit, Walston was independently represented. The trustee in bankruptcy for Walston moved to disqualify the firm because of the firm's prior representation of Walston in the stockholder action.

In refusing to disqualify Perot's counsel, the *Allegaert* court said, "[i]ntegral to our conclusion that [Perot's lawyers] were not in a position to receive information intended to be withheld from [Perot] is the [lawyers'] continuous and unbroken legal relationship with their primary client [Perot]. In contrast with our earlier cases, the attorneys sought to be disqualified here have not changed sides from a former client to a current, adverse client." Id. at 251.

Allegaert can thus be distinguished from *Brennan's* on the following basis: First, so far as the duty of confidentiality is concerned, there was no reasonable expectation by Walston that information provided by it to Perot's lawyers was to be withheld from Perot. It was a joint defense where information was to be shared. Second, so far as the duty of loyalty is concerned, Walston knew that counsel's primary loyalty was to Perot. Indeed, in defending the stockholder's suit (the prior "matter") Walston was essentially a free rider on the Perot representation. Cf. M.R. 2.2.

See also C.A.M. v. E.B. Marks Music, Inc., 558 F.Supp. 57, 59 (S.D. N.Y.1983) (motion to disqualify denied where the prior representation had been joint and, as in *Allegaert*, "the attorneys . . . had a long-standing relationship with a primary client and briefly represented both parties when their interests apparently coincided . . . [T]he later representation of the primary client against the interests of the former joint client could not cause the disclosure of any secrets—there was no expectation that information would be concealed from the primary client."). See also Anderson v. Pryor, 537 F.Supp. 890, 895 (W.D.Mo. 1982).

Conventional doctrine is that a lawyer owes "equal" loyalty to every client. Does the notion of a "primary client" contradict this proposition?

The Comment to M.R. 2.2 says that "intermediation is improper when . . . impartiality cannot be maintained. For example, a lawyer who has represented one of the clients for a long period and in a variety of matters might have difficulty being impartial between that client and one to whom the lawyer has only recently been introduced."

The *Allegaert* court's ruling might be better justified by looking at the problem as one of consent. Walston consented to a joint representation with Perot in the stockholder suit, which challenged the agreement with Perot, where Perot and Walston had potentially conflicting interests. Walston waived this conflict when it consented to the joint representation. Later, in *Allegaert v. Perot*, Walston attempted to revoke that consent. Does this reading resolve the inconsistency between *Allegaert* and *Brennan's?*

Whatever the problems with the primary client theory, some courts rely on *Allegaert* for the proposition that there is no expectation of confidentiality between joint clients and hence no basis for subsequent disqualification of a lawyer representing one client against the other in a related transaction. For example, in American Special Risk Insurance Co. v. Delta America Insurance Co., 634 F.Supp. 112, 121 (S.D.N.Y. 1986), the district court, citing *Allegaert,* said:

> This Circuit has held, however, that the substantial relationship test is inapplicable where a law firm's alleged disqualification arises out of simultaneous representation of two clients if each client was aware of the other's relationship to the firm and had no reason to believe that confidences of one party would be withheld from the other.

See also Christensen v. FSLIC, 844 F.2d 694, 698 (9th Cir.1988) (collecting cases); Kempner v. Oppenheimer, 662 F.Supp. 1271, 1277 (S.D.N.Y. 1987) (collecting cases). But see Anchor Packing v. Pro–Seal, 688 F.Supp. 1215, 1217 (E.D.Mich.1988) (disapproving of this line of cases and adopting *Brennan's* approach); and United States v. Moscony, 697 F.Supp. 888, 891 (E.D.Pa.1988) (*Brennan's* approach is appropriate in criminal cases especially when parties are not sophisticated).

"Sophisticated Clients" Beware

Another factor noted by the *Allegaert* court was the sophistication of the parties involved: "[T]he parties were not only aware of their mutual relationship, but also were as sophisticated, perhaps, as the American corporate community can be." 565 F.2d at 251. Should the former client's sophistication be considered? Would the *Brennan's* court have given weight to that factor?

The Duty of Loyalty to a Former Client

In *Brennan's,* the Court recognizes two underlying concerns of the substantial relationship test: the duty to preserve confidences and the duty of loyalty to a former client. Lawyer Sprung is treated differently from Lawyer Wegmann because he has no duty of loyalty to clients whom he never represented.

Nevertheless, some courts seem to reduce the substantial relationship test to one designed solely to protect the former client's confidences. See, e.g., Analytica v. NPD Research, 708 F.2d 1263, 1266 (7th Cir.1983), where the court says two matters are considered to be substantially related "if the lawyer could have obtained confidential information in the first representation that would be relevant to the second." But most courts still recognize a duty of loyalty apart from the duty of confidentiality. The majority position appears to be that in deciding on whether to disqualify counsel, disloyalty—"changing sides"—will be considered, but alone it is insufficient to warrant disqualification. Keep in mind that this is a rule developed in disqualification decisions. A disciplinary body could decide that sanctions were warranted where a breach of loyalty was the "only" wrong.

Look again at the language of *Analytica* quoted above. The *Analytica* standard would seem to apply whether or not the matters are substantially related and hence could be read as *broader* than the "substantial relationship" test. That is, if the question is as *Analytica* states it, namely whether the lawyer "*could* have" obtained confidential information relevant to the second matter, does not that possibility exist no matter what the first matter involved? At the same time, the *Analytica* standard seems to require greater risk that confidences will have to be disclosed in order to prove that they might be used against the client. The Seventh Circuit cases are notable for this inversion of the substantial relationship test. For another example, see Lasalle Nat'l Bank v. County of Lake, 703 F.2d 252 (7th Cir.1983).

The underlying reason for reducing the successive conflict question to one of protecting confidences may be the courts' growing impatience with disqualification motions used for tactical purposes. If so, courts could resort to more frequent use of sanctions for frivolous motions to disqualify. See, for example, Optyl Eyewear Fashion Intern. Corp. v. Style Companies, Ltd., 760 F.2d 1045 (9th Cir.1985) where the court imposed sanctions against the lawyer after finding that the disqualification motion was brought in bad faith. In *Analytica* the Seventh Circuit imposed sanctions for frivolously resisting a motion to disqualify.

A still deeper problem is that the courts are not of one mind on whether to demand relatively strict loyalty to a former client, at the cost of requiring one or both parties to get new lawyers if they have a falling out, or to avoid that cost through a more relaxed standard of loyalty.

B. IMPUTED DISQUALIFICATION

Introduction: Rules and Problems

DR 5–105(D) provides that if any lawyer in a firm is disqualified from representing a client or being involved in a case, all the lawyers in the firm are disqualified. The courts have, however, created exceptions to this rule.

This rule proceeds on the legal fiction that those who practice together are "one lawyer." No matter how large the firm or how far away the offices, no matter how tangential the first lawyer's involvement, DR 5–105 specifies that if one lawyer is out, the firm is out. See, for example, the *Westinghouse* case printed in Chapter 7.

What is the rationale for this rule? First, lawyers who practice together talk to one another about their cases, and in doing so share client confidences. To protect confidences from being revealed or used in an improper manner, all lawyers who have had access to them are disqualified. The rule carries this possibility further, and presumes that confidences have been shared. Second, lawyers who practice together share professional and financial interests and are concerned with furthering each other's interest. Where a lawyer's interests suggest that her loyalty to the client will be impaired, her colleagues' loyalty can be similarly affected. Third, whether or not the first and second dangers are real in a particular case, their specter could cause clients and the public to lose confidence in the system of legal representation were the firm of a disqualified lawyer allowed to proceed.

The merit of the Code approach is that it is simple. But its problems are apparent in a world in which lawyers move with increasing frequency from firm to firm. A strict operation of the rule in this world creates what more than one commentator has called, legal "Typhoid Marys." Consider the following problems:

Mr. Gulliver is with First and First. Ms. First, a partner in the firm, represented Sewer Corp. in its suit against Bland Construction. Motor Corp. comes to First wanting to sue Sewer in a substantially related matter. The firm must turn down the case: Ms. First is disqualified so everyone in the firm is disqualified, including Mr. Gulliver who never worked on the Sewer trial.

Now Gulliver leaves First. He joins Second and Second, but when Motor was turned down by First, it went to the Second Firm which is now representing it against Sewer. Is the disqualification imputed to Gulliver when he was at First to be imputed to all the lawyers at Second? Must Second now drop the Motor case?

The first question to be answered in this problem is whether Gulliver remains disqualified after leaving First. The applicable rule is that a lawyer may not be involved in suing a former client in a substantially related matter. But is that rule engaged in this situation? Was Sewer Gulliver's client? The Model Code did not address this question.

The original conflicts provisions in the Model Rules and the provisions as amended in 1989 are somewhat ambiguous on whether and under what circumstances Gulliver would remain personally disqualified when he moved to the Second firm. Under M.R. 1.9(a), it seems that as long as Sewer can be considered Gulliver's former client,

Gulliver would be disqualified from opposing it in the same or a substantially related matter. But when is Sewer to be considered to have been Gulliver's client? At one extreme, M.R. 1.9(b), as amended, [M.R. 1.10(b) as originally adopted] * makes it clear that Sewer would be considered Gulliver's former client if Gulliver had "acquired information material to the matter" when at First. In this situation neither Gulliver nor any other lawyer at Second could proceed against Sewer in this matter; Second would have to drop the Motor case. But what if Gulliver while at First had learned no material confidences about Sewer or for that matter no confidences at all?

One reading of the Model Rules is that Gulliver is not considered as having represented Sewer (at all or in a substantially related matter) if no material confidences were learned. Another reading is, however, suggested by the original Comment to M.R. 1.10, now included in the Comment to M.R. 1.9. The Comment discusses the lawyer's duty of loyalty to the client (her obligation to avoid adverse representation in a related matter) separately from the duty to preserve confidences. It explains that this loyalty interest, while not requiring the new firm's disqualification, may nonetheless require that the individual lawyer refrain from opposing a former client even in cases where 1.9(b) [1.10(b)] would allow the firm to proceed, i.e., in cases where the lawyer had not actually acquired material confidences. Does this mean Gulliver is disqualified no matter how insignificant his involvement with the Sewer matter was while at First? According to the Comment to M.R. 1.9 [Comment to 1.10] the answer is no. The Comment specifically states that when the lawyer has acquired "no knowledge of information relating to a particular client of the firm" then that lawyer is not personally disqualified. The best reading of these provisions, then, is that Gulliver may be disqualified in some instances when Second is not, i.e., when he has been involved enough in the case to have been considered Sewer's lawyer but not enough to have learned any material confidences that he could pass on to Second. On the other hand, Gulliver may have had no contact or such insignificant contact with the Sewer matter while at First that he may work on the very same matter on behalf of Motor. The size of First and Gulliver's position at First would be two important factors in determining whether to allow him to proceed. Other factors are discussed in the *Nemours* case printed below.

This resolution is in accordance with the case law. See, e.g., Gas–A–Tron of Arizona v. Union Oil Co. of California, 534 F.2d 1322 (9th Cir.1976), cert. denied, 429 U.S. 861 (1976); Silver Chrysler Plymouth,

---

* In 1989, the ABA House of Delegates amended the conflicts provisions of the Model Rules. In effect, the amendments moved old M.R. 1.10(b) to new M.R. 1.9(b); made old M.R. 1.9(b) into new M.R. 1.9(c); and made old M.R. 1.10(c) into new M.R. 1.10(b). Because many states based their rule sections on the original numbering, we will indicate the original Model Rule section in brackets after the Model Rule section number as amended. Thus, new M.R. 1.9(b), will be referred to as M.R. 1.9(b) [1.10(b)]. The corresponding sections are not identical, but they are close enough that the analysis presented here is the same under either version of the Model Rules.

Inc. v. Chrysler Motors Corp., 518 F.2d 751 (2d Cir.1975). In both the *Gas–A–Tron* case and *Silver Chrysler,* the tainted lawyer had been an associate while at the first firm. The courts, evaluating the level of work by the associate, concluded that there was little or no possibility that the associate would have been privy to client confidences. See also Freeman v. Chicago Musical Instrument, 689 F.2d 715, 722 (7th Cir. 1982) (factors to be considered include the size of the firm, lawyer's area of specialization, and the lawyer's position in the firm).

M.R. 1.10(b) [1.10(c)] is exemplified by the next problem.

While Gulliver was at First, he defended Landlord in a suit brought by a tenant, charging that the building was unsafe. After Gulliver leaves First, the city housing department asks First to represent it in a suit against Landlord for violating the housing code, which provides for civil penalties. Can First take the suit now that Gulliver is gone?

While Gulliver was at First, the firm would have had to turn down the suit whether or not Gulliver had ever talked about the case to any of the lawyers at First, M.R. 1.10(a). However, after Gulliver has gone, whether First remains disqualified is decided under M.R. 1.10(b) [1.10(c)].

Under these provisions, First can take the case, even though it is substantially related to a case in which Gulliver represented the other side, if none of the lawyers still with the firm acquired confidential information about Landlord from Gulliver. See Novo Terapeutisk v. Baxter Travenol Laboratories, 607 F.2d 186 (7th Cir.1979).

NEMOURS FOUNDATION v. GILBANE

United States District Court, District of Delaware, 1986.
632 F.Supp. 418.

OPINION

FARNAN, DISTRICT JUDGE.

At this late juncture in a long and complicated proceeding the plaintiff, The Nemours Foundation ("Nemours"), has filed a motion to disqualify counsel for the defendant in this case, Pierce Associates, Inc. ("Pierce"). . . . In Nemours' motion to disqualify, filed on October 4, 1985, Nemours requests the disqualification of the entire firm of Biggs & Battaglia ("Biggs"), Pierce's local Wilmington counsel, from further representation of their client. Nemours alleges that Biggs has a conflict of interest due to the former involvement of one of its present associates in this litigation as a former associate of Howard M. Berg & Associates ("Berg"), counsel for Furlow [a co-party of Nemours'] and co-counsel for Nemours at the time.

BACKGROUND

Much of the factual background is not in dispute. Paul A. Bradley, the attorney whose former representation of Furlow has raised the issue of disqualification in this case, was admitted to the practice of law in February 1983 while he was employed at Berg. He began his employment there on September 7, 1982. Bradley became involved in the litigation in April 1984, when he assisted Howard M. Berg, who "made all decisions regarding the representation of Furlow." Bradley's responsibilities as a low-level associate involved preparing for a "mini-trial" among the parties in efforts to reach a settlement agreement. Bradley prepared the materials for a set of books to be distributed to the party participants and the arbitrator. Most of his consultation with experts concerned these materials. Bradley also reviewed documents for Berg's client, Furlow, which included documents produced by Nemours, the party moving for the disqualification of Biggs in this case. Bradley further attested in his affidavit submitted to the Court that, having reviewed thousands of documents, he presently (November 1, 1985) has no recollection of the content or existence of any documents that potentially were covered either by the work product doctrine or attorney-client privilege. To the best of his knowledge, Bradley's involvement in the Furlow case terminated after the end of the mini-trial. [3]

Bradley subsequently did not follow the litigation, review any discovery materials, or attend depositions concerning Furlow. He stated that he had no way to determine if any conversation he had while representing Furlow or any document involved in that case has been disclosed beyond the purview of the attorney-client privilege or work product doctrine. When he interviewed for a position with Biggs, he did not know of its involvement in the present litigation and had no conversation with anyone concerning his work for Furlow before being hired. [4]

It is apparent that Biggs was completely innocent of any knowledge of Bradley's involvement in the litigation, as was Bradley of Biggs' until Bradley met Jack Rephan, an attorney for Braude, Margulies, Sacks & Rephan ("Braude, Margulies"), Pierce's main counsel, when Rephan visited Biggs' offices approximately in May 1985. Bradley and his superiors at Biggs immediately decided that Bradley would have no contact with the Pierce litigation whatsoever and would not discuss it. Bradley himself resolved that he would not discuss the litigation or

3. Bradley stated that to the best of his knowledge he did not meet with Nemours' attorneys or their clients at any time after the mini-trial. He did attend a brief meeting to discuss settlement, but no attorneys from Nemours, Pierce, or other clients were present. Finally, he did some research on the proper form of Release and Stipulation of Dismissal to be filed with the Court.

4. Since then, Bradley's contacts with anyone involved in the litigation were limited to the following. He became aware that Biggs represented Pierce when he met Jack Rephan, of Braude, Margulies, Sacks & Rephan, at Biggs' offices, probably in May 1985. He merely greeted him and helped him carry several sealed boxes to an elevator; they did not discuss the litigation. On the same day, Victor F. Battaglia and Robert Beste, attorneys at Biggs, also became aware of Bradley's prior involvement. They briefly discussed only the fact of his representation of Furlow. All agreed, and Bradley was so advised, that he should not discuss the litigation with anyone. Finally, he walked a Pierce employee to a federal grand jury hearing after gaining permission from Victor Battaglia. To the best of his knowledge, the hearing had nothing to do with the Nemours and Pierce litigation.

prior representation of Furlow "in any way with anyone" at Biggs. He further attested that he has never been asked by anyone at Biggs or Braude, Margulies concerning his Furlow representation. He does not [know] nor . . . has [he ever] known the location of the Pierce files at Biggs.

Victor Battaglia described his firm's procedure of "screening" Bradley from the litigation. All attorneys in the Pierce litigation must report to him. Biggs has a central file room, but since the actions of the litigation were consolidated, and long before Bradley was hired, all Pierce files have been kept directly adjacent to Robert Beste's offices. Furthermore, the only documents in the file are pleadings and other documents filed and of record with the Court, and previous drafts of filed documents.

ANALYSIS

On this motion for disqualification of Biggs, this Court is faced with two major issues. The first question is whether Bradley's previous involvement on behalf of Furlow in this litigation calls for his disqualification. Pierce argues that an attorney-client relationship never existed between Bradley and Nemours and contends therefore that there is no conflict of interest. The Court must address this issue first to determine the extent of Bradley's own involvement in the litigation, a necessary step in addressing the second issue. The essential discordance between Nemours' and Pierce's positions centers on whether this involvement of Bradley, now associated with Biggs, requires the disqualification of the entire firm of Biggs, as Nemours argues it should. Biggs contends that it has effectively "screened off" Bradley from any involvement or contacts with the Nemours litigation. This defense has been commonly termed the "Chinese Wall" * defense. In ruling on this motion, the Court has coined the term "cone of silence" as a more accurate description of the ethical commands involved and the policies at stake.

· · ·

A. *Disqualification of Bradley*

Nemours alleges that the conflict of interest originates with Bradley, thus leading ultimately to the disqualification of Bradley and his firm. Bradley, as an associate at Berg, worked on the current litigation as counsel for Furlow. At that time, Furlow was a co-defendant of Nemours. As counsel for Furlow, Bradley was privy to confidences of both Furlow and Nemours as both planned "strategy sessions" in concert against Gilbane. This "commonality of interest" necessitated a sharing of work product, attorney-client privileges, and other confidential information. . . . After intense negotiations, Gilbane, Furlow, and Nemours entered a series of agreements to settle or to dismiss

---

* Editor's note: The term "Chinese Wall" can be interpreted as having an ethnic connotation, notwithstanding that it refers to an architectural phenomenon. We believe the more suitable term is "insulation wall."

claims. During this entire period, according to Nemours, the interests of Pierce—whose counsel is Biggs, Bradley's new employer—were adverse to those of Furlow. Applying the Rules to this set of facts, specifically Rule 1.6 on confidentiality, Bradley is disqualified because the information he gained from Nemours was confidential information which must be protected, because Nemours must be considered a "client" of Bradley. Under Rule 1.9, Bradley cannot represent a client whose interests are "materially adverse" to the interest of the former client.

Pierce argues that Nemours cannot be considered a former client of Bradley for purposes of Rules 1.6 and 1.9. Nemours was merely a co-party of Furlow. The presumption that confidential information has passed to an attorney, which arises in the context of the attorney-client relationship, therefore does not apply. Nemours must prove that confidential information actually did pass from Nemours to Bradley, which it has been unable to do. (D.I. 730 at 15.)

Analysis must begin with the Rules. Rule 1.9, which deals with conflict of interest, reads as follows:

Rule 1.9 Conflict of Interest: Former Client

A lawyer who has formerly represented a client in a matter shall not thereafter:

(a) represent another person in the same or a substantially related matter in which that person's interests are materially adverse to the interests of the former client unless the former client consents after consultation; or

(b) use information relating to the representation to the disadvantage of the former client except as Rule 1.6 would permit with respect to a client or when the information has become generally known.

Several requirements arise from this provision. First, the lawyer must have had an attorney-client relationship with the former client. Second, the present client's matter must either be the same as the matter the lawyer worked on for the first client, or a "substantially related" matter. Third, the interests of the second client must be materially adverse to the interests of the former client. Fourth, the former client must not have consented to the representation after consultation. The second part of the provision lists the conditions on the use of the information relating to representation of the former client.

Rule 1.7, which Rule 1.9 references, provides guidance for determining when the interests of two clients are adverse:

Rule 1.7 Conflict of Interest: General Rule

(a) A lawyer shall not represent a client if the representation of that client will be directly adverse to another client, unless:

(1) the lawyer reasonably believes the representation will not adversely affect the relationship with the other client; and

(2) each client consents after consultation.

(b) A lawyer shall not represent a client if the representation of that client may be materially limited by the lawyer's responsibilities to another client or a third person, or by the lawyer's own interests, unless:

(1) the lawyer reasonably believes the representation will not be adversely affected; and

(2) the client consents after consultation. . . .

This provision applies to both simultaneous representation of two clients, or successive representation, where the attorney-client relationship has been formally terminated, which characterizes the case at hand. The duty involved is one of loyalty to the client.

The Third Circuit has only begun to construe the Rules as applied to conflict of interest. See In Re Corn Derivatives Antitrust Litigation, 748 F.2d 157, 161–62 (3d Cir.1984), cert. denied, [472] U.S. [1008] (1985). The overwhelming bulk of precedent has been based on an interpretation of the Code. A brief review of the relevant portions of the Code is therefore necessary.

Canon 4 of the Code provides: "A lawyer should preserve the confidences and secrets of a client." Ethical Consideration 4–5 states:

EC 4–5 A lawyer should not use information acquired in the course of the representation of a client to the disadvantage of the client and a lawyer should not use, except with the consent of his client after full disclosure, such information for his own purposes. Likewise, a lawyer should be diligent in his efforts to prevent the misuse of such information by his employees and associates. Care should be exercised by a lawyer to prevent the disclosure of the confidences and secrets of one client to another, and no employment should be accepted that might require such disclosure.

In addition, Canon 9 states: "A lawyer should avoid even the appearance of professional impropriety." This provision does not appear in the Rules; and the Code did not contain a conflict of interest section such as Rule 1.9. Both Canons are usually combined to deal with a conflict of interest question arising from subsequent representation of interests adverse to a former client.

Courts interpreted the Code in such a manner that the test for a conflict of interest is not substantially different from that embodied in Rule 1.9. Furthermore, the Third Circuit has followed other circuits in beginning to discredit Canon 9 as an exclusive basis for disqualification, reflecting a more liberal treatment of this question. See In Re Corn Products Antitrust Litigation, 748 F.2d at 162.

Resolving the question of whether to disqualify counsel cannot be accomplished through mechanical means, but requires a careful balancing of the goals and objectives of professional conduct. "The chosen mode of analysis is to carefully sift 'all the facts and circumstances'." Pennwalt Corp. v. Plough, Inc., 85 F.R.D. 264, 269 (D.Del.1980); Akerly v. Red Barn System, Inc., 551 F.2d 539, 543 (3d Cir.1977). The Third Circuit has long refused to adopt a per se rule in questions of disqualification. *Akerly,* 551 F.2d at 543.

There is no doubt that Nemours must be considered a former "client" of Bradley for the purpose of determining whether a conflict of interest exists. Bradley himself stated that he reviewed confidential documents of Nemours when he represented Furlow in the litigation. Although there was no express attorney-client relationship, a fiduciary obligation, or "implied professional relation" existed nevertheless because Nemours disclosed information acting on the belief and expectation that such submission was made in order for Berg to render legal service to Nemours in furtherance of Nemours' interests. Westinghouse Elec. Corp. v. Kerr–McGee Corp., 580 F.2d 1311, 1319–20 (7th Cir.), cert. denied, 439 U.S. 955, 99 S.Ct. 353, 58 L.Ed.2d 346 (1978).[7]

Regarding the second requirement, under the old Code the Third Circuit adopted the "substantial relationship" test, now formally incorporated into the Rules, in determining when an attorney is prohibited from accepting a subsequent representation. Disqualification of counsel is required "where it appears that the subject matter of a pending suit in which the attorney represents an interest adverse to a prior employer is such that during the course of the former representation the attorney 'might have acquired substantially related material.' "

. . .

There is no doubt that the Pierce litigation in which the Biggs' firm is involved is substantially related to the matter in which Bradley was involved when he was representing Furlow; indeed, the matter is one and the same.

The third requirement of Rule 1.9 is also met: Pierce's interests are adverse to Nemours'. Finally, Nemours, the "former client," now moving for disqualification of Biggs, certainly has not consented to the continued representation of Pierce. Bradley is thus clearly disqualified from representing Pierce in this litigation.

B. *Disqualification of Biggs & Battaglia*

The next issue is whether the entire law firm of Biggs must be disqualified, given the disqualification of one of its associates. Pierce

---

7. There is no doubt that as far as Bradley's formal client, Furlow, was concerned, the confidences relayed to him from Furlow's co-party, Nemours, were "confidential" within this primary attorney-client relationship.

The relevant portion of Rule 1.6 which deals with confidentiality, reads: "(a) A lawyer shall not reveal information relating to representation of a client unless the client consents after consultation, except for disclosures that are impliedly authorized in order to carry out the representation, and except as stated in paragraph (b)." The Comment to Rule 1.6 indicates the scope of confidential information. The confidential rule "applies not merely to matters communicated in confidence by the client but also to all information relating to the representation, whatever its source." Such a source would certainly include a co-party such as Nemours.

argues that an effective screening mechanism is an acceptable alternative to disqualification of an entire law firm when one of its associates formerly represented a client whose interests are "substantially related," and adverse, to those of a present client of the law firm.

An attorneys' disqualification is normally "imputed" to the other attorneys in his law firm. Sections (a) and (b) of Rule 1.10, which governs cases of imputed disqualification, state:

Rule 1.10   Imputed Disqualification: General Rule

(a) While lawyers are associated in a firm, none of them shall knowingly represent a client when any one of them practicing alone would be prohibited from doing so by Rules 1.7, 1.8(c), 1.9 or 2.2.

(b) When a lawyer becomes associated with a firm, the firm may not knowingly represent a person in the same or a substantially related matter in which the lawyer, or a firm with which the lawyer was associated, had previously represented a client whose interests are materially adverse to that person and about whom the lawyer had acquired information protected by Rules 1.6 and 1.9(b) that is material to the matter. . . .

There is now an explicit exception to imputed disqualification. The Rules, unlike the Code, sanction the use of a screening mechanism in appropriate circumstances, specifically referring to former government attorneys. Rule 1.11 states: "A firm with which that lawyer is associated may undertake or continue representation in the matter only if the disqualified lawyer is screened from any participation in the matter and is apportioned no part of the fee therefrom." Rule 1.11(b). The policy supporting this rule is to enable the government to attract qualified lawyers and to prevent the disqualification rule from imposing too severe a deterrent against entering public service. Comment to Rule 1.11.

The Comment to Rule 1.10 indicates the firm intention of its draftsmen that a pragmatic approach is necessary to the question of vicarious disqualification. The Comment also extends the analysis of Rule 1.10 to disqualified lawyers in law firms generally, not only former government attorneys. In the section "Lawyers Moving Between Firms," the authors of the Rules adopt a "functional analysis" in determining questions of vicarious disqualification. The rigid formalism underlying Canon 9's injunction against an "appearance of impropriety" is strongly rejected in favor of a new philosophy of pragmatism which balances the expectations of confidentiality of a former client against the importance of allowing a client the representation of his choice and promoting the mobility of attorneys, particularly associates, from one private law firm to another. The language of the Comment merits extensive quotation:

Lawyers Moving Between Firms

When lawyers have been associated in a firm but then end their association, however, the problem is more complicated. The fiction that the law firm is the same as a single lawyer is no longer wholly realistic. There are several competing considerations. First, the client previously represented must be reasonably assured that the principle of loyalty to the client is not compromised. Second, the rule of disqualification should not be so broadly cast as to preclude other persons from having reasonable choice of legal counsel. Third, the rule of disqualification should not unreasonably hamper lawyers from forming new associations and taking on new clients after having left a previous association. In this connection, it should be recognized that today many lawyers practice in firms, that many to some degree limit their practice to one field or another, and that many move from one association to another several times in their careers. If the concept of imputed disqualification were defined with unqualified rigor, the result would be radical curtailment of the opportunity of lawyers to move from one practice setting to another and of the opportunity of clients to change counsel.

Reconciliation of these competing principles in the past has been attempted under two rubrics. One approach has been to seek per se rules of disqualification. For example, it has been held that a partner in a law firm is conclusively presumed to have access to all confidences concerning all clients of the firm. Under this analysis, if a lawyer has been a partner in one law firm and then becomes a partner in another law firm, there is a presumption that all confidences known by a partner in the first firm are known to all partners in the second firm. This presumption might properly be applied in some circumstances, especially where the client has been extensively represented, but may be unrealistic where the client was represented only for limited purposes. Furthermore, such a rigid rule exaggerates the difference between a partner and an associate in modern law firms.

The other rubric formerly used for dealing with vicarious disqualification is the appearance of impropriety proscribed in Canon 9 of the ABA Model Code of Professional Responsibility. This rubric has a two-fold problem. First, the appearance of impropriety can be taken to include any new client-lawyer relationship that might make a former client feel anxious. If that meaning were adopted, disqualification would become little more than a question of subjective judgment by the former client. Second, since "impropriety" is undefined, the term "appearance of impropriety" is question-begging. It therefore has to be recognized that the problem of imputed disqualification cannot be properly resolved either by simple analogy to a lawyer practicing alone or by the very general concept of appearance of impropriety.

A rule based on a functional analysis is more appropriate for determining the question of vicarious disqualification. Two functions are involved: preserving confidentiality and avoiding positions adverse to a client.

. . .

. . . In INA Underwriters Insurance Co. v. Rubin, 635 F.Supp. 1 (E.D.Pa.1983), the "Chinese Wall" defense was raised against a motion to disqualify a law firm. In that case, a client contacted a partner of the law firm Wolf, Block & Schorr ("Wolf, Block"). The client confided certain confidential information to the partner, but the partner subsequently refused to represent the client because he found that a conflict of interest existed. The court refused to apply an irrebuttable presumption that confidences were shared by the partners of Wolf, Block, and to impute the disqualification firm-wide. Id. at 3. There was no question that the partner who had met with the client was disqualified. The court approved of the screening of secret documents and firm members possessing knowledge of secrets and confidences in order to avoid disqualification of an entire firm. Id. at 4. The partner had never discussed the substantive content of his meeting with the client with any of the attorneys inside or outside the Wolf, Block firm. Id. at 5. A refusal to disqualify Wolf, Block in this case would not only maintain public confidence and integrity of the legal system, but also promote the policies of respecting a litigant's right to retain counsel of its choice and of enabling attorneys to practice without excessive restrictions. Id. at 5–6.

Before the adoption of the Rules, case law in other circuits [8] and scholarly commentary [9] had already adopted a liberalized approach based on a functional analysis. In the Second Circuit, where this approach has received its most extensive development, the test is whether the conduct of the disqualified attorney taints the underlying trial. Armstrong v. McAlpin, 625 F.2d 433, 444 (2d Cir.1980) (en banc), vacated on other grounds and remanded, 449 U.S. 1106, 101 S.Ct. 911, 66 L.Ed.2d 835 (1981). Disqualification if based solely on the appearance of impropriety cannot be justified as long as a firm's representa-

---

8. See Fred Weber, Inc. v. Shell Oil Co., 566 F.2d 602, 609 (8th Cir.1977), cert. denied, 436 U.S. 905, 98 S.Ct. 2235, 56 L.Ed.2d 403 (1978) (holding that every representation against a former client's co-defendant in a related matter raises an appearance of impropriety would unnecessarily restrict choice of counsel available to litigants); Woods v. Covington County Bank, 537 F.2d 804, 813 n. 12 (5th Cir.1976) (test is whether likelihood of public suspicion or obloquy outweighs social interests served by lawyer's continued participation in a particular case); Silver Chrysler Plymouth, Inc. v. Chrysler Motors Corp., 518 F.2d 751, 757 (2d Cir.1975) (underscoring importance of public's right to counsel of its choice and economic mobility).

9. See Liebman, The Changing Law of Disqualification: The Role of Presumption and Policy, 73 Nw.U.L.Rev. 996 (1979); Lindgren, Toward a New Standard of Attorney Disqualification, 1982 A.B.A. Found. Research J. 419 (1982); Comment, The Ethics of Moving to Disqualify Opposing Counsel for Conflict of Interest, 1979 Duke L.J. 1310 (1979); Note, The Chinese Wall Defense to Law–Firm Disqualification, 128 U.Pa.L.Rev. 677 (1980); Note, A Dilemma in Professional Responsibility: The Subsequent Representation Problem, 50 UMKC L.Rev. 165 (1982).

tion does not pose a threat to the integrity of the trial process. Id. As the court in *McAlpin* stated:

> We recognize that a rule that concentrates on the threat of taint fails to correct all possible ethical conflicts. . . . However, absent a threat of taint to the trial, we continue to believe that possible ethical conflicts surfacing during a litigation are generally better addressed by the "comprehensive disciplinary machinery" of the state and federal bar [citation omitted] or possibly by legislation.

Id. at 445–46; Board of Education of New York City v. Nyquist, 590 F.2d 1241, 1246 (2d Cir.1979). A court should only reluctantly order disqualification because of the immediate adverse effect on the client of separating him from counsel of his choice. *Nyquist,* 590 F.2d at 1246. Such motions for disqualification are often made for tactical reasons, and even when made in the best of faith, inevitably cause delay.

Several circuits have extended this functional analysis to create a rebuttable presumption of shared confidences among attorneys in a law firm in order to avoid vicarious disqualification. . . .

The factual circumstances of Lemaire v. Texaco, Inc., 496 F.Supp. 1308 (E.D.Tex.1980), closely resemble those of the case at bar. In that case, an attorney switched law firms after having represented one party in a lawsuit to the limited extent of filing initial pleadings. His new law firm represented the opposite side in the *same* litigation. The screening was established immediately, even before the attorney accepted the position with the new firm. The attorney went to great lengths to insure that he would have no connection with any facet of the lawsuit. He also made certain he would receive no part of any attorneys' fees collected in the case or share in its expenses.[10] The lawsuit was complex and very expensive to prepare. There was no other law firm in the area qualified or willing to take on the litigation. Id. at 1309. The court found that any appearance of impropriety was greatly outweighed by the plaintiffs' right to have counsel of their choice. Id. at 1310.

There is no substantial reason against extending the exception to vicarious disqualification from the case of a former government attorney to private attorneys generally although the complex of policy factors differs somewhat in the two situations:

> Once it is admitted that a Chinese Wall can rebut the presumption of imputed knowledge in former government attorney cases, it becomes difficult to insist that the presumption is irrebuttable when the disqualified attorney's previous employment was private and not public. To hold fast to such a proposition would logically require a belief that privately employed attorneys are inherently incapable of being effectively screened, as though they were less trustworthy or more voluble than their ex-Government counter-

---

10. See Rule 1.11(b).

parts. If former government attorneys can be screened effectively, it follows that former private attorneys can be too.

INA Underwriters Insurance Co. v. Rubin, 635 F.Supp. at 5 (quoting Note, The Chinese Wall Defense To Law–Firm Disqualification, 128 U.Pa.L.Rev. 677, 701 (1980)).

The Court holds that an appropriate screening mechanism, in the proper circumstances, may rebut the presumption of shared confidences that arises under Rule 1.10 in cases where the disqualified attorney's conflict of interest originated in private practice. The Court prefers to refer to this screening procedure figuratively as a "cone of silence" [11] rather than a "Chinese Wall." The conical image, a metaphor adopted from popular television, more appropriately describes the responsibility of the *individual* attorney to guard the secrets of his former client. He is commanded by the ethical rules to seal, or encase, these particular confidences within his own conscience. The term "Chinese Wall" is suggestive of attempts in the context of a large law firm to physically cordon off attorneys possessing information from the other members of the firm who represent clients whose interests are adverse to interests of these attorneys' former clients. See Analytica, Inc. v. NPD Research, Inc., 708 F.2d 1263, 1269 (7th Cir.1983). Such an approach tends to cast a shadow of disrepute on attorneys separated in this manner from their professional colleagues. The implicit assumption is that the wall, if high and thick enough, will resist an errant attorney's lack of discretion, and calm public mistrust through prophylaxis. A firm of more moderate size must therefore erect a wall of greater impenetrability. Instead, the Court believes that the more logically consistent, honest, and straightforward approach is to credit members of the legal profession with a certain level of integrity. This emphasis on the ethical rules themselves, rather than a presumption that they will be circumvented, should more effectively promote public respect for the bar. In effect, the Rules enjoin the attorney to guard his client's secrets in an affirmative and deliberate manner, through self-imposed silence. Canon 4 and Rule 1.6, which mandate maintenance of a client's confidences, have an independent significance. Baglini v. Pullman, 412 F.Supp. 1060, 1064 n. 11 (E.D.Pa.), aff'd, 547 F.2d 1158 (3d Cir.1976). Moreover, the trend among courts now to rule out an "appearance of impropriety" as the sole basis for disqualification strongly supports this increased emphasis on the ethical rule of confidentiality. *McAlpin*, 625 F.2d at 444; *Silver Chrysler Plymouth*, 518 F.2d at 757.

On the other hand, certain objective circumstances, including the timing and physical characteristics of the screening, will in many cases require disqualification of an entire firm. The evidence of faithfulness to Rule 1.6 is only one factor in a balancing of the policy factors

11. As explained at greater length later in this opinion, in this case, Bradley determined on his own initiative not to speak to anyone concerning the Furlow–Nemours representation. This self-imposed silence began immediately upon his gaining knowledge of the adverse representation at Biggs.

identified above against the likelihood that confidences will be violated. The size of the firm remains an important consideration, as well as the nature of the prior involvement of the tainted attorney and the extensiveness of the screening.   The test is one that integrates subjective reliance on the Rules manifested by the attorney's "cone of silence," with objective evidence that the Rules are being followed.

As in *Rubin* and *Lemaire,* Biggs' and Bradley's deliberateness and speed in establishing a "cone of silence" in the instant case similarly help support denial of the motion to disquaify. The circumstances of this case strongly support such a finding. Bradley himself is required by Rule 1.6 to maintain the confidences of his former client. The Court harbors no doubt based on the present affidavits that he thus far has not violated this ethical norm. If he should disclose any information, although he claims that he has no recollection of any substantive confidences, he can be subject to the disciplinary machinery of the state bar. *McAlpin,* 625 F.2d at 446. The Court's primary task at this juncture is to ensure a fair and just trial. Id. at 445–46; *Nyquist,* 590 F.2d at 1246. Following Rule 1.6, Bradley immediately sealed himself in a "cone of silence," resolving not to say anything concerning the substance of any communication, documents, or information to which he may have had access. In addition, Bradley's present lack of access to the information helps to reinforce his fidelity to Rule 1.6. When he changed firms, Bradley did not personally retain any notes or documents with which to refresh his recollection. (Id. at ¶ 6.) Furthermore, the information he reviewed when he was with the Berg firm was primarily non-confidential and his memory of this information is now fading. The importance of the ethical precept against disclosure of client confidences as a prophylactic safeguard in instances where violation of confidences is possible was recognized by the district court in Baglini v. Pullman, 412 F.Supp. at 1064 n. 11. See Silver Chrysler Plymouth, Inc. Chrysler Motors Corp., 518 F.2d 751, 757 (2d Cir.1975) (Canon 9 should not override delicate balance created by Canon 4).

Supplementing Bradley's own self-imposed silence, Biggs has established an effective screening mechanism which has been in place ever since Bradley's former involvement was discovered. No information was disclosed to other Biggs attorneys up to that time or since then. Bradley does not know where the Pierce files are located at Biggs. These files are not contained in Biggs' central filing system but are segregated in separate file cabinets, all adjacent to one partner's office. Only pleadings and correspondence are located in Biggs' offices. Although Biggs would be considered a medium-size firm by Wilmington standards, the limited nature of Bradley's contact with his "former client" and knowledge of the litigation effectively counterbalance this factor.[12]

12. As reported by the law firms themselves, as of March 1986, Biggs & Battaglia had 16 attorneys; Richards, Layton & Finger and Morris, Nichols, Arsht & Tunnell, two of Wilmington's largest law firms, had 52 and 43 attorneys, respectively, in Wilmington.

Another factor indicating that the confidences and secrets of Nemours will remain inviolate is the extent of Bradley's previous involvement in the litigation. Bradley was not the lead counsel in this litigation when he was at Berg. He had only recently joined Berg after becoming a member of the Delaware Bar,[13] and was assigned the duties which typically characterize the life of a young associate in his position. In addition, his involvement was brief, lasting only about four months, and ended approximately eight months before he changed firms. The attorney's degree of prior involvement, whether he controlled strategy, whether he was an associate or partner, and whether he shared legal fees from his firm's representation are all important factors in evaluating the effectiveness of a "cone." [14]

Furthermore, the policies identified in the Comment to Rule 1.10 would be promoted by a decision denying disqualification in this case. As of October 1985, in the entire State of Delaware there were currently 856 attorneys in private practice, 710 of whom practice in New Castle County. Of the 710 attorneys, over 280, or over forty percent, work for only ten Wilmington law firms. Eleven different law firms have been involved directly in this case and eight of these are in the "top ten." Attorney mobility, especially among young associates, would be severely restricted if a per se rule against a "cone of silence" were adopted. The small number of private firms in Wilmington of substantial size, combined with the facts and circumstances of this case, cry out for a flexible approach to vicarious disqualification.

In addition, Pierce would be considerably prejudiced by the disqualification of Biggs at this point in the litigation, shortly before trial is scheduled to begin on March 31, 1986. When Pierce attempted to obtain local counsel in Wilmington, all the major law firms in Wilmington either were already representing parties or believed that a conflict existed. Jack Rephan, attorney for Braude, Margulies, stated that he was not aware of any other office in Delaware of "sufficient abilities or facilities equipped to represent Pierce" in this litigation other than Biggs, after the other firms were found to have a conflict of interest. This large, complex litigation requires a large law office locally located with sufficient facilities and manpower to adequately represent Pierce's interests. The Court has scheduled three full months for the trial. Moreover, an "excellent working relationship" has developed between Pierce and its local counsel. An abrupt withdrawal by Biggs would substantially prejudice Pierce in this litigation.[19]

13. Bradley became a member of the Delaware Bar in 1983, having graduated from law school in 1981. 1 Martindale–Hubbell Law Directory 3408B (1985).

14. As an associate, Bradley would receive only his fixed, annual salary.

19. Indeed, if Biggs & Battaglia were to be disqualified in the circumstances of this case, it is quite possible that in view of the realignment of the parties which resulted in the disqualification of Bradley, other firms should be disqualified, including counsel for the moving party on this motion.

Gilbane and Pierce were originally aligned together and shared confidential information. Through settlement, Gilbane is now aligned with Nemours. The technical disquali-

In contrast, Nemours fails to adduce any convincing evidence of prejudice to its interests resulting from Biggs' continued representation of Pierce. Nowhere in presenting its argument does Nemours allege the slightest disadvantage or harm. Certainly, the fact that Nemours was only a co-party of Bradley's primary client has some significance. Furthermore, this is not the case of a partner who, as a major strategist, must be quarantined from contact with other members of his firm who are involved in a case from which he is disqualified. This representation of Pierce by Biggs therefore has no tendency to "taint the underlying trial." *McAlpin,* 625 at 444; *Nyquist,* 590 at 1246. This fact, in combination with the harm that would accrue to Pierce should Biggs be required to withdraw, and the other powerful arguments of policy, all support denial of Nemours' motion to disqualify.

In addendum, the Court takes note of a factor weighing against Nemours' motion involving possible delay. Courts have been extremely reluctant to disqualify attorneys when there is a possibility that a motion was made primarily for strategic purposes in a litigation. Even when made in the best of faith, such motions inevitably cause delay. *McAlpin* at 444. It is possible—but by no means proven—that counsel for Nemours knew already in April 1985 that Bradley had joined Biggs.[20] Nemours raised this issue five months later, in September. Shortly before that, Nemours had lost a motion to compel. The total absence of any prejudice to Nemours of Bradley's association with Biggs . . . tends to strengthen the appearance of mere delay and harassment as the overriding motive for the plaintiff's motion to disqualify. Nevertheless, the evidence is not sufficient to show that delay was an intentional element. The other factors standing alone are sufficient to withstand a motion to disqualify.

Questions and Comments

Why was Bradley disqualified? Why wasn't Biggs disqualified? Why was it necessary for Bradley to maintain a "cone of silence"? Why did the court bother to switch metaphors? See Employers Insurance of Wausau v. Albert D. Seeno Construction Co., 692 F.Supp. 1150, 1165 (N.D.Cal.1988) (using "ethical wall," noting that some find "Chinese Wall" offensive and others confuse it with a flimsy paper structure instead of the Great Wall of China). Does the court place too much emphasis on Bradley's personal integrity? Does the "cone" metaphor give insufficient emphasis to the responsibilities of other lawyers in the firm? See M.R. 5.1 and M.R. 5.2

In Atasi Corp. v. Seagate Technology, 847 F.2d 826, 831–832 (Fed. Cir.1988) (interpreting the law in the Ninth Circuit), the court held that neither, in its words, a "Chinese Wall" nor a "cone of silence" could

fications resulting from this realignment would rapidly cause this litigation to become unmanageable.

20. In April 1985, notices were sent to all members of the Delaware Bar that Bradley had joined the Biggs firm.

allow the firm to proceed. In the process of so holding the court described the "cone of silence" as a screening method in which "the attorney switching firms, but not the other members of the [new] firm, agrees not to share confidences of prior clients with his new associates." Is this what the *Nemours* court had in mind? Screening is discussed further in the notes following the *Panduit* case printed below.

A novel approach to the reimputation problem was suggested by the court in City of Cleveland v. Cleveland Electric Illuminating Co., 440 F.Supp. 193, 211 (N.D.Ohio 1976), affirmed without opinion, 573 F.2d 1310 (6th Cir.1977). The court held that in cases involving imputed disqualification of a second firm by a "tainted" lawyer who had been vicariously disqualified because one of his former partners had handled a particular matter, the presumption that the lawyer had access to confidential information about the client should apply only when the lawyer's practice was in the same area of concentration as that of the former partner who handled the case.

This dispenses with inquiry into whether the disqualified lawyer has actual knowledge of confidences or not. But it is both too broad and too narrow.

It is too broad in that a litigation department in a large firm may be organized in such a way that makes communications between lawyers on different litigation "teams" highly unlikely. It is too narrow in that the corporate department in a firm might have its offices right next to those of the litigators and information on cases might be routinely exchanged in the halls. Furthermore, the managing partner or other senior partners might routinely be apprised of the developments in all cases, whatever department is handling the case.

To avoid the disclosure of confidences during the inquiry into whether the tainted lawyer has knowledge, courts look at the firm's size; the lawyer's position in the firm (partners are judged more likely than associates to have actual confidences on the cases of others in the firm); the formal and informal patterns of communication among those who work at the firm; the procedures on access to client files; the number of the firm's lawyers involved in the original matter; and the testimony of lawyers, both the lawyers involved in the original case as to whether they discussed it with the tainted lawyer, and the testimony of the tainted lawyer as to whether she has any information about the original matter.

Here again, outcomes depend to an important extent on the judge's own prior experience in practice and her sensitivity to "purity" versus "mobility".

Conflicts Created by Paralegals and Secretaries Moving Between Firms

In Kapco Mfg. Co., Inc. v. C & O Enterprises, Inc., 637 F.Supp. 1231 (N.D.Ill.1985), a secretary from one law firm moved to the opponent's law firm. Kapco moved to disqualify C & O's lawyers based on this secretary's move. The court held that the same conflict rules and tests applied when the conflict was created by a non-lawyer changing firms as those that apply when lawyers move. Note that the litigation was ongoing in *Kapco*, so the tainted person would have been disqualified under M.R. 1.7, not 1.9.

While secretaries and paralegals may move from one firm to another with some frequency, as the court noted in *Kapco*, there is little case law on the subject. The court in *Kapco* found only two other cases which dealt with the conflicts of non-lawyer personnel, Williams v. Trans World Airlines, Inc., 588 F.Supp. 1037 (W.D.Mo.1984); and Swanson v. Wabash, Inc., 585 F.Supp. 1094 (N.D.Ill.1984). As the court in *Kapco* says, "the courts in both cases took the disqualification motions seriously and applied analysis similar to those applied in attorney-transfer cases." 637 F.Supp. at 1236.

In footnote 11 of the *Kapco* decision, 637 F.Supp. at 1236, the court remarks that Kapco failed to cite any "fact-relevant cases [but] to its credit, C & O" brought these cases, which helped Kapco's case, to the court's attention. Note that one of the cases was a decision of the Northern District of Illinois, the court hearing the Kapco case, and the other was a decision of another district court in the same circuit as the Kapco court. Did C & O have a duty to bring both to the court's attention? See Rule 3.3 and the discussion of this rule in Ch. 5 above.

PANDUIT CORP. v. ALL STATES PLASTIC MANUF. CO.

United States Court of Appeals, Federal Circuit, 1984.
744 F.2d 1564.

PER CURIAM.

This is an appeal from an order of the United States District Court for the Northern District of Illinois (No. 76 C 4012), entered by Judge Grady on September 16, 1983. The district court disqualified Robert Conte and the firm of Laff, Whitesel, Conte & Saret (the "Laff Firm") from representing appellant, All States Plastic Manufacturing Co., Inc. ("All States"). We reverse-in-part, vacate-in-part, and remand.

Background

The Laff Firm has been patent counsel for All States since prior to the inception of the instant case in late 1976. The instant suit involves the alleged infringement by All States of Panduit Corporation's ("Panduit") U.S. Patent Nos. 3,537,146 (the '146 patent) and 3,660,869 (the '869 patent). The claimed inventions relate to one-piece cable ties. These self-locking devices, molded from nylon, are designed to encircle and hold together a bundle of electrical wires or similar items.

Shortly before the filing of the instant suit, Bowthorpe–Hellermann, Ltd. ("Bowthorpe"), a British company that manufactures and markets one-piece cable ties, filed suit against All States, charging infringement of its U.S. Patent No. 3,486,201.[1] Since the Bowthorpe lawsuit, also filed in the Northern District of Illinois, involves similar issues, all parties involved in these two lawsuits agreed to conduct joint discovery. The joint discovery has resulted in approximately 13 depositions and All States has received over 5,000 documents in each case. The joint discovery has been stayed pending the outcome of this appeal.

In addition, All States filed a counterclaim in the instant case in mid–1978, alleging that Panduit had conspired with Bowthorpe and Bowthorpe's wholly-owned U.S. subsidiary, Tyton Corporation, to compete unfairly in violation of Sections 1 and 2 of the Sherman Act and Section 3 of the Clayton Act. Discovery on the counterclaim has been stayed pending resolution of the patent infringement issues. The Laff Firm is also representing All States in the Bowthorpe lawsuit. In addition, Judge Grady is presiding over both cases.[2]

In July 1981, Panduit filed a motion to disqualify the Laff Firm. The motion is based on an alleged conflict of interest created by the merger on July 1, 1981, of the law firm of Robert F.I. Conte Ltd. with the Laff Firm, which brought Robert Conte into the firm. From 1965 to 1975, Conte was an attorney with Ladas & Parry in its Chicago office, working under an employment contract during the entire period. He became a "special partner" in 1972, which entitled him to certain perquisites, such as membership in the Union League Club of Chicago, but he did not share in the equity or management of the firm. Ladas & Parry specializes in international patent work and, at that time, also had offices in New York, Los Angeles, Paris, and London.

During 1969–1975, the Chicago office of Ladas & Parry was retained by Panduit's counsel, David Vogel of Prangley, Dithmar, Vogel, Sandler & Stotland, to handle Panduit's foreign patent work. The Panduit work amounted to several hundred thousand dollars for which Vogel was billed.

Prior to June 1, 1971, Ladas & Parry was not a law firm, but rather was a service organization for lawyers, doing business under the name Langner, Parry, Card and Langner. The firm, before and after 1971, prepared, filed, and prosecuted foreign patent applications through foreign associates. During the period 1969–1975, the firm filed approximately 170 Panduit applications, counterparts of seven U.S. applications; 29 counterparts of the '146 patent and 23 of the '869 patent.

In addition, Ladas & Parry was involved in *inter partes* patent proceedings between Panduit and Bowthorpe or a company related to Bowthorpe, such as patent oppositions where the validity of certain of Panduit's foreign patent applications was contested. In the period 1969–1975, Panduit and Bowthorpe were involved in 17 adversarial

1. Bowthorpe–Hellermann, Ltd. v. All States Plastic Mfg. Co., No. 76 C 3574 (N.D.Ill. filed 1976).

2. In late 1978, Panduit filed suit against Dennison Manufacturing Co., Inc., alleging infringement of the '146 and '869 patents. Panduit Corp. v. Dennison Mfg. Co., No. 78 C 4993 (N.D.Ill. filed Dec. 14, 1978). This case has also been assigned to Judge Grady and has been consolidated for trial with the instant case on the patent validity issue.

patent proceedings overseas, at least a few of which were patent opposition proceedings involving counterparts of the subject patents.

Mr. John Chrystal, presently the senior partner in the Ladas & Parry's Chicago office, has at all times been in charge of its work for Panduit. The firm continues to maintain foreign Panduit patent registrations, work which is not considered to involve any Panduit confidences. In the critical period prior to 1975, Chrystal was assisted on the Panduit matters by two other attorneys, Thomas Peterson and Richard Streit. Since Conte's technical expertise was in chemical engineering, his work at Ladas & Parry primarily involved matters in the chemical field. While with Ladas & Parry, Conte was never assigned to or worked on any Panduit matters, never reviewed or studied any Panduit files or documents, and never met with any Panduit personnel. Nor is it asserted that he was ever consulted informally on any Panduit matter.

When Conte left Ladas & Parry to form the firm of Kolar & Conte in 1976, he took substantial business with him, and he sued under his employment contract for moneys due, resulting in a settlement. In 1980 he organized the firm of Robert F.I. Conte Ltd., and, in July, 1981, he merged that practice with the Laff Firm.

Though the present litigation was filed in 1976, discovery was still being carried on in 1981. On June 18, 1981, All States served a subpoena on Ladas & Parry seeking all files maintained on behalf of Panduit. On July 10, 1981, All States took the deposition of Richard Streit, a Ladas & Parry partner, in connection with these documents. Conte attended the Streit deposition with Charles Laff. No charge was made for his services because two others of the firm were attending. He attended, he states, to gain experience in such litigation techniques. Subsequently, Panduit's counsel was informed by telephone that Conte was coming over to inspect the 170 Ladas & Parry files which had been produced at the Streit deposition. Conte testified he suggested that he make the inspection because he was familiar with Ladas & Parry's filing system and could more quickly identify files that might contain more than routine matters. Having learned in the interim that Conte had been with Ladas & Parry during the period when that firm had been actively handling Panduit matters, Panduit's counsel refused to permit Conte to inspect the files. In response to this objection, Mr. Laff informed Panduit's counsel that Conte would no longer be involved in the case, and he has not been, except for preparing affidavits in connection with this motion. All States asserts he has been "screened" since that time. On July 27, 1981, Panduit filed a motion to disqualify the Laff Firm from further representation of All States.

District Court Proceeding

The district court initially determined that the matters handled by Ladas & Parry were substantially related to the present litigation. In an order dated November 16, 1982, the district court stated its preliminary impression that upon finding substantial relatedness, disqualification was required if only because of the appearance of impropriety. However, in light of the more recent Seventh Circuit decisions discussed infra, the court concluded that that ground was insufficient; that the court had to make a finding as to whether Conte had actual knowledge; that actual knowledge was presumed from the substantial relationship; and that All States had the burden of proving, clearly and effectively, that Conte had received no confidences. As a result, an evidentiary hearing was held for this purpose.

To show that Conte acquired Panduit confidences at Ladas & Parry, Chrystal testified that he, Conte, and other members of the firm regularly had lunch together at the Union League Club in Chicago. Chrystal and Conte dispute the frequency of the lunches but, at a minimum during 1972–1975, when Conte was a special partner, it would have been at least once a month.

Although he was unable to recall a specific instance or a specific topic discussed with Conte, Chrystal nonetheless testified that Panduit matters, especially the overseas patent opposition proceedings, were discussed frequently because it was unusual to have so many going on at one time. Chrystal's testimony was generally corroborated by Thomas Peterson, although he too could not recall specifically that Conte was present at any of these discussions.

The district court ruled that any specific confidences known to Mr. Chrystal could not be disclosed, recognizing that this created a dilemma to All States with respect to proving that Conte received no confidences. However, Chrystal was permitted to identify general areas of confidences. In addition to the opposition matters, he recalled two others, one in 1969 relating to replacing a German associate whose work was not satisfactory and one relating to a French matter which was of public record. He could not remember passing on these confidences, or any other, to Mr. Conte. His testimony essentially was that he must have shared Panduit confidences with Conte because of the frequency of the lunches and because he was like a broken record repeatedly talking about the Panduit oppositions. His only specific recollection of consulting with Conte on any matter was asking him about how to bill on a time basis since Ladas & Parry, prior to organization as a law firm, simply charged flat fees for particular services.

Conte testified that he does not recall ever receiving any Panduit confidences while at Ladas & Parry. In addition, he testified that he has no present recollection of any Panduit confidences, if he received any, and that he has never communicated to anyone at the Laff Firm any Panduit confidences. Further, Mr. Laff testified that no Panduit confidences were received from Conte.

After hearing the parties' testimony, and an expert's testimony regarding All States' possible expense, if it were to change counsel, the trial judge stated:

My decision is governed primarily by the decision of the Seventh Circuit in Freeman v. Chicago Musical Instrument Company [689 F.2d 715 (1982)].

. . .

I have already held in my order of November 16, 1982, that there is a substantial relationship between the matters which were being worked on by Ladas & Parry and the subject matter of the instant lawsuit. The mere appearance of impropriety which I was prepared to hold existed in this case without even going to the question of whether there was any actual imparting of confidential information is, under the Freeman case, insufficient to warrant disqualification. There must be more than the mere appearance of impropriety. There must be actual possession of confidential information by the attorney whose disqualification is sought.

Such actual possession of confidential information is presumed to exist upon a showing of the substantial relationship. However, this presumption can be rebutted. The attorney whose disqualification is sought has the burden of rebutting the presumption. Under the Freeman case, that attorney has the burden of, quote, "clearly and effectively," closed quote, rebutting the presumption.

What is it that he must rebut? He must rebut the presumption that he had confidential information, or, in other words, he must prove that he did not have knowledge of the confidences of the client.

It is important to note that the burden is not simply that of proving that there is no present recollection of any confidences of the client. Indeed, that distinction is pivotal in this case. What the attorney must prove is that he never received any confidential information whether or not he presently remembers either the confidential information or whether he received it.

. . .

This case really turns on the burden of proof. If it were Panduit's burden to prove that Conte received and presently retains confidential information, Panduit would lose. That, however, is not the burden. It is All States' burden to prove that Conte never received confidential information in the first place, and I find that the evidence does not clearly and effectively establish that proposition.

In summary, the district court made the following four findings of fact:

One, All States has not proved clearly and effectively that Conte never received any confidential information concerning matters relevant to this case while he was with the firm of Ladas & Parry.

Secondly, All States has proved clearly and effectively that Mr. Conte has no present recollection of any such confidential information.

Third, *All States has proved clearly and effectively that Mr. Conte has not communicated to anyone at the Laff Firm any confidential information concerning Panduit which he may have received while at the Ladas & Parry firm.* [Emphasis added.]

Fourth, All States has not proved clearly and effectively that there is no possibility of an inadvertent use of such confidential information by Mr. Conte should he at some time in the future recollect that information.

On the basis of these findings, the district court concluded that Conte and the Laff Firm must be disqualified as counsel for All States. It also noted that the disqualification imposed a very substantial economic hardship on All States in light of the testimony that it would take at least $30,000 for new counsel to acquire the necessary knowledge in order to adequately represent All States. Moreover, the trial judge believed that the likelihood of actual prejudice to Panduit, if the Laff Firm remained as counsel, would be very slight.

All States urged that the court allow the Laff Firm to continue under an order that screened Conte from the case. In denying that remedy the court reasoned that it could not possibly find as a matter of fact that Conte had not already inadvertently passed on some confidence.

Because the court felt "there is some likelihood that the Court of Appeals will disagree with my findings and conclusions", and "in the interest of doing the least harm to anyone," it ordered the Laff Firm to do no more work on the case until the disqualification matter was resolved on appeal and stayed proceedings.

. . .

When we review procedural matters that do not pertain to patent issues, we sit as if we were the particular regional circuit court where appeals from the district court we are reviewing would normally lie. We would adjudicate the rights of the parties in accordance with the applicable regional circuit law. . . . Where the regional circuit court has spoken on the subject, we must apply the law as stated. . . . Where the regional circuit court has not spoken, we need to predict how that regional circuit would have decided the issue in light of the decisions of that circuit's various district courts, public policy, etc. . . .

Accordingly, in order not to violate the spirit of our enabling legislation and in order to minimize confusion and conflicts, we shall decide the disqualification order of the instant appeal in light of Seventh Circuit law.

III

Disqualification

A. *Policy Considerations Underlying Disqualification*

. . .

. . . Fortunately we have the benefit of a recent Seventh Circuit case heard in Banc, Novo Terapeutisk Laboratorium A/S v. Baxter Travenol Laboratories, Inc., 607 F.2d 186, 206 USPQ 769 (7th Cir.1979), which, obviously, is controlling. In *Novo,* the facts in support of disqualification were at least as strong as those before us; nevertheless a disqualification order was set aside. More recently, a panel of the Seventh Circuit in *Freeman* set aside a disqualification order *as a matter of law* on the ground that the principles in *Novo* had not been properly applied. The results, as well as the language, in these recent cases indicate that the Seventh Circuit considers the right of a party to select counsel of his choice to be a matter of significant importance, which will not be disturbed unless a specifically identifiable impropriety *has occurred.* See also Whiting Corp. v. White Machinery Corp., 567 F.2d 713 (7th Cir.1977) (no disqualification). . . .

B. *Presumptions Underlying Disqualification*

In ruling on a disqualification motion directed to an individual and a firm, all cases which we have reviewed in the Seventh Circuit show that the court analyzes disqualification of the firm separately from the individual and carefully weighs each step in each disqualification. However, the movant for disqualification has several presumptions working in his favor.

First, proof by the movant of a base fact, the existence of a so-called "substantial relationship" between past work and the suit at hand, gives rise to a presumption that an attorney who actually did the past work received confidences relevant to the present litigation. Second, there is a presumption that attorneys within a firm share each other's confidences, so that knowledge will be imputed from one to the other.

In the decision under review, no clear distinction was drawn between the above two presumptions. Indeed, Panduit's brief totally confuses the two, invoking the presumption arising from a substantial relationship, and the extremely strict burden of proof to overcome it, directly against Conte. The district court also inextricably intertwined the two presumptions into a single presumption against Conte. The case before us, however, does not fit into the simple pattern of an attorney who had worked on Panduit matters moving to another firm, which would make the case comparable to the above cited *LaSalle* case, for example. Panduit's analysis would be apropos only if Chrystal rather than Conte had moved to the Laff Firm. Proof of the substantial relationship here gave rise to a presumption against Chrystal, not Conte. Moreover, Chrystal and the client Panduit are not in an adversarial relationship. (Cf. *Novo*, 607 F.2d at 197). Chrystal's knowledge is being *imputed* to Conte. *Freeman*, 689 F.2d at 723. No Panduit confidences could have been obtained by Conte as a result of *work* by him on Panduit matters since he never performed such work. Further, the district court held that Panduit failed to prove that Conte actually received any Panduit confidences. Nevertheless, based on the fact that Conte and Chrystal were in the same firm, confidences have to be *imputed* from Chrystal to Conte unless Conte effectively rebutted the sharing presumption.

A presumption of having received confidences from *having worked* on relevant related matters is difficult to overcome. Indeed, it is attackable only on the facts with respect to the nature of the earlier work.[19] In accordance with Seventh Circuit precedent, the district court refused to allow Chrystal to divulge specific confidences that he knew. *Novo*, 607 F.2d at 196. While All States appears to have attempted to prove that Chrystal knew only matters that were of public record, we cannot say that the court erred in any way in finding a substantial relationship between the past Panduit work of Chrystal and the present litigation. Cf. *Novo*, 607 F.2d at 196.

With respect to disqualification of Conte, the district court held that the presumption against him could be rebutted if he could prove that he never received any confidential information. We will discuss Conte's disqualification again later. At this juncture the point to be made is that Conte was disqualified vicariously because of Chrystal's work not because of his own work. The Laff Firm was then disqualified solely because of the "sharing" presumption. It is significant, however, that underlying the presumption invoked against the Laff Firm is Conte's *imputed* knowledge.

IV.

The Laff Firm Disqualification

A. *Reimputing Imputed Knowledge*

While the Seventh Circuit has not expressed itself specifically on the imputation of knowledge from one firm to another through a *vicariously* disqualified attorney[21], the panel in *Freeman* cited with

---

19. See LaSalle National Bank v. County of Lake, 703 F.2d 252, 255–256 (7th Cir.1983) which delineates a three-part test for determining whether or not the prior work and the present litigation are substantially related and speaks of "the very strict standard of proof" to rebut it. This presumption may be close to irrebuttable. See *Novo*, 607 F.2d at 196, 197.

21. As described in Attorney's Conflict of Interests: Representation of Interest Adverse to that of Former Client, 55 B.U.L.Rev. 61, 70 n. 51 (1975):

This pattern of imputation, one of several possible patterns, is presented in Laskey Bros. v. Warner Bros. Pictures, Inc., 224 F.2d 824, 827 (2d Cir.1955), cert. denied, 350 U.S. 932 [76 S.Ct. 300, 100 L.Ed. 814] (1956). Courts have stopped short of adopting a double imputation theory. See, e.g., American Can Co. v. Citrus Feed Co., 436 F.2d 1125, 1129–30 (5th Cir.1971). The double imputation theory would work as follows: Attorney A of Firm 1 represents Client C. The receipt of confidential information is imputed to Attorney B of Firm 1, who did not participate in the representation.

approval the Fifth Circuit case of American Can Company v. Citrus Feed Co., 436 F.2d 1125 (5th Cir.1971). Where the basis for granting a disqualification order was multiple presumptions, the Fifth Circuit reversed, holding:

> However, new partners of a vicariously disqualified partner, to whom knowledge has been imputed during a former partnership, are not necessarily disqualified: they need show only that the vicariously disqualified partner's knowledge was imputed, not actual. . . .

> If these ethical principles are applied to the instant case, it becomes evident that disqualification of Miller and the Covington firm is unnecessary. Indeed, resort to so drastic a measure would not only be unwise, but would also set disturbing precedent. If the Prossers' rationale were accepted, imputation and consequent disqualification could continue *ad infinitum*. It is not surprising, then, that the courts have carefully limited their travels in this area.

436 F.2d at 1129.

While Chrystal and his partner, Peterson, testified concerning numbers of luncheons with Conte and the general tenor of conversations at the firm luncheons, such testimony does not alter the fact that Conte's knowledge is imputed, not actual. The testimony added nothing of substance to the presumption itself. The presumption that members of a firm share confidences arises simply because lawyers frequently discuss the matters on which they are working with other members of their firm. However, there is no dispute that Conte never worked on any Panduit matters, and his knowledge of Panduit affairs is, therefore, *imputed* knowledge. Thus, under the rationale of *American Can*, the Laff Firm would be entitled to prevail since knowledge cannot be *imputed* to the Laff Firm based on knowledge *imputed* to Conte.

B. *Standard To Overcome Shared Knowledge*

Alternatively, even if the Seventh Circuit were to approve the reimputation of imputed knowledge, the record here does not support Panduit's motion against the Laff Firm under independent established principles of that circuit.

The effect of a presumption of fact, here the fact of shared confidences, is to place upon the opposing party the burden of establishing

Attorney B leaves Firm 1 and joins Firm 2. Under the single imputation theory, Attorney B cannot represent a party opposing C even though he has left Firm 1. The double imputation theory would impute the receipt of confidential information, already imputed to Attorney B, to Attorney D of Firm 2, so that Attorney D would be foreclosed from representing an interest adverse to C's. The double imputation theory would invent conflicts where none exist. However, if there were actual disclosure to Attorney D, he should surely withdraw, although his withdrawal would not be based on a double imputation theory.

the nonexistence of that fact.[22] The burden on the opposing party, however, is limited to *production* of evidence. The burden of *persuasion* on the existence of the presumed fact remains throughout on the party invoking the presumption.[23] The movant for disqualification, as on any other motion, bears the ultimate burden.

A presumption does not enjoy the status of evidence. If a finding on the evidence is made that a presumed fact has been effectively rebutted, the presumed fact ceases to exist. It does not linger on to be weighed against the evidence. If evidence is provided which falls short of meeting the threshold of rebuttal, the presumed fact retains its viability. Hence, the standard to establish the nonexistence of the presumed fact may be critical.

Under Seventh Circuit law, to rebut a presumption of shared confidences within a firm, the district court is required to find:

> [W]hether the knowledge of the "confidences and secrets" of [the client of the first firm] which [the attorney] brought with him *has been* passed on to or *is likely to be* passed on to the members of the [second] firm. [Emphasis added.]

Schiessle [v. Stephens], 717 F.2d [417] at 421 [(7th Cir.1983)].

The record in this case discloses that the district court initially made the following finding:

> Third, All States has proved clearly and effectively that Mr. Conte has not communicated to anyone at the Laff firm any confidential information concerning Panduit which he may have received while at the Ladas & Parry firm.

This finding effectively negated the imputation of knowledge to the Laff Firm at the time the firm was disqualified. During the subsequent argument on screening Conte, rather than disqualifying the Laff Firm, the district court felt compelled to qualify that finding as follows:

> I am going to have to modify that finding. The more we talk about this case, the more refined it becomes, but I cannot possibly find as a matter of fact *that he [Conte] has not already inadvertently passed on some confidence.* There is no way of my knowing that. [Emphasis added.]

It is in the standard stated above that the district court erred as to the Laff Firm. An *absolute* finding of no *possible* inadvertent sharing of confidences is not required to establish an effective rebuttal. The proof of a negative renders certainty virtually impossible. If such were the requirement, disqualification would have been mandated in the *Novo* case. There, a partner in a firm, Mr. Cook, worked for a particular client (Baxter–Travenol). Upon leaving the firm six months later, Cook filed suit on behalf of Baxter–Travenol against Novo. Novo hired

22. FRE Rule 301, Notes of Advisory Committee on Proposed Rules. See, generally, McCormick, Evidence § 345 (2d ed. 1972).

23. Fed.R.Evid.Rule 301, Notes of Committee on the Judiciary, Senate Report No. 93–1277.

Cook's former firm, and Baxter–Travenol moved for the firm's disqualification. With respect to the six month interim, the presumption of shared confidences was applied. It would have been impossible to hold with certainty that confidences were not inadvertently disclosed to the firm by Cook. Indeed, Cook's affidavit averred that some client confidences were passed on. 607 F.2d at 196, n. 4. A panel of the court, which first heard the appeal, resolved doubts in favor of disqualification. The Seventh Circuit, in banc, overturned that holding on the basis of affidavits from the firm members that they received no confidences. There was no evidence from Cook that they did, specifically with respect to the subject matter of the suit. The presumption was held to be overcome.

Here, we have comparable, if not stronger, facts for no disqualification. The presumption against the Laff Firm would not be as difficult to overcome as in *Novo* since one of the circumstances which affects the likelihood of confidences being passed on is that Conte was not shown to have any confidences. His taint is vicarious. Cook's taint was direct. In any event, Laff, like Cook's former partners, credibly testified, per the district court, that no confidences were received. Conte credibly testified, per the district court, that he passed on no confidences. The district court's error was in requiring *absolute certainty* that no confidences had been *inadvertently* shared. A legal requirement of that magnitude makes the presumption effectively irrebuttable, contrary to the law of the Seventh Circuit. *Novo,* 607 F.2d at 197; *Freeman,* 689 F.2d at 723. As Panduit acknowledges in its brief here, the standard is *likelihood* not *certainty,* and all of the circumstances must be weighed in determining such likelihood.

C. *Screening*

Despite the trial court's "complete satisfaction" that the Laff Firm received no confidences through Conte, disqualification of the firm was required, in that court's view, because of the absence of a screen or wall *at the time* Conte got there. Panduit cites as authority for the correctness of this proposition *LaSalle National Bank v. County of Lake,* supra. Contrary to the holding of the court and Panduit's argument, the absence of screening is not fatal to All States' position. As illustrated in the in banc *Novo* case, the presumption of sharing between partners of a firm can be overcome by testimonial evidence, despite the absence of screening. The district court failed to appreciate that evidence of voluntary screening procedures is simply one type of evidence that may overcome the presumption of shared confidences. Thus, the question of the Laff Firm disqualification cannot be disposed of simply by the absence of screening. The question before the district court was whether, considering all the evidence, it was *likely* that confidences had been passed to the firm. In the face of the district court's finding that the Laff firm had *received no confidences* from Conte up to the time of the hearing, it was error to find that it was "too late" to formally endorse screening procedures.

Nowhere in Seventh Circuit opinions has proof of *formal screening* been delineated as the *sine qua non* of establishing the nonexistence of the presumed fact that confidences have been shared. Within the factual context of *LaSalle,* 703 F.2d at 259, the court merely opined that a *timely* screening arrangement might have prevented disqualification in that case.

Similarly, in *Schiessle,* the relevant inquiry was whether it was likely that confidences had been shared. Interpreting its own *LaSalle* case, the Seventh Circuit stated in *Schiessle* that "the presumption of shared confidences *could* be rebutted by demonstrating [specific institutional mechanisms]" and that the determination "*must* be made on a case-by-case basis". 717 F.2d at 421 (emphasis added). The court concluded in *Schiessle* that the absence of a wall to screen an attorney with direct, rather than imputed, knowledge was dispositive in that case.

The shared confidences presumption is fully rebutted by a finding of the nonexistence of the presumed fact, as made here at trial. Since *Schiessle* must be read with *Novo,* there is no reason to conclude that the passage in *Schiessle* regarding institutional mechanisms being in place at the time the tainted attorney joined the firm is a requirement. Quite the contrary, the context of *Schiessle* and its predecessors renders it more likely that the court was merely expressing a willingness to consider whatever evidence is presented to rebut the presumption.

In any event, in *Novo* the presumption of shared confidences was overcome despite six months of a continued partnership relationship without a wall to prevent sharing. A rule that screening is the exclusive means of rebutting the presumption that confidences have been shared, *regardless of independent evidence,* cannot rest on *LaSalle* or *Schiessle.*

Presumptions of fact have been created to assist in certain circumstances where direct proof of a matter is for one reason or another rendered difficult. They arise out of considerations of fairness, public policy, and probability, and are useful devices for allocating the burden of production of evidence between the parties. However, derived as they are from considerations of fairness and policy, they must not be given mechanical application. Thus, with each presumption in the chain utilized in this case, we must not lose sight of the Seventh Circuit's view that attorney disqualification as a prophylactic device should not be imposed unless "absolutely necessary". We must not give undue dignity to a procedural tool and fail to recognize the realities of the particular situation at hand.

One of the realities accompanying this particular disqualification is that reversal of the district court will likely result in *no prejudice* to Panduit. The district court analyzed the prejudice to Panduit from the Laff Firm remaining in the case as follows:

> The possibility of prejudice resides entirely in the prospect of Mr. Conte recovering whatever memory he might perchance recover

concerning some confidential information he may or may not have received at some remote time in the past. The probability that any such revival of memory would materially assist Mr. Laff or any other member of the Laff firm at this stage of this litigation seems to me to be very small.

On the other hand, the prejudice to All States is catastrophic. Its long standing counsel, a relationship established before this case began, is no longer available and could not even consult on transfer of the case to another firm. The estimate of costs in 1981 for bringing in new counsel was $30,000–$50,000, no doubt now substantially more. Other pending litigation will also be affected. The *balancing* of interests at the time of the hearing did not require disqualification of the Laff Firm.

V.

The Conte Disqualification

With respect to Conte, the district court order is vacated.

The impropriety of Conte's disqualification was urged by All States to negate the basis for disqualification of the Laff Firm. However, the Laff Firm should not have been disqualified in any event since the presumption as to the firm had been overcome regardless of the ruling on Conte.

If it were urged that Conte be allowed to stay in the case, we would have to remand for reconsideration because an incorrect legal presumption was applied against him. Cf. *Freeman*, supra. However, in view of All States' position on appeal, we remand to the district court for an appropriate order formalizing procedures which will screen Conte from involvement in these and related proceedings.

. . .

Questions

Should Conte have been disqualified? What about the Laff firm? The court refers to Conte's knowledge of confidences as "imputed." Didn't the evidence show that confidences had actually been shared with him? What difference should it make, if any, that the confidences learned were learned by actually working on the former matter rather than by casual conversations with members of the firm?

In *Panduit* the court, quoting from the *Schiessle* case, says that the question to be asked when a tainted lawyer moves to a new firm is: "[W]hether the knowledge of the 'confidences and secrets' of [the client of the first firm] which [the attorney] brought with him has been passed on to or is likely to be passed on to the members of the [second] firm."

How is this question different from the question to be asked under the Model Rules? Which standard does the *Panduit* court end up using? Is the *Schiessle* formulation of the test better than that in the Model Rules?

Screening

In *Panduit,* the court holds that evidence of formal screening is only one of several ways to establish that the second firm remains untainted despite the presence of one "tainted" lawyer.

Formal screening, otherwise known as building an "insulation wall" or establishing a "cone of silence," refers to physical and procedural barriers established in a firm to prevent the tainted lawyer from transmitting information or receiving information on a particular matter, which that lawyer is disqualified from handling. What screening is designed to prove, according to the *Panduit* court, is that confidences have not been transmitted from the tainted lawyer to the other lawyers in the firm. And this, the court holds, may be shown in other ways, e.g., testimony from the lawyers involved that no confidences were shared.

But in *Panduit,* there was not only no formal screening at the start of the suit, lawyer Conte actually worked on this case, even if only briefly. When the tainted lawyer has actually been involved, should any evidence be allowed to outweigh the presumption that the rest of the firm is now tainted?

If the *Panduit* court is right that the question is whether information has been transferred, why not use screening to cure all conflicts within a firm? Isn't the logic of screening to prevent taint as expansive as imputation is to attribute taint? Why couldn't a firm establish "screens" between all matters being worked on by different lawyers in the firm?

Why was screening rejected in *Westinghouse?* See Chapter 7 above.

Screening has been accepted in cases of lawyers moving between government and private practice, see *Armstrong,* printed below and M.R. 1.11(a). Where the conflict arises between private clients, the prevailing rule is that screening will not prevent imputed disqualification unless the lawyer joining the firm is disqualified vicariously rather than through personal contact with the former client's representation. See Schiessle v. Stephens, 717 F.2d 417 (7th Cir.1983); Cheng v. GAF Corp., 631 F.2d 1052 (2d Cir.1980); Amoco Chemicals Corp. v. D.C. MacArthur, 568 F.Supp. 42 (N.D.Ga.1983); Yaretsky v. Blum, 525 F.Supp. 24 (S.D.N.Y.1981).

There is, however, dissatisfaction with the difficulties that the imputation rule creates. These difficulties are especially significant for young lawyers, who are more likely to move than their older colleagues. A lawyer seeking to move from one firm to another will have to account for all her prior involvements in representation and have those checked against the prospective firm's list of pending clients and matters. This makes it important for young lawyers to keep an accurate record of the matters on which they have worked. It also suggests that young lawyers should keep their noses out of cases being handled by their firms in which they have no direct involvement.

Both *Nemours* and *Panduit* recognize that the nonscreening rule may be too rigorous. Courts may more readily permit screening where there was acquiescence by the opposing party or where the conflict arose from an unusual or unforeseeable chain of events. See, e.g., Manning v. Waring, Cox, James and Sklar, 849 F.2d 222 (6th Cir.1988); Cox v. American Cast Iron Pipe Co., 847 F.2d 725 (11th Cir.1988); Geisler v. Wyeth Laboratories, 716 F.Supp. 520 (D.Kan.1989). Other courts continue the rigorous stance against screening. See, e.g., Atasi Corp. v. Seagate Technology, 847 F.2d 826, 831–832 (Fed.Cir.1988) (interpreting Ninth Circuit law).

Where do the courts get authority to permit screening in situations in which the ethical rules do not permit it?

Pennsylvania modified M.R. 1.10 to permit screening of lawyers moving between private firms in the same way as M.R. 1.11(a), see discussion of that rule below, permits screening of former government lawyers entering private practice. The version of the Rules adopted by the District of Columbia Court of Appeals specifically addresses the problems of law students moving between firms. The rules provide that law students are bound to keep the former client's confidences, D.C. Rule 1.6(g); but that the new firm is not disqualified, D.C. Rule 1.10(b). The D.C. Rules do not explicitly require that the firm implement screening procedures in this situation, but it would seem the prudent course.

The Model Rules do not depend on whether material confidences were actually passed from the tainted lawyer to others in the second firm. If the tainted lawyer has such confidences the firm cannot proceed. Screening might still be advisable and even necessary under the Model Rules, if the tainted lawyer—despite the fact that she has no material confidential information—is still disqualified under M.R. 1.9(a). See p. 661 above.

On screening in the private lawyer context see Morgan, Screening the Disqualified Lawyer: The Wrong Solution to the Wrong Problem, 10 U. Arkansas Little Rock L.Rev. 37 (1987/88); and Brodeur, Building Chinese Walls: Current Implementation and a Proposal for Reforming Law Firm Disqualification, 7 Rev. of Litigation 167 (1988).

Conflicts When Law Firms Merge

The conflicts problems arising when a lawyer moves from one firm to another are compounded when two firms merge. In a merger, all the current clients of each firm become the current clients of the surviving firm under M.R. 1.7, and the former clients of both firms come within the purview of M.R. 1.9. In dealing with law firm mergers, the courts have refused to allow a firm simply to dump one of the clients who will not consent to a conflict and indeed have said that notice to the affected clients should be given when the negotiations reach the stage that merger has "reasonable likelihood." See, e.g., In re Eastern Sugar Antitrust Litigation, 697 F.2d 524 (3d Cir.1982); Picker Intern. v. Varian Associates, 869 F.2d 578 (Fed.Cir.1989). Also see the discussion of curing simultaneous conflicts in Chapter 7 above.

C. GOVERNMENT LAWYERS AND THE REVOLVING DOOR

Statutes and Government Regulations

There are federal statutes regulating conflicts of interest on the part of present and former government employees generally. See 18 U.S.C. §§ 203–209. In addition, there are regulatory provisions specially governing lawyers as such and lobbying as such, the latter a professional activity in which many lawyers engage. Thus, 28 C.F.R. §§ 45.735 *et seq.* governs employees and former employees of the Department of Justice. § 45.735–2(a) requires all Department of Justice employees to "conduct themselves in a manner that creates and maintains respect for" the Department and the government. § 45.735–5 provides that no Department employee shall "participate personally and substantially" in any matter in which she or her immediate family or business association has a financial interest, subject to narrow qualifications. § 45.745–7(a) prohibits a former Department employee from any appearance in or communication concerning any matter in which the employee "participated personally and substantially as an employee." § 45.735–7(b) imposes a two year post-employment prohibition on being involved in any matter that "was actually pending under his official responsibility as an employee within a period of one year prior to the termination of such responsibility." § 45.735–7(c) imposes a two year post-employment prohibition on executive level employees from advising or aiding in any matter in which they "participated personally or substantially," and a one year prohibition on such employees representing anyone in any matter "pending before the Department or in which it has a substantial and direct interest."

§ 45.735–6 prohibits a Department employee from assisting in matters against the government. § 45.735–8 prohibits receiving compensation apart from government salary; § 45.735–9 prohibits outside employment; § 45.735–10 prohibits "improper use" of confidential official information; § 45.735–11 restricts investments; § 45.735–12 generally prohibits fees for lectures or the like on subjects related to Department activities and limits activity in political fund-raising; § 45.735–14 restricts receiving gifts and entertainment; § 45.735–14(a) regulates receipt of travel expenses; §§ 45.735–22 and 45.735–27 impose extensive financial reporting requirements. Other agencies have similar regulations, see, e.g. 17 C.F.R. § 200.735 (SEC); 16 C.F.R. § 4.1 (FTC); 31 C.F.R. § 10.26 (IRS).

The federal statutory conflict of interest provisions, reformulated in 1963, include 18 U.S.C. §§ 203, 205, 207, 208 and 209. In general these provisions are mirrored in the regulations governing the Department of Justice, but the statutory prohibitions have criminal sanctions.

They are summarized in 28 C.F.R. 45.735–1 Appendix. Also see the conflicts rules in the Integrity in Procurement Act, 41 U.S.C. § 423.

The Federal Lobbying Act, 2 U.S.C. §§ 261–270, requires that anyone "receiving any contributions" in order to "influence, directly or indirectly, the passage or defeat of any legislation" by Congress must register. The statute was construed, and a challenge to its constitutionality on the basis of the First Amendment rejected, in United States v. Harriss, 347 U.S. 612, 74 S.Ct. 808 (1954). Any person covered by the Act must file a quarterly report, Report Pursuant to Federal Regulation of Lobbying Act, covering receipts and expenditures.

Persons who act as "agent of a foreign principal" are also subject to the Foreign Agents Registration Act, 22 U.S.C. §§ 611–621, and implementing regulations, 28 C.F.R. § 5.100. Both are administered by the Department of Justice, with which such an agent must register, thereafter file reports every six months, and comply with record-keeping requirements. In Meese v. Keene, 481 U.S. 465, 107 S.Ct. 1862 (1987), the Court upheld the Foreign Registration Act against a challenge that its use of the term "political propaganda" to trigger its requirements violated the First Amendment.

Virtually every state has some kind of statutory provisions governing conflict of interest on the part of state and municipal employees and those acting on behalf of government agencies. See, e.g., Ariz.Rev. Stat.Ann. § 38–504; Fla.Stat.Ann. § 112.313; Iowa Code Ann. § 68B.7; N.J.Stat.Ann. § 52:13D–12; N.Y. Pub.Off.Law § 73. See also Council of State Governments, Campaign Finance, Ethics and Lobby Law Blue Book 1986–87 (1986).

In United States v. Nofziger, 878 F.2d 442 (D.C.Cir.1989), Nofziger had been convicted for violating § 207(c) of the Ethics in Government Act, which provides:

> Whoever, [being a covered government employee], within one year after such employment has ceased, knowingly acts as agent or attorney for, or otherwise represents, anyone other than the United States in any formal or informal appearance before, or, with the intent to influence, makes any oral or written communication on behalf of anyone other than the United States, to—
>
> (1) the department or agency in which he served as an officer or employee, or any officer or employee thereof, and
>
> (2) in connection with any . . . particular matter, and
>
> (3) which is pending before such department or agency or in which such department or agency has a direct and substantial interest—
>
> shall be fined not more than $10,000 or imprisoned for not more than two years, or both.

Nofziger served as Assistant to the President for Political Affairs in the Reagan White House. After resigning, he established a political consulting firm. It was charged that Nofziger had lobbied White House officials on behalf of three clients less than one year after leaving his White House post. Nofziger claimed that, while he knowingly lobbied the White House, the government had not proved that he did so with *knowledge* that the White House had a "direct and substantial interest" in the matters and therefore the requisite intent under the statute had not been proven. Reread the statute quoted above, does "knowingly" modify the "communications" clause? The government argued that it did not. The court adopted Nofziger's reading and reversed his conviction, stating that the government's reading of the statute "would impose strict liability on a lobbyist who is misinformed." Doesn't the court's interpretation put a premium on staying misinformed? Why would the lobbyist be communicating with the agency with the intent to influence it if she did not think it had a "direct and substantial interest" in the matter? Should the government have to prove this as a separate element apart from the lobbying activity itself? Judge Edwards filed a forceful dissent in *Nofziger*. 878 F.2d at 454.

In addition to statutes and regulations governing members of the Executive Branch, many legislatures have rules that govern their members with restrictions that may implicate lawyers who are members of the legislature or who have dealings with legislators. The following are the principal provisions of the rules governing the House of Representatives. They seem remarkably porous compared to the rules governing the Executive Branch. House Rule XLIII—Code of Official Conduct:

There is hereby established by and for the House of Representatives the following code of conduct, to be known as the "Code of Official Conduct":

1. A Member, officer, or employee of the House of Representatives shall conduct himself at all times in a manner which shall reflect creditably on the House of Representatives.

2. A Member, officer, or employee of the House of Representatives shall adhere to the spirit and the letter of the Rules of the House of Representatives and to the rules of duly constituted committees thereof.

3. A Member, officer, or employee of the House of Representatives shall receive no compensation nor shall he permit any compensation to accrue to his beneficial interest from any source, the receipt of which would occur by virtue of influence improperly exerted from his position in the Congress.

4. A Member, officer, or employee of the House of Representatives shall not accept gifts (other than personal hospitality of an individual or with a fair market value of $50 or less) in any calendar year aggregating $100 or more in value, directly or indirectly, from any person (other than from a relative of his) having a direct interest in legislation before the Congress or who is a foreign national (or agent of a foreign national). Any person registered under the Federal Regulation of Lobbying Act of 1946

(or any successor statute), any officer or director of such registered person, and any person retained by such registered person for the purpose of influencing legislation before the Congress shall be deemed to have a direct interest in legislation before the Congress.

5.   A Member, officer, or employee of the House of Representatives shall accept no honorarium for a speech, writing for publication, or other similar activity, from any person, organization, or corporation in excess of the usual and customary value for such services.

6.   A Member of the House of Representatives shall keep his campaign funds separate from his personal funds. He shall convert no campaign funds to personal use in excess of reimbursement for legitimate and verifiable prior campaign expenditures and he shall expend no funds from his campaign account not attributable to bona fide campaign purposes.

· · ·

The Model Code and the Government Lawyer's Conflicts

As explained in Chapter 7, both the ABA Code of Professional Responsibility and the Model Rules of Professional Conduct apply to government and private lawyers alike.

DR 9–101 provides that a lawyer shall not accept employment in a private matter upon which she acted as a judge or in which she had substantial responsibility while a public employee. This rule disqualifies a lawyer from subsequent representation of a private party in a matter in which the lawyer had substantial responsibility while with the government, *even if the private party is on the "same side" as the government.* This is broader than the general rule on subsequent representation of private clients developed in the case law and codified in M.R. 1.9(a), which applies only when the present client's interests are *adverse* to the interests of the former client, i.e., when the lawyer has "switched sides." Why the broader rule for government lawyers? What are the interests that this broader rule is designed to protect?

DR 5–105(D) says that when one lawyer is disqualified the whole firm is disqualified. When read together with DR 9–101, this would require the disqualification of the entire firm in any case in which the former government lawyer had substantial responsibility. However, the ABA, the courts, and state ethics committees interpreted these rules to allow firms to proceed if the disqualified former government lawyer was screened from participation.

It was thought that former government lawyers might find it difficult to obtain subsequent employment in a private firm, if by hiring them the firm would end up disqualified in a significant number of cases. As a further consequence, it was feared that government service would be less attractive to lawyers; the government (it is argued) can attract top legal talent despite uncompetitive salaries because the experience will make a lawyer valuable to a private firm later.

ABA FORMAL OPINION 342
November 24, 1975

. . .

The policy considerations underlying DR 9–101(B) have been thought to be the following: the treachery of switching sides; the safeguarding of confidential governmental information from future use against the government; the need to discourage government lawyers from handling particular assignments in such a way as to encourage their own future employment in regard to those particular matters after leaving government service; and the professional benefit derived from avoiding the appearance of evil.

There are, however, weighty policy considerations in support of the view that a special disciplinary rule relating only to former government lawyers should not broadly limit the lawyer's employment after he leaves government service. Some of the underlying considerations favoring a construction of the rule in a manner not to restrict unduly the lawyer's future employment are the following: the ability of government to recruit young professionals and competent lawyers should not be interfered with by imposition of harsh restraints upon future practice nor should too great a sacrifice be demanded of the lawyers willing to enter government service; the rule serves no worthwhile public interest if it becomes a mere tool enabling a litigant to improve his prospects by depriving his opponent of competent counsel; and the rule should not be permitted to interfere needlessly with the right of litigants to obtain competent counsel of their own choosing, particularly in specialized areas requiring special, technical training and experience.

. . .

Although a precise definition of "matter" as used in the Disciplinary Rule is difficult to formulate, the term seems to contemplate a discrete and isolatable transaction or set of transactions between identifiable parties. Perhaps the scope of the term "matter" may be indicated by examples. The same lawsuit or litigation is the same matter. The same issue of fact involving the same parties and the same situation or conduct is the same matter. By contrast, work as a government employee in drafting, enforcing or interpreting government or agency procedures, regulations, or laws, or in briefing abstract principles of law, does not disqualify the lawyer under DR 9–101(B) from subsequent private employment involving the same regulations, procedures, or points of law; the same "matter" is not involved because there is lacking the discrete, identifiable transactions or conduct involving a particular situation and specific parties.[21]

21. "Many a lawyer who has served with the government has an advantage when he enters private practice because he has acquired a working knowledge of the department in which he was employed, has learned the procedures, the governing substantive and statutory law and is to a greater or lesser degree an expert in the field in which he was engaged. Certainly this is perfectly proper and ethical. Were it not so, it would be a

The element of DR 9–101(B) most difficult to interpret in light of the underlying considerations, pro and con, is that of "substantial responsibility."

. . .

As used in DR 9–101(B), "substantial responsibility" envisages a much closer and more direct relationship than that of a mere perfunctory approval or disapproval of the matter in question. It contemplates a responsibility requiring the official to become personally involved to an important, material degree, in the investigative or deliberative processes regarding the transactions or facts in question. Thus, being the chief official in some vast office or organization does not *ipso facto* give that government official or employee the "substantial responsibility" contemplated by the rule in regard to all the minutiae of facts lodged within that office. Yet it is not necessary that the public employee or official shall have personally and in a substantial manner investigated or passed upon the particular matter, for it is sufficient that he had such a heavy responsibility for the matter in question that it is unlikely he did not become personally and substantially involved in the investigative or deliberative processes regarding that matter. With a responsibility so strong and compelling that he probably became involved in the investigative or decisional processes, a lawyer upon leaving the government service should not represent another in regard to that matter. To do so would be akin to switching sides, might jeopardize confidential government information, and gives the appearance of professional impropriety in that accepting subsequent employment regarding that same matter creates a suspicion that the lawyer conducted his governmental work in a way to facilitate his own future employment in that matter.

. . .

The extension by DR 5–105(D) of disqualification to all affiliated lawyers is to prevent circumvention by a lawyer of the Disciplinary Rules. Past government employment creates an unusual situation in which inflexible application of DR 5–105(D) would actually thwart the policy considerations underlying DR 9–101(B). . . .

When the Disciplinary Rules of Canons 4 and 5 mandate the disqualification of a government lawyer who has come from private practice, his governmental department or division cannot practicably

distinct deterrent to lawyers ever to accept employment with the government. This is distinguishable, however, from a situation where, in addition, a former government lawyer is employed and is expected to bring with him and into the proceedings a personal knowledge of a particular matter," the latter being thought to be within the prescription of former Canon 36; Allied Realty of St. Paul v. Exchange National Bank of Chicago, 283 F.Supp. 464 (D.Minn.1968), aff'd. 408 F.2d 1099 (8th Cir.1969). See also B. Manning, Federal Conflict of Interest Law 204 (1964).

A contrary interpretation would unduly interfere with the opportunity of a former lawyer to use his expert technical legal skills, and the prospect of such unnecessary limitations on future practice probably would unreasonably hinder the recruiting efforts of various local, state and federal governmental agencies and bodies.

. . .

be rendered incapable of handling even the specific matter. Clearly, if DR 5–105(D) were so construed, the government's ability to function would be unreasonably impaired. Necessity dictates that government action not be hampered by such a construction of DR 5–105(D). The relationships among lawyers within a government agency are different from those among partners and associates of a law firm. The salaried government employee does not have the financial interest in the success of departmental representation that is inherent in private practice. This important difference in the adversary posture of the government lawyer is recognized by Canon 7: the duty of the public prosecutor to seek justice, not merely to convict, and the duty of all government lawyers to seek just results rather than the result desired by a client. The channeling of advocacy toward a just result as opposed to vindication of a particular claim lessens the temptation to circumvent the disciplinary rules through the action of associates. Accordingly, we construe DR 5–105(D) to be inapplicable to other government lawyers associated with a particular government lawyer who is himself disqualified by reason of DR 4–101, DR 5–105, DR 9–101(B), or similar Disciplinary Rules. Although vicarious disqualification of a government department is not necessary or wise, the individual lawyer should be screened from any direct or indirect participation in the matter, and discussion with his colleagues concerning the relevant transaction or set of transactions is prohibited by those rules.

Likewise, DR 9–101(B)'s command of refusal of employment by an individual lawyer does not necessarily activate DR 5–105(D)'s extension of that disqualification. The purposes of limiting the mandate to matters in which the former public employee had a substantial responsibility are to inhibit government recruitment as little as possible and enhance the opportunity for all litigants to obtain competent counsel of their own choosing, particularly in specialized areas. An inflexible extension of disqualification throughout an entire firm would thwart those purposes. So long as the individual lawyer is held to be disqualified and is screened from any direct or indirect participation in the matter, the problem of his switching sides is not present; by contrast, an inflexible extension of disqualification throughout the firm often would result in real hardship to a client if complete withdrawal of representation was mandated, because substantial work may have been completed regarding specific litigation prior to the time the government employee joined the partnership, or the client may have relied in the past on representation by the firm.

. . .

Our conclusion is further supported by the fact that DR 5–105(C) allows the multiple representation that is generally forbidden by DR 5–105(A) and (B), where all clients consent after full disclosure of the possible effect of such representation. DR 5–105(A) and (B) deals, of course, with much more egregious contingencies than those covered by DR 9–101(B). It is unthinkable that the drafters of the Code of Professional Responsibility intended to permit the one afforded protection by DR 5–105(A) and (B) to waive that protection without also permitting the one protected by DR 9–101(B) to waive that less-needed protection. Accordingly, it is our opinion that whenever the government agency is satisfied that the screening measures will effectively isolate the individual lawyer from participating in the particular matter and sharing in the fees attributable to it, and that there is no appearance of significant impropriety affecting the interests of the government, the government may waive the disqualification of the firm under DR 5–105(D). In the event of such waiver, and provided the firm also makes its own independent determination as to the absence of particular circumstances creating a significant appearance of impropriety, the result will be that the firm is not in violation of DR 5–105(D) by accepting or continuing the representation in question.

. . .

Questions and Comments

Is the definition of "matter" provided in Opinion 342 broad enough? Too broad? This issue is discussed further in *SIPC v. Vigman,* printed later in this chapter, and the notes following it.

In New York State Bar Association, Opinion 502 (Jan. 17, 1979), the ethics committee addressed the meaning of "personally and substantially." The committee ruled that a former prosecutor may represent a criminal defendant who was indicted while the lawyer was still with the district attorney's office as long as the lawyer did not have access to confidential information on the matter.

Here again we encounter the reductionist approach, equating the conflict rules with a confidentiality test. Notice that the former deputy district attorney had switched sides. Should a government lawyer have a residual duty of loyalty, for example, not to represent any defendant against whom a prosecution had been commenced while the lawyer was in the prosecutor's office? All of the cases and rules concerning government revolving door conflicts speak of the importance of the public's perception that the government's business is being conducted with integrity. Is "personally and substantially" given a broader reading in Opinion 342 than in N.Y. Opinion 502?

Read DR 9–101. Is it "unthinkable" that the drafters of the Code intended to permit a private client to waive the protections of DR 5–105(A) and (B) and not to permit the government the option of waiving DR 9–101(B)? Is the government as client the only "one protected" by DR 9–101(B)? What about the public at large? M.R. 1.11(a) also permits the government to waive the individual lawyer's disqualification. If consent is either not requested or not granted, the firm may still continue the representation provided the disqualified lawyer is isolated from all involvement in the case. Unlike Opinion 342, however, M.R. 1.11(a) does not require the government's consent to the screening. The firm's only obligation is to promptly notify the government agency involved so that it may monitor the firm's compliance with the rule's dictates on screening the lawyer. Is Opinion 342's requirement of consent to the screening a better rule?

The District of Columbia Bar's version of DR 9–101 was different from the Model Code's. Prompt notice to the government of the screening was required, consent was not. The D.C. Bar's proposed version of M.R. 1.11(a) continues the notice-not-consent rule, although like its predecessor D.C. DR 9–102(C), it sets out more specifically than M.R. 1.11(a) what constitutes adequate notice. M.R. 1.11(a)(2) states only that "written notice" must be provided the government so that it can ensure compliance with the screening. In contrast D.C. DR 9–102(C) requires the personally disqualified lawyer to file with the government agency involved and serve on all other parties to the proceeding a signed document attesting that she will not participate in or discuss the matter with any other lawyer in the firm and will not share in any fees attributable to the matter. In addition, at least one other lawyer from the disqualified lawyer's firm must file with the government and serve on all other parties to the proceeding a signed document attesting that all affiliated lawyers are aware that the disqualified lawyer must be screened and describing the screening procedures which the firm is implementing.

Where screening is allowed in cases involving private clients, see e.g., *Nemours,* supra, should the courts require that similar documents be filed with the court or the opposing party?

In reading the *Armstrong* case printed below, consider how much weight the court placed on the government's consent to the representation.

Should screening be allowed to cure all imputed conflicts with the government? Only those in which the government and the private client are on the "same side?" Is the appearance of impropriety in fact greater when the government and private lawyer are on the same side than when the former government lawyer's firm is representing a private client adverse to the government? Does the court in *Armstrong,* the next principal case, view screening as a cure-all?

ARMSTRONG v. McALPIN

United States Court of Appeals, Second Circuit, 1980, En Banc.
625 F.2d 433, vacated, 449 U.S. 1106, 101 S.Ct. 911, 66 L.Ed.2d 835 (1981).

Before KAUFMAN, CHIEF JUDGE, and FEINBERG, MANSFIELD, MULLIGAN, OAKES, TIMBERS, VAN GRAAFEILAND, MESKILL and NEWMAN, CIRCUIT JUDGES.*

FEINBERG, CIRCUIT JUDGE (with whom KAUFMAN, CHIEF JUDGE, and MANSFIELD, OAKES and TIMBERS, CIRCUIT JUDGES, concur):

---

* The order granting en banc reconsideration of this appeal was filed on December 12, 1979. Judge Gurfein, who was a member of the en banc court, unfortunately died on December 16, 1979. Prior to his death, he did not have the opportunity to vote on the merits of the appeal. Judge Kearse, subsequent to December 12, 1979, disqualified herself.

. . .

. . . . Clovis McAlpin and Capital Growth Real Estate Fund, Inc., two of numerous defendants in a suit seeking over $24 million for violation of federal securities laws, appeal from an order of the United States District Court for the Southern District of New York, Henry F. Werker, J., denying their motion to disqualify the law firm representing plaintiffs. . . .

I. *The Facts*

Appellants' motion to disqualify is based on the prior participation of Theodore Altman, now a partner in the law firm representing plaintiffs-appellees, in an investigation of and litigation against appellants conducted when he was an Assistant Director of the Division of Enforcement of the Securities and Exchange Commission (the SEC). In September 1974, after a nine-month investigation, the SEC commenced an action in the United States District Court for the Southern District of New York against Clovis McAlpin and various other individual and institutional defendants. The complaint alleged that McAlpin and the other defendants had looted millions of dollars from a group of related investment companies, referred to here collectively as the Capital Growth companies; McAlpin was the top executive officer of these companies. The SEC suit sought, among other things, the appointment of a receiver to protect the interests of shareholders in the Capital Growth companies. When McAlpin fled to Costa Rica and certain other defendants failed to appear, the SEC obtained a default judgment; in September 1974, Judge Charles E. Stewart appointed Michael F. Armstrong, the principal appellee in this appeal, as receiver of the Capital Growth companies. See SEC v. Capital Growth Company, S.A. (Costa Rica) et al., 391 F.Supp. 593 (S.D.N.Y.1974).

One of Armstrong's principal tasks as receiver for the Capital Growth companies is to recover all moneys and property misappropriated by defendants; to further this task, Armstrong was authorized to initiate litigation in the United States and abroad. In October 1974, Judge Stewart granted Armstrong's request to retain as his counsel the New York firm of Barrett Smith Schapiro & Simon.[1] Shortly after the appointment of Armstrong, the SEC made its investigatory files available to him, in accordance with its practice, we are informed in its brief, of assisting "the efforts of receivers who have been appointed by the courts in Commission law enforcement actions." Cf. SEC v. Everest Managment Corp., 475 F.2d 1236, 1240 (2d Cir.1972). The Barrett Smith firm reviewed these files, conducted its own investigation for the receiver, and assisted him in taking possession of various Capital Growth properties in the continental United States and in Puerto Rico. For the next year and a half, we are told, Barrett Smith devoted approximately 2,600 hours to assisting the receiver, which included the

---

1. Armstrong was a partner of that firm, which is now Barrett Smith Schapiro Simon & Armstrong.

services of five partners and eight associates; a little over half of this time was spent preparing for litigation.

In early 1976, however, the receiver and Barrett Smith became aware of a potential conflict of interest involving an institutional client of Barrett Smith that might become a defendant in litigation brought by the receiver. Thus, despite Barrett Smith's substantial investment of time, the receiver concluded that it was necessary to substitute litigation counsel. The task, however, was not an easy one; McAlpin had fled to Costa Rica with most of the assets of the Capital Growth companies and hence the funds available to Armstrong to secure new counsel were quite limited.[2] It was therefore necessary to find a firm that could not only handle difficult litigation in Costa Rica and in the United States, but would also commit itself to conclude the task, even if little or no interim compensation was available.[3] Moreover, it was important to retain a law firm large enough to cope with the immense paper work soon to be generated by the firms that would probably represent the institutional defendants.[4]

Because of these considerations, appellees assert, the receiver focused on firms already involved in litigation against Robert L. Vesco, who, like McAlpin, had fled to Costa Rica rather than face possible prosecution for numerous alleged securities fraud violations. After abortive negotiations with two such firms, the receiver in April 1976 retained the law firm of Gordon Hurwitz Butowsky Baker Weitzen & Shalov, the firm that is the target of appellants' disqualification motion. According to Armstrong, the Gordon firm was chosen in part because one partner, David M. Butowsky, was then Special Counsel to International Controls Corporation and was involved in legal work in Costa Rica relating to the alleged Vesco defalcations, while another partner had specialized experience in prosecuting complex fraud cases. In accepting the representation, the Gordon firm agreed to "conduct all Capital Growth litigation through to a conclusion" even if the receiver could not compensate the firm as the litigation progressed.

In October 1975, some seven months before the receiver obtained substitute counsel for Barrett Smith, Theodore Altman ended his nine-year tenure with the SEC to become an associate with the Gordon firm. At the time of his resignation, Altman had been an Assistant Director of the Division of Enforcement for three years, and had about twenty-five staff attorneys working under him. As a high-ranking enforcement officer of the SEC, Altman had supervisory responsibility over numerous cases, including the Capital Growth investigation and litigation. Although he was not involved on a daily basis, he was generally aware of the facts of the case and the status of the litigation. The

2. Cash on hand was then about $200,000; it is apparently not much more now.

3. Up to that time, neither Barrett Smith nor the receiver had been awarded any fees; subsequently, there were some interim allowances for Barrett Smith but Armstrong as yet has received no compensation.

4. After the receiver's complaint was subsequently filed, some of the largest and most prestigious New York firms appeared for the various defendants.

SEC's complaint was prepared and filed by the staff of the New York Regional Administrator, and the litigation was handled by the New York office. Altman's name appeared on the SEC complaint, although he did not sign it.

At the time that Altman joined the Gordon firm, the receiver had no reason to know that Altman had left the SEC or to be aware of his new affiliation. Subsequently, during the initial meetings with the Gordon firm, Armstrong first learned that Altman had recently become associated with the firm. Both the Gordon firm and Barrett Smith researched the question of the effect of Altman's prior supervisory role in the SEC suit. The two firms concluded that under applicable ethical standards discussed in Part IV of this opinion, Altman should not participate in the Gordon firm's representation of the receiver, but that the firm would not be disqualified if Altman was properly screened from the case. The matter was brought to the attention of Judge Stewart, who nonetheless authorized the receiver to retain the Gordon firm. Shortly thereafter, the firm asked the SEC if it had any objection to the retention, and was advised in writing that it did not, so long as Altman was screened from participation. Barrett Smith then turned over its litigation files to the Gordon firm, including those received from the SEC; in September 1976, the receiver filed the action by plaintiffs-appellees against defendants-appellants that gave rise to this appeal.[5]

In June 1978, almost two years after the commencement of this action, appellants filed their motion to disqualify the Gordon firm because of Altman's prior activities at the SEC. In December 1978, Judge Werker, to whom the case had been reassigned, denied the motion. In his opinion, the judge concluded that the Gordon firm had carried out the letter and spirit of the relevant bar association ethical rulings, that the firm's representation of the receiver was not unethical and did not threaten the integrity of the trial, and that appellants had suffered no prejudice as a result of the representation. . . .

. . .

IV. *The Merits*

In his thorough opinion refusing to disqualify the Gordon firm, Judge Werker reviewed the facts set forth in Part I of this opinion and carefully analyzed the ethical problem defendants had raised. He noted that Altman was concededly disqualified from participating in the litigation under Disciplinary Rule 9–101(B) of the American Bar Association Code of Professional Responsibility. That Rule prohibits an attorney's private employment in any matter in which he has had substantial responsibility during prior public employment.[16] The judge

---

5. A more complete statement of the underlying facts in this action is set forth in Armstrong v. McAlpin, [1978 Transfer Binder] Fed.Sec.L.Rep. ¶ 96,323 (S.D.N.Y.1978), which deals with defendants' motion to dismiss the amended complaint.

16. Disciplinary Rule 9–101(B) provides:

then considered the effect of Disciplinary Rule 5–105(D), which deals with disqualification of an entire law firm if one lawyer in the firm is disqualified.[17] This issue had been considered by both the American Bar Association (the ABA) and the Committee on Professional and Judicial Ethics of The Association of the Bar of the City of New York (the Association). The ABA, in its Formal Opinion No. 342, had recognized that "[p]ast government employment creates an unusual situation in which an inflexible application of D.R. 5–105(D) would actually thwart the policy considerations underlying D.R. 9–101(B)," 62 ABA Journal 517, 520 (1976), and concluded that, absent an appearance of significant impropriety, a government agency could waive Rule 5–105(D), if adequate screening procedures effectively isolated the former government lawyer from those members of his firm handling the matter. . . .

Judge Werker then carefully examined the screening of Altman by the Gordon firm, noting that: . . .

> [N]othing before this court indicates that Altman, while employed by the SEC, formed an intent to prosecute a later action involving Growth Fund. Indeed, sworn affidavits reveal that he has never participated in any fashion whatever in the Gordon firm's representation of the Receiver, nor has he shared in the firm's income derived from prosecution of this action. And . . . Altman and his two partners Velie and Butowsky have attested under penalty of perjury that Altman has never discussed the action with other firm members. These statements are uncontradicted by defendants and provide a basis for *not* imputing Altman's knowledge to other members of the firm. . . .

On this rehearing en banc, we are favored with briefs not only from the parties but also from the United States,[18] the Securities and Exchange Commission, the Interstate Commerce Commission, the Federal Maritime Commission, the Commodities Futures Trading Commission and twenty-six distinguished former government lawyers now employed as practicing attorneys, corporate officers, or law professors, all attesting to the importance of the issues raised on appeal. Thus, the United States asserts that a "decision to reject screening procedures is certain to have a serious, adverse effect on the ability of Government legal offices to recruit and retain well-qualified attorneys"; . . . the latter may fear that government service will transform them into legal

A lawyer shall not accept private employment in a matter in which he had substantial responsibility while he was a public employee.

17. Disciplinary Rule 5–105(D) provides:

If a lawyer is required to decline employment or to withdraw from employment under a Disciplinary Rule, no partner, or associate, or any other lawyer affiliated with him or his firm, may accept or continue such employment.

18. The brief of the United States also states that it presents the views of the Federal Trade Commission, the Civil Aeronautics Board, the Federal Energy Regulatory Commission, and the Federal Legal Council, a committee consisting of the General Counsels of fifteen executive branch agencies and chaired by the Attorney General of the United States.

"Typhoid Marys," [19] shunned by prospective private employers because hiring them may result in the disqualification of an entire firm in a possibly wide range of cases. The amici also contend that those already employed by the government may be unwilling to assume positions of greater responsibility within the government that might serve to heighten their undesirability to future private employers. Certainly such trends, if carried to an extreme, may ultimately affect adversely the quality of the services of government attorneys.

. . .

. . . . [T]he current uncertainty over what is "ethical" underscores for us the wisdom, when considering such issues, of adopting a restrained approach that focuses primarily on preserving the integrity of the trial process. We expressed this view in Board of Education v. Nyquist, 590 F.2d 1241 (2d Cir.1979), in which we reviewed at length our precedents on attorney disqualification and pointed out:

> Our reading of the cases in this circuit suggests that we have utilized the power of trial judges to disqualify counsel where necessary to preserve the integrity of the adversary process in actions before them. In other words, with rare exceptions disqualification has been ordered only in essentially two kinds of cases: (1) where an attorney's conflict of interests in violation of Canons 5 and 9 of the Code of Professional Responsibility undermines the court's confidence in the vigor of the attorney's representation of his client, . . . or more commonly (2) where the attorney is at least potentially in a position to use privileged information concerning the other side through prior representation, for example, in violation of Canons 4 and 9, thus giving his present client an unfair advantage. . . . But in other kinds of cases, we have shown considerable reluctance to disqualify attorneys despite misgivings about the attorney's conduct. . . . This reluctance probably derives from the fact that disqualification has an immediate adverse effect on the client by separating him from counsel of his choice, and that disqualification motions are often interposed for tactical reasons. . . . And even when made in the best of faith, such motions inevitably cause delay. . . .

. . . Although appellants assert that the trial will be tainted by the use of information from Altman, we see no basis on the record before us for overruling the district court's rejection of that claim. Using the *Nyquist* analysis, there is certainly no reason to fear any lack of "vigor" by the Gordon firm in representing the receiver; this is not a case where a law firm, by use of a "Chinese wall," is attempting to justify representation of conflicting interests at the same time. . . . Nor is the Gordon firm "potentially in a position to use privileged information" obtained through prior representation of the other side. And finally, the receiver will not be making unfair use of information obtained by Altman as a government official, since the SEC files were

19. Kesselhaut v. United States, 555 F.2d 791, 793 (Ct.Cl.1977) (per curiam).

turned over to the receiver long before he retained the Gordon firm and Altman has been entirely screened from all participation in the case, to the satisfaction of the district court and the SEC.[24]   Nor is there any reason to believe that the receiver retained the Gordon firm because Altman was connected with it [25] or that Altman had anything to do with the retention.   If anything, the presence of Altman as an associate at that time was a problem, not a benefit, for the Gordon firm, as the district court, the receiver and the Gordon firm all apparently recognized.

Thus, because the district court justifiably held that the Gordon firm's representation of the receiver posed no threat to the integrity of the trial process, disqualification of the firm can only be based on the possible appearance of impropriety stemming from Altman's association with the firm.   However, as previously noted, reasonable minds may and do differ on the ethical propriety of screening in this context. But there can be no doubt that disqualification of the Gordon firm will have serious consequences for this litigation;   separating the receiver from his counsel at this late date will seriously delay and impede, and perhaps altogether thwart, his attempt to obtain redress for defendants' alleged frauds.   Under the circumstances, the possible "appearance of impropriety is simply too slender a reed on which to rest a disqualification order . . . particularly . . . where . . . the appearance of impropriety is not very clear."   *Nyquist,* supra, 590 F.2d at 1247.   Thus, we need not resolve the ethical propriety of the screening procedure used here at this time as long as the district court justifiably regarded it as effective in isolating Altman from the litigation.

. . .

Questions and Comments

The decision in *Armstrong* was vacated after Firestone Tire & Rubber Co. v. Risjord, 449 U.S. 368, 101 S.Ct. 669 (1981), which held that denials of motions to disqualify are not appealable orders under 28 U.S.C. § 1291.   *Armstrong* is, however, still cited as authority and its reasoning is accepted by other circuits.   See, e.g., Telectronics Proprietary Ltd. v. Medtronic, Inc., 836 F.2d 1332, 1335 (Fed.Cir.1988).

How does *Armstrong* differ from Opinion 342?

The Model Rules and the Government Lawyer's Conflicts

Under the Model Rules, lawyers who move between the government and private practice are bound by the conflicts rules applicable to

24.   The case therefore is entirely distinguishable from General Motors Corp. v. City of New York, 501 F.2d 639 (2d Cir.1974), where an attorney who had substantial responsibility over an antitrust litigation against General Motors Corporation while he was employed by the Antitrust Division of the Justice Department later accepted employment as plaintiff's attorney in a private antitrust action against the same defendant for substantially the same conduct.

25.   Altman was then an associate, although he is now a partner.

all lawyers. Thus, M.R. 1.7 applies not only to private lawyers but to government and former government lawyers, as does M.R. 1.9, as originally adopted, and M.R. 1.9(a) and (c), as amended in 1989. In addition, the special provisions in M.R. 1.11 apply to lawyers moving between private and government practice. See the Comments to these rules, which make it clear that while M.R. 1.11 only applies to former and present government lawyers, M.R. 1.6, 1.7, and 1.9 apply to all lawyers, government and former government lawyers included.

M.R. 1.11(a) does two things: first, for the individual lawyer formerly with the government and now in private practice, it augments the prohibitions on subsequent representation found in M.R. 1.9; second, for the firm which hires a lawyer formerly with the government, it limits disqualification by imputation.

As to the individual lawyer now in private practice, who formerly worked for the government, M.R. 1.11(a) provides that where the lawyer participated in the matter *personally and substantially* while working for the government, the lawyer may not later represent a private client in connection with that matter unless the government agency consents or other law expressly permits the representation.

Like its predecessor provision in the Code, M.R. 1.11(a) applies whether or not the present client's interests are adverse to the former client (the government). The Model Rules provision, unlike the Model Code, adds the adverb "personally" to describe the kind of involvement that will trigger the rule. What difference does this make? Consider the examples provided in Opinion 342.

Remember that even though the lawyer's present involvement may not be prohibited by M.R. 1.11(a), the former government lawyer must also make sure that M.R. 1.9(a) does not prohibit the representation. M.R. 1.9(a) does not require "personal and substantial" involvement in the former representation before it is triggered. Thus, when the present client's interests are adverse to those of the government, the former government lawyer's disqualification is broader.

Consent from the appropriate government agency (the former client) allows the individual lawyer to proceed under M.R. 1.11(a). As with consent under M.R. 1.9(a), the government's consent under M.R. 1.11(a) does not waive the government's right to preservation of its confidences. The lawyer's duty to preserve the government's confidences under M.R. 1.9(c) and M.R. 1.6 remains in effect unless expressly waived.

M.R. 1.11(a) provides that when a lawyer is disqualified under this subsection (because she participated personally and substantially in the matter while with the government), the entire firm is disqualified unless:

(1) the disqualified lawyer is screened from any participation in the matter and is apportioned no part of the fee therefrom; and

(2) written notice is promptly given to the appropriate government agency to enable it to ascertain compliance with the provisions of this rule.

Notice to, not consent of, the government agency is required before the firm may proceed. The government's consent is necessary for the *individual* lawyer to participate (to avoid screening) but is unnecessary once the firm screens the lawyer. Compare the approach in Opinion 342.

New Jersey's version of 1.11 provides two separate bases for disqualifying the former government lawyer. The first tracks M.R. 1.11(a): the lawyer is disqualified if she was personally and substantially involved in the matter while with the government. If the lawyer is disqualified on these grounds, the entire firm is disqualified, i.e., screening will not cure the conflict. The second basis for disqualification, N.J. Rule 1.11(b), is "appearance of impropriety." If the lawyer is disqualified on this ground, the firm may proceed with the representation provided the lawyer is screened and written notice is given to the government.

SECURITIES INVESTOR PROTECTION CORP. (SIPC) v. VIGMAN

United States District Court, Central District of California, 1984.
587 F.Supp. 1358.

MEMORANDUM OPINION AND ORDER

TASHIMA, DISTRICT JUDGE.

This is an action brought by the Securities Investor Protection Corporation ("SIPC") . . . The complaint names seventy-five individual and corporate defendants and alleges numerous violations of § 10(b) of the Securities Exchange Act of 1934 (the "Exchange Act"), 15 U.S.C. §§ 78a *et seq.*, and Rule 10b–5 promulgated thereunder, the Racketeer Influenced and Corrupt Organizations Act, 18 U.S.C. §§ 1961 *et seq.* ("RICO"), fraud and breaches of fiduciary duty under California common law. . . . I address here, the motion of defendant Isadore Diamond, joined in by five other defendants, to disqualify SIPC's counsel.

BACKGROUND

Gerald E. Boltz and Charles R. Hartman are members of the law firm of Rogers & Wells and counsel of record for plaintiff SIPC in this action. Both attorneys formerly were employed by the Securities and Exchange Commission ("SEC" or the "Commission"). Boltz was employed as an attorney by the SEC for approximately 20 years, from 1959 until 1979. From 1972 until 1979, he was Regional Administrator of the SEC's Los Angeles Regional Office. Hartman was employed as an attorney by the SEC for approximately 11 years, from 1969 to 1980. From 1972 until 1980, he was assigned to the SEC's Los Angeles

Regional Office, where he held the position of regional counsel from 1976 to 1980.

During the early 1970s, two related proceedings were instituted by the SEC against, among others, certain of the defendants named in this action. The first was a Commission administrative proceeding brought by the SEC's Washington Office in March, 1971. . . . The second was a civil injunctive action filed in this court by the SEC's Los Angeles Regional Office [in 1973]. . . . The gravamen of the complaint in that action was the alleged fraudulent manipulation of the common stock of DCS Financial Corporation ("DCS"). Although the scope of the responsibilities and actions of Boltz and Hartman in those proceedings is in dispute, it is uncontested that Boltz signed the complaint and trial brief in the 1973 civil action and that Hartman appeared as trial counsel for the SEC in that action.

The complaint in the instant action, filed July 22, 1983, was signed by Boltz and lists Rogers & Wells and, among others, Hartman as attorneys, for plaintiff SIPC. Like the 1973 civil action and the 1971 administrative proceeding, plaintiff alleges the manipulation of a number of securities. The instant action, however, alleges an extremely elaborate scheme, encompassing the manipulation of seven securities on the over-the-counter market, including the securities of Bunnington Corp. ("Bunnington"), the company into which DCS had merged. As stated, the complaint charges numerous violations of the anti-manipulative provisions of the Exchange Act and RICO, as well as other violations of law. Certain of the claimed violations are based on asserted securities manipulations which occurred prior to the 1971 administrative proceeding and the 1973 civil action.

Defendants seek to disqualify Boltz, Hartman and Rogers & Wells from further representing SIPC in this action on the ground that continued representation by these former government attorneys in a matter connected to their government work contravenes the ethical standards of the legal profession.

I. THE APPLICABLE STANDARD OF PROFESSIONAL RESPONSIBILITY

Defendants contend that Boltz and Hartman's representation of SIPC in this action violates Rule 1.11(a) of the American Bar Association's ("ABA") recently adopted Model Rules of Professional Conduct (1983) ("Model Rules"). Rule 1.11(a) provides:

(a) Except as law may otherwise expressly permit, a lawyer shall not represent a private client in connection with a matter in which the lawyer participated personally and substantially as a public officer or employee, unless the appropriate government agency consents after consultation. No lawyer in a firm with which that lawyer is associated may knowingly undertake or continue representation in such a matter unless:

(1) the disqualified lawyer is screened from any participation in the matter and is apportioned no part of the fee therefrom; and

(2) written notice is promptly given to the appropriate government agency to enable it to ascertain compliance with the provisions of this Rule.[1]

Since SIPC does not contend that Boltz and Hartman have been screened from participation in this action, disqualification of either of these attorneys would require that Rogers & Wells also be disqualified. Model Rule 1.11(a)(1).

The district court has primary responsibility for controlling the conduct of attorneys practicing before it. Trone v. Smith, 621 F.2d 994, 999 (9th Cir.1980). Although the ABA does not establish rules of law that are binding on this Court, it is the Court's prerogative to disqualify counsel based on contravention of the ABA Model Rules. Paul E. Iacono Structural Eng'r, Inc. v. Humphrey, 722 F.2d 435 (9th Cir.), cert. denied, [464] U.S. [851], 104 S.Ct. 162, 78 L.Ed.2d 148 (1983) (former DR 9–101(B) and Canon 9 ["avoiding appearance of impropriety"] sufficient basis to disqualify former National Labor Relations Board attorney from representing union in private suit similar to one he had prosecuted for the Board); In re Coordinated Pretrial Proceedings, 658 F.2d 1355 (9th Cir.1981) (former Canon 9 can be sole basis of disqualification order). This is true, despite the fact that neither this Court's Local Rules nor the Rules of Professional Conduct of the State Bar of California expressly refers to the ABA Model Rules. As the Ninth Circuit has recently stated:

> Despite the deletion in 1975 of a reference to the ABA Model Code in the Rules of Professional Conduct of the State Bar of California . . . the California courts continue to rely on the Model Code in addressing issues not covered precisely by the Rules of Professional Conduct of the State Bar of California.

. . . But see People v. Ballard, 104 Cal.App.3d 757, 761, 164 Cal.Rptr. 81 (1980) (dictum) ("conduct of California attorneys is governed by California Rules of Professional Conduct" not ABA Model Code).

Because California courts have consistently looked to the Model Code, the predecessor of the Model Rules, as a source of ethical principles governing the conduct of California lawyers, I conclude that Rule 1.11(a) is an appropriate standard to apply in this case. See Local Rule 2.5.1 (requiring lawyers to comply with "decisions of any court applicable" to "standards of professional conduct required of members of the State Bar of California"). As noted, Rule 1.11(a) is substantially similar to former DR 9–101(B). Thus, California attorneys are, or should be, apprised of the standard of responsibility encompassed by

---

1. Except for the provision allowing representation when "the appropriate government agency consents after consultation," Rule 1.11(a) is similar to former Disciplinary Rule ("DR") 9–101(B), which provided that "[a] lawyer shall not accept private employment in a matter in which he had substantial responsibility while he was a public employee." Model Code of Professional Responsibility DR 9–101(B) (1979). See also footnote 9, ante.

the rule, from decisions of California and federal courts applying former DR 9–101(B).[2]

SIPC contends that Rule 1.11(a) was meant to apply only to "switching sides" cases, that is, situations where a former government attorney seeks to represent a private litigant whose interests are adverse to the government. SIPC argues that such a limitation is supported by the rule's allowance of an otherwise prohibited representation when "the appropriate government agency consents after consultation." I disagree. Nowhere in the Model Rules, the Comments, or the ABA draft proposals is there support for limiting Rule 1.11(a) to switching sides cases. Although there is no lengthy discussion of the "government consent" provision in the Comment accompanying Rule 1.11, the ABA has explained the provision as follows:

> The direct disqualification of a former government lawyer under Paragraph (A) may be waived by the former agency in proper circumstances. Waiver may be in the public interest. See Woods v. Covington County Bank, 537 F.2d 804 (5th Cir.1976); General Motors Corp. v. City of New York, 501 F.2d 639 (2d Cir. 1974).

ABA, Notes, Proposed Alternative Model Rules at 306 (May 30, 1981) ("1981 Draft Notes").

Neither *Woods* nor *General Motors* involved an attorney switching sides. In fact, the focus in both of these cases was not on whether or not an attorney had switched sides, but instead, was on avoiding the "appearance of impropriety." In *General Motors,* the City of New York brought an action against a bus manufacturer alleging an unlawful nationwide monopoly. One of the City's attorneys formerly had been employed by the Department of Justice and during that time had substantial responsibility in the investigatory and preparatory stages of a similar antitrust action against the same manufacturer. The court, in disqualifying the attorney from further representation of the City, noted that the purpose behind former Canon 9 and DR 9–101(B), as stated in ABA Formal Opinion No. 37 (1931), was to avoid:

> the manifest possibility . . . [that a former government lawyer's] action as a public legal official might be influenced (or open to the charge that it had been influenced) by the hope of later being employed privately to *uphold* or *upset* what he had done.

501 F.2d at 649 (emphasis in the original). The court further recognized that its responsibility was:

> to preserve a balance, delicate though it may be, between an individual's right to his own freely chosen counsel . . . and the need to maintain the highest ethical standards of professional

---

2. Although the ABA Model Rules were not adopted until Aug. 2, 1983, 11 days after this action was commenced, they are the appropriate standard against which to test the *continued* representation of SIPC. Moreover, as the ensuing discussion will indicate, the outcome of the analysis under former Canon 9 and DR 9–101(B) would not differ.

responsibility. This balance is essential if the public's trust in the integrity of the Bar is to be preserved.

Id., quoting *Emle Indus., Inc.* v. *Patentex, Inc.,* 478 F.2d 562, 564–65 (2d Cir.1973). The disqualification was not based on actual impropriety, but in order to avoid the appearance of impropriety and to safeguard the "public's trust." *Id.*

In *Woods,* the Fifth Circuit found no such danger of public mistrust. There, a former naval reserve attorney, during service, had investigated a securities fraud allegedly perpetrated on returning ex-prisoners of war ("POWs") on behalf of the POWs. He later represented the POWs in a private fraud action. The district court's disqualification order was reversed because, the court concluded, the attorney's conduct could not conceivably impugn the public's trust in the Navy or the legal profession. This was due, in large part, to the fact that

> as a legal assistance officer . . . [the attorney] did not possess any investigative authority beyond that available to a private lawyer. . . . Neither is there any allegation that [the attorney] ever held himself out to be an investigating officer acting on behalf of the United States Navy or as having any special governmental authority.

537 F.2d at 817.

The 1981 Draft Notes' citation to *Woods* and *General Motors* makes it apparent that the drafters of the Model Rules did not intend that Rule 1.11(a) be limited to switching sides cases. In fact, the 1981 Draft Notes, at 303, states directly that "a former government lawyer may be prohibited from representing private parties in a related matter even though it is not adverse to the government," citing *Woods.* Thus, the ABA considered that in certain circumstances, such as presented in *Woods,* a former government attorney's representation of a private client may be in the public interest. This is the reason why Rule 1.11(a) permits a discretionary waiver by the former agency of disqualification in such a situation. SIPC's contention that the "government consent" provision was meant to limit the application of Rule 1.11(a) to switching sides cases is contrary to the drafters' reliance on *Woods* and *General Motors* and, therefore, must be rejected. I now turn to an examination of the substantive aspects of the rule.[3]

3. SIPC argues that this motion is governed by Model Rule 1.11(b), rather than Rule 1.11(a). Rule 1.11(b) provides:

> Except as law may otherwise expressly permit, a lawyer having information that the lawyer knows is confidential government information about a person acquired when the lawyer was a public officer or employee, may not represent a private client whose interests are adverse to that person in a matter in which the information could be used to the material disadvantage of that person. A firm with which that lawyer is associated may undertake or continue representation in the matter only if the disqualified lawyer is screened from any participation in the matter and is apportioned no part of the fee therefrom.

Possible disqualification under this rule is independent of and in addition to any basis for disqualification under Rule 1.11(a). Because I conclude that disqualification is required under Rule 1.11(a), I do not reach the question of whether Rule 1.11(b) also applies.

II. APPLICATION OF RULE 1.11(a)

A. *Agency Consent*

As indicated, Rule 1.11(a) appears to allow an otherwise prohibited representation by a former government attorney when "the appropriate government agency consents after consultation." When, at the hearing on the motion, the Court confirmed that agency consent had not been sought, SIPC was directed to consult with the Commission to ascertain whether it would consent to the continued representation of SIPC by Boltz and Hartman. The SEC was then contacted by Rogers & Wells, as well as a number of other counsel in this action. The Commission has declined to give its consent, stating:

> [T]he Commission believes that as a general matter, a policy of waiving the personal disqualification of former Commission lawyers to permit them to participate in the matters which they handled while on the staff could undermine the public's confidence in the activities of the Commission's lawyers. After reviewing the factors relevant to this case, the Commission sees nothing unique in this situation which would warrant deviating from that general principle. Therefore, the Commission has determined that it would not waive any disqualification personal to Messrs. Boltz and Hartman, pursuant to Rule 1.11(a).[4]

The Commission's declination to waive personal disqualification in this case must be accepted as that agency's discretionary determination, as contemplated by the rule, that this is not a situation where waiver of disqualification would be in the public interest. However, it remains to be considered whether the predicate requirements for the application of Rule 1.11(a) are here present.[5]

B. *Same Matter*

Although the ABA Model Rules do not define the term "matter" as used in Rule 1.11(a), it can be said that a matter includes a "discrete, identifiable transaction or conduct involving a particular situation and specific parties." See ABA Formal Opinion No. 342 (1975). Opinion No. 342 provides the following examples:

> The same lawsuit or litigation is the same matter. The same issue of fact involving the same parties and the same situation or conduct is the same matter. . . . [T]he same "matter" is not involved [when] . . . there is lacking the discrete, identifiable transaction or conduct involving a particular situation and specific parties.

---

4. The Commission's determination was communicated to counsel in a letter signed by its General Counsel. A copy of that letter, dated February 28, 1984, is appended hereto.

5. As explained in the SEC's letter, the Commission has "made no determination" that this action and the 1973 civil action "are the same particular matter and that Messrs. Boltz and Hartman had personal and substantial responsibility for both matters."

SIPC contends that, under this definition, the 1973 civil action is not the same matter as the instant action. However, examination of the instant complaint belies this contention. In paragraph 200 of the complaint, in support of the first claim for violation of RICO, plaintiffs allege:

> that at various times prior to November, 1967, *and thereafter, Vigman . . . and Diamond* participated in a fraudulent scheme to manipulate the prices of various securities, including . . . *DCS Corporation (a corporation subsequently merged with Bunnington) . . . Said conduct violated Section 10(b) of the Exchange Act and Rule 10b–5.*

(Emphasis added.) In paragraph 211 of the complaint, plaintiffs further allege:

> that between November, 1967 and January, 1971, in furtherance of the racketeering enterprise, Vigman, Diamond, and others engaged in a scheme to defraud the public in violation of the Securities Act, the Exchange Act and Rule 10b–5. This scheme involved the placement of unregistered securities into the marketplace and the subsequent manipulation of the price of those securities for the benefit of the RICO Defendants.

The complaint also alleges that defendant Vigman, despite being barred from the securities business on November 1, 1967, "continued to exercise control over Newport Securities Corp.", as well as a number of issuers, including Bunnington, and that the racketeering enterprise was carried out through, *inter alia,* Newport Securities.

It must be remembered that the subject of the 1973 civil action was the alleged manipulation of DCS stock by, among others, Vigman and Diamond (defendants here) in violation of, *inter alia,* § 10(b) of the Exchange Act and Rule 10b–5. Although the subject of the 1973 civil action largely was alleged manipulations occurring in 1972, the complaint in the 1973 civil action also alleged fraudulent manipulation of securities "since about September 15, 1970."

It is evident that paragraphs 200, 208, 211 and 212 of the instant complaint refer to the same matter that was the subject of the 1973 civil action. Although this is not a situation where the subsequent complaint was "lifted ad haec verba" from the SEC complaint, *General Motors,* 501 F.2d at 650, I find that a discrete series of transactions involving a specific situation and specific parties in the 1973 civil action is part and parcel of a subsequent, broader allegation of widespread securities fraud and racketeering in the case at bench. The essence of the complaint here is that, since 1967, Vigman, Diamond and others have engaged in a sophisticated conspiracy to manipulate the price of securities. Thus, the complaint includes among its allegations, the alleged manipulation of the price of DCS stock by, among others, Diamond and Vigman, which allegation was the precise subject of the 1973 civil action. Therefore, I find that Boltz and Hartman are representing SIPC "in connection with a matter" which the SEC prosecuted in the 1973 civil action, within the meaning of Rule 1.11(a).[7]

C. *Personal and Substantial Participation*

SIPC argues that neither Boltz nor Hartman personally and substantially participated in the 1973 civil action. However, it is uncontroverted that Boltz signed both the complaint and the trial brief in that action. Although in his declaration Boltz states that his signatures "merely reflect a general SEC practice and policy that a Regional Administrator should personally sign the initial complaint in any action filed by that office," his argument ignores that plain requirement of F.R.Civ.P. 11. At the time Boltz signed the complaint and trial brief, Rule 11 provided that "[t]he signature of an attorney constitutes a certificate by him that he has read the pleading; that to the best of his knowledge, information, and belief there is good ground to support it." The Ninth Circuit has interpreted this language to require an attorney, before filing a civil action, "to make an investigation to ascertain that it has at least some merit, and further to ascertain that the damages sought appear to bear a reasonable relation to the injuries actually sustained." Rhinehart v. Stauffer, 638 F.2d 1169, 1171 (9th Cir.1979). See also Kinee v. Abraham Lincoln Sav. & Loan Ass'n, 365 F.Supp. 975 (E.D.Pa.1973). Therefore, when Boltz, as Regional Administrator, signed the complaint and trial brief, he assumed, as a matter of law, the personal and substantial responsibility of ensuring that there existed good ground to support the SEC's case and that it had, at least, some merit.[9] The assumption and proper discharge of that responsibility required his personal and substantial participation in the action. That Boltz had such responsibility under law is further indicated by former Rule 11's provision that an attorney who violated the rule "may be subjected to appropriate disciplinary action." I, thus, find that Boltz had personal and substantial responsibility over and participation in the 1973 civil action within the meaning of Rule 1.11(a).[10] Cf. Telos, Inc. v. Hawaiian Tel. Co., 397 F.Supp. 1314, 1316 n. 11 (D.Haw.1975)

---

7. Because of this finding, it is unnecessary to and I do not reach the question of whether this action also involves the same matter as the 1971 administrative proceeding.

9. One reason the Model Rule employs the term "participated personally and substantially" is because the term "substantial responsibility" used in former DR 9–101(B), "could disqualify the former head of a large governmental agency from private employment with respect to any matter arising during his tenure. See Cleveland v. Cleveland Elec. Illum. Co., 440 F.Supp. 193 (N.D.Ohio 1977); ABA Formal Opinion 342 (1975) [other citations omitted]." Boltz's disqualification here is not based on his "substantial responsibility" as Regional Administrator of the SEC's Los Angeles Regional Office, but on his personal substantial responsibility and participation in the 1973 civil action as an attorney who, by signing the complaint and trial brief and other actions personally participated substantially in the 1973 civil action. An attorney who personally signs the pleadings in an action is not immunized from Rule 11's imposition of personal responsibility because he also happens to be the head of a governmental office.

10. Further evidence of Boltz's personal participation in the 1973 civil action is found in the response of the SEC staff attorney who deposed defendant Diamond to Diamond's request for a copy of his deposition transcript: "Mr. Boltz has asked me to assure you on behalf of the [SEC] staff" that such a copy would be provided.

("Signing a complaint, is, . . . by itself, except in rare circumstances, the exercise of substantial responsibility" under former DR 9–101(B).).

With respect to Hartman, it is not contested that he appeared at the trial as counsel of record on each day of the three-day trial in the 1973 civil action. However, Hartman contends that his role at the trial merely was to supervise an attorney-colleague at the SEC, who had no prior trial experience. Hartman further declares that all of the legal work in the 1973 civil action, "including both the actual preparation and the trial itself, was performed by" the other trial attorney.

Be that as it may, it is unlikely that an experienced attorney would or could effectively and properly supervise an inexperienced colleague without familiarizing himself with the facts of the case and the applicable law. To this end, Hartman no doubt had access to records, both public and confidential, relating to the case. It is difficult to conceive how an experienced attorney could carry out the type of supervisory role assigned to Hartman without becoming familiar with the evidence to be presented both by and against the SEC and conferring with and advising his less-experienced colleague during the course of the three-day trial. Therefore, I find that Hartman also had personal and substantial responsibility over and participation in the 1973 civil action within the meaning of Rule 1.11(a).

III. CONCLUSION

Because courts have differed as to whether the somewhat subjective standard of the "appearance of impropriety" under former Canon 9 and DR 9–101 was an appropriate one to guide the conduct of lawyers, Model Rule 1.11(a) "sets forth more specifically the circumstances in which concern for public confidence in government necessitates disqualification of a government lawyer." 1981 Draft Notes at 304. The concerns addressed, however, remain the same. The specific circumstances requiring disqualification under Rule 1.11(a) have been met here. Because I find that Boltz and Hartman are representing a private client in connection with a matter in which both of them participated personally and substantially while employed by the SEC, and because the Commission has declined to consent to such representation, these attorneys and Rogers & Wells must be disqualified from further representation of SIPC in this action. Of course, this ruling is intended in no way to suggest any actual wrongdoing on the part of the attorneys involved or their law firm. Rather, this ruling is intended to effectuate the prophylactic purpose of Rule 1.11(a). See *General Motors Corp.,* 501 F.2d at 649.

ORDER

IT IS ORDERED that Gerald E. Boltz, Charles E. Hartman and the law firm of Rogers & Wells are forthwith disqualified from further representing plaintiff Securities Investor Protection Corporation in this action. SIPC is granted 30 days within which to engage new counsel and to substitute such counsel as its attorneys of record. All proceedings in this action are stayed until such new counsel are substituted in or for 30 days, whichever is the shorter period. Until substitution, Rogers & Wells remains as attorney of record and is authorized to attend to any required "housekeeping" or administrative matters.

APPENDIX

SECURITIES AND EXCHANGE COMMISSION
WASHINGTON, D.C. 20549

February 28, 1984

Stephen R. Carley, Esq.
Rogers & Wells
261 South Figueroa Street
Los Angeles, California 90012

> Re: Securities Investor Protection Corp. et al. v. Vigman et al.
> Case No. 83–4742 AWT (C.D.Cal. July 22, 1983).

Dear Mr. Carley:

The Commission has authorized me to inform you that, after considering your request that it waive any personal disqualification of Gerald E. Boltz and Charles R. Hartman, pursuant to Rule 1.11(a) of the American Bar Association's Model Rules of Professional Conduct, to permit them to continue their legal representation of the Securities Investor Protection Corporation, it has declined to do so. I would appreciate your conveying the Commission's determination to the court. By copy of this letter, I am notifying the proponents of the disqualification motion, and the other parties to this litigation, of the Commission's decision.

After a hearing on January 9, 1984, on a motion to disqualify Messrs. Boltz and Hartman, and Rogers & Wells as counsel for SIPC, filed by Isadore Diamond and joined in by Magnetic Technologies, Inc., in the above-captioned case, Judge A. Wallace Tashima directed counsel for SIPC to consult with the Securities and Exchange Commission to determine whether the Commission would, pursuant to Rule 1.11(a), waive any personal disqualification of Messrs. Boltz and Hartman. Subsequently, by letter dated January 10, 1984, you requested that the Commission consent to such a waiver to permit Messrs. Boltz and Hartman to continue their legal representation of SIPC.

In reviewing this matter, the Commission has considered only the question of waiver of disqualification personal to Messrs. Boltz and Hartman, and has assumed for purposes of a response to the court's inquiry that the predicate requirements for the applicability of Model Rule 1.11(a), i.e., that the captioned action and the earlier *SEC v. Newport Securities Inc.* action are the same particular matter and that Messrs. Boltz and Hartman had personal and substantial responsibility for both matters. It has, therefore, made no determinations with respect to those issues.

The question presented in connection with this request is one of first impression for the Commission. As you know, the Model Rules have only been recently adopted. Prior American Bar Association restrictions on post-government employment included no proviso permitting consent by the former government client to a representation which was prohibited by existing ethical rules.*

A major premise underlying the disqualification rule applicable to former government employees is the recognition that lawyers for the government have the opportunity to abuse their governmental positions by conducting the government's business in a manner designed to advance their post-government careers. Therefore, a rule which prohibits former government lawyers from participating, after leaving government service, in matters for which they had responsibility while government employees discourages the thought of future employment from intruding in decisionmaking by the government lawyer. Of equal importance, such a rule serves to maintain public confidence in the objectivity of government lawyers, and that their conduct, on the public's behalf, is not motivated by self-interest.

The Commission recognizes that the participation of Messrs. Boltz and Hartman in the present action will not, in a narrow sense, harm the Commission. Moreover, the Commission has no reason to believe that any actions which Messrs. Boltz and Hartman took while in the Commission's employ were motivated by considerations related to their post-government careers. Nonetheless, the Commission believes that as a general matter, a policy of waiving the personal disqualification of former Commission lawyers to permit them to participate in matters which they handled while on the staff could undermine the public's confidence in the activities of the Commission's lawyers. After reviewing the factors relevant to this case, the Commission sees nothing unique in this situation which would warrant deviating from that general principle. Therefore, the Commission has determined that it would not waive any disqualification personal to Messrs. Boltz and Hartman, pursuant to Rule 1.11(a).

Very truly yours,

/s/ Daniel L. Goelzer/ms
Daniel L. Goelzer
General Counsel

---

* While Model Rule 1.11(a) permits a government agency to waive the personal disqualification of its former lawyers, 18 U.S.C. 207, the federal post-employment statute would, if applicable, presumably eliminate any such discretionary action by a federal agency. While authoritative interpretations of Section 207 are the province of the Office of Government Ethics and the Department of Justice, it appears that Section 207 does not apply in this instance.

The Definition of "Matter"

The court in *SIPC* says that the Model Rules do not define the word "matter" as used in M.R. 1.11(a). The court is in error in this respect. M.R. 1.11(d) says:

> As used in this used in this rule, the term "matter" includes:

> (1) any judicial or other proceeding, application, request for a ruling or other determination, contract, claim, controversy, investigation, charge, accusation, arrest or other particular matter involving a specific party or parties; and

> (2) any other matter covered by the conflict of interest rules of the appropriate government agency.

The court in *SIPC* uses the definition of matter found in ABA Formal Opinion 342, supra. Compare the court's quote from Opinion 342 with the definition in M.R. 1.11(d).

The Department of Justice, in its comments to the Kutak Commission's draft of the Model Rules, argued that "matter" should be defined "to conform to ABA Formal Opinion 342, where it was limited to activities akin to litigation between identifiable parties." It also argued that the final version of the Model Rules should make clear that the definition of "matter" does not include "such prior government activities as drafting proposed legislation, participation in rulemaking, or reviewing government contracts [because an] overly broad categorization of disqualifying activity could impede government hiring significantly." Letter from Assistant Attorney General Jonathan C. Rose to Robert J. Kutak, July 23, 1982, page 2.

Are these activities included in the definition adopted as M.R. 1.11(d)?

Government Consent

If the lawyers for SIPC had formerly represented another private party against Vigman, they could represent SIPC now because M.R. 1.9 only applies when interests of the former and present clients are adverse. When consent was requested in *SIPC,* the SEC refused on the basis of its general policy. Is the SEC's general policy wise? What would be wrong with a policy to grant consent, absent special circumstances, whenever the lawyer was on the same side of the matter in the private case as she was when she worked for the government?

When the Former Client is Another Level of Government

An oft-cited case, discussed in *SIPC,* involving "same side" representation by a former government lawyer is General Motors Corp. v.

City of New York, 501 F.2d 639 (2d Cir.1974). In that case the lawyer while working for the federal government helped develop an antitrust case against General Motors. Later, in private practice, he was retained by New York City to handle a similar antitrust case against General Motors. The court held that the lawyer was disqualified because his prior involvement in the matter was substantial and his arrangement with New York City (he was hired on a contingent fee basis) was private employment. The fact that New York City was on the "same side" as the Federal Government was not enough to eliminate the "appearance of impropriety".

ABA Formal Opinion 342 states that the restrictions on former government lawyers should not apply if the new employer is another government agency. Footnote 18 of that opinion says that this construction is consistent with *General Motors* because in that case the court found that the lawyer's employment by the city constituted private employment. How does working on a contingent basis turn the government employment into private employment?

The Comment to M.R. 1.11 takes up this issue directly:

> When the client is an agency of one government, that agency should be treated as a private client for purposes of this Rule if the lawyer thereafter represents an agency of another government, as when a lawyer represents a city and subsequently is employed by a federal agency.

What about a lawyer who transfers from one agency of government to another agency of the same government? Should one agency of government be treated as the same client as another agency of government—thereby mooting conflict questions? Would your answer change if the first "agency" was the Congress and the second "agency" was the White House legal team?

Confidential Government Information

As used in M.R. 1.11(b), the phrase "confidential government information" protects the confidences of *third* parties, not the confidences of the government itself, which are protected by M.R. 1.6. M.R. 1.11(b) provides that a lawyer who, by virtue of her former government employment, has "confidential government information about a person . . . may not represent a private client whose interests are adverse to that person in a matter in which the information could be used to the material disadvantage of that person." The government has no power to waive this provision.

The trigger for M.R. 1.11(b) is not whether the *matters* are the same, but whether the lawyer has confidential government information about a third party. Confidential government information is defined in M.R. 1.11(e) as "information which has been obtained under governmental authority and which, at the time this rule is applied, the government is prohibited by law from disclosing to the public or has a legal privilege not to disclose, and which is not otherwise available to the public."

In light of M.R. 1.11(b), consider again the question of whether one level of government should be treated as a private client with respect to 1.11(a)'s prohibitions. Consider again whether one agency of government should be considered a private client with respect to former employment by a different agency of the same government. In thinking about the latter point, keep in mind that government agencies are not free to share information gathered about private parties with other agencies at their own discretion. Other law may restrict the transfer of information between government agencies. See, e.g., Fed.R.Crim.P. 6(e).

Note, Professional Ethics in Government Side–Switching, 96 Harv. L.Rev. 1914 (1983), examines the complicated ethical questions raised when the government changes its position in a lawsuit, moving from one side of the controversy to another—usually due to a change in administrations. This question is examined more closely in Chapter 9 below at pp. 804–805, 815.

Moving From Private Practice into Government Service

M.R. 1.11(c)(1) governs situations where a lawyer moves from private practice into government service. It is a counterpart to 1.11(a) and like that provision applies even if the present client (the government) is on the "same side" as the former client. The exception in M.R. 1.11(c) allows the present government lawyer to proceed in the same matter if law expressly allows *or* if "no one is, or by lawful delegation may be, authorized to act in the lawyer's stead in the matter." This exception prevents the conflicts rules from paralyzing the government in those rare cases where the only person able to take the case for the government has a conflict.

M.R. 1.11(c)(1) has no consent provision. Whether the government lawyer can proceed on the *same side* of a matter in which she worked for a private client is not determined by whether the private client consents. Whether a government lawyer can proceed in a matter in which her former private client's interests are *adverse* to the government, is governed by M.R. 1.9(a). Moreover, whenever a government lawyer proceeds in a matter she handled while in private practice M.R. 1.9(c) and M.R. 1.6 protect the former private client's confidences.

Generally see Rotunda, Ethical Problems in Federal Agency Hiring of Private Attorneys, 1 Geo. J. Legal Ethics 85 (1987).

Can the Government be Disqualified by Imputation?

If one lawyer in the government is disqualified because of prior representation of a private client (or for any other reason), is the entire office disqualified?

M.R. 1.11(c) is silent on the question. M.R. 1.10 is inapplicable to government law departments. Hence, there is no rule prohibiting a government law department (e.g., a prosecutor's office or a city counsel's office) from proceeding when one of its lawyers is disqualified. Nor is there any rule prescribing the manner in which such an office could proceed in this situation, e.g., by screening.

Would it nevertheless be prudent for a government law office to screen a lawyer who had formerly represented a private client against whom the office is now engaged?

The case law in this area arises primarily out of criminal trials. Typically, the defendant seeks to disqualify the state prosecutor's office (or the U.S. Attorney's office) on the ground that one of the lawyers in that office formerly represented the accused or a co-defendant or a witness in connection with the same case. Most state courts hold that the government should be allowed to proceed as long as the disqualified lawyer is not personally involved. Florida v. Cote, 538 So.2d 1356 (Fla. App.1989); People v. Lopez, 155 Cal.App.3d 813, 202 Cal.Rptr. 333 (1984); State v. Laughlin, 232 Kan. 110, 652 P.2d 690 (1982); Pisa v. Commonwealth, 378 Mass. 724, 393 N.E.2d 386 (1979); Commonwealth v. Miller, 281 Pa.Super. 392, 422 A.2d 525 (1980). Where the state prosecutor has multiple offices, courts sometimes require that the case be handled by an office in a different location.

Some cases suggest that the entire government might be disqualified, People v. Shinkle, 51 N.Y.2d 417, 415 N.E.2d 909, (1980); and Collier v. Legakes, 98 Nev. 307, 646 P.2d 1219 (1982). In *Shinkle,* the Chief Assistant District Attorney in Sullivan County, the prosecuting office, had formerly been with the Legal Aid Society, where he had been actively involved with the representation of the defendant in the same matter. In vacating the conviction, the New York Court of Appeals implied that a special prosecutor would have to be appointed to reprosecute.

The federal courts have refused to require that the entire United States Attorney's office be disqualified because of one disqualified lawyer. See, e.g., United States v. Caggiano, 660 F.2d 184 (6th Cir. 1981); In re Grand Jury Proceedings, 700 F.Supp. 626 (D.P.R.1988); United States v. Newman, 534 F.Supp. 1113 (S.D.N.Y.1982). Also see Grand Jury Subpoena of Rochin, 873 F.2d 170 (7th Cir.1989), discussed in Chapter 7 at p. 617 above.

If the disqualified prosecutor has not been properly screened, the whole office may be disqualified. For example, in Arkansas v. Dean Foods Prods. Inc., 605 F.2d 380 (8th Cir.1979) the state's entire antitrust division was disqualified from prosecuting an individual, who had been the client of the division's new chief when the chief was in private practice. Compare United States v. Weiner, 578 F.2d 757 (9th Cir. 1978), where defendant moved to disqualify the U.S. Attorney's Office in a securities case because his former lawyer was now working for the SEC. The court denied the motion, finding that the size and complexity of the two government offices made any imputation of knowledge inappropriate.

Other Conflicts Rules for Those in Public Service

M.R. 1.11(c)(2) prohibits government lawyers from negotiating "with any person who is involved as a party or as attorney for a party in a matter in which the lawyer is participating personally and substantially." M.R. 1.12 governs the conflicts faced by former judges or arbitrators. On the ethical responsibilities of law clerks, see Note, The Law Clerk's Duty of Confidentiality, 129 U.Pa.L.Rev. 1230 (1981).

D. REMEDIES

FIRST WISCONSIN MORTGAGE TRUST v. FIRST WISCONSIN CORP.

United States Court of Appeals, Seventh Circuit, 1978, En Banc.
584 F.2d 201.

PELL, CIRCUIT JUDGE.

The ultimate, and apparently first impression, issue in this appeal, stated as simply as possible is whether, when attorneys are judicially determined to have been disqualified to represent a client because of prior simultaneous representation of that client's adversary in litigation, the written product of lawyer work [1] performed during the period of disqualification may be made available to successor counsel. The answer to this issue, in our opinion, is not a per se preclusion but must be a flexible one based upon an examination of the particular facts of the case under consideration.

I.

The plaintiff, First Wisconsin Mortgage Trust (Trust), is a real estate investment trust which was established in 1971 under the sponsorship of the defendant First Wisconsin Corporation (FWC) with a public offering following. Trust was advised on its investments by the defendant First Wisconsin Mortgage Company (Advisor), a wholly owned subsidiary of FWC. Advisor was staffed by employees of the mortgage loan division of the defendant First Wisconsin National Bank (Bank), also a subsidiary of FWC. FWC was jointly involved in various loan transactions with Bank. We ordinarily herein will refer collectively to FWC and its subsidiaries as "defendants."

From the time Trust was established the law firm of Foley & Lardner (Foley) was general counsel to Trust as well as general counsel to FWC and its subsidiaries.

Commencing in 1973 serious loan defaults occurred, a problem which increased in momentum in 1974. Apparently Foley began to

---

1. Throughout this litigation, the parties and the district court have used the generic term "work product" to describe the written work which the defendants desire their present counsel to receive and which the plaintiff contends should not be delivered, a position accepted by the district court. While "work product" as a term probably encompasses substantially broader and more legally sophisticated writings than the routine analyses here in controversy, see Hickman v. Taylor, 329 U.S. 495, 67 S.Ct. 385, 91 L.Ed. 451 (1947), we shall use the term here for convenience of reference.

represent Trust and Bank in the workout of some of the problem loans, but in early 1974 Foley recommended that Trust retain separate counsel to represent it in connection with the problem loans. At that time Trust retained Sonnenschein, Carlin, Nath & Rosenthal (Sonnenschein) as special counsel to represent the Trust with regard to the problem loans. Following retention of Sonnenschein, Trust asserted claims against the defendants, and threatened to file suit thereon. Adversary negotiations followed between the Trust represented by Sonnenschein and defendants represented by Foley. At one point in June 1974 a partial agreement was executed but it apparently did not resolve the underlying disputes. In September 1974 Foley resigned as general counsel to Trust. Indications of the filing of suit by Trust and negotiations between Foley and Sonnenschein to resolve the controversy continued through the winter months of 1974–75. These were not met by success and the present suit was filed in March 1975 with Trust claiming that the defendants violated certain sections of the Federal Securities Laws and Regulations.

Throughout most of 1974 and early 1975, 15 Foley lawyers engaged in an extensive analysis and review of some 300 real estate investment transactions, this being the work product which is the subject matter of the present dispute. There is no indication of any formal objection during the pre-suit adversary negotiations on the part of Trust or its counsel as to Foley representing the defendants. However, immediately following the filing of the suit, Foley, by letter, requested the consent of Trust to its representation of the defendants, which consent was refused by Trust. In June 1975 Sonnenschein advised Foley that if that firm did not withdraw voluntarily, Trust would move its disqualification which in fact was done on August 1, 1975. Defendants opposed the motion on the principal ground that the work done by Foley for Trust did not substantially relate to the issues in the lawsuit. The motion for disqualification was granted on November 16, 1976. First Wisconsin Mortgage Trust v. First Wisconsin Corp., 422 F.Supp. 493 (E.D.Wis. 1976).

On December 15, 1976, Foley withdrew and Mayer, Brown & Platt (Mayer) entered that firm's appearance for the defendants in this action. . . .

Shortly thereafter defendants formally moved the district court for authorization to request access to the Foley work product. This motion was denied on June 14, 1977. First Wisconsin Mortgage Trust v. First Wisconsin Corp., 74 F.R.D. 625 (E.D.Wis.1977). The defendants filed a timely notice of appeal of the work product order and also requested the district court to certify the order for interlocutory appeal under 28 U.S.C. § 1292(b), which certification request was denied on September 15, 1977, subsequent to the filing of the defendants-appellants' original brief in this court. Plaintiffs' August 17, 1977, motion to dismiss the appeal for lack of jurisdiction was taken under advisement by the court together with the merits at oral argument. By a 2–1 decision this court affirmed the district court order on February 24, 1978. First Wisconsin

Mortgage Trust v. First Wisconsin Corp., 571 F.2d 390 (7th Cir.1978). Subsequently upon the granting of the petition to that effect, the case was reheard by the court en banc.

II.

In the opinion of the three-judge panel originally hearing this case, the first issue considered was the plaintiffs' motion to dismiss the appeal for lack of jurisdiction. The entire panel was of the opinion that the appeal was properly before this court. No purpose is served by restating the previous opinion of the court on the matter of jurisdiction. That portion of the prior opinion is therefore adopted as the opinion of the court sitting en banc and part II of the court's prior opinion, 571 F.2d at 392–96, is incorporated herein by reference.

III.

Turning to the merits of this appeal, we do so with the underlying assumption that the disqualification of Foley was correct, the appeal having been dismissed.

That which the defendants seek to secure from the attorneys formerly representing them in the present litigation is, as described by the defendants, the "written work product, consisting essentially of summaries of loan files relating to more than 300 complex transactions, and an explanation limited to an identification of the documents reviewed."

Beginning in 1974 a number of Foley attorneys were engaged in analyzing the various claims being asserted on behalf of Trust and analyzing the loan files regarding such claims. This work continued after suit was filed. The analysis of the loan files was conducted by a team of 15 Foley lawyers for more than a year prior to the ultimate disqualification of that firm in November 1976.

Neither the district court in its opinion, nor the plaintiff in its brief or at oral argument has contradicted the defendants' contention that the loan file summaries are the result of routine lawyer work of a type which any competent lawyer, by spending the substantial time which would be required, could accomplish just as well as did Foley. The work product came into being for the benefit of the defendants. It may be safely assumed that the work was not performed gratuitously by Foley but rather on a compensated fee basis. There is no challenge to the defendants' assertion that the preparation of the loan file summaries was not aided by any confidential information acquired by the Foley lawyers through their prior relationship with Trust. Indeed, it appears that the summaries are no different than they would have been if made in their entirety by lawyers who were strangers to all of the parties.

The district court in its opinion under review here, while noting the contention that no confidential information was involved, in effect found this to be of no significance. . . .

As we read the district court's opinion in this respect, it is saying that because the Foley firm was disqualified from the time litigation was instituted, and in all probability from the very beginning of its representation of the defendants on the matter which ultimately went into litigation, any work performed during this entire period is automatically tainted by the disqualification and is unavailable to the party for whom the work was performed. This, of course, constitutes a sanction for representation subsequently determined to be improper without any independent basis therefor related to the work itself.

In our opinion, such an automatic or per se equation of denial of the work product to the disqualification of representation is not good law and the application of such a rule without more requires reversal. No doubt it will frequently be that the lawyer who is unfortunate enough to become involved in the Goodwin Sands of simultaneously representing clients whose interests either are or thereafter come into conflict, and who ceases representation of one of the clients, will find that the work performed during the period subject to disqualification will have aspects of confidentiality or other unfair detriment to the former client arising from the very fact of the knowledge and acquaintanceship acquired during the period of the prior representation. This does not mean, however, that this is always the situation, or even that it is frequently so. We see no reason for an irrebuttable presumption merely from dual representation in the conflict context to the effect that whenever cause of disqualification exists any lawyer work thereafter is lost work irrespective of its nature or any other pertinent factors.

The present case presents a particularly strong case for justifying a flexible rule in that the order of disqualification did not occur until 15 months after the motion for that purpose. The practical effect of this time frame is that once a motion of disqualification is filed the work performed thereafter is subject to the risk of automatically being wasted work to the detriment of the client. . . . Unfortunately the practical effect might well be to impose a moratorium upon trial preparation for such period of time as it might take to rule upon a motion for disqualification.

A secondary aspect of this matter is that litigation must be ongoing, and the counsel representing the party prior to an ultimate disqualification is confronted with other aspects of the litigation as it proceeds, such as filing responsive pleadings, answering interrogatories, addressing requests for admissions, and production of documents, and in taking part in depositions. In the present case, all of these procedures, other than the work product, which were performed by Foley on behalf of the defendants have been left extant without challenge by Trust.

. . .

With this background in mind, we deem it appropriate to observe that in our opinion a lawyer who is charged with impropriety, here a disqualifying conflict of interest, should not, if he or she reasonably and in good conscience denies the charge, be expected forthwith to withdraw from the representation. Indeed, proper representation of the client might seem to militate against such precipitous action, suggesting instead a vigorous resistance where in good faith it is believed that impropriety does not exist. Leveling the charge of impropriety at opposing counsel, which if sustained would require withdrawal, should not be a standard part of counsel's offensive armament to be used routinely or without reasonable and good faith belief in its necessity. In the present case, we must also observe that we have no basis for discerning lack of good faith on the part of either charging or resisting counsel.

. . .

In the present case the raw materials which Foley had examined and analyzed were loan files which were equally available to the plaintiff for examination and analysis. The work product, the analyses, if "tainted" in the present case are only so by virtue of the application of a per se sanction flowing from the disqualification, and relating back in extent to the beginning of the cause for disqualification. They are not "tainted" by virtue of having been based upon confidential knowledge or other advantage gained during or from the dual representation.

Trust also cites Cord v. Smith, 338 F.2d 516 (9th Cir.1964). We read this case as saying that the disqualified attorney, once disqualified, should not act by way of consultation or advice outside the court to the former client, a result of disqualification which would seem logically to follow and which would not seem to be arguable. We do not read the case, however, as going farther to say that work product which had been achieved during the period prior to the determination of disqualification necessarily is lost to client in whose behalf the work product was produced.

The most recent case coming to our attention, and one decided since the original opinion of this court, is International Business Machines Corporation v. Levin, 579 F.2d 271 (3d Cir.1978). In that case, the . . . court . . . stated what we deem to be an important guiding principle in cases of the present type, namely, that "disqualification in circumstances such as these where specific injury to the moving party has not been shown is primarily justified as a vindication of the integrity of the bar." at 283. . . .

. . .

. . . [W]e have no particular quarrel with the test proposed by the dissent that the cases would "turn upon whether there exists a reasonable possibility of confidential information being used in the formation of, or being passed to substitute counsel through, the work product in question." The dissent after stating this test then proceeds in part II.

C., although first asserting that the possibility of Foley's using confidential information in its work on this case is "inescapable," to engage in speculation as to confidential information which "possibly," or as a "possibility," or even as "a distinct possibility," and finally as "highly probable," could have tainted the work product in question.

The difficulty here, however, is that this contention is made only in the dissenting opinion. Trust was in a position to know whether such possibilities existed, but the argument advanced by the concededly competent counsel now representing Trust contains no such contentions. The record in the case before us, and that is the only case we now need to decide, is devoid of any showing, either directly or by necessary implication, that the routine lawyer work bore the imprint of confidentially acquired or secret information.

· · ·

Comments

In EZ Paintr Corp. v. Padco, Inc., 746 F.2d 1459 (Fed.Cir.1984), two lawyers of the law firm representing Padco had formerly been members of the firm representing EZ Paintr. The court disqualified Padco's firm and limited the turn-over of work product from the disqualified law firm to successor counsel to that prepared before the two tainted lawyers joined the firm. See also Capital City Publishing Co. v. Trenton Times Corp., 1983 WL 1958, 1984–1 Trade Cas. (CCH) P65, 955 (D.C.N.J.1983) (not reported in F.Supp.).

What about consultation between the disqualified firm and substitute counsel? In IBM v. Levin, 579 F.2d 271, 281 (3d Cir.1978), the court upheld the district court's disqualification order, allowing disqualified counsel to turn over work product to and consult with new counsel. In Williams v. TWA, 588 F.Supp. 1037, 1610 (W.D.Mo.1984), the court allowed portions of the disqualified firm's work product to be turned over to new counsel but, citing *IBM v. Levin*, limited consultation to that necessary to explain the work product. See also Manoir–Electroalloys Corp. v. Amalloy Corp., 711 F.Supp. 188, 196 (D.N.J.1989) (where no reason to assume disqualified firm had confidential information, court allowed disqualified lawyers to discuss case with potential successor counsel, turn over its work product, and confer with substitute counsel for sixty days after retention).

On access to work product see also: Developments in the Law—Conflicts of Interests in the Legal Profession, 94 Harv.L.Rev. 1015, 1484–1486 (1981); Comment, The Availability of the Work–Product of a Disqualified Attorney: What Standard?, 127 U.Pa.L.Rev. 1607 (1979); Comment, Access to Work Product of Disqualified Counsel, 46 U.Chi.L. Rev. 443 (1979).

Chapter IX

WHO IS THE CLIENT?

A. INDIVIDUAL OR ENTERPRISE

Introductory Note

A lawyer is required to communicate and confer with the client, M.R. 1.4; to keep the client's secrets, M.R. 1.6 and DR 4–101; to abide by the client's decision on whether to accept a settlement offer, M.R. 1.2(a). When a lawyer represents an entity rather than an individual to whom are these duties owed?

When a lawyer represents a corporation, is communicating with the Chief Executive Officer always sufficient? Should the lawyer ever insist on communicating with the Board? The shareholders?

When the CEO communicates with the lawyer is the attorney-client privilege personally held by the CEO or may the corporation waive it against the CEO's wishes? Who may waive the privilege on the corporation's behalf?

These questions confront a lawyer for an organization. They also confront lawyers for partnerships, lawyers for trustees and other fiduciaries, and lawyers for the government. The Code provides little guidance on these difficult questions. EC 5–18, the Code's primary provision on this subject, states:

> A lawyer employed or retained by a corporation or similar entity owes his allegiance to the entity and not to a stockholder, director, officer, employee, representative, or other person connected with the entity. In advising the entity, a lawyer should keep paramount its interests and his professional judgment should not be influenced by the personal desires of any person or organization. Occasionally, a lawyer for an entity is requested by a stockholder, director, officer, employee, representative, or other person connected with the entity to represent him in an individual capacity; in such case the lawyer may serve the individual only if the lawyer is convinced that differing interests are not present.

When organizational peace reigns and all the organization's agents lawfully fulfill their responsibilities to the entity, there is little problem deciding who personifies the client: it is the person designated by the organization's powers-that-be to deal with the lawyer. The problems arise when the person designated to speak for the client acts in a way that may harm the entity or when there is infighting over control of the entity. Who personifies the client then?

MEEHAN v. HOPPS

District Court of Appeal, First District, Division 1, California, 1956.
144 Cal.App.2d 284, 301 P.2d 10.

BRAY, JUSTICE.

This is an appeal from a certain order in an action brought by respondents as plaintiffs, against appellants as defendants, for an accounting and other relief on behalf of the policyholders, creditors and stockholders of the Rhode Island Insurance Company, in which it is charged that Stewart B. Hopps, former director, member of the executive committee and chairman of the board of the company, dominated and managed the company's affairs for his own personal gain in violation of his fiduciary duties. Defendants moved the trial court to restrain and enjoin the Providence, Rhode Island, law firm of Edwards & Angell, . . . from further participation in the case and from disclosing information pertaining thereto. The motion was based upon the alleged dual relationship of Edwards & Angell towards Hopps and a claim that Hopps had turned over to that firm as his lawyers certain files, documents and other information which plaintiffs have used and have threatened to use against him in the present action. After a hearing the motion was denied. Defendants appeal.

. . .

The Law.

With legislative authority the Board of Governors of the State Bar of California have formulated rules of professional conduct approved by the Supreme Court. These rules are binding upon all members of the State Bar. Bus. and Prof.Code § 6077.[4] Applicable here are Rule 5: "A member of the State Bar shall not accept employment adverse to a client or former client, without the consent of the client or former client, relating to a matter in reference to which he has obtained confidential information by reason of or in the course of his employment by such client or former client"; Rule 7: "A member of the State Bar shall not represent conflicting interests, except with the consent of all parties concerned." Section 6068, Business and Professions Code, provides: It is the duty of an attorney "(e) To maintain inviolate the confidence, and at every peril to himself to preserve the secrets, of his client."

As the law is clear, we deem it unnecessary to cite the many cases holding that an attorney who attempts to use against the interests of his former client information gained while the attorney-client relationship existed, may be enjoined from so doing.

4. The firm of Edwards & Angell are the attorneys for the receiver, and the attorneys of that firm representing the receiver in the action were admitted by the trial court to the California State Bar for the purpose of participating in this case. None of them appear of record on this appeal.

The question first to be determined is:

1. Had There Been an Attorney–Client Relationship Between Counsel and Hopps?

The determination of that question is one of law. De Long v. Miller, 133 Cal.App.2d 175, 178, 283 P.2d 762. However, where there is a conflict in the evidence the factual basis for the determination must first be determined, and it is for the trial court to evaluate the evidence. Id., 133 Cal.App.2d at page 179, 283 P.2d at page 764.

On the question of whether counsel ever represented Hopps as his attorney, the evidence is directly conflicting. Concededly the firm never charged nor received payment from Hopps for any services whatever. The services which Hopps claims were for him personally were paid for by Rhode Island. Soon after Hopps became connected with the company, counsel ceased to act as general counsel for it. Thereafter they were employed on special matters from time to time. At the time counsel first met Hopps they were working for Rhode Island on a merger of the Merchants Insurance Company into the former. Rhode Island's chairman asked counsel to draw a contract for the employment of Hopps, which was done. Hopps claims that the attorney drawing the contract advised him as well as the company. The attorney denied this and claimed that Hopps consulted his own lawyer, Farber, exclusively concerning the contract. Hopps testified that he confided in and was advised by counsel concerning his personal involvement in the affairs of Rhode Island; that he turned over to counsel his personal files; that Attorney Winsor of the firm was a friendly advisor and legal confidant and familiar with Hopps' personal affairs; that the firm undertook to represent Hopps' personal interest in the California controversy [5] and in a number of other matters. We deem it unnecessary to detail the evidence concerning the matters testified to by Hopps as showing a personal attorney and client relationship between him and counsel. Suffice it to say that evidence to the contrary on all matters was presented by Edwards & Angell. The question is primarily one of credibility. The trial court obviously disbelieved Hopps.

There are four matters in which appellants particularly claim that counsel acted personally for Hopps.

(1) The preparation of the employment contract between Rhode Island and Hopps. While Hopps does not claim that he employed counsel in this behalf but that Gilman, of counsel, advised him personally, Gilman denied this. Gilman had been handling for Rhode Island a proposed merger of Merchants Insurance Company with it. Watson, Rhode Island's chairman, asked Gilman to draw the employment contract. Gilman conferred with both Hopps and Watson, sending copies of the contract when prepared to both. In the letter to Hopps accompa-

---

5. This was a conflict between the Insurance Commissioner of California and Rhode Island, see Rhode Island Ins. Co. v. Downey, 95 Cal.App.2d 220, 212 P.2d 965, in which the actions of Hopps were looked upon with disfavor by the commissioner.

nying the proposed contract Gilman stated that if it was not satisfactory to Hopps Gilman would take up with Watson any proposed changes.
It frequently happens that one retained by a client to draft an agreement between him and another, will send such agreement to the other,
asking for the latter's suggestions concerning it, which suggestions the
drafter will take up with his client. This statement did not convert
Gilman's relationship from attorney for Rhode Island to attorney for
Hopps in any respect. The agreement was not to become effective
unless the merger was made, and provided that Hopps was to have the
right to be interested in the Merchants Insurance Company's dealing
with Rhode Island and was only required to give part of his time to the
latter. Winsor, of counsel, called on Hopps in New York in connection
with the merger. None of these matters changed counsel's relationship
as attorney for Rhode Island into attorney for Hopps as well. In his
deposition Hopps stated that the work done by counsel on the employment contract was done for Rhode Island. At the trial he retracted
that statement. . . .

   (2) Approximately nine years after the contract was drawn, counsel
were employed by Rhode Island in connection with a controversy with
Cuban interests. It involved nine companies and individuals including
Hopps and Rhode Island on the American side, and seven on the Cuban
side. It was actually a fight for control. Although the controversy had
been going on for approximately seven years, counsel had nothing to do
with it until approximately three months prior to its settlement. At
Watson's request, counsel were employed to represent Rhode Island.
At counsel's request Hopps prepared and gave them data concerning
the background and history of the controversy and his interest in it.
One of the most important problems was whether a proxy held by
Hopps or those held by the Cuban interests should prevail. Hopps
prepared memoranda concerning these, sending copies to Rhode Island's executive committee as well as to counsel. Counsel advised
Rhode Island that only Hopps' proxy could be considered. The fact that
counsel so advised, and the other matters they did in connection with
the controversy, did not make them attorneys for Hopps.

   (3) The Pioneer Equitable Settlement. This involved a dispute
between Rhode Island on one side, the Pioneer Equitable and other
companies and an individual on the other. Hopps had interests on both
sides. There were a number of lawyers representing Rhode Island in
this matter including counsel, who were employed by Rhode Island as
special counsel in connection with a suit over custodian funds included
in the controversy. Counsel denied Hopps' assertion that their special
duty in the controversy involved any consideration by them of Hopps'
personal interests nor any advice to him concerning them.

   (4) The California controversy. As above stated, this was a controversy between Rhode Island and the Insurance Commissioner of California. . . . In addition to proceedings in the federal court, counsel
endeavored to work out a settlement of the controversy with the
commissioner. Richards, of counsel, after consultation with Hopps and

the obtaining of data from Hopps and other company officers, went to California for that purpose. Richards was told by the California authorities that the commissioner objected to Hopps' association with the company. Richards testified that he told them that he would not discuss personalities, but wanted to work out an arrangement by which the company could continue in business in California. During the negotiations in California, Hopps came out as well as other members of counsel, and together they prepared memoranda to be submitted to the commissioner's counsel. Here again there was nothing done by counsel or information received by them, which in anywise made them attorneys for Hopps. While they refused to agree to Hopps' removal from a position of authority in the company, or even to discuss such a change, they were not representing Hopps in so doing, but as attorneys for the company were refusing to discuss the matter of the removal of its president.

Appellants point out that the "contemporaneous record" is replete with instances where Hopps presented memoranda and material to counsel and spent considerable time in conference with counsel, all to assist them in the preparation of the various proceedings in which they were engaged for the corporation. These are matters which Hopps' position as an officer of the corporation, and particularly one who dictated, or at least was instrumental in determining, the policy of the corporation in the particular matter, required him to give the corporation.

Disregarding the testimony of Hopps, as we are required to do on this appeal, we can find nothing in the record to show any relationship of attorney and client between Hopps and counsel, nor that he gave them any data, or disclosed to them any information which he as an officer of the company was not required by his position to do, nor which they as attorneys for the company in the matters entrusted to them, were not entitled to receive.

2. Effect of Representation of the Company.

Appellant has not cited, nor have we found, any case holding that an attorney for a corporation is disqualified from representing it in an action brought by it against one of its officers, nor that in such an action the attorney may not use information received from such officer in connection with company matters. The attorney for a corporation represents it, its stockholders and its officers in their representative capacity. He in nowise represents the officers personally. It would be a sorry state of affairs if when a controversy arises between an attorney's corporate client and one of its officers he could not use on behalf of his client information which that officer was required by reason of his position with the corporation to give to the attorney.

Kingman, of counsel, testified that on May 26, 1950, White, the then president of the company, came to counsel's office and informed him that the company would have to go into receivership and that Hopps stated that he was going to get counsel appointed as co-counsel for the receiver with another firm of attorneys. . . . The fact that counsel, as attorney for the receiver, requested and received Hopps' cooperation in certain receivership matters, that prior to their appointment as receiver, counsel on behalf of the company had prepared an answer in which it alleged that the officers, directors and agents of the company were not at fault, in nowise affected their right to represent the receiver, nor to participate in an action in which the receiver claims that Hopps, one of the officers, was at fault. If Hopps' action in arranging for the appointment did not constitute a consent to counsel being appointed attorneys for the receiver and acting in all respects as their duty as attorneys for the receiver required, such action indicates at least that Hopps originally did not consider that counsel had been his personal attorneys nor that he had disclosed to them any information over and above what his position with the company required him to disclose.

Cases cited by appellants where attorneys were enjoined from proceeding against former clients are easily distinguishable from our case. In all of them the relationship of attorney and client actually had existed between the attorney and the party against whom the attorney was now acting. . . . Consolidated Theatres v. Warner Bros. Cir. Man. Corp., 2 Cir., 1954, 216 F.2d 920: An attorney who had been in the office of the law firm defending a motion picture producer in antitrust litigation attempted to represent an exhibitor's anti-trust damage suit against the producer. United States v. Bishop, 6 Cir., 1937, 90 F.2d 65: An attorney represented the government on the first trial of an action by a veteran on a war risk policy. On the second trial of the same issue he attempted to represent the veteran. Watson v. Watson, 1939, 171 Misc. 175, 11 N.Y.S.2d 537: A wife sued to annul a marriage on the ground of the husband's previous conviction of a crime. The attorneys who had defended the husband in the criminal proceeding and who had obtained from him the history of his life attempted to represent the wife in the annulment action. The other cases cited by appellants relate to situations where the attorney either had represented the person whom he was now appearing against in the same matter or one connected with it or had advised other counsel representing the person he was now proceeding against. In none of the cases was there a situation where the attorney for a corporation was appearing for the corporation adversely to a former officer thereof.

Assuming that some of the information obtained from Hopps by counsel as representative of the corporation is that upon which the receiver's contention that Hopps dominated the corporation, its officers and companies, to its damage, is partially based, nevertheless such fact would not prevent counsel from representing either the corporation or the receiver in a controversy with Hopps nor from using that information against him. . . . If this were true, then the attorney representing a corporation in any given matter becomes the personal attorney of each stockholder because the attorney's actions benefiting the corporation likewise benefit the stockholder. Such relationship would disqualify the attorney from acting adversely to the stockholder concerning that particular matter in any controversy between the stockholder and a third party, but obviously would not prevent the attorney from representing the corporation in any controversy between it and the stockholder. As attorneys for the corporation, counsel's first duty is to it. Likewise, as an officer of the corporation, it was Hopps' duty to disclose to it all information necessary for its purposes. To hold that the giving of such information in that more or less intimate relationship which necessarily must exist between an officer of the corporation and its attorneys would prevent the corporation attorneys from thereafter using it in favor of the corporation in litigation against the officer, would be unfair to the corporation and its stockholders, and would violate the above mentioned very important precept, namely, that the attorney's first duty is to his client. . . .

Questions and Comments

The rule in *Meehan* that a lawyer for a corporation represents the corporation and not the individual officers, directors or shareholders is the general rule. See EC 5–18 and M.R. 1.13(a). As the court notes in *Meehan,* the working relationship between counsel and the managing officers of a company can easily blur the distinction (in the mind and actions of lawyer and corporate official alike) between representing the company and representing the individual. M.R. 1.13(d) requires that a lawyer for an organization provide corporate officers or other constituents something like a Miranda warning about who it is the lawyer represents whenever "it is apparent that the organization's interests are adverse to those of the constituents with whom the lawyer is dealing." Would this have helped in the *Meehan* case?

When the lawyer negotiated the employment contract between Hopps and the corporation, was he acting as lawyer for both parties? What must an officer show to prove that the organization's lawyer also represented her as an individual?

Note on *E.F. Hutton & Co. v. Brown*

In E.F. Hutton & Co. v. Brown, 305 F.Supp. 371 (S.D.Tex.1969), the court disqualified the firm representing Hutton on the ground that previously the firm had jointly represented Brown, a former vice-president of Hutton, as an individual. The firm claimed that it had only represented the company and that its dealings with Brown were in his official capacity as an officer of Hutton.

As vice-president of Hutton, Brown had authorized a loan to Hurbraugh to be secured by Westec common stock. Shortly after the loan was made the SEC suspended trading in Westec stock because of suspected trading illegalties. This resulted in legal difficulties for Hutton, including an SEC investigation and a number of civil suits. One of the key issues in the suits was whether Brown knew that the loan would be used to purchase stock. Brown was twice called to testify about this matter. Hutton's lawyers discussed with him his forthcoming testimony and told him that they would accompany him to the hearings. At both hearings, Brown was asked if the lawyers with him were his lawyers, and he responded that they were. Thereafter, Hutton fired Brown and sued him for negligence in authorizing the Hurbraugh loan. When Brown claimed that his communications with Hutton's lawyers were privileged, the lawyers argued that his having identified them as his counsel at the hearings surprised them because they had previously explained to Brown that they represented Hutton and not him individually. (Brown disputed this.) The lawyers had not corrected Brown's assertion at either hearing.

The court placed great emphasis on these facts, stating:

> An attorney's appearance in a judicial or semi-judicial proceeding creates a presumption that an attorney-client relationship exists between the attorney and the person with whom he appears. This presumption shifts to Hutton, the party denying the existence of the relationship, the burden of persuasion. When the relationship is also evidenced by the entry of a formal appearance by the attorney on behalf of the person with whom he appears, the presumption becomes almost irrebuttable . . .

Id. at 387.

The fact that Brown had not paid the lawyers' fee and that he had never asked the firm to represent him were held not to overcome the relationship implied by the conduct of the lawyers at the hearings.

Hutton's lawyers argued that they represented Brown only in his official capacity, arguing that at the time of the hearings the interests of Hutton and Brown were identical, that Brown was present only as Hutton's spokesperson, and that they went with him to fulfill their duties to Hutton. The court rejected these arguments: (1) The SEC was investigating both Hutton and Brown, hence Brown testified both as Hutton's agent and as an individual. (2) Even if Hutton's and Brown's interests were identical, the fact that Hutton needed counsel did not imply that Brown did not need counsel as an individual. (3) It was unlikely that Brown's and Hutton's interests coincided at the time of the hearings; therefore, saying they represented Brown meant Brown as an individual. The court further found that Brown's belief that he was represented individually was reasonable, given the failure of counsel to correct the record and the fact that Hutton faced civil penalties, but Brown faced a potential prison term.

On the ramifications of its holding, the court observed:

> [N]ot all corporate counsel appearing with corporate officers who are called to testify will risk disqualification. Only those counsel who permit the officer to believe that they represent him individually will disable themselves from appearing in subsequent litigation against him. And it is eminently proper to disqualify these, for

they are the persons who are in a position, and have the obligation, to ensure that there is no misunderstanding by the officer.

Id. at 398.

Compare United States v. Keplinger, 776 F.2d 678 (7th Cir.1985), where a corporate officer, who had been convicted of mail and wire fraud, claimed that evidence admitted against him should have been excluded under the attorney-client privilege. The corporation's lawyers had accompanied him to a meeting with the FDA, and FDA officials had referred to the lawyers as "your counsel." The court distinguished *Hutton* on the grounds that the lawyers had not entered a formal appearance as counsel, and that the officer's subjective belief that counsel was representing him as an individual was not sufficient to demonstrate that an attorney-client relationship existed: "no individual attorney-client relationship can be inferred without some finding that the potential client's subjective belief is minimally reasonable." 776 F.2d at 701. See also Bernstein v. Crazy Eddie, Inc., 702 F.Supp. 962, 988 (E.D.N.Y.1988).

In *Hutton,* the court said that corporate lawyers who find themselves in situations where the corporate officer might misconstrue the lawyer's participation as individual representation have two options:

> First, counsel might have elected to make themselves available to represent both Brown and Hutton. Had they done so, their duty to both of their potential clients would have required them to inform each fully. The extent of disclosure necessary would be governed by the reason for requiring counsel to disclose: to enable each potential client to make a reasoned choice. In the context of the two investigatory hearings at which Brown testified, full disclosure would have required counsel to apprise each potential client of the existence of any potential conflict, to advise each of the consequences of a joint representation, to explain to each the serious consequences which could occur to either or both as a result of Brown's testimony at the hearings, and to inform each that either was free to retain independent counsel. Only then would either Hutton or Brown have been in a position to make a knowing waiver of its or his right to retain independent counsel.

> Counsel's second option was to inform Brown that when they appeared at the hearings, they would do so solely on Hutton's behalf, and that if Brown had any interest which failed to coincide with some interest of Hutton's his interest would go unprotected unless he employed personal counsel. By so advising Brown, they would have prevented an attorney-client relationship between themselves and him from arising.

305 F.Supp. 396–97.

If Hutton's lawyers had exercised option one, the court implies that they would not have been disqualified from suing Brown in this case. Is that correct, in light of M.R. 1.9 and the *Brennan's* case in Chapter 8 above? See Cooke v. Laidlaw, Adams & Peck, 126 A.D.2d 453, 510

N.Y.S.2d 597 (App.Div.1987) (firm that had jointly represented corporation and officer disqualified from representing corporation against the now-former officer involving matter substantially related to joint representation even if no confidences were in fact communicated to lawyer by officer).

Who Controls the Corporation's Attorney–Client Privilege?

Corporations like natural persons may claim an attorney-client privilege. See Upjohn v. United States, 449 U.S. 383, 101 S.Ct. 677 (1981), printed in Chapter 4 above. This privilege belongs to the corporation, not individual corporate officers, see Citibank N.A. v. Andros, 666 F.2d 1192, 1195 (8th Cir.1981); In re Grand Jury Proceedings, 434 F.Supp. 648, 650 (E.D.Mich.1977), aff'd, 570 F.2d 562 (6th Cir. 1978); United States v. Piccini, 412 F.2d 591, 593 (2d Cir.1969), cert. denied, 397 U.S. 917 (1970).

In CFTC v. Weintraub, 471 U.S. 343, 105 S.Ct. 1986 (1985), the issue was whether the trustee for a bankrupt corporation could waive the privilege on the corporation's behalf and against the wishes of the former directors of the debtor. Weintraub had been counsel to the now-bankrupt company. When called before the Commodity Future Trading Corporation to testify about the company's transactions, he refused citing attorney-client privilege. The trustee in bankruptcy then waived the privilege on the corporation's behalf, but former officers intervened and attempted to assert it.

The Supreme Court held that the trustee, as the company's current management, controlled the privilege on the company's behalf. The former directors argued that vesting control of the privilege with the trustee would leave shareholders' interests unprotected or at least always subservient to the interests of creditors. The court pointed out that the trustee had fiduciary duties that ran to both creditors and shareholders. The court acknowledged that the privilege could be used by trustees in favor of creditors at the expense of shareholders, but said this was "in keeping with the hierarchy of interests created by the bankruptcy laws." 471 U.S. at 344, 105 S.Ct. at 1989.

What about communications, prior to the filing of bankruptcy between corporate management and bankruptcy counsel? Can the bankruptcy trustee waive the privilege as to those communications? In Gekas v. Pipin, 69 B.R. 671 (D.C.Ill.1987), Pipin argued that communications to secure bankruptcy advice were an exception to the general rule in *Weintraub*. He argued that the trustee is the agent of the debtor's unsecured creditors and that the company, as a separate entity, is entitled to separate legal representation in bankruptcy. The court rejected this argument, pointing out that *Weintraub* was grounded on the proposition that the trustee assumed a role analogous to the management of a solvent corporation.

A Privilege for Individual Corporate Officers?

Unlike the court in *Meehan,* the court in *Hutton* found an attorney-client relationship between the corporate officer and corporate counsel. Nevertheless, *Hutton* also held that the officer had no privilege to assert against the company:

> Brown gave information to counsel concerning the Hurbraugh loan transaction long before counsel appeared with him at the SEC and bankruptcy hearings. As a corporate officer, Brown's duty to his corporate employer required him to furnish this information to counsel at Hutton's request. In fact, because Brown obtained his knowledge within the scope of his position as an officer of Hutton, the information which he conveyed to counsel was, as a matter of law, already known to Hutton. The attorney-client privilege is therefore not available to Brown against Hutton, since all information he gave to counsel already was known to Hutton, and since Brown gave the information to counsel knowing that counsel, in turn, would convey it to Hutton's New York management.

> 305 F.Supp. at 400–01.

The *Hutton* court offered three grounds for denying Brown the privilege: (1) he gave the information before he was being represented as an individual; (2) since he had a duty to give counsel the information, what was known to him in his official capacity was, under law, already known to the company; and (3) he gave the information with the understanding that Hutton would be privy to it. Together these reasons suggest that a corporate officer, who had been represented as an individual and joint client with the corporation, may never be able to assert a privilege against the corporation itself. Several courts so hold. See, e.g., *Piccini,* supra, 412 F.2d at 593; Polycast Technology Corp. v. Uniroyal Inc., 125 F.R.D. 47, 49 (S.D.N.Y.1989); In re O.P.M. Leasing Services, Inc., 13 B.R. 64, 67–68 & n. 11 (S.D.N.Y.1981), aff'd, 670 F.2d 383 (2d Cir.1982).

But other courts have held that the officer sometimes may assert the privilege against the corporation. See, e.g., Diversified Industries, Inc. v. Meredith, 572 F.2d 596 (8th Cir.1977); In re Grand Jury, 434 F.Supp. 648 (E.D.Mich.1977), aff'd, 570 F.2d 562 (6th Cir.1978). See also Eureka Investment Corporation, N.V. v. Chicago Title Insurance Co., 743 F.2d 932, 936 (D.C.Cir.1984); Odmark v. Westside Bankcorporation, Inc., 636 F.Supp. 552 (W.D.Wa.1986).

In In the Matter of Bevill, Bresler & Schulman, 805 F.2d 120 (3d Cir.1986), the court held that a personal attorney-client privilege could not be asserted against the corporation as to communications made by the officer about matters within the officer's "roles and functions" within the corporation. The court, however, recognized the possibility that the officers could have a personal attorney-client privilege as to communications "not related to their role as officers of the corporation." Id. at 125. For this proposition and for the test to determine the scope of any such personal privilege, the district court in *Bevill* cited In re Grand Jury Investigation No. 83–30557, 575 F.Supp. 777 (N.D.Ga. 1983). 805 F.2d at 123 (explaining with apparent approval the district court's reasoning).

In *In re Grand Jury* supra, the court held that the corporate officers who claim a personal attorney-client privilege must show: (1) that they approached counsel for the purpose of seeking legal advice; (2) that they made it clear that they were seeking advice as individuals; (3) that counsel dealt with them as individuals, knowing that a possible conflict could arise; (4) that their conversations were confidential; and (5) "that the substance of their conversation did not concern matters within the company or the general affairs of the company." 575 F.Supp. at 780.

This test is difficult to meet, particularly the last requirement. This may explain why those courts accepting the concept of such a personal privilege rarely sustain its invocation. Is the *Bevill/Grand Jury* test consistent with the general rules on privilege between joint clients? Review the note on this subject in Chapter 4 above at pp. 228–229.

YABLONSKI v. UNITED MINE WORKERS OF AMERICA

United States Court of Appeals, District of Columbia Circuit,
1971. 448 F.2d 1175.

Before McGOWAN, ROBINSON and WILKEY, CIRCUIT JUDGES.

PER CURIAM:

This is an action under § 501 of the Labor–Management Reporting and Disclosure Act[1] brought by the late Joseph A. Yablonski and 48 other members of the United Mine Workers of America against the UMWA and three named officers—Boyle, President; Titler, Vice President; Owens, Secretary–Treasurer—asking for an accounting of UMWA funds disbursed by them and for restitution of funds allegedly misappropriated and misspent.

No trial on the merits has been had. The issue on this appeal is whether the law firm regularly representing the UMWA, who originally entered an appearance for the UMWA and the three individual officer-defendants, should be allowed to continue its representation of the UMWA after it withdrew as counsel for the individual defendants. The District Court found that the regular UMWA outside counsel was not disqualified from continuing its representation in this action, but

---

1. 29 U.S.C. § 501(b) (1964) provides *inter alia:*

When any officer, agent, shop steward, or representative of any labor organization is alleged to have violated the duties declared in subsection (a) of this section and the labor organization or its governing board or officers refuse or fail to sue or recover damages or secure an accounting or other appropriate relief within a reasonable time after being requested to do so by any member of the labor organization, such member may sue such officer, agent, shop steward, or representative in any district court of the United States or in any State court of competent jurisdiction to recover damages or secure an accounting or other appropriate relief for the benefit of the labor organization.

for reasons enunciated infra we hold that in the particular circumstances of this case such representation should be discontinued.

After the action was filed in December 1969, appellant-plaintiffs filed in May 1970 a motion to disqualify counsel on the grounds (1) that the compensation of the regular UMWA counsel would continue to come from the UMWA treasury and (2) that there existed a conflict between the UMWA and the individual defendant officers. A month later the UMWA counsel withdrew as counsel for the individual defendants but remained as counsel for the UMWA, which the District Court sustained as proper.

At the outset of the lawsuit the then counsel for all defendants set about with commendable diligence to delineate the real issues of the lawsuit, filing in behalf of the UMWA and the three individual defendants answers setting forth all customary general defenses, and filing 34 pages of interrogatories to develop more fully the scope of the case.

The appellants argue that this period of six months' prior representation in this same suit disqualifies the regular union outside counsel to continue its representation of the UMWA, even after its withdrawal as counsel for the three individual officer-defendants. With this we do not agree. It has been inferentially held that one lawyer can properly represent all defendants if a suit appears groundless, and that separate counsel is required only in a situation where there is a potential conflict between the interests of the union and those of its officers. We regard the actions of the regular UMWA counsel during its six-month representation of both the union and its officers as an effort to ascertain the exact nature of the lawsuit and protect the interests of all defendants, and by our ruling herein do not imply any censure of counsel's action during this period of joint representation. But there does exist in our judgment a more serious barrier to the continued representation of the UMWA by its regular outside counsel in this particular lawsuit.

I. *Effect of Other Litigation in Which Regular UMWA–Counsel Represent Defendant President Boyle*

Of far more concern is the existence of other litigation in which the regular UMWA counsel is representing Boyle, sometimes in conjunction with representation of the union, at other times not.

(1) The "reinstatement" or "reprisal" case—one of four "election" cases brought by Joseph A. Yablonski against the UMWA and its officers, alleging that the reassignment or severance of plaintiff Yablonski from certain union duties was a reprisal for his running for president against the incumbent Boyle. After the death of Yablonski the trial court dismissed the case as moot, and this action is on appeal in this court. Appellants here claim that if this court should hold that the trial court was wrong in dismissing the reprisal case as moot, then appellee Boyle may subsequently be required to pay substantial punitive damages to the estate of Yablonski, and thus Boyle has a personal,

as distinguished from a union, interest in that appeal. Although initially the union and its officers were represented by the union general counsel in the District Court, the regular UMWA outside counsel represented both the UMWA and Boyle personally on the motion to dismiss as moot, and continues such representation on appeal in this court.

(2) Denial of attorney's fees—as an outgrowth of the UMWA election cases, attorneys for "the Yablonski group" applied for attorney's fees to be paid by the union, which the District Court denied, finding that "no malfeasance on the part of the officers has yet been established." These four cases are now on appeal. The regular UMWA counsel represents both the union and the individual officer-defendants here and did so on the merits in two of the cases in the District Court (the "*Journal*" and "fair election" cases, paragraph 3 infra) and on the motions to dismiss in all four cases, where the issue originally was the compliance of the incumbent officers with the Labor–Management Reporting and Disclosure Act. This series of cases is alleged to be related to the case at bar, inasmuch as paragraph 13 of the complaint herein alleges that Boyle and the other individual officer-defendants employed counsel to defend them on charges of breach of trust and paid such counsel from UMWA funds, the regular outside UMWA counsel here involved being one of those whose representation and compensation is being challenged in this present suit.

(3) The "*Journal*" and "fair election" cases—during the UMWA election campaign candidate Yablonski claimed that the union newspaper was being used to promote the candidacy of incumbent President Boyle. On appeals in this court the regular UMWA counsel represented Boyle and the union, although in one aspect in the District Court which was severed and consolidated with the instant case, whether Boyle should be made to pay for some of the costs of printing of the *Journal,* the regular UMWA counsel does not represent Boyle.

(4) Blankenship v. Boyle—a group of retired miners sued the Trustees of the UMWA Welfare and Retirement Fund of 1950, one of the Three Trustees being Boyle, alleging that the Fund had been mismanaged by the Trustees. Boyle was charged with using his position as a Trustee to increase pension benefits to assist his re-election campaign. The District Court ordered his removal as Trustee and this court has recently refused to stay the effectiveness of that order, although not deciding the appeal on the merits. Regular UMWA counsel represents Boyle individually in all three of the capacities in which he is sued, as Trustee of the Fund, President of the UMWA, and Director of the National Bank of Washington, as well as representing the union.

We have listed and briefly described the above actions of record in which the regular UMWA counsel represents Boyle individually. Each of these has been minutely examined by appellees' counsel to demonstrate that in no instance is the representation of Boyle individually in conflict with the good faith representation of the UMWA in this case;

in effect, that the interests of the UMWA and of Boyle individually are the same. We are assured that if any conflict should arise appellees' counsel would be prompt to withdraw as counsel to the UMWA in this case.

While the issues involved in each of the individual cases, and the past or present existence or nonexistence of any conflict, are relevant to the propriety of the regular UMWA counsel continuing its representation of the union in the case at bar, yet we do not think that this analysis is determinative of the real problem here. It is undeniable that the regular UMWA counsel have undertaken the representation of Boyle individually in many facets of his activities as a UMWA official, as a Trustee of the Fund, as a Director of the Bank owned 74% by the union. With strict fidelity to this client, such counsel could not undertake action on behalf of another client which would undermine his position personally. Yet, in this particular litigation, counsel for the UMWA should be diligent in analyzing objectively the true interests of the UMWA as an institution without being hindered by allegiance to any individual concerned.

We are not required to accept at this point the charge of the appellants that the "true interest" of the union is aligned with those of the individual appellants here; this may or may not turn out to be the fact. But in the exploration and the determination of the truth or falsity of the charges brought by these individual appellants against the incumbent officers of the union and the union itself as a defendant, the UMWA needs the most objective counsel obtainable. Even if we assume the accuracy of the appellee's position at the present time that there is no visible conflict of interest, yet we cannot be sure that such will not arise in the future.

Whether facts are discovered and legal positions taken which would create such a conflict of interest between the UMWA position and the position of the individual defendant Boyle may well be determined by the approach which counsel for the UMWA takes in this case. We think that the objectives of the Labor–Management Reporting and Disclosure Act [8] would be much better served by having an unquestionably independent new counsel in this particular case. The public

8. 29 U.S.C. § 401 (1964) sets forth the congressional declaration of findings, purposes and policy of the LMRDA, including *inter alia* the statement that "in order to accomplish the objective of a free flow of commerce it is essential that labor organizations, employers, and their officials adhere to the highest standards of responsibility and ethical conduct in administering the affairs of their organizations. . . ." The legislative history of the Act makes plain that a major congressional objective was to provide union members, as well as the Government in the public interest, with a variety of means to ensure that officials of labor organizations perform their duties in accordance with fiduciary standards. Both the Senate and House reports relating to the Act stressed the importance of such standards, the Senate Committee noting that:

Labor organizations are creations of their members; union funds belong to the members and should be expended only in furtherance of their common interest. A union treasury should not be managed as the private property of union officers, however well intentioned, but as a fund governed by fiduciary standards appropriate to this type of organization. The members who are the real owners of the money and property of the organization are entitled to a full accounting of all transactions interest requires that the validity of appellants' charges against the UMWA management of breach of its fiduciary responsibilities be determined in a context which is as free as possible from the appearance of any potential for conflict of interest in the representation of the union itself.

II. *Objective Determination of the UMWA's Institutional Interest*

Counsel for the appellees here have stressed the "institutional interest" of the UMWA in all of the issues raised, and particularly the institutional interest of the union in "repose." Counsel's interpretation of the "institutional interest" of the union appears to have been broad enough to authorize UMWA counsel to undertake practically everything worthwhile in the defense of this lawsuit. After the withdrawal of the regular union counsel from representation of Boyle individually in this case, the individual practitioner selected to represent Boyle has apparently contributed little to the defense.

By far the strongest laboring oar has been stroked by the regular UMWA counsel on behalf of the union. On oral argument appellees' counsel stated that it had prepared 94 pages of answers to interrogatories, that the individual practitioner representing Boyle had agreed they should do this, as the UMWA had a definite interest that all questions as to the conduct of union affairs previously were accurately answered and that the accurate answers were to be found in the union records. We can see the UMWA interest in having such interrogatories answered accurately, but we would think that since it is the individual defendants who are charged with the misconduct, their counsel would be the one to initiate and to carry the burden. . . .

In the crucial area of discovery matters, clearly representing the vast bulk of the effort expended by the parties defendant at this stage of the litigation, UMWA counsel have prepared 174 pages of answers to plaintiffs' initial interrogatories which were directed to all defendants, while counsel for the individual defendants, until 2 April 1971, some 7½ months after the interrogatories were originally served, had contented himself with filing 2 pages of answers for each individual defendant, a total of 6 pages. On 2 April 1971 counsel finally filed additional answers on behalf of defendant Boyle; however, as of the

involving their property. (S.Rep. No. 187, 86th Cong. 1st Sess. 8 (1959), U.S.Code Cong. & Admin.News, p. 2324; see also H.R. No. 741, 86th Cong., 1st Sess. 7, 8 (1959).

The House Committee strongly expressed its concern that:

Some trade unions have acquired bureaucratic tendencies and characteristics. The relationship of the leaders of such unions to their members has in some instances become impersonal and autocratic. In some cases men who have acquired positions of power and responsibility within unions have abused their power and forsaken their responsibilities to the membership and to the public. The power and control of the affairs of a trade union by leaders who abuse their power and forsake their responsibilities inevitably leads to the elimination of efficient, honest and democratic practices within such union, and often results in irresponsible actions which are detrimental to the public interest. (H.R. No. 741, 86th Cong., 1st Sess. 6 (1959).

Appellants' complaint in the instant case alleges a state of affairs existing within the leadership of the UMWA of the magnitude of that which the House Report condemned.

date of argument of this appeal, answers on behalf of the other individual defendants had not been filed.

. . .

. . . It appears that in 18 months of representation (6 months for both the UMWA and Boyle individually, and 12 months for the UMWA alone), the regular UMWA counsel has not brought forth a single issue on which the UMWA and the Boyle individual interest have diverged.

We think the analogy of the position of a corporation and its individual officers when confronted by a stockholder derivative suit is illuminating here.[10] We believe it is well established that when one group of stockholders brings a derivative suit, with the corporation as the nominal defendant and the individual officers accused of malfeasance of one sort or another, the role of both the corporate house counsel and the regular outside counsel for the corporation becomes usually a passive one. Certainly no corporate counsel purports to represent the individual officers involved, neither in the particular derivative suit nor in other litigation by virtue of which counsel necessarily must create ties of loyalty and confidentiality to the individual officers, which might preclude counsel from the most effective representation of the corporation itself. The corporation has certain definite institutional interests to be protected, and the counsel charged with this responsibility should have ties on a personal basis with neither the dissident stockholders nor the incumbent officeholders.

Purportedly a stockholder derivative suit is for the benefit of the corporation, even though the corporation is a nominal defendant, just as the appellants here assert (yet to be proved) that their action is for the benefit of the UMWA and that the individual incumbent officers are liable to the union itself for their alleged misdeeds. And, under established corporate law, if the individual officers are successful in the defense of a suit arising out of the performance of their duties as corporate officers, then they may justifiably seek reimbursement from the corporation for the costs of their successful defense.

In the ordinary case the action taken here by the regular UMWA counsel in the District Court might well have been the proper one, i.e., after establishing the nature of the lawsuit by interrogatories and filing answers on behalf of both the union and the individual officers in order fully to protect the position of all parties, then to step aside as counsel for the individual defendants and continue the representation of the union. But this particular case is a derivative action for the benefit of the union, and furthermore must be viewed in its relationship to this entire complex of numerous cases already pending or decided in this and the District Courts in which the regular UMWA counsel has already undertaken the representation of Boyle individually. Each and every one of these cases either directly arises out of or is directly

10. See Phillips v. Osborne, 403 F.2d 826, 831 (9th Cir.1968); Int'l Bhd. of Teamsters, etc. v. Hoffa, 242 F.Supp. 246, 251 (D.D.C.1965). Indeed, as appellees themselves noted in a motion filed in the court below "The action by Mr. Yablonski and others is a derivative action on behalf of the union. . . ."

connected with the struggle for power in the UMWA being waged by the Yablonski group on one side and the incumbent officers headed by President Boyle on the other. In this situation, the best interests of the UMWA and the purposes of the Labor–Management Reporting and Disclosure Act will be much better served by the disqualification of the regular union counsel in this particular suit and its continued representation of the individual Boyle in the other lawsuits.

We are cognizant that any counsel to represent the UMWA selected by President Boyle will be to some degree under his control. But such counsel will still only have one client—the UMWA—to represent in matters growing out of the union's affairs. Such counsel would never be professionally obligated to consider Boyle's personal interests, because they would not be representing him individually in related matters. And the extent of their labors would be gauged by the need to protect the UMWA position in this litigation. . . .

. . .

―――――――――

Epilogue

Following the decision printed above, the firm withdrew from representation of the UMWA, and UMWA's in-house general counsel and his staff attorneys entered appearances on behalf of the union. The Yablonski group immediately moved to disqualify these lawyers, but the District Court denied the motion. The Court of Appeals in a sharply critical opinion overturned the ruling and disqualified counsel, Yablonski v. United Mine Workers, 454 F.2d 1036 (D.C.Cir.1971). In this second opinion, the court said:

> The record now reveals a new arrangement for union counsel which in final analysis does not differ essentially from the older [one]. . . . UMWA general counsel and three members of his staff are representing or have represented to some extent union officers who are accused of wrongdoing in this case. One staff member is the son of one of such officers, and another is the son of a nonparty officer whom the charges conceivably could implicate. Atop that, three of the five attorneys are themselves named in appellants' complaint as recipients of payments allegedly made by officers in breach of fiduciary duties.

> Considerably more is both charged and largely denied, but merely to recite only these several uncontested circumstances is to demonstrate satisfactorily that house counsel as a group do not fit the specifications we previously laid down for those who would undertake representation of UMWA in this cause. They simply are not "unquestionably independent new counsel" whose contemplated appearance would enable resolution of the issues "in a context which is as free as possible from the appearance of any potential for conflict of interests in the representation of the union itself." It follows that the license the District Court gave them to

remain union counsel is a grave departure from the terms of our prior mandate . . .

The district court's ruling [was apparently based on its] belief that "a passive role" was in store for UMWA in this case. . . .

. . . [T]here is no predicate for a present assumption that UMWA must or will remain an inactive party. UMWA may, but is not inexorably bound to, take and maintain a detached position on the merits . . .

Much of appellees' presentation is devoted to attempted justification of UMWA's representation by its house counsel on the ground that its institutional interests as a union coincide with the individual defensive interests of the officers who are sued. That approach puts the cart before the horse . . .

. . .

. . . [A] sine qua non of permissible union representation . . . is the absence of any duty to another that might detract from a full measure of loyalty to the welfare of the union. House counsel no less than outside counsel must survive that test . . .
Id. at 1040–42.

Afterwards:

In 1969, on New Year's Eve, Joseph Yablonski, a dissident official of the United Mine Workers union, was murdered along with his wife and daughter on the orders of the union's president [Boyle.]

In 1973 William Prater, a union official who was one of the three men who had conspired to assassinate Yablonski—his role being to transfer union pension funds to the triggerman in payment for the assassination—pleaded guilty to conspiracy to injure a United States citizen in the exercise of his federal rights, in violation of 18 U.S.C. § 241 . . .

Prater v. United States Parole Commission, 802 F.2d 948, 949 (7th Cir.1986).

The Role of Corporate Counsel in Shareholder Derivative Suits

The law of corporations generally contemplates an orderly relationship of shareholders, directors and officers. In *Yablonski* and in all situations resulting in a shareholders derivative suit, this model has broken down: shareholders, or some of them, suing the directors, or some of them, in the name of the corporation and to enforce an obligation allegedly due the corporation. Somewhere in the fray stands counsel to the corporation, either an outside law firm or "inside" lawyers employed by the corporation on a full-time basis. Whom does the lawyer represent and what difference does it make?

In a derivative suit, the minority shareholders formally place themselves in the shoes of the corporation to enforce a corporate right. As the court points out in *Yablonski,* the corporation is a defendant in name only, see Ross v. Bernhard, 396 U.S. 531, 90 S.Ct. 733 (1970); the real defendants are the current management, officers and perhaps also majority shareholders, i.e., those with control of the corporation.

Yablonski states that corporate counsel's proper role in a derivative suit is to protect the corporation's interests, as distinct from the interests of either the director-defendants or the plaintiff-shareholders. Corporate counsel should not jointly represent the corporation and either the director-defendants or the plaintiff-shareholders; the corporation is entitled to "independent counsel." Nevertheless, the court approves counsel's having jointly represented all defendants in the initial stages of the lawsuit. Why?

Many courts allow joint representation when the plaintiffs' suit appears to lack merit. This is seen as necessary to avoid nuisance suits. See, e.g., Schwartz v. Guterman, 109 N.Y.Misc. 1004, 441 N.Y.S. 2d 597, 598 (1981), ("In a meritless . . . suit [retaining] separate counsel for the corporation . . . may delay the matter and cause a needless expense, ultimately borne by the shareholders."); In re Kinsey, 294 Or. 544, 660 P.2d 660, 669 (1983) (counsel may represent all defendants if the suit is "patently sham or patently frivolous."). See also Hausman v. Buckley, 299 F.2d 696, 699 (2d Cir.1962) (representation during preliminary stages when interests of corporation and officers coincided was proper).

Other courts have questioned the "meritless" lawsuit standard. In Lewis v. Shaffer Stores Company, 218 F.Supp. 238, 240 (S.D.N.Y.1963), the court stated, "I have no doubt that . . . [the law firm for the defendants believes] in good faith that there is no merit to this action. Plaintiff, of course, vigorously contends to the contrary. The court cannot and should not attempt to pass upon the merits at this stage." Held: the corporation should retain independent counsel for the litigation.

In Cannon v. United States Acoustics Corporation, 398 F.Supp. 209 (N.D.Ill.1975), aff'd in relevant part, 532 F.2d 1118 (7th Cir.1976), a leading case on this issue, the court concluded that a lawyer should be disqualified from simultaneously representing the corporation and the individual management and officer defendants:

> . . . [T]his is a derivative shareholder action against four officer-directors and two corporations. The complaint alleges that certain directors misappropriated monies of the corporation and violated federal and state securities laws. These are serious charges. If they are proved, the corporations stand to gain substantially. The [Code of Professional Responsibility] unquestionably prohibits one lawyer from representing multiple clients when their interests are in conflict. The code goes so far as to say that if the clients' interests are potentially differing, the preferable course is for the lawyer to refuse the employment initially. . . .

> . . . Nevertheless, defendants' counsel argue there is no present conflict and should one arise they will withdraw their

representation of the individual defendants and represent only the corporations. There are a number of problems with this solution. First, the complaint on its face establishes a conflict that cannot be ignored despite counsel's good faith representations. Second, counsel overlooks the hardship on the court and the parties if in the middle of this litigation new counsel must be obtained because a conflict arises. Lastly, although counsel offers to withdraw its representation of the individual defendants and remain counsel for the corporations if a conflict should arise, the appropriate course . . . is for the corporation to retain independent counsel. Under this procedure, once counsel has examined the evidence, a decision can be made regarding the role the corporation will play in the litigation. This decision will be made without the possibility of any influence emanating from the representation of the individual defendants, and will also eliminate the potential problem of confidences and secrets reposed by the individual defendants being used adverse to their interests by former counsel should new counsel have had to have been selected under the approach suggested by defense counsel. This solution, concededly, is not without its disabilities. The corporations' rights to counsel of their choice are infringed and in a closely held corporation, as here, the financial burden is increased. Nevertheless, on balance, the corporations must obtain independent counsel. . . .

398 F.Supp. at 220.

See also Messing v. FDI, Inc., 439 F.Supp. 776, 772 (D.N.J.1977); Murphy v. Washington American League Baseball Club, Inc., 324 F.2d 394 (D.C.Cir.1963); Henn, Corporations § 370 (2d ed. 1970); Developments in the Law: Conflicts of Interest in the Legal Profession, 94 Harv.L.Rev. 1244, 1339–40 (1981).

In contrast to *Cannon* the Comment to the M.R. 1.13 suggests that joint representation is presumptively valid:

The question can arise [in a shareholder derivative suit] whether counsel for the organization may defend such an action. The proposition that the organization is the lawyer's client does not alone resolve the issue. Most derivative actions are a normal incident of an organization's affairs, to be defended by the organization's lawyer like any other suit. However, if the claim involves serious charges of wrongdoing by those in control of the organization, a conflict may arise between the lawyer's duty to the organization and the lawyer's relationship with the board. In those circumstances, Rule 1.7 governs who should represent the directors and the organization.

Under corporate law, however, a derivative suit is predicated on failure of the board to take legal action appropriate to protect the corporation. Such inaction, if it occurred, necessarily involves at least serious neglect. Isn't that "wrongdoing"?

There is some support in the case law for the Comment's approach. See Selama–Dindings Plantations, Ltd. v. Durham, 216 F.Supp. 104 (S.D.Ohio 1963), aff'd, 337 F.2d 949 (6th Cir.1964); Otis & Co. v. Pennsylvania R. Co., 57 F.Supp. 680 (E.D.Pa.1944), aff'd, 155 F.2d 522 (3d Cir.1946) (per curiam). But these cases are of older vintage. Almost all of the more recent cases find joint representation improper, except for suits that clearly lack merit on their face. See, e.g., In re Kinsey, 294 Or. 544, 660 P.2d 660 (1983), and the cases cited in *Cannon,* 398 F.Supp. at 218–19. But see Robinson v. Snell's Limbs and Braces, 538 So.2d 1045, 1048 (La.App.1989) (law firm could represent corporation and individual director-defendants in derivative suit because the corporation is only a nominal defendant; "its true interest lies with the plaintiff shareholder. . . . Therefore [corporate counsel] represents only the interests of the individual directors who have allegedly harmed the corporation and the plaintiff's counsel actually represents the interests of the corporation. . . ." The court cited M.R. 1.13). Does this analysis make sense?

The Comment to M.R. 1.13 may reflect the continuing practice and ethic of the corporate bar, many of whom assume that joint representation is proper except where the charges against the corporate defendants are of the most serious nature. See, e.g., ABA Professional Responsibility, A Guide for Attorneys: Shipman, Professional Responsibilities of the Corporations Lawyer, p. 280 (1978) (criticizing the holding in *Cannon:* "This opinion is troublesome, for it is common practice for the corporation's counsel to defend officers and directors in a derivative action, with the corporation being represented in the action by independent counsel. Such procedure seems proper, especially where the officers and directors have relied upon corporation counsel's advice, as the attorney should be allowed to defend his work and advice."). See also Morril, Legal Ethics: "Everything a Lawyer Needs to Know and Should Not Be Afraid to Ask," 348 PLI/Lit 231 (1988) ("Although a few commentators have urged a different rule, [cites omitted], a lawyer may represent both the corporation and individual officers or directors named as defendants in a derivative suit. *Selama* [supra]; *Otis* [supra].")

Can there be an "institutional interest" of the organization, referred to in *Yablonski,* that is not voiced by a specific "constituent," either stockholder, officer or director? Could that institutional interest be voiced by the corporation's lawyer against *both* the plaintiff-stockholder and the defendant-directors and officers?

"Switching Sides" in a Derivative Suit: Representing the Shareholders Against Management

Because shareholders' derivative suits are brought on behalf of the corporation, it has been argued that corporate counsel would not be switching sides, i.e., opposing a former client, if she subsequently represented shareholders in a derivative suit. Most courts considering this argument have rejected it. See, e.g., Richardson v. Hamilton

International Corporation, 469 F.2d 1382 (3d Cir.1972); Doe v. A. Corp., 330 F.Supp. 1352 (S.D.N.Y.1971), aff'd sub nom. Hall v. A. Corp., 453 F.2d 1375 (2d Cir.1972). But see Jacuzzi v. Jacuzzi, 218 Cal.App.2d 24, 32 Cal.Rptr. 188, 191 (Dist.Ct.App.1963) (a former attorney for the Jacuzzi company could represent shareholders in a derivative suit that sought to restore assets to the corporation; the attorney acted "for the benefit of the corporation he previously represented," and therefore, "is not representing an interest adverse to the corporation.").

How would the Model Rules resolve this question? How would the corporate bar do so?

Choosing Independent Counsel for the Corporation

After the first *Yablonski* case, the president of the union, Boyle, selected new counsel for the union who were no more independent of his influence than the counsel they were replacing. Should the court have appointed counsel instead of leaving it to Boyle? Order the board of the corporate defendant (here, the union) to delegate to a group of independent directors, i.e., directors not implicated in the present action, the power to appoint and work with corporate counsel?

While there is some authority for court appointment of counsel on behalf of the organization-client, see Rowen v. LeMars Mutual Insurance Co., 230 N.W.2d 905 (Iowa 1975); Niedermeyer v. Niedermeyer, 1973 WL 419, CCH Fed.Sec.L.Rep. 94,123 (D.Or.1973) (not reported in F.Supp.), most courts agree with the court in *Yablonski* that this is too great an interference in the corporation's governance, see, e.g., *Cannon* supra, and Lewis v. Shaffer Stores Company, 218 F.Supp. 238 (S.D.N.Y. 1963).

In Messing v. FDI, 439 F.Supp. 776 (D.N.J.1977), after regular corporate counsel was disqualified, the corporation appointed an ad hoc committee to select and work with new counsel for the corporation; the committee consisted of the two directors who were not parties to the case. The corporation then sought the court's approval of this arrangement while the plaintiffs sought to have the court itself appoint counsel. The court declined to approve or disapprove of the committee plan:

> direct[ing] only that the corporation resolve this problem as it would any other issue as to which the existence of interested directors renders the usual corporate decision-making process unavailable. Of course, the directors may request this or any other court with jurisdiction over the matter to relieve them of this duty . . . If they are disqualified from acting on this or on any other matter, then it is for them, in the first instance, to devise a method to accommodate the need to continue the corporate enterprise while refraining from participating in any corporate decision in which they might have a personal interest. They act, or fail to act, at their peril.

Id. at 783–84.

Should a board, the majority of whose members are named as defendants in a derivative suit, be permitted to appoint a committee to direct the litigation for the corporation, usually referred to as a "special litigation committee"? Almost all courts have approved this solution because a contrary rule would permit one shareholder to incapacitate the entire board by leveling charges against a majority of its members. See, e.g., Hasan v. Clevetrust Realty Investors, 729 F.2d 372 (6th Cir. 1984) (applying Massachusetts law); Joy v. North, 692 F.2d 880 (2d Cir. 1982) (applying Connecticut law); Lewis v. Anderson, 615 F.2d 778 (9th Cir.1979) (applying California law); Abbey v. Control Data Corp., 603 F.2d 724 (8th Cir.1979) (applying Delaware law); Grossman v. Johnson, 89 F.R.D. 656, 662–63 (D.Mass.1981) (applying Maryland law); Zapata v. Maldonaldo, 430 A.2d 779 (Del.1981); Auerbach v. Bennett, 47 N.Y.2d 619, 419 N.Y.S.2d 920, 393 N.E.2d 994 (1979); see also 13 Fletcher's Cyclopedia of Corporations, § 5963 (1984). But see Miller v. Register and Tribune Syndicate, Inc., 336 N.W.2d 609 (Iowa 1983) (holding that when a majority of board members are named defendants, the board may not appoint "independent" people to serve on a litigation committee because they would not be independent enough). The *Miller* court relied in part on § 7.03 of Tentative Draft No. 1 of the Principles of Corporate Governance and Structure: Restatement and Recommendations (April 1, 1982) of the American Law Institute. This draft was not approved by the ALI. More significant, in later drafts the *Miller* rule is specifically rejected. See Principles of Corporate Governance Analysis and Recommendations, § 7.10 Comment F (Tent. Draft No. 9, April 14, 1989). See also Alford v. Shaw, 320 N.C. 465, 358 S.E.2d 323, 326 (1987) (rejecting *Miller* and withdrawing prior decision, 318 N.C. 289, 349 S.E.2d 41 (1986), endorsing *Miller*).

There is, however, division on the deference to be given the judgments of special litigation committees. Contrast *Auerbach v. Bennett* supra, holding under New York law that judicial scrutiny of the recommendations of special litigation committees is limited to questioning the committee's good faith, thoroughness and independence; with *Joy v. North* supra, where the Second Circuit, applying Connecticut law, held that courts should examine the committee's recommendation and make an independent determination of whether the action is likely to harm the corporation rather than help it. *Zapata,* supra takes an intermediate position, and most courts describe the choice as one between the *Auerbach* deferential approach and the more interventionist *Zapata* approach. *Joy* has not been followed.

In Abella v. Universal Leaf Tobacco Co., 546 F.Supp. 795, 799 (E.D. Va.1982), applying Virginia law, the court stated:

> . . . The Delaware Supreme Court [in *Zapata*] showed its sensitivity to the danger of giving minority shareholders the power to embroil the corporation in ill-founded litigation . . . as well as the danger of allowing the board of directors to appoint a few "good ol boys" as a special litigation committee and to be accordingly whitewashed pursuant to the majority rule. While the Court

recognizes the limitations of its own expertise in applying its business judgment . . . it also recognizes the relative ease with which a committee could construct a record of apparently diligent investigation after having predetermined the outcome of the investigation. The Court is persuaded that the *Zapata* approach adequately safeguards the competing interests at stake. . . .

See Alford v. Shaw, 320 N.C. 465, 358 S.E.2d 323, 325–26 (1987) ("recent trend among courts faced with [*Auerbach–Zapata*] choice . . . is away from *Auerbach*" and toward *Zapata*).

Commentators have also been critical of the *Auerbach* approach. See, e.g., Brudney, The Independent Director: Heavenly City or Potemkin Village, 95 Harv.L.Rev. 597 (1982); Dent, The Power of Directors to Terminate Shareholder Litigation: The Death of the Derivative Suit?, 75 Nw.U.L.Rev. 96 (1980). See also Gevurtz, Who Represents the Corporation? In Search of a Better Method for Determining the Corporate Interest in Derivative Suits, 46 U.Pitt.L.Rev. 265 (1985) (arguing that the corporate interest is not protected by either the board of directors, the plaintiff shareholder, other shareholders or the court, and proposing that the court appoint a litigation panel composed of neutral third parties to make decisions concerning the litigation, including who should represent the corporation). But see Johnson and Siegel, Corporate Mergers: Redefining the Role of Target Directors 136, U.Pa.L.Rev. 315 (1987) (arguing that *Zapata* approach is inappropriate in judging committee's decisions in takeover situation).

The Attorney–Client Privilege in Derivative Suits: Garner v. Wolfinbarger

As *Weintraub*, p. 738 above, makes clear, the corporation's current management controls the privilege and may waive it despite the objections of present or former constituents. But can current management assert the privilege against constituents, e.g., shareholders?

In *Garner v. Wolfinbarger*, 430 F.2d 1093 (5th Cir.1970), cert. denied, 401 U.S. 974 (1971), on remand, 56 F.R.D. 499 (S.D.Ala.1972), the Fifth Circuit recognized an exception to the corporation's attorney-client privilege, holding that shareholder-plaintiffs in derivative suits may gain access to information protected by the corporation's attorney-client privilege if they can "show cause why [the privilege] should not be invoked in the particular instance." 430 F.2d at 1103–04. This amorphous exception is referred to as a "good cause" exception and has been widely recognized. See, e.g., Quintel Corp. v. Citibank, 567 F.Supp. 1357, 1363–64 (S.D.N.Y.1983); Panter v. Marshall Field & Co., 80 F.R.D. 718, 722–23 (N.D.Ill.1978); Cohen v. Uniroyal, Inc., 80 F.R.D. 480, 482–85 (E.D.Pa.1978); In re Transocean Tender Offer Sec. Litig., 78 F.R.D. 692, 695–97 (N.D.Ill.1978); Valente v. Pepsico, 68 F.R.D. 361, 366–68 (D.Del.1975).

The *Garner* court reasoned that where management is charged with a breach of fiduciary responsibility, accountability to shareholders justifies interference with confidentiality. The court also reasoned that as constituents of the corporation, shareholders were somewhat similar to joint clients of the lawyer, noting that the privilege is unavailable among joint clients.

The question is how broad the exception should be, i.e., what is "good cause." *Garner* listed various factors to be considered:

— the number of shareholders bringing the claim against the corporation and the percentage of stock they represent;

— the bona fides of the shareholders;

— the nature of the shareholders' claim and whether it is obviously colorable;

— whether the information is vital to the shareholders and whether it is available from other sources;

— whether the shareholders' claim alleges that corporate officers acted criminally, or illegally but not criminally, or in a way that is of doubtful legality;

— whether the communication related to past or to future actions, i.e., whether the communications might have been part of an ongoing fraud;

— whether the communication concerns advice about the litigation itself;

— the extent to which the shareholders are fishing for information;

— the risk of revelation of trade secrets or other information in whose confidentiality the corporation has an interest beyond the present litigation.

430 F.2d at 1104.

Most courts have held that *Garner* allows shareholders access upon a showing of good cause even if their suit is "direct" rather than derivative. See, e.g., *Cohen v. Uniroyal,* supra; *Bailey v. Meister Brau, Inc.,* supra (*Garner* approach followed in federal securities lawsuit brought by individual plaintiff on his own behalf).

But see Weil v. Investment/Indicators, Research & Management, Inc., 647 F.2d 18, 23 (9th Cir.1981) ("Weil is not currently a shareholder of the Fund, and her action is not a derivative suit. The *Garner* plaintiffs sought damages from other defendants in behalf of the corporation, whereas Weil seeks to recover damages . . . for herself and members of her proposed class. *Garner's* holding and policy rationale simply do not apply here.").

See also Note, The Attorney–Client Privilege in Shareholder Litigation: The Need for a Predictable Standard, 9 Loy.U.Chi.L.J. 731 (1978) (arguing that the criteria in *Garner* for determining good cause are vague and overbroad); Developments in the Law—Privileged Communication: III. Attorney–Client Privilege, 98 Harv.L.Rev. 1501 (1985) (arguing that the *Garner* exception be abandoned: courts should rely exclusively on the crime/fraud exception to get at those communications that corporate managers should not be allowed to shield from shareholders or others).

Is the *Garner* exception broader than the crime/fraud exception to the attorney-client privilege? It is difficult to prove that communications were made with the intent to further a fraud or crime. How would shareholders demonstrate that? The crime/fraud exception may be too narrow for the purposes envisioned by *Garner*. *Garner* seeks to ensure that the attorney-client privilege is asserted in the best interests of the organization rather than for the benefit of management. It is, in other words, concerned with bad faith in asserting the privilege not bad faith in communicating with counsel for illegal purpose.

After the Supreme Court's decision in *Upjohn,* printed in Chapter 4 above, affirming the corporation's strong interest in frank and confidential communications with counsel, some commentators predicted the demise of *Garner*. See, e.g., Kirby, New Life for the Corporate Attorney–Client Privilege in Shareholder Litigation, 69 A.B.A.J. 174 (1983); Sexton, A Post–Upjohn Consideration of Corporate Attorney–Client Privilege, 57 N.Y.U.L.Rev. 443 (1982). But see Ward v. Succession of Freeman, 854 F.2d 780, 785 (5th Cir.1988) ("*Upjohn* does not undermine . . . *Garner* "); Lewis, Garner is Alive and Well in Securities Litigation, 69 A.B.A.J. 903 (1983). In fact, the *Garner* rationale has been extended by the courts outside the shareholder/corporation context to allow others to whom a fiduciary duty is owed to gain access to communications between the fiduciary and her counsel. This development is discussed in the notes to *Fickett* below at pp. 781–783.

Garner is inapplicable to communications with counsel about the derivative suit itself. In re LTV Securities Litigation, 89 F.R.D. 595 (N.D.Tex.1981) (*Garner* exception does not apply to "after-the-fact" communications concerning offenses already completed). See also In re International Sys. & Controls Corp., 693 F.2d 1235 (5th Cir.1982) (refusing to apply *Garner* to the lawyer's work-product concerning the pending litigation).

Rule 501 of the Federal Rules of Evidence provides that the rules of privilege "shall be governed by the principles of the common law as they may be interpreted by the courts of the United States in the light of reason and experience." The *Garner* rule was developed on this authority. Several state courts have used their general common law power to adopt *Garner* as state law. See, e.g., Hoopes v. Carota, 74 N.Y.2d 716, 544 N.Y.S.2d 808, 543 N.E.2d 73 (1989) (adopting *Garner* approach to determine whether beneficiaries of a trust plan may gain access to communications between the plan's trustee and his attorney); Neusteter v. The District Court of Denver, 675 P.2d 1 (Colo.1984) (adopting the "good cause" exception of *Garner* and applying it to accountant-client privilege). California however has refused to follow *Garner,* holding that the California statute on the attorney-client privilege does not empower the courts to carve out exceptions. See Dickerson v. Superior Court of Santa Clara County, 135 Cal.App.3d 93, 185 Cal.Rptr. 97 (1982); and Hoiles v. Superior Court of Orange County, 157 Cal.App.3d 1192, 204 Cal.Rptr. 111, 114–15 (1984).

Protections for Corporate Officers and Agents

Business Judgment Rule

Corporate directors and other top corporate officials are protected in large measure from the legal risks of their decisions. First, there is the judicially developed "business judgment rule" that shields directors from liability based on mere bad judgment. See generally ALI, Principles of Corporate Governance § 4.01 (Tent. Draft No. 3, 1984). This rule is justified on three grounds: (1) shareholders voluntarily take the risk of bad business judgment when they choose to invest in a particular corporation; (2) litigation conducted with the benefit of hindsight is a poor device for evaluating business judgments; and (3) the law should not induce overly cautious decision-making, which may adversely affect profits. See Joy v. North, 692 F.2d 880 (2d Cir.1982). However, as the court in *Joy* states:

> [T]he business judgment rule extends only as far as the reasons which justify its existence. Thus, it does not apply in cases, e.g., in which the corporate decision lacks a business purpose, see Singer v. Magnavox, 380 A.2d 969 (Del.Supr.1977), is tainted by a conflict of interest, Globe v. Electric Co., 224 N.Y. 483, 121 N.E. 378 (1918), is so egregious as to amount to a no-win decision, Litwin v. Allen, 25 N.Y.S.2d 667 (N.Y.Co.Sup.Ct.1940), or results from an obvious and prolonged failure to exercise oversight or supervision. McDonnell v. American Leduc Petroleums, Ltd., 491 F.2d 380 (2d Cir.1974).
>
> 692 F.2d at 886.

Also see Note, False Halo: The Business Judgment Rule in Corporate Control Contests, 66 Tex.L.Rev. 843 (1988) (arguing that court should repudiate the rule in most takeover cases).

Indemnification and Insurance

Second, corporate officers are protected by contracts that provide for indemnification from the corporation, for liability insurance, or for both. For example, Delaware law allows corporate officers and agents to receive indemnification for the costs of defending (and liability that results from) civil actions brought against them by third parties as long as the officer or agent "acted in good faith and in a manner he reasonably believed to be in or not opposed to the best interests of the corporation." As to criminal prosecutions, the officer can be indemnified for lawyer's costs and fines as long as the officer "had no reasonable cause to believe his conduct was unlawful." 8 Del.Code § 145(a); see also Model Business Corp. Act § 5(b) (1982).

When the suit is brought by shareholders instead of third-parties, the law in many states, while still allowing indemnification of officers, is more restrictive. The Delaware approach is common: officers may be indemnified for defending against and liability arising from a shareholder derivative suit if the officers acted in good faith and not opposed to the corporation's interest and *were not negligent or responsible for other misconduct related to their corporate duties.* 8 Del.Code § 145(c) (emphasis added). While on its face this approach seems more restrictive, Delaware and some other states allow indemnification beyond the limits of the statute if a by-law, contract, or vote of disinterested directors or shareholders provides for extended indemnification. See, e.g., 8 Del.Code § 145(f). Hence statutes of the Delaware type are referred to as "nonexclusive."

At the other end of the spectrum are states, such as Connecticut, that have exclusive statutes, i.e., the terms of which cannot be varied by corporate by-laws, and that provide for indemnification of the costs of defending against charges of misconduct only if the defendant directors or officers secure a successful outcome or if, in the case of a judgment against the corporation, the court approves indemnification. See Conn.Gen.Stat.Ann. § 33-320a(b).

Where indemnification might not be available—for willful misconduct or bad faith or because of statutory restrictions—many states allow corporations to protect officials through insurance. See, e.g., 8 Del.Code § 145(g); and Model Business Corp. Act § 5(g) (1979). Commercially available insurance does not, however, provide coverage for willful misconduct.

Federal law may preclude broad indemnification. For example, the Foreign Corrupt Practices Act prohibits direct or indirect reimbursement of fines imposed on individuals for willful violations, 15 U.S.C. § 78dd-Z(g)(3). The SEC takes the position that public policy does not permit a corporation to indemnify a director against liability for misrepresentations or omissions in registration statements, 17 C.F.R. § 229.512, although this prohibition does not apply to insurance coverage, Fed.Sec.L.Rep. (CCH) P77,636 (1968).

The SEC also requires a company that indemnifies officials for violations of the securities laws to state that the SEC believes such indemnification is "against public policy . . . and is, therefore, unenforceable." 17 C.F.R. § 229.510. For cases supporting the SEC's position see Globus v. Law Research Serv., Inc., 287 F.Supp. 188, 199 (S.D. N.Y.1968), aff'd in part and rev'd in part, 418 F.2d 1276 (2d Cir.1969); and Heizer Corp. v. Ross, 601 F.2d 330, 334 (7th Cir.1979). For discussion of director and officer liability see, Kraakman, Corporate Liability Strategies and the Cost of Legal Controls, 93 Yale L.J. 857 (1984); Coffee, Beyond the Shut-Eyed Sentry: Toward a Theoretical View of Corporate Misconduct and an Effective Response, 63 Va.L.Rev. 1099 (1977); and Corporate Governance and Directors' Liabilities: The Legal, Economic, and Sociological Analysis of Corporate Social Responsibility (K. Hopt & G. Teubner eds. 1984).

The "Reliance on Counsel" Defense

Another protection against legal risks available to corporate officers and agents is the "reliance on counsel" defense. Good faith reliance on advice of counsel allows corporate officers to escape liability for acts taken in their official capacity if it negates relevant intent. This defense puts a premium on an opinion that shields the officer and may encourage "opinion shopping." See Hawes & Sherrard, Reliance on Advice of Counsel as a Defense in Corporate and Securities Cases, 62 Va.L.Rev. 1 (1976); Reliance on Counsel's Advice as Defense to Securities Law Violations Discussed by Longstreth, [July–Dec.1981] Sec.Rec. & L.Rep. (BNA) No. 633 (Dec. 16, 1981).

Model Rule 1.13, The Organization as Client

M.R. 1.13(a) states that the lawyer represents the organization not its constituents. M.R. 1.13(b) addresses what a lawyer should do when a constituent, e.g., an officer or employee, is acting in a way that may legally harm the organization. The text of M.R. 1.13(b) begins:

> (b) If a lawyer for an organization knows that an officer, employee or other person associated with the organization is engaged in action, intends to act or refuses to act in a matter related to the organization that is a violation of a legal obligation to the organization, or a violation of law which reasonably might be imputed to the organization, the lawyer shall proceed as is reasonably necessary in the best interest of the organization. . . .

Notice that only acts harmful to the *organization* trigger the rule: the act must either be a violation of a legal obligation, e.g., a fiduciary duty or contractual obligation, to the organization; or a violation of law, but one that might reasonably be imputed to the organization.

Assuming the rule is triggered, M.R. 1.13(b) continues.

> In determining how to proceed, the lawyer shall give due consideration to the seriousness of the violation and its consequences, the scope and nature of the lawyer's representation, the responsibility in the organization and the apparent motivation of the person involved, the policies of the organization concerning such matters and any other relevant considerations. . . .

The rule states a condition for any action by the lawyer: "Any measure taken shall be designed to minimize disruption of the organization and the risk of revealing information relating to the representation to persons outside the organization."

What may the lawyer do? The rule has a non-exhaustive list ("such measures may include among others"):

> (1) asking reconsideration of the matter;
>
> (2) advising that a separate legal opinion on the matter be sought for presentation to appropriate authority in the organization; and
>
> (3) referring the matter to higher authority in the organization, including, if warranted by the seriousness of the matter, referral to the highest authority that can act in behalf of the organization as determined by applicable law.

What should the lawyer do if the highest authority (which, in the case of a corporation, is usually the board of directors) refuses to act in the best interests of the corporation to prevent the harm?   Should the lawyer tell the shareholders?   A government agency?   The proposal of the Kutak Commission (Revised Final Draft M.R. 1.13(c), June 30, 1982) provided that the lawyer's options:

> may include revealing information, otherwise protected by Rule 1.6 *only if* the lawyer reasonably believes that:
>
> (1) the highest authority in the organization has acted to further the personal or financial interests of members of that authority which are in conflict with the interest of the organization; *and*
>
> (2) revealing the information is necessary in the best interest of the organization.   (emphasis added)

This proposal was rejected by the ABA House of Delegates and M.R. 1.13(c) as adopted reads:

> If, despite the lawyer's efforts in accordance with paragraph (b), the highest authority that can act on behalf of the organization insists upon action, or a refusal to act, that is clearly a violation of law, and is likely to result in substantial injury to the organization, the lawyer may resign in accordance with Rule 1.16.

Does this rule sufficiently protect the lawyer from liability under other law?   Recall the standards in *Benjamin* and *Greycas,* printed in Chapter 2 above, and the *OPM* case in Chapter 4.   Consider this question in reading the following summary and the notes that follow it.   Also see Gillers, Model Rule 1.13(c) Gives the Wrong Answer to the Question of Corporate Counsel Disclosure, 1 Geo.J.Leg. Ethics 289 (1987).

For a step-by-step analysis of the rules governing corporate internal investigations, see Kershen, Ethical Issues for Corporate Counsel in Internal Investigations: A Problem Analyzed, 13 Okla.City U.L.Rev. 1 (1988).   For an exploration of various models of the lawyer's role in an internal investigation, see Gruenebaum and Oppenheimer, Special Investigative Counsel: Conflicts and Roles, 33 Rutgers L.Rev. 865 (1981).

Note on *In re Carter and Johnson*

The following excerpt from Krane, The Attorney Unschackled: SEC Rule 2(e) Violates Clients' Sixth Amendment Right to Counsel, 57 Notre Dame Lawyer 50, 59–63 (1981) provides a summary of the facts and holding in In re Carter and Johnson, 1981 Fed.Sec.L.Rep. P82, 847 (SEC 1981).

STEVEN C. KRANE, "THE ATTORNEY UNSHACKLED: SEC RULE 2(E) VIOLATES CLIENTS' SIXTH AMENDMENT RIGHT TO COUNSEL"

57 Notre Dame Lawyer 50, 59–63 (1981).*

. . .

Perhaps William R. Carter (Carter) and Charles J. Johnson, Jr. (Johnson) were the only two people for whom the decision in *In re Carter & Johnson* was worth the nearly two year wait from the date of the Initial Decision of the Administrative Law Judge (ALJ).[60] The ALJ found that Carter and Johnson had engaged in "unethical" and "improper" professional conduct [61] despite their allegation that the terms are unconstitutionally vague. In its decision, the SEC recognized that:

> [t]he ethical and professional responsibilities of lawyers who become aware that their client is engaging in violations of the securities laws have not been so firmly and unambiguously established that we believe all practicing lawyers can be held to an awareness of generally recognized norms.

Without stating that the conduct of Carter and Johnson was in fact professional and ethical,[64] the SEC proceeded to "hereby giv[e] notice of its interpretation of 'unethical or improper professional conduct' as that term is used in rule 2(e)(1)(ii)."

The case involved the collapse of the National Telephone Company (National), which leased telephone equipment systems to commercial customers under long-term leases. National required a substantial initial cash outlay to finance the equipment and its marketing and installation before lease payments began. Accordingly, National was forced to seek outside financing to provide working capital until lease payments began. National obtained financing with conditions designed to prevent overexpansion of operations. These funds were insufficient, and National filed for bankruptcy in 1975.

During this period, National was represented by Carter and Johnson. National issued a misleading press release that concealed its precarious cash position, and filed overstated earnings and revenue figures with the SEC. Despite Carter and Johnson's repeated warnings that the company was violating the securities laws, National's chairman issued the questionable information. The case against Carter and Johnson centered around their obligation to go beyond attempted

---

* Copyright © 1981 by Notre Dame Law Review, University of Notre Dame. Reprinted with permission.

60.   . . . In re Carter & Johnson, Initial Decision (Mar. 7, 1979), reprinted in 494 Sec. Reg. & L.Rep. (BNA) F–1 (1979).

61.   17 C.F.R. § 201.2(e)(1)(ii) (1981).

64.   The new standards set forth by the SEC were not valid retroactively; Carter and Johnson were held not to have violated the standards merely because the standards did not exist at the time of their conduct.

persuasion of a corporate officer when that officer refused to heed advice of counsel.

The ALJ found that Carter and Johnson's failure to go to the National board of directors was in itself a breach of professional responsibility. The ALJ stated:

> The matter of counsel responsibility when confronted with irregular or illegal client activity involves a delicate balance between judgment and courage. Counsel needs to guard against falling prey to blandishments of client [*sic*] by accepting repeated evasion and rationalization, or worse, to allow himself to be drawn into or become a party to the illegal activity. Decision concerning the point at which further persuasion in the face of client defiance becomes futile cannot be postponed indefinitely. To drift may be as culpable as to connive. At some point it becomes necessary to take a stand.

Unfortunately, the ALJ did not define either the "some point" or what "stand" was required to be taken. That, in essence, was the purpose of the *Carter & Johnson* decision, and the SEC did indeed attempt to clarify the nebulous rule 2(e) standard.

Even in the narrow *Carter & Johnson* context, the SEC's delineation of professional responsibility deserves particular attention. The SEC stated:

> When a lawyer with *significant responsibilities* in the effectuation of a company's compliance with the disclosure requirements of the federal securities laws becomes aware that his client is engaged in a *substantial and continuing* failure to satisfy those disclosure requirements, his continued participation violates professional standards unless he takes *prompt steps* to end the client's noncompliance.

There are three steps to the SEC's analysis of noncompliance problems, and each is subject to variable interpretations. First, which attorneys have "significant responsibilities" in a client's compliance program? Presumably, the senior partner in charge of the client's affairs would fall within this definition. Perhaps a junior partner or senior associate to whom was delegated responsibility for "effectuation of a company's compliance with the disclosure requirements of the federal securities laws" would also fall within the rubric of "significant responsibilities." But what of the junior associate who is given responsibility for the preparation of the more mechanical and repetitive documents to be filed with the SEC? How significant must the responsibilities be before an attorney will be subject to liability for failure to take "prompt steps" to remedy the situation?

The SEC has given significantly more guidance in defining the other two variables in the *Carter & Johnson* test. A "substantial and continuing failure" to satisfy disclosure requirements is not "isolated disclosure action or inaction" on the part of the client. However, "there may be isolated disclosure failures that are *so serious* that their correction becomes a matter of primary professional concern." Although the SEC has merely substituted one variable, "so serious," for another, "substantial and continuing," attorneys can at least be sure that they must take "prompt steps" after more than one occurrence of inaccurate disclosure. Nevertheless, the SEC has left itself room for imaginative applications of rule 2(e).

The critical question of the *Carter & Johnson* test is what constitutes the taking of "prompt steps" to end a client's noncompliance. The SEC states that while "counselling accurate disclosure" may be sufficient for awhile, "there comes a point at which a reasonable lawyer must conclude that his advice is not being followed, or even sought in good faith, and that his client is involved in a continuing course of violating the securities laws." At that point, the SEC requires that an attorney "take further, more affirmative steps" to clear himself of an inference of cooption into the client's scheme. What steps will satisfy this obligation is not clear, although the SEC suggests that an attorney might resign, but not prematurely, or that he might approach the board of directors or other management personnel to enlist their aid. These are merely suggested courses of action for an attorney; the ultimate standard is barely more lucid than was "unethical or improper professional conduct:"

> What is required, in short, is *some prompt action,* [though not necessarily successful] that leads to the conclusion that the lawyer is engaged in efforts to correct the underlying problem, rather than having capitulated to the desires of a stong-willed, but misguided client. . . . So long as a lawyer is acting in *good faith* and exerting *reasonable efforts* to prevent violations of the law by his client, his professional obligations have been met.

The "conclusion" referred to in the opinion, which will decide whether an attorney is suspended or disbarred, will of course be made by the SEC.

. . . .

Aftermath

The SEC staff had hoped for a stronger ruling from the Commission, perhaps imposing an affirmative duty of disclosure on lawyers faced with client intransigence. The SEC issued a request for comments on the rule laid down in *Carter/Johnson*, Sec. Act Release No. 6344, Sec.Exchange Act Release No. 18106 (Sept. 21, 1981), in which it stated that the following rule taken from *Carter/Johnson* would apply for all conduct occurring after February 28, 1981 and would remain the rule unless modified by the SEC: "What is required, in short, is some prompt action that leads to the conclusion that the lawyer is engaged in efforts to correct the underlying problem, rather than having capitulated to the desires of a strong-willed, but misguided client."

The ABA submitted a response drafted by its Section of Corporation, Banking and Business Law, 37 Bus.Law. 915 (1982), challenging the SEC's authority to discipline lawyers under Rule 2(e) and the standard of conduct in the *Carter/Johnson* case. After the comment period, the SEC took no further official action on the release.

Many other commentators were critical of the SEC's use of 2(e) in cases like *Carter/Johnson*, arguing that lawyers would become overcautious in order to protect themselves from liability, which would in turn result in clients keeping more and more information from their lawyers. See, e.g., Miller, The Distortion and Misuse of Rule 2(e), 7 Sec. Reg.L.J. 54, 59 n. 13 (1979); Note, SEC Disciplinary Proceedings Against Attorneys Under Rule 2(e), 79 Mich.L.Rev. 1270, 1275–77, 1285 (1981); Krane, The Attorney Unshackled: SEC Rule 2(e) Violates Clients' Sixth Amendment Right to Counsel, supra. See also dissents of SEC Commissioner Roberta Karmel: *In the Matter of Darrel L. Nielson*, Securities Exchange Act Release No. 16479 (Jan. 10, 1980); *In the Matter of Bernard J. Coven*, Securities Exchange Act Release No. 16448 (Dec. 21, 1979); *In the Matter of Richard D. Hodgin*, Securities Exchange Act Release No. 16225 (Sept. 27, 1979); and her articles, Karmel, Regulation by Prosecution, The SEC v. Corporate America (1982); Daley and Karmel, Attorneys' Responsibilities: Adversaries at the Bar of the SEC, 24 Emory L.J. 747 (1975); and Karmel, Attorneys' Securities Law Liabilities, 27 Bus.Law. 1153 (1972). (Karmel, a longstanding opponent of the SEC's use of Rule 2(e) was an SEC Commissioner at the time *Carter/Johnson* was decided, but recused herself because she formerly had been a partner with the law firm that had represented some of the directors of National Telephone.)

The SEC continues to assert that it had the authority to issue and enforce 2(e), but it has brought very few cases against lawyers and has refrained from articulating standards of conduct for securities lawyers. See Nelson, "Hushed SEC Voice Adds Little to Legal Ethics Debate," Legal Times, Commentary and Insight (May 16, 1983) ("[T]he SEC has done virtually nothing to articulate its position . . . since it decided the *Carter and Johnson* case").

After the collapse of the company in *Carter/Johnson* (National Telephone), the SEC brought charges against all the directors, including the non-officer or "outside" directors of the company. The SEC issued a release stating that "[t]he outside directors of National were aware during the fall of 1974 and the winter and spring of 1975 of significant facts concerning National's troubled financial condition. Moreover they were aware of the optimistic nature of the company's public disclosures, disclosures which were in direct contrast with the true state of the company's affairs. Under these circumstances the company's outside directors had an affirmative duty to see to it that proper disclosures were made." See Report of Investigation in the Matter of National Telephone Co., Inc. Relating to Activities of the Outside Directors . . . [1977–78 Transfer Binder] Fed.Sec.L.Rep. (CCH) P81,410, 88,878.

As former SEC Director of Enforcement, Stanley Sporkin, put it:

> The Commission was not saying that the directors of a company are responsible for proofreading every line of every press release and periodic filing made by the company. Rather, the Commission was cautioning that at a time of distress in a company's existence, the directors have an affirmative duty to ensure that the marketplace is provided accurate and full disclosures concerning the basic liability of the company and the continuity of its operations. *Directors cannot play the role of the ostrich.* Directors cannot simply say, "We are not going to do anything." They have a duty and a responsibility. Directors who are smart may try to defend themselves by saying, "We relied on the company's management and counsel to take care of these problems."

> Sporkin, Symposium: Southeastern Conference on Corporate and Securities Law I. SEC Enforcement and Corporate Responsibility: SEC Enforcement and the Corporate Board Room, 61 N.C.L. Rev. 455, 458 (1983) (emphasis added).

What were the responsibilities of the law firm in *Carter/Johnson* to the non-officer directors? What if a law firm represented such a director as a client? Did the law firm have a fiduciary relationship with these directors? See the *Fassihi* case printed below.

The Reality of Practice and Alternatives to the "Organization as Client"

In the real world of practice corporate lawyers often see the client as management (the real-life people who run the company), not some abstract entity. Does M.R. 1.13 and its Comment adequately deal with this reality?

There are at least two readily apparent alternatives to the "organization as client" approach. See generally FitzGibbon, Professional Ethics, Organizing Corporations 7–8 (ABA Problems in Professional Responsibility Monograph No. 3, 1982). The first treats the constituents, not the organization, as the client—in effect as joint clients. If the lawyer perceives a conflict among the constituents, e.g., the board and the shareholders or the board and the CEO, the lawyer is to withdraw and may not represent any of the constituents in subsequent matters substantially related to the work done on behalf of the joint clients. Given the reality of corporate infighting and shareholder derivative suits, this theory could result in a succession of lawyers for any one corporation, which would deprive the corporation of the benefit of sustained representation over time. It would also undercut whatever autonomy a lawyer might have as corporate counsel. It might also mean the end of the institution of in-house counsel.

The second theory conceives of corporate counsel as lawyer "for the situation," empowered to act to further the best interests of all concerned as the lawyer perceives those interests. The lawyer would function like a mediator among the various factions, ultimately deciding on the legal course that best serves the corporation, conceived as the embodiment of these various interests. This approach, if taken to its conclusion, divests management of control of the corporation's legal actions and places enormous power in the hands of "disinterested" lawyers. Its conception of the corporate lawyer as sage seems at odds with the real world.

The "organization as client" approach embodied in Rule 1.13 may conflict with the real corporate world as experienced by the lawyer and in some cases is difficult to translate into action. However, it is grounded in both the law of corporations and the law of agency. The law of corporations recognizes the corporation as a "person" capable of holding privileges and entering into relationships. See Dartmouth College v. Woodward, 17 U.S. (4 Wheat.) 518, 636 (1819); New Colonial Ice Co. v. Helvering, 292 U.S. 435, 442, 54 S.Ct. 788, 791 (1933). And the law of agency describes and delineates the relationships among agents that serve a common principal (the lawyer, the CEO, the directors, etc. . . . and the corporation). See Restatement Second of Agency generally and § 1 Comment e (on the lawyer as agent) (1958); F. Mechem, Outlines of the Law on the Law of Agency, particularly § 12(a), 76 (4th ed. 1952). See also Fletcher, Cyclopedia of the Law of Private Corporations, §§ 275, 437, 466.3, 483 (rev. perm ed. 1982). This grounding in other law at least provides a structure of legal relationships in which to locate the lawyer's role. Second, corporate and agency law bridge between theory and fact in corporate functions in the same way that the corporate lawyer must bridge between theory and action in professional responsibility.

Reality's intrusion on the idea of "organization as client" is perhaps most acute when one person dominates the organization. For example, in *Carter/Johnson* Hart was controlling stockholder, CEO, chairman of the board, president and treasurer of National. Should this make a difference in the lawyer's analysis of who the client is? If not, what can the lawyer who is faced with such a dominant figure do to ensure some measure of independence? The *OPM* case, reprinted in Chapter 4 above, is another instance of the dominant figure in an organization acting to harm it. Would M.R. 1.13 have suggested a different course of conduct for the lawyers in that case?

Mediating Among Competing Interests Within an Organization

Corporations and other organizations may become battlefields of conflicting interests. How much involvement by the lawyer is appropriate?

Consider, for example, the question posed in ABA Informal Opinion 1056 (1968): Is it proper for corporation counsel to advise the president of the corporation on how to conduct an upcoming election of directors to frustrate a minority attempt to gain representation on the board. The committee, advising that such advice was appropriate, said:

In acting as counsel for a corporation a lawyer not only may but should give legal advice to its officers in all matters relating to the corporation as long as they are in office, except in situations where to his knowledge the interests of the officers are adverse to the interests of the corporation and the giving of the advice would be contrary to the interests of the corporation.

Would M.R. 1.13 or its Comment suggest a different conclusion? How is a lawyer to judge when the "giving of such advice would be contrary to the interests of the corporation?"

Questions such as that posed by Opinion 1056 are infrequently presented to courts or disciplinary boards. Something has to go very wrong before the lawyer's decisions on such matters are reviewed in a formal setting. Even then, the lawyer's decisions are unlikely to be second-guessed except in egregious cases. Courts and disciplinary boards justifiably perceive that they cannot recreate the inner workings of organizations and their relationships with counsel. The reality that confronts corporate counsel is too idiosyncratic, amorphous, and dynamic to dissect in an adversary proceeding.

This is not to suggest that courts should ignore gross misconduct. If the courts will not examine gross misconduct by lawyers, who will?

Note on *Financial General Bankshares, Inc. v. Metzger*

In Financial General Bankshares, Inc. v. Metzger, 523 F.Supp. 744 (D.D.C.1981), rev'd, 680 F.2d 768 (D.C.Cir.1982), the District Court found that attorney Metzger had breached his fiduciary and ethical duties to his client, Financial General Bankshares, Inc., (FG), by secretly engaging in attempts to seize or sell control of the company. The "Watergate group", a minority group of shareholder/directors, was dissatisfied with current management and planned to seize control of the company. Without advising current management, Metzger, also a shareholder in FG, attended and participated in these planning sessions. He devised a plan to sell FG to a European bank and wrote to potential purchasers of FG that: "I am generally familiar with the structure of FG and the legal problems which might interest a potential purchaser—have gun will travel." 523 F.Supp. at 756. Metzger became counsel to a group of Middle Eastern investors seeking to buy substantial blocks of FG stock. The court held that his involvement with the Watergate group violated "the requirement that a corporate advisor remain neutral when confronted with an internecine conflict", citing Canon 5 of the Model Code; several ABA opinions, including 1056 supra, and *Yablonski,* supra. Id. at 765. The court rejected Metzger's claim that his status as a shareholder gave him the right "to express his views on the management of the company", stating:

> . . . Had he not also been an attorney for the corporation, he would, indeed, have been free to join the Watergate group. . . .

> Because "what is in the best interests of the corporation" generally furthers an individual's interests as a stockholder, the

lawyer-shareholder combination is not prohibited. ABA Informal Opinion 1057 (1968). But the combination is subject to the limits set forth in DR 5–101. . . . When an attorney's privileges as a shareholder collide with his obligations as a lawyer for the company . . ., the lawyer's professional obligations predominate. Formal Opinion 86 (1932). At that point, the attorney should advise the corporate client to seek outside counsel. ABA Informal Opinion 1057 (1968). If that is not appropriate, the attorney should relinquish his privileges as a shareholder, ABA Opinion 86 (1932) or resign.

Id. at 767.

The court also found that Metzger's representation of the Middle Eastern investors, which he did not disclose to FG, involved a conflict of interest and that he violated his duty to keep FG's confidences by using its shareholder list to solicit potential investors. Although Metzger obtained the list as a shareholder, not as FG's lawyer, the court found the list was a "secret" of the client's under the Model Code and that making use of it to harm current management was a breach of the lawyer's duty to his client. The court ordered Metzger to disgorge the legal fees paid him by FG while he was violating his duties to it, $80,284, and to pay to FG an equal amount as punitive damages for his egregious misconduct.

The Court of Appeals reversed, Financial General Bankshares, Inc. v. Metzger, 680 F.2d 768 (D.C.Cir.1982), and reproved the district court for assuming jurisdiction of this issue:

In this case, after the federal securities law claims had been settled or dismissed . . ., the District Court retained pendent jurisdiction over common law claims that one defendant, an attorney, had breached his fiduciary duty to the plaintiff, his client. The court held a three-day trial and issued a lengthy decision dealing with novel and difficult issues of local law. No court of the District of Columbia has provided any guidance regarding the standards defining an attorney's fiduciary duties, the construction of the conflict of interest provisions of the Code of Professional Responsibility, or the remedies for breach. Under these circumstances, we find that the District Court abused its discretion in exercising pendent jurisdiction over the local claims. . . .

. . .

Having concluded that Metzger had violated common law standards of fiduciary duty, the District Court also broke new ground in imposing a remedy . . . The District Court cited no District of Columbia cases, and we have discovered none, which award a monetary remedy to a client for an attorney's breach of fiduciary duty in the absence of proven pecuniary loss to the client or proven financial gain to the attorney.

Id. at 769, 771–72.

The Court of Appeals noted that in settling the underlying dispute, the corporation agreed not to oppose the defendant's takeover attempt. In exchange, the defendants agreed to offer a premium price for the company's shares: "The tender offer contemplated by the settlement has now been successfully completed. The Middle Eastern investors are in control of Financial General Bankshares, Inc." Id. at n. 5. The extensive notes by the court on the resolution of the internecine battle adds an "all's well that ends well" flavor to the opinion.

Although the Court of Appeals said that there were no District of Columbia precedents, in Wolf v. Weinstein, 372 U.S. 633, 641, 83 S.Ct. 969, 975 (1963), the Supreme Court said: "[It is a] historic maxim of equity that a fiduciary may not receive compensation for services tainted by disloyalty or conflict of interest." *Wolf* involved a bankruptcy proceeding, but the courts have consistently affirmed their inherent powers to disallow improper fees apart from the bankruptcy law. See, e.g., Berner v. Equitable Office Building Corp., 175 F.2d 218 (2d Cir. 1949); Chicago & W. Towns R.R. v. Friedman, 230 F.2d 364 (7th Cir. 1956). These precedents have been applied in other contexts. See, e.g., In re Eastern Sugar Antitrust Litigation, Pantry Pride Inc. v. Finley, Kumble, 697 F.2d 524 (3d Cir.1982).

The problem of client identity is central in hostile corporate takeovers. See generally Symposium: The Role of Counsel in Corporate Acquisitions and Takeovers: Conflicts and Complications, 39 Hastings L.J. 571 (1988). In Ward v. Succession of Freeman, 854 F.2d 780, 784–85 (5th Cir.1988), the court recognized that the interests of management and shareholders differ when a tender offer is made. Management seeks to conserve corporate assets by not paying too much for the stock and shareholders seek to transfer their stock at the highest price. Nevertheless, the court held that *Garner* applies to tender offer situations.

> . . . [W]hen all is said and done management is not managing for itself. The representative and the represented have a mutuality of interest in the representative's freely seeking advice. . . . This is not to say that management does not have allowable judgment in putting advice to use. But management judgement must stand on its merits, not behind an ironclad veil of secrecy which under all circumstances preserves it from being questioned by those for whom it is, at least in part, exercised.

Id. at 785, quoting *Garner*, supra 430 F.2d at 1101.

Having found that *Garner* applies, the court denied the plaintiffs' access to the communication because they had not demonstrated "good cause." Also see In re Diasonics, 110 F.R.D. 570 (D.Colo.1986) (shareholders of acquiring corporation could gain access to communications between officers of acquired corporation and the acquired corporation's counsel made while acquired corporation was subsidiary of acquiring corporation even though communications concerned rescinding the acquisition and acquisition was later rescinded). On the inner workings of corporate bureaucracies, see Robert Jackall, Moral Mazes: The World of Corporate Managers (1988) (focusing on mid-level management and managers near the top at the divisional level); and Hazard, Ethics and Politics in the Corporate World, 6 Yale J. on Reg. 155 (1989) (reviewing Jackall's book).

The Lawyer's Relationship to the Board of Directors

Is M.R. 1.13 as adopted a "board as client" concept more than "organization as client"?

Compare the approach suggested by the American Trial Lawyers in the American Lawyer's Code of Conduct, Rule 2.5, with M.R. 1.13.

ALCC Rule 2.5:

> A lawyer representing a corporation shall, as early as possible in the lawyer-client relationship, inform the board of directors of potential conflicts that might develop among the interests of the board, corporate officers, and shareholders. The lawyer shall receive from the board of directors instructions in advance as to how to resolve such conflicts, and shall take reasonable steps to ensure that officers with whom the lawyer deals, and the shareholders, are made aware of how the lawyer has been instructed to resolve conflicts of interest.

The comment explains:

> One of the conundrums of professional ethics has been the responsibility of a corporate lawyer who learns from a corporate official that the official has engaged in illegal conduct, either against or on behalf of the company. In informing the lawyer, the official assumes a confidential relationship. Nevertheless, the lawyer may feel compelled to inform the board of directors, which is generally regarded as the embodiment of the corporate entity. If the board fails to take appropriate action, however, the lawyer may then feel an obligation to inform the shareholders (although the general public will then learn about the problem, to the likely disadvantage of the company). As the question is frequently posed, who is the lawyer's client in such circumstances?

> Although it has not been generally recognized, the problem is basically a familiar and relatively simple one of conflict of interest. The lawyer's difficulty is insoluble only because the lawyer has failed to inform the board of the readily foreseeable conflicts of interest and to receive guidance in advance. On the basis of the board's instructions, the lawyer can then make sure that each interested party is informed in advance and is thereby in a position to seek adequate protection.

> For example, one board might prefer to maximize candor between its officers and the lawyer, and therefore, instruct the lawyer to honor the officers' confidences, even in reporting to the board. The shareholders would then be in a position to approve or

disapprove that policy, or to relinquish their shares. Another board might prefer to know everything the lawyer knows. In that event the officers would be on notice that they might want to consult personal counsel before disclosing certain information to corporate counsel . . .

Is this comment consistent with the principle that as fiduciaries of the corporation, corporate officers have a duty to reveal "awkward" information to counsel or the board of directors?

The American Trial Lawyer Association's approach suggests that it would be appropriate for the board of directors to agree to be kept uninformed. Would such an agreement be consistent with the directors' duties under corporation law? Consistent with the regulatory scheme in securities law?

Calif.Rule of Prof.Conduct 3–600 provides:

If, despite the member's actions in accordance with Paragraph (B), the highest authority that can act on behalf of the organization insists upon action or a refusal to act that is a violation of law and is likely to result in substantial injury to the organization, the member's response is limited to the member's right, and, where appropriate, duty to resign in accordance with Rule 3–700.

In the Discussion of this Rule, it is stated: "Rule 3–600 is not intended to enmesh members in the intricacies of the entity and aggregate theories of partnerships." What does this mean?

The Lawyer as Plaintiff

May the corporation lawyer who owns shares in the corporation sue the corporation as a plaintiff-shareholder after terminating representation of the company?

In Doe v. A. Corp., 330 F.Supp. 1352 (S.D.N.Y.1971), aff'd sub nom. Hall v. A. Corp., 453 F.2d 1375 (2d Cir.1972), Doe had been an attorney with the law firm that represented the A corporation; he had worked on A corporation business and had had access to its confidential files. Two weeks before he left the firm, he bought one share of A corporation stock. He admitted that he bought this stock for the purpose of trying to oust current management by initiating a shareholder-derivative suit. He further conceded that "every fact alleged in the complaint" was acquired by him through his employment as A's lawyer. The court held: "[I]f an attorney believes that executives of a corporate client are engaging in wrongful conduct, he may disclose this to the corporation's board of director; but he infringes Canon 4 [of the Code of Professional Responsibility] if he himself institutes suit. ABA Opinion 202 (1940)." 330 F.Supp. at 1355.

In Hull v. Celanese Corp., 513 F.2d 568 (2d Cir.1975), Hull, an employee of Celanese, brought suit against the company alleging sex-based discrimination under Title VII of the Civil Rights Act of 1964. Delulio was a member of Celanese's in-house counsel staff, who had done some work on the Hull suit for Celanese. Delulio contacted Hull's lawyers and asked them to represent her in the lawsuit as another plaintiff. Celanese sought to disqualify the firm based on the risk that confidential information received by Delulio in her role as the corporation's lawyer would be used by the firm against Celanese. The firm argued that in its dealings with Delulio it had "cautioned [her] not to reveal any information received in confidence as an attorney for Celanese, but rather to confine her revelations . . . to the facts of her own case." Id. at 571. The court, after commending the firm for the care it had taken, disqualified it from representing either plaintiff, and then added that its decision "should not be read to imply that either Hull or Delulio cannot pursue her claim of employment discrimination." Id. at 572.

How would Delulio's new lawyer proceed?

The Lawyer as Member of the Board of Directors

The Comment to M.R. 1.7 reads in part:

A lawyer for a corporation or other organization who is a member of its board of directors should determine whether the responsibilities of the two roles may conflict. The lawyer may be called on to advise the corporation in matters involving actions of the directors. Consideration should be given to the frequency with which such situations may arise, the potential intensity of the conflict, the effect of the lawyer's resignation from the board and the possibility of the corporation's obtaining legal advice from another lawyer for such situations. If there is material risk that the dual role will compromise the lawyer's independence of professional judgment the lawyer should not serve as a director.

In Informal Opinion 930 (1966), the ABA was asked whether a lawyer for a bank may also serve on its board. The Committee in a short opinion approved of the dual role. The Committee's conclusion was that this was a common practice "which to our knowledge has not been criticized" and that it did not involve the representation of conflicting interests.

Lawyers who serve in dual roles as outside counsel and member of the client's board of directors may jeopardize the attorney-client privilege. The privilege is not available for information communicated to or learned by counsel through membership on the board. See, e.g., Securities and Exchange Commission v. Gulf & Western Industries, Inc., 518 F.Supp. 675 (D.D.C.1981).

Some firms prohibit their members from sitting on the boards of client corporations; others have lawyers on the boards of almost all clients.

B. ALMOST CLIENTS

FASSIHI v. SOMMERS

Court of Appeals of Michigan, 1981.
107 Mich.App. 509, 309 N.W.2d 645.

PER CURIAM.

. . . In his complaint, plaintiff asserted that he was a 50% shareholder, officer, and director of Livonia Physicians X–Ray, P.C., a professional medical corporation. The various allegations included breach of the attorney-client relationship, breach of fiduciary, legal, and ethical duties, fraud, and legal malpractice. Defendant filed a motion for summary judgment on the basis that . . . no attorney-client relationship existed with plaintiff. This motion was denied. . . .

Following the trial court's order denying defendant's motion for summary judgment, plaintiff deposed attorney Donald Epstein. However, during the deposition Epstein repeatedly refused to answer questions, claiming an attorney-client privilege. Plaintiff moved for an order compelling discovery, but the trial court denied the motion . . . This order also extended to both parties the opportunity to take an interlocutory appeal from the denial of their respective motion.

This Court granted leave to take the interlocutory appeals . . .

The following factual recitation comes from plaintiff's complaint and the statement of facts appearing in his brief. Since we are obligated to consider the facts in the light most favorable to the nonmoving party when passing on a motion for summary judgment . . . we are hereinafter setting forth this favorable picture.

In the summer of 1973, plaintiff, a radiologist practicing medicine in Ohio, was asked by Dr. Rudolfo Lopez to come to Michigan and join him in the practice of radiology at St. Mary's Hospital in Livonia. In August, 1973, the doctors formed a professional corporation known as Livonia Physicians X–Ray. Each doctor owned 50% of the stock, was an employee of the corporation, and received an identical salary. Plaintiff contends that the by-laws adopted by the two shareholders made each of them a member of the Board of Directors and that the two of them constituted the entirety of the board. Dr. Lopez was president of the corporation, and Dr. Fassihi was the secretary-treasurer.

Shortly after the corporation was organized, plaintiff sought and obtained medical staff privileges at St. Mary's. For a period of approximately 18 months, the doctors practiced together at the hospital in the radiology department.

Some time on or before June 4, 1975, Dr. Lopez decided that he no longer desired to be associated with plaintiff. Consequently, Lopez requested that the attorney for the professional corporation, the defendant, ascertain how plaintiff could be ousted from Livonia Physicians X–Ray.

On or about June 6, 1975, defendant's agent, Donald Epstein, Esquire, personally delivered to plaintiff a letter dated June 4, 1975, purporting to terminate his interest in the professional corporation. The letter stated that this termination followed a meeting of the board of directors.[2] Plaintiff denies that any such meeting ever occurred. On June 9, 1975, plaintiff went to St. Mary's to perform his duties as a staff radiologist. At this time officials at the hospital told him that, due to his "termination" from the professional corporation, he was no longer eligible to practice at St. Mary's.

Dr. Lopez had an agreement with St. Mary's Hospital prior to plaintiff's association with Livonia Physicians X–Ray giving him personal and sole responsibility for staffing the radiology department. This agreement necessitated membership in Livonia Physicians X–Ray, P.C.

Defendant was responsible for drafting all the agreements pertaining to membership in the professional corporation. Defendant, and specifically Donald Epstein, had knowledge of the arrangements between Dr. Lopez and the hospital but never disclosed these facts to plaintiff. Plaintiff finally states that defendant has represented both Lopez individually and the professional corporation without disclosing to him this dual representation.

This case presents us with the difficult question of what duties, if any, an attorney representing a closely held corporation has to a 50% owner of the entity, individually.[3] This is a problem of first impression in Michigan.

We start our analysis by examining whether an attorney-client relationship exists between plaintiff and defendant. . . .

A corporation exists as an entity apart from its shareholders, even where the corporation has but one shareholder. . . . While no Michigan case has addressed whether a corporation's attorney has an attorney-client relationship with the entity's shareholders, the general proposition of corporate identity apart from its shareholders leads us to conclude, in accordance with decisions from other jurisdictions, that the attorney's client is the corporation and not the shareholders. . . .

2. Whether or not the by-laws of the professional corporation made Drs. Fassihi and Lopez the sole directors of the organization, Donald Epstein in a deposition contended that a Joseph Carolan was a third director. Mr. Carolan was apparently the business manager of Livonia Physicians X–Ray. We assume that at least defendant considers him a proper director. Otherwise, it would have been impossible for Lopez to effect his scheme of terminating Fassihi's association with the professional corporation as Fassihi would have undoubtedly opposed the plan. In any case, a corporate arrangement whereby one 50% shareholder can oust the other 50% shareholder—whether individually or with the assistance of a third director—seems highly unusual and comes to us on a stipulated hypothetical for purposes of this appeal.

3. See L. Greenhouse, In Corporate Law, Who's the Client? The New York Times, Sunday, February 15, 1981, p. 20 E.

Although we conclude that no attorney-client relationship exists between plaintiff and defendant, this does not necessarily mean that defendant had no fiduciary duty to plaintiff. The existence of an attorney-client relationship merely establishes a per se rule that the lawyer owes fiduciary duties to the client.

A fiduciary relationship arises when one reposes faith, confidence, and trust in another's judgment and advice. Where a confidence has been betrayed by the party in the position of influence, this betrayal is actionable, and the origin of the confidence is immaterial. . . . Furthermore, whether there exists a confidential relationship apart from a well defined fiduciary category is a question of fact. . . . Based upon the pleadings, we cannot say that plaintiff's claim is clearly unenforceable as a matter of law.

Plaintiff asserts that he reposed in defendant his trust and confidence and believed that, as a 50% shareholder in Livonia Physicians X–Ray, defendant would treat him with the same degree of loyalty and impartiality extended to the other shareholder, Dr. Lopez. In his complaint plaintiff states that he was betrayed in this respect. Specifically, plaintiff asserts that he was not advised of defendant's dual representation of the corporate entity and Dr. Lopez personally.[5] Plaintiff also alleges that he was never informed of the contract between Lopez and St. Mary's which gave Lopez sole responsibility in the staffing of the radiology department and, more importantly, that defendant actively participated with Lopez in terminating plaintiff's association with the corporation and using the Lopez–St. Mary's contract to his detriment.

In support of his position that he has an attorney-client relationship with defendant, plaintiff cites a number of cases standing for the proposition that the corporate veil will be pierced where the corporate identity is being used to further fraud or injustice. . . . These cases are not factually similar to the instant matter as they involve claims against a corporate principal attempting to protect himself from personal liability through the corporate entity. At the same time, these cases are instructive as they point out the difficulties in treating a closely held corporation with few shareholders as an entity distinct from the shareholders. Instances in which the corporation attorneys stand in a fiduciary relationship to individual shareholders are obviously more likely to arise where the number of shareholders is small. In such cases it is not really a matter of the courts piercing the corporate entity. Instead, the corporate attorneys, because of their close interaction with a shareholder or shareholders, simply stand in confidential relationships in respect to both the corporation and individual shareholders.[6]

5. The Code of Professional Responsibility and Canons DR 5–105 requires full disclosure of dual representation of parties to the clients involved and forbids dual representation in some circumstances.

6. Although factually different, Prescott v. Coppage, 266 Md. 562, 296 A.2d 150 (1972), is illuminating in its discussion of an attorney's obligations to third parties apart from a

In addition to the claim for breach of fiduciary duties, plaintiff contends that his complaint states a cause of action for fraud. The elements of fraud are: (1) a material representation which is false; (2) known by defendant to be false, or made recklessly without knowledge of its truth or falsity; (3) that defendant intended plaintiff to rely upon the representation; (4) that, in fact, plaintiff acted in reliance upon it; and (5) thereby suffered injury. Hyma v. Lee, 338 Mich. 31, 37, 60 N.W.2d 920 (1953); Cormack v. American Underwriters Corp., 94 Mich. App. 379, 385, 288 N.W.2d 634 (1979). The false material representation needed to establish fraud may be satisfied by the failure to divulge a fact or facts the defendant has a duty to disclose. An action based on the failure to disclose facts is one for fraudulent concealment. . . .

Plaintiff's fraudulent concealment claim is premised on defendant's failure to divulge its dual representation of Livonia Physicians X–Ray and the failure of defendant to disclose the existence of the contract between Dr. Lopez and St. Mary's Hospital. We agree with plaintiff that, irrespective of any other duty, defendant would have an obligation to divulge its dual representation of the corporation and Dr. Lopez individually. The failure to divulge this fact might serve as the basis for a fraudulent concealment action. We cannot agree, however, that defendant had an obligation to divulge the existence or contents of the Lopez–St. Mary's Hospital contract to plaintiff. Defendant's knowledge of this contract arose out of a confidential attorney-client relationship between [it] and Dr. Lopez.[7] This attorney-client relationship prohibited defendant from divulging facts learned during the course of representation of Dr. Lopez unless Lopez waived his right to the attorney-client privilege. While defendant should have, and likely did, consider the effect that its relationship with Lopez might have on the representation of the corporation and incidentally plaintiff, as a 50% shareholder, officer, and director, it was not prohibited from representing both if its employees' independent professional judgment on behalf of either would not likely be adversely affected by representation of the other. Code of Professional Responsibility and Canons DR 5–105(C).

· · ·

We now turn to the issue of whether defendant has a privilege to refuse to answer questions relative to communications concerning the ouster of plaintiff from the corporation. Defendant contends that these communications are privileged because they were made on behalf of the majority of the board of directors and the attorney-client privilege belongs to the control group.

specific attorney-client relationship. In *Prescott*, the Maryland court found that the attorney owed a duty to a preferred creditor on a third-party beneficiary theory. The question in any given case is whether, irrespective of an actual attorney-client relationship, plaintiff has pled sufficient allegations tending to show some legal duty on the part of the attorney to him personally.

7. This is not to say that Dr. Lopez's personal failure to divulge the existence of his contract with St. Mary's Hospital could not serve as the basis for a fraudulent concealment claim.

We hold that under defendant's own argument, the attorney-client privilege may not be asserted against plaintiff. As a member of the board of directors, plaintiff was a member of the corporate control group. See Diversified Industries, Inc. v. Meredith, 572 F.2d 596 (CA 8, 1977). Thus, with respect to any communications defendant had with Dr. Lopez while representing the corporation, as opposed to Lopez personally, plaintiff, as a member of the control group, is equally entitled to this information.

Additionally, defendant acknowledges that the attorney-client privilege does not protect communications made for the purpose of perpetrating a fraud. See Garner v. Wolfinbarger, 430 F.2d 1093 (CA 5, 1970). Although plaintiff's complaint does not use the magic word "fraud", the gist of his complaint rests on a species of fraud. Plaintiff asserts that defendant, while under the guise of representing the corporation, conspired to withhold information from him which he had a right to have as a 50% shareholder and member of the board of directors and to wrongfully deprive him of the benefits of a business opportunity. These allegations were sufficient to defeat the invocation of the attorney-client relationship pursuant to the fraud exception.

. . .

Questions and Comments

Compare *Fassihi* to *Meehan*. Would the *Fassihi* court have found on the facts in *Meehan* that the corporation's law firm owed fiduciary duties to Hopps during Hopps' tenure as chairman of the board? After the bankruptcy? Does not the CEO of a large publicly-held corporation "repose faith, confidence, and trust in [corporate counsel's] judgment and advice" as Fassihi did? Is a fiduciary relationship thus created between corporate counsel and the CEO? Between corporate counsel and the shareholders? See Schaeffer v. Cohen, Rosenthal, Price . . ., 405 Mass. 506, 541 N.E.2d 997, 1002 (1989), in which the court stated in dicta:

> [T]here is logic in the proposition that, even though counsel for a closely held corporation does not by virtue of that relationship alone have an attorney-client relationship with the individual shareholders, counsel nevertheless owes each shareholder a fiduciary duty. See *Fassihi*, . . . for a well-reasoned opinion supporting that view. Just as an attorney for a partnership owes a fiduciary duty to each partner, it is fairly arguable that an attorney for a close corporation owes a fiduciary duty to the individual shareholders.

Does the same logic extend to lawyers for publicly owned corporations?

The court in *Fassihi* found no attorney-client relationship between Fassihi and the corporation's law firm, but held that the firm nevertheless owed this 50% shareholder fiduciary duties, which presumably it breached by helping to oust him from the corporation and keeping important information from him. Also see Adell v. Sommers,

Schwartz, Silver and Schwartz, P.C., 170 Mich.App. 196, 428 N.W.2d 26, 29 (1988) (lawyers for partnership owe fiduciary duties to limited partners). This is doctrinally consistent with the proposition that a lawyer for a corporation represents it and not any of its constituents, but is unclear as to the extent of the responsibility. If the lawyer's duties are essentially the same as those owed a client, would it not be clearer to call it a client relationship?

A number of courts simply hold that a lawyer representing a closely-held corporation also represents the individual shareholders as joint clients. In re Banks, 283 Or. 459, 584 P.2d 284 (1978), involved a closely-held family corporation that had been dominated by one family member during most of its history. Other family members subsequently wrested control of the corporation, and the corporation's lawyers brought suit against him on their behalf. The court held that "in closely held . . . corporations where the operator of the corporation either owns or controls the stock in such a manner that it is reasonable to assume that there is no real reason for him to differentiate in his mind between his own and corporate interests," the lawyer for the corporation owes that person the same duty not to represent conflicting interests that she would owe a client. In In re Brownstein, 288 Or. 83, 602 P.2d 655, 657 (1979), the Oregon court went one step further:

> Where a small, closely held corporation is involved, and in the absence of a clear understanding with the corporate owners that the attorney represents solely the corporation and not their individual interests, it is improper for the attorney thereafter to represent a third party whose interests are adverse to those of the stockholders and which arise out of a transaction which the attorney handled for the corporation. In actuality, the attorney in such a situation represents the corporate owners in their individual capacities as well as the corporation unless other arrangements are clearly made.

In Rosman v. Shapiro, 653 F.Supp. 1441, 1445 (S.D.N.Y.1987), the court held that it is reasonable for a 50% shareholder in a closely held corporation, where there is only one other shareholder, to believe that the lawyer for the corporation "is in effect his own individual attorney." Is this consistent with *Meehan?*

See also Margulies v. Upchurch, 696 P.2d 1195 (Utah 1985) (lawyer for partnership may be found to have an attorney-client relationship with limited partners that would preclude him from suing them as individuals). See also Woods v. Superior Court of Tulare County, 149 Cal.App.3d 931, 197 Cal.Rptr. 185 (1983); In re Bowman Trading Co., Inc., 99 A.D.2d 459, 471 N.Y.S.2d 289 (App.Div.1984); In the Matter of Nulle, 127 Ariz. 299, 620 P.2d 214 (1980); Opdyke v. Kent Liquor Mart, Inc., 40 Del.Ch. 316, 181 A.2d 579 (1962).

Should the courts find "joint clients" in some circumstances and a fiduciary relationship in others? What facts should be important in making this determination? Cf. Stainton v. Tarantino, 637 F.Supp.

1051, 1077 (E.D.Pa.1986) (in deciding whether attorney/client relationship exists with individual partners, jury should consider whether individual partners confided in, relied on and had partnership counsel perform legal services for them as individuals; if no attorney/client relationship, no fiduciary duty either). These questions are examined further in the notes following the next case and in the Hazard article on Triangular Relationships printed below at p. 784.

As *Fassihi* demonstrates, the question of "whistle-blowing" can readily arise in a partnership, business or closely held corporation, where one of the entrepreneurs seeks to defraud or otherwise exploit another. Ass'n Bar City of New York Op. No. 1986–2 states that an attorney representing a limited partnership represents the partnership entity; that the duty to the entity includes responsibilities to the limited partners; and hence that the attorney, upon discovering that a general partner has committed acts adversely affecting the interests of limited partners, may disclose those facts to the limited partners. In the course of the analysis, the opinion states:

> In a situation where the "governing body" of the entity is implicated in the improper act, however, disclosure to persons such as shareholders or partners outside of the "governing body" may be warranted in order to allow them to protect their interests if the governing body could not reasonably be expected to do so.

The conclusion is that the attorney "may disclose his knowledge of the general partner's actions to the limited partners so that they will be able to take steps to protect their interests."

This analysis is based upon the "entity as client" concept and obviously can be applied to a corporate entity. If the lawyer has authority to disclose to the limited partners, or stockholders as the case may be, as a matter of agency law she may have a duty to do so, at least in that she can be liable for resulting damages if she does not.

See Roberts v. Heim, 123 F.R.D. 614, 625 (D.N.Cal.1988) (limited partners are clients of the partnership's counsel for purposes of the attorney-client privilege because both counsel and the general partners have a fiduciary duty to make full disclosure of material facts to their beneficiaries (the limited partners), and withholding such information would constitute fraud).

FICKETT v. SUPERIOR COURT OF PIMA COUNTY

Court of Appeals of Arizona, Division 2, 1976.
27 Ariz.App. 793, 558 P.2d 988.

OPINION

HOWARD, CHIEF JUDGE.

Petitioners are defendants in a pending superior court action filed by the present conservator (formerly guardian) of an incompetent's estate against the former guardian and petitioners, attorneys for the former guardian. The gravamen of the complaint was that petitioner

Fickett, as attorney for the former guardian, was negligent in failing to discover that the guardian had embarked upon a scheme to liquidate the guardianship estate by misappropriation and conversion of the funds to his own use and making improper investments for his personal benefit.[1]

Petitioners filed a motion for summary judgment contending that, as a matter of law, since there was no fraud or collusion between the guardian and his attorney, the attorney was not liable for the guardian's misappropriation of the assets of the guardianship estate. In opposing the motion for summary judgment, the present conservator conceded that no fraud or collusion existed. His position, however, was that one could not say as a matter of law that the guardian's attorney owed no duty to the ward. The respondent court denied the motion for summary judgment and petitioners challenge this ruling by special action.

The general rule for many years has been that an attorney could not be liable to one other than his client in an action arising out of his professional duties, in the absence of fraud or collusion. 7 Am.Jur.2d, Attorneys at Law, § 167. In denying liability of the attorney to one not in privity of contract for the consequences of professional negligence, the courts have relied principally on two arguments: (1) That to allow such liability would deprive the parties to the contract of control of their own agreement; and (2) that a duty to the general public would impose a huge potential burden of liability on the contracting parties. An annotation of cases dealing with an attorney's liability to one other than his immediate client for the consequences of negligence in carrying out his professional duties may be found in Annot., 45 A.L.R.3d 1181 et seq.

We cannot agree with petitioners that they owed no duty to the ward and that her conservator could not maintain an action because of lack of privity of contract. We are of the opinion that the better view is that the determination of whether, in a specific case, the attorney will be held liable to a third person not in privity is a matter of policy and involves the balancing of various factors, among which are the extent to which the transaction was intended to affect the plaintiff, the foreseeability of harm to him, the degree of certainty that the plaintiff suffered injury, the closeness of the connection between the defendant's conduct and the injuries suffered, the moral blame attached to the defendant's conduct, and the policy of preventing future harm. Biakanja v. Irving, 49 Cal.2d 647, 320 P.2d 16 (1958); Lucas v. Hamm, 56 Cal.2d 583, 15 Cal.Rptr. 821, 364 P.2d 685 (1961); Heyer v. Flaig, 70 Cal.2d 223, 74 Cal.Rptr. 225, 449 P.2d 161 (1969); Licata v. Spector, 26 Conn.Sup. 378, 225 A.2d 28 (1966); Donald v. Garry, 19 Cal.App.3d 769, 97 Cal.Rptr. 191 (1971).

1. The facts of the guardian's misconduct can be found in the case of In Re Guardianship of Styer, 24 Ariz.App. 148, 536 P.2d 717 (1975). There we affirmed a judgment surcharging the guardian in the sum of $378,789.62.

We believe that the public policy of this state permits the imposition of a duty under the circumstances presented here. In the case of In re Fraser, 83 Wash.2d 884, 523 P.2d 921 (1974), the Supreme Court of Washington in considering a complaint concerning an attorney's refusal to withdraw as attorney for a client-guardian, stated:

"The respondent maintains and we agree that under the circumstances he would not have been justified in withdrawing as counsel until such time as the guardian had secured the agreement of some other attorney to take over the handling of the guardianship. As the respondent suggests, *the attorney owes a duty to the ward, as well as to the guardian.* Since the guardian in this case manifested a greater interest in obtaining money for herself than in serving the interest of the ward, it would have been hazardous to the interest of the ward to turn the assets of her small estate over to the guardian.

In In re Michelson, 8 Wash.2d 327, 335, 111 P.2d 1011, 1015 (1941), we said:

'It must be borne in mind that the real object and purpose of a guardianship is to preserve and conserve the ward's property for his own use, as distinguished from the benefit of others.'

We think that under the circumstances of this case, the respondent cannot be faulted for refusing to abandon the ward at the guardian's request." 523 P.2d at 928. (Emphasis ours)

We are of the opinion that when an attorney undertakes to represent the guardian of an incompetent, he assumes a relationship not only with the guardian but also with the ward. If, as is contended here, petitioners knew or should have known that the guardian was acting adversely to his ward's interests, the possibility of frustrating the whole purpose of the guardianship became foreseeable as did the possibility of injury to the ward. In fact, we conceive that the ward's interests overshadow those of the guardian. We believe the following statement in *Heyer v. Flaig,* supra, as to an attorney's duty to an intended testamentary beneficiary is equally appropriate here:

"The duty thus recognized in *Lucas* stems from the attorney's undertaking to perform legal services for the client but reaches out to protect the intended beneficiary. We impose this duty because of the relationship between the attorney and the intended beneficiary; public policy requires that the attorney exercise his position of trust and superior knowledge responsibly so as not to affect adversely persons whose rights and interests are certain and foreseeable.

Although the duty accrues directly in favor of the intended testamentary beneficiary, the scope of the duty is determined by reference to the attorney-client context. Out of the agreement to provide legal services to a client, the prospective testator, arises the duty to act with due care as to the interests of the intended beneficiary. We do not mean to say that the attorney-client contract for legal services serves as the fundamental touchstone to fix the scope of this direct tort duty to the third party. The actual circumstances under which the attorney undertakes to perform his legal services, however, will bear on a judicial assessment of the care with which he performs his services." 74 Cal.Rptr. at 229, 449 P.2d at 165.

We, therefore, uphold the respondent court's denial of petitioners' motion for summary judgment since they failed to establish the absence of a legal relationship and concomitant duty to the ward.

. . .

Lawyers for Fiduciaries

Fickett requires a lawyer who represents a fiduciary to make reasonable efforts to discover whether the fiduciary is breaching her duties to the beneficiary. What should a lawyer do upon discovering such a breach?

Corporations have fiduciary responsibilities to their shareholders. May a lawyer for a corporation be sued by shareholders for failing to discover (and stop) corporate fraud? Does *Fickett* provide additional guidance to the lawyer for a corporation that is dominated by one person?

In *Carter/Johnson*, see p. 760 above, the outside directors retained counsel of their own as the situation at the company grew worse. What obligation, if any, would that lawyer have to the company?

See Dobris, Ethical Problems for Lawyers Upon Trust Terminations: Conflicts of Interests, 38 U.Miami L.Rev. 1 (1983), for a thoughtful analysis of conflicts where the lawyer represents the trustee.

The Attorney–Client Privilege of a Fiduciary

As discussed in the notes after *Yablonski,* the corporation's attorney-client privilege may be pierced on a showing of good cause by shareholders suing on behalf of the corporation. See the discussion of *Garner v. Wolfinbarger* above at p. 753. The rationale of *Garner* has been extended beyond the shareholder-corporation context to other beneficiary/fiduciary situations, allowing beneficiaries access to information otherwise protected by the attorney-client privilege in suits alleging breach of fiduciary duties.

In Valente v. Pepsico, Inc., 68 F.R.D. 361 (D.Del.1975), the minority shareholders in Wilson Co. brought suit against Pepsico, which was the majority shareholder, alleging violations of the securities laws. The court found that *Garner* was relevant because a majority shareholder owes fiduciary responsibilities, just as a corporation, does, to minority shareholders. The court held that the minority shareholders could gain access to communications between Pepsico and its lawyers that touched upon the interests of the minority and the duties owed to them.

"A fiduciary owes the obligation to his beneficiaries to go about his duties without obscuring his reasons from the legitimate inquiries of the beneficiaries." Id. at 370. The court stated that the purpose of the privilege, to encourage frank communication between lawyer and client, was outweighed by the "more general and important right of those who look to fiduciaries to safeguard their interests to be able to determine the proper functioning of the fiduciary." Id. n. 16.

In Quintel Corp., N.V. v. Citibank, N.A., 567 F.Supp. 1357 (S.D.N.Y. 1983), Gajria contracted with Citibank to be his agent in acquiring certain investment property. His suit alleged that Citibank breached its fiduciary duties to him in acquiring the property. The court, in applying *Garner* to allow Gajria access to communications between Citibank and its lawyers, said:

> . . . Here as in *Garner,* Citibank and Gajria had a mutuality of interest in the consummation of the acquisition on the most advantageous terms. Citibank acted not for itself but for Gajria, in similar fashion to corporate management's actions taken on behalf of the corporations shareholders. Here as in *Garner* . . ., the fiduciary's duty to exercise its authority without veiling its reasons from the grantor of that authority outweighs the fiduciary's interest in the confidentiality of its attorney's communications. The *Garner* rule stems not only from the general proposition that a beneficiary is entitled to know how the authority he has granted has been exercised but on the recognition that because of the mutuality of interest between the parties, the faithful fiduciary has nothing to hide from his beneficiary.

Id. at 1363.

See also Aguinaga v. John Morrell & Co., 112 F.R.D. 671, 681 (D.Kan. 1986) (*Garner* applies to allow union members access to communications between union counsel and union leadership); Donovan v. Fitzsimmons, 90 F.R.D. 583 (N.D.Ill.1981) (*Garner* rule allows the Secretary of Labor, suing a pension fund on behalf of the fund's beneficiaries, access to communications between the pension fund trustee and its lawyers). Compare In re Atlantic Financial Management Securities Litigation, 121 F.R.D. 141, 146 (D.Mass.1988) ("Without a showing of a fiduciary relationship, the *Garner* exception does not apply."); and In re Colocotronis Tanker Securities Litigation, 449 F.Supp. 828 (S.D.N.Y.1978) (*Garner* exception inapplicable between parties to an arms-length contract). Should *Garner* allow individuals who allege the government has violated its trust to discover communications of government lawyers upon a showing of good cause?

See also Note, The Attorney–Client Privilege in Class Actions: Fashioning an Exception to Promote Adequacy of Representation, 94 Harv.L.Rev. 947 (1984) (arguing that a *Garner*-like exception be created for class members who seek access to communication between class representatives and counsel).

Commentators have argued that a broad interpretation of *Garner* "effectively swallows the rule . . . ." See Developments in the Law— Privileged Communication: III. Attorney–Client Privilege, 98 Harv.L. Rev. 1501, 1527 (1985) (which argues that *Garner* be abandoned altogether in favor of the crime/fraud exception to the attorney-client privilege). What are the dangers of allowing beneficiaries access to their fiduciaries' conversations with counsel? If the faithful fiduciary has "nothing to hide" from his beneficiary, why must the beneficiary show good cause before gaining access to the confidential communications between lawyer and fiduciary?

Some courts have held that the fiduciary does not have a privilege to assert against the beneficiary, i.e., that the beneficiary is a joint client for purposes of the privilege. See, e.g., Roberts v. Heim, 123 F.R.D. 614 (N.D.Cal.1988) (limited partners are joint clients of lawyer for partnership for purposes of the privilege); United States v. Evans, 796 F.2d 264, 265–66 (9th Cir.1986) (pension trustee may not assert privilege against pension plan beneficiaries because "trustee is not the real client in the sense that he is personally being served"); Washington–Baltimore Newspaper Guild v. Washington Star Co., 543 F.Supp. 906 (D.D.C.1982) (beneficiaries of an employees' benefit plan granted access to communications between the plan's administrators and their lawyers without requiring a showing of good cause). Note that in California the courts have held that they are precluded by statute from adopting *Garner*. Hence, in that state beneficiaries would be denied access to fiduciary-lawyer communications unless the court found that beneficiaries were joint clients, whereupon the joint client exception to the privilege would provide free access. See *Roberts v. Heim*, supra (limited partners are joint clients; decided under federal common law but court notes that result would be the same under California law); and Hoiles v. Superior Court of Orange County, 157 Cal.App.3d 1192, 204 Cal.Rptr. 111, 115 n. 4 (1984).

In *Valente*, supra, the court shifted the burden to the fiduciary, requiring that it show why the privilege should not yield. Is this middle position between *Garner* and no privilege a better alternative?

The privilege still protects communications between fiduciary and lawyer that do not relate to the fiduciary relationship, or that occur after the fiduciary relationship has been terminated. What about communications between the fiduciary and counsel about forming the fiduciary relationship, which by definition occur before the fiduciary relationship actually exists? Compare *Quintel*, 567 F.Supp. at 1364 ("Prior to the investor's entry on the scene the important mutuality of interest is absent since Citibank's interest is in putting together a proposal that it can sell to the investor, an interest not shared by the investor"; the privilege holds); with *Roberts v. Heim*, supra (limited partners may later gain free access to these communications). Should communications between the fiduciary and its lawyers about the extent of its obligations to the beneficiary be available to the beneficiary under *Garner*? The court in *Quintel* said yes, stating that such communications were made "as part of and in furtherance of . . . fiduciary obligations."   567 F.Supp. at 1357.

GEOFFREY C. HAZARD JR., "TRIANGULAR LAWYER RELATIONSHIPS: AN EXPLORATORY ANALYSIS"
1 Georgetown Journal of Legal Ethics 15 (1987).*

I. Introduction

This article examines the nature of a lawyer's responsibilities where the lawyer's client has a special legal relationship with another party that modifies the lawyer's "normal" professional responsibilities. This legal relationship is termed "triangular," denoting the coexistence of a linkage of legal responsibility between the lawyer's client and a third person along with a linkage of professional responsibility between the lawyer and the client. The combination results in a special legal relationship between the lawyer and the third person.

. . .

This exploration focuses on two types of triangular relationships. The first involves a client in a fiduciary relationship to a third party. The classic example is that of a lawyer representing a guardian in matters relating to the guardian's responsibilities to a ward. In that relationship, the client-guardian has a set of strong and well defined legal obligations. Given these obligations, what are the legal obligations of the lawyer to the ward?

The lawyer→guardian→ward triangular relationship can be diagrammed:

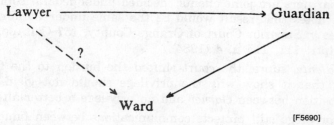

[F5690]

The second type of triangular relationship involves a third party who owes fiduciary duties to the lawyer's client, and the third party rather than the client is the one with whom the lawyer deals ordinarily. The classic situation is that of a lawyer who represents a corporation but who, in the ordinary course of professional service, deals with the corporation's officers, directors, and employees. To simplify terminology, we can treat the corporate officers, directors, and employees as a single category, even though important differences exist in their legal relationships to the corporation. Thus simplified, the corporate lawyer triangular relationship can be designated as lawyer→corporation←officer.

* Copyright © 1987 by the Georgetown Journal of Legal Ethics.

The lawyer-corporation-officer triangular relationship can be diagrammed:

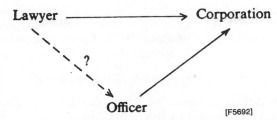

[F5692]

The difference in the vectors of obligation in these two triangular relationships is important. In the lawyer→guardian→ward triangular relationship, the ward is the dependent person and the obligee of the guardian, but the guardian is the dependent person and the primary obligee of the lawyer. In the lawyer→corporation←officer triangular relationship, the corporation is the dependent entity and the obligee of both the lawyer and the corporate officer. This structural difference in obligations can help identify and define the lawyer's role in the two triangular relationships.

These two basic triangles can be used to analyze other triangular relationships that arise throughout law practice. It may be that some triangular relationships cannot be categorized according to these two basic types; certainly all the relationships categorized under one of these types are not identical to each other in all important respects. Hence, this article does not explore all the implications of analysis "triangularity." It is addressed to the classic examples of the two basic types, but further study may indicate that this can be applied to all triangular relationships.

Other triangular relationships can be classified into the two basic types:

I.	II.
Classic	*Classic*
Lawyer→Guardian→Ward	Lawyer→Corporation←Officer
Others	*Others*
Lawyer→General Partner→Partnership	Lawyer→Partnership←General Partner
Lawyer→Govt. Employee→Govt.	Lawyer→Govt.←Govt. Employee
Lawyer→Union Officer→Union	Lawyer→Union←Union Officer
Lawyer→Director→Corp.	Lawyer→Ward←Guardian

As the foregoing chart depicts, whether a triangular relationship falls into one or the other of the two basic categories depends on which party is the lawyer's client. If the lawyer represents the *guardian,* for example, the relationship is lawyer→guardian→ward and is of the first basic type. On the other hand, if the lawyer represents the *ward,* the relationship is lawyer→ward←guardian and is of the second basic type. Similarly, a lawyer retained to represent a corporate officer or director rather than the corporation falls under the first basic type, whereas the normal corporate lawyer relationship is lawyer→corporation←director and falls under the second basic type.

. . .

II. Traditional Concepts for Defining a Lawyer's Responsibilities

A. Three Possible Relationships

Part of the difficulty posed by triangular lawyer relationships lies in the traditional limitations in the definition of a lawyer's responsibilities. Generally, those responsibilities recognize only three relationships that a lawyer may have. One is with a client; the second is with the court; and the third is with a third party. In substance and orientation, these relationships differ from each other radically. In moral and existential quality, they are strangely alike in their radical simplicity. They characterize the lawyer's "relevant other" respectively as something like friend, father, and foe.

1. Clients

In the relationship with a client, the lawyer is required above all to demonstrate loyalty. For the present discussion it is unnecessary to describe the dimensions of this duty of loyalty in detail. The duty includes maintaining diligent preference for the client's interests with the sole purpose of maximizing them—"zeal"—and doing so with sedulous protection of the client's secrets and confidences. Charles Fried analogized this relationship to that of "friend." [17] Although the analogy to friendship is imperfect in many important details, it is generally satisfactory. A client is one to whom the lawyer is friend, indeed friend as distinguished from "foe."

The relationship is otherwise largely unstructured, however. The lawyer's efforts may go as far as the law allows one person to act on behalf of another. The conventional statement of the duty of loyalty requires that, if the client so demands, the lawyer pursue the representation to the "bounds of the law." Except for this exterior boundary of legality and a few technical particulars, the direction and purpose of the lawyer's activity in the lawyer-client relationship are legally undefined. The lack of any such structure allows maximum flexibility, which in turn facilitates the partisan purpose of the lawyer-client relationship.

. . .

Not only is the lawyer-client relationship legally unstructured, aside from the requirement that it be "within the bounds of the law," but it is also enveloped in secrecy. The duty of confidentiality prohibits the lawyer from revealing anything about the client's affairs to anyone else—even the client's family—except as necessary to carry out endeav-

17. Fried, The Lawyer as Friend: The Moral Foundations of the Lawyer–Client Relationship, 85 Yale L.J. 1060 (1976).

ors on the client's behalf. . . . The lawyer-client relationship in practice is an essential instrument in many undertakings at the margin of legality, with consequent implication of the lawyer in transactions that could beget disapproval, disgust, and ostracism if they were brought into open view by others. In serving a client, the lawyer is largely shielded from such informal social controls because his or her work is largely done in secret. The low visibility of the lawyer's work with clients permits the lawyer to operate largely free of legal and social restraint.

The structure of the lawyer's relationship with a client thus is legally both amorphous and secret. Subject to the client's approval and "within the limits of the law," the lawyer operates in something of a legal vacuum in working for a client, especially compared to the working environment, for example, of a securities underwriter, an accountant, or a policeman. Similar immunity from general social norms and scrutiny is enjoyed only by undercover agents, political go-betweens, and Cayman Island bankers.

2. Courts

The second of the lawyer's legal relationships, in the traditional conception, is with the court. The basic proposition posits that "A lawyer is an officer of the court." As an officer of the court the lawyer's duty is to play by the rules of the litigation game. The rules of the game are the laws of procedure and evidence—rules about pleading, discovery, objections, appeals, etc. In substance, these rules impose little constraint, short of fraud, on the advocate's role. As long as an advocate speaks through a complaint, brief, oral argument, or other forensic medium, he or she is permitted to assert anything not plainly frivolous or knowingly false. Rule 11 of the Federal Rules of Civil Procedure qualifies this freedom in the federal courts by requiring some due diligence in investigating facts. More generally, under the "duty of candor" the lawyer is obliged, notwithstanding his or her duty to the client, to tell the truth in statements made to the court and to refrain from offering submissions on a client's behalf that the lawyer knows are false or frivolous.

. . .

Once the advocate has met the minimal requirements of due diligence and candor when speaking on his or her own behalf, however, the substantive license is nearly wide open. The lawyer is accorded economic and moral immunity from the costs and consequences of the representation. . . .

Although the lawyer's substantive responsibility to the court is minimal, the formal aspects of that relationship—the law of procedure and the rules of evidence—are highly detailed and exacting. The law of procedure and rules of evidence prescribe the parties' conduct in relationship to each other. Thus, rule 8 of the Federal Rules of Civil Procedure provides: "A pleading which sets forth a claim for relief

. . . shall contain . . . a short and plain statement of the claim showing that the pleader is entitled to relief. . . ." While this rule is addressed formally to the parties, it is addressed implicitly to the advocate and reflexively to the advocate's legal relationship with the judge. Because of this rule, an advocate cannot convey the nature of his client's cause to the judge in just any simple and convenient way, such as sending the judge a letter. The advocate may present the cause only in a complaint formulated and filed according to rule 8. . . .

The advocate's relationship to the judge is not only controlled by an elaborate structure of legal rules but is also under the continuous surveillance of a suspicious monitor, opposing counsel. . . .

There is a further peculiarity about the lawyer's relationship to the court. The task in which the lawyer and the judge are engaged—along with the lawyer's client and the opposing lawyer and his client—is a game of make-believe. The game is litigation—the presentation of evidence and argument to establish facts and rules for resolving the dispute between the parties. The game is real in its "internal" manifestations, because it involves real energy, real emotion, real credibility, and real expenditures. It is also real in its "external" consequences, because there are winners and losers; real money passes according to the outcome. The immediate game itself, however, is one of make-believe. Concerning the facts, the law proceeds on the normative fiat of its own officials. The "facts found" by the court are taken as truth by force of law, no matter what Heaven or the litigants know the "true facts" to be. Similarly, the substantive rules governing the dispute are artifacts of a political process made authoritative by law. In the immediate sense, the law is what the judges say it is. Under the rules of the litigation game, these legal constructs pass for truth and justice.

Morally and existentially, the relationship between advocate and judge is the converse of the lawyer's relationship to a client. The lawyer's role as an officer of the court is as legally structured and visible as the role of law office counselor is legally unstructured and secretive. The relationship with the court is governed by a tight formal matrix that closely regulates all of the lawyer's moves; the relationship with the client is governed only by a broad fiduciary formula that permits almost any arrangement within the limits of the law. The domain of advocate and judge is a theatrical stage in which every act and utterance is ex officio and the end product is an "official story." The domain of counselor and client is, or is supposed to be, an intimate, frank, trusting friendship, where the "client must feel free to discuss whatever he wishes" and the "lawyer should be fully informed of all the facts of the matter. . . ."

3. Third Party

The third kind of lawyer's relationship is that with a third party. In general, a third party is entitled to very little from the lawyer. If Brougham's dictum about the duty of the advocate is taken as the measure of the lawyer's legal duty to anyone but the client, a lawyer owes a third party nothing. The law concerning a lawyer's obligations to others is hard indeed, but not quite that hard. Against a lawyer, a third party is entitled to the protection of the criminal law and the law of fraud. . . . Rules against abusive litigation, such as rule 11 of the Federal Rules of Civil Procedure are essentially corollaries of the rule against fraud.

B. Inadequacy of Conceptual Premises

The established conceptual system thus allows for only three parties with whom the lawyer may have a professional relationship: client, court, third party. As we shall see, the most difficult problems in triangular relationships are those in which the lawyer is performing a counseling function as distinct from the function of advocate. In counseling situations one thing is clear: none of the relevant others is a judge. Under the established scheme, that reduces the conceptual possibilities from three to two. The lawyer's relationship to the other person—the ward or the corporate officer—must be characterized as either that between lawyer and client or that between lawyer and third party.

This is a stark choice. If the relationship is characterized as that with a client, then the duties of loyalty, zealous partisanship, and confidentiality are fully engaged. To say that when the lawyer represents a guardian he or she thereby also represents the ward, or that when a lawyer represents a corporation he or she also represents its corporate officers, is to implicate very serious practical and conceptual difficulties, indeed contradictions.

This becomes clear when we consider that, if a lawyer is deemed to represent both guardian and ward, or both corporation and corporate officer, then the following problems would arise.

1. Conflict of Interest in Current Representation

The conflicts of interest rules governing concurrent representation would determine whether the lawyer could concurrently represent the guardian and the ward, and the corporation and its officer. Guardian and ward, and corporation and corporate officer, necessarily have some potentially serious conflicts of interest. If a lawyer representing a guardian also represents the ward, and if a low threshold of sensitivity is used in applying the conflicts test, potential conflict between the two clients would always exist. As a result, a lawyer could *never* represent a guardian because that representation would necessarily entail the conflicting representation of the ward. The same would be true of corporate representation.

2. Conflict of Interest Regarding Former Client

The conflicts of interest rules regarding former clients would determine whether a lawyer could continue representation of the guardian after a dispute arose concerning the guardian's performance of his or her responsibility as such. A lawyer cannot represent one client against a former client in a matter that is the "same or substantially related." Hence, if a lawyer were deemed to represent both guardian and ward and if at any point the ward disputed the guardian's accounts, the lawyer would not only have to cease "representing" the ward but would also have to cease representing the guardian as well. The same would be true in corporate representation.

3. Confidential Communications

Communications and confidential information concerning the guardianship would be governed by the rule as to "confidences and secrets" among multiple clients. In general, a lawyer engaged in multiple representation may not withhold from one of the clients confidences and secrets that have been obtained from or on behalf of the other. If this rule were applied on the premise that guardian and ward are both considered clients, everything the guardian confided to the lawyer would have to be made available to the ward. The same would be true in the corporate situation.

4. Attorney–Client Privilege

The corollaries of attorney-client privilege that apply in multiple representation would govern the situation of guardian and ward and that of corporation and officer. Both guardian and ward, or both corporation and corporate officer, would be joint holders of the privilege. Thus the privilege could be claimed by both, could be waived by either, and would be inoperative between them. For example, a disgruntled former corporate employee could freely report corporate legal confidences to third parties. The same would be true in the situation of guardian and ward.

The courts have rightly hesitated to embrace the foregoing implications. They have been confused, however, in knowing where to stop or even where to start. They evidently recognize that the lawyer in these triangular relationships has special protective responsibilities to the person who is not the client, but they do not wish to say that these responsibilities include the whole package owed to a client. Under the conventional conceptual system, the alternative is to say that the lawyer's relationship to the other person is that of lawyer and third party. In the guardian-ward situation, this would mean that the ward is merely a stranger. The same would be true of the corporate lawyer's responsibility to a corporate director, officer, or employee.

To treat the ward or the corporate officer as a mere stranger is unappealing and incoherent. It is unappealing because it affords the ward or the corporate employee, insofar as the lawyer is concerned, only the cold comfort provided by the laws of crime and fraud. It is incoherent in the guardianship situation because it calls for the lawyer as agent of the guardian to have an arm's length relationship with one to whom the guardian has an intimate and exacting fiduciary duty.

That makes no sense under basic principles of the law of agency. Under the law of agency, the duty of an agent of the principal (i.e., the lawyer representing the guardian) to a third person (i.e., the ward) is a function of the duty of the principal (i.e., the guardian) to that person. To treat the ward as a stranger vis-à-vis the lawyer disregards that interconnection.

In the corporate situation an even more complicated set of difficulties is presented if the corporate officer is treated as a mere stranger. For one thing, the corporate officer is effectively the personification of the corporate client for most ordinary legal purposes. Corporate counsel and the corporate officer must maintain an intimacy that substantially replicates that between counsel and a flesh and blood client. It is simply impossible to hold that a person who is, in fact, a confidential intimate shall nevertheless be regarded in law as a total stranger. Moreover, under the law of agency, some kind of protective responsibility is owed by the principal to the agent in matters within the scope of the agency. A corporation owes a responsibility to its employees, sometimes something like that of guardian to ward. Thus, whatever the relationship between a corporation and its director, officer, or employee, it is not that of one stranger to another.

The alternative relationships, lawyer-client and lawyer-third party, are starkly different in substance. They are oddly similar, however, in one qualitative respect: Both are relatively unmodulated, uncomplicated, polarized relationships. A client is a friend, for whom the lawyer legally may do anything within the limits of the law of crime and fraud. A third party is a foe, to whom the lawyer legally may do anything within those same limits. Neither relationship involves graduations, intermediacies, thresholds, degrees of scrutiny—none of the rebuttable presumptions, conditions precedent or subsequent, prima facie requirements, or other differentiations that the law uses ubiquitously in other domains. Tort law, for example, distinguishes between fraud, recklessness, ordinary care, highest care, and strict liability; contract law distinguishes between invitation, offer, conditions precedent and subsequent, executory contract, mutual promises, and injurious reliance. . . . The law at large thus readily conceives modulated relationships. Indeed, modulation of relationships between the polar types of friend and foe is mostly what substantive law is about.

This kind of modulation is absent in the legal definition of relationships between lawyer and client and between lawyer and third party. The very simplicity of these autonomies fits them for application in relationships of contentious struggle, particularly in litigation and zero sum negotiation, where they are safe for being simple. A lawyer's relationship to his or her client carries only minimal obligations to others and is normally characterized by almost unambiguous fidelity. A lawyer's relationship to third parties is one of almost equally unambiguous antagonism—a mirror image. Neither relationship imposes more than minimal responsibility on the lawyer for defining the situation and structuring the relationships within it. Neither requires facility in accommodating conflicting interests, or much resiliency in interpersonal relationships, or even much self-control. Neither the advocate nor the negotiator is required to ask whether the client's present interests are more complex and more ambivalent than simply winning. Neither is required to ask whether the client's long-range interest may be defeated by immediate victory. The only judgment required is essentially tactical—how much to commit with what chance of winning. The attitude generally nurtured is that which Vince Lombardi cultivated in another professional calling, "Winning isn't everything, it's the only thing." Of course, Lombardi was addressing postadolescent males about playing football.

Such a simplistic normative premise is inadequate for defining the relationship between a lawyer and the guardian's ward or between a corporation's counsel and the corporation's directors, officers, and employees. The complex interdependencies in the[se] . . . situations do not lend themselves to analysis in terms of friend or foe.

The inadequacy of these premises no doubt explains why the responses of courts and scholars to lawyer triangular relationships have been so baffled and baffling. Lacking an adequate conceptual system to address the problem, the courts have done what courts always do in such circumstances: They adhere to bad concepts and get poor results, or, as in the *Fickett* and *Yablonski* cases, they reach what may be good results but improvise on concepts. A variation of this technique is to marshal miscellaneous "factors," factors found in all the problematic situations, and then to maintain that the correct solution depends on "all the factors." . . . [See e.g., the list of factors to be considered in deciding whether shareholder's may gain access to the corporation's confidential communications with counsel. *Garner v. Wolfinbarger.*

.   .   .

IV.   Toward Better Conceptualizations

.   .   .

Neither the concept of "client" nor that of "third party" appropriately engages the complexities of triangular relationships, even a simple one such as that of guardian and ward involved in *Fickett v. Superior Court*. The client in such a triangular situation is not a person alone—the A of classical legal hypotheticals, where "A, the owner of Blackacre" does something to or is done something by B. One who has become another's guardian is no longer A but has become "A encumbered by duties to B." So long as the relationship between A and B exists, and for some purposes even after it ends, A is not a legal monad. Rather A is a member of an "institution," (as said in *Yablonski v. United Mine Workers*), that has a "whole purpose," (as said in *Fickett*). In legal terms, a guardian as such is an officeholder constituted by law, by court appointment as in the *Fickett* case or by private contractual designation. So also, and more obviously, the corporate director, officer, or employee is an officeholder constituted by legally sanctioned private ordering, and is a member of an "institution" that has a "whole purpose." As a matter of law, both guardian and corporate officer are not persons but personages, individuals who act in legal capacities.

The relationship between the lawyer and the client in a triangular relationship is not one of complete confidentiality and intimacy. In consultations relating to the representation, the interests of a third party—the ward or the corporation—are always in contemplation. The consultations indeed are unintelligible except by reference to the needs, vulnerabilities, expectations, and history of the "relevant other." That being so, there is a special meaning in fact and in law to everything that both the fiduciary and the lawyer do and say. "Confidence," "trust," "accountability," "care," "prudent regard" as concerns the ward are the terms in which the law will interpret the guardian's words, acts, and documents. Those of the lawyer will also have to be interpreted in those terms.

Because the law imputes such meaning to the behavior of both the fiduciary and the lawyer, and because the lawyer knows or is deemed to know the law, the lawyer is in a position to interpret what he or she and the guardian are doing as a court might interpret them. Because the lawyer *can* interpret what is being done in the same way a court would, the law expects that the lawyer *will* in fact have done that, and accordingly assess whether the requisite care and bona fides have been manifested.[48] And if a day of reckoning comes concerning the guardian's performance in office, any conflict over whether that performance was full and fair cannot be simply a dispute between the guardian and the ward. The question also will arise, as in *Fickett* and *Yablonski,* as to what the lawyer had been doing.

The vocabulary and metaphorical geometry used in analyzing the "normal" lawyer-client relationship contemplate an intimate dyad of lawyer and client, facing outward toward an alien and presumptively hostile world of third parties. That vocabulary and geometry misdescribes relationships between a lawyer, a client who is a legal personage, and a third person whose very existence defines that personage. The problem is to develop concepts and vocabulary that intelligibly address relationships where the lawyer must care about two parties.

One method is to specify core or paradigm cases where the correct result is "intuitively" clear, and then to develop exceptions and qualifications. Another method is definition by exclusion—identifying the exceptions and qualifications first and then working at what remains in the middle. In this inquiry the latter procedure is used. First, it identifies, along one boundary, situations where the relationship between lawyer, client, and "relevant other" ought to be assimilated to that which "normally" obtains between lawyer, client, and "arms length" third party. Second, it considers, along another boundary, situations where the relationship can be assimilated to another "nor-

---

48. See Hazard, Rectification of Client Fraud: Death and Revival of a Professional Norm, 33 Emory L.J. 271, 282–283 (1984).

mal" case, that of a lawyer's joint representation of multiple clients. Finally, it considers the more complicated intermediate cases.

A. Client Openly Adverse to the "Other"

There are cases where a lawyer in a triangular situation has the same "arm's length" position vis-à-vis the "relevant other" as a lawyer "normally" should have on behalf of a client. The clearest is where the lawyer, not having been involved previously, is retained to represent a guardian or a corporate officer in litigation concerning that person's performance of duties. The specification that the lawyer has *no* previous involvement with the guardian or corporate officer indicates that the lawyer has not incurred any responsibility in the transaction prior to the litigation.

In the case of a guardianship, litigation could involve a proceeding initiated by the ward against the guardian, either an independent suit or a motion in the guardianship proceeding to surcharge or remove the guardian. Litigation could involve an objection by the ward to a periodic accounting submitted by the guardian; such an accounting is essentially a request by the guardian for a declaratory judgment of exoneration and is therefore a surcharge proceeding with the parties reversed. The guardian risks legal condemnation, financial loss, civic disgrace, and moral obloquy. This being the guardian's legal exposure, the guardian is entitled to vigorous marshalling of evidence tending to show he did not violate his trust, and he is entitled to vigorous argument for a favorable definition of his legal obligations. By the same token, the lawyer is obliged to make zealous efforts on the guardian's behalf; hold in confidence information garnered for the representation; and abstain from conflicting representation in the matter.

There should be no equivocation or confusion about the nature of lawyer-client relationship and the lawyer's duties in this situation. An action for surcharge is a legal claim against the guardian in his or her individual capacity for alleged wrong committed in the course of an official capacity. The potential financial loss, moral obloquy, and civic disgrace faced by the guardian are real individual interests. Persons with that kind of exposure are entitled to legal representation, which means full service advocacy.

The same analysis applies where a lawyer, not previously involved, is retained to represent a corporate director, officer, or employee. Ordinarily, that kind of representation is arranged only when there is a significant possibility that the interests of the director, officer, or employee may diverge from the corporation's interests. When this possibility exists, there is also a risk that there will be legal or informal recrimination on behalf of the corporation. Persons with that kind of exposure are likewise entitled to full service advocacy.

The same analysis again applies where a lawyer, not previously involved, is retained to represent the corporation against a corporate director, officer, or employee to redress malfeasance in office. That was the situation in *Yablonski,* where the derivative suit sought to redress the officer's misspending of organization funds. The holding in *Yablonski* that the organization is entitled to the zeal of an uncompromised advocate is correct.

A second almost equally clear case of a normal "arm's length" relationship involves the lawyer retained to represent someone nominated as guardian or corporate officer in negotiating the terms and conditions of the office. Again by hypothesis, the lawyer has not represented "the guardianship" or the corporation. If the nominee takes on the office, then he or she will have the fiduciary duties it entails—the duty to avoid self-interested transactions, the duty to use the care required in protecting the interests of the "relevant other," etc. While the general terms of these duties attach to the office, important details may be specified by contract and are therefore matters for potential negotiation. It is familiar hornbook learning that a fiduciary may contract for the duty of care to be recklessness rather than negligence; that broader rather than narrower discretion may be conferred; that certain otherwise applicable legal formalities may be waived, etc. A nominee for the office is entitled to legal advice about these obligations of the office, to unfettered assistance in negotiating the terms upon which it is undertaken, and to walk away from the deal if, upon due consultation with legal counsel, the terms appear unacceptable. . . . The situation is the same where the lawyer represents one of the parties in other kinds of proposed special relationships: prenuptial agreements, partnership agreements, formation of corporate ventures, corporate employment contracts, etc.

A third clear case of "arm's length" representation is where a lawyer with no prior involvement is brought into negotiations for termination or reformation of the special relationship. Again by the hypothesis the lawyer has not been involved in the conduct of the relationship, but only in negotiations concerning whether or not it should be continued.

Opening such negotiations signals that continuation of the fiduciary relationship has been transformed from an assumption—a presupposed characteristic of the relationship—into an unresolved contingency. That signal divides the relationship into two aspects. In past and pending transactions, the fiduciary remains subject to established obligations. Even in this respect, however, those duties are being performed "on notice" that the fiduciary for whatever reason is dissatisfied or fearful or tired or sees a better use of time, and in any event may not long continue to perform. For the other party, the ward or the corporation as the case may be, being "on notice" signifies that the fiduciary's protective service may cease; that a final accounting may be imminent; and that there is a risk of "exit opportunism." The fiduciary's legal duties continue but their fulfillment is pervaded by legal uncertainty, emotional disengagement, and usually some distrust. Lots of human relationships are like that, however, and legally the fiduciary is still bound ex officio.

In the other aspect of the relationship, however, the lawyer has been retained concerning whether and on what terms the parties should continue their relationship in the future. This potential transformation is intelligible only if interpreted as a negotiation between the fiduciary in his or her original individual capacity and the ward or the corporation, wherein the subject of negotiation is the future existence of the fiduciary's distinct legal capacity. In those negotiations the person occupying the fiduciary office stands at arm's length with the ward, and the role of the lawyer is correspondingly "normal."

The foregoing cases are quite clear as a matter of legal concept and analysis. There is, of course, an element of unreality in hypothesizing such unambiguous facts. The unreality is greatest in the third case, where it is hypothesized that the lawyer is brought in only for negotiations between the guardian and ward or corporation and officer about continuing their relationship. In reality it is unlikely that things would happen this way. Much more likely, the lawyer handling negotiations over continuation of a guardianship relationship would have been involved while the relationship was ongoing, quite possibly from its inception. The corporate situations hypothesized are also abstractions. A lawyer representing the corporation in negotiations with a corporate officer or employee is likely to have had some prior involvement in the relationship between the corporation and the officer.

Recognition of this element of unreality serves, however, to establish an important point: One problem in thinking through the lawyer's responsibilities in triangular relationships is that the relationship may not be continuously triangular. In various stages and circumstances the link of special responsibility between the client and the "relevant other" may become contingent, openly or otherwise. When this contingency becomes imminent the relationship threatens to become antipodal, with the client and lawyer on one side and the "relevant other" on the other. . . . *If* the relationship becomes openly adverse, the lawyer "knows no other duty" than to the client. But when does a triangular relationship threaten to become contingent and antipodal? We will return to that question presently.

B. Normal Protective Relationship

While the positions of the fiduciary and the "relevant other" are openly adverse in some situations, normally the fiduciary's protective responsibility is unambiguous. In the normal legal relationship between guardian and ward, or between corporation and corporate director, officer, or employee, the legal purpose of the relationship is being fulfilled and the fiduciary is conforming his or her conduct to legal requirements.

The lawyer's task in this normal situation is to assist the fiduciary in meeting his or her legal obligations, and to help minimize legal risks to the relationship from outside forces, such as persons with competing claims on the assets or the tax collector. Toward these ends the lawyer supplies advice and employs legally recognized techniques that further the undertaking. Thus, the lawyer provides the forms and procedures for board action in the corporation, for the proprieties where a director has a conflict of interest that disqualifies him or her from voting on a corporate matter, etc. In the guardianship, the lawyer similarly safeguards the proprieties. The lawyer represents the guardian *in taking care* of the ward—the "whole purpose of the relationship," to use the phrase from *Fickett*. In the corporate situation, the corporate counsel works with the corporate director, officer, or employee *in taking care* of the corporation's "institutional interests," to use the phrase from *Yablonski*. Neither a "guardianship" nor a "corporation" has material existence or autonomous identity. They are legal events, artifacts of the lawyer's endeavors in the representation. The relationship itself is an evolving legal event that the lawyer's services continuously create.

The closest analogy for this kind of representation is joint representation in which a lawyer represents two or more closely connected parties, one of whom serves as spokesperson. In a typical example, the lawyer represents "the partnership" or "the partners" but on a day-to-day basis deals with the managing partner. A variation involves a lawyer who jointly represents both members of a marital community in its financial affairs but on a day-to-day basis deals only with one of the spouses. In many guardianships and trusts, the guardian or trustee voluntarily or by direction consults with the ward or beneficiary, and to that extent makes their relationship into something of a partnership. In the corporate situation, while the law carefully specifies that the client is the corporation as an entity, the lawyer nevertheless has responsibilities to various corporate "constituents" and deals on a day-to-day basis with several corporate officials.

The "joint" character of the representation in a triangular relationship is reflected, in reality if not legal form, in the lawyer's employment contract. In a guardianship, the lawyer's employment is determined by the guardian but his or her fee is chargeable to the guardianship estate. Managerially, the contract is with the guardian; economically, the burden of the fee rests on the ward. In the corporate situation, the lawyer's employment is determined by a corporate official but the cost of the legal fee or salary is borne by the corporation, the dependent party. Thus, on the client side, the engagement of the lawyer is close to a joint enterprise legally and practically.

· · ·

In view of these characteristics of the functioning triangular relationship, the lawyer's responsibilities may well be analogized to multiple representation. The key rules are those of confidentiality and loyalty. In multiple representation, the rule of confidentiality includes all within the group and excludes all outside it. In the corporate situation, the rule of confidentiality applies to information the corporate lawyer obtains from corporate "constituents" in the course of the representation, as does the corresponding rule of attorney-client privilege.[51] The same principle would apply to information provided to a lawyer for a partnership and ought to apply to information received from a ward by a lawyer or a guardian.

Concerning the principle of loyalty, a lawyer may serve two or more clients in the same matter if they do not have adverse interests. In a triangular relationship in the normal state, the interests of the nonlawyer participants are not adverse; both, therefore, may be considered to be clients.

Conceptualizing both the "relevant others" as clients, and the lawyer as engaged in multiple representation, seems entirely natural when the triangular relationship is in its normal state. The question is whether there are reasons for refusing to conceptualize it in this way. Only one reason exists for such hesitancy: the implications that follow if the triangular relationship ceases to be normal and instead becomes antagonistic.

The principal implications of treating this situation as one of multiple representation have been suggested earlier. Under standard doctrine, in multiple representation each client has the full rights of a client, including the power over confidentiality and the right to enforce the conflict of interest rules against the lawyer. Thus, if the corporate officer is treated in all respects as a client, then confidences he or she has imparted to the lawyer would not be usable against him or her *after* the normal triangular relationship has collapsed and the corporation and its officers become legal antagonists.[54] If the corporate officer is treated as a client in all respects, upon the collapse of his or her relationship with the corporation, the officer could then insist that the corporate lawyer not represent the corporation against him or her.[55] These are undesirable corollaries and their specter is a weighty objection.

This weighty objection indicates that the multiple representation concept should not operate fully once the triangular relationship has collapsed; indeed, that is the recognized rule. Ordinarily upon collapse of the relationship, the lawyer may continue to represent the person or entity that was his client in the full and formal sense, even though representation entails a position adverse to the other member of the

51. Upjohn Co. v. United States, 449 U.S. 383 (1981) (attorney-client privilege covers employee responses to questionnaires and interview notes of counsel).

54. The corporate officer does not have that right. E.g., Lane v. Chowning, 610 F.2d 1385 (8th Cir.1979) (defendant bank's attorney has no obligation to plaintiff-officer to refrain from using information acquired in representing bank).

55. The corporate officer does not have that right either. E.g., Meehan v. Hopps, 144 Cal.App.2d 284, 301 P.2d 10 (1956) (attorney not precluded from representing client-corporation against officer where no prior attorney-client relationship existed between counsel and officer).

triangle.[56] If both were treated as clients in the strict sense, that option would not be available.[57] The law should continue to recognize the lawyer's authority to continue representation of a guardian or a corporation after the relationship with the other party becomes antagonistic. On the other hand, the possibility that a triangular relationship might collapse into antagonism is an insufficient reason for rejecting the multiple representation analogy while the triangular relationship is still intact. It is also insufficient reason for denying the "relevant other" some of the rights of a full-fledged former client if the relationship does collapse, particularly where the lawyer had not made the ground rules clear earlier.[59]

C. Ambivalent and Unstable Situations

A triangular relationship may, then, be analyzed in two ways regarding the lawyer. One of the parties can be regarded as the client and the other as the third party, or both can be regarded as clients. Each interpretation fits traditional concepts and terminology, and each implies a firm set of legal consequences. While both interpretations are plausible, they result in radically different definitions of the lawyer's responsibilities. Under one interpretation the "relevant other" is like a friend, under the second the "relevant other" is like a foe.

The obvious conclusion is that the problem cannot be analyzed usefully in terms of the structure of the relationship. That is, nothing very useful can be found in the proposition that in a guardianship relationship the guardian *is* the client and the ward *is not*, or in the proposition that in the corporate relationship the corporation *is* the client and the director or officer *is not*. Under normal circumstances, the most appropriate interpretation of the relationship between lawyer and guardian and ward is that the latter are both clients of the lawyer, subject to a rule of precedence among them when it comes to managing their own relationship and in dealing with the lawyer. So also in

---

56. E.g., Commodity Futures Trading Comm'n v. Weintraub, 471 U.S. (1985) (trustee of corporation in bankruptcy has power to waive corporation's attorney-client privilege with respect to communications that took place before filing petition in bankruptcy); Lane v. Chowning, 610 F.2d. 1385 (8th Cir.1979); Meehan v. Hopps, 144 Cal.App.2d 284, 301 P.2d 10 (1956).

57. E.g., Opdyke v. Kent Liquor Market, Inc., 40 Del.Ch. 316, 181 A.2d 579 (1962) (attorney who organized and was retained by three man corporation owed fiduciary duty to stockholders, breached fiduciary duty to minority stockholder by buying majority stock to which minority shareholder had claim, and held stock as constructive trustee for minority stockholder).

59. Compare Model Rule Rule 1.13 (Organization as Client), . . . with E.F. Hutton & Co. v. Brown, 305 F.Supp. 371 (S.D.Tex.1969) (in-house counsel who had represented corporate officer in his individual capacity in prior separate litigation disqualified from representing corporation in negligence action against officer); see G. Hazard & W. Hodes, The Law of Lawyering 243–244, 262–264 (1985) (discussing fairness to nonclients within an organization and the *Miranda*-type warning required by rule 1.13(d)); but cf. W.T. Grant Co. v. Haines, 531 F.2d 671 (2d Cir.1976) (court has discretion to allow outside counsel to represent corporation in antitrust action against former employee even if counsel has had allegedly improper communication with employee unrepresented by counsel).

normal circumstances, the most appropriate interpretation of the relationship between lawyer and corporation and corporate constituents is that the latter are all clients of the lawyer, again subject to a rule of precedence among them when it comes to managing the enterprise and dealing with the lawyer. Nevertheless, when the relationship between the parties is about to collapse, the most appropriate legal interpretation is that they are antagonists as far as the lawyer is concerned. The vectors described earlier indicate the order of precedence.

The difference between a "normal" triangular relationship and one contaminated by antagonism does not lie in the *structure* of the relationship. Until finally resolved or dissolved, the structure is ambiguously triangular, with the nonlawyer parties being fellow clients, or antipodal, with the nonlawyer parties being antagonists. The proper interpretation depends not on structure but on process—what has happened within the relationship. The relevant set of happenings include, above all, what the lawyer has done in the relationship.

In *Fickett*, the lawyer had done nothing when he should have been doing something. The "something" he should have been doing was neither mysterious nor extraordinary. If he had adhered to normal lawyer practice followed in a normal guardian representation, he would have satisfied himself that the guardian had at least some idea of the responsibilities concerning investments and of the requirements for periodic accounting, and would have activated the procedure for submitting such accounts. If the guardian had approached him to confide that some of the investments were irregular, normal lawyer practice would suggest that the lawyer should have said something like, "That could involve very serious difficulties." The lawyer would thereby not commit himself to representing the guardian versus the ward, or vice versa; the lawyer would only be suggesting the urgent need for redefinition of the relationship between the guardian and the ward. He or she should do nothing to further or conceal the guardian's misfeasance, because the law provides that doing so would constitute fraudulent conduct on the lawyer's part. If the guardian persisted in misconduct, under accepted standards of practice the lawyer could withdraw and advise the ward of the fact of withdrawal.

In *Yablonski*, the organization's lawyer did things when the situation was such that "the role of . . . counsel . . . becomes usually a passive one." [61] The lawyer should not have assisted the president in defending colorable claims of malfeasance toward the organization. If the lawyer had adhered to proper practice in this abnormal situation, he or she would have advised the president to get independent legal representation and perhaps have advised the board to get other independent representation for the organization. Indeed, as the law has now evolved, any other course by the lawyer could be regarded as furthering or concealing the president's malfeasance.

61. *Yablonski,* 448 F.2d at 1179.

V. Conclusion

The critical problem the lawyer faces in triangular relationships is that his or her professional responsibilities depend unavoidably on what the other two parties do for and to each other. The lawyer's duty cannot adequately be defined, as it normally is, by specificying *ex ante* the identity of "the client." Neither of the "relevant others" is a legally freestanding person in the standard conceptual sense of "client." The guardian is not an individual alone but a person whose legal identity is expressed in terms of legal responsibilities ex officio. The corporation is not an individual at all, but exists only in law and through personification by others who act ex officio. If the other parties to the relationship conduct themselves as the law contemplates they should, then all the "relevant others" collectively can be considered "the client." That principle is already well established for corporations,[62] and there seems to be no reason not to think of guardianships and other triangular relationships in the same way. On the other hand, if the dominant party is guilty of misconduct toward the dependent one and if the lawyer behaves as though everything were still normal, the lawyer would then have at least an ethical problem and quite possibly legal liability.

Triangular relationships are legal artifacts, the creation of a legal process orchestrated by the lawyer. They collapse when lawyers fail to recognize, intercept, and mitigate legal derelictions by the dominant actors. Whether a triangular relationship is viable or headed for collapse is primarily a question of legal interpretation that the lawyer is uniquely situated to answer.

The lawyer can see and act. Depending on what he or she sees and does, the dominant actor may have to be treated as something less than a client simplicitor and the lawyer himself or herself as something different from one who "knows no other duty." That definition of role entails being an active, visible participant in the transaction and exercising independent judgment. Such deportment does not fit the conventional mold.

C. LAWYERS FOR THE GOVERNMENT

Introductory Note

Who is the client of the government lawyer? Possible contenders include: the agency head; the chief executive officer, e.g., the Governor or President; the legislature as the elected representatives of the public; the "public."

One way to begin the analysis is to ask who is the counterpart for the government lawyer of the CEO in the corporate lawyer's world? Of the board of directors? Of the shareholders? For a lawyer in the Justice Department is the Attorney General analogous to the CEO?

---

62. Upjohn Co. v. United States, 449 U.S. 383 (1981).

Does the answer depend on whether the lawyer is concerned about illegal acts on the part of the Attorney General? Is the "public" comparable to shareholders? What duties, if any, does the lawyer owe to Congress? For a lawyer at the Securities and Exchange Commission, is the Commission akin to a board of directors?

As these questions demonstrate, the analogy to corporations is imperfect. Corporations are private organizations subject to public law and usually have a limited purpose (e.g., making money) and a limited ultimate constituency (e.g., the shareholders). Governments are themselves instruments of public law whose purpose cannot be expressed in a single formula. Further, the federal government, state governments and many local governments are organized on the basis of separation of powers, not integrated under one "board of directors." Finally, the public's interest is more amorphous than the shareholders' interest. While the law artificially reduces shareholders' interest to law-abiding profitability, reduction of the public's interest to a corruption-free, law-abiding government is simplistic.

Case Law

Case law on the identity of the government lawyer's client is sparse.

In Humphrey v. McLaren, 402 N.W.2d 535 (Minn.1987), the state attorney general's office brought suit against the former executive director of a state agency, the Public Employees Retirement Association (PERA), to recover state funds the director allegedly misappropriated. The former executive director, McLaren, sought to disqualify the attorney general's office on the ground that it had represented him during his tenure at PERA. A state statute made the attorney general's office legal counsel to PERA. The court refused to disqualify the attorney general's office, stating that even the individual lawyer who had advised PERA during McLaren's tenure would have been free to sue him now. The court, citing Minnesota's version of M.R. 1.13 and its Comment, held that the agency (and in some cases the entire government) was the client, not the individual head of the agency. This opinion is consistent with the holding in *Meehan,* supra. Also see United States v. Troutman, 814 F.2d 1428 (10th Cir.1987) (no impermissible conflict when state attorney general assisted United States attorneys in prosecution of state official). But is it a satisfactory resolution?

President Nixon had promised Archibald Cox independence to conduct an investigation into whether members of the executive branch had been involved in the break-in at Democratic headquarters at the Watergate Building and had further broken the law by trying to cover-up their involvement. When it was learned that President Nixon had taped conversations in the Oval Office, Cox sought access to these tapes. Judge Sirica ordered the tapes turned over to the court for in-camera review, after which the court would transmit unprivileged portions to

Cox for use before the grand jury. The Court of Appeals sustained Judge Sirica's order, Nixon v. Sirica, 487 F.2d 700 (D.C.Cir.1973).

> [The President] decided to avoid a "constitutional crisis" by declining to appeal the decision and ordered Cox, as "an employee of the executive branch," not to pursue the matter further. Declining to follow the court's order, he proposed instead to provide White House "summaries" of the tapes. Cox rejected the offer, and on October 20, in what has become known as the "Saturday Night Massacre," the President accepted the resignation of Attorney General Elliot Richardson when he refused to fire Cox, then fired Deputy Attorney General Ruckelshaus when he refused to fire Cox, and finally persuaded Solicitor General Robert H. Bork to fire Cox and [many] of his staff of ninety investigators.

Cushman, Cases in Constitutional Law (7th ed. 1989) at 79.

The outcry over these events compelled President Nixon to appoint a new special prosecutor, Leon Jaworski. The tapes were turned over to the new special prosecutor. As an ensuing consequence, President Nixon resigned.

To ensure the independence of future prosecutors investigating the executive branch, Congress passed the Ethics in Government Act, 28 U.S.C. §§ 591 et seq. This statute gives a three-judge panel the power to appoint an independent counsel to investigate and prosecute members of the executive branch in lieu of the Department of Justice and further provides that the Attorney General may remove a special prosecutor only by "personal action . . . and only for good cause, physical disability, mental incapacity, or any other condition that substantially impairs the performance of such independent counsel's duties." Upon such removal, the Attorney General must submit a report to the three-judge panel and to the Judiciary Committees of the House and Senate. See Morrison v. Olson, 487 U.S. 654, 108 S.Ct. 2597 (1988) (holding that the independent counsel provisions of this statute are constitutional). It is interesting to ponder who is the client of the independent counsel.

By statute, 28 U.S.C. § 518, the Solicitor General of the United States has authority to decide whether to petition the Supreme Court to review decisions in lower courts ruling against Government agencies and departments. The Solicitor General may be removed from office by the President. See United States v. Providence Journal Co., 485 U.S. 693, 108 S.Ct. 1502 (1988) (attorney appointed by district court to prosecute criminal contempt charges cannot represent the United States before the Supreme Court without authorization from the Solicitor General, who declined to give such authorization). Cf. Ethics in Government Act, 28 U.S.C. § 594(a)(9) (authorizing independent counsel to appear before "any court of competent jurisdiction . . . in the name of the United States").

The authority of the attorney general of a state varies considerably from state to state. In People ex rel. Deukmejian v. Brown, 29 Cal.3d

150, 172 Cal.Rptr. 478, 624 P.2d 1206 (1981), the California Attorney General sought a writ of mandamus to prevent the Governor from enforcing an employee relations statute which the Attorney General alleged was unconstitutional. The Governor moved to enjoin the litigation. The court granted the Governor's motion, holding that the Attorney General could not bring such a case on his own authority. Contrast Feeney v. Commonwealth, 373 Mass. 359, 366 N.E.2d 1262 (1977), holding that the Massachusetts Attorney General could seek review against the objections of the the the head of the affected agency, the Governor and the Massachusetts legislature (both houses of which passed resolutions asking that review not be sought) of a lower court decision holding that the state's civil service preference for veterans unconstitutionally discriminated against women. For cases in accord with *Deukmejian* see Manchin v. Browning, 296 S.E.2d 909 (W.Va. 1982); and Arizona State Land Dept. v. McFate, 87 Ariz. 139, 348 P.2d 912 (1960). In accord with *Feeney* are State ex rel. Howard v. Oklahoma Corp. Commission, 614 P.2d 45 (Okl.1980); Connecticut Commission on Special Revenue v. Connecticut Freedom of Information Commission, 174 Conn. 308, 387 A.2d 533 (1978). Also see Stevens, Can the State Attorney General Represent Two Agencies Opposed in Litigation? 2 Geo.J.Legal Ethics 757 (1989).

Several factors apparently contribute to the sparsity of case law. First, whereas in the corporate context the issue of final authority usually arises when various constituents are fighting for control of the corporation, in government such a struggle normally plays out politically rather than through litigation. Second, standing requirements and requirements of justiciability, e.g., the political question doctrine, may bar a suit to challenge whether the government (as an entity) is being adequately represented. Third, under prevailing state administrative law, litigation in other forms is readily available to resolve disputed substantive questions of official authority, for example a taxpayers' or citizens' suit. Suits in this form ordinarily would not expose conflict between the agency and the lawyer representing it. If the lawyer agrees with the agency, she will defend the suit; otherwise either the suit will be acquiesced in or some other government lawyer will be assigned to defend the agency position.

Hypotheticals

To examine the government lawyer's situation consider the following two hypotheticals. What, if anything, does M.R. 1.13 contribute to the analysis?

(1) In 1979 the Justice Department's Civil Rights Division intervened on behalf of the plaintiffs in an action against the Main City Fire Department to compel the city to implement an affirmative action hiring plan to correct past discrimination against blacks and hispanics. In 1981, after President Carter is defeated by President Reagan, the suit is still in the discovery stage. The new head of the Civil Rights Division orders the staff lawyer to seek court permission to withdraw

the government's brief on behalf of the plaintiffs and to intervene instead on behalf of the Fire Department. The lawyer sincerely believes that "truth, justice, and the law" are with the plaintiffs. What should the lawyer do?

(2) A staff attorney in the Internal Revenue Service is investigating a private foundation, which he suspects of tax fraud. He discovers that the foundation is supplying money to the Contras and that a White House aide has been a fundraiser for the project, in apparent violation of a law. The staff attorney reports this to his department head who checks with the Deputy Commissioner. After two weeks, the Deputy instructs the department head (orally, of course):

> I have consulted with the Department of Justice and have been instructed that your office should not pursue this investigation for national security reasons. Of course, the details of this conversation should not be discussed with the staff attorney or anyone else; it is confidential and involves national security matters. Just tell him that we will handle this matter.

The staff attorney is told to drop the investigation. It is September.

In November the Contragate disclosures begin. The Attorney General and all White House personnel state that up until the last week in October they had no knowledge, nor any reason to suspect, any government involvement in supplying money to the Contras. The foundation under investigation by the staff attorney is described as a key player in the matter.

What should the staff attorney and the department head do? Should they have done something different in September?

The Scope section of the Model Rules states:

> Under various legal provisions, including constitutional, statutory and common law, the responsibilities of government lawyers may include authority concerning legal matters that ordinarily reposes in the client in private client-lawyer relationships. For example, a lawyer for a government agency may have authority on behalf of the government to decide upon settlement or whether to appeal from an adverse judgment. Such authority in various respects is generally vested in the attorney general and the state's attorney in state government, and their federal counterparts, and the same may be true of other government law officers. Also, lawyers under supervision of these officers may be authorized to represent several government agencies in intragovernmental legal controversies in circumstances where a private lawyer could not represent multiple private clients. They also may have authority to represent the "public interest" in circumstances where a private lawyer would not be authorized to do so. These Rules do not abrogate any such authority.

The Comment to Rule 1.13 states:

> The duty defined in this Rule applies to governmental organizations. However, when the client is a governmental organization, a different balance may be appropriate between maintaining confidentiality and assuring that the wrongful official act is prevented or rectified, for public business is involved . . . Therefore, defining precisely the identity of the client and prescribing the resulting obligations of such lawyers may be more difficult in the government context. Although in some circumstances the client may be a specific agency, it is generally the government as a whole. For example, if the action or failure to act involves the head of a bureau, either the department of which the bureau is a part or the government as a whole may be the client for purpose of this Rule. Moreover, in a matter involving the conduct of government officials, a government lawyer may have authority to question such conduct more extensively than that of a lawyer for a private organization in similar circumstances. This Rule does not limit that authority.

FEDERAL ETHICAL CONSIDERATIONS
4.1–4.3, 5.1, 8.1–8.3

Reprinted in Poirer, "The Federal Government Lawyer and
Professional Ethics," 1974.
60 A.B.A.J. 1541.

Canon 4. A Lawyer Should Preserve the Confidences and Secrets of a Client.

F.E.C.–4–1. If, in the conduct of official business of his department or agency, it appears that a fellow employee of the department or agency is revealing or about to reveal information concerning his own illegal or unethical conduct to a federal lawyer acting in his official capacity the lawyer should inform the employee that a federal lawyer is responsible to the department or agency concerned and not the individual employee and, therefore, the information being discussed is not privileged.

F.E.C.–4–2. If a fellow employee volunteers information concerning himself which appears to involve illegal or unethical conduct or is violative of department or agency rules and regulations which would be pertinent to that department's or agency's consideration of disciplinary action, the federal lawyer should inform the individual that the lawyer is responsible to the department or agency concerned and not the individual employee.

F.E.C.–4–3. The federal lawyer has the ethical responsibility to disclose to his supervisor or other appropriate departmental or agency official any unprivileged information of the type discussed above in F.E.C.–4–1 and 2.

. . .

Canon 5. A Lawyer Should Exercise Independent Professional Judgment on Behalf of a Client.

F.E.C.–5–1. The immediate professional responsibility of the federal lawyer is to the department or agency in which he is employed, to be performed in light of the particular public interest function of the department or agency. He is required to exercise independent professional judgment which transcends his personal interests, giving consideration, however, to the reasoned views of others engaged with him in the conduct of the business of the government.

. . .

Canon 8. A Lawyer Should Assist in Improving the Legal System.

F.E.C.–8–1. The general obligation to assist in improving the legal system applies to federal lawyers. In such situations he may have a higher obligation than lawyers generally. Since his duties include responsibility for the application of law to the resolution of problems incident to his employment there is a continuing obligation to seek improvement. This may be accomplished by the application of legal considerations to the day-to-day decisional process. Moreover it may eventuate that a federal lawyer by reason of his particular tasks may have insight which enhances his ability to initiate reforms, thus giving rise to a special obligation under Canon 8. In all these matters paramount consideration is due the public interest.

F.E.C.–8–2. The situation of the federal lawyer which may give rise to special considerations, not applicable to lawyers generally, include certain limitations on complete freedom of action in matters relating to Canon 8. For example, a lawyer in the Office of the Chief Counsel of the Internal Revenue Service may reasonably be expected to abide, without public criticism, with certain policies or rulings closely allied to his sphere of responsibility even if he disagrees with the position taken by the agency. But even if involved personally in the process of formulating policy or ruling there may be rare occasions when his conscience compels him publicly to attack a decision which is contrary to his professional, ethical or moral judgment. In that event, however, he should be prepared to resign before doing so, and he is not free to abuse professional confidences reposed in him in the process leading to the decision.

F.E.C.–8–3. The method of discharging the obligations imposed by Canon 8 may vary depending upon the circumstances. The federal lawyer is free to seek reform through the processes of his agency even if the agency has no formal procedure for receiving and acting upon suggestions from lawyers employed by it. Such intra-agency activities may be the only appropriate course for him to follow if he is not prepared to leave the agency's employment. However, there may be situations in which he could appropriately bring intra-agency problems to the attention of other federal officials (such as those in the Office of Management and Budget or Department of Justice) with responsibility and authority to correct the allegedly improper activities of the employ-

ing agency. Furthermore, it may be possible for the lawyer to participate in bar association or other activities designed to improve the legal
system within his agency without being involved in a public attack on
the agency's practices, so long as the requirement to protect confidences
is observed.

Sound policy favors encouraging government officials to invite and
consider the views of counsel. This tends to prevent the adoption of
illegal policies. Even where there are choices between legal alternatives, the lawyer's viewpoint may be valuable in affecting the choice.
Lawyers in federal service accordingly should conduct themselves so as
to encourage utilization of their advice within the agencies, retaining at
all times an obligation to exercise independent professional judgment,
even though their conclusions may not always be warmly embraced.
The failure of lawyers to respect official and proper confidences discourages this desirable resort to them.

. . .

FEDERAL BAR ASSOCIATION, OPINION 73-1
32 Fed.B.J. 71 (1973).*

1. Under what circumstances may a federally employed lawyer
    disclose information concerning a Government official of any
    rank which would reveal corrupt, illegal, or grossly negligent
    conduct?

2. If disclosure may be properly made, to whom may it be made?

3. Who is the client of a Government attorney in the Executive or
    Legislative branches of Government?

. . .

A few remarks as to terminology are in order. . . . In defining
the terms "corrupt, illegal or grossly negligent" conduct, as used in the
opinion, and in judging whether particular conduct comes within those
terms, special care is required. The "corrupt" conduct referred to in
the request for an opinion was construed to be venal conduct in
violation of law and duty, engaged in for personal gain or the gain of
another, the gain ordinarily being of a pecuniary or other valuable
nature which is measurable. Defining "illegal" conduct was not so
easy for such conduct is often subject to reasonable differences of
opinion as to its legality. The profession as well as the courts are
constantly troubled and at odds about whether particular conduct is
legal or not. For purposes of this opinion "illegal" conduct is divided
into two general categories. One consists of the willful or knowing
disregard of or breach of law, other than of a corrupt character, the
latter type of illegal conduct having been separately defined. The
second category of illegal conduct was considered to be that about
which the lawyer may hold a firm position as to its illegality but which
he nevertheless recognizes is in an area subject to reasonable differences of professional opinion as to its legality. Conduct which is

---

* Reprinted with permission of the Federal Bar Association.

"grossly negligent" would seem not to lend itself to greater clarification than those words themselves indicate.

．．．

Assuming the described conduct to have occurred, answers to the three questions can be more clearly developed by considering first the question posed as to who is the client of the federally employed lawyer in the Executive and Legislative branches of the government. Problems of disclosure involved in the other questions should be considered in light of the answer to the client question.

The client problem also divides according to the duties involved. There is the government lawyer who is designated to represent another in government service against whom proceedings are brought of a disciplinary, administrative or personnel character, including a court-martial. The answer to the client question in these situations seems clear. The person the lawyer is designated to represent is the client. The usual attorney-client relationship arises, with its privilege and professional responsibility to protect and defend the interest of the one represented.

The more usual situation of the federally employed lawyer, however, is that of the lawyer who is a principal legal officer of a department, agency or other legal entity of the Government, or a member of the legal staff of the department, agency, or entity.[1] This lawyer assumes a public trust, for the government, over-all and in each of its parts, is responsible to the people in our democracy with its representative form of government. Each part of the government has the obligation of carrying out, in the public interest, its assigned responsibility in a manner consistent with the Constitution, and the applicable laws and regulations. In contrast, the private practitioner represents the client's personal or private interest. In pointing out that the federally employed lawyer thus is engaged professionally in the furtherance of a particular governmental responsibility we do not suggest, however, that the public is the client as the client concept is usually understood. It is to say that the lawyer's employment requires him to observe in the performance of his professional responsibility the public interest sought to be served by the governmental organization of which he is a part.

Proceeding upon the foregoing background, the client of the federally employed lawyer, using the term in the sense of where lies his immediate professional obligation and responsibility, is the agency where he is employed, including those charged with its administration insofar as they are engaged in the conduct of the public business. The relationship is a confidential one, an attribute of the lawyer's profession which accompanies him in his government service. This confidential relationship is usually essential to the decision-making process to which the lawyer brings his professional talents. Moreover, it encourages

---

1. In the course of this opinion . . . we use the term "agency" as a matter of convenience to include "Department" or other governmental entity.

resort to him for consultation and advice in the on-going operations of the agency.

The relationship above described gives rise to the question whether or to what degree the attorney-client privilege known to private practice attaches with respect to those to whom the government lawyer is professionally obligated in the conduct of the public business. No all-inclusive answer to the problem of the privilege is attempted herein, not only because no concrete factual situation has been posed, but also because the questions as submitted call for consideration of the privilege only as it bears upon the problem of disclosure. In that context the following is submitted.

The Committee does not believe there are any circumstances in which corrupt conduct may not be disclosed by the federally employed lawyer, apart from those situations to which we have referred in which the lawyer has been designated to defend an individual in a proceeding against him with respect to a personal problem.

In other instances of corruption the ethical aspect of the answer merges with the legal. Section 535 of Title 28 of the United States Code provides:

> (b) Any information, allegation, or complaint received in a department or agency of the executive branch of the Government relating to violations of Title 18 [the federal criminal code] involving Government officers and employees shall be expeditiously reported to the Attorney General by the head of the department or agency, unless—
>
> > (1) the responsibility to perform an investigation with respect thereto is specifically assigned otherwise by another provision of law; or
> >
> > (2) as to any department or agency of the Government, the Attorney General directs otherwise with respect to a specified class of information, allegation, or complaint.
>
> (c) This section does not limit—
>
> > (1) the authority of the military departments to investigate persons or offenses over which the armed forces have jurisdiction under the Uniform Code of Military Justice (chapter 47 of Title 10); or
> >
> > (2) the primary authority of the Postmaster General to investigate postal offenses.

In addition to this statute, there is House Concurrent Resolution No. 175 of July 11, 1958, 72 Stat. B12, entitled "Code of Ethics for Government Service." Its provisions have been made applicable to the entire Executive branch by Regulations of the Civil Service Commission, 5 C.F.R. § 735.10.[2] The Resolution provides: "Any person in the

---

2. The legislative history of the Resolution (S.Rep. No. 1812, 85th Cong.2d Sess. (1958)) states it is intended only as a guide and "creates no new law . . . and establishes no legal restraints on anyone."

Government service should: 9. Expose corruption wherever discovered." . . .[3]

Reading section 535 of Title 28 of the United States Code with the Joint Resolution and the Civil Service Commission Regulations, corrupt conduct and other illegal conduct of a criminal character, that is, the willful or knowing disregard of or breach of law, in either the Legislative or Executive branch may be disclosed by the federally employed lawyer, that is, reported to the "head of the department or agency" or other governmental entity, who shall report it to the Attorney General. If the head officer referred to is involved, the report in our opinion may be made directly to the Attorney General, or other appropriate official of the Department of Justice.[4]

With respect to the second category of illegal conduct, conduct about which there may be reasonable differences of opinion as to its legality, and grossly negligent conduct, the Committee considers the problem to be different. Ordinarily there is no need of disclosure of such conduct beyond the personnel of the agency where it arises. Differences of opinion as to the legality of action are often unavoidable in the process of arriving at a course of action to be recommended or adopted. The lawyer may not deem the decision reached or the action taken to be legally sound, but in the situations in which the question arises it may not be misconduct at all. Moreover, when we turn particularly to the grossly negligent category, one must consider that the particular conduct may be accidental by a person ordinarily careful. There should usually be an adequate remedy in the public interest calling for no disclosure beyond the immediate persons involved, including if need be other members of the agency. In all of these matters there may be regulations of the agency pointing to the course which should be followed. These should be observed unless for some very good reason the lawyer deems them inapplicable. In any event, the opportunity to correct these matters should first be within the agency itself.

Something more needs to be said. The confidential relationship of the lawyer with those entitled to consult with and be advised by him varies in degree according to the subject matter. It is one thing in the area of national security or the conduct of foreign affairs, for example, and quite another if there is involved, for example, a dispute over the validity of a particular order of the National Labor Relations Board.

3. Id.

4. The Committee adds at this point a strong recommendation that the federally employed lawyer, for himself personally and for his ability to assist others in his agency, acquaint himself with the full content of 5 C.F.R. § 735.10. This section provides that each employee shall acquaint himself with each statute that relates to his ethical and other conduct as an employee of his agency and of the Government, and that the agency itself shall direct the attention of its employees, by specific reference in agency regulations issued under this Part 735, which is concerned with employee responsibilities and conduct, to each statute relating to the ethical and other conduct of employees of that agency, as well as to a listed number of provisions respecting employee conduct, including Chapter 11 of Title 18 U.S.C., which is concerned, *inter alia* with conflicts of interest.

The diversity of situations is almost innumerable. It is to be borne in mind throughout that ours is an open society insofar as compatible with the orderly and effective conduct of government. This follows from the nature of the relationship of our Government with the people, and it has been given legislative recognition in recent years by the Freedom of Information Act, with its limited exemptions from the obligation of disclosure. Moreover, the government lawyer cannot be a refuge for the corrupt or looked upon as a secret repository for illegal or grossly negligent conduct of the business of the Government. There is a dividing line between conduct which falls in the area of strict confidentiality and that which falls within the area of appropriate public knowledge. This line cannot accurately be drawn except upon consideration of a particular factual situation, and even then not always easily or accurately drawn, certainly not to the satisfaction of all. Accordingly, the Committee feels obliged to limit its answer respecting disclosure to acceptance of the principle that disclosure beyond the confines of the agency or other law enforcing or disciplinary authorities of the Government is warranted only in the case when the lawyer, as a reasonable and prudent man, conscious of his professional obligation of care, confidentiality and responsibility, concludes that these authorities have without good cause failed in the performance of their own obligation to take remedial measures required in the public interest. In the absence of a concrete situation upon which to pass judgment as to the ethical course which should be followed we go no further than to adopt the above stated ethical principle. We think it appropriate for us to affirm the position that honesty and faithfulness is the prevailing rule in the Government service, and we warn against applying the principle we have stated to any situation without that care and sense of responsibility which is the hallmark of the legal profession at its best. Such care would call for resort by the lawyer himself to a trustworthy advisor as to the course to be followed. The ultimate decision, however, remains with him.

· · · ·

Questions

Do the Federal Ethical Considerations resolve the question of who is the client? Are they consistent with the approach of M.R. 1.13?

How would the authors of 73–1 resolve the hypothetical concerning the foundation that contributed to the Contras, above at p. 805?

For a critique of Opinion 73–1, see Lawry, Who is the Client of the Federal Government Lawyer? An Analysis of the Wrong Question, 37 Fed.Bar.J. 61 (1979). Also see Josephson and Pearce, To Whom Does the Government Lawyer Owe the Duty of Loyalty When the Clients are in Conflict, 29 Howard L.J. 539 (1986).

ERIC SCHNAPPER, "LEGAL ETHICS AND THE GOVERNMENT LAWYER"

32 The Record 649 (1977).*

I

All litigation presents to some degree, real though not always perceived, a conflict between each attorney's responsibility as a representative of his or her client and as an officer of the court. Winning the case and seeing that justice is done must be inconsistent goals for counsel on at least one side in a case, if not on both. However substantial this problem may be regarded, it is certainly more complex for counsel for the government. Unlike a private attorney subject to dismissal for ignoring a client's wishes, counsel for the government often has, subject to the variables of intragovernmental relations, the power to take a course of action or accept a settlement contrary to the wishes of the agency officials involved. In addition, government counsel owes some arguable duty to the opposing party, not only as a citizen and taxpayer of the entity for which he or she works, but also because that party seeks to invoke the same laws as those which he or she is committed, in theory if not by oath, to enforce. The relationship of agency officials to government counsel is not that of client and attorney in any ordinary sense, for the identities and desires of those officials may vary with popular opinion, the vote of the electorate, or the whims of their superiors, while the law to which both officials and counsel owe their allegiance remains unaltered.

Although attitudes on this problem vary significantly among and within government law offices, the general practice of government counsel seems to be to refrain from making any independent judgment on the merits of the agency's position, or to argue for that position even when the lawyer believes it is wrong.

Three related explanations are commonly advanced by government attorneys for resolutely defending whatever conduct, or advancing whatever claim, the agency involved may prefer. It is urged that the agency is entitled to a lawyer, that the agency's theory or argument should be ruled on by a court rather than by government counsel, and that no harm can come of pressing the agency's case since the courts will ultimately resolve the matter correctly. While legitimate considerations underlie each of these contentions, none is sufficient to absolve counsel for the government from his or her responsibility to scrutinize the validity of the conduct or contention he or she is asked to defend in court.

The suggestion that government bodies are entitled to counsel has a heady Sixth Amendment ring to it, but there is less here than meets the eye. The issue at the outset is not a right to counsel, but a right to unlimited free representation by counsel with the prestige and re-

---

* Copyright © 1977 by Eric Schnapper.

sources of an attorney general's or corporation counsel's office. No one denies the right of a public employee to retain private counsel and litigate in his or her own name any legal theory, however fanciful, he or she may favor, subject to establishing the requisite standing. Whether such special counsel should be provided at public expense depends on whether, to use an admittedly troublesome phrase, the "real party" is the state or city or merely a whimsical or lawless public employee. . . . The decision whether an agency or official is "entitled" to government counsel seems to turn on whether the disputed conduct in fact represents public policy, bearing in mind that even the policies of a high official are not public policies if in violation of public law, or the private whims of one or more government employees. Thus, this line of reasoning provides no foundation for a general obligation on the part of government counsel to represent the views of agency officials, but merely supports a duty to represent agency officials when they are right.

The second argument does have some independent weight. In our adversary system courts are created for resolving disputes of law and legally significant disputes of fact, and are frequently an optimal forum for doing so. Any action which cuts off such contentions from reaching the courts prevents the mode of resolution generally regarded as most fair and definitive. . . .

The argument that litigation can be cavalierly and endlessly pursued on behalf of public agencies without social cost is manifestly unsound. Any litigation places burdens on the opposing side, which, unlike the state officials, usually is not receiving free representation, and that often irreparable burden seems progressively less conscionable as the state or city contention becomes less substantial. In many cases continued litigation will entail a delay in the awarding of necessary relief. If in these cases the private party prevails on the merits, the public policy and thus true state interest will have been found to be on its side, and thus to have suffered because of continued representation of the views of one or more public employees. . . .

Finally, it must be noted that government counsel has alternatives to either arguing whatever position is preferred by agency officials or asserting a view or agreeing to a settlement contrary to their wishes. An attorney general believing a view erroneous but entitled to consideration in court can seek to arrange for that view to be presented by special outside counsel or agency house counsel; in such a case the attorney general could take no position or perhaps file an amicus brief against the agency. Government counsel can choose to present an argument expressly explained to be an agency contention on which counsel takes no position. Where the agency has taken a position government counsel believes unsound, but there are other parties in the litigation prepared to defend it, counsel enjoys some freedom to decline to take a stand on the issue. If the position of an attorney general's or corporation counsel's office is subject to ultimate control by a governor or mayor, an attorney who believes the position taken to be erroneous can and usually should decline to have his or her name placed on the brief involved. Each of these responses serves to protect for other cases the independence and stature of an attorney general's or corporation counsel's office and provides a method short of the more drastic step of imposing a settlement for putting pressure on agency officials to reconsider a questionable stance.

. . .

Questions and Comments

What suggestions might Schnapper have for the government lawyer in the Main City Fire Department hypothetical, above at pp. 804–805?

In the initial stages of Washington v. Seattle School District No. 1, 458 U.S. 457, 102 S.Ct. 3187 (1982); see Seattle School District No. 1 v. Washington, 473 F.Supp. 996 (W.D.Wash.1979), aff'd, 633 F.2d 1338 (9th Cir.1980), the Federal Government intervened on the side of the local school district, supporting the district's attempt to overturn a state law that prevented the district from adopting a voluntary school busing plan. By the time the case made its way to the Supreme Court, President Reagan had replaced President Carter and the Government was fighting school busing plans. Accordingly, the government switched sides, filing a brief supporting the state law. The school district argued that the Justice Department should be disqualified from further representation of the government because the government lawyers had had access to the school district's confidences during the time of cooperation. The Supreme Court noted the change in the government's position, but did not address the ethical or legal issues raised. 458 U.S. at 471, 102 S.Ct. at 3195.

This case and the ethical issues it raises are discussed in Note, Professional Ethics in Government Side–Switching, 96 Harv.L.Rev. 1914 (1983), which argues for disqualification of government lawyers in cases where the government cooperates with one party and then switches sides to cooperate with that party's adversary. The Note urges the adoption of a rebuttable presumption that confidences of a former ally were shared with the government and a rebuttable presumption that other lawyers in the government were privy to the confidences possessed by their colleagues, i.e., limited imputed disqualification.

Should disqualification of the individual government lawyers be limited to those cases when the government has been aligned with another party that it now seeks to oppose?

SISSELA BOK, *SECRETS* (1982)

pp. 213–227 "Whistleblowing and Leaking." *

. . . The alarm of the whistleblower is meant to disrupt the status quo: to pierce the background noise, perhaps the false harmony, or the imposed silence of 'business as usual.' Three elements, each jarring, and triply jarring when conjoined, lend acts of whistleblowing special urgency and bitterness: dissent, breach of loyalty, and accusation.

Like all *dissent,* first of all, whistleblowing makes public a disagreement with an authority or a majority view. But . . . whistleblowing has the narrower aim of casting light on negligence or abuse, of alerting the public to a risk and of assigning responsibility for that risk.

. . .

In the second place, the message of the whistleblower is seen as a *breach of loyalty* because it comes from within. . . . Loyalty to colleagues and to clients comes to be pitted against concern for the public interest and for those who may be injured unless someone speaks out. Because the whistleblower criticizes from within, his act differs from muckraking and other forms of exposure by outsiders. Their acts may arouse anger, but not the sense of betrayal that whistleblowers so often encounter.

The conflict is strongest for those who take their responsibilities to the public seriously, yet have close bonds of collegiality and of duty to clients as well. They know the price of betrayal. They know, too, how organizations protect and enlarge the area of what is concealed, as failures multiply and vested interests encroach. And they are aware that they violate, by speaking out, not only loyalty but the hierarchy as well.

It is the third element of *accusation,* of calling "foul" from within, that arouses the strongest reactions on the part of the hierarchy. The charge may be one of unethical or unlawful conduct on the part of colleagues or superiors. Explicitly or implicitly, it singles out specific groups or persons as responsible: as those who know or should have known what was wrong and what the dangers were, and who had the capacity to make different choices. . . .

. . .

. . . [B]ecause of the elements of dissent, breach of loyalty, and accusation, the tension between concealing and revealing is great. It may be intensified by an urge to throw off the sense of complicity that comes from sharing secrets one believes to be unjustly concealed, and to achieve peace of mind by setting the record straight at last . . .[1]

. . .

[T]he three elements mentioned earlier: dissent, breach of loyalty, and accusation . . . impose certain requirements: of judgment and accuracy in dissent, of exploring alternative ways to cope with impro-

1. Judith P. Swazey and Stephen R. Scheer suggest that when whistleblowers expose fraud in clinical research, colleagues respond more negatively to the whistleblowers who report the fraudulent research than to the person whose conduct has been reported. See "The Whistleblower as a Deviant Professional: Professional Norms and Responses to Fraud in Clinical Research," Workshop on Whistleblowing in Biomedical Research, Washington D.C. 1981, to be published.

prieties that minimize the breach of loyalty, and of fairness in accusation. . . . Consider, for example, the following situation:

An attorney for a large company manufacturing medical supplies begins to suspect that some of the machinery sold by the company to hospitals for use in kidney dialysis is unsafe, and that management has made attempts to influence the federal regulatory personnel to overlook these deficiencies.

The attorney brings these matters up with a junior executive, who assures her that he will look into the matter and convey them to the chief executive if necessary. When she questions him a few weeks later, however, he tells her that all the problems have been taken care of, but offers no evidence, and seems irritated at her desire to learn exactly where the issues stand. She does not know how much further she can press her concern without jeopardizing her position in the firm.

The lawyer in this case has reason to be troubled, but does not yet possess sufficient evidence to blow the whistle. She is far from being as sure of her case as . . . [were] the engineers [who exposed safety hazards in the San Francisco mass transportation system, BART,] whose professional expertise allowed them to evaluate the risks of the faulty braking system . . .

.   .   .

Before deciding to speak out publicly, however, it is important . . . to consider whether the existing avenues for change within the organization have been sufficiently explored. By turning first to insiders for help, one can often uphold both sets of loyalties and settle the problem without going outside the organization. The engineers in the BART case clearly tried to resolve the problem they saw in this manner, and only reluctantly allowed it to come to public attention as a last resort. . . .

It *is* disloyal to colleagues and employers, as well as a waste of time for the public, to sound the loudest alarm first. . . .

The third element in whistleblowing—accusation—is strongest whenever efforts to correct a problem without going outside the organization have failed, or seem likely to fail. Such an outcome is especially likely whenever those in charge take part in the questionable practices . . ..

. . . Here, the very notion of what is in the public interest is at issue . . ..

.   .   .

Must the whistleblower who speaks out openly also resign? . . . In practice . . . they know that retaliation, forced departure, perhaps blacklisting, may be sufficient risks at times so that it may be wise to resign before sounding the alarm: to resign in protest, or to leave quietly, secure another post, and only then blow the whistle.

.   .   .

For those who are concerned about a situation within their organization, it is therefore preferable to seek advice before deciding either to go public or to remain silent. But the more corrupt the circumstances, the more dangerous it may be to consult colleagues, and the more likely it is that those responsible for the abuse or neglect will destroy the evidence linking them to it. And yet, with no one to consult, the would-be whistleblowers themselves may have a biased view of the state of affairs; they may see corruption and conspiracy where none exists, and choose not to consult others when in fact it would have been not only safe but advantageous to do so.

Questions and Comments

How important is the whistleblower's intent in judging the propriety of her disclosure?

Many states have enacted laws protecting government employee whistleblowers from retaliatory action. See, e.g., Cal.Gov.Code § 10543; Colo.Rev.Stat. 24–50.5–101; Me.Rev.Stat.Ann. tit. 26, § 831; N.Y. Labor Law § 740; Ohio Rev.Code Ann. § 4113.51; 43 Pa.Cons. Stat. § 1421.

Does a whistleblower statute supersede or nullify the ethical obligations otherwise governing a government lawyer?

In addition to the whistleblower statutes, the First Amendment protects the speech of federal, state and local government employees. In Pickering v. Board of Education, 391 U.S. 563, 574, 88 S.Ct. 1731, 1738 (1968), the Supreme Court held that an individual's exercise of his "right to speak on issues of public importance may not furnish the basis for his dismissal from public employment." Also see Rankin v. McPherson, 483 U.S. 378, 383, 107 S.Ct. 2891, 2896 (1987) (government employer may not discipline an "employee on a basis that infringes that employee's constitutionally protected interest in freedom of speech"). In Connick v. Myers, 461 U.S. 138, 103 S.Ct. 1684 (1983), the Court discussed the limits on this doctrine. Myers was a deputy district attorney who had circulated a questionnaire about internal office procedures regarding transfers and office morale; she was about to be transferred. The Court emphasized that the questionnaire focused not on "evaluat[ing] the performance of the office but rather [on] gather[ing] ammunition for another round of controversy with [Myers'] superiors." Id. at 148, 103 S.Ct. at 1691. Had the questionnaire involved the office's conduct of a particular case could the prosecutor have been disciplined under M.R. 3.6? See *In the Matter of Hinds*, reprinted in Chapter 10 below.

Government Lawyers Representing Individual Government Employees

In Dunton v. County of Suffolk, 729 F.2d 903 (2d Cir.1984), modified 748 F.2d 69 (2d Cir.1984), Dunton brought a suit under 42 U.S.C. § 1983 against a Suffolk County police officer and the county. Dunton charged that the officer had beaten him up after having found him in a car with the officer's wife. The County Attorney represented both defendants. At trial, the lawyer argued that the County was not liable because the officer was not acting within the scope of his employment but was an "irate husband." This argument prevailed; the County was found not liable and the officer, liable. The Second Circuit remanded for a new trial based on an impermissible conflict of interest on the part of the County Attorney. While the Court of Appeals refused to ban all joint representation in such situations, it emphasized that the "district court is under a duty to ensure that the client fully appreciates his situation." Id. at 908. See also Clay v. Doherty, 608 F.Supp. 295, 305 (N.D.Ill.1985) ("both lawyer and judge must guard against any threatened interests . . . in the *Dunton*-type cases.").

Under Monell v. New York City Department of Social Services, 436 U.S. 658, 98 S.Ct. 2018 (1978), liability may be imposed on a municipality under 42 U.S.C. § 1983 for violation of civil rights resulting from the "execution of a government's policy or custom, whether made by its lawmakers or by those whose edicts or acts may fairly be said to represent official policy." Id. at 693, 98 S.Ct. at 2037. When city employees are sued as individuals along with the city, the city can avoid liability by arguing that the employees' conduct was not city "policy or custom" but individual misconduct, and the individual employee may avoid liability by arguing that her actions were taken pursuant to official policy, i.e., the employee enjoys qualified immunity.

Where employees may raise qualified immunity as a defense, courts generally have allowed joint representation only when the municipality embraces the employees' acts as municipal policy. Even in those situations, the court may require proof that the individual defendants have been adequately and fully informed of the potential conflict and its effect on the representation. See, e.g., Mangella v. Keyes, 613 F.Supp. 795 (D.C.Conn.1985). Within these contours, municipalities still rely on joint representation. Compare Shadid v. Jackson, 521 F.Supp. 87 (E.D.Tex.1981) (disqualifying government lawyer from representing individual defendants without inquiring whether defenses would be incompatible), with Coleman v. Smith, 814 F.2d 1142, 1147–48 (7th Cir.1987) (expressing reservations about the broad language condemning joint representation in *Dunton*).

Also see Suffolk County Patrolmen's Benevolent Association Inc. v. County of Suffolk, 751 F.2d 550 (2d Cir.1985) (upholding procedure creating panel of three independent lawyers from which police officers who were co-defendants with the county in civil rights actions had to choose counsel in order to get the county to reimburse their attorneys' fees).

None of these cases address whether the government, as opposed to the employee, could adequately consent to the joint representation; whether the decision to embrace the employee's acts, i.e., to waive a defense, was made free from conflict; or whether the government would be adequately defended. Who would have standing to challenge the government's consent to the joint representation? Do these concerns justify a per se rule?

Other materials on the government lawyer's responsibilities include: Miller, Ethics in a System of Checks and Balances, 54 U.Chi.L. Rev. 1293 (1987); Comment, Government Employee Disclosure of Agency Wrongdoing: Protecting the Right to Blow the Whistle, 42 U.Chi.L. Rev. 530 (1975); Fahy, Special Ethical Problems of Counsel for the Government, 33 Fed.Bar J. 331 (1974); Weinstein, Some Ethical and Political Problems of a Government Lawyer, 18 Me.L.Rev. 155 (1966); L. Huston, A. Miller, S. Krislov & R. Dixon, Jr., Roles of the Attorney General of the United States (1968); and C. Horsky, The Government Lawyer (1952).

D. LAWYERS FOR A CLASS

Introductory Note

"Experience teaches that it is counsel for the class representatives, and not the named parties, who direct and manage [class] actions. Every experienced federal judge knows that any statement to the contrary is sheer sophistry." Greenfield v. Villager Industries, Inc., 483 F.2d 824, 832 n. 9 (3d Cir.1973).

Lawyer/client relationships can be arrayed according to how closely they resemble the paradigm of the individual client who defines the objectives of the representative: lawyers for partnerships and small businesses are closest to the paradigm, then corporation lawyers, then government lawyers and finally lawyers for a class.

As the Model Rules acknowledge, the lawyer for the government often acts as both client and lawyer at least in the office of state's attorney. However, the government lawyer is not free to make choices for the client because political constraints mean that public policies—the objectives of the representation—are never solely matters for the lawyer. Within accepted policy limits the government lawyer may have free rein, but at the limits the government lawyer still has a client.

Lawyers for a class, on the other hand, often construct the client by defining the objectives of the representation. A class often is defined in terms of a legal theory formulated by the lawyer. While the lawyer for a class appears in the mask of agent, the client may be solely the lawyer's creation and may exist only to serve the lawyer's ends.

DEBORAH L. RHODE, "CLASS CONFLICTS IN CLASS ACTIONS"

34 Stan.L.Rev. 1183 (1982).*

A fundamental premise of American adjudicative structures is that clients, not their counsel, define litigation objectives. Thus, the Ameri-

* Copyright © 1982 by the Board of Trustees of the Leland Stanford Junior University.

can Bar Association's current and proposed ethical codes both emphasize that an attorney must defer to the client's wishes on matters
affecting the merits of legal action.   However, by presupposing an
individual client with clearly identifiable views, these codes elide a
frequent and fundamental difficulty in class action proceedings.   In
many such cases, the lawyer represents an aggregation of litigants with
unstable, inchoate, or conflicting preferences.   The more diffuse and
divided the class, the greater the problems in defining its objectives.

This article examines those problems in one selected context:
plaintiff class actions seeking structural reforms in public and private
institutions.   Such cases merit special attention on two grounds.   First,
the often indeterminate quality of relief available makes conflicts
within plaintiff classes particularly likely.   Most school desegregation,
employment discrimination, prison reform, and related cases present no
obvious single solution flowing ineluctably from the nature of the
violation.   Nor will all class members alleging unlawful conduct agree
on what should be done about it.   Moreover, the prominence of institutional reform litigation vests these intra-class cleavages with particular
significance.   Such cases account for a high percentage of all class suits
and an even greater proportion of legal claims attracting widespread
societal concern.   Thus, institutional reform litigation provides a useful
paradigm for analyzing some of the most vexing issues in class representation.

In exploring these issues, this article takes one central proposition
for granted.   On the whole, institutional reform class actions have
made and continue to make an enormous contribution to the realization
of fundamental constitutional values—a contribution that no other
governmental construct has proven able to duplicate.   That contention
has been defended at length elsewhere, and the arguments need not be
recounted here.   Thus, the following discussion should not be taken to
suggest that institutional reform class actions are misused or misconceived, or that there are preferable alternatives.   The point, rather, is
that the framework in which such actions proceed could benefit from
both conceptual and mechanical refurbishing.

Much of the renovation required concerns our concept of class
representation.   In particular, we need a more coherent theory of class
interests and of the role plaintiff preferences should play in defining
class objectives.   As a first cut at reconceptualization, this article posits
a theory of representation mandating full disclosure of, although not
necessarily deference to, class sentiment.   A central premise is that the
class as an entity has interests that may not be coextensive with the
preferences of its current membership.   Often those able to register
views will be insufficiently disinterested or informed to speak for the
entire constituency of present and future class members who will be
affected by the court's decree.   Nonetheless, preferences matter, not
because they are conclusive of class interests, but because their disclosure is critical to the efficacy and legitimacy of judicial intervention.

.   .   .

I. Intra–Class Conflicts and Disclosure Obligations

A. A Taxonomy of Conflicts

. . .

The importance, complexity, and protracted character of structural reform lawsuits create opportunities for conflict at every stage of litigation. Class members who prefer the certainty of the status quo to the risks of judicial rearrangement may oppose litigation from the outset. For example, some parents who anticipate busing or closure of institutional facilities as a consequence of legal intervention will prefer to never initiate proceedings. So too, minority employees have feared retaliation by coworkers and management, or loss of job-related advantages in the aftermath of Title VII actions. . . .

Far more common, however, are schisms that surface during settlement or remedial deliberations. Often when a suit is filed, plaintiffs will not have focused on issues of relief. The impetus for the action will be a general sense that rights have been infringed or needs ignored, rather than a shared conviction about the appropriate remedy. Thus, there may be consensus only on relatively abstract questions— that ghetto schools are bad, institutional conditions unbearable, or special education programs inadequate. During the liability phase of litigation, class members may not be sufficiently informed or interested to participate in decisionmaking. However, once it becomes clear that some relief will be forthcoming, factions emerge. Also, where proceedings are protracted, changes in legal doctrine, contested practices, or plaintiff preferences can create new sources of dissension.

School desegregation cases provide the most well-documented instances of conflict. Both commentators and litigators have described in some detail the balkanization within minority communities over fundamental questions of educational policy. Dispute has centered on the relative importance of integration, financial resources, minority control, and ethnic identification in enriching school environments. Constituencies that support integration in principle have disputed its value in particular settings where extended bus rides, racial tension, or white flight seem likely concomitants of judicial redistricting. . . .

Comparable cleavages arise in various other institutional reform contexts. Parents challenging the adequacy of existing bilingual or special education programs have differed over whether mainstreaming or upgrading separate classes represents the better solution. Suits involving rights of the disabled have divided their families over whether to demand institutional improvement or creation of community care alternatives. . . . In employment cases, controversy has centered on tradeoffs between back-pay awards and prospective relief, the formula used to compute damages, and the means chosen to restructure hiring, promotion, and transfer systems.

Moreover, as with any form of collective litigation, parties often differ in their amenability to compromise and their assessment of particular proposals. Given the uncertainty of outcome and indeterminacy of relief in many institutional reform class actions, risk-averse plaintiffs will often be prepared to make substantial concessions. Other class members will prefer to fight, if not to the death, at least until the Supreme Court denies certiorari. Particularly where the proffered settlement provides generously for a few named plaintiffs, or where some individuals have special reasons for wanting expeditious relief, dissension may arise within the ranks. And, as the following discussion will suggest, all of these problems are compounded by class counsels' own interests and by a doctrinal framework that fails to raise, let alone resolve, the most difficult issues. . . .

II. The Participants' Roles in Disclosing Conflict: Rules and Realities

. . .

B. Class Counsel

A familiar refrain among courts and commentators is that lawyers assume special responsibilities in class litigation. According to one circuit court of appeals, the duty to ensure adequate representation rests "primarily upon counsel for the class . . . in addition to the normal obligations of an officer of the court, and . . . counsel to parties of the litigation, class action counsel possess, in a very real sense, fiduciary obligations to those not before the court." Principal among those duties is the responsibility to apprise the trial judge of conflicting interests that may warrant separate representation or other corrective measures.

Although unobjectionable in concept, that role definition has frequently proved unworkable in practice. To be sure, many attorneys make considerable efforts to appreciate and accommodate the broadest possible spectrum of class sentiment. . . . [But] where the range and intensity of divergent preferences within the class are unlikely to surface without counsel's assistance, he often has strong prudential and ideological reasons not to provide it. One need not be a raving realist to suppose that such motivations play a more dominant role in shaping attorneys' conduct than Rule 23's directives and the accompanying judicial gloss.

1. Prudential interests.

An attorney active in institutional reform class actions is subject to a variety of financial, tactical, and professional pressures that constrain his response to class conflicts. Of course, none of these constraints is unique to this form of litigation. And the intensity of such pressures varies considerably depending, inter alia, on the sources of funding and organizational support for particular cases. Nonetheless, it is important to identify, in generic form, the range of prudential interests that can affect counsel's management of internecine disputes, and the inadequacy of conventional correctives.

The most patent of these interests arises from the financial under-pinnings of institutional reform litigation. Support for such cases derives largely from limited public interest funding and from court-awarded counsel fees to prevailing parties. Among the factors affecting the attorney's fee award are the relief obtained, the costs of attaining it, and the number of other counsel who have contributed to the result. Given the expense of institutional reform class actions, few litigators can remain impervious to fee-related considerations or organizational budget constraints. And flushing out dissension among class members can prove costly in several respects.

For example, opposing parties often seek to capitalize on class dissension by filing motions for decertification. If such efforts prove successful, class counsel may lose a substantial investment that he cannot, as a practical matter, recoup from former class members. At a minimum, such motions result in expense, delay, and loss of bargaining leverage, and deflect resources from trial preparation. Certification disputes may also trigger involvement of additional lawyers, who would share the limelight, the control over litigation decisions and, under some circumstances, the resources available for attorneys' fees.

Exposing conflict can also impede settlement arrangements that are attractive to class counsel on a number of grounds. As in many other litigation contexts, attorneys often have a bias to settle not shared by their clients. Since institutional reform plaintiffs generally do not underwrite the costs of litigation, their primary interest is in the result attained; the time and effort necessary to attain it are of less concern. Yet from the attorney's perspective, a modest settlement may generate a result "bearing a higher ratio to the cost of the work than a much larger recovery obtained only after extensive discovery, a long trial and an appeal." For example, if the prospects for prevailing on the merits are uncertain, some plaintiffs will see little to lose and everything to gain from persistence. That viewpoint may be inade-quately aired by class counsel, who has concerns for his reputation as well as competing claims on his time and his organization's resources to consider.

The potential for attorney-client conflicts is compounded when a proposed settlement makes extremely generous, or totally inadequate, provision for class counsel. Of course a lawyer may attempt to avoid compromising influences by refusing to discuss fees until agreement on all other issues is final. However, that strategy is not necessarily in anyone's interest if it inhibits favorable settlement offers, and many defendants are reluctant to compromise without some understanding of their total liability. Moreover, in an escalating number of civil rights cases, defendants have sought to make settlement on the merits condi-tional on counsel's waiver or curtailment of claims to statutory compen-sation. . . .

A final set of problems emerges in test-case litigation. In some instances, counsel may be reluctant to espouse positions that are at odds with those he has taken or intends to take in other proceedings or that could establish an unwelcome precedent. Moreover, test-case litigation often generates settlement biases directly converse to those discussed above. Once a lawyer has prepared a claim with potentially significant impact, he may be disinclined to settle. He almost certainly would not share some plaintiffs' enthusiasm for pre- or post-trial agreements promising generous terms for the litigants but little recognition and no precedential value for similarly situated victims. Few professionals, class attorneys included, can make decisions wholly independent of concerns about their careers and reputations among peers, potential clients, and funding sources. Litigating well-publicized institutional reform cases can provide desirable trial experience, generate attractive new cases, legitimate organizational objectives in the eyes of private donors, and enhance attorneys' personal standing in the legal community. Where such rewards are likely, counsel may tend to discount preferences for a low-visibility settlement, particularly if it falls short of achieving ideological objectives to which he is strongly committed. . . .

    2. Ideological interests.

. . .

Relying on case histories from Boston, Atlanta, and Detroit, Derek Bell submits that NAACP attorneys' "single-minded commitment" to maximum integration has led them to ignore a shift in priorities among many black parents from racial balance to quality education.

Similar indictments have been leveled against attorneys in other civil rights contexts. For example, in 1974, a number of parents and guardians brought suit in behalf of all present and future residents of Pennsylvania's Pennhurst facility for the retarded. Class counsel took the position that his obligations ran solely to the residents, and that their interests dictated Pennhurst's closure and replacement with community facilities. Accordingly, counsel made little effort to expose or espouse the views of parents and guardians preferring institutionalization. Indeed, according to one of the lawyers subsequently involved, class counsel sought to avoid "stir[ring] people up" by deemphasizing the possibility of Pennhurst's closure in his out-of-court statements. After the district judge ordered removal of Pennhurst residents to community facilities, a systematic survey of their parents and guardians revealed that only 19% of respondents favored deinstitutionalization. Accounts of other civil rights litigation suggest that *Pennhurst* is not an isolated example.

It does not follow, of course, that attorneys in these and comparable cases failed to represent class interests. Much depends on who one views as appropriate spokesmen for the class and how broadly one defines "interest." . . . [P]arents are often poorly situated to speak for all children who will be affected by judicial decree. But neither is an attorney with strong prudential or ideological preferences well positioned to decide which class members or guardians deserve a hearing and which do not. And one critical problem with existing class action procedures is that they fail to assure adequate disclosure of counsel's own interests or of countervailing client concerns. . . .

[Discussion is omitted concerning limitations in the two most common procedural approaches to class conflicts. The current pluralist approach—which is to rely on separate counsel for separate interests—may, in some instances, exacerbate problems of delay, expense, manageability, and accountability. In other contexts, that strategy can bias results toward those with the organizational acumen and financial resources to make themselves heard. The majoritarian alternative is to provide for direct class participation through plebiscites and public hearings. Yet that approach cannot adequately respond to circumstances where those registering preferences are uniformed, unrepresentative, or unresponsive to the needs of most current or future class members. For example, the complexity of remedial tradeoffs may be difficult to convey to large constituencies. And parents whose children will bear the short term costs of certain desegregation and deinstitutionalization remedies may be poorly situated to evaluate their long-range benefits.

However, granting these difficulties, the article considers various strategies to encourage more reflective resort to pluralist or majoritarian strategies in appropriate circumstances. Among other things, courts could be required to make a record concerning their responsiveness to class conflicts. To assist judicial determinations, class counsel could submit statements detailing contacts with class members, and attorneys' fee awards might be structured to create greater incentives for lawyer-client communication.]

IV. Alternatives and Apologia

. . .

C. The Bounded Potential of Procedural Solutions

The ultimate effect of procedural reforms is difficult to predict. There remains the possibility that greater reliance on separate counsel or court-appointed experts will simply increase the numbers of platonic guardians involved in institutional reform litigation. And requiring fact-finders to make more detailed records in support of their conclusions has had mixed success in other contexts. According to Joseph Sax, "emphasis on the redemptive quality of [such] procedural reform" in administrative decisionmaking is "about nine parts myth and one part coconut oil." Yet while systematic data are lacking, most commentators would probably agree with Richard Stewart's less dire assessment. In his view, forcing the decisionmaker to "direct attention to factors that may have been disregarded" has in some instances proved of real prophylactic value.

Moreover, clearer mandates to class counsel than those provided by existing procedural and ethical rules could serve important socialization functions. Concededly, asymmetrics between class interests and preferences will often force counsel to function more as a Burkean trustee than instructed delegate. Even so, it should be possible to recast that trusteeship role to encompass more explicit fiduciary obligations to dissenting constituencies. Requiring attorneys to record contacts with the class and perceptions of conflict would, if nothing else, narrow their capacity for self-delusion about whose views they were or were not representing. Explicit professional obligations, even those unlikely to trigger any formal sanction, often affect behavioral norms simply by sensitizing individuals to the full implications of their conduct.

. . .

To be sure, none of the proposals outlined here can guarantee better results in [institutional reform cases]. But that conclusion, if disconcerting, is not necessarily damning. Given the values at issue in institutional reform cases, conflicts are an ineradicable feature of the legal landscape. Virtually all of the pluralist and majoritarian deficiencies that impede judicial management of such conflicts would arise with equal force if the underlying issues were addressed in legislative or bureaucratic settings. Indeed, one of the strongest justifications for those governance structures is equally available to class actions: While we cannot depend on disinterested and informed judgment by any single group of decisionmakers, we can at least create sufficient procedural checks and balances to prevent the worst abuses.

Moreover, to acknowledge that the formal mandates governing class actions promise far more than they deliver is not to condemn the pretense. No hypothesized procedures can insure that all class interests will be "adequately represented" or that counsel will single-mindedly pursue his "client's" objectives. But the risks of abandoning either fiction may be too great.

No matter how faulty the enforcement mechanism, such mandates serve important legitimating functions. Broad injunctions concerning client autonomy and adequate representation allow us to affirm the individual's right to be heard without in fact paying the entire price. Giving overly fixed content to those terms could propel us toward some generic prescription that raises more difficulties than it resolves. An unqualified embrace of pluralism would entail problems of increased expense and diminished effectiveness. To totter towards majoritarianism would require confrontation with the awkward fact that paternalism is often offensive in principle but desirable in practice. Like other "white lies" of the law, those governing class adjudication have spared us such discomfitting choices by masking certain "weak spots in our intellectual structure."

[And, given the extraordinary achievements of this form of litigation, that is a useful, if sometimes unbecoming, role.]

Questions and Comments

Rule 23(a)(4) of the Federal Rules of Civil Procedure provides, inter alia, that the parties representing the class must "fairly and adequately protect the interests of the class." This provision has been applied to class counsel as well as the named representatives of the class. In *Wagner v. Lehman Brothers Kuhn Loeb Inc.*, 646 F.Supp. 643 (N.D.Ill. 1986), counsel for the class engaged in unethical conduct: offering to pay a witness a percentage of any recovery in exchange for favorable testimony; and interviewing the opposing party without informing that party's counsel. The court held that this unethical conduct barred the lawyer from representing the class:

> . . . An inquiry into the character of counsel for the class-representative is also necessary because he stands in a fiduciary relationship with the absent class. See, e.g., *Greenfield v. Villager Industries, Inc.*, 483 F.2d 824, 832 (3d Cir.1973); *Stavrides v. Mellon National Bank & Trust Co.*, 60 F.R.D. 634, 637 (W.D.Pa.1973) . . .

> . . .

> . . . In the majority of the reported decisions, examination of counsel's character focuses on his ethical behavior and the attorney's professional responsibility. See, e.g., *Halverson v. Convenient Food Mart, Inc.*, 458 F.2d 927, 931 (7th Cir.1972); *Brame v. Ray Bills Finance Corp.*, 85 F.R.D. 568, 577 (N.D.N.Y.1979). Reference to counsel's unethical and improper actions is sufficient to find that he cannot adequately represent the putative class in accordance with his fiduciary duties. See *Taub v. Glickman*, 14 Fed.R.Serv.2d 847, 849 (S.D.N.Y.1970) (court denied class certification because of attorney's improper conduct without even finding an actual violation of any disciplinary rule).

646 F.Supp. at 661–62.

Should the court make this kind of inquiry in every class action—acting as guardian for the absent class in deciding whether to "hire" the particular lawyer? The court's failure to inquire in every class action may be partly justified by the assumption that deficiencies in the class counsel's competence or integrity will be brought out by the opposing party in the class certification process, which is an adversary proceeding. For an example of the court allowing the opposing party to inquire into the class lawyer's character, see *Stavrides v. Mellon National Bank & Trust Co.*, 60 F.R.D. 634 (W.D.Pa.1973). Is it always in the opposing party's interest to challenge class counsel?

One commentator has suggested that a *Garner*-like exception to the attorney-client privilege be adopted to protect the interests of absentee class members. See Note, The Attorney–Client Privilege in Class Actions: Fashioning an Exception to Promote Adequacy of Representation, 97 Harv.L.Rev. 947 (1984).

Would this proposal meet the problems addressed by Rhode? If the *Garner* exception were available in class actions before the case had been resolved on the merits, how would the court ensure that the opposing party did not become the primary beneficiary of the invasion of the class' confidences? Should the exception be limited to class members challenging a settlement or attorney's fees?

The Bounds of Paternalism

Professor Rhode's article focuses on one kind of class action: institutional reform litigation. Is her conclusion also applicable to other types of class actions, e.g., a class derivative action brought by the shareholders of a company or a mass tort class suit such as that by the victims of the chemical leak in Bhopal India?

Does it matter that in the latter two types of cases the lawyer is hoping to make a profit out of the proceeds of the suit? Should we be more concerned with the lawyer's interest in making a profit than her interest in seeing ideological goals realized?

See Garth, Nagel and Plager, The Institution of the Private Attorney General: Perspectives from an Empirical Study of Class Action Litigation, 61 S.Cal.L.Rev. 353 (1988), distinguishing between the "social advocate" and the "legal mercenary" in terms of creativity in legal strategy (the mercenary prefers not to experiment), mobilization of the class (the mercenary prefers it to be inert), obtaining certification of the class (the mercenary may not be interested unless it will increase settlement value), and settlement approach (the mercenary is interested in the fee, the social advocate in the decree).

DERRICK A. BELL, JR., "SERVING TWO MASTERS: INTEGRATION IDEALS AND CLIENT INTERESTS IN SCHOOL DESEGREGATION LITIGATION"
85 Yale L.J. 470, 471–72, 485–87, 504–05 (1976).*

. . .

The espousal of educational improvement as the appropriate goal of school desegregation efforts is out of phase with the current state of the law. Largely through the efforts of civil rights lawyers, most courts have come to construe Brown v. Board of Education [2] as mandating "equal educational opportunities" through school desegregation plans aimed at achieving racial balance, whether or not those plans will improve the education received by the children affected. To the extent that "instructional profit" accurately defines the school priorities of black parents in Boston and elsewhere, questions of professional responsibility are raised that can no longer be ignored:

2. 347 U.S. 483 (1954).

How should the term "client" be defined in school desegregation cases that are litigated for decades, determine critically important constitutional rights for thousands of minority children, and usually involve major restructuring of a public school system? How should civil rights attorneys represent the often diverse interests of clients and class in school suits? Do they owe any special obligation to class members who emphasize educational quality and who probably cannot obtain counsel to advocate their divergent views? Do the political, organizational, and even philosophical complexities of school desegregation litigation justify a higher standard of professional responsibility on the part of civil rights lawyers to their clients, or more diligent oversight of the lawyer-client relationship by the bench and bar?

As is so often the case, a crisis of events motivates this long overdue inquiry. The great crusade to desegregate the public schools has faltered. There is increasing opposition to desegregation at both local and national levels (not all of which can now be simply condemned as "racist"), while the once vigorous support of federal courts is on the decline. New barriers have arisen—inflation makes the attainment of racial balance more expensive, the growth of black populations in urban areas renders it more difficult, an increasing number of social science studies question the validity of its educational assumptions.

Civil rights lawyers dismiss these new obstacles as legally irrelevant. Having achieved so much by courageous persistence, they have not waivered in their determination to implement *Brown* using racial balance measures developed in the hard-fought legal battles of the last two decades. This stance involves great risk for clients whose educational interests may no longer accord with the integration ideals of their attorneys. Indeed, muffled but increasing criticism of "unconditional integration" policies by vocal minorities in black communities is not limited to Boston. Now that traditional racial balance remedies are becoming increasingly difficult to achieve or maintain, there is tardy concern that racial balance may not be the relief actually desired by the victims of segregated schools.

This article will review the development of school desegregation litigation and the unique lawyer-client relationship that has evolved out of it. It will not be the first such inquiry. During the era of "massive resistance," Southern states charged that this relationship violated professional canons of conduct. A majority of the Supreme Court rejected those challenges, creating in the process constitutional protection for conduct that, under other circumstances, would contravene basic precepts of professional behavior. The potential for ethical problems in these constitutionally protected lawyer-client relationships was recognized by the American Bar Association Code of Professional Responsibility, but it is difficult to provide standards for the attorney and protection for the client where the source of the conflict is the attorney's ideals. The magnitude of the difficulty is more accurately gauged in a much older code that warns: "No servant can serve two masters: for either he will hate the one, and love the other; or else he will hold to one, and despise the other."

.   .   .

II. Lawyer–Client Conflicts: Sources and Rationale

.   .   .

3. *The Atlanta Case*

Prior to Detroit, the most open confrontation between NAACP views of school integration and those of local blacks who favored plans oriented toward improving educational quality occurred in Atlanta. There, a group of plaintiffs became discouraged by the difficulty of achieving meaningful desegregation in a district which had gone from 32 percent black in 1952 to 82 percent black in 1974. Lawyers for the local NAACP branch, who had gained control of the litigation, worked out a compromise plan with the Atlanta School Board that called for full faculty and employee desegregation but for only limited pupil desegregation. In exchange, the school board promised to hire a number of blacks in top administrative positions, including a black superintendent of schools.

The federal court approved the plan. The court's approval was apparently influenced by petitions favoring the plan's adoption signed by several thousand members of the plaintiffs' class. Nevertheless the national NAACP office and LDF lawyers were horrified by the compromise. The NAACP ousted the Atlanta branch president who had supported the compromise. Then, acting on behalf of some local blacks who shared their views, LDF lawyers filed an appeal in the Atlanta case. The appeal also raised a number of procedural issues concerning the lack of notice and the refusal of the district court to grant hearings on the Compromise Plan. These issues gave the Fifth Circuit an opportunity to remand the case to the district court without reaching the merits of the settlement agreement. Undaunted, LDF lawyers again attacked the plan for failing to require busing of whites into the predominantly black schools in which a majority of the students in the system were enrolled. But the district court's finding that the system had achieved unitary status was upheld by the same Fifth Circuit panel.

.   .   . NAACP opposition to the Atlanta Compromise Plan was not deterred by the fact that local leaders, including black school board members, supported the settlement. Defending the Compromise Plan, Dr. Benjamin E. Mays, one of the most respected black educators in the country, stated:

> We have never argued that the Atlanta Compromise Plan is the best plan, nor have we encouraged any other school system to adopt it. This plan is the most viable plan for Atlanta—a city school system that is 82 percent Black and 18 percent white and is

continuing to lose whites each year to five counties that are more than 90 percent white.

. . .

More importantly, Black people must not resign themselves to the pessimistic view that a non-integrated school cannot provide Black children with an excellent educational setting. Instead, Black people, while working to implement *Brown*, should recognize that integration alone does not provide a quality education, and that much of the substance of quality education can be provided to Black children in the interim.

. . .

B. *Alternatives to the Rigidity of Racial Balance*

. . .

Idealism, though perhaps rarer than greed, is harder to control. Justice Harlan accurately prophesied the excesses of derailed benevolence, but a retreat from the group representational concepts set out in *Button* would be a disaster, not an improvement. State legislatures are less likely than the ABA to draft standards that effectively guide practitioners and protect clients. Even well intentioned and carefully drawn standards might hinder rather than facilitate the always difficult task of achieving social change through legal action. And too stringent rules could encourage officials in some states to institute groundless disciplinary proceedings against lawyers in school cases, which in many areas are hardly more popular today than they were during the massive resistance era.

Client involvement in school litigation is more likely to increase if civil rights lawyers themselves come to realize that the special status accorded them by the courts and the bar demands in return an extraordinary display of ethical sensitivity and self-restraint. The "divided allegiance" between client and employer which Justice Harlan feared would interfere with the civil rights lawyer's "full compliance with his basic professional obligation" has developed in a far more idealistic and thus a far more dangerous form. For it is more the civil rights lawyers' commitment to an integrated society than any policy directives or pressures from their employers which leads to their assumptions of client acceptance and their condemnations of all dissent.

. . .

Questions and Comments

How much of Bell's critique is unique to class actions and how much is equally applicable to any lawyer/client relationship where the lawyer is "independent" of (not paid by) a client who is a member of a disadvantaged group? How much more respectful of their clients' wishes are public defenders? Or *pro bono* lawyers for individual clients? Are the problems inherent in these "unequal" relationships merely exacerbated by the class action form?

Other articles questioning the traditional lawyer/client relationship as a model for class action lawyers in public interest law or lawyers representing disadvantaged individuals include: Note, Petitioning and the Empowerment Theory of Practice, 96 Yale L.J. 569 (1987); Yeazell, From Group Litigation to Class Action Part II: Interest, Class, and Representation, 27 U.C.L.A.L.Rev. 1067 (1980); Simon, The Ideology of Advocacy . . ., 1978 Wis.L.Rev. 29; Alschuler, The Defense Attorney's Role in Plea Bargaining, 84 Yale L.J. 1179 (1975). See also Bersoff, Representation for Children in Custody Decisions: All That Glitters is not Gault, 15 J.Fam.L. 27, 33–34 (1976).

For a case of shareholder class members challenging the class lawyer's claim for attorney fees, see In re Fine Paper Antitrust Litigation, 98 F.R.D. 48 (E.D.Pa.1983), rev'd, 751 F.2d 562 (3d Cir.1984). This case is infamous for the patronage system that developed among the scores of plaintiffs' lawyers for the various classes represented, for the scale of the alleged padding of fees and expenses, and for the animosity that developed between the two lead counsel. A good discussion of this case can be found in Coffee, Rescuing the Private Attorney General: Why the Model of the Lawyer as Bounty Hunter Is Not Working, 42 Md.L.Rev. 215 (1983).

JOHN C. COFFEE, JR., "UNDERSTANDING THE PLAINTIFF'S ATTORNEY: THE IMPLICATIONS OF ECONOMIC THEORY FOR PRIVATE ENFORCEMENT OF LAW THROUGH CLASS AND DERIVATIVE SUITS"

86 Col.L.Rev. 669 (1986).*

INTRODUCTION

Probably to a unique degree, American law relies upon private litigants to enforce substantive provisions of law that in other legal systems are left largely to the discretion of public enforcement agencies. This system of enforcement through "private attorneys general" is most closely associated with the federal antitrust and securities laws and the common law's derivative action, but similar institutional arrangements have developed recently in the environmental, "mass tort," and employment discrimination fields. The key legal rules that make the private attorney general a reality in American law today, however, are not substantive but procedural—namely, those rules that establish the fee arrangements under which these plaintiff's attorneys are compensated.[2] Inevitably, these rules create an incentive structure that either encourages or chills private enforcement of law.

. . .

2. Four such legal rules are critical to our current system of private enforcement and are largely unique to the American legal system. First and oldest is the "American rule," under which each side bears its own legal expenses. See Alyeska Pipeline Serv. Co. v. Wilderness Soc'y, 421 U.S. 240 (1975). Economic analysis suggests that the effect of this rule is to increase the incentive to bring an action that has a relatively low prospect

I. THE INCENTIVE TO LITIGATE IN CLASS AND DERIVATIVE ACTIONS

. . .

A. *Principal and Agent: Who's in Control?*

In theory, a fundamental premise of American legal ethics is that clients, not their attorneys, should define litigation objectives.[21] Yet, in the context of class and derivative actions, it is well understood that the actual client generally has only a nominal stake in the outcome of the litigation. Empirical studies have shown this,[22] and courts, when dissatisfied with the performance of plaintiff's attorneys, are prone to emphasize that the plaintiff's attorney has no "true" identifiable client.[23] Despite these grumblings, our legal system has long accepted, if somewhat uneasily, the concept of the plaintiff's attorney as an entrepreneur who performs the socially useful function of deterring undesirable conduct. This acceptance is manifested in a variety of ways: by permitting the attorney to advance the expenses of the litigation and receive reimbursement only if successful; [24] by sometimes permitting the attorney to settle a class or derivative action over the objections of

of success at trial. See Shavell, Suit, Settlement, and Trial: A Theoretical Analysis Under Alternative Methods for the Allocation of Legal Costs, 11 J.Legal Stud. 55 (1982).

Second, the "common fund" doctrine entitles a plaintiff who creates a fund that benefits others to recover attorney's fees out of the fund based on principles of unjust enrichment. This doctrine is an exception to the traditional "American rule." See Boeing Co. v. Van Gemert, 444 U.S. 472, 478–81 (1980). The "common fund" doctrine has long governed the award of attorney's fees in derivative suits and securities class actions. See Hornstein, The Counsel Fee in Stockholder's Derivative Suits, 39 Colum.L.Rev. 784 (1939).

Third, the contingent fee, which has long been permitted in the United States, see Findlater, The Proposed Revisions of DR 5–103(B): Champerty and Class Actions, 36 Bus. Law. 1667, 1669–70 (1981), enables a plaintiff's attorney to undertake litigation as a joint venturer with the client.

The final rule involves statutory "attorney fee shifting." Over the last several decades, a host of statutes have been enacted that authorize an award of attorney's fees to a successful plaintiff's attorney. One recent survey found 1,974 such statutes at the state level alone and suggested that fee shifting is now at least as common as the traditional "American rule." See Note, State Attorney Fee Shifting Statutes: Are We Quietly Repealing the American Rule?, Law & Contemp.Probs., Winter 1984, at 321.

21. See Model Rules of Professional Conduct Rule 1.2(a) (1983) ("A lawyer shall abide by a client's decisions concerning the objectives of representation. . . ."); see also Rhode, Class Conflicts in Class Actions, 34 Stan.L.Rev. 1183, 1183 (1982) (noting difficulties in applying principle of client control to context of class litigation).

22. The Wood Report, which surveyed nearly 1400 derivative actions filed in several New York state and federal courts during the 1930s and early 1940s, reported that the representative plaintiff typically had very small stakes in the outcome. See F. Wood, [Survey and Report Regarding Stockholders' Derivative Suits (1984)] at 45–46. More recent empirical research has not challenged this finding. See Garth, Nagel & Plager, Empirical Research and the Shareholder Derivative Suit: Toward a Better–Informed Debate, Law & Contemp. Probs., Summer 1985, at 137, 142–43.

23. See Piambino v. Bailey, 757 F.2d 1112, 1144 (11th Cir.1985); Foster v. Boise–Cascade, Inc., 420 F.Supp. 674, 681 (S.D.Tex.1976), aff'd, 577 F.2d 335 (5th Cir.1978).

24. See Model Rules of Professional Conduct Rule 1.8(e)(1) (1983) (lawyer "may advance court costs and expenses of litigation, the repayment of which may be contingent on the outcome of the matter"); Findlater, supra note 2, at 1669.

the actual client who is serving as representative of the class,[25] and by allowing the use of fee formulas that view "the lawyer as a calculating entrepreneur regulated by calculating judges."[26] Thus, although our law publicly expresses homage to individual clients, it privately recognizes their limited relevance in this context.

Although this legal structure is largely unparalleled in other common law systems, it has its obvious advantages. First, it enables clients who are dispersed or have suffered relatively small injuries to receive legal representation without incurring the substantial transaction costs of coordination. Absent such a system, a classic "free rider" problem would arise because litigation is a form of "public good" in which the benefits of an action accrue to persons who are not required to bear their share of the action's costs. This means that litigation would be predictably underfunded, from the clients' perspective, if the clients had to take collective action. Second, because the attorney as private enforcer looks to the court, not the client, to award him a fee if successful, the attorney can find the legal violation first and the client second. In principle, this system should encourage the attorney to invest in search costs and seek out violations of the law that are profitable for him to challenge, rather than wait passively for an aggrieved client to arrive at his door. Thus, the attorney becomes a "bounty hunter"—or, less pejoratively, an independent monitoring force—motivated to prosecute legal violations still unknown to prospective clients.

However, this system also creates the potential for both opportunism and overenforcement. The first of these dangers arises because, in economic terms, there are high "agency costs" associated with class and derivative actions.[30] To be sure, the magnitude of these costs will vary depending upon a variety of factors. In much "public interest" litigation, the structure of the "public interest" law firm—in particular,

25. See Morris, A View of Representative Actions, Derivative and Class, from a Plaintiff's Attorney's Vantage Point, 3 Del.J.Corp.L. 273, 276 (1978) (discussing conflict between attorney and client in Saylor v. Livesay, 274 F.Supp. 253 (S.D.N.Y.1967), rev'd on other grounds, 391 F.2d 965 (2d Cir.1968)).

It is generally recognized that counsel's fiduciary obligation runs to the class and not simply to the named plaintiff. Thus, courts have sided with class counsel where conflicts arise between counsel and the lead plaintiff in a class action. See Greenfield v. Villager Indus., Inc., 483 F.2d 824, 832 n. 9 (3d Cir.1973); Handler, Edgar & Settle, Public Interest Law and Employment Discrimination, *in* Public Interest Law: An Economic and Institutional Analysis 251, 274 (1978) (discussing claimed ability of public interest law firms to manage litigation without client direction); Rhode, supra note 21, at 1202–04.

26. Leubsdorf, [The Contingency Factor in Attorney Fee Awards, 90 Yale L.J. 473 (1981)] at 481 (discussing courts' rationale for granting attorneys a contingency bonus in addition to fees calculated under the lodestar formula).

. . .

30. The term "agency costs" refers to both the costs the principal must incur to keep an agent loyal and to the losses that occur as a result of agent disloyalty that are not worth preventing. See Jensen & Meckling, Theory of The Firm: Managerial Behavior, Agency Costs and Ownership Structure, 3 J.Fin.Econ. 305, 308–09 (1976). Once "agency costs" become very high, it is simpler to view attorneys as independent actors, even though they remain, to some degree, ultimately accountable to their clients.

its independent board, its more limited ability to pay out earnings to its attorneys, and its need to raise funds from donors in the future—may substitute for client control and produce substantial monitoring of attorney opportunism. In other areas, such as employment discrimination litigation, client control may be relatively stronger than in the typical class action either because of a greater financial injury per client (thereby encouraging closer monitoring of the attorney) or because of a subjective, nonmonetary component to the injury that produces the same effect.[31]

The second danger—overenforcement—arises because the unconstrained attorney may be motivated to sue where the client would not.[32] Although the rational plaintiff's attorney would consider only the immediate payoff, the client may be concerned about the longer-term effects of litigation. For example, a plaintiff's attorney might commence a derivative suit against a corporation's officers and directors for a negligent business decision whenever the expected settlement would justify a fee that covered the attorney's opportunity costs. The shareholders, however, might rationally fear that such litigation would make directors excessively risk averse in the long-run.[33] . . .

What happens when client control is so weak as to make the attorney virtually an independent entrepreneur? In some areas of contemporary litigation, the pattern is typically one of the lawyer finding the client, rather than vice versa. A principal characteristic of these areas is that plaintiff's attorneys typically have low search costs. That is, plaintiff's attorneys can discover the existence of potentially meritorious legal claims at low cost to themselves. As an entrepreneur who is compensated only when successful, the plaintiff's attorney bears the costs of failure and seeks to minimize those costs by free riding on the monitoring efforts of others. The classic illustration of this pattern is in the field of antitrust enforcement, where private antitrust class

---

31. A plaintiff may be motivated by a belief that he is contributing to an important social movement in a civil rights, employment discrimination, or environmental class action, but it is doubtful that such "psychic income" is a significant factor in an antitrust or securities class action, or in a derivative suit.

32. See Landes & Posner, [The Private Enforcement of Law, 4 J. Legal Stud. 1 (1945)] at 15 (arguing that because the price paid to the private enforcer does not decline once an optimum level of enforcement is achieved, there will be an excessive level of enforcement activity). On a more practical level, this problem of overenforcement can arise in a derivative action because the fee award is based on the gross recovery. Such a formula does not reflect the actual net recovery, if any, to the corporation after subtraction of the corporation's own litigation expenses, the indemnification payments made to the individual defendants, and the imputed costs associated with lost executive time.

33. This author has argued elsewhere that directors make "poor cost avoiders" with respect to corporate losses flowing from negligent decision making and hence can be rendered excessively risk averse (in terms of the desires of shareholders, who hold diversified portfolios). See Coffee, Litigation and Corporate Governance: An Essay on Steering Between Scylla and Charybdis, 52 Geo.Wash.L.Rev. 789, 801–03 (1984). Another example might be a derivative suit brought by a small shareholder to enjoin questionable corporate payments in foreign countries. Although the payments may be illegal and injurious to United States foreign policy interests, they could be highly profitable to the corporation, and it is far from clear that shareholders collectively desire that such illegal action be enjoined.

actions have tended to piggyback on a prior governmental proceeding (such as a grand jury indictment or a Federal Trade Commission proceeding). . . . The mass tort, such as an airplane crash or a toxic disaster, provides another obvious example. Similarly, a publicized takeover attempt may lead to a "greenmail" transaction, the adoption of a "poison pill," or some other defensive measure by the board of directors of a target corporation, thereby indicating the potential for a derivative suit.

. . .

Once the plaintiff's attorney has decided to bring suit, identifying and securing a nominal client is often only a necessary procedural step that seldom poses a substantial barrier for the experienced professional. In the securities and derivative suit areas, there are well-known individuals who possess broad (but thin) securities portfolios and have served as the lead plaintiff in numerous previous class actions. . . .

As a normative matter, such a description of the attorney-client relationship may seem offensive to those accustomed to viewing the relationship as a fiduciary one. Yet for analytical purposes, one better understands the behavior of the plaintiff's attorney in class and derivative actions if one views him not as an agent, but more as an entrepreneur who regards a litigation as a risky asset that requires continuing investment decisions. Furthermore, a purely fiduciary perspective is misleading because it assumes that the client's preferences with respect to when an action should be settled are exogenously determined, when, in fact, they are largely influenced by the fee award formula adopted by the court. The real question, then, is what fee award formula should courts choose? This question cannot be sensibly answered by considering only the client's interest. Rather, social costs must also be analyzed.

B. *The Disparity Between the Private and Social Incentive to Litigate*

In a stimulating article, Professor Shavell contends that the private and social incentives to bring suit bear no necessary relationship to each other.[44] In particular, the social costs of litigation can often exceed the private costs because the parties to the action do not bear the costs of the judicial system. Under these circumstances, an externality arises because the private conduct that is encouraged imposes net costs on society. . . . Professor Shavell's analysis suggests that there is likely to be an excessive incentive to litigate. . . .

. . . Historically, courts have awarded plaintiff's attorneys in class and derivative actions fees that have ranged between twenty and thirty percent of recoveries.[51] Moreover, fee awards have not been a

44. See Shavell [The Social Versus the Private Incentive to Bring Suit in a Costly Legal System, 11 J. Legal Stud. 333, 334 (1982).]

51. For discussion of fee awards in securities class actions and derivative suits, see supra note 26. In the antitrust context, where there is statutory fee shifting in favor of plaintiffs, a recent Georgetown University study found that plaintiff's attorney's fees averaged 20.2% ($58,000) of the total recovery in non–Multi–District Litigation (non-

constant percentage of recoveries, but rather have tended to decline as recovery size increases, thereby inclining plaintiff's attorneys to settle more "cheaply" as the damages involved increase.

If we assume that the plaintiff's attorney acts as a rational entrepreneur in deciding to bring, maintain, or settle litigation, it follows that investment in class and derivative actions will tend to be underfunded in terms of the clients' preferences. The key point is that the litigation stakes are asymmetric, with the defendant focusing on the judgment or settlement and the plaintiff's attorney focusing on the fee, which is typically a declining percentage of the recovery. . . .

C. *Policy Responses*

If [the analysis thus far] implies that private enforcement of law will be underfunded so long as the plaintiff's attorney is compensated on a percentage of the recovery basis, what policy responses are appropriate? One answer might be to employ the lodestar formula, which essentially compensates plaintiff's attorneys for their time at their normal billing rates. In fact, however, the lodestar formula may exacerbate the problem of cheap settlements. By severing the fee award from the settlement's size, this formula facilitates the ability of defendants and the plaintiff's attorneys to arrange collusive settlements that exchange a low recovery for a high fee award. In addition, the lodestar formula essentially places the court in the position of a public utility commission that regulates the "fair" return the attorney receives by both determining the attorney's normal billing rate and assessing whether the attorney's time was reasonably expended. At a minimum, such an undertaking imposes a substantial burden on the already overloaded judicial system, thus increasing the earlier noted disparity between the social and private costs of litigation.[62]

In light of the lodestar formula's deficiencies, it is worth asking what other alternatives can be imagined. An economic answer might

MDL), but that their fee award fell to an average level of 8.3% ($4,000,000) in typical Multi–District Litigation (MDL) cases. See S. Salop & L. White, Private Antitrust Litigation: An Introduction and Framework 14–15 (Sept. 1985) (unpublished manuscript) (copy on file at the offices of the Columbia Law Review). This substantial difference may be attributable to the much larger size of the recovery in MDL cases ($48,000,000 versus $287,000 in non-MDL cases). Id. For purposes of this Article, the MDL context seems the more accurate proxy for class action litigation in which the clients are unable to constrain their attorney. In any event, a plaintiff's attorney who sees a fee award of about 8% to 10% of the expected recovery has far less incentive to invest in the action than do the defendants who bear the full cost of the settlement or final judgment (including, in the latter case, the plaintiff's attorney's fee as well).

62. For example, in the *Fine Paper* antitrust litigation, the district court spent 41 hearing days reviewing the fee petitions and considering challenges to them. Thereafter, the court wrote a lengthy opinion of over 100 pages. See Coffee, [Rescuing the] Private Attorney General . . . 42 Md.L.Rev. 215 (1983)] at 255 n. 94. But the Third Circuit partially reversed the district court, thus requiring even further litigation. See In re Fine Paper Antitrust Litig., 98 F.R.D. 48 (E.D.Pa.1983), rev'd in part, 751 F.2d 562 (3d Cir. 1984). When the fee petition hearing consumes nearly as much judicial time as the litigation of the substantive merits, it appears that the tail has begun to wag the dog. Such a case well illustrates Professor Shavell's thesis that litigation receives a public subsidy. See Shavell, supra note [44].

be to eliminate the principal-agent relationship entirely by permitting the plaintiff's attorney to acquire all the client's rights in the action.[63] The beauty of this approach is that the attorney is given the incentive to expend effort up to the socially optimal position . . .

.   .   .

Given that this . . . approach seems unpromising, other less perfect methods of alleviating the externality caused by the principal-agent problem must be examined. It is at this point of searching for "second best" solutions that we reencounter the contemporary debate over treble damages.   .   .   .

[A] multiple damages formula, however, generates considerably more deterrence than the compensatory damages equilibrium.   .   .   . [M]ultiple damages can be said to overdeter because they cause defendants to restrain their output even when further production would produce gains in excess of social costs. On the other hand, this additional deterrent may be thought desirable as a means of offsetting the low risk of detection that accompanies many forms of illegal behavior.

.   .   .

.   .   . A more sensible response might be to apply the standard prescription of neoclassical economics that the "law should mimic the market." In the class action context, that would mean attempting to award the fee that informed private bargaining, if it were truly possible, might have reached. The simplest way for the law to duplicate the bargain that informed parties would reach if agency costs were low is to look to fee award levels in actions brought by sophisticated private parties under the same or comparable statutes. For example, the Georgetown study of antitrust enforcement found that the fees awarded in large class actions averaged 8.3%, but rose to 20.2% in non-class action cases. This latter context might serve as the appropriate proxy to which courts should look when setting fees in antitrust class actions, where private negotiation among informed parties is impossible.[77] . . . Moreover, the preceding analysis suggests that the most logical answer to this problem of premature settlement would be to base fees on a graduated, increasing percentage of the recovery formula—one that operates, much like the Internal Revenue Code, to award the plaintiff's attorney a marginally greater percentage of each defined increment of the recovery. While this approach cannot be said to eliminate the inevitable tension between the interests of plaintiff's attorneys and their clients in class actions, it can at least partially counteract the tendency for premature settlements.

63. Professor Scott concludes that for the "most effective enforcement, the recovery in its entirety should go to the attorney. . . ." Scott, [Corporate Law and the . . . Corporate Governance Project, 35 Stan.L.Rev. 927 (1940)], at 941 n. 43.

77. After determining the fee award percentage in the most comparable area of private litigation, courts should also adjust that percentage upward to compensate the class action plaintiff's attorney for assuming the additional risk associated with a contingent fee payment arrangement.

Principal-agent problems will persist, however, and their existence implies that there can be no socially optimal suit preclusion equilibrium . . . [T]he most feasible answer to the attorney's inadequate incentive to fund litigation probably involves some combination of multiple damages, an increasing percentage of the recovery formula, and higher fee awards. Although such a policy is clearly feasible, it brings us back to the predictable response that enhancing the plaintiff's attorney's incentive may also invite extortion and "strike suits."

III. THE PLAINTIFF'S ATTORNEY'S INCENTIVES: TOWARD AN ECONOMIC MODEL

. . . This Part examines four different explanations of why a rational plaintiff's attorney would bring an action having little probability of success at trial. This analysis then sets the stage for a discussion of what reforms, if any, are justified.

A. *The Cost Differential Explanation*

Professors Rosenberg and Shavell have explained the nuisance action in terms of a cost differential that may exist between plaintiffs and defendants.[93] When it is costlier for defendants to litigate than plaintiffs, even a frivolous action may possess some settlement value because obtaining the dismissal of such an action, they argue, imposes more costs on defendants than plaintiffs. Essentially, plaintiffs know that they can impose substantially greater litigation expenses on defendants than the plaintiffs will incur themselves. As a result, they can extort some form of payment (typically in the form of a fee award) as the price for not subjecting defendants to this greater expense . . .

Still, the existence of a cost differential favoring the plaintiff does not necessarily imply that the case will be settled on terms more favorable than the litigation odds would dictate. If the defendant officers and directors in a derivative suit or securities class action view themselves as "repeat players," they may believe that yielding to extortion in this fashion will only expose them to future litigation. Hence, they may behave strategically and insist on going to trial. . . .

. . .

(A) more basic problem with the cost differential explanation that involves the now familiar concept of asymmetric stakes. Put simply, the cost differential may be more than offset by a benefit differential that both favors defendants and tends to decrease the value of an action to the private enforcer. Indeed, even a two-to-one cost differential favoring the plaintiff will be offset by the fact that the plaintiff's attorney's fee award tends to be no more than twenty to thirty percent of the total settlement. To illustrate, suppose that it would cost the defendants $200,000 to prepare for trial while the plaintiff's side need

---

93. See Rosenberg & Shavell, [A Model in Which Suits Are Brought for Their Nuisance Value, 5 Int'l Rev.L. & Econ. 3 (1985)] at 4–5, 9–10.

spend only $100,000. Holding aside the action's possible merit, the maximum the defendants would pay to avoid this expenditure is something less than $200,000. Yet even from a $200,000 settlement, the plaintiff's attorney would receive only $40,000 to $60,000—a fee award that may not cover his own opportunity costs, particularly if the defendants' dilatory conduct compels the plaintiff's attorney to expend more time on the action than he anticipated. This is a curious form of extortion when the plaintiff's attorney's threat, if carried out, could cause him more harm than the defendants. Of course, if a collusive settlement can be arranged between the plaintiff's attorney and the defendants, then this scenario for the nuisance action may make sense, but the source of the problem has now shifted, because collusion and extortion are different phenomena.

. . .

B.   *A Portfolio Theory Perspective*

In those areas of litigation where client control over the plaintiff's attorney is weak, a disparity seems likely to exist between the adversaries' respective attitudes toward risk. As much as the asymmetric character of the stakes, this factor could explain the apparent "optimism" of the plaintiff's attorney in the face of a low rate of litigated victories. As a starting point, it seems reasonable to hypothesize that plaintiff's attorneys are typically repeat players who are accustomed to facing litigation risks. In contrast, the only study on the rate of litigation against corporate personnel suggests that, whether the action is a securities class action or a derivative suit, defendants (especially the individual defendants) are not accustomed to being sued. Thus, even if the stakes were equal, this differential in the parties' relative familiarity with litigation could explain why "one-shot" defendants would behave in a more risk averse fashion than their more legally experienced adversaries.[99] In addition, there is a distinct possibility that plaintiff's attorneys, being a self-selected population, may be disproportionately composed of risk preferrers who are willing to gamble on winning one large recovery.

More importantly, plaintiff's attorneys may possess a superior ability to spread their risks. As a professional litigator, and thus a repeat player, the typical plaintiff's attorney is likely to handle a number of cases simultaneously. The attorney thus has a portfolio of investments in litigation; in contrast, the typical defendant is a one-shot player. This contrast is similar to that between a fully diversified investor and an investor who holds only a single speculative asset. . . .

[T]he solo practitioner may be able to spread risks without affiliating with others through a "second best" technique that may help explain the phenomenon of nuisance suits. Although the individual

---

99. See Galanter, Why the "Haves" Come Out Ahead: Speculations on the Limits of Legal Change, 9 Law & Soc'y Rev. 95, 99–100 (1974).

attorney who handles securities or derivative actions cannot effectively litigate a sufficient number of actions to achieve efficient diversification, such an attorney can deliberately bring a large number of actions and devote relatively little time or energy to any single case. To be sure, this low intensity strategy means that each individual suit will have a lower expected value than it would have had if more time, effort, and money had been invested in its preparation. Yet this litigation strategy does permit risk spreading. In this light, the classic nuisance action—that is, a slapdash action that is inadequately researched and prepared and on which little attorney time is expended—may be less an extortionate attempt to exploit the cost differential that favors plaintiff's attorneys than a means of achieving the only form of risk spreading available to plaintiff's attorneys in small firms. In effect, such attorneys may restrict their investment of time and money in any individual case just as intelligent speculators may adopt self-imposed trading rules that limit their investment in any one stock.

· · ·

C. *Strategic Behavior*

If we recognize that plaintiff's attorneys are "repeat players" who may manage a portfolio of actions, and thus might rationally make litigation decisions based on their portfolio-wide impact, another explanation comes into focus for the apparent excessive optimism of plaintiff's attorneys and their low rate of litigated victories: such an attorney may gain a long-term advantage by demonstrating a willingness to go to trial. Although a refusal to accept a reasonable settlement offer may be illogical in terms of an individual case, such a refusal may signal a plaintiff's attorney's toughness at bargaining, which could enhance his position in future settlement negotiations. Willingness to go to trial distinguishes this attorney from others who seldom try their cases. Even more importantly, a litigated victory may significantly enhance a lawyer's reputation; thereafter, the attorney becomes known within the profession as "the guy who won the Amalgamated Widget case."

For plaintiff's attorneys, reputation has special importance because they are not associated with an institutional firm that possesses its own prestige. Also, because the "ad hoc" plaintiff's firm that assembles to litigate a major class action is only loosely organized, the reputations of the plaintiff's attorneys will affect their rank and seniority in the firm. Predictably, an attorney who is granted membership on the steering committee that runs the plaintiffs' side of the action will be more highly compensated than an attorney who simply conducts discovery for the plaintiffs' team—even in the unlikely event that both work an equivalent number of billable hours.[117] . . .

---

117. In part, this incentive for plaintiff's attorneys to hold a senior position in an "ad hoc" firm arises because they are more likely to obtain fee petition approval if they are visible to the court and to receive a contingency bonus under the lodestar formula. As The American Lawyer succinctly stated in describing the *Fine Paper* case: "Titles were a

D.　*The Problem of Collusion: Litigation As a Non–Zero Sum Game*

The principal-agent problem that is endemic to class and derivative actions implies that there are three sets of interests involved in these actions: those of the defendants, the plaintiffs, and the plaintiff's attorneys.　Often, the plaintiff's attorneys and the defendants can settle on a basis that is adverse to the interests of the plaintiffs.　At its worst, the settlement process may amount to a covert exchange of a cheap settlement for a high award of attorney's fees.　Although courts have long recognized this danger and have developed some procedural safeguards intended to prevent collusive settlements, these reforms are far from adequate to the task.[121]

Indeed, in some areas, the law seems almost to have institutionalized a process which ensures that a case will be settled on a basis that need not closely reflect the litigation odds.　The derivative action supplies the best example.　Under well-established rules, the corporation pays the plaintiff's attorney's fees when the action produces a substantial benefit to the corporation.　Correspondingly, the corporation is permitted to indemnify defendant corporate officials for their legal expenses incurred in connection with a derivative action.　Many large corporations have adopted by-laws authorizing such indemnification to the full extent permitted by law, and virtually every corporation listed on a national securities exchange purchases liability insurance for its corporate officials covering such legal expenses.　Restrictions exist, however, on the availability of both insurance and indemnification: typically, the corporation may not indemnify a defendant's litiga-

valued commodity, since lawyers in 'leadership' roles can more easily petition the court for fee 'multipliers,' allowing them to double or triple their normal hourly billings." Reading *Moody's* at $682 an Hour, Am.Law., Jan. 1982, at 31, col. 2.

121.　Judge Henry Friendly observed that "[a]ll the dynamics conduce to judicial approval of [the] settlement[ ]" once the adversaries have agreed.　See Alleghany Corp. v. Kirby, 333 F.2d 327, 347 (2d Cir.1964) (Friendly, J., dissenting), aff'd en banc by equally divided court, 340 F.2d 311 (2d Cir.1965), cert. dismissed, 384 U.S. 28 (1966).　Although the case law may require full and elaborate judicial review before a settlement is approved, it is doubtful that courts have much incentive to be very demanding.　Their deferential attitude is probably best expressed by one recent decision which acknowledged that: "In deciding whether to approve this settlement proposal, the court starts from the familiar axiom that a bad settlement is almost always better than a good trial."　In re Warner Communications Sec. Litig., 618 F.Supp. 735, 740 (S.D.N.Y.1985).　Empirical evidence also suggests that judicial monitoring of class action settlements is relatively slack.　See Rosenfield, An Empirical Test of Class–Action Settlement, 5 J. Legal Stud. 113, 119 (1976) (settlements of class action suits tend to result in monetary bonuses to attorneys at the expense of class' interests).　Indeed, not only do courts lack any incentive to oppose proposed settlements, but unless an objector appears on the scene, they have little independent access to information about the merits of the settlement.　For a recent critical review of the adequacy of existing procedures, see Note, Derivative Suit Settlements: In Search of a New Lodestar, Law & Contemp. Probs., Summer 1985, at 229. Even when a settlement is rejected, the result may only be to continue a seemingly interminable action.　In this regard, Piambino v. Bailey, 757 F.2d 1112 (11th Cir.1985), is depressingly instructive.　In *Piambino,* the circuit court in 1985 justifiably overturned an obviously improper settlement that was reached in 1977 of an action commenced in 1973. Thus, a dozen years after the action's commencement, the matter is still pending and the ultimate outcome is not yet in sight.　The fact that the decision appears to have been justified hardly proves that a judicial approval requirement is sufficient to deal with the problem of cheap settlements.

tion expenses when he has been "adjudicated" to have breached a duty to the corporation. Also, as a matter of both law and insurance contract provisions, insurance does not cover liability for fraud or unfair self-dealing. Hence, powerful pressures to settle exist because each side can assure itself that its legal fees will be reimbursed in the wake of a settlement. . . . .

. . .

Notwithstanding this logical description of how the principal adversaries can settle collusively at the expense of the shareholders, experienced litigators will dispute the accuracy of this account. They will respond that in their entire experience they have never seen anyone offer or agree to swap a high fee award for a low recovery. Indeed, this response is probably accurate, because there is one further nuance that must be understood in order to comprehend settlement dynamics. This factor involves the impact of the now prevailing method of awarding attorney's fees. The lodestar formula compensates the attorney based essentially on the time the attorney expends on the action, rather than simply awarding the attorney a percentage of the recovery. While some have criticized the lodestar formula on the ground that it encourages an attorney to expend excessive time on an action (because it equates time with money), this analysis misses the formula's real impact. Essentially, the lodestar formula enables collusion to occur on an implicit, rather than explicit, basis. Collusion becomes structural, not actual, because the fee award is no longer a simple function of the recovery.

To see this, consider the position of a plaintiff's attorney who invests a year's effort in preparing a case for trial. Assume the case has an expected value to the class of $4,000,000 (meaning that the plaintiffs would reject any lesser settlement and take their chances at trial). Assume further that the attorney historically would have received a fee award of $1,000,000 based on a percentage of the recovery benchmark of twenty-five percent, but that today the attorney is instead compensated based on the time reasonably expended on the action. Assume finally that on the eve of trial, the attorney has already expended sufficient time to justify a $1,000,000 fee award on an hourly basis, and that there is also a substantial litigation risk that the judgment (if the attorney goes to trial) will be adverse to his side (in which case the attorney will receive nothing). If defendants now offer a settlement of only $2,000,000, there is little reason for the attorney to decline this settlement, even though the plaintiffs would prefer to hold out for $4,000,000. That is, when fees are based on the lodestar formula, the plaintiff's attorney receives the same fee award under the proposed settlement as if the plaintiffs had won a much larger victory at trial. In addition, the attorney avoids the substantial risk of an adverse decision. . . . .

Once polite collusion becomes possible in this manner, it affects the quality of the cases that plaintiff's attorneys will bring in the long run.

Plaintiff's attorneys have less reason to screen their cases and may bring weak cases whose settlement value, when based simply on the litigation odds, would not normally cover the attorneys' opportunity costs. Defendants will sometimes resist settlement in these cases; for example, they may see a reputational injury or view themselves as repeat players. As a result, the cases that go to trial will be disproportionately weak ones for plaintiffs, given defendants' strong motivation to settle any case other than a frivolous one. Once again, litigated cases will constitute a very biased sample of all cases that are filed, and so will tell us little about the meritoriousness of the average case.

Collusion can also occur in ways that depend more on the defendants' behavior than on that of the plaintiff's attorneys. By several techniques, individual defendants can seek to transmute their personal liability into corporate liability. Derivative actions against corporate officials are frequently brought in tandem with class actions against the corporation that allege violations of the federal securities laws. In such instances, the individual defendants may find it in their interest to offer a generous settlement on the claims brought against the corporation in return for a cheap settlement of the derivative action against themselves. Plaintiff's attorneys may see little reason to resist this offer because their duty (as they perceive it) is to maximize the plaintiff class' recovery, not to administer punishment. Thus, plaintiff's attorneys can be relatively indifferent to the issue critical to the defendants: namely, who pays. This pattern of transmuting individual liability into corporate liability can even arise in class actions that essentially allege insider trading by corporate executives. . . . Eventually, settlements that shift these costs from officers to their corporations both rob the law of its deterrent impact and, paradoxically, force shareholders, who are the intended beneficiaries of the substantive legal standard, to bear the costs of the actions.

E. *Perverse Reforms: The Curious Impact of Proposals to Curb "Frivolous" Litigation*

Although the preceding analysis does not refute the possibility of extortionate litigation, it does suggest that the collusion hypothesis has greater explanatory power. Against this backdrop, the impact of various proposals to control frivolous actions can be better understood. Historically, corporate law has relied on two principal methods of chilling nuisance actions: (1) the legislative attempt, which arose in the 1940s, to curtail derivative actions by requiring that plaintiffs post a security for expenses bond as a precondition to maintaining a derivative action, and (2) the more recent judicial acceptance, largely dating from the 1970s, of the special litigation committee as a means by which a corporation's board of directors can effect the dismissal of a derivative action without substantive judicial review.

What is the impact of each of these legal rules on the plaintiff's attorney? Essentially, a security for expenses bond represents a form of partial fee shifting. Hence, it should tend to discourage actions having a low probability of success at trial. Although the bond requirement will clearly discourage underfinanced plaintiff's attorneys, it may have less impact on better financed attorneys if they anticipate that collusive settlements are possible. So long as the adversaries find it in their interest to settle rather than fight, and settle on a basis not necessarily closely related to the litigation odds, then any proposal that relies at bottom on partial fee shifting can be expected to have only a limited impact on the incidence of derivative actions.

In contrast, the judicial acceptance of the special litigation committee significantly tilts the litigation odds against plaintiffs. Recent cases have permitted a board of directors, even if all of its members are legitimate defendants in a nonfrivolous case, to appoint two or three new directors to the board and constitute them as the special committee to review the action. On the evidence to date, it appears that these committees almost invariably recommend to dismiss derivative suits. . . . In principle, this development would seem to signal the death of the derivative suit. Yet the frequency of derivative actions has increased.[142] What explains this?

From this Article's perspective, the economic impact of the special litigation committee on "entrepreneurial" plaintiff's attorneys may be chiefly to change their tactics by reducing the investment that they will make in any action. The special litigation committee device is notoriously expensive and time-consuming: it may well cost over $1,000,000 for special counsel and other out-of-pocket expenses, and take an average of two years to terminate an action. The very pendency of an action may also have various negative consequences for the corporation or the defendants. As a result, a plaintiff's attorney may be able to underbid the cost of the committee procedure. . . . An alternative open to the corporation is to bribe the plaintiff's attorney to settle the action—for example, by offering $250,000 in legal fees and a nonpecuniary cosmetic settlement. This latter course is cheaper and faster for the defendants than the special litigation committee technique, but it creates an incentive for further extortionate actions to be brought. To the extent that the defendants are repeat players or see reputational injury in settling, they may resist. Yet indirect evidence suggests that both strategies are frequently employed today, with cheap settlements being as popular as the technique of special litigation committee review and dismissal.

---

142. According to insurance industry data, liability claims under director and officer insurance policies have risen dramatically. The Wyatt Company reports that in 1984, 18.5% of the companies they surveyed experienced such a claim against their directors, up from 7.1% in 1974. See Schatz, [Focus on Corporate Boards: Directors Feel the Legal Heat, N.Y.Times, Dec. 15, 1985] at F13, col. 2; see also Myrick & Ochipinti, Corporate Officers, Directors Face Rise in Suits, Legal Fees, Legal Times, Feb. 4, 1985, at 3, col. 1 (noting 10% increase in derivative litigation between 1982 and 1984). Multiple factors can explain this rise: the increased frequency of highly visible transactions, such as golden parachutes and takeover defenses, the increased number of attorneys, and the increased detectability of insider trading violations because of new techniques and technologies available to the SEC.

Ex ante, the lesson that the profit-maximizing plaintiff's attorney should learn from this set of incentives is not to invest heavily in a single case. Because the litigation odds are stacked against them, plaintiff's attorneys may find that they can stay in business only by underbidding the cost of the special litigation committee. To do this and still earn an acceptable profit, they must radically reduce their costs and attempt to exploit the differential between their litigation costs and those of the defendants. The irony, then, is that although the special litigation committee device is intended to discourage nuisance actions, it may have the perverse effect of making the nuisance action the most rational strategy for plaintiff's attorneys to pursue. Indeed, as the plaintiff's attorneys' profit margin is eroded, a Gresham's law effect may take hold as "bad" plaintiff's attorneys begin to drive out the "good." Plaintiff's attorneys who are unwilling to engage in collusive settlements, or who have high opportunity costs, may simply leave the field, abandoning it either to those with lower opportunity costs or those less able to redeploy their invested human capital to some related field of litigation.

. . .

CONCLUSION

Whether called a "private attorney general" or a "bounty hunter," the plaintiff's attorney in class and derivative actions has long been a controversial figure. Claims that such actions disproportionately result in extortionate or collusive settlements are not new, but an understanding of why such outcomes may occur requires that we move beyond character assassination and identify those legal rules that permit the parties to settle on a basis unrelated to an action's litigation odds. . . .

More generally, this Article has argued that good intentions often make bad law. An attraction of the lodestar formula is that it treats plaintiff's attorneys just like other lawyers by compensating them based on their time expended at their normal billing rates. Although this approach succeeds in disguising the fact that the plaintiff's attorney is different from other attorneys (because high agency costs make plaintiff's attorneys independent entrepreneurs), it simultaneously exacerbates the problem of collusion. Ironically, the cost of a purely fiduciary perspective, then, is to make matters significantly worse.

. . .

What reforms make sense, then? If one wishes to economize on the judicial time that is today invested in monitoring class and derivative litigation, the highest priority should be given to those reforms that restrict collusion and are essentially self-policing. The percentage of the recovery fee award formula is such a "deregulatory" reform because it relies on incentives rather than costly monitoring. Ultimately, this "deregulatory" approach is the only alternative to converting the courts into the equivalent of public utility commissions that oversee the plaintiff's attorney and elaborately fix the attorney's "fair" return.

There are, however, no easy victories. If the law seeks to restrict collusive settlements by moving in the direction of a percentage of the recovery fee formula, then a corollary is that the law will tend to encourage premature settlements. To compensate for such underfunding, the law could make greater use of multiple damage formulas, or award substantially higher fees or prejudgment interest on such fees. More to the point, courts could employ a marginally increasing percentage of the recovery fee formula; as a benchmark, courts should determine the level of fees sophisticated individual plaintiffs pay their attorneys in the most comparable field of litigation, and then the fee should be adjusted upward to compensate the attorney for incurring the additional risk of representing the class on a contingent fee basis. These options, if politically feasible at all, would surely extend the life and increase the cost of the typical litigation, and could potentially result in overdeterrence. These tradeoffs can be debated across a variety of specific contexts, but such a debate should focus on what is truly relevant. For too long, the dominant themes in the debate over private enforcement have involved the integrity of plaintiff's attorneys and the alleged excessiveness of their fees. Such digressions miss the key point that it is the current structure of the law that encourages collusion and invites low level extortion.

. . .

Private enforcement of law has its inevitable flaws, which are largely rooted in the principal-agent problems that attend class and derivative litigation. These problems are only aggravated so long as we repress the fact that the plaintiff's attorney is different from other attorneys, both in terms of the extent of the conflict and the potential for opportunism. Once this is recognized, the basic goal of reform should be to reduce the agency costs incident to this attorney-client relationship. While various means to this end are possible—including multiple damages, more realistic fee award standards that attempt to mimic what private bargaining would have produced had it been feasible, and the use of an increasing percentage of the recovery formula—all should be understood as responses to this agency cost problem and debated in that light. At times, these responses may produce overdeterrence, but in such cases the appropriate answer is then to revise the substantive legal standard, not to create more constraining procedural rules. Because it applies across the board, the law of procedure can only accomplish limited objectives and cannot respond surgically to specific problems in a narrow range of litigation. When we instead attempt to revise procedure to chill "excessive" litigation, the result is likely to be to transfer wealth between plaintiffs and defendants.

This view of private enforcement as less flawed than frustrated requires some explanation of how things got this way. The cynic might argue that frustration seldom occurs by accident and that powerful social forces have quietly combined to undercut the private attorney general concept. Perhaps, there is some truth to this claim, but a more balanced, fuller account probably should begin with how we think about law and lawyers. Even the most practical litigator or judge is often the slave of some defunct law professor who taught him to think of the lawyer as a fiduciary. Convenient and comforting as it is to view the attorney only through this nostalgic lens of fiduciary analysis, a fixation on this mode of analysis is likely to blind us to the real issues relating to the incentives and misincentives that the law today creates for the plaintiff's attorney. Sadly, to call a lawyer a fiduciary is too often to end the analysis, not begin it.

The Costs of Monitoring the Lawyer's Conduct

Class counsel who generates a monetary recovery for the class—a "common fund"—is entitled to attorney's fees from the fund, subject to court approval. See Boeing Co. v. Van Gemert, 444 U.S. 472, 478, 100 S.Ct. 745 (1980).

In the Report of the Third Circuit Task Force, on Attorneys' Fees, reprinted above in Chapter 6, the task force stated:

> Of primary concern in dealing with fund-in-court cases is solving the problem raised when a class action lawyer secures a recovery for his clients and then proceeds to file a fee petition seeking compensation from those very same funds. In these situations, the plaintiffs' attorney's role changes from one of a fiduciary for the clients to that of a claimant against the fund created for the clients' benefit. The perspective of the judge also changes because the court must now monitor the disbursement of the fund and act as a fiduciary for those who are supposed to benefit from it, since typically no one else is available to perform that function—the defendant has no interest in how the fund is distributed and the plaintiff class members rarely become involved. Note that neither of these concerns arise in the statutory fee context, which continues to be an adversary proceeding until resolution, except when a statutory fee case is 'converted' into a fund case by settlement.

Protection of the class in fee awards imposes an enormous burden on the courts in reviewing the hourly rates, hourly activities, and expenditures of the lawyers on behalf of the class. See the *Fine Paper Litigation* supra. To impose on courts a duty of still closer scrutiny would transform the adversary process and might push the judiciary beyond its effective capability.

Would more detailed ethical rules help? See Waid, Ethical Problems of the Class Action Practitioner: Continued Neglect by the Drafters of the Proposed Model Rules of Professional Conduct, 27 Loy.L.Rev. 1047 (1981). Can courts or disciplinary boards monitor the "market" in named representatives?

Lawyer Financing of Class Actions

DR 5–103(B) of the Model Code provides that a lawyer may advance court costs and litigations expenses, "provided the client remains ultimately liable for such expenses." M.R. 1.8(e) removes the requirement that the client remain liable, allowing the lawyer to advance costs that can be recouped only if the client is successful on the merits. The major reason for this change was to permit "private attorney general" class actions, in which no single member of the class can fund the action but the lawyer would be willing to do so when there is a strong enough probability of success. See Lynch, Ethical Rules in Flux: Advancing Costs of Litigation, 7 Litigation 19 (1981). For criticism of the change see Findlater, The Proposed Revision of DR 5–103(B): Champerty and Class Actions, 36 Bus.Law 1667 (1981).

Coffee approves of M.R. 1.8(e), arguing that it vindicates the enforcement of law and results in greater access to courts, and suggests that the rules should allow the lawyer to acquire property interests in class litigation. On the funding of mass tort litigation, see Johnson, Ethical Limitations on Creative Financing of Mass Tort Class Actions, 54 Brooklyn L.Rev. 539 (1988).

The Value of Myth

Rhode argues that the myth of the lawyer as fiduciary for the class has some value at least in institutional reform litigation. Coffee, on the other hand, argues that the myth leads to faulty analysis of the problem of conflicts in class actions and worse, to misguided "reform" proposals, which, if enacted, might exacerbate the problems they are designed to cure. Does Coffee's critique of the myth of fiduciary apply to "public interest" lawyers and their clients? See *Evans v. Jeff D.* printed in Chapter 6.

Class Counsel Communicating With the Class

As soon as a class action is filed, the lawyer usually wishes to solicit potential class members to increase the likelihood of certification. Before and after certification, the lawyer has an interest in contacting class members to gather evidence and to discourage opting-out, for once a class is certified eligible members are counted "in" unless they opt-out. See Fed.R.Civ.P. 23(c)(2)(a). By such contacts the lawyer strengthens the class' case, which in turn maximizes the potential award and increases the lawyer's fee. The Comment to M.R. 7.2 on advertising states that "[n]either this Rule nor Rule 7.3 [on direct solicitation] prohibits communications authorized by law, such as notice to members of a class in class action litigation." May the court, however, prohibit such solicitation?

Gulf Oil Corp. v. Bernhard, 452 U.S. 89, 101 S.Ct. 2193 (1981), was a class action brought by black employees charging race discrimination. Gulf was hoping that employees would opt out of the class action and instead accept a back-pay award which Gulf had negotiated with the

EEOC in a conciliation agreement. Gulf petitioned the court for an order limiting the named plaintiffs and their lawyers from communicating with potential class members, alleging that counsel was telling potential class members that they could double their recovery by joining the suit and rejecting the back-pay offer. Without corroborating Gulf's allegations, the district court issued an order barring both the parties and their lawyers from communicating with the class without court approval.

The Supreme Court, while acknowledging the potential for abuse, held that the trial court had abused its discretion: "[A]n order limiting communications between parties and potential class members should be based on a clear record and specific findings that reflect a weighing of the need for a limitation and the potential interference with the rights of the parties." 452 U.S. at 101. The order in this case had thwarted the plaintiff's ability to form a class and maintain the action, thereby violating Rule 23. While the Court did not decide the case on First Amendment grounds, as the Court of Appeals had done, 604 F.2d 499 (5th Cir.1979), it said that any order limiting communications should be "carefully drawn . . . to limit speech as little as possible . . ." Id. at 102.

See also Rossini v. Ogilvy & Mather, Inc., 798 F.2d 590 (2d Cir.1986) (upholding an order restricting communications between class counsel and the class against a challenge under *Gulf Oil v. Bernhard*).

E. WHO IS THE OPPOSING PARTY?

WRIGHT v. GROUP HEALTH INSURANCE HOSPITAL

Supreme Court of Washington, en banc 1984.
103 Wn.2d 192, 691 P.2d 564

DOLLIVER, JUSTICE.

The question presented in this appeal is whether, in connection with events leading to a medical malpractice action, a defendant hospital corporation may prohibit its current employees from conducting ex parte interviews with plaintiffs' attorneys. The trial court held these interviews would violate CPR DR 7–104(A)(1). We reverse.

I

This appeal arose out of plaintiffs' medical malpractice action pending against Group Health Hospital (Group Health) and Dr. Kevin Schaberg, its employee. In the malpractice action, plaintiffs allege defendant employees of Group Health, including Dr. Schaberg, committed medical malpractice in the care and management of Mrs. Wright during labor and delivery of her son Jeffrey.

Group Health is a large Seattle-based health care cooperative. When a medical malpractice action is brought against it, Group Health has a policy of giving the following instructions to the individuals involved in the care of the plaintiff/patient. Group Health advises these employees that its outside counsel represents Group Health in the action; the employees will be contacted by and should fully cooperate with this law firm; their communications with the law firm are confidential; and they are not to discuss the case with anyone other than said law firm. This notice is given to the pertinent employees even if they were not currently employed by Group Health.

During the course of discovery in the malpractice action, plaintiffs' attorney asked for the addresses and telephone numbers of nurses involved in the care of Mrs. Wright. The information was provided with the understanding that such nurses were to be regarded as clients of the law firm and that plaintiffs would make no effort to contact these nurses ex parte. Group Health's attorneys asserted these ex parte interviews were barred by the attorney-client privilege and the disciplinary rules. Plaintiffs' attorney disagreed and moved for a protective order declaring he had both the legal and ethical right to interview ex parte both current and former Group Health employees so long as they were not management employees.

The trial court denied plaintiffs' motion for a protective order. The court affirmed the defendant corporation's right to give a blanket instruction to its *current* nonparty employees not to have ex parte contacts with plaintiffs' attorneys. The court held these interviews would violate CPR DR 7–104(A)(1). . . .

II

Group Health argues that as a corporation represented by counsel, its current and former employees are "clients" of the law firm for purposes of the attorney-client privilege. To preserve the confidences and secrets protected by the privilege, Group Health argues its employees should not be discoverable plaintiffs on an ex parte basis. We disagree.

The attorney-client privilege, RCW 5.60.060(2), provides that an attorney shall not, without the consent of his client, be examined as to any *communication* made by the client to him, or his advice given thereon in the course of professional employment. While the attorney-client privilege may in certain instances extend to lower level employees not in a "control group", Upjohn Co. v. United States, 449 U.S. 383, 101 S.Ct. 677, 66 L.Ed.2d 584 (1981), the privilege extends only to protect communications and not the underlying facts. This distinction was noted by the *Upjohn* Court:

> "[T]he protection of the privilege extends only to *communications* and not to facts. A fact is one thing and a communication concerning that fact is an entirely different thing. The client cannot be compelled to answer the question, 'What did you say or write to the attorney?' but may not refuse to disclose any relevant fact within his knowledge merely because he incorporated a statement of such fact into his communication to his attorney."

Upjohn Co., at 395–96, 101 S.Ct. at 685–86 (quoting Philadelphia v. Westinghouse Elec. Corp., 205 F.Supp. 830, 831 (E.D.Pa.1962)).

In *Upjohn* the "communication" was the correspondence between the corporate employee and corporate counsel. At issue was the applicability of the privilege to the employee. In the present case, plaintiffs' attorney does not seek to discover a *communication* by a Group Health employee. Indeed, there is no communication which Group Health claims is privileged. Plaintiffs' attorney seeks to interview Group Health employees to discover *facts* incident to the alleged medical malpractice, not privileged corporate confidences.

We hold the attorney-client privilege does not in itself bar plaintiffs' attorney from interviewing defendant corporation's employees.

III

Group Health next argues all of its current and former employees are "parties" within the meaning of CPR DR 7–104(A)(1) and the rule would be violated if plaintiffs' counsel attempted to contact Group Health's employees.

CPR DR 7–104(A) provides:

During the course of his representation of a client a lawyer shall not:

(1) Communicate or cause another to communicate on the subject of the representation with a *party* he knows to be represented by a lawyer in that matter unless he has the prior consent of the lawyer representing such other party or is authorized by law to do so.

·   ·   ·

(Italics ours.)

A

CPR DR 7–104(A)(1) (rule) is based on the American Bar Association original version of Canon 9, which was superseded by the adoption of the American Bar Association of the Code of Professional Responsibility in 1970. Leubsdorf, Communicating with Another Lawyer's Client: The Lawyer's Veto and the Client's Interest, 127 U.Pa.L.Rev. 683, 685 n. 10 (1979) (Leubsdorf). The original Canon 9 read:

A lawyer should not in any way communicate upon the subject of controversy with a party represented by counsel; much less should he undertake to *negotiate* or *compromise* the matter with him, but should deal only with his counsel. . . . (Italics ours.) ABA Canons of Professional Ethics 9 (1908); H. Drinker, *Legal Ethics* 201 (1953); Leubsdorf, supra.

The official historical purposes of the rule and its predecessor Canon 9 were two-fold: preserving the proper functioning of the legal system and shielding the adverse party from improper approaches.

ABA Comm. on Professional Ethics and Grievances, Formal Op. 108 (1934). Others characterized the historical purposes of the rule as preventing attorneys from "stealing clients" (H. Drinker, *Legal Ethics,* at 190), or to proscribe attorney contacts with represented parties so they would not diminish potential contingent fees by negotiating unfavorable settlements directly with clients. Note, DR 7–104 of the Code of Professional Responsibility Applied to the Government "Party", 61 Minn.L.Rev. 1007, 1010 (1977) (Note, Government "Party"). In more recent years, however, the purpose of the rule has been said to shield the represented client from improper approaches. Note, Government "Party", supra. See also State v. Thompson, 206 Kan. 326, 330, 478 P.2d 208 (1970). The general thrust of the rule is to prevent situations in which a represented party may be taken advantage of by adverse counsel; the presence of the party's attorney theoretically neutralizes the contact. See Kurlantzik, The Prohibition on Communication with an Adverse Party, 5 Conn.B.J. 136, 145–46 (1977).

B

Plaintiffs' attorney does *not* seek ex parte contacts with Group Health's employee, Dr. Schaberg, who *is* a joined party in this action. Rather, plaintiffs seek to interview ex parte nurses and other Group Health personnel all of whom are *not* parties in the malpractice action. While easily identifiable in litigation between private parties, the scope of CPR DR 7–104(A)(1) is less clear when one party is a corporation, as is Group Health. In this context the crucial issue is: Which of the corporate party's employees should be protected from approaches by adverse counsel?

In our adversarial legal system, a policy conflict arises when a corporation attempts to use CPR DR 7–104(A)(1) defensively so as to prevent an adverse attorney from interviewing its employees ex parte. On the one hand, there is the need of the adverse attorney for information which may be in the exclusive possession of the corporation and may be too expensive or impractical to collect through formal discovery. On the other hand is the corporation's need to protect itself for the traditional reasons justifying the rule. For discussion of the conflicting interests, see generally IBM Corp. v. Edelstein, 526 F.2d 37, 41–43 (2d Cir.1975) (judge's order requiring that ex parte interviews of defendant government employees be transcribed exceeded trial court's authority because informal witness interviews serve important fact-finding function); Leubsdorf, supra at 695; Note, Government "Party", supra at 1013–16. In attempting to balance the conflicting policies, courts, bar associations, and commentators have struggled with the issue whether a corporate party's employee should be considered a "party". The decisions may be classified as follows.

Some authorities declare CPR DR 7–104(A)(1) does *not* bar ex parte interviews with *any* of a corporate party's employees who were witnesses to the acts or omissions giving rise to the action. These authorities, moreover, do not require the consent of adverse counsel in advance of these interviews. ABA Comm. on Professional Ethics and Grievances, Formal Op. 117 (1934) (plaintiff's attorney may interview defendant store's employees in connection with plaintiff's slip and fall in defendant's store); Los Angeles Cy. Bar Ass'n, Op. 234 (1956), digested in O. Maru, Digest of Bar Association Ethics Opinions 66 (1970) (hereinafter 1970 Digest); Michigan State Bar Ass'n, Op. 141 (1951), reprinted in 38 Mich.St.B.J. 181 (1959) (permissible to interview defendant corporation's clerks who had witnessed or were involved in accident causing injury without obtaining consent of opposing counsel); New York City Bar Ass'n, Op. 331 (1935), digested in 1970 Digest, at 279 (same).

Other authorities *conditionally* permit an adverse attorney to interview ex parte employees of a corporate party. These authorities distinguish

> officers and directors with power to bind the corporation and employees lacking such power to bind. The former tend to be considered parties while the latter are considered witnesses . . .

Lawyers' Manual on Professional Conduct (ABA/BNA) 71:314 (1984). This appears to be the American Bar Association's most recent approach. The Bar held that non-party employees can be interviewed ex parte so long as they cannot

> commit the corporation because of their authority as corporate officers or employees or for some other reason the law cloaks them with authority . . . as the alter egos of the corporation . . .

Lawyers' Manual on Professional Conduct, supra (quoting ABA Comm. on Professional Ethics and Grievances, Informal Op. 1410 (1978)). Accord, Comment, Model Rules of Professional Conduct, Rule 4.2 (1983) (persons having a managerial responsibility on behalf of the organization); Los Angeles Cy. Bar Ass'n, Op. 369 (1977), digested in O. Maru, 1980 Supplement to the Digest of Bar Association Ethics Opinions 75–76 (1982) (distinguishing employees with "authority to negotiate", whose admissions are valid, and who have access to confidential corporate information); . . . . One commentator argues the rule should be extended not only to the corporation's "managing agents" but to all employees through whom the corporation speaks. Leubsdorf, supra at 695.

Other authorities define "party" based on the employee's relationship to the matter in which the attorney is seeking information, i.e., is the employee merely a witness or is the act or omission of the employee imputed to the corporation for purposes of civil liability. See, e.g., Texas State Bar Ass'n, Op. 342 (1968), digested in 1970 Supplement, at 297 (no ex parte interviews if employee is person whose acts or omissions led to the lawsuit); . . . Comment, Model Rules of Professional Conduct, Rule 4.2 (1983) (rule prohibits communication with any other person whose act or omission in connection with that matter may be imputed to the organization for purposes of civil or criminal liability).

Finally, one authority appears to proscribe completely ex parte interviews with a corporate party's employees. New York Cy. Year Book, Op. 528 (1965), digested in 1970 Digest, at 241–42.

One court interpreting the rule rejected a fixed test for determining whether a corporate employee was a "party". Rather, the court held the interviewing government attorneys were "sensitive" to the ethical considerations because they identified themselves as adverse attorneys and instructed the corporate employees in advance that they had the right to an attorney during the interview. Nevertheless, the court directed there could be no ex parte interviews of the company's president, chairman, or plant managers. In re FMC Corp., 430 F.Supp. 1108, 1110–11 (S.D.W.Va.1977). Another court, analyzing a case in which the government was the defendant, stressed the vital First Amendment interest in contacting ex parte the government's employees. Vega v. Bloomsburgh, 427 F.Supp. 593 (D.Mass.1977); see generally Leubsdorf, supra at 694–95.

C

We hold the best interpretation of "party" in litigation involving corporations is only those employees who have the legal authority to "bind" the corporation in a legal evidentiary sense, i.e., those employees who have "speaking authority" for the corporation. This interpretation is consistent with the declared purpose of the rule to protect represented parties from the dangers of dealing with adverse counsel. Leubsdorf, supra at 686–88. A flexible interpretation of "parties", moreover, advances the policy of keeping the testimony of employee witnesses freely accessible to both parties. . . . We find no reason to distinguish between employees who in fact witnessed an event and those whose act or omission caused the event leading to the action. It is not the purpose of the rule to protect a corporate party from the revelation of prejudicial facts. . . . Rather, the rule's function is to preclude the interviewing of those corporate employees who have the authority to *bind* the corporation. H. Drinker, Legal Ethics 201 (1953).

D

We hold *current* Group Health employees should be considered "parties" for the purposes of the disciplinary rule if, under applicable Washington law, they have managing authority sufficient to give them the right to speak for, and bind, the corporation. Since former employees cannot possibly speak for the corporation, we hold that CPR DR 7–104(A)(1) does not apply to them.

The "managing-speaking" agent test has its roots in agency and evidence law. The well established test is a flexible one under the circumstances of each case. . . .

Group Health asserts the agency law "managing-speaking" agent test is archaic since the United States Supreme Court has adopted, in *Upjohn,* a flexible "client" test extending coverage to many nonmanagerial employees. Group Health argues the "flexible" test in United States v. Upjohn Co., 449 U.S. 383, 101 S.Ct. 677, 66 L.Ed.2d 584 (1981) should apply to CPR DR 7–104(A)(1) in determining whether corporate employees are "parties" for purposes of the rule.

While Group Health is correct in noting that both the attorney-client privilege and the disciplinary rules share the mutual goals of "furthering the attorney-client relationship", the *policies* represented by these two rules are different. In enunciating a flexible "control group" test, the *Upjohn* Court was expanding the definition of "clients" so the laudable goals of the attorney-client privilege would be applicable to a greater number of corporate employees. The purpose of the disciplinary rule, on the other hand, is to protect the corporation so its agents who have the authority to prejudice the entity's interest are not unethically influenced by adverse counsel. Thus, the purpose of the managing-speaking agent test is to determine who has the *authority* to bind the corporation. . . .

. . . The policy reasons necessitating the "flexible" test in *Upjohn* are not present here. A corporate employee who is a "client" under the attorney-client privilege is not necessarily a "party" for purposes of the disciplinary rule.

Group Health contends the evidentiary rules governing speaking authority of agents serve a hearsay reliability function and should not be used in the "managing agent" determination. While it is true an agent's admissions and statements against a principal are considered "reliable", the more "satisfactory justification" of the evidence rule is that admissions by agents "are the *product of the adversary system,* sharing, though on a lower and nonconclusive level, the characteristics of admissions in pleadings or stipulations." (Italics ours.) E. Cleary, McCormick on Evidence § 262, at 629 (2d ed. 1972). The policies behind the speaking agent determination and the speaking agent distinction of CPR DR 7–104(A)(1) are not inconsistent.

E

Since we hold an adverse attorney may, under CPR DR 7–104(A)(1), interview ex parte nonspeaking/managing agent employees, it was improper for Group Health to advise its employees not to speak with plaintiffs' attorneys. An attorney's right to interview corporate employees would be a hollow one if corporations were permitted to instruct their employees not to meet with adverse counsel. This opinion shall not be construed in any manner, however, so as to *require* an employee of a corporation to meet ex parte with adverse counsel. We hold only that a corporate party, or its counsel, may not *prohibit* its non-speaking/managing agent employees from meeting with adverse counsel.

The case is remanded to the trial court with instructions that Group Health's cautioning letters be revoked as to the relevant employees and that appropriate relief be accorded consistent with this opinion. . . .

Questions and Comments

The court in *Wright* describes the various interpretations that might be given to the term "party" as used in M.R. 4.2 and DR 7–104(A)(1). These interpretations range from prohibiting ex parte contact with any agents of the opposing party to prohibiting contact only with the control group of the corporation. What reasons does the court give for defining "party" as it does? Why does the court reject the definition of "party" provided in *Upjohn?*

How is the attorney to decide whom the court will consider a party, given the flexible approach in *Wright?* In Mills Land and Water Co. v. Golden West Refining Co., 186 Cal.App.3d 116, 230 Cal.Rptr. 461 (1986), the court, while approving the flexible approach of *Wright,* held that the lawyer could not make a unilateral decision about who was to be considered the opposing party for purposes of the communication rule: the court, not the attorney, must decide the issue. In *Mills,* lawyers opposing the Mills Corporation conducted an ex parte interview with a director of the Mills Company, who had formerly served as Mills' President but had been forced out in a management fight. Mills' counsel conceded that they could not represent the director because of a conflict of interest, but argued that his position as a director and majority shareholder made him a constituent of the company. The court agreed, reasoning that directors should be considered constituents because of their access to communications between counsel for the corporation and the board. The court specifically reserved the question of whether a shareholder, who was not also a director, could qualify as a constituent of the opposing corporation.

In Morrison v. Brandeis University, 125 F.R.D. 14 (D.Mass.1989), the court rejected the approach in *Wright.* The court criticized *Wright* for adopting a test based on Fed.R.Civ.P. 32(a)(1), which provides that a deposition of "anyone who at the time of taking the deposition was an officer, director or managing agent . . . of a . . . corporation which is a party may be used by an adverse party . . . for any purpose." According to the court in *Morrison:*

> [T]he problem with the test is that Rule 801(d)(2)(D), F.R.Evid., is far broader than Rule 32(a)(2), Fed.R.Civ.P., and does not limit the admissibility of statements against a corporation to statements made by its officers, directors or managing agents. Rather, it permits the admission by a party-opponent against a party of "a statement made by that party's agent or servant concerning a matter within the scope of the agency or employment, made during the existence of the relationship." One can envision a factual situation in which an agent or servant who is not a member of the "control group" but who, as a result of his employment and within

the scope of his employment, had far greater knowledge and involvement in a situation which might result in liability to his corporate employer such that "effective representation" for the corporation would require that that employee be considered a "party" as the term is used in DR 7–104(A)(1). Under the "control group" test, the employee would not be a party for purposes of DR 7–104(A)(1) unless the definition of the term "managing agent" could be stretched to cover him.

Id. at 16–17.

The court acknowledged that the *Wright* court had no need to consider the broad federal rule of evidence and that Washington had no evidence rule of similar breadth.

Morrison adopted instead a case-by-case balancing approach, emphasizing that lawyers would be bound by the strictures of DR 7–104(A) (1) or M.R. 4.2 unless authorized by a court to make direct contact otherwise prohibited by the ethics rules. Id. at 18 n. 1. *Morrison* involved a civil rights suit brought by an instructor against Brandeis University alleging racial and gender discrimination in its denial of her tenure. Under the court's balancing approach, plaintiff's counsel was allowed to contact University professors who participated in the tenure decision. The court found that these people were in the "control group" or were persons whose statements could be admitted against the university, but that this was outweighed by the plaintiff's need for the information and the unlikelihood that these people would speak freely in front of university counsel. Compare Chancellor v. Boeing Co., 678 F.Supp. 250 (D.Kan.1988) (citing *Wright* and *Upjohn,* the court denied plaintiff's counsel ex parte contact with employees involved in denying plaintiff's promotion). See Miller and Calfo, Ex Parte Contact with Employees and Former Employees of a Corporate Adversary: Is it Ethical?, 42 Bus.Law. 1053 (1987).

When the Opposing Party Is a Class

In Kleiner v. First National Bank of Atlanta, 751 F.2d 1193 (11th Cir.1985), the bank's counsel tried to get members of the opposing class to opt out of the suit. The bank claimed that the First Amendment protected these communications with the members of the class, citing Gulf Oil Corp. v. Bernhard, 452 U.S. 89, 101 S.Ct. 2193 (1981), discussed above at pp. 850–851. The court distinguished *Gulf* on the ground that the speech in that case, between class counsel and the class, was associational and thus entitled to more protection under the First Amendment than the speech in *Kleiner,* which was commercially-motivated and thus subject to greater regulation. Is this distinction persuasive? Contrast In re School Asbestos Litigation, 842 F.2d 671 (3d Cir.1988) (applying *Gulf* to hold that an order which restricted defendants' communications on school asbestos matters with any group reasonably believed to include a member of the plaintiff class was overbroad).

In Haffer v. Temple University, 115 F.R.D. 506 (E.D.Pa.1987), a class of women students brought an action against Temple University alleging sex discrimination in the intercollegiate athletic program. Temple's counsel and an associate director in its athletic department distributed a memo to class members at Temple attempting to dissuade women athletes from taking part in the suit. The memo argued the importance of loyalty to the school. Temple's lawyer also telephoned two class members to dissuade them from meeting with class counsel. The court sanctioned Temple and its counsel for communicating with members of the class directly and for attempting to discourage them from cooperating with class counsel. Also see Tedesco v. Mishkin, 629 F.Supp. 1474 (S.D.N.Y.1986) (sanctioning lawyer for communicating directly with opposing class members and for communicating in a misleading and coercive manner).

When the Opposing Party Is the Government

DR 7–104(A)(1) and M.R. 4.2, prohibiting communication with the opposing party unless the opposing lawyer consents, both provide that such communication is permissible when "authorized by law". The Comment to M.R. 4.2 explains: "Communications authorized by law include, for example, the right of a party to a controversy with a government agency to speak with government officials about the matter." Also see Cal.Rule of Prof.Cond. 2–100(C)(1) (expressly excepting from the rule against direct communication, "communication with a public officer, board, committee or body"). The First Amendment protects the right to petition the government for a redress of grievances. Does this mean that the government lawyer has no right to control access to her client's agents to prevent them from making adverse disclosures? See M.R. 3.4(f).

That government lawyers may deny an opposing lawyer access to some government agents to prevent adverse admissions outside of the discovery process, and correlatively that opposing counsel may be prohibited from directly communicating with some agents of the government, has been generally assumed by the courts, see, e.g., Frey v. Department of Health and Human Services, 106 F.R.D. 32, 35 (E.D.N.Y. 1985). In *Frey,* the court held that the opposing party must be allowed direct access to all government employees except those "who are the 'alter egos' of the entity, that is, those individuals who can bind it to a decision or settle controversies on its behalf." Id. The court observed that "while for most litigation purpose the law treats a government entity just like any other party, . . . unlike a corporate party, the government also has a duty to advance the public's interest in achieving justice, an ultimate obligation that outweighs its narrower interest in prevailing in a law suit." Id. at 36. See also Vega v. Bloomsburgh, 427 F.Supp. 593, 595 (D.Mass.1977) (state's attempt to bar its employees from communicating with opposing counsel impermissibly infringed on the state employee's First Amendment rights where there was no showing that any of the employees' "interests are adverse to those of the plaintiffs, or for that matter consistent with those of the defendants"). Also see Fusco v. City of Albany, 134 Misc.2d 98, 509 N.Y.S.2d 763 (1986) (state freedom of information law authorized direct contact with government employees without prior consent of the government's lawyers).

Chapter X

REGULATION OF THE PRACTICE OF LAW

A. ADMISSION TO PRACTICE

Historical Sketch of the American Legal Profession

In their beginnings, the colonies had few trained lawyers and their citizens had to deal with legal formalities as best they could. In the absence of a regulatory system, anyone can be a lawyer who can use a set of legal forms and maintain a position in argument. Some of the early colonists certainly could do that. In the absence of regulation, someone who did so more or less regularly for money could call himself a practicing lawyer. So much the better if one had, or pretended to have had, some kind of practice experience in the mother country, for example, being a justice of the peace. For history of the earliest beginnings of the English Legal Profession in the 12th Century, see Symposium, 5 Law and History Rev. 1 (1987).

The practice of law, however, has been a regulated vocation almost from the time that an identifiable legal profession emerged in this country. As the political economy of the colonies expanded from 1620 to 1776, a legal professional evolved, concentrated in the wealthier and more populous colonies. The skills of practice were acquired primarily by the means by which technical knowledge was usually transmitted in those days—apprenticeship with an established practitioner. Apprenticeship was essentially a contract whereby tutelage was provided by the master in return for scut work by the apprentice, such as scrivening documents and running errands. The apprenticeship system could accommodate only a limited number of new entrants, and therefore restrained competition within the profession. Quality of training necessarily varied widely. The system undoubtedly favored sons and nephews of existing practitioners, as in the modern apprenticeship systems in skilled trades such as those of plumber and electrician. In time, weight was given to years of college education in place of apprenticeship years.

Burrage, Revolution and the Collective Action of the French, American, and English Legal Professions, 13 Law & Social Inquiry 225 (1988), has an excellent summary of the history of the American legal profession. Concerning the colonial period, the author says, at p. 243:

> Seven colonies required periods of apprenticeship, ranging from three years in Delaware to seven in New York and New Jersey. New York and Massachusetts granted some exemption for college education and also set additional requirements for those wishing to practice as barristers in the higher courts. New Jersey, imitating

the English bar, had a third, higher coopted order of serjeants.*
Virginia and South Carolina, with sizable number of lawyers, had
no formal training requirements, probably because a large proportion of lawyers in both colonies qualified at the Inns of Court in
London.   Virginia seems to have expected those not trained in
London, and certainly those who wished to appear in the higher
courts, to serve a four-year apprenticeship.   In sum, the principle
of a specialist, trained, select bar seems to have been accepted in
the majority of the colonies.   However, it is not always clear
whether the bar admission rules were imposed by the governor and
the courts or by the practitioners themselves.   Only in Massachusetts do we know for certain that the bar devised, administered,
and enforced its own admission rules.

There is little record of attempts to practice by those who lacked
the requisite training, what is today called unauthorized practice of
law.   Theoretically, someone who represented himself to be trained as a
lawyer, but who was not, would be subject to an action for deceit or
perhaps malpractice.   See Wolfram, Modern Legal Ethics § 5.6.1 (1986).
However, that remedy is costly and worth pursuing only if damages can
be both proved and collected.   An alternative to a deceit action by the
client could be a suit by the bar to enjoin unauthorized practice by the
unlicensed practitioner.   As the law of unfair competition stood until
the 20th century, however, members of the bar probably would have
had no right of action against someone pretending to be qualified as a
lawyer.   See Handler, False and Misleading Advertising, 29 Yale L.J.
22 (1929).

In the 20th Century it was made a statutory offense for a person
not a lawyer to engage in law practice.   That prohibition is in turn a
basis for injunctive proceedings by the bar to prevent such practice.
See *Florida Bar v. Brumbaugh,* printed later in this chapter.   Before
these statutes, the bar could do little to prevent untrained people from
doing law office work, such as conveyancing and giving legal advice.
The bar also could not prevent informal practice in the justice of the
peace courts.   However, those trained in law practice apparently had
two effective controls on law practice by those not admitted to the bar.
One was ostracism.   Thus, nonlawyers would be excluded from the
formal and informal associations of practitioners, hence would be shut
out from professional lore and professional gossip.   Then as now this
kind of access—being a member of "the club"—is important.   Second,
and relatedly, courts of general jurisdiction had control over the right
to appear on behalf of others.   Admission before the court in turn
would be granted only to those recognized by their professional peers,
through the apprenticeship system.   From an early date the key to
entry into the profession was admission before the trial court of general
jurisdiction under the auspices of the apprenticeship system.   This

---

* "Serjeants" refers to serjeants at law, a small order of highest level barristers which
had originated in medieval times and became obsolescent in the 18th Century.

system apparently was fairly effective at the time the Constitution was adopted in 1787.

However, populist sentiment emanating from the American and French Revolutions culminated in what was subsequently called the Jacksonian revolution. In 1801 Georgia required that admission to practice law be allowed simply on application to court; Ohio in 1802 abrogated all requirements for admission; Tennessee in 1809; South Carolina in 1812. Deregulation gained momentum over the next four decades. As summarized in Burrage, supra, 13 Law & Social Inquiry at 249, 252:

> In one way or another, therefore, most states reduced or eliminated mandatory requirements for admission to the bar during the first half of the 19th century . . .
>
> The reduction or elimination of bar admission requirements had a disastrous effect on professional organization, leading to the collapse of all existing bar associations. The Suffolk County Bar Association, the leading organization in Massachusetts, dissolved in 1836 . . . The only exception was the Philadelphia Bar Association, which originated in 1802 as a law library but later became a professional body. However, it exercised these functions only among an elite, never seeking to extend its authority over all lawyers in the city or county . . .
>
> The repeal of bar admission rules and the collapse of bar associations prevented the American profession from remaining as a small, closed, aloof, and largely self-recruiting status group . . .
>
> This process of opening legal practice to members of lower socioeconomic classes probably . . . must have accelerated everywhere with the mushrooming of university and private commercial night schools after the Civil War. As a result, the American legal profession . . . became a heterogeneous occupational category whose "members," if that is the right word, were stratified by their social and ethnic origins, law schools they attended, and places of work. Since they could no longer look to practitioners' organizations to confer distinctive professional honors or titles, they were obliged to earn their status like everyone else in American society by their educational qualifications, their incomes, and their lifestyles.

Is Burrage's description of the American legal profession as a "heterogenous occupational category" accurate today? For a review of historical sources on the American legal profession, see Maru, Research on the Legal Profession c. 1 (2d ed. 1986).

Women, Blacks and Other Minorities in the Profession

Women

The history of women in the legal profession through the 19th Century is essentially a story of frustration and exclusion. It is recounted in K. Morello, The Invisible Bar: The Woman Lawyer in America, 1638 to the Present (1986). The socio-legal attitude sustaining exclusion was stated in the high Victorian age by Justice Bradley, concurring in Bradwell v. State, 83 U.S. (16 Wall.) 130 (1873). That decision affirmed denial of admission to the Illinois bar of Myra Bradwell, who surely was better qualified than most of her contemporaries. Justice Bradley said:

> [T]he civil law, as well as nature herself, has always recognized a wide difference in the respective spheres and destinies of man and woman . . . The natural and proper timidity and delicacy which belongs to the female sex evidently unfits it for many of the occupations of civil life. The constitution of the family organization, which is founded in the divine ordinance, as well as in the nature of things, indicates the domestic sphere as that which properly belongs to the domain and functions of womanhood . . . So firmly fixed was this sentiment in the founders of the common law that it became a maxim of that system of jurisprudence that a woman had no legal existence separate from her husband, who was regarded as her head and representative in the social state; and, notwithstanding some recent modifications of this civil status, many of the special rules of law flowing from and dependent upon this cardinal principle still exist in full force in most States . . . This very incapacity was one circumstance which the Supreme Court of Illinois deemed important in rendering a married woman incompetent fully to perform the duties and trusts that belong to the office of an attorney and counsellor.

83 U.S. (16 Wall.) at 141 (Bradley, J., concurring).

For an analysis of long term demographic trends in the legal profession, giving special attention to gender, see Halliday, Six Score Years and Ten: Demographic Transitions in the American Legal Profession, 1950–1980, 20 Law & Soc'y Review 53 (1986). The available data indicate that the number of women lawyers rose from less than a dozen in 1870 to about 1,000 in 1910 but was still less than 10,000 by 1960. The increase in numbers whereby women have become a significant proportion of the profession has occurred since the 1960's. From 1973 to 1983, the size of the profession doubled; the number of women lawyers increased sevenfold. Fossum, Women in the Law: A Reflection on Portia, 69 A.B.A.J. 1388, 1389 (1983).

Another demographic study is Curran, Rosich, Carson & Puccetti, Supplement to the Lawyer Statistical Report: The U.S. Legal Profession in 1985, Am.Bar Foundation (1986). Curran and her associates provide a breakdown of employment data indicating that a higher fraction of women than of men have law jobs in government (other than judiciary) and in legal education, and that the fraction in private law firms is lower for women than men. Within private firm settings, women are somewhat more heavily concentrated in sole practice and in very large firms (51 lawyers and more). Correlatively, women are disproportionately fewer in small and middle-sized firms. This pattern may reflect that engaging in sole practice doesn't depend so much on others, and that big firms tend to be more self-conscious about their hiring practices. Sole practice may allow greater control over one's life, or constitute the residual form of professional employment when other possibilities are unsatisfactory, or both. The significance of the big firms is suggested by Judge Judith Kaye in her reflective analysis, Women Lawyers in Big Firms: A Study in Progress Toward Gender Equality, 57 Fordham L.Rev. 111, 113 (1988):

> First, the big firms are most familiar to me from my own decades in private practice and from public reports, and these are for the most part the sources of my information. Second, I am convinced that what seems to be happening in the big firms is symptomatic of something more pervasive—that is exactly why there is so much publicity about them—and that these firms are in fact a superb example of our halting progress toward gender equality in the workforce. The big firms cast a giant shadow, in terms of public perceptions of the profession, parallels in other fields, and standards within the legal community. Their every uptick reverberates widely . . . [T]he actual influence of the big firms and their alumni—many of them general counsels of major corporations—extends far beyond their numbers. If any change should be made, they have the creativity to devise solutions and the resources to implement them.

Nonetheless, as of 1988 the percentage of women partners in large law firms ranged no higher than 13 percent and typically was in the range of 5–10 percent. See N.Y. Times Magazine, March 6, 1988, p. 75.

The number of women on law school faculties in tenured or tenure-track position increased by about 50% in the six years between 1980 and 1986, from 10.8% to 15.9%. Chused, The Hiring and Retention of Minorities and Women on American Law School Faculties, 137 U.Pa.L. Rev. 537, 548 (1988) (study sponsored by the Society of American Law Teachers (SALT); faculty members at 149 schools, over 85% of those American Association of Law School (AALS) member institutions, returned survey questionnaires) (hereinafter SALT study). This survey directly depicts the situation of women in law teaching and inferentially that of women in law practice. In evaluating this increase several caveats are in order, as Chused points out: "About one-fifth of the reporting law schools currently maintain faculties in which the proportion of women remains below the national average of six years ago. The 'high prestige' institutions are heavily represented among these laggard institutions. Legal writing, moreover, may be on its way to becoming a 'woman's job'." Id. "Sixty-three of the 149 reporting schools had contract legal writing positions [as opposed to tenure track positions]. The median size of these 63 legal writing staffs were three. Typically, two of the three were women." Id. at 538 n. 7. Women have experienced difficulties in receiving tenure, as anecdotal evidence attests. See, e.g., Angel, Women in Legal Education: What its Like to be

Part of a Perpetual First Wave or the Case of the Disappearing Women, 61 Temp.L.Q. 799 (1988); "Women Face Hurdles as Professors," National Law Journal, October 24, 1988, p. 1; and Chused, Faculty Parenthood: Law School Treatment of Pregnancy and Child Care, 35 J.Legal Educ. 568, 584 (1985). The SALT data showed that tenure and departure rates:

> were almost identical for men and women. This uniformity, however, masks several troubling trends. Schools with a low proportion of women on their tenured faculty grant tenure to women at lower rates than to men, while schools with higher proportions of women among their tenured ranks grant tenure to women at higher rates than to men. The presence of a certain size core of tenured women on a faculty significantly improves the likelihood that junior level women will successfully leap the tenure hurdle.
>
> Id. at 550.

Chused writes:

> There are a number of possible explanations for this outcome. The presence of a few tenured women may result in "mentoring" relationships with younger female faculty more successful than those young men typically establish with their senior peers. Tenured women in general, or newly tenured women in particular, may vote negatively in tenure cases less frequently than men. Or, perhaps, once a group of women have crossed the tenure threshold, men begin to view the tenure process differently. Regardless of cause, it is apparent that some schools have moved much more rapidly than others to integrate women into all levels of their faculties. Although larger longitudinal studies are necessary to confirm these trends, the over-representation of high prestige schools among low-progress institutions suggests that tenure may be a serious problem for many women now working on "big name" faculties.
>
> Id. at 552.

The presence of senior women and the number of such women in firms and other practice settings may similarly affect the career progression of junior women and undoubtedly has an effect on how sensitive others in the workplace are to sexist attitudes and practices. On women in legal academia, see Menkel–Meadow, Women as Law Teachers: Toward the Feminization of Legal Education, in Essays on the Application of a Humanistic Perspective to Law Teaching (1981).

Gender bias in the courtroom against women lawyers and women litigants has received attention by state court judges and state, local and women bar associations. In 1980 the NOW Legal Defense Fund in cooperation with the National Association of Women Judges created the National Judicial Education Program to Promote Equality for Women and Men in the Courts. In 1984, New Jersey became the first state to issue a report on gender bias in the courts, largely due to the efforts of Superior Court Judge Marilyn Loftus and New Jersey Chief

Justice Robert Wilentz. Other states have since undertaken studies of the problem, including Arizona, California, Florida, Illinois, Massachusetts, and Rhode Island. New York issued a report in 1986 which concluded that "gender bias," defined as "[d]ecisions made or actions taken because of weight given to preconceived notions of sexual roles rather than upon a fair and unswayed appraisal of merit as to each person or situation," is "pervasive". It operates against not only women lawyers but women litigants and court personnel. "[P]roblems are perpetuated by some attorneys' and judges' misinformed belief that complaints by women are contrivances of overwrought imaginations and hypersensitivities. More was found . . . than bruised feelings resulting from rude and callous behavior. Real hardships are borne by women." (Is suffering callous behavior not a real hardship? What audience is addressed by such terms as "bruised feelings?" Is this itself a problem? Smart politics?)

As shown in the New York report, women litigants are accorded less credibility because of their gender and face a judiciary poorly informed and in many cases misinformed about matters integral to the welfare of women. As to women lawyers, the study found that they must brave a "verbal and psychological obstacle course" in the courtroom. Examples of overt sexism include: being ordered not to use Ms. and to use her husband's last name, not her own, under threat of "sleep[ing] in the county jail tonight" New York Times, July 14, 1988 (comments made by United States District Court Judge Teitelbaum to attorney Barbara Wolvowitz who was trying a race discrimination case in federal court); being told by a judge "I don't think ladies should be lawyers" and being asked what "her husband thought of her working here." Blodgett, I Don't Think that Ladies Should be Lawyers, 72 A.B. A.J. 48 (1986) (reporting comments made by a Illinois state court judge to a woman lawyer from Mayer, Brown & Platt of Chicago in 1986); being referred to as "lawyerette" and "attorney generalette," Complaint Concerning the Honorable John J. Kirby, 354 N.W.2d 410 (Minn. 1984) (censuring state court judge for these remarks). Generally see Note, Gender Bias in the Judicial System, 61 So.Calif.L.Rev. 2193 (1988).

DEBORAH L. RHODE, "PERSPECTIVES ON PROFESSIONAL WOMEN"
40 Stan.L.Rev. 1163 (1988).*

. . .

In a variety of studies, female students have also expressed lower expectations for occupational success than males and have attached greater priority to relational aspects of employment such as opportunities for helping others than to opportunities for money, status and power. Family and peer pressure can also skew vocational choices and discourage career decisions that would compete with domestic responsibilities, require geographic mobility, or bring wives greater prestige and income than their husbands. Such pressures can be particularly intense within certain class, race, and ethnic groups.

Disparities between traits associated with femininity and traits associated with vocational achievement further reinforce these gender socialization processes. A wide array of experimental and clinical evidence indicates that profiles of successful professionals conflict with profiles of normal or ideal women. The aggressiveness, competitiveness, dedication, and emotional detachment traditionally presumed necessary for advancement in the most prestigious and well-paid occupations are incompatible with traits commonly viewed as attractive in women: cooperativeness, deference, sensitivity, and self-sacrifice. Despite substantial progress toward gender equality over the last several decades, these gender stereotypes remain remarkably resilient. Females aspiring to nontraditional or high-status positions remain subject to a familiar double bind. Those conforming to traditional characteristics of femininity are often thought lacking in the requisite assertiveness and initiative, yet those conforming to a masculine model of success may be ostracized in work settings as bitchy, aggressive, and uncooperative. As long as aspiring women are found wanting either as professionals or as women, they face substantial disincentives to aspire . . .

Of particular significance are the sexes' different priorities concerning family responsibilities. Although cultural commitments to equal opportunity in vocational spheres have steadily increased, these sentiments have not translated into equal obligations in domestic spheres. Most studies have indicated that women still perform about 70 percent of the family tasks in an average household. Employed wives spend about twice as much time on homemaking demands as employed husbands; men married to women with full-time jobs devote only 1.4 hours a week more to domestic duties than other husbands. When time spent in paid labor and domestic labor is combined, employed males average two hours less per day than employed females, and a disproportionate amount of male homemaking contributions involve relatively enjoyable activities such as playing with the children . . . Women, particularly social and ethnic minorities, are also far more likely to become single parents, with all the associated demands. In the late 1980s, females headed 90 percent of the nation's singleparent households, and women of color were disproportionately likely to have such responsibilities . . .

Not only do women bear the vast majority of family obligations, they do so in occupational environments designed by and for men. As a result, career success has often meant compromise of caretaking values.

Female employees unwilling to make that sacrifice have paid a demanding professional price . . .

. . . [E]lite professionals tend to impose longer and more unpredictable working hours, and are particularly resistant to extended leaves, part-time or flexible-time shifts, and home work. That resistance springs from a variety of sources. Many clients and colleagues object to the inconveniences and the apparent lack of commitment among employees working nonconventional hours . . .

Extended hours, unpredictable schedules, and frequent travel mesh poorly with childrearing responsibilities. Yet for women "on the road to success," no detours from standard workplace obligations are advisable . . .

The self, it appears, should conform to a male model with a vengeance . . .

Unconscious gender bias can operate on three levels: (1) prototypes, the images associated with members of a particular occupation; (2) schema, the personal characteristics and situational factors that are used to explain conduct; and (3) scripts, definitions of appropriate behavior in a given situation. Thus, when a female applicant for a given position (e.g., litigator) does not fit the evaluator's prototype (e.g., aggressive male), her credentials will be judged with greater skepticism. Many explanatory schema embody similar stereotypes: Men's success is more likely to be explained in terms of ability and their failure in terms of luck, while women's achievement is more often attributed to luck or effort and their failures ascribed to inability. Since evaluations of ability are most crucial in hiring and promotion decisions, these attribution biases entrench gender hierarchies. So too, the scripts defining appropriate social behavior often reflect patterns of gender dominance, deference, and accommodation. For example, in group conversation, male participants tend to speak and interrupt more often, and to hold the floor for longer periods than females. Women are expected not only to talk less but also to allow more interruptions, and those who deviate from their accustomed role provoke negative evaluations. Once again, these perceptual prejudices create a double bind: Women who conform to accepted stereotypes will appear to have less to contribute and less leadership potential than the male colleagues, while women who take a more assertive stance risk appearing arrogant, aggressive, and abrasive. How to seem "demure but tough" is particularly difficult when standards vary among those whose opinions are most critical. In male-dominated cultures, women are subject to criticism for being "too feminine" and not "feminine enough."

Unconscious gender prejudices affect not only the evaluation of individual performance, they also affect the performance itself. As both experimental and longitudinal studies have repeatedly demonstrated, low expectations of achievement frequently become self-fulfilling prophecies. Individuals often signal their assumptions in subtle or not so subtle ways. These forms of negative feedback, including lower salaries and less demanding assignments, can adversely affect self-confidence and job performance.　Such consequences then reinforce the initial expectations, and a self-perpetuating cycle continues . . .

Comments

The problems encountered by women lawyers and the responses to these problems are mirrored in the experience of women in other fields, such as medicine and college teaching.　See P. Glazer and M. Slater, Unequal Colleagues (1987).

Practicing women and women in academia have changed the focus in many substantive legal areas, in some areas have changed what is considered worthy of debate in law, and have challenged the ground rules of traditional legal debate itself.　See, e.g., Resnick, On the Bias: Feminist Reconsiderations of the Aspirations for our Judges, 6 So.Calif. L.Rev. 1877 (1988); Minow, Foreword: Justice Engendered, 107 Harv.L. Rev. 10 (1987); Estrich, Rape, 95 Yale L.J. 1087 (1986); Finley, Transcending Equality Theory: A Way Out of the Maternity and the Workplace Debate, 86 Colum.L.Rev. 1118 (1986); Law, Rethinking Sex and the Constitution, 132 U.Pa.L.Rev. 955 (1984); Minow, "Forming Underneath Everything that Grows:" Toward a History of Family Law, 1985 Wisc.L.Rev. 819; Olsen, Statutory Rape: A Feminist Critique of Rights Analysis, 63 Tex.L.Rev. 387 (1984); C. MacKinnon, Sexual Harassment of Working Women: A Case of Sex Discrimination (1979). Generally see Menkel–Meadow, Excluded Voices: New Voices in the Legal Profession Making New Voices in the Law, 42 U.Miami L.Rev. 29 (1987); Scales, The Emergence of Feminist Jurisprudence: An Essay, 95 Yale L.J. 1373 (1986); and R. Jack and D. Jack, Moral Vision and Professional Decisions: The Changing Values of Women and Men Lawyers (1989).

There has developed a large literature by and about women in the profession, ranging from statistical demographics to recount of personal experience.　For a comprehensive bibliography, see Grech & Jacobs, Women and the Legal Profession: A Bibliography of Current Literature, 44 The Record 215 (March 1989), covering the following subheadings:　General, Bar Association Participation, Biographies, History, Networking, Part–Time Lawyering, Rise to Partnership, Studies and Reports, Surveys and Statistics, Women in the Study of Law, Women Judges.

Women's situation in the contemporary legal profession has greatly enlarged the matters considered relevant to lawyers' social roles and personal psychology, not only for women but for men as well.　Moreover, there are very great differences among women, and among men, as well as between women and men, concerning "prototypes," "schema," and "scripts."　Any universal description of male lawyers unavoidably approaches a stereotype.　Many men, even among those who have become lawyers, care much more about their family life than others.　For example, one of the attractions of certain staff legal jobs is that they do not involve irregular hours, unpredictable schedules and heavy travel, and allow more time for nonprofessional life. So also many men are much more concerned with maintenance of group cohesion than fully articulating differences of opinion. Men so inclined may be better "deal makers" and law firm managing partners than "hired gun" types. Some male lawyers are actually good listeners.

Correlatively, many women lawyers are intensely interested in legal and philosophical ideas; are attracted to the excitement of competitive interaction; are uninterested in most or all aspects of domestic life and nurturing children. These differences among women appear to have more fully emerged in the discussions about women in the legal profession than have the corresponding differences among men. The relative silence of and about men in this respect is partly the product of male prototypes, schema, and scripts. Males from an early age learn to talk less about matters of feeling and identity. When they do talk about such matters, males tend to speak indirectly, facetiously, and in cliches, punctuated by occasional outbursts of feeling from the depths. However, male lawyers would resist being described as coy or emotional.

Blacks

The history of blacks in the law essentially parallels that of women, except that the pattern of events since the 1960's has been morally more equivocal and far less encouraging to those who believe in "natural progress" toward human equality in opportunity and life realization. The history of other minorities in the legal profession, particularly Hispanics and Asians, has not been as well developed.

The basic work on blacks in the legal profession is Segal, Blacks in the Law (1985) *:

Through the first half of the twentieth century, and even beyond, to become a black lawyer in America required an extraordinary measure of courage, determination, and vision. To most blacks it was a goal that seemed to defy social and economic realities. Indeed, at the turn of the century W.E.B. Du Bois found that physicians and lawyers together comprised only 1.5 percent of the black population. According to the 1910 United States census, there were then only 798 black lawyers in the country, and by 1940 there were a mere 1,925—one black lawyer for every 13,000 blacks in America.

During those years blacks who did manage to become lawyers found themselves in a profession that was pervaded by racism and fundamentally segregated. Until 1937 there was no black federal judge in the nation, and even then it was a term appointment in the Virgin Islands; until 1949, none on a United States Circuit Court; until 1961, none on a United States District Court; and until 1967, none on the United States Supreme Court. Until 1936, blacks were not admitted to "white" law schools. Until 1943 color had to be stated on applications to the American Bar Association. Until 1946 there was no black teacher on the faculty of predominantly white law schools . . .

Legal Education

Between 1877 and 1935 Howard [University Law School] was the only substantial source of legal education for blacks in the United States. During this period no black could obtain a legal education in an approved law school anywhere south of Washington, D.C.

During the next twelve years three other currently functioning accredited black law schools, all state institutions and all in the South, came into existence. The first of these was North Carolina Central University Law School in Durham, North Carolina, founded in 1939. The next two, both founded in 1947, were Texas Southern University Law School in Houston, Texas, and Southern University Law School in Baton Rouge, Louisiana. Howard and these three state black law schools have trained the majority of black lawyers in the nation.

Not content with the perpetuation of a situation that limited blacks to black law schools, skilled black advocates instituted suits beginning in the middle 1930s on the reasoning that blacks were entitled to a common education forum with whites if they were to practice the same law. Under the leadership of Charles H. Houston, and later Thurgood Marshall, and under the auspices of the NAACP Legal Defense and Educational Fund, a series of lawsuits were filed to obtain for blacks the right to attend predominantly white southern law schools. When Houston and Marshall took up the fight to enable Donald Murray, a 1934 black graduate of Amherst College, to enter the University of Maryland Law School, legal barriers restricting admission of blacks to white law schools began to fall, but only after persistent and effective advocacy produced court orders mandating this result . . .

Undoubtedly, the decision of the United States Supreme Court in *Brown v. Board of Education,* handed down in 1954, had some significant impact on the thinking of white law schools . . .

After this milestone was reached, changes came more rapidly. By the late 1960s most law schools, spurred on by the civil rights legislation and by the argument that minority leaders could benefit the country in numerous ways, had initiated minority recruitment and admissions programs . . .

Overt policies of racial discrimination in admissions were not the only barriers that potential black law students had to overcome. Many blacks grew up in deprived environments and did not receive in early life the educational opportunities that would allow them to compete in higher education . . .

Parents deliberately discouraged their children from entering the legal profession. They were skeptical of the black lawyer's ability to obtain justice in the courts; they realized that a large proportion of the black community chose white lawyers to represent them; and they knew that black lawyers frequently had to associate themselves with white lawyers and split fees if they wanted clients.

The discouragement facing potential black lawyers graphically appears in the advice given to Malcolm X when he discussed his career plans with his high school teacher and adviser:

". . . Malcolm, you ought to be thinking about a career. Have you been giving it thought?"

". . . I've been thinking I'd like to be a lawyer."

". . . Malcolm, one of life's first needs is for us to be realistic . . . You've got to be realistic about being a nigger. A lawyer—that's no realistic goal for a nigger."

In addition to family opposition, educational handicaps, and humiliating conditions diverting blacks from a career in the law, there was the problem of the high costs of both undergraduate and law school education . . .

In the mid–1960s a number of philanthropic organizations attempted to spur the interest of blacks in becoming lawyers by making grants to reduce the financial barriers to their entering law school . . .

That the increased financial aid and remedial programs detailed above were successful to a significant degree is clear from the dramatic increases in black enrollment in law schools all over the country during the late 1960s and early 1970s. In 1965, Harvard Law School estimated that of the approximately 65,000 law students in accredited law schools in the nation, there were no more than 700 black students, or approximately 1 percent. By 1972 the 4,423 black students constituted 4.3 percent of all students attending accredited law schools in the country, and by the 1976–77 school year there were 5,503 black students, or about 4.7 percent of the total, in approved law schools.

In the succeeding three school years, however, black enrollment leveled off instead of continuing in its prior record of steady growth . . .

Professional Associations

Although blacks have not yet achieved anything near proportional representation in the legal profession, the situation has improved markedly since *Brown v. Board of Education* (1954). Before that legal turning point, black attorneys were virtually isolated professionally. Opportunities to work with white colleagues or to represent white clients were almost nonexistent. Moreover, many blacks who needed legal representation feared that black lawyers would be unsuccessful against a white lawyer and before a white judge, regardless of the ability or the quality of the performance of the black lawyers. Those blacks who did retain black lawyers were usually too poor to furnish a lucrative practice. Black lawyers were largely confined to petty criminal cases and were rarely given the opportunity to prove their ability in other areas of the law.

In varying degrees this problem of professional segregation has beset black lawyers throughout the century. In 1912, racism within the legal community was so rampant that a storm arose over the "inadvertent" election of the first three black attorneys to the American Bar Association by its Executive Committee. When the Executive Committee discovered that it had unknowingly elected three members "of the colored race," the committee rescinded its prior action, stating that "the settled practice of the Association has been to elect only white men to membership." . . .

In 1925, twelve black lawyers from around the nation (eleven men and one woman) met in Des Moines, Iowa, to organize and incorporate the National Bar Association (NBA). Although not restricting its membership to race, the NBA was designed to be, and became, the chief professional association of black lawyers . . .

In 1981, the NBA estimated that there were 12,000 black lawyers, of whom about 8,000 belonged to the NBA. From an American Bar Foundation estimate of a total of 535,000 lawyers in the United States in 1980, it appears that black lawyers comprise a little more than 2.2 percent of the American lawyer population . . .

Segal, pp. 1–7, 16–19.

As Segal's study demonstrates, a "black lawyer," like all lawyers, lives and practices in a specific practice setting, in a specific community, during a specific historical period. Law practice tends to be highly localized, being bound up in an immediate socio-political context and tied to specific economic possibilities. Segal accordingly has subchapters on individual black lawyers and on several cities in which black lawyers were concentrated, including Atlanta, New York, Philadelphia, and Washington, D.C. Of Philadelphia, for example, she writes:

Aaron Mossell was the first black to graduate from the University of Pennsylvania Law School. Born in Hamilton, Ontario, the son of a free Black who migrated to Canada to avoid having his children reared in a slave state, he returned to Philadelphia after the Emancipation. He entered Lincoln University (situated near) as an undergraduate and then matriculated at the University of Pennsylvania Law School, from which he graduated in 1888. After he was admitted to the Philadelphia Bar on February 18, 1893, he began the practice of law. He and John Wesley Parks later formed a partnership and practiced law together, apparently successfully.

Mossell was the father of the distinguished lawyer, Sadie Tanner Mossell Alexander . . .

The 1910 census reported that there were thirteen black lawyers in Philadelphia . . . [F]rom 1909 to 1945, a period of thirty-six years, only twenty black lawyers (nineteen males and one female) were admitted to the Philadelphia Bar.

A remarkable number of these twenty lawyers went on to achieve success in the profession and to attain judgeships and other public offices, thereby doing a great deal to enhance the standing of the black lawyer in Philadelphia.

Herbert E. Millen had the distinction of being the first black judge in Philadelphia when he became judge of the Municipal Court in 1948. Raymond Pace Alexander, husband of Sadie T.M. Alexander, gave up a lucrative law practice in 1958 to become the first black judge on the Court of Common Pleas, the trial court of general jurisdiction . . . He was also Chief Counsel for the NAACP and was elected and reelected to the Philadelphia City Council in the 1950s. Robert N.C. Nix, Sr. was elected to fill the unexpired term of a Philadelphia Congressman in 1958 and served in the House of Representatives until January 1, 1979. J. Austin Norris, after a successful career as a newspaper publisher in Pittsburgh, returned to the practice of law in Philadelphia and started a law firm that produced its own corps of talented black lawyers, several of whom became judges and high-level public officials. Among these are: A. Leon Higginbotham, Jr., United States Court of Appeals for the Third Circuit; Clifford Scott Green, United States District Court for the Eastern District of Pennsylvania; Robert W. Williams, Jr., Commonwealth Court of Pennsylvania; Doris M. Harris and Harvey N. Schmidt, Court of Common Pleas of Philadelphia; William F. Hall, United States Magistrate; and William H. Brown, III . . .

As the times and circumstances changed, a different occupational picture developed. Offers from white sole practitioners, from law firms and corporations, and from federal and state governments, which were unknown to the oldest cohort, became routine for the youngest cohort. Offers from black practitioners and black firms, which were the major employers of the oldest cohort, decreased proportionately in the youngest cohort, while white law firms and corporations vied for the services of the outstanding black law school graduates . . .

But what happened to the black lawyers in Philadelphia who received no offers from major firms? . . .

Of the seventeen who had received no offers, seven became sole practitioners; seven took posts with government (three city, one state, and three federal); one went with a black sole practitioner; and one with a white firm . . .

Segal, pp. 28–33, 76–77.

Comments

For more general background, see also Davis, The American Negro Reference Book (1966); Goldman, A Portrait of the Black Lawyer in Chicago (1972); Kluger, Simple Justice (1977). Also see Littlejohn & Hobson, Black Lawyers, Law Practice, and Bar Associations—1844 to 1970: A Michigan History, 33 Wayne L.Rev. 1625 (1987).

Despite the greater opportunity that blacks now have for entry into the legal profession, their life chances in the profession remain precarious. In particular, the number of blacks making partner in predominantly white firms is small and perhaps not increasing. The black experience in legal academia has been equally bleak. According to the SALT study, supra, "[in] 1986–87, a typical law school faculty had thirty-one members . . . [o]f these . . . thirty were white, one was black, Hispanic or other minority . . ." Chused, 137 U.Pa.L.Rev. at 538. In 1980, blacks constituted 2.8% of the faculty at white-operated law schools. By 1986, the figure had risen only to 3.7%. Id. Compare the increase in the same period for women, supra; for Hispanics the percentage went from .5 to .7; and for other minorities from .5 to 1.0%. "The data . . . demonstrate that minority professors in general, and black professors in particular, tend to be tokens if they are present at all. . . . In sheer numbers, the increase has been very small . . . only thirty-five more tenured black professors . . . than there were in 1981." 137 U.Pa.L.Rev. at 539. On the experience of blacks in legal academia, see Haines, Minority Law Professors and the Myth of Sisyphus: Consciousness and Praxis Within the Special Teaching Challenge in American Law Schools, 10 Nat'l Black L.J. 247 (1988); R. Delgado, Minority Law Professors' Lives: The Bell–Delgado Survey (Institute for Legal Studies Working Papers Series 39, Oct. 1988); Lawrence, Minority Hiring in AALS Law Schools, 20 U.S.F.L.Rev. 429 (1986); Bell, Application of the "Tipping" Point Principle to Law Faculty Hiring Policies, 10 Nova L.J. 319 (1986); Bell, Strangers in Academic Paradise: Law Teachers of Color in Still White Law Schools, 20 U.S.F.L.Rev. 385 (1986).

An adequate explanation of the precarious situation of black lawyers in the white-controlled institutions of the legal profession would cover American social history for the last three decades. In the final analysis, however, racism remains a potent force, both as an attitude of whites (and other non-black ethnic groups) and as a response by blacks. Consider the following two statements: Hazard, Permissive Affirmative Action for the Benefit of Blacks, 1987 U.Ill. L.Rev. 379, 385 (1987):

> Simply put, while most Americans avow and genuinely believe in the principle of equality, most white Americans still consider black people as such to be obnoxious and socially inferior. This prevalent attitude is generally and appropriately called racism. "Racism" is to be distinguished from "racists." These days only a small discredited minority of Americans are willing to say explicit-

ly that they regard blacks as inherently obnoxious and inferior. We have no racists in this country, or only a handful of them, because being a self-acknowledged racist has become socially and politically impermissible. To be sure, many white Americans will acknowledge that "everyone has his prejudices" or that "every individual is different." Most white Americans know individual blacks with whom they get along and some whom they like and some whom they respect. Most white Americans, in my observation, try to be fair and try to do the right thing in specific dealings with blacks, at least where they do not feel threatened. Nevertheless, most white Americans do not have the same positive attitude toward blacks that they have to others in general, or even that they have toward whites who are quite different from themselves in respects other than race.

The attitude of American whites toward racial minorities other than blacks has often been similarly negative. I refer particularly to the attitude of white Anglo–Saxon Protestants toward Native Americans, Asians, and Hispanics, and in different degree toward Jews and Southern and Eastern European ethnics. Viewed in broad historical and social perspectives, however, the attitude toward blacks has been qualitatively different—more persistent, more manifest, and more resistant to eradication. From one individual white to another this negative attitude is more or less intense, more or less repressed psychologically, and more or less consistently suppressed in behavior. But it is there.

Lawrence, The Id., the Ego, and Equal Protection: Reckoning with Unconscious Racism, 39 Stan.L.Rev. 317–318 (1987):

It is 1948. I am sitting in a kindergarten classroom at the Dalton School, a fashionable and progressive New York City private school. My parents, both products of a segregated Mississippi school system, have come to New York to attend graduate and professional school. They have enrolled me and my sisters here at Dalton to avoid sending us to public school in our neighborhood where the vast majority of the students are black and poor. They want us to escape the ravages of segregation, New York style.

It is circle time in the five-year old group, and the teacher is reading us a book. As she reads, she passes the book around the circle so that each of us can see the illustrations. The book's title is *Little Black Sambo*. Looking back, I remember only one part of the story, one illustration: Little Black Sambo is running around a stack of pancakes with a tiger chasing him. He is very black and has a minstrel's white mouth. His hair is tied up in many pigtails, each pigtail tied with a different color ribbon. I have seen the picture before the book reaches my place in the circle. I have heard the laughter of my classmates. There is a knot in the pit of my stomach. I feel panic and shame. I do not have the words to articulate my feelings—words like "stereotype" and "stigma" that might help cathart the shame and place it outside of me where it began.

But I am slowly realizing that, as the only black child in the circle, I have some kinship with the tragic and ugly hero of this story—that my classmates are laughing at me as well as at him. I wish I could laugh along with my friends. I wish I could disappear.

I am in a vacant lot next to my house with black friends from the neighborhood. We are listening to Amos and Andy on a small radio and laughing uproariously. My father comes out and turns off the radio. He reminds me that he disapproves of this show that pokes fun at Negroes. I feel bad—less from my father's reprimand than from a sense that I have betrayed him and myself, that I have joined my classmates in laughing at us.

I am certain that my kindergarten teacher was not intentionally racist in choosing *Little Black Sambo*. I knew even then, from a child's intuitive sense, that she was a good, well-meaning person. A less benign combination of racial mockery and profit motivated the white men who produced the radio show and played the roles of Amos and Andy. But we who had joined their conspiracy by our laughter had not intended to demean our race.

A dozen years later I am a student at Haverford College. Again, I am a token black presence in a white world. A companion whose face and name I can't remember seeks to compliment me by saying, "I don't think of you as a Negro." I understand his benign intention and accept the compliment. But the knot is in my stomach again. Once again, I have betrayed myself.

This happened to me more than a few times. Each time my interlocutor was a good, liberal, white person who intended to express feelings of shared humanity. I did not yet understand the racist implications of the way in which the feelings were conceptualized. I am certain that my white friends did not either. We had not yet grasped the compliment's underlying premise: To be thought of as a Negro is to be thought of as less than human. We were all victims of our culture's racism. We had all grown up on *Little Black Sambo* and Amos and Andy.

Another ten years pass. I am thirty-three. My daughter, Maia, is three. I greet a pink-faced, four-year-old boy on the steps of her nursery school. He proudly presents me with a book he has brought for his teacher to read to the class. "It's my favorite," he says. The book is a new edition of *Little Black Sambo*.

———

Other Minorities

Until the 1970s, the minority group most affected by discrimination in the legal profession had been Jews. Jews in small number have been members of the American legal profession since the 19th Century.

Beginning with the large immigration from central and eastern Europe at the end of the 19th Century, a substantial fraction of whom were Jews, the established legal profession became uneasy, widely hostile, and discriminatory. Similar attitudes were manifested toward Catholics as such and Irish, Italians, and Poles as such, but with less intensity. The same holds for all ethnic minorities in one degree or another. See generally Auerbach, Unequal Justice: Lawyers and Social Change in Modern America (1976). At least since the mid–1970s, however, discrimination appears to have sharply declined in the legal profession, as much or more than in other vocational groups, as against people of European heritage.

Discrimination and differentials in opportunity evidently persist as against Hispanics, Asians and other ethnic minorities. Gay and lesbian lawyers must also confront discrimination and barriers to entry into the "establishment" legal institutions in this country as must lawyers who are physically disabled. The high average academic achievement of many Asians has improved their competitive position, but also engenders fear of competition. The moral challenge remains.

In 1984 the American Bar Association created a Task Force on Minorities in the Legal Profession. The Task Force submitted a report dated January 10, 1986, the principal recommendations of which were as follows:

1. The American Bar Association adopt a ninth goal to read as follows:

"Goal 9: To promote full and equal participation in the profession by minorities and women."

2. The Association create a commission on opportunities for minorities in the profession.

3. The Association takes concrete actions with regard to the hiring, recruitment, promotion and advancement of minority lawyers and minority law students and graduates . . .

5. The Association maintain cooperative working relationships with the national, state and local minority and majority bar associations and implement and carry out joint programs and projects . . .

6. The Association takes concrete actions with regard to legal education for minorities . . .

8. The Association adopt procedures to encourage minority lawyers and law students to join the Association, participate in its activities and receive its benefits . . .

10. The Association should amend section 6.8(a)(1) of its constitution to permit the Hispanic National Bar Association to have a delegate to the House of Delegates.

The ABA appointed a Commission on Minorities in the legal profession to carry out these recommendations. Through 1989 the Commission had undertaken a variety of programs toward this end.

The Co–Reporters for the Task Force were Professors Edward Little-john of Wayne State Law School and Leonard Rubinowitz of Northwest-ern Law School. They are collaborating on a study whose working title is Lawyers of Color: Racial and Ethnic Minorities in the Legal Profes-sion. Until that study is published the sources on the situation of ethnic minorities in the profession will remain fragmentary.

Modern Admission Standards

Introductory Note

Admission to the practice of law today takes the form of admission before the highest court of the state, except in New York and perhaps a few other states, where it takes the form of admission to a lower court. Admission to the court carries with it the right of audience (i.e., to present matters on behalf of clients) in all courts of the jurisdiction, and to engage in law office practice.

A parallel procedure governs admission to practice in federal courts. Admission to practice in a state does not of itself result in admission to practice in the federal courts in that state. Rather, a motion for admission to the federal court must be made. Separate admission is required to each United States District Court, to each United States Court of Appeals, and to the Supreme Court of the United States. The basic requirement for admission to federal court is that the applicant have been admitted in a state. However, local federal court rules often require in addition a period of practice experi-ence, participation in a number of trials, proof of familiarity with federal procedure, or a combination of such requirements. See Wolf-ram, Modern Legal Ethics §§ 15.2 et seq. (1986).

Today, admission to practice in a state generally entails three requirements: (1) completion of the curriculum at an accredited law school; (2) passing a bar examination; and (3) meeting a requirement of "good character." Until invention of the bar examination in the latter half of the 19th century, admission required satisfying a judge that the applicant was conversant with the law, providing proof of good charac-ter, and, in some states, fulfilling an apprenticeship requirement. As noted in the Historical Background, above, the apprenticeship system yielded uneven product under the best of circumstances. "Good charac-ter" was often interpreted to mean acceptability to the local establish-ment in the bench and bar. The requirement that the applicant demonstrate knowledge of the law could mean almost anything. In Baldwin, Flush Times of Alabama and Mississippi (1858), a reminis-cence of the year 1836 by a lawyer who later was a member of the California Supreme Court, the author recalled that the judge adminis-tered his rite of passage by "asking not a single legal question . . ." The modern admissions process may leave much to be desired, but it displaced a system that was uneven, frequently indifferent to any matters of qualification, and often discriminatory against newcomers in society.

Accredited Law Schools

Comprehensive data on law schools, law school enrollments, and bar admissions requirements are compiled in ABA, Section of Legal Education and Admissions to the Bar, A Review of Legal Education in the United States, Fall, 1988, Law Schools and Bar Admissions Requirements (1989). Bar admission requirements are compiled in ABA Section of Legal Education and Admissions to the Bar and National Conference of Bar Examiners, Comprehensive Guide to Bar Admission Requirements 1989 (1989). Law Schools have an organization called the Association of American Law Schools, established in 1900 with the encouragement of the ABA. See generally Stevens, Law School: Legal Education in America from the 1850s to the 1980s (1983); AALS, Report of the AALS Long Range Planning Committee—May 1989.

Most law schools in this country are reviewed for accreditation by the American Bar Association, in cooperation with the Association of American Law Schools. Accreditation by the ABA requires maintenance of specified standards as to curriculum, law library, classroom facilities, and faculty. Compliance is enforced by periodic inspections and by the sanction of withdrawal of accreditation. The standards permit a substantial range in faculty-student ratio, pedagogical procedure (e.g., "lecture" versus "Socratic method"), clinical instruction, training in legal writing and research, subject matter of courses, and relative balance between theory and "nuts and bolts." See ABA Section of Legal Education and Admissions to the Bar, A Review of Legal Education in the United States (1977); Note, ABA Approval of Law Schools, 72 Mich.L.Rev. 1134 (1974); and Boyer and Cramton, American Legal Education: An Agenda for Research and Reform, 59 Cornell L.Rev. 221 (1974); White, Legal Education in the Era of Change: Law School Autonomy, 1987 Duke L.J. 292.

According to the rules in every state, accreditation of a law school by the ABA constitutes accreditation for purposes of fulfilling that state's requirement of graduation from an approved law school. A few states such as California separately accredit law schools, so that a law school may be accredited for purposes of admission by a state such as California but not for purpose of admission in other states. A number of states still permit completion of study in a law office instead of completion of law school. This pathway, essentially an apprenticeship, was pursued by Justice Robert Jackson (Supreme Court of the United States, 1941 to 1954) and a good many others in his generation. It is pursued by few people today. As a practical matter, graduation from an accredited law school is a requirement for admission to the bar.

Bar Examination

With very limited exceptions, a second requirement for admission to practice is passing the bar examination. One or two states recognize a "diploma privilege" under which graduation from a law school in the state fulfills the requirement of legal knowledge.

The legitimacy of the bar examination has often been disputed but remains generally accepted. It is acknowledged that the examination tests only part of the skills required to be a lawyer, and may test them imperfectly. However, it produces documentary evidence that can be reviewed without revealing the applicant's identity and which can be compared with the performance of other applicants. The alternatives would be an interview system, in which personal identity would be important, or an apprenticeship system, in which personal identity would be even more important, or no qualifications test at all. In modern times the latter has been considered unacceptable.

At certain periods, notably during the 1930s, it was contended that the general "fail" rate on the bar examination had been raised in order to restrain competitive entry into the profession. The last controversy of that kind appears to have occurred in California in the 1950s. However, in the 1960s and 1970s two sometimes related challenges were made to the bar examination. One was that the grading of essays was subjective and therefore arbitrary and therefore required judicial review. The other was that the bar examination results were systematically adverse to Blacks, Hispanics, and other racial minorities.

Judicial review of bar examination answers has been uniformly rejected, once the courts have been satisfied that grading of the examination is "blind" and conducted by a structured procedure. As for the subjectivity in grading even where grading is "blind," one response by the admissions authorities is simply to give an applicant who fails the right to repeat the examination. The theory is that any subjectivity is unlikely as a statistical matter to repeat itself against the same applicant. This approach has been sustained several times, for example in Lucero v. Ogden, 718 F.2d 355 (10th Cir.1983), cert. denied, 465 U.S. 1035 (1984) (challenge to the Colorado bar examination). The lower court's opinion, adopted by the Court of Appeals, stated:

> Although the plaintiff asks for "an adversary hearing, an unbiased judge or hearing examiner, the opportunity to argue the facts and cross examine the other party, and the right to present evidence,"
> . . . there is nothing to indicate that any of these procedures would be any more effective in detecting grading errors than the absolute right to retake the examination.

> 718 F.2d at 358.

Poats v. Givan, 651 F.2d 495 (7th Cir.1981), sustained an Indiana rule limiting an applicant to four attempts to pass the bar examination. The constitutional legitimacy of the current type of bar examination thus seems beyond serious legal challenge.

The problem of disparate impact of the bar examination on Blacks and Hispanics has been raised in a number of states, including California, New York and Pennsylvania. The most systematic challenge appears to have been that litigated in Delgado v. McTighe, 522 F.Supp. 886 (E.D.Pa.1981), involving the Pennsylvania bar examination. The court's extensive opinion recites the background of earlier investigations of the Pennsylvania bar examination and the procedures for administering the examination in Pennsylvania in the years 1972–1976. The Pennsylvania examination had the modern format of one day of short answer questions through the Multistate Bar Examination and one day of essay questions formulated and graded by the state's bar examiners. The court found that the essay questions were graded "blind," that errors in grammar and spelling were not counted negatively, and that the examiners had established an adequate system of internal procedures for reviewing grades initially given. The court placed heavy reliance on an outside study commissioned by the Pennsylvania Board of Bar Examiners, based on the 1972 examination. The salient findings of the study were:

> In July of 1972 there were 43 black candidates, of whom 34, or 79%, were admitted to the Bar. The lack of success of the 9 who failed was due more to failure on the Essay than on the MBE [Multistate Bar Examination].

> When the scores of the black candidates were compared with those of the whites, differences were found on both the Essay and the MBE. The average for the whites was higher on each test, and there were more high scores among the whites. On both the Essay and the MBE the poorest candidates as well [as] the best were white candidates; thus the blacks were found to be a more homogeneous group than the whites.

> A further analysis showed a significant fact about the nature of the law schools attended by the blacks. Of 43 candidates who took the test during July 1972, 12 had attended predominantly black law schools, and only 50% passed. The other 31 candidates had attended predominantly white law schools and 90% passed. A much larger percentage of those who attended white law schools were well prepared than of those who attended black law schools.

> The fact that, as groups, the blacks and whites had different distributions of scores on both the Essay and the MBE makes the setting of the passing score a vital matter. If the distributions were the same the effect of setting a passing score would be to pass and to fail an equal proportion of each group. However, because of the differences in the distributions of scores, whatever passing score is selected will result in a difference in the proportions passed. This is shown by the table below.

[Ed. note: To interpret the following chart, notice that if MBE test score 150 is a "pass," then 91% of black applicants fail to pass and 76% of white applicants fail to pass; if test score 130 is a "pass," then 56% of blacks fail compared with 19% of whites, etc. Notice also that the perceived justness of the test might be different if the MBE pass score was 120 (almost 40% black fail, less than 10% white) than if the pass score was 150 (only 10% black pass but only 25% whites). A pass score resulting in 75% failure among all applicants would almost certainly be politically untenable. The pass rates for the Pennsylvania bar examination in the period were: July, 1972: 98%; February, 1973: 84%; July, 1973: 95%. See 522 F.Supp. at 891.]

PASS–FAIL POINT AND BLACK WHITE FAILURES

	MBE Percent Failing			ESSAY Percent Failing	
Score	Black	White	Score	Black	White
170		100	90		100
160	100	95	80	100	88
150	91	76	70	82	45
140	80	44	60	36	17
130	56	19	50	9	5
120	39	7	40	0	1.5
110	24	2			
100	11	.5			
90	3	.2			
80	0	.2			

No matter where the passing point is set, except at the very bottom, more blacks than whites will be failed.

The remedy for this situation is beyond the scope of the present inquiry. It seems clear, however, that further improvement in the Bar examination itself, through further increasing the reliability and the validity of the test, will not change the situation.

522 F.Supp. at 893–894.

The court found that the disproportionate failure rate was not due to purposeful discrimination or to any invidious standards or grading procedures. *Delgado* appears to be the last court challenge to bar examinations on the ground of discriminatory impact.

Character and Fitness

In addition to meeting educational requirements and passing the written bar examination, admission to the bar requires fulfillment of a "character and fitness" requirement. See generally Rhode, Moral Character as a Professional Credential, 94 Yale L.J. 491 (1985). Traditionally, proof was supplied through affidavits from people personally acquainted with the applicant, a mechanism still used. The standard implicitly to be met has always been indeterminate if not completely vacuous. At some places and times, it apparently was applied to assure that only young people of proven upright character would be admitted. It was unclear how a young person who had not yet undergone the strain of practice could show the capacity to handle such strain, but to character committees "good background" was always propitious. At various times and places the requirement effectively screened out or deterred application by women and blacks and inhibited applications by Irish, Jews and others of recent immigrant origin.

At various times and places the character and fitness requirement was a basis for inquiring into an applicant's political beliefs, particularly Communism during the period from 1947 to 1970. Many serious people thought such inquiry within limits made sense, on the ground that it would be difficult to be "an officer of the court" if one actually believed that law was inherently oppressive. Other serious people thought that there was no correlation between political radicalism, including membership in the Communist Party, and predisposition to violate standards of professional conduct. Moreover, excluding political radicals from law practice would change the pool of lawyers available to take various types of cases, particularly cases involving political radicals. That in turn would also change the kinds of causes and arguments that would be taken to the courts. At all events, inquiries into radical political beliefs were often administered with high anxiety and were resisted on constitutional grounds.

The result was a series of decisions by a closely divided Supreme Court that have imposed some restraints on the subject matter and procedure of such inquiries. Schware v. Board of Bar Examiners of New Mexico, 353 U.S. 232, 77 S.Ct. 752 (1957), involved an applicant who was denied admission because of prior membership in the Communist Party and related activities, including participation in the 1930s in shipyard strikes that became embittered and violent; numerous arrests; use of aliases; and recruiting volunteers for the anti–Franco forces in the Spanish Civil War. Schware quit the Communist Party in 1940, served honorably in the Army, and entered the state university law school in 1950, graduating in 1953. In support of his application he offered testimony of his rabbi, his attorney, and the faculty, fellow students, and staff at the law school. No contrary evidence was offered. The bar committee nevertheless denied him admission: "Taking into consideration the use of aliases by the applicant, his former connection with subversive organizations, and his record of arrests, he has failed to satisfy the Board as to the requisite moral character." The Supreme Court of New Mexico upheld the denial. The Supreme Court reversed, saying:

> Any qualification must have a rational connection with the applicant's fitness or capacity to practice law . . . There is nothing in the record which suggests that Schware has engaged in any conduct in the past 15 years which reflects adversely on his character . . . During the period when Schware was a member, the Communist Party was a lawful political party . . . Assuming that some members of the Communist Party during the period from 1932 to 1940 had illegal aims and engaged in illegal activities, it cannot automatically be inferred that all members shared their evil purposes or participated in their illegal conduct . . . There is no evidence in the record which rationally justifies a finding that Schware was morally unfit to practice law.

353 U.S. at 239, 244, 246–47, 77 S.Ct. at 756, 759, 760.

The "rational connection" rule remains the law.

The more difficult issue was the constitutionality of questioning that sought to establish a connection between membership in the Communist Party and fitness to practice law. This issue first arose in Konigsberg v. State Bar of California, 353 U.S. 252, 77 S.Ct. 722 (1957) (*Konigsberg I*), decided the same day as *Schware*. In the hearing on his application for admission, Konigsberg presented favorable character evidence by law teachers, friends, a rabbi, and a monsignor. He was asked whether he had been a member of the Communist Party, but refused to answer on First Amendment grounds. The Bar Examiners declined to approve his application, grounding their decision on Konigsberg's failure affirmatively to establish his good character as distinct from his refusal to answer questions about his Party membership. The Supreme Court in a 5–4 decision reversed the denial of his application:

> Serious questions of elemental fairness would be raised if the Committee had excluded Konigsberg simply because he failed to answer questions without explicitly warning him that he could be barred for this reason alone . . .

> If . . . the Board barred Konigsberg solely because of his refusal to respond to its inquiries into his political associations and his opinions about matters of public interest, then we would be compelled to decide far-reaching and complex questions relating to freedom of speech, press and assembly.

353 U.S. at 261, 77 S.Ct. at 727.

The court's opinion interweaves three questions: (1) The burden of proof—whether Konigsberg had to show that there was no substantial doubt as to his character, or the Committee had to show there was such doubt; (2) The Constitutional propriety of the Committee asking about Konigsberg's membership in the Communist Party; and (3) The significance of such membership as proof of deficient moral character.

These questions could have been asked in this order: (1) Is present membership in the Communist Party, as of the early 1950s, evidence of deficient moral character? (2) Assuming present membership is such evidence, can the Bar Examiners ask the applicant whether he presently holds such membership? (3) If the applicant is asked the question and refuses to answer, has he failed to carry his burden of proof?

Resolution of the second and third questions seems not very difficult if the first question is resolved affirmatively—that membership in the Communist Party in the 1950s was probative of indifference to a lawyer's professional obligations. The argument for this affirmative was as follows: The Communist Party was committed to violent overthrow of capitalist regimes; membership in the Party constituted an affirmation of that commitment; and a person making that affirmation probably could not be relied on to represent clients "within the limits of the law." However, there were counter considerations. First, it does not follow that membership in an organization involves affirmation of all of the organization's purposes, nor does it follow that affirmation of a general political purpose (to overthrow capitalist regimes) signifies indifference to immediate legal obligations imposed by such a regime. Second, there is a First Amendment argument that, even if membership in the Communist Party is probative of a predisposition to ignore a lawyer's professional obligations, the fact of membership is constitutionally privileged information that the government cannot inquire into. Cf. NAACP v. Alabama, 357 U.S. 449, 78 S.Ct. 1163 (1958). That is, the bar examiners could no more ask an applicant to disclose membership in organizations than they could require him to incriminate himself. See Matter of Anonymous Attorneys, 41 N.Y.2d 506, 393 N.Y.S.2d 961, 362 N.E.2d 592 (1977), printed below. Third, disclosure of membership in the Communist Party, even if it did not preclude admission to the bar, could have disastrous effect on the applicant's professional career, a consideration not to be ignored. The Supreme Court in *Konigsberg I* did not address these issues, however, Justice Harlan in dissent said:

> The court decides the case as if the issue were whether the record contains evidence demonstrating as a factual matter that Konigsberg had a bad moral character. I do not think that is the issue. The question before us . . . is whether it violates the Fourteenth Amendment to decline to certify . . . an applicant who . . . [refuses] to answer questions relevant to his fitness under valid standards, and who is therefore deemed . . . to have failed to carry his burden of proof to establish that he is qualified.

> 353 U.S. at 279–280, 77 S.Ct. at 737.

On remand, the California Bar Examiners asked Konigsberg whether he was presently a member of the Communist Party, indicating clearly that refusal to answer would be regarded as obstruction of necessary inquiry into his fitness to practice law. Konigsberg refused to answer on the ground that the question was impermissible under the First Amendment. The Supreme Court by 5–4 vote affirmed denial of admission, Konigsberg v. State Bar of California, 366 U.S. 36, 81 S.Ct. 997 (1961) (*Konigsberg II*). In an opinion by Harlan, J., the Court held that the question of Party membership was legitimate even if its being asked might have some chilling effect on speech:

> General regulatory statutes, not intended to control the content of speech but incidentally limiting its unfettered exercise, have not been regarded as the type of law the First Amendment forbade Congress or the States to pass, when they have been found justified by subordinating valid governmental interests, prerequisite to constitutionality which has necessarily involved a weighing of the governmental interest involved . . .

> It would indeed be difficult to argue that a belief, firm enough to be carried over into advocacy, in the use of illegal means to change the form of the State or Federal Government is an unimportant consideration in determining the fitness of applicants for a

profession in whose hands so largely lies the safekeeping of this country's legal and political institutions.

366 U.S. at 50–52, 81 S.Ct. at 1007.

A case involving essentially the same issue, decided the same day as *Konigsberg II* by the same 5–4 vote, was In re Anastaplo, 366 U.S. 82, 81 S.Ct. 978 (1961). Justice Harlan there stated for the Court:

> Where, as with membership in the bar, the State may withhold a privilege available only to those possessing the requisite qualifications, it is of no constitutional significance whether the State's interrogation of an applicant on matters relevant to these qualifications—in this case Communist Party membership—is prompted by information which it already has about him from other sources, or arises merely from a good faith belief in the need for exploratory or testing qualification of the applicant.

366 U.S. at 90, 81 S.Ct. at 983.

Justice Black, along with Chief Justice Warren and Justices Douglas and Brennan, bitterly dissented in both cases, stating in *In re Anastaplo*:

> Consider the following remarks of Anastaplo to the Committee—remarks the sincerity of which the majority does not deny:
>
> > "I speak of a need to remind the bar of its traditions and to keep alive the spirit of dignified but determined advocacy and opposition. This is not only for the good of the bar, of course, but also because of what the bar means to American republican government. The bar when it exercises self-control is in a peculiar position to mediate between popular passions and informed and principled men, thereby upholding republican government. Unless there is this mediation, intelligent and responsible government is unlikely. The bar, furthermore, is in a peculiar position to apply to our daily lives the constitutional principles which nourish for this country its inner life. Unless there is this nourishment, a just and humane people is impossible. The bar is, in short, in a position to train and lead by precept and example the American people."
>
> These are not the words of a man who lacks devotion to "the law in its broadest sense."
>
> The majority, apparently considering this fact irrelevant because the State might possibly have an interest in learning more about its Bar applicants, decides that Anastaplo can properly be denied admission to the Bar by purporting to "balance" the interest of the State of Illinois in "having lawyers who are devoted to the law in its broadest sense" against the interest of Anastaplo and the public in protecting the freedoms of the First Amendment, concluding, as it usually does when it engages in this process, that "on balance" the interest of Illinois must prevail. If I had ever doubted that the "balancing test" comes close to being a doctrine of govern-

mental absolutism—that to "balance" an interest in individual liberty means almost inevitably to destroy that liberty—those doubts would have been dissipated by this case. For this so-called "balancing test" . . . here proves pitifully and pathetically inadequate to cope with an invasion of individual liberty so plainly unjustified that even the majority apparently feels compelled expressly to disclaim "any view upon the wisdom of the State's action."

366 U.S. at 110–111, 81 S.Ct. at 993–994 (Black, J., dissenting).

The issue came up for reconsideration in a set of three cases in 1971, Baird v. State Bar of Arizona, 401 U.S. 1, 91 S.Ct. 702 (1971); Application of Stolar, 401 U.S. 23, 91 S.Ct. 713 (1971); and Law Students Civil Rights Research Council v. Wadmond, 401 U.S. 154, 91 S.Ct. 720 (1971). All three cases were decided 5–4, with Justice Potter Stewart being the decisive vote. He wrote the opinion in Wadmond, stating:

It is . . . well settled that Bar examiners may ask about Communist affiliations as a preliminary to further inquiry into the nature of the association and may exclude an applicant for refusal to answer.

401 U.S. at 165–166, 91 S.Ct. at 728.

The relationship between organization memberships and fitness to practice law, however, is complicated even today. Consider whether it would be proper for the bar examiners to inquire into, or to attach significance to, membership in an anti-abortion organization that publicly professes "direct action" against abortion clinics.

There have been no subsequent Supreme Court decisions applying the "rational connection" standard to questions in character and fitness inquiries. Among the challenges that state courts have considered are to questions concerning homosexuality, In re N.R.S., 403 So.2d 1315 (Fla.1981) (impermissible to inquire into sexual preference), and psychological abnormalities, Florida Board of Bar Examiners Re: Applicant, 443 So.2d 77 (Fla.1983) (inquiry proper). Clearly proper subjects of inquiry include previous criminal convictions, financial dealings that have been legally questioned, and involvement in litigation.

Professor Rhode's comprehensive empirical study, supra, documents the character and fitness inquiry in operation. The following matters are considered significant but not decisive and hence a basis for more intensive inquiry: criminal record, drug or alcohol abuse, repeated traffic offenses, dishonesty in business transactions, plagiarism and other cheating in school, unauthorized practice of law, psychiatric treatment, and nondisclosure or false statements on the bar admission questionnaire. See 94 Yale L.J. at 533–536. These would all seem to comport with the "rational connection" standard. Professor Rhode's findings suggest that the character and fitness inquiry is generally administered on a sensible basis, if one that may involve exasperating detail. Perhaps the most serious criticism is not that the inquiry into character for admission to practice is absolutely too rigorous, but that it is far more rigorous than the standards used for disciplining those already inside the bar. See 94 Yale L.J. at 546.

Residency

Many states for many years required that a person seeking to be lawyer be a resident of the state, or affirm an intention to become a resident upon admission, or both. These restrictions were particularly rigorous in states adjacent to large metropolitan centers, the fear being competition from the city lawyers, and "sunshine" states such as Florida and Arizona, the fear being that senior lawyers from other states would come there to retire and engage in incidental practice. These restrictions were challenged on grounds of Equal Protection and the Privileges and Immunities Clause. In Supreme Court of New Hampshire v. Piper, 470 U.S. 274, 105 S.Ct. 1272 (1985), a requirement of residency for admission was held to violate the Privileges and Immunities Clause. In Supreme Court of Virginia v. Friedman, 487 U.S. 59, 108 S.Ct. 2260 (1988), on the same basis the Court held invalid a Virginia provision allowing a lawyer from another state to be admitted in Virginia by motion, without having to take the bar examination, only if the lawyer had become a resident and affirmed the intention to practice full time in Virginia. Then in Barnard v. Thorstenn, 109 S.Ct. 1294 (1989), the court invalidated a rule of the Virgin Islands requiring for admission that the applicant reside for a year in the Islands and affirm an intention to reside there. In this decision the Court said:

> Petitioners offer five justifications for the residency requirements of Rule 56(b), which track the reasons recited by the District Court. First, petitioners contend that the geographical isolation of the Virgin Islands, together with irregular airline and telephone service with the mainland United States, will make it difficult for nonresidents to attend court proceedings held with little advance notice. Second, petitioners cite the District Court's finding that the delay caused by trying to accommodate the schedules of nonresidents attorneys would increase the massive caseload under which that court suffers. Third, petitioners contend that delays in publication and lack of access to local statutes, regulations, and court opinions will prevent nonresident attorneys from maintaining an adequate level of competence in local law. Fourth, petitioners argue that the Virgin Islands Bar does not have the resources for adequate supervision of a nationwide bar membership. Finally, petitioners exert much energy arguing that the residency requirements of Rule 56(b) are necessary to apply Local Rule 16 in a strict and fair manner. That rule requires all active members of the Bar to represent indigent criminal defendants on a regular basis. See V.I. Code Ann., Tit. 5, App. V, Rule 16. We find none of these justifications sufficient to meet the Virgin Island's burden of demonstrating that the discrimination against nonresidents by Rule

56(b) is warranted by a substantial objective and bears a close or substantial relation to that objective.

109 S.Ct. at 1299.

Meanwhile, the Court invalidated a local rule of a United States District Court which imposed a residency requirement for admission to that federal court. The ground for the ruling was not the Privileges and Immunities Clause but the Court's inherent supervisory power over the lower federal courts. Frazier v. Heebe, 482 U.S. 641, 107 S.Ct. 2607 (1987). Taken together, the *Piper* line of cases seems to eliminate a residency requirement. However, a lawyer can be required to maintain an office where papers can be served on her. Generally see Note, Invalidation of Residency Requirements for Admission to the Bar: Opportunities for General Reform, 23 U.Rich.L.Rev. 231 (1989).

Admission Pro Hac Vice

By long established practice, a lawyer admitted in one jurisdiction may be permitted by a court of another jurisdiction to participate in a specific case. Normally, permission is sought through a motion by a lawyer already admitted to the court. This is called admission pro hac vice. A typical situation is bringing in a trial specialist from out of state to present a particularly difficult or important matter. Most courts have specific rules concerning such admissions and the rules often impose the requirement that a locally admitted lawyer also be associated in the case. See generally Brakel and Loh, Regulating the Multistate Practice of Law, 50 Wash.L.Rev. 699 (1975); Annot., 20 A.L.R. 4th 855 (1983).

In Leis v. Flynt, 439 U.S. 438, 99 S.Ct. 698 (1979), an out of state lawyer claimed a right to appear in behalf of a criminal defendant (Larry Flynt of *Hustler* fame) without being admitted pro hac vice, on the ground that the right to practice constituted a constitutionally protected interest that other states had to recognize. This contention was rejected. Pro hac vice admission is still required for a lawyer to appear in a court to which she has not been regularly admitted. However, a court's refusal to admit pro hac vice a lawyer who meets the standard requirements may amount to a violation of the client's constitutional right to be represented by a lawyer of her choice. It certainly could result in reversible error. See Herrmann v. Summer Plaza Corp., 201 Conn. 263, 513 A.2d 1211, 1214 (1986), quoting an earlier Connecticut decision:

The right to have counsel of one's own choice, although not absolute, is important enough to require a legitimate state interest before a person can be deprived of that right. See . . . United States v. Curcio, 694 F.2d 14, 23 (2d Cir.1982) . . . In this period of greater mobility among members of the bar and the public, and the corresponding growth in interstate business, a court should reluctantly deny an application to appear pro hac vice . . .

Unauthorized Practice of Law

FLORIDA BAR v. BRUMBAUGH

Supreme Court of Florida, 1978.
355 So.2d 1186.

PER CURIAM.

The Florida Bar has filed a petition charging Marilyn Brumbaugh with engaging in the unauthorized practice of law, and seeking a permanent injunction prohibiting her from further engaging in these allegedly unlawful acts. We have jurisdiction under our constitutional authority to adopt rules for the practice and procedure in all the courts of this state. Article V, Section 2(a), Florida Constitution (1968). We now issue an injunction, delineating in this opinion those acts of respondent which we deem to constitute the unauthorized practice of law, and ordering her to stop such activities.

Respondent, Marilyn Brumbaugh, is not and has never been a member of the Florida Bar, and is, therefore, not licensed to practice law within this state. She has advertised in various local newspapers as "Marilyn's Secretarial Service" offering to perform typing services for "Do–It–Yourself" divorces, wills, resumes, and bankruptcies. The Florida Bar charges that she performed unauthorized legal services by preparing for her customers those legal documents necessary in an uncontested dissolution of marriage proceeding and by advising her customers as to the costs involved and the procedures which should be followed in order to obtain a dissolution of marriage. For this service, Ms. Brumbaugh charges a fee of $50.

Of course, we must determine whether the Florida Bar has presented sufficient evidence in the record before us to prove that respondent has engaged in the unauthorized practice of law. But, in cases such as this, the Florida Supreme Court is not confined to act solely in its judicial capacity. In addition, it acts in its administrative capacity as chief policy maker, regulating the administration of the court system and supervising all persons who are engaged in rendering legal advice to members of the general public. Such authority carries with it the responsibility to perform this task in a way responsive to the needs and desires of our citizens. This principle has long been our goal. In State v. Sperry, 140 So.2d 587, 595 (Fla.1962), we noted:

> The reason for prohibiting the practice of law by those who have not been examined and found qualified to practice is frequently misunderstood. It is not done to aid or protect the members of the legal profession either in creating or maintaining a monopoly or closed shop. It is done to protect the public from being advised and represented in legal matters by unqualified persons over whom the judicial department can exercise little, if any, control in the matter of infractions of the code of conduct which, in the public interest, lawyers are bound to observe.

The Florida Bar as an agent of this Court, plays a large role in the enforcement of court policies and rules and has been active in regulating and disciplining unethical conduct by its members. Because of the natural tendency of all professions to act in their own self interest, however, this Court must closely scrutinize all regulations tending to limit competition in the delivery of legal services to the public, and determine whether or not such regulations are truly in the public interest. Indeed, the active role of state supreme courts in the regulation of the practice of law (when such regulation is subject to pointed reexamination by the state court as policy maker) is accorded great deference and exemption from federal interference under the Sherman Act. Bates v. State Bar of Arizona, 433 U.S. 350, 97 S.Ct. 2691, 2698, 53 L.Ed.2d 810 (1977).

The United States Supreme Court has recently decided issues which may drastically change the practice of law throughout the country, especially with regards to advertising and price competition among attorneys. Bates v. State Bar of Arizona, supra; Goldfarb, et al. v. Virginia State Bar, 421 U.S. 773, 95 S.Ct. 2004, 44 L.Ed.2d 572 (1975). In addition, the Supreme Court has affirmed the fundamental constitutional right of all persons to represent themselves in court proceedings, Faretta v. California, 422 U.S. 806, 95 S.Ct. 2525, 45 L.Ed.2d 562 (1975). In *Faretta*, the Supreme Court emphasized that an attorney is merely an assistant who helps a citizen protect his legal rights and present his case to the courts. A person should not be forced to have an attorney represent his legal interests if he does not consent to such representation. It is imperative for us to analyze these cases and determine how their holdings and the policies behind them affect our regulation of the legal profession in this state.

With regard to the charges made against Marilyn Brumbaugh, this Court appointed a referee to receive evidence and to make findings of fact, conclusions of law, and recommendations as to the disposition of the case. The referee found that respondent, under the guise of a "secretarial" or "typing" service prepares, for a fee, all papers deemed by her to be needed for the pleading, filing, and securing of a dissolution of marriage, as well as detailed instructions as to how the suit should be filed, notice served, hearings set, trial conducted, and the final decree secured. The referee also found that in one instance, respondent prepared a quit claim deed in reference to the marital property of the parties. The referee determined that respondent's contention that she merely operates a typing service is rebutted by numerous facts in evidence. Ms. Brumbaugh has no blank forms either to sell or to fill out. Rather, she types up the documents for her customers after they have asked her to prepare a petition or an entire set of dissolution of marriage papers. Prior to typing up the papers, respondent asks her customers whether custody, child support, or alimony is involved. Respondent has four sets of dissolution of marriage papers, and she chooses which set is appropriate for the particular customer. She then types out those papers, filling in the blank spaces with the appropriate information. Respondent instructs her customers how the papers are to be signed, where they are to be filed, and how the customer should arrange for a final hearing.

Marilyn Brumbaugh, who is representing herself in proceedings before this Court, has made various objections to the procedure and findings of fact of the referee. Respondent alleges that the referee has an inherent conflict of interest because he is a lawyer and a member of The Florida Bar. She asserts that "all lawyers have a property interest in this case, because they have been making money, running typing services, without proper licenses." She further alleges that the referee did not provide her with a proper hearing, that he threw her in jail for pleading the Fifth Amendment, and denied her her constitutional right to a jury trial. Respondent argues that she has never held herself out as an attorney, and has never professed to have legal skills. She does not give advice, but acts merely as a secretary. She is a licensed counselor, and asserts the right to talk to people and to let her customers make decisions for themselves. Finally, respondent contends that her civil rights have been violated, and that she has been denied the right to make an honest living.

This case does not arise out of a complaint by any of Ms. Brumbaugh's customers as to improper advice or unethical conduct. It has been initiated by members of The Florida Bar who believe her to be practicing law without a license. The evidence introduced at the hearing below shows that none of respondent's customers believed that she was an attorney, or that she was acting as an attorney in their behalf. Respondent's advertisements clearly addressed themselves to people who wish to do their own divorces. These customers knew that they had to have "some type of papers" to file in order to obtain their dissolution of marriage. Respondent never handled contested divorces. During the past two years respondent has assisted several hundred customers in obtaining their own divorces. The record shows that while some of her customers told respondent exactly what they wanted, generally respondent would ask her customers for the necessary information needed to fill out the divorce papers, such as the names and addresses of the parties, the place and duration of residency in this state, whether there was any property settlement to be resolved, or any determination as to custody and support of children. Finally, each petition contained the bare allegation that the marriage was irretrievably broken. Respondent would then inform the parties as to which documents needed to be signed, by whom, how many copies of each paper should be filed, where and when they should be filed, the costs involved, and what witness testimony is necessary at the court hearing. Apparently, Ms. Brumbaugh no longer informs the parties verbally as to the proper procedures for the filing of the papers, but offers to let them copy papers described as "suggested procedural education."

The Florida Bar argues that the above activities of respondent violate the rulings of this Court in The Florida Bar v. American Legal and Business Forms, Inc., 274 So.2d 225 (Fla.1973), and The Florida Bar

v. Stupica, 300 So.2d 683 (Fla.1974). In those decisions we held that it is lawful to sell to the public printed legal forms, provided they do not carry with them what purports to be instructions on how to fill out such forms or how to use them. We stated that legal advice is inextricably involved in the filling out and advice as to how to use such legal forms, and therein lies the danger of injury or damage to the public if not properly performed in accordance with law. In *Stupica,* supra, this Court rejected the rationale of the New York courts in New York County Lawyer's Association v. Dacey, 28 A.D.2d 161, 283 N.Y.S.2d 984, reversed and dissenting opinion adopted 21 N.Y.2d 694, 287 N.Y.S.2d 422, 234 N.E.2d 459 (N.Y.1967), which held that the publication of forms and instructions on their use does not constitute the unauthorized practice of law if these instructions are addressed to the public in general rather than to a specific individual legal problem. The Court in *Dacey* stated that the possibility that the principles or rules set forth in the text may be accepted by a particular reader as solution to his problem, does not mean that the publisher is practicing law. Other states have adopted the principle of law set forth in *Dacey,* holding that the sale of legal forms with instructions for their use does not constitute unauthorized practice of law. See State Bar of Michigan v. Cramer, 399 Mich. 116, 249 N.W.2d 1 (1976); Oregon State Bar v. Gilchrist, 272 Or. 552, 538 P.2d 913 (1975). However, these courts have prohibited all personal contact between the service providing such forms and the customer, in the nature of consultation, explanation, recommendation, advice, or other assistance in selecting particular forms, in filling out any part of the forms, suggesting or advising how the forms should be used in solving the particular problems.

Although persons not licensed as attorneys are prohibited from practicing law within this state, it is somewhat difficult to define exactly what constitutes the practice of law in all instances. This Court has previously stated that:

> . . . . if the giving of such advice and performance of such services affect important rights of a person under the law, and if the reasonable protection of the rights and property of those advised and served requires that the persons giving such advice possess legal skill and a knowledge of the law greater than that possessed by the average citizen, then the giving of such advice and the performance of such services by one for another as a course of conduct constitute the practice of law.

Sperry, supra, 140 So.2d at 591.

This definition is broad and is given content by this Court only as it applies to specific circumstances of each case. We agree that "any attempt to formulate a lasting, all encompassing definition of 'practice of law' is doomed to failure 'for the reason that under our system of jurisprudence such practice must necessarily change with the ever-changing business and social order.'" State Bar of Michigan v. Cramer, supra, 399 Mich. 116, 249 N.W.2d at 7.

In determining whether a particular act constitutes the practice of law, our primary goal is the protection of the public. However, any limitations on the free practice of law by all persons necessarily affects important constitutional rights. Our decision here certainly affects the constitutional rights of Marilyn Brumbaugh to pursue a lawful occupation or business. Prior v. White, 132 Fla. 1, 180 So. 347 (1938); State ex rel. Fulton v. Ives, 123 Fla. 401, 167 So. 394 (1936); State ex rel. Davis v. Rose, 97 Fla. 710, 122 So. 225 (1929). Our decision also affects respondent's First Amendment rights to speak and print what she chooses. In addition, her customers and potential customers have the constitutional right of self representation, *Faretta,* supra, and the right of privacy inherent in the marriage relationship, Roe v. Wade, 410 U.S. 113, 93 S.Ct. 705, 35 L.Ed.2d 147 (1973); Boddie v. Connecticut, 401 U.S. 371; 91 S.Ct. 780, 28 L.Ed.2d 113 (1971). All citizens in our state are also guaranteed access to our courts by Article I, Section 21, Florida Constitution (1968). Although it is not necessary for us to provide affirmative assistance in order to ensure meaningful access to the courts to our citizens, as it is necessary for us to do for those incarcerated in our state prison system, Bounds v. Smith, 430 U.S. 817, 97 S.Ct. 1491, 52 L.Ed.2d 72 (1977), we should not place any unnecessary restrictions upon that right. We should not deny persons who wish to represent themselves access to any source of information which might be relevant in the preparation of their cases. There are numerous texts in our state law libraries which describe our substantive and procedural law, purport to give legal advice to the reader as to choices that should be made in various situations, and which also contain sample legal forms which a reader may use as an example. We generally do not restrict the access of the public to these law libraries, although many of the legal texts are not authored by attorneys licensed to practice in this state. These texts do not carry with them any guarantees of accuracy, and only some of them purport to update statements which have been modified by subsequently enacted statutes and recent case law.

The policy of this Court should continue to be one of encouraging persons who are unsure of their legal rights and remedies to seek legal assistance from persons licensed by us to practice law in this state. However, in order to make an intelligent decision as whether or not to engage the assistance of an attorney, a citizen must be allowed access to information which will help determine the complexity of the legal problem. Once a person has made the decision to represent himself, we should not enforce any unnecessary regulation which might tend to hinder the exercise of this constitutionally protected right. However, any restriction of constitutional rights must be "narrowly drawn to express only the legitimate state interests at stake." *Roe v. Wade,* supra, NAACP v. Button, 371 U.S. 415, 438, 83 S.Ct. 328, 340, 9 L.Ed.2d 405 (1963). "And if there are other reasonable ways to achieve those goals with a lesser burden on constitutionally protected activity, a state may not choose the way of greater interference. If it acts at all, it must choose less drastic means. Shelton v. Tucker, 364 U.S. 479, 488, 81 S.Ct. 247, 252, 5 L.Ed.2d 231 (1960).

It is also important for us to consider the legislative statute governing dissolution of marriage in resolving the question of what constitutes the practice of law in this area. Florida's "no fault" dissolution of marriage statute clearly has the remedial purpose of simplifying the dissolution of marriage whenever possible. Section 61.001, Florida Statutes (1975) states:

(1) This chapter shall be liberally construed and applied to promote its purposes.

(2) Its purposes are:

(a) To preserve the integrity of marriage and to safeguard meaningful family relationships;

(b) To promote the amicable settlement of disputes that have arisen between parties to a marriage;

(c) To mitigate the potential harm to the spouses and their children caused by the process of legal dissolution of marriage.

Families usually undergo tremendous financial hardship when they decide to dissolve their marital relationships. The Legislature simplified procedures so that parties would not need to bear the additional burden of expensive legal fees where they have agreed to the settlement of their property and the custody of their children. This Court should not place unreasonable burdens upon the obtaining of such divorces, especially where both parties consent to the dissolution.

Present dissolution procedures in uncontested situations involve a very simplified method of asserting certain facts required by statute, notice to the other parties affected, and a simple hearing where the trial court may hear proof and make inquiries as to the facts asserted in those pleadings.

The legal forms necessary to obtain such an uncontested dissolution of marriage are susceptible of standardization. This Court has allowed the sale of legal forms on this and other subjects, provided that they do not carry with them what purports to be instructions on how to fill out such forms or how they are to be used. *The Florida Bar v. American Legal and Business Forms, Inc.*, supra; *The Florida Bar v. Stupica*, supra. These decisions should be reevaluated in light of those recent decisions in other states which have held that the sale of forms necessary to obtain a divorce, together with any related textual instructions directed towards the general public, does not constitute the practice of law. The reasons for allowing the sale of such legal publications which contain sample forms to be used by individuals who wish to represent themselves are persuasive. *State Bar of Michigan v. Cramer*, supra, reasoned that such instructional material should be no more objectionable than any other publication placed into the stream of commerce which purports to offer general advice on common problems and does not purport to give a person advice on a specific problem particular to a designated or readily identified person. In Bates v. State Bar of Arizona, 433 U.S. 350, 364, 97 S.Ct. 2691, 2699, 53 L.Ed.2d 810 (1977) the Supreme Court discussed at length the substantial interests in the free flow of commercial speech. The Court said that the choice between the dangers of suppressing information and the dangers arising from its free flow is precisely the choice "that the First Amendment makes for us." There the Court, in approving legal advertising, reasoned that the state cannot assume a paternalistic approach which rests in large part on its citizens being kept in ignorance. The Court stated that we must assume that this information is not in itself harmful, and "that people will perceive their own best interests if only they are well enough informed, and that the best means to that end is to open the channels of communication rather than to close them."

Although there is a danger that some published material might give false or misleading information, that is not a sufficient reason to justify its total ban. We must assume that our citizens will generally use such publications for what they are worth in the preparation of their cases, and further assume that most persons will not rely on these materials in the same way they would rely on the advice of an attorney or other persons holding themselves out as having expertise in the area. The tendency of persons seeking legal assistance to place their trust in the individual purporting to have expertise in the area necessitates this Court's regulation of such attorney-client relationships, so as to require that persons giving such advice have at least a minimal amount of legal training and experience. Although Marilyn Brumbaugh never held herself out as an attorney, it is clear that her clients placed some reliance upon her to properly prepare the necessary legal forms for their dissolution proceedings. To this extent we believe that Ms. Brumbaugh overstepped proper bounds and engaged in the unauthorized practice of law. We hold that Ms. Brumbaugh, and others in similar situations, may sell printed material purporting to explain legal practice and procedure to the public in general and she may sell sample legal forms. To this extent we limit our prior holdings in *Stupica* and *American Legal and Business Forms, Inc.* Further, we hold that it is not improper for Marilyn Brumbaugh to engage in a secretarial service, typing such forms for her clients, provided that she only copy the information given to her in writing by her clients. In addition, Ms. Brumbaugh may advertise her business activities of providing secretarial and notary services and selling legal forms and general printed information. However, Marilyn Brumbaugh must not, in conjunction with her business, engage in advising clients as to the various remedies available to them, or otherwise assist them in preparing those forms necessary for a dissolution proceeding. More specifically, Marilyn Brumbaugh may not make inquiries nor answer questions from her clients as to the particular forms which might be necessary, how best to fill out such forms, where to properly file such forms, and how to present necessary evidence at the court hearings. Our specific holding with regard to the dissolution of marriage also applies to other unauthorized legal assistance such as the preparation of wills or real estate transaction documents. While Marilyn Brumbaugh may legally sell forms in these areas, and type up instruments which have been completed by clients, she must not engage in personal legal assistance in conjunction with her business activities, including the correction of errors and omissions.

Accordingly, having defined the limits within which Ms. Brumbaugh and those engaged in similar activities may conduct their business without engaging in the unauthorized practice of law, the rule to show cause is dissolved.

It is so ordered.

OVERTON, C.J., and ADKINS, BOYD and HATCHETT, JJ., concur.

. . .

Legal Remedies Against Unauthorized Law Practice

Given that the practice of law is a licensed vocation, it follows that one who is not a licensed lawyer may be subject to legal consequences for providing legal assistance to others. The minimum legal consequence would be application of the law of fraud. Thus, a person who is not a licensed lawyer may not represent herself as being a lawyer. See, e.g., People v. Schreiber, 250 Ill. 345, 95 N.E. 189 (1911). A further legal consequence is that an unlicensed person rendering legal services would be held to a licensed lawyer's standard of care and competence, whatever what might be. See Biakanja v. Irving, 49 Cal.2d 647, 320 P.2d 16 (1958) (will drafting). Another consequence could be that legal remedies could not be invoked by such a person to recover fees for the services rendered. See, e.g., Ames v. Gilman, 51 Mass. (10 Metc.) 239 (1845); cf. Gesellschaft Fur Drafhtlose Telegraphie M.B.H. v. Brown, 78 F.2d 410 (D.C.App.1935) (lawyer barred from recovering fees for services rendered in violation of ethical standards). The unlicensed person could be enjoined from practicing law on the principle supporting injunction against a public nuisance. See, e.g., State v. Scopel, 316 S.W.2d 515 (Mo.1958) (injunction against unlicensed practice of medicine); Prosser and Keeton on Torts § 90 (5th ed. 1984). Practicing law without a license has been treated as contempt of court, e.g., In re Root, 173 Kan. 512, 249 P.2d 628 (1952). Finally, it may be defined as a crime. See Rhode, Policing the Professional Monopoly, 34 Stan.L.Rev. 1, 11 n. 39 (1981) (collection of state statutes).

What is "Practice of Law"?

Observe that Brumbaugh did not present herself as a lawyer, quite the contrary. Nor was it contended that her services, whatever they were, fell below the standard of care and competence of lawyers performing services in similar matters. There is no indication that Brumbaugh had sought to use legal remedies to collect for her services;

apparently her customers were satisfied enough to have paid her. The court does not say so, but Florida makes practicing law without a license a criminal offense. West's Fla.Stat.Ann. § 454.23. That legislative proscription is an adequate basis for injunctive relief according to general legal principles, see Prosser and Keeton on Torts, supra.

The difficult question concerning unauthorized practice of law is that of defining the activities which constitute the "practice of law," not of fashioning remedies against it. The Model Rules of Professional Conduct and the Code of Professional Conduct prohibit a lawyer from assisting the unauthorized practice of law. See Rule 5.5; DR 3–101(A). These provisions do not define the term, however. That has been a matter of ad hoc decision, as the opinion in *Brumbaugh* indicates.

The best general accounts of the bar's attempts to suppress unauthorized practice of law are Christensen, The Unauthorized Practice of Law, 1980 Am.Bar Found.Res.J. 159, primarily an historical analysis, and Rhode, Policing the Professional Monopoly, supra, primarily an empirical study of contemporary bar association enforcement practice.

Christensen's study records that systematic efforts to suppress activities asserted to constitute the practice of law began in the early 20th Century and focussed on title companies. The title companies examined real estate titles and issued policies insuring against defects in title in connection with conveyances. This service directly competed with the function of lawyers who issued opinions as to title in connection with conveyances. In the 1920s the focus was on automobile liability insurance companies that sought to provide legal representation to their insureds through salaried staff attorneys in defending auto accident litigation. This competed with independent law firms that undertook such representation on retainer by the insurance companies. Other conflicts concerned the activities of collection agencies in bringing litigation to enforce debts, the activities of accountants in preparation of tax returns, and the activities of real estate brokers in closing real estate transactions. A recent case involves pension fund counseling. See In re Florida Bar, 355 So.2d 766 (Fla.1978).

The organized bar also negotiated "treaties" with other professional associations, such as real estate brokers and accountants, to define the boundaries of the respective areas of practice. The treaty-making process has succumbed to threats from the Justice Department that such arrangements are in restraint of trade. See Wolfram, Modern Legal Ethics 826 (1986). The ABA does, however, maintain contact with representatives from these other professions through the ABA National Conference Groups, the "groups" (committees) include the National Conference Group of: Lawyers and Certified Public Accountants; Lawyers and Collection Agencies; Lawyers and Life Insurance Companies; and Lawyers and Realtors. Each of these groups includes an equal number of ABA representatives and representatives of the relevant other professional associations. For example, the group on

Lawyers and Realtors Agencies has five ABA representatives and five representatives from the National Association of Realtors.

The boundaries of "practice of law" for purposes of enforcing the licensure requirement remain very indistinct and vary from one state to another. The location of the boundaries is the product of interaction between the organized bar and competing service-providers, state law as formulated by state courts, constitutional law as formulated by the Supreme Courts, inter-professional detente, and market forces. In Florida and Colorado, for example, the bar associations have been fairly aggressive, whereas in some other jurisdictions they have been nearly dormant. In general, the state courts act only in response to bar association initiatives, as in *Brumbaugh.* When the state courts have been asked to suppress activity as unauthorized practice of law, they have in general sided with the bar's position. The scope of state proscription of unauthorized practice had been significantly limited by Supreme Court decisions applying the First Amendment, to provision of legal services, as the *Brumbaugh* opinion recognizes.

Observe that deference to First Amendment concerns led the court in *Brumbaugh* to recognize that a nonlawyer could disseminate written "how to" materials, including not only legal forms but instructions about using the forms. However, she may not give oral advice. Is oral utterance not protected by the First Amendment? What if Brumbaugh had made video tapes of "instructions"? Interestingly, concerning the problem of lawyer solicitation of clients, the Supreme Court has drawn a line between sending out written materials to clients, which is protected by the First Amendment and personal contact with clients, which is not. See *Shapero v. Kentucky State Bar,* printed below.

Case law has said that a matter having legal ramifications requires a lawyer's involvement only when it involves "difficult or doubtful legal questions." Gardner v. Conway, 234 Minn. 468, 48 N.W.2d 788 (1951); Agran v. Shapiro, 127 Cal.App.2d Supp. 807, 273 P.2d 619 (1954). Suppose Brumbaugh had made an arrangement with a lawyer under which any of her clients who had questions about filling out the forms could call the lawyer. Would participating in such an arrangement constitute a violation on the part of the lawyer of M.R. 5.5? That Rule provides that a lawyer may not assist a person who is not a member of the bar in the performance of an activity that constitutes the unauthorized practice of law.

Could a lawyer operate a service like that which Brumbaugh provided, calling it a "People's Law Center" or the like, having all intake and basic work done by paralegals such as Brumbaugh, and having a lawyer involved only when the paralegal considers such involvement necessary? Many law firms operate a high volume practice in such matters as divorce, real estate closings, workers' compensation claims, and bankruptcy. In these firms, and in legal services organizations representing the poor, intake and basic work is done by paralegals, with the lawyers involved only as necessary. Compare the Comment to M.R. 5.3:

> Lawyers generally employ assistants in their practice, including secretaries, law student interns, and paraprofessionals. Such assistants, whether employees or independent contractors, act for the lawyer in rendition of the lawyer's professional services.

Why didn't Brumbaugh get together with a lawyer to set up her service on such a basis? Perhaps it was because she loathed lawyers. Perhaps it was also because of the prohibition in M.R. 5.4, and the substantially identical provisions of DR 3–102(A) and DR 3–103(A), which prohibit a lawyer from sharing "legal fees" with a nonlawyer or forming a partnership with a nonlawyer. As a nonlawyer, she could have been an employee of a law firm but not a partner.

There is reason to think that potential clients, particularly those of lower and middle socio-economic status, fear lawyers and are quite unsure how to deal with them. That fear may have been why Brumbaugh's service appealed to her customers. Does the court take that possibility into account? What could be done to respond to that kind of fear?

"Unauthorized" Practice of Business Law

It is well known that all large accounting firms, including "the big eight," have large inhouse legal staffs. These lawyers help in the services that the accounting firms provide their clients. It is well known that all large banks have legal departments that help in the financial services that banks provide their customers. It is well known that all large corporations have legal departments that help in corporate operations. All these forms of legal service give legal shape to transactions involving the clients or customers of these organizations.

Are these business organizations involved in the "unauthorized practice of law"? The technical answer has been that the corporation is engaged in unauthorized practice if its lawyers provide legal assistance to *others,* such as the corporation's customers. However, the corporation can provide legal assistance to *itself* without thereby engaging in practice of law. This conclusion has never been fully reconciled with the proposition that law department lawyers are treated as full-fledged practitioners for purposes of the attorney-client privilege. That is, corporate law department attorneys are regarded as rendering legal advice to someone (the corporation) for purposes of the attorney-client privilege, but are not regarded as providing legal services to that someone for purposes of the unauthorized practice of law prohibition. See Upjohn Co. v. United States, 449 U.S. 383, 101 S.Ct. 677 (1981).

There is, however, a political explanation of why accounting firms, banks and corporations are allowed to employ lawyers as they do. "In house" legal services are regarded as more efficient by the businesses that pay for them and these businesses have enough political clout to block the bar from interfering. Until the 1950s, the bar maintained substantial influence in defining what is "the practice of law." However, in the early 1960s the bar suffered defeats from which lessons could be learned. A well publicized instance is concisely described in Marks, The Lawyers and the Realtors: Arizona's Experience, 49 A.B.A.J. 139 (1963) *:

> For many years real estate brokers in Arizona have prepared instruments incidental to real estate sales; the conventional deposit receipt and agreement, serving as the preliminary agreement between the parties; the deed, and the note and mortgage or contract for the sale of real estate; and sundry other documents. Title insurance is used extensively in Arizona and the title companies, when employed as escrow agents by the parties, have often prepared the instruments of conveyance . . .

> The companion cases of State Bar of Arizona v. Arizona Land Title & Trust Company and Lohse v. Hoffman [90 Ariz. 76, 366 P.2d 1 (1961), opinion on rehearing, 91 Ariz. 293, 371 P.2d 1020 (1962)] . . . were commenced by the integrated State Bar of Arizona, and certain attorneys individually and as members of the State Bar Committee on Unauthorized Practice, as plaintiffs, against five land title and trust companies and a real estate firm, as respective defendants in the two actions.

> The complaint against the title companies alleged that the defendants, acting through their employed attorneys and other agents, in connection with the conduct of their business, had been regularly and continuously preparing, drafting and formulating documents affecting title to real property for their "clients, patrons and customers" and giving legal advice regarding such transactions and instruments, all of which constituted the unauthorized practice of law . . .

> A unanimous court held for the Bar on all issues . . .

> The impact of the decision was explosive on both sides; the Bar hailing it as a colossus of progress in the field of unauthorized practice, and the realtors roundly condemning it as an infamous fiat that would result in the elimination of their livelihoods.

> The realtors reacted swiftly with a radical and novel device: They obtained 107,420 signatures on an initiative petition designed to place on the November ballot the following proposed amendment to the Constitution of the State of Arizona:

> Section 1: Any person holding a valid license as a real estate broker or a real estate salesman regularly issued by the Arizona State Real Estate Department when acting in such capacity as broker or salesman for the parties, or agent for one of the parties to a sale, exchange or trade, or the renting and leasing of property, shall have the right to draft or fill out and

complete, without charge, any and all instruments, incident thereto including, but not limited to, preliminary purchase agreements and earnest money receipts, deeds, mortgages, leases, assignments, releases, contracts for sale of realty, and bills of sale . . .

The basic [argument] of the realtors was:

1. Brokers have been preparing instruments for years without cost to the public, and doing so competently.

2. Lawyers are primarily interested in raising their incomes through the vehicle of forcing parties to real estate transactions to employ them.

3. This is only the beginning of an onslaught by the Bar against victims of the unauthorized practice drive: insurance companies, banks, accountants, architects, etc., will soon be attacked.

4. By its opposition to the proposed amendment the organized Bar seeks to deprive parties to a transaction of their freedom of choice to employ attorneys or not, according to their wishes.

5. The cost of real estate transactions would be unnecessarily increased to benefit lawyers, at the public's expense.

The thrust of the Bar's counterattack was:

1. The state constitution should not be corrupted by turning it into a vehicle for promoting special interests.

2. Realtors are legally untrained and therefore incompetent to prepare instruments of conveyance. The public interest is of paramount importance.

3. The real motive of the realtors is to enact into law a system which will make it less likely that a sale might be lost because of the intervention of an attorney's advice.

4. Lawyers earn relatively small fees in connection with the typical residential or small business transaction (which would be most affected by the amendment). If the brokers are really interested in saving the public's money, let them reduce their huge commissions.

5. Conversely, the larger professional fees are to be earned as a result of litigation due to improperly prepared instruments.

Each side drew its allies: The title companies, as parties in the actions, supported the amendment. The Arizona Association of Certified Public Accountants supported the Bar . . .

On November 6, 1962, the controversial amendment was passed by an overwhelming majority of the votes. [For the amendment 224,177; against the amendment 61,316.]

. . .

Compare the political arguments in the Arizona Constitutional initiative, described above, with the legal arguments in the court's opinion in *Brumbaugh.*

Meeting Lawyer's Standard of Competence

Ms. Brumbaugh could probably prove that her services met the standard of competence of the practicing bar in the kind of services she was providing. If she could, what is the objection to her providing those services?

B. DISCIPLINARY ENFORCEMENT

Disciplinary Procedure

Introductory Note

The old regime of disciplinary procedure is described in Hazard and Beard, A Lawyer's Privilege Against Self–Incrimination in Professional Disciplinary Proceedings, 96 Yale L.J. 1060, 1063–65 (1987):

> Since the beginning of the nineteenth century, most American jurisdictions have required one who acts as a lawyer for others to be licensed. In the older parlance, and in the Hohfeldian sense, the practice of law is a "privilege," i.e., a capacity that is not an incident of citizenship but is conferred by law on a limited number of people who meet specified requirements . . .
>
> The term "privilege" has long been used as a predicate in analysis of the rules governing both admission to practice and lawyer discipline. The leading treatise on law practice of the early twentieth century . . . stated:
>
>> The right to practice law is not a natural inherent right, but one which may be exercised only upon proof of fitness, through evidence of the possession of satisfactory legal attainments and fair character. The privilege of practicing law is not open to all, but is a special personal franchise limited to persons of good moral character, with special qualifications . . . [E. Thornton, A Treatise on Attorneys at Law 22–23 (1914)].
>
> Under traditional legal doctrine, this characterization implied that constitutional law would require only a modicum of procedural formality for revocation of an attorney's license . . .
>
> According to Thornton, a petition for disbarment was to set forth verified allegations specifying with reasonable particularity the misconduct for which disbarment was sought. If the court found the allegations sufficient in law, it would ordinarily issue an order against the lawyer in question, directing him to show cause why he should not be disbarred. The burden of proof thus was on the attorney to prove his innocence. There was little or no pretrial discovery. Appellate review was nominally available, but the tenor of the decisions suggests that a lawyer found guilty of an offense

warranting disbarment had little chance of obtaining reversal on either substantive or procedural grounds . . .

The Supreme Court has considered remarkably few cases involving lawyer disciplinary proceedings, particularly compared with the number of bar admission cases it has considered. This suggests that the bar itself supports protective procedural standards in disciplinary matters, whatever its views might be on the rights of new applicants. The principal Supreme Court cases are *Ruffalo* and *Spevack v. Klein.*

In re Ruffalo, 390 U.S. 544, 88 S.Ct. 1222 (1968), involved charges that the respondent lawyer solicited personal injury claims to be brought under the Federal Employers Liability Act, and hired a railroad employee to investigate claims against the railroad by which the investigator was employed. The Court invalidated a disbarment based on a charge that was added only after the evidence had been received at the disciplinary hearing:

> [The lawyer] is entitled to procedural due process, which includes fair notice of the charge . . . These are adversary proceedings of a quasi-criminal nature . . . The charge must be known before the proceedings commence. They become a trap if . . . the charges are amended on the basis of testimony of the accused. He can then be given no opportunity to expunge the earlier statements and start afresh.

390 U.S. at 550–551, 88 S.Ct. at 1225–26.

Spevack v. Klein, 385 U.S. 511, 87 S.Ct. 625 (1967), held that a lawyer could not be disbarred for refusing to produce records in a disciplinary proceeding concerning solicitation of personal injury cases. The decision rested on the ground that the privilege against self-incrimination of the Fifth Amendment conferred protection against being compelled to give evidence in a disciplinary matter that could expose the lawyer to incrimination in a criminal prosecution. The premise was that the 5th Amendment protects against being compelled to produce records, because producing records is in effect being "compelled . . . to be a witness against himself" within the 5th Amendment. That premise, however, has since been overruled by Fisher v. United States, 425 U.S. 391, 96 S.Ct. 1569 (1976), see Chapter 4 above. However, still apparently sound are the propositions in *Spevack* that (1) a lawyer cannot be disciplined for failure to respond in a disciplinary proceeding when the failure consists of invoking a constitutional privilege, and (2) the Fifth Amendment may be invoked in a disciplinary proceeding to avoid giving incriminating testimony.

Lawyer disciplinary procedure now adheres to a "due process" model. In most jurisdictions, the procedure is similar to a civil proceeding tried to a judge rather than a jury, with a preliminary prosecutorial review to determine probable cause. Hazard and Beard, supra, 96 Yale L.J. at 1066–67:

> First, there is a required screening by the disciplinary agency to determine whether lodging a formal charge would be warranted.

Functionally, this resembles the probable cause hearing in criminal procedure. It screens out those complaints for which the evidence is insufficient to get to a trier of fact, and synthesizes the evidence when it meets the sufficiency test, in the latter case laying the foundation for possible "plea bargaining." The second variation from the civil procedure model concerns discovery. In some jurisdictions, the accused lawyer has the same rights of discovery as are available in civil actions in the trial court of general jurisdiction, but the prevailing pattern gives the accused only informal access to the prosecution's dossier. Third, except in Texas and Georgia, there is no right to a jury trial.

The prevailing model thus may be described as a relatively formal version of administrative law procedure. Its elements include:

— The benefit of pre-charge screening by the disciplinary enforcement agency;

— The right to notice and a statement of the charge or grievance;

— The right to formal or informal discovery;

— The right to assistance of counsel;

— The rights to subpoena witnesses and evidence, to cross-examine adverse witnesses, and to exclude evidence inadmissible under the rules of evidence;

— The requirement of proof by a preponderance of the evidence or, in some cases, by clear and convincing evidence; and

— The right to judicial review.

A model procedure recommended by the American Bar Association has been widely adopted, with relatively minor variations from state to state. See Am.Bar Ass'n, Standards for Lawyer Discipline and Disability Proceedings (1979).

Typical of the disciplinary structure and procedure is that of New Jersey, described in Middlesex County Ethics Committee v. Garden State Bar Ass'n, 457 U.S. 423, 425–427, 102 S.Ct. 2515, 2518–19 (1982):

The Constitution of New Jersey charges the State Supreme Court with the responsibility for licensing and disciplining attorneys admitted to practice in the State. Art. 6, Sec. 2, Par. 3. Under the rules established by the New Jersey Supreme Court, promulgated pursuant to its constitutional authority, a complaint moves through a three-tier procedure. First, local District Ethics Committees appointed by the State Supreme Court are authorized to receive complaints relating to claimed unethical conduct by an attorney. New Jersey Court Rule 1:20–2(d). At least two of the minimum of eight members of the District Ethics Committee must be nonattorneys. Complaints are assigned to an attorney member of the Committee to report and make a recommendation. Rule 1:20–2(h). The decision whether to proceed with the complaint is made by the person who chairs the Ethics Committee. If a complaint is issued by the Ethics Committee it must state the name of the Complainant, describe the claimed improper conduct, cite the relevant rules, and state, if known, whether the same or a similar complaint has been considered by any other Ethics Committee. The attorney whose conduct is challenged is served with the complaint and has 10 days to answer.

Unless good cause appears for referring the complaint to another Committee member, each complaint is referred to the member of the Committee who conducted the initial investigation for review and further investigation, if necessary. The Committee member submits a written report stating whether a prima facie indication of unethical or unprofessional conduct has been demonstrated. The report is then evaluated by the chairman of the Ethics Committee to determine whether a prima facie case exists. Absent a prima facie showing, the complaint is summarily dismissed. If a prima facie case is found, a formal hearing on the complaint is held before three or more members of the Ethics Committee, a majority of whom must be attorneys. The lawyer who is charged with unethical conduct may have counsel, discovery is available, and all witnesses are sworn. The panel is required to prepare a written report with its findings of fact and conclusions. The full Committee, following the decision of the panel, has three alternatives. The Committee may dismiss the complaint, prepare a private letter of reprimand, or prepare a presentment to be forwarded to the Disciplinary Review board. Rule 1:20–2(o).

The Disciplinary Review Board, a statewide board which is also appointed by the Supreme Court, consists of nine members, at least five of whom must be attorneys and at least three of whom must be nonattorneys. The Board makes a de novo review. Rule 1:20–3(d)(3). The Board is required to make formal findings and recommendations to the New Jersey Supreme Court.

All decisions of the Disciplinary Review Board beyond a private reprimand are reviewed by the New Jersey Supreme Court. Briefing and oral argument are available in the Supreme Court for cases involving disbarment or suspension for more than one year. Rule 1:20–4.

Jurisdiction to Impose Discipline

On the question of disciplinary authority over lawyers admitted to practice before a federal court, compare Waters v. Barr, 103 Nev. 694, 747 P.2d 900 (1987) (state court asserting disciplinary authority over Government prosecutors), with Kolibash v. West Virginia Bar Committee on Legal Ethics, 872 F.2d 571 (4th Cir.1989) (disciplinary proceeding commenced in state tribunal removable to federal court under 28 U.S.C. § 1442). See also Theard v. United States, 354 U.S. 278, 77 S.Ct. 1274

(1957); Comment, Disbarment in the Federal Courts, 85 Yale L.J. 975 (1977).

On inter-state disciplinary jurisdiction, see M.R. 8.5.

Obligation to Report Misconduct

M.R. 8.3(a) of the Rules of Professional Conduct requires a lawyer to report to appropriate disciplinary authority "a violation of the rules of professional conduct that raises a substantial question as to that lawyer's honesty, trustworthiness or fitness as a lawyer in other respects." M.R. 8.3(b) imposes a counterpart obligation regarding misconduct by a judge. DR 1–103(A) goes further, requiring report of any violation by another lawyer.

These obligations are not generally observed. There may be justification for not reporting when a lawyer is representing a client in seeking redress against another lawyer for malpractice and reporting the violation would inhibit reaching a settlement. However, it is clearly a violation for a lawyer to agree not to report another lawyer's violation. Such an agreement could constitute or approximate extortion if it is done in connection with exacting a payment from the second lawyer. In re Himmel, 125 Ill.2d 531, 533 N.E.2d 790 (1988), involved a one year suspension of a lawyer nominally on the ground of his failure to report another lawyer's misconduct. The court failed to attach specific significance to the underlying transaction. In that transaction, Himmel had been retained to recover funds that the other lawyer had converted from the client while previously representing her. Himmel, acting on a contingent fee basis, obtained an agreement whereby the other lawyer agreed to pay far in excess of the amount converted in return for a promise not to report the matter to the disciplinary authority. While it seems clear that Himmel was guilty of extortion and abetting concealment of professional misconduct, imposing a heavy sanction on failure to report as such has sent shock waves. The court stated that it was no defense that Himmel had learned about the other lawyer's violation in connection with a representation aimed at civil redress from the lawyer. Generally see the discussion of the ethical duty to report misconduct and the *Himmel* case in Chapter 3 above at pp. 153–154.

IN THE MATTER OF ANONYMOUS ATTORNEYS

Court of Appeals of New York, 1977.
41 N.Y.2d 506, 393 N.Y.S.2d 961, 362 N.E.2d 592.

PER CURIAM.

The sole issue before the court is whether incriminating testimony given by an attorney, following a grant of immunity, may be used as evidence against him in a disciplinary proceeding.

The appellants, attorneys admitted to practice in the State of New York, were called to testify before a Grand Jury investigating alleged irregularities in the fixing of traffic tickets in the City Court of Buffalo.

The District Attorney requested that they execute waivers of immunity which they declined to do, and the Grand Jury then voted them full immunity pursuant to CPL 50.10. The Grand Jury probe resulted in an indictment against certain officials and, subsequently, the appellants, still retaining immunity, testified at the trial of these officials. Thereafter, they were served with a petition and notice of motion instituted by the respondent Bar Association seeking to have them disciplined for their involvement in the activity concerning which they had testified. After service of the petitions, the appellants commenced an action in the Federal District Court seeking an injunction against prosecution of these disciplinary proceedings. The respondent's motion to dismiss the Federal action was granted on the ground of insufficiency under the abstention doctrine of Younger v. Harris, 401 U.S. 37, 91 S.Ct. 746, 27 L.Ed.2d 669, and that dismissal was affirmed (Anonymous J. v. Bar Assn. of Erie County, 2 Cir., 515 F.2d 435, cert. den., 423 U.S. 840, 96 S.Ct. 71, 46 L.Ed.2d 60). Thereafter, appellants moved in the Appellate Division for an order dismissing the petitions on the ground that they had been granted immunity from any penalties or forfeitures arising out of the transactions concerning which they had testified. The Appellate Division denied the motion to dismiss and granted leave to appeal to this court on a certified question. We affirm the order of the Appellate Division and answer the certified question in the affirmative.

Initially, we confront the question of statutory construction of the immunity statute. The appellants were granted immunity pursuant to and defined in CPL 50.10 which provides that: "A person who has been a witness in a legal proceeding, and who cannot, except as otherwise provided in this subdivision, be convicted of any offense or subjected to any penalty or forfeiture for or on account of any transaction, matter or thing concerning which he gave evidence therein, possesses 'immunity' from any such conviction, penalty or forfeiture. A person who possesses such immunity may nevertheless be convicted of perjury as a result of having given false testimony in such legal proceeding, and may be convicted of or adjudged in contempt as a result of having contumaciously refused to give evidence therein." The appellants strongly urge that the possible sanctions flowing from the disciplinary proceeding constitute a "penalty or forfeiture" within the meaning of the statute. Without doubt the sanctions which may be imposed in such proceedings may have serious consequences resulting in impairment of repute, loss of clientele, or, in the case of disbarment, loss of license to practice a profession which is their very source of livelihood. Although serious in consequence, these sanctions are not penalties or forfeitures within the meaning of the Criminal Procedure Law. The penalties and forfeitures encompassed by this immunity are those imposed or sought to be imposed as punishment upon conviction for a criminal offense committed in violation of the Penal Law or other statute of the State. . . . We hold that disciplinary sanctions are not punishment within the meaning of section 50.10. As Judge Cardozo explained in Matter of

Rouss (supra, 221 N.Y. pp. 84–85, 116 N.E. p. 783): "Membership in the bar is a privilege burdened with conditions. A fair private and professional character is one of them. Compliance with that condition is essential at the moment of admission; but it is equally essential afterwards [citations omitted]. Whenever the condition is broken, the privilege is lost. To refuse admission to an unworthy applicant is not to punish him for past offenses. The examination into character, like the examination into learning is merely a test of fitness. To strike the unworthy lawyer from the roll is not to add to the pains and penalties of crime." Whether the practice of law is termed a privilege (*Matter of Rouss,* supra) or a right (Matter of Levy, 37 N.Y.2d 279, 282, 372 N.Y.S.2d 41, 44, 333 N.E.2d 350, 352) disciplinary sanctions imposed for misconduct are not criminal penalties under the statute.

Immunity does not protect against all private consequences of the facts or involvement revealed by testimony given under its shelter. And some people, because of their relationship with government, may suffer governmentally imposed consequences of a serious nature (see Uniformed Sanitation Men Assn. v. Commissioner of Sanitation, 2 Cir., 426 F.2d 619, cert. den., 403 U.S. 917, 91 S.Ct. 2223, 29 L.Ed.2d 693, Note, Immunity Statutes and the Constitution, 68 Col.L.Rev. 959). The criterion is whether the sanctions are imposed in the context of a criminal proceeding, covered by immunity, or whether such subsequent proceedings are civil in nature where immunity does not necessarily extend. Disciplinary proceedings against an attorney for professional misconduct have consistently been held not to be criminal proceedings but rather are those which serve to protect the court and society from the practice of law by persons who fail to maintain the necessary standards of integrity and probity (. . ., Chilingirian, State Disbarment Proceedings and the Privilege Against Self–Incrimination, 18 Buffalo L.Rev. 489). The immunity statute, prohibiting use of covered testimonial evidence in criminal proceedings, does not bar the use of such evidence in disciplinary proceedings brought against an attorney on the grounds of misconduct; and this has been the established law in this State for over 40 years (Matter of Solovei, 250 App.Div. 117, 121, 293 N.Y.S. 640, 644, affd., 276 N.Y. 647, 12 N.E.2d 802).

The appellants also contend that the Fifth Amendment privilege against self incrimination precludes the use of any immunity-clothed statements in a disciplinary proceeding. The appellants were concededly granted transactional immunity in return for their Grand Jury and trial testimony. They assert that their testimony was compelled by the grant of immunity arguing that subsequent refusal would result in contempt charges and as such must be coextensive with the privilege against self incrimination which it replaced and that privilege must be deemed to protect against the use of compelled self-incriminating statements in disciplinary proceedings. This argument has a surface attractiveness that dissipates under analysis.

The Fifth Amendment provides that no person "shall be compelled *in any criminal case* to be a witness against himself" (emphasis added), and the State Constitution assures this privilege in the very same language (N.Y. Const., art. I, § 6). These constitutional protections forbid the State from compelling incriminating answers which may be used in any criminal proceedings but they permit "that very testimony to be compelled if neither it nor its fruits are available for such use" (Lefkowitz v. Turley, 414 U.S. 70, 84, 94 S.Ct. 316, 325, 38 L.Ed.2d 274; Kastigar v. United States, 406 U.S. 441, 92 S.Ct. 1653, 32 L.Ed.2d 212). Where immunity coextensive with the privilege against self incrimination is granted, the courts have the power to compel testimony by the use of civil contempt and coerced imprisonment (Lefkowitz v. Turley, supra; Shillitani v. United States, 384 U.S. 364, 86 S.Ct. 1531, 16 L.Ed. 2d 622; Matter of Rushkin v. Detken, 32 N.Y.2d 293, 344 N.Y.S.2d 933, 298 N.E.2d 101; see People v. Ianniello, 21 N.Y.2d 418, 288 N.Y.S.2d 462, 235 N.E.2d 439, cert. den., 393 U.S. 827, 89 S.Ct. 90, 21 L.Ed.2d 98). The Supreme Court has held that "immunity from use and derivative use is coextensive with the scope of the privilege against self incrimination, and therefore is sufficient to compel testimony over a claim of the privilege" (Kastigar v. United States, supra, 406 U.S. p. 453, 92 S.Ct. p. 1661). The New York Statute goes further and provides full transactional immunity (Matter of Gold v. Menna, 25 N.Y.2d 475, 307 N.Y.S.2d 33, 255 N.E.2d 235; Pitler, New York Criminal Practice under the CPL, p. 241). Thus, the appellants are clothed with full transactional immunity which immunizes them against prosecutions for any and all *crimes* to which their testimony might relate.

The constitutional protection does not, however, extend to its use in other than criminal proceedings. It is certain that the privilege against self incrimination may be asserted in any situation where the testimony may ultimately be used in a criminal proceeding against the person testifying (Matter of Gault, 387 U.S. 1, 47–48, 87 S.Ct. 1428, 18 L.Ed.2d 527), but where immunity bars such use the testimony is nonetheless admissible in other noncriminal hearings such as those involving disciplinary charges. The salient question is whether that proceeding is a criminal case within the purview of the Fifth Amendment. A criminal case is "one which may result in sanctions being imposed upon a person as a result of his conduct being adjudged violative of the criminal law. The essence of state bar disciplinary proceedings, however, is not a resolution regarding the alleged criminality of a person's acts, but rather a determination of the moral fitness of an attorney to continue in the practice of law. Although conduct which could form the basis for a criminal prosecution might also underlie the institution of disciplinary proceedings, the focus is upon gauging an individual's character and fitness, and not upon adjudging the criminality of his prior acts or inflicting punishment for them" (Matter of Daley, 7 Cir., 549 F.2d 469, 474). In urging a contrary position, appellants rely on cases which are not here applicable. In Spevack v. Klein, 385 U.S. 511, 87 S.Ct. 625, 17 L.Ed.2d 574 the Supreme Court held that an attorney could not be disciplined solely on the ground that he had asserted his privilege against self incrimination. The threat of disbarment for the mere exercise of the privilege was viewed as an unconstitutional compulsion to waive the privilege without a coextensive protection against the ultimate use of those statements in a criminal proceeding. Likewise in Garrity v. New Jersey, 385 U.S. 493, 87 S.Ct. 616, 17 L.Ed.2d 562 certain police officers made incriminating statements during an inquiry concerning the fixing of traffic tickets. The statements were made under the threat that if they refused to respond to the questions put to them, they would be removed from office. Since no immunity was granted, the Supreme Court considered those threats coercive, negating any apparent waiver of the privilege against self incrimination and the statements were thus declared inadmissible in a later criminal action against them. Further, in Gardner v. Broderick, 392 U.S. 273, 88 S.Ct. 1913, 20 L.Ed.2d 1082 the court held that refusal to waive the privilege could not be grounds for termination of a police officer's employment. In all of these cases testimony was being compelled by threats of disbarment or the loss of employment without a guarantee that the statements would not later be used in criminal proceedings. The Fifth Amendment and our State Constitution prohibit such coercion. But these decisions in no way imply that once immunity coextensive with the privilege is granted, the statements may not be used in a disciplinary hearing. When assurance is made that the statements cannot be used in a related criminal action, the constitutional privilege is satisfied and no more is required. Further use of the information does not offend the essential purposes of the privilege but guarantees the proper opportunity for the pursuit of other public values.

The State has a compelling interest in regulating our system of justice to assure high standards of professional conduct. Sanctions imposed in that capacity are distinct and apart from penalties and forfeitures stemming from criminal proceedings. Once the constitutional guarantee that no person "shall be compelled in any criminal case to be a witness against himself" is assured by a grant of immunity, the State may act, and indeed must act, in its supervisory capacity to assure that those standards are maintained.

Accordingly, the order of the Appellate Division should be affirmed and the certified question answered in the affirmative.

STATE EX REL. OKLAHOMA BAR ASSOCIATION v. PORTER

Supreme Court of Oklahoma, 1988.
766 P.2d 958.

HARGRAVE, VICE CHIEF JUSTICE.

Presently before the Court is a disciplinary matter brought against E. Melvin Porter upon a grievance filed by District Judge Ralph G. Thomspon. After a hearing the Professional Responsibility Trial Panel found that E. Melvin Porter violated the mandatory strictures of 5 O.S.A. Ch. I, App. 3 (1981), D.R. 1–102(A)(5), (6) providing:

"(A) A lawyer shall not:

. . .

(5) Engage in conduct that is prejudicial to the administration of justice.

(6) Engage in any other conduct that adversely reflects upon his fitness to practice law."

As disclosed by the evidence taken in the hearing before the Professional Responsibility Trial Panel, the finding of misconduct arises from statements made by respondent regarding United States District Judge Ralph G. Thompson. The comments were made immediately after the judge had presided over the trial and sentencing of respondent's client, Bernard J. McIntyre. The statements were made out of court, in public, to the news media. Respondent admitted the comments were referable to the Judge.

"He showed all the signs of being a racist" in addition to "I've never tried a case before him that I felt I got an impartial trial out of him."

"He showed all the signs of being a racist during the trial. He never talked to me. He always talked to Mr. Gotcher. He only talked to me when he had to. And if he wants to practice his racism that way that's his business."

The complainant Bar Association called the respondent as its witness at the hearing on the complaint. During this testimony, respondent admitted making the statements. He also outlined his experiences as a trial lawyer before the judge. He stated that these experiences had led him to believe the remarks were justified. After calling respondent and introducing various exhibits, complainant rested its case. The respondent put on its case, calling one witness, John D. Berry, Executive Director of the Oklahoma County Bar Association, and rested without further testimony. Thereafter the complainant attempted to call rebuttal witnesses. These witnesses were offered to rebut evidence elicited from respondent when called to the stand to testify as the Bar Association's witness. After prolonged debate the trial panel ruled that complainant would not be allowed to put on witnesses to rebut the evidence given by Mr. Porter in the Bar's case-in-chief, nor would the entire case be reopened. On these two issues the panel's ruling appears in the record as follows:

". . . . while you do have the right to offer rebuttal witnesses there are limitations with regard to what can be rebutted. The panel is going to hold that you would not be permitted to rebut evidence presented by Senator Porter who was called as your witness."

The Trial Panel cannot be held to have erred in refusing the offered rebuttal evidence. Middlebrook v. Imler, Tenny and Kugler, M.D.s, 713 P.2d 572 (Okl.1985):

" . . . Rebuttal evidence is that class of evidence which has become relevant only by virtue of evidence *introduced* by the adverse party, and its function is to explain or repel evidence of the adverse party (citations omitted). In this instance, the offered testimony is not rebuttal matter for it has no relation to repelling evidence of the adverse party. (emphasis added) . . .

In testimony and by exhibits the respondent asserted in his defense that the remarks were truly descriptive of the official conduct of the district judge in question. The respondent also asserted he had been selectively prosecuted, that the complaint here considered violated his right to free speech under the First Amendment to the United States Constitution, that the disciplinary regulations at issue are vague and indefinite, and that respondent's rights under 42 U.S.C. § 1983 had been violated.

One trial master recommended the respondent be found innocent of all charges of misconduct. Two masters concurred in findings of fact and conclusions. Summarized, the findings and conclusions disclose the following: The respondent established by unrefuted evidence that he had subjectively formed an opinion based upon experiences which he perceived as providing him with a rational basis for having concluded that the remarks he made had a factual basis. Additionally, the two trial masters found the respondent exceeded the bounds of proper conduct for an attorney; that action subjects him to discipline under the code of professional responsibility, and the respondent did not have the constitutional right to make these utterances. A member of the legal profession is subject to reasonable restraint in his professional behavior exceeding those which exist in respect to the general public. The trial masters also found that the respondent had not met his burden of demonstrating the affirmative defense of selective prosecution. They further found the regulations governing the matter imposed upon respondent a duty to uphold respect for the law, and respondent's actions were professionally indefensible whether or not he believed them to be supported by a factual basis. The respondent's actions are specifically prohibited and were known by respondent to be likely to bring discredit upon the courts of this state and nation and upon a jurist actively engaged in a well-publicized trial. These two masters additionally found the constitutionality of the restriction imposed by the disciplinary rules was beyond the purview of the Trial Panel.

In the light of the findings the trial panel made individual recommendations. Trial master Don Simmons, the lay member, recommended that respondent be found innocent of all charges. Trial master Kenneth E. Holmes recommended that the respondent be suspended from the practice of law for a period of 60 days and that costs of the proceeding be taxed to the respondent. Trial master Darven L. Brown recommended that respondent receive a public censure and that costs of the proceeding be taxed against him.

The Bar Association recommended to the trial panel that the respondent receive a public censure. The complainant states in its brief to this Court that the respondent's refusal to demonstrate remorse for his actions warrants an order of suspension.

I

The Supreme Court of the State of Oklahoma has spoken to the question of an attorney's criticism of individuals holding judicial office. An examination of these cases leads to the conclusion that this Court has always looked at the nature of the accusation and has carefully avoided censuring attorneys for speech in the absence of a showing of falsity. In certain respects these opinions foreshadow constitutional interpretation established decades later. In the early case of State Bar Commission v. Sullivan, 35 Okl. 745, 131 P. 703 (1912), the State Bar Commission brought an original action for the disbarment of P.M. Sullivan. There it was alleged that the defendant had been guilty of gross misconduct and violations of his duty and obligations as an attorney and counselor at law, in that he falsely, maliciously and without reasonable justification or excuse caused to be printed and published a pamphlet entitled "A Criminal Combine". This pamphlet described the Governor, Attorney General, the Supreme Court, district clerks, district attorneys and referees, as perjurers, murder plotters, and crooks galore. . . . It was charged the filing of this pleading was malicious and designed to slander and libel the defendants and bring contempt, ridicule and hatred to the courts of this state. The opinion notes an attorney may be disbarred for issuing out of court statements designed to willfully, purposely and maliciously misrepresent the courts and judges of the state, and bring them into disrepute, thereby lessening the respect due to them.[2] In reaching this conclusion, the Court recognized the effect of the principles of freedom of speech on the case. The opinion recognizes the role of truth in assessing a violation of the duties of an attorney and counselor at law. The Court implicitly found that the statements made were untrue and expressly stated the statements were willfully and maliciously made to misrepresent the position of the courts. *State Bar Commission v. Sullivan,* supra, does not stand for the proposition that an attorney may be sanctioned for any out of court statement critical of the courts or an individual judge. The case states an attorney is liable to suffer the ultimate punishment of professional excommunication where false accusations are willfully made with the specific intent to misrepresent the position of the court, or bring the courts into disrespect and lessen the respect rightfully due them. . . .

2. This is the precept referred to in certain law references. See 12 A.L.R.3rd 1408 at 1431.

. . . The law of Oklahoma has shown concern from the earliest times with the balance between a citizen's duties as an attorney and his right to speak freely on matters of public concern accorded to all people under our constitutional system of government. . . .

. . .

The Court again examined the propriety of disciplining an attorney for remarks critical of the courts and judiciary in State v. Nix, 295 P.2d 286 (Okl.1956). There the Bar Association had enumerated three charges of misconduct. Two were held to be privileged utterances made on the Senate floor. The third incident was in a television interview. The Court said the remarks on television, although mostly of his comment or opinion, in places went beyond comment and amounted to a reflection on the named court. In determining that such conduct merited a public censure, the Court noted the absence of any showing in the record of justification. That absence of justification in this context referable to the issue of factual support for the statement made:

"... The remarks under the circumstances were indiscreet, ill-advised and unbecoming, and under the facts as disclosed by the record in this case wholly unjustified, and the respondent is hereby censured and reproved for the statement made on the telecast." State v. Nix, supra, at 293. . . .

II

The parties now before the Court agree that the latest authority from the United States Supreme Court on this matter is In Re Sawyer, 360 U.S. 622, 79 S.Ct. 1376, 3 L.Ed.2d 1473 (1959). We note the existence of In Re Snyder, 472 U.S. 634, 105 S.Ct. 2874, 86 L.Ed.2d 504 (1985), as does respondent. Although that case presented the issue now before the Court, *Snyder* was decided upon the facts without constitutional analysis. In *Sawyer,* the petitioner made a speech during the trial of an action in federal court. In that speech Sawyer referred to "horrible and shocking" things that occurred during the trial, stated a fair trial was impossible, and made other derogatory statements about the proceedings. For such conduct Sawyer was suspended for a year by the Supreme Court of the Territory of Hawaii, which was affirmed by the United States Court of Appeals for the Ninth Circuit. The Supreme Court reversed with the Justices issuing separate opinions. Five members of the Court found the evidence insufficient to support the conclusion that the petitioner's speech impugned the integrity of the judge presiding at the trial. (The five Justices being Warren, C.J., Black, Douglas, Brennan and Stewart, JJ.) . . . *In Re Sawyer,* supra, 360 U.S. at 631 and 632 and 635 and 636, 79 S.Ct. at 1380 and 1381 and 1382 and 1383 . . .:

"We start with the proposition that lawyers are free to criticise the state of the law. Many lawyers say that the rules of evidence relative to the admission of statements by those alleged to be co-

conspirators are overbroad. . . . Others disagree. But all are free to express their views on these matters, and no one would say that this sort of criticism constituted an improper attack on the judges who enforced such rules and who presided at the trials. This is so, even though the existence of questionable rules of law might be said in a sense to produce unfair trials. Such criticism simply cannot be equated with an attack on the motivation or the integrity or the competence of the judges. And surely permissible criticism may as well be made to a lay audience as to a professional; oftentimes the law is modified through popular criticism; . . ."

"But it is said that while it may be proper for an attorney to say the law is unfair or that judges are in error as a general matter, it is wrong for counsel of record to say so during a pending case. The verbalization is that it is impermissible to litigate by day and castigate by night. See [In re Sawyer,] 260 F.2d, [189] at 202 [(9th Cir.1958)]. This line seems central to the Bar Association's argument, as it appears to have been to the reasoning of the court below, and the dissent here is much informed by it, but to us it seems totally to ignore the charges made and the findings. The findings were that petitioner impugned the integrity of Judge Wiig and made an improper attack on his administration of justice in the Honolulu trial. A lawyer does not acquire any license to do these things by not being presently engaged in a case. They are equally serious whether he currently is engaged in litigation before the judge or not. We can perceive no ground whereby the pendency of litigation might be thought to make an attorney's out-of-court remarks more censurable, other than they might tend to obstruct the administration of justice. Remarks made during the course of a trial might tend to such obstruction where remarks made afterwards would not. . . . Judge Wiig remained equally protected from statements impugning him, and petitioner remained equally free to make critical statements that did not cross that line. . . ."

Two precepts are drawn from these excerpts that are worthy of further consideration. The first is that an attorney is free to criticise the institution of the law in this country or the wisdom and efficacy of the rules of law which control the exercise of judicial power. Contrarily, criticism by an attorney amounting to an attack on the motivation, integrity or competence of a judge whose responsibility it is to administer the law may be under certain circumstances properly censurable. There is a certain unresolved tension between this teaching and the precepts first discussed five years after *Sawyer,* supra, in New York Times Co. v. Sullivan, 376 U.S. 254, 84 S.Ct. 710, 11 L.Ed.2d 686 (1964). *New York Times Co. v. Sullivan,* supra, and the line of cases flowing therefrom, it would seem, places rather less stress upon the social utility of shielding a public official from criticism than is evident in

Sawyer, supra, and more emphasis upon preservation of the integrity of the institution rather than the personality occupying that office.

The United States Supreme Court was faced with this same issue in the case of *In Re Snyder,* supra. In this action attorney Snyder had been suspended from the practice of law in the federal court for the Eighth Circuit for six months for a statement made out of court in a letter to the staff of a district judge which was deemed disrespectful by the Chief Judge of the United States Court of Appeals for the Eighth Circuit. In full, the letter reads as follows:

"In the first place, I am appalled by the amount of money which the federal court pays for indigent criminal defense work. The reason that so few attorneys in Bismarck accept this work is for that exact reason. We have, up to this point, still accepted the indigent appointments, because of a duty to our profession, and the fact that nobody else will do it.

Now, however, not only are we paid an amount of money which does not even cover our overhead, but we have to go through extreme gymnastics even to receive the puny amounts which the federal courts authorize for this work. We have sent you everything we have concerning our representation, and I am not sending you anything else. You can take it or leave it.

Further, I am extremely disgusted by the treatment of us by the Eighth Circuit in this case, and you are instructed to remove my name from the list of attorneys who will accept criminal indigent defense work. I have simply had it.

Thank you for your time and attention." 472 U.S. at 637, 105 S.Ct. at 2877.

The Eighth Circuit had determined that this letter in conjunction with an unspecified refusal to show continuing respect for the court demonstrated conduct prejudicial to the administration of justice. North Dakota Code of Professional Responsibility, D.R. 1–102(A)(5) and the American Bar Association Model Code of Professional Responsibility (1980), D.R. 1–102(A)(5). The Supreme Court found it unnecessary to examine the free speech issue tendered, and held that criticism of the administration of the Criminal Justice Act was not cause for discipline or suspension. In reference to the concededly harsh tone of the letter the Court said:

". . . a single incident of rudeness or lack of professional courtesy—in the context here—does not support a finding of contemptuous or contumacious conduct, or a finding that a lawyer is not presently fit to practice law in the federal courts; nor does it rise to the level of 'conduct unbecoming a member of the bar' warranting suspension from practice." . . .

III

. . .

The speech activity for which respondent is called to answer for here is plainly at the center of the protective umbrella of the First Amendment. Freedom of speech, press, assembly and the right to petition the government for a redress of grievances share a common core purpose of assuring freedom of communication on matters relating to the functioning of government. Richmond Newspapers, Inc. v. Virginia, 448 U.S. 555, 100 S.Ct. 2814, 65 L.Ed.2d 973 (1980):

". . . Plainly it would be difficult to single out any aspect of government of higher concern and importance to the people than the manner in which criminal trials are conducted; . . ." *Richmond,* supra, at 448 U.S. 575 [100 S.Ct. 2826].

The regulation sought to be upheld by this proceeding prohibits a certain class of citizens, attorneys, from speaking on certain subjects, criticism of the judiciary. This concern with limiting what subjects may be spoken to by which speakers is absolutely inimical to the principles of the First Amendment. In the realm of protected speech, the government is constitutionally disqualified from dictating the subject about which persons may speak and the speakers who may address a public issue. First National Bank of Boston v. Bellotti, supra, Police Department v. Mosley, 408 U.S. 92, 92 S.Ct. 2286, 33 L.Ed.2d 212 (1972).

The inquiry here made must also take into account rights other than the right of the speaker to communicate. The counterpoint to the right to speak is the right of the listener to receive a free flow of information. The First Amendment goes beyond protection of the press and individual self-expression to prohibit the government from limiting the stock of information from which members of the public may draw. *First National Bank of Boston v. Bellotti,* supra. State ex rel. Department of Transportation v. Pile, 603 P.2d 337 (1979), cert. denied 453 U.S. 922, 101 S.Ct. 3158, 69 L.Ed.2d 1004 (1981). This concomitant right to receive information has been referred to as a freedom to listen. The freedom of speech necessarily protects the right to receive that information. Martin v. City of Struthers, 319 U.S. 141, 63 S.Ct. 862, 87 L.Ed. 1313 (1943), Stanley v. Georgia, 394 U.S. 557, 89 S.Ct. 1234, 22 L.Ed.2d 542 (1969). . . .

. . .

. . . Where, as here, a prohibition is directed at speech itself, and the speech is ultimately related to the process of self government, the state may prevail only upon showing a subordinating interest which is compelling. *First National Bank of Boston v. Bellotti,* supra, Bates v. Little Rock, 361 U.S. 516, 80 S.Ct. 412, 4 L.Ed.2d 480 (1960). The means chosen to further this intention, if compelling, still must be narrowly tailored to avoid unnecessary abridgement of the right of free speech. *First National Bank of Boston v. Bellotti,* supra, Buckley v. Valeo, 424 U.S. 1, 96 S.Ct. 612, 46 L.Ed.2d 659 (1976), NAACP v.

Button, 371 U.S. 415, 83 S.Ct. 328, 9 L.Ed.2d 405 (1963), Shelton v. Tucker, 364 U.S. 479, 81 S.Ct. 247, 5 L.Ed.2d 231 (1960).

The analysis used to weigh an offered compelling interest that would justify a significant impairment of the First Amendment is outlined in Elrod v. Burns, 427 U.S. 347, 96 S.Ct. 2673, 49 L.Ed.2d 547 (1976). In summary, that analysis shows a significant impairment of First Amendment rights must survive exacting scrutiny, even if the impairment arises indirectly from the questioned regulation. A mere showing of state interest is insufficient; the interest must be paramount, of vital importance, and the burden is on the government to show its existence. Further it is not enough to show a rational relationship between the means chosen and the end sought to be accomplished. The advance of the subordinating interest must outweigh the loss of protected rights and the government must employ means closely drawn to avoid unnecessary abridgement. If the state has open to it a less drastic method of satisfying its legitimate interest it may not validly choose a legislative scheme that broadly stifles the exercise of fundamental personal liberties. Elrod v. Burns, supra, 427 U.S. at 362 through 363, 96 S.Ct. at 2684 through 2685.

The detriment caused by this disciplinary rule to protected rights, visited upon the attorney speaking on issues regarding governmental affairs is substantial, although personal. However, the public at large also experiences curtailment of its First Amendment privileges. Through application of this rule the public is deprived of its right to receive information about the workings of its governmental functionaries from those precisely situated to be ultimately familiar with the operation of the judicial branch of government. The right of the public to receive this information occupies a critical citadel of the First Amendment rights. We have not been shown, nor can we at present conceive, of an interest sufficiently imperative to justify such a restriction of core First Amendment rights, at least where the statements made are not shown to be incorrect statements of fact. In the record before this Court no evidence was introduced to demonstrate that the statements were false or that they were insincerely uttered by a speaker having no basis upon which to found them. . . .

. . .

. . . In keeping with the high trust placed in this Court by the people, we cannot shield the judiciary from the critique of that portion of the public most perfectly situated to advance knowledgeable criticism, while at the same time subjecting the balance of government officials to the stringent requirements of the *New York Times Co. v. Sullivan,* supra, and its progeny.

False speech does not foster First Amendment protection, Time v. Pape, 401 U.S. 1015, 91 S.Ct. 1248, 28 L.Ed.2d 552 (1971), because there is no constitutional value in false statements of fact. Keeton v. Hustler Magazine, Inc., 465 U.S. 770, 104 S.Ct. 1473, 79 L.Ed.2d 790 (1984). See also, Herbert v. Lando, 441 U.S. 153, 99 S.Ct. 1635, 60 L.Ed.2d 115

(1979). There is no First Amendment protection afforded remarks critical of the judiciary when those statements are false. The state has an interest in suppressing false statements of fact referenced to the judiciary originating from members of the Bar. Disseminating false statements of fact in reference to the judiciary can be prejudicial to the administration of justice and is properly a subject for discipline under D.R. 1–102(A)(5). Misinformation from the Bar is detrimental to the public weal for the same reason that the access to information from that source may not be impeded. Members of the Bar possess, and are perceived by the public as possessing, special knowledge of the workings of the judicial branch of government. Critical remarks from the Bar thus have more impact on the judgment of the citizen than similar remarks by a layman would be calculated to have. . . .

. . . Although not precisely raised by the record before the Court, it is proper to note that the considerations which dictate that First Amendment protection be afforded to ultimately false statements shown to be made in good faith such as in St. Amant v. Thompson, 390 U.S. 727, 88 S.Ct. 1323, 20 L.Ed.2d 262 (1968), face a differing analysis in this context. The First Amendment protection afforded attorney criticism of the judiciary here is not based on the attorney's right to communicate freely. Here the First Amendment consideration held to be paramount is the public's right to receive information from a class of persons most intimately familiar with the administration of the judiciary. False information emanating from that source is inimical to the same extent that true information from the Bar on the subject benefits society. The public has a right to expect that attorneys be held to stringent standards when divulging information and commenting on legal affairs touching upon issues of self government.

The record is devoid of any attempt to show that the statements complained of are false. In the absence of a showing of falsity the statement must be held to be speech on vital issues of self government protected by the First Amendment. We thus hold that D.R. 1–102(A) (5), (6) cannot be construed to sanction the expressive activity before the Court. Similarly discipline under 5 O.S.A. Ch. I, App. 3 (1981), D.R. 8–102(B) is not warranted by virtue of the absence of any showing of falsity.

IV

At this point it is necessary to remind the profession that First Amendment license to comment is broader than the traditional correct demeanor expected of an officer of the court. Nothing said in this opinion changes those expectations. Remarks of the sort being now considered are indeed disrespectful, exhibiting a definite lack of the polish expected of the true professional and they remain uncondoned. It is expected that counselors will maintain the honor of the profession and the decorum properly expected of an officer of this court. Nothing less than precisely proper decorum and conduct is expected by this

Court of members of the Bar. We view the remarks here examined to be extremely bad form while in the same breath we hold them to be protected. Each member of the Bar should remember that as an attorney, all have sworn: ". . . to act in the office of attorney of this Court according to best learning and discretion, and with all good fidelity as well to the court and to client." [5]

Therefore it should be a personal point of honor for each attorney to keep faith with himself and the oath he has taken, cognizant of the fact that one's own word and professional pride should be a sufficient principle upon which to base one's conduct. . . .

OPALA, JUSTICE, concurring in judgment.

I concur in today's opinion only insofar as it holds that the respondent may not be disciplined for constitutionally protected utterances that fall under the rubric of political speech. See in this connection, In re Snyder, 472 U.S. 634, 646–647, 105 S.Ct. 2874, 2882, 86 L.Ed.2d 504 [1985] and Comment, The First Amendment and Attorney Discipline for Criticism of the Judiciary: Let the Lawyer Beware, 15 N.Ky.L.Rev. 129 [1988]. Even if, after an initial rejection of its evidence—a ruling I deem correct—the Bar had followed up with a formal and particularized offer to prove that the respondent's remarks were false in fact, no discipline would be imposable here. Respondent's constitutional freedom of speech does not depend on the truth of it's content.

IN THE MATTER OF HINDS, AN ATTORNEY AT LAW

Supreme Court of New Jersey, 1982.
90 N.J. 604, 449 A.2d 483.

HANDLER, J.

. . .

I

. . . Hinds has been a member of the New Jersey Bar since 1973. He has been active and prominent as a lawyer in civil rights causes and has a national reputation for his work as Director of the National Conference of Black Lawyers (hereinafter "NCBL"), a capacity in which he served for five years until 1978. In 1973 Joanne Chesimard, a black woman reputed to be a militant radical, was accused of killing a New Jersey State trooper. Following her arrest, Chesimard was brought to trial after a long series of delays. Hinds represented Chesimard during this pretrial period in several federal civil actions concerning the legality and general conditions of her incarceration by the State. Hinds apparently did not, however, represent Chesimard at her criminal trial.

5. From 5 O.S.1981 § 2, as appearing on the Oklahoma attorney's license to practice.

Chesimard finally went on trial for murder in 1977 in the Superior Court, Law Division, in New Brunswick. After observing the initial phases of the trial and while the jury was still being impaneled, Hinds called a press conference at his New Brunswick office on January 20, 1977. In an article appearing January 21, 1977, in the *New York Daily News* under the headline, "Joanne Loses 2 Rounds in Trial Transfer," it was reported that:

> . . . Lenox [sic] Hinds, an attorney also representing Mrs. Chesimard, said the defense team wanted the case moved to another court because in New Brunswick "what we are seeing is legalized lynching."

> He said he was speaking for the defense team because its members were "gagged" by [the trial judge] whom he accused of asking prospective jurors self-serving questions which he said were leading to "the creation of a hangman's court."

An article appearing in the *Newark Star–Ledger* on the same date reported that Hinds had referred to the Chesimard trial as "a travesty." The article further quoted Hinds as saying that the trial judge "does not have the judicial temperament or the racial sensitivity to sit as an impartial judge" in Chesimard's trial, and that "[i]t was only after the trial began that we began to have fears that what we are seeing is a legalized lynching."

Also, a television reporter covering the press conference for the New Jersey Public Broadcasting Authority (Channel 52) recorded the following exchange:

> Hinds: "We feel that it is a kangaroo—it will be a kangaroo court unless the judge recluses [sic] himself and that will be the very minimum."

> Reporter: "And a kangaroo court means a guilty verdict?"

> Hinds: "That's correct."

The Middlesex County Ethics Committee (now the District VIII Ethics Committee) authorized an investigation to determine whether Hinds' statements constituted a violation of any disciplinary rules. . . . [I]t was recommended that Hinds be charged with violating two disciplinary rules: DR 1–102(A)(5), which prohibits attorneys from "[e]ngag[ing] in conduct . . . prejudicial to the administration of justice;" and DR 7–107(D), which provides that

> [d]uring the selection of a jury or a trial of a criminal matter, a lawyer or law firm associated with the prosecution or defense of a criminal matter shall not make or participate in making an extrajudicial statement that he expects to be disseminated by means of public communication and that relates to the trial, parties, or issues in the trial or other matters that are reasonably likely to interfere with a fair trial. . . .

. . . .

II

. . .

A restriction on free speech can survive judicial scrutiny under the First Amendment only if certain fundamental and stringent conditions are satisfied. First, the limitation must "further an important or substantial governmental interest unrelated to the suppression of expression." Procunier v. Martinez, 416 U.S. 396, 413, 94 S.Ct. 1800, 1811, 40 L.Ed.2d 224, 240 (1974). Second, the restriction must be "no greater than is necessary or essential to the protection of the particular governmental interest involved." Id. . . .

Like other citizens, attorneys are entitled to the full protection of the First Amendment, even as participants in the administration of justice. See R.M.J., [455] U.S. [191], [198–204], 102 S.Ct. 929, 935–38, 71 L.Ed.2d 64, 70–75 (1982); Konigsberg v. State Bar, 353 U.S. 252, 273, 77 S.Ct. 722, 733, 1 L.Ed.2d 810, 825 (1957). Cf. Richmond Newspapers, Inc. v. Virginia, 448 U.S. 555, 100 S.Ct. 2814, 65 L.Ed.2d 973 (1980) (reaffirming right of public access to trials). Since DR 7–107 purports to restrict the free speech rights of attorneys, its validity turns upon the application of conventional First Amendment standards. . . .

Attorneys occupy a special status and perform an essential function in the administration of justice. Because attorneys are "officers of the court" with a special responsibility to protect the administration of justice, courts have recognized the need for the imposition of some reasonable speech restrictions upon attorneys. "The interest of the states in regulating lawyers is especially great since lawyers are essential to the primary governmental function of administering justice, and have historically been 'officers of the courts.'" Goldfarb v. Virginia State Bar, 421 U.S. 773, 792, 95 S.Ct. 2004, 2016, 44 L.Ed.2d 572, 588 (1975). Cf. Standards Relating to Fair Trial and Free Press, ABA Project on Minimum Standards for Criminal Justice at 82 (1968) (hereinafter "ABA Project") (lawyers have a "fiduciary obligation to the courts"). . . .

This interest in trial fairness is particularly acute in the criminal context. There, the problem of preserving the basic fairness and integrity of the proceeding is of constitutional dimension because the defendant's right to a fair trial is guaranteed in the Sixth Amendment of the federal Constitution. Some courts, including the Supreme Court, have even held that the criminal defendant's constitutional right to a fair trial must take precedence over free speech. See, e.g., Estes v. Texas, 381 U.S. 532, 540, 85 S.Ct. 1628, 1632, 14 L.Ed.2d 543, 549 (1965) (defendant's right to a fair trial is "the most fundamental of all freedoms"): [Chicago Council of Lawyers v.] Bauer, 522 F.2d [242] at 248 [(7th Cir.1975)]; [United States v.] Tijerina, 412 F.2d [661] at 667 [(10th Cir.1969)]; Hirschkop v. Virginia State Bar, 421 F.Supp. 1137, 1146–47 (E.D.Va.1976). Cf. Gannett Co., Inc. v. DePasquale, 443 U.S. 368, 99 S.Ct. 2898, 61 L.Ed.2d 608 (1979) (press may sometimes be excluded from pretrial hearings in a criminal case); Branzburg v. Hayes, 408 U.S. 665, 92 S.Ct. 2646, 33 L.Ed.2d 626 (1972) (journalists have no absolute First Amendment right to refuse to disclose their sources or other confidential information when asked to do so by a grand jury). . . .

Some guidance in this regard is furnished by the Supreme Court's landmark decisions concerning prejudicial trial publicity. See Sheppard v. Maxwell, 384 U.S. 333, 86 S.Ct. 1507, 16 L.Ed.2d 600 (1966); *Estes* [supra].

In *Estes,* the Supreme Court stressed the paramount importance of protecting the defendant's right to a fair trial. The opinion noted: "We have always held that the atmosphere essential to the preservation of a fair trial—the most fundamental of all freedoms—must be maintained at all costs." Id. at 540, 85 S.Ct. at 1632, 14 L.Ed.2d at 549.

In *Sheppard,* the Supreme Court observed:

Effective control of [counsel]—concededly within the court's power—might well have prevented the divulgence of inaccurate information, rumors, and accusations that made up much of the inflammatory publicity. . . .

. . . [W]here there is a reasonable likelihood that prejudicial news prior to trial will prevent a fair trial, the judge should continue the case until the threat abates, or transfer it to another county not so permeated with publicity. . . . If publicity during the proceedings threatens the fairness of the trial, a new trial should be ordered. But we must remember that reversals are but palliatives; the cure lies in those remedial measures that will prevent the prejudice at its inception. The courts must take such steps by rule and regulation that will protect their processes from prejudicial outside interferences. Neither prosecutors, counsel for defense, the accused, witnesses, court staff nor enforcement officers coming under the jurisdiction of the court should be permitted to frustrate its function. Collaboration between counsel and the press as to information affecting the fairness of a criminal trial is not only subject to regulation, but is highly censurable and worthy of disciplinary measures. (384 U.S. at 361–63, 86 S.Ct. at 1521–1522 (dictum)).

Thus, the Supreme Court targeted the evil as public speech that creates "a reasonable likelihood . . . (of) prevent(ing) a fair trial." Id. . . .

Many courts have upheld the constitutional validity of the "reasonable likelihood" standard for limiting lawyer extrajudicial comments during criminal trials. See, e.g., *Hirschkop,* 594 F.2d at 368–70; . . .

Other courts have rejected the "reasonable likelihood" test and have applied a traditional First Amendment analysis, holding that the Constitution protects an attorney's right to make extrajudicial statements, except when those comments create a "clear and present danger" or a "serious and imminent threat" to the administration of justice. See, e.g., *Bauer,* 522 F.2d at 249; . . . See also Model Rules of

Professional Conduct, ABA Commission of Evaluation of Professional Standards at 270, 275 (Alt.Draft 1981) (recommending change in standard to proscribe only those comments that have a "substantial likelihood of materially prejudicing" the trial, with change intended to incorporate "clear and present danger" test); ABA Standards 1978, supra (recommending change to "clear and present danger" test and suggesting constitutional invalidity of present standard); Note, "Professional Responsibility—Trial Publicity—Speech Restrictions Must Be Narrowly Drawn," 54 Texas L.Rev. 1158 (1976).

We are satisfied that the clear and present danger formulation is not constitutionally compelled when the subject of the restriction is the extrajudicial speech of attorneys participating in criminal trials. The clear and present danger test is neither more precise nor more certain in meaning than is the reasonable likelihood test. While the clear and present danger test may be stricter than the reasonable likelihood standard, strictness does not import more precision or imply greater clarity. . . .

Contrary to Hinds' assertions, the reasonable likelihood standard is susceptible of objective measurement. It is expressed in straightforward language, in terminology that is commonly and frequently used in communications. Younger [v. Smith], 30 Cal.App.3d [138] at 163–64, 106 Cal.Rptr. [225] at 241–42 [(1973)]. Whether a particular utterance creates a reasonable likelihood of affecting trial fairness will depend upon the special circumstances of each case. This inquiry involves a careful balancing and consideration of all relevant factors. Cf. Landmark [Communications, Inc., v. Virginia], 435 U.S. [829] at 842–43, 98 S.Ct. [1535] at 1543–1544 (such balancing required in a "free press" situation). These factors can include such matters as the nature of the statement, the timing of the statement, the extent to which the information has been publicized, the nature of the proceeding and its vulnerability to prejudicial influence, the attorney's status in the case, the lawyer's unique position as an informed and accurate source of information in the case, and the effect of unrestricted comment on the interest of the litigants and the integrity of the proceeding.[4] See Note,

4. . . . Several commentators have suggested that criminal defense attorneys should not be subject to the same strict speech limitations as prosecutors. See, e.g., Freedman and Starwood, "Prior Restraints on Freedom of Expression by Defendants and Defense Attorneys: Ratio Decidendi v. Obiter Dictum," 29 Stan.L.Rev. 607 (1977); Hirst, "Silence Orders—Preserving Political Expression by Defendants and Their Lawyers," 6 Harv.Civ. Rts.—Civ.Lib.L.Rev. 595, 604, 606–08 (1976); Isaacson, "Fair Trial and Free Press: An Opportunity for Coexistence," 29 Stan.L.Rev. 561, 568–70 (1977); Kaplan, "Of Babies and Bathwater," 29 Stan.L.Rev. 621, 625 n. 13 (1977); Comment, "Professional Ethics and Trial Publicity: Another Constitutional Attack on DR 7–107—Hirschkop v. Snead," 14 U.Rich.L.Rev. 231, 225–236 (1979). These commentators essentially reason that the constitutional guarantee of a fair trial belongs to the defendant alone, not the prosecution. See U.S. Const., Amends. IV, V, VI. Thus, regulations restricting free speech in this context should be tailored to advance the defendant's constitutionally protected interest in a fair trial. Moreover, they point out that "the scales of justice . . . are weighed extraordinarily heavy against an accused after his indictment." Bauer, 522 F.2d at 250, quoted in Freedman and Starwood, 29 Stan.L.Rev. at 611. Therefore, they conclude that the defendant and his counsel need access to the public to combat the stigma of an indictment.

"A Constitutional Assessment of Court Rules Restricting Lawyer Comment on Pending Litigation," 65 Cornell L.Rev. 1106, 1120–21 (1980); Model Rules 1981, supra at 275–76.

. . . While the administration of criminal justice is a governmental responsibility, it cannot be accomplished through fiat or authoritarian methods. Its proper functioning depends upon all who participate in the process. *Sheppard,* 384 U.S. at 361–62, 86 S.Ct. at 1521–1522. It utilizes adversarial, not inquisitorial, techniques. Lawyers in criminal cases represent opposing parties and conflicting interests. They must, therefore, discharge their professional responsibilities ethically as well as skillfully. They must do so according to carefully prescribed rules within a procedural framework designed to assure due process and fairness to both the accused and the public. The sole objective of this system is to secure justice. The benchmark of its success is the reaching of a just result based solely on properly adduced, competent evidence that is relevant to the truth of the criminal charges.

These considerations, in our view, require ethical constraints upon attorneys. These must include reasonable restrictions upon their extrajudicial speech to discourage and prevent extraneous matters from being insinuated into a criminal case. Such outside influences, if left unchecked, could divert the search for truth and wreck the intricate machinery of the criminal justice system. The reasonable likelihood test expressed in DR 7–107(D) is necessary and essential to the achievement of these objectives . . .

· · ·

III

· · ·

. . . The attorney's status in the case is highly relevant and may indeed be determinative on the question of whether he has violated DR 7–107(D). The prohibition of DR 7–107(D) does not apply unless the speech is made by an attorney "associated with" the criminal trial. . . .

Attorneys of record clearly fall within the class of lawyers who have a special connection with the case. Such attorneys have direct responsibility for the representation of parties and the actual conduct of a trial. They are individuals who have confidential information and an intimate knowledge of the merits of the prosecution. Their views are invested with particular credibility and weight in light of their positions. Hence, their statements relating to the trial are likely to be considered knowledgeable, reliable and true.

When extrajudicial statements of defense attorneys are prohibited, the interest sought to be protected is not simply the right of the accused to a fair trial. Defense attorneys are also silenced because of the government's interest in the "fair administration of justice" and basic "integrity of judicial processes." *Hirschkop,* 594 F.2d at 362, 376. As we have noted, this is a significant interest which justifies speech restrictions on attorneys associated with the case, whether as prosecutor or defense counsel.

The question remains whether an attorney who is not an attorney of record but is closely "associated with" the trial in other ways can be subject to the rule's sanctions. . . .

We are satisfied that DR 7–107(D) was intended to be applied to attorneys who have such an association with the defense of a criminal trial that extrajudicial statements made by them about the proceedings have a unique capacity for prejudicial impact upon the trial process. Accordingly, we now hold that under DR 7–107(D) an attorney who cooperates with the defense of a criminal prosecution on a regular and continuing basis, provides legal assistance in connection with the defense of a criminal charge, and holds himself out to be a member of the defense team is to be considered "associated with" the defense for purposes of invoking this disciplinary rule.

. . .

IV

Although we determine that DR 7–107(D) is constitutional, under the circumstances of this case, we conclude that Hinds should not be found in violation of the rule. We do so for two reasons. First, there is sufficient doubt as to the underlying facts regarding Hinds' relationship with the Chesimard defense to prevent an ultimate conclusion from being drawn on this important issue. . . .

Our second and primary reason for refusing to apply DR 7–107(D) in this instance is based on elementary fairness. This is the first time we have addressed the question of whether an attorney in Hinds' position would be considered "associated with" a case for purposes of falling within the rule's coverage. Furthermore, as already pointed out, this decision also constitutes the first time we have explained the balancing test to be applied for determining whether the extrajudicial speech of an attorney associated with an ongoing criminal trial is reasonably likely to interfere with a fair trial. We therefore deem it appropriate that DR 7–107(D) be applied prospectively only and that Hinds be given the benefit of this ruling. . . .

. . .

V

Since we have determined that DR 7–107(D), as construed by us in this decision, is to be given prospective effect only and, therefore, should not be applied to Hinds, the question arises whether he can nevertheless be punished under DR 1–102(A)(5). This disciplinary rule sanctions attorney conduct that is "prejudicial to the administration of justice." . . .

. . . . The New Jersey cases disclose a pattern of applying DR 1–102(A)(5) in conjunction with other more specific disciplinary rules to sanction attorney misconduct. See, e.g., In re Clark, 83 N.J. 458, 416 A.2d 851 (1980) (also violating DR 6–101, 9–102); Wilson, 81 N.J. 451, 409 A.2d 1153 (also violating DR 9–102). And on those few occasions when the rule has served as the sole basis for discipline, it has been applied only in situations involving conduct flagrantly violative of accepted professional norms. See, e.g., In re Schleimer, 78 N.J. 317, 394 A.2d 359 (1978) (false swearing). Thus, the rule's broad language proscribing acts "prejudicial to the administration of justice" takes on sufficient definition to pass constitutional muster, given these prior judicial determinations narrowing its scope to particularly egregious conduct. See Committee on Professional Ethics v. Durham, 279 N.W.2d 280 (Iowa 1979). . . .

Comments

In addition to First Amendment protection of a lawyer's statements, statements made in the course of representation of a client are protected by common law privilege. There is an absolute privilege for statements made in or reasonably related to a judicial proceeding. See Restatement Second of Torts § 586; Prosser & Keeton on Torts § 114 (5th ed. 1984); e.g., DeVivo v. Ascher, 228 N.J.Super. 453, 550 A.2d 163 (1988) ("We . . . favor a broad interpretation of the phrase 'in the course of a judicial proceeding.' "). There is a qualified privilege for statements in the course of representation outside of judicial proceedings. See Restatement Second of Torts § 595, Comment d; Prosser & Keeton, supra, § 115. See the discussion of these privileges in Chapter 5 above at p. 430.

Effectiveness of Disciplinary Enforcement

The procedural protections afforded lawyers in disciplinary proceedings are substantial. The effectiveness of the enforcement process has been something else. In 1970, the American Bar Association sponsored a study of lawyer discipline by a special committee headed by former Supreme Court Justice Tom C. Clark. The "Clark Committee Report," as it is commonly called, found that the disciplinary machinery in most jurisdictions was in poor shape: inadequate staff, poor record keeping, feeble prosecution, erratically functioning grievance committees, and other defects. It also found that the sanctions were unequal and generally mild relative to the heinousness of offenses. The report called for comprehensive reform, including enlarged staff resources, more hospitable concern for complainants, speedier preliminary investigations and trial, and better calibrated sanctions. See ABA, Special Committee on Evaluation of Disciplinary Enforcement (1970).

The course of events since the Clark Committee has not been smooth. Most jurisdictions have introduced reforms along the lines recommended in the Clark Report. At the same time, the volume and backlog of disciplinary cases has rapidly increased in many jurisdictions, sometimes overwhelming the disciplinary system, as in California in the 1980's. The bar takes some satisfaction in its efforts to improve disciplinary enforcement, but many people within the bar and in the general public remain profoundly dissatisfied. In 1988, the Connecticut Judicial Department created a special committee to look into the situation in that state. Among other things, the committee held open meetings at which members of the public could express their feelings. Members of the Committee expressed shock at the volume and vehemence of the witnesses' criticism of lawyer ethics, and the frustration and outrage that people felt at being unable to get recourse against misconduct and mistreatment by their lawyers, including overcharging, procrastination, refusal to respond, evasion and lying. The authors of this book, as observers of the profession, believe that this kind of public opinion is typical throughout the country.

Consider the two assessments of the disciplinary system that follow.

T. McPIKE AND MARK HARRISON, "LAWYER DISCIPLINE SINCE 1970," IN ALI–ABA, LAW PRACTICE QUALITY EVALUATION: AN APPRAISAL OF PEER REVIEW AND OTHER MEASURES TO ENHANCE PROFESSIONAL PERFORMANCE
(September 10–12, 1987).*

The accusation that the legal profession isn't doing enough to discipline unethical lawyers is a perennial complaint by the public and the press. The criticism is unfair, unjustified by the record, and unsupported by the facts.

The lawyer disciplinary practices have been transformed in the last 17 years from what was called in 1970 a "scandalous situation" to a sophisticated, effective system of self regulation today.

Consider the facts:

- Disciplinary agency budgets for 42 of 54 jurisdictions reporting to the ABA totaled over $26 million in 1985 compared to under $2 million in funds to reimburse clients wronged by unethical lawyers.

- The number of sanctions imposed for ethics violations has increased nationally in all categories by 122 percent from 1979 to 1985.

- The ABA Standards for Lawyer Discipline and Disability Procedures provide a detailed set of guidelines for state disciplinary systems; 47 states revised their disciplinary rules after the standards were published in 1979.

- The ABA National Disciplinary Data Bank has been distributing names of lawyers for 15 years to prevent a lawyer who was disbarred in one state from moving to another state to practice law.

Of primary importance, however, is the attitude that has developed among lawyers about lawyer discipline. Twenty-nine states have public members on their disciplinary boards. Of those states, 11 have been evaluated by the ABA, and it turns out that the lawyer members of the boards are more likely to find misconduct and to vote for a stronger sanction than non-lawyer members.

From 24 evaluations and hundreds of interviews with lawyers, clients, judges, and others, it is clear that there is a new understanding about professional discipline. It is understood to be fundamental to the profession's duty to the public. The old attitude of tolerance for professional misconduct ("there but for the grace of God go I") is in hasty retreat.

"A Scandalous Situation"

In 1970 the ABA Special Committee on Evaluation of Disciplinary Enforcement, better known as the Clark Committee after its chairman, former U.S. Supreme Court Justice Tom Clark, stated:

> After three years of studying lawyer discipline throughout the country, this Committee must report the existence of a scandalous situation that requires the immediate attention of the profession.

The ABA House of Delegates had established the Clark Committee in 1967 "to assemble and study information relevant to all aspects of professional discipline."

Justice Clark's committee did a thorough job. It began by surveying disciplinary authorities, which at the time consisted of local and county as well as state agencies. The disciplinary agency at the time was usually a bar association. There were few independent bodies. After completing the survey, the committee held hearings nationwide.

What the committee learned was deeply disturbing. To emphasize the urgency of its call for action, the committee's 1970 report, which has come to be called the Clark Report, detailed the problems it had uncovered:

> With few exceptions, the prevailing attitude of lawyers toward disciplinary enforcement ranges from apathy to outright hostility. Disciplinary action is practically nonexistent in many jurisdictions; practices and procedures are antiquated; many disciplinary agencies have little power to take effective steps against malefactors.

> The committee has found that in some instances disbarred attorneys are able to continue to practice in another locale; that lawyers convicted of federal income tax violations are not disciplined; that lawyers convicted of serious crimes are not disciplined until after appeals from their convictions have been concluded, often a matter of three or four years, so that even lawyers convicted of serious crimes, such as bribery of a governmental agency

employee, are able to continue to practice before the very agency whose representative they have corrupted;

[T]hat even after disbarment lawyers are reinstated as a matter of course; that lawyers fail to report violations of the Code of Professional Responsibility committed by their brethren, much less conduct that violates the criminal law; that lawyers will not appear or cooperate in proceedings against other lawyers but instead will exert their influence to stymie the proceedings;

[T]hat in communities with a limited attorney population disciplinary agencies will not proceed against prominent lawyers or firms and that, even when they do, no disciplinary action is taken, because the members of the disciplinary agency simply will not make findings against those with whom they are professionally and socially well acquainted; and that, finally, state disciplinary agencies are undermanned and underfinanced, many having no staff whatever for investigation or prosecution of complaints.

With the filing of the Clark Report, the legal profession found itself in a novel and uncomfortable position. Criticism of lawyers' self-regulation traditionally had come from the public and at a local level. But now the profession was faced with evidence of a nationwide pattern of lawyers tolerating professional misconduct, and this time the charges were not prompted by disgruntled clients or the press but by a committee of nationally prominent lawyers. Local reforms quite plainly would not remedy the ills uncovered in the Clark Report.

A Total Restructuring

The Clark Committee called for what amounted to a total restructuring of many state disciplinary systems, the abolition of local systems, and the creation of a permanent national body to assist states in reform.

Some other recommendations of the Clark Report were:

- Discipline in each state should be centralized under the state supreme court.
- Procedural steps should be reduced to a minimum.
- Full-time disciplinary counsel should be used instead of volunteers.
- Procedures should be established to remove attorneys incapacitated by senility, mental illness, drug or alcohol addiction.
- Mechanisms should be developed for reciprocal discipline.
- Procedures should be developed for interim suspensions of lawyers convicted of serious crimes pending appeal.
- Jury trials should be eliminated in disciplinary cases.
- Disciplinary proceedings should be public following the formal hearing.

- A national discipline data bank should be established to collect and disseminate disciplinary information.

Prompt Reforms

Implementation of the Clark Committee's recommendations began immediately. The ABA formed the Special Committee on the Coordination of Disciplinary Enforcement in 1970. The next year an ABA Center for Professional Responsibility, an administrative center to support the special committee, was established. The need for a permanent committee was apparent by 1973, and the special committee was succeeded by the Standing Committee on Professional Discipline . . .

Many Accomplishments

The discipline and professional responsibility efforts of the ABA since 1973 and of the states since 1977 have cost more than $130 million. Here is what has been accomplished with these funds:

- Since 1979, when the standards were published, 48 states and the District of Columbia have made major revisions in their rules.

- According to a 1983 ABA survey, the majority of states comply with a majority of the ABA standards. These reforms include non-lawyers on hearing boards, immunity for witnesses and complainants, procedures designed to minimize delay, interim suspension rules, disability removal procedures, and others.

- Twenty-four jurisdictions have had their systems carefully examined by an ABA evaluation team to assist in improving operations. They are District of Columbia, Idaho, Minnesota, Mississippi, Texas, New Jersey, New Mexico, Florida, New York, Colorado, Delaware, Georgia, Nevada, Arizona, North Dakota, Alaska, Illinois, Virginia, Utah, Ohio, Wisconsin, Oklahoma, Oregon, Louisiana.

- Forty-eight states have established client security funds that have paid millions of dollars to injured clients.

- A professional disciplinary counsel bar has been created, so that now 47 states and the District of Columbia have fulltime disciplinary counsel.

- A national reporter for disciplinary and professional responsibility case law, developed jointly by the ABA and the Bureau of National Affairs, is published biweekly.

- The National Conference of Bar Examiners utilizes the National Discipline Data Bank to screen applicants referred to it, preventing lawyers disbarred in one state from continuing practice elsewhere.

- Disciplinary enforcement continues to expand as systems become more professional and the number of lawyers increases.

From 1978 to 1985 sanctions increased nationally by 122 percent in all categories.

- Some larger states, for example California, have sophisticated enforcement, such as lawyer probation departments, and others, like Illinois, have fully computerized recordkeeping.

- In February 1986 the ABA adopted Standards for Imposing Lawyer Sanctions to assist courts in determining what sanction a lawyer should receive for specific misconduct and to ensure that the public will be adequately protected. Several state supreme courts have already referred to the standards in disciplinary opinions. . . .

GEOFFREY C. HAZARD, Jr., "DISCIPLINARY PROCESS NEEDS MAJOR REFORMING"

National Law Journal, August 1, 1988, p. 13.*

HALT [Help Abolish Legal Tyranny] is a non-profit activist organization whose aim is improving the quality and integrity of the legal profession. That description would also fit the American Bar Association, so it is important to note that HALT is not quite the same as the ABA. Although concerned about the legal profession, and having lawyers as part of its constituency, HALT seeks to improve the profession from the outside rather than the inside.

Recently HALT issued a report on the state of disciplinary enforcement throughout the country. Its primary findings were:

— In many jurisdictions there is prolonged delay between a grievance and a disposition. Serious cases usually take a couple of years. Meanwhile, the lawyer continues to practice.

— Investigatory and prosecutorial resources are in short supply compared with the demand. If enforcement were made more rigorous, the imbalance would be worse.

— Complainants are not given an encouraging reception nor moral support. The button for the disciplinary machinery often is difficult to locate. The proceedings themselves are invisible to the general public, owing to the requirement that they be kept confidential until a sanction is imposed.

— Sanctions generally are mild. Many cases get plea-bargained down to minor dispositions. Even in serious cases the authorities, including the reviewing courts, are sympathetic to lawyer infirmities. Lawyers who have cheated and lied to clients, including lying about their cheating, may get off with a short suspension if they can prove they were alcoholics, or were having marital problems, or other mitigating circumstances.

The total effect, according to HALT, is a system that is overburdened, more or less fortuitous in its outcomes, cool toward the rage and frustration of victims, and lenient when measured by the premise that professional misconduct is a serious matter.

Sound familiar? The conclusions drawn by HALT are not greatly different from those of the Clark Committee twenty years ago.

The uncertain condition of disciplinary enforcement thus persists. This, despite the fact that almost all jurisdictions have substantially expanded and improved their disciplinary machinery over the years since the Clark Report. What is happening?

A partial explanation is that the number of lawyers has greatly increased over the same period, at a rate paralleling the increase in disciplinary resources. Moreover, the expansion of the bar has been at the low end of the professional population in terms of age and experience. Younger and more inexperienced lawyers are probably no more prone to misbehavior than older ones. However, they probably are more vulnerable to temptation and to being caught if they succumb.

Another factor is the "due process explosion" in disciplinary procedure. Disciplinary procedure used to be drum-head justice, partly because it was invoked only in clearcut cases. However, the procedure has become elaborate—preliminary investigation, probable cause hearing, adversarial trial in contested cases, and judicial review where serious sanctions were involved. . . . In short, the typical case unit in disciplinary matters has become larger than it used to be.

Another likely factor in the disciplinary crunch is that lawyers are now more willing to report miscreant colleagues and to testify against them. In the old days, they usually just turned their backs, a powerful sanction when the bar was an intimate group.

Still another factor may be that more lawyers are willing to take ethical risks than they used to be. Many people nowadays see pervasive decline in conformity to legal standards throughout our society. There is no reason to think lawyers are immune from this tendency.

Finally, improvement in the disciplinary machinery itself probably contributes to the problem. When disciplinary enforcement was largely nominal so were the enforcement statistics. This phenomenon mirrors the truism in criminal justice that improvement in law enforcement results in higher reported crime rates.

In all these respects, the disciplinary system is eerily similar to the criminal justice system as it operates in white collar offenses. Indeed, perhaps we should analyze the disciplinary system as if it were a quasi-criminal system involving a special category of white collar law enforcement. Such a characterization is implicit in one of HALT's principal recommendations, that administration of the disciplinary system be moved outside the bar and be placed in a public agency, like other regulatory enforcement.

The HALT report implies that relocating enforcement jurisdiction from the bar to a public agency would substantially improve the machinery's performance. Such a change could make for some improvement.   It seems likely that reviewing judges could then recognize that lawyer discipline deals with white-collar crime and miscreancy instead of simple waywardness within a fraternity.   Moreover, legislatures might provide more financial resources to an agency under their scrutiny than one under the aegis of the legal profession.   Perhaps a public agency would incline toward more publicity and show more solicitude toward victims.   If these influences combined, the result could be substantial strengthening of the disciplinary process and enhancement of its deterrent effects.

There would be little loss to the bar in such a reallocation of disciplinary jurisdiction.   The disciplinary system is already beyond the direct supervision of the organized bar, except the few jurisdictions where the profession is still an essentially fraternal group.   On a day-to-day basis the disciplinary machinery is in the hands of the professional staff, who do the investigations, make the charging decisions, and prosecute the cases that have to go the whole route.   A change in jurisdiction would not much affect those routines, and the system would remain remote from the daily concerns of the large majority of the practicing bar. . . .

Perhaps there is need to reexamine basic premises and to consider more radical reforms.   For example, lawyers could be required to be members of associations that would themselves be answerable in some way for misconduct of their members.   There is now a rule that members of firms must monitor ethical performance within the firm. Model Rule 5.1 provides: "A partner in a law firm shall make reasonable efforts to ensure that the firm has in effect measures giving reasonable assurance that all lawyers in the firm conform to the rules of professional conduct."   What if every lawyer had to maintain membership in an association that had such a responsibility?

Comments

Another assessment is the thoughtful study Martyn, Lawyer Competence and Lawyer Discipline: Beyond the Bar?, 69 Georgetown L.J. 705 (1981), focusing on the problem of policing against incompetence. Professor Martyn concludes that the bar has not been successful in dealing with incompetence and is unlikely to be so, and hence that either the remedy of civil malpractice suits or more pervasive public regulation will be needed.   This is much the same conclusion as in the HALT report, summarized above.   However, the malpractice remedy operates more or less randomly and more intensive public regulation seems an unlikely prospect.   If the principal justification for licensure is protection against incompetence (as distinct from lawyer dishonesty, which is covered by criminal law in any event), and if effective policing against incompetency remains unattainable, what is the justification for licensure?

A specific problem of great seriousness in the legal profession is incompetence and other misconduct resulting from substance abuse.

For a review of the alcohol problem, see Bloom and Wallinger, Lawyers and Alcoholism: Is It Time for a New Approach?, 61 Temple L.Rev. 1409 (1988), which includes references to the related problem of drug abuse.

For a descriptive survey of studies of regulation of the legal profession, see Maru, Research on the Legal Profession, c. 4 (2d ed. 1986). Also see Garth, Rethinking the Legal Profession's Approach to Collective Self–Improvement: Competence and the Consumer Perspective, 1983 Wisc.L.Rev. 639; and Levinson, Professional Responsibility Issues in Administrative Adjudication, 2 B.Y.U.J.Pub.L. 219 (1988).

C. REGULATION OF THE PROFESSION BY INSTITUTIONAL CONTROLS

Note on Legal Structure of Law Practice

As Justice O'Connor suggests in her dissent in *Shapero v. Kentucky State Bar,* printed below, being a "lawyer" is a distinct social identity. A practitioner of law is someone who: (1) graduated from an accredited law school, and thus underwent the socialization process of legal education; (2) successfully passed the bar admission requirements, and has a certificate to prove it, whereby marking herself off from the large majority of the white collar workforce that does not have such a certificate; (3) primarily is engaged in work that is done exclusively or primarily by lawyers, including preparing and conducting various kinds of litigation and negotiating and documenting various kinds of contracts; (4) spends her day in lawyer work settings, particularly independent law firms and the law departments of government agencies and business corporations; and (5) talks and thinks "law" in shop talk, at professional meetings, in schmoozing with peers after work, and in response to conversational gambits at cocktail parties.

Legal Protection of Competition

Being a lawyer is sustained and influenced by complex institutional structures, far beyond admission requirements and the disciplinary system. Even in the absence of admission requirements and the disciplinary system, the practice of law would still be subject to general legal controls that operate on lawyers along with everyone else. These controls include criminal law, contract law, and tort law, including the law of malpractice. Throughout the materials in this book we have seen these general legal controls applied to lawyers. See, e.g., *United States v. Benjamin,* Chapter 2 above (mail fraud, securities fraud); *Fassihi v. Sommers,* Chapter 9 above (fiduciary duty). Indeed, many of the central provisions in the Rules of Professional Conduct and the Code of Professional Responsibility reflect or correspond to general rules of common law, particularly the law of agency. These rules of law would continue to operate in the absence of specific regulation of the legal profession and would protect clients and third persons even if

there were no restrictions on admission to practice law and no disciplinary machinery.

Second, if common law at large did not provide adequate protection
against misconduct by an unregulated legal profession, entrepreneurs
could come forward to turn such a lamentable situation into opportunity.
The legal profession's monopoly of the practice of law may be seen as the
result of such entrepreneurship. In the absence of their legal monopoly,
lawyers would be subject to competition from other institutions that
could provide equivalent services. The potential for such competition is
sustained by the common law rule that trades and businesses generally
are open to competition, which is as much a legal rule as any regulatory
provision. Hence, the question is not whether the legal profession
should be "unregulated" but whether there should be special legal
controls on lawyers and, if so, what kind.

Indirect Legal Controls on the Lawyer's Workplace

Law practice is also subject to indirect controls that have legal
foundations. Particularly influential on the lawyer's environment are
the atmosphere and routines in the law firm or law department in
which the lawyer works day to day; in other law firms and law
departments with which the lawyer interacts in her day to day work
and by whom she might be employed if she changes jobs; in the courts
and the government agencies with whom the lawyer interacts; and in
the bar associations in which the lawyer participates. These institutions—the firms, the government agencies, and the bar associations—
all have political structures and agendas and are subject to economic
incentives and constraints. They all have cultural characteristics. For
example, some law firms are high pressure and earn high incomes;
others are not. Some are very "pro bono" oriented; others are not.
Some courts where lawyers appear are well managed and on top of
their calendars; others are bogged down and chaotic. Some government agencies that lawyers have to deal with have high technical
competence and high esprit de corps; others are sluggish and incompetent. Together, these institutions are the matrix of life in which the
lawyer tries to accomplish professional tasks, adjusts to the realities of
practice, and takes on her professional identity.

Systematic studies of careers in law are relatively few. One can
imagine studies that take samples from cohorts of graduates from a
cross-section of law schools ("elite," "national," state university, "local,"
etc.) at various years (1960, 1970, 1980, for example) and track their
employment patterns over the years. Such studies would show what
kinds of jobs graduates begin with (firms, prosecutor offices, sharing
office space, etc.), when and where they shift jobs, and when they more
or less settle into a permanent career. In 1985, seven law schools
cooperated in such a study but only on the condition that the data not
correlate the schools with their graduates. The schools were Boston
College, Boston University, Columbia, University of Connecticut, Harvard, Northeastern, and Suffolk. Key findings were that:

— 70% remain in the same metropolitan area in which they took their first law job;

— about 80% of law school graduates remain in law practice or a law-related vocation such as government;

— 40% were in a work setting other than a private law firm;

— 75% of those who had been out 25 years had made at least one job change.

Those more than 15 years out will have had on the average two or three different jobs. The ones most likely still to be in the same work setting where they started are those who joined large law firms (and were the survivors) and those who started in sole practice. See L. Vogt, From Law School Career, Harvard Law School Program on the Legal Profession (May, 1986) ("Career Paths Study").

The best conceptual formulation of lawyer employment in terms of the structure of law practice is in Heinz and Laumann, Chicago Lawyers: The Social Structure of the Bar (1983). A valuable study focussing on large law firms is Nelson, The Changing Structure of Opportunity: Recruitment and Careers in Large Law Firms, 1983 Am. Bar Found.Res.J. 109. See also Hedegard, Causes of Career–Relevant Interest Changes Among First–Year Law Students: Some Research Data, 1982 Am. Bar Found.Res.J. 787; Hirsch, Are You on Target?, 12 Barrister 17 (1985) (survey of lawyers' job satisfaction); Sander and Williams, Why are There So Many Lawyers? Perspectives on a Turbulent Market, 14 Law & Social Inquiry 431 (1989). Compare D. Kennedy, Legal Education and the Reproduction of Hierarchy: A Polemic Against the System (1983) (critical legal theory perspective); R. Abel, Lawyers, in Lipson and Wheeler, eds., Law and the Social Sciences (1988) (same); and Handler, The Lawyer and His Community: The Practicing Bar in a Middle–Sized City (1967). In most of these studies there is a tendency to treat all lawyers with similar backgrounds as more or less the same, disregarding differences within various "sectors" of the legal profession and among individuals. That there are sharp individual differences is suggested by recalling the backgrounds of some Supreme Court Justices. For example, Chief Justice Earl Warren was a graduate of the law school of the University of California, Berkeley, and Justice William Brennan was a graduate of Harvard Law School, while Chief Justice Warren Burger was a graduate of William Mitchell Law School and Justice Sandra Day O'Connor went to Stanford Law School, and Governors Cuomo of New York and Deukmejian of California went to St. Johns at the same time. This diversity probably proves something, but exactly what?

A full account of the lawyer's vocation matrix would have to include a political, economic, sociological, and historical analysis of American legal institutions. Obviously, we do not have time for that here. We simply emphasize that an adequate account of the vocation of "lawyer" would extend that far, and we incorporate by reference whatever the student has come to know about these aspects of the law.

However, all the institutions constituting the lawyer's vocational matrix also have legal structures. Institutions such as law firms, courts and bar associations do not simply exist. They have been created by law or with the authority of law, they have legal powers that can impinge on lawyers, and they are legally accountable in one way or another. See, e.g., *Hishon v. King & Spalding* (law firm); *Shapero v. Kentucky State Bar* (bar association), both printed below. See Model Rules 5.1–5.3.

The legal aspects of this institutional structure are as much a part of the system of professional regulation as are the rules governing admission to practice or those of professional discipline. For example, among the important institutional influences on law practice is the character of the courts in which a litigation lawyer practices and in which a transaction lawyer has to anticipate the transaction may ultimately be litigated. Contrast in this respect the Supreme Court of the United States, whose opinions make up a large part of today's law school curriculum, and the trial court in a state where judges are elected by popular vote. Suppose a lawyer had a case involving the publishability of a literary work alleged to be pornographic, for example. Would she handle the matter differently if she took it over after certiorari had been granted by the Supreme Court, as compared with the situation of a client who could not afford to litigate beyond a preliminary injunction in front of the local trial court? It would of course make all the difference in the world, or at least all the difference in the United States. Among the differences: The Supreme Court is the Supreme Court, not a one-person local trial judge; the Supreme Court is an instrument of the United States Government, and its judges have tenure effectively for life; the state trial judge faces an election in the near future, and has to worry about the local news media and being able to raise campaign funding if necessary; the Supreme Court will have amicus briefs from all sectors of the national intelligentsia, while the state trial judge may have nothing more than poorly drafted briefs by practitioners who have never before handled a First Amendment case. All these aspects of the case are "legal"—the rules governing tenure of the judges, the rules defining the participants in the litigation, and the character of the forum that determines the kinds of argument that are submitted.

The institutions most directly influencing the lawyer are her situation of employment and her relationship to professional colleagues. Consider, first, the lawyer's employment situation: While a lawyer's relationship with a client can be terminated by the client at any time and without reason, M.R. 1.16, it does not necessarily follow that the lawyer's employment relationship with a firm or law department similarly is merely "at will." Compare *Hishon v. King & Spalding*, printed below. Did the court in *Herbster*, also printed below, recognize the complexities of the situation before it?

HISHON v. KING & SPALDING

Supreme Court of the United States, 1984.
467 U.S. 69, 104 S.Ct. 2229, 81 L.Ed.2d 59.

CHIEF JUSTICE BURGER delivered the opinion of the Court.

We granted certiorari to determine whether the District Court properly dismissed a Title VII complaint alleging that a law partnership discriminated against petitioner, a woman lawyer employed as an associate, when it failed to invite her to become a partner.

I

A

In 1972 petitioner Elizabeth Anderson Hishon accepted a position as an associate with respondent, a large Atlanta law firm established as a general partnership. When this suit was filed in 1980, the firm had more than 50 partners and employed approximately 50 attorneys as associates. Up to that time, no woman had ever served as a partner at the firm.

Petitioner alleges that the prospect of partnership was an important factor in her initial decision to accept employment with respondent. She alleges that respondent used the possibility of ultimate partnership as a recruiting device to induce petitioner and other young lawyers to become associates at the firm. According to the complaint, respondent represented that advancement to partnership after five or six years was "a matter of course" for associates "who receive[d] satisfactory evaluations" and that associates were promoted to partnership "on a fair and equal basis." Petitioner alleges that she relied on these representations when she accepted employment with respondent. The complaint further alleges that respondent's promise to consider her on a "fair and equal basis" created a binding employment contract.

In May 1978 the partnership considered and rejected Hishon for admission to the partnership; one year later, the partners again declined to invite her to become a partner. Once an associate is passed over for partnership at respondent's firm, the associate is notified to begin seeking employment elsewhere. Petitioner's employment as an associate terminated on December 31, 1979.

B

Hishon filed a charge with the Equal Employment Opportunity Commission on November 19, 1979, claiming that respondent had discriminated against her on the basis of her sex in violation of Title VII of the Civil Rights Act of 1964, 78 Stat. 241, as amended, 42 U.S.C. § 2000e et seq. Ten days later the Commission issued a notice of right to sue, and on February 27, 1980, Hishon brought this action in the United States District Court for the Northern District of Georgia. She sought declaratory and injunctive relief, backpay, and compensatory damages "in lieu of reinstatement and promotion to partnership." This, of course, negates any claim for specific performance of the contract alleged.

The District Court dismissed the complaint on the ground that Title VII was inapplicable to the selection of partners by a partnership. 24 FEP Cases 1303 (1980). A divided panel of the United States Court of Appeals for the Eleventh Circuit affirmed. 678 F.2d 1022 (1982). We granted certiorari, 459 U.S. 1169, 103 S.Ct. 813, 74 L.Ed.2d 1012 (1983), and we reverse.

II

At this stage of the litigation, we must accept petitioner's allegations as true. A court may dismiss a complaint only if it is clear that no relief could be granted under any set of facts that could be proved consistent with the allegations. Conley v. Gibson, 355 U.S. 41, 45–46 (1957). The issue before us is whether petitioner's allegations state a claim under Title VII, the relevant portion of which provides as follows:

"(a) *It shall be an unlawful employment practice for an employer—*

"(1) to fail or refuse to hire or to discharge any individual, or otherwise *to discriminate against any individual with respect to his* compensation, *terms, conditions, or privileges of employment, because of such individual's* race, color, religion, *sex,* or national origin." 42 U.S.C. § 2000e–2(a) (emphasis added).

A

Petitioner alleges that respondent is an "employer" to whom Title VII is addressed.[3] She then asserts that consideration for partnership was one of the "terms, conditions, or privileges of employment" as an associate with respondent.[4] See § 2000e–2(a)(1). If this is correct, respondent could not base an adverse partnership decision on "race, color, religion, sex, or national origin."

Once a contractual relationship of employment is established, the provisions of Title VII attach and govern certain aspects of that relationship.[5] In the context of Title VII, the contract of employment may be written or oral, formal or informal; an informal contract of employment may arise by the simple act of handing a job applicant a

3. The statute defines an "employer" as a "person engaged in an industry affecting commerce who has fifteen or more employees for each working day in each of twenty or more calendar weeks in the current or preceding calendar year," § 2000e(b), and a "person" is explicitly defined to include "partnerships," § 2000e(a). The complaint alleges that respondent's partnership satisfies these requirements.

4. Petitioner has raised other theories of Title VII liability which, in light of our disposition, need not be addressed.

5. Title VII also may be relevant in the absence of an existing employment relationship, as when an employer *refuses* to hire someone. See § 2000e–2(a)(1). However, discrimination in that circumstance does not concern the "terms, conditions, or privileges of employment," which is the focus of the present case.

shovel and providing a workplace. The contractual relationship of employment triggers the provision of Title VII governing "terms, conditions, or privileges of employment." Title VII in turn forbids discrimination on the basis of "race, color, religion, sex, or national origin."

Because the underlying employment relationship is contractual, it follows that the "terms, conditions, or privileges of employment" clearly include benefits that are part of an employment contract. Here, petitioner in essence alleges that respondent made a contract to consider her for partnership.[6] Indeed, this promise was allegedly a key contractual provision which induced her to accept employment. If the evidence at trial establishes that the parties contracted to have petitioner considered for partnership, that promise clearly was a term, condition, or privilege of her employment. Title VII would then bind respondent to consider petitioner for partnership as the statute provides, i.e., without regard to petitioner's sex. The contract she alleges would lead to the same result.

Petitioner's claim that a contract was made, however, is not the only allegation that would qualify respondent's consideration of petitioner for partnership as a term, condition, or privilege of employment. An employer may provide its employees with many benefits that it is under no obligation to furnish by any express or implied contract. Such a benefit, though not a contractual *right* of employment, may qualify as a "privileg[e]" of employment under Title VII. A benefit that is part and parcel of the employment relationship may not be doled out in a discriminatory fashion, even if the employer would be free under the employment contract simply not to provide the benefit at all. Those benefits that comprise the "incidents of employment," S.Rep. No. 867, 88th Cong., 2d Sess., 11 (1964),[7] or that form "an aspect of the relationship between the employer and employees," Chemical & Alkali Workers v. Pittsburgh Plate Glass Co., 404 U.S. 157, 178, 92 S.Ct. 383, 397, 30 L.Ed.2d 341 (1971),[8] may not be afforded in a manner contrary to Title VII.

---

6. Petitioner alleges not only that respondent promised to consider her for partnership, but also that it promised to consider her on a "fair and equal basis." This latter promise is not necessary to petitioner's Title VII claim. Even if the employment contract did not afford a basis for an implied condition that the ultimate decision would be fairly made on the merits, Title VII itself would impose such a requirement. If the promised consideration for partnership is a term, condition, or privilege of employment, then the partnership decision must be without regard to "race, color, religion, sex, or national origin."

7. Senate Report No. 867 concerned S.1937, which the Senate postponed indefinitely after it amended a House version of what ultimately became the Civil Rights Act of 1964. See 110 Cong.Rec. 14602 (1964). The Report is relevant here because S.1937 contained language similar to that ultimately found in the Civil Rights Act. It guaranteed "equal employment opportunity," which was defined to "include all the compensation, terms, conditions, and privileges of employment." S.Rep. No. 867, 88th Cong., 2d Sess., 24 (1964).

8. *Chemical & Alkali Workers* pertains to § 8(d) of the National Labor Relations Act (NLRA), which describes the obligation of employers and unions to meet and confer regarding "wages, hours, and other terms and conditions of employment." 61 Stat. 142, as amended, 29 U.S.C. § 158(d). The meaning of this analogous language sheds light on the Title VII provision at issue here. We have drawn analogies to the NLRA in other

Several allegations in petitioner's complaint would support the conclusion that the opportunity to become a partner was part and parcel of an associate's status as an employee at respondent's firm, independent of any allegation that such an opportunity was included in associates' employment contracts. Petitioner alleges that respondent's associates could regularly expect to be considered for partnership at the end of their "apprenticeships," and it appears that lawyers outside the firm were not routinely so considered.[9] Thus, the benefit of partnership consideration was allegedly linked directly with an associate's status as an employee, and this linkage was far more than coincidental: petitioner alleges that respondent explicitly used the prospect of ultimate partnership to induce young lawyers to join the firm. Indeed, the importance of the partnership decision to a lawyer's status as an associate is underscored by the allegation that associates' employment is terminated if they are not elected to become partners. These allegations, if proved at trial, would suffice to show that partnership consideration was a term, condition, or privilege of an associate's employment at respondent's firm, and accordingly that partnership consideration must be without regard to sex.

B

Respondent contends that advancement to partnership may never qualify as a term, condition, or privilege of employment for purposes of Title VII. First, respondent asserts that elevation to partnership entails a change in status from an "employee" to an "employer." However, even if respondent is correct that a partnership invitation is not itself an offer of employment, Title VII would nonetheless apply and preclude discrimination on the basis of sex. The benefit a plaintiff is denied need not *be* employment to fall within Title VII's protection; it need only be a term, condition, or privilege *of* employment. It is also of no consequence that employment as an associate necessarily ends when an associate becomes a partner. A benefit need not accrue before a person's employment is completed to be a term, condition, or privilege of that employment relationship. Pension benefits, for example, qualify as terms, conditions, or privileges of employment even though they are received only after employment terminates. Arizona Governing Committee for Tax Deferred Annuity & Deferred Compensation Plans v. Norris, 463 U.S. 1079, 103 S.Ct. 3492, 77 L.Ed.2d 1236 (1983) (opinion of Marshall, J.). Accordingly, nothing in the change in status that advancement to partnership might entail means that partnership consideration falls outside the terms of the statute. See Lucido v. Cravath, Swaine & Moore, 425 F.Supp. 123, 128–129 (SDNY 1977).

Title VII contexts, see Franks v. Bowman Transportation Co., 424 U.S. 747, 768–770, 96 S.Ct. 1251, 1266–1267, 47 L.Ed.2d 444 (1976), and have noted that certain sections of Title VII were expressly patterned after the NLRA, see Albemarle Paper Co. v. Moody, 422 U.S. 405, 419, 95 S.Ct. 2362, 2372, 45 L.Ed.2d 280 (1975).

9. Respondent's own submissions indicate that most of respondent's partners in fact were selected from the ranks of associates who had spent their entire prepartnership legal careers (excluding judicial clerkships) with the firm.

Second, respondent argues that Title VII categorically exempts partnership decisions from scrutiny. However, respondent points to nothing in the statute or the legislative history that would support such a *per se* exemption.[10] When Congress wanted to grant an employer complete immunity, it expressly did so.[11]

Third, respondent argues that application of Title VII in this case would infringe constitutional rights of expression or association. Although we have recognized that the activities of lawyers may make a "distinctive contribution . . . to the ideas and beliefs of our society," NAACP v. Button, 371 U.S. 415, 431, 83 S.Ct. 328, 337, 9 L.Ed.2d 405 (1963), respondent has not shown how its ability to fulfill such a function would be inhibited by a requirement that it consider petitioner for partnership on her merits. Moreover, as we have held in another context, "[i]nvidious private discrimination may be characterized as a form of exercising freedom of association protected by the First Amendment, but it has never been accorded affirmative constitutional protections." Norwood v. Harrison, 413 U.S. 455, 470, 93 S.Ct. 2804, 2813, 37 L.Ed.2d 723 (1973). There is no constitutional right, for example, to discriminate in the selection of who may attend a private school or join a labor union. Runyon v. McCrary, 427 U.S. 160, 96 S.Ct. 2586, 49 L.Ed.2d 415 (1976); Railway Mail Assn. v. Corsi, 326 U.S. 88, 93–94, 65 S.Ct. 1483, 1487–1488, 89 L.Ed. 2072 (1945).

III

We conclude that petitioner's complaint states a claim cognizable under Title VII. Petitioner therefore is entitled to her day in court to prove her allegations. The judgment of the Court of Appeals is reversed, and the case is remanded for further proceedings consistent with this opinion.

It is so ordered.

10. The only legislative history respondent offers to support its position is Senator Cotton's defense of an unsuccessful amendment to limit Title VII to businesses with 100 or more employees. In this connection the Senator stated:

"[W]hen a small businessman who employs 30 or 25 or 26 persons selects an employee, he comes very close to selecting a partner; and when a businessman selects a partner, he comes dangerously close to the situation he faces when he selects a wife." 110 Cong. Rec. 13085 (1964); accord, 118 Cong.Rec. 1524, 2391 (1972).

Because Senator Cotton's amendment failed, it is unclear to what extent Congress shared his concerns about selecting partners. In any event, his views hardly conflict with our narrow holding today: that in appropriate circumstances partnership consideration may qualify as a term, condition, or privilege of a person's employment with an employer large enough to be covered by Title VII.

11. For example, Congress expressly exempted Indian tribes and certain agencies of the District of Columbia, 42 U.S.C. § 2000e(b)(1), small businesses and bona fide private membership clubs, § 2000e(b)(2), and certain employees of religious organizations, § 2000e–1. Congress initially exempted certain employees of educational institutions, § 702, 78 Stat. 255, but later revoked that exemption, Equal Employment Opportunity Act of 1972, § 3, 86 Stat. 103.

JUSTICE POWELL, concurring.

I join the Court's opinion holding that petitioner's complaint alleges a violation of Title VII and that the motion to dismiss should not have been granted. Petitioner's complaint avers that the law firm violated its promise that she would be considered for partnership on a "fair and equal basis" within the time span that associates generally are so considered. Petitioner is entitled to the opportunity to prove these averments.

I write to make clear my understanding that the Court's opinion should not be read as extending Title VII to the management of a law firm by its partners. The reasoning of the Court's opinion does not require that the relationship among partners be characterized as an "employment" relationship to which Title VII would apply. The relationship among law partners differs markedly from that between employer and employee—including that between the partnership and its associates.[2] The judgmental and sensitive decisions that must be made among the partners embrace a wide range of subjects.[3] The essence of the law partnership is the common conduct of a shared enterprise. The relationship among law partners contemplates that decisions important to the partnership normally will be made by common agreement, see, e.g., Memorandum of Agreement, King & Spalding, App. 153–164 (respondent's partnership agreement), or consent among the partners.

Respondent contends that for these reasons application of Title VII to the decision whether to admit petitioner to the firm implicates the constitutional right to association. But here it is alleged that respondent as an employer is obligated by contract to consider petitioner for partnership on equal terms without regard to sex. I agree that enforcement of this obligation, voluntarily assumed, would impair no right of association. . . .

Comments

In the aftermath of the *Hishon* decision at least three major questions remained unanswered: (1) Does Title VII regulate the relationship among partners? (2) Who is a partner for Title VII purposes? (3) Will the courts grant specific performance in a Title VII partnership case?

2. Of course, an employer may not evade the strictures of Title VII simply by labeling its employees as "partners." Law partnerships usually have many of the characteristics that I describe generally here.

3. These decisions concern such matters as participation in profits and other types of compensation; work assignments; approval of commitments in bar association, civic, or political activities; questions of billing; acceptance of new clients; questions of conflicts of interest; retirement programs; and expansion policies. Such decisions may affect each partner of the firm. Divisions of partnership profits, unlike shareholders' rights to dividends, involve judgments as to each partner's contribution to the reputation and success of the firm. This is true whether the partner's participation in profits is measured in terms of points or percentages, combinations of salaries and points, salaries and bonuses, and possibly in other ways.

As to the first question, Justice Powell's concurrence in *Hishon* states that the case does not regulate the relationship among partners. While the statements in that concurrence are dicta, they are still good dicta although their significance is limited by an emerging restrictive definition of "partner."

A person called a "partner" may nevertheless be an employee for purposes of fair employment practices. In EEOC v. Peat Marwick, Mitchell & Co., 775 F.2d 928 (8th Cir.1985), cert. denied, 475 U.S. 1046 (1986), the court ruled that the EEOC might subpoena records of Peat Marwick to determine whether or not nominal partners really were employees. In Hyland v. New Haven Radiology Associates, 794 F.2d 793 (2d Cir.1986), the court ruled that a professional corporation has no partners, only employees; hence New Haven Radiology, having taken the corporate form for tax purposes, could not assert that it was a partnership for Title VII purposes. See also Reiver v. Murdoch and Walsh P.A., 625 F.Supp. 998 (D.Del.1985), holding that whether a member of the board of directors of a professional corporation (law firm) is an employee is a triable question of fact. Both these last two cases reject the analysis in EEOC v. Dowd and Dowd, 736 F.2d 1177 (7th Cir.1984), which held that a professional corporation (law firm) was, in economic reality, a partnership for purposes of Title VII.

No case has specifically held that specific performance may be awarded to elect an employee to partnership in a law firm, although Price Waterhouse v. Hopkins, 109 S.Ct. 1775 (1989), discussed below, suggests that it is an available remedy. In Pyo v. Stockton State College, 603 F.Supp. 1278 (D.N.J.1985), the court held that it had authority to award tenure to a college professor in an appropriate case.

In *Price Waterhouse,* supra, Hopkins, described by partners at Price Waterhouse as "an outstanding professional . . . with strong character, independence, and integrity," was denied partnership in the accounting firm. Virtually all of the criticism of Hopkins had to do with her "interpersonal skills." She was described as "sometimes overly aggressive," "macho," as someone who "overcompensated for being a women." One partner advised her to take a course in "charm school" and another objected to "a lady using foul language." The Supreme Court held that the evidence was sufficient to establish that sexual stereotyping played a part in evaluating Hopkins' candidacy for partnership and that once a plaintiff establishes that her gender played a part in the employment decision, the burden shifts to the employer to show by a preponderance of evidence that it would have made the same decision had it not taken gender into account.

HERBSTER v. NORTH AMERICAN CO. FOR LIFE AND HEALTH INSURANCE

Appellate Court of Illinois, Second District, 1987.
150 Ill.App.3d 21, 103 Ill.Dec. 322, 501 N.E.2d 343, appeal denied, 114 Ill.2d 545,
108 Ill.Dec. 417, 508 N.E.2d 728, cert. denied, 484 U.S. 850, 108 S.Ct. 150,
98 L.Ed.2d 105.

JUSTICE STROUSE delivered the opinion of the court:

The plaintiff, Robert W. Herbster, a licensed attorney, brought suit for retaliatory discharge against his employer, North American Company for Life and Health Insurance (North American). The suit was premised on plaintiff's refusal to destroy or remove documents from North American's files which had been requested in law suits pending in the Federal court in Alabama against North American and other insurance companies. These documents were generated by North American in its actuarial department and contained information which, if made available to the Alabama plaintiffs, tended to support allegations of fraud in the sale of so-called flexible annuities sold by North American. On December 28, 1984, the trial court granted North American's motion for summary judgment. This appeal followed.

The plaintiff was employed as chief legal officer and vice-president in charge of the legal department for North American under an oral contract which was terminable at will. Plaintiff claimed that he was discharged for refusing to destroy or remove discovery information. He further alleged that if he had not refused, it would have constituted a fraud on the Federal court of Alabama and would have caused him to violate Rules 1–102(5) and 7–109(a) of the Code of Professional Responsibility (87 Ill.2d Rules 1–102(5) and 7–109(a)).

North American filed its motion for summary judgment charging that: (1) there was no genuine issue as to any material fact; (2) there was no cause of action for retaliatory discharge by an attorney who is terminated by his client; (3) plaintiff was discharged because of the quality of his work; and (4) they never ordered, demanded or directed plaintiff to destroy or remove any discovery information.

The trial court granted summary judgment to North American because of the attorney-client relationship. Plaintiff appeals.

There are two elements to a claim for retaliatory discharge: (1) the employer discharged the employee in retaliation for the employee's activities, and (2) the discharge was in contravention of a clearly mandated public policy. Midgett v. Sackett–Chicago, Inc. (1984), 105 Ill.2d 143, 148, 85 Ill.Dec. 475, 473 N.E.2d 1280; Palmateer v. International Harvester Co. (1981), 85 Ill.2d 124, 52 Ill.Dec. 13, 421 N.E.2d 876.

There is no question that there are public policy considerations in this case to support the second element of the tort. Supreme Court Rules would be contravened (87 Ill.2d Rules 1–102, 7–102(a)(3), and 7–109(a)); justice would be obstructed (see, e.g., Ill.Rev.Stat.1983, ch. 38, par. 31–4(a)); and destroying documents would be fundamentally incompatible with this State's broad discovery policies (Consolidation Coal Co. v. Bucyrus–Erie Co. (1982), 89 Ill.2d 103, 118, 59 Ill.Dec. 666, 432 N.E.2d 250). Clearly, these matters "strike at the heart of a citizen's social rights, duties, and responsibilities." Palmateer v. International Harvester Co. (1981), 85 Ill.2d 124, 130, 52 Ill.Dec. 13, 421 N.E.2d 876.

We must decide, however, whether an attorney, as general counsel and an employee of a corporation, is entitled to bring a claim for retaliatory discharge. . . .

. . . .

. . . Unlike the employees in the present retaliatory discharge cases, attorneys occupy a special position in our society. As professionals closely supervised by the Supreme Court of Illinois, their conduct is governed by State statutes and legal precedent. In representing clients in civil and criminal matters their authority is extremely broad. The attorney is placed in the unique position of maintaining a close relationship with a client where the attorney receives secrets, disclosures and information that otherwise would not be divulged to intimate friends. . . .

. . . .

Accordingly, the law places special obligations upon an attorney by virtue of this close relationship. Those obligations are referred to generally as the fiduciary duty of the attorney. It permeates all phases of the relationship, including the contract for employment. An attorney's duty to his client includes not taking advantage of the client's trust. An attorney must inform his client of all basic material facts affecting his employment. This protection of the client is so important that all transactions between an attorney and a client are subject to the closest scrutiny. . . .

. . . The general rule is that a client may terminate the relationship between himself and his attorney with or without cause. (Tobias v. King (1980), 84 Ill.App.3d 998, 1000, 40 Ill.Dec. 400, 406 N.E.2d 101.) This right is implied in every contract of employment and is deemed necessary because of the deeply embedded concept of the confidential nature of the relationship between the attorney and the client and the evil that would obviously be engendered by any friction or distrust. Rhoades v. Norfolk & Western Ry. Co. (1979), 78 Ill.2d 217, 228, 35 Ill. Dec. 680, 399 N.E.2d 969; Savich v. Savich (1957), 12 Ill.2d 454, 457–58, 147 N.E.2d 85.

. . . .

The mutual trust, exchanges of confidence, reliance on judgment and personal nature of the attorney-client relationship demonstrate the unique position attorneys occupy in our society. Attorneys are governed by different rules and have different duties and responsibilities than the employees in recent retaliatory discharge cases. Most employees do not have the mutuality of choice that is inherent in the professional relationship which attorneys enjoy. The attributes of the relationship are so important that we can not permit this expansion of the exception to the general rule which would have a serious impact on that relationship. The attorneys in their briefs and arguments focused on the privilege aspect of the relationship only. We find that all aspects are so necessary to our system of jurisprudence that extending this tort to the attorney-client relationship here is not justified. Accordingly, we hold that the tort of retaliatory discharge is not available to an attorney under these circumstances.

Affirmed.

Comments

See Gillers, Protecting Lawyers Who First Say No, 5 Georgia St.L. Rev. 1 (1988) (for a thoughtful critique of the decision in Herbster). Also see Reynolds, Wrongful Discharge of Employed Counsel, 1 Geo.J. Legal Ethics 553 (1988).

"Commercialization" of Law Practice: Advertising and Solicitation

SHAPERO v. KENTUCKY BAR ASSOCIATION
Supreme Court of the United States, 1988.
486 U.S. 466, 108 S.Ct. 1916, 100 L.Ed.2d 475.

JUSTICE BRENNAN announced the judgment of the Court and delivered the opinion of the Court as to Parts I and II and an opinion as to Part III in which JUSTICE MARSHALL, JUSTICE BLACKMUN, and JUSTICE KENNEDY join.

This case presents the issue whether a State may, consistent with the First and Fourteenth Amendments, categorically prohibit lawyers from soliciting legal business for pecuniary gain by sending truthful and nondeceptive letters to potential clients known to face particular legal problems.

I

In 1985, petitioner, a member of Kentucky's integrated Bar Association, see Ky.Sup.Ct. Rule 3.030 (1988), applied to the Kentucky Attorneys Advertising Commission [1] for approval of a letter that he proposed to send "to potential clients who have had a foreclosure suit filed against them." The proposed letter read as follows:

1. The Attorneys Advertising Commission is charged with the responsibility of "regulating attorney advertising as prescribed" in the Rules of the Kentucky Supreme Court. Ky.Sup.Ct. Rule 3.135(3) (1988). The Commission's decisions are appealable to the Board of Governors of the Kentucky Bar Association, Rule 3.135(8)(a), and are ultimately reviewable by the Supreme Court of Kentucky. Rule 3.135(8)(b). "Any attorney who is in doubt as to the propriety of any professional act contemplated by him" also has the option of seeking an advisory opinion from a committee of the Kentucky Bar Association, which, if formally adopted by the Board of Governors, is reviewable by the Supreme Court of Kentucky. Rule 3.530.

It has come to my attention that your home is being foreclosed on. If this is true, you may be about to lose your home. Federal law may allow you to keep your home by *ORDERING* your creditor [*sic*] to *STOP* and give you more time to pay them.

"You may call my office anytime from 8:30 a.m. to 5:00 p.m. for *FREE* information on how you can keep your home.

"Call *NOW,* don't wait. It may surprise you what I may be able to do for you. Just call and tell me that you got this letter. Remember it is *FREE,* there is *NO* charge for calling."

The Commission did not find the letter false or misleading. Nevertheless, it declined to approve petitioner's proposal on the ground that a then-existing Kentucky Supreme Court rule prohibited the mailing or delivery of written advertisements "precipitated by a specific event or occurrence involving or relating to the addressee or addressees as distinct from the general public." Ky.Sup.Ct. Rule 3.135(5)(b)(i).[2] The Commission registered its view that Rule 3.135(5)(b)(i)'s ban on targeted, direct-mail advertising violated the First Amendment—specifically the principles enunciated in Zauderer v. Office of Disciplinary Counsel of Supreme Court of Ohio, 471 U.S. 626, 105 S.Ct. 2265, 85 L.Ed.2d 652 (1985)—and recommended that the Kentucky Supreme Court amend its rules. Pursuing the Commission's suggestion, petitioner petitioned the Committee on Legal Ethics (Ethics Committee) of the Kentucky Bar Association for an advisory opinion as to the Rule's validity. See Ky. Sup.Ct. Rule 3.530; n. 1, supra. Like the Commission, the Ethics Committee, in an opinion formally adopted by the Board of Governors of the Bar Association, did not find the proposed letter false or misleading, but nonetheless upheld the Rule 3.135(5)(b)(i) on the ground that it was consistent with Rule 7.3 of the American Bar Association's (ABA) Model Rules of Professional Conduct (1984).

On review of the Ethics Committee's advisory opinion, the Kentucky Supreme Court felt "compelled by the decision in *Zauderer* to order [Rule 3.135(5)(b)(i)] deleted," 726 S.W.2d 299, 300 (1987), and replaced it with the ABA's Rule 7.3, which provides in its entirety:

"'A lawyer may not solicit professional employment from a prospective client with whom the lawyer has no family or prior professional relationship, by mail, in-person or otherwise, when a significant motive for the lawyer's doing so is the lawyer's pecuniary gain. The term 'solicit' includes contact in person, by telephone or telegraph, by letter or other writing, or by other communication directed to a specific recipient, but does not include letters addressed or advertising circulars distributed generally to persons not known to need legal services of the kind provided by the lawyer in

---

2. Rule 3.135(5)(b)(i) provided in full:

"A written advertisement may be sent or delivered to an individual addressee only if that addressee is one of a class of persons, other than a family, to whom it is also sent or delivered at or about the same time, and only if it is not prompted or precipitated by a specific event or occurrence involving or relating to the addressee or addressees as distinct from the general public."

a particular matter, but who are so situated that they might in general find such services useful.'" 726 S.W.2d, at 301 (quoting ABA, Model Rule of Professional Conduct 7.3 (1984)).

The court did not specify either the precise infirmity in Rule 3.135(5)(b) (i) or how Rule 7.3 cured it. Rule 7.3 like its predecessor, prohibits targeted, direct-mail solicitation by lawyers for pecuniary gain, without a particularized finding that the solicitation is false or misleading. We granted certiorari to resolve whether such a blanket prohibition is consistent with the First Amendment, made applicable to the States through the Fourteenth Amendment, and now reverse.

II

Lawyer advertising is in the category of constitutionally protected commercial speech. See Bates v. State Bar of Arizona, 433 U.S. 350, 97 S.Ct. 2691, 53 L.Ed.2d 810 (1977). The First Amendment principles governing state regulation of lawyer solicitations for pecuniary gain are by now familiar: "Commercial speech that is not false or deceptive and does not concern unlawful activities . . . may be restricted only in the service of a substantial governmental interest, and only through means that directly advance that interest." *Zauderer,* supra, 471 U.S., at 638, 105 S.Ct., at 2275 (citing Central Hudson Gas & Electric Corp. v. Public Service Comm'n of New York, 447 U.S. 557, 566, 100 S.Ct. 2343, 2351, 65 L.Ed.2d 341 (1980)). Since state regulation of commercial speech "may extend only as far as the interest it serves," *Central Hudson,* supra, at 565, 100 S.Ct., at 2351, state rules that are designed to prevent the "potential for deception and confusion . . . may be no broader than reasonably necessary to prevent the" perceived evil. In re R.M.J., 455 U.S. 191, 203, 102 S.Ct. 929, 937, 71 L.Ed.2d 64 (1982).

In *Zauderer,* application of these principles required that we strike an Ohio rule that categorically prohibited solicitation of legal employment for pecuniary gain through advertisements containing information or advice, even if truthful and nondeceptive, regarding a specific legal problem. We distinguished written advertisements containing such information or advice from in-person solicitation by lawyers for profit, which we held in Ohralik v. Ohio State Bar Assn., 436 U.S. 447, 98 S.Ct. 1912, 56 L.Ed.2d 444 (1978), a State may categorically ban. The "unique features of in-person solicitation by lawyers [that] justified a prophylactic rule prohibiting lawyers from engaging in such solicitation for pecuniary gain," we observed, are "not present" in the context of written advertisements. *Zauderer,* 471 U.S., at 641–642, 105 S.Ct., at 2277.

Our lawyer advertising cases have never distinguished among various modes of written advertising to the general public. See, e.g., *Bates,* supra (newspaper advertising); *id.,* 433 U.S., at 372, n. 26, 97 S.Ct., at 2703, n. 26 (equating advertising in telephone directory with newspaper advertising); *In re R.M.J.,* supra (mailed announcement cards treated same as newspaper and telephone directory advertisements). Thus, Ohio could no more prevent Zauderer from mass-mailing to a general population his offer to represent women injured by the Dalkon Shield than it could prohibit his publication of the advertisement in local newspapers. Similarly, if petitioner's letter is neither false nor deceptive, Kentucky could not constitutionally prohibit him from sending at large an identical letter opening with the query, "Is your home being foreclosed on?," rather than his observation to the targeted individuals that "It has come to my attention that your home is being foreclosed on." The drafters of Rule 7.3 apparently appreciated as much, for the Rule exempts from the ban "letters addressed or advertising circulars distributed generally to persons . . . who are so situated that they might in general find such services useful."

The court below disapproved petitioner's proposed letter solely because it targeted only persons who were "known to need [the] legal services" offered in his letter, 726 S.W.2d, at 301, rather than the broader group of persons "so situated that they might in general find such services useful." Generally, unless the advertiser is inept, the latter group would include members of the former. The only reason to disseminate an advertisement of particular legal services among those persons who are "so situated that they might in general find such services useful" is to reach individuals who *actually* "need legal services of the kind provided [and advertised] by the lawyer." But the First Amendment does not permit a ban on certain speech merely because it is more efficient; the State may not constitutionally ban a particular letter on the theory that to mail it only to those whom it would most interest is somehow inherently objectionable.

The court below did not rely on any such theory. See also Brief for Respondent 37 (conceding that "targeted direct mail *advertising*"—as distinguished from "*solicitation*"—"is constitutionally protected") (emphasis in original). Rather, it concluded that the State's blanket ban on all targeted, direct-mail solicitation was permissible because of the "serious potential for abuse inherent in direct solicitation by lawyers of potential clients known to need specific legal services." 726 S.W.2d, at 301. By analogy to *Ohralik*, the court observed:

> "Such solicitation subjects the prospective client to pressure from a trained lawyer in a direct personal way. It is entirely possible that the potential client may feel overwhelmed by the basic situation which caused the need for the specific legal services and may have seriously impaired capacity for good judgment, sound reason and a natural protective self-interest. Such a condition is full of the possibility of undue influence, over-reaching and intimidation." 726 S.W.2d, at 301.

Of course, a particular potential client will feel equally "overwhelmed" by his legal troubles and will have the same "impaired capacity for good judgment" regardless of whether a lawyer mails him an untargeted letter or exposes him to a newspaper advertisement—concededly constitutionally protected activities—or instead mails a targeted letter. The relevant inquiry is not whether there exist potential clients whose "condition" makes them susceptible to undue influence, but whether the mode of communication poses a serious danger that lawyers will exploit any such susceptibility. Cf. *Ohralik*, supra, 436 U.S., at 470, 98 S.Ct., at 1926 (Marshall, J., concurring in part and concurring in judgment) ("What is objectionable about Ohralik's behavior here is not so much that he solicited business for himself, but rather the circumstances in which he performed that solicitation and the means by which he accomplished it").

Thus, Respondent's facile suggestion that this case is merely "*Ohralik* in writing" misses the mark. In assessing the potential for overreaching and undue influence, the mode of communication makes all the difference. Our decision in *Ohralik* that a State could categorically ban all in-person solicitation turned on two factors. First was our characterization of face-to-face solicitation as "a practice rife with possibilities for overreaching, invasion of privacy, the exercise of undue influence, and outright fraud." *Zauderer*, supra, 471 U.S., at 641, 105 S.Ct., at 2277. See *Ohralik*, supra, 436 U.S., at 457–458, 464–465, 98 S.Ct., at 1919–1920, 1922–1923. Second, "unique . . . difficulties," *Zauderer*, supra, 471 U.S., at 641, 105 S.Ct., at 2277, would frustrate any attempt at state regulation of in-person solicitation short of an absolute ban because such solicitation is "not visible or otherwise open to public scrutiny." *Ohralik*, 436 U.S., at 466, 98 S.Ct., at 1924. See also ibid. ("[I]n-person solicitation would be virtually immune to effective oversight and regulation by the State or by the legal profession") (footnote omitted). Targeted, direct-mail solicitation is distinguishable from the in-person solicitation in each respect.

Like print advertising, petitioner's letter—and targeted, direct-mail solicitation generally—"poses much less risk of over-reaching or undue influence" than does in-person solicitation, *Zauderer*, 471 U.S., at 642, 105 S.Ct., at 2277. Neither mode of written communication involves "the coercive force of the personal presence of a trained advocate" or the "pressure on the potential client for an immediate yes-or-no answer to the offer of representation." Ibid. Unlike the potential client with a badgering advocate breathing down his neck, the recipient of a letter and the "reader of an advertisement . . . can 'effectively avoid further bombardment of [his] sensibilities simply by averting [his] eyes,'" *Ohralik*, supra, 436 U.S., at 465, n. 25, 98 S.Ct., at 1923, n. 25 (quoting Cohen v. California, 403 U.S. 15, 21, 91 S.Ct. 1780, 1786, 29 L.Ed.2d 284 (1971)). A letter, like a printed advertisement (but unlike a lawyer), can readily be put in a drawer to be considered later, ignored, or discarded. In short, both types of written solicitation "conve[y] information about legal services [by means] that [are] more conducive to reflection and the exercise of choice on the part of the consumer than is personal solicitation by an attorney." *Zauderer*, supra, 471 U.S., at 642, 105 S.Ct., at 2277. Nor does a targeted letter invade the recipient's privacy any more than does a substantively identical letter mailed at large. The invasion, if any, occurs when the lawyer discovers the recipient's legal affairs, not when he confronts the recipient with the discovery.

Admittedly, a letter that is personalized (not merely targeted) to the recipient presents an increased risk of deception, intentional or inadvertent. It could, in certain circumstances, lead the recipient to overestimate the lawyer's familiarity with the case or could implicitly suggest that the recipient's legal problem is more dire than it really is. Similarly, an inaccurately targeted letter could lead the recipient to believe she has a legal problem that she does not actually have or, worse yet, could offer erroneous legal advice. See, e.g., Leoni v. State Bar of California, 39 Cal.3d 609, 619–620, 217 Cal.Rptr. 423, 429, 704 P.2d 183, 189 (1985), summarily dism'd, 475 U.S. 1001, 106 S.Ct. 1170, 89 L.Ed.2d 290 (1986).

But merely because targeted, direct-mail solicitation presents lawyers with opportunities for isolated abuses or mistakes does not justify a total ban on that mode of protected commercial speech. See In re R.M.J., 455 U.S., at 203, 102 S.Ct., at 937. The State can regulate such abuses and minimize mistakes through far less restrictive and more precise means, the most obvious of which is to require the lawyer to file any solicitation letter with a state agency, id., at 206, 102 S.Ct., at 939, giving the State ample opportunity to supervise mailings and penalize actual abuses. The "regulatory difficulties" that are "unique" to in-person lawyer solicitation, *Zauderer,* supra, 471 U.S., at 641, 105 S.Ct., at 2277—solicitation that is "not visible or otherwise open to public scrutiny" and for which it is "difficult or impossible to obtain reliable proof of what actually took place," *Ohralik,* supra, 436 U.S., at 466, 98 S.Ct., at 1924—do not apply to written solicitations. The court below offered no basis for its "belie[f] [that] submission of a blank form letter to the Advertising Commission [does not] provid[e] a suitable protection to the public from overreaching, intimidation or misleading private targeted mail solicitation." 726 S.W.2d, at 301. Its concerns were presumably those expressed by the ABA House of Delegates in its comment to Rule 7.3:

> "State lawyer discipline agencies struggle for resources to investigate specific complaints, much less for those necessary to screen lawyers' mail solicitation material. Even if they could examine such materials, agency staff members are unlikely to know anything about the lawyer or about the prospective client's underlying problem. Without such knowledge they cannot determine whether the lawyer's representations are misleading." ABA, Model Rules of Professional Conduct, pp. 93–94 (1984).

The record before us furnishes no evidence that scrutiny of targeted solicitation letters will be appreciably more burdensome or less reliable than scrutiny of advertisements. See *Bates,* 433 U.S., at 379, 97 S.Ct., at 2706; id., at 387, 97 S.Ct., at 2711 (Burger, C.J., concurring in part and dissenting in part) (objecting to "enormous new regulatory burdens called for by" *Bates*). As a general matter, evaluating a targeted advertisement does not require specific information about the recipient's identity and legal problems any more than evaluating a newspaper advertisement requires like information about all readers. If the targeted letter specifies facts that relate to particular recipients (e.g., "It has come to my attention that your home is being foreclosed on"), the reviewing agency has innumerable options to minimize mistakes. It might, for example, require the lawyer to prove the truth of the fact stated (by supplying copies of the court documents or material that lead the lawyer to the fact); it could require the lawyer to explain briefly how she discovered the fact and verified its accuracy; or it could require the letter to bear a label identifying it as an advertisement, see id., at 384, 97 S.Ct., at 2709 (dictum); In re R.M.J., supra, 455 U.S., at 206, n. 20, 102 S.Ct., at 939, n. 20, or directing the recipient how to report inaccurate or misleading letters. To be sure, a state agency or bar association that reviews solicitation letters might have more work than one that does not. But "[o]ur recent decisions involving commercial speech have been grounded in the faith that the free flow of commercial information is valuable enough to justify imposing on would-be regulators the costs of distinguishing the truthful from the false, the helpful from the misleading, and the harmless from the harmful." *Zauderer*, supra, 471 U.S., at 646, 105 S.Ct., at 2279.

III

The validity of Rule 7.3 does not turn on whether petitioner's letter itself exhibited any of the evils at which Rule 7.3 was directed. See *Ohralik*, 436 U.S., at 463–464, 466, 98 S.Ct., at 1922–1923, 1923. Since, however, the First Amendment overbreadth doctrine does not apply to professional advertising, see *Bates*, supra, 433 U.S., at 379–381, 97 S.Ct., at 2706–2707 we address respondent's contentions that petitioner's letter is particularly overreaching, and therefore unworthy of First Amendment protection. Id., at 381, 97 S.Ct., at 2707. In that regard, respondent identifies two features of the letter before us that, in its view, coalesce to convert the proposed letter into "high pressure solicitation, overbearing solicitation," which is not protected. First, respondent asserts that the letter's liberal use of underscored, uppercase letters (e.g., "Call *NOW*, don't wait"; "it is *FREE*, there is *NO* charge for calling") "fairly shouts at the recipient . . . that he should employ Shapero." Id., at 19. See also Brief in Opposition 11 ("Letters of solicitation which shout commands to the individual, targeted recipient in words in underscored capitals are of a different order from advertising and are subject to proscription"). Second, respondent objects that the letter contains assertions (e.g., "It may surprise you what I may be able to do for you") that "stat[e] no affirmative or objective fact," but constitute "pure salesman puffery, enticement for the unsophisticated, which commits Shapero to nothing."

The pitch or style of a letter's type and its inclusion of subjective predictions of client satisfaction might catch the recipient's attention more than would a bland statement of purely objective facts in small type. But a truthful and nondeceptive letter, no matter how big its type and how much it speculates can never "shou[t] at the recipient" or "gras[p] him by the lapels," as can a lawyer engaging in face-to-face solicitation. The letter simply presents no comparable risk of over-reaching. . . .

To be sure, a letter may be misleading if it unduly emphasizes trivial or "relatively uninformative fact[s]," In re R.M.J., supra, at 205, 102 S.Ct., at 938 (lawyer's statement, "in large capital letters, that he was a member of the Bar to the Supreme Court of the United States"), or offers overblown assurances of client satisfaction, cf. In re Von Wiegen, 63 N.Y.2d 163, 179, 481 N.Y.S.2d 40, 49, 470 N.E.2d 838, 847 (1984) (solicitation letter to victims of massive disaster informs them that "it is [the lawyer's] opinion that the liability of the defendants is clear"), cert. denied, 472 U.S. 1007, 105 S.Ct. 2701, 86 L.Ed.2d 717 (1985); *Bates,* supra, 433 U.S., at 383–384, 97 S.Ct., at 2709 ("advertising claims as to the quality of legal services . . . may be so likely to be misleading as to warrant restriction"). Respondent does not argue before us that petitioner's letter was misleading in those respects. Nor does respondent contend that the letter is false or misleading in any other respect. Of course, respondent is free to raise, and the Kentucky courts are free to consider, any such argument on remand.

The judgment of the Supreme Court of Kentucky is reversed and the case is remanded for further proceedings not inconsistent with this opinion.

It is so ordered.

JUSTICE WHITE, with whom JUSTICE STEVENS joins, concurring and dissenting in part.

I agree with Parts I and II of the Court's opinion, but am of the view that the matters addressed in Part III should be left to the state courts in the first instance.

JUSTICE O'CONNOR, with whom CHIEF JUSTICE REHNQUIST and JUSTICE SCALIA join, dissenting.

Relying primarily on Zauderer v. Office of Disciplinary Counsel of Supreme Court of Ohio, 471 U.S. 626, 105 S.Ct. 2265, 85 L.Ed.2d 652 (1985), the Court holds that States may not prohibit a form of attorney advertising that is potentially more pernicious than the advertising at issue in that case. I agree with the Court that the reasoning in *Zauderer* supports the conclusion reached today. That decision, however, was itself the culmination of a line of cases built on defective premises and flawed reasoning. As today's decision illustrates, the Court has been unable or unwilling to restrain the logic of the underlying analysis within reasonable bounds. The resulting interference with important and valid public policies is so destructive that I believe the analytical framework itself should now be reexamined.

I

Zauderer held that the First Amendment was violated by a state rule that forbade attorneys to solicit or accept employment through advertisements containing information or advice regarding a specific legal problem. See id., at 639–647, 105 S.Ct., at 2276–2280. I dissented from this holding because I believed that our precedents permitted, and good judgment required, that we give greater deference to the States' legitimate efforts to regulate advertising by their attorneys. Emphasizing the important differences between professional services and standardized consumer products, I concluded that unsolicited legal advice was not analogous to the free samples that are often used to promote sales in other contexts. First, the quality of legal services is typically more difficult for most laypersons to evaluate, and the consequences of a mistaken evaluation of the "free sample" may be much more serious. For that reason, the practice of offering unsolicited legal advice as a means of enticing potential clients into a professional relationship is much more likely to be misleading than superficially similar practices in the sale of ordinary consumer goods. Second, and more important, an attorney has an obligation to provide clients with complete and disinterested advice. The advice contained in unsolicited "free samples" is likely to be colored by the lawyer's own interest in drumming up business, a result that is sure to undermine the professional standards that States have a substantial interest in maintaining.

. . .

II

. . .

A standardized legal test has been devised for commercial speech cases. Under that test, such speech is entitled to constitutional protection only if it concerns lawful activities and is not misleading; if the speech is protected, government may still ban or regulate it by laws that directly advance a substantial governmental interest and are appropriately tailored to that purpose. See Central Hudson Gas & Electric Corp. v. Public Service Comm'n of New York, 447 U.S. 557, 566, 100 S.Ct. 2343, 2351, 65 L.Ed.2d 341 (1980). Applying that test to attorney advertising, it is clear to me that the States should have considerable latitude to ban advertising that is "*potentially* or demonstrably misleading," In re R.M.J., 455 U.S. 191, 202, 102 S.Ct. 929, 937, 71 L.Ed.2d 64 (1982) (emphasis added), *as well as* truthful advertising that undermines the substantial governmental interest in promoting the high ethical standards that are necessary in the legal profession.

Some forms of advertising by lawyers might be protected under this test. Announcing the price of an initial consultation might qualify, for example, especially if appropriate disclaimers about the costs of other services were included. Even here, the inherent difficulties of policing such advertising suggest that we should hesitate to interfere with state rules designed to ensure that adequate disclaimers are included and that such advertisements are suitably restrained.

As soon as one steps into the realm of prices for "routine" legal services such as uncontested divorces and personal bankruptcies, however, it is quite clear to me that the States may ban such advertising completely. The contrary decision in *Bates* was in my view inconsistent with the standard test that is now applied in commercial speech cases. Until one becomes familiar with a client's particular problems, there is simply no way to know that one is dealing with a "routine" divorce or bankruptcy. Such an advertisement is therefore inherently misleading if it fails to inform potential clients that they are not necessarily qualified to decide whether their own apparently simple problems can be handled by "routine" legal services. Furthermore, such advertising practices will undermine professional standards if the attorney accepts the economic risks of offering fixed rates for solving apparently simple problems that will sometimes prove not to be so simple after all. For a lawyer to promise the world that such matters as uncontested divorces can be handled for a flat fee will inevitably create incentives to ignore (or avoid discovering) the complexities that would lead a conscientious attorney to treat some clients' cases as anything but routine. It may be possible to devise workable rules that would allow something more than the most minimal kinds of price advertising by attorneys. That task, however, is properly left to the States, and it is certainly not a fit subject for constitutional adjudication. Under the Central Hudson test, government has more than ample justification for banning or strictly regulating most forms of price advertising.

. . . Soliciting business from strangers who appear to need particular legal services, when a significant motive for the offer is the lawyer's pecuniary gain, always has a tendency to corrupt the solicitor's professional judgment. This is especially true when the solicitation includes the offer of a "free sample," as petitioner's proposed letter does. I therefore conclude that American Bar Association Model Rule of Professional Conduct 7.3 (1984) sweeps no more broadly than is necessary to advance a substantial governmental interest. . . .

III

The roots of the error in our attorney advertising cases are a defective analogy between professional services and standardized consumer products and a correspondingly inappropriate skepticism about the States' justifications for their regulations.

. . . The best arguments in favor of rules permitting attorneys to advertise are founded in elementary economic principles. See, e.g., Hazard, Pearce, & Stempel, Why Lawyers Should Be Allowed to Advertise: A Market Analysis of Legal Services, 58 N.Y.U.L.Rev. 1084 (1983). Restrictions on truthful advertising, which artificially interfere with the ability of suppliers to transmit price information to consumers, presumably reduce the efficiency of the mechanisms of supply and demand. Other factors being equal, this should cause or enable suppliers (in this case attorneys) to maintain a price/quality ratio in some of their services that is higher than would otherwise prevail. Although one could probably not test this hypothesis empirically, it is inherently plausible. Nor is it implausible to imagine that one effect of restrictions on lawyer advertising, and perhaps sometimes an intended effect, is to enable attorneys to charge their clients more for some services (of a given quality) than they would be able to charge absent the restrictions.

Assuming *arguendo* that the removal of advertising restrictions should lead in the short run to increased efficiency in the provision of legal services, I would not agree that we can safely assume the same effect in the long run. The economic argument against these restrictions ignores the delicate role they may play in preserving the norms of the legal profession. While it may be difficult to defend this role with precise economic logic, I believe there is a powerful argument in favor of restricting lawyer advertising and that this argument is at the very least not easily refuted by economic analysis.

One distinguishing feature of any profession, unlike other occupations that may be equally respectable, is that membership entails an ethical obligation to temper one's selfish pursuit of economic success by adhering to standards of conduct that could not be enforced either by legal fiat or through the discipline of the market. There are sound reasons to continue pursuing the goal that is implicit in the traditional view of professional life. Both the special privileges incident to membership in the profession and the advantages those privileges give in the necessary task of earning a living are means to a goal that transcends the accumulation of wealth. That goal is public service, which in the legal profession can take a variety of familiar forms. This view of the legal profession need not be rooted in romanticism or self-serving sanctimony, though of course it can be. Rather, special ethical standards for lawyers are properly understood as an appropriate means of restraining lawyers in the exercise of the unique power that they inevitably wield in a political system like ours. . . .

Imbuing the legal profession with the necessary ethical standards is a task that involves a constant struggle with the relentless natural force of economic self-interest. It cannot be accomplished directly by legal rules, and it certainly will not succeed if sermonizing is the strongest tool that may be employed. Tradition and experiment have suggested a number of formal and informal mechanisms, none of which is adequate by itself and many of which may serve to reduce competition (in the narrow economic sense) among members of the profession. A few examples include the great efforts made during this century to improve the quality and breadth of the legal education that is required for admission to the bar; the concomitant attempt to cultivate a subclass of genuine scholars within the profession; the development of bar associations that aspire to be more than trade groups; strict disciplinary rules about conflicts of interest and client abandonment; and promotion of the expectation that an attorney's history of voluntary public service is a relevant factor in selecting judicial candidates.

Restrictions on advertising and solicitation by lawyers properly and significantly serve the same goal. Such restrictions act as a concrete, day-to-day reminder to the practicing attorney of why it is improper for any member of this profession to regard it as a trade or occupation like any other. There is no guarantee, of course, that the restrictions will always have the desired effect, and they are surely not a sufficient means to their proper goal. Given their inevitable anticompetitive effects, moreover, they should not be thoughtlessly retained or insulated from skeptical criticism. Appropriate modifications have been made in the light of reason and experience, and other changes may be suggested in the future.

In my judgment, however, fairly severe constraints on attorney advertising can continue to play an important role in preserving the legal profession as a genuine profession. Whatever may be the exactly appropriate scope of these restrictions at a given time and place, this Court's recent decisions reflect a myopic belief that "consumers," and thus our nation, will benefit from a constitutional theory that refuses to recognize either the essence of professionalism or its fragile and necessary foundations. Compare, e.g., *Bates,* 433 U.S., at 370–372, 97 S.Ct., at 2702–2703, with id., at 400–401, and n. 11, 97 S.Ct., at 2717–2718, and n. 11 (Powell, J., concurring in part and dissenting in part). In one way or another, time will uncover the folly of this approach. I can only hope that the Court will recognize the danger before it is too late to effect a worthwhile cure.

First Amendment Protection of Lawyer Advertising

The landmark cases putting First Amendment protection around lawyer advertising began with Bates v. State Bar of Arizona, 433 U.S. 350, 97 S.Ct. 2691 (1977), involving a newspaper advertising of a legal clinic that offered "legal services at very reasonable rates." Such truthful advertising was held protected by the "commercial speech" component of the First Amendment. In Ohralik v. The Ohio State Bar Ass'n, 436 U.S. 447, 98 S.Ct. 1912 (1978), the Supreme Court upheld disciplinary sanctions against a lawyer who had personally gone to the home of a person involved in an automobile accident, and also visited her in the hospital, to solicit the lawyer's employment for a personal injury case. However, in In re Primus, 436 U.S. 412, 98 S.Ct. 1893 (1978), the Court upheld "in person" solicitation carried out by a lawyer for a civil rights organization seeking a plaintiff who would bring a civil rights "test case." Zauderer v. Office of Disciplinary Counsel, 471 U.S. 626, 105 S.Ct. 2265 (1985), held that lawyers could use "targeted" newspaper advertisements. The newspaper advertisement in that case invited Dalkon Shield claimants to contact the attorney concerning possible personal injury claims.

In the meantime, In re R.M.J., 455 U.S. 191, 102 S.Ct. 929 (1982), upholding First Amendment protection for circulating professional announcements to potential clients, indicated that it would be valid to require any such written communications to be labeled as an "advertisement." See 455 U.S. at 206, fn. 20, 102 S.Ct. at 939, fn. 20.

In the 1983 version of the Model Rules of Professional Conduct, the American Bar Association adopted the provision on advertising in M.R. 7.3 that was involved in the *Shapero* case. This version of M.R. 7.3 allowed lawyers to send "non-targeted" letters, but not "targeted" ones and represented rejection of a recommendation by the Kutak Commission that "targeted" letters be permitted along with newspaper advertisements, circulars distributed by a general mailing, and other forms of written communication. In any event, Model Rules 7.1 and 7.2 make all advertising subject to requirements of truthfulness. The Rules also require that a lawyer maintain copies of all written solicitations for a reasonable period, such as a year, following their dissemination. This was to allow enforcement authorities to verify the text of any such communications.

After the decision in *Shapero* invalidated M.R. 7.3 as promulgated in 1983, the ABA amended Model Rules 7.2 and 7.3. The text of amended Model Rules 7.2 and 7.3 is as follows:

Rule 7.2   Advertising

(a) Subject to the requirements of Rules 7.1 and 7.3, a lawyer may advertise services through public media, such as a telephone directory, legal directory, newspaper or other periodical, outdoor advertising, radio or television, or through written or recorded communication.

(b) A copy or recording of an advertisement or communication shall be kept for two years after its last dissemination along with a record of when and where it was used.

(c) A lawyer shall not give anything of value to a person for recommending the lawyer's services, except that a lawyer may pay the reasonable cost of advertisements or communications permitted by this rule and may pay the usual charges of a not-for-profit lawyer referral service or other legal service organization.

(d) Any communication made pursuant to this rule shall include the name of at least one lawyer responsible for its content.

———

Rule 7.3   Direct Contact with Prospective Clients

(a) A lawyer shall not by in-person or live telephone contact solicit professional employment from a prospective client with whom the lawyer has no family or prior professional relationship when a significant motive for the lawyer's doing so is the lawyer's pecuniary gain.

(b) A lawyer shall not solicit professional employment from a prospective client by written or recorded communication or by in-person or telephone contact even when not otherwise prohibited by paragraph (a), if:

(1) the prospective client has made known to the lawyer a desire not to be solicited by the lawyer; or

(2) the solicitation involves coercion, duress or harassment.

(c) Every written or recorded communication from a lawyer soliciting professional employment from a prospective client known to be in need of legal services in a particular matter, and with whom the lawyer has no family or prior professional relationship, shall include the words "Advertising Material" on the outside envelope and at the beginning and ending of any recorded communication.

(d) Notwithstanding the prohibitions in paragraph (a), a lawyer may participate with a prepaid or group legal service plan operated by an organization not owned or directed by the lawyer which uses in-person or telephone contact to solicit memberships or subscriptions for the plan from persons who are not known to need legal services in a particular matter covered by the plan.

———

It will be noted that M.R. 7.3(c) adopts the suggestion in *In re R.M.J.* that the First Amendment does not preclude a requirement that advertising material be labeled as such. Also, M.R. 7.3(a) differentiates between in-person solicitation resulting in pecuniary gain and other solicitation. This attempts to track *Ohralik* and *In re Primus,* supra.

It would seem that *Shapero* has pretty well settled the law. All forms of written communication are protected by the First Amendment, subject to the requirement that they be truthful and that they not be harassing. On the other hand, in-person solicitation by lawyers seeking fee-paying cases may validly be prohibited, as held in *Ohralik.* In-person solicitation is prohibited in every state and it is very likely that the prohibition will continue, subject to the exception recognized in *In re Primus.*

Although the law may be settled that lawyer advertising and written solicitation are protected by the First Amendment, the thesis developed by Justice O'Connor in her dissent in *Shapero* has implications that reach much further. The practice of law is a social institution performing unique functions in the administration of justice. Indeed, the unique place of legal services in our social order was one of the premises advanced in the decisions sustaining lawyer advertising. See Bates v. State Bar of Arizona, 433 U.S. 350 at 376, 97 S.Ct. 2691 at 2705 (1977), and *Zauderer,* where the court said:

Nor does the traditional justification for restraints on solicitation—the fear that lawyers will "stir up litigation"—justify the restriction imposed on this case . . . Over the course of centuries, our society has settled upon civil litigation as a means for redressing grievances, resolving disputes, and vindicating rights when other means fail . . . The State is not entitled to interfere with that access by denying its citizens accurate information about their legal rights.

471 U.S. at 642–43, 105 S.Ct. at 2277.

Direct Legal Controls on "Commercialization"

As a social institution, the practice of law and the organization of the bar are sustained by legal rules. This book is an exposition of those legal rules. Particular note may be taken of the requirements that a lawyer attend law school, pass the bar examination, and maintain competence of at least a minimal level. As Justice O'Connor's opinion indicates, the rule against advertising and solicitation helped sustain the special character of the practice of law. Another example of a rule having that effect is the custom in most other countries that an advocate, as well as a judge, must wear a black robe in court. One could say that having to wear a black robe involves suppression of one's freedom of expression, while at the same time recognizing that the rule "says something" about the nature of the advocate's function.

Other kinds of rules could more rigorously inhibit the "commercialization" of law practice. Lawyers could be prohibited from engaging in any other vocation or business as long as they are engaged in law practice. Lawyers could be prohibited from holding public office or corporate directorships if they are also engaged in practice. They could be prohibited from forming law firms of "bureaucratic" size, for example larger than 20 members. (English barristers still are required to be sole practitioners; 30 years ago the largest firm in many states was no bigger than 20 lawyers.)

The present character of American law practice is significantly shaped by the *absence* of rules against the foregoing kinds of "commercialization" and "bureaucratization." Justice O'Connor does not mention these rules in her dissent in *Shapero*. Does allowing advertising "commercialize" the legal profession in different ways than allowing lawyers to sit on corporate boards? Are different social-economic interests involved?

"Professionalism"

On the complex and subtle concept of "professionalism," and the professionalism of lawyers in particular, a classic statement is Parsons, The Professions and Social Structure (rev. ed. 1954). Another valuable analysis by a leading sociologist is Friedson, Professional Powers: A Study of the Institutionalization of Formal Knowledge (1986). See also Morgan, The Fall and Rise of Professionalism, 19 U.Rich.L.Rev. 451

(1985); Luban, The "Noblesse Oblige" Tradition in the Practice of Law, 41 Vand.L.Rev. 717 (1988); Nelson, Ideology, Practice and Professional Autonomy: Social Values and Client Relationships in the Large Firm Practice, 37 Stan.L.Rev. 503 (1985); American Bar Ass'n Commission on Professionalism, ". . . In the Spirit of Public Service;" A Blueprint for the Rekindling of Lawyer Professionalism (1986).

Solicitation of Another Firm's Clients

Subject to the restrictions on in-person solicitation in provisions such as M.R. 7.3, and subject to the prohibition in M.R. 4.2 against dealing directly with an opposing party, a lawyer is legally free to suggest to a prospective client that she switch lawyers. This would not constitute tortious interference with a contract relationship, because the client has a right to discharge a lawyer at any time, see *Herbster v. North American Company,* above. However, additional problems are presented where a lawyer leaves a firm and seeks to take clients with her. The law previously had been protective of the firm in such situations. See Alder, Barish, Daniels, Levin & Creskoff v. Epstein, 482 Pa. 416, 393 A.2d 1175 (1978). However, recognition of the client's interest in a choice of lawyers, and consequently the need to protect the lawyer's right to compete for clients, is leading to much less protection of the law firm. See Johnson, Solicitation of Law Firm Clients by Departing Partners and Associates, 50 U.Pitt.L.Rev. 1 (1988); see also Terry, Ethical Pitfalls and Malpractice Consequences of Law Firm Breakups, 61 Temple L.Rev. 1055 (1988).

Compulsory Membership in the Bar

LATHROP v. DONOHUE

Supreme Court of the United States, 1961.
367 U.S. 820, 81 S.Ct. 1826, 6 L.Ed.2d 1191.

MR. JUSTICE BRENNAN announced the judgment of the Court and an opinion in which THE CHIEF JUSTICE, MR. JUSTICE CLARK and MR. JUSTICE STEWART join.

The Wisconsin Supreme Court integrated the Wisconsin Bar by an order which created "The State Bar of Wisconsin" on January 1, 1957, under Rules and Bylaws promulgated by the court. . . .

. . .

. . . [T]he appellant, a Wisconsin lawyer, brought this action in the Circuit Court of Dane County for the refund of $15 annual dues for 1959 paid by him under protest . . .

. . .

The core of appellant's argument is that he cannot constitutionally be compelled to join and give support to an organization which has among its functions the expression of opinion on legislative matters and which utilizes its property, funds and employees for the purposes of influencing legislation and public opinion toward legislation. . . .

. . . The purposes of the organization are stated as follows in Rule 1, § 2: "to aid the courts in carrying on and improving the administration of justice; to foster and maintain on the part of those engaged in the practice of law high ideals of integrity, learning, competence and public service and high standards of conduct; to safeguard the proper professional interests of the members of the bar; to encourage the formation and activities of local bar associations; to provide a forum for the discussion of subjects pertaining to the practice of law, the science of jurisprudence and law reform, and the relations of the bar to the public, and to publish information relating thereto; to the end that the public responsibilities of the legal profession may be more effectively discharged." To achieve these purposes standing committees and sections are established. The Rules also assign the organization a major role in the State's procedures for the discipline of members of the bar for unethical conduct. . . .

. . .

The State Bar, through its Board of Governors or Executive Committee, has taken a formal position with respect to a number of questions of legislative policy. These have included such subjects as an increase in the salaries of State Supreme Court justices; making attorneys notaries public; amending the Federal Career Compensation Act, 37 U.S.C.A. § 231 et seq., to apply to attorneys employed with the Armed Forces the same provisions for special pay and promotion available to members of other professions; improving pay scales of attorneys in state service; court reorganization; extending personal jurisdiction over nonresidents; allowing the recording of unwitnessed conveyances; use of deceased partners' names in firm names; revision of the law governing federal tax liens; law clerks for State Supreme Court justices; curtesy and dower; securities transfers by fiduciaries; jurisdiction of county courts over the administration of *inter vivos* trusts; special appropriations for research for the State Legislative Council.

The standing committees, particularly the Committees on Legislation and Administration of Justice, and the sections have devoted considerable time to the study of legislation, the formulation of recommendations, and the support of various proposals. For example, the president reported in 1960 that the Committee on Legislation "has been extremely busy, and through its efforts in cooperation with other interested agencies has been instrumental in securing the passage of the Court Reorganization bill, the bill of the Judicial Council expanding personal jurisdiction, and at this recently resumed session a bill providing clerks for our Supreme Court, and other bills of importance to the administration of justice." Wis.Bar Bull., Aug. 1960, p. 41.

But it seems plain that legislative activity is not the major activity of the State Bar. The activities without apparent political coloration are many. The Supreme Court provided in an appendix to the opinion below, "an analysis of [State Bar] . . . activities and the public purpose served thereby." 10 Wis.2d at page 246, 102 N.W.2d at page 412. The court found that "The most extensive activities of the State Bar are those directed toward postgraduate education of lawyers," and that "Postgraduate education of lawyers is in the public interest because it promotes the competency of lawyers to handle the legal matters entrusted to them by those of the general public who employ them." . . .

This examination of the purposes and functions of the State Bar shows its multifaceted character, in fact as well as in conception. In our view the case presents a claim of impingement upon freedom of association no different from that which we decided in Railway Employes' Dept. v. Hanson, 351 U.S. 225, 76 S.Ct. 714, 100 L.Ed. 1112. We there held that § 2, Eleventh of the Railway Labor Act, 45 U.S.C. § 152, 45 U.S. C.A. § 152, subd. 11, . . . did not on its face abridge protected rights of association in authorizing union-shop agreements between interstate railroads and unions of their employees conditioning the employees' continued employment on payment of union dues, initiation fees and assessments. There too the record indicated that the organizations engaged in some activities similar to the legislative activities of which the appellant complains. See International Association of Machinists v. Street, 367 U.S. [740], at page 748, 81 S.Ct. [1784], at page 1789, note 5. In rejecting Hanson's claim of abridgment of his rights of freedom of association, we said, "On the present record, there is no more an infringement or impairment of First Amendment rights than there would be in the case of a lawyer who by state law is required to be a member of an integrated bar." 351 U.S. at page 238, 76 S.Ct. at page 721. Both in purport and in practice the bulk of State Bar activities serve the function, or at least so Wisconsin might reasonably believe, of elevating the educational and ethical standards of the Bar to the end of improving the quality of the legal service available to the people of the State, without any reference to the political process. It cannot be denied that this is a legitimate end of state policy. . . .

We are persuaded that on this record we have no sound basis for deciding appellant's constitutional claim insofar as it rests on the assertion that his rights of free speech are violated by the use of his money for causes which he opposes. . . . There is an allegation in the complaint that the State Bar had "used its employees, property and funds in active, unsolicited opposition to the adoption of legislation by the Legislature of the State of Wisconsin, which was favored by the plaintiff, all contrary to the plaintiff's convictions and beliefs," but there is no indication of the nature of this legislation, nor of appellant's views on particular proposals, nor of whether any of his dues were used to support the State Bar's positions. There is an allegation that the State Bar's revenues amount to about $90,000 a year, of which $80,000 is derived from dues, but there is no indication in the record as to how political expenditures are financed and how much has been expended for political causes to which appellant objects. . . .

We, therefore, intimate no view as to the correctness of the conclusion of the Wisconsin Supreme Court that the appellant may constitutionally be compelled to contribute his financial support to political activities which he opposes. . . . Upon this understanding we four vote to affirm. Since three of our colleagues are of the view that the claim which we do not decide is properly here and has no merit, and on that ground vote to affirm, the judgment of the Wisconsin Supreme Court is affirmed.

Affirmed.

MR. JUSTICE HARLAN, with whom MR. JUSTICE FRANKFURTER joins, concurring in the judgment.

. . .

For me, there is a short and simple answer to all of this. The Hanson case, 351 U.S. 225, 76 S.Ct. 714, 100 L.Ed. 1112, decided by a unanimous Court, surely lays at rest all doubt that a State may Constitutionally condition the right to practice law upon membership in an integrated bar association, a condition fully as justified by state needs as the union shop is by federal needs. Indeed the conclusion reached in *Hanson* with respect to compulsory union membership seems to be *a fortiori* true here, in light of the supervisory powers which the State, through its courts, has traditionally exercised over admission to the practice of law, . . .

MR. JUSTICE BLACK, dissenting.

. . .

The plurality decision to affirm the judgment of the Wisconsin courts on the ground that the issue in the case is not "shaped . . . as leanly and as sharply as judicial judgment upon an exercise of . . . [state] power requires" is, in my judgment, wrong on at least two grounds. First of all, it completely denies the appellant an opportunity to amend his complaint so as to "shape" the issue in a manner that would be acceptable to this Court. Appellant's complaint was dismissed by the Wisconsin courts, without giving him a chance to amend it and before he had an opportunity to bring out the facts in the case, solely because those courts believed that it would be impossible for him to allege any facts sufficient to entitle him to relief. The plurality now suggests, by implication, that the Wisconsin courts were wrong on this point and that appellant could possibly make out a case under his complaint. Why then is the case not remanded to the Wisconsin courts in order that the appellant will have at least one opportunity to meet this Court's fastidious pleading demands? The opinions of the Wisconsin courts in this case indicate that the laws of that State—as do the laws in most civilized jurisdictions—permit amendments and clarifications of complaints where defects exist in the original complaint which can be cured. And even if Wisconsin law were to the contrary, it is settled by the decisions of this Court that a federal right cannot be defeated merely on the ground that the original complaint contained a curable defect.[6] On this point, the judgment of the Court affirming the dismissal of appellant's suit, insofar as that judgment rests upon the plurality opinion, seems to me to be totally without justification, either in reason, in precedent or in justice.

. . . [T]he same reasons that led me to conclude that it violates the First Amendment for a union to use dues compelled under a union-shop agreement to advocate views contrary to those advocated by the workers paying the dues under protest lead me to the conclusion that an integrated bar cannot take the money of protesting lawyers and use it to support causes they are against. . . .

. . . I do not mean to suggest that the Wisconsin State Bar does not provide many useful and entirely lawful services. Quite the contrary, the record indicates that this integrated bar association, like other bar associations both integrated and voluntary, does provide such services. But I think it clear that these aspects of the Wisconsin State Bar are quite beside the point so far as this case is concerned. For a State can certainly insure that the members of its bar will provide any useful and proper services it desires without creating an association with power to compel members of the bar to pay money to support views to which they are opposed or to fight views they favor. . . .

Comments

In Hollar v. Government of the Virgin Islands, 857 F.2d 163, 168 (3d Cir.1988), the court concluded with respect to Lathrop v. Donohue that:

> As we read the various opinions in that case, seven justices, in effect, upheld the facial constitutional validity of the integrated state bar of Wisconsin against first amendment attack. The fact that those seven justices may have advanced various rationales in support of their conclusions does not diminish the precedential value of the case.

Accord, Levine v. Heffernan, 864 F.2d 457 (7th Cir.1988). Also see Keller v. State Bar of California, 47 Cal.3d 1152, 255 Cal.Rptr. 542, 767 P.2d 1020 (en banc) (1989), cert. granted, 110 S.Ct. 46 (1989) (mandatory bar could expend dues for legislative lobbying and amicus briefs on issues as to which members of the bar might have disagreement). Compare Schneyer, The Incoherence of the Unified Bar Concept: Generalizing From the Wisconsin Case, 1983 Am.Bar Found.Res.J. 1.

For a description of studies of the organized bar, see Maru, Research on the Legal Profession c. 5 (2d ed. 1986).

6. See, e.g., Brown v. Western R. of Alabama, 338 U.S. 294, especially at page 296, 70 S.Ct. 105, at page 106, 94 L.Ed. 100.

D. LEGAL REPRESENTATION OF THE POOR

Professional Obligation to Represent Poor People

The bar has long recognized some kind of an obligation on the part of its members to represent persons who need legal services but cannot afford them. Various rationales are offered. One is that, as an officer of the court, a lawyer has a concern that justice be done, and that representing an indigent person who requires legal assistance is an obvious way to act upon this concern. Another rationale is that the bar has a monopoly of law practice, and as a monopolist it should reallocate its monopoly profits to a manifest public need that is related to the monopoly. Another rationale is that representation of the poor is a special kind of continuing legal education that exposes the lawyer to the realities of justice as administered to the poor. For discussions of the "pro bono" obligation see Christensen, The Lawyer's Pro Bono Public Responsibility, 1981 Am.Bar Found.Res.J. 1; Hazard, The Lawyer's Pro Bono Obligation, in ABA Proceedings of the Second National Conference on Legal Services and the Public (1981); Shapiro, The Enigma of the Lawyer's Duty to Serve, 55 N.Y.U.L.Rev. 735 (1980); Smith, A Mandatory Pro Bono Service Standard—Its Time Has Come, 35 U.Miami L.Rev. 727 (1981). Compare M.R. 6.1.

Making the obligation of lawyers to represent the poor a legal one, as distinct from an ethical exhortation, encounters two difficult problems of feasibility. One arises from the fact that the law in which poor people typically become involved is a set of highly technical subjects with which most lawyers are unfamiliar. Most law schools do not teach these subjects, at least in an integrated way. Representation of indigent criminal defendants requires familiarity with criminal law and its practice. Representation of poor people in disputes with a welfare department requires familiarity with a complicated body of federal and state law and with local administrative practice in administering that law. The law of landlord and tenant, which affects many poor people, is similarly complicated. From a political-economic viewpoint, most poor people exist in a semi-socialist regime in which their lives are continuously dependent on government regulation and discretion. Hence, in most localities, certainly in all major cities, a very sophisticated system would be required to provide that every lawyer shall be on call for whatever may be the legal needs of the poor. These difficulties would be less severe, however, if the law governing the poor were as central to the law school curriculum as is corporation law, constitutional law or administrative law. As law school patterns stand, most lawyers enter law practice without a foundation in the subjects affecting the poor.

A related problem is equalizing the burden of service on all members of the bar. While the bar as a whole may have a monopoly of law practice, no single lawyer or law firm does. If the burden of discharging the collective responsibility were not equitably apportioned,

widely disparate burdens would be involved. Lawyers who had undertaken to learn a speciality in the "law of the poor" would be particularly vulnerable, and that would create perverse incentives to remain
unskilled in poverty law. The difficulties could be ameliorated if
lawyers were required, through continuing legal education and practice, to maintain competence in some field of "poverty law."

MALLARD v. UNITED STATES DISTRICT COURT FOR THE SOUTHERN DISTRICT OF IOWA et al.

Supreme Court of the United States, 1989.
__ U.S. __, 109 S.Ct. 1814, 104 L.Ed.2d 318.

JUSTICE BRENNAN delivered the opinion of the Court.

We are called upon to decide whether 28 U.S.C. § 1915(d) authorizes a federal court to require an unwilling attorney to represent an
indigent litigant in a civil case. We hold that it does not.

I

Section 1915(d) provides: "The court may request an attorney to
represent any [person claiming *in forma pauperis* status] unable to
employ counsel and may dismiss the case if the allegation of poverty is
untrue, or if satisfied that the action is frivolous or malicious." In
Nelson v. Redfield Lithograph Printing, 728 F.2d 1003, 1005 (1984), the
Court of Appeals for the Eighth Circuit ordered "the chief judge of each
district to seek the cooperation of the bar associations and the federal
practice committees of the judge's district to obtain a sufficient list of
attorneys practicing throughout the district so as to supply the court
with competent attorneys who will serve in pro bono situations," such
as *in forma pauperis* proceedings conducted under 28 U.S.C. § 1915.
The District Court for the Southern District of Iowa heeded the Court of
Appeals' command. Under the system in force since February 1986,
once the District Court has determined that an indigent party qualifies
for representation under § 1915(d), the Clerk of the Court forwards a
copy of the court file to the Volunteer Lawyers Project (VLP), a joint
venture of the Legal Services Corporation of Iowa and the Iowa State
Bar Association. The VLP keeps a copy of a roster prepared by the
District Court of all attorneys admitted to practice before the court and
in good standing. After deleting the names of lawyers who have
volunteered for VLP referrals of *pro bono* state court cases, the VLP
selects lawyers from the list nonalphabetically for § 1915(d) assignments.[1] Lawyers who are chosen under the plan may apply to the
District Court for reimbursement of out-of-pocket costs. They may also
keep any fee award provided by statute, but are not guaranteed even

---

1. In February 1986, the Iowa State Bar Association sent a letter to all lawyers
licensed to practice before the United States District Courts for the Northern and
Southern Districts of Iowa describing the referral system. According to the letter, 130
appointments were made between June 1984 and June 1985. The combined lists for both
Districts embraced roughly 3,500 lawyers. Each lawyer was eligible to be chosen every
third year, making her odds of being selected roughly one in nine in those years.

minimal compensation for their own services. The VLP assists lawyers assigned to litigate in areas of the law with which they are unfamiliar by providing written materials, holding periodic seminars, and facilitating consultations with experienced attorneys.

Petitioner Mallard was admitted to practice before the District Court in January 1987, and entered his first appearance the following month. In June 1987 he was asked by the VLP to represent two current inmates and one former inmate who sued prison officials under 42 U.S.C. § 1983, alleging that prison guards and administrators had filed false disciplinary reports against them, mistreated them physically, and endangered their lives by exposing them as informants. After reviewing the case file, Mallard filed a motion to withdraw with the District Court. In his motion, petitioner stated that he had no familiarity with the legal issues presented in the case, that he lacked experience in deposing and cross-examining witnesses, and that he would willingly volunteer his services in an area in which he possessed some expertise, such as bankruptcy and securities law. The VLP opposed petitioner's motion, claiming that he was competent, that he had an ethical duty to do whatever was necessary to try the case, and that permitting an exception to the rule of assignment would create a dangerous precedent. A Magistrate denied petitioner's motion.

Mallard then appealed to the District Court. Although he reiterated his unfamiliarity with § 1983 actions, he contended that he should be permitted to withdraw not because of his inexperience in interpreting the statute and its case law, but because he was not a litigator by training or temperament. Forcing him to represent indigent inmates in a complex action requiring depositions and discovery, cross-examination of witnesses, and other trial skills, Mallard asserted, would compel him to violate his ethical obligation to take on only those cases he could handle competently and would exceed the court's authority under § 1915(d). In an accompanying affidavit, Mallard added: "I do not like the role of confronting other persons in a litigation setting, accusing them of misdeeds, or questioning their veracity. Because of my reluctance to become involved in these activities, I do not feel confident that I would be effective in litigating a case such as the instant case."

Unmoved, the District Court upheld the Magistrate's decision. Based on the quality of petitioner's brief in support of his motion to withdraw, the court pronounced him competent, notwithstanding his very slight acquaintance with trial litigation. The court also held that § 1915(d) empowers federal courts to make compulsory appointments in civil actions. In November 1987, Mallard sought a writ of mandamus from the Court of Appeals for the Eighth Circuit to compel the District Court to allow his withdrawal. The Court of Appeals denied the petition without opinion. We granted certiorari to resolve a conflict among the Courts of Appeals over whether § 1915(d) authorizes compulsory assignments of attorneys in civil cases. . . . We now reverse.

II

. . . Section 1915(d)'s operative term is "request": "The court may request an attorney to represent" an indigent litigant. The import of the term seems plain. To request that somebody do something is to express a desire that he do it, even though he may not generally be disciplined or sanctioned if he declines. . . .

There is little reason to think that Congress did not intend "request" to bear its most common meaning when it used the word in § 1915(d). . . .

Perhaps the clearest proof that Congress did not intend § 1915(d) to license compulsory appointments of counsel is the contrast between that subsection and § 1915(c). Whereas § 1915(d) merely empowers a court to *request* an attorney to represent a litigant proceeding *in forma pauperis,* § 1915(c)—adopted at the very same time as § 1915(d)—treats court officers and witnesses differently: "The officers of the court *shall* issue and serve all process, and perform all duties in such cases. Witnesses *shall* attend as in other cases, and the same remedies shall be available as are provided for by law in other cases." (Emphasis added.) Congress evidently knew how to require service when it deemed compulsory service appropriate. Its decision to allow federal courts to *request* attorneys to represent impoverished litigants, rather than command, as in the case of court officers, that lawyers *shall* or *must* take on cases assigned to them, bespeaks an intent not to authorize mandatory appointments of counsel.

An examination of state statutes governing *in forma pauperis* proceedings at the time § 1915(d) became law bolsters this conclusion. By the late 19th century, at least 12 States had statutes permitting courts to assign counsel to represent indigent litigants. The Congress that adopted § 1915(d) was undoubtedly aware of those statutes, for the brief and otherwise unilluminating Report of the House Judiciary Committee states that the bill containing § 1915(d) was designed to enable persons unable to afford legal representation to avail themselves of the courts, as "[m]any humane and enlightened States" that had similar laws allowed them to do. H.R.Rep. No. 1079, 52nd Cong., 1st Sess., 2 (1892). None of those state statutes, however, provided that a court could merely *request* that an attorney serve without compensation. All of them provided instead that a court could *assign* or *appoint* counsel. . . .

. . . It is . . . significant that no reported decision exists in the above States prior to 1892 holding that a lawyer could not decline representation without compensation, see Shapiro, The Enigma of the Lawyer's Duty to Serve, 55 N.Y.U.L.Rev. 735, 749–762 (1980) (hereinafter Shapiro), for it suggests that Congress did not intend to replicate a system of coercive appointments when it enacted § 1915(d), particularly when it used the weaker verb "request" in place of the words "assign" or "appoint." English precedents from the 15th to the late 19th

century, on which the States apparently relied and which Congress
might have had in mind, were equally murky. Few appointments were
made in either civil or criminal cases; and although sergeants-at-law
were expected to represent indigent persons upon demand of the court,
they held public office and were court officers in a much fuller sense
than advocates who appeared before it. Again, no reported decisions
involve the imposition of sanctions on lawyers unwilling to serve. See
id., at 740–749. Professor Shapiro concludes: "To justify coerced,
uncompensated legal services on the basis of a firm tradition in England and the United States is to read into that tradition a story that is
not there." Id., at 753. . . .

This inference finds additional support in Congress' actions subsequent to § 1915(d)'s enactment. Every federal statute still in force that
was passed after 1892 and that authorizes courts to provide counsel
states that courts may "assign" or "appoint" attorneys, just as did the
1790 capital representation statute. See 18 U.S.C. § 3006A (1982 ed.
and Supp. V) (appoint; criminal defendant); 18 U.S.C. § 3503(c) (assign;
criminal defendant at deposition to preserve testimony); 18 U.S.C.
§ 4109 (appoint; proceeding to verify offender's consent to transfer to
or from United States); 25 U.S.C. § 1912(b) (appoint; Indian child
custody proceedings); 42 U.S.C. § 1971(f) (assign; defendant in voting
rights case); 42 U.S.C. § 2000a–3(a) (appoint; complainant seeking
injunction under civil rights laws); 42 U.S.C. § 2000e–5(f)(1) (appoint;
Title VII complainant); 42 U.S.C. § 3413(1) (assign; commitment of
narcotics addict); see also Fed.Rule Crim.Proc. 44 (assign; criminal
defendant); cf. 10 U.S.C. § 827 (courts-martial shall "detail" trial
counsel and defense counsel). Congress' decision to promulgate these
apparently coercive representation statutes when § 1915(d) was already
on the books and after it had been extended to cover criminal as well as
civil cases, see Act of June 25, 1910, Pub.L. 317, ch. 435, 36 Stat. 866,
suggests that § 1915(d)'s use of "request" instead of "assign" or "appoint" was understood to signify that § 1915(d) did not authorize
compulsory appointments. . . .

Contrary to respondent's assertion, construing § 1915(d) to allow
courts to ask but not compel lawyers to represent indigent litigants
does not render § 1915(d) a nullity. . . . Section 1915(d) may meaningfully be read to legitimize a court's request to represent a poor
litigant and therefore to confront a lawyer with an important ethical
decision; one need not interpret it to authorize the imposition of
sanctions should a lawyer decide not to serve in order to give purpose to
the provision.

. . .

. . . Nor do we express an opinion on the question whether the
federal courts possess inherent authority to require lawyers to serve.
Although respondent and its *amici* urge us to affirm the Court of
Appeals' judgment on the ground that the federal courts do have such
authority, the District Court did not invoke its inherent power in its

opinion below, and the Court of Appeals did not offer this ground for denying Mallard's application for a writ of mandamus. We therefore leave that issue for another day. . . .

So ordered.

. . .

JUSTICE STEVENS, with whom JUSTICE MARSHALL, JUSTICE BLACKMUN, and JUSTICE O'CONNOR join, dissenting.

. . . This case involves much more than the parsing of the plain meaning of the word "request" as used in 28 U.S.C. § 1915(d). This case also does not concern the sufficiency of the lawyer's reasons for declining an appointment or the sanctions that may be imposed on an attorney who refuses to serve without compensation. There are, of course, many situations in which a lawyer may properly decline such representation. He or she may have a conflict of interest, may be engaged in another trial, may already have accepted more than a fair share of the uncompensated burdens that fall upon the profession, or may not have the qualifications for a particular assignment. As this case comes to us, however, the question is whether a lawyer may seek relief by way of mandamus from the court's request simply because he would rather do something else with his time. For me, the answer is quite plain.

A few weeks ago we held that the Virgin Islands Bar could not exclude nonresidents from its membership. See Barnard v. Thorstenn, 489 U.S. ___, 109 S.Ct. 1294, 103 L.Ed.2d 559 (1989). In that case, we expressly recognized the legitimacy of the Bar's interest in requiring its entire membership to share in the burdens of providing representation to indigent defendants in criminal cases. Id., 109 S.Ct. at 1299. That recognition reflects the fact that a court's power to require a lawyer to render assistance to the indigent is firmly rooted in the authority to define the terms and conditions upon which members are admitted to the bar, Frazier v. Heebe, 482 U.S. 641, 107 S.Ct. 2607, 96 L.Ed.2d 557 (1987); United States v. Hvass, 355 U.S. 570, 78 S.Ct. 501, 2 L.Ed.2d 496 (1958), and to exercise "those powers necessary to protect the functioning of its own processes." Young v. United States ex rel. Vuitton et Fils S.A., 481 U.S. 787, 821, 107 S.Ct. 2124, 2144–2145, 95 L.Ed.2d 740 (1987) (Scalia, J., concurring in judgment). Cf. Sparks v. Parker, 368 So.2d 528 (Ala.), appeal dism'd, 444 U.S. 803, 100 S.Ct. 22, 62 L.Ed.2d 16 (1979) (rejecting constitutional challenges to compelled representation of indigent defendants). The lawyer's duty to provide professional assistance to the poor is part of the ancient traditions of the bar long recognized by this Court and the courts of the several States.[4] As

---

4. Justice Cardozo stated for the New York Court of Appeals:

" 'Membership in the bar is a privilege burdened with conditions.' The appellant was received into that ancient fellowship for something more than private gain. He became an officer of the court, and, like the court itself, an instrument or agency to advance the ends of justice. His co-operation with the court was due whenever justice would be imperiled if co-operation was withheld. He might be assigned as counsel for

Justice Field, then sitting on the California Supreme Court, declared more than a century ago:

> "[I]t is part of the general duty of counsel to render their professional services to persons accused of crime, who are destitute of means, upon the appointment of the Court, when not inconsistent with their obligations to others; and for compensation, they must trust to the possible future ability of the parties. Counsel are not considered at liberty to reject, under circumstances of this character, the cause of the defenseless, because no provision for their compensation is made by law." Rowe v. Yuba County, 17 Cal. 61, 63 (1860).

. . .

I attach no particular significance to the difference, if any, between the ordinary meaning of the word "request" used in § 1915(d) and "assign" and "appoint" used in the various state statutes. . . .

. . .

In context, I would therefore construe the word "request" in § 1915(d) as meaning "respectfully command." . . . Congress gave its endorsement to these judicial "requests," assuming that it would be "unthinkable" [9] for a lawyer to decline without an adequate reason.

I respectfully dissent.

Publicly Financed Legal Services

Background

Legal Aid in various forms began around 1900, sometimes as self-help associations of worker and immigrant groups, sometimes as charities. Through the 1950s legal aid programs were funded almost entirely by charity and subscription of members of the bar. The programs usually had a small staff, often one person, assisted by volunteers and law students. The agencies were few in number, located almost exclusively in major cities, thinly funded, relatively passive, concentrating on individual cases and having the aura of a charity. In the 1960s the Ford Foundation made legal aid a major undertaking and infused it with new money, new stature and new

the needy, in causes criminal or civil, serving without pay." People ex rel. Karlin v. Culkin, 248 N.Y. 465, 470–471, 162 N.E. 487, 489 (1928) (citation omitted). . . .

9. Justice Blackmar of the Missouri Supreme Court expressed precisely my sentiments in dissent from a decision denying the courts of that State the power to compel attorneys to represent indigents in civil cases:

"I have often served in court appointments, and I am sure that my brethren have also. When a judge said, 'help me out,' I really felt that I had no choice. Perhaps I had in mind the old army maxim that the commanding officer's desire is the subaltern's command. Perhaps I thought that the court could use its coercive power. I found, however, that judges were sensitive when good reasons for declining appointments were advanced, and were willing to explore alternatives. By issuing our absolute writ, we strip the respondent [the trial judge] of her bargaining power." State ex rel. Scott v. Roper, 688 S.W.2d 757, 773 (Mo.1985).

assertiveness. In 1964, the Economic Opportunity Act of President Lyndon Johnson's "Great Society" program contemplated and provided funding for a quantum leap in civil legal assistance. That Act was the origin of the Federal Legal Services Program, discussed more fully below.

Public defender programs originated in the western states, notably California, in the early part of this Century. They are publicly funded law offices providing representation to indigent criminal accused and to juveniles.

For general and historical background, see Brownell, Legal Aid in the United States (1951); Cheatham, A Lawyer When Needed (1963); Silverstein, Defense of the Poor in Criminal Cases in American State Courts (1965); Wald, Law and Poverty (1965); Carlin, Howard & Mesinger, Civil Justice and the Poor (1967); Christensen, Lawyers for People of Moderate Means (1970).

Federal Legal Services Program

The social reform potential visualized in the 1960s for the federal legal assistance program excited hopes of reformers and fears of conservatives, both probably exaggerated. The result was a political struggle for control of the program, involving the organized bar at various levels, political action groups, factions in Congress, and various agencies in the Government. Broadly speaking, the reformers sought to make legal aid programs a vehicle for structural legal reform, through test cases, class actions and legislative activity, in such areas as housing, civil rights, education, women's rights, and regulation of the workplace. The conservatives sought to maintain legal aid as a service program for needy individuals in such traditional matters as child support and custody, landlord-tenant disputes, debtor-creditor disputes, and securing welfare benefits. For one view at the time, see Carlin, Howard & Mesinger, supra; for another, see Hazard, Social Justice Through Civil Justice, 36 U.Chi.L.Rev. 242 (1970); Law Reforming in the Anti–Poverty Effort, 37 U.Chi.L.Rev. 242 (1970).

In 1974, a detente of sorts was reached. The federal legal services program was established on a permanent basis through the Legal Services Corporation Act, Pub.L. 93–355, 88 Stat. 378. However, the Act imposed various restrictions on the operations of the program and in the matters it could undertake. These restrictions have since been elaborated, each time in highly political battles. Parallel struggles occurred over the level of funding. President Reagan was strongly against any reformist tendency in legal aid and favored abolishing the Legal Services Corporation. Major bar associations, led by the American Bar Association, in company with various civil rights and other activist groups, held out for continuing the program. In the 1980s, the program continued on funding diminished by budget cuts and inflation. It seems fair to say that the federal legal aid program has emerged with modest funding, a traditional program, but on a more or less permanent basis. It also seems likely that from time to time disputes will be renewed over restrictions on program activities. See generally Cramton, Crisis in Legal Services for the Poor, 26 Vill.L.Rev. 521 (1981).

Legislative Controls

Lobbying

The 1974 Act prohibited use of LSC funds to "directly or indirectly" influence the passage or defeat of federal, state or local legislation or regulation except where "necessary to the provision of legal advice and representation with respect to such clients' legal rights and responsibilities" or where a government agency or legislative body or committee or member thereof requested assistance. Public Law 93–335, § 1007(a) (5). A recipient legal aid agency was also prohibited from using private funds for lobbying. The restriction on lobbying was relaxed somewhat in 1977, but tightened in appropriation statutes beginning in 1983. In 1984, LSC issued highly controversial regulations interpreting the lobbying restrictions. Congress responded by requiring that these regulations and all new regulations be submitted to the appropriations committee for review. When LSC did not realize its position, Congress prohibited LSC from implementing or enforcing either the 1984 or 1986 lobbying regulations. See Pub.L. 99–591. As of 1989, the situation remained in that posture.

Class Actions

The LSC Act requires that class actions be approved by the project director of a recipient agency in accordance with policies established by the agency's governing body. See § 1006(d)(5). Beginning with the 1983 appropriation statute, new restrictions were added, notably that prior to filing a class action against a government entity, the project director must determine that the government entity is unlikely to change the policy or practice in question, that the policy or practice will continue to adversely affect eligible clients, and that responsible efforts to resolve the matter without litigation have been unsuccessful or would be adverse to the interests of the clients.

Organizing

The LSC Act forbids use of LSC funds "to organize, assist to organize or encourage to organize or to plan for the creation or formation of, or the structuring of, any organization, association, coalition, alliance, federation, confederation or any similar entity." Pub.L. 93–355, § 1007(b)(6). Changes in 1977 somewhat relaxed this restriction.

Specific Causes

LSC funds may not be used to provide legal assistance with respect to abortions, desegregation of school systems, violations of military selective service act or military desertion, criminal proceedings, or political activity. "Political activity" is defined by the LSC Act to include any activity involving transportation of voters to the polls, voter registration activity other than legal advice or representation, and various partisan and election activities. The 1977 amendments prohibit a staff attorney from being a candidate in a partisan political election.

Fee–Generating Cases

LSC recipients may not provide legal assistance in any fee-generating case except in accordance with guidelines promulgated by LSC. See § 1007(b)(1); 45 C.F.R. § 1609.

E. ETHICAL CONTROLS ON JUDGES

Introductory Note

Judges are subject to statutory, common law, and ethical code regulations. For the federal courts the basic statute is 28 U.S.C. § 455. In 1972 the American Bar Association promulgated a Code of Judicial Conduct, which has subsequently been adopted in most states and by the Judicial Conference of the United States for governance of the United States Circuit and District Courts but not the Supreme Court. The Code has rules against conflict of interest on the part of judges and provisions on other matters. In addition, the Due Process Clause requirements for fair adjudication imposes standards of disinterestedness on judges. See Aetna Life Ins. Co. v. Lavoie, 475 U.S. 813, 106 S.Ct. 1580 (1986).

These requirements may be enforced through judicial disciplinary machinery and in some jurisdictions, including the federal system, by impeachment, and in other jurisdictions by refusal to reelect a judge. They may also be enforced by a motion for disqualification or recusal, as it is often called. For general background, see Braithwaite, Who Judges the Judges?, Am. Bar Found. (1971). See also Stolz, Judging Judges: The Investigation of Rose Bird and the California Supreme Court (1981). For legislative background of the Code of Judicial Conduct, see Thode, Reporter's Notes to the Code of Judicial Conduct (1973).

An authoritative application of judicial standards of conduct is Liljeberg v. Health Service Acquisition Corp., which follows.

LILJEBERG v. HEALTH SERVICES ACQUISITION CORP.

Supreme Court of the United States, 1988.
486 U.S. 847, 108 S.Ct. 2194, 100 L.Ed.2d 855.

JUSTICE STEVENS delivered the opinion of the Court.

In 1974 Congress amended the Judicial Code "to broaden and clarify the grounds for judicial disqualification." 88 Stat. 1609. The first sentence of the amendment provides:

"Any justice, judge, or magistrate of the United States shall disqualify himself in any proceeding in which his impartiality might reasonably be questioned." 28 U.S.C. § 455(a) as amended. . . .

. . .

I

In November 1981, respondent Health Services Acquisition Corp. [hereinafter HAI] brought an action against petitioner John Liljeberg, Jr., seeking a declaration of ownership of a corporation known as St. Jude Hospital of Kenner, Louisiana (St. Jude). The case was tried by Judge Robert Collins, sitting without a jury. Judge Collins found for Liljeberg and, over a strong dissent, the Court of Appeals affirmed. Approximately 10 months later, respondent learned that Judge Collins had been a member of the Board of Trustees of Loyola University while Liljeberg was negotiating with Loyola to purchase a parcel of land on which to construct a hospital. The success and benefit to Loyola of these negotiations turned, in large part, on Liljeberg prevailing in the litigation before Judge Collins.

Based on this information, respondent moved pursuant to Federal Rule of Civil Procedure 60(b)(6) to vacate the judgment on the ground that Judge Collins was disqualified under § 455 at the time he heard the action and entered judgment in favor of Liljeberg. Judge Collins denied the motion and respondent appealed. The Court of Appeals determined that resolution of the motion required factual findings concerning the extent and timing of Judge Collins' knowledge of Loyola's interest in the declaratory relief litigation. Accordingly, the panel reversed and remanded the matter to a different judge for such findings. On remand, the District Court found that based on his attendance at Board meetings Judge Collins had actual knowledge of Loyola's interest in St. Jude in 1980 and 1981. The court further concluded, however, that Judge Collins had forgotten about Loyola's interest by the time the declaratory judgment suit came to trial in January 1982. On March 24, 1982, Judge Collins reviewed materials sent to him by the Board to prepare for an upcoming meeting. At that time—just a few days after he had filed his opinion finding for Liljeberg and still within the 10–day period allowed for filing a motion for a new trial— Judge Collins once again obtained actual knowledge of Loyola's interest in St. Jude. Finally, the District Court found that although Judge Collins thus lacked actual knowledge during trial and prior to the filing of his opinion, the evidence nonetheless gave rise to an appearance of impropriety. . . .

. . .

II

. . .

Respondent filed its complaint for declaratory judgment on November 30, 1981. The case was tried by Judge Collins, sitting without a jury, on January 21 and January 22, 1982. At the close of the evidence, he announced his intended ruling, and on March 16, 1982, he filed a judgment (dated Mar. 12, 1982) and his findings of fact and conclusions of law. He credited Liljeberg's version of oral conversations that were disputed and of critical importance in his ruling.

During the period between November 30, 1981, and March 16, 1982, Judge Collins was a trustee of Loyola University, but was not conscious of the fact that the University and Liljeberg were then engaged in serious negotiations concerning the Kenner hospital project, or of the further fact that the success of those negotiations depended upon his conclusion that Liljeberg controlled the certificate of need. To determine whether Judge Collins' impartiality in the Liljeberg litigation "might reasonably be questioned," it is appropriate to consider the state of his knowledge immediately before the lawsuit was filed, what happened while the case was pending before him, and what he did when he learned of the University's interest in the litigation.

After the certificate of need was issued, and Liljeberg and HAI became embroiled in their dispute, Liljeberg reopened his negotiations with the University. On October 29, 1981, the Real Estate Committee sent a written report to each of the trustees, including Judge Collins, advising them of "a significant change" concerning the proposed hospital in Kenner and stating specifically that Loyola's property had "again become a prime location." The Committee submitted a draft of a resolution authorizing a University vice-president "to continue negotiations with the developers of the St. Jude Hospital." At the Board meeting on November 12, 1981, which Judge Collins attended, the trustees discussed the connection between the rezoning of Loyola's land in Kenner and the St. Jude project and adopted the Real Estate Committee's proposed resolution. Thus, Judge Collins had actual knowledge of the University's potential interest in the St. Jude hospital project in Kenner just a few days before the complaint was filed.

While the case was pending before Judge Collins, the University agreed to sell 80 acres of its land in Kenner to Liljeberg for $6,694,000. The progress of negotiations was discussed at a Board meeting on January 28, 1982. Judge Collins did not attend that meeting, but the Real Estate Committee advised the trustees that "the federal courts have determined that the certificate of need will be awarded to the St. Jude Corporation." Presumably this advice was based on Judge Collins' comment at the close of the hearing a week earlier, when he announced his intended ruling because he thought "it would be unfair to keep the parties in doubt as to how I feel about the case."

The formal agreement between Liljeberg and the University was apparently executed on March 19th. The agreement stated that it was not in any way conditioned on Liljeberg's prevailing in the litigation "pending in the U.S. District Court for the Eastern District of Louisiana . . . involving the obtaining by [Liljeberg] of a Certificate of Need," but it also gave the University the right to repurchase the property for the contract price if Liljeberg had not executed a satisfactory construction contract within one year and further provided for nullification of the contract in the event the rezoning of the University's adjoining land was not accomplished. Thus, the University continued to have an active interest in the outcome of the litigation because it was unlikely that Liljeberg could build the hospital if he lost control of the certificate of need; moreover, the rezoning was in turn dependent on the hospital project.

The details of the transaction were discussed in three letters to the trustees dated March 12, March 15, and March 19, 1982, but Judge Collins did not examine any of those letters until shortly before the Board meeting on March 25, 1982. Thus, he acquired actual knowledge of Loyola's interest in the litigation on March 24, 1982. As the Court of Appeals correctly held, "Judge Collins should have recused himself when he obtained actual knowledge of that interest on March 24." 796 F.2d, at 801.

In considering whether the Court of Appeals properly vacated the declaratory relief judgment, we are required to address two questions. We must first determine whether § 455(a) can be violated based on an appearance of partiality, even though the judge was not conscious of the circumstances creating the appearance of impropriety, and second, whether relief is available under Rule 60(b) when such a violation is not discovered until after the judgment has become final.

III

Title 28 U.S.C. § 455 provides in relevant part: [7]

"(a) Any justice, judge, or magistrate of the United States shall disqualify himself in any proceeding in which his impartiality might reasonably be questioned.

"(b) He shall also disqualify himself in the following circumstances:

. . .

"(4) He knows that he, individually or as a fiduciary, or his spouse or minor child residing in his household, has a financial interest in the subject matter in controversy or in a

7. Prior to the 1974 amendments, § 455 simply provided:

"Any justice or judge of the United States shall disqualify himself in any case in which he has a substantial interest, has been of counsel, is or has been a material witness, or is so related to or connected with any party or his attorney as to render it improper, in his opinion, for him to sit on the trial, appeal, or other proceeding therein." 62 Stat. 908.

The statute was amended in 1974 to clarify and broaden the grounds for judicial disqualification and to conform with the recently adopted ABA Code of Judicial Conduct, Canon 3C (1984). See S.Rep. No. 93–419, p. 1 (1973); H.R.Rep. No. 93–1453, pp. 1–2 (1974), U.S.Code Cong. & Admin.News 1974, p. 6351. The general language of subsection (a) was designed to promote public confidence in the integrity of judicial process by replacing the subjective "in his opinion" standard with an objective test. See S.Rep. No. 93–419, at 5 (1973); H.R.Rep. No. 93–1453, at 5, U.S.Code Cong. & Admin.News 1974, p. 6355.

party to the proceeding, or any other interest that could be substantially affected by the outcome of the proceeding.

. . .

"(c) A judge should inform himself about his personal and fiduciary financial interests, and make a reasonable effort to inform himself about the personal financial interests of his spouse and minor children residing in his household."

Scienter is not an element of a violation of § 455(a). The judge's lack of knowledge of a disqualifying circumstance may bear on the question of remedy, but it does not eliminate the risk that "his impartiality might reasonably be questioned" by other persons. To read § 455(a) to provide that the judge must know of the disqualifying facts, requires not simply ignoring the language of the provision—which makes no mention of knowledge—but further requires concluding that the language in subsection (b)(4)—which expressly provides that the judge must *know* of his or her interest—is extraneous. A careful reading of the respective subsections makes clear that Congress intended to require knowledge under subsection (b)(4) and not to require knowledge under subsection (a). Moreover, advancement of the purpose of the provision—to promote public confidence in the integrity of the judicial process, see S.Rep. No. 93–419, p. 5 (1973); H.R.Rep. No. 93–1453, p. 5 (1974)—does not depend upon whether or not the judge actually knew of facts creating an appearance of impropriety, so long as the public might reasonably believe that he or she knew. . . .

Contrary to petitioner's contentions, this reading of the statute does not call upon judges to perform the impossible—to disqualify themselves based on facts they do not know. . . .

. . . No one questions that Judge Collins could have disqualified himself and vacated his judgment when he finally realized that Loyola had an interest in the litigation. . . . Accordingly, even though his failure to disqualify himself was the product of a temporary lapse of memory, it was nevertheless a plain violation of the terms of the statute.

. . .

IV

Although § 455 defines the circumstances that mandate disqualification of federal judges, it neither prescribes nor prohibits any particular remedy for a violation of that duty. Congress has wisely delegated to the judiciary the task of fashioning the remedies that will best serve the purpose of the legislation. . . .

Section 455 does not, on its own, authorize the reopening of closed litigation. However, as respondent and the Court of Appeals recognized, Federal Rules of Civil Procedure 60(b) provides a procedure whereby, in appropriate cases, a party may be relieved of a final judgment.[10] In particular, Rule 60(b)(6), upon which respondent relies, grants federal courts broad authority to relieve a party from a final judgment "upon such terms as are just," provided that the motion is made within a reasonable time and is not premised on one of the grounds for relief enumerated in clauses (b)(1) through (b)(5). The rule does not particularize the factors that justify relief, but we have previously noted that it provides courts with authority "adequate to enable them to vacate judgments whenever such action is appropriate to accomplish justice," Klapprott v. United States, 335 U.S. 601, 614–615, 69 S.Ct. 384, 390, 93 L.Ed. 266 (1949), while also cautioning that it should only be applied in "extraordinary circumstances," Ackermann v. United States, 340 U.S. 193, 71 S.Ct. 209, 95 L.Ed. 207 (1950). Rule 60(b)(6) relief is accordingly neither categorically available nor categorically unavailable for all § 455 violations. We conclude that in determining whether a judgment should be vacated for a violation of § 455, it is appropriate to consider the risk of injustice to the parties in the particular case, the risk that the denial of relief will produce injustice in other cases, and the risk of undermining the public's confidence in the judicial process. We must continuously be in mind that "to perform its high function in the best way "justice must satisfy the appearance of justice.' " In re Murchison, 349 U.S. 133, 136, 75 S.Ct. 623, 625, 99 L.Ed. 942 (1955) (citation omitted). . . .

. . . The very purpose of § 455(a) is to promote confidence in the judiciary by avoiding even the appearance of impropriety whenever possible. See S.Rep. No. 93–419, at 5; H.R.Rep. No. 93–1453, at 5. Thus, it is critically important in a case of this kind to identify the facts that might reasonably cause an objective observer to question Judge Collins' impartiality. There are at least four such facts.

First, it is remarkable that the judge, who had regularly attended the meetings of the Board of Trustees since 1977, completely forgot about the University's interest in having a hospital constructed on its property in Kenner. The importance of the project to the University is indicated by the fact that the 80–acre parcel, which represented only about 40% of the entire tract owned by the University, was sold for $6,694,000 and that the rezoning would substantially increase the value of the remaining 60%. The "negotiations with the developers of the St. Jude Hospital" were the subject of discussion and formal action by the trustees at a meeting attended by Judge Collins only a few days before the lawsuit was filed.

10. Federal Rule Civil Procedure 60(b) provides in relevant part:

"On motion and upon such terms as are just, the court may relieve a party or a party's legal representative from a final judgment, order, or proceeding for the following reasons: (1) mistake, inadvertence, surprise, or excusable neglect; (2) newly discovered evidence which by due diligence could not have been discovered in time to move for a new trial under Rule 59(b); (3) fraud . . ., misrepresentation, or other misconduct of an adverse party; . . . or (6) any other reason justifying relief from the operation of the judgment. The motion shall be made within a reasonable time, and for reasons (1), (2), and (3) not more than one year after the judgment, order, or proceeding was entered or taken."

Second, it is an unfortunate coincidence that although the judge regularly attended the meetings of the Board of Trustees, he was not present at the January 28, 1982, meeting, a week after the 2–day trial and while the case was still under advisement. The minutes of that meeting record that representatives of the University monitored the progress of the trial, but did not see fit to call to the judge's attention the obvious conflict of interest that resulted from having a University trustee preside over that trial. These minutes were mailed to Judge Collins on March 12, 1982. If the Judge had opened that envelope when he received it on March 14th or 15th, he would have been under a duty to recuse himself *before* he entered judgment on March 16.

Third, it is remarkable—and quite inexcusable—that Judge Collins failed to recuse himself on March 24, 1982. A full disclosure at that time would have completely removed any basis for questioning the Judge's impartiality and would have made it possible for a different judge to decide whether the interests—and appearance—of justice would have been served by a retrial. Another 2–day evidentiary hearing would surely have been less burdensome and less embarrassing than the protracted proceedings that resulted from Judge Collins' nonrecusal and nondisclosure. Moreover, as the Court of Appeals correctly noted, Judge Collins' failure to disqualify himself on March 24, 1982, also constituted a violation of § 455(b)(4), which disqualifies a judge if he "knows that he, individually or as a fiduciary, . . . has a financial interest in the subject matter in controversy or in a party to the proceeding, or any other interest that could be substantially affected by the outcome of the proceeding." This separate violation of § 455 further compels the conclusion that vacatur was an appropriate remedy; by his silence, Judge Collins deprived respondent of a basis for making a timely motion for a new trial and also deprived it of an issue on direct appeal.

Fourth, when respondent filed its motion to vacate, Judge Collins gave three reasons for denying the motion, but still did not acknowledge that he had known about the University's interest both shortly before and shortly after the trial. Nor did he indicate any awareness of a duty to recuse himself in March of 1982.

These facts create precisely the kind of appearance of impropriety that § 455(a) was intended to prevent. The violation is neither insubstantial nor excusable. Although Judge Collins did not know of his fiduciary interest in the litigation, he certainly should have known. In fact, his failure to stay informed of this fiduciary interest, may well constitute a separate violation of § 455. See § 455(c). Moreover, providing relief in cases such as this will not produce injustice in other cases; to the contrary, the Court of Appeals' willingness to enforce § 455 may prevent a substantive injustice in some future case by encouraging a judge or litigant to more carefully examine possible grounds for disqualification and to promptly disclose them when discovered. It is therefore appropriate to vacate the judgment unless it can be said that respondent did not make a timely request for relief, or that it would otherwise be unfair to deprive the prevailing party of its judgment.

If we focus on fairness to the particular litigants, a careful study of Judge Rubin's analysis of the merits of the underlying litigation suggests that there is a greater risk of unfairness in upholding the judgment in favor of Liljeberg than there is in allowing a new judge to take a fresh look at the issues. Moreover, neither Liljeberg nor Loyola University has made a showing of special hardship by reason of their reliance on the original judgment. . . .

CHIEF JUSTICE REHNQUIST, with whom JUSTICE WHITE and JUSTICE SCALIA join, dissenting.

The Court's decision in this case is long on ethics in the abstract, but short on workable rules of law. The Court first finds that 28 U.S.C. § 455(a) can be used to disqualify a judge on the basis of facts not known to the judge himself. It then broadens the standard for overturning final judgments under Federal Rule of Civil Procedure 60(b). Because these results are at odds with the intended scope of § 455 and Rule 60(b), and are likely to cause considerable mischief when courts attempt to apply them, I dissent.

I

As detailed in the Court's opinion, § 455(a) provides that "[a]ny justice, judge, or magistrate of the United States shall disqualify himself in any proceeding in which his impartiality might reasonably be questioned." Section 455 was substantially revised by Congress in 1974 to conform with the recently adopted Canon 3C of the American Bar Association's Code of Judicial Conduct (1974). Previously, a federal judge was required to recuse himself when he had a substantial interest in the proceedings, or when "in his opinion" it was improper for him to hear the case. Subsection (a) was drafted to replace the subjective standard of the old disqualification statute with an objective test. Congress hoped that this objective standard would promote public confidence in the impartiality of the judicial process by instructing a judge, when confronted with circumstances in which his impartiality could reasonably be doubted, to disqualify himself and allow another judge to preside over the case. The amended statute also had the effect of removing the so-called "duty to sit," which had become an accepted gloss on the existing statute.

. . .

The purpose of § 455 is obviously to inform judges of what matters they must consider in deciding whether to recuse themselves in a given case. The Court here holds, as did the Court of Appeals below, that a judge must recuse himself under § 455(a) if he *should have known* of the circumstances requiring disqualification, even though in fact he did not know of them. I do not believe this is a tenable construction of subsection (a). A judge considering whether or not to recuse himself is necessarily limited to those facts bearing on the question of which he has knowledge. To hold that disqualification is required by reason of facts which the judge does *not* know, even though he should have known of them, is to posit a conundrum which is not decipherable by ordinary mortals. While the concept of "constructive knowledge" is useful in other areas of the law, I do not think it should be imported into § 455(a). . . .

See also Leubsdorf, Theories of Judging and Judicial Disqualification, 62 N.Y.U.L.Rev. 237 (1987).

Chapter XI

BECOMING AND BEING A LAWYER

Introductory Note

This coursebook is about the law and morals of a profession, the practice of law. The law consists of the regulations and common law directly addressing the lawyer's conduct, and the substantive and procedural law that is the material with which the lawyer works and in which her practice is embedded. The moral issues are the questions of right and wrong that are unresolved by the law or which arise because the law, as written or as administered, does not correspond to a sense of justice.

In the course of addressing these problems, the materials herein convey a great deal of information about the practice of law. It is not a systematic presentation, for this is not a coursebook in the demographics, sociology, or economics of the legal profession. Nevertheless, the cases report real-life vignettes in the practice of law and yield a composite picture that is fairly accurate. There are cameos of big firm practitioners, small firm and sole practitioners, corporate law department lawyers, lawyers in government practice, and prosecutors and defenders. There are men and women, and individuals of various ethnic, religious, and geographical backgrounds. Along with the other sources of information that a law student has, informal as well as formal, the whole is a reasonable description of the profession at work.

In very general terms, the professional activity of lawyers is directed primarily at protecting property and claims to property and wielding or seeking to deflect the coercive power of government. That is, law practice is concerned with the use of money and power. Yet the lawyer's relationship to money and power is secondary and mediatory. A lawyer is not an investment banker or a business entrepreneur, although many people trained as lawyers migrate into those lines of work. Nor is a lawyer a public official even though a lawyer is appropriately called, as in the Preamble to the Model Rules of Professional Conduct, "an officer of the legal system." A lawyer provides assistance to those who directly own or manage property and who directly exercise political authority. In doing so, a lawyer acts with loyalty to the client, but a loyalty qualified by responsibilities to the legal system.

As Canon 7 of the Code of Professional Responsibility states, "A lawyer should represent a client zealously within the bounds of the law." This seemingly simple axiom reveals the conflicting commitments involved in the practice of law. The practice of law is a continual encounter with such personal conflict.

990

What are the rewards of practice? Why go through the labor, and bear the opportunity costs, of preparing to practice law? Why pursue it afterwards? There are some obvious answers. Entry into the practice of law is fairly open to people of a wide range of backgrounds and talents, so long as they have relatively high levels of verbal facility, stamina, and diligence. It doesn't require capital or a constituency and can be entered even without social or political connections, although those certainly can help. Work in law practice generally has considerable variety and novelty, and often involves an inside view of fascinating and sometimes bizarre human affairs. It usually requires active use of a person's intelligence. Most kinds of practice involve a relatively high degree of autonomy—freedom from bureaucratic or direct regulatory control. Most practitioners make a decent living, certainly compared to the general population, and many achieve substantial influence in the councils of business, government or politics. Most will have had repeated satisfactions in using their abilities to help people out of messy situations.

So what are the discontentments in the practice of law, and how do they arise? The following materials seek to frame that problem and to suggest responses.

The first excerpt, from Gorgias, provides Socrates' moral critique of the lawyers of his day, rhetoricians, and more particularly, his moral challenge to law professors. Gorgias was the most famous rhetorician of his age; he practiced and taught. The word "gorgeous" is derived from his name, bearing witness to the beauty and power of his speech.

GORGIAS

Reprinted From the Dialogues of Plato, Translated Into English by B. Jowett
(D. Appleton and Co.: New York 1898).

. . .

Gorgias: Rhetoric, Socrates, is my art.

Socrates: Then I am to call you a rhetorician?

Gor. Yes, Socrates, and a good one too, if you would call me that which, in Homeric language, "I boast to be."

Soc. I should wish to do that.

Gor. Then pray do.

Soc. And are we to say that you make other men rhetoricians?

Gor. Yes, that is exactly what I profess to make them, not only at Athens, but in all places.

Soc. And will you continue to ask and answer questions, Gorgias, as we are at present doing, and reserve for another occasion the longer mode of speech which Polus was attempting? and will you keep your promise, and answer shortly the questions which are asked of you?

Gor. Some answers, Socrates, are of necessity longer; but I will do my best to make them as short as I can; for a part of my profession is that I can be as short as any one.

Soc. That is what is wanted, Gorgias; exhibit the shorter method now, and the longer one at some other time.

Gor. Well, I will; and I am sure that you will commend my brevity of speech as unrivaled.

Soc. Well, then, as you say that you are a rhetorician, and a maker of rhetoricians, what is the business of rhetoric in the sense in which I might say that the business of weaving is making garments— might I not?

Gor. Yes.

Soc. Might I not say, again, that the business of music is the composition of melodies?

Gor. Yes.

Soc. By Here, Gorgias, I admire the surpassing brevity of your answers.

Gor. Yes, Socrates, and I do think that I am good at that.

Soc. I am glad to hear it; answer me in like manner about rhetoric: what is the business of rhetoric?

Gor. Discourse.

Soc. What sort of discourse, Gorgias?—such discourse as would teach the sick under what treatment they might get well?

Gor. No.

Soc. Then rhetoric does not treat of all kinds of discourse?

Gor. Certainly not.

Soc. And yet rhetoric makes men able to speak?

Gor. Yes.

Soc. And to understand that of which they speak?

Gor. To be sure.

Soc. But does not the art of medicine, which we were just now mentioning, also make men able to understand and speak about the sick?

Gor. Certainly.

Soc. Then medicine also treats of discourse?

Gor. Yes.

Soc. Of discourse concerning diseases?

Gor. Certainly.

Soc. And does not gymnastic also treat of discourse concerning the good or evil condition of the body?

Gor. Very true.

Soc. And the same, Gorgias, is true of the other arts: all of them treat of discourse concerning the subject of which they are the arts.

Gor. That is evident.

Soc. Then why, if you call rhetoric the art which treats of discourse, and all the other arts treat of discourse, do you not call them arts of rhetoric?

Gor. Because, Socrates, the knowledge of the other arts has only to do with some sort of external action, as of the hand; but there is no such action of the hand in rhetoric which operates and in which the effect is produced through the medium of discourse. And therefore I am justified, as I maintain, in saying that rhetoric treats of discourse.

Soc. I do not know whether I perfectly understand you, but I dare say that I shall find out: please to answer me a question; you would allow that there are arts?

Gor. Yes.

Soc. And in some of the arts a great deal is done and nothing or very little said; in painting, or statuary, or many other arts, the work may proceed in silence; and these are the arts with which, as I suppose you would say, rhetoric has no concern?

Gor. You perfectly conceive my meaning, Socrates.

Soc. And there are other arts which work wholly by words, and require either no action or very little, as, for example, the arts of arithmetic, of calculation, of geometry, and of playing draughts; in some of which words are nearly coextensive with things: and in most of them predominate over things, and their whole efficacy and power is given by words: and I take your meaning to be that rhetoric is one of this sort?

Gor. Exactly.

Soc. And yet I do not believe that you really mean to call any of these arts rhetoric; although the precise expression which you used was, that rhetoric is an art of which the effect is produced through the medium of discourse; and an adversary who wished to be captious might take a fancy to say, "And so, Gorgias, you call arithmetic rhetoric." But I do not think that you would call arithmetic rhetoric, any more than you would call geometry rhetoric.

Gor. You are quite right, Socrates, in your apprehension of my meaning.

Soc. Well, then, let me have now the rest of my answer: seeing that rhetoric is one of those arts which works mainly by the use of words, and there are other arts which also use words, tell me what is that quality of words by which the effect of rhetoric is given: I will suppose some one to ask me about any of the arts which I was mentioning just now; he might say, "Socrates, what is arithmetic?" and I should reply to him as you replied to me just now, that arithmetic is one of those arts in which the effect is produced by words. And then he

would proceed: "Words about what?" and I should say, Words about
odd and even numbers, and how many there are of each. . . . And
suppose, again, I were to say that astronomy works altogether by
words—he would ask, "Words about what, Socrates?" and I should
answer, that the words of astronomy are about the motions of the stars
and sun and moon, and their relative swiftness.

Gor. Very true, Socrates; I admit that.

Soc. And now let us have from you, Gorgias, the truth about
rhetoric: which you would admit (would you not?) to be one of those
arts which operate and produce all their effects through the medium of
words?

Gor. True.

Soc. Tell me, I say, what are the words about? To what class of
things do the words which rhetoric uses relate?

Gor. To the greatest, Socrates, and the best of human things.

Soc. That again, Gorgias, is ambiguous; I am still in the dark: for
which are the greatest and best of human things? . . .

Gor. That, Socrates, which is truly the greatest good, being that
which gives men freedom in their own persons, and to rulers the power
of ruling over others in their several States.

Soc. And what would you consider this to be?

Gor. I should say the word which persuades the judges in the
courts, or the senators in the council, or the citizens in the assembly, or
at any other public meeting: if you have the power of uttering this
word, you will have the physician your slave, and the trainer your
slave, and the money-maker of whom you talk will be found to gather
treasures, not for himself, but for you who are able to speak and
persuade the multitude.

Soc. Now I think, Gorgias, that you have very accurately explained what you conceive to be the art of rhetoric; and you mean to
say, if I am not mistaken, that rhetoric is the artificer of persuasion,
having this and no other business, and that this is her crown and end.
Do you know any other effect of rhetoric over and above that of
producing persuasion?

Gor. No; the definition seems to me very fair, Socrates; for
persuasion is the crown of rhetoric.

Soc. Then hear me, Gorgias, for I am quite sure that if there ever
was a man who entered on the discussion of a matter from a pure love
of knowing the truth, I am one, and I believe that you are another.

Gor. What is coming, Socrates?

Soc. I will tell you: I am very well aware that I do not know what,
according to you, is the exact nature, or what are the topics of that
persuasion of which you speak, and which is given by rhetoric; although I have a suspicion both about the one and about the other. And
I am going to ask—what is this power of persuasion which is given by

rhetoric, and about what? But why, if I have a suspicion, do I ask instead of telling you? Not for your sake, but in order that the argument may proceed in such a manner as is most likely to elicit the truth. And I would have you observe, that I am right in asking this further question. If I asked, "What sort of a painter is Zeuxis?" and you said, "the painter of figures," should I not be right in asking, "What sort of figures, and where do you find them?"

Gor. Certainly.

Soc. And the reason for asking this second question would be, that there are other painters as well, who paint many other figures?

Gor. True.

Soc. But if there had been no one but Zeuxis who painted them, then you would have answered very well?

Gor. Certainly.

Soc. Now I want to know about rhetoric in the same way;—is rhetoric the only art which brings persuasion, or do other arts have the same effect? I mean to say this—Does he who teaches anything persuade of what he teaches or not?

Gor. He persuades, Socrates,—there can be no mistake about that.

Soc. Again if we take the arts of which we were just now speaking,—do not arithmetic and the arithmetician teach us the properties of number?

Gor. Certainly.

Soc. And therefore persuade us of them?

Gor. Yes.

Soc. Then arithmetic as well as rhetoric is an artificer of persuasion?

Gor. That is evident.

Soc. And if any one asks us what sort of persuasion, and about what,—we shall answer, of that which teaches the quantity of odd and even; and we shall be in a position to show that all the other arts of which we were just now speaking are artificers of persuasion, and of what kind of persuasion, and about what.

Gor. Very true.

Soc. Then rhetoric is not the only artificer of persuasion?

Gor. True.

Soc. Seeing, then, that not only rhetoric works by persuasion, but that other arts do the same, as in the case of the painter, a question has arisen which is a very fair one: Of what persuasion is rhetoric the artificer, and about what? is not that a fair way of putting the question?

Gor. I think that is.

Soc. Then, if you approve the question, Gorgias, what is the answer?

Gor. I answer, Socrates, that rhetoric is the art of persuasion in the courts and other assemblies, as I was just now saying, and about the just and unjust.

Soc. And that, Gorgias, was what I was suspecting to be your notion; yet I would not have you wonder if by and by I am found repeating a seemingly plain question; for as I was saying, I ask not for your sake, but in order that the argument may proceed consecutively, and that we may not get the habit of anticipating and suspecting the meaning of one another's words, and that you may proceed in your own way.

Gor. I think that you are quite right, Socrates.

Soc. Then let me raise this question; you would say that there is such a thing as "having learned"?

Gor. Yes.

Soc. And there is also "having believed"?

Gor. Yes.

Soc. And are the "having learned" and the "having believed," and are learning and belief the same things?

Gor. In my judgment, Socrates, they are not the same.

Soc. And your judgment is right, as you may ascertain in this way: If a person were to say to you, "Is there, Gorgias, a false belief as well as a true?" you would reply, if I am not mistaken, that there is.

Gor. Yes.

Soc. Well, but is there a false knowledge as well as a true?

Gor. No.

Soc. No, indeed; and this again proves that knowledge and belief differ.

Gor. That is true.

Soc. And yet those who have learned as well as those who have believed are persuaded?

Gor. That is as you say.

Soc. Shall we then assume two sorts of persuasion,—one which is the source of belief without knowledge, as the other is of knowledge?

Gor. By all means.

Soc. And which sort of persuasion does rhetoric create in courts of law and other assemblies about the just and unjust, the sort of persuasion which gives belief without knowledge, or that which gives knowledge?

Gor. Clearly, Socrates, that which only gives belief.

Soc. Then rhetoric, as would appear, is the artificer of a persuasion which creates belief about the just and unjust, but gives no instruction about them?

Gor. True.

Soc. And the rhetorician does not instruct the courts of law or other assemblies about just and unjust, but he only creates belief about them; for no one can be supposed to instruct such a vast multitude about such high matters in a short time?

Gor. Certainly not.

Soc. Come, then, and let us see what we really mean about rhetoric; for I do not know what my own meaning is as yet. When the assembly meets to elect a physician or a shipwright or any other craftsman, will the rhetorician be taken into counsel? Surely not. For at every election he ought to be chosen who has the greatest skill; and, again, when walls have to be built or harbors or docks to be constructed, not the rhetorician but the master workman will advise; or when generals have to be chosen and an order of battle arranged, or a position taken, then the military will advise and not the rhetoricians: would you admit that, Gorgias? As you profess to be a rhetorician and a maker of rhetoricians, I shall do well to learn the nature of your art from you. And here let me assure you that I have your interest in view as well as my own. For I dare say that some one or other of the young men present might like to become your pupil, and in fact I see some, and a good many too, who have this wish, but they would be too modest to question you. And therefore when you are interrogated by me, I would have you imagine that you are interrogated by them. "What is the use of coming to you, Gorgias?" they will say; "about what will you teach us to advise the State? about the just and unjust only, or about those other things also which Socrates has just mentioned?" How will you answer them?

Gor. I like your way of leading us on, Socrates, and I will endeavor to reveal to you the whole nature of rhetoric. You must have heard, I think, that the docks and the walls of the Athenians and the plan of the harbor were devised in accordance with the counsels, partly of Themistocles, and partly of Pericles, and not at the suggestion of the builders.

Soc. Certainly, Gorgias, that is what is told of Themistocles, and I myself heard the speech of Pericles when he advised us about the middle wall.

Gor. And you will observe, Socrates, that when a decision has to be given in such matters the rhetoricians are the advisers; they are the men who win their point.

Soc. I had that in my admiring mind, Gorgias, when I asked what is the nature of rhetoric, which always appears to me, when I look at the matter in this way, to be a marvel of greatness.

Gor. A marvel indeed, Socrates, if you only knew how rhetoric comprehends and holds under her sway all the inferior arts. And I will give you a striking example of this. On several occasions I have been with my brother Herodicus or some other physician to see one of his patients, who would not allow the physician to give him medicine, or apply the knife or hot iron to him; and I have persuaded him to do for me what he would not do for the physician just by the use of rhetoric.

And I say that if a rhetorician and a physician were to go to any city, and there had to argue in the Ecclesia or any other assembly as to which should be elected, the physician would have no chance; but he who could speak would be chosen if he wished, and in a contest with a man of any other profession the rhetorician more than any one would have the power of getting himself chosen, for he can speak more persuasively to the multitude than any of them, and on any subject. Such is the power and quality of rhetoric, Socrates. And yet rhetoric ought to be used like any other competitive art, not against every-body,—the rhetorician ought not to abuse his strength any more than a pugilist or pancratiast or other master of fence; because he has powers which are more than a match either for enemy or friend, he ought not therefore to strike, stab, or slay his friends. And suppose a man who has been the pupil of a palestra and is a skillful boxer, and in the fulness of his strength he goes and strikes his father or mother or one of his familiars or friends, that is no reason why the trainer or master of fence should be held in detestation or banished,—surely not. For they taught this art for a good purpose, as an art to be used against enemies and evil-doers, in self-defense, not in aggression, and others have perverted their instructions, making a bad use of their strength and their skill. But not on this account are the teachers bad, neither is the art in fault or bad in itself; I should rather say that those who make a bad use of the art are to blame. And the same holds good of rhetoric; for the rhetorician can speak against all men and on any subject, and in general he can persuade the multitude of anything better than any other man, but he ought not on that account to defraud the physician or any other artist of his reputation merely because he has the power; he ought to use rhetoric fairly, as he would also use his combative powers. And if after having become a rhetorician he makes a bad use of his strength and skill, his instructor surely ought not on that account to be held in detestation or banished. For he was intended by his teacher to make a good use of his instructions, and he abuses them. And therefore he is the person who ought to be held in detestation, banished, and put to death, and not his instructor.

Soc. You, Gorgias, like myself, have had great experience of arguments, and you must have observed, I think, that they do not always terminate to the satisfaction or mutual improvement of the disputants; but disagreements are apt to arise, and one party will often deny that the other has spoken truly or clearly; and then they leave off arguing and begin to quarrel, both parties fancying that their opponents are only speaking from personal feeling. And sometimes they will go on abusing one another until the company at last are quite annoyed at their own condescension in listening to such fellows. Why do I say this? Why, because I cannot help feeling that you are now saying what is not quite consistent or accordant with what you were saying at first about rhetoric. And I am afraid to point this out to you, lest you should think that I have some animosity against you, and that I speak, not for the sake of discovering the truth, but from personal feeling. Now if you are one of my sort, I should like to cross-examine you, but if not I will let you alone. And what is my sort? you will ask. I am one of those who are very willing to be refuted if I say anything which is not true, and very willing to refute any one else who says what is not true, and just as ready to be refuted as to refute; for I hold that this is the greater gain of the two, just as the gain is greater of being cured of a very great evil than of curing the evil in another. For I imagine that there is no evil which a man can endure so great as an erroneous opinion about the matters of which we are speaking; and if you claim to be one of my sort, let us have the discussion out, but if you would rather have done, no matter; let us make an end.

Gor. I should say, Socrates, that I am quite the man whom you indicate; but, perhaps, we ought to consider the audience, for, before you came, I had already given a long exhibition, and if we proceed the argument may run on to a great length. And therefore I think that we should consider whether we may not be detaining some part of the company when they are wanting to do something else.

Chærephon: You hear the audience cheering, Gorgias and Socrates, which shows their desire to listen to you, and for myself, Heaven forbid that I should have any business which would take me away from so important and interesting a discussion.

. . .

Soc. I may truly say . . . that I am willing, if Gorgias is.

Gor. After this, Socrates, I should be disgraced if I refused, especially as I have professed to answer all comers; in accordance with the wishes of the company, then, do you begin, and ask of me any question which you like.

Soc. Let me tell you then, Gorgias, what makes me wonder at your words; though I dare say that you may be right, and I may have mistaken your meaning. You say that you can make any man, who will learn of you, a rhetorician?

Gor. Yes.

Soc. Do you mean that you will teach him to gain the ears of the multitude on any subject, and this not by instruction but by persuasion?

Gor. Certainly.

Soc. You were saying, in fact, that the rhetorician will have greater powers of persuasion than the physician, even in a matter of health?

Gor. Yes, with the multitude,—that is.

Soc. That is to say, greater with the ignorant; for with those who know, he cannot be supposed to have greater powers of persuasion than the physician has.

Gor. Very true.

Soc. And if he is to have more power of persuasion than the physician, he will have greater power than he who knows?

Gor. Certainly.

Soc. Though he is not a physician,—is he?

Gor. No.

Soc. And he who is not a physician is obviously ignorant of what the physician knows?

Gor. That is evident.

Soc. Then, when the rhetorician is more persuasive than the physician, the ignorant is more persuasive with the ignorant than he who has knowledge? is not that the inference?

Gor. In the case which is supposed, yes.

Soc. And the same holds of the relation of rhetoric to all the other arts; the rhetorician need not know the whole truth about them; he has only to discover some way of persuading the ignorant that he has more knowledge than those who know?

Gor. Yes, Socrates, and is not this a great blessing?—not to have learned the other arts, but the art of rhetoric only, and yet to be in no way inferior to the professors of them?

Soc. Whether the rhetorician is or is not inferior on this account is a question which we will hereafter examine if the inquiry is likely to be of any service to us; but I would rather begin by asking, whether he is as ignorant of the just and unjust, base and honorable, good and evil, as he is of medicine and the other arts; I mean to say, does he know anything actually of what is good and evil, base or honorable, just or unjust in them; or has he only a way with the ignorant of persuading them that he not knowing is to be esteemed to know more than another who knows? Or must the pupil know and come to you knowing these things before he can acquire the art of rhetoric? And if he is ignorant, you who are the teacher of rhetoric will not teach him, for that is not your business, but you will make him seem to know them to the multitude, when he does not know them; and seem to be a good man, when he is not. Or will you be wholly unable to teach him rhetoric unless he knows the truth of these things first? What is to be said, Gorgias, about all this? I swear that I wish you would, as you were saying, reveal to me the power of rhetoric.

Gor. Well, Socrates, I suppose that if the pupil does chance not to know them, he will have to learn of me these things as well.

Soc. Say no more, for there you are right; and so he whom you make a rhetorician must know the nature of the just and unjust, either of his own previous knowledge, or he must be taught by you.

Gor. Certainly.

Soc. Well, and is not he who has learned carpentering a carpenter?

Gor. Yes.

Soc. And he who has learned music a musician?

Gor.   Yes.

Soc.   And he who has learned medicine is a physician, in like manner.   He who has learned anything whatever is that which his knowledge makes him.

Gor.   Certainly.

Soc.   And in the same way, he who has learned what is just is just?

Gor.   To be sure.

Soc.   And he who is just may be supposed to do what is just?

Gor.   Yes.

Soc.   And must not the rhetorician be just, and is not the just man desirous to do what is just?

Gor.   That is clearly the inference.

Soc.   Then the just man will surely never be willing to do injustice?

Gor.   That is certain.

Soc.   And according to the argument the rhetorician ought to be a just man?

Gor.   Yes.

Soc.   And will therefore never be willing to do injustice?

Gor.   Clearly not.

Soc.   But do you remember saying just now that the trainer is not to be accused or banished if the pugilist makes a wrong use of his pugilistic art; and in like manner, if the rhetorician makes a bad and unjust use of his rhetoric, that is not to be laid to the charge of his instructor, neither is he to be banished, but the wrong-doer himself who made a bad use of his rhetoric is to be banished—was not that said?

Gor.   Yes, that was said.

Soc.   And now it turns out that this same rhetorician can never have done any injustice.

Gor.   True.

Soc.   And at the very outset, Gorgias, there was an assertion made, that rhetoric treated of discourse, not about odd and even, but about just and unjust.   Is not that true?

Gor.   Yes.

Soc.   And I thought at the time, when I heard you saying this, that rhetoric, which is always discoursing about justice, could not possibly be an unjust thing.   But when you said, shortly afterwards, that the rhetorician might make a bad use of rhetoric, I noted with surprise the inconsistency into which you had fallen; and I said, that if you thought, as I did, that there was a gain in being refuted, there would be an advantage in discussing the question, but if not, I would leave off.   And in the course of our examination, as you will see yourself, the rhetorician has been acknowledged to be incapable of making an unjust use of rhetoric, or of unwillingness to do injustice. By the dog, Gorgias, there will be a great deal of discussion, before we get at the truth of all this.

Polus: And do you, Socrates, seriously incline to believe what you are now saying about rhetoric? What! because Gorgias was ashamed to deny that the rhetorician knew the just and the honorable and the good, and that he could teach them to any one who came to him ignorant of them, and then out of the admission there may have arisen a contradiction; you, as you always do, having recourse to your favorite mode of interrogation. For do you suppose that any one will ever say that he does not know, or cannot teach, the nature of justice? The truth is, that there is great want of manners in bringing the argument to such a pass.

Soc. Illustrious Polus, the great reason why we provide ourselves with friends and children is that when we get old and stumble a younger generation may be at hand, and set us on our legs again in our words and in our actions; and now, if I and Gorgias are stumbling, there are you a present help to us, as you ought to be; and I for my part engage to retract any error into which you may think that I have fallen—upon one condition.

Pol. What is that?

Soc. That you contract, Polus, the prolixity of speech in which you indulged at first.

Pol. What! Do you mean that I am not to use as many words as I please?

Soc. Only to think, my friend, that having come on a visit to Athens, which is the most free-spoken State in Hellas, you of all men should be deprived of the power of speech—that is hard indeed. But then look at my case: should not I be very hardly used if, when you are making a long oration and refusing to answer what you are asked, I may not go away, but am compelled to stay and listen to you? I say rather, that if you have a real interest in the argument, or, to repeat my former expression, have any desire to set me on my legs, take back again anything which you please; and in your turn ask and answer, like myself and Gorgias—refute and be refuted: for I suppose that you would claim to know what Gorgias knows?

Pol. Yes.

Soc. And you, like him, invite any one to ask you about anything which he likes, and you will know how to answer him?

Pol. To be sure.

Soc. And now, which will you do, ask or answer?

Pol. I will ask; and do you answer me, Socrates, the same question which Gorgias, as you suppose, is unable to answer: What is rhetoric?

Soc. Do you mean what sort of an art?

Pol. Yes.

Soc. Not an art at all, in my opinion, if I am to tell you the truth, Polus.

Pol. Then what, in your opinion, is rhetoric?

. . .

Soc. I should say a sort of routine or experience.

Pol. Then does rhetoric seem to you to be a sort of experience?

Soc. That is my view, if that is yours.

Pol. An experience of what?

Soc. An experience of making a sort of delight and gratification.

Pol. And if able to gratify others, must not rhetoric be a fine thing?

Soc. What are you saying, Polus? Why do you ask me whether rhetoric is a fine thing or not, when I have not as yet told you what rhetoric is?

Pol. Why, did you not tell me that rhetoric was a sort of experience?

Soc. As you are so fond of gratifying others, will you gratify me in a small particular?

Pol. I will.

Soc. Will you ask me what sort of an art is cookery?

Pol. What sort of an art is cookery?

Soc. Not an art at all, Polus.

Pol. What then?

Soc. I should say a sort of experience.

Pol. Of what? I wish that you would tell me.

Soc. An experience of making a sort of delight and gratification, Polus.

Pol. Then are cookery and rhetoric the same?

Soc. No, they are only different parts of the same profession.

Pol. And what is that?

Soc. I am afraid that the truth may seem discourteous; I should not like Gorgias to imagine that I am ridiculing his profession, and therefore I hesitate to answer. For whether or no this is that art of rhetoric which Gorgias practises I really do not know: from what he was just now saying, nothing appeared of what he thought of his art, but the rhetoric which I mean is a part of a not very creditable whole.

Gor. A part of what, Socrates? Say what you mean, and never mind me.

Soc. To me then, Gorgias, the whole of which rhetoric is a part appears to be a process, not of art, but the habit of a bold and ready wit, which knows how to behave to the world: this I sum up under the word "flattery"; and this habit or process appears to me to have many other parts, one of which is cookery, which may seem to be an art, and, as I maintain, is not an art, but only experience and routine: another part is rhetoric, . . . And Polus may ask, if he likes, for he has not as yet been informed, what part of flattery is rhetoric: he did not see that I had not yet answered him when he proceeded to ask a further question,—Whether I do not think rhetoric a fine thing? But I shall not tell him whether rhetoric is a fine thing or not, until I have first answered, "What is rhetoric?" For that would not be right, Polus; but I shall be happy to answer, if you will ask me, What part of flattery is rhetoric?

Pol. I will ask, and do you answer: What part of flattery is rhetoric?

Soc. Will you understand my answer? Rhetoric, according to my view, is the shadow of a part of politics.

Pol. And noble or ignoble?

Soc. Ignoble, as I should say, if I am compelled to answer, for I call what is bad ignoble,—though I doubt whether you understand what I was saying before.

Gor. Indeed, Socrates, I cannot say that I understand myself.

Soc. I do not wonder at that; for I have not as yet explained myself, and our friend Polus, like a young colt as he is, is apt to run away.

Gor. Never mind him, but explain to me what you mean by saying that rhetoric is the shadow of a part of politics.

Soc. I will try, then, to explain my notion of rhetoric, and if I am mistaken, my friend Polus shall refute me. Are there not bodies and souls?

Gor. There are.

Soc. And you would further admit that there is a good condition of either of them?

Gor. Yes.

Soc. Which condition may not be really good, but good only in appearance? I mean to say, that there are many persons who appear to be in good health, and whom only a physician or trainer will discern at first sight not to be in good health.

Gor. True.

Soc. And this applies not only to the body, but also to the soul: in either there may be that which gives the appearance of health and not the reality?

Gor. Yes, certainly.

Soc. And now I will endeavor to explain to you more clearly what I mean: the soul and body being two, have two arts corresponding to them: there is the art of politics attending on the soul; and another art attending on the body, of which I know no specific name, but which may be described as having two divisions, one of which is gymnastic, and the other medicine. And in politics there is a legislative part, which answers to gymnastic, as justice does to medicine; and they run into one another, justice having to do with the same subject as legislation, and medicine with the same subject as gymnastic, yet there is a difference between them. Now, seeing that there are these four arts which are ever ministering to the body and the soul for their highest good, flattery, knowing or rather guessing their natures, has distributed herself into four shams or simulations of them; she puts on the likeness of one or other of them, and pretends to be that which she simulates, and has no regard for men's highest interests, but is ever making pleasure the bait of the unwary, and deceiving them into the belief that she is of the highest value to them. Cookery simulates the disguise of medicine, and pretends to know what food is the best for the body; and if the physician and the cook had to enter into a competition in which children were the judges, or men who had no more sense than children, as to which of them best understands the goodness or badness of food, the physician would be starved to death. A flattery I deem this and an ignoble sort of thing, Polus, for to you I am now addressing myself, because it aims at pleasure instead of good. And I do not call this an art at all, but only an experience or routine, because it is unable to explain or to give a reason of the nature of its own applications. And I do not call any irrational thing an art; if you dispute my words, I am prepared to argue in defense of them.

Cookery, then, as I maintain, is the flattery which takes the form of medicine, and the art of tiring [cosmetics], in like manner, takes the form of gymnastic, and is a knavish, false, ignoble, and illiberal art, working deceitfully by the help of lines, and colors, and enamels, and garments, and making men affect a spurious beauty to the neglect of the true beauty which is given by gymnastic.

I would rather not be tedious, and therefore I will only say, after the manner of the geometricians (for I think that by this time you will be able to follow),

As the art of tiring : gymnastic :: cookery : medicine; or rather—

As tiring : gymnastic :: sophistry : legislation; and—

As cookery : medicine :: rhetoric : justice.

And this, I say, is the natural difference between them, but by reason of their near connection, the sphere and subject of the rhetorician is apt to be confounded with that of the sophist; neither do they know what to make of themselves, nor do other men know what to make of them. For if the body presided over itself, and were not under the guidance of the soul, and the soul did not discern and discriminate between cookery and medicine, but the body was made the judge of them and the rule of judgment was the bodily delight which was given by them, then the word of Anaxagoras, that word with which you, friend Polus, are so well acquainted, would come true: chaos would return, and cookery, health, and medicine would mingle in an indiscernible mass. And now I have told you my notion of rhetoric, which is in relation to the soul what cookery is to the body. I may have been inconsistent in making a long speech, when I would not allow you to discourse at length. But I think that I may be excused, as you did not understand me, and could make no use of my shorter answer, and I had to enter into an explanation. And if I show an equal inability to make use of yours, I hope that you will speak at equal length; but if I am able to understand you, let me have the benefit of your brevity, for this is only fair; and now this answer of mine is much at your service.

Pol. What do you mean? Do you think that rhetoric is flattery?

Soc. Nay, I said a part of flattery; if at your age, Polus, you cannot remember, what will you do by and by, when you get older?

Pol. And are the good rhetoricians meanly regarded in States, under the idea that they are flatterers?

Soc. Is that a question or the beginning of a speech?

Pol. I am asking a question.

Soc. Then my answer is, that they are not regarded at all.

Pol. How not regarded? Have they not very great power in States?

Soc. Not if you mean to say that power is a good to the possessor.

Pol. And I do mean to say that.

Soc. Then, in that case, I think that they have the least power of all the citizens. . . .

. . .

Soc. Well then, I say to you that here are two questions in one, and I will answer both of them. And I tell you, Polus, that rhetoricians and tyrants have the least possible power in States, as I was just now saying; for they do nothing, as I may say, of what they will, but only what they think best.

Pol. And is not that a great power?

Soc. Polus has already denied that.

Pol. Denied? Nay, that is what I affirm.

Soc. By the—what do you call him?—not you, for you say that great power is a good to him who has the power.

Pol. I do.

Soc. And would you maintain that if a fool does what appears best to him he does what is good, and would you call this great power.

Pol. I do not say that.

Soc. Then you must prove that the rhetorician is not a fool, and that rhetoric is an art and not a flattery,—that is the way to refute me; but if you leave me unrefuted, then the rhetoricians who do what they think best in States, and the tyrants, will be deprived of this power: for you assume that power is a good thing, and yet admit that the power which is exercised without understanding is an evil.

Questions

How do the tone and "rules" of the dialogue as conducted by Socrates differ from the "Socratic method" used in law school? What values are implicit in Socrates' style? In the "Socratic method"?

Gorgias concedes that if a student does not know the right and wrong of those things upon which he will argue, it is the law professor's responsibility to teach the student this. Do you agree?

Is the practice of law a "routine" or "experience" as Socrates called "rhetoric"? Does Socrates' critique apply only to lawyers acting as advocates? What arguments in defense of a lawyer's role would a modern lawyer make that Gorgias did not? Are they more persuasive than the ones offered in the dialogue?

Introductory Note on Asylums

Goffman's project in Asylums was the examination of "total institutions," e.g., prisons, monasteries, and mental hospitals. The institutions in which lawyers train and work are not "total." Law schools, which come closest to his model, allow "inmates" to interact more or less freely with the outside world. Law firms, corporations and government bureaucracies are all further along the spectrum, controlling the lives of "inmates" and "staff" by less obvious, although not necessarily less effective, means. Finally, the court system is obviously not a "total" institution. While some of its participants, judges and court personnel, are more or less "fixed" participants, lawyers, plaintiffs, defendants and jurors are transitory actors—although at least the lawyers are often repeat players. There are, however, two factors that make the connection between courts and total institutions closer than it might appear at first. One, the power of courts, in civil and criminal matters, is dependent on their ability to transform people into inmates of total institutions. The power of law in the end *is* the power of total institutions. The court system may therefore be seen as the portal to society's involuntary total institutions. Second, courts, while ostensibly "open" to the public, are not open in the sense that Grand Central Station is open. The court wields enormous power on all within its domain—lawyers, litigants, jurors and even spectators to a lesser degree—are expected to play by special rules and act in accordance with roles not appropriate in other settings.

Despite the sometimes striking parallels between legal institutions and total institutions, it is important to remember an important distinction. Most "inmates" in legal institutions retain active membership in other "institutions" or communities—families, ethnic and religious groups, community-organizations, political parties etc. . . .— which serve as continuing sources of traditions, norms, and commitments that provide grounds by which the individual may critique, resist and revise the institutions of law.

ERVING GOFFMAN, ASYLUMS (1961) *
pp. 3–18, 44–45, 60–65, 99.

INTRODUCTION

I

Social establishments—institutions in the everyday sense of that term—are places such as rooms, suites of rooms, buildings, or plants in which activity of a particular kind regularly goes on. In sociology we do not have a very apt way of classifying them. Some establishments, like Grand Central Station, are open to anyone who is decently behaved; others, like the Union League Club of New York or the laboratories at Los Alamos, are felt to be somewhat snippy about who is let in. Some, like shops and post offices, have a few fixed members who provide a service and a continuous flow of members who receive it. Others, like homes and factories, involve a less changing set of participants. . . . In this book another category of institutions is singled out and claimed as a natural and fruitful one because its members appear to have so much in common—so much, in fact, that to learn about one of these institutions we would be well advised to look at the others.

II

Every institution captures something of the time and interest of its members and provides something of a world for them; in brief, every institution has encompassing tendencies. When we review the different institutions in our Western society, we find some that are encompassing to a degree discontinuously greater than the ones next in line. Their encompassing or total character is symbolized by the barrier to social intercourse with the outside and to departure that is often built right into the physical plant, such as locked doors, high walls, barbed wire, cliffs, water, forests, or moors. These establishments I am calling *total institutions,* and it is their general characteristics I want to explore.

The total institutions of our society can be listed in five rough groupings. First, there are institutions established to care for persons felt to be both incapable and harmless; these are the homes for the blind, the aged, the orphaned, and the indigent. Second, there are places established to care for persons felt to be both incapable of looking after themselves and a threat to the community, albeit an unintended one: TB sanitaria, mental hospitals, and leprosaria. A third type of total institution is organized to protect the community against what are felt to be intentional dangers to it, with the welfare of the persons thus sequestered not the immediate issue: jails, penitentiaries, P.O.W. camps, and concentration camps. Fourth, there are institutions purportedly established the better to pursue some worklike task and justifying themselves only on these instrumental grounds: army barracks, ships, boarding schools, work camps, colonial compounds, and large mansions from the point of view of those who live in the servants' quarters. Finally, there are those establishments designed as retreats from the world even while often serving also as training stations for the religious; examples are abbeys, monasteries, convents, and other cloisters. . . .

Before I attempt to extract a general profile from this list of establishments, I would like to mention one conceptual problem: none of the elements I will describe seems peculiar to total institutions, and none seems to be shared by every one of them; what is distinctive about total institutions is that each exhibits to an intense degree many items in this family of attributes. In speaking of "common characteristics," I will be using this phrase in a way that is restricted but I think logically defensible. At the same time this permits using the method of ideal types, establishing common features with the hope of highlighting significant differences later.

III

A basic social arrangement in modern society is that the individual tends to sleep, play, and work in different places, with different co-participants, under different authorities, and without an over-all rational plan. The central feature of total institutions can be described as a breakdown of the barriers ordinarily separating these three spheres of life. First, all aspects of life are conducted in the same place and under the same single authority. Second, each phase of the member's daily activity is carried on in the immediate company of a large batch of others, all of whom are treated alike and required to do the same thing together. Third, all phases of the day's activities are tightly scheduled, with one activity leading at a prearranged time into the next, the whole sequence of activities being imposed from above by a system of explicit formal rulings and a body of officials. Finally, the various enforced activities are brought together into a single rational plan purportedly designed to fulfill the official aims of the institution.

Individually, these features are found in places other than total institutions. For example, our large commercial, industrial, and educational establishments are increasingly providing cafeterias and free-time recreation for their members; use of these extended facilities remains voluntary in many particulars, however, and special care is taken to see that the ordinary line of authority does not extend to them. Similarly, housewives or farm families may have all their major spheres of life within the same fenced-in area, but these persons are not collectively regimented and do not march through the day's activities in the immediate company of a batch of similar others.

The handling of many human needs by the bureaucratic organization of whole blocks of people—whether or not this is a necessary or effective means of social organization in the circumstances—is the key fact of total institutions. From this follow certain important implications.

When persons are moved in blocks, they can be supervised by personnel whose chief activity is not guidance or periodic inspection (as in many employer-employee relations) but rather surveillance—a seeing to it that everyone does what he has been clearly told is required of him, under conditions where one person's infraction is likely to stand out in relief against the visible, constantly examined compliance of the others. Which comes first, the large blocks of managed people, or the small supervisory staff, is not here at issue; the point is that each is made for the other.

In total institutions there is a basic split between a large managed group, conveniently called inmates, and a small supervisory staff. Inmates typically live in the institution and have restricted contact with the world outside the walls; staff often operate on an eight-hour day and are socially integrated into the outside world. Each grouping tends to conceive of the other in terms of narrow hostile stereotypes, staff often seeing inmates as bitter, secretive, and untrustworthy, while inmates often see staff as condescending, highhanded, and mean. Staff tends to feel superior and righteous; inmates tend, in some ways at least, to feel inferior, weak, blameworthy, and guilty.

Social mobility between the two strata is grossly restricted; social distance is typically great and often formally prescribed. Even talk across the boundaries may be conducted in a special tone of voice . . . Although some communication between inmates and the staff guarding them is necessary, one of the guard's functions is the control of communication from inmates to higher staff levels . . . Just as talk across the boundary is restricted, so, too, is the passage of information, especially information about the staff's plans for inmates. Characteristically, the inmate is excluded from knowledge of the decisions taken regarding his fate. Whether the official grounds are military, as in concealing travel destination from enlisted men, or medical, as in concealing diagnosis, plan of treatment, and approximate length of stay from tuberculosis patients, such exclusion gives staff a special basis of distance from and control over inmates.

All these restrictions of contact presumably help to maintain the antagonistic stereotypes. Two different social and cultural worlds develop, jogging alongside each other with points of official contact but little mutual penetration. Significantly, the institutional plant and name come to be identified by both staff and inmates as somehow belonging to staff, so that when either grouping refers to the views or interests of "the institution," by implication they are referring (as I shall also) to the views and concerns of the staff.

The staff-inmate split is one major implication of the bureaucratic management of large blocks of persons; a second pertains to work.

In the ordinary arrangements of living in our society, the authority of the work place stops with the worker's receipt of a money payment; the spending of this in a domestic and recreational setting is the worker's private affair and constitutes a mechanism through which the authority of the work place is kept within strict bounds. But to say that inmates of total institutions have their full day scheduled for them is to say that all their essential needs will have to be planned for. Whatever the incentive given for work, then, this incentive will not have the structural significance it has on the outside. There will have to be different motives for work and different attitudes toward it. This is a basic adjustment required of the inmates and of those who must induce them to work.

. . .

There is an incompatibility, then, between total institutions and the basic work-payment structure of our society. Total institutions are also incompatible with another crucial element of our society, the family. Family life is sometimes contrasted with solitary living, but in fact the more pertinent contrast is with batch living, for those who eat and sleep at work, with a group of fellow workers, can hardly sustain a meaningful domestic existence. Conversely, maintaining families off the grounds often permits staff members to remain integrated with the outside community and to escape the encompassing tendency of the total institution.

. . .

THE INMATE WORLD

I

It is characteristic of inmates that they come to the institution with a "presenting culture" (to modify a psychiatric phrase) derived from a "home world"—a way of life and a round of activities taken for granted until the point of admission to the institution. . . . Whatever the stability of the recruit's personal organization, it was part of a wider framework lodged in his civil environment—a round of experience that confirmed a tolerable conception of self and allowed for a set of defensive maneuvers, exercised at his own discretion, for coping with conflicts, discreditings, and failures.

. . .

The full meaning for the inmate of being "in" or "on the inside" does not exist apart from the special meaning to him of "getting out" or "getting on the outside." In this sense, total institutions do not really look for cultural victory. They create and sustain a particular kind of tension between the home world and the institutional world and use this persistent tension as strategic leverage in the management of men.

II

The recruit comes into the establishment with a conception of himself made possible by certain stable social arrangements in his home world. Upon entrance, he is immediately stripped of the support provided by these arrangements. In the accurate language of some of our oldest total institutions, he begins a series of abasements, degradations, humiliations, and profanations of self. His self is systematically, if often unintentionally, mortified. He begins some radical shifts in his *moral career,* a career composed of the progressive changes that occur in the beliefs that he has concerning himself and significant others.

The processes by which a person's self is mortified are fairly standard in total institutions; analysis of these processes can help us to see the arrangements that ordinary establishments must guarantee if members are to preserve their civilian selves.

The barrier that total institutions place between the inmate and the wider world marks the first curtailment of self. In civil life, the sequential scheduling of the individual's roles, both in the life cycle and in the repeated daily round, ensures that no one role he plays will block his performance and ties in another. In total institutions, in contrast, membership automatically disrupts role scheduling, since the inmate's separation from the wider world lasts around the clock and may continue for years. Role dispossession therefore occurs. In many total institutions the privilege of having visitors or of visiting away from the establishment is completely withheld at first, ensuring a deep initial break with past roles and an appreciation of role dispossession. . . . I might add that when entrance is voluntary, the recruit has already partially withdrawn from his home world; what is cleanly severed by the institution is something that had already started to decay.

Although some roles can be re-established by the inmate if and when he returns to the world, it is plain that other losses are irrevocable and may be painfully experienced as such. It may not be possible to make up, at a later phase of the life cycle, the time not now spent in educational or job advancement, in courting, or in rearing one's children. A legal aspect of this permanent dispossession is found in the concept of "civil death": prison inmates may face not only a temporary loss of the rights to will money and write checks, to contest divorce or adoption proceedings, and to vote but may have some of these rights permanently abrogated.

The inmate, then, finds certain roles are lost to him by virtue of the barrier that separates him from the outside world. The process of entrance typically brings other kinds of loss and mortification as well. We very generally find staff employing what are called admission procedures, such as taking a life history, photographing, weighing, fingerprinting, assigning numbers, searching, listing personal possessions for storage, undressing, bathing, disinfecting, haircutting, issuing institutional clothing, instructing as to rules, and assigning to quarters.

Admission procedures might better be called "trimming" or "programming" because in thus being squared away the new arrival allows himself to be shaped and coded into an object that can be fed into the administrative machinery of the establishment, to be worked on smoothly by routine operations. . . .

Because a total institution deals with so many aspects of its inmates' lives, with the consequent complex squaring away at admission, there is a special need to obtain initial co-operativeness from the recruit. Staff often feel that a recruit's readiness to be appropriately deferential in his initial face-to-face encounters with them is a sign that he will take the role of the routinely pliant inmate. The occasion on which staff members first tell the inmate of his deference obligations may be structured to challenge the inmate to balk or to hold his peace forever. Thus these initial moments of socialization may involve an "obedience test" and even a will-breaking contest; an inmate who shows defiance receives immediate visible punishment, which increases until he openly "cries uncle" and humbles himself.

An engaging illustration is provided by Brendan Behan in reviewing his contest with two warders upon his admission to Walton prison:

"And 'old up your 'ead, when I speak to you."

" 'Old up your 'ead, when Mr. Whitbread speaks to you," said Mr. Holmes.

I looked round at Charlie. His eyes met mine and he quickly lowered them to the ground.

"What are you looking round at, Behan? Look at me."

. . .

I looked at Mr. Whitbread. "I am looking at you," I said.

"You are looking at Mr. Whitbread—what?" said Mr. Holmes.

"I am looking at Mr. Whitbread."

Mr. Holmes looked gravely at Mr. Whitbread, drew back his open hand, and struck me on the face, held me with his other hand and struck me again.

My head spun and burned and pained and I wondered would it happen again. I forgot and felt another smack, and forgot, and another, and moved, and was held by a steadying, almost kindly hand, and another, and my sight was a vision of red and white and pity-coloured flashes.

"You are looking at Mr. Whitbread—what, Behan?"

I gulped and got together my voice and tried again till I got it out. "I, sir, please, sir, I am looking at you, I mean, I am looking at Mr. Whitbread, sir."

Admission procedures and obedience tests may be elaborated into a form of initiation that has been called "the welcome," where staff or inmates, or both, go out of their way to give the recruit a clear notion of his plight. As part of this rite of passage he may be called by a term such as "fish" or "swab," which tells him that he is merely an inmate, and, what is more, that he has a special low status even in this low group.

The admission procedure can be characterized as a leaving off and a taking on, with the midpoint marked by physical nakedness. Leaving off of course entails a dispossession of property, important because persons invest self feelings in their possessions. Perhaps the most significant of these possessions is not physical at all, one's full name; whatever one is thereafter called, loss of one's name can be a great curtailment of the self.

Another clear-cut expression of personal inefficacy in total institutions is found in inmates' use of speech. One implication of using words to convey decisions about action is that the recipient of an order is seen as capable of receiving a message and acting under his own power to complete the suggestion or command. Executing the act himself, he can sustain some vestige of the notion that he is self-determining. Responding to the question in his own words, he can sustain the notion that he is somebody to be considered, however slightly. And since it is only words that pass between himself and the others, he succeeds in retaining at least physical distance from them, however unpalatable the command or statement.

The inmate in a total institution can find himself denied even this kind of protective distance and self-action. Especially in mental hospitals and political training prisons, the statements he makes may be discounted as mere symptoms, with staff giving attention to non-verbal aspects of his reply. Often he is considered to be of insufficient ritual status to be given even minor greetings, let alone listened to. Or the inmate may find that a kind of rhetorical use of language occurs: questions such as, "Have you washed yet?" or, "Have you got both socks on?" may be accompanied by simultaneous searching by the staff which physically discloses the facts, making these verbal questions superfluous. And instead of being told to move in a particular direction at a particular rate, he may find himself pushed along by the guard, or pulled (in the case of overalled mental patients), or frog-marched. . . .

VI

Although there are solidarizing tendencies such as fraternalization and clique formation, they are limited. Constraints which place inmates in a position to sympathize and communicate with each other do not necessarily lead to high group morale and solidarity. In some concentration camps and prisoner-of-war installations the inmate cannot rely on his fellows, who may steal from him, assault him, and squeal on him, leading to what some students have referred to as anomie. In mental hospitals, dyads and triads may keep secrets from the authorities, but anything known to a whole ward of patients is likely to get to the ear of the attendant. (In prisons, of course, inmate organization has sometimes been strong enough to run strikes and short-lived insurrections; in prisoner-of-war camps, it has sometimes been possible to organize sections of the prisoners to operate escape channels; in concentration camps there have been periods of thoroughgoing underground organization; and on ships there have been mutinies; but these concerted actions seem to be the exception, not the rule.) But though there is usually little group loyalty in total institutions, the expectation that group loyalty should prevail forms part of the inmate culture and underlies the hostility accorded those who break inmate solidarity. . . . The same inmate will employ different personal lines of adaptation at different phases in his moral career and may even alternate among different tacks at the same time.

First, there is the tack of "situational withdrawal." The inmate withdraws apparent attention from everything except events immediately around his body and sees these in a perspective not employed by others present. This drastic curtailment of involvement in interactional events is best known, of course, in mental hospitals, under the title of "regression." . . .

Secondly, there is the "intransigent line": the inmate intentionally challenges the institution by flagrantly refusing to co-operate with staff. The result is a constantly communicated intransigency and sometimes high individual morale. Many large mental hospitals, for example, have wards where this spirit prevails. Sustained rejection of a total institution often requires sustained orientation to its formal organization, and hence, paradoxically, a deep kind of involvement in the establishment. Similarly, when staff take the line that the intransigent inmate must be broken (as they sometimes do in the case of hospital psychiatrists prescribing electroshock or military tribunals prescribing the stockade), then the institution shows as much special devotion to the rebel as he has shown to it. Finally, although some prisoners of war have been known to take a staunchly intransigent stance throughout their incarceration, intransigence is typically a temporary and initial phase of reaction, with the inmate shifting to situational withdrawal or some other line of adaptation.

A third standard alignment in the institutional world is "colonization": the sampling of the outside world provided by the establishment is taken by the inmate as the whole, and a stable, relatively contented existence is built up out of the maximum satisfactions procurable within the institution. Experience of the outside world is used as a point of reference to demonstrate the desirability of life on the inside, and the usual tension between the two worlds is markedly reduced, thwarting the motivational scheme based upon this felt discrepancy which I described as peculiar to total institutions. Characteristically, the individual who too obviously takes this line may be accused by his fellow inmates of "having found a home" or of "never having had it so good." The staff itself may become vaguely embarrassed by this use that is being made of the institution, sensing that the benign possibilities in the situation are somehow being misused. Colonizers may feel obliged to deny their satisfaction with the institution, if only to sustain the counter-mores supporting inmate solidarity. They may find it necessary to mess up just prior to their slated discharge to provide themselves with an apparently involuntary basis for continued incarceration. Significantly, the staff who try to make life in total institutions more bearable must face the possibility that doing so may increase the attractiveness and likelihood of colonization.

A fourth mode of adaptation to the setting of a total institution is that of "conversion": the inmate appears to take over the official or staff view of himself and tries to act out the role of the perfect inmate. While the colonized inmate builds as much of a free community for himself as possible by using the limited facilities available, the convert takes a more disciplined, moralistic, monochromatic line, presenting himself as someone whose institutional enthusiasm is always at the disposal of the staff. In Chinese P.O.W. camps, we find Americans who became "Pros" and fully espoused the Communist view of the world. In army barracks there are enlisted men who give the impression that they are always "sucking around" and always "bucking for promotion." In prisons there are "square johns." In German concentration camps, a long-time prisoner sometimes came to adapt the vocabulary, recreation, posture, expressions of aggression, and clothing style of the Gestapo, executing the role of straw boss with military strictness. . . .

The alignments that have been mentioned represent coherent courses to pursue, but few inmates seem to pursue any one of them very far. In most total institutions, most inmates take the tack of what some of them call "playing it cool." This involves a somewhat opportunistic combination of secondary adjustments, conversion, colonization, and loyalty to the inmate group, so that the inmate will have a maximum chance, in the particular circumstances, of eventually getting out physically and psychologically undamaged. Typically, the inmate when with fellow inmates will support the counter-mores and conceal from them how tractably he acts when alone with the staff.[124] Inmates who play it cool subordinate contacts with their fellows to the higher claim of "keeping out of trouble"; they tend to volunteer for nothing; and they may learn to cut their ties to the outside world just enough to give cultural reality to the world inside but not enough to lead to colonization.

. . .

An interesting institutional ceremony, often connected with the annual party and the Christmas celebration, is the institutional theatri-

124. This two-facedness is very commonly found in total institutions. In the state mental hospital studied by the writer, even the few elite patients selected for individual psychotherapy, and hence in the best position to espouse the psychiatric approach to self, tended to present their favorable view of psychotherapy only to the members of their intimate cliques. For a report on the way in which army prisoners concealed from fellow offenders their interest in "restoration" to the Army, see the comments by Richard Cloward in Session Four of New Perspectives for Research on Juvenile Delinquency, eds. Helen L. Witmer and Ruth Kotinsky, U.S. Dept. of Health, Education, and Welfare, Children's Bureau Publication No. 356 (1956), especially p. 90.

cal. Typically the players are inmates and the directors of the production are staff, but sometimes "mixed" casts are found. The writers are usually members of the institution, whether staff or inmate, and hence the production can be full of local references, imparting through the private use of this public form a special sense of the reality of events internal to the institution. Very frequently the offering will consist of satirical skits that lampoon well-known members of the institution, especially high-placed staff members. If, as is frequent, the inmate community is one-sexed, then some of the players are likely to perform in the costume and burlesqued role of members of the other sex. Limits of license are often tested, the humor being a little more broad than some members of the staff would like to see tolerated. . . .

Questions

How do law schools use admission procedures and obedience tests to initiate recruits? Why are these techniques necessary? What lines of adaptation have you used in your career as a law student? Why? Have you perceived among your fellow students variations on the lines of adaptation described by Goffman? What values does the structure of law school inculcate? Are these necessary for "good" lawyering? What changes in law school would you suggest?

What are the admission procedures and obedience tests used by law firms and other institutions in which lawyers work? Are there similar lines of adaptation present? In what ways are clients like inmates in the lawyer's office? Since neither the model of inmate or staff works well to describe the client in a law firm, how would you go about describing the client's relationship to the institution?

How are lawyers like inmates in the courts? How are they like staff? What role do the litigants play in the court system? The jurors?

The Legal Profession's Messages About Professional Responsibility

In an article entitled, Law School Instruction in Professional Responsibility: A Curricular Paradox, 1979 Amer. Bar Found.J. 247, Professor Ronald Pipkin argues that many law school courses in professional responsibility actually "desensitize students to legal ethics." He begins by identifying the manifest and latent hierarchy of courses in law schools. The manifest hierarchy identifies important courses by such official indicators as the number of credits assigned to each course, and whether a course is required or elective. The latent hierarchy is "less visible, less explicitly rationalized, and may either reinforce or work at cross-purposes to the official . . . manifest structure. The latent hierarchies are communicated to students through the content of instruction, cues from the faculty, advice from practitioners and other students, feedback from the job market, bar exams and so forth." Id. at 252–53. Pipkin argues that the latent hierarchy works to undercut whatever importance the manifest hierarchy assigns to courses in professional responsibility.

Pipkin interviewed students at seven law schools in the academic year 1975–76. His data showed that students perceived courses in professional responsibility as requiring less time, as substantially easier, as less well taught, and as a less valuable use of class time. His data further suggested that courses in professional responsibility were held in low intellectual esteem in large measure because they were more likely to be taught by discussion method than by either lecture or the socratic method. Generally, courses taught by the socratic method were considered by students to be the most intellectually demanding, with courses taught by lecture coming in second and courses, no matter what the subject, taught by discussion coming in a poor third. Although students perceived professional responsibility as highly relevant to their later careers as practicing lawyers, a course's perceived relevance to life as a lawyer was irrelevant to how much time students expended on the course or whether they saw the course as intellectually challenging.

How does law school communicate messages about the importance of professional responsibility? If professional responsibility has come up in other courses, how has the subject been treated by the professor? Was professional responsibility a theme that ran through your law school career? How do employers treat the subject? Fellow students? How have these messages affected your attitude toward professional responsibility?

ROBERT W. GORDON, "THE IDEAL AND THE ACTUAL IN THE LAW"

In Gawalt, Ed., The New High Priests.
Lawyers in Post–Civil War America (1984).*

· · ·

[We can think of lawyers] as having "ideal interests" as well as material ones, and as struggling to work out a relationship between their beliefs and their practices—between the ideal and the actual— with which they could live in comfort. Lawyers are perhaps . . . double agents. They have obligations to a universal scheme of order, "the law," understood as some fairly coherent system of rules and procedures that are supposed to regulate social life in accordance with prevailing political conceptions of the good.

The law, to put this another way, is an artificial utopia of social harmony, a kind of collectively maintained fantasy of what society would look like if everyone played by the rules. But lawyers are also supposed to be loyal toward and advance the interests of clients pursuing particular ends. The lawyer's job, thus, is to mediate between the universal vision of legal order and the concrete desires of his clients, to show how what the client wants can be accommodated to the utopian scheme. The lawyer, thus, has to find ways of squeezing the client's plan of action into the legally recognized categories of approved conduct. Of course, the law's view of the client's reality is often a highly distorted one, since its categorizing forms are administratively manageable only if they drastically abstract and simplify from that reality, and legitimate only if they seem to be part of the system of universal normative order. Even so, the lawyer's job is selling legitimacy: reassurance to the client and its potential regulators, investors, or business partners that what it wants to do is basically all right; and the lawyer cannot deliver unless she can make plausible arguments rationalizing her client's conduct within the prevailing terms of legal discourse. She must, in short, be able to understand the day-to-day world of the client's transactions and deals as somehow approximating, in however decayed or imperfect a form, the ideal or fantasy world of legal order.

Reform-minded lawyers of 1870 had no trouble perceiving that their world was, from this point of view, in lots of trouble. The articulate ones are most easily described as modified or pragmatic classical liberals, that is, their ideal society was one in which (adult male) individuals were left free to pursue self-interest within a framework of property rights, exchange rules, and public order guaranteed by law—rules of general application, treating individuals as formally equal, and impartially and predictably applied. . . . Within their ideal scheme of order, all participants had definitely bounded rights and powers—the individual vis-à-vis other individuals and the state, the states vis-à-vis one another and the federal government, the separate branches of government vis-à-vis one another—which it was the role of the judiciary, the natural arbiter of the system as well as a player in it, to enforce.

Yet this scheme had for some years—since the '50s or '60s, depending on whether one blamed the railroads or Reconstruction—been in a process of total breakdown. Liberal lawyers analyzed the breakdown much as other reformers did, except that they were more prone to see it as the result of *legal* failure that was remediable by legal reform. The present evils could be summed up as lack of generality in framing laws, and lack of predictability and impartiality in applying them. Southern black codes, debtor's stay laws, legislation relieving municipalities from contracted bond obligations, handouts of subsidies, exemptions, and privileges to railroad corporations—all had in common the vice of *particularly* favoring or disfavoring special classes of citizens. Impartiality of application had been subverted by patronage appointments or machine-controlled election of corrupt judges or officials. Predictability was undermined by the same factors, as well as by sloppiness in statutory draftsmanship, judicial decision making, and administration of procedural rules, and by the wild variety of law-making jurisdictions.

The lawyers proposed to restore all this unruly mess to the dominion of the rule of law. . . .

[H]igh-minded lawyers were embarked on a practical program of reform. As leaders of the bar, they belonged to a tradition, communicated through endless reiteration in formal speeches, of patrician Whig aspirations to play a distinctive role in American society as a Third Force in politics (in fact the role of "the few" in classical republican theory), mediating between capital and labor, between private acquisitiveness and democratic redistributive follies; thus, they kept looking for social stages on which to enact the role of Tocqueville's lawyer-aristocrats. . . .

Note on the Ideal in the Law

Gordon suggests that the leaders of the New York bar of the 1870's faced a conflict between their idealized conception of the law and their role in its administration, on the one hand, and the seamy actuality they confronted in everyday life on the other hand. It seems clear that the same contradictions are confronted by all lawyers, not just those in New York or a century ago.

Gordon refers to the underlying wish to "enact the role of Tocqueville's lawyer-aristocrats." In this he is referring to Tocqueville's famous observation:

Men who have made a special study of the laws and have derived therefrom habits of order, something of a taste for formalities, and an instinctive love for a regular concatenation of ideas are naturally strongly opposed to the revolutionary spirit and to the ill-considered passions of democracy.

Study and specialized knowledge of the law give a man a rank apart in society and makes of lawyers a somewhat privileged intellectual class. The exercise of their profession daily reminds them of this superiority; they are the masters of a necessary and not widely understood science; they serve as arbiters between the citizens . . . Add that they naturally form *a body* . . .

So, hidden at the bottom of a lawyer's soul one finds the tastes and habits of an aristocracy.

deTocqueville, Democracy in America, P. II, Ch. 8.

Do the professed ideals of the legal profession concerning its own role reflect Tocqueville's description of the profession? Do both remain an accurate portrayal of the professional ideal?

Following are several different statements about the role of lawyers, all of them now classics. The excerpts from Hoffman, *A Course of Legal Study,* are representative of his views on a range of subjects concerning law practice, which were presented as lectures to those about to enter the profession. Note both the similarity of some of his propositions to modern-day ethical formulations, and also the loftily high-minded position he assumed to take. It is difficult to imagine that he actually acted out the role he describes, but it is easy to imagine that he *believed* he did. At any rate, the same tone persisted in the Canons of Professional Ethics adopted by the American Bar Association in 1908, which remained the ABA's official position until 1970. Thus, compare Hoffman's *Resolution III,* regarding the lawyer's proper attitude toward the courts, with Canon 1 of the 1908 Canon:

> It is the duty of the lawyer to maintain towards the Courts a respectful attitude, not for the sake of the temporary incumbent of the judicial office, but for the maintenance of its supreme importance . . .

So also, compare Hoffman's *Resolution XIV* with the recitals in Canon 15 of the 1908 Canons:

> Nothing operates more certainly to create or to foster popular opinion against lawyers as a class, and to deprive the profession of that full measure of public esteem and confidence which belongs to the proper discharge of its duties than does the false claim, often set up by the unscrupulous in defense of questionable transactions, that it is the duty of the lawyer to do whatever may enable him to succeed in winning his client's cause.

The Brandeis address, given in 1905, also has become a classic. By that time, the legal profession's mode of practice was well into the revolutionary change from being almost entirely sole practice, or partnerships made up of two or occasionally three lawyers, into modern form where practice in firms predominates. Moreover, the practice of the emergent firms was by then increasingly devoted to affairs of corporate enterprise rather than to the business and property affairs of individuals. Brandeis' address was one of the most forceful, if not the earliest, in decrying the subservience of law practice to corporate interests. Consistent with the traditional rhetoric of the profession, Brandeis related the special position of the profession to the Constitution and the rule of law. However, he described the unique competence of lawyers to be "judgment," rather than knowledge of the law, as Tocqueville had said, or the role of officer of the court, as Hoffman had suggested. Although he presented a different concept of the lawyer's unique competence, Brandeis nevertheless reaffirmed the ideal of the lawyer's autonomy, particularly in issues relating to social justice.

The third excerpt is an address by Justice, later Chief Justice, Harlan Fisk Stone. The address created quite a stir because it was a lamentation on the fallen state of the bar from one who stood at the pinnacle of the legal establishment. Observe how Stone also derives a unique position for the legal profession from the Constitution, and, on this basis, attributes to lawyers a special competence and responsibility in matters of public policy. Was this claim subsequently vindicated by the Warren Court's activist Constitutional interpretation? Did that activism have roots arising from sectors of the legal profession that had little connection to the sector of the bar that Stone was talking about? Is there some kind of relationship between the idea of protecting corporate property through legal devices and protecting equality of citizenship through legal devices? Is the concept of such a relationship one that would readily occur to lawyers as a body, but be unlikely to occur either to businessmen or to oppressed minorities or the average citizen? Could some such idea be the basis of the ideology of the legal profession? Or is it the profession's lie?

DAVID HOFFMAN, A COURSE OF LEGAL STUDY (1836)

Resolutions in Regard to Professional Deportment

. . .

III. To all judges, when in court, I will ever be respectful: they are the Law's viceregents; and whatever may be their character and deportment, the individual should be lost in the majesty of the office.

. . .

V. In all intercourse with my professional brethren, I will be always courteous. No man's passions shall intimidate me from asserting fully my own, or my client's rights; and no man's ignorance or folly shall induce me to take any advantage of him; I shall deal with them all as honourable men, ministering at our common altar.

. . .

X. Should my client be disposed to insist on captious requisitions, or frivolous and vexatious defences, they shall be neither enforced nor countenanced by me. And if still adhered to by him from a hope of pressing the other party into an unjust compromise, or with any other motive, he shall have the option to select other counsel.

XI. If, after duly examining a case, I am persuaded that my client's claim or defence (as the case may be,) cannot, or rather ought not, to be sustained, I will promptly advise him to abandon it. To press it further in such a case, with the hope of gleaning some advantage by an extorted compromise, would be lending myself to a dishonourable use of legal means, in order to gain a *portion* of that, the *whole* of which I have reason to believe would be denied to him both by law and justice.

XII. I will never plead the Statute of Limitations, when based on the *mere efflux of time;* for if my client is conscious he owes the debt; and has no other defence than the *legal bar,* he shall never make me a partner in his knavery.

XIV. My client's conscience, and my own, are distinct entities; and though my vocation may sometimes justify my maintaining as facts, or principles, in doubtful cases, what may be neither one nor the other, I shall ever claim the privilege of solely judging to what extent to go. In *civil* cases, if I am satisfied from the evidence that the *fact* is against my client, he must excuse me if I do not see as he does, and do not press it; and should the *principle* also be wholly at variance with sound law, it would be dishonourable folly in me to endeavor to incorporate it into the jurisprudence of the country, when, if successful, it would be a gangrene that might bring death to my cause of the succeeding day.

XV. When employed to defend those charged with crimes of the deepest dye, and the evidence against them, whether legal, or moral, be such as to leave no just doubt of their guilt, I shall not hold myself privileged, much less obliged, to use my endeavors to arrest, or to impede the course of justice . . . & c. Persons of atrocious character, who have violated the laws of God and man, are entitled to no such special exertions from any member of our pure and honourable profession; and indeed, to no intervention beyond securing to them a fair and dispassionate investigation of the *facts* of their cause, and the due application of the law; all that goes beyond this, either in manner or substance, is unprofessional, and proceeds, either from a mistaken view of the relation of client and counsel, or from some unworthy and selfish motive, which sets a higher value on professional display and success, than on truth and justice, and the substantial interests of the community.

LOUIS D. BRANDEIS, THE OPPORTUNITY
IN THE LAW (1905)

In Brandeis, Business—A Profession (1914).

I assume that in asking me to talk to you on the Ethics of the Legal Profession, you do not wish me to enter upon a discussion of the relation of law to morals, or to attempt to acquaint you with those detailed rules of ethics which lawyers have occasion to apply from day to day in their practice. What you want is this: Standing not far from the threshold of active life, feeling the generous impulse for service which the University fosters, you wish to know whether the legal profession would afford you special opportunities for usefulness to your fellow-men, and, if so, what the obligations and limitations are which it imposes. I say special opportunities, because every legitimate occupation, be it profession or business or trade, furnishes abundant opportunities for usefulness, if pursued in what Matthew Arnold called "the grand manner." It is, as a rule, far more important *how* men pursue their occupation than *what* the occupation is which they select.

For centuries before the American Revolution the lawyer had played an important part in England. His importance in the State became much greater in America. One reason for this, as deTocqueville indicated, was the fact that we possessed no class like the nobles, which took part in government through privilege. A more potent reason was that with the introduction of a written constitution the law became with us a far more important factor in the ordinary conduct of political life than it did in England. Legal questions were constantly arising and the lawyer was necessary to settle them. But I take it the paramount reason why the lawyer has played so large a part in our political life is that his training fits him especially to grapple with the questions which are presented in a democracy.

The whole training of the lawyer leads to the development of judgment. His early training—his work with books in the study of legal rules—teaches him patient research and develops both the memory and the reasoning faculties. He becomes practiced in logic; and yet the use of the reasoning faculties in the study of law is very different from their use, say, in metaphysics. The lawyer's processes of reasoning, his logical conclusions, are being constantly tested by experience. He is running up against facts at every point. Indeed it is a maxim of the law: Out of the facts grows the law; that is, propositions are not considered abstractly, but always with reference to facts . . .

If the lawyer's practice is a general one, his field of observation extends, in course of time, into almost every sphere of business and of life. The facts so gathered ripen his judgment. His memory is trained to retentiveness. His mind becomes practiced in discrimination as well as in generalization. He is an observer of men even more than of things. He not only sees men of all kinds, but knows their deepest secrets; sees them in situations which "try men's souls." He is apt to become a good judge of men . . .

His experience teaches him that nearly every question has two sides; and very often he finds—after decision of judge or jury—that both he and his opponent were in the wrong. The practice of law creates thus a habit of mind, and leads to attainments which are distinctly different from those developed in most professions or outside of the professions. These are the reasons why the lawyer has acquired a position materially different from that of other men. It is the position of the adviser . . .

[B]y far the greater part of the work done by lawyers is done not in court, but in advising men on important matters, and mainly in business affairs. In guiding these affairs industrial and financial, lawyers are needed, not only because of the legal questions involved, but because the particular mental attributes and attainments which the legal profession develops are demanded in the proper handling of these large financial or industrial affairs. The magnitude and scope of these operations remove them almost wholly from the realm of "petty trafficking" which people formerly used to associate with trade. The questions which arise are more nearly questions of statesmanship. The relations created call in many instances for the exercise of the highest diplomacy. The magnitude, difficulty and importance of the problems involved are often as great as in the matters of state with which lawyers were formerly frequently associated. The questions appear in a different guise; but they are similar. The relations between rival railroad systems are like the relations between neighboring kingdoms. The relations of the great trusts to the consumers or to their employees is like that of feudal lords to commoners or dependents . . .

It is true that at the present time the lawyer does not hold as high a position with the people as he held seventy-five or indeed fifty years ago; but the reason is not lack of opportunity. It is this: Instead of holding a position of independence, between the wealthy and the people, prepared to curb the excesses of either, able lawyers have, to a large extent, allowed themselves to become adjuncts of great corporations and have neglected the obligation to use their powers for the protection of the people. We hear much of the "corporation lawyer," and far too little of the "people's lawyer." The great opportunity of the American Bar is and will be to stand again as it did in the past, ready to protect also the interests of the people . . .

For nearly a generation the leaders of the Bar have, with few exceptions, not only failed to take part in constructive legislation designed to solve in the public interest our great social, economic and industrial problems; but they have failed likewise to oppose legislation prompted by selfish interests. They have gone further in disregard of common weal. They have often advocated, as lawyers, legislative measures which as citizens they could not approve, and have endeavored to justify themselves by a false analogy. They have erroneously assumed that the role of ethics to be applied to a lawyer's advocacy is the same where he acts for private interests against the public, as it is in litigation between private individuals.

The ethical question which laymen most frequently ask about the legal profession is this: How can a lawyer take a case which he does not believe in? The profession is regarded as necessarily somewhat immoral, because its members are supposed to be habitually taking cases of that character. As a practical matter, the lawyer is not often harassed by this problem; partly because he is apt to believe, at the time, in most of the cases that he actually tries; and partly because he either abandons or settles a large number of those he does not believe in. But the lawyer recognizes that in trying a case his prime duty is to present his side to the tribunal fairly and as well as he can, relying upon his adversary to present the other side fairly and as well as he can. Since the lawyers on the two sides are usually reasonably well matched, the judge or jury may ordinarily be trusted to make a decision as justice demands.

But when lawyers act upon the same principle in supporting the attempts of their private clients to secure or to oppose legislation, a very different condition is presented . . .

Here, consequently, is the great opportunity in the law. The next generation must witness a continuing and ever-increasing contest between those who have and those who have not. The industrial world is in a state of ferment . . . The labor movement must necessarily progress. The people's thought will take shape in action; and it lies with us, with you to whom in part the future belongs, to say on what lines the action is to be expressed; whether it is to be expressed wisely and temperately, or wildly and intemperately; whether it is to be expressed on lines of evolution or on lines of revolution. Nothing can better fit you for taking part in the solution of these problems, than the study and preeminently the practice of law. Those of you who feel drawn to that profession may rest assured that you will find in it an opportunity for usefulness which is probably unequalled. There is a call upon the legal profession to do a great work for this country.

HARLAN FISK STONE, "THE PUBLIC INFLUENCE OF THE BAR"
48 Harv.L.Rev. 1 (1934).*

. . .

We meet at a time when, as never before in the history of the country, our most cherished ideals and traditions are being subjected to searching criticism. The towering edifice of business and industry, which had become the dominating feature of the American social structure, has been shaken to its foundations by forces, the full significance of which we still can see but dimly. . . .

[If] tradition and history are guides . . . we may rightly look to the Bar for leadership in the preservation and development of American institutions. Specially trained in the field of law and government, invested with the unique privileges of his office, experienced in the world of affairs, and versed in the problems of business organization and administration, to whom, if not to the lawyer, may we look for guidance in solving the problems of a sorely stricken social order?

No tradition of our profession is more cherished by lawyers than that of its leadership in public affairs. We dwell upon the part of lawyers in the creation of the Federal Constitution and in the organization of the national government and of our federal and state judicial systems. The role they played in politics and government in the first half of the last century is a familiar part of our history. . . . In a very real sense they were guardians of the law, cherishing the legitimate influence of their guild as that of a profession charged with public duties and responsibilities. . . . Yet candor would compel even those of us who have the most abiding faith in our profession, and the firmest belief in its capacity for future usefulness, to admit that in our own time the Bar has not maintained its traditional position of public influence and leadership. Although it tends to prove the point, it is not of the first importance that there are fewer lawyers of standing serving in the halls of legislatures or in executive or administrative posts than in earlier days. Public office is not the only avenue to public influence. Representatives of other professions in public position have always been comparatively few, but wherever questions of professional concern to them touch the public interest, they are nevertheless profoundly influential. In matters of sanitation and public health, in great public undertakings involving engineering knowledge and skill, we place ourselves unreservedly in their hands. . . . [M]ost laymen, at least, would deny that there is today a comparable leadership on the part of lawyers, or a disposition of the public to place reliance upon their leadership where the problems of government touch the law.

. . . While it has not inherited the completely independent status of the English bar, to no other group in this country has the state granted comparable privileges or permitted so much autonomy. No other is so closely related to the state, and no other has traditionally exerted so powerful an influence on public opinion and on public policy. That influence in the past has been wielded chiefly in the courts, in the forum of local communities, in legislative halls, in the councils of government. In all its varying aspects, it has been most potent when public questions have been closely associated with legal questions in whose discussion the lawyer was peculiarly at home, and when, with a developed consciousness of its social responsibility, it was inevitable that the Bar should draw upon all its special knowledge and skill and resourcefulness for their solution.

In appraising the present-day relationship of the lawyer to his community, we cannot leave out of account either the altered character of public questions or the change in the function which the lawyers, as a class, are called upon to perform. It was in 1809 when Jefferson wrote: "We are a rural farming people; we have little business and few manufactures among us, and I pray God it will be a long time before we have much of either." Profound changes have come into American life since that sentence was penned. . . .

.   .   .

The changed character of the lawyer's work has made it difficult for him to contemplate his function in its new setting, to see himself and his occupation in proper perspective. No longer does his list of clients represent a cross section of society; no longer do his contacts make him the typical representative and interpreter of his community. The demands of practice are more continuous and exacting. He has less time for reflection upon other than immediate professional undertakings. He is more the man of action, less the philosopher and less the student of history, economics, and government.

The rise of big business has produced an inevitable specialization of the Bar. The successful lawyer of our day more often than not is the proprietor or general manager of a new type of factory, whose legal product is increasingly the result of mass production methods. More and more the amount of his income is the measure of professional success. More and more he must look for his rewards to the material satisfactions derived from profits as from a successfully conducted business, rather than to the intangible and indubitably more durable satisfactions which are to be found in a professional service more consciously directed toward the advancement of the public interest. Steadily the best skill and capacity of the profession has been drawn into the exacting and highly specialized service of business and finance. At its best the changed system has brought to the command of the business world loyalty and a superb proficiency and technical skill. At its worst it has made the learned profession of an earlier day the obsequious servant of business, and tainted it with the morals and manners of the market place in its most anti-social manifestations. In any case we must concede that it has given us a Bar whose leaders, like its rank and file, are on the whole less likely to be well rounded professional men than their predecessors, whose energy and talent for public service and for bringing the law into harmony with changed conditions have been largely absorbed in the advancement of the interests of clients.

. . .

. . . The loss and suffering inflicted on individuals, the harm done to a social order founded upon business and dependent upon its integrity, are incalculable. There is little to suggest that the Bar has yet recognized that it must bear some burden of responsibility for these evils. . . .

We must remember, nevertheless, that the very conditions which have caused specialization, which have drawn so heavily upon the technical proficiency of the Bar, have likewise placed it in a position where the possibilities of its influence are almost beyond calculation. The intricacies of business organization are built upon a legal framework which the current growth of administrative law is still further elaborating. Without the constant advice and guidance of lawyers business would come to an abrupt halt. And whatever standards of conduct in the performance of its function the Bar consciously adopts must at once be reflected in the character of the world of business and finance. Given a measure of self-conscious and cohesive professional unity, the Bar may exert a power more beneficent and far reaching than it or any other non-governmental group has wielded in the past.

. . . Before it can function at all as the guardian of public interests committed to its care, there must be appraisal and comprehension of the new conditions and the changed relationships of the lawyer to his clients, to his professional brethren and to the public. That appraisal must pass beyond the petty details of form and manners which have been so largely the subject of our codes of ethics, to more fundamental consideration of the way in which our professional activities affect the welfare of society as a whole. . . .

. . .

[T]he Bar must assume the responsibility of consciously bringing its conduct to conform to new standards fitting the times in which we live. And unless history reverses itself the cooperation and support of leaders of the Bar will not be wanting. . . .

. . .

Note on the Satisfactions of Practice

The following is a condensation of an article based on the findings of a National Survey of Career Satisfaction/Dissatisfaction, conducted under the auspices of the American Bar Association. Following the Hirsch article is a table that relates overall satisfaction in practice to position in practice, years in practice and gender. Observe that law practice is not regarded by lawyers as being all wine and roses, but on the other hand that the level of satisfaction seems pretty high in this age of discontent. Observe also how intellectual challenge is salient in the sources of satisfaction. That ties back to Tocqueville's observation, quoted supra, that "study and specialized knowledge of the law give a man a rank apart in society and makes of lawyers a somewhat privileged intellectual class."

The last piece is from a book on legal ethics that was based on discussions by practicing lawyers. It analyzes the relationship between what a client might want to do and what a lawyer might give the client. Observe that in handling this relationship, the lawyer has both an intellectual and an ethical challenge. Would it be fair to say that one of the most difficult intellectual challenges facing the lawyer is how to handle the ethical challenges that practice involves? Is effectively coping with those challenges perhaps a source of satisfaction in the practice of law?

RONALD L. HIRSCH, "ARE YOU ON TARGET?"

The Barrister Magazine, Vol. 12, No. 1, p. 17 (1985).*

. . .

In an effort to accurately study the state of the profession, the Young Lawyers Division, with the generous support of the ABA Board of Governors, undertook the first comprehensive survey of the legal profession: the National Survey of Career Satisfaction/Dissatisfaction.

A random probability sample of 3,018 lawyers of all ages was drawn from both ABA member and nonmember lists totalling 569,706 lawyers. The sampled individuals were sent a lengthy survey covering many aspects of their work environment, job history, educational background, health and psychological profile and basic demographics. . . .

. . .

. . . The good news is that the overall level of dissatisfaction is less than was expected, albeit still substantial: 16 percent of all lawyers (25 percent of junior associates and staff attorneys) are dissatisfied.

However, despite the high level of overall satisfaction, the survey confirms that there are serious problems in the workplace, even for those who are satisfied overall. Problems concerning training, feedback from superiors, time for one's nonwork life, among others, are widespread throughout the profession. Also, serious problems concerning control of work, office intrigue, and even financial reward exist in many firms and other job settings.

Another way of looking at problems within the profession is to look at the 25 percent of all lawyers planning to change jobs within the next two years. When we look at those in private practice who plan to change, the data is astonishing: Only 26 percent plan to look for a job in private practice and 31 percent plan to look at non-legal positions. Further, almost no one currently in a large firm wants to stay in one, and few lawyers want to move to one.

. . .

In looking at this data, we see that junior associates in most firms and lawyers in general in 2–3 man firms are far more dissatisfied than those in other positions and settings. And women are far more dissatisfied generally, regardless of position.

* Copyright © 1985 by the American Bar Association.

However, although being a junior associate and being a woman account for a small amount of the variation in satisfaction levels, it is the particular mix of positive and negative work environment factors that primarily accounts for satisfaction or dissatisfaction.

. . .

INTELLECTUAL CHALLENGE CONQUERS ALL

Just what are these positive and negative factors? The most important positive factor is the existence of intellectual challenge in the job.

The results of this analysis are also supported by other data from the survey. In looking at the data on why people choose law as a career, as well as the factors important to their overall feeling about their jobs, intellectual challenge was by far the single most important factor—for both men and women. If one then looks at the job descriptor for intellectual challenge, we find that the overwhelming majority find the amount of challenge to be either great or somewhat so.

As a result, 60 percent are satisfied with the extent of challenge present in their jobs, 27 percent feel neutral, and only 14 percent are dissatisfied. Clearly, the overwhelmingly satisfactory presence of intellectual challenge in their jobs is enough to overcome the various negative aspects of their jobs. The result: an overall feeling of satisfaction in most cases.

After intellectual challenge, the next most important positive factor contributing to job satisfaction is the presence of a warm and personal work atmosphere. Other important factors are opportunity to advance, treatment by superiors as a professional colleague and control over one's work.

Two other positive factors, although not significant statistically, are both the substantive and activity mix—client contact, memo writing, court appearances—in a lawyer's job.

There is a popular belief that many lawyers, especially junior associates, are very dissatisfied with the mix of their work, that many are stuck in library stacks, and that others work on one big case for years. Although such cases obviously do exist, the survey found that such cases are relatively rare. The survey also found, not surprisingly, that those lawyers who have a good mix of activities were significantly more satisfied overall than either those lawyers who were acting as "drones," doing mostly research and memo writing and other nonclient-contact work, as well as those lawyers who had a very heavy concentration in activities such as trials, court appearances and depositions. In total, only 5 percent of all attorneys find the substantive mix of their work unattractive, and only 9 percent find the mix of activities to be unattractive.

WHY ARE WOMEN MORE DISSATISFIED?

Why, then, are so many more women lawyers dissatisfied? The answer is that women experience far more negative work environments in a number of critical areas. Significantly more women report that their job atmosphere is not warm and personal, that advancement is not determined by the quality of work, that they have no control over the cases they handle, that tension is high, and that they have virtually no time for themselves. Finally, the income of women lawyers is far below that of their male counterparts in most situations. Thus, even though their intellectual challenge is almost as high as reported by men, the other positive factors are not present to the same extent—and various negative factors are more pronounced.

NEGATIVE FACTORS: POLITICS AND PERSONAL TIME

On the negative side, the most important factor for lawyers is the existence of political intrigue and backbiting, followed by an extreme lack of time for themselves. A high score on these factors results in an attorney being dissatisfied, regardless of position or setting.

One frequent complaint about the practice of law is that it is all-consuming to the exclusion of one's personal life. A severe problem is identified by the survey in the area of vacation time. Although most lawyers have relatively generous vacation allowances, the comparison between time allowed and time taken shows that far less time is taken.

Thus, we find that 40 percent of all lawyers are dissatisfied with the amount of vacation they are able to take. This should not be surprising. Given the number of hours that lawyers regularly work, 1 or 2 weeks vacation a year is not enough to recover and replenish one's physical and mental reservoirs.

The survey shows that many lawyers work long hours: 11 percent work in excess of 240 hours a month, while 44 percent of all lawyers work in excess of 200 hours a month. Twenty percent felt that their hours were unattractive, while 34 percent felt neutral. "Hours worked" includes all activities that were considered by the respondent or his employer to be part of the job, regardless of whether defined as "billable" or not.

One surprising fact is the comparison of the hours worked by junior associates with those of senior associates and partners. Conventional wisdom is that junior associates work longer hours than others. However, . . . junior associates in fact work slightly less hours, with senior associates shouldering the heaviest burden. It is also interesting to note that solo practitioners work less than lawyers in firms, which is probably a function of the amount of work they have.

. . .

TRAINING AND FEEDBACK: TOO INFREQUENT

The survey also supports the often-heard statement that supervision within firms is very poor. Forty-seven percent of junior associates reported negatively on the extent of supervision—whether defined as feedback on work, or provision of instruction and training. Only 14–17 percent of junior associates report receiving frequent training and feedback from superiors. However, although many attorneys complain about this problem, . . . only 21 percent report dissatisfaction with this individual factor and it is rather unimportant in its effect on overall satisfaction.

IS MONEY THE NAME OF THE GAME?

Lawyers have a reputation in American folklore for being an avaricious group who will do anything for money. However, the survey shows that the majority of lawyers earn far less than many would expect. Further, in spite of the fact that 41 percent are dissatisfied with their earnings, most of these attorneys are still satisfied overall with their jobs. Money, then, is not the name of the game. The amount of financial reward, although a factor of some importance in its effect on overall satisfaction, did not account for a large degree of variation in satisfaction.

Thus, 45 percent of all lawyers report job incomes under $45,000.
. . .

Although the general public might not find these salaries bad, the expectations of most people who go to law school and work very hard in their practices are not being met.

. . .

DISSATISFACTION AFFECTS LAW FIRM PROFITS

Many lawyers feel that law firms could care less if their attorneys are dissatisfied or not; as long as the work gets out, that's all that matters. However, the findings of the survey show clearly that it is in a firm's enlightened self-interest to do what it can to increase lawyer satisfaction, the reason being that dissatisfaction increases lawyer turnover and decreases lawyer productivity.

Twenty-five percent of all attorneys plan to change jobs within the next two years; as a lawyer's satisfaction decreases or dissatisfaction increases, the likelihood of his changing jobs increases dramatically. However, . . . it is not only malcontents that change jobs. Even those who score neutral on the satisfaction scale have an uncomfortably large propensity to change jobs. This is again the result of the complex interaction of work environment factors, with many attorneys having considerable dissatisfaction with various aspects of the workplace—even though they overall feel satisfied or neutral.

. . .

Of those in private practice, 11 percent of partners, 26 percent of senior associates and 35 percent of junior associates plan to change within the next two years. The economic impact of the loss of a partner or a senior associate cannot help but be substantial. However, there is also economic impact in the loss of associates after they get to the point where they can truly start to "earn their keep," especially when, as in most reported cases, they leave their firms because they are dissatisfied with the firm rather than that the firm is dissatisfied with them. All the time, effort and money that firms have invested in individuals is lost.

ANALYSIS OF HIRSCH DATA BY ROBERT L. NELSON
Project Director, American Bar Foundation

Mean Satisfaction Level by Law Position,
Years in Practice, and Sex

(1 to 5 scale: 1 = very sat.; 5 = very dissat.)

Years in Practice

Law Position	1–4 yrs		5–9 yrs		10+yrs		Total		
	Male	Female	Male	Female	Male	Female	Male	Female	(n)
Solos, 2–3	2.04	2.43	2.18	2.23	2.18	3.00	2.14	2.41	(368)
4–30 lawyers	1.95	2.46	1.93	2.62	1.69	2.33	1.89	2.48	(447)
31+ lawyers	2.32	2.74	2.21	2.64	1.67	2.00	2.10	2.68	(244)
Government	2.34	2.75	2.05	2.29	1.88	1.67	2.08	2.54	(196)
Corp./Other	2.00	1.78	2.23	2.06	1.73	3.00	1.97	1.95	(171)
(n)	(383)	(153)	(361)	(78)	(436)	(15)	(1180)	(246)	(1426)

significant effects: law position, years in practice, sex, interaction of law position and years in practice

Range: Males 10 years or more in practice,
  large firm: 1.67
to
Females 10 years or more in practice,
  solo practice or corp./other: 3.00

GEOFFREY C. HAZARD, Jr., ETHICS IN THE PRACTICE OF LAW (1978)
c. 10, pp. 136–149.[*]

. . .

Many courses of action taken by a client are "wrong" at least in the exacting sense that they are not what would be done by a supremely moral person unconcerned with costs. If this were the standard by which a lawyer should judge whether to continue his association with a client, there would be few of either clients or lawyers.

Ethically sensitive lawyers are very much concerned about clients who refuse to follow advice, particularly when it concerns a serious matter of right and wrong. This concern contradicts both the popular lore that the lawyer is simply a tool of his client and the professional dogma that the client's conduct is never morally imputable to his legal adviser. For the skillful lawyer, the question is not what to do if the client refuses to follow advice on an important matter but how to give the advice so that it will not be refused.

In considering this question, it should be kept in mind what a lawyer may include in the advice he gives a client. Legal advice takes the form of a suggestion concerning a course of action that might or should be pursued or avoided, with a supporting explanation. The explanation is the heart of the matter, for otherwise the advice amounts to nothing more than a Delphic pronouncement. A legal adviser's explanation can include one or more of the following elements:

— A report of the text of the law as it stands.

— An estimate of how key provisions of the law properly should be interpreted (if the advice is given within the government) or will likely be interpreted by the officials responsible for its administration (if the advice is given outside the government).

— An estimate of the likelihood that a serious effort will be made to invoke the rule in question.

— A projection of the best, worst, and intermediate situations that could result as a consequence of the rule's being invoked.

— An appraisal of the significant consequences of possible courses of action, whether they will provoke retaliation, etc.

— A judgment whether the recommended course of action is in some less pragmatic sense good or right.

. . .

The rules governing the legal adviser's role thus can be summed up by saying that his advice can comment upon a proposed course of conduct in terms of the letter of the law, its pragmatic implications, and its moral rightness. The question therefore is not what kind of explanation a legal adviser is permitted to give his client when rendering advice; the question is what kind he should give. This depends on what the lawyer seeks to achieve in giving his advice.

The beginning point is that a client is not obliged to follow legal advice, or even to seek it. An attorney-client relationship is not one of tutelage. The client is assumed to be an autonomous person capable of making his or its own decisions. He or it is assumed to be responsible for his or its courses of action. . . .

. . .

From the viewpoint of both the client and the legal adviser, then, the theory is essentially that legal advice is delivered on a take it or leave it basis. Underlying this concept is not only the legal idea that the client is autonomous and the attorney a bystander but an image of client and lawyer. The image, here as elsewhere in the professional ethics of the bar, is mid-Victorian. The setting involves two individuals between whom "a matter" is under consideration. Both are adults, both free agents in their respective stations in life; the "matter" is separable in time and space from what has gone before and what may eventuate later. The advice is given and received; the client acts; and that is that.

Given the image, the theory makes sense. In modern setting . . . the theory's suitability is not so clear. Organizational clients are not obliged to seek legal advice but they do so as a matter of routine. The routine is supported by several practical necessities. The transactions of large corporations and agencies are generally large in size or frequent in repetition, so that the added cost of obtaining a legal check-out is relatively low. These organizations are relatively vulnerable to legal sanctions, especially if the sanction of political criticism is included, when they find themselves on the wrong side of legality. The responsible management officials of these organizations may themselves be personally liable, financially or politically, for legally wrongful or invalid actions. Furthermore, when the organization is a government agency, the question of legality is often simultaneously a question of agency jurisdiction and competence. If these considerations do not amount to a legal obligation to seek legal advice, taken together they come close to it.

. . .

The legal adviser in such a situation surely is not clothed with the immunity of a pure bystander. But what sort of responsibilities does he have?   . . .

. . . The point is made by suggesting that it is one thing to represent a sometime murderer, quite another to be on retainer to the Mafia.

Thus, the question has to be faced: Is a lawyer responsible for the conduct of a regular client?   . . .

The obvious answer for the adviser whose advice is ignored is that he can resign. In some circumstances that is the only honorable course to be followed, but it is impractical as a response to all except fundamental disagreements. More important, though not often recognized by the critics of legal and other advisers to corporations, the sanction of resignation involves some ethical problems of its own. If taken seriously, it should be applicable only when any right-thinking adviser would resign. But this is to say that such a client ought to have no right-thinking adviser at all, at least until the client redirects his conduct so that it would no longer be objectionable to a right-thinking adviser. There are situations in which it seems proper that the client should suffer that kind of penalty, for example if he insists on fabricating evidence or carrying out a swindle. But if the case is less extreme than this, the sanction of resignation is too severe. It implies that the client should have to function without proper guidance, or perhaps cease functioning at all, because its managers do not see fit to follow the advice of its advisers.

If this were the consequence that should ensue from a client's refusal to follow advice, it would mean that the advice was in effect peremptory—not an informed suggestion but a command. When an adviser's advice is in effect peremptory, however, the result is a reversal of the underlying structure of responsibility. . . . The adviser becomes the ultimate arbiter and the client a subordinate. If the reversal of responsibilities becomes permanent, as it must if the adviser is deemed responsible for all critical decisions, the erstwhile adviser now becomes principal and we are back at the beginning. Furthermore, in the meantime the nominal principal has the excuse that he was merely following directions and so is not responsible for action taken in his name. Putting the point differently, when responsibility is transferred to an adviser, it is also transferred from his principal.

. . .

But somewhere there is a stopping place. If it is clear that a lawyer cannot be held responsible for everything his client does, it is equally clear that he must assume responsibility at some point. The reasons he must do so are at least threefold. First, he owes a client the responsibility of putting himself on the line; at a critical juncture nothing but an implicit threat of resignation will persuade the client that the advice in question is of utmost seriousness. Second, the lawyer owes it to himself as a matter of self-respect; a lawyer with regular clients takes on their reputation, no matter what the canons say. Third, he has to maintain his reputation for professional competence. The practice of law largely involves persuading people to do things that are very unpleasant; a lawyer who cannot induce his client to do what must be done is almost certainly incapable of exercising such persuasion on others.

The way in which the lawyer assumes responsibility for the client's conduct is to give peremptory advice. Peremptory advice is in form like any other legal advice—a suggestion coupled with a supporting statement of reasons. Its tenor, however, is such that the recipient can disregard it only if he is foolish or if the advice itself is misguided.

. . .

The fact that it is possible to give peremptory advice is, ultimately, the explanation of why a lawyer is responsible at some point for his client's conduct. The fact that the lawyer has to speak as adviser and not as principal explains why that point is reached only when the legal question is virtually unarguable. In the end, the boundary between a proposition that is legally arguable and one that is not pretty well conforms to the boundary between fundamental right and wrong in everyday life, wherever that is. A good lawyer has to know where it is. A lawyer who does not know where it is also does not know when to keep open the client's options and when to close them, and therefore how to give good advice when it is most needed.

INDEX

References are to Pages

†